WHAT IS Psychology? ESSENTIALS

Ellen Pastorino

Valencia Community College

Susann Doyle-Portillo

Gainesville State College

 WADSWORTH
CENGAGE Learning™

Australia • Canada • Mexico • Singapore • Spain
United Kingdom • United States

WADSWORTH
CENGAGE Learning™

What Is Psychology? Essentials
Ellen Pastorino, Susann Doyle-Portillo

Publisher: Linda Schreiber

Senior Editor: Jaime Perkins

Senior Development Editor: Kristin Makarewycz

Assistant Editor: Paige Leeds

Editorial Assistant: Sarah Worrell

Associate Media Editor: Rachel Guzman

Executive Marketing Manager: Kimberly Russell

Marketing Manager: Elisabeth Rhoden

Marketing Assistant: Molly Felz

Executive Marketing Communications
Manager: Talia Wise

Project Manager, Editorial
Production: Mary Noel

Creative Director: Rob Hugel

Art Director: Vernon T. Boes

Print Buyer: Karen Hunt

Permissions Editors: Margaret Chamberlain-
Gaston, Deanna Ettinger

Production Service: Lachina Publishing Services

Text Designer: Marsha Cohen

Photo Researcher: Roman Barnes

Copy Editor: Margaret C. Tropp

Cover Designer: Robert Russell

Cover Image: Robert Russell

Compositor: Lachina Publishing Services

For product information and technology assistance, contact us at
Cengage Learning Customer & Sales Support, 1-800-354-9706

For permission to use material from this text or product,
submit all requests online at **www.cengage.com/permissions**
Further permissions questions can be emailed to
permissionrequest@cengage.com

Library of Congress Control Number: 2008938411

Student Edition:

ISBN-13: 978-0-495-59673-8

ISBN-10: 0-495-59673-6

Casebound Edition:

ISBN-13: 978-0-495-60399-3

ISBN-10: 0-495-60399-6

Loose-leaf Edition:

ISBN-13: 978-0-495-60398-6

ISBN-10: 0-495-60398-8

Wadsworth
10 Davis Drive
Belmont, CA 94002-3098
USA

Cengage Learning is a leading provider of customized learning solutions with office locations around the globe, including Singapore, the United Kingdom, Australia, Mexico, Brazil, and Japan. Locate your local office at: **www.cengage.com/international**.

Cengage Learning products are represented in Canada by Nelson Education, Ltd.

To learn more about Wadsworth, visit **www.cengage.com /wadsworth**

Purchase any of our products at your local college store or at our preferred online store **www.ichapters.com**

Printed in Canada
1 2 3 4 5 6 7 12 11 10 09 08

For Christian, Andrew, and Scott. Thank you for sharing the wonders of the male psyche! You have made me a better mom, a better teacher, and have enriched my life with beauty and laughter. I am so proud of the young men that you are becoming. Never stop loving, learning, and dreaming.

—Ellen Pastorino

For Eulalio Ortiz Portillo who is the love of my life, as well as one of my greatest teachers.

—Susann Doyle-Portillo

About the Authors

Ellen E. Pastorino (Ph.D., Florida State University, 1990) is a developmental psychologist who established her teaching career at Gainesville State College in Georgia. As a tenured professor she created and developed the college's Teaching and Learning Center, working with faculty to promote student learning. For the past 11 years she has been teaching at Valencia Community College in Orlando, Florida. Here, too, she has worked with faculty in designing learning-centered classroom practices. Ellen has won numerous teaching awards, including the University of Georgia Board of Regents Distinguished Professor, the NISOD Excellence in Teaching Award, and Valencia's Teaching and Learning Excellence Award. Ellen has published articles in *The Journal of Adolescent Research* and *Adolescence*, and actively participates in many regional and national teaching conferences. However, her main passion has always been to get students excited about the field of psychology. Ellen is a member of the Association for Psychological Science (APS) and currently serves as Valencia's Endowed Chair in Social Sciences. Ellen has authored test banks, instructor manuals, and student study guides. While working as a consultant for IBM Corporation she developed numerous educational materials for teachers and students. Her current interests include assessment, inclusion, service learning, and reaching underprepared students. Ellen strives to balance her professional responsibilities with her love of physical fitness and family life.

Susann M. Doyle–Portillo, a professor of psychology at Gainesville State College for the past 14 years, earned her Ph.D. in Social Cognition in 1994 from the University of Oklahoma. Prior to her doctoral program, Susann earned bachelor's degrees in engineering and psychology. This exposure to both the hard sciences and the social sciences helped to ground her firmly in the experimental tradition of psychology. She has published articles in *Social Cognition* and *Contemporary Social Psychology*, but the main focus of her career has and will always be teaching. During her tenure at Gainesville State College, Susann has earned a reputation as an excellent but challenging instructor. Her annual teaching evaluations regularly rank her performance as being "superior" and "excellent" and she has three times been listed in *Who's Who Among America's Teachers*. Susann is also actively engaged in student learning outside of the classroom. One of her major goals is to help students learn by getting them involved in conducting original research. In addition to her teaching, Susann is also heavily involved in the assessment of general education at Gainesville State College. In this role, she has helped colleagues across her institution to develop and implement performance-based assessments of learning outcomes in their courses.

BRIEF Contents

Contents

Chapter 1
What Is Psychology? 2

Chapter 2

How Does Biology Influence
Our Behavior? 36

Chapter 3
How Do We Sense and Perceive Our World? 74

Chapter 4
Consciousness: Wide Awake, in a Daze, or Dreaming? 118

Chapter 5
How Do We Learn? 156

Chapter 6
How Does Memory Function? 196

Chapter 7
Cognition, Language, and Intelligence: How Do We Think? 232

Chapter 8
Motivation and Emotion: What Guides Our Behavior? 272

Chapter 9
How Do People Grow, Change, and Develop? 312

Chapter 10
Social Psychology: How Do We Understand and Interact With Others? 364

Chapter 11
Health, Stress, and Coping: How Can You Create a Healthy Life? 408

Chapter 12
What Is Personality and How Do We Measure It? 444

Chapter 13
What Are Psychological Disorders, and How Can We Understand Them? 478

Chapter 14
What Therapies Are Used to Treat Psychological Problems? 522

Preface

Together, we have over 30 years of experience teaching Introductory Psychology. We each teach 4–6 sections of Introductory or General Psychology each and every semester—it is our bread and butter, so to speak. So, it's a good thing that Introductory Psychology is also our favorite course. Contrary to what many may think of professors teaching the same course over and over, it never grows old for us. Teaching General Psychology allows us to touch on many different aspects of our fascinating field and to work with diverse students from all walks of life, such that no two classes are ever alike.

The uniqueness of each class is just one of the challenges that keep us excited about teaching this course. There are others. General Psychology classes are often full of students who are just beginning their academic careers—some are fresh from high school—others are returning, non-traditional students who've been out of the classroom for several years. They come to us with the desire to learn about psychology, but often they face serious obstacles. Some are overworked in their personal lives. Some have lingering academic deficiencies. And most expect learning to be easier than we know it to be. As such, a big part of our mission is to help students overcome these obstacles and obtain success.

Getting students to read their textbook in preparation for lectures and exams is one of the biggest problems we face as instructors. Like many professors, our experience has been that few students read assigned chapters prior to lecture, and some even fail to read the chapters by the time they take exams. For years, we have tried various methods of motivating students to read—pop quizzes, reading quizzes, test questions from material in the book but not covered in lecture, and so on. None of these methods seemed to have much of an impact on students.

Students' free time is, of course, in short supply. And when they do have free time, reading a textbook doesn't always seem like an attractive option. Students often find their texts difficult to read, boring, and full of content that is far removed from the concerns of their daily lives. One of us overheard students speaking before class the second week of the semester. One student asked those sitting around him if they had read the reading assignment—most replied they had not. He then said, "I read it, but man I have no idea what they were saying in that chapter!" If we want students to read their textbooks, we will have to give them books that they will *want* to read, and that means giving them a book that they can understand and one that *they* find relevant enough to be worth the time it takes to read. That is why we've written this text. Our goal was to write a textbook that students would find interesting to read, easy to read, and memorable.

Unlocking Curiosity in Students by Making Psychology Interesting

One of the best ways to motivate students to read is to capture their curiosity from the very beginning. Any good psychologist knows that personal relevance is one aspect of information that is very likely to capture our interest and attention. To capitalize on this, each chapter opens with the story of one of our former students who has found the information in that chapter useful in his or her work, studies, or personal life. These stories serve as testimonials from our students to our readers. If they see that their peers have found value in the material, readers may be motivated to see for themselves the ways in which psychology is relevant to their own lives.

Our *You Asked* feature also gives voice to what students actually want to know about psychology. As we were writing this text, we asked our students to share with us the questions that they had about psychology. These questions then became a guide to us as we wrote each chapter. By ensuring that we address points that are of interest to students, we help encourage students to read.

Making Psychology Relevant for All People

There is little doubt that students learn best when they become personally invested in the material that they are reading and studying. However, for this to occur, students must actually find the material to be applicable to *their* lives. Given that today's college students are a diverse group of people, writing a text that is relevant to today's students means writing a text that embraces their diversity. We have written our book with this in mind.

Throughout our text, we have used examples of real people (such as those whose stories open each chapter) who reflect the diversity seen in our classrooms. Where applicable, we have cited and highlighted research that reflects many aspects of diversity, including gender differences, racial diversity, sexual orientation, cultural diversity, age differences, and facing physical and/or mental health challenges. In all, we reference people from nearly 100 countries and/or cultural groups.

Countries and Cultural Groups Referenced in What Is Psychology? Essentials

Afghanistan	Africa	African Americans
Alaskan Natives	American Indians	Austria
American Navajos	Americans	Argentina
Asian Americans	Asians	Australia
Bashi people of Africa	Belgium	Brazil
Britain	Canada	Central America
China	Croatia	Czech Republic
Denmark	El Salvador	England
Estonia	Finland	Dominican Republic
Eskimo peoples	Ethnic Hawaiian peoples	Europe
European Americans	France	Gabonese
Germany	Great Britain	Greece
Hungary	Hindi peoples	Hispanics
Hispanic-Americans	Hong Kong	India
Indonesia	Iran	Ireland
Iraq	Islamic peoples	Israel
Italy	Jamaica	Japan
Japanese-Americans	Jewish peoples	Kenya
Korea	Korean Americans	Latin Americans
Latvia	Lithuania	Latino
Mauritania	Mayan peoples	Mexican Americans
Mexico	Morocco	Multi-racial peoples
Native Americans	New Zealand	Nicaragua
Northern America	Norway	Oceania
Pacific-Islanders	Philippines	Poland
Portugal	Protestant peoples	Puerto Rico
Quebecois	Russia	Setswana
Seventh Day Adventists	Slovakia	South Africa
South America	South Korea	Southeast Asia
Spain	Sweden	Swiss
Thailand	Turkey	United States
Urban peoples	West Africa	Western culture
Western Europe	Whites	Wales

Making Psychology Accessible Without Dumbing It Down

Motivating a student to read the text is, of course, a primary concern of professors. But reading the text does no good if the student does not understand what he or she has read. The student comment we mentioned previously is very telling. He read the assignment, but he did not understand it. We doubt this did much to encourage him to read his next reading assignment! A major goal of this text is to bring psychology to the student by making it understandable and to do so without sacrificing content. We believe that it is not necessary to condescend to students to get them to understand. Rather, you just have to explain difficult concepts thoroughly and clearly.

Engaging Narrative Writing Style

Throughout the text, we have adopted an engaging narrative writing style that will not intimidate students. Difficult concepts (e.g., neural transmission, classical conditioning) are given extended description and many examples are used to illustrate and clarify our points. The language we use in the text strongly reflects the way we speak to our students during class. We also include a pronunciation glossary so students will know how to correctly pronounce the more difficult, unfamiliar terms. We attempted to use our prose to tell students the *story* of psychology, as opposed to a mere litany of theories and research findings. We believe we have succeeded. Throughout the process of writing this text, many faculty reviewers and students have consistently praised our writing style for its clarity and accessibility. One reviewer commented that it was obvious that this text was written by authors who have spent much time in the classroom in front of students.

Enhancing Motivation and Learning by Making Psychology Practical

A key point in getting students to read a text and retain what they've read is making the material applicable to their lives. When information is associated with the self, it becomes more easily retrieved from memory. So, when students can see how psychology relates to their personal lives, they are much more likely to find it interesting and a lot less likely to forget it. Throughout the text, we have made a concerted effort to use practical, everyday examples to illustrate the concepts of psychology.

Psychology Applies to Your World

What Is Psychology? Essentials includes *Psychology Applies to Your World*, a feature that emphasizes the personal relevance of psychology by showing students that an understanding of psychology can help them to better understand their world. *Psychology Applies to Your World* topics include how to get a good night's sleep (Chapter 4), the obesity epidemic (Chapter 8), televised violence (Chapter 10), and using taste aversion to help people cope with chemotherapy and alcoholism (Chapter 5).

Neuroscience Applies to Your World

Another applied feature is *Neuroscience Applies to Your World*, which shows students the many ways in which understanding our biology can give us better insight into our mental processes and behavior. Each *Neuroscience Applies to Your World* feature pairs an interesting photo with a caption describing how biological functioning relates to some aspect of behavior or cognition. For example, in Chapter 2, we discuss whether or not eating certain foods can affect mood via their effects on nervous system functioning. In Chapter 14, we discuss biomedical therapies that can be used to treat people suffering from substance abuse problems. And in Chapter 5, we discuss the connections among genes, brain chemicals, hyperactivity in the brain, and one's tendency to suffer from migraines.

Enhancing Student Learning by Encouraging Active Learning and Self-Assessment

Many of our students learn best when they engage in active rather than passive learning. We have made a concerted effort to get students *involved* with the material as they read. By remaining engaged, students will be more motivated to read, and they will likely retain the information in memory much better.

Your Turn – Active Learning

The *Your Turn – Active Learning* feature asks students to do hands-on activities to illustrate important chapter concepts. Active learning not only encourages students to see the personal relevance of the material, it also helps students elaborate the material in memory by connecting it to personal experience. Examples of *Your Turn – Active Learning* activities include having students examine their attributional biases when making judgments about celebrities (Chapter 10), illustrating the nonverbal nature of procedural memories by having students explain how to engage in certain skills (Chapter 6), and having students practice progressive muscle relaxation as a means of illustrating systematic desensitization techniques (Chapter 14).

Let's Review!

Another feature, *Let's Review!*, appears after each major section of the chapter. *Let's Review!* allows students to actively assess their learning by asking them to apply the material of the preceding section to answer several multiple choice questions. Most of the *Let's Review!* questions are application questions that apply the material to practical situations. For example, in Chapter 10, *Social Psychology: How Do We Understand and Interact with Others?*, we use the following question to test the student's understanding of attribution theory:

> Jasper was quick to assume that Susan was intelligent when he saw that she earned an "A" on her last psychology exam. However, when Jasper earned an "A" on his history test, he was not so quick to assume that he was intelligent. Which of the following biases in social cognition *best* explains Jasper's behavior?
>
> **a.** The fundamental attribution error
>
> **b.** The self-serving bias
>
> **c.** The social desirability bias
>
> **d.** The actor-observer bias

To answer this question, the student must not only understand the different attribution biases, but he or she must also be able to think analytically about them in applying these concepts to a very common student-oriented scenario.

You Review

What Is Psychology? Essentials also includes a *You Review* feature in each chapter that is a table that summarizes a body of content from the chapter. For example, in Chapter 11 the symptoms of sexually transmitted infections are summarized. In Chapter 7 gender differences on some cognitive tasks are highlighted.

Stop, Look, and Learn

Students also tend to learn best when information is frequently rehearsed and encoded in smaller batches. To facilitate frequent rehearsal, we have included a new *Stop, Look, and Learn* feature in each chapter. *Stop, Look, and Learn* is a mid-chapter visual summary of the material found in the first part of the chapter. By providing students with this review, we encourage them to begin integrating the material into an overall understanding of the chapter even as they are reading the chapter for the first time.

What Do You Know? Assess Your Understanding

In addition to the *Let's Review!* questions at the end of each major section of the chapter, we have also included a more extensive self-assessment for students at the end of each chapter. This assessment, *What Do You Know? Assess Your Understanding*, is a twenty-question multiple choice practice test (with the answers provided at the bottom of the page) that allows students to evaluate their retention and understanding of the entire chapter. By self-assessing, students can better judge which concepts and/or sections of the chapter they should target for further study.

Look Back at What You've Learned

A visual summary of the chapter, entitled *Look Back at What You've Learned*, is also included in the end-of-chapter material to allow students to truly *see the big picture* of the chapter. In *Look Back at What You've Learned*, all the major concepts and theories of the chapter are brought together in a graphical format. This tool will be especially helpful to students who prefer to learn through visual means.

Available Supplements

Instructor Resources

Annotated Instructor's Edition
ISBN: 0-495-60411-9

Annotations include Technology Tips, Teaching Tips, and Discussion Tips, many of which have been shown to be effective teaching tools by the authors in their own classes. Web addresses for the technology topics are referenced in the Annotated Instructor's Edition and the full web links can be found on the Instructor's Resource website.

Instructor's Resource Manual
ISBN: 0-495-60316-3

Written by Thomas Hancock, Gainesville State College. A comprehensive resource, the Instructor's Manual contains tools for each chapter of the text. The contents include lecture topics, activities, student projects, journal prompts, web links, video suggestions, and handouts.

PowerLecture™ CD-ROM (with JoinIn™ and ExamView®)
ISBN: 0-495-60318-X

This one-stop digital library, lecture, and class preparation tool contains ready-to-use slides in Microsoft® PowerPoint® (written by Christine Vanchella, Ph.D.), as well as the full Instructor's Manual and Test Bank in Microsoft Word® format. PowerLecture brings together all of your media resources in one place, including an image library with graphics from the book itself, video clips, and more. PowerLecture also includes ExamView testing software with all the test items from the printed Test Bank in electronic format, enabling you to create customized tests in print or online, as well as JoinIn Student Response System, offering instant assessment and better student results.

Test Bank
ISBN: 0-495-60317-1

Written by Clayton L. Teem II, Gainesville State College, Ellen Pastorino, and Susann Doyle-Portillo. The Test Bank includes over 200 questions for each text chapter (multiple choice, true/false, and essay).

ABC Videos: Introductory Psychology
Volume I ISBN: 0-495-50306-1
Volume II ISBN: 0-495-59637-X
Volume III ISBN: 0-495-60490-9

Available to adopters, these ABC videos feature short, high-interest clips about current studies and research in psychology. These videos are perfect to start discussions or to enrich lectures. Topics include brain damage, measuring IQ, sleep patterns, obsessive-compulsive disorder, obedience to authority, rules of attraction, and much more.

WebTutor™
WebCT Printed Access Card ISBN: 0-495-83713-X
Blackboard Printed Access Card ISBN: 0-495-83714-8

The ultimate in online course management! Available on WebCT® and Blackboard®. With the text-specific, preformatted content and total flexibility of WebTutor you can easily create and manage your own course website! "Out of the box" or customizable, this versatile online tool is preloaded with content from this text, including sample syllabi, additional quizzing, and more, organized by text chapter. Customize the content in any way you choose, from uploading images and other resources, to adding web links, to creating your own practice materials.

Student Supplements

Study Guide
ISBN: 0-495-60315-5

Written by Susann Doyle-Portillo and Ellen Pastorino specifically to accompany *What Is Psychology? Essentials*, the *Study Guide* offers students the following for each chapter:

- *Learning Objectives*
- *Chapter Overview* narrative chapter summary
- *Chapter Outline* with space for student note taking
- A *Key Points* list of important terms, definitions, and examples
- *Fill-in Review of the Chapter*, a fill-in-the-blank activity
- *Use It or Lose It!*, an application activity that requires students to use what they've learned in the chapter
- *Self-Check* quizzes using true/false and multiple choice questions
- *Short Answer Question* essay questions over chapter content
- *Label the Diagram* activity in which students label a diagram from the text
- *You Review*, a review activity that requires students to fill in information from the *You Review* text tables

CengageNOW™
Printed Access Card ISBN: 0-495-80503-3
Instant Access Code ISBN: 0-495-80502-5
www.cengage.com/login

This interactive online resource is the most exciting assessment-centered learning tool ever offered for this course. Through a series of diagnostic Pre- and Post-Tests (written by Dan Muhwezi) that you can assign, as well as media-rich Personalized Study Plans and the Cengage Learning eBook, students discover those areas of the text where they need to focus their efforts.

Also included with CengageNOW is the Psychology Resource Center, a powerful teaching and learning tool that brings psychology to life with a full library of original and classic video clips plus interactive learning modules tied to all of the topics covered in an introductory psychology course. Organized by topic, the Psychology Resource Center is easy to navigate by students to find learning resources and instructors will also find it an amazing lecture resource to easily stream multimedia into their classrooms.

While students can use CengageNOW with no instructor setup or involvement, an Instructor Gradebook is available to monitor student progress.

Book Companion Website
www.cengage.com/psychology/pastorino

Students will have access to a rich array of teaching and learning resources. There are chapter-correlated study tools, such as tutorial quizzes, a pronunciation glossary, flash cards, Internet exercises, web links, and more.

Writing Papers in Psychology: A Student Guide to Research Papers, Essays, Proposals, Posters, and Handouts
ISBN-10: 0-534-53331-0
ISBN-13: 978-0-534-53331-1

This brief, inexpensive, and easy-to-use "how-to" manual has helped thousands of students in psychology and related fields with the task of writing term papers and reports. This best seller includes a wealth of information and has been updated to reflect the latest APA Style Manual.

Writing With Style: APA Style Made Easy
ISBN-10: 0-495-09972-4
ISBN-13: 978-0-495-09972-7

This accessible and invaluable workbook-style reference guide will help your students smoothly make the transitions from writing for composition classes to writing for psychology classes. In her Third Edition of *Writing With Style*, author Lenore T. Szuchman quickly and succinctly provides the basics of style presented by the Fifth Edition of the APA's Publication Manual. Dr. Szuchman's years of experience teaching writing-intensive courses give her an inside track on the trouble spots students often encounter when writing papers and dealing with APA style. Her students play a large part in tailoring this guide's exercises to ensure an effective learning experience. This unique workbook format offers both a quick reference to APA style and interactive exercises that give students a chance to practice what they've learned.

Challenging Your Preconceptions: Thinking Critically About Psychology
ISBN-10: 0-534-26739-4
ISBN-13: 978-0-534-26739-4

This supplement supports the development of critical thinking skills necessary to success in the introductory psychology course. The chapter sequence mirrors the organization of the typical introductory psychology course. In the first chapter, the author identifies seven characteristics of critical thinkers, and in the following chapters he dissects a challenging issue in the discipline and models critical thinking for the reader. Each chapter concludes with an analysis of the process, exercises for the student, and extensive references. This useful volume supports the full semester of the course.

Critical Thinking in Psychology: Separating Sense from Nonsense

ISBN-10: 0-534-63459-1
ISBN-13: 978-0-534-63459-1

Do your students have the tools to distinguish between the true science of human thought and behavior from pop psychology? John Ruscio's book provides a tangible and compelling framework for making that distinction. Because we are inundated with "scientific" claims, the author does not merely differentiate science and pseudoscience, but goes further to teach the fundamentals of scientific reasoning on which students can base their evaluation of information.

Cross-Cultural Perspectives in Introductory Psychology

ISBN-10: 0-534-54653-6
ISBN-13: 978-0-534-54653-6

With its 27 carefully selected cross-cultural articles, this book enriches the introductory psychology course—helping students to better understand the similarities and differences among the peoples of the world as they relate to psychological principles, concepts, and issues.

Introduction to Positive Psychology

ISBN-10: 0-534-64453-8
ISBN-13: 978-0-534-64453-8

This brief paperback presents in-depth coverage of the relatively new area of positive psychology. Topically organized, it looks at how positive psychology relates to stresses and health within such traditional research areas as developmental, clinical, personality, motivational, social, and behavioral psychology.

Acknowledgments

Writing a college textbook has been an exhausting yet rewarding experience. We are ordinary community college professors who teach four to six classes every semester, so we are often writing in whatever free time we have—weekends, nights, and holidays. We do not live in a "publish or perish" environment. Instead we are valued for our contributions to student learning and service to our institutions. Yet, we have grown so much as educators and psychologists in tackling

this project. This would not have been possible without the support of many people who deserve our acknowledgement.

We would like to thank Tim Grogan at Valencia Community College, and Chuck Karcher, Amy Reeder, and Dean Michael Stoy from Gainesville State College for their administrative support. Our deepest gratitude and thanks also go out to the great people who have helped with both the development of *What Is Psychology? 2e* and this *Essentials* edition: Michele Sordi, Jaime Perkins, Kristin Makarewycz, Kimberly Russell, Liz Rhoden, Nicole Lee Petel, Mary Noel, Vernon Boes, Rachel Guzman, Paige Leeds, Sarah Worrell, Roman and Kate Barnes, and everyone else at Cengage/Wadsworth and Lachina Publishing who help make these texts the best possible learning tools for students everywhere.

We also would like to thank the following reviewers for their insightful comments and expert guidance in developing this text:

Brenda J. Beagle
John Tyler Community College

Amy A. Bradshaw
Embry-Riddle Aeronautical University

Wendy Brooks
College of the Desert

Adria DiBenedetto
Quinnipiac University

Kimberley Duff
Cerritos College

Jean M. Egan
Asnuntuck Community College

Kimberly Fairchild
Manhattan College

Keith D. Foust
Shasta College

Laura Fry
Coconino Community College

Terry Lyn Funston
Sauk Valley Community College

Andrea Goldstein
Keiser University

Pete Gram
Pensacola Junior College

Julie A. Gurner
Community College of Philadelphia

Jill Haasch
Glenville State College

Sean C. Hill
Lewis and Clark Community College

Bobby Hutchison
Modesto Junior College

Michael Leffingwell
Tarrant County College, NE Campus

John Lu
Concordia University Irvine

George Martinez
Somerset Community College

Robin P. McHaelen
University of Connecticut, School of Social Work

Antoinette R. Miller
Clayton State University

Nancy Murray
Vermont Technical College

Linda Petroff
Central Community College

Andrea Rashtian
California State University Northridge

Illeana P. Rodriguez
Triton College

Gwendolyn Scott
University of Houston-Downtown

Ronald W. Stoffey
Kutztown University of Pennsylvania

Eva Szeli
Arizona State University

Jeff Wachsmuth
Napa Valley College

We would also like to thank our friends and colleagues at Gainesville State College and Valencia Community College for their support and latitude over the past decade. Special gratitude goes to the students who helped shape this text by offering their stories, insights, and curiosities about psychology to our readers: Amber Brandt, Franco Chevalier, Daniel, Diana Flores, Pamela Hunter, Edgar Lituma, Tamara Stewart, Tyler Larko, Joshua Kennedy, Carolanne Parker, Megan Arispe, Paige Redmon, Jonathan Gantes, Jean-Paul Eslava, Cristofer Arthurs, Brooke Landers, Heather Lacis, Zach Veatch, Joseph Vickers, Jeff Wright, Cristian Caceres, Erica Breglio, Karen Arevalo, Candace Kendrick, Christie Knight, Emily Phillips, Amber Maner, Nick Tatum, Holly Sosebee, Rebecca Mboh, Erick Hernandez, Cassidy Turner, Taylor Evans, Pam Lively, Clinton Blake Roberts, Bredron Lytle, Ally Burke, Angel Rosa-Rivera, Bianca Vaughan, Brittany Bryant, Brittany Teller, Carla Belliard, Charlotte Anderson, Christian Forero, Danie Lipschutz, David Melendez, Dierdra Torres, Emmanuel Cotto, Erika Larkins, Jaelynn Packer, Jennifer Deane, Jesse Madonna, Jose Moreno, Junior Louis, Justen Carter, Katiria Mejia, Kayla Campana, Keiran Siddiqi, Kiara Suarez, Kristin MacPherson, Laura Fernandez, Lesley Manzano, Lisandra Machado, Melissa Tyndale, Michael Horsfall, Nick DeGori, Niesha Hazzard, Paola Chavez, Ramon Velez, Rebecca Cantarero, Richard Nieves, Saqib Abbas, Sarah Knych, Sheila Quinones, Susy Alvarez, Takese McKenzie, Tiffany Slowey, Victor Ocasio, Yanilsa Osoria, Michelle Lewis, Tawnya Brown, Crystal Athas Thatcher, Micaiah Frazier, and Mayra Rosario.

We would also like to thank the thousands of other students we have worked with over the years. In your own way, each of you has helped us to become better teachers and better people. Our hope is that this book will touch many other students and foster an interest in and passion for psychology.

Finally, we would like to thank our families. Susann would like to thank her husband, Eddie, for his loving support and for selflessly allowing her to put work first on far too many occasions. Ellen would like to thank her husband, Dave, for his technical assistance, his tireless rereading of material, and his patience and support through all the frustration, deadlines, and apprehension. Love is indeed something that you do.

1

What Is PSYCHOLOGY?

© Simon Jarratt/Corbis

It was the first day of the new college semester. Parking as usual was a challenge. Christian finally found a spot, parked his car, and headed toward the campus buildings. While grabbing a coffee at the college café, he ran into his friend Andrew. "Hey, man, what's up?" he asked. "Not much," Andrew replied. "Just getting java before I head to class." "What are you taking?" Christian asked. "Well, I've got a math class and a music appreciation class tomorrow. Today, I've got oceanography and introduction to psychology. I'm heading to the psych class now." Christian smiled, "Cool, dude, I've got that psych class too." The two students grabbed their coffees and headed toward the psychology building, continuing their conversation. Andrew asked, "What do you think the course will be about?" "Probably how you feel about things. Ought to be an easy A—like being with Dr. Phil all semester," Christian joked. Andrew laughed. "Yeah, I guess we'll see how screwed up we are and get a lot of therapy." "Speak for yourself," Christian kidded. "I figure it's just commonsense stuff, things your parents and grandparents have been telling you since you were a kid. Shouldn't be too hard." Andrew nodded his head in agreement as they arrived at the college classroom. "Let's take a seat in the back, so we don't have to share our feelings too much," Christian whispered. "Sure thing," Andrew replied. The two young men found a seat in the back and waited for the class to begin.

© David Young-Wolff/Alamy

Many students hold misconceptions about the field of psychology.

What Is Psychology?

Learning Objectives

- Identify common misconceptions about the field.
- Define psychology.

Welcome to the world of **psychology**, the scientific study of behavior and mental processes. But what exactly does that include? Behavior includes actions, feelings, and biological states. Mental processes include problem solving, intelligence, and memory, to name just a few. Psychology is a science because psychologists conduct research in accord with the **scientific method**. They analyze the behavior of humans as well as other species.

Psychology is probably one of the few disciplines in which students come to the first class believing they already know much about the topic. We see psychologists and psychiatrists on talk shows (Dr. Phil, Dr. Drew) and listen to them on the radio. We frequently see them depicted on television (*The Sopranos, Monk*) and in the movies (*Basic Instinct 2, Running with Scissors, I, Robot, Prime*). Many of these portrayals are quite entertaining, but they do not always represent psychology accurately. As a result, the public image of the discipline tends to be distorted.

The purpose of this textbook is to help you develop a deeper understanding of psychology. In this chapter, we explain what psychologists do, how they think, and where they work. It is a general overview of the field of psychology, an introduction to the more specific areas of psychology discussed in subsequent chapters. We describe how psychology became a science, and what the field is like today. We also describe the goals of psychological research and how psychologists study behavior.

Each chapter begins with former students relating how psychological principles and concepts have helped them better understand their jobs, their relationships, and their world. We hope that by reading these real-life stories, you will find psychological topics easier to understand and will be better able to apply psychological principles and concepts to your own life.

Correcting Common Misconceptions About the Field of Psychology

You are probably reading this book because you have enrolled in a general psychology course. Your expectations of what you will learn have been influenced by your general impressions of psychology. Much of the psychological information presented in the media focuses on practitioners, therapy, and helping others, and you—like the students in the opening section—may have the impression that psychology is all about how you feel and how you can feel better. It is true that many psychologists (around 55%) counsel or otherwise treat clients, yet many of these professionals hold a doctorate degree in psychology, which required that they study scientific methodology and complete a considerable amount of research.

Psychology is rooted in scientific research. The information in this book is research based. Every idea put forward in the field is subject to scientific study. You will notice that many statements in this text are followed by names and years in parentheses—for example, (Pastorino, 2009). These text citations refer to the scientific studies on which the stated conclusions are based, with the researcher names(s) and date of the study. The complete research citations (■ FIGURE 1.1) can be found in the reference section at the end of the book.

A psychologist's explanation of a particular behavior is generally presented as a theory. A **theory** is an explanation of why and how a behavior occurs. It does not explain a particular

psychology the scientific study of behavior and mental processes

scientific method a systematic process used by psychologists for testing hypotheses about behavior

theory an explanation of why and how a behavior occurs

behavior for all people, but it provides general guidelines that summarize facts and help us organize research on a particular subject.

We all, at times, fancy ourselves as psychologists. We interact with people all the time, we observe others' behaviors, and we have our own personal experiences. Therefore, we might naturally think that we already know a lot about psychology. People often behave the way we think they will behave, so psychology seems as though it is just common sense. However, we often overlook the examples of behavior that don't confirm our expectations or support our preexisting beliefs. Psychologists systematically test their ideas about behavior using the prescribed methods and procedures we will describe later in this chapter.

Consider this example. In heterosexual relationships, who do you believe falls in love more quickly, men or women? Many people in our culture believe that women are more emotional, so you might assume that women would tend to fall in love more quickly. However, psychological research suggests that men are generally quicker to fall in love (Kanin, Davidson, & Scheck, 1970). As you can see, the commonsense conclusion is in error. Psychological findings do not always confirm our everyday observations about behavior. By objectively measuring and testing our ideas and observations about behavior, we can determine which ideas are more likely to stand up to scientific scrutiny.

Most students entering a general psychology class, like Christian and Andrew, expect to focus on diagnosing and treating mental disorders. Although some psychologists specialize in mental illness, many others work in academic settings, in the business world, in education, or in government agencies. Psychology is an extremely diverse field, and new specialties are appearing each year. Psychologists are interested in numerous topics, including learning, memory, aging, development, gender, motivation, emotion, sports, criminal behavior, and many other subjects. We cannot cover every area of psychology in this textbook, but we will give you an overview of the main areas of psychological research.

> **APA Style:**
>
> **Author, A. A., Author, B. B., & Author, C. C. (Year). Title of article:**
>
> **Subtitle of article. _Title of Periodical or Journal, Vol #_, pages.**
>
> Example:
>
> Snibbe, A. C. (2003). Cultural psychology: Studying the exotic other.
>
> _APS Observer, 16_, 30–32.

FIGURE 1.1 Reference Citations in Psychology

The References section at the end of this book lists the complete source for each citation. Here is the APA style format for psychological references. The citation for this particular reference would appear in the text as (Snibbe, 2003).

You Asked...

What exactly do psychologists do, other than treat mental disorders or help people cope?

PAOLA CHAVEZ, STUDENT

Who do you believe falls in love more quickly in heterosexual relationships, men or women? Psychological findings do not always confirm our commonsense notions.

Psychology Will Teach You About Critical Thinking

As you can see from the misconceptions we've poked holes in, psychology requires critical thinking, and psychological theories generally don't definitively explain the behavior of all people. To think like a psychologist, you must analyze and evaluate information. You must be able to distinguish true psychological information from _pseudoscience_. Pseudoscientific findings sound persuasive, but they are not necessarily based on scientific procedures. Their conclusions may go far beyond the scope of their actual data. For example, have

Anne Ackermann/Getty Images

you ever heard that people use only 10% of their brains? Many college students believe this false statement despite evidence that shows it is not true (Higbee & Clay, 1998). To think like a psychologist, you must be skeptical rather than accepting about explanations of behavior.

Critical thinking involves analyzing concepts and applying them to other situations. To foster these abilities, *Let's Review!* sections at the end of each main topic offer several questions to test your understanding of the concepts just presented, because learning is easier when you can digest information in small amounts. The *What Do You Know? Assess Your Understanding* at the end of the chapter helps you test your knowledge further.

Because we all engage in behavior, much of the information in this text will have application to your life. We all dream, remember, like or dislike others, are motivated, have high or low self-esteem, suffer from bouts of depression, behave aggressively, help others, learn, perceive, and use our senses. Consequently, we recommend that you apply the material in this text to your own behavior as much as possible. This will increase your interest in the text, and you will study more effectively.

Let's Review!

In this section we defined psychology. For a quick check of your understanding, answer these questions.

1. Which of the following statements is *true*?
   a. Psychology is just common sense.
   b. Psychologists only study abnormal behavior.
   c. Psychologists know why people behave the way that they do.
   d. Psychologists test ideas about behavior according to the scientific method.

2. Which of the following topics would a psychologist most likely study?
   a. Weather patterns in Africa
   b. Memory changes in adults
   c. Causes of the Vietnam War
   d. All of the above

Answers 1. d; 2. b

The Origins of Psychology

Learning Objective

- Describe the early schools of psychology and identify the major figures that influenced its development.

Psychology has been described as having "a long past but only a short history" (Ebbinghaus, 1910, p. 9). Although psychology did not formally become a science until the 1870s, people have always been interested in explaining behavior. The roots of psychology can be traced back to philosophy and medicine in ancient Egypt, Greece, and Rome. Although these issues were not considered "psychological" at the time, doctors and philosophers debated many of the same issues that concern modern psychologists.

Early Approaches: Structuralism, Functionalism, and Psychoanalysis

Traditionally, psychology's birth is linked with the establishment by Wilhelm Wundt of the first psychology laboratory in 1879 in Leipzig, Germany. However, the focus of psychology was not the same in every country, resulting in a field that was broad and complex, with many avenues of exploration.

WILHELM WUNDT AND STRUCTURALISM

For Wilhelm Wundt (1832–1920), the goal of psychology was to study conscious processes of the mind and the body. He wanted to know what thought processes enabled us to experience the external world. In particular, Wundt attempted to detail the *structure* of our mental experiences. Like a chemist who questions what elements combine to create different substances, Wundt questioned what elements, when combined, would explain mental processes. Wundt's view that mental experiences were created by different elements is referred to as **structuralism**, a term coined not by Wundt but by his student Edward Titchener. To identify the structure of thought, Wundt used a process known as **introspection**, a self-observation technique. Trained observers were presented with an event and asked to describe their mental processes. The observations were repeated many times. From these introspections, Wundt and his students identified two basic mental processes: sensations and feelings.

YOUR TURN – ACTIVE LEARNING

To illustrate the nature of introspection, look at the photo of the object below. If you were asked to describe this object, what would you say? How do you know that the object is a potato? Does the object fit your visual image or memory of a potato? That is, does it look like a potato? If it were in front of you right now, how else might you conclude it is a potato? Does it smell like a potato, taste like a potato, and feel like a potato? Using your senses, you deduce that the object before you is a potato.

Apply the technique of introspection to determine how you know what this object is.

© David Young-Wolff/PhotoEdit

Wundt's research went beyond introspection and structuralism to encompass a very broad view of psychology. He conducted detailed studies on color vision, visual illusions, attention, and feelings. He also influenced the field of psychology through his students, many of whom went on to establish psychology departments and laboratories in the United States.

WILLIAM JAMES AND FUNCTIONALISM

William James (1842–1910) had visited Wundt's laboratory but did not share Wundt's focus on introspection and mental processes. Rather, James came to believe that psychological processes developed through the process of *evolution*, an idea that was then quite new. Evolution refers to the development of a species—the process by which, through a series of changes over time, humans have acquired behaviors and characteristics that distinguish them from other species. For James, the question was not what elements contribute to one's experience but rather what *function* does the event serve for

structuralism an early psychological perspective concerned with identifying the basic elements of experience

introspection observing one's own thoughts, feelings, or sensations

William James (1842–1910) is associated with functionalism.

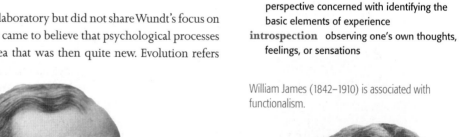

Wilhelm Wundt (1832–1920) wanted to know what psychological processes enable us to experience the external world. His approach today is referred to as structuralism.

© Bettmann/Corbis

© Bettmann/Corbis

Darwin's finches illustrated the interaction between genes and adaptation to the environment. The different species originated from common ancestors (genes), yet differences in their beaks arose as they adapted to different food supplies on each island.

the person or animal. How does a particular behavior help an organism adapt to its environment and thereby increase its chances of surviving and reproducing? James's perspective on psychology became known as **functionalism**.

Functionalism's focus on the adaptive value of behavior was influenced by Charles Darwin's theory of evolution. Darwin's theory speculated that certain behaviors or traits that enhance survival are *naturally selected*. For example, Darwin had collected several different types of birds in the Galapagos Islands. The birds were all about the same size but had different beaks (see photo). Through research with other scientists in London, Darwin discovered that the birds were all finches but that each species was uniquely related to a specific island. Darwin thought that the different species had been formed from a small number of common ancestors. The differences in their beaks could be attributed to adapting to different food supplies on each island. According to James, if human behavior is naturally selected like Darwin's finches' beaks, it is important for psychologists to understand the function, or survival value, of a behavior.

Functionalism was not the whole of James's work in the young field of psychology. James suggested applications of psychology to teaching, creating the field of *educational psychology*. The James-Lange theory of emotion, formulated by James and a Danish physiologist, Carl Lange, at about the same time, describes how physical sensations give rise to emotions (more on this in Chapter 8). In addition, James published books on religious experiences and philosophy. James's open-mindedness also influenced psychology when he became intrigued by the unorthodox ideas of a Viennese physician named Sigmund Freud.

SIGMUND FREUD AND PSYCHOANALYTIC THEORY

Sigmund Freud is probably the best known historical figure in psychology, more familiar to students than Wundt or James. Freud's ideas permeate Western culture in music, media, advertising, art, and humor—a testament to his influence and importance.

As a European Jew, the only professions open to Freud (1856–1939) were law and medicine. Freud opted for medicine, focusing on neurology and disorders of the nervous system. He began seeing people with all kinds of "nervous" disorders, such as an intense fear of horses or heights or the sudden paralysis of an arm. He began asking patients to express any and every thought that occurred to them, no matter how trivial or unpleasant. Freud theorized that encouraging patients to say whatever came to mind allowed them to recall forgotten memories that seemed to underlie their problems. This process, known today as *free association*, is one element of *psychoanalysis*, a therapy that Freud developed.

From these experiences, Freud came to believe that the *unconscious* plays a crucial role in human behavior. For Freud, the unconscious was that part of the mind that includes impulses, behaviors, and desires that we are unaware of but that influence our behavior. Until this time, much of psychology had focused on conscious mental processes.

Freud's focus on the unconscious was unique and led to his formulation of **psychoanalytic theory**. According to this theory, humans are similar to animals in that they possess basic sexual and aggressive instincts that motivate behavior. However, unlike animals, humans can reason and think,

functionalism an early psychological perspective concerned with how behavior helps people adapt to their environment

psychoanalytic theory Sigmund Freud's view that emphasizes the influence of unconscious desires and conflicts on behavior

Charles Darwin's theory of natural selection influenced the beginnings of psychological research.

Sigmund Freud's (1856–1939) focus on the unconscious was unique and led to his formulation of psychoanalytic theory.

especially as they mature. In childhood we learn to use these conscious reasoning abilities to deal with and to suppress our basic sexual and aggressive desires so that we can be viewed approvingly by others. For Freud, the conflict between the conscious reasoning part of the mind and the unconscious instinctual one was key to understanding human behavior. Although controversial, Freud's theory dominated European psychology. However, in the early 1900s in the United States Freud's ideas were overshadowed by another approach called *behaviorism*.

Behaviorism: A True Science of Psychology

In the 1920s, in the United States functionalism was slowly being replaced by a school of thought referred to as **behaviorism**. A growing number of psychologists believed that in order for psychology to be taken seriously as a "true" science, it must focus on observable behavior and not on the mind. You can't see the mind or what a person thinks; you can only see what a person does. Behaviorists believed that only overt, observable behaviors could truly be measured consistently from person to person. One of the most vocal proponents of this school of thought was John B. Watson (1878–1958).

JOHN WATSON'S BEHAVIORISM

Watson was influenced by Russian physiologist Ivan Pavlov's studies of digestion in dogs. While measuring and analyzing the first process of digestion (salivation), Pavlov noticed that his dogs started to salivate before he gave them meat powder. When the experiments first started, the salivation had occurred only *after* the dogs were given the meat powder. To further study this curious change in response, Pavlov performed experiments to train the dogs to salivate to other nonfood stimuli. (You will learn more about Pavlov's classic experiments in Chapter 5.)

Pavlov's experiments were important to Watson as examples of how behavior is the product of stimuli and responses. To further his point, Watson and his associate, Rosalie Rayner, performed an experiment on a 9-month-old infant named Albert. Watson first presented Little Albert with a white rat. Albert played with the white rat and showed no fear of it. Knowing that infants do fear loud noises, Watson paired the two stimuli, first presenting the rat to Albert and then presenting a loud gong sound behind Albert's head. Little Albert reacted to the loud noise with the startle, or fear, response. Over and over again, Watson repeated the procedure of pairing the two stimuli—presenting the rat followed by the loud gong. Then, when Watson presented the rat to Albert with no gong, the infant responded with the startle response. Watson had conditioned Little Albert to fear a white rat, a rat that Albert had played with earlier without fear. This demonstrated for Watson that observable stimuli and responses should be the focus of psychology. Unfortunately for Watson, a personal scandal resulted in his dismissal as the chair of the psychology department at Johns Hopkins University (Buckley, 1989).

© Michael Newman/PhotoEdit

Can you identify the Freudian symbols in this advertisement?

behaviorism a psychological perspective that emphasizes the study of observable responses and behavior

Ivan Pavlov's studies illustrated that behavior is the product of stimuli and responses.

© History of American Psychology, U. of Akron, Akron, Ohio

John Watson (1878–1958) believed in behaviorism—that only observable stimuli and responses should be studied by psychologists.

© Bettmann/Corbis

B. F. Skinner's (1904–1990) behaviorism emphasizes the influence of consequences on behavior.

B. F. SKINNER AND BEHAVIORAL CONSEQUENCES

Despite Watson's departure from psychology, behaviorism remained strong in the United States, partially due to the work of B. F. Skinner (1904–1990). Skinner, like Watson, believed that psychology should focus on observable behavior. But Skinner added a dimension to Watson's framework: *consequences*. Skinner believed that psychologists should look not only at the stimuli in the environment that cause a particular response but also at what happens to a person or animal after the response—what Skinner called the consequences of a behavior. To illustrate consequences, let's look at Little Albert's behavior from Skinner's perspective. Once Albert was afraid of the rat, how would he act when he saw it? If Albert moved away from the rat, his behavior effectively reduced his fear. Feeling less fear or anxiety is a good (positive) consequence, or outcome. Whenever Albert saw the fearsome rat again, he probably moved away even faster. Skinner asserted that positive consequences, such as the reduction of Albert's anxiety, would lead him to engage in the same behavior again. Negative consequences, or outcomes that are not liked, would lessen Albert's desire to engage in the behavior again. We know these processes as *reinforcement* and *punishment*, topics that are explored further in Chapter 5.

Beyond Behaviorism: Humanism and Cognitive Psychology

Behaviorism was a dominant force in American psychology until the 1960s. By that time, it became evident that this one theory could not account for all behaviors. This criticism, combined with the social climate of the times, opened the door for other views on behavior and a willingness to explore topics previously ignored.

THE HUMANISTS

Discontent with behaviorism and the social upheaval of the 1960s led to a growing interest in an approach toward treatment called **humanism**. Many psychologists did not accept that humans were governed by stimuli and responses, with no will of their own to change their behavior. In the 1960s, societal values were rapidly changing, and the civil rights movement and the Vietnam War sparked widespread civil disobedience. Many young Americans were endorsing women's rights, free love, and free will. Psychology was changing too, and humanists emphasized that everyone possesses inner resources for personal growth and development. The goal of humanistic therapy, therefore, would be to help people use these inner resources to make healthier choices and thus lead better lives. Humanism stressed the free will of individuals to choose their own patterns of behavior. Well-known humanists include Abraham Maslow and Carl Rogers. You will read more about their ideas in Chapters 8 and 12.

COGNITIVE PSYCHOLOGY

While humanism was changing how psychologists were treating clients, changes were also occurring in research psychology. Researchers were becoming disenchanted with the limits of testing stimuli, responses, and consequences in the laboratory, and there was renewed interest in the study of mental processes. Research expanded to subjects such as memory, problem solving, and decision making. However, unlike the earlier functionalism and structuralism, this new study of mental processes was based much more on experimental methods. Acknowledging that mental processes are not directly observable to the eye, scientists believed that reasonable inferences about mental processes could be made from performance data. For example, in studying memory processes in children, a researcher can ask children what strategies or techniques they use to remember a list of items. If children using a particular strategy (Strategy A) remember more compared to children using a different strategy (Strategy B), then one can infer that there must be something about Strategy A that facilitates memory. This conclusion is reasonable even though we can't directly see the children use the techniques. Such reasoning led to much experimental research on mental processes, or *cognition*. By the 1980s the study of cognitive processes, **cognitive psychology**, was a part of mainstream psychology.

humanism a psychological perspective that emphasizes the personal growth and potential of humans

cognitive psychology the study of mental processes such as reasoning and problem solving

biological perspective focuses on physical causes of behavior

Let's Review!

In this section we discussed the early theories of psychology. For a quick check of your understanding, answer these questions.

1. Javier wants to know how aggression helps a person adapt to the environment. Which historical approach is Javier emphasizing?
   a. Structuralism   c. Functionalism
   b. Psychoanalysis   d. Humanism

2. Karena believes that elements, when combined, can explain our mental processes. Which historical approach is Karena emphasizing?
   a. Structuralism   c. Functionalism
   b. Psychoanalysis   d. Humanism

3. Which of the following persons would be least likely to emphasize the influence of stimuli and responses on behavior?
   a. John Watson   c. Rosalie Rayner
   b. Carl Rogers   d. B. F. Skinner

Answers 1. c; 2. a; 3. b

Psychology in the Modern World

Learning Objectives

- Differentiate between the modern perspectives of psychology and understand the nature of the eclectic approach.

- Describe the training of a psychologist and discriminate among the different specialty areas of the profession.

Given the historical sketch of psychology we have just provided, it is probably no surprise to learn that modern psychology is a very broad profession. Not everyone agreed on how to explain behavior then, just as many debate the causes of behavior today. Many modern perspectives are an extension of the historical schools of thought. Here we discuss seven orientations or perspectives on behavior (■ FIGURE 1.2): *biological, evolutionary, cognitive, psychodynamic, behavioral, sociocultural,* and *humanistic.*

Modern Perspectives and the Eclectic Approach

Psychologists who adopt a **biological perspective** toward behavior look for a physical cause for a particular behavior. Genetics, chemical imbalances, and brain functioning are often the focus of this perspective (discussed more fully in Chapter 2). For example, knowing how the brain monitors motor behavior has enabled neuroscientists to develop devices to assist people with severe motor deficits or spinal cord injuries (Srinivasan, Eden, Mitter, & Brown, 2007).

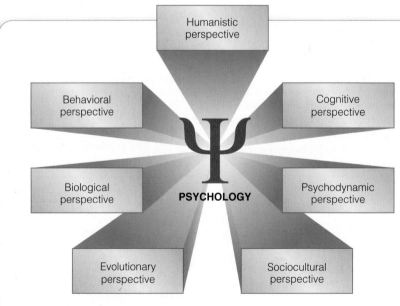

FIGURE

1.2 Psychological Perspectives

Just as a photograph or a piece of art can be examined from many different angles, so too can behavior. We call these angles perspectives. Each offers a somewhat different picture of why people behave as they do. Taken as a whole, these perspectives underscore the complex nature of behavior.

Neuroscience Applies to Your World:

Restoring and Enhancing Motor Movement

With EEG technology and other methods, neuroscientists have been able to measure how a person's body movement causes nerve cells in the brain to fire. They can then use this information to design prosthetic devices, such as robotic arms, that work in much the same way. These appliances can help improve the functioning of people with spinal cord injuries and other severe motor deficits.

© Brad Wrobleski/Masterfile

Very closely aligned to the biological perspective is the **evolutionary perspective**. This approach is similar to the biological approach in that the cause of behavior is biological. However, this is where the similarity ends. The evolutionary perspective proposes that natural selection is the process at work. Behaviors that increase your chances of surviving are favored or selected over behaviors that decrease your chances of surviving. Remember James's functionalism? One could say that James was an early evolutionary psychologist. Similarly, this approach analyzes whether a particular behavior increases a person's ability to adapt to the environment, thus increasing the chances of surviving, reproducing, and passing one's genes on to future generations.

A **cognitive perspective** explains behavior as the product of thoughts and interpretations based on memory, expectations, beliefs, problem solving, or decision making. A cognitive view focuses on how people process information and on how that process may influence behavior. For example, in explaining depression, a cognitive approach focuses on how people who are depressed think and perceive the world differently from people who are not depressed. You will learn more about cognitive processes in Chapters 6 and 7, when we discuss such topics as memory, problem solving, thinking, decision making, intelligence, and language.

The **psychodynamic perspective** is a collective term that refers to those assumptions about behavior originally conceived by Freud, which have been modified by his followers.

evolutionary perspective focuses on how evolution and natural selection cause behavior

cognitive perspective focuses on how mental processes influence behavior

psychodynamic perspective focuses on internal unconscious mental processes, motives, and desires that may explain behavior

The psychodynamic view focuses on internal, often unconscious mental processes, motives, and desires or childhood conflicts to explain behavior. For example, in the Virginia Tech shooting in 2007, Seung-Hui Cho entered several campus buildings and shot at teachers and classmates, killing 32 people and wounding many others before committing suicide. The psychodynamic view might suggest that Seung-Hui had some frustrated desires or unresolved childhood conflicts that erupted into hostility and anger that he unleashed on his classmates and professors. These conflicts and frustrated desires also may explain why Seung-Hui was not able to control his hostile feelings—feelings that everyone has from time to time but does not act upon.

The **behavioral perspective** focuses on external causes of behavior. It looks at how stimuli in our environment and/or the rewards and punishments we receive influence our behavior. This approach suggests that behavior is learned and is influenced by other people and events. For example, if a student studies and then aces an exam, that reward may encourage her to study again the next time. If she only gets an average score, merely passing the test may not be rewarding enough to encourage the student to study for future exams. This perspective stems from Watson's and Skinner's behaviorist views (more on this in Chapter 5).

The **sociocultural perspective** adopts a wider view of the impact of the environment on behavior. It suggests that your society or culture influences your actions. Consider the fact that the United States has one of the highest teenage pregnancy rates among countries in the developed world. The sociocultural perspective would attribute this phenomenon to aspects of society such as sexual values, changes in family structure, or the lack of connectedness among people in neighborhoods and communities. Countries that have lower teenage pregnancy rates, such as Japan, may have experienced fewer or altogether different social changes. Sociocultural views will be evident throughout this textbook when differences due to culture, income level, or gender are highlighted.

The **humanistic perspective** explains behavior as stemming from your choices and free will. These choices are influenced by your self-concept (how you think of yourself) and by your self-esteem (how you feel about yourself). This view of the self and feelings toward the self direct you to choose certain behaviors over others. For example, if you see yourself as a low achiever in school, you may be less likely to take challenging courses or to apply yourself in the courses that you do take. Humanistic views of behavior are explored in Chapters 12 and 14.

Most psychologists do not rigidly adhere to just one of these perspectives but are likely to take what is referred to as an **eclectic approach** to explain behavior. This eclectic approach integrates or combines several perspectives to provide a more complete, yet complex picture of behavior. ■ YOU REVIEW 1.1 illustrates these approaches and shows how a combined approach gives a more expansive understanding of behavior than any single approach could.

Specialty Areas in Psychology

In addition to the various approaches or perspectives psychologists take, they also study a range of different aspects of behavior, which correspond to specialty areas of psychology. A number of these specialty areas are depicted in ■ TABLE 1.1, but keep in mind that there are many more. This diversity stems from the complexity of behavior and the interrelatedness of different areas. What a developmental psychologist studies, for example, is connected to and may have an impact on the work of social, clinical, and educational psychologists.

You Asked...

What different fields of psychology are there?   NICK DEGORI, STUDENT

behavioral perspective focuses on external, environmental causes of behavior

sociocultural perspective focuses on societal and cultural factors that may influence behavior

humanistic perspective focuses on how an individual's view of him- or herself and the world influences behavior

eclectic [ee-KLECK-tic] **approach** integrates and combines several perspectives when explaining behavior

Looking at Anxiety From Modern Perspectives

Psychologists can examine behavior from many different perspectives.

APPROACH	PERSPECTIVE
Biological	Anxiety is related to chemicals in the body or to genetics (heredity).
Evolutionary	Anxiety is an adaptive response that prepares one to respond to potential threats in the environment. This response helps humans survive because it warns them of danger and thereby helps them avoid situations or people that may harm them. However, in modern times, these threats tend to be ongoing: traffic jams, crowding, and the hectic pace of consumerism.
Cognitive	Anxiety is a reflection of the way people think. For example, people who are anxious may worry that everything will go wrong or engage in more pessimistic thinking than people who are not anxious.
Psychodynamic	Anxiety is the product of unresolved feelings of hostility, guilt, anger, or sexual attraction experienced in childhood.
Behavioral	Anxiety is a learned behavior much like Albert's fear of the white rat. It is a response that is associated with a specific stimulus or a response that has been rewarded.
Sociocultural	Anxiety is a product of a person's culture. In the United States, more women than men report being anxious and fearful, and this gender difference results from different socialization experiences. Men in the United States are raised to believe that they must not be afraid, so they are less likely to acknowledge or report anxiety. Women do not experience this pressure to hide their fears, so they are more likely to tell others that they are anxious and to seek treatment.
Humanistic	Anxiety is rooted in people's dissatisfaction with their real self (how they perceive themselves) as compared to their ideal self (how they want to be).
Eclectic	Anxiety stems from various sources depending on the individual. One person may be prone to anxiety because many people in his family are anxious and he has learned to be anxious from several experiences. Another person may be anxious because she is dissatisfied with herself and believes that everything always goes wrong in her life.

Gender, Ethnicity, and the Field of Psychology

In the early development of psychology, women and minorities generally were not allowed to receive graduate degrees even if they completed all the requirements. Despite these constraints and many other societal hurdles, several women and minority members contributed significantly to the field. In 1894, Margaret Washburn (1871–1939) became the first woman to be awarded a doctorate in psychology (Furumoto, 1989). Mary Calkins (1863–1930) became the first female president of the American Psychological Association in 1905. She studied at Harvard University with William James and performed several studies on the nature of memory. Christine Ladd-Franklin (1847–1930) studied color vision in the early 1900s. Karen Horney (1885–1952) focused on environmental and cultural factors that influence personality development (see Chapter 12).

Few degrees were awarded to minority students in the early 1900s. Gilbert Haven Jones (1883–1966) was the first African American to earn a doctorate in psychology—in Germany in 1909. Francis Sumner (1895–1954) was the first African American to receive a doctorate

Table 1.1 Specialty Areas in Psychology

SPECIALTY AREA	TOPICS OF INTEREST
Experimental psychology	Conducts research on sensation, perception, learning, motivation, and emotion.
Developmental psychology	Researches how we develop cognitively, socially, and emotionally over the life span.
Biopsychology	Researches the biological processes that underlie behavior, including genetics and heredity, chemicals in the brain, and hormones in the body.
Personality psychology	Researches how people differ in their individual traits, how people develop personality, whether personality traits can be changed, and how these qualities can be measured.
Social psychology	Researches how our beliefs, feelings, and behaviors are influenced by others, whether in the classroom, on an elevator, on the beach, on a jury, or at a football game.
Cognitive psychology	Studies mental processes such as decision making, problem solving, language, and memory.
Industrial/organizational (I/O) psychology	Examines the relationship between people and their work environments. May study issues such as increasing job satisfaction or decreasing employee absenteeism, or focus on understanding the dynamics of workplace behavior, such as leadership styles or gender differences in management styles.
Human factors psychology	Researches human capabilities as they apply to the design, operation, and maintenance of machines, systems, and environments to achieve optimal performance.
Forensic psychology	Works with mental health issues within the context of the legal system. May study a certain type of criminal behavior such as rape or murder, or may be asked to determine a person's competence to stand trial.
Cross-cultural psychology	Investigates cultural similarities and differences in psychological traits and behaviors.
Health psychology	Researches ways to promote health and prevent illness. May be concerned with issues such as diet and nutrition, exercise, and lifestyle choices that influence health.
Educational psychology	Researches how people learn and how variables in an educational environment influence learning. May develop materials and strategies to enhance learning.
Clinical psychology	Researches, assesses, and treats children, adolescents, and adults who are experiencing difficulty in functioning or who have a serious mental health disorder such as schizophrenia.
Counseling psychology	Researches, assesses, and treats children, adolescents, and adults who are experiencing adjustment difficulties.
School psychology	Assesses students' psychoeducational abilities and shares test results with teachers and parents to help them make decisions regarding the best educational placement for students.
Sports psychology	Investigates the mental and emotional aspects of physical performance.

in psychology from a university in the United States (in 1920) and is known as the father of African American psychology. Inez Prosser was the first African American female to be awarded a doctorate in psychology, in 1933 (Benjamin, Henry, & McMahon, 2005). Albert Sidney Beckham (1897–1964), whose studies focused on the nature of intelligence, established the first psychology laboratory at an all-Black institution of higher learning, Howard University. His wife, Ruth Howard, earned her psychology doctorate in 1934.

Have times changed for women and minorities in psychology? Women have indeed made great progress in the field of psychology. From 1920 to 1974, 23% of doctorates in

Known as the father of African American psychology, in 1920 Francis Sumner (1895–1954) was the first African American to receive a doctorate from a U.S. university.

The first woman to be awarded a doctorate in psychology was Margaret Washburn (1871–1939).

psychology went to women (APA, 2000b), and from 1960 to 1999 the greatest percentage increase in science and engineering doctorates earned by women was in psychology (NSF, 2006). Currently, far more women than men earn psychology degrees. In 2000, nearly 75% of students doing graduate-level work in psychology were women (Pate, 2001), and in 2005, 68% of the doctorates were awarded to women (Hoffer et al., 2006). Educational gains have to some extent been followed by progress in the careers of women in psychology. In 2003, 47% of the full-time psychology faculty at degree-granting institutions were women (U.S. Department of Education, 2005). However, female psychology faculty are less likely than males to be promoted to the rank of full professor. In a faculty salaries survey conducted by the APA in 2001, women represented only 25% of full professors yet held more than 50% of the lower ranks of assistant professor and lecturer (APA Research Office, 2001). In U.S. graduate departments of psychology, only 30% of tenured faculty members are women (APA Research Office, 2003). Although psychology has become more fully open to both men and women at the educational level, inequities at the professional level still exist.

Likewise, although the numbers of racial and ethnic minorities in psychology have increased, progress has been slow. While approximately 33% of the U.S. population are minorities (U.S. Census Bureau, 2006b), only 20% of newly enrolled students to graduate schools in psychology were minorities (APA Research Office, 2004). Between 1976 and 1993, close to 8% of all doctorates in psychology were awarded to minorities (APA, 1997); by 2005, that number had increased to almost 19% (Hoffer et al., 2006). This means that more than 8 out of 10 psychology doctorates are granted to Whites, regardless of gender. Despite increases in advanced degrees awarded to minorities, they are still underrepresented as faculty in colleges. In 2003, only 16% of all full-time psychology faculty members were minorities (U.S. Department of Education, 2005). The APA has established several programs to attract more minorities to the field of psychology. Only through efforts such as these will the field become as diversified in people as it is in scope.

Psychology Applies to Your World:

Training to Be a Psychologist

The majority of psychologists hold a doctorate in psychology—usually a Ph.D. (Doctor of Philosophy), sometimes a Psy.D. (Doctor of Psychology). A Ph.D. program focuses more on research, whereas the Psy.D. focuses more on clinical training. To obtain either doctorate, psychologists must first complete a bachelor's and a master's degree. The road to a doctoral degree is long, usually five to seven years after the undergraduate degree. Most doctoral programs require extensive study of research methods and statistics, and most require that students do some form of research.

Those who study psychology to the point of a bachelor's or master's degree aren't excluded from the profession. A bachelor's degree in psy-

You Asked...

What do you need to do to become a psychologist?

JOSE MORENO, STUDENT

chology may qualify you to assist psychologists in mental health centers or rehabilitation and correctional programs, or to serve as a research assistant. Without additional academic training, the opportunities for advancement in the profession are limited (Appleby, 1997), but 20% of students who graduate with a bachelor's degree in psychology do find work in social services or public relations. The skills an undergraduate psychology major acquires are valued by employers in business, industry, and government (APA, 2000a). As you can see in ■ FIGURE 1.3, psychology is a popular degree among undergraduate students.

A master's degree typically requires two to three years of graduate work. Master's-level psychologists may administer tests, conduct research, or counsel patients under the supervision of a doctoral-level psychologist. In a few states, they may be able to practice independently. They may teach in high schools or community colleges, work in corporate human resource departments, or work as school psychologists.

A large percentage of psychologists affiliated with colleges and universities teach and do research. Psychologists also work in school systems, hospitals, business, and government; others are in private practice treating clients (Pion, 1991; ■ FIGURE 1.4). Psychologists perform many functions in many different roles. Their job descriptions may include conducting research, counseling clients, and teaching college courses.

A related profession is *psychiatry*. A psychiatrist holds a medical degree (M.D.) and then specializes in mental health. A psychiatrist's graduate work includes a medical internship and residency, followed by training in the treatment of mental health disorders. As medical practitioners, psychiatrists have extensive training in the use of therapeutic drugs; they may dispense or prescribe medication and order medical procedures such as brain scans.

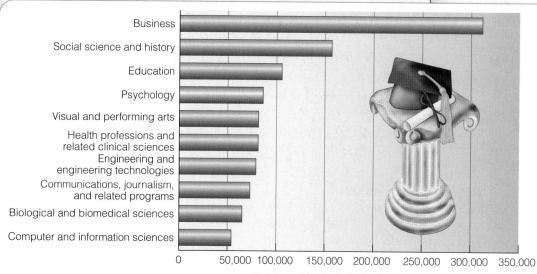

Number of bachelor's degrees awarded

> **You Asked...**
>
> *Do most psychologists own a clinic?*
>
> CHRISTIAN FORERO, STUDENT

FIGURE

1.3

Undergraduate Degrees in Psychology

Psychology is a popular undergraduate degree. It ranked fourth following business, social sciences and history, and education in number of degrees awarded in 2004–2005.

(Data from U.S. Department of Education, National Center for Education Statistics, 2006.)

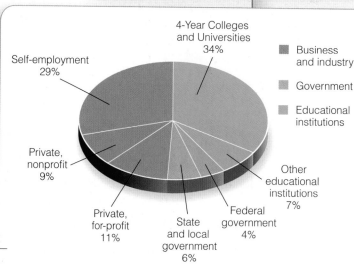

FIGURE

1.4

Work Settings of Psychologists

A large percentage of psychologists affiliated with colleges and universities teach and do research. Psychologists also work in school systems, hospitals, nonprofit organizations, and government, or are self-employed in private practice in which they see and treat clients.

Source: National Science Foundation (NSF)/Division of Science Resources Studies, 2003 Survey of Doctorate Recipients. Special tabulation for the American Psychological Association (APA), July 2007. Compiled by APA Center for Psychology Workforce Analysis and Research (CPWAR), August 2007.

Let's Review!

In this section we discussed modern psychological perspectives, described the training that is necessary to be a psychologist, and surveyed a number of the specialty areas of psychology. For a quick check of your understanding, answer these questions.

1. Which modern psychological perspective emphasizes the importance of thought processes as the bases for understanding behavior?
   a. Behavioral   c. Sociocultural
   b. Humanistic   d. Cognitive

2. Which of these modern perspectives most emphasizes external causes of behavior?
   a. Biological   c. Psychodynamic
   b. Behavioral   d. Evolutionary

3. Which of the following professionals is most likely to prescribe medication for a mental health disorder?
   a. A clinical psychologist   c. A biopsychologist
   b. A psychiatrist   d. An experimental psychologist

4. A psychologist who studies individual differences in shyness is probably from which specialty area?
   a. Cognitive   c. Developmental
   b. Social   d. Personality

Answers: 1. d; 2. b; 3. b; 4. d

Stop, LOOK, and LEARN

What Is Psychology?

- **Psychology** is the scientific study of behavior and mental processes.

- Early psychologists adopted several approaches:

  - **Structuralism:** identify the elements of mental processes

  - **Functionalism:** identify the purpose of behavior

William James
© Bettmann/Corbis

  - **Psychoanalysis:** uncover unconscious motivations

  - **Behaviorism:** examine the influence of the environment

- Today, psychology is a field of diverse perspectives:

  - **Biological:** physical aspects of behavior

© History of American Psychology, U. of Akron, Akron, Ohio
John Watson

  - **Evolutionary:** how behavior helps us to adapt and survive

  - **Cognitive:** the influence of mental processes on behavior

  - **Psychodynamic:** the influence of unconscious forces on behavior

  - **Behavioral:** the influence of the environment on behavior

  - **Sociocultural:** studies behaviors across diverse groups and cultures

  - **Humanistic:** behavior stems from choices and free will

- Most psychologists take an **eclectic approach**, integrating several perspectives to explain behavior.

- Psychologists also study diverse behaviors. These specialty areas are quite broad, including clinical and counseling psychology, experimental and developmental psychology, industrial/organizational psychology, and sports psychology, to name a few.

Psychological Research: Goals, Hypotheses, and Methods

- Identify the goals of psychological research.

- Understand the steps of the scientific method and distinguish between predictive and causal hypotheses.

- Discuss the advantages and disadvantages of observational, correlational, and experimental research methods and the types of conclusions that can be drawn from each strategy.

Learning Objectives

The Goals of Psychology

Though psychologists in various specialty areas study and emphasize different aspects of behavior, they all share similar goals. The main goals of psychology and psychological research are:

- To describe behavior
- To predict behavior
- To explain behavior
- To control or change behavior

Description involves observing events and describing them. Typically, description is used to understand how events are related to one another. For example, you may notice that your health club tends to get more crowded in the months of January, February, and March. It seems you have to wait longer to use the weight machines or that there are more people in the yoga classes. This observation describes an event.

If you observe that two events occur together rather reliably or with a general frequency or regularity, you can make *predictions* about or anticipate what events may occur. From your observations, you may predict that the health club will be more crowded in January. You may arrive earlier for a parking spot or to get a place in the Power Yoga class.

Although it may be known that two events regularly occur together, that doesn't tell us what caused a particular behavior to occur. Winter months do not cause health clubs to become crowded. These two events are related, but one event does not cause the other. Therefore, an additional goal of psychology is to *explain* or understand the causes of behavior. As stated previously, psychologists usually put forth explanations of behavior in the form of theories. A theory is an explanation of why and how a particular behavior occurs. We introduced seven types of explanations, or perspectives, earlier in the chapter. For example, how do we explain higher health club attendance in the winter months? Is it a behavior that is influenced by the environment? Perhaps health clubs are more crowded because the weather makes outdoor exercise more difficult. Perhaps it is more influenced by motivation as many people at the start of a new year resolve to work out more. Is it a behavior that is influenced by our biology? As these ideas are tested, more and more causes and predictors of behavior are discovered. Some of these explanations or theories will be modified, some will be discarded, and new ones will be developed.

The purpose behind explaining and understanding the causes of behavior is the final goal of psychology, *controlling* or *changing* behavior. One needs to understand what is causing a behavior in order to change or modify it. For example, let's say that the weather is a factor in health club attendance. Health clubs could offer outdoor fitness activities beginning in mid-March to prevent declining enrollment. Many psychologists go into the field in the hope of improving society. They may want to improve child care, create healthier work environments, or reduce discrimination in society. Such sentiments reflect the goal of control and underscore the potential impact of good research. ■ FIGURE 1.5 summarizes the goals of psychology.

Describe Behavior

Observe events and behaviors, then look at how events might be related.

Example: The researcher observes that the health club is more crowded in January, February, and March.

Predict Behavior

Predict what events or behaviors may occur, based on their relationship.

Example: Colder months predict higher health club attendance.

Explain Behavior

Suggest and test an explanation (in the form of a hypothesis).

Examples:
• The health club is full because the weather makes outdoor exercise more difficult.
• The health club is full because many people make New Year's resolutions to be physically fit, but give up by the end of March.

Control or Change Behavior

By explaining and understanding the causes of behavior, psychologists can create programs or treatments to control or change the behaviors.

Example: If people give up on fitness after three months, develop incentives to offer during March to remain physically active. If the weather is a factor, sponsor outdoor fitness activities beginning in mid-March.

FIGURE

1.5 Goals of Psychology

Psychologists attempt to describe, predict, explain, and ultimately control or change behavior.

prediction an expected outcome of how variables will relate
hypothesis an educated guess

Psychologists Are Scientists: The Scientific Method

The purpose of psychological research is to test ideas about behavior. As previously stated, researchers use the scientific method when testing ideas about behavior. The scientific method is a set of rules for gathering and analyzing information that enables you to test an idea or hypothesis. All scientists adhere to these same steps even though they may use different techniques within each step. The decisions the scientist makes at each step of the scientific method will ultimately affect the types of conclusions that can be made about behavior.

How can the scientific method be used to meet the goals of psychology? Let's say that you have an interest in understanding beer drinking among college students. You want to make some predictions (a goal of psychology) about beer drinking. You use the scientific method to test this idea, as outlined in ■ FIGURE 1.6.

1. *Define and describe the issue to be studied.* You might hypothesize that college students who buy pitchers of beer tend to drink more than college students who purchase bottles of beer (a **prediction**). You study previous research in scientific journals on alcohol consumption.

2. *Form a testable hypothesis.* Students who buy pitchers of beer tend to drink more than students who buy beer in bottles. This **hypothesis** must be phrased in a way that can be objectively measured—that is, in such a way that another person can come along and test the same hypothesis to verify or *replicate* your results.

3. *Choose an appropriate research strategy.* You choose a group of people to observe (college students) and a research method that allows you to measure objectively how much beer students who buy pitchers drink versus how much beer students who buy bottles drink. You decide where your study will be conducted. Will it be in the environment where the behavior naturally occurs (such as the local college bar) or will it be in a laboratory (a more controlled setting)? You decide who you will use as *participants*. Will you use animals or humans? If using humans, how will they be selected? If using animals, what species will you use?

4. *Conduct the study to test your hypothesis.* Run the study and collect the data based on the decisions in steps 1–3.

5. *Analyze the data to support or reject your hypothesis.* Analysis of data is usually conducted using statistics. If the result does not support your hypothesis, you can revise it or pose a new one. If the results do support your hypothesis, you can make additional predictions and test them. Geller, Russ, and Altomari (1986) actually included this prediction in a larger

study on beer drinking among college students and found support for the hypothesis that buying pitchers was associated with consuming larger amounts of beer.

No matter which goal of psychology you are addressing, the process is the same. The goal merely influences the decisions that you make when testing an idea through the scientific method. If your goal is description or prediction, your hypothesis will state what you expect to observe or what relationships you expect to find. Your research strategy will then be designed to measure observations or relationships, and your analysis of the data will employ statistics that enable you to support or refute your hypothesis. It is in this way that the scientific method allows us to test the ideas of psychology.

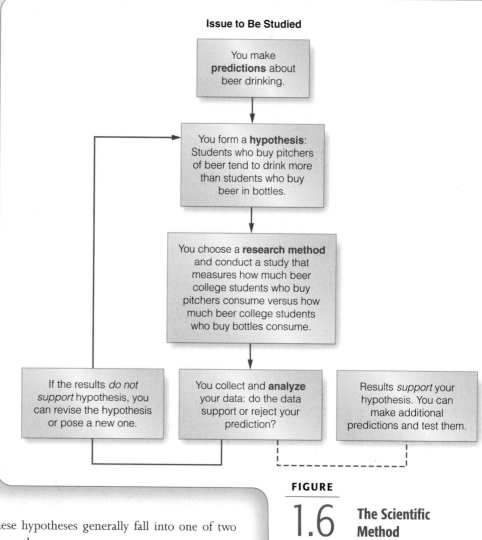

FIGURE

1.6 **The Scientific Method**

The scientific method enables researchers to test ideas about behavior.

Psychologists Ask Questions: Hypotheses

As you have seen, one of the first steps of the scientific method is to formulate a question or hypothesis about behavior. These hypotheses generally fall into one of two categories: predictive hypotheses and causal hypotheses.

Predictive hypotheses make a specific set of predictions about the relationships among variables. They are used to address two goals of psychology: description and prediction. The previous example on beer drinking among college students illustrated a predictive hypothesis: The study predicted that students who buy pitchers of beer tend to drink more than students who buy beer in bottles. Predictive hypotheses are made when the researcher measures the variables of interest but does not manipulate or control the variables in the study. Because the researcher does not control the variables, conclusions of research studies that test predictive hypotheses are limited. The conclusions can only state what was observed, or what variables appear to be related to one another. They cannot be used to draw cause-and-effect conclusions. To do this, you must form and test a causal hypothesis.

Causal hypotheses specifically state how one variable will influence another variable. Causal hypotheses state our ideas about the causes of behavior and in many ways influence the theories that are formulated to explain behavior. Causal hypotheses can be tested only when the researcher is able to control or manipulate the main variables in a study. The researcher sets up different conditions in a study and then observes whether or not there is a change in behavior because of the different conditions. As you will soon see, causal hypotheses can only be tested by means of an experiment. To test a causal hypothesis, a researcher must be able to conclude how one variable affects or causes a change in another variable.

predictive hypothesis an educated guess about the relationships among variables
causal hypothesis an educated guess about how one variable will influence another variable

Psychologists Strategize: Research Methods

You Asked...

How do psychologists study people?

KEIRAN SIDDIQI, STUDENT

Once you have stated a hypothesis, the next step in the research process is to decide on a research strategy and a way of selecting participants. The type of hypothesis you make (predictive or causal) typically determines which research methods you can employ. You are more likely to use some research methods to test predictive hypotheses and to use other methods to test causal hypotheses.

Naturalistic observations, case studies, and correlational research are used to test predictive hypotheses. All of these methods are used when the researcher cannot control or manipulate the main variables in the study. Each method has its advantages and disadvantages, which we will discuss in a moment.

In a perfect world, researchers would include every person they are interested in studying. This is termed the **population of interest**. It is impossible to test everyone, so researchers select a portion, or subset, of the population of interest called a **sample**. Because the sample will be used to make inferences or judgments about the entire population, the sample should reflect the whole population as much as possible; that is, it should be a *representative sample*. Random sampling of participants ensures a representative sample. In a *random sample*, every member of the population has an equal chance of being selected to participate in the study; thus, *sampling bias* is not introduced into the research.

The more representative the sample is, the more the results will generalize to the population of interest. But random sampling is not always possible. Consequently, psychological research often uses *samples of convenience*, or groups of people who are easily accessible to the researcher. The students in your psychology course are a sample of convenience. In fact, much psychological research relies on using college students as the sample of convenience! In the United States only 24% of those over the age of 25 have college degrees, so these samples probably do not represent people from all walks of life (Snibbe, 2003).

population of interest the entire universe of animals or people that could be studied

sample the portion of the population of interest that is selected for a study

naturalistic observation observing behavior in the environment in which the behavior typically occurs

NATURALISTIC OBSERVATIONS

Naturalistic observations are research studies that are conducted in the environment in which the behavior typically occurs. For example, Belsky, Woodworth, and Crnic (1996) wanted to investigate if the quality of family interaction identifies which families have more difficulty managing their firstborn sons at 2 years of age. The researchers measured family interaction by observing the parents and their toddlers on two occasions around dinnertime—an environment that naturally produces child management issues. The researcher in a naturalistic study is a recorder or observer of behavior who then describes or makes predictions about behavior based on what he or she has observed. Because the researcher does not control events in a naturalistic study, it is not possible to pinpoint the causes of behavior. Therefore, naturalistic studies are predominately used to get at the goals of description and prediction. The observations of Belsky et al. (1996) suggest that the child's temperament, the parents' personalities, and the quality of the parents' marriage were just three of nine measurements that predicted which families might have more difficulty controlling their toddlers.

While naturalistic observation does allow a researcher to paint a picture of behavior as it normally occurs, researchers need to consider the influence of *reactivity*. Consider the example of studying childhood aggression by observing students on a school playground. What might happen if you were to simply enter the playground, sit down, and start writing about what you saw? The

A school playground could be an environment for naturally observing children's behaviors.

© Ariel Skelley/Corbis

children might behave differently because of your presence and/or their awareness that they are being observed; as a result, your observations of aggression might not be reliable or true. Consequently, when conducting a naturalistic observation, researchers attempt to minimize reactivity. In this way, they can be sure that they are observing the true behavior of their participants.

CASE STUDIES

A **case study** is an in-depth observation of one participant. The participant may be a person, an animal, or even a setting such as a business or a school. As with naturalistic observation, in case studies researchers do not control any variables but merely record or relate their observations. Case studies provide in-depth information on rare and unusual conditions that we might not otherwise be able to study. However, the main disadvantage of the case study method is its limited applicability to other situations. It is very difficult to take one case, especially a rare case, and say that it applies to everyone. In other words, case studies lack **generalizability**; because of this, the conclusions that are drawn from case studies are limited to the topic being studied.

CORRELATIONAL STUDIES

Correlational studies test the relationship, or **correlation**, between two or more variables—television watching and violent behavior, or depression and gender, for example. The researcher does not control variables but rather measures them to see if any reliable relationship exists between them. For example, if we were to measure your weight (one variable), what other variable might show a relationship to your weight? Your height? Your calorie consumption? Your gender? Your age? Your life expectancy? If you were to measure all of these variables, you might find that all of them vary in relation to weight. These relationships are correlations.

Researchers often conduct surveys, questionnaires, and interviews and attempt to establish correlations when tabulating their results. They measure many variables and then use statistics to see if any two variables are related. If you have ever filled out a questionnaire, participated in a phone interview, or completed a survey, you have participated in a correlational study. You were probably asked many questions such as your age, income level, gender, race, and what products you buy or how you feel about a particular issue or candidate. Your responses are then sorted by these attributes to see if, for instance, men are more likely than women to buy a particular product or vote for a certain candidate.

Correlational data are used to make predictions and test predictive hypotheses. Knowing which people are more likely to buy a product enables a company to market its product more effectively and perhaps devise new strategies to target individuals who are not buying its products. Similarly, knowing which behaviors are related to a higher frequency of illness enables a psychologist to predict who is more at risk for physical or mental illness.

The strength of a correlation is measured in terms of a *correlation coefficient*, which is a number that tells us the strength of the relationship between two factors. Correlation coefficients range from −1.00 to +1.00. The closer the correlation coefficient is to −1.00 or +1.00, the stronger the correlation, or the more related the two variables are. The closer the correlation coefficient is to 0, the weaker the correlation—that is, one variable does not reliably predict the other variable. For example, in a study on the quality of parent–infant relationships and the degree of later problem behavior in their children, Rothbaum, Rosen, Pott, and Beatty (1995) found a −.50 correlation between the mother's quality of attachment to the infant and later problem behavior in the child. The correlation between the father's quality of attachment to the infant and later problem behavior was −.15. The higher correlation found with mothers suggests that the quality of the mother–child relationship is a better predictor of subsequent problem behavior than is the quality of the father–child relationship. Generally, the stronger the correlation is between two variables the more accurate our predictions are, but perfect (+1.00 or −1.00) correlations never happen in psychology. Human behavior is too complex for such perfect relationships to occur.

case study an in-depth observation of one participant

generalizability [jen-er-uh-lies-uh-BILL-uh-tee] how well a researcher's findings apply to other individuals and situations

correlation [cor-ruh-LAY-shun] the relationship between two or more variables

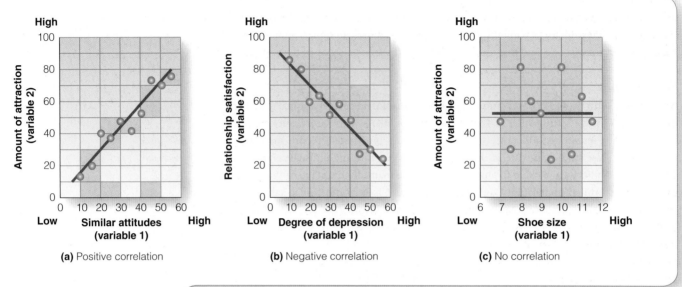

(a) Positive correlation   **(b)** Negative correlation   **(c)** No correlation

1.7 Correlation

Correlation, a research method used for prediction, shows how two variables are related.

FIGURE

1.8 Correlation Does Not Mean Causation

When two variables are correlated or related, it does not mean that we know *why* they are related. It could be that high academic achievement causes high self-esteem. However, it is equally likely that high self-esteem causes high academic achievement. It is also possible that a third variable, such as genetics, causes both high self-esteem and high academic achievement, resulting in a relationship between the two variables. Correlation can only be used for making predictions, not for making cause-and-effect statements.

The sign before the correlation coefficient tells us how the variables relate to one another (■ FIGURE 1.7). A **positive correlation** means that as one variable increases, the second variable also tends to increase, or as one variable decreases, the other variable tends to decrease. In both cases, the variables are changing in the *same* direction. An example of a positive correlation is marijuana use and lung cancer. As marijuana use increases, so does the likelihood of developing lung cancer (Caplan & Brigham, 1990; "Marijuana as Medicine," 1997).

In a **negative correlation**, as one variable increases the other variable tends to decrease in what is referred to as an *inverse* relationship. Notice that the variables are changing in *opposite* directions. An example of a negative correlation is exercise and anxiety. The more people exercise, the less anxiety they tend to experience (Morgan, 1987). Or consider the negative correlation between relationship satisfaction and depression. As relationship satisfaction increases, feelings of depression decrease (Beach, Sandeen, & O'Leary, 1990).

Correlational studies enable researchers to make predictions about behavior, but they do not allow us to draw cause-and-effect conclusions (■ FIGURE 1.8). For example, there is a positive correlation between academic achievement and self-esteem. Students who have high academic achievement also tend to have high self-esteem. Similarly, students who have low academic achievement tend to have low self-esteem. High academic achievement may cause an increase in self-esteem. However, it is just as likely that having high self-esteem causes one to do better academically. There may be a third variable, such as the parents' educational level or genetics, that actually causes the relationship between academic achievement and self-esteem. A correlational study does not tell us which of these explanations is correct. The only research method that permits us to draw cause-and-effect conclusions is the experiment.

Academic achievement and self-esteem are correlated.

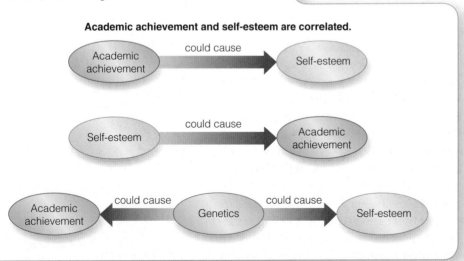

EXPERIMENTS

While several types of research methods are used to test predictive hypotheses, only one research method can test a causal hypothesis: the **experiment**. We will discuss several features of the experiment, including its advantages and disadvantages.

Necessary Conditions for an Experiment

Two main features characterize an experiment. First, the variables in the study are controlled or manipulated. Second, participants are randomly assigned to the conditions of the study. When these two conditions have been met, causal conclusions *may* be drawn.

The point of the experiment is to manipulate one variable and see what effect this manipulation has on another variable (■ FIGURE 1.9). These variables are termed the independent and dependent variables, respectively. The **independent variable** is the variable that the experimenter manipulates; it is the cause in the experiment. The **dependent variable** measures any result

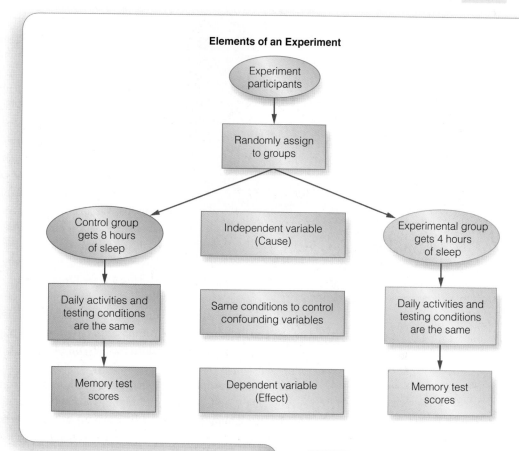

Elements of an Experiment

of manipulating the independent variable; it is the effect in the experiment. Suppose, for example, that we want to study the effects of sleep deprivation. Specifically, we hypothesize that sleep deprivation causes deficits in memory. This is a causal hypothesis that can be tested with an experiment. We decide to manipulate the amount of sleep participants receive to see if it has any effect on memory. In this example, the amount of sleep is our independent variable. Some participants will be allowed to sleep 8 hours per night for the week of our study. Others will be allowed to sleep only 4 hours each night. The experimenter has set, or controlled, the amount of sleep (the independent variable) at two levels: 8 hours and 4 hours. Each day of our study we measure the participants' memory (the dependent variable) by having them complete several memory tasks. At the end of the study, we compare the memory scores of those participants who received 8 hours of sleep with those who received only 4 hours of sleep.

To be sure that it is the amount of sleep affecting memory and not something else, we need to be sure that we have controlled any variable (other than the independent variable) that may influence this relationship. These potentially problematic variables are called **confounding variables**. What variables might we need to control? Maybe age influences one's memory or how one handles sleep deprivation. If either of these is true, we would want to control the age of our participants. We also would want to make sure that participants had not used any substances known to affect memory or the sleep cycle prior to their participation in the experiment. Consequently, we would control for this variable too.

Both groups must be treated the same except for the amount of sleep they receive, so the researcher sets the conditions of the experiment to be the same for both groups. For example, every participant should complete the memory tasks at the same time of day, and every participant should complete the same memory tasks. The criteria for scoring the memory tasks must be the same as well. The instructions for completing the tasks must be the

FIGURE 1.9 Elements of an Experiment

The two main ingredients of an experiment are (1) that the variables in the study are controlled or manipulated and (2) that participants are randomly assigned to the conditions of the study. When these two conditions have been met, causal conclusions *may* be drawn.

positive correlation a relationship in which increases in one variable correspond to increases in a second variable

negative correlation a relationship in which increases in one variable correspond to decreases in a second variable

experiment a research method that is used to test causal hypotheses

independent variable the variable in an experiment that is manipulated

dependent variable the variable in an experiment that measures any effect of the manipulation

confounding variable any factor other than the independent variable that affects the dependent measure

By studying behavior in a lab environment, researchers are better able to control the variables in an experiment.

same. The lighting, temperature, and other physical features of the room in which the participants sleep and complete the memory tasks should be the same for all participants. Our purpose is to design a study in which we manipulate the independent variable to see its effect on the dependent variable. If we control any potentially confounding variables that influence this relationship and find a difference in the dependent variable between our groups, that difference is most likely due to the independent variable, and we have established a cause-and-effect relationship.

If the experimenter does not control a confounding variable, we now have more than one variable that could be responsible for the change in the dependent variable: the independent variable and the confounding variable. When this occurs, the researcher is left with an alternative explanation for the results. The change in the dependent variable could have been caused by the independent variable, but it also could have been caused by the confounding variable. Consequently, causal conclusions are limited.

Let's not forget the second condition necessary for an experiment—how participants are assigned to the conditions of the independent variable. We must be sure that there are no differences in the composition of our groups of participants. Psychologists eliminate this problem through **random assignment** of participants to the conditions of the study. In our example on sleep and memory, assigning all the males in the sample to the 4-hour sleep condition and all the females to the 8-hour sleep condition would create a confounding variable. Gender differences might have an effect on memory scores. It may be that gender (the confounding variable) rather than sleep deprivation (the independent variable) is the cause of a difference in memory. To eliminate the influence of such confounding variables, experimenters randomly assign participants to conditions. Each participant has an equal chance of being placed in either condition. Male participants are just as likely to be assigned to the 4-hour condition as they are to the 8-hour condition, and the same is true for female participants. In this way, any participant variable that has the potential to influence the research results is just as likely to affect one group as it is the other. Without random assignment, confounding variables could affect the dependent variable. This is typically what occurs in quasi-experiments.

A **quasi-experiment** is in some ways like an experiment. The researcher manipulates the independent variable and sets the other conditions to be the same for both groups. However, the second requirement for an experiment—randomly assigning participants to conditions—has not been met. Quasi-experiments use existing groups of people who differ on some variable. For example, suppose you want to see if smoking cigarettes during pregnancy causes lower-birth-weight babies. For ethical reasons, you cannot assign some pregnant women to smoke and prevent others from smoking. Instead, for your smoking condition, you must select pregnant women who already smoke. These women may differ on other variables when compared to pregnant women who do not smoke. For example, their eating habits may differ. As a result, a confounding variable (the diet of the mothers) rather than smoking could cause a difference in the dependent variable (the birth weight of the offspring). Because quasi-experiments do not meet the conditions necessary for a "true" experiment, causal conclusions based on these designs should be made cautiously.

Advantages and Disadvantages of Using Experiments Experiments have several advantages. First, it is only through experimentation that we can approach two of the goals of psychology: explaining and changing behavior. An experiment is the only research method that enables us to determine cause-and-effect relationships. This advantage makes interpreting research results less ambiguous. In an experiment, we attempt to eliminate any confounding variables through experimenter control and random assignment of participants to groups. These techniques enable us to draw clearer conclusions from research results.

random assignment participants have an equal chance of being placed in any condition of the study

quasi-experiment a research study that is not a true experiment because participants are not randomly assigned to the different conditions

Experiments also have disadvantages. First, experiments do not address the first two goals of psychology: describing and predicting behavior. These are often the first steps in understanding behavior, and naturalistic observation and correlational studies are quite useful for doing this. Second, in an attempt to control confounding variables, experiments conducted in laboratory settings may create an artificial atmosphere. It is then difficult to know if the same result would occur in a more natural setting. This may be another reason to conduct naturalistic observations or correlational studies. Third, sometimes employing the experimental method is simply not possible for ethical or practical reasons. As we mentioned in the case of quasi-experiments, we cannot force people to be randomly assigned to a condition that would harm them (such as smoking) or that does not pertain to them (such as having high blood pressure). Psychologists must follow certain ethical guidelines and practices when conducting research. We turn our attention to this topic next.

Let's Review!

In this section we detailed the goals of psychology, outlined the steps of the scientific method, and described methods of research. For a quick check of your understanding, answer these questions.

1. Theories are used for which goal of psychology?
   a. To describe
   b. To explain
   c. To predict
   d. To observe

2. When we know that two events regularly occur together, which goal of psychology can be met?
   a. Predicting behavior
   b. Changing behavior
   c. Understanding behavior
   d. Explaining behavior

3. As an educational psychologist, you might use naturalistic observations of college students in a test-taking environment to get at which of psychology's goals?
   a. Change behavior
   b. Predict behavior
   c. Explain behavior
   d. Describe behavior

4. In an experiment on attitudes, participants are given either positive or negative information about a speaker and then asked to evaluate the effectiveness of the speaker. In this experiment, what is the independent variable?
   a. The effectiveness of the speaker
   b. The type of information the participant is given
   c. Attitude change
   d. The speaker

5. The more hours that students work, the less successful they are academically. This is an example of a _____ correlation.
   a. zero
   b. positive
   c. perfect
   d. negative

Answers 1. b; 2. a; 3. d; 4. b; 5. d

Ethical Issues in Psychological Research

Learning Objective

- Describe the main ethical principles that guide psychologists as they conduct research.

Generally, psychologists affiliated with universities and colleges cannot conduct research unless their research proposal has passed review by an **Institutional Review Board (IRB)**. The function of the IRB is to ensure that the research study being proposed conforms to a set of ethical standards or guidelines.

Ethical Guidelines for Participants

The American Psychological Association (APA), one of the main professional organizations for psychologists, has taken the lead in establishing ethical guidelines, or professional behaviors that psychologists must follow. These guidelines, the "Ethical Principles of Psychologists and

Institutional Review Board (IRB)
a committee that reviews research proposals to ensure that ethical standards have been met

Code of Conduct" (APA, 2002), address a variety of issues, including general professional responsibility, clinical practice, psychological testing, and research. Here we look at the guidelines psychologists must follow when conducting research with humans and animals. The ethical duties of psychologists who treat clients are discussed in Chapter 14.

A fundamental principle of ethical practice in research is **informed consent**. Researchers inform potential participants of any risks during the informed consent process, establishing a clear and fair agreement with research participants prior to their participation in the research study (APA, 2002). This agreement clarifies the obligations and responsibilities of the participants and the researchers and includes the following information:

- The general purpose of the research study, including the experimental nature of any treatment
- Services that will or will not be available to the control group
- The method by which participants will be assigned to treatment and control groups
- Any aspect of the research that may influence a person's willingness to participate in the research
- Compensation for or monetary costs of participating
- Any risks or side effects that may be experienced as a result of participation in the study

Prospective participants are also informed that they may withdraw from participation in the study at any time, and they are informed of any available treatment alternatives. In addition, the researcher agrees to maintain **confidentiality**. Personal information about participants obtained by the researcher during the course of the investigation cannot be shared with others unless explicitly agreed to in advance by the participant or as required by law or court order.

It is not always possible to fully inform participants of the details of the research, as it may change their behavior. For this reason, psychologists sometimes use *deception* in their research. For example, suppose we wanted to research student cheating. If we tell participants we are studying cheating behavior, it will likely influence their behavior. If we tell participants we are investigating student–teacher behavior, we can measure student cheating more objectively. However, the use of deception must be justified by the potential value of the research results. Moreover, deception can be used only when alternative procedures that do not use deception are unavailable.

If participants have been deceived in any way during the course of a study, the researcher is obligated to debrief participants after the experiment ends. **Debriefing** consists of full disclosure by the researcher to inform participants of the true purpose of the research. Any misconceptions that the participant may hold about the nature of the research must be removed at this time.

Consider the following classic research study. In the 1960s, Stanley Milgram (1963) set out to determine if the average person could be induced to hurt others in response to orders from an authority figure. (You will read more about Milgram's research in Chapter 10.) Participants were deceived into believing that they were participating in a research study on learning rather than on obedience. Participants were told that they would be playing the role of a "teacher" in the experiment. Participants were introduced to a "learner" who was then led to a separate room. The teacher's job was to administer electric shocks to the learner every time the learner made a mistake, in an effort to help the learner better learn a list of words. In reality, the participant was not actually shocking the learner. The learner's responses were prerecorded on a tape, but the participants did not know this and believed that they were, indeed, shocking the learner.

Despite the fact that participants believed the learner to be ill or worse, most of them continued to follow the experimenter's orders. A full 65% of the participants shocked the learner all the way up to the highest shock level! During the procedure, Milgram's par-

informed consent research participants agree to participate after being told about aspects of the study

confidentiality researchers do not reveal which data were collected from which participant

debriefing after an experiment, participants are fully informed of the nature of the study

Although Stanley Milgram debriefed his participants, he still caused them psychological harm. Such a study violates current ethical standards of psychological research.

Obedience © 1965, Stanley Milgram

ticipants exhibited emotional distress. Although Milgram debriefed his participants after the study, he still violated the ethical principle of psychological harm. He was criticized for exposing participants to the trauma of the procedure itself and for not leaving the participants in at least as good a condition as they were prior to the experiment (Baumrind, 1964). Because of these ethical problems, a study such as this would not be approved today.

We should also note that for years the primary focus in research was on white males. Women and minorities were largely ignored or neglected when studying psychological issues. Many minority and female as well as male psychologists have contributed to the field of psychology by addressing these shortcomings and designing research that looks specifically at the behaviors of minorities and women.

Ethical Guidelines for Animal Research

Animal studies have advanced our understanding of many psychological issues, including the importance of prenatal nutrition, our treatment of brain injuries, and our understanding of mental disorders (Domjan & Purdy, 1995). Psychologists must meet certain standards and follow ethical guidelines when conducting research with animals. Psychological research using animal subjects must also be approved by an IRB. Less than 10% of all psychological studies involve animal subjects, and these consist mainly of rodents and birds (APA, 1984). Animals must be treated humanely and in accord with all federal, state, and local laws and regulations. Researchers are responsible for the daily comfort, housing, cleaning, feeding, and health of animal subjects. Discomfort, illness, and pain must be kept at a minimum, and such procedures can only be used if alternative procedures are not available. Moreover, harmful or painful procedures used on animals must be justified in terms of the knowledge that is expected to be gained from the study. Researchers must also promote the psychological well-being of some animals that are used in research, most notably primates (APA, 2002).

In the chapters that follow, we will detail more specifically psychological research in the main subfields of psychology. For example, in the next chapter, we start with the biological processes that underlie all behavior. Each chapter will prepare you for mastering the concepts of the next chapter, and we frequently remind you of concepts presented in earlier chapters to help you connect the information. A *Look Back at What You've Learned* concludes each chapter. It will help you remember the topics and concepts that have been introduced and further your understanding of how these concepts relate to one another.

Let's **Review!**

As a quick check of your understanding of ethical considerations in research, answer these questions.

1. Dr. Kwan is performing case study research. She should be most concerned with which of the following ethical principles?

    a. Deception   **c.** Debriefing

    b. Physical harm   **d.** Confidentiality

2. Which of the following is *not* an ethical guideline psychologists must follow when conducting research?

    a. Paying participants for their participation

    b. Informed consent

    c. Freedom from harm

    d. Confidentiality

Answers 1. d; 2. a

Studying THE **Chapter**

Key Terms

psychology (4)
scientific method (4)
theory (4)
structuralism (7)
introspection (7)
functionalism (8)
psychoanalytic theory (8)
behaviorism (9)
humanism (10)
cognitive psychology (10)
biological perspective (11)
evolutionary perspective (12)
cognitive perspective (12)
psychodynamic perspective (12)

behavioral perspective (13)
sociocultural perspective (13)
humanistic perspective (13)
eclectic approach (13)
prediction (20)
hypothesis (20)
predictive hypothesis (21)
causal hypothesis (21)
population of interest (22)
sample (22)
naturalistic observation (22)
case study (23)
generalizability (23)
correlation (23)

positive correlation (24)
negative correlation (24)
experiment (25)
independent variable (25)
dependent variable (25)
confounding variable (25)
random assignment (26)
quasi-experiment (26)
Institutional Review
    Board (IRB) (27)
informed consent (28)
confidentiality (28)
debriefing (28)

What Do You Know? Assess Your Understanding

Test your retention and understanding of the material by answering the following questions.

1. Which of the following is *not* true about psychology?
   a. Psychology is just common sense.
   b. Psychology is just the study of mental illness.
   c. Psychology has no connection with everyday life.
   d. All of the above

2. Which of the following topics would a psychologist have the least interest in?
   a. Learning
   b. Sexuality
   c. Weather patterns
   d. Color perception

3. The _____ perspective in psychology stresses the importance of looking at the influence of unconscious drives and motives on behavior and mental processes.
   a. functionalism
   b. structuralism
   c. psychoanalytic
   d. behaviorist

4. Dr. Babar is a psychologist who studies how people's eating habits help them adapt to and survive in their environments. Dr. Babar is emphasizing which psychological perspective?
   a. Evolutionary
   b. Structuralism
   c. Humanism
   d. Behaviorism

5. Many modern psychologists follow the _____ approach to psychology, in that they do not adhere strictly to any one psychological perspective.
   a. pragmatic
   b. functional
   c. common sense
   d. eclectic

6. Which of the following is the most likely educational attainment of the majority of psychologists?
   a. Doctorate degree
   b. Master's degree
   c. Bachelor's degree
   d. Associate's degree

7. Dr. Warren is a psychologist who studies chemicals in the brain. Dr. Warren is approaching psychology from the _____ perspective.
   a. cognitive
   b. eclectic
   c. biological
   d. sociocultural

8. Dr. Barrios is a psychologist who studies how people change over time. Dr. Barrios is most likely a _____ psychologist.
   a. cognitive
   b. biological
   c. social
   d. developmental

9. Dr. Grogan studies how psychological principles can be applied in the workplace. Dr. Grogan is most likely a(n) _____ psychologist.
   a. organizational
   b. clinical
   c. social
   d. health

10. Dr. Pi wants to test the hypothesis that smoking marijuana impairs one's ability to remember information. What type of hypothesis is Dr. Pi interested in testing?
    a. Predictive
    b. Causal
    c. Correlational
    d. Biological

11. The first African American to earn a doctorate in psychology was _____.
    a. Karen Horney
    b. Mary Calkins
    c. Gilbert Haven Jones
    d. Sidney Beckham

12. Today, who earns most of the doctorates in psychology?
    a. Men
    b. Women
    c. African Americans
    d. Asian Americans

13. Which of the following is *not* a goal of psychology?
    a. To describe behavior
    b. To change behavior
    c. To explain behavior
    d. To eliminate free will

14. Which of the following best defines the nature of a theory?
    a. An explanation of why a behavior occurs
    b. A statement of fact
    c. An untestable assumption
    d. A prediction

15. The hypothesis that the number of rapes will increase during the summer months is an example of a(n) _____ hypothesis.

  a. causal
  b. predictive
  c. untestable
  d. nonscientific

16. Dr. Vaz conducted an experiment in which she randomly assigned her participants to one of two conditions. In the first condition, the participants were shown visual images of common objects and then one hour later asked to recall as many of the objects as they could remember. In the second condition, the participants heard the names of the same objects and then one hour later were asked to recall as many of the objects as they could. Dr. Vaz then compared the number of items recalled for these two groups of participants. In this experiment, the independent variable is _____.

  a. the number of items recalled
  b. whether the participants saw or heard the objects
  c. the sex of the subjects
  d. the room in which the participants were tested

17. Dr. Ling is studying helping behavior in children. Every day, he goes to the local playground at 3 P.M., sits on the sidelines, and records the number of times one child helps another, the sex of the child who helps, and the sex of the child who is helped.

Dr. Ling is using which research method in his study?

  a. An experiment
  b. A case study
  c. A naturalistic observation
  d. A quasi-experiment

18. A confounding variable _____.

  a. measures the effect of the independent variable
  b. is the variable that is manipulated by the experimenter
  c. has no effect on the dependent variable
  d. is any factor other than the independent variable that affects the dependent variable

19. The longer the commute for a student to a college campus, the less likely he or she is to complete a degree. This is an example of a _____.

  a. positive correlation
  b. negative correlation
  c. zero correlation
  d. case study

20. Dr. Eden tells potential participants of any risks they may experience prior to their participation in his research study. Dr. Eden is following the ethical guideline of _____.

  a. deception
  b. confidentiality
  c. informed consent
  d. debriefing

Answers: 1. d; 2. c; 3. c; 4. a; 5. d; 6. a; 7. c; 8. d; 9. a; 10. b; 11. c; 12. b; 13. d; 14. a; 15. b; 16. b; 17. c; 18. d; 19. b; 20. c

Online Resources

CENGAGENOW™ Personalized Study

www.cengage.com/login

Go to www.cengage.com/login to link to CengageNOW, your online study tool. First take the **Pre-Test** for this chapter to get your **Personalized Study Plan**, which will identify topics you need to review and direct you to online resources. Then take the **Post-Test** to determine what concepts you have mastered and what you still need work on.

 What Is Psychology? Essentials Book Companion Website

www.cengage.com/psychology/pastorino

Visit your book companion website, where you will find more resources to help you study. Resources include learning objectives, Internet exercises, quizzing, flash cards, and a pronunciation glossary.

Look Back
AT **WHAT** YOU'VE LEARNED

To think like a psychologist, you must be skeptical about explanations of behavior, rather than accepting of them. **Psychology** is:

- NOT simply giving advice
- NOT just "common sense"
- NOT limited to studying mental illness

How Did Psychology Become a Science?

Wilhelm Wundt

Sigmund Freud

B. F. Skinner

- Psychology became a distinct field of scientific study when Wilhelm Wundt established the first psychology laboratory, in Germany, in 1879. Wundt studied the elements that explained mental processes (**structuralism**).

- William James's focus was on how particular behaviors helped people adapt to their environment (**functionalism**).

- Sigmund Freud, one of the most famous people to influence psychology, believed the key to understanding behavior was uncovering unconscious motivations (**psychoanalysis**).

- John Watson and B. F. Skinner emphasized the need to study observable behavior and the influence of the environment on behavior (**behaviorism**).

- Carl Rogers emphasized free will and personal growth in determining behavior (**humanism**).

- **Cognitive** psychology seeks to understand key mental processes such as memory, problem solving, and decision making.

What Are the Goals of Psychological Research?

- To describe behavior
- To predict behavior
- To explain behavior
- To control or change behavior

What IS PSYCHOLOGY?

- Psychologists typically have a doctorate in psychology, which usually involves 5–7 years of postgraduate study and research beyond the undergraduate (bachelor's) degree.

- Modern psychological perspectives include:

  - **Biological**, which examines the physiological contributions to behavior

  - **Evolutionary**, which looks at how behaviors may be genetically programmed to help us adapt better for survival

  - **Psychodynamic**, which focuses on internal, often unconscious, mental processes, motives, and desires or childhood conflicts to explain behavior

  - **Behavioral**, which focuses on external causes of behavior, such as how stimuli in the environment and/or rewards and punishments influence our behavior

  - **Cognitive**, which focuses on how people process information and on how that process may influence behavior

  - **Sociocultural**, which researches behaviors across ethnic groups and nations

  - **Humanistic**, which explains behavior as stemming from choices and free will

- Most psychologists today embrace an **eclectic** approach to studying and understanding behavior.

- There are dozens of specialty areas in psychology, including:

  - Developmental psychology (which studies child and adult development)

  - Social psychology (which examines ways in which we are influenced by others)

  - Industrial/organizational psychology (which looks at behavior in the workplace)

  - Experimental psychology (which performs research on sensation, perception, and learning)

- Clinical or counseling psychologists practice therapy to assist people with mental health problems.

- Although the numbers of women and ethnic minorities in psychology have increased, they are still underrepresented as faculty in colleges.

History of American Psychology, U. of Akron, Akron, Ohio

History of American Psychology, U. of Akron, Akron, Ohio

© Laura Dwighty/PhotoEdit

- Psychologists form **predictive** and **causal hypotheses**, and then conduct research using the **scientific method**.

- Predictive hypotheses are tested by **naturalistic observation**, **case studies**, and **correlational studies**.

- Causal hypotheses are tested by **experiments** in which variables are controlled and care is taken to survey a **random sample** of a **population of interest**.

- To assure humane conduct of experiments, the American Psychological Association has established a strict set of ethical guidelines that must be followed when researchers study animals and humans.

2

HOW DOES Biology Influence OUR BEHAVIOR?

- Billions of Neurons: Communication in the Brain

- Neurotransmitters: Chemical Messengers in the Brain

- The Structure of the Nervous System

- The Brain and Spine: The Central Nervous System

- The Endocrine System: Hormones and Behavior

One day Pamela H., a police officer from the Atlanta area, came home from work to find her teenage son behaving strangely. He was bursting with energy as he excitedly told her about his sudden ability to read people's minds. At first, she attributed this strange claim to a joke, but over the days and weeks his behavior became more bizarre and frightening. He began to hear voices that no one else heard, and he began to fear that others, including Pamela, were trying to hurt him. Soon his behavior spiraled out of control, and he had to be remanded for a psychological evaluation. He was diagnosed as having schizophrenia, a mental illness related to chemical imbalances in the brain. People suffering from schizophrenia often suffer from hallucinations (e.g., hearing voices that aren't really there) and delusions (e.g., believing that others are trying to harm them), as well as other symptoms that make it difficult to function in everyday life.

In an effort to better help her son and others, Pamela later resigned her position with the police force and returned to school to study social work. As part of her psychology class, Pamela studied the same material that you will study in this chapter. She learned about the chemicals or neurotransmitters that regulate brain functioning and their relationships to mental illnesses like schizophrenia. She learned that controlling her son's illness hinged on finding the correct medication to rebalance the chemical environment of his brain and that it was not the result of poor parenting. After studying this chapter, Pamela found that she was better able to participate in her son's treatment. It was easier for her to communicate with his doctors, to do her own research on schizophrenia and the medications used to treat it, and to feel deeper compassion for those suffering from mental illnesses. Even if you never find yourself in a situation like Pamela's, the knowledge that you gain as you study this chapter will give you a deeper understanding of the workings of your own brain and the way in which it influences your behavior. We'll start this journey of discovery by looking at how the brain communicates information throughout our bodies.

© Susann Doyle-Portillo

The understanding of the brain that Pamela Hunter gained in her psychology class helped her deal with her son's illness.

Billions of Neurons: Communication in the Brain

- Describe the basic structure of a neuron, including the axon, dendrites, and synapse.

- Explain what an action potential is, and describe how it moves down the axon and across the synapse.

- Describe the processes of excitation and inhibition at the synapse.

You Asked...

How is the brain connected to psychology? JEAN-PAUL ESLAVA, STUDENT

Psychologists are very interested in understanding the brain because the brain has a direct impact on both our mental processes and our behavior. For everything from breathing to thinking, we rely on our bodies to enable us to perform the tasks of daily life. We do not question that our brain will somehow store the information we just learned in psychology class, and that on exam day it will retrieve that information. We take for granted that we will be able to walk, to talk, to play baseball, and to maintain a constant body temperature and a steady heart rate. But how are such everyday miracles accomplished? How does your brain know when you need to eat or sleep? How does your brain tell the muscles of your arm to contract so you can throw a baseball? In short, how does the brain communicate?

The brain communicates with itself and the rest of the body over networks of specialized information-carrying cells called **neurons**. Neurons use a sophisticated communication system to conduct the signals that allow us to control our bodies. For example, when you touch a hot stove, neurons in your fingertips send information up your arm to your spinal column. In response to this possible threat, signals are sent back out from the spine to the muscles of your arm. The result is a quick, reflexive jerking of your arm away from the hot stove (■ FIGURE 2.1).

It is estimated that an adult human brain contains roughly 100 billion neurons. Although 100 billion seems like a great many cells, our brains contain even more of another type of cell, **glia cells**. Glia cells were once thought to merely provide support functions, such as providing nutrients and removing wastes, for the neurons

neurons [NUR-ons] cells in the central nervous system that transmit information

glia [GLEE-uh] **cells** brain cells that provide support functions for the neurons

3 In the spinal cord, information travels from **sensory neurons** to **motor neurons**.

4 **Motor neurons** send information from your spinal cord to your arm muscles, signaling them to contract, jerking your hand away.

Spinal cord (cross section)

2 **Sensory neurons** send information from your (hot) fingertips up your arm and to your spinal cord.

Courtesy of William L. Breneman

1 You touch the hot stove; the heat registers in your skin's sensory receptors.

FIGURE 2.1 **The Neurons Involved in a Reflex**

When you touch a hot stove, neurons in your fingertips send information up your arm to your spinal column. In response to this possible threat, signals are sent out from the spine to the muscles of your arm. The result is a quick, reflexive jerking of your arm away from the hot stove.

of the brain. However, recent research suggests that glia cells may play a more critical role in the brain by working to directly regulate the signals that neurons send to one another (Huang & Bergles, 2004; Overstreet, 2005; Volterra & Steinhauser, 2004). Although scientists do not yet understand the full role of the glia cells, we have abundant evidence of the importance of glia cells to normal brain functioning.

For starters, glia cells help maintain the chemical environment of the neuron, and they help repair neural damage after injuries. However, one of their most important functions is the formation of **myelin**. Myelin is a whitish, fatty, waxy substance that coats many neurons. This protective coating insulates and speeds up neural signals. Much like rubber or plastic insulation on an electrical cord, myelin helps the signal get where it is going quickly. Myelinated neurons can conduct signals much faster than unmyelinated neurons. To appreciate what myelin does for neural communication, let's look at what happens when myelin is lost due to illness.

Multiple sclerosis (MS) is one disease that attacks and destroys the myelin insulation on neurons (Chabas et al., 2001). People with MS have difficulty controlling the actions of their body and have sensory problems, including numbness and vision loss. When myelin breaks down, neural signals are greatly slowed down or halted altogether. Initially, movement becomes difficult; as the disease progresses, voluntary movement of some muscles may become impossible. Sensory systems such as vision may also fail because incoming signals from the eye do not reach the vision-processing parts of the brain. Life often becomes very challenging for people with MS as the "orders" sent to and from the brain are delayed or lost along the way.

Without myelin our nervous system cannot function properly—our neurons cannot carry information efficiently from one point to another. As psychologists, we are particularly interested in understanding how healthy neurons send signals throughout the nervous system. Before we can examine how neurons transmit signals, however, we must first examine the anatomy of neural cells and how they connect with one another in the nervous system.

Actress Teri Garr suffers from multiple sclerosis, a disease that results in destruction of myelin. As the myelin is destroyed, patients may suffer from a variety of neurological symptoms, including difficulty moving and sensory loss.

© Reuters/Corbis

The Anatomy of the Neuron

Like any cell in the body, the neuron has a **cell body** that contains a nucleus (■ FIGURE 2.2). The cell body is somewhat similar in shape to a fried egg with the nucleus being the yolk. Like the nucleus of any cell, the nucleus of the neuron contains **DNA** (deoxyribonucleic acid), the chemical that contains the genetic blueprint that directs the development of the neuron. Growing out of the cell body are branchlike structures called **dendrites** (from the Greek word for tree branch). The dendrites receive incoming signals from other neurons. For ease of understanding, we will refer to the dendrite end of the neuron as the *head* of the cell.

Growing out of the other end of the cell body is a long tail-like structure called an **axon**, which carries signals away from the cell body. We will refer to the axon end of the neuron as the *tail* end of the cell. When a neuron is insulated with myelin, it is the axon that is covered, or *myelinated*. As you can see in Figure 2.2, myelin does not continuously cover the entire length of a neuron's axon. Rather, the myelin covers segments of the axon with a *myelin sheath*. Axons vary in length from a few hundred micrometers to many centimeters, depending on where in the nervous system they are located. Axons in the brain are typically very short (1 millimeter or less), whereas other axons in the body, such as those that extend down the legs, can be almost a meter in length (Purves et al., 1997).

The tail end of the axon splits into separate branches (Figure 2.2). At the end of each branch is an axon bulb that contains small storage pouches called *vesicles* that hold **neurotransmitters**, the chemical messengers that carry signals across the synapse. A **synapse** is the junction between two neurons where the axon bulb of one neuron comes into close proximity with specialized *receptor sites* on another neuron.

myelin [MY-eh-lynn] fatty, waxy substance that insulates portions of some neurons in the nervous system

cell body the part of the neuron that contains the nucleus and DNA

DNA the chemical found in the nuclei of cells that contains the genetic blueprint that guides development in the organism

dendrites [DEN-drights] branchlike structures on the head of the neuron that receive incoming signals from other neurons in the nervous system

axon [AXE-on] the long tail-like structure that comes out of the cell body of the neuron and carries action potentials that convey information from the cell body to the synapse

neurotransmitters [NUR-oh-trans-mitters] chemical messengers that carry neural signals across the synapse

synapse [SIN-aps] the connection formed between two neurons when the axon bulb of one neuron comes into close proximity with the dendrite of another neuron

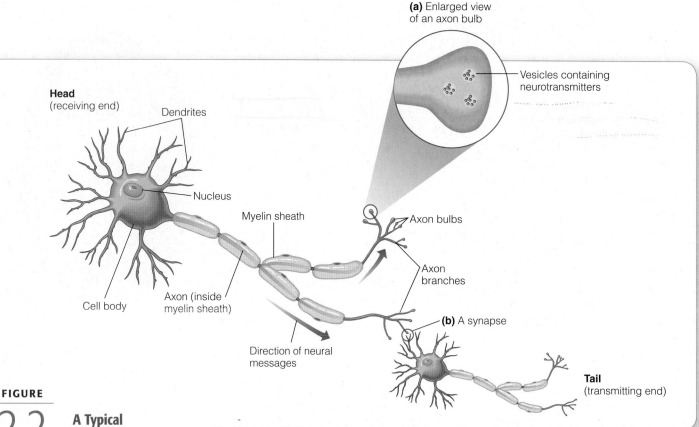

(a) Enlarged view of an axon bulb

Vesicles containing neurotransmitters

Head (receiving end)

Dendrites

Nucleus

Myelin sheath

Axon bulbs

Axon branches

Cell body

Axon (inside myelin sheath)

Direction of neural messages

(b) A synapse

Tail (transmitting end)

FIGURE

2.2 A Typical Neuron

The arrows indicate the flow of information from the dendrites on the head of the neuron to the axon bulbs at the tail of the neuron. Neurons may have many dendrites and axon branches, and some neurons are insulated with myelin, which helps speed up neural signals in the neuron.

From Gaudin and Jones, Human Anatomy and Physiology, Fig 11.3a, p. 263. Reprinted by permission of the author.

The neural structure of the brain is extremely complex, and synapses can occur at several places along a neuron (e.g., dendrites, axon, or cell body). However, for simplicity's sake we will discuss only a simple *head-to-tail* synapse. In this type of synapse, the axon bulb on the tail end of the first neuron is in close proximity to specialized receptor sites on the dendrites on the head of a second neuron (■ FIGURE 2.3). You will notice that the first neuron, called the **presynaptic neuron**, does not physically touch the second neuron, called the **postsynaptic neuron**. At a synapse, there is a measurable gap between the presynaptic and postsynaptic neurons.

Humans have an extremely large number of synapses. Current estimates of the number of synapses range between trillions and quadrillions. Think about this for a moment. How is it possible for humans to have a quadrillion synapses but only 100 billion neurons? It's possible because the neurons of the brain do not synapse in a one-to-one fashion. Rather, each neuron can synapse with up to 10,000 other neurons (Bloom, Nelson, & Lazerson, 2001). Look again at the neurons in Figure 2.3. Synapses can occur at any place along any of the dendrites of these neurons. The vast network of neurons that results from all of these synapses gives our nervous system the ability to generate and send the messages that are necessary to govern our bodies. Let's take a closer look at how these signals are generated within the neuron and how the signals jump across the synapse as they travel through the nervous system.

Signals in the Brain: How Neurons Fire Up

presynaptic neuron [pre-sin-AP-tic NUR-on] the neuron that is sending the signal at a synapse in the nervous system

postsynaptic neuron [post-sin-AP-tic NUR-on] the neuron that is receiving the signal at a synapse in the nervous system

Neural signals underlie much of the action in our bodies—breathing, movement, using our senses, and so on. To understand how these neural signals are generated within a neuron, we must first understand the chemical environment of the neuron. Understanding brain chemistry is important because the brain uses *electrochemical* energy that is produced by charged

2.3 Detail of a Synapse

A synapse is formed when the axon bulb of one neuron comes in close proximity to the receptors on the dendrites of the postsynaptic neuron.

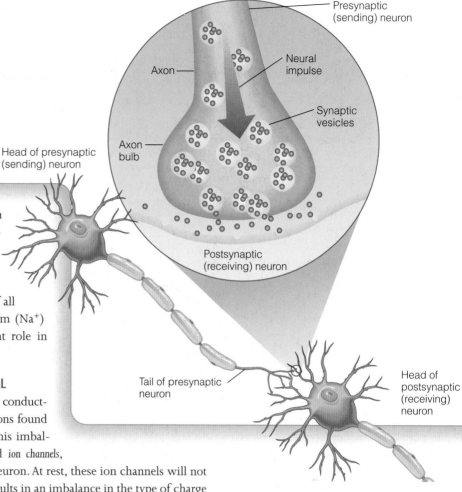

particles called **ions** to send neural signals. Brain tissue is made up largely of densely packed neurons and glia cells. Brain tissue is surrounded by a constant bath of body fluid that contains many different ions. Some of these ions are positively charged, whereas others carry negative charges. Of all the different ions found in our body fluids, sodium (Na^+) and potassium (K^+) play a particularly important role in allowing our neurons to send signals.

THE NEURON AT REST: THE RESTING POTENTIAL

When a neuron is at rest, meaning it is not actively conducting a signal, there is an imbalance in the types of ions found inside and outside the cell walls of the neuron. This imbalance exists because openings in the axon, called *ion channels*, allow only some ions to pass into and out of the neuron. At rest, these ion channels will not allow sodium (Na^+) to enter the neuron, which results in an imbalance in the type of charge that is found inside and outside of the neuron. If you look at ■ FIGURE 2.4, you'll see that at rest, the charge inside the neuron is more negative than the charge outside of the neuron.

This difference in the charges found inside and outside of the neuron is referred to as the neuron's **resting potential**. In mammals, the resting potential is about −70 millivolts (a millivolt, mv, is 1/1000 of a volt). This means that when resting, the inside of the neuron is about 70 mv more *negative* than the outside of the neuron. Although it is far less than 1 volt in magnitude, the resting potential is an important driving force in creating neural signals.

ions [EYE-ons] charged particles that play an important role in the firing of action potentials in the nervous system

resting potential potential difference that exists in the neuron when it is resting (approximately −70 mv in mammals)

2.4 Resting Potential

When a neuron is at rest, the ion channels do not allow large sodium ions (Na^+) to enter the cell. As a result of the high concentration of Na^+, the predominant charge on the outside of the neuron is positive. The predominant charge inside the neuron is negative because of the high concentration of negatively charged ions found there. This difference in charge between the inside and the outside of the cell is called the resting potential.

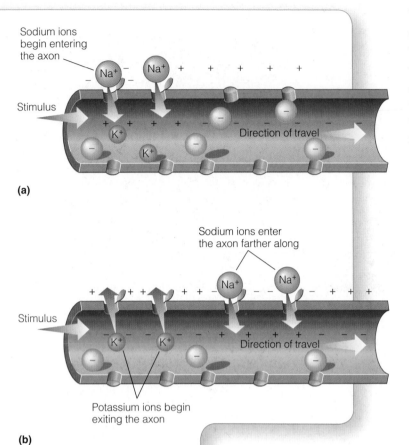

(a)

(b)

FIGURE

2.5   Action Potential

The action potential shown here (a) occurs all the way down the axon and is how we send neural signals in our nervous system. As the action potential travels down the axon (b), the sodium channels close and potassium (K⁺) channels open, allowing potassium to leave the cell. As the K⁺ leaves the cell, the inside of the cell becomes more negative. Potassium will continue to leave the cell until the neuron has returned to its resting potential.

Source: Modified from Starr & Taggart (1989).

threshold of excitation   potential difference at which a neuron will fire an action potential (–55 mv in humans)

action potential   neural impulse fired by a neuron when it reaches –55 mv

all-or-none fashion   all action potentials are equal in strength; once a neuron begins to fire an action potential, it fires all the way down the axon

refractory period   brief period of time after a neuron has fired an action potential in which the neuron is inhibited and unlikely to fire another action potential

THE NEURON IN ACTION: REACHING THE THRESHOLD OF EXCITATION AND FIRING AN ACTION POTENTIAL

When a neuron receives input from other neurons, these incoming signals enter at the dendrites and travel across the cell body to the axon. These signals can make the inside of the cell more positive or more negative. If the incoming signals make the inside of the neuron more positive, the inside of the neuron may become positive enough to reach the neuron's **threshold of excitation** (about –55 mv in mammals). When the threshold of excitation is reached, the ion channels along the axon suddenly open and allow Na⁺ ions to enter the cell. As Na⁺ ions flood into the cell, the inside of the neuron becomes rapidly more and more positive. This is how a neuron fires. These "firings" or neural impulses within the neuron are called **action potentials** (■ FIGURE 2.5a).

All neural impulses are equally strong: If a neuron reaches threshold and fires an action potential, the neural signal will reach the synapse. A neuron firing an action potential is like firing a gun. You either shoot or you don't, and once the shot is fired, it's not going to stop in midair! Because all action potentials are equally strong and because, once fired, they will reach the synapse, action potentials are said to fire in an **all-or-none fashion**.

RETURNING TO THE RESTING POTENTIAL: THE REFRACTORY PERIOD

As the action potential travels to the end of the axon, the inside of the axon becomes more and more positive as Na⁺ floods into the neuron. As the inside of the neuron becomes increasingly positive, additional ion channels open along the axon and begin to pump positive potassium ions (K⁺) *out* of the cell. This removal of potassium (K⁺) from the neuron works to once again make the inside of the neuron more negatively charged (because *positive* ions are leaving the cell). Potassium will continue to leave the neuron until the neuron's original resting potential (–70 mv) is restored (Figure 2.5b). As the neuron is returning to its resting potential, it will experience a very brief (a few milliseconds) **refractory period** during which it is unable to fire another action potential.

So far, we've looked at how a neural signal travels down the axon, but what happens when the action potential hits the axon bulb at the end of the axon? How does the signal get across the synapse?

Jumping the Synapse: Synaptic Transmission

When the action potential reaches the axon bulb of the presynaptic (sending) neuron, it causes the release of neurotransmitters into the synapse. The neurotransmitter molecules float in the fluid-filled synapse (■ FIGURE 2.6). Some of them will quickly drift across the synapse and come into contact with the tulip-shaped receptor sites lined up on the dendrites of the postsynaptic (receiving) neuron.

Each type of neurotransmitter has a specific molecular shape, and each type of receptor site has a specific configuration. Only certain types of neurotransmitters open specific receptor sites. Just as you must have the correct key to open a lock, a particular receptor site will be activated only by a specific neurotransmitter. When a neurotransmitter finds the correct

FIGURE

2.6

Neurotransmitters Carry the Signal Across the Synapse

The neurotransmitter is released in the synapse from the axon bulb of the presynaptic neuron. The neurotransmitters travel across the synapse and bind with receptor sites on the postsynaptic neuron.

Head of presynaptic (sending) neuron

Head of postsynaptic (receiving) neuron

Tail of presynaptic neuron

receptor site on the postsynaptic neuron, it *binds* with the receptor site and causes a change in the electrical potential inside the postsynaptic neuron (Figure 2.6).

EXCITATION AND INHIBITION

In some instances, the neurotransmitter will cause **excitation** in the postsynaptic cell. Excitation occurs when the neurotransmitter makes the postsynaptic cell *more* likely to fire an action potential. Excitatory neurotransmitters move the postsynaptic neuron closer to its threshold of excitation by causing the postsynaptic neuron to become more positive on the inside. Excitation is very important because it ensures that messages will continue onward through the nervous system after they cross the synapse.

However, sometimes we need to stop the message from continuing onward. This process is called **inhibition**. Inhibition occurs when the neurotransmitter makes the postsynaptic cell *less* likely to fire an

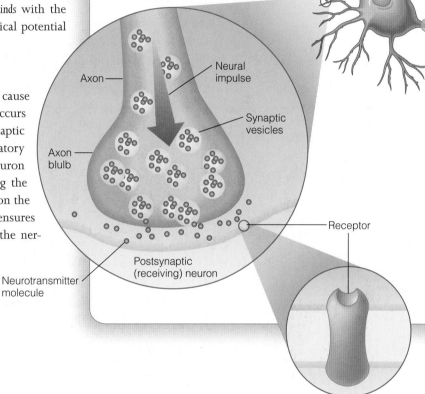

Axon

Neural impulse

Axon blulb

Synaptic vesicles

Receptor

Postsynaptic (receiving) neuron

Neurotransmitter molecule

Just as one must cock a gun again after firing, neurons must return to their resting potential before they can send more action potentials. The brief period of time it takes for the neuron to return to its resting potential is known as the refractory period.

© Colin Anderson/Brand X/Corbis

Just as we must use the correct key to open a lock, a neuron can be stimulated only when the correct neurotransmitter binds with its receptor sites.

© Network Productions/Index Stock Imagery

excitation when a neurotransmitter depolarizes the postsynaptic cell and it becomes more likely to fire an action potential

inhibition when a neurotransmitter further polarizes the postsynaptic cell and it becomes less likely to fire an action potential action potential. As you may have guessed, inhibitory neurotransmitters cause the inside of the postsynaptic cell to become more negative, moving it away from its threshold of excitation.

Because of the complexity of the brain, a single postsynaptic cell can simultaneously receive excitatory and inhibitory signals from a great number of presynaptic neurons. So, how does the postsynaptic cell know whether or not to fire an action potential and send the signal down the line? All the incoming signals converge on the axon, which acts like an adding machine, summing up the excitatory and inhibitory signals. Only when the sum of the signals moves the resting potential at the axon to threshold (−55 mv) will the neuron fire an action potential. If the threshold is not reached, the signal simply does not go any farther at this time.

YOUR TURN – ACTIVE LEARNING

The function of excitation in the nervous system is pretty clear. Excitation starts actions in the nervous system. But why do we need inhibition in the nervous system? Simply put, inhibition is required to slow down and shut off certain processes in the nervous system. Try this demonstration: Bend your arm at the elbow and touch your shoulder with your fingers. As you do this, feel the muscles on the top of your upper arm contract (excitation) while the muscles on the bottom of your upper arm relax (inhibition). If you only had the capacity for excitation, you could not bend your arm in this fashion. You would only be able to stiffen it!

Some everyday activities, such as touching your shoulders, require both inhibition and excitation in the nervous system. Some muscles must be contracted, or excited, while others must be relaxed, or inhibited, to accomplish this feat.

© David Young-Wolff/PhotoEdit

Excitation◀

Inhibition▶

Cleaning Up the Synapse: Reuptake

When neurotransmitters cross the synapse to bind with postsynaptic receptor sites, not all of these floating neurotransmitters will find available receptors to bind with. What happens to the neurotransmitters left in the synapse? Neurotransmitters are removed from the synapse and returned to the presynaptic neuron by a process called **reuptake**. Reuptake accomplishes two goals. First, it resupplies the presynaptic neuron with neurotransmitters so that the next signal sent by the neuron can also jump the synapse. Second, reuptake clears the synapse of neurotransmitters, thereby ensuring that just the right amount of excitation or inhibition occurs in the postsynaptic neuron.

When neurotransmitters bind with receptor sites, they cause either excitation or inhibition. Afterward, the molecules either dislodge from the receptor site or are broken down by specialized chemicals called *enzymes* and cleared away. If reuptake did not occur, once the receptor sites were cleared out other unattached neurotransmitters in the synapse would bind with the sites, causing further excitation or inhibition. This duplication of signals could

reuptake   process through which unused neurotransmitters are recycled back into the presynaptic neuron

Let's Review!

For a quick check of your understanding of how neurons generate and send signals, answer these questions.

1. Suki's dentist gave her a drug that froze the sodium ion channels along Suki's neural axons. What is the likely effect of this drug?

   a. Suki's neurons will fire more action potentials than normal.

   b. Suki's neurons will fire stronger action potentials.

   c. Suki's neurons will fire weaker action potentials.

   d. Suki's neurons will fail to fire action potentials.

2. Sabrina has contracted a disease that is destroying her myelin sheath. What effect would you expect this disease to have on the functioning of Sabrina's nervous system?

   a. It will speed up the neural signals traveling through her nervous system.

   b. It will slow down the neural signals traveling through her nervous system.

   c. It won't affect the functioning of her nervous system in any measurable way.

   d. Her nervous system will speed up and slow down in a random fashion.

3. A drug that causes potassium ions to leave one's neurons is likely to produce what type of effect on the neuron?

   a. Increased firing

   b. Excitation

   c. Inhibition

   d. Both excitation and inhibition

Answers 1. d; 2. b; 3. c

cause confusion or dysfunction in the nervous system. Therefore, reuptake is essential to healthy functioning of our brain and nervous system.

Later in this chapter, you will see that some beneficial drugs act on the body by altering this process of reuptake. In fact, as we will see in Chapter 4, most drugs have their effect in the body at the synapse. For now, let's turn our attention to the types of neurotransmitters and their basic influence on behavior.

Neurotransmitters: Chemical Messengers in the Brain

- List the major neurotransmitters, and describe the functions they may influence.

Learning Objective

Well over 60 different chemical compounds have been identified as neurotransmitters (Bradford, 1987), and researchers continue to investigate more substances that may affect neural signaling. For example, some forms of the female sex hormone *estrogen* that regulate certain aspects of reproduction in the body have recently been shown to also behave like neurotransmitters in the brain (Balthazart & Ball, 2006). A complete review of all known neurotransmitters is well beyond the scope of this text, but we will look at the ones that most influence our moods and behavior.

Acetylcholine: Memory and Memory Loss

Acetylcholine (ACh) was the first neurotransmitter discovered. In the early part of the 20th century, ACh was found to inhibit the action of the heart and to excite skeletal muscles. Today,

acetylcholine [uh-see-til-COE-leen] **(ACh)** neurotransmitter related to muscle movement and perhaps consciousness, learning, and memory

ACh is thought to play a role in awareness or consciousness and in memory (Perry, Walker, Grace, & Perry, 1999). This hypothesized role in memory comes primarily from the discovery that during the course of their disease, Alzheimer's patients suffer loss of functioning in neurons that release ACh into their synapses (Thatcher, Bennett, & Reynolds, 2006). Because Alzheimer's disease is associated with both memory loss and the loss of ACh action in the brain, it appears that ACh *may* help the brain store and/or process memories.

Dopamine, Serotonin, and Norepinephrine: Deepening Our Understanding of Mental Illness

Another neurotransmitter, **dopamine**, appears to influence processes such as movement, learning, attention, and motivation. Dopamine may influence motivation by making some activities, such as sex and eating, very pleasurable or rewarding for us. The reward produced by dopamine may even play a role in the development of certain types of substance abuse (see Chapter 4; Nestler & Carlezon, 2006; Schmidt & Pierce, 2006).

Parkinson's disease is associated with the loss of neurons in an area of the brain richest in dopamine. Drugs used to treat Parkinsonian symptoms work to indirectly increase the amount of dopamine in the brain. Care must be used in administering such drugs, though, because too much dopamine in the brain produces some very troubling symptoms—in particular, symptoms similar to those of schizophrenia, the serious psychiatric disorder that Pamela's son suffered from in our opening story (for more information on schizophrenia, see Chapter 13). Drugs used to treat schizophrenia block the action of dopamine at the synapse. Regulating brain chemistry is not simple. As you might imagine, prolonged use of dopamine-blocking drugs can cause Parkinsonian-like side effects. Think about it. Too little dopamine, and one suffers from Parkinson's disease; too much dopamine, and the result is schizophrenic symptoms. It appears that healthy functioning requires just the right amount of dopamine in the brain.

Mental health may depend on having proper levels of other neurotransmitters as well. The neurotransmitter **serotonin** is thought to play a role in many different behaviors, including sleep, arousal, mood, eating, and pain perception. A lack of serotonin in the brain has been linked to several mental and behavioral disorders (e.g., depression). Drugs that increase the action of serotonin at the synapse by preventing its reuptake are called *selective serotonin reuptake inhibitors* (SSRIs). Prozac and other SSRIs have been used to successfully treat depression, eating disorders, compulsive behavior, and pain. However, not all drugs that act on serotonin are therapeutic. The illegal drug *MDMA* (or *ecstasy*, as it is commonly known) may actually reduce

> **You Asked...**
>
> *What effects do serotonin and norepinephrine have on the brain?*
>
> CRISTOFER ARTHURS, STUDENT

dopamine [DOPE-uh-mean]
neurotransmitter that plays a role in movement, learning, and attention

serotonin [ser-uh-TOE-nin]
neurotransmitter that plays a role in many different behaviors, including sleep, arousal, mood, eating, and pain perception

© Stephen Jaffe/AFP/Getty Images

Actor Michael J. Fox and boxer Mohammed Ali both suffer from Parkinson's disease, a degenerative disease that results in decreased dopamine action in the brain, which causes tremors and other neurological symptoms.

By inhibiting the reuptake of serotonin, Prozac increases the amount of serotonin activity in the synapse, which may reduce depressive symptoms in some patients and allow them to once again enjoy the pleasurable moments of their lives.

serotonin action in the brain (Xie et al., 2006). This loss of serotonin action may account for reports of depression following ecstasy highs in some users (see Chapter 4).

Also related to depression is **norepinephrine (NOR)**, a neurotransmitter thought to play a role in regulating sleep, arousal, and mood. Some drugs that alleviate depression have an effect on NOR as well as on serotonin. NOR may also play a role in the development of synapses during childhood and recovery of functioning after brain injury (Phillipson, 1987).

GABA and Glutamate: Regulating Brain Activity

Gamma amino butyric acid (GABA) is thought to regulate arousal, our general level of energy and alertness. It is estimated that one-third of all synapses and most inhibitory synapses in the brain use GABA as their neurotransmitter. Therefore, it appears that GABA plays an essential role in normal brain function. Loss of GABA in the brain can produce seizures, because without GABA's inhibitory effects, arousal levels become too high. Some anticonvulsant drugs work by lessening the effects of enzymes that destroy GABA molecules (Purves et al., 1997). GABA may also play a role in mediating anxiety. Rats injected with drugs that increase GABA action in certain parts of the brain demonstrate fewer anxiety-related behaviors (e.g., Degroot, 2004), and drugs that increase GABA action in the brain are often used to calm and sedate humans. These drugs include benzodiazepines such as Valium, barbiturates (Phenobarbital), and alcohol. We will discuss treatment of anxiety again in Chapter 14.

Whereas GABA is the chief inhibitory neurotransmitter, **glutamate** is the chief excitatory neurotransmitter in the brain. More than 50% of all synapses in the brain use glutamate as a neurotransmitter, and without it many brain processes would not take place. Ironically, glutamate can also be a deadly force in the brain. When physical brain damage affects glutamate-bearing neurons, glutamate molecules may be released in large quantities from the damaged neuron. Large amounts of extracellular glutamate can cause brain cell death as the neurons literally become excited to death when the glutamate spreads to neighboring neurons and causes them to fire a frenzy of action potentials. It appears that in the brain too much excitation is a very bad thing!

norepinephrine [nor-ep-in-EF-rin] **(NOR)** neurotransmitter that plays a role in regulating sleep, arousal, and mood

gamma amino butyric [GAM-ma uh-MEAN-oh bee-you-TREE-ick] **acid (GABA)** the body's chief inhibitory neurotransmitter, which plays a role in regulating arousal

glutamate [GLUE-tuh-mate] the chief excitatory neurotransmitter in the brain, found at more than 50% of the synapses in the brain

Endorphins: Pain and Pleasure in the Brain

Have you ever heard the term *endorphin*? If you have, what was the context? If you are like most people, your first exposure to endorphins was probably in the context of exercise or physical injuries. **Endorphins** are neurotransmitters that are chemically very similar to the class of narcotic drugs called *opiates* (e.g., opium, heroin, morphine, and codeine). Endorphins are released in the central nervous system during times of stress, such as physical exertion or physical injury, to protect us from pain. Because endorphins block pain messages in the central nervous system, we feel less pain and a mild sense of euphoria when they are released. Endorphins may be one of the reasons that physical activity makes us feel physically and mentally better (Fichna, Janecka, Piestrzeniewicz, Costentin, & do Rego, 2007).

Endorphins may also play a role in making other activities, such as eating, pleasurable (Hayward, Schaich-Borg, Pintar, & Low, 2006). Does this mean that eating tasty foods such as chocolate gives you an endorphin "high"? For some answers, check out *Neuroscience Applies to Your World*.

We hope that you now have a basic understanding of the role that neurotransmitters play in allowing our neurons to communicate with one another (see ■ YOU REVIEW 2.1). Our next step is to take a look at how this neural signaling fits into the structure of the nervous system.

Stockbyte/Getty Images

Exercise can lead to the release of endorphins, producing feelings of pleasure and well-being that are sometimes called a "runner's high."

endorphins [in-DOOR-fins]
 neurotransmitters that act as a natural painkiller

Neuroscience Applies to Your World:

Food and Mood

Can eating chocolate improve a person's mood? Recently, the mass media have reported widely on the health benefits of eating high-quality chocolate. Cocoa, a major ingredient in chocolate, contains chemicals called *flavonoids*, and recent research indicates that flavonoids may reduce high blood pressure and lower the risk of heart disease (see Dyer, 2006). Others have suggested that eating chocolate may improve our mood state by causing the release of endorphins, natural pain-killing neurotransmitters, in the brain. When released, endorphins block pain signals and produce a sense of euphoria. However, before you start pigging out on chocolate, there are a few things to keep in mind. For example, it is likely that chocolate's mood-enhancing effect is due more to the fact that it tastes good than to the chemicals found in chocolate (Macht & Mueller, 2007). In fact, eating many palatable foods will cause the release of endorphins (Benton & Donohoe, 1999). Given this, and given that chocolate is high in fat and sugar (which can lead to obesity), we might do better to find other, healthier "comfort" foods. In fact, preliminary cross-cultural research has suggested that as sugar consumption increases in a country, so does the prevalence of depression (Westover & Marangell, 2002). So, when enjoying your chocolate (and other sweets), think moderation!

Image Source Black/Alamy

Some Neurotransmitters, Their Functions, and Related Diseases and Clinical Conditions

You Review 2.1

NEUROTRANSMITTER	FUNCTIONS	RELATED DISEASES AND CLINICAL CONDITIONS
Acetylcholine	Excites skeletal muscles; inhibits heart action; memory	Alzheimer's disease
Dopamine	Movement; learning; attention; motivation and reward	Parkinson's disease; schizophrenia; substance abuse
Serotonin	Sleep; arousal; mood; eating; pain perception	Depression; obsessive compulsive disorder; some eating disorders; chronic pain
Norepinephrine	Sleep; arousal; mood	Depression
GABA	Chief inhibitor; regulates arousal	Some anxiety disorders; some seizure disorders
Glutamate	Chief excitatory neurotransmitter; many diverse functions	Neural death following head injuries
Endorphins	Suppression of pain; eating; cardiovascular functioning	Some indication of a link to mood

Let's Review!

We've described some of the major neurotransmitters and the roles they may play in our functioning. For a quick check of your understanding, answer these questions.

1. Lamont developed a disease that reduces the amount of serotonin in his brain. What symptoms would you expect Lamont to have?

   a. Hallucinations
   b. Trouble with his motor skills
   c. Symptoms of depression
   d. Seizures

2. Jackson is a normal, healthy adult man. Jackson's brain likely contains more _____ than any other neurotransmitter.

   a. glutamate   c. dopamine
   b. GABA   d. acetylcholine

3. Sasha has been drinking an herbal tea that she believes boosts her body's ability to manufacture acetylcholine. Why do you suppose Sasha is so interested in drinking this tea?

   a. She is trying to improve her memory.
   b. She is trying to treat her depression.
   c. She is hoping it will help her have more energy.
   d. She is hoping it will help her sleep better.

Answers 1. c; 2. a; 3. a

The Structure of the Nervous System

- Describe the major parts of the nervous system and what types of information they process.

Our **nervous system** is the vast, interconnected network of all the neurons in our body. Every single facet of our body's functioning and our behavior is monitored and influenced by the nervous system. The nervous system is arranged in a series of interconnected subsystems, each with its own specialized tasks. At the broadest level, the nervous system is divided into the brain and spinal cord, known as the **central nervous system (CNS)**, and the remaining components of the nervous system, referred to collectively as the **peripheral nervous system (PNS)** (■ FIGURE 2.7). We will discuss the function of the CNS later when we discuss the brain, but first let's take a closer look at the PNS.

> **You Asked...**
>
> *How does the brain communicate with the body?*
>
> BROOKE LANDERS, STUDENT

nervous system an electrochemical system of communication within the body that uses cells called neurons to convey information

central nervous system (CNS) the brain and the spinal cord

peripheral nervous system (PNS) all of the nervous system except the brain and spinal cord

sensory neurons neurons that transmit information from the sense organs to the central nervous system

motor neurons neurons that transmit commands from the brain to the muscles of the body

Sensing and Reacting: The Peripheral Nervous System

The functions of the PNS are twofold. First, the PNS must ensure that the CNS is informed about what is happening inside and outside our body. To this end, the PNS is equipped with **sensory neurons** that convey information to the CNS from the outside world, such as sights and sounds, as well as information from our internal world, such as aches and pains. Second, the PNS acts out the directives of the CNS. The PNS is equipped with **motor neurons** that

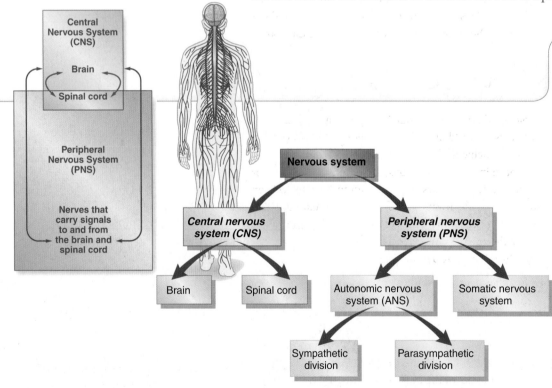

FIGURE 2.7 The Human Nervous System

The nervous system is divided into the central nervous system (CNS, shown in blue) and the peripheral nervous system (PNS, shown in red). Together the central and peripheral nervous system affect virtually all of our bodily functions. The PNS can be further subdivided into the somatic NS (governs voluntary action and sensory functioning) and the autonomic NS (governs involuntary organ functioning). The autonomic NS can be further subdivided into the parasympathetic NS (governs organs in calm situations) and the sympathetic NS (governs organs during times of stress).

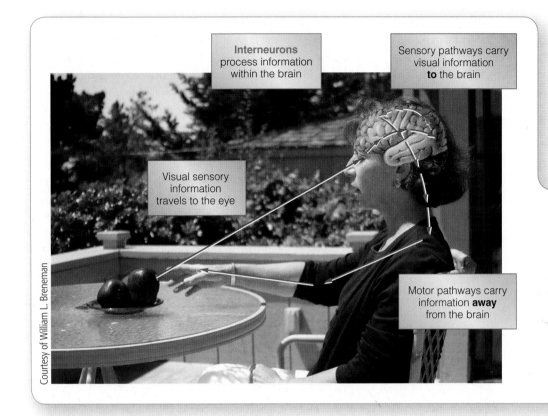

Interneurons process information within the brain

Sensory pathways carry visual information **to** the brain

Visual sensory information travels to the eye

Motor pathways carry information **away** from the brain

FIGURE

2.8 **Sensory and Motor Pathways**

Reaching for an apple involves sensory pathways (shown in red), motor pathways (shown in blue), and interneuron pathways (shown in green).

carry signals from the CNS to our muscles. For example, when you see a juicy apple, the sensory neurons of your eye send this information upward to the part of the brain that processes visual information. Here the brain recognizes the apple, and you decide to eat the apple. The brain then sends signals downward to the motor neurons of your hand and arm, which, in turn, direct you to reach out and grasp the apple with your hand (■ FIGURE 2.8). In this fashion, the sensory pathways send sensory information *to* the spinal cord and brain, and the motor pathways carry "orders" *away* from the brain and spinal cord to the rest of the body.

Voluntary Action: The Somatic Nervous System

Traditionally, psychologists and physiologists have further subdivided the neurons of the PNS into two subsystems: the somatic nervous system and the autonomic nervous system (Purves et al., 1997). The **somatic nervous system** includes those neurons that control the skeletal muscles of the body that allow us to engage in voluntary actions. For example, reaching for an apple requires the activation of the somatic nervous system. The brain makes the decision to reach for the apple, then this "order" is sent downward, across the motor neurons of the somatic nervous system that control the muscles of the arm. The arm muscles react to the orders from the CNS, and you reach for the apple. The functioning of the somatic nervous system enables us to control our bodies in a deliberate and flexible manner.

Involuntary Actions: The Autonomic Nervous System

Although controlling body movements is important, it is equally advantageous to have some processes in the body controlled automatically and involuntarily. The neurons of the **autonomic nervous system** control the smooth muscles of the internal organs, the muscles of the heart, and the glands. By automatically regulating organ functions, the autonomic nervous

somatic nervous system branch of the peripheral nervous system that governs sensory and voluntary motor action in the body

autonomic nervous system branch of the peripheral nervous system that primarily governs involuntary organ functioning and actions in the body system frees up our conscious resources and enables us to respond quickly and efficiently to the demands placed on us by the environment. Imagine how hard life would be if you had to remember to breathe, tell your heart to beat, and remind your liver to do its job! You would have little energy and attention left for thinking and learning, let alone responding quickly to threatening situations. Thankfully, we have the autonomic nervous system to regulate our organ functions, and it is equipped with separate divisions to help us survive in an ever-changing and sometimes dangerous world.

THE PARASYMPATHETIC NERVOUS SYSTEM

The **parasympathetic** division of the autonomic nervous system operates mainly under conditions of relative calm. As you read this page, it is very likely that your parasympathetic nervous system is primarily responsible for regulating the functions of your internal organs. When the parasympathetic nervous system is active, heart rate, blood pressure, and respiration are kept at normal levels. Blood is circulated to the digestive tract and other internal organs so that they can function properly, and your pupils are not overly dilated. Your body is calm, and everything is running smoothly. But if threat arises in the environment, this will quickly change. During times of stress, the sympathetic system takes over primary regulation of our organ functions from the parasympathetic system.

THE SYMPATHETIC NERVOUS SYSTEM

The **sympathetic** division of the autonomic nervous system springs into action under conditions of threat or stress. The sympathetic nervous system evolved to protect us from danger. When it is activated, heart rate increases, breathing becomes more rapid, blood pressure increases, digestion slows, muscle tissue becomes engorged with blood, the pupils dilate, and the hair on the back of the neck stands up. All of these changes help to prepare us to defend our body from threat. For this reason, the actions of the sympathetic nervous system are often referred to as the *fight or flight* response. The increased cardiovascular activity quickly pumps oxygenated blood away from internal organs and to the muscles of the arms and legs so that the animal or person can swiftly attack, defend itself, or run away. Once the danger is past, the parasympathetic system resumes control, and heart rate, respiration, blood pressure, and pupil dilation return to normal. Because the sympathetic nervous system plays an important role in our response to stress, it also plays an important role in our health. We explore this connection in Chapter 11.

parasympathetic nervous system branch of the autonomic nervous system most active during times of normal functioning

sympathetic nervous system branch of the autonomic nervous system most active during times of danger or stress

Let's Review!

We have described the structure of the nervous system, including the central and peripheral nervous systems. For a quick check of your understanding, answer these questions.

1. Juanita was hiking in the woods when she stumbled upon a rattlesnake. Immediately after she saw the snake, which division of the nervous system was most likely in control of Juanita's internal organ functions?

    a. Parasympathetic
    b. Sympathetic
    c. Endocrine
    d. Spinal

2. Moving your arm is an example of a behavior that is governed by which branch of the nervous system?

    a. Somatic nervous system
    b. Autonomic nervous system

    c. Sympathetic nervous system
    d. Parasympathetic nervous system

3. The sensory neurons in your fingertips are part of the _____ nervous system.

    a. central
    b. peripheral
    c. autonomic
    d. sympathetic

Answers 1. b; 2. a; 3. b

How Does Biology Influence Our Behavior?

- **Neurons** carry information throughout the nervous system. The important parts of the neuron include the **dendrites**, **cell body**, **axon**, and **myelin**. Neurons form connections with one another called **synapses**.

- An **action potential**, or neural impulse, fires when a neuron reaches −55 mv, its **threshold of excitation**, and sodium ions are allowed to flood into the cell through the ion channels in the axon.

- **Neurotransmitters**, such as **dopamine** and **serotonin**, carry the signal to the **postsynaptic neuron**.

- The nervous system is divided into several branches:

The Brain and Spine: The Central Nervous System

- Be able to locate the hindbrain, midbrain, and forebrain, list their parts, and explain what they do.

- Describe brain-imaging techniques and other ways we can study the brain, and explain their advantages and limitations.

Learning Objectives

The structures of the brain are composed largely of neurons and glia cells. These structures are organized into three regions: the hindbrain, the midbrain, and the forebrain. The **hindbrain** sits directly above the spinal cord and is named for its position at the bottom of the brain (■ FIGURE 2.9). The hindbrain is the most "primitive" part of the brain, involved in the most basic life-sustaining functions. The hindbrain makes up a good portion of the *brainstem*, a series of brain structures that are essential for life. Even small amounts of damage to the brainstem can be life-threatening.

hindbrain primitive part of the brain that comprises the medulla, pons, and cerebellum

The **forebrain** resides in the top part of the skull and regulates complex mental processes such as thinking and emotional control. It is the largest region of the brain and includes structures that regulate many emotional, motivational, and cognitive processes. Without this well-developed forebrain, humans would not have the mental abilities such as problem solving, thinking, remembering, and using language.

Between the hindbrain and the forebrain is the **midbrain**, which acts as a connection between the more basic functions of the hindbrain and the complex mental processes of the forebrain. Without the midbrain, the hindbrain could not supply the forebrain with the neural impulses it needs to remain active and to keep us conscious. Now that we have a feel for the overall organization of the brain, let's examine the components and functions of these structures.

The Hindbrain

Simply put, without the functioning of the hindbrain, we would die (Wijdicks, Atkinson, & Okazaki, 2001). The hindbrain consists of three structures: the medulla, the pons, and the cerebellum. The **medulla** sits at the top of the spinal column at the point where the spinal cord enters the base of the skull (■ FIGURE 2.10). The medulla regulates heartbeat and respiration, and even minor damage to the medulla can result in death from heart or respiratory failure. It also plays a role in sneezing, coughing, vomiting, swallowing, and digestion.

The **pons** sits above the medulla, where the brainstem bulges inside the skull (Figure 2.10). Like the medulla, the pons is crucial to life. The pons plays a role in respiration, consciousness, sleep, dreaming, facial movement, sensory processes, and the transmission of neural signals from one part of the brain to another. The pons acts as a "bridge" for neural signals; in particular, sensory information coming from the right and left sides of the body crosses through the pons before moving on to other parts of the brain. If the pons becomes damaged, the "bridge" is out, and serious sensory impairments can result.

The final part of the hindbrain is the **cerebellum**. The cerebellum is the large, deeply grooved structure at the base of the brain (Figure 2.10). The cerebellum is necessary for bal-

forebrain brain structures, including the limbic system, thalamus, hypothalamus, and cortex, that govern higher-order mental processes

midbrain brain structure that connects the hindbrain with the forebrain

medulla [meh-DOO-luh] part of the hindbrain that controls basic, life-sustaining functions such as respiration, heart rate, and blood pressure

pons hindbrain structure that plays a role in respiration, consciousness, sleep, dreaming, facial movement, sensory processes, and the transmission of neural signals from one part of the brain to another

cerebellum hindbrain structure that plays a role in balance, muscle tone, and coordination of motor movements

FIGURE

2.9 The Human Hindbrain, Midbrain, and Forebrain

The human hindbrain (shown in blue) governs basic and life-sustaining functions. The midbrain (shown in red) connects the lower structures of the hindbrain with the higher structures of the forebrain. The forebrain (shown in tan) governs complex processes such as cognition, sensory processing, and the planning and execution of behaviors.

ance, muscle tone, and the performance of motor skills (Seidler et al., 2002). It may also play a critical role in the learning of motor skills (Hikosaka, Nakamura, Sakai, & Nakamura, 2002) and the execution of certain behaviors (Walker, Diefenbach, & Parikh, 2007). Damage to the cerebellum leads to loss of balance and coordination. Alcohol impairs the functioning of the cerebellum (as well as the functioning of some important forebrain structures), producing the familiar symptoms of staggering, clumsiness, and slowed reaction time. Police officers assess these behaviors when they give motorists a field sobriety test of balance, coordination, and reaction time. Can you see why drinking and driving don't mix?

FIGURE 2.10 The Brain and Its Structures

This figure shows the cortex and the subcortical structures of the brain.

Without the cerebellum we would not be able to accomplish tasks such as learning to ride a bicycle.

© Peter Hvizdak/The Image Works

reticular activating system (RAS) part of the midbrain that regulates arousal and plays an important role in attention, sleep, and consciousness

limbic system system of structures, including the amygdala and hippocampus, that govern certain aspects of emotion, motivation, and memory

cerebral cortex thin, wrinkled outer covering of the brain in which high-level processes such as thinking, planning, language, interpretation of sensory data, and coordination of sensory and motor information take place

cerebral hemispheres right and left sides of the brain that to some degree govern different functions in the body

amygdala [uh-MIG-duh-luh] part of the limbic system that plays a role in our emotions of fear and aggression

The Midbrain

The midbrain structures connect the hindbrain with the more sophisticated forebrain. For psychologists, one of the most interesting midbrain structures is the **reticular activating system (RAS)** or *reticular formation*. The RAS, located near the pons, is a network of neurons that extends from the hindbrain region into the midbrain. The RAS serves primarily to regulate arousal levels (Kinomura, Larsson, Gulyas, & Roland, 1996), thereby playing an important role in attention, sleep, and consciousness (Izac, 2006). The RAS functions as a type of "on switch" for the high-level thinking centers of the forebrain. Additionally, the RAS appears to play a role in regulating cardiovascular activity, respiratory functioning, and body movement.

The Forebrain

The forebrain contains several groups of structures that function as subsystems. The structures of the **limbic system** govern emotional and motivational processes, and other forebrain structures govern sensory processing and motivation. The wrinkled and folded external surface of the brain, the **cerebral cortex**, governs high-level processes such as cognition and language. In ■ FIGURE 2.11 you can see that the forebrain is divided into right and left **cerebral hemispheres**. For the most part, forebrain structures are duplicated in the right and left hemispheres.

The Limbic System

The series of forebrain structures collectively called the *limbic system* regulates some of our basic emotional reactions. Two limbic structures are located deep in the central region of the brain, above the hindbrain and beneath the cerebral cortex: the amygdala and the hippocampus (■ FIGURE 2.12).

The **amygdala** is an almond-shaped structure located almost directly behind the temples. The amygdala governs the emotions of fear and aggression (Sah, Faber, Lopez De Armentia, & Power, 2003). More specifically, the amygdala may play a role in the way we perceive and respond to emotion-evoking stimuli (Adolphs, 2002; Isenberg et al., 1999). Studies

FIGURE

2.11 The Cerebral Hemispheres

The brain is divided into right and left hemispheres. The outside covering of the hemispheres, the cortex, is where the higher-order processing in the brain takes place.

Left cerebral hemisphere   Right cerebral hemisphere

Frontal lobes

Parietal lobes

Occipital lobes

have found that participants with damage to their amygdala have a difficult time making accurate judgments about others' mood states by looking at their facial expressions. This is especially true when participants are making judgments about other people's level of fear and anger (Adolphs, Tranel, & Damasio, 1998; Graham, Devinsky, & LaBar, 2007).

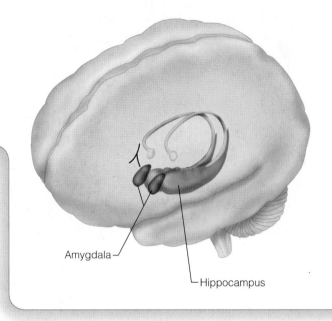

FIGURE 2.12 **The Limbic System**

Limbic system structures, including the amygdala and the hippocampus, process specific aspects of emotion and memory.

Amygdala

Hippocampus

Recently, researchers have shown that persons suffering from *autism* or *Asperger syndrome*, psychological disorders characterized by severe deficits in social behavior, experience abnormal patterns of amygdala activation when perceiving fear in other people's faces (Ashwin, Baron-Cohen, Wheelwright, O'Riordan, & Bullmore, 2006). Studies like these suggest that the amygdala may play an essential role in helping us size up social situations and, in turn, regulate our emotional reactions to these situations.

The **hippocampus**, a structure related to learning and memory, is the final structure of the limbic system that we will describe (Figure 2.12). Much of what we know about the function of the hippocampus is from case studies of people who have suffered damage to the hippocampus. One of the first case studies of such damage occurred in the early 1950s. Scoville and Milner (1957) reported the case of a young man named H. M. who had severe, uncontrollable epilepsy. H. M.'s epilepsy did not respond to medication and threatened his health as well as his lifestyle. In a last-ditch effort to reduce the severity of H. M.'s seizures, doctors decided to take the drastic measure of destroying part of H. M.'s brain with surgically produced lesions. The doctors cut neurons in the limbic system, hoping to check the rampant electrical current that occurs when an epileptic has a seizure. The surgery performed on H. M. destroyed his hippocampus.

The surgery did reduce the intensity of H. M.'s seizures, but it also appeared to produce some devastating and unexpected side effects. Shortly after the surgery, it became apparent that H. M. was suffering from *anterograde amnesia*, the inability to store new memories. H. M. could hold information in consciousness the way we briefly hold a phone number in mind while we dial, and his memory for events that occurred prior to the surgery remained intact. But H. M. was unable to form new memories for concepts and events. He would forget conversations seconds after they occurred. He was unable to learn new facts. Oddly, though, H. M. could store new motor skills (for example, he could learn new dance steps), but later he would have no recollection of having ever executed the new skill. Imagine waking up one day and knowing how to do a dance that you don't remember ever having danced!

It appears from H. M.'s case that the hippocampus plays an essential role in forming memories of concepts and events but not in learning new skills. Should we assume that H. M.'s case proves conclusively that the hippocampus is needed for normal memory functioning? The answer, of course, is "No," because one case study proves nothing. Have other studies supported the findings of the H. M. case study?

Since H. M.'s surgery, a large number of subsequent case studies and controlled animal experiments have supported the hypothesis that the hippocampus is important to learn-

© Jose Luis Pelaez, Inc,/Corbis

The amygdala plays a role in emotions such as fear and aggression.

hippocampus [HIP-po-CAM-puss] part of the brain that plays a role in the transfer of information from short- to long-term memory

© Peter Turnley/Corbis

Researchers (Maguire, Woollett, & Spiers, 2006) found that some regions of the hippocampus in London taxi drivers were larger than the same hippocampal regions in the brains of London bus drivers. These results suggest that certain regions of the hippocampus may enlarge as a cab driver uses his or her brain to memorize complicated street maps of an entire city such as London.

ing and memory. For example, researchers used brain-imaging techniques to compare the hippocampi of London taxi drivers with those of London bus drivers. They found that certain areas of the hippocampus were enlarged in the taxi drivers, but not in the bus drivers. Furthermore, the number of years a participant had been driving a taxi was positively correlated with the size of certain hippocampal areas. These data *suggest* that portions of the hippocampus enlarged as the taxi drivers memorized complicated maps of the entire city. For bus drivers, who only had to memorize a small number of bus routes, length of time driving did not correlate with the size of their hippocampus (Maguire, Woollett, & Spiers, 2006). Keep in mind, however, that this research is merely correlational in nature. For example, from this research alone, it is impossible to tell if the differences seen in the taxi drivers' hippocampi were directly *caused* by memorizing the maps or by some other activity. For example, perhaps taxi drivers spend more time talking to passengers than bus drivers and this influenced their hippocampal development. This is just one of many possibilities that need further investigation.

> ### You Asked...
>
> *I would like to know more about stress and its effects on the brain.*
>
> TAMARA STEWART, STUDENT

A similar debate concerns the relationship between the amount of stress we experience and hippocampal size. Studies have shown that certain hormones released during times of stress can damage hippocampal tissue (Sapolsky, 2000) and that people who have suffered from prolonged stress (such as combat or childhood abuse) have smaller hippocampi (Sapolsky, 2002). At first glance, the conclusion looked simple—stress shrinks the hippocampus. However, it's not that simple. A recent study found that combat veterans who suffered from *posttraumatic stress disorder* did have smaller hippocampi—but so did their identical twin brothers who never faced combat! This finding suggests that having a smaller hippocampus to begin with may predispose one to developing posttraumatic stress (Gilbertson et al., 2002). Further studies are being conducted to try to isolate exactly how stress affects the structure of the hippocampus *and* how the hippocampus affects our reaction to stress (e.g., Weidenmayer et al., 2006).

THE THALAMUS AND HYPOTHALAMUS

The *thalamus* and the *hypothalamus* of the forebrain may have similar names, but they have distinctly different functions. The **thalamus** plays a role in the attention we pay to things that stimulate our senses (Michael, Boucart, Degreef, & Goefroy, 2001), and it functions as a relay station for information coming from our senses to the brain (see Chapter 3). Except for our sense of smell, input from our senses first travels to the thalamus before being sent on to the appropriate part of the cortex for further processing. Without a properly functioning thalamus, we would suffer serious problems, including sensory impairment.

Nestled below the thalamus is the **hypothalamus** (the prefix *hypo* means "below"). The hypothalamus maintains **homeostasis** in the body, a state of internal equilibrium across a variety of bodily systems. In maintaining homeostasis, the hypothalamus is responsible for monitoring and regulating body temperature, thirst, hunger, sleep, autonomic nervous system functioning, and some sexual and reproductive functions, and can change hormone levels in the bloodstream. To maintain homeostasis, the hypothalamus must ultimately motivate us to engage in certain behaviors. For example, when our body needs fuel, the hypothalamus motivates us with hunger. When we need sleep, the hypothalamus makes us sleepy, and we

thalamus [THAL-uh-muss] part of the forebrain that functions as a sensory relay station

hypothalamus [high-poe-THAL-uh-muss] part of the forebrain that plays a role in maintaining homeostasis in the body, involving sleep, body temperature, sexual behavior, thirst, and hunger; also the point where the nervous system intersects with the endocrine system

homeostasis [hoe-mee-oh-STAY-suss] an internal state of equilibrium in the body are motivated to go to bed. No other part of the nervous system plays a more central role in physiological motivation, a topic we will return to in Chapters 4 and 8. Without the hypothalamus, we would not know when to engage in the behaviors that keep our bodily systems in balance.

The Cortex

The most noticeable structure on the external surface of the brain is the cerebral cortex, or simply the cortex. The cortex is the thin (approximately 2 mm thick), wrinkled layer of tissue that covers the outside of the cerebral hemispheres, or the two sides of the brain (■ FIGURE 2.13). The cortex is arguably the most sophisticated part of the brain and is responsible for the highest levels of processing: cognition and mental processes such as planning, decision making, perception, and language. It is the cortex that gives us our humanness. It is no coincidence that the human cortex is the most developed of all known creatures and that humans also have the most highly developed cognitive skills of all known species. Compare the photographs in Figure 2.13. Notice that the human cortex is very folded and convoluted, whereas the cat's brain is much less so. The folds allow for more cortical surface area within the confines of the skull cavity. A cat has proportionately less cortical area than a human does, and this reduction in cortex translates into fewer cognitive abilities for the cat.

THE LOBES OF THE CORTEX AND LATERALIZATION IN THE BRAIN

The human cortex is divided into four distinct physical regions called *lobes*. These are the **frontal lobe**, the **parietal lobe**, the **occipital lobe**, and the **temporal lobe** (■ FIGURE 2.14a). The lobes of the cortex are structurally symmetrical in both hemispheres of the brain, meaning that the brain has both right and left frontal lobes, right and left temporal lobes, and so on. However, the functions of the right and left lobes are often somewhat different. Functions are *lateralized*, or found in only one hemisphere of the brain, for a couple of reasons. First, the lobes of the brain tend to be wired in a *contralateral* fashion, with the right side of the brain governing the left side of the body and the left side of the brain governing the right side of the body. Although contralateral wiring is the norm in the brain, some neural pathways carry information to and from the body to the same hemisphere of the brain.

Lateralization in the brain is also evident in that the right and left hemispheres process somewhat different types of information (Stephan et al., 2003). For example, most people process language largely in the left hemisphere. Although some people have major language

frontal lobe cortical area directly behind the forehead that plays a role in thinking, planning, decision making, language, and motor movement

parietal [puh-RYE-it-ull] **lobe** cortical area on the top sides of the brain that play a role in touch and certain cognitive processes

occipital [ox-SIP-it-ull] **lobe** cortical area at the back of the brain that plays a role in visual processing

temporal [TEM-por-ull] **lobe** cortical area directly below the ears that play a role in auditory processing and language

Human

Domestic cat

© Leetsma/Custom Medical Stock Photo

© Wally Welker, U. of Wisconsin/Madison

FIGURE

2.13

Cortex of a Human Brain and a Cat Brain

Note how much more convoluted, or folded, the human brain is compared to the cat brain. Many of the higher-order processes that humans engage in, such as language and thinking, are processed in the cortex.

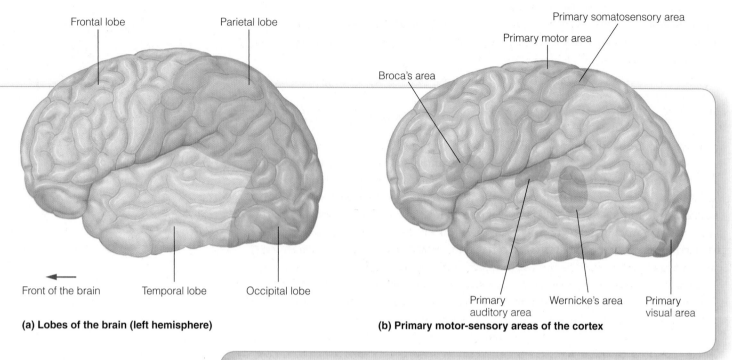

(a) Lobes of the brain (left hemisphere)

(b) Primary motor-sensory areas of the cortex

FIGURE

2.14 The Human Brain

(a) The lobes of the brain. (b) The language centers of the brain are generally found in the left hemisphere. Wernicke's area in the left temporal lobe allows us to comprehend speech. Broca's area in the left frontal lobe allows us to produce speech.

From Gaudin and Jones, Human Anatomy and Physiology, *Fig. 12.2, p. 294. Reprinted by permission of the author.*

Wernicke's [WURR-neh-kees] **area**
    a region of the left temporal lobe that plays a role in the comprehension of speech
Broca's [BRO-kuz] **area**   a region in the left frontal lobe that plays a role in the production of speech
corpus callosum [COR-puss cal-OH-sum]
    a thick band of neurons that connect the right and left hemispheres of the brain

centers in the right hemisphere, and some have major language centers in both hemispheres, for the average person language is located in the left hemisphere. As a result, when people suffer major damage to the left hemisphere (as from a stroke), their ability to use language often suffers. Two examples illustrate this hemispheric specialization of language.

When people suffer damage to **Wernicke's area** in the left temporal lobe, they are unable to understand spoken language. When damage is severe in **Broca's area** in the left frontal lobe (Figure 2.14b), patients are unable to produce understandable speech (Geschwind, 1975; Geschwind & Levitsky, 1968). When the damage is confined to the right side of the brain, patients usually remain able to understand and produce speech, but they have some difficulty processing certain types of spatial information (such as judging the distance between two objects). Differences in the linguistic and spatial processing of the left and right hemispheres once led scientists to conclude broadly that the hemispheres of the brain processed very different categories of information: they surmised that the left hemisphere processed verbal information and the right hemisphere processed spatial information.

However, more recent studies have suggested that the left and right hemispheres of the brain may not divide up their functions as neatly as once thought. In their review of previous brain research, Beeman and Chairello (1998) report that the right hemisphere also seems to process some of the more subtle aspects of language, such as atypical uses of words (e.g., calling a person a "pig"). Newer research also indicates that both hemispheres process different aspects of spatial information (see Chabris & Kosslyn, 1998, for a review). To sum up, we are coming to understand that the hemispheres accomplish tasks, such as language and processing spatial information, by working together and performing complementary functions.

THE CORPUS CALLOSUM: ARE WOMEN'S BRAINS LESS LATERALIZED THAN MEN'S?

Whether the hemispheres process different information or merely different aspects of the same information, they must have some means of coordinating the information they process. The **corpus callosum** is a dense band of neurons that sits just below the cortex along the midline of the brain (Banich & Heller, 1998; Figure 2.10). This band physically connects the right and left cortical areas and ensures that each hemisphere "knows" what the other hemisphere is doing. The corpus callosum passes information back and forth between the right and left hemispheres, allowing us to integrate these somewhat independent functions. Without the corpus callosum, the right and left cortices would function independently and in ignorance of each other.

> **You Asked...**
>
> *What is different in the male's brain compared with the female's?*
>
> ZACH VEATCH, STUDENT

Some studies have suggested that certain areas of the corpus callosum may be larger in women than in men (Delacoste-Utamsing & Holloway, 1982). However, this size difference is controversial (Ankey, 1992; Driesen & Raz, 1995; Morton & Rafto, 2006). Some researchers have suggested that the difference may have less to do with gender than with brain size; that is, larger corpora callosa (the plural of corpus callosum) may be found in people with smaller brains, regardless of gender (Jäncke & Steinmetz, 2003). If this is true, men with small brains may also have large corpora callosa. Furthermore, some argue that having a larger corpus callosum allows for more connections between hemispheres, resulting in a brain that is less lateralized and more integrated (Reite et al., 1995). Does this mean that because women tend to have smaller brains, they also have larger corpora callosa and more integrated brain function than men? It's hard to say right now. Although these ideas sound plausible, some researchers suggest that having a larger corpus callosum may not actually lead to less lateralization in the brain (Kimura, 2000). It's clear that more research will have to be done before we fully understand how gender, the corpus callosum, and brain lateralization are related.

THE SPLIT BRAIN

Physicians have at times willfully disrupted communication between the hemispheres by destroying the corpus callosum in the human brain. Such a drastic measure is taken in cases where people suffer from severe, uncontrollable epilepsy. In severe epilepsy, abnormal electrical activity can build up in one hemisphere and spread across the corpus callosum to engulf the opposite hemisphere. This short-circuiting of both hemispheres produces a severe, life-threatening seizure called a *grand mal seizure*. If drugs cannot control the seizures, surgery may be performed to cut the corpus callosum and thereby contain the short-circuiting to one hemisphere only. The patient still suffers from seizures, but they are not as severe. Patients who have had this surgery are referred to as having **split brains** because their hemispheres are no longer connected by neural pathways. Split-brain patients provide scientists with an opportunity to study the lateralization of the brain.

Working with split-brain patients, researchers have a chance to study the functioning of each hemisphere independent of the other. For example, split-brain research helped researchers conclude that the left hemisphere enables us to produce speech (■ FIGURE 2.15). Researcher Michael Gazzaniga (1967) briefly flashed pictures of familiar objects to the right and left visual fields of split-brain patients and asked them to identify the objects (Figure 2.15). When an object is briefly presented to the right peripheral field of vision, the resulting visual information is sent directly to the left hemisphere of the brain. Because Broca's area is in the left hemisphere for most people, Gazzaniga found that the average split-brain person could verbally identify the object. But what about an object presented to the patient's left peripheral field of vision? When an object is briefly shown on the far left side, the resulting visual information is sent directly to the right hemisphere of the brain. Recall that most people do not have a Broca's area in their right hemisphere. In a normal brain, the information travels from the right hemisphere across the corpus callosum to the language centers in the left hemisphere. However, in a split-brain individual this cannot happen. Without the corpus callosum, Gazzaniga's split-brain patients could not transmit the knowledge of what they were seeing to the language centers in their left hemisphere. The right brain knew what the

split brain a brain with its corpus callosum severed; sometimes done to control the effects of epilepsy in patients who do not respond to other therapies

(a) Visual pathways in the brain

Left visual field   Right visual field

"Cup"

Language center

Normal brain

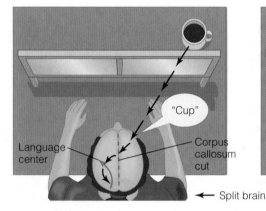

"Cup"

Language center

Corpus callosum cut

?

← Split brain →

(b) Split brain

FIGURE 2.15

A Typical Split-Brain Study

In a typical split-brain experiment, an image is flashed to a split-brain person's right or left visual field, and she is asked to identify the object in the image. When the image is flashed to the person's right visual field, she is able to name it; but when it is flashed to her left visual field, she is unable to name it because the information cannot travel to the language centers in the left hemisphere.

objects were, but it could not inform the "speaking" left brain! Predictably, the split-brain patients were unable to name the objects they saw in their left visual fields. Interestingly, in this situation split-brain patients were able to point to the objects in a drawing—provided they used their left hand (which is controlled by the right brain.) Split-brain research has helped us to begin sorting out the relative contributions that the right and left hemispheres make to everyday cognitive processes.

The Specialization of Function in the Lobes of the Cortex

Just as there is specialization in the hemispheres of the brain, there is also specialization within the different lobes of the brain. About 25% of the total surface area of the cortex is dedicated to motor and sensory functions such as vision, hearing, movement, and tactile sensation. Specific motor-sensory areas can be found in all the lobes of the brain (frontal, parietal, occipital, and temporal). The remaining 75% of the cortical area is thought to be devoted to higher-order processes that involve the integration of information, such as thinking, planning, decision making, and language. Collectively, this 75% is referred to as the **association cortex** because these areas are presumed to involve the association of information from the motor-sensory areas of the cortex.

We do not yet have a complete understanding of the functions of specific areas of the association cortex. Often, damage to the association areas produces general changes and deficits in behavior. However, stimulation of specific areas of the association cortex does not usually lead to specific, predictable physical reactions. It is thought that the association cortex plays a role in general cognition, such as planning and decision making. Where applicable, we will discuss the known functions of the association areas for the specific lobes of the brain.

THE FRONTAL LOBE

The frontal lobe is the area of the cortex that lies closest to the forehead (Figure 2.14a). Much of the frontal lobe is association cortex. We know more about the association areas of the frontal lobe than any other lobes. Broca's area in the association area of the left frontal lobe is, as previously mentioned, involved in the production of speech. It also appears that the frontal lobe association areas play a role in cognitive processes such as attention, problem solving, judgment, the planning and executing of behavior, and certain aspects of personality.

These cognitive functions are illustrated in a famous case study from the history of psychology. In 1848 a railway worker named Phineas Gage suffered severe trauma to his *prefrontal cortex* (the association area at the very front part of the frontal lobe) when a metal rod was shot through his head in an explosion. The rod entered his left cheek and shot out of the top of his head. Although he survived his injuries, they resulted in some dramatic personality changes. Whereas Gage had been a calm, responsible man prior to his injuries, he became impulsive, emotionally volatile, and irresponsible afterward. Because the prefrontal cortex is important for the regulation of emotion (Davidson, Putman, & Larson, 2000), the damage to Gage's brain robbed him of his ability to control his emotions, make good judgments, and execute planned behaviors (Damasio, Grabowski, Frank, Galaburda, & Damasio, 1994). Phineas Gage was no longer himself, but he could still move and speak because the motor-sensory areas of his frontal lobe were undamaged.

At the back of the frontal lobe (behind the prefrontal cortex) lies the **motor cortex**, a narrow band of cortex that allows us to execute motor movements. The motor cortex on the right side of the brain affects movement on the left side of the body, and vice versa. Additionally, specific points along the motor cortex correspond to particular points on the body. ■ FIGURE 2.16a is a rendering of a *homunculus*, a humorous mapping of body parts onto their appropriate motor cortical points. If stimulation were applied to these points along the motor cortex, the result would be movement of the corresponding body part. During brain surgery, surgeons may apply electrical stimulation to the brain before making incisions in the cortical tissue; the patient's subsequent movements or other responses indicate where their instruments are located along the motor cortex (and other areas). Without such precautionary measures, a physician could accidentally cause paralysis with a misplaced cut along the motor cortex.

THE PARIETAL LOBE

As with the frontal lobe, much of the parietal lobe is association cortex, but we know less about the specific functions of these association areas. One possibility is that parts of the parietal lobe may play a role in reading (Newman & Tweig, 2001). Damage to the lower areas of the parietal lobe can be associated with deficits in reading ability (Diamond, Scheibel, & Elson, 1985). We have a better understanding of the role that the parietal lobe plays in sensation. A thin strip of the parietal lobe plays a role in our sense of touch, pressure, and pain. This strip, called the **somatosensory cortex**, lies directly behind the motor cortex, along the leading edge of the parietal lobe (Figure 2.14b). The somatosensory cortex is wired much like the motor cortex, and specific points along the somatosensory cortex correspond to particular points on the body (Figure 2.16b). Damage to the somatosensory cortex often results in numbness of the corresponding body part.

THE OCCIPITAL LOBE

The occipital lobe of the brain is located at the very back of the skull, above the cerebellum. Much of the occipital lobe is dedicated to processing visual information. The visual cortex (Figure 2.14b) of the occipital lobe is composed of layers of tissue that contain long axonal fibers. An action potential is stimulated in specialized cells of the **visual cortex** when our eyes see specific types of visual stimuli in the outside world. For instance, some cells begin to fire only when we see lines, and other cells fire only when we see circular shapes. Like a computer, our brain integrates all the incoming neural impulses from these specialized cells in the visual cortex to enable us to perceive what we are viewing. Without the operation of the visual cortex, our brain could not make sense of what our eyes see and we would be functionally blind.

THE TEMPORAL LOBE

The temporal lobe is in front of the occipital lobe and just below the parietal and frontal lobes—roughly behind our ears inside the skull. Not surprisingly, one of the major functions of the temporal lobe is the processing of auditory information, or hearing. The temporal lobe areas devoted to hearing are the **auditory cortex**, located on the upper edge of the tempo-

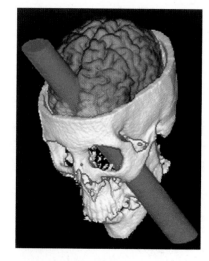

Phineas Gage was a responsible, mild-mannered worker on a railway construction crew until a rod like this one was shot through his head in a freak accident. Gage survived, but he was never the same. The damage to Gage's prefrontal cortex coincided with dramatic changes in his personality. The once calm Gage became emotionally volatile and difficult. As a result, he was unable to perform his former job with the railroad.

Reprinted with permission from Damasio, H., Grabowski, T., Frank, R., Galaburda, A. M., & Damasio, A. R. (1994). The return of Phineas Gage: The skull of a famous patient yields clues about the brain. *Science*, 264, 1102–1105. © 1994, AAAS.

association cortex areas of the cortex involved in the association or integration of information from the motor-sensory areas of the cortex

motor cortex a strip of cortex at the back of the frontal lobe that governs the execution of motor movement in the body

somatosensory [so-MAT-oh-SEN-sor-ee] **cortex** a strip of cortex at the front of the parietal lobe that governs the sense of touch

visual cortex a region of cortex found at the back of the occipital lobe that processes visual information in the brain

auditory cortex a region of cortex found in the temporal lobe that governs the processing of auditory information in the brain

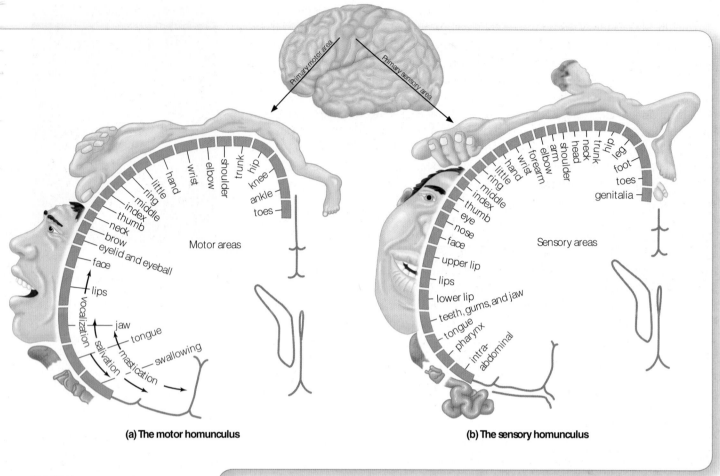

(a) The motor homunculus

(b) The sensory homunculus

FIGURE

2.16

Motor and Sensory Homunculi

Homunculi are humorous depictions of the localization of function on the cortex.

From Penfield and Rasmussen, The Cerebral Cortex of Man, © 1950 Macmillan Library Reference. Renewed 1978 by Theodore Rasmussen. Reprinted by permission of The Gale Group.

ral lobe (Figure 2.14b). In addition to the auditory cortex, the left temporal lobe of most people contains Wernicke's area. As we've already seen, Wernicke's area is responsible for the comprehension of speech. Persons who have suffered major damage to Wernicke's area often cannot understand the meaning of spoken words. They hear the words, but they can't make sense of them.

The association areas of the temporal lobe are also very important to everyday functioning. The inner surface of the temporal lobes appears to be very important to the processing of memory. This should not be surprising because this area of the temporal lobe has direct connections with the hippocampus. Other association areas of the temporal lobe are thought to play a role in the integration of diverse sensory information. For example, the temporal lobe helps with the integration of the sight, texture, and sound generated as we bite into an apple (Diamond, Scheibel, & Elson, 1985).

Now that you have learned about the structure and function of the brain, we hope that you are suitably impressed. We have merely begun to explore the function of our nervous system in this chapter, and scientists are far from completely understanding this amazing system. As research continues, scientists learn more about how our physiology influences our thoughts and behaviors. Luckily, researchers have a great deal of modern technology to help them learn about the brain. You can learn more about these technologies in *Psychology Applies to Your World*.

These technologies have helped doctors and psychologists gain a better understanding of how the brain works to regulate and control our mental processes and behavior. Through the use of these technologies, we have learned that the human nervous system is an extremely impressive and important network. However, the nervous system is not the only communication system within the body. We turn now to the other major communication network, the endocrine system.

Psychology Applies to Your World:

Technologies for Studying the Brain

Recently, a friend of ours hit her head in a car accident. As a precaution, doctors ordered an MRI of her brain. An MRI, or magnetic resonance imaging scan, allows doctors to see a detailed picture of the brain. If our friend had suffered serious damage from the injury, it would have shown up on the MRI. Luckily, the MRI showed no serious damage from the accident, but there was another surprise on the MRI. It showed that despite having no troubling symptoms, she had a very large tumor growing in her brain. Without the MRI, the tumor would have gone undiagnosed until she began suffering from serious symptoms; at that point, it might have been too late to do much for her. We are happy to report that shortly after discovering the tumor doctors were able to quickly remove most of it, and she is now recovering nicely.

You Asked...

How many ways are there to study the brain? JOSEPH VICKERS, STUDENT

Both doctors and psychologists use technologies like MRIs for studying the brain. Some of these procedures allow researchers to examine only the structure of the brain, whereas others indicate which areas of the brain are most active at a given moment. Because these techniques can be used on living brain tissue, they can give researchers important information about the specific behavioral functions that are governed by particular areas of the brain. The table to the right summarizes some of the most useful technologies available for helping us to better understand the inner workings of the brain: *CAT scans, MRIs, PET scans, fMRIs,* and *EEGs.*

Common Techniques for Studying the Brain and Examples of Their Usage

TECHNIQUE FOR STUDYING THE BRAIN	DESCRIPTION
COMPUTERIZED AXIAL TOMOGRAPHY (CAT SCAN) © Custom Medical Stock Photo	Multiple X-ray beams are passed through the brain from different angles. A computer then analyzes the X-rays that exit the head and uses this information to build a very detailed picture of the brain and its structures. CAT scans can be used to diagnose tumors, strokes, certain diseases, and the structural features of the brain.
MAGNETIC RESONANCE IMAGING (MRI) S & I/Photo Researchers, Inc.	A magnetic field is used to excite the atoms in the body, and the energy emitted by these atoms is used to construct a highly detailed computer-generated picture of the brain's structure.
POSITRON EMISSION TOMOGRAPHY (PET SCAN) Tim Beddow/Photo Researchers, Inc.	Radioactive glucose (the brain's fuel source) is injected into the bloodstream. The computer measures which areas of the brain are most active and consuming the most glucose.
FUNCTIONAL MRI (fMRI) © Lester Lefkowitz/Corbis	Uses MRI technology to track which neurons in the brain are most active at a given moment by examining the energy released by hemoglobin molecules in the bloodstream.
ELECTROENCEPHALOGRAPHY (EEG) CC Studio/Photo Researchers, Inc.	Measures changes in electrical voltage at points along the scalp and yields information on gross patterns of brain activation.

Let's Review!

This section dealt with the structure and function of the hindbrain, midbrain, and forebrain. The hindbrain is primarily involved in life-sustaining functions, and the midbrain connects the hindbrain with the sophisticated structures of the forebrain. The function of the cortex and lateralization of the cortex were also described. For a quick check of your understanding, answer these questions.

1. Damage to which of the following brain structures would be most likely to cause death?

    a. Frontal lobe
    b. Amygdala
    c. Medulla
    d. Hippocampus

2. Billy suffered a stroke on the left side of his brain. Most of his left frontal lobe was destroyed. What symptoms would you most expect to see in Billy as a result of this damage?

    a. Paralysis on the right side of his body and an inability to speak
    b. Paralysis on the right side of his body and an inability to understand speech

    c. Paralysis of his left leg, partial deafness, and stuttering
    d. Paralysis on the left side of his body and an inability to understand speech

3. Juanita suffered a brain injury that left her with an inability to store new memories for events and concepts. Which part of Juanita's brain was most likely damaged?

    a. Hippocampus
    b. Hypothalamus
    c. Thalamus
    d. Midbrain

Answers 1. c; 2. a; 3. a

The Endocrine System: Hormones and Behavior

Learning Objective

- Explain how the endocrine system works, and list the endocrine glands.

We have seen that because of its electrochemical nature, the nervous system is especially good at quickly conveying information within the body. It is the speed of the nervous system that enables us to react quickly to changes in our environment. Messages are sent, decisions are made, and actions are taken—all accomplished with the speed of firing action potentials. At times, however, we require communication within the body that is slower and produces more long-lasting effects. In these circumstances, the endocrine system is called into action.

You Asked...

Why do our hormones affect our behavior so much?

DIANA FLORES, STUDENT

The endocrine system is a chemical system of communication that relies on the action of specialized organs called **endocrine glands** that are located throughout the body (■ FIGURE 2.17). When stimulated, endocrine glands release chemicals called **hormones** into the bloodstream. These hormones circulate through the bloodstream until they reach other organs in the body. Our internal organs are equipped with special receptor sites to accept these hormones.

The endocrine system is considerably slower than the nervous system in relaying messages because it relies on blood circulating through the veins and arteries of the cardiovascular system to transport hormones throughout the body. The stimulation created by hormones,

endocrine [EN-doe-crin] **glands** organs of the endocrine system that produce and release hormones into the blood

hormones chemical messengers of the endocrine system

FIGURE
2.17
Major Endocrine Glands of the Body

The glands of the endocrine system make and release hormones into the bloodstream.

From Starr and McMillan, Human Biology, *2nd ed., p. 271, © 1997 Wadsworth. Art by Kevin Somerville.*

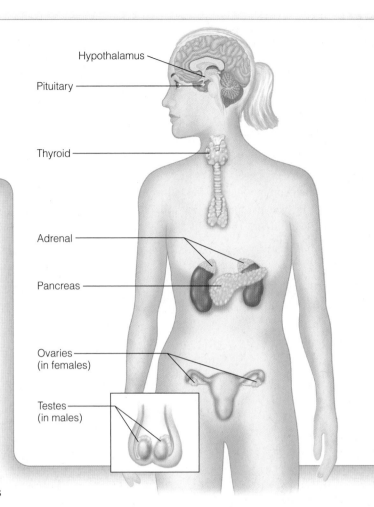

however, tends to last longer than the stimulation caused by action potentials at the synapse. Some of the bodily processes that are heavily influenced by hormonal activity include sexual activity, eating, sleeping, general physiological arousal, and growth.

Communication between the nervous and endocrine systems takes place through the hypothalamus and its connection with the **pituitary gland**. The pituitary gland, situated in the vicinity of the limbic system under the hypothalamus (Figure 2.17), is responsible for regulating hormone release in all the other endocrine glands. When the endocrine system is called into action, the hypothalamus sends a signal to the pituitary gland. The pituitary gland then releases hormones that travel through the bloodstream to the other endocrine glands, stimulating them to release the hormones they produce into the bloodstream. These hormones circulate to their target organs, where they bring about specific changes in the functioning of these organs.

Our bodies are equipped with a great number of peripheral endocrine glands (see Figure 2.17). Probably the best known endocrine glands are the *ovaries* and *testes*, which are necessary for sexuality and reproduction. Ovaries are the female sex glands, located in the abdominal cavity. Ovaries are directly responsible for the production of female eggs (ova) and the release of female sex hormones, or **estrogens**. Testes are the male sex glands, located in the testicles. Testes produce male sex cells (sperm) and male hormones, or **androgens**.

The *adrenal glands* sit just above the kidneys in both males and females and are important for regulating arousal and sexual behavior, among many things. When the sympathetic nervous system becomes active during times of stress, the inside of the adrenal glands, or the **adrenal medulla**, releases norepinephrine and epinephrine (also known as *adrenaline*) into the body's bloodstream, where they function as hormones. The sudden flooding of the bloodstream with these hormones causes the familiar sympathetic reactions of increased heart rate, blood pressure, and respiration.

The outside of the adrenal glands, or the **adrenal cortex**, produces *adrenal androgens*, which are male sex hormones found in both males and females. These androgens control many aspects of our sexual characteristics and basic physiological functioning. The adrenal cortex also interacts with the immune system to help protect us from infection and disease.

The nervous and endocrine systems are nothing short of amazing in their intricate structure and function. Without these systems we would not be able to control our bodies, think, feel, and interact with our environment. After studying this chapter, we hope you are suitably impressed with the wonder of your own biology. In the next chapter, we will explore the areas of sensation and perception, the study of how we sense and perceive information from the outside world.

pituitary [peh-TOO-uh-tare-ee] **gland** master gland of the endocrine system that controls the action of all other glands in the body

estrogens [ESS-tro-jens] a class of female hormones

androgens [ANN-dro-jens] a class of male hormones

adrenal [uh-DREEN-ull] **medulla** center part of the adrenal gland that plays a crucial role in the functioning of the sympathetic nervous system

adrenal cortex outside part of the adrenal gland that plays a role in the manufacture and release of androgens, and therefore influences sexual characteristics

Let's Review!

This section described the endocrine system and its relationship to the nervous system. For a quick check of your understanding, answer these questions.

1. The _____ releases male sex hormones in the body.
   a. adrenal cortex
   b. adrenal medulla
   c. hippocampus
   d. ovary

2. A malfunction in which of the following endocrine glands would be most disruptive to the overall functioning of the endocrine system?
   a. Ovaries/testes
   b. Thalamus
   c. Pituitary
   d. Adrenal

3. Juanita was just frightened by a snake. Which of the following endocrine glands most likely played the biggest role in her response to danger?
   a. Testes
   b. Adrenal cortex
   c. Ovaries
   d. Adrenal medulla

Answers 1. a; 2. c; 3. d

Studying
THE Chapter

Key Terms

neurons (38)	threshold of excitation (42)	endorphins (48)
glia cells (38)	action potential (42)	nervous system (50)
myelin (39)	all-or-none fashion (42)	central nervous system (CNS) (50)
cell body (39)	refractory period (42)	peripheral nervous system (PNS) (50)
DNA (39)	excitation (43)	sensory neurons (50)
dendrites (39)	inhibition (43)	motor neurons (50)
axon (39)	reuptake (44)	somatic nervous system (51)
neurotransmitters (39)	acetylcholine (ACh) (45)	autonomic nervous system (51)
synapse (39)	dopamine (46)	parasympathetic nervous system (52)
presynaptic neuron (40)	serotonin (46)	sympathetic nervous system (52)
postsynaptic neuron (40)	norepinephrine (NOR) (47)	hindbrain (53)
ions (41)	gamma amino butyric acid (GABA) (47)	forebrain (54)
resting potential (41)	glutamate (47)	midbrain (54)

medulla (54)

pons (54)

cerebellum (54)

reticular activating system (RAS) (56)

limbic system (56)

cerebral cortex (56)

cerebral hemispheres (56)

amygdala (56)

hippocampus (57)

thalamus (58)

hypothalamus (58)

homeostasis (58)

frontal lobe (59)

parietal lobe (59)

occipital lobe (59)

temporal lobe (59)

Wernicke's area (60)

Broca's area (60)

corpus callosum (60)

split brain (61)

association cortex (62)

motor cortex (63)

somatosensory cortex (63)

visual cortex (63)

auditory cortex (63)

endocrine glands (66)

hormones (66)

pituitary gland (67)

estrogens (67)

androgens (67)

adrenal medulla (67)

adrenal cortex (67)

What Do You Know? Assess Your Understanding

Test your retention and understanding of the material by answering the following questions.

1. The _____ system is an electrochemical system of communication in the body.
   a. nervous
   b. endocrine
   c. hormonal
   d. All of the above

2. The resting potential of a neuron is roughly _____.
   a. −55 mv
   b. +55 mv
   c. −70 mv
   d. +70 mv

3. The _____ of the neuron receive(s) incoming signals from other neurons in the nervous system.
   a. axon
   b. myelin
   c. axon bulb
   d. dendrites

4. Freddy was startled by a car backfiring outside. The increased heart rate and blood pressure that accompanied Freddy's startle response were most likely due to activation of Freddy's _____ nervous system.
   a. sympathetic
   b. parasympathetic
   c. somatic
   d. voluntary

5. There tends to be a(n) _____ of _____ in the brains of people suffering from Alzheimer's disease.
   a. excess; dopamine
   b. lack; dopamine
   c. excess; acetylcholine
   d. lack; acetylcholine

6. Drugs that are used to treat depression often _____ the action of _____ in the brain.
   a. increase; serotonin
   b. decrease; serotonin
   c. increase; GABA
   d. decrease; GABA

7. The chief excitatory neurotransmitter in the brain is _____.
   a. acetylcholine
   b. dopamine
   c. GABA
   d. glutamate

8. An excitatory neurotransmitter makes the post-synaptic neuron _____ likely to fire an action potential by making the inside of the postsynaptic neuron more _____.
   a. more; positive
   b. less; positive
   c. more; negative
   d. less; negative

9. Rachael cut her finger while cooking. Which neurotransmitter would be most useful in alleviating her pain?
   a. Dopamine
   b. Endorphin
   c. Norepinephrine
   d. GABA

10. The largest area of the brain's cortex is the _____ cortex.
    a. somatosensory
    b. auditory
    c. motor
    d. association

11. Our ability to detect anger and fear in others is likely influenced by which part of the brain?
    a. Hippocampus
    b. Amygdala
    c. Thalamus
    d. Hypothalamus

12. Loss of balance and coordination when drunk is most likely due to alcohol's effects on which part of the brain?
    a. Thalamus
    b. Hippocampus
    c. Cerebellum
    d. Broca's area

13. The _____ allows the right and left hemispheres of the brain to communicate.
    a. pons
    b. medulla
    c. corpus callosum
    d. limbic system

14. Mike was in a car accident in which he suffered massive damage to his left frontal lobe. What types of impairments would you most expect to see in Mike as a result of this damage?
    a. Paralysis on his right side
    b. Numbness on his right side
    c. An inability to comprehend speech
    d. Blindness in his right visual field

15. Damage to Broca's area would likely produce what effect?
    a. An inability to comprehend speech
    b. An inability to produce speech
    c. Paralysis on the right side of the body
    d. Both a and b

16. The master gland of the endocrine system is the _____ gland.
    a. hippocampus
    b. pituitary
    c. adrenal medulla
    d. adrenal cortex

17. During times of stress, the endocrine system is most likely to release _____.
    a. androgens
    b. estrogens
    c. adrenaline
    d. dopamine

18. Male sex hormones are called _____.
    a. estrogens
    b. androgens
    c. testosterone
    d. adrenalines

19. A split-brain operation is done to control _____.
    a. seizures
    b. depression
    c. schizophrenia
    d. pain

20. Visual information is processed in the _____ lobe of the brain.
    a. temporal
    b. occipital
    c. parietal
    d. frontal

Answers: 1. A; 2. C; 3. D; 4. A; 5. D; 6. A; 7. D; 8. A; 9. B; 10. D; 11. B; 12. C; 13. C; 14. A; 15. B; 16. B; 17. C; 18. B; 19. A; 20. B.

Online Resources

CENGAGENOW™ Personalized Study

www.cengage.com/login

Go to www.cengage.com/login to link to CengageNOW, your online study tool. First take the **Pre-Test** for this chapter to get your **Personalized Study Plan**, which will identify topics you need to review and direct you to online resources. Then take the **Post-Test** to determine what concepts you have mastered and what you still need work on.

 What Is Psychology? Essentials Book Companion Website

www.cengage.com/psychology/pastorino

Visit your book companion website, where you will find more resources to help you study. Resources include learning objectives, Internet exercises, quizzing, flash cards, and a pronunciation glossary.

Look Back
AT WHAT YOU'VE LEARNED

The nervous system is organized into a hierarchy of systems:

How Do Neurons Communicate?

- **Neurons** use electrochemical energy to generate **action potentials** that travel to the end of the neuron and cause the release of **neurotransmitters**.

- Action potentials or neural signals are fired when a neuron is depolarized enough to reach their **threshold of excitation** (−55 mv).

- Neurotransmitters are chemical compounds that carry signals across neurons. Some of the key neurotransmitters are **acetylcholine**, **dopamine**, **serotonin**, **norepinephrine**, **endorphin**, **GABA**, and **glutamate**.

- Neurotransmitters play significant roles in regulating behavior and mood.

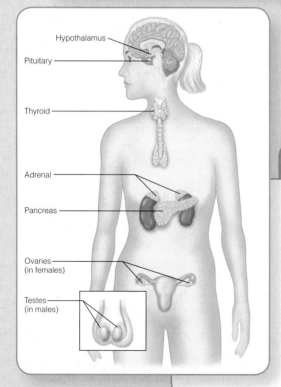

What Is the Endocrine System?

The endocrine system contains glands that release chemical messengers—**hormones**—into the bloodstream. Compared to the nervous system, the endocrine system is slower and more long-lasting in its effects.

Anne Ackerman/Getty Images

What Are the Structure and Function of the Brain?

- The brain is divided into three key regions: the **hindbrain**, the **midbrain**, and the **forebrain**. The forebrain regulates higher-order processes such as thinking and emotional control.

- The brain regulates motor activity, sensation and perception, emotions, our ability to learn and remember, and all the other elements of human behavior.

- The **cerebral cortex** is a thin layer of wrinkled tissue that covers the outside of the brain and is most responsible for the cognition, decision making, and language capabilities that are unique to humans.

© JLP/Jose Luis Pelaez/zefa/Corbis

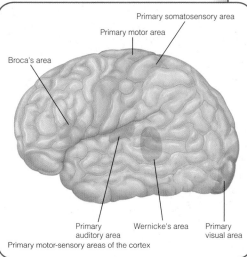

Primary motor-sensory areas of the cortex

- The brain is divided into right and left hemispheres. The left hemisphere generally governs the right side of the body, whereas the right hemisphere governs the left side of the body.

- To assist in studying the brain and its functioning, technology such as CAT scans, MRIs, fMRIs, PET scans, and EEGs are all important tools.

S & I/Photo Researchers, Inc.

3

HOW DO WE Sense AND Perceive OUR WORLD?

DAJ/Getty Images

Understanding how sensation and perception occur is very useful to a number of professions. For example, one of our former students, Edgar Lituma, uses these areas of psychology on a daily basis in his work as an artist and graphic designer. Simply put, his art is about creating perceptions in people. Much of Edgar's work centers on designing elements that will be used in advertisements. One of his favorite areas is motion graphics or animated graphics such as those that you might see in videos, TV, or on the Internet. In creating graphics for ads, Edgar must understand how people sense and perceive color, texture, shape, motion, and so on. This understanding is important because being able to predict how the public will perceive an image or video is crucial to Edgar's ability to convey his client's intended message. In fact, Edgar recently told us, "If you want to get into a motion graphics department without using psychology, you won't get very far. You have to be able to predict people's reactions." Check out one of Edgar's art pieces, Chicken Hormonia, on page 85. As you study this chapter, you too will gain important insight into how we use our senses to experience and understand the world around us. We'll begin by looking at how psychologists measure sensation and perception.

© KB Bishi

Edgar Lituma uses his knowledge of sensation and perception in his work as a graphic artist.

Measuring Sensation and Perception

- Explain the concepts of absolute threshold, just noticeable difference (jnd), and subliminal perception.

To read this page, you must first focus your conscious awareness or **attention** on the page and be able to *see* the images printed on it. Seeing is an example of what psychologists call **sensation**. In sensation, sense organs of the body, such as the eyes, convert environmental energy, such as the light that is bouncing off the book page, into neural signals that the brain can then process. Sensation—in this case, seeing—is the first step to getting information into our minds. After sensation, you must *understand* what the images printed on the page mean. **Perception** occurs when you interpret the meaning of the information gathered through your senses.

Psychologists who study sensation and perception are most interested in understanding how we process sensory stimuli such as sights, sounds, and smells. For instance, what occurs when you look at an apple? How does your mind interpret the color of the light bouncing off the surface of the apple? Why do some apples appear to be greenish-red and others appear to be deep ruby red? What makes the different notes of a musical piece sound different? What physical properties of a food make it taste sweet or bitter? Questions like these are the focus of the branch of psychology called **psychophysics**.

> ### You Asked...
>
> *Can testing on people's senses and perceptions be that scientific, or is it just opinion?*   JEFF WRIGHT, STUDENT

Absolute Thresholds

One of the fundamental questions psychophysicists have sought to answer concerns the limits of human sensory capabilities. How faint a light can humans see? How soft a tone can we hear? Psychophysicists have conducted many experiments to answer these questions. These experiments typically involve presenting stimuli of gradually increasing or decreasing intensity (along with some trials on which the stimulus is not presented at all). Participants are asked to report whether they can detect the presence of the stimulus. In this way psychophysicists establish an *absolute threshold*. **Absolute threshold** is defined as the minimum intensity of a stimulus that can be detected 50% of the time. This 50% mark is used because the level of the stimulus required for it to *just* be perceived varies from trial to trial and from person to person during an experiment. ■ TABLE 3.1 lists the approximate established absolute thresholds for the five senses, described in familiar descriptive terms.

The Just Noticeable Difference and Weber's Law

In addition to establishing absolute thresholds for the senses, psychophysicists have tried to establish the minimum *change* in the intensity of a stimulus that can be detected 50% of the time. This barely noticeable change in the stimulus is referred to as the *difference threshold* or the **just noticeable difference (jnd)**. In the early 1800s, psychophysicist Max Weber discovered an interesting characteristic of the jnd, known as **Weber's law**. According to this law, for each of our five senses, the amount of change in the stimulus that is necessary to produce a jnd depends on the intensity at which the stimulus is *first* presented. For example, if you

attention   conscious awareness; can be focused on events that are taking place in the environment or inside our minds

sensation   the process through which our sense organs convert environmental energies such as light and sound into neural impulses

perception   the process through which we interpret sensory information

psychophysics   the study of how the mind interprets the physical properties of stimuli

absolute threshold   the minimum intensity of a stimulus at which participants can identify its presence 50% of the time

just noticeable difference (jnd)   the minimum change in intensity of a stimulus that participants can detect 50% of the time

Weber's [VAY-bers] **law**   a psychological principle that states that for each of our five senses, the amount of change in the stimulus that is necessary to produce a jnd depends on the intensity at which the stimulus is first presented add one additional teaspoon of salt to a very salty pot of soup, it will probably not be noticeable. But that same teaspoon of salt added to a less salty pot of soup may be very noticeable. Weber's law helps explain some of the subjectivity we experience in sensation. Under some conditions, one teaspoon of salt won't make a difference to our enjoyment of a recipe. Under other conditions, it might.

Processing Without Awareness: Subliminal Stimulation of the Senses

Absolute thresholds and just noticeable differences describe the limits of our conscious awareness of sensations. But is sensation always a conscious experience? Or is it possible that we might be affected by sensory stimuli even when we are unaware of sensing them? **Subliminal** perception, the unconscious perception of stimuli, became a topic of many debates in the late 1950s when a man named James Vicary attempted to use subliminal persuasion to convince moviegoers at a public theater to buy more popcorn and soda. Vicary flashed messages such as "Eat popcorn" and "Drink Coca-Cola" between the frames of a movie at a speed so fast that moviegoers did not have time to consciously perceive the messages. Because the messages were flashed so briefly, the moviegoers never consciously saw anything other than the movie.

Vicary reported that as a result of his "experiment," concession sales rose 18%. As it turns out, James Vicary admitted in 1962 that he had not conducted a true experiment. The data that he collected were so few that they could not be used for scientific purposes (Epley, Savitsy, & Kachelski, 1999; Pratkanis, 1992). After Vicary's attempts at subliminal persuasion, researchers began to carefully examine the effects of subliminal persuasion both in the real world and in the laboratory. To date, most studies have failed to yield convincing evidence for the effectiveness of subliminal persuasion (see Pratkanis, Epley, Savitsky, & Kachelski, 2007).

Table 3.1 Descriptions of the Absolute Thresholds for the Five Senses

Sense		Absolute Threshold
Vision		A candle seen from 30 miles away on a clear, dark night.
Hearing		A ticking watch that is 20 feet away in an otherwise quiet room.
Smell		One drop of perfume diffused in a three-room apartment.
Taste		One teaspoon of sugar dissolved in 2 gallons of water.
Touch		The wing of a bumblebee falling on one's cheek from a distance of 1 centimeter.

subliminal when the intensity of a stimulus is below the participant's absolute threshold and the participant is not consciously aware of the stimulus

There is no good scientific evidence to suggest that moviegoers can be coerced into buying refreshments through subliminal persuasion.

GDT/Getty Images

Extrasensory Perception: Can Perception Occur Without the Five Senses?

As with subliminal perception, scientific research casts serious doubts on the existence of *extrasensory perception* (ESP), sometimes also referred to as *psi*. ESP is the purported ability to acquire information about the world without using the known senses—for example, the ability to read people's minds or see the future. Most of the scientific tests of ESP involve the Ganzfeld procedure, a procedure in which one participant acts as a *sender* who tries to send a message to another participant acting as a *receiver* in another room. Although a few of these studies have suggested that some people may be better at sending and receiving such telepathic messages, the vast majority fail to support the existence of ESP (Milton & Wiseman, 2001).

Very recently, researchers have used neuroimaging to investigate whether ESP exists. Researchers Samuel Moulton and Steven Kosslyn (2008) had participants engage in a modified version of the Ganzfeld procedure. During the experiment, the receiver had to guess which of two images on a computer screen was being sent by the sender in another room. As the receivers made these judgments, their brains were scanned using fMRI technology. Moulton and Kosslyn found that the receivers guessed the correct image only about 50% of the time (no better than chance alone). Furthermore, the fMRIs showed no differences in brain functioning between the trials resulting in correct and incorrect responses. Moulton and Kosslyn interpret these results as powerful evidence against the existence of ESP.

Now that we have a basic understanding of how psychologists measure the limits of our sensory abilities, we will examine how our bodies accomplish the process of sensation.

Let's Review!

This section has given you a quick overview of some important aspects of measuring sensation and perception—absolute threshold, just noticeable difference, and subliminal stimulation of the senses. For a quick check of your understanding, answer these questions.

1. Jerry wants to sweeten his iced tea. He adds one teaspoon of sugar, but the tea does not taste sweet to him. When Jerry adds one more teaspoon of sugar, he finds that the tea now tastes sweet—but just barely. Two teaspoons of sugar seem to correspond to Jerry's _____.
   a. just noticeable difference
   b. absolute threshold
   c. k value
   d. stimulus threshold

2. If your tea already tastes sweet to you, the minimum amount of sugar that you would have to add to your tea to make it taste sweeter corresponds to your _____.
   a. just noticeable difference
   b. absolute threshold

   c. k value
   d. stimulus threshold

3. According to Weber's law, who will most likely notice the addition of one more teaspoon of sugar in a glass of iced tea?
   a. Joni, whose tea has no sugar in it
   b. Bill, who has two teaspoons of sugar in his tea
   c. Sarafina, who has three teaspoons of sugar in her tea
   d. All of these people will be equally likely to notice the difference.

Answers 1. b; 2. a; 3. a

Vision: The World Through Our Eyes

Our eyes are at the front of our skulls, so you might assume that vision is a direct transfer from object to eye to brain. Vision is more complicated than that, however, and researchers have studied vision more than the other senses. To understand vision, we'll look at the properties of light that apply to vision, the anatomy of the eye, the layers of the retina, and how we process visual information in the brain.

How Vision Works: Light Waves and Energy

When we see an object, what we really see are the light waves that are reflected off the surface of the object. Thus, a blue shirt appears blue because blue is the only color of light that is reflected by the shirt. The shirt absorbs all other colors of light. As we'll see, the specific characteristics of the shirt's color and brightness are all determined by the physical characteristics of the particular light energy that is bouncing off the shirt.

MEASURING LIGHT: WAVELENGTH AND AMPLITUDE

■ FIGURE 3.1 depicts the electromagnetic spectrum, which includes visible light. Electromagnetic energies, including light, result from disturbances in the electrical and magnetic fields that exist in the universe. Like all electromagnetic energies, light waves are characterized by their **wavelength** and **amplitude**. The wavelength of light is the distance between the

wavelength a physical property of some energies that corresponds to the distance between wave peaks

amplitude a physical property of some energies that corresponds to the height of wave peaks

FIGURE 3.1 **The Visible Spectrum of Light**

Reprinted with permission: Galanter, Eugene (1962). "Contemporary Psychophysics" in New Directions in Psychology. R. Brown, E. Galanter, E. H. Hess, & G. Mandler (eds.). New York: Holt, Rinehart, & Winston., p. 97.

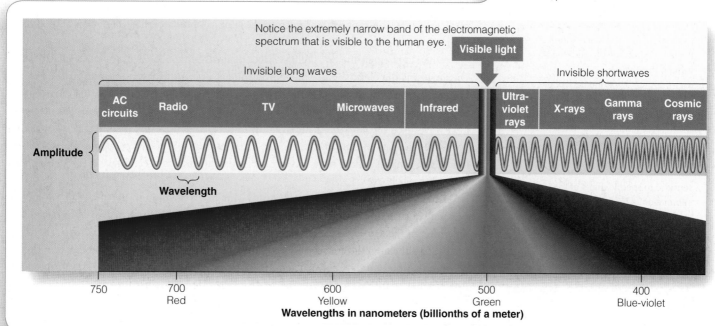

Notice the extremely narrow band of the electromagnetic spectrum that is visible to the human eye.

Visible light

Invisible long waves   Invisible shortwaves

| AC circuits | Radio | TV | Microwaves | Infrared | Ultra-violet rays | X-rays | Gamma rays | Cosmic rays |

Amplitude

Wavelength

750   700   600   500   400
Red   Yellow   Green   Blue-violet

Wavelengths in nanometers (billionths of a meter)

peaks of consecutive waves. The amplitude of the light wave is the height of each wave peak. These distances are typically measured in nanometers (nm).

The human eye cannot sense all electromagnetic energy. In fact, the **visible spectrum** for humans is only a very narrow band of the electromagnetic spectrum that spans from about 360 nm to 750 nm (Figure 3.1). Other species can sense electromagnetic wavelengths that are beyond the human visible spectrum. Some snakes sense infrared rays, allowing them to sense other animals' body heat (Sinclair, 1985). Some insects, fish, reptiles, birds, and other vertebrates are able to sense ultraviolet rays (Boulcott & Braithewaite, 2005). If you are hiking through the woods, keep in mind that certain animals may be able to see you before you see them!

PROPERTIES OF LIGHT: HUE, BRIGHTNESS, AND SATURATION

Although our eyes cannot sense much of the electromagnetic spectrum, we are capable of seeing millions of different combinations of color, richness, and brightness of light (Bornstein & Marks, 1982; Kleiner, 2004). The wavelength of the light wave corresponds to the color or **hue** of the light we see. Shorter wavelengths correspond to cool colors such as blues and purples; longer wavelengths correspond to warmer colors such as yellows and reds (Figure 3.1). The amplitude of the light wave corresponds to its **brightness**. The higher the amplitude of the light wave, the brighter the color we perceive. One other characteristic of light, **saturation**, corresponds to the purity of the light. Light that consists of a single wavelength will produce the most saturated, or richest, color. Light that is a mixture of wavelengths produces less saturated colors. For example, pure blue light is high in saturation, but a mixture of blue and white light produces a less saturated blue light.

For vision to occur, our eyes must be able to convert the electromagnetic waves of the visible spectrum into action potentials that our brains can process. In the next section, we will look at the anatomy of the eye to get a feel for how this conversion occurs.

The Anatomy of the Outer Eye

The process of vision begins with the parts of the eye we can readily see: the clear cornea that covers the iris, the colored part of your eye, and the pupil, the opening in the iris. From there, light is eventually focused on the retina at the back of your eye. The white part, the sclera, is a supporting structure that doesn't play a part in the processing of visual information.

When light enters the eye, the first structure it passes through is the *cornea* (■ FIGURE 3.2). The cornea is the clear, slightly bulged-out outer surface of the eye. It protects the eye and begins the focusing process. The light that is reflected from an object in the environment must eventually be focused on the rear surface of the eye if we are to see the object clearly. As light waves pass through the material of the cornea, they slow down and bend—just as they do when they pass through a camera lens. This bending of light waves plays an essential role in focusing images on the back of your eye. A damaged cornea can make it impossible for a person to see clearly.

Directly behind the cornea is the **pupil**. This black opening in the center of your eye is not really a structure. Rather, it is an opening, or aperture, through which light passes into the center of the eye. Light cannot pass through the white part of the eye, the *sclera*. Therefore, it must pass through the cornea and pupil to enter the eye. The *iris*, the colored part of the eye surrounding the pupil, is constructed of rings of muscles that control the size of the pupil. In dimly lit conditions, the iris relaxes to dilate the pupil, allowing the maximum amount of light into the eye. In brightly lit conditions, the iris constricts to close the pupil, thus reduc-

visible spectrum the spectrum of light that humans can see

hue the color of a light

brightness the intensity of light; it corresponds to the amplitude of the light waves

saturation the purity of light; pure light or saturated light consists of a single wavelength

pupil the hole in the iris through which light enters the eye

lens the part of the eye that lies behind the pupil and focuses light rays on the retina

accommodation the process through which the lens is stretched or squeezed to focus light on the retina

retina the structure at the back of the eye that contains cells that convert light into neural signals

rods the light-sensitive cells of the retina that pick up any type of light energy and convert it to neural signals

cones the cells of the retina that are sensitive to specific colors of light and send information to the brain concerning the colors we are seeing

optic nerve the structure that conveys visual information away from the retina to the brain

blindspot the point where the optic nerve leaves the retina, where there are no rods or cones ing the amount of light entering the eye so as not to overwhelm the light-sensitive cells in the eye.

Directly behind the iris and the pupil is the **lens** of the eye. The lens is a clear structure that is attached to the eye with strong *ciliary muscles*. The lens of the eye is rather like the lens of a camera—its job is to bring the light waves entering the eye into sharp focus on the back of the eye. The lens of the eye is somewhat soft and flexible. As the ciliary muscles stretch the lens, it changes shape, or undergoes **accommodation**, so that the image passing through it is focused properly.

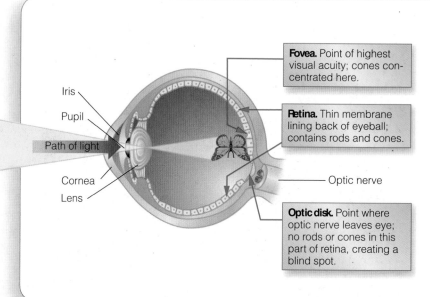

Fovea. Point of highest visual acuity; cones concentrated here.

Retina. Thin membrane lining back of eyeball; contains rods and cones.

Optic nerve

Optic disk. Point where optic nerve leaves eye; no rods or cones in this part of retina, creating a blind spot.

Iris
Pupil
Path of light
Cornea
Lens

FIGURE

3.2   **The Anatomy of the Eye**

The Retina: Light Energy to Neural Messages

Once the light waves have been focused on the back of the eye, conversion of light waves into neural impulses occurs in the **retina**, the surface that lines the inside of the back of the eyeball. In the retina, specialized cells called **rods** and **cones** convert light into neural signals. Without these cells, vision would not be possible.

THE ANATOMY OF THE RETINA

The diagram in ■ FIGURE 3.3 shows a cross section of the layers in the human retina. The *ganglion cells* are on the surface of the retina, followed by successive layers of *amacrine, bipolar*, and *horizontal cells*, and finally the light-sensitive rods and cones. Look closely at Figure 3.3 and you will see that the light entering the eye must filter through all the layers of the retina before finally striking the rods and cones.

Incoming light passes unimpeded through the transparent layers of the retina to reach the rods and cones, which convert the light energy into neural impulses. These signals travel back out to the ganglion cells on the surface of the retina. Along the way, the horizontal, bipolar, and amacrine cells funnel and consolidate the neural information from the rods and cones so that we can see a unified, coherent image. The signals that reach the ganglion cells in the top layer of the retina are to some degree summaries of the visual information from the rods and cones.

THE OPTIC NERVE AND THE BLINDSPOT

Once the neural impulses reach the ganglion cells, they exit the retina and travel to the brain via the **optic nerve**, which is composed of the axons of the ganglion cells (see Figures 3.2 and 3.3). The optic nerve actually exits the retina on the *surface* of the retina; there are no light-sensitive rods or cones at the point where the optic nerve leaves the retina. With no rods or cones at this spot, each of our eyes has a **blindspot**, which is a point in our visual field that we cannot see.

Luckily, however, our blindspots do not pose much of a problem. For one thing, the blindspot is at the side of our visual field, where we normally do not bring objects into focus in the first place (see Figure 3.2). If the blindspot were located at the *fovea* (the point directly behind the pupil), it is possible that we would be much more aware of it. Another reason is that we have two eyes. Whatever part of the world we miss seeing because of the blindspot in our left eye we see with our right eye, and vice versa.

Ray Hendley/Indexstock

Vision problems can strike at any age. Nearsightedness, or not seeing distant objects well, is common at all ages. Another condition, *presbyopia,* is more common after middle age. Presbyopia occurs when, as we age, the lens of the eye becomes more rigid and the eye is less able to accommodate to close objects. Because of presbyopia, many middle-aged and older adults need reading glasses or bifocals.

The back of the retina, which lines the back interior surface of the eye

Rods   Cones

Rod (R) and cone receptors (C)

Horizontal cells (H)

Bipolar cells (B)

Amacrine cells (A)

Ganglion cells (G)

Optic nerve fibers

Light rays entering from the outer eye

Omikron/Photo Researchers, Inc.

FIGURE

3.3

A Cross Section of the Retina

Above is a schematic of the retina with the rods shown in purple and the cones in pink. To the right is an electron micrograph of the retina showing the rods and cones.

From "Organization of the Primate Retina," by J. E. Dowling and B. B. Boycott, in Proceedings of the Royal Society of London, 16, Series B, 80–111. Copyright © 1966 by the Royal Society.

THE RODS AND CONES

The rods and cones that line the inside layer of the retina play different roles in the process of vision. The rods, which are long and skinny, are sensitive to all colors of light, but they do not transmit information about color to the brain (see Figure 3.3). You can think of the rods as being black-and-white receptors. If you had only rods in your retina, you'd see everything in black and white. We see the world in color because of the cone cells in the retina. The cones, which are shorter and fatter than the rods, are responsible for transmitting information about color to the brain.

Relative to rods, the cones of the eye require a higher intensity of light to become activated. Because of this, we do not have good color vision in dimly lit situations. Think about driving at night. When light levels are not very intense, it may be possible to see objects in the distance, but impossible to discern their color. In each eye you have about 100 million rods but only about 5 million cones (Matlin & Foley, 1997). Having so many rods and so few cones in the retina indicates that perceiving shape and form takes precedence over perception of color. If you think about it for a minute, this arrangement makes sense. Which information would you need first: to see the shape of a car speeding toward you in the dark, or to see the color of the car? Your first concern would be seeing the car to avoid a collision!

In addition to being differentially sensitive to light energy, the rods and cones of the eye are not distributed evenly across the surface of the retina. The highest concentration of cones is at the fovea, with fewer and fewer cones toward the peripheral edges of the retina. The density of rods follows the opposite pattern, with the highest concentration at the peripheral edges of the retina and fewer and fewer rods as you move toward the fovea. This arrangement means that our best color vision is for objects placed directly in front of us, whereas our color vision for objects seen out of the corners of our eyes (in our peripheral vision) is very poor.

TURNING LIGHT ENERGY INTO NEURAL MESSAGES

The rods and cones of the eye are able to convert light into neural impulses because they contain light-sensitive **photopigments**, chemicals that are activated by light energy. When a rod is not receiving light input, its photopigment molecules are stable. However, when light strikes the rod, this incoming light energy splits the photopigments apart (McNaughton, 1990). As the photopigments break up, they set off a complex chain of chemical reactions that change the rate at which the neurons of the visual system fire action potentials. The brain uses the pattern of these action potentials to interpret what we are seeing.

Eddie Hironaka/Getty Images

Because cones require more light energy than rods, it can be difficult to discriminate among colors at night. Even though you can clearly make out the shapes of the oncoming cars, you may not be able to discern their color.

photopigments light-sensitive chemicals that create electrical changes when they come into contact with light

dark adaptation the process through which our eyes adjust to dark conditions after having been exposed to bright light

light adaptation the process through which our eyes adjust to bright light after having been exposed to darkness

Adapting to Light and Darkness

Have you ever had to wait at the back of a dark movie theater for your eyes to adjust before you could find your seat? This type of adaptation is referred to as **dark adaptation**. It also takes our eyes a while to adapt to sudden increases in light brightness, or undergo **light adaptation**.

Dark and light adaptation are accomplished, in part, by changes in pupil size. Unfortunately, the amount of dilation and constriction that our pupils can accomplish is limited, and they alone cannot fully account for the adaptations we experience. Another mechanism of adaptation is found in the photopigments themselves. If you were to enter a completely darkened room, no light would enter your eyes and no photopigments would break down. After remaining in these darkened conditions for a period of time, the photopigment levels in your eyes would build up because they are not being broken down by light. This is what occurs when we sleep at night. With a large store of photopigments, your eyes are very sensitive to light. If someone were to suddenly turn on the lights in the bedroom, you would experience a bright flash of light and perhaps even pain as the large number of available photopigments makes your eyes very sensitive to the light. It would take about one minute for your eyes to adjust to the light (Hood & Finkelstein, 1986).

The process of dark adaptation is the opposite of what occurs during light adaptation. Under normal daytime lighting conditions, we constantly use our photopigments to see our surroundings. So, at any given moment during the day, a certain percentage of our photopigments are broken down. If you suddenly enter a darkened theater after being in bright daylight, you will not have enough photopigments to be able to see well. It will take more than 30 minutes for your photopigment levels to build up completely (Hood & Finkelstein, 1986). This is why you may have to stand, popcorn in hand, at the back of the darkened theater for several minutes before you can find your seat!

When you step out of the darkness into bright light, you may experience a flash of pain as the built-up photopigment in your eyes reacts all at once to the bright light.

How We See Color

Like the rods, the cones of the retina also contain photopigments. However, there is an important distinction between the photopigments in the rods and cones. All rods contain the same photopigment. In

Jack Wild/Getty Images

FIGURE

3.4

Primary Colors of Paint and Light

Mixing paint is not the same as combining colors of light.

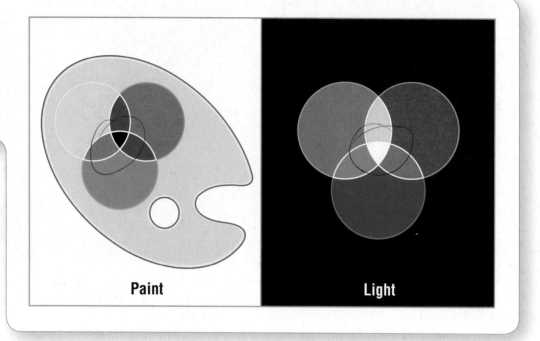

Paint   Light

contrast, there are three different types of cones, each containing a slightly different photopigment. Having different types of photopigments in our cones is one reason we see color.

THE COLORS OF LIGHT

You may have learned in elementary school about three primary colors (red, yellow, and blue) from which all other colors can be made. This is true when you are talking about paint or crayons that actually reflect the color of light that we see. However, mixing colored light is different from mixing colors of paints or crayons. The primary colors of light are *red, green, and blue*. All other colors of light can be made from these three colors. If you mix all the primary colors of light together, you get white light. In contrast, if you mixed red, blue, and yellow paint together, you would get black paint (■ FIGURE 3.4). When we describe color vision and combinations of colors, remember to think in terms of *light*, and not in terms of paint.

THE TRICHROMATIC THEORY OF COLOR VISION

By now, we hope that some of you have made the connection between the three primary colors of light and the three different types of cones in our retinas. Could it be that each type of cone detects the presence of a different primary color of light? This is the central assumption of the **trichromatic theory of color vision**.

The exact origin of the trichromatic theory of color vision is not really known (Rushton, 1975; Wasserman, 1978). Most psychologists credit Hermann von Helmholtz (1821–1894) with proposing this theory in the mid-1800s. According to the trichromatic theory, we have three different types of cones in our eyes, each of which contains a slightly different photopigment that makes the cell particularly sensitive to a certain wavelength of light.

One type of cone is particularly sensitive to long wavelengths of light (red), another is very sensitive to medium wavelengths of light (green), and the third is most sensitive to short wavelengths of light (blue). Notice that these colors correspond to the primary colors of light. These differentially sensitive cones give our brain a means of knowing what color of light we are seeing at any particular moment (Wald, 1964).

For example, if the brain receives input that the red cones are very active and the green and blue are not very active, the brain knows you are seeing the color red. This same logic can

trichromatic [try-crow-MAT-ick] **theory of color vision**   the idea that color vision is made possible by the presence of three different types of cones in the retina that react respectively to either red, green, or blue light be applied to seeing the color green and blue, but how does it apply to seeing nonprimary colors? All colors of light are some combination of red, green, and blue light (see Figure 3.4). So, the brain processes the proportions of red, green, and blue cones that are firing intensely to know what color you are seeing.

> **You Asked...**
>
> *Why do some people have color blindness with only certain colors?*   PAIGE REDMON, STUDENT

COLOR BLINDNESS: DOES EVERYONE HAVE THREE TYPES OF CONES?

Research in the last decade or so suggests that some people with normal color vision may have more than three types of cones. The presence of additional types of cones may cause some people to perceive colors differently than others do (Nathans, Merbs, Sung, Weitz, & Wang, 1992; Neitz, Neitz, & Jacobs, 1993). There is also abundant evidence that some people have fewer than three types of cones. **Color blindness,** or the inability to see one or more colors, is often the result of missing cones in the retina. A particularly common type of color blindness is red–green color blindness, a disorder that occurs in approximately 8% of males in the United States who are born missing either red or green cones. Similar levels of color blindness have been seen in specific populations of males in Turkey and Greenland, whereas lower levels of color blindness have been found among males in Colombia, Spain, and Italy. The fact that rates of color blindness vary across genetically disparate populations suggests a genetic basis to the disorder (see Citirik, Acaroglu, Batman, & Zilelioglu, 2005). The red–green color-blind person has only blue and red cones or blue and green cones in his retina. The lack of red (or green) cones results in an inability to discriminate between red and green. At a stoplight, a red–green color-blind person must look at the position of the red and green lights, because the lights appear to be the same color.

Although trichromatic theory explains certain aspects of color vision, it does not explain all aspects of vision. Trichromatic theory cannot explain *negative afterimages.* To understand what an afterimage is, try this demonstration.

color blindness a condition in which a person cannot perceive one or more colors because of a lack of specific cones in the retina

On the left is a colorful piece of art, *Chicken Hormonia,* by our former student Edgar Lituma. On the right is what this piece of art would look like if you were missing all of your cones.

© Edgar Lituma

© Edgar Lituma

FIGURE

3.5 Negative Afterimages

See text for instructions.

YOUR TURN – ACTIVE LEARNING

Get a blank sheet of paper and set it aside. Stare at the black dot in the center of ■ FIGURE 3.5 without blinking or moving your eyes. Continue staring for 60 to 90 seconds. Then quickly move your gaze to the blank sheet of white paper. What do you see? You should see the image of a green shamrock with a yellow border on the blank sheet of white paper. The shamrock is a negative afterimage. Notice that the colors you see in the afterimage are different from the colors in the original. Why would you see different colors in your afterimage? Simply having different types of cones cannot explain this phenomenon. So, what does explain afterimages?

THE OPPONENT-PROCESS THEORY OF COLOR VISION

The **opponent-process theory** proposes a different type of color-sensitive cell in the visual system, a cell that is sensitive to two colors of light. There are thought to be three types of opponent-process cells in our visual system: red/green, yellow/blue, and black/white. The key to opponent-process theory is that these cells can detect the presence of only one color at a time. The colors *oppose* each other so that the opponent-process cell cannot detect the presence of both colors at the same time. For example, a red/green cell can detect either red or green light at any one time. If you shine a red light in the eye, the red/green cells tell our brain that we are seeing red. If you shine a green light in the eye, the red/green cells tell our brain that we are seeing green. But these red/green cells cannot detect red and green at the same time. Opponent-process theory is consistent with the finding that if we simultaneously shine red and green lights into your eye, you will likely see a neutral shade that is neither red nor green (Hurvich & Jameson, 1957/2000).

Opponent-process theory can explain the phenomenon of negative afterimages. Recall the demonstration you tried with Figure 3.5. After staring at the red and blue shamrock, you saw a green and yellow afterimage. Opponent-process theory proposes that as you stared at the red and blue shamrock, you were using the red and blue portions of the opponent-process cells. After a period of 60–90 seconds of continuous staring, you expended these cells' capacity to fire action potentials. In a sense, you temporarily "wore out" the red and blue portions of these cells. Then you looked at a blank sheet of white paper. Under normal conditions, the white light would excite *all* of the opponent-process cells. Recall that white light contains all colors of light. But, given the exhausted state of your opponent-process cells, only parts of them were capable of firing action potentials. In this example, the green and yellow parts of the cells were ready to fire. The light reflected off the white paper could excite only the yellow and green parts of the cells, so you saw a green and yellow shamrock.

TRICHROMATIC THEORY OR OPPONENT-PROCESS THEORY?

We've seen that trichromatic theory and opponent-process theory each explain certain aspects of color vision. So, which theory is correct? Both theories seem to have merit. It is generally believed that these two theories describe processes that operate at different places in the visual system (Hubel, 1995).

Trichromatic theory does a good job of explaining color vision at the level of the rods and cones. Opponent-process theory best explains the processing of color vision beyond the level of the rods and cones. Evidence suggests that opponent processing may occur at the level of the ganglion cells (Dacey, 2000; DeValois & DeValois, 1975); the amacrine, horizontal, and bipolar cells of the retina; or even in the visual cortex (see Conway & Livingstone, 2005). In the next section, we will trace the path that visual information takes as it leaves the retina and enters the brain.

opponent-process theory proposes that we have dual-action cells beyond the level of the retina that signal the brain when we see one of a pair of colors

The Visual Pathways of the Brain

Once the rods and cones of the retina convert light into neural signals, this information begins its journey into the visual cortex of the brain. Along the way, visual information is continually processed and combined to ultimately give us a coherent perception of what we see in the environment. The bipolar, horizontal, and amacrine cells gather the information from the rods and cones and funnel it to the ganglion cells. The ganglion cells join together to form the optic nerve, which carries visual information into the brain.

Visual information from the right side of the body travels to the left hemisphere, and information from the left side travels to the right hemisphere. The point at which the optic nerve from the left eye and the optic nerve from the right eye cross over is called the **optic chiasm**. From the optic chiasm, most visual information travels to the *thalamus* before traveling to the visual cortex, where specialized cells interpret the input (see ■ FIGURE 3.6). Some of the cells in the visual cortex function as **feature detectors** that fire only when they receive input that indicates we are looking at a particular shape, color, angle, or other visual feature. We have feature detectors for many different specific features of visual stimuli (Conway, 2003; Hubel, 1995; Hulbert, 2003; Seiffert, Somers, Dale, & Tootell, 2003; Xiao, Wang, & Felleman, 2003). The visual cortex and other parts of the brain gather information from our various feature detectors and combine it to give us a coherent picture of whatever it is we are seeing (Lumer, Friston, & Rees, 1998; Murray, Olshausen, & Woods, 2003).

DO MEN AND WOMEN SEE THE WORLD DIFFERENTLY?

Recent evidence suggests that when it comes to processing visual information, men and women see things differently. Females tend to be better at discriminating one object from another (Overman, Bachevalier, Schuhmann, & Ryan, 1996), naming colors (Bornstein, 1985), and processing facial expressions accurately (McClure, 2000). Females also tend to show a preference for using many colors and seem to prefer warm colors to cool ones. Males tend to be better at processing moving objects and the spatial aspects of objects (Alexander, 2003).

Researcher Gerianne Alexander (2003) has argued that these gender differences in visual processing are neurological and that they have evolved to facilitate the performance of traditional male/female roles in society. In many societies, males have historically hunted for food, whereas women have gathered crops and nurtured their children. By being able to discriminate among objects and colors well, females are well suited to gathering food. For example, good color vision allows you to see a ripe fig among the green leaves of a tree. A preference for warm colors (skin tones of all races tend to be warm) and faces may also predispose women to care for their young. On the other hand, male facility in processing movement and spatial information may have helped them perform hunting duties.

However, keep in mind that both color preference and gender roles may also be highly influenced by the particular culture in which a boy or girl is raised. For example, in many cultures, products marketed to girls are often colored with bright, warm colors. Worldwide, girls' toys often involve babies, fashion, cooking, nurturing, and other

optic chiasm the point in the brain where the optic nerve from the left eye crosses over the optic nerve from the right eye

feature detectors specialized cells in the visual cortex that fire only when they receive input that indicates we are looking at a particular shape, color, angle, or other visual feature

---

FIGURE

3.6

The Visual Pathways in the Brain

Visual information from your right side travels to the visual cortex on the left side of the brain, and information from your left side travels to the visual cortex on the right side.

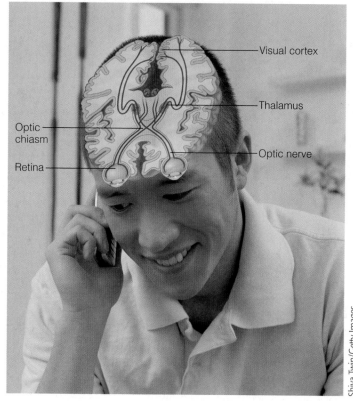

Visual cortex

Thalamus

Optic chiasm

Optic nerve

Retina

Shiva Twin/Getty Images

domestic themes, whereas toys marketed to boys frequently involve vehicles, weaponry, and darker, cooler colors. Thus, observed differences in gender roles and color preferences may simply reflect what we teach our children to prefer. We'll have more to say about gender roles and gender differences in Chapter 9. For now, let's turn our attention to our other senses.

Let's Review!

In this section, we discussed vision, including the physical properties of light, the anatomy of the eye and the retina, how we adapt to light and dark, how we see color, and the role of the brain in vision. For a quick check of your understanding, answer these questions.

1. Jared was born with no cones in his retina. How will this condition affect Jared?
   a. He will be blind.
   b. He will not be able to see black or white.
   c. He will see the world in shades of black and white.
   d. His vision will not be affected.

2. Which theory *best* explains why Sara would see flashes of red light after eight hours of working on a computer monitor that has a green and black screen?
   a. The opponent-process theory
   b. The trichromatic theory
   c. The rod-and-cone theory
   d. The theory of red–green color blindness

3. You have just returned to a darkened theater after a trip to the concession stand. Now you have a problem—you can't find your seat in the dark. Knowing what you do about vision, which of the following would *most likely* help you to find your seat?
   a. Stare straight ahead at the seats.
   b. Search for your seat out of the corner of your eye.
   c. Go back out into the bright light and allow your eyes to deplete their photopigments.
   d. Cross your eyes and search for your seat.

Answers 1. c; 2. a; 3. b

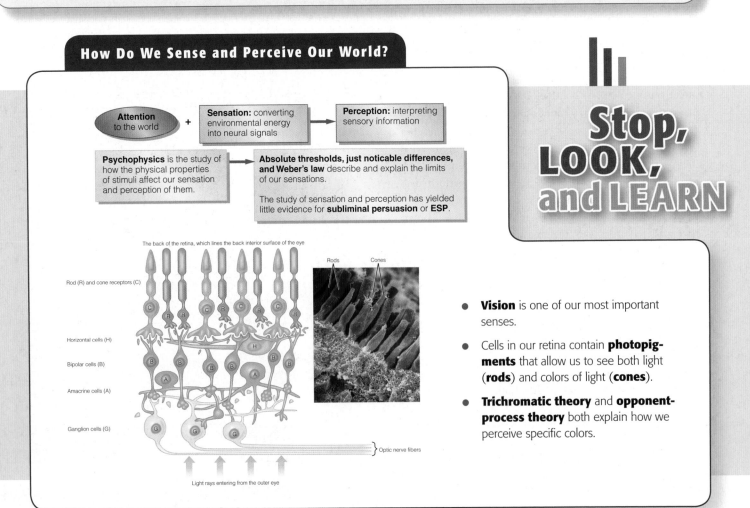

How Do We Sense and Perceive Our World?

Attention to the world + **Sensation:** converting environmental energy into neural signals → **Perception:** interpreting sensory information

Psychophysics is the study of how the physical properties of stimuli affect our sensation and perception of them. → **Absolute thresholds, just noticeable differences, and Weber's law** describe and explain the limits of our sensations.

The study of sensation and perception has yielded little evidence for **subliminal persuasion** or **ESP**.

The back of the retina, which lines the back interior surface of the eye

Rod (R) and cone receptors (C)

Horizontal cells (H)

Bipolar cells (B)

Amacrine cells (A)

Ganglion cells (G)

Rods   Cones

Optic nerve fibers

Light rays entering from the outer eye

Stop, LOOK, and LEARN

- **Vision** is one of our most important senses.

- Cells in our retina contain **photopigments** that allow us to see both light (**rods**) and colors of light (**cones**).

- **Trichromatic theory** and **opponent-process theory** both explain how we perceive specific colors.

Hearing: The World We Hear

Like vision, hearing is one of our most important senses; much of what we learn in life depends on these two senses. Additionally, hearing plays an important role in our ability to communicate with others. To understand hearing, we will describe the physical properties of sound waves, the anatomy of the ear, and how our brain processes sound.

Vibration and Sound: A Noisy Environment Can Lead to Hearing Loss

Sounds, such as a human voice, produce waves of compressed air that our ears convert to neural impulses. Like light waves, sound waves have their own psychophysical properties. A sound wave has both peaks and valleys (■ FIGURE 3.7).

A **cycle** includes the peak of the wave and the valley that immediately follows it (Figure 3.7a). Counting the number of cycles in a given time frame allows us to determine the **frequency** of a sound wave. Traditionally, the frequency of sound waves is measured in hertz (Hz), or the number of cycles completed per second. A sound wave with a frequency of 1000 Hz would complete 1,000 cycles per second. The **loudness** of the sound we hear, measured in **decibels (dB)**, corresponds to the amplitude of a sound wave (Figure 3.7b). The higher the amplitude, the more pressure is exerted on the eardrum, and the louder the sound is.

The frequency of a sound wave corresponds to the **pitch** of the sound we perceive: the higher the frequency, the higher the pitch. The average young adult can perceive sounds that range from a low of 20 Hz to a high of 20000 Hz (Gelfand, 1981). For example, we can hear the low pitch of a foghorn and the high pitch of a mosquito's wings. We lose some of this range as we age, however, particularly our ability to hear high pitches. Some young people have capitalized on this by downloading ultra-high-pitched "mosquito" ringtones for their cell phones so that parents and other adults will be unaware of incoming calls and text messages. Tones above 16000 Hz go unheard by people as young as 24!

Those of us who live and work in noisy environments may be even more likely to suffer hearing loss as we age. For instance, people who live in North American urban areas experience greater age-related hearing loss than do people who live in quiet rural areas of Africa (Bennett, 1990). Luckily, most of the everyday sounds we hear fall well below the 20000-Hz level. In fact, unless the gradual deterioration impairs our ability to hear sounds at 1800 Hz and below, our ability to comprehend speech should remain pretty much intact (Welford, 1987).

Nonetheless, you would do well to protect your hearing. Age-related hearing damage can be made much worse by exposure to loud noises. For example, typical rock concert volumes

cycle a physical characteristic of energy defined as a wave peak and the valley that immediately follows it

frequency a physical characteristic of energy defined as the number of cycles that occur in a given unit of time

loudness the psychophysical property of sound that corresponds to the amplitude of a sound wave

decibels [DESS-uh-bells] **(dB)** the unit of measure used to determine the loudness of a sound

pitch the psychophysical property of sound that corresponds to the frequency of a sound wave

FIGURE 3.7 **The Amplitude and Frequency of Sound Waves**
The frequency, or number of cycles per second, determines the sound's pitch. The higher the wave's frequency, the higher the sound's pitch will be (a). The height, or amplitude, of a sound wave determines its loudness. Higher amplitudes correspond to louder sounds (b).

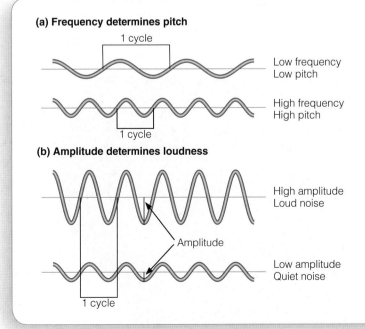

(a) Frequency determines pitch

1 cycle
— Low frequency Low pitch

1 cycle
— High frequency High pitch

(b) Amplitude determines loudness

— High amplitude Loud noise

Amplitude

— Low amplitude Quiet noise

1 cycle

cochlea [COCK-lee-uh] the curled, fluid-filled tube that contains the basilar membrane in the inner ear

basilar membrane the structure in the cochlear duct that contains the hair cells, which convert sound waves into action potentials

hair cells neurons that grow out of the basilar membrane and convert sounds waves into action potentials

You Asked...

How does our ear work?

CRISTIAN CÀCERES, STUDENT

of 120 dB can damage your hearing in as little as 15 minutes. Good rules of thumb are that if your hearing feels different immediately after exposure to a loud noise, you were likely exposed to damaging levels of sound; and a safe headphone volume should allow you to still hear conversations taking place around you.

The Anatomy and Function of the Ear

The very outside of the *outer ear* is called the *pinna* (■ FIGURE 3.8). This is the part of the body normally referred to as the ear and earlobe. The pinna acts as a funnel to gather sound waves. After being gathered by the pinna, sound waves are channeled through the *auditory canal*, where sounds are amplified and then strike the membrane at the end of the auditory canal, the *eardrum*.

The eardrum, or tympanic membrane, is a very thin membrane that vibrates as the incoming sound waves strike it, much as the head of a drum vibrates when a drumstick strikes it. The three bones of the *middle ear* that are directly behind the eardrum are the *hammer, anvil,* and *stirrup* (Figure 3.8). These very small bones mechanically amplify the vibrations coming from the eardrum and transmit them to the inner ear. The middle ear connects to the *inner ear* at the point where the stirrup rests against the *oval window* (Figure 3.8). The oval window is found on the outer end of the **cochlea**, one of the major components of the inner ear. The cochlea is a coiled, fluid-filled tube about 1.4 inches long that resembles a snail (Matlin & Foley, 1997). It is here that sound waves are turned into neural impulses.

If you were to uncoil the cochlea, you would see that it resembles a flexible tube that is closed off at the end. The inside of the tube contains a fluid-filled canal called the *cochlear duct* (■ FIGURE 3.9). The floor of the cochlear duct is lined with the **basilar membrane**. Growing out of the basilar membrane are specialized **hair cells** that convert sound wave energy into neural impulses.

Incoming sound waves cause the bones of the middle ear to vibrate (Figures 3.8 & 3.9). The vibration of the stirrup against the oval window sets up a pressure wave inside the fluid-filled cochlea. As this wave travels through the cochlea, the cochlear duct begins to ripple. Inside the cochlear duct, the traveling wave ripples across the hair cells, causing them to begin sending neural impulses.

FIGURE

3.8 The Anatomy of the Ear

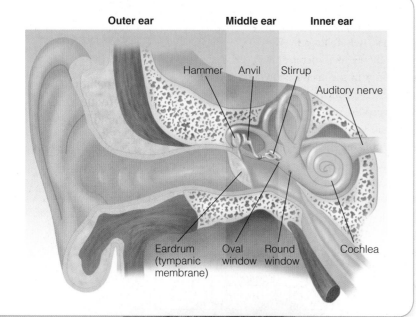

Outer ear | Middle ear | Inner ear

Hammer | Anvil | Stirrup

Auditory nerve

Eardrum (tympanic membrane) | Oval window | Round window | Cochlea

The pinna is much more than a place to hang an earring. It helps funnel sound waves into the ear canal.

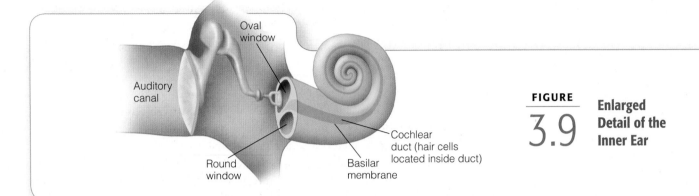

FIGURE 3.9 Enlarged Detail of the Inner Ear

The Auditory Pathways of the Brain

Once the hair cells convert sound into neural impulses, these impulses must be sent to the brain for further processing. Attached to the end of the cochlea is the **auditory nerve** (Figure 3.8). The bundled neurons of the auditory nerve gather the information from the hair cells to relay it to the brain. ■ FIGURE 3.10 shows the path that auditory information takes from the ears to the brain. Notice that auditory information from each ear reaches both sides of the brain.

The auditory cortex has the capacity to decode the meanings of the sounds we hear. Our next task is to examine how the brain perceives, or makes sense of, the auditory information it receives from the ears. We'll begin by looking at several theories that explain our ability to perceive pitch.

auditory nerve the nerve that carries information from the inner ear to the brain

FIGURE 3.10 The Auditory Pathways in the Brain

PLACE THEORY OF PITCH PERCEPTION

Hermann von Helmholtz, who is credited with the trichromatic theory of color vision, also studied pitch perception. Helmholtz contributed to our understanding of sound perception with his **place theory** of pitch perception (1863/1930), which proposes that sounds of different frequencies excite different hair cells at particular points along the basilar membrane. According to place theory, the brain receives information on pitch from the location, or *place*, on the basilar membrane that is being most excited by incoming sound waves. Evidence suggests that place theory may indeed explain some of our ability to perceive pitch.

In the late 1950s, Georg von Békésy conducted some important studies using pure tones, made up of single sound waves, which revealed that different pitches caused the most vibration at different points along the basilar membrane (Békésy, 1960). Low-frequency sounds activate the far end of the basilar membrane the most. High-frequency sounds cause the most activation at the front part of the basilar membrane, near the oval window. Hair cells at the front of the basilar membrane are most vulnerable to damage, explaining why age-related hearing loss occurs first for high pitches.

Although Békésy's research on place theory does describe some of our ability to perceive pitch, he only tested pure tones composed of a single frequency. He did not test tones of other *timbres*, meaning tones made up of multiple frequencies. This is important since most of the sounds we hear in life are a mixture of frequencies. When place theory is tested using complex sounds rather than pure tones, it does not fare as well as it does in explaining perception of pure tones (Matlin & Foley, 1997).

FREQUENCY THEORY OF PITCH PERCEPTION

Frequency theory proposes that our brain receives information about pitch directly from the frequency at which the hair cells are firing (Rutherford, 1886; Wever, 1949/1970). An incoming sound wave will cause the hair cells to fire action potentials at a frequency that is equal to the frequency of the sound wave. For example, a sound wave at 500 Hz would cause the hair cells to fire 500 action potentials per second; a sound wave at 750 Hz would produce 750 action potentials per second.

Frequency theory is a very simple concept, but it has a severe limitation. Hair cells can fire only at a maximum rate of 1,000 action potentials per second (1000 Hz), yet we can hear sounds in the range of 20–20000 Hz. Frequency theory obviously falls short in explaining perception of pitches over 1000 Hz.

VOLLEY THEORY OF PITCH PERCEPTION

Volley theory is an updated version of frequency theory that seeks to explain perception of sounds over 1000 Hz (Wever, 1949/1970). According to volley theory, "teams" of hair cells work together to give us the perception of sounds over 1000 Hz. For example, let's say you hear a tone of 3000 Hz (a pitch higher than human speech). No single hair cell can fire at 3000 Hz, but three hair cells, each firing at 1000 Hz, can work together as a group to tell your brain that you are hearing a 3000-Hz tone.

DUPLICITY THEORY: AN INTEGRATION

Volley theory seems adequate to explain pitch perception, but we still have to deal with place theory, which also seems to explain some aspects of our perception. Recall that Georg von Békésy (1960) found that different pitches excite different parts of the basilar membrane. Volley theory cannot explain why this would be the case. So, what is going on in our ears? Is it the place or the frequency of the excited hair cells that tells us what pitch we are hearing? It may well be *both*.

place theory proposes that our brain decodes pitch by noticing which region of the basilar membrane is most active

frequency theory proposes that our brain decodes pitch directly from the frequency at which the hair cells of the basilar membrane are firing

volley theory proposes that our brain decodes pitch by noticing the frequency at which groups of hair cells on the basilar membrane are firing

Today it is widely believed that we perceive pitch through a combination of volley theory and place theory. This combination of perceptual processes is called **duplicity theory**. Researchers strongly suspect that frequency and place information work together to give us pitch perception, but we don't yet understand exactly how these two mechanisms work together.

duplicity theory proposes that a combination of volley and place theory explains how our brain decodes pitch

You Review 3.1

Theories of Pitch Perception

THEORY	DESCRIPTION
Place theory	Different pitches of sound activate specific regions of the basilar membrane more than others. Pitch perception occurs when the brain notices which portions of the basilar membrane are being most excited by incoming sound waves.
Frequency theory	The hair cells of the basilar membrane fire action potentials at a rate equal to the frequency of the incoming sound wave. The brain determines pitch by noticing the rate at which the hair cells are firing. This theory explains only perception of pitches up to 1000 Hz, the maximum firing rate of a hair cell.
Volley theory	Similar to frequency theory, this theory states that groups of hair cells fire as teams to give us the perception of pitches over 1000 Hz. For example, three hair cells each firing at 1000 Hz together yield the perception of a 3000-Hz tone.
Duplicity theory	This theory states that a combination of frequency and place information is used in pitch perception. Exactly how these sources of information are integrated in the brain is still being investigated.

Let's Review!

In this section, we looked at the process of hearing: the psychophysics of sound, the anatomy of the ear, the brain's role in hearing, and theories of pitch perception. For a quick check of your understanding, answer these questions.

1. Jack is 58 years old and having trouble with his hearing. He has spent his life working around noisy machinery without any ear protection. Knowing what you do about hearing, what type of hearing loss is Jack *most likely* experiencing?
   a. Total deafness
   b. Deafness for low pitches
   c. Deafness for medium pitches
   d. Deafness for high pitches

2. By turning up the volume on your stereo, you are changing the _____ of the sound waves being emitted by the stereo.
   a. amplitude
   b. wavelength
   c. pitch
   d. width

3. _____ theory proposes that pitch is perceived when the brain locates the region of the basilar membrane that is firing the most action potentials.
   a. Frequency
   b. Basilar
   c. Place
   d. Volley

Answers 1. d; 2. a; 3. c

Taste, Smell, Touch, and the Body Senses

- Explain the processes involved in taste, smell, touch, and the body senses.

Taste: Information From the Tongue

For most of us, the senses of taste and smell are interconnected. These two senses are called chemical senses, because they require that certain chemicals come into direct contact with our sense organs. Vision and hearing don't require such direct contact; you can perceive visual and auditory stimuli at a distance. But for taste, or **gustation**, to occur, certain chemicals in foods and other substances must be dissolved in our saliva and come into direct contact with the sense organ commonly know as the tongue. For smell, chemicals in the nearby air—from food or other substances—must come into contact with cells in the nasal cavity.

PROPERTIES OF TASTE: THE FOUR—OR FIVE—TASTES

It is widely believed that humans are sensitive to at least four different types of tastes: bitter, sweet, salty, and sour (Bartoshuk & Beauchamp, 1994). It makes good sense that our tongues are designed to detect these tastes, because they are associated with certain types of foods that have implications for our survival (Scott & Plata-Salaman, 1991). For example, sweet flavors are associated with foods and bitter tastes with poisons.

In addition to these four basic tastes, some researchers have proposed that humans may be sensitive to a fifth taste called *umami*, or glutamate (Rolls, 2000). Umami is a meaty, brothy flavor that is more common in Asian foods than it is in Western cuisine (MSG, or monosodium glutamate, is a common ingredient in Asian dishes). So, Westerners are not likely to be as familiar with umami's flavor as they are with the other basic tastes. Nonetheless, preliminary studies indicate that the ability to taste umami exists (Damak et al., 2003; Hodson & Linden, 2006).

FROM TONGUE TO TASTE: HOW DO WE EXPERIENCE FLAVOR?

When you look at your tongue in the mirror, you normally see a bunch of little bumps lining its surface. We'll guess that you were taught to refer to these visible bumps as taste buds. This is incorrect—the bumps you see are the **papillae** of the tongue. Your **taste buds** actually reside in the pits between the papillae (■ FIGURE 3.11). Your taste buds are what convert the chemicals in the foods you eat into the neural impulses that convey taste information to your brain. Most people have between 2,000 and 5,000 taste buds on their tongue (Miller & Bartoshuk, 1991). Unlike some types of sensory cells, taste buds can regenerate. This is important because we damage our taste buds on a regular basis. Have you ever eaten a very hot slice of pizza and as a result lost some of your sense of taste for a few days? You probably killed many of your taste buds with that molten mozzarella, and you had to wait for them to grow back!

Many researchers believe that, like the cones of the eye, different taste buds seem to be maximally sensitive to one of the four basic flavors (Shallenberger, 1993). Thus, taste perception on the tongue appears to work very much like color perception in the retina. If the brain is informed that the "sweet taste buds" are very active, we taste a sweet flavor. If the "sour taste buds" are most active, we taste something sour. If all flavors are some combination of sweet, salty, sour, bitter, and perhaps umami, the presence of four or five types of taste buds is sufficient to explain our taste perception (Chandrashekar, Hoon, Ryba, & Zuker, 2006).

gustation [gus-TAY-shun] the sense of taste
papillae [puh-PILL-ee] bumps on the tongue that many people mistake for taste buds
taste buds the sense organs for taste that are found between the papillae on the tongue

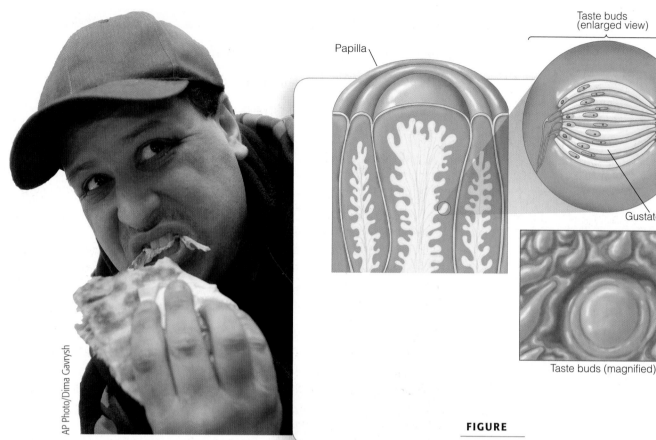

Papilla

Taste buds
(enlarged view)

Gustatory cell

Taste buds (magnified)

AP Photo/Dima Gavrysh

If you burn your taste buds with a slice of hot pizza, you will experience temporary loss of taste sensation until the taste buds grow back.

FIGURE

3.11 Papilla and Taste Buds

Taste buds are the sensory receptors for taste. Contrary to popular belief, the bumps on our tongues are not taste buds—they are papillae. Our taste buds are located next to the papillae on the tongue.

However, a good deal of our ability to taste certain flavors depends on where on the tongue the substance is placed. The different types of taste buds are concentrated in certain locations. Over the years, there has been significant disagreement as to exactly where these areas of sensitivity are located, although there is more agreement on the sweet and sour tastes. Sweet tastes are best detected at the front of the tongue and sour tastes on the sides; salty tastes are thought to be detected best near the front of the tongue (Shallenberg, 1993).

You may be surprised to learn that the center of the tongue lacks taste buds. You won't taste flavors that are placed directly in the center of your tongue. In a sense, this region of the tongue is like the blindspot in the eye—no taste sensation can occur here (Matlin & Foley, 1997). Despite this taste blindspot, we still manage to taste the foods we eat because chewing distributes food across the tongue.

Of course, only after your brain has done its part can you become consciously aware of the flavor of your food. Each taste bud is connected to a neuron that receives input from the taste bud. These neurons join together to form three nerves. One nerve gathers input from the front of the tongue, another from the back of the tongue, and a third from the throat. These nerves travel to the medulla and the pons of the brainstem before conveying the taste information to the thalamus. Like most sensory information, taste information travels from the thalamus to the "thinking" part of the brain, the cortex. Most of the taste information ends up in the somatosensory cortex of the parietal lobe, but some of the information is diverted to the limbic system before reaching the cortex. It's here in the cortex that we perceive the flavor of our food. But why do some foods taste good to us while others taste terrible?

Psychology Applies to Your World:

Why Don't We All Like the Same Foods?

Have you ever found yourself discussing where to go for dinner with your friends, only to find that everyone has a different opinion on which type of food you should have? One wants pizza; another loves sushi; another hates sushi but loves burgers. Sound familiar? What accounts for the wide variation in taste preferences that humans experience? Why does one person love spicy foods while another prefers bland tastes?

As it turns out, several factors affect our taste preferences. One of these is age. We lose some of our taste buds permanently with age. This may contribute to the diminished sense of taste that is often seen in older adults (Nordin, Razani, Markison, & Murphy, 2003). With fewer active taste buds, it might appear that older people would tend to prefer richly flavored foods. In fact, some people have proposed that diets enriched with intensely flavored foods may help maintain elders' appetites. However, studies have shown that this strategy may not always work (Essed, van Staveren, Kok, & de Graaf, 2007).

© Bios/Peter Arnold, Inc.

Culture is another factor in taste preferences. For example, the spouse of one of your authors is from El Salvador, where iguana meat is considered a treat enjoyed mostly by the wealthy. In the United States, iguanas are more likely to be kept as pets than eaten. Why do food preferences vary across cultures? One reason is that the availability of food sources dictates what a particular people *can* eat. Central Americans eat iguana meat today partly because their ancestors once ate the wild iguanas that roamed there. Every culture must take advantage of the food sources at its disposal, and hunger can make foods taste better, especially when those foods provide needed nutrients (Mobini, Chambers, & Yeomans, 2007).

Religious values and traditions also shape cultural food preferences. Many of the world's religions influence the diet of their followers. For example, Jews and Muslims will not eat pork, Hindus do not eat beef, and Seventh Day Adventists frown upon the use of certain spices (Grivetti, 2000). These taste preferences are passed from generation to generation as parents teach children to follow their religious values.

Many of our individual food preferences develop through learning—some of it very early in life. Research shows that the foods a mother eats can affect the flavor of her breast milk, and exposure to these flavors during breast-feeding can affect her child's later taste preferences (Mennella & Beauchamp, 1991). Being exposed to a variety of flavors in infancy tends to make infants more open to new and novel foods (Gerrish & Mennella, 2001).

Although the influence of learning on food preferences is strong, evidence also suggests that biological factors can affect our sense of taste. Prior to menopause, women's ability to taste fluctuates with hormonal levels, and after menopause ability to taste declines (Prutkin et al., 2000). There are also some genetic variations in the ability to taste. Some people, called *supertasters,* have a higher than average number of taste buds and are able to strongly taste a bitter compound called 6-n-propylthiocuracil (PROP). In contrast, *nontasters* perceive very little or no bitterness from PROP (Bartoshuk, 2000). Nontasters have been shown to eat a wider variety of foods than supertasters do (Azar, 1998; Pasquet, Obeerti, Ati, & Hladik, 2002). Compared to nontasters, female PROP tasters tend to eat more fat and less fruit in their diets (Yackinous & Guinard, 2002). Supertasters may avoid some foods that are rich in cancer-fighting compounds but also have bitter flavors (e.g., Brussels sprouts).

The ability to taste another chemical, phenylthiocarbamide (PTC), has also been linked to health. Researchers have recently discovered that PTC nontasters find cigarette smoking more rewarding than PTC tasters, and therefore may be more at risk for nicotine addiction (Snedecor, Pomerleau, Mehringer, Ninowski, & Pomerleau, 2006).

Finally, our sense of taste is not influenced solely by our culture, early learning, or taste buds. Our sense of taste is also heavily dependent on our sense of smell (Shepard, 2006). If you've ever tried to taste food when you've had a bad cold, you know that your sense of smell makes a significant contribution to taste and that clogged nasal passages tend to make food taste bland.

Smell: Aromas, Odors, and a Warning System

Olfaction, our sense of smell, has adaptive value. Smells can alert us to danger. The ability to smell smoke enables us to detect a fire long before we see flames. The rotten smell of spoiled food warns us not to eat it. Without such odoriferous warnings, we could easily find ourselves in harm's way.

Like our sense of taste, our sense of smell is a chemical sense. Odors come from airborne chemicals that are diffused in the air. When we inhale these molecules into our nose, we may experience smelling the substance. Compared with our other senses, our sense of smell is quite sensitive. Recall from our earlier discussion of sensory thresholds that we can detect the presence of a single drop of perfume in a three-room apartment (see Table 3.1). When it comes to discriminating between odors, we can detect roughly 500,000 different scents (Cain, 1988), and we can identify by name about 10,000 different smells (Lancet et al., 1993). Yet, despite these impressive abilities, when compared to other animals, humans do not fare so well. Dogs, for example, are much better at detecting odors.

The inability to smell also limits the ability to taste.

THE MYSTERY OF SMELL

Researchers have not been able to determine precisely how our sense of smell works. Of the senses we have described to this point, smell is by far the least understood. What we do know is that we are able to smell because of a special piece of skin that lines the top of the nasal cavity (■ FIGURE 3.12). This special piece of skin, the **olfactory epithelium,** probably contains only a few hundred different types of odor receptors (Lancet et al., 1993). When we breathe in odor-laden air, the odor molecules reach the receptors in the olfactory epi-

olfaction the sense of smell
olfactory epithelium [ole-FACT-uh-ree epp-ith-THEEL-ee-um] a special piece of skin at the top of the nasal cavity that contains the olfactory receptors

Olfactory nerve

Olfactory bulb

Receptor cells
in olfactory
epithelium

Tongue

FIGURE

3.12

The Anatomy of the Nose

Odors in the form of airborne chemicals are inhaled into the nasal cavity, where sensory cells in the olfactory epithelium convert them into neural signals.

thelium and stimulate these cells. This stimulation accomplishes the conversion of odor into smell, but just how our brain understands what we smell is not well understood at this time (Matlin & Foley, 1997). One theory, **lock-and-key theory**, proposes that olfactory receptors are excited by odor molecules in much the same way that neurotransmitters excite receptor sites on the postsynaptic neuron (Amoore, 1970). According to lock-and-key theory, specific odor molecules have the power to "unlock" or excite certain olfactory receptors in the olfactory epithelium.

Once the cells of the epithelium have converted odor into neural impulses, these signals travel across the *olfactory nerve* to the *olfactory bulb* of the brain. The olfactory bulb is located just below the bottom edge of the frontal lobe of the brain (see Figure 3.12). The olfactory bulb processes incoming information before sending it on to other parts of the brain. Some olfactory information goes directly to the primary smell cortex, in the temporal lobes of the brain.

Other olfactory information is sent to both the cortex and the limbic system. Recall from Chapter 2 that the limbic system regulates emotional and motivational activity. The limbic system seems to be heavily involved in the processing of olfactory information. This may explain the strong emotional reactions we often have to certain smells. For example, the smell of one of your favorite childhood meals may conjure up beloved memories of your childhood. Are there particular smells that bring back emotionally charged memories for you?

lock-and-key theory proposes that olfactory receptors are excited by odor molecules in a fashion that is similar to how neurotransmitters excite receptor sites

PHEROMONES: ARE SOME ODORS SEXY?

Some researchers believe that humans have yet another sense somewhat related to smell. This sense, the *vomeronasal sense,* is well documented in animals (Doty, 2001). Many animals communicate with each other via airborne chemicals called **pheromones**. Pheromones are produced by glands in the animal's body and dispersed into the air, where other animals then inhale them. Such animals are equipped with vomeronasal organs that can detect the presence of inhaled pheromones. Perhaps you have seen a cat inhale deeply through its open mouth—a process called cat's *flehmen.* The cat is passing pheromone-laden air over special organs, called Jacobson's organs, in the roof of its mouth. These organs can detect the presence of pheromones. The presence of such an organ in humans has been the subject of controversy, but at least one study has found evidence that some people have vomeronasal organs in their nasal cavities (Won, Mair, Bolger, & Conran, 2000). There is also some suggestion that a little-known cranial nerve (cranial nerve 0, or CN0), found in humans and many other vertebrates, may play a role in the detection of pheromones. CN0 travels from the nasal cavity to the brain, including areas of the brain known to be involved in sexual behavior (see Fields, 2007).

Do pheromones affect human sexual behavior? Perhaps. For example, when women are exposed to pheromones in the underarm secretions of another woman, their menstrual cycle tends to synchronize with the other woman's cycle (Larkin, 1998; Stern & McClintock, 1998). When women are exposed to a pheromone that is released from men's hair follicles, they tend to increase their social interactions with males (Miller, 1999). Other pheromones found in men's sweat tend to improve a woman's mood state (Monti-Bloch, Diaz-Sanchez, Jennings-White, & Berliner, 1998). Current evidence, however, does not support the idea that pheromone-laden perfumes can make one wildly attractive to the opposite sex. It's more likely the case that the vomeronasal sense is just one of the senses involved in sexuality.

© Joe McDonald/Visuals Unlimited

Many mammals use pheromones to communicate with each other. This cat is passing pheromone-laden air over vomeronasal organs in the roof of its mouth.

▬▬▬ Touch: The Skin Sense

Touch is associated with many of life's pleasurable experiences. Feeling a friendly pat on the back can certainly enhance our social interactions. Sexual activity depends heavily on our ability to feel touch. But our ability to sense with our skin also affects our survival. Through our skin we feel touch, temperature, and pain.

Our keen sense of touch originates in our skin. Our skin is composed of several layers that contain touch receptors. The inner layer, the **dermis**, contains most of the touch receptors (■ FIGURE 3.13). Our skin's outer layer is the **epidermis**, which consists of several layers of dead skin cells. The epidermis also contains touch receptors, especially in areas of the skin that do not have hair, such as the fingertips.

We have different types of receptors for touch, temperature, and pain (Figure 3.13). We know more about the function of the touch receptors than we do about the pain and temperature receptors. Pressure on the skin pushes against the axons of the touch receptors. This causes a change in the axonal membrane's permeability to positive ions, allowing them to enter the cell (Loewenstein, 1960). As you recall from Chapter 2, as positive ions enter a cell, the cell becomes more likely to fire an action potential. If the touch is intense enough to allow the receptors to reach threshold, neural impulses will be fired. These impulses travel to the spinal cord, and then to the brain. In the brain, the signals enter the thalamus and then go on to the somatosensory cortex of the parietal lobe. Some signals, particularly those indicat-

> ### You Asked...
>
> *What makes us able to feel different things with our hands?*
>
> ERICA BREGLIO, STUDENT

pheromones [FAIR-uh-moans] airborne chemicals that are released from glands and detected by the vomeronasal organs in some animals and perhaps humans

dermis the inner layer of the skin

epidermis the outer layer of the skin

Neuroscience Applies To Your World:

People Who Can't Feel Pain

Although unpleasant, pain does serve a purpose. Pain warns us of disease and damage to our bodies and thereby helps us avoid danger. The usefulness of pain is illustrated clearly in the cases of people who suffer from a rare genetic disorder that makes them unable to feel pain. In one such case, researchers discovered a 10-year-old boy working as a street performer in northern Pakistan (Cox et al., 2006). To earn money, the boy would "entertain" crowds by piercing his arms with knives and walking on burning coals. He was able to do these things because he was unable to perceive pain. In addition to such "performances," his inability to feel pain led him to engage in other risky behaviors, which tragically led to his premature

Peter Ginter/Getty Images

death at age 14 from injuries sustained after jumping off a house roof.

Before his death, researcher James Cox and his colleagues studied the boy and other Pakistani families in which several members were insensitive to pain. Curiously, although these people could not feel pain, they could still perceive hot, cold, pressure, and tickling. The researchers did thorough physical exams on these individuals and found that, other than their lack of pain perception, they were generally healthy. The pain-insensitive family members, they discovered, have a rare genetic mutation that disables some of the sodium channels on the neurons that carry pain signals throughout the body. Recall that for a neuron to fire a neural signal or action potential, positive sodium ions (Na+) must enter the neuron though tiny ion channels in the neuron's outer membrane (see Chapter 2, p. 42). These defective ion channels do not allow sodium to enter the neuron, rendering the neuron unable to send pain signals. By studying people who suffer from this condition, researchers hope not only to find a way to help pain-insensitive individuals avoid harm but also to learn more about how to develop better pain-relieving drugs for those of us who do feel pain.

ing the presence of threatening stimuli, go to the limbic system as well as the somatosensory cortex (Coren, Ward, & Enns, 1999). Once the signals reach the somatosensory cortex, our brain interprets the sensation and directs us to take the appropriate action.

The Body Senses: Experiencing the Physical Body in Space

So far, we have covered what are referred to as the five senses: vision, hearing, taste, smell, and touch. Do we possess other senses? The answer is "Yes," but this time, we're not talking

FIGURE

3.13

Anatomy of the Skin and Its Receptors

Different types of skin receptors pick up different types of stimulation.

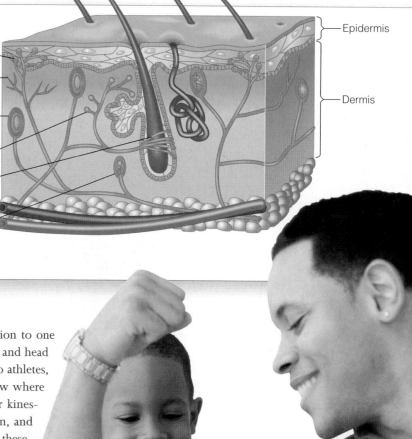

Merkel's disks (touch)

Free nerve endings (pain)

Meissner's corpuscle (touch)

Krause's end-bulb (uncertain function)

Nerve endings around hair follicle (movement of hair)

Pacinian corpuscle (pressure)

Epidermis

Dermis

about ESP. We are referring to the body senses, the senses that help us experience our physical bodies in space: kinesthesis and the vestibular sense.

KINESTHESIS

Kinesthesis refers to the ability to sense the position of our body parts in space and in relation to one another. As you walk, you are aware of where your arms, legs, and head are in relation to the ground. Kinesthetic sense is important to athletes, especially to gymnasts and high divers. It allows them to know where their bodies are as they execute their routines and dives. Our kinesthetic sense uses information from the muscles, tendons, skin, and joints to keep us oriented at all times. The information from these sources is processed in the somatosensory cortex and the cerebellum of the brain (see Chapter 2).

THE VESTIBULAR SENSE

Another important body sense is our sense of balance, or **vestibular sense**. The vestibular system uses input from the semicircular canals and the vestibular sacs of the inner ear to keep us balanced (■ FIGURE 3.14). These structures are filled with a fluid gel that surrounds hair cells much like those in the cochlea. When your head moves in any direction, the gel inside these structures moves in the opposite direction. The movement of the gel bends the hair cells and stimulates them to send neural impulses to the brain, which then uses these signals to determine the orientation of your head. Our vestibular system allows us to do such everyday tasks as walking, driving a car, and bending over to pick up a pencil from the floor. Without our vestibular sense, we would simply topple over.

Rapid movements of your head, such as those you experience on spinning carnival rides, can overstimulate the vestibular system. Such movements can cause a violent wave action in the fluid gel of the vestibular system. When the gel crashes against the sensory cells, the result can be dizziness and nausea. People vary with respect to the degree of vestibular stimulation that they can comfortably tolerate.

You now have a working knowledge of how our sensory organs convert environmental energies into neural impulses. Our next topic is perception, or how we make sense of all of this sensory information.

© Jose Luis Pelaez Inc/Blend Images/Corbis

kinesthesis [kin-ess-THEE-sis] the ability to sense the position of our body parts in relation to one another and in relation to space

vestibular [ves-STIB-you-lar] **sense** the sense of balance

3.14 The Vestibular Organs

The vestibular system helps us balance our body by monitoring the position and acceleration of our head as we move. To accomplish this, a gel-like fluid in the semicircular canals, saccule, and utricle presses against hair cells much like those found in the cochlea of the inner ear. When the hair cells of the vestibular system are moved, they signal the brain with information about the orientation of our head in three-dimensional space.

Based on S. Iurato (1967). Submicroscopic Structure of the Inner Ear. Pergamon Press.

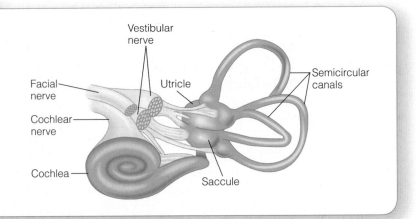

Nick Laham/Getty Images

Our vestibular sense keeps us balanced, and the kinesthetic sense allows this skateboarder to perform intricate moves without falling.

Let's Review!

This section explained the chemical senses, taste and smell; touch; and the body senses, kinesthesis and the vestibular sense. For a quick check of your understanding, answer these questions.

1. Which of the following is *not* thought to be a taste for which your tongue has receptors?
   a. Salty
   b. Sour
   c. Acidic
   d. Bitter

2. Spinning around and around on a carnival ride is most likely to affect which of your senses?
   a. Taste
   b. Touch
   c. Smell
   d. Vestibular sense

3. Which of your senses would be *least likely* to be affected when you have a bad head cold?
   a. Taste
   b. Touch
   c. Smell
   d. Vestibular sense

Answers 1. c; 2. d; 3. b

Perception: Interpreting Sensory Information

- Describe top-down and bottom-up perceptual processing and explain the differences between them.

- Give an overview of perceptual constancy theories and how we perceive depth.

At the beginning of this chapter, we defined perception as *the interpretation of sensory information*. That's it in a nutshell. When you look at your friend's face, light bounces off his or her face. This light strikes your retina, and the rods and cones convert the light into neural impulses. Sensation is complete. But now your brain must interpret the meaning of the neural impulses so you will recognize your friend's face. The fact that you believe you are seeing your friend's face and not, say, a dog or a cat, is the result of perceptual processes in your brain. But how does your brain know that you are seeing your friend's face?

Using What We Know: Top-Down Perceptual Processing

Top-down perceptual processing occurs when we use previously gained knowledge to help us interpret a stimulus. Let's go back to the example of perceiving your friend's face. When you see a face that you recognize, what leads you to this recognition? Your memory helps you understand the "meaning" of the face you see. You know that faces usually contain two eyes, a nose, a mouth, and so on. Furthermore, you know how your friend's particular eyes, nose, and other features look. This stored knowledge allows you to quickly perceive the face of a friend.

> **You Asked...**
>
> *Why can two people look at one thing and have it be different to them?* JEAN-PAUL ESLAVA, STUDENT

top-down perceptual processing
perception that is guided by prior knowledge or expectations

Top-down perceptual processing can also fill in parts of a stimulus that are missing from our actual sensation of it. For example, look at ■ FIGURE 3.15. You cannot see this man's left leg or his feet, but you probably assume that they are there. Your knowledge of the human body tells you that the odds are slim that he is actually missing the limbs you cannot see. Consequently, in perceiving this picture, you implicitly assume that the "missing" leg and feet do, in fact, exist. This effect is so strong that later when you recall this picture, you might even remember having seen the missing limbs—right down to the type of shoes the man was "wearing."

Unfortunately, this "filling-in" of missing details can sometimes lead to mistakes in perception. Because people have different knowledge and expectations about the world, two people can witness the same event and yet perceive it differently. This can be a real problem in eyewitness accounts of crimes (see also Chapter 6). What if the correct identification of a suspect depended on accurately remembering what he was wearing? Or recall-

FIGURE 3.15 **Top-Down Perceptual Processing**

When you perceive the image in this photograph, your knowledge of the human body leads you to have certain expectations about the man in this picture. Because of top-down processing, you do not perceive that this man is missing his feet or parts of his legs.

PM Images/Getty Images

ing the color of her eyes? In the real world, this can be a serious problem. In fact, one study showed that a majority of the falsely convicted people being studied had been mistakenly identified by eyewitnesses (Wells & Olson, 2003).

Building a Perception "From Scratch": Bottom-Up Perceptual Processing

What do we do when we have very little or no stored knowledge to help us perceive a stimulus? We use a different perceptual process, one that does not rely on stored knowledge or expectations of the stimulus. In **bottom-up perceptual processing**, the properties of the stimulus itself are what we use to build our perception of that stimulus.

Your Turn – Active Learning

Look at ■ FIGURE 3.16. What do you see? With few clues about what this stimulus is, you cannot easily use your knowledge to help you perceive it. The stimulus is too ambiguous. Without top-down processing, you are forced to use bottom-up processes to perceive the stimulus. You build your perception of the picture by piecing together your perceptions of the many different components that make up this stimulus. You perceive the lines, curves, dots, shaded areas, and shapes. You then try to fit these components together to figure out what the drawing means. Most people find it very difficult to figure out what Figure 3.16 is using only bottom-up perceptual processes!

If you are ready to give up and try top-down perceptual processing, look at ■ FIGURE 3.19 (p. 106). Now turn back to Figure 3.16. You will likely find that you can now readily perceive the image in Figure 3.16. You now have knowledge of what to look for, so perception becomes much easier. Your knowledge of what the picture is guides the way you piece together the components of the stimulus. When you switch to top-down processing, the picture of the cow becomes almost obvious.

FIGURE 3.16 Top-Down Versus Bottom-Up Processing

What is this picture? With no expectations to guide your perception, you are forced to rely mainly on bottom-up processes. Because the picture is ambiguous, bottom-up processes do not lead to a quick recognition of the stimulus. Now turn to Figure 3.19 (p. 106), which will enable you to engage your top-down perceptual processes. After looking at Figure 3.19, you should be able to quickly recognize the figure in this picture because you now have expectations to guide your perception.

In the course of a typical day, we probably use both top-down and bottom-up perceptual processes continually. We use bottom-up processes to piece together perceptions of ambiguous stimuli and top-down processes to tell us what we can expect to perceive in certain situations. Perception can be complicated in a three-dimensional world that is full of shapes and forms. To make perception even more complicated, our bodies do not remain stationary during perception. We move. The objects we perceive sometimes move. As a result, the information our senses receive from our world is highly variable. Our perceptual processes must be able to deal with these dynamic conditions. So how do we organize and make sense of our perceptions?

Understanding What We Sense: Perceiving Size, Shape, and Brightness

bottom-up perceptual processing perception that is not guided by prior knowledge or expectations

One of the phenomena encountered in interpreting sensory data is that of *perceptual constancy*. When you look at a visual stimulus, the image it projects on your retina is highly influenced by the perspective from which you view the object. Yet your perception of the object is not as

(a)   (b)   (c)   (d)

Matthias Clamer/Getty Images

Matthias Clamer/Getty Images

dependent on perspective as your sensation is. For example, if you view a friend from a distance of 3 feet, an image of a certain size is projected onto your retina. If you move away and view the same friend from a distance of 6 feet, a smaller image is projected on your retina. Your *sensation* has changed, but you will not perceive that your friend has shrunk. In this case, your brain appears to step in to correct your perception, to give you a *constant* perception of the objects that you see in the world. There is evidence that our brains correct not only for *size* constancy, but also for *shape constancy, brightness constancy,* and *color constancy* (■ FIGURE 3.17).

Depth Perception: Sensing Our 3-D World With 2-D Eyes

Another perceptual challenge is depth perception. The world we view is three-dimensional, but the image it projects onto our retina is two-dimensional, like a photograph. Somehow our brains must be able to determine depth from the information our eyes receive from the outside world. What makes this possible?

BINOCULAR DEPTH PERCEPTION

One way that we perceive depth is through binocular depth cues. The term *binocular* means "two-eyed." **Binocular depth cues** rely on information from both eyes—specifically, information based on **retinal disparity**. Retinal disparity refers to the fact that, because our eyes are set a few centimeters apart, each eye sees a slightly different view of the world. Retinal disparity is greatest for objects that are close to us, and less for objects that are distant (■ FIGURE 3.18). Thus, the amount of retinal disparity we experience is a function of the distance from which we view an object. Our brain uses the amount of retinal disparity we experience to calculate how far the object is from us, enabling us to perceive depth in the world.

MONOCULAR DEPTH CUES

Binocular disparity is an important depth cue, but it is not the only way we perceive depth. If it were, we would be in serious trouble if we lost the use of one eye. We also would not be able to perceive depth in paintings or photographs. Luckily, we have another means of depth perception that requires the use of only one eye: **monocular depth cues**.

Many of you may have learned about monocular depth cues when you began drawing and painting as a child. Because a canvas has no depth, all parts of the painting are the same distance from the viewer's eyes, and retinal disparity does not help us perceive depth. So how

FIGURE

3.17 Perceptual Constancies

(a) The shape of the image this door projects onto the retina changes dramatically as the orientation of the door changes. Yet we still perceive that the door is rectangular because of shape constancy. (b) Even though the size of the image this person projects onto the retina shrinks as he walks away, because of size constancy we do not perceive that he is shrinking. (c) The coal may reflect more light in the sun than the paper does in the shade, yet we still perceive that the paper is brighter than the coal because of brightness constancy. (d) Even though this apple is in the shade, we still perceive it as being red because of color constancy.

binocular [bye-NOCK-you-lar] **depth cues** depth cues that utilize information from both eyes

retinal disparity a binocular depth cue that uses the difference in the images projected on the right and left retinas to inform the brain about the distance of a stimulus

monocular depth cues depth cues that require information from only one eye

FIGURE

3.18 Binocular Depth Cues

The brain uses retinal disparity, or the degree to which the images projected on the right and left retinas differ from each other, to calculate how far away an object is. The farther away the object, the smaller the degree of retinal disparity.

FIGURE

3.19 Solution to the Problem in Figure 3.16

After looking at this picture, can you easily find the cow in Figure 3.16?

Gestalt [gush-TALLT] **approach** a psychological school of thought originating in Germany that proposed that the whole of a perception must be understood rather than trying to deconstruct perception into its parts

figure–ground a Gestalt principle of perception that states that when we perceive a stimulus, we visually pull the figure part of the stimulus forward while visually pushing backward the background, or ground, part of the stimulus

closure a Gestalt principle of perception that states that when we look at a stimulus, we tend to see it as a closed shape rather than lines

proximity a Gestalt principle of perception that states that we tend to group close objects together during perception

similarity a Gestalt principle of perception that states that we tend to group like objects together during perception

do we perceive depth in paintings and photographs? We use cues such as the *relative size* of objects and *interposition* to tell us which objects are farther away. ■ TABLE 3.2 describes some of the most useful monocular depth cues.

Perceptual constancy and depth perception are both important components of our perceptual processing. But how do we perceive the cylindrical shape of a soda can or the rectangular shape of a shoebox? To understand this level of perceptual processing, we will examine theories of form perception.

Perceiving Form: The Gestalt Approach

One influential approach to understanding form perception is the **Gestalt approach**. According to the Gestalt approach, the whole of a perception is greater than the sum of its parts. In fact, the word *Gestalt* is German for "whole form." According to the Gestaltists, when you look at your friend's face, the resulting perception is not merely a sum of the angles, curves, shapes, and lines that make up the face; rather, you perceive the stimulus *as a whole*. In this case, you perceive a face because your mind has implicitly grouped all of the stimuli that make up that face into a coherent whole.

One of the major contributions of Gestalt theory is a series of perceptual laws that attempt to explain how our minds automatically organize perceptual stimuli together to produce the perception of a whole form (Wertheimer, 1923). One of the most important Gestalt concepts of perceptual organization is **figure–ground**. When you look at your world, you see a multitude of objects or figures that seem to stand away from the background. For instance, your professor standing at the blackboard is a *figure* against the blackboard or *ground*. ■ FIGURE 3.20 shows figure–ground in action. You should have two different perceptions of this picture, depending on what you visually pull forward as the *figure* and what you push back as the *ground*. When you focus on the light parts as the figure, you see a skull. When you focus on the dark parts of the figure, you see a young woman.

Another Gestalt principle is **closure**. When we perceive a stimulus such as the one in ■ FIGURE 3.21, we tend to mentally fill in, or *close*, the object. The stimulus is not a complete triangle, but nearly everyone will perceive it as complete. According to the principle of closure, we have a preference for viewing solid shapes as opposed to lines.

The Gestalt principles of **proximity** and **similarity** help explain how we group objects together. These rules state that we group together stimuli that are close to each other, or proximal, and also stimuli that are similar (■ FIGURE 3.22). As you read this page, you are

Table 3.2 Monocular Depth Cues

Monocular Depth Cue	Description	Example
Interposition	More distant objects are partially hidden by closer objects.	© Robert Estall/ Corbis
Height on the horizon	More distant objects are placed higher on the horizon than closer objects.	© Richard T. Nowitz/ Corbis
Relative size	More distant objects are seen as smaller than closer objects of the same size.	© W. Cody/Corbis
Texture gradient	More distant objects have less texture or detail than closer objects.	© Corbis
Aerial perspective	More distant objects are hazier and blurrier than closer objects.	© Sylvain Grandadam/Getty Images
Linear perspective	Converging lines indicate distance or depth.	© Corbis
Motion parallax	More distant objects appear to move more slowly than closer objects as we pass by them.	© Steven Lam/Getty Images

© Rykoff Collection/Corbis

FIGURE

3.20 **Figure–Ground**

What do you see when you look at this picture? Depending on how you use the perceptual rule of figure–ground, you may see a skull or a young woman.

good continuation a Gestalt principle of perception that states that we have a preference for perceiving stimuli that seem to follow one another as part of a continuing pattern

FIGURE

3.21 **Closure**

According to the Gestaltists, we tend to mentally fill in, or close, solid forms during perception.

continually using proximity to discriminate between the words that make up the sentences. Without proximity, you would see a mass of letters, but you would not know where one word ends and another begins.

The final Gestalt principle that we will look at is **good continuation**. The principle of good continuation states that we prefer to perceive stimuli that seem to follow one another as being part of a continuing pattern (■ FIGURE 3.23). Camouflage works on the principle of good continuation. Can you see the hidden animal in Figure 3.23b? This animal's very survival depends on its predator's use of good continuation!

(a) Grouping based on proximity

(b) Grouping based on similarity

FIGURE

3.22   The Gestalt Rules of Similarity and Proximity

Perceiving Form: Feature Detection Theory

Feature detection theory states that we have cells in our visual cortex that fire only in response to certain stimuli. Researchers studied this theory in animals, using electrodes to measure the activity of single neurons in the visual cortex. With an electrode in place, the researchers presented the animal with a certain visual stimulus, such as a bar of light, then checked to see whether the neuron fired. Through a process of elimination, the researchers determined what particular stimulus was needed to cause the specific neuron to fire (Hubel & Weisel, 1965).

Using this approach, researchers have found that some cells of the cortex respond to particular combinations of lightness and darkness, lines of differing thickness, location, and orientation (Hubel & Wiesel, 1979). The neurons that fire only when certain visual stimuli are presented may work as feature detectors. Presumably, the human brain also has feature detectors, and by noticing which of our feature-detecting neurons are firing, our brain determines the form of the stimulus we are viewing. Consider, for example, how feature detectors could help us perceive the geometric shape of a square. As you know, a square is made up of two parallel horizontal lines and two parallel vertical lines. If each of these four lines is detected by a different set of feature-detecting neurons, two detectors for vertical lines and two detectors for horizontal lines, then our brain can deduce that we are looking at a square.

Feature detection research holds much promise, but it is difficult to conduct (Hubel, 1990). Each neuron of the visual system has to be tested to determine what feature it detects. Mapping the entire visual system of feature detectors is likely to take a long time!

feature detection theory a theory of perception that proposes the existence of feature detectors, cortical cells that fire only when we see certain visual stimuli such as shapes, colors of light, or movement

FIGURE

3.23   Two Instances of Good Continuation

Good continuation ensures that we perceive continuous patterns in the world. This perceptual principle is vital to the survival of the animal in (b).

(a)

(b)

Let's Review!

This section described perception and perceptual organization, including top-down and bottom-up perception; ways that our brain corrects our perception to give us perceptual constancy; how our brain uses monocular and binocular depth cues to perceive depth; and two theories of form perception. For a quick check of your understanding, answer these questions.

1. Jamal was a witness to a bank robbery. Although he did not clearly see the robber's face, Jamal assumed that the robber was a man. What is the *most likely* reason for Jamal's assumption?
   a. Bottom-up perceptual processing
   b. Top-down perceptual processing
   c. Gestalt perceptual processing
   d. Feature detection processing

2. If you went blind in one eye, which depth cue would you lose?
   a. Motion parallax
   b. Interposition
   c. Retinal disparity
   d. Textural gradient

3. A brain tumor in your occipital lobe might result in distorted visual perception. This result is *most consistent* with which theory of perception?
   a. Feature detection theory
   b. Gestalt theory of perceptual organization
   c. Top-down perceptual processing theory
   d. Bottom-up perceptual processing theory

Answers 1. b; 2. c; 3. a

How Accurate Are Our Perceptions?

- Describe some of the common perceptual illusions we experience and explain their causes.

- Explain how culture affects perception.

Learning Objectives

One of our students once had a frightening experience in which he misinterpreted a visual stimulus. He was driving in the mountains of northern Georgia when he passed a bear on a distant hillside. The bear was standing on its hind legs, towering over the 20-foot-tall pine trees that surrounded it. But the student knew that this was very unlikely, so he turned his car around and went back for another look. On closer inspection of the scene, he saw that all of the pine trees on the mountainside were newly planted saplings, about 3 feet high. The bear that towered over them was only an average-sized Georgia black bear! Our student was able to go back and correct his perception, but this is not always the case. We may never discover that we have misperceived a situation. Why do we sometimes misperceive our world?

Because of top-down processing, it would take a long time to accurately perceive this laptop computer in the road. We simply don't expect to see laptop computers in the middle of the highway; therefore, our perception is slowed down.

ThinkStock/Getty Images

Errors Due to Top-Down Processing: Seeing What We Expect to See

Why do you think the student misperceived the size of the black bear? The key to his misperception of the bear was in his misperception of the size of the pine trees. We would explain this in terms of top-down processing. When driving through the mountains, most Georgians do not expect to see hillsides of baby trees. It's more typical to see mountainsides covered with mature pine trees that can be well over 20 feet tall. Because this is the normal expectation, the student simply took for granted that the trees were a mature height. It wasn't until he saw the pine trees up close that he realized that his top-down processing had failed him. Because he misperceived the trees, he also misperceived the height of the bear.

Errors Due to Perceptual Constancy: Tricks of the Brain

Errors that are caused by top-down processing relate to the knowledge and the expectations we have of our world. Misperceptions occur for other reasons, too. Sometimes we misperceive things when our brain's attempts to give us perceptual constancy go awry.

THE MOON ILLUSION

Have you ever noticed that the moon appears to be much larger as it rises over the horizon than when it is directly overhead? Many people think it is because the earth is closer to the moon when it is at the horizon, but this is not true. The answer lies in our brain's attempt to correct for what it thinks is a mistake in perception. The moon projects the same size image on our retina when it is on the horizon as it does when it is directly overhead. But when the moon is on the horizon, many interposition cues, such as trees and buildings that stand between the moon and us, indicate distance to our brain. When we view the moon directly overhead, however, there are no interposition cues to indicate distance. Consequently, our brain thinks the moon is farther away when it is on the horizon. The logic involved is this: If the moon is farther away on the horizon, but it still projects the same size image on the retina as the moon overhead, then the moon on the horizon must actually be bigger than the moon overhead. The brain tries to "fix" the inconsistency by inflating our perception of the size of the moon on the horizon (Kaufman & Rock, 1989). Curiously, you can undo the moon illusion by facing away from the moon, bending over, and looking at the moon from between your legs. In this position, the brain does not try to fix the inconsistency, and the illusion disappears.

THE PONZO ILLUSION

This same logic underlies the Ponzo illusion. Lines of equal length that lie across converging lines appear to be unequal in length (■ FIGURE 3.24). In the Ponzo illusion, linear perspective and height on the horizon cues tell the brain that the top line is farther away than the bottom one. Yet both lines project the same size image on the retina. In an attempt to maintain size constancy, the brain inflates our perception of the top line's length, thus causing the illusion that the top line is longer than the bottom line. This illusion occurs even though we do not consciously perceive that the line on top is farther away (Gillam, 1980).

THE MÜLLER-LYER ILLUSION

Size constancy probably also plays a role in the Müller-Lyer illusion (■ FIGURE 3.25; Coren, Porac, Aks, & Morikawa, 1988). In this illusion, our perception of the length of the vertical line segments changes, depending on the direction of the arrows at either end of the line. When the arrows extend away, the line looks longer.

FIGURE

3.24 **The Ponzo Illusion**

Line segments A and B are both the same length, but we perceive that A is longer than B.

The Ponzo Illusion

FIGURE

3.25 **The Müller-Lyer Illusion**

In the Müller-Lyer illusion, the line in (a) is perceived as being shorter than the line in (b), even though they are of equal length. The Müller-Lyer illusion is often seen in rectangular, "carpentered" buildings. The vertical line in the outside corner (c) looks shorter than the vertical line in the inside corner (d)—yet they are the same length. Architects use the Müller-Lyer illusion to create certain perceptions of their buildings.

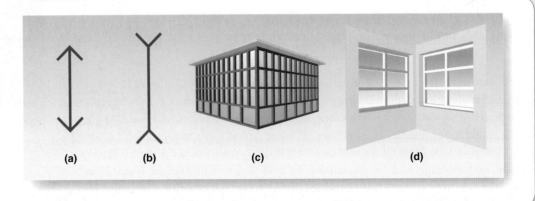

(a)   (b)   (c)   (d)

Although researchers are not quite sure why the Müller-Lyer illusion occurs, it is thought that the arrows serve as depth cues, much as we might find in the inside and outside corners of a building. If you look at Figure 3.25c, you can see that this type of corner produces a surface that is closer to the viewer than the recessed corner in Figure 3.25d. These depth cues may set off a process of compensation for size consistency that is very similar to those found in the moon illusion and the Ponzo illusion.

> ### You Asked...
>
> *How has society affected our perceptions of what we see?*
>
> KAREN AREVALO, STUDENT

Cultural Factors in Perception

As we've discussed, your beliefs and expectations of the world can influence your top-down perceptual processing. Given that culture and environment influence many of our beliefs and expectations (remember our student and the Georgia bear?), it stands to reason that culture and environment also affect perception. The Müller-Lyer illusion is a good example of this type of influence.

People who live in "carpentered" environments, where many of the buildings are wood-framed rectangular structures, have much experience with the architectural angles that produce the Müller-Lyer illusion. Is it possible that these people also experience the Müller-Lyer illusion to a greater degree than those who've lived their lives in "noncarpentered" worlds (where rectangular structures are rare)? This seems to be the case. The Bashi people of Africa traditionally live in round dwellings. When compared to Europeans, the Bashi are often found to be less susceptible to the Müller-Lyer illusion (Bonte, 1962). A similar effect has been found among American Navajos. When traditional Navajos who live in round homes called *hogans* were compared to Navajos who grew up in rectangular buildings, the former were found to be less likely to experience the Müller-Lyer illusion (Pedersen & Wheeler, 1983). These studies suggest that our perceptions are influenced by elements in our culture that prepare us to see the world in a particular way.

People who grow up in *noncarpentered* environments, where structures tend to be like this round *hogan,* are less likely to experience the Müller-Lyer illusion.

Rob Crandall/The Image Works

Let's Review!

The material in this section dealt with errors in perception and several common perceptual illusions. For a quick check of your understanding, answer these questions.

1. Leahannaba grew up in a culture where most of the structures were dome-shaped huts. Compared to someone from New York City, which optical illusion is Leahannaba less likely to experience?
   a. Ponzo illusion
   b. Müller-Lyer illusion
   c. Moon illusion
   d. All of the above

2. Last night, Samantha noticed that the moon looked huge as it rose above the horizon. Later, when the moon was overhead, it did not look nearly as large to her. Which of the following is a primary cause of this illusion?
   a. Perceptual constancies
   b. Top-down processing
   c. Bottom-up processing
   d. Binocular depth cues

3. When you look down the railroad tracks, the tracks appear to converge even though they are parallel. This illusion is the result of which perceptual process?
   a. Monocular depth cues
   b. Binocular depth cues
   c. Top-down processing
   d. Subliminal perception

Answers 1. b; 2. a; 3. a

Studying THE Chapter

Key Terms

attention (76)
sensation (76)
perception (76)
psychophysics (76)
absolute threshold (76)
just noticeable difference (jnd) (76)
Weber's law (76)
subliminal (77)
wavelength (79)
amplitude (79)
visible spectrum (80)
hue (80)
brightness (80)
saturation (80)
pupil (80)
lens (81)
accommodation (81)

retina (81)
rods (81)
cones (81)
optic nerve (81)
blindspot (81)
photopigments (83)
dark adaptation (83)
light adaptation (83)
trichromatic theory of color vision (84)
color blindness (85)
opponent-process theory (86)
optic chiasm (87)
feature detectors (87)
cycle (89)
frequency (89)
loudness (89)
decibels (dB) (89)

pitch (89)
cochlea (90)
basilar membrane (90)
hair cells (90)
auditory nerve (91)
place theory (92)
frequency theory (92)
volley theory (92)
duplicity theory (92)
gustation (94)
papillae (94)
taste buds (94)
olfaction (96)
olfactory epithelium (97)
lock-and-key theory (98)
pheromones (99)
dermis (99)
epidermis (99)

kinesthesis (101)

vestibular sense (101)

top-down perceptual
    processing (103)

bottom-up perceptual
    processing (104)

binocular depth cues (105)

retinal disparity (105)

monocular depth
    cues (105)

Gestalt approach (106)

figure–ground (106)

closure (106)

proximity (106)

similarity (106)

good continuation (107)

feature detection
    theory (108)

What Do You Know? Assess Your Understanding

Test your retention and understanding of the material by answering the following questions.

1. _____ is the conversion of environmental energies into neural impulses.
   a. Sensation
   b. Perception
   c. Absolute threshold
   d. The jnd

2. _____ is the branch of psychology that studies how the physical properties of stimuli correspond to the sensory experience of these stimuli.
   a. Physiological psychology
   b. Perception psychology
   c. Psychophysics
   d. Psychodynamics

3. According to Weber's law, a teaspoon of sugar added to an already sweet glass of tea will be _____ noticeable than a teaspoon of sugar added to a glass of tea that has no sugar to begin with.
   a. less
   b. more
   c. equally
   d. Weber's law does not tell us what to expect in this situation.

4. The visible spectrum spans from _____ to roughly _____ in humans.
   a. 640 nm; 875 nm
   b. 543 nm; 981 nm
   c. 402 nm; 750 nm
   d. 360 nm; 750 nm

5. The brightness of a light we perceive corresponds to the _____ of the light wave.
   a. purity
   b. amplitude
   c. wavelength
   d. frequency

6. The eye's _____ undergoes _____ to focus an image of what we see on our retina.
   a. iris; constriction
   b. pupil; constriction
   c. lens; accommodation
   d. sclera; accommodation

7. _____ in the _____ of the retina allow us to see color.
   a. Neurotransmitters; cones
   b. Photopigments; cones
   c. Neurotransmitters; rods
   d. Photopigments; rods

8. According to the trichromatic theory of color vision, we have _____ for _____, _____, and _____ light.
   a. cones; red; green; blue
   b. cones; red; green; yellow
   c. rods; red; green; blue
   d. rods; red; green; yellow

9. The _____ of a sound corresponds to the _____ of a sound wave.
   a. loudness; frequency
   b. pitch; frequency
   c. loudness; cycle
   d. pitch; amplitude

10. When we hear a sound, _____ cells on the _____ _____ convert sound waves into neural signals.
   a. cone; vestibular canal
   b. rod; cochlea
   c. hair; basilar membrane
   d. hair; vestibular canal

11. The _____ of the brain processes visual information before it travels to the cortex.
    a. thalamus
    b. hypothalamus
    c. olfactory bulb
    d. cerebellum

12. Jonas, a retired jet engine mechanic, is 65 years old. Lately he's been experiencing some hearing loss. From what you know about hearing and exposure to loud sounds, what would you predict about Jonas's hearing loss?
    a. He will have the most trouble hearing low-pitched sounds.
    b. He will have the most trouble hearing medium-pitched sounds.
    c. He will have the most trouble hearing high-pitched sounds.
    d. He will most likely be completely deaf.

13. To date, the most widely accepted theory of pitch perception is _____ theory.
    a. place
    b. volley
    c. frequency
    d. duplicity

14. If you want to be sure to taste the full flavor of a piece of chocolate, where should you avoid placing the chocolate on as you taste it?
    a. The front of the tongue
    b. The center of the tongue
    c. The right side of the tongue
    d. The back of the tongue

15. Ultimately, most taste information is processed in the _____ cortex of the brain.
    a. somatosensory
    b. occipital
    c. temporal
    d. motor

16. When your cat breathes deeply through his open mouth, he is likely using his _____ sense.
    a. vomeronasal
    b. olfactory
    c. vestibular
    d. kinesthetic

17. Karina goes to a Halloween party where she meets a man who is wearing a monster mask that covers his entire face. Later, when her best friend asks her to describe the man, she describes him as being "good-looking" even though she never actually saw his face. Which of the following best explains Karina's perception of the man?
    a. Good continuation
    b. Closure
    c. Bottom-up perceptual processing
    d. Top-down perceptual processing

18. Mike was in an accident that injured his right eye. Although he'll recover, he must wear an eye patch for the next two weeks. During this time, Mike's doctor will not allow him to drive a car. Mike's doctor is most likely concerned with disturbances to Mike's _____.
    a. vestibular system
    b. binocular depth cues
    c. monocular depth cues
    d. kinesthetic system

19. In which of the following situations, would you be most likely to use bottom-up perceptual processing?
    a. When viewing a piece of abstract art composed of nothing but paint splatters on a canvas.
    b. When reading your best friend's bad handwriting.
    c. When trying to watch a movie in a crowded theater where your view of the screen is obstructed by the people sitting in front of you.
    d. When reading the daily news on the Internet.

20. What do the moon illusion and the Ponzo illusion have in common?
    a. They both occur because of binocular depth cues.
    b. They both occur because of perceptual constancies.
    c. They both occur because of cultural influences.
    d. They both occur because of bottom-up perceptual processes.

Answers: 1. a; 2. c; 3. a; 4. d; 5. b; 6. c; 7. b; 8. a; 9. b; 10. c; 11. a; 12. c; 13. d; 14. b; 15. a; 16. a; 17. d; 18. b; 19. a; 20. b.

Online Resources

CENGAGE**NOW**™ **Personalized Study**

www.cengage.com/login

Go to www.cengage.com/login to link to CengageNOW, your online study tool. First take the **Pre-Test** for this chapter to get your **Personalized Study Plan**, which will identify topics you need to review and direct you to online resources. Then take the **Post-Test** to determine what concepts you have mastered and what you still need work on.

 What Is Psychology? Essentials Book Companion Website

www.cengage.com/psychology/pastorino

Visit your book companion website, where you will find more resources to help you study. Resources include learning objectives, Internet exercises, quizzing, flash cards, and a pronunciation glossary.

CHAPTER 3

Look Back AT **WHAT** YOU'VE **LEARNED**

GDT/Getty Images

How Do We See the World?

- Light is electromagnetic energy, measured primarily by **wavelength** and **amplitude**. Wavelength = **hue**; amplitude = **brightness**.

- The **visible spectrum** of light is the narrow band we are able to see. Some animals are able to see a much broader spectrum.

How Do We Measure Sensation and Perception?

- **Psychophysics** is the branch of psychology that studies how we process sensory stimuli.

- Psychophysicists conduct experiments to determine the **absolute threshold** and **just noticeable difference (jnd)** of each of the five senses.

  - **Weber's law** is the relationship between the original intensity of a stimulus and the amount of change that is required to produce a jnd.

  - When sensory stimuli are too weak in intensity to reach absolute threshold, the stimuli are said to be **subliminal**.

  - There is little evidence for the existence of ESP.

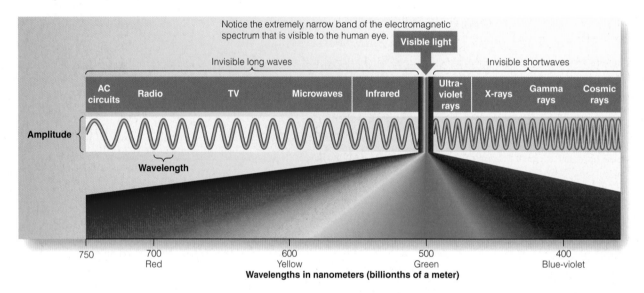

Notice the extremely narrow band of the electromagnetic spectrum that is visible to the human eye. **Visible light**

Invisible long waves | Invisible shortwaves

AC circuits | Radio | TV | Microwaves | Infrared | Ultra-violet rays | X-rays | Gamma rays | Cosmic rays

Amplitude

Wavelength

750 / Red | 700 | 600 / Yellow | 500 / Green | 400 / Blue-violet

Wavelengths in nanometers (billionths of a meter)

- In the **retina** of the eye, specialized cells known as **rods** and **cones** convert light into neural impulses, which eventually travel to the brain via the **optic nerve**.

- The **trichromatic theory of color vision** and the **opponent-process theory** are both used to explain how we process color.

- **Color blindness** is the inability to see certain colors, and is often the result of missing cones in the retina.

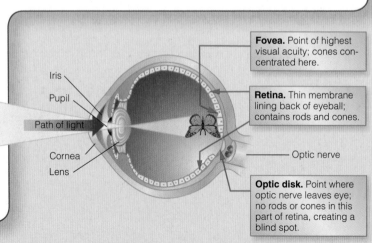

Iris
Pupil
Path of light
Cornea
Lens

Fovea. Point of highest visual acuity; cones concentrated here.

Retina. Thin membrane lining back of eyeball; contains rods and cones.

Optic nerve

Optic disk. Point where optic nerve leaves eye; no rods or cones in this part of retina, creating a blind spot.

HOW DO WE **Sense** AND **PERCEIVE OUR WORLD?**

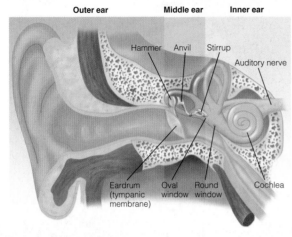

Outer ear | Middle ear | Inner ear

Hammer Anvil Stirrup Auditory nerve

Eardrum (tympanic membrane) Oval window Round window Cochlea

How Do We Hear?

- Sounds are produced by waves of compressed air. **Frequency = pitch**; amplitude = **loudness**.

- The eardrum, or tympanic membrane, is a very thin membrane in the middle ear that vibrates to incoming sounds. It begins transmitting those sounds through the small bones to the **hair cells** of the fluid-filled **cochlea**, where neural impulses are generated.

- The **auditory nerve** carries the sounds we hear into the brain.

How Do We Taste, Smell, Touch, and Use Our Bodies to Sense?

- Humans are sensitive to at least four tastes: bitter, sweet, sour, and salty.

- The **taste buds**, which reside in the pits between the **papillae** on your tongue, convert the chemicals in the foods you eat into neural impulses.

- The sense of smell operates by converting odors captured by a special piece of skin that lines the top of the nasal cavity to neural impulses that travel via the olfactory nerve to the olfactory bulb in the brain.

- Many animals (and perhaps humans) have a vomeronasal system that allows them to communicate with other animals via airborne chemicals known as **pheromones**.

- The sense of touch originates in the skin, with the inner layer—the **dermis**—containing most of the touch receptors.

- **Kinesthesis** refers to our ability to sense the position of our body parts in space and in relation to one another.

- The **vestibular sense** monitors the position of our head in space and helps us to stay balanced.

© Corbis

Perception: How Do We Interpret Sensory Information?

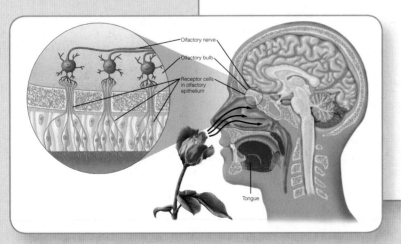

Olfactory nerve
Olfactory bulb
Receptor cells in olfactory epithelium
Tongue

- **Top-down perceptual processing** refers to using previously gained knowledge to interpret a sensory stimulus.

- **Bottom-up perceptual processing** refers to using properties of the stimulus itself to form our perception of a stimulus.

- Perceptual constancies, depth cues, and **feature detection** are among the mental shortcuts we automatically employ to assist in perceiving stimuli.

- Perceptual errors can occur for a variety of reasons. They are often due to misapplied expectations that lead us to think we have seen or heard something that we have not.

4

Consciousness: Wide Awake, IN A Daze, OR DREAMING?

- Sleep, Dreaming, and Circadian Rhythm

- Hypnosis: Real or Imagined?

- Psychoactive Drugs

© Image Source Black/Alamy

Altered states are relevant to our everyday lives. For example, Micaiah Frazier is a 17-year-old college student, majoring in biology, in the hopes of pursuing a medical degree after college. Micaiah frequently hears students bragging about how little sleep they get, but after learning about sleep, he knows how important it is to get adequate sleep after studying. He expects that sleep will be a low priority in medical school, but knows that without it he will not do as well academically and his grades will suffer. He has seen the effect that disruptive sleeping has had on his mother, an overnight nurse. Working all night and trying to sleep during the day affected her physically and mentally. It reinforced for Micaiah the value of sleep for a sound mind and body.

Micaiah also sees the usefulness in knowing about psychoactive drugs. He realizes that drugs don't just affect the body; they affect one's behavior, thoughts, and emotions. He hopes that this knowledge will help him identify patients who are addicted to drugs. He feels that patients should be especially aware of the potential for some prescribed drugs to alter consciousness. Micaiah has also witnessed negative effects of drugs in his job as a valet cashier at a five-star resort. Micaiah often sees valets attempt to persuade intoxicated guests not to drive as they are a danger to themselves and others. He believes that alcohol's effects make them lose perspective on the long-term consequences of their behavior.

Like Micaiah, we all experience altered states of consciousness. **Consciousness,** in psychological terms, includes the feelings, thoughts, and aroused states of which we are aware. This chapter examines the levels or gradations of consciousness itself—when you are not fully awake, alert, aware, or perhaps of sound mind. For example, psychologists have done quite a bit of research in three areas: sleep, hypnosis, and the effects of various psychoactive drugs. By closely examining these states, we may better understand our behavior and the behavior of those around us. We will start with the altered state we all experience—sleep.

M. Frazier

After learning about states of consciousness in his psychology class, Micaiah Frazier can see the relevance of sleep and psychoactive drugs to his current job and future career.

119

Sleep, Dreaming, and Circadian Rhythm

- Discuss why we sleep and what factors influence the amount of sleep we need.

- Describe the sleep stages we progress through during a typical night of sleep.

- Compare and contrast the different theories on dreaming.

- Describe and distinguish among sleep disorders, including insomnia, narcolepsy, sleep apnea, sleepwalking, night terrors, and enuresis.

Many of us never question what goes on in our bodies and minds as we sleep. But sleep offers plenty of behaviors for psychologists to explore. First, we will look at *why* we sleep and what occurs in our brains and bodies as we sleep. We will then explore the purpose of dreams and whether dreams have meaning. We will conclude by describing different types of sleep disorders. We caution you that just reading about sleep can make you drowsy!

Functions of Sleep: Why Do We Sleep, and What If We Don't?

What would happen if you tried to stay awake? William C. Dement, a pioneer in sleep research, actually tried this experiment himself. Dement's lack of sleep made him a danger to himself and others, but he was not in danger of dying from lack of sleep. Eventually he fell asleep. In the same way that you cannot hold your breath until you die, you cannot deprive yourself of all sleep. Sleep always wins. We drift into repeated microsleeps (Goleman, 1982). A **microsleep** is a brief (3- to 15-second) episode of sleep that occurs in the midst of a wakeful activity. We are typically unaware of its occurrence unless we are behind the wheel of a car, steering a ship, or flying a plane. In such circumstances, microsleeps could cause a disaster. Yet microsleeps appear to help us survive by preventing total sleep deprivation.

Sleep ensures our continued physical and mental health in several ways.

consciousness [CON-shis-nus] feelings, thoughts, and aroused states of which we are aware

microsleep brief episode of sleep that occurs in the midst of a wakeful activity

- *Sleep restores body tissues and facilitates body growth.* Sleep allows your immune system, nervous system, and organs time to replenish lost reserves and energy and to repair any

It is estimated that more than 24,000 deaths occur annually in accidents caused directly or in part by drowsy drivers.

© Tom Carter/PhotoEdit

cellular damage. This prepares the body for action the next day and ensures the continued health of the body. Sleep also activates growth hormone, which facilitates physical growth during infancy, childhood, and the teen years (Gais, Hullemann, Hallschmid, & Born, 2006; Szentirmai et al., 2007). Lack of adequate sleep can also affect energy levels, often making us feel drowsy and fatigued (Oginska & Pokorski, 2006).

- *Sleep increases immunity to disease.* During sleep, the production of immune cells that fight off infection increases. Therefore, your immune system is stronger when you receive the appropriate amount of sleep (Beardsley, 1996; Lange, Dimitrov, Fehm, Westermann, & Born, 2006; Motivala & Irwin, 2007). When you deprive your body of sleep, your natural immune responses are reduced (Irwin, Clark, Kennedy, Christian Gillin, & Ziegler, 2003). This is in part why you are encouraged to sleep and rest when you are ill. This effect on immunity occurs after as few as two days of not sleeping or even several days of partial sleep deprivation (Heiser et al., 2000; Irwin et al., 1996; Ozturk et al., 1999; Rogers, Szuba, Staab, Evans, & Dinges, 2001). For college students, this may mean you are more susceptible to colds and flu at midterm and final exam time. You are more likely to sleep less at these times, thereby decreasing your immune system's ability to combat illnesses. Fortunately, after a night or several nights of recovery sleep, your natural immune functions return to normal (Irwin et al., 1996; Ozturk et al., 1999). Sleeping truly is good medicine.

- *Sleep keeps your mind alert.* When people do not get enough sleep, they are more likely to be inattentive and easily distracted (Jennings, Monk, & van der Molen, 2003; Kahol et al., 2008; Kendall, Kautz, Russo, & Killgore, 2006; Koslowsky & Babkoff, 1992). Sleep makes your body more sensitive to norepinephrine—the neurotransmitter that keeps you alert during the day (Chapter 2; Steriade & McCarley, 1990).

- *Sleep helps learning and memory.* When you sleep, information that you have reviewed or rehearsed is more likely to be remembered (Fogel, Smith, & Cote, 2007; Gais, Lucas, & Born, 2006; Karni, Tanne, Rubenstein, Askenasy, & Sagi, 1994; Stickgold & Walker, 2007; Walker & Stickgold, 2004). Chapter 6 offers an in-depth look at memory processing, but a few simple statements here will help you understand the connection between sleep and memory.

    - In order to get information into your memory, you must *encode* it, or do something to remember the information. This may mean repeating the information over and over again, visualizing the information, or associating it with a personal experience. When information is thoroughly encoded, it can be more easily transferred to long-term memory so that we can retrieve it later.

    - Sleep allows you to better store material that was actually processed (that is, encoded well enough) during studying. Information that you can't readily retrieve in the morning probably wasn't encoded well enough, and you will need to study it again. You can see the advantage of a good night's sleep before an exam.

    - Sleep's connection to memory processing may also explain why problem solving seems to improve after a night's sleep (Ellenbogen, Hu, Payne, Titone, & Walker, 2007). You may think about a problem repeatedly during the day, frustrated by your inability to find a solution. The next day you awaken with a solution in mind. This suggests that pertinent details about the problem are processed during sleep. The phrase "sleep on it" really does have merit.

- *Sleep enhances your mood.* Sleep activates many chemicals that influence your emotions and mood. Consequently, if you are deprived of sleep, you are more likely to be irritable, cranky, and unhappy, in addition to being tired (Boivin et al., 1997; Durmer & Dinges, 2005).

Research also suggests that sleep may have evolved as a necessary behavior for humans (Hirshkowitz, Moore, & Minhoto, 1997; Webb, 1983). When humans lived in caves, it was dangerous for them to go out at night to hunt for food because they had very little night vision and were relatively small compared to other species. If they did go outside at night, they were likely to be the food for larger predators. Humans who stayed inside the cave at night were more likely to survive and produce offspring. Over time, these offspring may have adapted to the pattern of nighttime sleeping and daytime hunting and gathering.

As you can see, sleep is a necessity, not a luxury. Sleep offers many benefits to our functioning and ensures that we will be healthy, alert, and happy.

How Much Sleep Do We Need?

People show differences in the amount of sleep they need. Here are some sleep factors and facts:

- *Age.* The older we get, the less sleep we need (■ FIGURE 4.1). Babies require a lot of sleep, between 16 and 18 hours a day. Preschoolers require less sleep, about 10 to12 hours a day, typically including a midday nap. Teenagers and young adults need less sleep than children, but they still require 8 to 10 hours of sleep a night. However, just one in five teenagers gets an optimal 9 hours of sleep on school nights (National Sleep Foundation, 2006). On average, college students sleep 6.1 hours—2 hours less than they need—each night (Maas, 1998). One study of 191 undergraduates found that the majority exhibited some form of sleep disturbance (Buboltz, Brown, & Soper, 2001). Adults, on average, sleep 6.8 hours a night on weekdays (National Sleep Foundation, 2005).

- *Lifestyle (Environment).* Our habits and our environment also influence the amount of sleep we need or get. If you were raised in a home in which everyone was up early on the weekends to do chores, you adapted to a different sleep schedule than someone who slept until 10 A.M. or noon on weekends. In one study of college students, good sleepers were more likely to have regular bedtime and rise time schedules than poorer sleepers (Carney, Edinger, Meyer, Lindman, & Istre, 2006). Keep in mind, too, that stressors and responsibilities change as we get older. Living on one's own, parenting, or job responsibilities also bring about changes in our sleep schedule.

- *Genetics.* Genes may also play a role in the amount of sleep that each of us requires. For example, studies that measured the sleep patterns of identical twins compared to fraternal twins found more similar sleep needs among identical twins (Webb & Campbell, 1983). Additional research also suggests that genes may influence our propensity to be either "night owls" or "early birds." Some people may be genetically predisposed to get up early in the morning and go to bed earlier, whereas others may prefer getting up later and going to bed later (Guthrie, Ash, & Bendapudi, 1995; Mongrain, Lavoie, Selmaoui, Paquet, & Dumont, 2004; Tankova, Adan, & Buela-Casal, 1994). Learn your propensity toward morningness or eveningness by completing the brief scale in Your Turn – Active Learning.

FIGURE

4.1 Age Differences in Sleep Needs

Newborns sleep an average of 16 hours a day. Preschoolers require less sleep, about 10 to 12 hours. Most teenagers and adults require 8 hours.

From "Ontogenetic Development of Human Sleep-Dream Cycle," by H. P. Roffwarg, J. N. Muzino, and W. C. Dement, Science, 1966, 152:604–609. Copyright 1966 by the AAAS. Reprinted by permission.

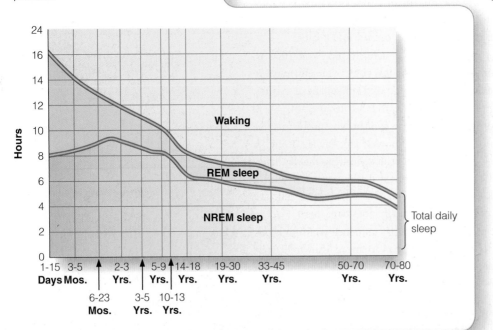

YOUR TURN – ACTIVE LEARNING

Answer the following questions, then add up the values to get your total score. Compare your total score with the key at the end to get an idea of your chronotype.

Morningness–Eveningness Scale

QUESTION	ANSWER	VALUE
If you were entirely free to plan your evening and had no commitments the next day, at what time would you choose to go to bed?	8 P.M.–9 P.M.	5
	9 P.M.–10:15 P.M.	4
	10:15 P.M.–12:30 A.M.	3
	12:30 A.M.–1:45 A.M.	2
	1:45 A.M.–3 A.M.	1
You have to do 2 hours of physically hard work. If you were entirely free to plan your day, in which of the following periods would you choose to do the work?	8 A.M.–10 A.M.	4
	11 A.M.–1 P.M.	3
	3 P.M.–5 P.M.	2
	7 P.M.–9 P.M.	1
For some reason you have gone to bed several hours later than normal, but there is no need to get up at a particular time the next morning. Which of the following is most likely to occur?	Will wake up at the usual time and not fall asleep again	4
	Will wake up at the usual time and doze thereafter	3
	Will wake up at the usual time but will fall asleep again	2
	Will not wake up until later than usual	1
You have a 2-hour test to take that you know will be mentally exhausting. If you were entirely free to choose, in which of the following periods would you choose to take the test?	8 A.M.–10 A.M.	4
	11 A.M.–1 P.M.	3
	3 P.M.–5 P.M.	2
	7 P.M.–9 P.M.	1
If you had no commitments the next day and were entirely free to plan your own day, what time would you get up?	5 A.M.–6:30 A.M.	5
	6:30 A.M.–7:45 A.M.	4
	7:45 A.M.–9:45 A.M.	3
	9:45 A.M.–11 A.M.	2
	11 A.M.–12 P.M.	1
A friend has asked you to join him twice a week for a workout in the gym. The best time for him is between 10 P.M. and 11 P.M. Bearing nothing else in mind other than how you normally feel in the evening, how do you think you would perform?	Very well	1
	Reasonably well	2
	Poorly	3
	Very poorly	4
One hears about "morning" and "evening" types of people. Which of these types do you consider yourself to be?	Definitely a morning type	6
	More a morning than an evening type	4
	More an evening than a morning type	2
	Definitely an evening type	0

MORNINGNESS–EVENINGNESS SCALE	
Definitely morning type	32–28
Moderately morning type	27–23
Neither type	22–16
Moderately evening type	15–11
Definitely evening type	10–6

(Adapted from A Self Assessment Questionnaire to Determine Morningness–Eveningness in Human Circadian Rhythms, by J. A. Horne and O. Ostberg, International Journal of Chronobiology, 1976, Vol. 4, 97–110.)

Circadian Rhythm and the Biological Clock

Our cycle of sleep is also greatly influenced by our biological clocks. For example, if you were put in a cave and had no cues as to time—no watches, light, or clocks—your body would exhibit a natural rhythm of sleeping and waking that closely resembles a 24- to 25-hour cycle. This phenomenon is referred to as a **circadian rhythm**. This circadian rhythm is programmed by a group of brain cells in the hypothalamus called the **suprachiasmatic nucleus (SCN)** (Zee & Manthena, 2007). The SCN works very much like an internal clock—signaling other brain areas when to be aroused (awake) to start the day and when to shut down (sleep) for the day.

How does the SCN know when it is time to be awake or asleep? The SCN is very responsive to light changes and takes its cues from your eyes. When your eyes transmit light information to the SCN, they are in essence telling it whether it is light or dark outside (■ FIGURE 4.2). The light information helps the SCN direct the release of **melatonin**, the hormone that facilitates sleep. Melatonin regulates your circadian rhythm and helps you get to sleep. As darkness increases, so does the production of melatonin in your body (Arendt, 2006; Brzezinski, 1997). For this reason, it is called the "Dracula hormone" because it comes out at night.

A significant amount of research now suggests that a developmental change in our intrinsic sleep–wake cycle occurs during puberty (Carskadon, Acebo, & Jenni, 2004; Jenni, Achermann, & Carskadon, 2005; Munch et al., 2005; Taylor, Jenni, Acebo, & Carskadon, 2005). Changes in melatonin secretion and light sensitivity alter the timing of our cycle. We are more likely to want to stay up later in the evening and sleep longer in the morning. Although teenagers' social calendars often strengthen this tendency, the fact that part of this change is developmental in nature does have serious implications for high school starting times and adolescent academic performance.

circadian rhythm [sir-KAY-dee-un RI-thum] changes in bodily processes that occur repeatedly on approximately a 24- to 25-hour cycle

suprachiasmatic [sue-pra-kigh-as-MAT-ick] **nucleus (SCN)** a group of brain cells located in the hypothalamus that signal other brain areas when to be aroused and when to shut down

melatonin [mel-uh-TONE-in] hormone in the body that facilitates sleep

FIGURE 4.2 Circadian Rhythm, Sleep, and the Brain

The suprachiasmatic nucleus (SCN) takes its cues from the light that is transmitted to your eyes. The light information helps the SCN direct the release of melatonin, the "Dracula hormone" that helps you to get to sleep.

Adapted from Starr and McMillan, Human Biology *(2nd ed.), p. 271, © 1997 Wadsworth.*

Light

Suprachiasmatic nucleus

Light → SCN → Lowered levels of melatonin → Awake

No light → SCN → Release of melatonin → Sleep

"WEEKEND LAG" AND JET LAG

Many of us disrupt our circadian rhythm on a weekly basis. We attempt to maintain a routine sleep schedule on weekdays, going to bed around the same time every night so that we can get up in the morning for work or school. Then the weekend comes, and many of us stay up later and "sleep in" on the weekends. Then Sunday night arrives. We may have the best intentions—getting to bed at a decent hour so that we'll get enough sleep to meet the demands of our Monday schedules. But instead, we toss and turn, look at the clock, and wonder when we are going to fall asleep. When Monday morning comes, we feel tired. We may hit the snooze button several times, oversleep, or take a long shower to help us wake up. Why? Because we just asked our internal clock to reset itself by three, four, or more hours! Disrupting our circadian rhythm to this extent makes us irritable, tired, less attentive, and moody.

Our circadian rhythm must also be reset to adapt to the one-hour time change that takes place in the fall and spring in most parts of the United States and in many other countries. It must also be reset when we travel to different time zones, and we may experience *jet lag* as we adjust. On average, for each hour of time change, it takes one day to reset our circadian rhythm.

Sleeping on the plane may help to reduce jet lag when traveling to other time zones.

WORKING THE NIGHT SHIFT

Our body's circadian rhythm also has implications for shift work. In many professions (police work, firefighting, airline flight crew, medical care, and the military), people may be assigned to work 8-, 12-, or even 24-hour shifts, at varying times on different days. When you work Sunday and Monday nights, but Tuesday through Thursday mornings, it is more difficult for your body to reset its circadian rhythm. This disruption can impair your thinking and your health. Shift workers in general report more sleep disturbances; more hormonal irregularities (for women); more accidents, injuries, and illnesses; and decreased cognitive performance (Berger & Hobbs, 2006; Haus & Smolensky, 2006; Kahol et al., 2008; Rouch, Wild, Ansiau, & Marquie, 2005; Sharma, 2007). If late night or early morning shifts are regular, then your body can adapt to the new rhythm. However, if the shift hours are constantly changing, your circadian rhythm is disrupted, and your sleep benefits diminish. Hence, you may be less alert, more easily distracted, and more prone to mental errors.

Paula Bronstein/Getty Images

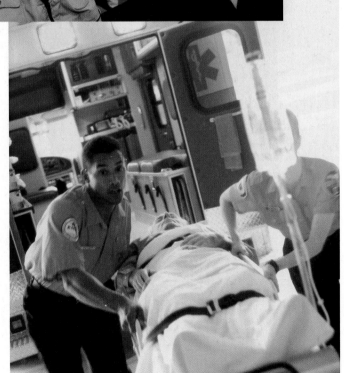

Shift work may interfere with normal sleep patterns, affecting job performance.

Stages of Sleep: What Research Tells Us

You Asked...

What happens during sleep?

SAQIB ABBAS, STUDENT

Using electroencephalogram (EEG) technology, sleep researchers have identified five stages of sleep. Recall from Chapter 2 (p. 37) that EEGs examine the electrical activity of relatively large areas of the brain. These brain waves are then plotted on graph paper or a computer screen. The patterns the brain waves create give researchers an image of our brain activity when we are awake and when we are asleep (■ FIGURE 4.3).

When we are awake and alert, our brain (as measured by an EEG) emits *beta* waves. Beta brain waves are rapid, with a high number of cycles per second. This indicates frequent impulses of electrical activity in the brain. When we are awake but relaxed, our brain emits *alpha* waves. Alpha waves are somewhat slower and less frequent than beta waves. As we sleep, our brain-wave patterns change in a predictable sequence.

If you watch someone sleep, you will notice that at times the person's eyes move under the eyelids, showing rapid eye movement (REM). At other times during sleep, such eye movement is absent. From such observations, researchers have identified two distinct sleep patterns: **non-REM sleep** and **REM sleep**. When your eyes do not move during sleep, it is referred to as non-rapid-eye-movement, or non-REM, sleep. The state in which our eyes do move is called rapid-eye-movement, or REM, sleep. During these two states of sleep, our bodies and brains are experiencing very different activities.

non-REM sleep relaxing state of sleep in which the person's eyes do not move

REM sleep active state of sleep in which the person's eyes move

FIGURE

4.3

Brain Activity During Wakefulness and the Various Stages of Sleep

Electroencephalogram technology records brain-wave activity during wakefulness and the various stages of sleep. When awake but relaxed, the brain emits alpha waves. Brain activity during non-REM sleep progressively slows from theta waves (stage I) to delta waves (stage IV). REM sleep is characterized by rapid brain waves. The brain slides also differentiate slow-wave sleep, REM sleep, and wakefulness. Notice that your brain looks as though it is awake while you are in REM sleep! The brain slides labeled "awake" and "REM sleep" look very similar, whereas the portion labeled "slow wave sleep," which comprises stages III and IV, looks quite different.

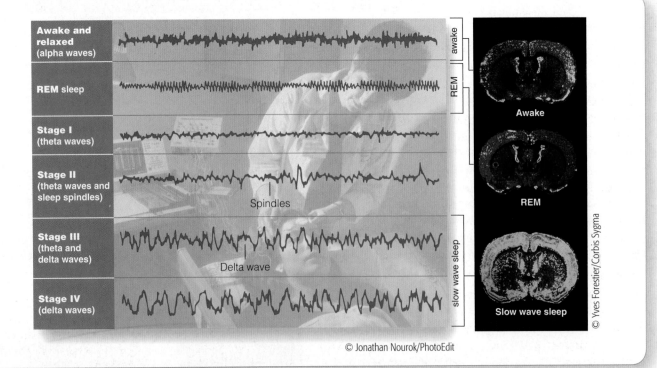

Awake and relaxed (alpha waves)

REM sleep

Stage I (theta waves)

Stage II (theta waves and sleep spindles)

Spindles

Stage III (theta and delta waves)

Delta wave

Stage IV (delta waves)

awake

REM

slow wave sleep

Awake

REM

Slow wave sleep

© Yves Forestier/Corbis Sygma

© Jonathan Nourok/PhotoEdit

Non-REM sleep is a progressively relaxed state. In contrast, REM sleep is very active. During a night of sleep, our bodies and brains move back and forth between states of relaxation and activity until we wake up in the morning (Armitage, 1995; Dement & Kleitman, 1957). The sleep cycle begins with non-REM sleep.

THE FOUR STAGES OF NON-REM SLEEP

When we fall asleep, our bodies and brains progress through a series of four stages of non-REM sleep.

- *Stage I sleep* is a light sleep and is characterized by *theta* waves. Notice in Figure 4.3 that theta waves are slower and less frequent than beta or alpha waves. During this stage, your breathing and heart rates slow down. You may experience sensations such as falling or floating. You can easily awaken from stage I sleep, which typically lasts from 1 to 7 minutes.

- *Stage II sleep* is characterized by *sleep spindles* (see Figure 4.3), a pattern of slower theta waves sporadically disrupted by bursts of electrical activity. During stage II sleep, breathing, muscle tension, heart rate, and body temperature continue to decrease. You are clearly asleep. Recent findings suggest that stage II sleep spindles help us process both simple and complex motor skills that we have learned (Fogel & Smith, 2006; Fogel et al., 2007; Kuriyama, Stickgold, & Walker, 2004).

- *Stage III sleep* is a short transitional stage of sleep when you begin showing *delta* brain-wave patterns. Delta waves are large, slow brain waves. When a consistent pattern of delta waves emerges, you have entered stage IV sleep.

- *Stage IV sleep* is referred to as deep sleep. The body is extremely relaxed. Heart rate, respiration, body temperature, and blood flow to the brain are reduced. Growth hormone is secreted. It is believed that during this deep sleep, body maintenance and restoration occur (Porkka-Heiskanen et al., 1997). For example, your proportion of deep sleep increases after a day of increased physical activity (Horne & Staff, 1983). Deep sleep is also associated with strengthening your memory of learned facts (Carey, 2007). It is difficult to awaken people from deep sleep. When they are awakened, they may be disoriented or confused.

REM SLEEP: DREAM ON

After deep sleep, your brain and body start to speed up again. You cycle back through stages III and II of non-REM sleep, then enter REM (rapid-eye-movement) sleep. REM sleep is a very active stage. Your breathing rate increases, and your heart beats irregularly. Blood flow increases to the genital area and may cause erections in males (Somers, Phil, Dyken, Mark, & Abboud, 1993). However, your muscle tone significantly decreases, leaving the muscles extremely relaxed and essentially paralyzed. Figure 4.3 shows that your REM brain-wave patterns are similar to your brain-wave patterns when you are awake. The brain slides labeled "awake" and "REM sleep" look almost exactly alike! You can see that the portion labeled "slow wave sleep," which comprises stages III and IV, looks quite different.

REM sleep is intimately connected to dreaming. Although you can dream in some form in all sleep stages, dreams during REM sleep are more easily recalled. More than 80% of people awakened from REM sleep report dreaming (Hirshkowitz et al., 1997). The body paralysis that occurs during REM prevents you from acting out your dreams. However, in rare instances, people do not experience the paralysis that normally accompanies REM sleep. This condition, which mainly affects older men, is referred to as **REM behavior disorder**. People with REM behavior disorder may thrash about while in REM sleep, causing harm to themselves or others (Gugger & Wagner, 2007; Plazzi et al., 1997).

The purpose of REM sleep is constantly being questioned. Some studies indicate a connection between REM sleep and memory processing. People who are deprived of REM sleep

REM behavior disorder a condition in which normal muscle paralysis does not occur, leading to violent movements during REM sleep and dreaming are less likely to recall complex information learned earlier in the day than are people who were not deprived of REM sleep (Chollar, 1989: Karni et al., 1994). REM-deprived people also report having difficulty concentrating when they awaken. These findings have led researchers to speculate that REM sleep—and perhaps dreaming—facilitates the storage of memories as well as mental strategies that are useful to us (Rauchs et al., 2004). At the same time, REM appears to help us "discard" information that is trivial or less important to us (Crick & Mitchison, 1995; Smith, 1995). Other research shows no relationship between time spent in REM sleep and memory problems (Siegel, 2001). The exact connection between REM sleep and memory continues to be investigated (Carey, 2007).

Another curiosity of REM sleep is referred to as **REM rebound**. When people lose REM sleep because of medications, drugs, or sleep deprivation, they make up for it on subsequent nights by spending more time dreaming (Dement, 1960).

A Typical Night's Sleep

A typical night of sleep consists of cycling through non-REM stages and REM sleep (Figure 4.3). We progress through stages I, II, III, and IV of non-REM sleep. We revisit stages III and II of non-REM sleep. We then enter REM sleep. After a brief period in REM sleep, we begin the cycle again, starting with the non-REM stages. The pattern repeats throughout the night. One complete cycle of non-REM and REM sleep takes about 90 minutes. But notice from ■ FIGURE 4.4 that as the night progresses we spend less time in deep sleep and more time in REM sleep. This means that the memory of learned facts and body-restoring functions of deep sleep take place early on, during the first few cycles of sleep. After these early cycles, we spend longer in REM sleep. So if you are not getting enough sleep, you will miss out on the longest period of REM sleep. On average, we spend around 20% of our total sleep time in REM sleep. Thus, if you sleep 8 hours a night, you spend roughly 90 minutes in REM sleep.

DREAMING: THE NIGHT'S WORK

Although not all of us remember our dreams when we awaken, everyone progresses through dream states during sleep. Dreams do show some similarities in content from one culture to another. For example, dream themes that focus on basic needs (sex, aggression, and death) seem to be universal. Other content seems to be specific to a particular culture. For instance, today's Alaskan natives may have dreams that include snowmobiles, but their ancestors of 100 years ago obviously did not. People dream about what they know, which is influenced by the culture in which they live (Price & Crapo, 2002).

> **You Asked...**
>
> *Do dreams have meaning?*
>
> LISANDRA MACHADO, STUDENT

REM rebound loss of REM sleep is recouped by spending more time in REM on subsequent nights

FIGURE 4.4 A Typical Night of Sleep

As the night progresses, we spend less time in deep sleep and more time in REM sleep.

Sigmund Freud's *Interpretation of Dreams*

One of the most controversial and best-known theories of dreaming is Sigmund Freud's. In his *Interpretation of Dreams* (1900/1980), Freud called dreams "the royal road to the unconscious." According to Freud, dreams allow us to express fears and sexual and aggressive desires without the censorship of our conscious thought processes. Having straightforward dreams about these "unacceptable" desires would cause us anxiety. Instead, we dream in symbols that represent our unconscious desires. For Freud, dreams contained both **manifest content** and **latent content**. The manifest content of a dream is what you recall when you awaken. The latent, or hidden, content of the dream is the symbolic interpretation. For example, a young girl may dream of coming home from school one day to find the house deserted. She runs from room to room, looking for her parents or some sign that they will be returning soon (manifest content). Such a dream among children may signify the anxiety of being left alone, deserted, uncared for, or unprotected (latent content).

Fred Basset   By Alex Graham

Dreams as Coping, Evolutionary Defense, or Just Biology at Work

Many psychologists have challenged Freud's theory of dreaming and have proposed alternative explanations for why we dream. For example, the *continuity hypothesis* suggests that dreaming is a way of coping with daily problems and issues. We dream about everyday experiences and current concerns in an effort to resolve these issues (Cartwright, 1993; Pesant & Zadra, 2006). In this view, dreams are not as symbolic as Freud suggested. *Memory theory* suggests that dreams are a way to consolidate information and to get rid of trivial details in our memories (Eiser, 2005; Porte & Hobson, 1996). From this viewpoint, dreams represent a function of memory.

The **threat simulation theory** (**TST**) suggests an evolutionary function of dreams. TST proposes that dreaming is an ancient biological defense mechanism that allows us to experience potentially threatening situations so that we can rehearse our responses to these events. Although studies do show that childhood trauma or recurrent dreams are associated with a greater number of threatening dream events, not all of our dreams involve themes of survival (Valli et al., 2005; Zadra, Desjardins, & Marcotte, 2006).

A biologically based theory is the **activation–synthesis theory** (Hobson & McCarley, 1977). This theory suggests that dreaming is just a consequence of the highly aroused brain during REM sleep, when the brain shows activation of millions of random neural impulses. The cortex of the brain attempts to create meaning out of these neural impulses by synthesizing them into familiar images or stories based on our stored memories. These images and stories may reflect our past, our emotions, our personal perspectives, and information accessed during waking (Hobson, Pace-Schott, & Stickgold, 2000), but they have no hidden "Freudian" meaning. However, because we are the ones who integrate these images into a plot, the story line may provide us with insights about ourselves (McCarley, 1998).

Obviously, our understanding of the purpose and meaning of dreaming is incomplete. Dreams aside, sleep research indicates that not everyone always gets a good night's sleep. Some of us exhibit sleep disturbances, our next topic of discussion.

Sleep Disorders: Tossing and Turning—and More

It is estimated that 95% of Americans suffer from a **sleep disorder**, or a disturbance in the normal pattern of sleep, at some point in their lives (Dement & Vaughan, 1999). Sleep disorders also affect approximately 25% to 40% of children and adolescents (Meltzer & Mindell, 2006).

manifest content according to Freud, what the dreamer recalls on awakening

latent content according to Freud, the symbolic meaning of a dream

threat simulation theory (TST) suggests that dreaming is an ancient biological defense mechanism that allows us to repeatedly simulate potentially threatening situations so that we can rehearse our responses to these events

activation–synthesis theory suggests that dreams do not have symbolic meaning, but are the by-product of the brain's random firing of neural impulses during REM sleep

sleep disorder a disturbance in the normal pattern of sleeping

INSOMNIA: THERE IS HELP!

Insomnia, the most commonly reported sleep disorder, is the inability to get to sleep and/or stay asleep. Occasional insomnia is quite common, with as many as 50% of adults reporting insomnia at some time in their lives (Nowell, Buysse, Morin, Reynolds, & Kuper, 1998). Insomnia is associated with a multitude of factors including stress, coping with the loss of a loved one, a change in sleep schedule, obesity, chronic pain, drug abuse, anxiety, or depression (Roth, Krystal, & Lieberman, 2007).

Insomnia can be treated medically using antianxiety or depressant medication. However, long-term use of these drugs may lead to dependence and serious side effects, including memory loss, fatigue, and increased sleepiness. Chronic insomnia is best treated with a combination of taking medication for a limited time and following the sleep guidelines described in the *Psychology Applies to Your World* box.

insomnia   a sleep disorder in which a person cannot get to sleep and/or stay asleep

Psychology Applies to Your World:

How Can You Get the Sleep You Need?

Nondrug treatments to improve sleep or reduce insomnia focus on following several guidelines that have evolved from our study of sleep (Bootzin & Rider, 1997; Roth, Krystal, & Lieberman, 2007):

> **You Asked...**
>
> *Are there ways to avoid insomnia? Are there ways to help it?*
>
> KAYLA CAMPANA, STUDENT

- Establish a regular sleep–wake cycle to work with your body's circadian rhythm. Go to bed at the same time every evening and wake up at the same time every morning. Even if you have difficulty falling asleep at night, continue to get up at the same time each morning.

- Avoid long naps during waking hours. Naps can disrupt your circadian rhythm. But what about children who take daily naps and adults who "power nap" or use siestas? Children's naps and siestas typically occur at the same time every day and thereby work with, rather than against, the circadian rhythm. Power naps are short periods of rest (15–20 minutes) that are relaxing and can reenergize the body and mind. Because they are short, they generally do not interfere with our sleep cycles.

- Don't use your bed for anything other than sleeping. Do not eat, study, work, or watch television in bed. The bed should be associated only with sleeping.

- If you can't get to sleep after 15 minutes, get up and do something that you think will make you tired enough to get to sleep, such as reading (but not in your bed). Then try again to fall asleep.

- Avoid sleeping pills, alcohol, cigarettes, and caffeine. These are all drugs that can interfere with your natural sleep cycle by disrupting REM sleep. A glass of milk before bedtime, however, may be helpful. Milk helps the body produce serotonin, a neurotransmitter that facilitates sleep (see Chapter 2).

- Exercise during the day can promote good sleep. But avoid physical workouts within an hour of bedtime. Your body should be relaxed prior to sleeping.

NARCOLEPSY AND CATAPLEXY

Narcolepsy, a rare sleep disorder that affects approximately 140,000 to 250,000 Americans, occurs when a person falls asleep during alert times of the day (Zeman et al., 2004). This is not the same as a microsleep, though. The person with narcolepsy experiences brief periods of REM sleep that may be accompanied by muscle paralysis, a condition called *cataplexy*. Cataplexy occurs in about 70% of people with narcolepsy (APA, 2000a). People with narcolepsy may fall down or otherwise injure themselves during these episodes. Narcolepsy is thought to stem from a loss of neurons in the hypothalamus of the brain. These neurons are responsible for producing a chemical called *hypocretin* that helps to control the sleep–wake cycle (Siegel & Boehmer, 2006; Zeitzer, Nishino, & Mignot, 2006). Those with the condition typically take *modafinil* to improve wakefulness (Becker, Schwartz, Feldman, & Hughes, 2004; Gallopin, Luppi, Rambert, Frydman, & Fort, 2004; Roth, Schwartz, et al., 2007) and *sodium oxybate*, the only FDA-approved medication for cataplexy (Thorpy, 2007).

SLEEP APNEA AND SIDS

Sleep apnea is a disorder in which a person stops breathing while sleeping. In an attempt to get air, people with sleep apnea often emit loud snores or snorts that may awaken them or their partners. This pattern may occur hundreds of times during the night. People afflicted may feel sluggish, tired, irritable, or unable to concentrate the next day because of the nighttime sleep disruption (Naegele et al., 1995). Obesity and the use of alcohol or sedatives increase one's chances of developing sleep apnea (Ball, 1997; Resta et al., 2001). Once diagnosed, sleep apnea may be treated in various ways. If obesity is a factor, a weight-loss program is the first treatment. In addition, a nasal mask (called a Continuous Positive Airway Pressure, or CPAP, device) that blows air into the nose can be worn at night. Wearing mouth retainers can help in some cases. In severe cases, removing the tonsils or surgery to alter the position of the jaw can be performed (Saskin, 1997). Considerable evidence suggests a genetic basis for sleep apnea (Chiang, 2006; Polotsky & O'Donnell, 2007). Estimates of sleep apnea in the general population range from 3% to 28% (Chiang, 2006).

Sleep apnea has been suggested as one cause of *sudden infant death syndrome* (SIDS), or "crib death," when apparently healthy babies die while they are sleeping. They stop breathing for reasons that are not yet understood. SIDS affects babies at an average age of 4 months. African American and American Indian babies are at greater risk than White or Hispanic babies, and the risk is higher for males than for females (Lipsitt, 2003).

SLEEPWALKING: WAKE ME UP!

Sleepwalking, or somnambulism, occurs during non-REM stage IV sleep. People with this disorder get up and walk around during deep sleep, sometimes performing actions that make them appear to be awake. They may cook, eat, open doors, or engage in minimal conversation. Because sleepwalkers are asleep, they may injure themselves or others. Wake them up or guide them back to bed. They may be initially disoriented or confused, but you will not do harm by awakening them. It is estimated that between 1% and 15% of the general population sleepwalk. It is more common in children than in adults (National Sleep Foundation, 2004).

NIGHT TERRORS AND ENURESIS

Night terrors also occur during non-REM stage IV, or deep sleep. Although night terrors can occur anytime in one's life, they are more commonly reported in children between the ages of 4 and 12, and in older adults with various neurological and cognitive disorders such as Parkinson's disease and elderly dementia (Abad & Guilleminault, 2004). During night terrors, people awaken in an apparent state of fear. Their heart rates and breathing are rapid,

narcolepsy [NAR-co-lep-see] a rare sleep disorder in which a person falls asleep during alert activities during the day

sleep apnea [APP-nee-uh] a sleep disorder in which a person stops breathing during sleep

sleepwalking a sleep disorder in which a person is mobile and may perform actions during stage IV sleep

night terrors very frightening non-REM sleep episodes

and they may scream loudly and sit up in bed, wide-eyed with terror. People rarely recall the incident in the morning (Hartmann, 1981). An attack may last 5 to 20 minutes. In the United States, an estimated 1% to 6% of children experience night terror episodes. For adults, estimates are less than 1% (APA, 2000a).

Why night terrors occur is still a mystery, although the disorder does tend to run in families (Guilleminault, Palombini, Pelayo, & Chervin, 2003). Keep in mind that people who are having night terrors do not know what is occurring. Simply reassure the person that everything is all right and to go back to sleep. Night terrors are different from nightmares. **Nightmares** are brief scary dreams that typically occur during REM sleep and are often recalled in vivid detail in the morning.

Enuresis is bedwetting, but it does not refer to the occasional nighttime bedwetting that is common among young children. Enuresis is diagnosed when a child who is at least 5 years old wets his or her bed or pajamas at least twice a week over a three-month period (APA, 2000a). It is estimated that 15–20% of 5-year-olds are enuretic at least once a month, but by adolescence the prevalence of enuresis decreases to about 1%. Enuresis is more common in males, and tends to run in families. Nearly 75% of children with enuresis have biological relatives who had the disorder (Ondersma & Walker, 1998). Such a high percentage suggests that enuresis may be inherited. However, the behavior may also occur during times of stress, such as when a new sibling is born or familial conflict is high, and may accompany night terrors. Do not scold or punish a child for wetting the bed. Children do not wet the bed on purpose or as an unconscious expression of anger. Several treatment methods are available, and most children outgrow the behavior (Berry, 2006).

Gender and Ethnic Differences in Sleep

Sleep research has also investigated the degree to which gender and ethnicity influence sleep. Several studies have found that men report needing less sleep than women to function at their best, and that women are more likely than men to sleep 8 hours or more. Women are also more likely than men to report daytime sleepiness and needing 30 minutes or more to fall asleep (National Sleep Foundation, 2005; Oginska & Pokorski, 2006). One research study (Adan & Natale, 2002) has also indicated potential gender differences in the circadian rhythm of males and females. In the area of sleep disorders, two consistent gender differences have emerged. Insomnia tends to be more frequent in women (Morlock, Tan, & Mitchell, 2006; Roberts, Roberts, & Chan, 2006; Voderholzer, Al-Shajlawi, Weske, Feige, & Riemann, 2003; Zhang & Wing, 2006), and snoring and sleep apnea are more common in men (Jordan & McEvoy, 2003).

Only a limited number of studies have compared sleep variables across ethnic groups. Those that have suggest that African Americans sleep worse than European Americans. They report poorer sleep quality and report taking longer to fall asleep (Durrence & Lichstein, 2006). However, African Americans are more likely to live in urban areas, a variable that is also associated with poorer sleep quality (Haie & Do, 2007). African American, American Indian, and Hispanic adults are also at higher risk for sleep apnea, although these observed ethnic differences are mainly explained by higher rates of obesity among these groups (Fiorentino, Marler, Stepnowsky, Johnson, & Ancoli-Israel, 2006; Villaneuva, Buchanan, Yee, & Grunstein, 2005).

In summary, sleep is as necessary to our survival as food and shelter. Sleep refuels our bodies and minds, preparing us for the challenges of the next day. When we skip sleep, change our sleep cycle, or experience disturbances in our sleep, we are more likely to feel irritable, tired, and less alert.

nightmare   a brief scary REM dream that is often remembered

enuresis [en-your-REE-sus]   a condition in which a person over the age of 5 shows an inability to control urination during sleep

Let's Review!

This section described why we sleep, the stages of sleep, theories of dreaming, and some common sleep disorders. For a quick check of your understanding, answer these questions.

1. Ronnie has a dream that he is being chased by a golden goose. He is told that this reflects his anxiety about impregnating women. This analysis represents the _____ of his dream.
   a. manifest content
   b. latent content
   c. activation synthesis
   d. mental reprogramming

2. Maria falls asleep in the middle of playing tennis or golf, or while watching an exciting movie. Maria is most likely suffering from which sleep disorder?
   a. Narcolepsy
   b. Insomnia
   c. Sleep apnea
   d. Enuresis

3. Which of the following is not characteristic of REM sleep?
   a. Rapid eye movements
   b. Paralysis of body musculature
   c. Shortening periods as the night progresses
   d. Increased heart rate

4. Hap is at a workshop and falls asleep. He is relaxed and his brain-wave pattern shows long waves—but not delta waves—interrupted by short bursts of electrical activity. Hap is in what stage of sleep?
   a. Stage I
   b. Stage II
   c. Stage IV
   d. REM

5. Which of the following statements about sleep is false?
   a. Sleep patterns change with age.
   b. Everyone needs at least 8 hours of sleep a night.
   c. Some people are night owls whereas others are early birds.
   d. Circadian rhythms influence the sleep cycle.

Answers 1. b; 2. a; 3. c; 4. b; 5. b

Consciousness: Wide Awake, in a Daze, or Dreaming?

- Sleep restores body tissues, increases immunity to disease, keeps mind alert, helps process memories and enhances mood. **Circadian rhythm** is programmed by brain cells in the hypothalamus called the **suprachiasmatic nucleus (SCN)**. Light information directs the SCN to release the hormone **melatonin**, which helps you get to sleep. A typical night of sleep starts with cycling through **non-REM sleep** and **REM sleep**.

Stop, LOOK, and LEARN

Light
Suprachiasmatic nucleus

Light → SCN → Lowered levels of melatonin → Awake
No light → SCN → Release of melatonin → Sleep

Hours of sleep

- Sleep disorders:
  - **Insomnia**: inability to get to sleep or stay asleep; most common sleep disorder
  - **Sleep apnea**: person stops breathing while asleep
  - **Narcolepsy**: person falls asleep during alert times of the day
  - **Sleepwalking**, **night terrors**, and **enuresis** (bedwetting): occur during non-REM stage IV sleep

- Dream theories:
  - Continuity hypothesis: Dreams help cope with daily problems.
  - Freud: Dreams reflect unconscious desires.
  - Memory theory: Dreams consolidate information.
  - **Threat simulation theory**: Dreams allow us to rehearse responses to threats.
  - **Activation-synthesis theory**: Dreams result from a highly aroused brain during REM sleep.

Hypnosis: Real or Imagined?

Learning Objectives

- Detail the experience of hypnosis and explain several theories about how hypnosis occurs.

- Distinguish between what hypnosis can and cannot do for you.

This section describes the experience of hypnosis, explains several ideas about how hypnosis occurs, and explains what hypnosis can and cannot do for you. Not all psychologists are hypnotists, and not all hypnotists are psychologists. **Hypnosis** is a method occasionally used by researchers and psychologists (and frequently by hypnotists) to create a state of heightened suggestibility in others.

You Asked...

How does hypnosis work?

LAURA FERNANDEZ, STUDENT

Typically, if you are undergoing hypnosis, you are asked to focus on an object, an image, or the hypnotist's voice. For several minutes, you are told that you are getting sleepy and becoming more relaxed (Druckman & Bjork, 1994). You don't fall asleep. EEG brain-wave patterns of hypnotized people show an increase in alpha waves, but this isn't followed by the non-REM pattern of sleep stages discussed earlier (Graffin, Ray, & Lundy, 1995). After inducing you into this relaxed hypnotic state, the hypnotist makes suggestions about what you are seeing, feeling, or perceiving. For example, one suggestion might be to lift your left arm over your head. A more complex suggestion might be that your eyelids feel as though they are glued shut and you cannot open them. Although accounts vary widely, many hypnotized people report that they feel as though they are floating or that their bodies are sinking. Under hypnosis, they remain in control of their bodies and are aware of their surroundings (Kirsch & Lynn, 1995).

hypnosis a state of heightened suggestibility

Hypnotic Susceptibility

Not everyone can be hypnotized. You have to want to be hypnotized and believe it will work for you.

You Asked...

What kind of people does hypnosis work on? DANIE LIPSCHUTZ, STUDENT

Hypnotic *susceptibility* is the ability to become hypnotized. Some people have a low degree of susceptibility—they cannot be hypnotized easily. Others have a high susceptibility, meaning that they can be hypnotized easily. One well-known standard test for measuring the degree to which people respond to hypnotic suggestions is the *Stanford Hypnotic Susceptibility Scale*. The scale assesses your suggestibility to certain tasks while in a state of hypnosis with a trained hypnotist. The tasks range from pulling apart your interlocked fingers to hallucinating the presence of a buzzing fly.

Contrary to what you may have seen on television or in the movies, research using such measures has found that not everyone can be hypnotized. The critical factor appears to be whether you want to be hypnotized, rather than the skill of the hypnotist (Kirsch & Lynn, 1995). About 10% of adults are extremely difficult to hypnotize (Hilgard, 1982).

© AP Photo/News Tribune/Stephen Brooks

People who are easily hypnotized tend to be better able to focus their attention (Crawford, Brown, & Moon, 1993; Egner, Jamieson, & Gruzelier, 2005; Raz, 2005), have vivid imaginations (Silva & Kirsch, 1992; Spanos, Burnley, & Cross, 1993), and have positive expectations about hypnosis (Bates, 1994). Hypnotic suggestibility does not appear to be related to such factors as intelligence, gender, sociability, or gullibility (Kirsch & Lynn, 1995).

Explaining Hypnosis: Is It an Altered State?

Currently, there are two theories explaining hypnosis: dissociation theory and the response set theory. Ernest Hilgard's (1977, 1992) **dissociation theory** suggests that hypnosis is truly an altered state of consciousness: a person feels, perceives, and behaves differently than in a conscious state. To dissociate means to split or break apart. Hilgard maintains that under hypnosis, your consciousness divides into two states. One level of your consciousness voluntarily agrees to behave according to the suggestions of the hypnotist. However, at the same time, a *hidden observer* state exists. This hidden observer is aware of all that is happening.

We all engage in dissociation at times. Have you ever driven to a familiar location and realized when you arrived that you couldn't consciously remember driving there? Have you ever dissociated in a class—paying attention to the lesson while at the same time doodling or mentally organizing the rest of your day? If you have experienced any of these behaviors, then you are familiar with the concept of dissociation. Hilgard believes that hypnosis works in much the same way, allowing the person to attend to the hypnotist's suggestions while still being aware of what is happening through the hidden observer.

In a classic demonstration, Hilgard hypnotized participants and suggested that they would feel no pain. The participants were then instructed to submerge one arm in ice-cold water. When Hilgard asked them whether they felt pain, the participants replied "No." However, when they were asked to press a key with their other hand if they felt pain, the participants did so. On one level, they agreed with the hypnotist that there was no pain, while at the same time a part of them indicated that there was pain (Hilgard, Morgan, & MacDonald, 1975).

Another view, the **response set theory of hypnosis** (Kirsch, 2000; Kirsch & Lynn, 1997; Lynn, 1997), asserts that hypnosis is *not* an altered state of consciousness. Rather, hypnosis is merely a willingness to respond appropriately to suggestions. Several studies do support that people's response expectancies influence their responsiveness to hypnosis (Benham, Woody, Wilson, & Nash, 2006; Milling, Reardon, & Carosella, 2006). Highly hypnotizable people enter hypnosis with the intention of behaving as a "hypnotized person" and hold the expectation that they will succeed in following the hypnotist's suggestions. Their intentions and expectations trigger their positive response to being hypnotized. Nonhypnotized participants show behaviors similar to those of hypnotized people, such as behaving in strange ways or acting like a young child, simply because they are willing to do what the hypnotist asks them to do (Dasgupta, Juza, White, & Maloney, 1995; Kirsch, 1994).

The debate over whether hypnosis is truly an altered state continues (Holroyd, 2003; Rainville & Price, 2003). Unfortunately, hypnosis has acquired a reputation for doing some things that it cannot. Let's look at these myths and realities of hypnosis.

What Hypnosis Can and Cannot Do

In an attempt to separate fact from fiction, psychologists have researched the effects of hypnosis. To date, research reveals the following:

- *Relieving Pain.* One of the best documented uses for hypnosis is pain relief (Clay,

You Asked...

Does hypnosis work?

SUSY ALVAREZ, STUDENT

dissociation [dis-so-see-AYE-shun] **theory**
Hilgard's proposal that hypnosis involves two simultaneous states: a hypnotic state and a hidden observer

response set theory of hypnosis asserts that hypnosis is not an altered state of consciousness, but a cognitive set to respond appropriately to suggestions

1996; Wiechman Askay & Patterson, 2007). Under hypnosis, clients relax, which reduces pain, and/or distract themselves from the pain by focusing on more pleasing and pain-free scenarios. Hypnosis has been used to minimize pain in childbirth, to block pain during medical or dental treatments, and to relieve chronic pain from arthritis and from migraine headaches (Chaves, 1994; Liossi, White, & Hatira, 2006; Nolan, Spanos, Hayward, & Scott, 1995; Pinnell & Covino, 2000). This pain relief is more pronounced for people who have a high susceptibility to hypnosis (Bates, 1994). Hypnosis does not reduce the sensation of pain. The pain is still there, but hypnosis changes a person's subjective experience of pain so that it is more bearable (Rainville, Duncan, Price, Carrier, & Bushnell, 1997).

- *Curing Addictions.* Posthypnotic suggestions have proven less successful for treating addictions or self-control behaviors, even in people with a high susceptibility to hypnosis (Bowers & LeBaron, 1986). Although hypnosis has been used as a treatment to stop smoking, nail biting, overeating, gambling, alcoholism, and other addictions, it has proven no more successful than other treatments at controlling these behaviors (Bates, 1994; Green & Lynn, 2000). Self-control behaviors such as smoking and alcoholism are some of the most difficult behaviors to change, and hypnosis doesn't appear to have an advantage over other types of treatment (Rabkin, Boyko, Shane, & Kaufert, 1984).

- *Enhancing or Recovering Memory.* One of the most controversial applications of hypnosis has been in the area of memory enhancement. Research in this area has focused on two key issues: age regression and recovered memories.

  - *Age regression* refers to a person's reliving earlier childhood experiences. Numerous studies on age regression demonstrate that under hypnosis, adults act the way they *expect* children to behave (Spanos, 1996). They may write, sing, or behave like a child, but it is more like an adult playing the role of a child. Their behavior is not different from that of nonhypnotized people who are asked to behave like a child (Nash, 1987).

  - A *recovered memory* is one in which a person recalls repressed events or information, such as events from a crime scene or from one's childhood. Being in a relaxed state may facilitate recall under certain circumstances. However, research reveals that hypnotized people may also recall untrue events. For this reason, information gathered under hypnosis is not permissible in a court of law in the United States, Canada, Australia, or Great Britain. People are more suggestible under hypnosis, and consequently their memories are more likely to be influenced by the suggestions, tone, hints, questions, and remarks of the hypnotist. They may recall just as many events that did not occur as events that did, and they may also be more prone to distort information (Scoboria, Mazzoni, & Kirsch, 2006; Scoboria, Mazzoni, Kirsch, & Milling, 2002). For these reasons, the use of hypnosis in the area of memory enhancement should be viewed with skepticism (Gibson, 1995; McConkey, 1995; Perry, 1997).

- *Enhancing Physical Performance.* Hypnosis does not create superhuman capacities. However, being in a relaxed state such as hypnosis can enhance physical performance. The person can more readily visualize optimal performance and reduce self-doubt or nerves. This enhancement can also be achieved through other techniques, such as deep muscle relaxation and guided imagery (Druckman & Bjork, 1994).

- *Decreasing Anxiety and Enhancing Psychotherapy.* Hypnosis has proven useful in decreasing fears and anxieties for people with a high susceptibility to hypnosis (Saadat et al., 2006). Clinicians sometimes use hypnosis in therapy to help their clients solve problems or cope with bodily symptoms such as headaches or stomach pains that appear to be related to psychological stress. Hypnosis has been helpful in reducing pain and tension. Again, it is most effective for clients who have a high susceptibility to hypnosis (Kirsch, Montgomery, & Sapirstein, 1995).

To summarize, hypnosis does not endow us with superhuman strength, allow us to reexperience childhood events, or improve the accuracy of our memories. However, hypnosis may be of some benefit in decreasing pain, promoting relaxation, and perhaps enhancing therapy for *some* people. These benefits are not universal. The person must want to be hypnotized and have positive beliefs about hypnosis.

Let's Review!

This section detailed the experience of hypnosis, presented theories about how hypnosis occurs, and discussed what hypnosis can and cannot do for you. For a quick check of your understanding, answer these questions.

1. Research on hypnosis suggests that it is *least* helpful for which of the following?
   a. Pain relief   **c.** Quitting smoking
   b. Reduction of anxiety   **d.** Childbirth

2. Which of the following statements about hypnosis is *false*?
   a. Everyone can be hypnotized.
   b. Hypnosis is real; people are not just faking it.
   c. Memories recalled under hypnosis are not always accurate.
   d. Not all psychologists agree as to whether hypnosis is an altered state of consciousness.

3. Cecilia has been hypnotized and told that she will not feel pain in her right hand. Her right hand is then immersed in freezing cold water. According to the dissociation theory of hypnosis, what part of Cecilia will report feeling pain?
   a. The secret hypnotist
   b. The posthypnotic suggester
   c. The conscious self
   d. The hidden observer

Answers 1. c; 2. a; 3. d

Psychoactive Drugs

- Define tolerance and substance dependence, and explain how psychoactive drugs work.

- Identify depressants, stimulants, and hallucinogens, and describe the effects these types of drugs have on behavior.

Psychoactive drugs are substances that influence the brain and thereby a person's behavior. Over the past 25 years, millions of teenagers and children in the United States have routinely been educated about the effects of drugs. The most popular of these programs, Drug Abuse Resistance Education, or DARE, began in 1983. Yet despite widespread education programs, many misperceptions about drugs still exist. For example, name the three most widely used psychoactive drugs in American society. The three drugs most commonly used by Americans over the age of 12 are alcohol, nicotine, and caffeine (see ■ FIGURE 4.5)—substances that are all legal for adults to use (SAMHSA, 2006).

In 2006, more than 45% of people in the United States age 12 or older admitted to having tried an illegal substance at some time in their lives. Illicit drug use is highest among young adults between the ages of 18 and 25, and is higher in males than in females (SAMHSA, 2007). Substance use in the United States also varies considerably by ethnic group (■ FIGURE 4.6; SAMHSA, 2007). Multiracial and American Indian/Alaskan Native groups have the highest rates of illegal drug use, and Asians have the lowest. We will discuss the most frequently used drugs and their effects, and describe how these drugs work and how they cause damage.

psychoactive drugs substances that influence the brain and thereby the behavior of individuals

FIGURE

4.5 Drug Use in the United States

Caffeine, alcohol, and nicotine (the active ingredient in cigarettes) are the three most commonly used psychoactive drugs in the United States.

Source: SAMHSA, Office of Applied Studies, *National Survey on Drug Use and Health, 2006.*

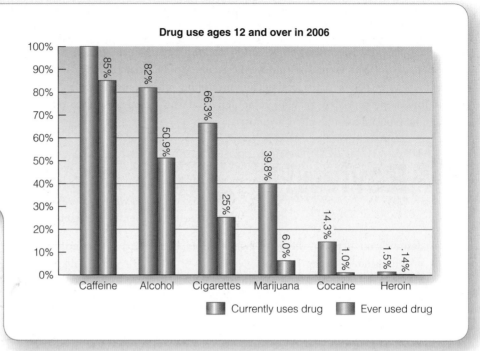

Drug use ages 12 and over in 2006

Caffeine: 100%, 85%
Alcohol: 82%, 50.9%
Cigarettes: 66.3%, 25%
Marijuana: 39.8%, 6.0%
Cocaine: 14.3%, 1.0%
Heroin: 1.5%, .14%

■ Currently uses drug ■ Ever used drug

Drug Tolerance, Substance Dependence, and Substance Abuse

In order to understand the effects of psychoactive drugs, it is important to establish the scientific meaning of two specific drug terms: tolerance and substance dependence.

Tolerance has to do with the amount of a drug required to produce its effect. After repeated use of a drug, it is usually the case that more and more of it is needed to achieve its initial effect (APA, 2000a). For example, when someone first drinks alcohol, he or she may have one beer or one glass of wine and get a buzz from it. However, after drinking alcohol frequently, this person will require more beers or glasses of wine to achieve the same effect. This person has increased his or her tolerance for alcohol.

tolerance a condition in which after repeated use, more of a drug is needed to achieve the same effect

Drug Abuse Resistance Education has had little effect on young people's use of drugs.

However, with the development of tolerance, the difference between a safe dose and a potentially harmful dose, called the *margin of safety*, narrows. Some drugs (like barbiturates) have a very narrow, or small, margin of safety; that is, their too-high, toxic dose differs only slightly from their too-low, ineffectual dose. In order to obtain the same level of intoxication, a user who has developed tolerance may raise his or her dose to a level that may result in coma or death—the too-high, toxic dose.

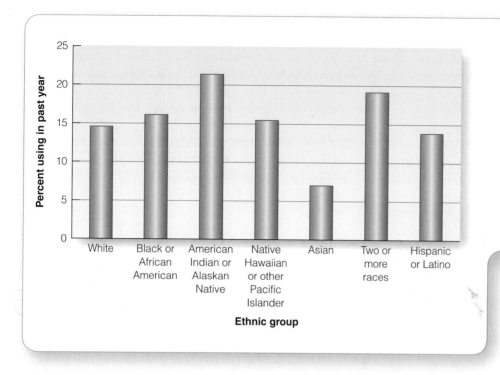

FIGURE

4.6

Ethnicity and Illicit Drug Use

Substance use in the United States varies considerably by ethnic group. Multiracial and American Indian/Alaskan Native groups have the highest rates of illegal substance abuse; Asians have the lowest incidence.

Source: SAMHSA, Office of Applied Studies, *Results from the 2006 National Survey on Drug Use and Health: National Findings, 2007.*

Related to tolerance is **substance dependence**, which occurs when someone is either physically or psychologically reliant on a drug's effects. Typically, dependence is operating when the person stops using the drug and experiences **withdrawal symptoms**. Withdrawal symptoms may include physical symptoms such as vomiting, shaking, sweating, physical pain, hallucinations, or headaches. People may also experience behavioral withdrawal symptoms when they are deprived of responses or rituals, such as injecting a drug or lighting a cigarette, that help them cope with negative emotions (Baker, Japuntich, Hogle, McCarthy, & Curtin, 2006; Siegel, 2005). Not all drugs produce the same withdrawal symptoms. In many cases, people continue to use a drug just to ward off the unpleasantness of the withdrawal effects or emotional distress. Psychologists typically use the term **substance abuse** to indicate that someone has lost control over his or her drug use.

How Drugs Work: Biology, Expectations, and Culture

Psychoactive drugs alter your state of functioning by interfering with the normal workings of the nervous system. Some drugs slow down normal brain activity, whereas others speed it up. Typically, drugs achieve these effects by interfering with or mimicking neurotransmitters in the brain (Chapter 2).

> ### You Asked...
>
> *What do drugs really do to humans?*   JOSE MORENO, STUDENT

Psychological factors also influence a drug's effect. Exposure to stress or trauma increases a person's vulnerability to drug dependence (Goeders, 2004). Environmental stimuli such as where a drug is taken or whether drug paraphernalia are present become associated with drug taking and later trigger the craving for the drug sensation (Crombag & Robinson, 2004; Siegel, 2005). If you expect a drug to alter your behavior in a particular way, you are more likely to change your behavior to fit your expectations. For example, in several studies people who believed that they had consumed alcohol behaved as if they had been drinking alcohol (Leigh, 1989). Whether or not they had actually consumed it, their behavior was influenced by their expectations about the effects of alcohol (Abrams & Wilson, 1983; McMillen, Smith, & Wells-Parker, 1989).

Is the behavior of these fans due to alcohol or to their expectations of alcohol?

substance dependence a condition in which a person needs a drug in order to maintain normal functioning

withdrawal symptoms physical or behavioral effects that occur after a person stops using a drug

substance abuse loss of control over one's drug use

One's culture also influences drug use. For example, rates of alcohol abuse are very low in China, where traditional beliefs scorn alcohol use or behaving as if one is under the influence of alcohol. People in China are not only less likely to drink alcohol, they are also less likely to advertise the fact that they have been drinking. In contrast, Korean men have a high rate of alcohol abuse, and Korean Americans have higher rates of alcohol use than other Asian American subgroups (SAMHSA, 2006). Their culture encourages drinking in social situations (Helzer & Canino, 1992).

The variety of psychoactive drugs in use today can be classified into four main groups: depressants, opiates, stimulants, and hallucinogens. ■ YOU REVIEW 4.1 provides a summary comparing the effects of these drugs. We'll begin with depressants.

You Review 4.1

Psychoactive Drugs and Their Effects

The four groups of substances most often leading to dependence are (1) depressants, (2) opiates, (3) stimulants, and (4) hallucinogens.

Substance	Trade Names; Street Names	Medical Uses	Route of Administration	Main Effects
DEPRESSANTS				
Alcohol	Beer, wine, liquor	Antidote for methanol poisoning, antiseptic	Oral, topical	Relaxation; lowered inhibitions; impaired reflexes, motor coordination, and memory
Barbiturates	Nembutal, Seconal, Phenobarbital; **Barbs**	Anesthetic, anticonvulsant, sedative, relief of high blood pressure	Injected, oral	Anxiety relief, euphoria, severe withdrawal symptoms
Benzodiazepines	Librium, Rohypnol, Valium, Xanax; **roofies, tranks**	Antianxiety, sedative, sleeping disorders	Injected, oral	Anxiety relief, irritability, confusion, depression, sleep problems
OPIATES				
Codeine	Tylenol with codeine, Fiorinal with codeine	Pain relief, antitussive	Injected, oral	Euphoria, constipation, loss of appetite
Heroin	**Horse, smack**	None	Injected, smoked, sniffed	Euphoria, pain control, constipation, loss of appetite
Methadone	Amidone, Methadose	Pain relief, treatment for opiate dependence	Injected, oral	Relief from withdrawal symptoms, constipation, loss of appetite
Morphine	Roxanol	Pain relief	Injected, oral, smoked	Euphoria, pain control
Opium	Laudanum; **Dover's Powder**	Pain relief, antidiarrheal	Oral, smoked	Euphoria

Substance	Trade Names; Street Names	Medical Uses	Route of Administration	Main Effects
STIMULANTS				
Caffeine	Coffee, teas, sodas, chocolates	Treatment for migraine headaches	Oral	Alertness, insomnia, loss of appetite, high blood pressure
Nicotine	Nicorette gum, Nicotrol; **cigars, cigarettes, snuff**	Treatment for nicotine dependence	Smoked, sniffed, oral, transdermal	Alertness, calmness, loss of appetite
Cocaine	**coke, crack, rock, snow, blow**	Local anesthetic; vasoconstrictor in Europe	Injected, smoked, sniffed	Increased energy, excitation, insomnia, loss of appetite, mood swings, delusions, paranoia, heart problems
Amphetamine	Dexedrine; **Black beauties, crosses**	ADHD, obesity, narcolepsy	Injected, oral, smoked, sniffed	Increased alertness and energy, insomnia, loss of appetite, delusions, paranoia
Methamphetamine	**Crank, crystal, ice**	ADHD, short-term aid to weight loss	Injected, oral, smoked, sniffed	Mood elevation, alertness, insomnia, loss of appetite, anxiety, paranoia
MDMA	**Adam, Ecstasy, XTC**	None	Oral	Increased insight and emotion, muscle tension, sleep problems, anxiety, paranoia
HALLUCINOGENS				
Marijuana	**Grass, herb, pot, reefer, weed, sinsemilla**	Glaucoma, nausea from chemotherapy In 2005, U.S. Supreme Court ruled against medical use	Oral, smoked	Relaxation, altered perceptions, sleep problems, paranoia, amotivation
Phencyclidine	PCP; **Angel dust, hog**	Anesthetic (veterinary)	Injected, oral, smoked	Euphoria, unpredictable moods, hostility
LSD	**Acid, microdot**	None	Oral	Altered perceptions, distortion of senses, panic reactions, flashback effects

Alcohol and Other Depressants

Depressant drugs interfere with brain functioning by inhibiting or slowing normal neural functioning. In low doses, depressants often reduce anxiety and cause a feeling of well-being, or a "nice buzz." This may be why many people mistakenly believe that alcohol is an "upper." In high dosages, depressants can cause blackouts, coma, or death. Anna Nicole Smith's fatal overdose in 2007 and Heath Ledger's death in 2008 are just two examples of people whose deaths were attributed in part to overdoses of depressants. Depressants are usually grouped into alcohol, barbiturates, and sedatives.

HEALTH EFFECTS OF ALCOHOL

Alcohol affects the neurotransmitter GABA, which is related to anxiety levels. In low dosages, alcohol may make one feel more sociable and relaxed. Alcohol also depresses the functioning of the cerebral cortex. So, in addition to feeling calm and relaxed, we are more likely to shed our inhibitions in regard to our thoughts and behaviors (Koob & Bloom, 1988; Stahl, 1996). When we drink alcohol, we are more willing to be silly or aggressive, share our emotions, or engage in behaviors that we would think twice about if we were sober.

Alcohol also inhibits the functioning of the brain stem, impairing motor skills and coordination. Reaction time and reflexes are slowed. When your tolerance is exceeded, your speech becomes slurred and your judgment is impaired. It is also harder for your brain to process information and to form new memories (Givens, 1995; Tsai, Gastfriend, & Coyle, 1995). Alcohol may cause *memory blackouts*—after a heavy night of drinking, you cannot remember the events of the night before. Chronic alcohol use can lead to *Korsakoff's syndrome*, a memory disorder caused by a deficiency of vitamin B (thiamine). The person who is an alcoholic often substitutes alcohol for more nutritious foods, which results in numerous vitamin deficiencies. Unfortunately, these memory deficits tend to be irreversible.

Because drinking alcohol results in reduced inhibitions, people are more likely to engage in sexual activity (Cooper, 2002). But alcohol impairs sexual performance. It makes it more difficult for a male to get and maintain an erection. The ability to achieve orgasm is also hampered by the effects of alcohol. We may think and feel that we are better lovers when under the influence of alcohol, but in reality we are not.

Women who drink alcohol and become intoxicated on a regular basis during pregnancy put their unborn child at risk for **fetal alcohol syndrome (FAS)**. Ingested alcohol does cross the placenta. Children born with FAS tend to have low birth weight; exhibit limb, head, and facial deformities; and suffer brain abnormalities that retard intellectual functioning and cause difficulties in learning, memory, problem solving, and attention (Ikonomidou et al., 2000; Kumada, Jiang, Cameron, & Komuro, 2007; Young, 1997). Because of the negative effects of alcohol on prenatal development, even moderate drinking during pregnancy is not recommended.

Does everyone experience the same effects from alcohol? No. The degree to which each of us experiences these effects depends on several factors. For example, alcohol has either more or less effect depending on your tolerance level: the higher your tolerance, the more alcohol you can consume before feeling its effects. Another factor is the rate of consumption. The faster you drink, the faster the alcohol is absorbed into the blood, increasing the alcohol's effect. Gender influences alcohol's effect as well. Metabolic and weight differences between males and females make it easier for male bodies to tolerate higher levels of alcohol (York & Welte, 1994).

depressants drugs that inhibit or slow down normal neural functioning

fetal alcohol syndrome (FAS) a birth condition resulting from the mother's chronic use of alcohol during pregnancy; characterized by facial and limb deformities and mental retardation

Alcohol's effect on motor coordination can be seen in a police sobriety test.

© Corbis

ALCOHOL AND GENETICS

Research suggests a possible genetic factor in alcohol's effect. Studies of twins show that if one identical twin is an alcoholic, the other twin has almost a 40% chance of developing a drinking problem. Rates for fraternal twins are much lower (Prescott et al., 1994). Research on sons of alcoholic fathers also suggests a possible genetic predisposition to alcohol dependence. The sons are likely to have an overall higher tolerance for alcohol, requiring more alcohol before feeling its effects, and are therefore at greater risk for abusing alcohol (Schuckit & Smith, 1997). More recently, researchers have located specific strands of genes that regulate the function of GABA. These genes vary across individuals and may contribute to a person's vulnerability to alcoholism (Edenberg & Foroud, 2006; Krystal et al., 2006; Soyka et al., 2008).

Cultural studies also support a possible genetic link. For instance, in some ethnic groups such as Japanese and Chinese, drinking alcohol can cause facial flushing. This sudden reddening of the face is a genetic trait that rarely occurs in Europeans. The physical and social discomfort of facial flushing tends to reduce the rate of alcohol consumption and alcoholism in these groups. People in ethnic groups that do not experience facial flushing are more likely to become alcoholics (Helzer & Canino, 1992).

However, environmental factors such as learning also play a role. Children of alcoholics have an increased risk of developing alcoholism that cannot be attributed solely to genetics. As adults, they are more likely to cope with personal or work-related stress by imitating the behavior of their alcoholic parent (Blane, 1988; Rivers, 1994). Clearly, the effects of alcohol and whether or not one becomes an abuser of alcohol depend on the interaction among genetic, cultural, individual, and environmental factors.

SOCIAL COSTS OF ALCOHOL USE

Alcohol dependence is devastating to individuals, families, and society in general. According to the National Highway Transportation Safety Administration, approximately 40% of all traffic deaths in the United States are alcohol related (NHTSA, 2003). Alcohol-impaired driving is highest for people between the ages of 21 and 24 and more common for males than for females (Centers for Disease Control and Prevention, 2002; Chou et al., 2006). More than half of rapists report that they drank alcohol before committing their crime. In college campus surveys, alcohol plays a role in the majority of sexual assaults and rapes. More than half of spousal abuse incidents involve alcohol (Adler & Rosenberg, 1994; Camper, 1990; Seto & Barbaree, 1995). Millions of children who live with alcoholic parents are also seriously affected. High levels of conflict—as well as physical, emotional, and sexual abuse—are likely in these households (Mathew, Wilson, Blazer, & George, 1993). Alcohol abuse also has economic costs. Alcohol abuse is associated with excessive absenteeism, lost productivity at work, and higher rates of on-the-job injury. These costs tend to be significantly higher for heavy drinkers (Fisher, Hoffman, Austin-Lane, & Kao, 2000; Gorsky, Schwartz, & Dennis, 1988; Jones, Casswell, & Zhang, 1995). Alcohol-related car accidents cost about $51 billion each year in the United States (Blincoe et al., 2002). Alcohol, contrary to the beer commercials, is indeed dangerous to our health and our society.

Alcohol has devastating effects on families.

© AP/Jack Kustron

Getty Images

The combined effects of pain medications and depressant drugs were a major factor in the accidental death of actor Heath Ledger in 2008.

Never leave drinks unattended at a party because they can be spiked with psychoactive drugs. Special drink coasters can be used to detect unwanted additives. When dipped into your drink, they change colors if something has been added to your drink.

© AP/Wide World Photos

BARBITURATES AND SEDATIVES

Barbiturates, commonly called "downers," are a category of depressants that are typically prescribed to reduce anxiety or to induce sleep. Well-known barbiturate drugs include Nembutal and Seconal. Sedatives or tranquilizers are also prescribed to reduce anxiety. They include a class of drugs called the *benzodiazepines*, including Valium and Xanax. Both types of depressants have effects similar to alcohol. In small dosages, they slow the nervous system, promoting relaxation. In high dosages, though, they severely impair motor functioning, memory, and judgment. Like alcohol, these drugs influence the functioning of the neurotransmitter GABA (Barbee, 1993). When these drugs are taken in combination with alcohol, they are potentially lethal because they can cause suppression of those brain areas that control breathing and heart rate, which can lead to unconsciousness, coma, or death.

You may have heard of the tranquilizer called Rohypnol ("roofies"), commonly known and used as a *date rape drug*. It is placed in a woman's drink at a party or club without her knowledge or consent, and the combined effect of alcohol and Rohypnol renders her unconscious. In this state she is then sexually assaulted or raped. In the morning, because of the drugs' effects on memory, she may not recall the event (Navarro, 1995).

When used as prescribed, barbiturates and sedatives can be helpful in the short-term treatment of anxiety disorders and sleeping problems such as insomnia. However, long-term use of tranquilizers leads to memory loss and actually heightens anxiety. When the effect of the drug has worn off, the body goes into "overdrive" to overcome its depressing effects (McKim, 1997). Withdrawal from these drugs can be brutal and includes convulsions, hallucinations, and intense anxiety.

Neuroscience Applies to Your World:

Psychoactive Drugs and General Anesthesia

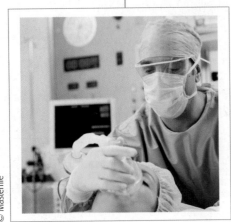

© Masterfile

Many people who have surgery receive general anesthesia, in which a combination of barbiturate, sedative, and narcotic drugs are used to induce unconsciousness and immobility, block pain, and cause you to forget the surgery and the time right after it. These drugs may be administered as injections or as inhaled gases. General anesthetics affect the whole brain and the entire body. The 2007 horror movie *Awake* dramatizes a condition called *anesthesia awareness,* in which general anesthetics fail and the person can hear or feel what is happening to him or her during surgery. Anesthesia awareness is actually quite rare, affecting roughly 2 out of every 1,000 surgery patients (Pollard, Coyle, Gilbert, & Beck, 2007; Sebel et al., 2004). In an attempt to minimize the amount of drugs given during surgery, neuroscientists are currently investigating safer, site-specific anesthetic drugs.

Opiates (Narcotics): Morphine, Codeine, Opium, and Heroin

The **opiates**, or narcotics, are drugs that are used to treat pain by mimicking pain-inhibiting neurotransmitters in the body such as endorphins. Opiates include morphine, codeine, opium, and heroin, although heroin is not considered or prescribed as a medicine. While depressing some brain areas, these drugs create excitation in other brain areas. In addition to blocking pain, they produce a feeling of pleasure that is almost like floating on a cloud or being in a dreamlike state (Bozarth & Wise, 1984). The opiates are extremely addictive, causing dependence within a few weeks. When you take opiates, your brain recognizes an abundance of pain inhibitors in the body and decreases its own production of endorphins. So when the effect of the opiate wears off, you feel your earlier pain *and* the absence of pleasure, and will want another, larger dose (Hughes et al., 1975; Zadina, Hackler, Ge, & Kastin, 1997). It is for this reason that narcotic administration is so closely monitored by health professionals.

Physical withdrawal symptoms related to opiate use include hot and cold flashes, cramps, sweating, and shaking. These symptoms typically last anywhere from 4 to 7 days, but they are not life-threatening. What is life-threatening is the risk of overdose. Street concentrations of narcotic drugs such as heroin and opium can vary widely. In addition, a person's sensitivity to opiates may fluctuate on a daily basis (Gallerani et al., 2001). The user never knows, therefore, if the concentration of drug he or she is taking will exceed the body's ability to handle it. There is an added risk of contracting HIV/AIDS and hepatitis C from using contaminated needles because opiates are often injected into a vein.

Currently, many heroin addicts are treated with the chemical methadone or buprenorphine. Each reduces the unpleasantness of the withdrawal symptoms yet does not produce the intense high of heroin. They are both equally effective in treating heroin dependence (Fiellin, Friedland, & Gourevitch, 2006; Payte, 1997; Vigezzi et al., 2006).

Stimulants: Legal and Otherwise

The **stimulants** include drugs that interfere with brain functioning by speeding up normal brain activity. Five stimulant substances we will review are caffeine, nicotine, cocaine, amphetamines, and MDMA (Ecstasy).

CAFFEINE: JAVA JITTERS

Because many of us wake up each morning reaching for that cup of coffee or that can of Monster to get us going, we may not even consider caffeine a mind-altering drug. Yet caffeine is a psychoactive drug because of its effects on the brain. It is perhaps the most frequently used psychoactive drug in the world. Caffeine is an active ingredient in coffee, tea, sodas, some energy drinks, chocolate, migraine headache medications, and diet pills. It stimulates the brain by blocking neurotransmitters (primarily adenosine) that slow down our nervous system and cause sleep (Julien, 1995). In small doses, caffeine gives us a boost, keeping us more alert and helping us focus. It helps problem solving and decreases reaction time (Warburton, 1995). However, in large doses, caffeine can "wire" you, causing insomnia, upset stomach, racing heartbeat, nervousness, and irritability.

Regular caffeine use can lead to dependence. If you suddenly stop drinking coffee or kick your cola habit, you will likely experience headaches, irritability, tiredness, and flu-like symptoms (Schuh & Griffiths, 1997). These withdrawal symptoms, even if they aren't severe, can last a week. Excessive caffeine use increases the risk of high blood pressure and encourages the development of fibroid cysts in women's breasts. Pregnant women in particular should reduce caffeine intake because high amounts of caffeine are associated with an increased risk of miscarriage and have been linked with birth defects (Infante-Rivard, Fernandez, Gauthier, David, & Rivard, 1993).

opiates [OH-pee-ates] painkilling drugs that depress some brain areas and excite others

stimulants drugs that speed up normal brain functioning

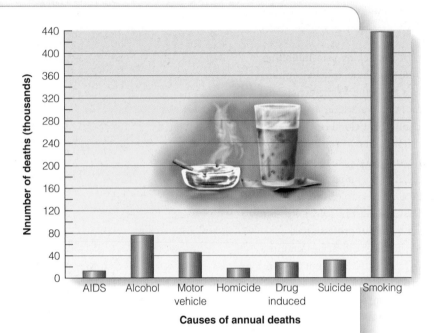

Y-axis: Nnumber of deaths (thousands)
X-axis categories: AIDS, Alcohol, Motor vehicle, Homicide, Drug induced, Suicide, Smoking

Causes of annual deaths

FIGURE 4.7 Causes of Annual Deaths in the United States

Cigarette smoking causes more deaths in the United States than AIDS, alcohol, motor vehicle accidents, homicides, suicides, and other drug use combined.

Sources: (AIDS, Motor Vehicles, Homicide, Drug Induced, Suicide) NCHS National Vital Statistics Reports, Volume 54, Number 19, "Deaths: Preliminary Data for 2004," 2006; (Alcohol) CDC MMWR, 53(37): 866–870, "Alcohol-Attributable Deaths and Years of Potential Life Lost–United States, 2001," 2004; (Smoking) CDC MMWR, 54(25): 625–628, "Annual Smoking-Attributable Mortality, Years of Potential Life Lost, and Productivity Losses–United States, 1997–2001," 2005.

NICOTINE: A REALLY BAD HABIT

Nicotine, the active ingredient in tobacco and the source of a smoker's craving for cigarettes, is a powerful stimulant. Tobacco use is the most preventable cause of death in the United States. More than 430,000 deaths result each year from tobacco use, at an annual price tag of more than $167 billion in health-related economic costs (Centers for Disease Control and Prevention, 2005). As seen in ■ FIGURE 4.7, tobacco-related deaths exceed deaths from AIDS, alcohol, motor vehicle accidents, drug overdoses, murders, and suicides combined! Tobacco use has been linked to lung cancer, throat cancer, emphysema, and heart disease (Noah & Robinson, 1997).

Most adult smokers started smoking before the age of 18, and every day more people under the age of 18 become regular smokers (Johnston, O'Malley, Bachman, & Schulenberg, 2006). Although the percentage of people in the United States who smoke has decreased considerably over the last 50 years, 23.9% of adult men and 18.1% of adult women continue to smoke regularly (Centers for Disease Control and Prevention, 2006b). The percentages are slightly higher for adults ages 18–25 years (25%) (SAMHSA, 2007). American Indians have the highest rates of tobacco use; African American and Southeast Asian men also have high rates of smoking. Asian American and Hispanic women have the lowest rates (Centers for Disease Control and Prevention, 2006a; SAMHSA, 2006).

Nicotine affects several neurotransmitters in the brain. It influences acetylcholine and glutamate such that in low doses, nicotine improves attention and memory (McGehee, Heath, Gelber, Devay, & Role, 1995). Nicotine also elevates dopamine levels, leading to feelings of pleasure and reward (Pidoplichko, DeBiasi, Williams, & Dani, 1997). In high doses, nicotine causes vomiting, diarrhea, sweating, and dizziness. Yet users quickly develop a tolerance to nicotine.

Withdrawal from chronic nicotine use rivals withdrawal from other abused drugs such as cocaine, morphine, and alcohol (Epping-Jordan, Watkins, Koob, & Markou, 1998). Withdrawal symptoms, lasting anywhere from 2 to 6 weeks, include headaches, irritability, stomach upset, difficulty sleeping, and an intense craving for the drug. This indeed illustrates the power of dependence.

COCAINE AND CRACK

Cocaine and its derivative, crack, are powerful and dangerous stimulant drugs. Snorted, smoked, or injected, cocaine is quickly absorbed into the body and thus reaches the brain rapidly. Cocaine blocks a protein, called the dopamine transporter (DAT), which helps the reuptake of dopamine into the neuron. Because reuptake is blocked, free dopamine in the brain increases (Hummel & Unterwald, 2002; Nestler, 2006; Williams & Galli, 2006).

The buildup of dopamine produces an instant surge of arousal, a feeling of pleasure and optimism. Appetite decreases, but heart rate, blood pressure, and alertness increase. When the effect of the cocaine wears off, the person "crashes," showing decreased energy and depressed mood. This

Nicotine is an addictive substance that makes it difficult for young people to quit smoking once they have started.

low creates an intense craving for the drug that sets up a cycle of continued use and dependence (Gawin, 1991). High doses of cocaine (relative to one's tolerance) can cause paranoia, sleeplessness, delusions, seizures, strokes, and potentially cardiac arrest (Lacayo, 1995). Users who are dependent on cocaine may lose interest in their usual friends and activities, lose weight, and have chronic sore throats and difficulty sleeping; there may also be a noticeable change in their finances.

Health effects of repeated use of cocaine include chronic nosebleeds, damage to nasal cartilage (from snorting), and respiratory and heart problems. Miscarriages are common for pregnant women who use cocaine. If the pregnancy continues, the infant is more likely to be born premature and, as a newborn, must be weaned from the effects of the drug. However, the long-term impact of prenatal exposure to cocaine continues to be in question. Earlier research indicated that by school age, children with prenatal exposure to cocaine were more likely to be hyperactive and to show delayed language learning and disorganized thinking (Konkol, Murphey, Ferriero, Dempsey, & Olsen, 1994; Lester et al., 1991; Mayes, Bornstein, Chawarska, & Haynes, 1996). However, recent research suggests that the home environment may play a stronger role in a child's development than prenatal cocaine exposure (Arendt et al., 2004; Hurt, Brodsky, Roth, Malmud, & Giannetta, 2005; Kilbride, Castor, & Fuger, 2006). For example, Hurt and colleagues (2005) have followed a group of 135 urban school children, 62 with prenatal exposure to cocaine and 73 without. Now in the fourth grade, children from both groups have shown similar poor school performance. In both groups, children with successful school performance were more likely to have come from better home environments.

AMPHETAMINES

Amphetamines, called "uppers" or "speed," have effects similar to those of cocaine. However, the high produced by these drugs is less intense but generally lasts longer (a few hours). Currently, the most abused form of amphetamine is *methamphetamine*, commonly called crystal meth, ice, chalk, or crank. According to the 2005 National Survey on Drug Use and Health (NSDUH), 4.3% of the U.S. population age 12 or over has used crystal meth at least once (SAMHSA, 2006). Approximately 4.1% of college students and 8.3% of young adults between the ages of 19 and 28 have tried methamphetamine (NIDA & University of Michigan, 2006).

Methamphetamine, like cocaine, affects dopamine, serotonin, and norepinephrine levels in the brain (Volkow et al., 2001). The result is enhanced mood and pleasure, energy, alertness, and reduced appetite. Heart rate and blood pressure also increase. Like cocaine, methamphetamine also leads to a crash to low energy levels, paranoia, and depressed mood when the effects of the drug have subsided. However, methamphetamine remains present in the brain longer than cocaine. It not only blocks the reuptake of dopamine but also increases the release of dopamine, leading to a more toxic effect (NIDA, 2006b). Continued use results in insomnia, paranoia, agitation, confusion, violent behavior, memory loss, and dependence. Methamphetamine use can also cause strokes, cardiovascular problems, and extreme anorexia. An overdose can cause coma and death. Users who inject the drug and share needles are also at risk for acquiring HIV/AIDS and hepatitis C (Bezchlibnyk-Butler & Jeffries, 1998).

MDMA (ECSTASY)

In its "pure" form, Ecstasy is called MDMA, but street Ecstasy, Adam, or XTC typically contains other drugs such as amphetamine, ketamine, caffeine, and ephedrine (Walters, Foy, & Castro, 2003). MDMA's use dramatically increased as a "club drug" in the 1990s and early 2000s, particularly among college students and young adults. In 2006, 5% of people over the age of 12 reported using Ecstasy at some point in their lives (SAMHSA, 2007). In the United States, use is also spreading beyond predominately European American youth to African American and Hispanic populations (Boeri, Sterk, & Elifson, 2004; Maxwell & Spence, 2003), and Ecstasy has become a popular drug among urban gay males (NIDA, 2006a).

Taken orally, usually in a tablet or a capsule, Ecstasy enhances mood and energy levels and heightens users' sensations. Users report increased self-confidence, increased feelings of love and warmth toward others, emotional openness, and lack of inhibition (Fry & Miller, 2002). The effect begins very fast, within half an hour of consumption, and lasts approximately 3 to 6 hours. Negative effects of Ecstasy use are insomnia, teeth clenching, nausea, increase in heart rate and blood pressure, fatigue, and blurred vision. Most of these negative effects subside within 24 hours. Paranoia, depression, drug craving, overheating, cardiac problems, kidney failure, seizures, strokes, and/or loss of touch with reality may also occur (Bezchlibnyk-Butler & Jeffries, 1998).

While MDMA increases the activity of several neurotransmitters in the brain, it is the serotonin pathway that has received the most attention. Ecstasy binds to the serotonin transport protein such that the availability of free serotonin increases (Britt & McCance-Katz, 2005; Colado, O'Shea, & Green, 2004). The long-term effects of Ecstasy use on the human brain have not yet been determined (Cowan, 2007). It also is unclear whether Ecstasy has properties of the hallucinogens. Users regularly report hallucinations, but it is impossible to know whether they have really been using pure MDMA or have bought low doses of LSD instead.

hallucinogens [huh-LOO-sin-no-gens] drugs that simultaneously excite and inhibit normal neural activity, thereby causing distortions in perception

THC (tetrahydrocannabinol) [tet-rah-high-dro-can-NAH-bin-all] the active ingredient in marijuana that affects learning, short-term memory, coordination, emotion, and appetite

Hallucinogens: Distorting Reality

Hallucinogens are drugs that interfere with brain functioning by both exciting and inhibiting the nervous system. These contrasting effects often cause distortions in perception, or *hallucinations*. Hallucinogenic substances include marijuana, PCP, and LSD.

MARIJUANA

Marijuana, also called pot, reefer, or weed, is a mild hallucinogen. It rarely, if ever, leads to overdoses that cause death (Zimmer & Morgan, 1997). Although the United States federal government does not recognize the medical use of marijuana, thirteen states currently allow for its medicinal use. It has been prescribed for medical conditions such as glaucoma, chronic pain, and nausea from cancer chemotherapy and has been found moderately effective in clinical trials for muscle spasms and multiple sclerosis (Croxford, 2003; Grinspoon & Bakalar, 1995; Iverson, 2003; Klein & Newton, 2007). It is also the most widely used illegal substance in the United States, with 40% of people over the age of 12 reporting having tried the drug. Past-year usage is highest among 16- to 25-year-olds, and males report higher usage than females. American Indians report the highest use and Asian Americans the lowest (SAMHSA, 2006, 2007).

The active ingredient in marijuana is **THC (tetrahydrocannabinol)**. THC is absorbed by the lungs and produces a high that lasts for several hours. THC binds to the neurotransmitter called anandamide that influences learning, short-term memory, motor coordination, emotions, and appetite—behaviors that are all affected when people are high on marijuana (Matsuda, Lolait, Brownstein, Young, & Bonner, 1990). In low doses, THC makes users feel good and experience vivid sensations. THC also slows reaction time and impairs judgment and peripheral vision. For this reason, marijuana users are just as dangerous driving a car or operating machinery as users of other drugs. Marijuana use also interferes with memory, disrupting both the formation of memories and the recall

Although controversy continues over the medicinal uses of marijuana, smoking pot increases one's chances of respiratory problems and lung damage.

Uriel Sinai/Getty Images

of information (Pope & Yurgelun-Todd, 1996; Ranganathan & D'Souza, 2006). Its stimulation of appetite and increased sensitivity to taste may result in an attack of the "munchies." In high doses, THC may produce hallucinations, delusions, paranoia, and distortions in time and body image (Hanson & Venturelli, 1998). Controversy still exists over whether marijuana use leads to dependence. Many people maintain that it does not; others report mild withdrawal symptoms when marijuana use is stopped (de Fonseca, Carrera, Navarro, Koob, & Weiss, 1997; Grinspoon, Bakalar, Zimmer, & Morgan, 1997; Stephens, Roffman, & Simpson, 1994; Vandrey, Budney, Hughes, & Liguori, 2008; Wickelgren, 1997).

Studies on long-term users of marijuana have shown long-lasting cognitive effects including impaired attention, learning, and motor coordination (Pope & Yurgelun-Todd, 1996; Volkow, Gillespie, Mullani, & Tancredi, 1996). However, permanent structural changes in the brain have not been identified with chronic use (Quickfall & Crockford, 2006). Marijuana also has serious long-term health effects. Because it is typically smoked, users may experience respiratory problems such as bronchitis and lung damage.

PCP

PCP is sold on the street by such names as angel dust and rocket fuel. Sherm, killer joints, or KJs are names that refer to PCP poured over cigarettes or marijuana joints. PCP can be eaten, snorted, smoked, or injected. Although the use of PCP has declined steadily since 1979, in 2006, 2.7% of people over the age of 12 reported having tried PCP, with males again outnumbering females (SAMHSA, 2007).

PCP has hallucinogenic properties as well as stimulant and depressant effects. These unpredictable effects often lead to distress, mood swings, and confusion. PCP inhibits the neurotransmitter glutamate, which is involved in the perception of pain, responses to the environment, and memory. In low doses, PCP produces a sudden increase in blood pressure, pulse rate, and breathing. Flushing, profuse sweating, and numbness of the limbs may also occur. Out-of-body experiences and the sensation of walking on a spongy surface are also reported. In higher doses, PCP causes a drop in blood pressure, pulse rate, and respiration. This may be accompanied by nausea, vomiting, blurred vision, drooling, loss of balance, and dizziness. Hallucinations, confusion, paranoia, and garbled speech also result. Users may become severely disoriented or suicidal and may therefore be a danger to themselves or others. Seizures, coma, or death may also occur (Rudgley, 1998).

Using PCP can lead to dependence. Users often crave the feelings of strength, power, and invulnerability and the escape from thinking that PCP brings. Long-term use of PCP is associated with memory loss and difficulty in speaking and thinking, and may lead to permanent changes in fine motor abilities (NIDA, 2001).

LSD

LSD (lysergic acid diethylamide), more commonly referred to as acid, is the most potent perception-altering drug known. In 2006, 9.5% of people over the age of 12 reported having tried LSD at some time in their lives; males were more likely to have tried the drug than females (SAMHSA, 2007). LSD's effects typically begin 30 to 90 minutes after ingestion and can last anywhere from 6 to 12 hours.

Users of LSD may experience increased blood pressure and heart rate, dizziness, loss of appetite, and nausea, but the drug's main effects appear to be emotional and sensory. Even at very low doses, LSD causes bizarre hallucinations, distortions in time and body image, and intense emotions that together are often referred to as "tripping." Emotions may shift rapidly from fear to happiness, and the user may seem to experience several emotions at once. Colors, smells, sounds, and other sensory stimuli seem highly intensified and may even blend in what is known as *synesthesia*, in which a person seems to hear or feel colors and see sounds (NIDA, 2001). These effects are due to LSD's resemblance to the neurotransmitter serotonin (Aghajanian, 1994). LSD stimulates serotonin receptors, influencing perceptions, emotions, and sleep. However, whether one's "trip" is pleasant or unpleasant is unpredictable and depends on the user's expectations and mood. On good trips, users experience enjoyable sensations, but bad trips produce terrifying thoughts and feelings, including fears of insanity, death, or losing control. Although withdrawal symptoms from LSD have not been documented, users quickly develop tolerance (Miller & Gold, 1994; NIDA, 2001).

Two long-term effects of LSD in some users are *persistent psychosis* and *hallucinogen persisting perception disorder* (HPPD), more commonly referred to as "flashbacks." Persistent psychosis is a long-lasting psychotic-like state after the trip has ended. It may include dramatic mood swings, visual disturbances, and hallucinations. These effects may last for years and can affect people who have no history or other symptoms of a psychological disorder. HPPD, or flashbacks, is a reexperiencing of the sensations originally produced by the LSD hours, weeks, or even years after its initial use. It typically consists of visual disturbances, such as seeing bright or colored flashes and trails attached to moving objects (NIDA, 2001). The causes of persistent psychosis and HPPD are not known. Additional lasting side effects may include short-term memory loss, paranoia, nightmares, and panic attacks (Gold, 1994).

Despite the different effects of the drugs discussed, they all have one thing in common: they alter our state of consciousness—in sometimes unpredictable, and occasionally tragic, ways. Although much is still unknown about many of these drugs, it is clear that the long-term negative effects outweigh the short-term high and feelings of well-being that they produce. By understanding these effects, you may well avoid or prevent their abuse in the future.

Let's Review!

This section has detailed the nature of psychoactive drugs—from caffeine to heroin—including how they work and their effects. As a quick check of your understanding, answer these questions.

1. Which category of drugs mainly has its effects by interfering with the neurotransmitter dopamine?
   a. Stimulants
   b. Hallucinogens
   c. Depressants
   d. Opiates

2. Rolanda takes a drug that raises her blood pressure and heart rate, makes her feel euphoric and excited, and suppresses her appetite. Rolanda in all likelihood has *not* taken _____.
   a. cocaine
   b. alcohol
   c. methamphetamine
   d. crack

3. Which of the following drugs is *least* likely to lead to physical withdrawal symptoms?
   a. Marijuana
   b. Heroin
   c. Alcohol
   d. Nicotine

4. The designer drug Ecstasy, or MDMA, produces effects similar to what two categories of drugs?
   a. Stimulants and depressants
   b. Hallucinogens and depressants
   c. Stimulants and hallucinogens
   d. Opiates and depressants

5. Which of the following categories of drugs produces the most intense withdrawal effects once the person stops using the drug?
   a. Hallucinogens
   b. Barbiturates
   c. Stimulants
   d. a and c

Answers 1. a; 2. b; 3. a; 4. c; 5. b

Studying THE **Chapter**

Key Terms

consciousness (119)
microsleep (120)
circadian rhythm (124)
suprachiasmatic nucleus
   (SCN) (124)
melatonin (124)
non-REM sleep (126)
REM sleep (126)
REM behavior disorder (127)
REM rebound (128)
manifest content (129)
latent content (129)
threat simulation theory
   (TST) (129)

activation-synthesis
   theory (129)
sleep disorder (129)
insomnia (130)
narcolepsy (131)
sleep apnea (131)
sleepwalking (131)
night terrors (131)
nightmare (132)
enuresis (132)
hypnosis (134)
dissociation theory (135)
response set theory of
   hypnosis (135)

psychoactive drugs (137)
tolerance (138)
substance dependence (139)
withdrawal symptoms (139)
substance abuse (139)
depressants (142)
fetal alcohol syndrome (FAS) (142)
opiates (145)
stimulants (145)
hallucinogens (148)
THC (tetrahydrocannabinol) (148)

What Do You Know? Assess Your Understanding

Test your retention and understanding of the material by answering the following questions.

1. Which of the following is not a benefit of sleep?
  a.   Increased alertness
  b.   Memory processing
  c.   Decreased immunity to disease
  d.   Enhanced mood

2. Juno is 62 and Athena is 22. Which of these women requires more sleep at night?
  a.   Juno
  b.   Athena
  c.   Both women require the same amount of sleep.
  d.   Juno needs more non-REM sleep, and Athena needs more REM sleep.

3. Alfred is just falling asleep. His brain waves most likely resemble _____ waves.
  a.   beta   c.   sleep spindle
  b.   delta   d.   theta

4. Which of the following brain waves is most likely to occur during stage IV sleep?
  a.   Beta   c.   Delta
  b.   Alpha   d.   Theta

5. Benita often wakes up in the morning feeling very tired, despite sleeping 9–10 hours. Her husband has noticed that she often emits loud snores and seems to have erratic breathing while she is sleeping. Benita most likely has which sleep disorder?
  a.   Narcolepsy   c.   Night terrors
  b.   Sleep apnea   d.   Enuresis

6. Recent research suggests a relationship between the sleep spindles of stage II sleep and _____.
  a.   processing of motor skills
  b.   body restoration
  c.   storage of memories
  d.   growth hormone

7. Dr. Surrell believes that dreaming evolved to help us rehearse potentially harmful events. Dr. Surrell is endorsing which dream theory?
   a. Freudian theory
   b. Activation synthesis theory
   c. Continuity hypothesis
   d. Threat simulation theory

8. When Kaitlin wakes up in the morning, she recalls having a dream that toads were invading her room. According to Freud, Kaitlin's recall is an example of _____.
   a. manifest content   c. survival themes
   b. latent content   d. the continuity hypothesis

9. Why is melatonin referred to as the "Dracula hormone"?
   a. Because it decreases during the day
   b. Because it increases at night
   c. Both a and b
   d. Neither a nor b

10. EEG-brain wave patterns of people who are hypnotized show an increase in _____ waves.
    a. theta   c. beta
    b. delta   d. alpha

11. Which of the following is not a documented use of hypnosis?
    a. Decreasing anxiety
    b. Relieving pain
    c. Recovering memories
    d. Enhancing therapy

12. People who are easily hypnotized tend to have which of the following traits?
    a. Positive expectations about hypnosis
    b. Higher intelligence
    c. Higher sociability
    d. All of the above

13. Which of the following drugs is not a stimulant?
    a. Cocaine   c. Caffeine
    b. Nicotine   d. Alcohol

14. Paz now needs more alcohol to get high than she did when she first started drinking. Paz has developed _____ alcohol.
    a. substance abuse for
    b. tolerance to
    c. withdrawal from
    d. substance dependence for

15. Howie has been using methamphetamine for several months now. If he stops taking the drug, which of the following is he most likely to experience?
    a. Paranoia   c. Reduced appetite
    b. Enhanced mood   d. High energy

16. Which of the following variables influences a drug's effects?
    a. How much of the drug is taken
    b. Your tolerance to the drug
    c. Your expectations about the drug's effects
    d. All of the above

17. The feeling of well-being that results from most illicit drug use is due to the activity of which of the following neurotransmitters?
    a. Dopamine   c. Acetylcholine
    b. Serotonin   d. Endorphins

18. After taking LSD several months ago, Sven still experiences visual disturbances and dramatic mood swings. Sven is most likely experiencing _____.
    a. flashbacks   c. persistent psychosis
    b. twittering   d. tweaking

19. While at a nightclub one weekend, Aoki had a drug slipped into her drink that made her "pass out" and have no recall of the events of the evening. What type of drug was most likely put in Aoki's drink?
    a. Hallucinogen   c. Stimulant
    b. Sedative   d. Opiate

20. Which of the following drugs is most likely to be prescribed to reduce pain?
    a. Stimulant   c. Hallucinogen
    b. Depressant   d. Opiate

Answers: 1. c; 2. b; 3. d; 4. c; 5. b; 6. a; 7. d; 8. a; 9. c; 10. d; 11. c; 12. a; 13. d; 14. b; 15. a; 16. d; 17. a; 18. c; 19. b; 20. d

■ **Online Resources**

CENGAGE**NOW**™ **Personalized Study**

www.cengage.com/login

Go to www.cengage.com/login to link to CengageNOW, your online study tool. First take the **Pre-Test** for this chapter to get your **Personalized Study Plan**, which will identify topics you need to review and direct you to online resources. Then take the **Post-Test** to determine what concepts you have mastered and what you still need work on.

    What Is Psychology? Essentials Book Companion Website

www.cengage.com/psychology/pastorino

Visit your book companion website, where you will find more resources to help you study. Resources include learning objectives, Internet exercises, quizzing, flash cards, and a pronunciation glossary.

Look Back
AT WHAT YOU'VE
LEARNED

Consciousness includes the feelings, thoughts, and aroused states in which we are aware. Altered states of consciousness occur when we sleep, are hypnotized, or take any psychoactive drug.

What Happens When We Sleep?

- When teenagers and adults get at least 8 hours of sleep, the benefits include restored body tissues, body growth, immunity to disease, an alert mind, processing of memories, and enhanced mood.

- The **circadian rhythm** is a natural rhythm of sleep and waking programmed by a group of brain cells in the hypothalamus called the **suprachiasmatic nucleus**.

- A typical night of sleep involves cycling through two states of sleep: **non-REM sleep**, which progressively relaxes the person; and **REM** (rapid-eye-movement) **sleep**, which is very active.

- Freud believed that dreams allow us to express fears and desires without conscious censorship. Many psychologists and psychiatrists dispute Freud's emphasis on sex and aggression in interpreting dreams.

- **Threat simulation theory** proposes that dreaming is an evolved defense mechanism that allows us to rehearse our responses to threatening situations.

- **Activation-synthesis theory** suggests that dreaming is just a consequence of the highly aroused brain during REM sleep.

- **Insomnia** is the inability to get to sleep or to stay asleep. It is the most common sleep disorder.

- Other sleep disorders include **sleep apnea**, in which a person stops breathing while asleep, and a rarer condition called **narcolepsy**, in which a person falls asleep during alert times of the day.

Consciousness: WIDE AWAKE, IN A DAZE, OR DREAMING?

What Is Hypnosis?

- **Hypnosis** is a technique used to create a state of heightened suggestibility. Hypnosis usually involves being asked to mentally focus on an object, image, or the hypnotist's voice, thus inducing a highly relaxed state.

- Hypnotic susceptibility varies greatly and does not seem to be related to intelligence, gender, or sociability. People who are easily hypnotized tend to be better able to focus their attention, have vivid imaginations, and have positive expectations about hypnosis.

- Hypnosis has been shown to be effective for some people in providing pain relief and decreasing anxiety. It has not been shown to be as effective in curing addictions or recovering accurate memories.

© AP Photo/News Tribune/Stephen Brooks

What Are the Effects of Psychoactive Drugs?

- **Psychoactive drugs** are substances that influence the brain and therefore the behavior of a person.

- Drug **tolerance** refers to the amount of a drug required to produce its effects. After repeated use of a drug, more of it is usually needed to achieve its initial effect.

- **Substance dependence** refers to a person's need of a drug in order to function emotionally and/or physically.

- **Depressants** such as alcohol, sedatives, and barbiturate drugs interfere with brain functions by inhibiting or slowing normal neural function.

- **Opiates** such as morphine, codeine, and opium are used to treat pain by mimicking the effects of neurotransmitters such as endorphins.

- **Stimulants** are drugs such as caffeine, nicotine, cocaine, and amphetamines that interfere with brain functioning by speeding up normal brain activity.

- **Hallucinogens**, including marijuana and LSD, are drugs that interfere with brain functioning by simultaneously exciting and inhibiting normal neural activity. These contrasting effects often cause disruptions in perception or hallucinations.

© Corbis

5

HOW DO WE LEARN?

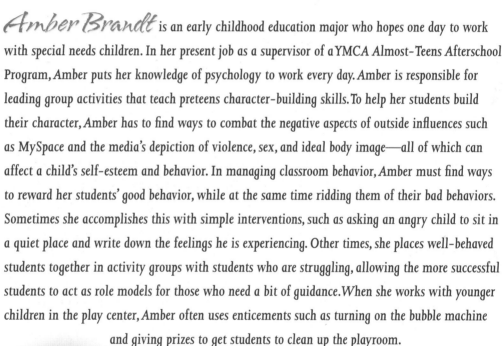

- Learning in Its Simplest Form: Habituation

- Classical Conditioning: Learning Through the Association of Stimuli

- Operant Conditioning: Learning From the Consequences of Our Actions

- Social Learning or Modeling

Amber Brandt is an early childhood education major who hopes one day to work with special needs children. In her present job as a supervisor of a YMCA Almost-Teens Afterschool Program, Amber puts her knowledge of psychology to work every day. Amber is responsible for leading group activities that teach preteens character-building skills. To help her students build their character, Amber has to find ways to combat the negative aspects of outside influences such as MySpace and the media's depiction of violence, sex, and ideal body image—all of which can affect a child's self-esteem and behavior. In managing classroom behavior, Amber must find ways to reward her students' good behavior, while at the same time ridding them of their bad behaviors. Sometimes she accomplishes this with simple interventions, such as asking an angry child to sit in a quiet place and write down the feelings he is experiencing. Other times, she places well-behaved students together in activity groups with students who are struggling, allowing the more successful students to act as role models for those who need a bit of guidance. When she works with younger children in the play center, Amber often uses enticements such as turning on the bubble machine and giving prizes to get students to clean up the playroom.

As you will see in reading this chapter, Amber's methods are applications of the learning theories developed by psychologists. After mastering this material, we bet that you too will find many ways to apply this material in your personal life. Understanding how we learn is the first step to changing behavior in ourselves and others.

© Susann Doyle-Portillo

© blickwinkel/Alamy

Amber Brandt puts her knowledge of learning into practice at her job working with Almost-Teens at the YMCA.

Learning in Its Simplest Form: Habituation

Our favorite definition of learning states that **learning** *is a relatively permanent change in behavior, or the potential for behavior, that results from experience.* Learning results from many experiences in life. We learn concepts and skills in school. We learn from watching others. And we learn certain skills, like riding a bike, by doing them. Learning may show up in our behavior (as when we ride a bike), or it may not (as when we get a speeding ticket even though we've learned that speeding is wrong). Learning may stay with us for years (as with riding a bike), or it may only linger for a while (as when we drive the speed limit for only a few weeks after getting a ticket).

> **You Asked...**
>
> *Does everyone have the ability to learn?*   CANDACE KENDRICK, STUDENT

All healthy humans have the capacity for some form of learning. In this chapter we will look at four common types of learning, beginning with what is widely thought to be the simplest form of learning that we engage in—habituation.

Paying Attention and Learning to Ignore: Orienting Reflexes and Habituation

Suppose you are sitting in class, listening to your psychology professor and taking notes. All of a sudden there is a loud banging noise directly outside your classroom. What would your very first reaction to the unexpected noise be? If you are like most people, you would immediately stop listening to the lecture and turn your head in the direction of the noise. This very normal response is called an **orienting reflex** (Pavlov, 1927/1960). Orienting reflexes occur when we stop what we are doing to orient our sense organs in the direction of unexpected stimuli.

In our example, the stimulus was auditory, but this doesn't have to be the case. If you were standing in line to buy coffee and someone poked you in the back, you would most likely turn to see what the person wanted. If you were having dinner in a restaurant and someone began to take pictures using a flash camera, you would likely look in the direction of the flashes of light. In short, we exhibit the orienting reflex to any type of novel stimulus.

learning a relatively permanent change in behavior, or behavior potential, as a result of experience

orienting reflex the tendency of an organism to orient its senses toward unexpected stimuli

This dog is orienting its ears toward a novel sound. In humans as in dogs, orienting reflexes allow us to respond quickly to potential dangers.

YOUR TURN – ACTIVE LEARNING

If you have a pet cat or dog, you can demonstrate an orienting reflex for yourself. The next time your pet is preparing to take a nap, stay out of sight, but make a soft whistling noise. Notice how your pet's ears prick up and how they orient toward you in an attempt to locate the sound. This is an orienting reflex.

Why do you think we exhibit orienting reflexes? What is the benefit of automatically paying attention to novel stimuli? If you said "self-protection," you would be correct. Orienting reflexes allow us to quickly gather information about stimuli that could

© isobel flynn/Alamy

potentially be threatening. For instance, that banging noise in the hallway could be a student dropping her books, or it could be a fight. In the case of a fight, you may want to take steps to ensure that the fight doesn't affect you in a negative way. By orienting your senses toward the event, you can quickly assess what, if any, action is needed to protect yourself.

The benefit of having orienting reflexes is limited, though. Suppose that after looking up at the sound of the banging, you see that it is only a worker hammering as he installs a new bulletin board in the hallway. You would likely return your attention to the psychology lecture. If the banging noise continues, your tendency to look up at the noise in the hall would steadily decrease. In other words, your orienting reflex would diminish over time. This decrease in responding to a stimulus as it is repeated over and over is called **habituation**.

After people live in this house for a while, habituation will ensure that they barely even notice the sounds of jets like this one as they take off and land.

Despite its name, habituation does not refer to forming a habit. Instead, habituation ensures that we do not waste our energy and mental resources by responding to irrelevant stimuli. In our previous example, after you have established that the noise in the hallway is not threatening, there is no reason to keep looking. If you did keep exhibiting the orienting reflex, you would needlessly miss part of your psychology lecture and waste energy that could be spent more usefully.

Almost all creatures, including those with very simple nervous systems, seem to have the capacity for habituation (Harris, 1943). This universality implies that habituation is the simplest type of learning seen in living things (Davis & Egger, 1992). Habituation can be seen in newborn infants (Lavoie & Desrochers, 2002; Rose, 1980) and even in fetuses (Van Heteren, Boekkooi, Jongsma, & Nijhuis, 2000). Recent studies have suggested that the cerebellum, which is part of the more primitive hindbrain (see Chapter 2), plays a role in certain instances of habituation (Frings et al., 2006). These findings seem to indicate the primitive nature of habituation.

The Benefits of Habituation

To get a better feel for the value of habituation, imagine what life would be like if you could *not* habituate. Without habituation, you would reflexively respond to every sight, sound, touch, and smell you encountered every time you encountered it. You would not be able to ignore these stimuli. Think of how this would limit your ability to function. Every time the worker hammered the bulletin board in the hall, your attention would move away from the lecture and toward the hall. You certainly would not learn much psychology under these circumstances! With habituation, you get the best of both worlds. You can respond to novel stimuli that may pose a danger, and you can also ignore stimuli that have been checked out and deemed to be harmless. Habituation gives you flexibility in that you don't have to continue to respond to a stimulus. Habituation may also serve to protect our brains from overstimulation, as you can see in *Neuroscience Applies to Your World*. But does this mean that once you have habituated to a stimulus, you must ignore it forever?

habituation [huh-bit-chew-AYE-shun] the tendency of an organism to ignore repeated stimuli

Neuroscience Applies to Your World:

What Causes Migraines?

Many people suffer from intense headaches called migraines. These debilitating headaches are frequently characterized by severe pain on one side of the head and can be associated with sensitivity to light, nausea, or vomiting. Some migraine sufferers also experience visual disturbances, called auras, which signal the impending onset of a migraine. In searching for the causes of migraines, researchers have uncovered some interesting information. First, having a specific genetic marker called the MTHFR C677T is correlated with a higher likelihood of having migraines, especially migraines with auras. This genetic marker is also associated with having higher levels of a chemical called homocysteine in the body (see de Tommaso et al., 2007). Second, researchers have also discovered that migraine sufferers often appear to have a lessened ability to habituate to stimuli. For example, migraine sufferers showed less ability than non–migraine sufferers to habituate to a stressful sound (Huber, Henrich, & Gündel, 2005). This suggests that migraine suffers may have less ability to tune out stressful stimuli, which may lead to hyperactivity in the brain that results in migraine pain. In fact, when migraine sufferers are taught to increase their levels of habituation to environmental stimuli, they tend to experience fewer migraine attacks (see Kropp, Siniatchkin, & Gerber, 2002). Studies like these suggest that one function of habituation may be to protect our nervous system from sensory overload.

© Itani/Alamy

Dishabituation

Another aspect of this flexibility is that you can also stop habituating when the circumstances warrant it. **Dishabituation** occurs when an organism begins to respond more intensely to a stimulus to which it has previously habituated. Let's return to our example of the worker in the hallway. Although you find the hammering distracting at first, you soon habituate to the sound. Then, after several minutes of ignoring the steady hammering, you hear a new sound. The worker has turned on a radio at a rather high volume. Will you ignore this sound, too? No, you likely will not. Because the quality of the stimulus has changed dramatically, you will dishabituate. You will again find yourself orienting toward the hallway. This new sound is too dissimilar to the hammering, and you have to check it out. Once you recognize that it is the worker's radio (and that it poses no threat), you will likely habituate to this new sound as well as to the hammering.

A change in the quality of the stimulus is not the only thing that can cause dishabituation. So can the passage of time. For instance, if the worker took an hour-long lunch break

dishabituation [DIS-huh-bit-chew-AYE-shun] to begin re-responding to a stimulus to which one has been habituated and then went back to hammering, you might briefly dishabituate to the hammering. This would not last long, however—after just a few bangs of the hammer, you would reenter habituation and return your attention to the lecture. As you can see, adaptive functioning is a balance of responding—habituating and dishabituating at the appropriate time.

Practical Applications of Habituation

One practical application of habituation is the use of habituation training for people who suffer from chronic motion sickness, or vertigo. For some vertigo sufferers, simple tasks like working at a computer may be impossible. Physical therapists often use habituation techniques to help people overcome chronic motion sickness. By repeatedly exposing clients to the stimulation that produces motion sickness, the therapist can gradually train these clients to habituate, or stop responding, to some of the visual and vestibular signals that would normally cause them to feel sick (Yardley & Kirby, 2006). Similar techniques have been used to train pilots and astronauts to do their jobs without experiencing motion sickness (e.g., Bagshaw, 1985).

Habituation is quite important to everyday life, but it is still a very simple type of learning. Habituation does not explain the bulk of the learning that we engage in during our lifetime, such as learning to play tennis or ride a bike. Nor does habituation explain how we come to associate certain emotions and physiological reactions with certain stimuli, such as learning to fear snakes or feeling happy when we smell Grandma's perfume. For explanations of these more complex events, we will have to turn our attention to more sophisticated and complex types of learning, discussed in the next section.

Let's Review!

This section has given you an overview of the simplest type of learning, habituation, and the related concepts of orienting reflexes and dishabituation. For a quick check of your understanding, answer these questions.

1. Which of the following is an example of habituation?
   a. Juan was teasing the family dog when it bit him. Because of the pain of the bite, Juan learned not to tease the dog again.
   b. Teresa was trying to learn to knit. At first, Teresa had to consciously think about what she was doing, but after practicing for 3 hours, Teresa could knit without thinking about it.
   c. Janel just bought a new puppy. At first, the dog's barking was distracting to Janel as she tried to watch TV, but after a while Janel did not notice the puppy's barking.
   d. Kerry loved her boyfriend very much. Now that they have broken up, every time she hears his favorite song on the radio, Kerry starts to cry.

2. Fido the puppy tilts his head up and sniffs the air as he smells his owner cooking dinner in the kitchen. Fido is exhibiting _____.
   a. habituation
   b. dishabituation
   c. an orienting reflex
   d. a & c

3. Which of the following would likely have the capacity for habituation?
   a. A 3-month-old human baby
   b. An adult monkey
   c. An adult dog
   d. All of the above

Answers 1. c; 2. c; 3. d

Classical Conditioning: Learning Through the Association of Stimuli

- Describe Pavlov's studies of classical conditioning.
- Define classical conditioning and discuss the factors that affect it.
- Explain how classical conditioning occurs in humans.
- Describe the process through which classically conditioned responses are removed.

The discovery of classical conditioning was something of an accident. In Russia around the turn of the 20th century, a physiologist named Ivan Pavlov (1849–1936) was doing research on the digestive processes of dogs (for which he would eventually win a Nobel Prize). Pavlov was investigating the role that salivation plays in digestion. He had surgically implanted devices in the cheeks of dogs so that he could measure how much saliva they produced. His experimental method was to place the dog in a harness, present the dog with some food, and then measure the amount of saliva the dog produced (see ■ FIGURE 5.1).

While conducting these studies, Pavlov noticed that sometimes the dogs began to salivate *before* the food was presented to them. Sometimes the mere sight of the food dish or the sound of the approaching experimenter was enough to produce salivation. So what was going on here? Why would a dog start to salivate when it heard footsteps or saw an empty food bowl? Pavlov reasoned that the dog had learned to *associate* certain cues or stimuli with the presentation of food. To the dog, the approach of footsteps had come to mean that food was soon going to appear. Consequently, the dog had become *conditioned*, or taught, to respond to the footsteps the same way that it responded to the food—by salivating. Unwittingly, Pavlov had discovered a learning process, one that became extremely influential in psychology.

Pavlov began to investigate the learning process itself. He systematically paired different stimuli with food to see which could be conditioned to produce the reflexive response of salivation. In one of these investigations, Pavlov sounded a buzzer just before he gave the dog some food. He repeated these trials several times while measuring the amount of saliva the dog produced. After repeated pairing of the buzzer and the food, the dog soon began to salivate on hearing the buzzer—even on trials in which *the food was not presented after the buzzer sounded!* The dog had become conditioned to associate the buzzer with the presentation of food. As a result, the buzzer had taken on the same power as food to cause the dog to salivate.

unconditioned stimulus (US) a stimulus that naturally elicits a response in an organism

unconditioned response (UR) the response that is elicited by an unconditioned stimulus

neutral stimulus (NS) a stimulus that does not naturally elicit an unconditioned response in an organism

FIGURE 5.1 Pavlov's Original Experiment

The dog was held in the harness and food was placed before it. The presence of the food (unconditioned stimulus, or US) caused the dog to salivate (unconditioned response, or UR). After a while, cues in the laboratory situation (lights, sounds, or sights) became conditioned stimuli (CS) that also caused the dog to salivate (conditioned response, or CR).

The Elements of Classical Conditioning

conditioned stimulus (CS) a stimulus that elicits a conditioned response in an organism

conditioned response (CR) the response that is elicited by a conditioned stimulus

The process of learning that Pavlov discovered is commonly referred to as *classical conditioning*, or *Pavlovian conditioning*. We will define it in a minute, but first let's look at the process that produces a conditioned response.

1. *The Unconditioned Stimulus and Response.* In order to classically condition a person or animal, you must begin with a stimulus that naturally and reliably causes some response in the organism. Because this stimulus naturally causes the reflexive response, it is referred to as an **unconditioned stimulus (US)**, and the response it evokes is called an **unconditioned response (UR)**. The term *unconditioned* refers to the fact that the association between the stimulus and the response is not learned. In Pavlov's case, the food was the unconditioned stimulus, and salivation was the unconditioned response. You do not need to teach a dog to salivate when food is presented. Instead, salivation occurs naturally when a dog sees food. ■ TABLE 5.1 gives some more examples of US–UR pairs that could be used in classical conditioning.

2. *The Neutral Stimulus.* The next step is the selection of a **neutral stimulus (NS)** that does *not* naturally elicit the unconditioned response. In Pavlov's case, the neutral stimulus used was a buzzer. Prior to training or conditioning, a dog would not be likely to salivate when it heard a buzzer. Therefore the buzzer is said to be *neutral.* It has no power to naturally cause the UR.

3. *Pairing the Neutral and Unconditioned Stimuli.* The third step is to systematically pair the neutral stimulus with the unconditioned stimulus. Pavlov accomplished this by repeatedly sounding the buzzer (NS) just prior to presenting the dog with the food (US). Through this repeated association of the US and the NS, the NS eventually loses its neutrality. In Pavlov's case, the dog began to salivate when the buzzer was presented without the food. At this point, classical conditioning had occurred because the buzzer was no longer neutral. The buzzer had become a **conditioned stimulus (CS)** that had the power to produce the **conditioned response (CR)** of salivation (■ FIGURE 5.2).

Summing up classical conditioning in a nice, neat definition is a bit awkward but nonetheless extremely important. Once, when one of us asked a student to define classical conditioning, she replied, "What Pavlov did with his dogs." This isn't, of course, a definition of classical conditioning. It does reflect the

Table 5.1 Some Examples of US-UR Pairs

Unconditioned Stimulus (US)	Unconditioned Response (UR)	
A puff of air to the eye	Eye blink	
Ingestion of a toxin	Nausea	
Being stuck with a pin	Flinching away from pin	
Sour food placed on the tongue	Salivation	
A light shone in the eye	Pupil contraction	
A blow to the knee	Knee-jerk reflex	

Michael L. Abramson/Time Life Pictures/Getty Images

© David Young-Wolff/ PhotoEdit

Jose Luis Pelaez/ Getty Images

Medioimages/Photodisc/Getty Images

Altrendo images/Getty Images

Michael Donne/Photo Researchers, Inc.

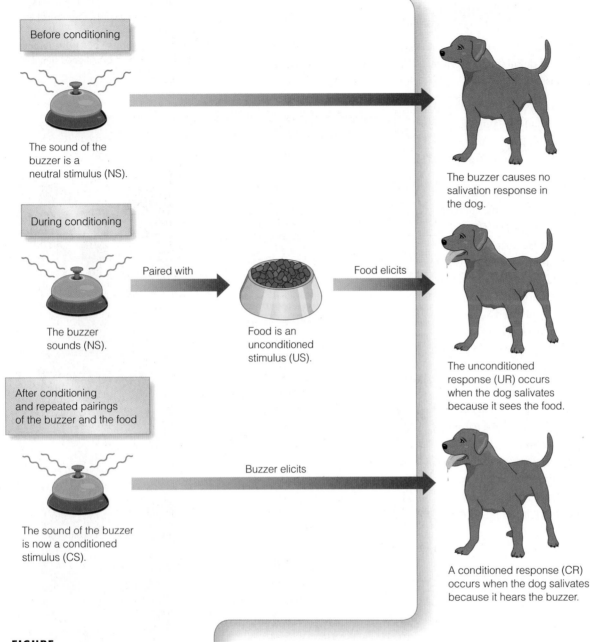

Before conditioning

The sound of the buzzer is a neutral stimulus (NS).

The buzzer causes no salivation response in the dog.

During conditioning

The buzzer sounds (NS).

Paired with

Food is an unconditioned stimulus (US).

Food elicits

The unconditioned response (UR) occurs when the dog salivates because it sees the food.

After conditioning and repeated pairings of the buzzer and the food

The sound of the buzzer is now a conditioned stimulus (CS).

Buzzer elicits

A conditioned response (CR) occurs when the dog salivates because it hears the buzzer.

FIGURE

5.2

Pavlov's Classical Conditioning Procedure

Before conditioning, the neutral stimulus has no power to cause the response. After repeated pairings of the neutral stimulus with an unconditioned stimulus, which naturally elicits an unconditioned response, the neutral stimulus becomes a conditioned stimulus with the power to elicit the response—now called the conditioned response.

student's difficulty in trying to understand the concept of classical conditioning apart from Pavlov's particular demonstration of it, however. Keep in mind that to truly understand a concept, you must be able to define it in abstract terms as well as give an example of it. So here goes.

We would define **classical conditioning** as *learning that occurs when a neutral stimulus is paired with an unconditioned stimulus that reliably causes an unconditioned response, and because of this association, the neutral stimulus loses its neutrality and takes on the same power as the unconditioned stimulus to cause the response.* This definition may seem a bit complex, but classical conditioning is actually a fairly simple process. It merely involves learning to associate two stimuli, the unconditioned stimulus and the neutral stimulus. Through this association, the neutral stimulus becomes a conditioned stimulus (■ YOU REVIEW 5.1). In the next section, we will examine some of the factors that affect the strength of the association.

Classical Conditioning   **You Review 5.1**

Abbreviation	Term	Definition
US	Unconditioned stimulus	A stimulus that naturally and reliably evokes a response in the person or animal
UR	Unconditioned response	The response that is naturally and reliably elicited by the unconditioned stimulus
NS	Neutral stimulus	A stimulus that does not initially elicit the unconditioned response in the person or animal
CS	Conditioned stimulus	A stimulus that was once neutral but, through association with the unconditioned stimulus, now has the power to elicit the response in the animal or person
CR	Conditioned response	After conditioning has occurred, the response that is elicited in the person or animal by the conditioned stimulus

Factors Affecting Classical Conditioning

Exactly what is being learned in classical conditioning? We said that the organism learns to associate the NS/CS with the US. This is true, but what is the nature of this association? Why do these two particular stimuli become associated? Why did Pavlov's dog associate the buzzer with the food instead of associating other stimuli from the situation with the food? Why didn't the dog begin to salivate when it heard the laboratory door open, or when the laboratory lights turned on? Why did it wait for the buzzer? To answer these questions, psychological researchers have experimentally examined different facets of the relationship between the NS/CS and the US.

RELATIONSHIP IN TIME: CONTIGUITY

One variable that emerged from this research as an important factor in classical conditioning is contiguity. **Contiguity** refers to the degree to which the NS/CS and US occur close together in time. Generally speaking, for classical conditioning to occur, the NS/CS and the US must be separated by only a short period of time (Klein, 1987; Wasserman & Miller, 1997). If the interval between the presentation of the NS/CS and the US is too long, the two stimuli will not be associated, and conditioning will not occur. If Pavlov had sounded the buzzer and then 3 hours later given the dog some food, imagine what would have happened. It is very unlikely that the dog would have been conditioned to salivate when it heard the buzzer!

Studies have shown that in most cases, if the US lags behind the NS/CS by more than a few seconds, conditioning will not be as strong as it could have been (Church & Black, 1958;

classical conditioning learning that occurs when a neutral stimulus is repeatedly paired with an unconditioned stimulus; because of this pairing, the neutral stimulus becomes a conditioned stimulus with the same power as the unconditioned stimulus to elicit the response in the organism

contiguity [con-teh-GYU-eh-tee] the degree to which two stimuli occur close together in time

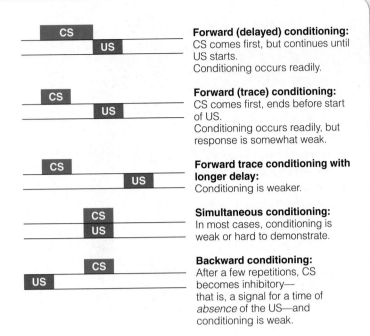

Forward (delayed) conditioning:
CS comes first, but continues until US starts.
Conditioning occurs readily.

Forward (trace) conditioning:
CS comes first, ends before start of US.
Conditioning occurs readily, but response is somewhat weak.

Forward trace conditioning with longer delay:
Conditioning is weaker.

Simultaneous conditioning:
In most cases, conditioning is weak or hard to demonstrate.

Backward conditioning:
After a few repetitions, CS becomes inhibitory—that is, a signal for a time of *absence* of the US—and conditioning is weak.

FIGURE

5.3

Possible Placements of the CS and the US in Classical Conditioning

Relative positions of the CS and US are shown for five different versions of classical conditioning: forward delayed, forward trace, forward trace with longer delay, simultaneous, and backward conditioning.

Noble & Harding, 1963; Smith, Coleman, & Gormezano, 1969). The exact length of the optimal time interval varies depending on what response is being conditioned.

Another aspect of contiguity is the relative placement of the NS/CS and the US in time—in other words, whether the NS/CS precedes the US or follows it. Imagine if Pavlov had first given the dog the food and *then* sounded the buzzer. In that case the dog would not have been as likely to associate the food with the buzzer. ■ FIGURE 5.3 shows the five major ways to place the NS/CS and the US in classical conditioning. Of these placements, *delayed conditioning* produces the strongest conditioning, and *backward conditioning* produces the weakest conditioning (Klein, 1987).

CONSISTENCY AND RELIABILITY: CONTINGENCY

Although contiguity is necessary for conditioning, it alone does not guarantee that conditioning will occur. Conditioning also requires **contingency**, which refers to the degree to which the NS/CS reliably signals that the US is going to be presented. If the NS/CS does not reliably predict the onset of the US, then conditioning will not occur (Bolles, 1972; Rescorla, 1967). For example, if Pavlov had sometimes fed the dog after sounding the buzzer and sometimes fed the dog without sounding the buzzer, conditioning would have been weakened. This inconsistency would not send the dog a clear message that the buzzer meant food was coming. Therefore, the dog would be less likely to salivate on hearing the buzzer. Given that both contiguity and contingency are necessary for strong classical conditioning, the best way to ensure strong conditioning is to consistently present only one NS/CS immediately before presenting the US.

The process of classical conditioning seems a bit complex, doesn't it? It also seems as if it could occur only in a laboratory (where stimuli could be systematically paired)—but this is not true. Classical conditioning occurs frequently in everyday life. In fact, each of us has probably felt the effects of classical conditioning many times. For example, we have been classically conditioned to have certain emotional reactions in our lives. You may feel happy when you smell a perfume that reminds you of your mother. You may feel fear when you see a snake.

As we look at classical conditioning in the real world, keep in mind the general definition of classical conditioning, and try to generate your own examples of real-world classical conditioning. By doing this, you will increase your understanding and retention of this material—both of which will help you on exam day!

Real-World Classical Conditioning

As you will recall, the starting point for classical conditioning is a preexisting US–UR relationship. Because of the nature of most unconditioned stimulus–unconditioned response relationships (see Table 5.1), the types of responses that can be classically conditioned usually fall into two categories: *emotional responses* and *physiological responses*.

CLASSICAL CONDITIONING OF EMOTIONAL RESPONSES

The classical conditioning of emotional responses was clearly demonstrated in a famous—now infamous—set of experiments conducted by John B. Watson and his student Rosalie Rayner in the early 1900s (Watson & Rayner, 1920). Watson set out to show that classical conditioning could be used to condition fear responses in a child. Because Watson used

contingency [con-TINGE-en-see] the degree to which the presentation of one stimulus reliably predicts the presentation of the other an 11-month-old boy named Albert, the experiments are now commonly referred to as the "Little Albert" experiments.

In the Little Albert experiments, Watson classically conditioned Albert to fear a white rat. To do this, Watson first gave Albert a white lab rat and allowed him to play with it. In the beginning, the rat was an NS for Albert because it did not cause him to be afraid. A few minutes after giving Albert the rat, Watson made a very loud noise by striking a piece of metal with a hammer. As with most 11-month-olds, a loud noise such as this was a US for Albert that reliably produced the UR of frightening Albert and making him cry. Over and over, Watson repeated this sequence of presenting the rat (NS), then making the noise (US), with the result that Albert would become afraid and cry (UR).

Can you see the parallels here between what Watson and Rayner were doing to Albert and what Pavlov did with his dogs? In the same way that Pavlov conditioned his dogs to salivate at the sound of the buzzer, Watson conditioned Albert to fear a white rat by associating the rat with a frightening noise. After several trials of pairing the noise and the rat, all Watson had to do to get Albert to cry was to show him the rat. Because the rat had been paired with the noise, the rat lost its neutrality and became a CS that was able to evoke the CR of fear.

In the Little Albert experiments, John B. Watson and his assistant, Rosalie Rayner, classically conditioned Albert to fear a white lab rat.

Emotional reactions such as fear are also classically conditioned outside of the laboratory. For example, one of us once had a professor who had an intense fear of bees because earlier in his life, several bees had stung him after he accidentally disturbed a beehive. In this case of classical conditioning, the multiple bee stings were a US that elicited the UR of fear. The bees were initially an NS, but because they were paired with the bee stings, they became a CS that could produce the CR of fear. From that day onward, all the professor had to do was to see a bee to feel intense fear.

In fact, the professor's fear of bees was so great that it spread to other insects as well. Not only was he afraid of bees, he was also afraid of wasps, yellow jackets, and any other flying insect that could sting. In psychological terms, his fear had undergone **stimulus generalization**, which occurs when stimuli that are similar to the CS have the same power to elicit the CR even though they have never been paired with the US. The professor had never been stung by a wasp, yet he feared them because they are similar to bees.

Stimulus generalization also occurred in the Little Albert experiments. After being conditioned to fear the rat, Albert also exhibited fear when presented with a dog, a rabbit, a fur coat, and a fake white Santa Claus beard. His fear of white rats had generalized to several furry things (Watson & Rayner, 1920). This may leave you wondering what happened to Little Albert. Did he suffer through life as a result of his conditioned phobias? Unfortunately, not much is known about Albert's fate. His mother withdrew him from the program and moved away before Watson and colleagues could remove the fear they had conditioned in Albert—leaving future psychologists to debate the ethics of Watson and Rayner's research.

Unlike what happened to Little Albert, all classically conditioned responses do not necessarily generalize. The opposite process, **stimulus discrimination**, often occurs. In stimulus discrimination, the conditioned response occurs in response to a particular conditioned stimulus, but it does not occur in response to other stimuli that are similar to the conditioned stimulus. For instance, a woman who works in the reptile house at the zoo is probably not afraid of most

stimulus generalization responding in a like fashion to similar stimuli

stimulus discrimination responding only to particular stimuli

Phobias are classically conditioned responses. A fear-producing encounter with a stimulus can result in the stimulus—a needle—becoming a conditioned stimulus that elicits fear.

snakes, but if she found herself face to face with a poisonous king cobra, she would likely feel afraid. Sometimes, knowing when to discriminate and when to generalize is important to survival!

CLASSICAL CONDITIONING OF PHYSIOLOGICAL RESPONSES: TASTE AVERSION

Emotions are not the only responses that can be classically conditioned. Pavlov's original demonstrations of classical conditioning show a physiological response, salivation. But what other kinds of physiological responses can be classically conditioned? Table 5.1 (p. 163) gives a list of some of the US–UR relationships that could form the basis of classical conditioning. Of these, one of the most important and common is the classical conditioning of nausea.

Have you ever eaten a food that you liked and soon after become sick to your stomach with the flu, food poisoning, motion sickness, or some other ailment? Then, after recovering from your sickness, did you find the sight, smell, or even the idea of that food nauseating? If you answered "yes" to both of these questions, you have experienced what psychologists call classically conditioned **taste aversion**.

One of the authors can vividly remember going through this type of conditioning as a child. After she ate a big dessert of peppermint ice cream, she came down with a severe case of tonsillitis that was accompanied by nausea and vomiting. After she recovered from the tonsillitis, it was *years* before she could even think about peppermint ice cream without feeling queasy. The same author regularly holds an informal contest in her classes to see who has had the longest-running taste aversion. The current record stands at more than 20 years!

> ### You Asked...
>
> *Why are some things easier to learn than others?*   CHRISTIE KNIGHT, STUDENT

It seems that taste aversion is something that we learn with particular ease (Garcia & Koelling, 1966). Taste aversion is unique in two ways. First, it often occurs with only one pairing of the NS/CS and the US. Unlike most cases of classical conditioning, in taste aversion a single pairing of the food (NS/CS) and the virus (US) is usually sufficient to cause strong conditioning. The second difference is that in taste aversion, the interval between the NS/CS and the US can be very long. Intervals as long as 24 hours can result in conditioning (Garcia, Ervin, & Koelling, 1966; Logue, 1979). Because taste aversion is an exception to some of the rules of conditioning, some psychologists believe that our genes biologically predispose or prepare us to learn taste aversion easily (Seligman, 1970).

By learning taste aversion easily, we are better able to avoid certain poisonous plants and substances. Once something has made us sick, we want no part of it in the future. No doubt the ability to learn taste aversion quickly, and consequently to avoid poisonous substances, has survival value. Therefore, through natural selection, genes that enabled our ancestors to learn taste aversion quickly would have been retained because animals with those genes—human and non-human—would have lived, whereas those with a sluggish response to taste aversion would likely die. Taste aversion is widely seen in many species of animals (Garcia, 1992).

In fact, because many other species are also susceptible to taste aversion, it can be used to help control the pesky nature of some animals. In the western United States, coyotes like to sneak into sheep pastures and kill sheep rather than hunt for food in the wild. In the past, frustrated sheep ranchers would be very tempted to either shoot the coyotes on sight or poison them. But thanks to psychologists, ranchers now have a more humane and ecologically sound alternative—using taste aversion to condition the coyotes to dislike sheep as a food source. They slaughter a few sheep and treat

taste aversion classical conditioning that occurs when an organism pairs the experience of nausea with a certain food and becomes conditioned to feel ill at the sight, smell, or idea of the food

Classically conditioned taste aversions can be used to change the food preferences of many people and animals, including coyotes.

© Stuart Ellins

their carcasses with a chemical that causes nausea in coyotes. These tainted carcasses are then left out for the coyotes to eat. Because the coyotes can't pass up a free meal, they eat the sheep and get very sick to their stomachs. After they recover, they want nothing to do with sheep because of conditioned taste aversion (Gustavson & Garcia, 1974)!

YOUR TURN – ACTIVE LEARNING

You can use taste aversion to help yourself eat more healthily. Think of a food that you frequently overindulge in, but wish you wouldn't (e.g., pizza, candy). Several times a day, imagine a delicious serving of this food. While thinking of this food, also think of something disgusting such as a bunch of worms squirming on your chosen food. If you repeat this procedure for several weeks, you may find yourself less motivated to indulge in this food! In a different approach, psychologists have classically conditioned children to like healthful vegetables by pairing new vegetable flavors with the flavor of sugar to produce liking. After repeatedly pairing the vegetables (NS/CS) with pleasant-tasting sugar (US), the children were conditioned to also like the vegetables (UR/CR). After conditioning, the children exhibited liking for the vegetables even when sugar was not present (Havermans & Jansen, 2007). So, initially sprinkling a little brown sugar on carrots might be just the ticket to get children to willingly eat their carrots in the future.

Psychology Applies to Your World:

Using Taste Aversion to Help People

Taste aversion is also applicable in several therapeutic settings. One such application is in the treatment of alcoholism. The idea behind this **aversion therapy** is to condition a taste aversion to alcohol. The client takes the drug Antabuse. If he or she then drinks alcohol, the result is intense nausea and headache, which often leads to conditioned taste aversion. One of the authors' (Doyle-Portillo's) father underwent such a treatment for his alcoholism. As a result of the treatment, the smell of any alcohol made him nauseous. Family members even had to stop wearing alcohol-based cologne in his presence for fear of making him sick!

Aversion therapy has been shown to be modestly helpful in motivating people with alcoholism to remain abstinent (Smith, Frawley, & Polissar, 1997). However, it does not represent a "cure" for alcoholism. In one study, only 20% of the people with alcoholism tested remained abstinent for 1 year after being treated with aversion therapy alone (Landabaso et al., 1999). So, although aversion therapy may be a useful part of a comprehensive treatment program, it should not be the only treatment used for alcoholism (Finn, 2003; Hunt, 2002).

(continued)

© Martyn F. Chilmaid/Photo Researchers, Inc.

Therapists can use classically conditioned taste aversion to help people who suffer from alcoholism overcome their desire to drink.

aversion therapy a type of therapy that uses classical conditioning to condition people to avoid certain stimuli

Another application of taste aversion is in helping people undergoing chemotherapy for cancer and other diseases. Chemotherapy drugs often cause intense nausea. If a patient receiving chemotherapy experiences nausea after eating foods that he would normally eat, there is a strong possibility that he will develop a conditioned taste aversion to those foods. This could severely affect the quality of the patient's life both during and after undergoing chemotherapy as he may develop multiple taste aversions over the course of treatment. One solution to this problem is to give the patient a novel food prior to undergoing chemotherapy. Because novel flavors are more easily associated with feelings of illness than familiar flavors are (c.f., Batsell, 2000), novel foods can act as *scapegoats* for the patients' regularly eaten foods. For example, patients given *halva* (a Middle Eastern sweet; Andresen, Birch, & Johnson, 1990) or strongly flavored candy (Broberg & Bernstein, 1987) prior to undergoing chemotherapy later experienced less taste aversion for the foods of their regular diet. Because the novel foods eaten just prior to chemotherapy were more strongly associated with their nausea, the patients' conditioned taste aversion for the novel foods was stronger than that for the familiar foods. Because novel foods can be easily avoided, the patients should be better able to resume their normal eating patterns after chemotherapy.

By having chemotherapy patients consume a *scapegoat* food prior to undergoing chemotherapy, doctors can help ensure that the taste aversion patients suffer after chemotherapy is for the scapegoat food and not for their normal diet.

Extinction of Classically Conditioned Responses

Let's assume that you had the misfortune of developing a classically conditioned taste aversion to your favorite food because you ate this food just before you became ill with the flu. Furthermore, let's assume that you wanted to be able to eat your favorite food again without feeling sick to your stomach. How would you go about ridding yourself of your acquired taste aversion?

In classical conditioning, **extinction**, or removal of the conditioned response, can be brought about by presenting the conditioned stimulus to the participant without also presenting the unconditioned stimulus. In our example, extinction would begin when you ate your favorite food (CS) and you did not have the flu (US). When the CS is presented alone, it no longer predicts the onset of the US, and the CR decreases. Years later, your author finally got over her taste aversion to peppermint ice cream after she took a job in a restaurant that sold a great deal of it. After scooping many scoops of peppermint ice cream, she found that the sight and smell of it no longer made her feel sick. It wasn't long before she was even able to eat peppermint ice cream without a problem.

Pavlov's experiments with dogs also included extinction trials with the dogs. ■ FIGURE 5.4 shows the **acquisition**, or learning, curve for the CR and the extinction curve for the CR in Pavlov's experiment. As you can see from this figure, the CR of salivation to the buzzer was acquired over several trials in which the CS and the US were paired. In the extinction trials, the buzzer was sounded but no food was presented, and there was a fairly steady decrease in the CR. In other words, the dog became less and less likely to salivate when it heard the buzzer.

> **You Asked...**
>
> *Once you learn something, how long does it stick with you if you never use what you learn? Will it still last for a while, or does it fade quickly?*   TYLER LARKO, STUDENT

extinction the removal of a conditioned response

acquisition the process of learning a conditioned response or behavior

spontaneous recovery during extinction, the tendency for a conditioned response to reappear and strengthen over a brief period of time before re-extinguishing

Does this mean that once a response has been extinguished, it is gone forever? Note that the extinction curve in Figure 5.4 does not show a completely continuous pattern of decrease in the CR. Sometimes, after a response has been extinguished, there will be a temporary increase in the CR. This phenomenon, called **spontaneous recovery**, can occur at any point during extinction (e.g., Troisi, 2003), or even after the response has been completely extinguished. Let's go back to our example of taste aversion for peppermint ice cream. Today, although your author does not have an active, ongoing taste aversion for peppermint ice cream, every now and again when she thinks of peppermint ice cream, she will feel a bit sick. Thankfully, her spontaneous recovery doesn't last long. She soon reenters extinction, and she can think of peppermint ice cream and even eat it without a trace of nausea.

What do you suppose would happen if she happened to eat some peppermint ice cream on a hot day and suffered from a *small* amount of heat-induced nausea? Do you think her taste aversion to peppermint ice cream would return? It is likely that it would. In fact, responses that are extinguished are usually reacquired more easily than they were acquired in the first place. Extinction does *not* mean that we forget that there once was a connection between the CS and the US; it simply means that the CR is less likely to occur when the CS is presented.

So far, we have seen that learning can occur through habituation and classical conditioning—learning processes that both result in rather simplistic behaviors. In the next section, we'll examine how we learn more complex behaviors through reward and punishment.

FIGURE

5.4 The Phases of Classical Conditioning

These plots show the number of conditioning trials on the *x* axis and the strength of the conditioned response on the *y* axis. During acquisition, the response increases in strength as a function of the number of times the CS and US have been paired together. During extinction, the CS is presented without the US, which leads to a decrease in the strength of the CR. Note that during extinction, sometimes there is a temporary increase in the strength of the CR even though the CS has not been recently presented with the US. This is called spontaneous recovery.

Let's Review!

This section has given you a brief overview of some of the important issues in classical conditioning. As a quick check of your understanding, answer these questions.

1. Which of the following is an example of classical conditioning?
   a. Damon learns to ride a bike by watching his older brother.
   b. Sally dislikes the smell of rose perfume because her crabby third-grade teacher used to wear rose perfume.
   c. After 20 minutes in the day-care center, Ralph barely notices the squealing of the children at play.
   d. Ted never speeds after receiving a $500 fine for speeding.

2. Which of the following is a US–UR pair?
   a. Receiving money–happiness
   b. An electric shock to the finger–jerking one's finger away
   c. Receiving a promotion–working overtime
   d. Seeing a snake–fear

3. Janna, a real estate agent, desperately wants to sell a home. She tells the owner to place a pan of vanilla extract in the oven and heat it just before the prospective buyers arrive to look at the house. Janna knows that the smell of vanilla in the house will increase the chance that the buyers will like the house because they have been classically conditioned to respond favorably to the smell of vanilla. In this example, what is the CR?
   a. The pleasant emotions evoked by the smell of vanilla
   b. The smell of vanilla
   c. The memory of Grandma baking cookies at Christmas
   d. The house

Answers 1. b; 2. b; 3. a

Stop, LOOK, and LEARN

Habituation: The Simplest Form of Learning

Habituation occurs when we stop responding to repetitive stimuli.

Dishabituation occurs when we resume orienting to a stimulus to which we had previously habituated.

Orienting reflexes cause us to automatically respond to unexpected stimuli.

Classical Conditioning: The Conditioning of Emotional and Physiological Responses

Unconditioned Stimulus

Being with your significant other

Unconditioned Response

You feel happy

Neutral Stimulus + Unconditioned Stimulus

Your significant other's cologne + Being with your significant other

Unconditioned Response

You feel happy

Conditioned Stimulus

Your significant other's cologne

Conditioned Response

You feel happy

Bruce Laurance/Getty Images

Operant Conditioning: Learning From the Consequences of Our Actions

- Explain the law of effect and the experiments that led to its discovery.

- Describe the contributions that B. F. Skinner made to the study of operant conditioning.

- Describe the phases of operant conditioning.

- Describe the factors that affect the process of operant conditioning.

- Describe generalization, discrimination, and shaping as they relate to operant conditioning.

- Describe the decisions that must be made when applying operant conditioning in the real world.

Learning Objectives

Suppose you are sitting in your psychology class, listening to a lecture, when your professor asks the class a question. For some reason, you raise your hand to answer the question even though you have never made a comment in this class before. The professor calls on you, and you give the correct answer. In response to your answer, the professor smiles broadly and praises you for giving such an accurate and insightful answer.

How do you think this scenario would affect you? As a result of the professor's reaction, would you be more or less likely to raise your hand in the future when she asked a question? If you are like most people, this type of praise would indeed encourage you to raise your hand in the future. But what would happen if, instead of praising you, she frowned and said that your answer was one of the stupidest she had ever heard. How would this reaction affect your behavior? Obviously, after such a cruel response, many of us would be very unlikely to answer any more questions in that professor's class!

Both of these examples illustrate another type of learning, called **operant conditioning**. In operant conditioning, *we learn from the consequences of our behavior*. In our example, being praised for answering a question makes one more likely to answer questions in the future; being called "stupid" makes one less likely to answer future questions. We will see that operant conditioning is a powerful means of learning that explains how we learn many of the important lessons in our lives. But first, we will begin by looking at how operant conditioning was discovered.

operant conditioning a type of learning in which the organism learns through the consequences of its behavior

E. L. Thorndike's Law of Effect

At about the same time that Ivan Pavlov was developing his theories about learning in Russia, American psychologist E. L. Thorndike (1874–1949) was busy conducting experiments on operant conditioning in New York. Thorndike was working with cats in specially constructed *puzzle boxes*. A puzzle box is a box with a lid or door that locks into place so that an animal can be locked inside. Once inside the box, the animal must activate some type of unlatching device to win its release. The device that unlatches the lid may be a rope pull, a pedal that needs to be pushed, or a switch that needs to be flipped. ■ FIGURE 5.5 shows a typical puzzle box with a foot-pedal release.

UNLOCKING THE PUZZLE OF LEARNING

In his research, E. L. Thorndike (1898) locked a hungry cat in one of these puzzle boxes and placed some food outside the box. Then he recorded how long it took the cat to figure out how to get out of the box. Once the cat activated the device and got out of the box, Thorndike would take the cat and place it back in the puzzle box. Over and over, Thorndike repeated this procedure of imprisoning the cat and measuring the time it took the cat to win its release.

FIGURE

5.5 Puzzle Box

This is an example of a puzzle box like those used by Thorndike. To get out of the box, the cat would have to pull the string or step on the pedal.

Thorndike observed in these studies that when the cat was first placed in the puzzle box, it thrashed around randomly until, by accident, it tripped the mechanism and got out of the box. However, after several more trials, the cat's behavior became less random, and the time it took to get out of the box declined. This decrease in the amount of time it took the cat to get out of the box indicated to Thorndike that *learning* was taking place: The cat was learning to associate its behavior with the consequences that its behavior brought about.

Based on what he observed in his puzzle box studies, Thorndike developed a principle of learning that he called the **law of effect**. The law of effect states that *in a given situation, behaviors that lead to positive, satisfying consequences will be strengthened, such that the next time the situation occurs, the behavior is more likely to be repeated*. In addition, the law of effect also states that *in a given situation, behaviors that lead to negative, discomforting consequences will be weakened, such that the next time the situation occurs, the behavior will be less likely to be repeated* (Thorndike, 1905).

RANDOM ACTIONS AND REINFORCEMENT

Let's examine the law of effect in terms of a hungry cat in a puzzle box. When the cat is first trapped in the box, it will likely perform many random behaviors. For instance, it may claw, hiss, bite at the bars, roll over on its back, or meow. But none of these behaviors will open the box. The cat's early responses to being stuck in the box are random or "trial-and-error." After some time, let's say that the cat happens to step on the foot pedal that opens the puzzle box and is able to get out to where the food is waiting. This particular random behavior has led to a consequence that is far more rewarding than any of the other random behaviors the cat has tried. The law of effect states that this particular response is strengthened, or *reinforced*, because it results in a reward. This process of **reinforcement** means that the rewarded behavior will become more likely in the future. The next time the cat is locked in the box, it will be more likely to step on the pedal than to try the other behaviors that did not lead to release on prior trials. Over many trials, the law of effect results in the cat's becoming more and more likely to step on the pedal and less and less likely to use other behaviors that were not reinforced in the past. The behaviors that were not rewarded—and therefore not reinforced—are likely to die out.

POSITIVE AND NEGATIVE REINFORCEMENT

The two types of reinforcement are *positive reinforcement* and *negative reinforcement* (see ■ YOU REVIEW 5.2). In **positive reinforcement**, the behavior leads to the *addition* of something pleasant to the organism's environment. For instance, Thorndike positively reinforced the cat for stepping on the pedal by giving the cat food when it got out of the puzzle box.

In **negative reinforcement**, the behavior is rewarded by the *removal* of something unpleasant from the organism's environment. In Thorndike's case, the cat was negatively reinforced for stepping on the pedal because this behavior led to the removal of its imprisonment in the puzzle box. (We are, of course, assuming that the hungry cat did *not* enjoy being trapped in the box.)

The difference between *punishment* and negative reinforcement is a point that gives many students great trouble because they tend to think that negative reinforcement is a type of punishment. This is not true! The "negative" in negative reinforcement refers to the fact that negative reinforcement *removes* something from the organism's environment; it does not refer to a negative or unpleasant consequence of the behavior. When you see the term *reinforcement*, keep in mind that reinforcement leads to an *increase* in behavior. **Punishment**, on the other hand, is an unpleasant consequence that leads to a *decrease* in behavior.

POSITIVE AND NEGATIVE PUNISHMENT

As you can see from You Review 5.2, punishment also comes in two varieties. **Positive punishment** occurs when a behavior results in the *addition* of something *unpleasant* to the organism's environment. For example, a puzzle box could be rigged to electrify the floor of the

law of effect a principle discovered by E. L. Thorndike, which states that random behaviors that lead to positive consequences will be strengthened and random behaviors that lead to negative consequences will be weakened

reinforcement the strengthening of a response that occurs when the response is rewarded

positive reinforcement strengthening a behavior by adding something pleasant to the environment of the organism

negative reinforcement reinforcing a behavior by removing something unpleasant from the environment of the organism

punishment the weakening of a response that occurs when a behavior leads to an unpleasant consequence

positive punishment weakening a behavior by adding something unpleasant to the organism's environment

The Four Consequences of Behavior   You Review 5.2

Reinforcement increases the likelihood of a behavior; punishment decreases it.

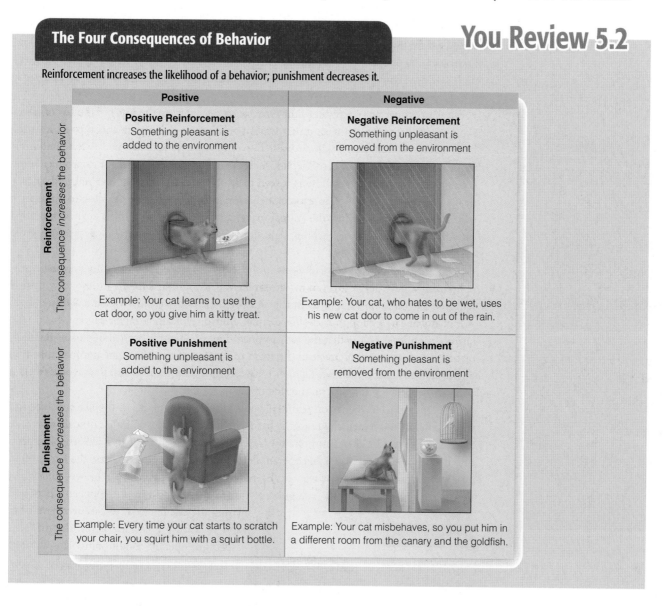

	Positive	**Negative**
Reinforcement — The consequence *increases* the behavior	**Positive Reinforcement** Something pleasant is added to the environment Example: Your cat learns to use the cat door, so you give him a kitty treat.	**Negative Reinforcement** Something unpleasant is removed from the environment Example: Your cat, who hates to be wet, uses his new cat door to come in out of the rain.
Punishment — The consequence *decreases* the behavior	**Positive Punishment** Something unpleasant is added to the environment Example: Every time your cat starts to scratch your chair, you squirt him with a squirt bottle.	**Negative Punishment** Something pleasant is removed from the environment Example: Your cat misbehaves, so you put him in a different room from the canary and the goldfish.

cage every time the cat stepped on the pedal. The cat would then be positively punished every time it stepped on the pedal because the resulting shock would add pain to the cat's environment.

In **negative punishment**, the behavior leads to the *removal* of something *pleasant* from the organism's environment. A puzzle box could be rigged so that when the cat presses the pedal, a drape falls over the cage, and the cat can no longer see outside the cage. If the cat enjoys seeing outside the cage, then stepping on the pedal would lead to negative punishment because it leads to the loss of a pleasant privilege for the cat. The effect of punishment is to decrease a behavior, regardless of whether the punishment is positive or negative.

B. F. Skinner and the Experimental Study of Operant Conditioning

Although E. L. Thorndike is generally credited with discovering the law of effect, American psychologist B. F. Skinner (1904–1990) is more commonly associated with the scientific study of operant conditioning. Skinner began to formally study operant conditioning

negative punishment weakening a behavior by removing something pleasant from the organism's environment in the late 1920s when he was a graduate student at Harvard University. During his long career—from the 1920s to the 1990s—Skinner made many significant contributions to our understanding of operant conditioning (Schultz & Schultz, 2000). Perhaps some of Skinner's most obvious contributions were to introduce new terminology and technology to the study of this type of learning.

It was Skinner who introduced the term *operant conditioning* to the study of the law of effect. Skinner felt that using the term *operant* was a good way to distinguish this type of learning from classical conditioning. Skinner wanted to emphasize the fact that in classical conditioning, the organism does not actively choose to operate on the environment to produce some consequence; rather, the response is forced from the animal. Thus, Skinner referred to classically conditioned behavior as *respondent* behavior. In contrast, Skinner wanted to emphasize that in operant conditioning, the animal makes a choice to respond to its environment in a certain way. In this type of learning, behavior *operates* on the environment to produce some consequence (Skinner, 1938).

Another of Skinner's contributions to the study of operant conditioning was the development of a new device that allows researchers to condition animals in less time than is required to condition an animal in a puzzle box. This device, now called a **Skinner box**, is a chamber large enough to house a small animal, typically a rat or pigeon. Inside the chamber is a lever or bar that the rat can press down. When the animal depresses the lever or bar, it receives reinforcement in the form of a pellet of food from an automatic feeding device attached to the chamber. Skinner boxes are also built for pigeons; the pigeon receives a reward by pecking at a disk on the side of the box.

To study operant behavior, Skinner would place a hungry rat in the Skinner box and wait for the rat to accidentally press the bar (which tends to happen rather quickly given the Skinner box's small size and simplicity). Once the rat pressed the bar, a pellet would drop into the chamber to reinforce this operant behavior. The rat was free to press the bar as often as it wanted and whenever it wanted. By recording the number of bar presses and when they occurred, Skinner could get a good picture of the acquisition of the operant behavior.

Using the Skinner box, researchers have been able to learn a great deal about the different aspects of operant conditioning. This advance in the methodology and apparatus for studying animal learning is one of B. F. Skinner's major contributions to psychology.

Photo Researchers, Inc. (both)

In these operant chambers, the animals can be reinforced with food for pressing the bar or pecking the disk. Skinner boxes such as these allow researchers to efficiently gather data on operant conditioning.

> ## You Asked...
>
> *Why do animals learn best through repetition?*   HEATHER LACIS, STUDENT

Skinner box a device created by B. F. Skinner to study operant behavior in a compressed time frame; in a Skinner box, an organism is automatically rewarded or punished for engaging in certain behaviors

Acquisition and Extinction

Two areas that Skinner explored were acquisition and extinction. You may recall from our discussion of classical conditioning that acquisition refers to the conditioning of a response and extinction refers to the loss of a conditioned response. As in classical conditioning, it is possible to plot acquisition and extinction curves for operantly conditioned behaviors. The rat learns that pressing the bar leads to obtaining food, and its tendency to press the bar increases. The intensity with which the rat presses the bar continues to increase until it reaches some maximum strength. For example, the rat can eat the pellets only so fast. Therefore, the number of times the rat will press the bar in a given time frame is limited by the speed at which it eats (■ FIGURE 5.6).

Extinction also occurs in operant conditioning, but it is caused by circumstances that differ from those that cause extinction in classical conditioning. In classical conditioning, extinction occurs because the CS is presented without the US. In operant conditioning, extinction occurs because the behavior is no longer reinforced (see Figure 5.6). Many of us hold jobs, and going to work is an example of an operantly conditioned response. We go to work because we expect to be reinforced for this behavior on payday. What would it take to extinguish your going-to-work behavior? The answer is simple, isn't it? All it would take is the removal of your reinforcement. If your boss stopped paying you, you would likely stop going to work! In operant conditioning, withholding the reinforcement that maintains the behavior causes the extinction of that behavior.

Like acquisition, extinction does not typically happen in one trial. Even if your boss failed to pay you on payday, you might very well return to work for a few days. In fact, you might even experience a temporary **extinction burst**, during which you worked *harder* in an attempt to obtain reward immediately after your boss withholds your pay (e.g., Galensky,

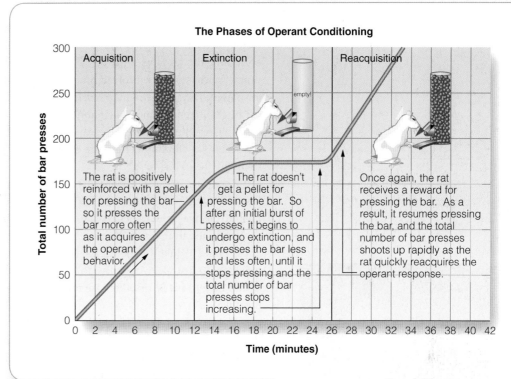

The Phases of Operant Conditioning

The rat is positively reinforced with a pellet for pressing the bar—so it presses the bar more often as it acquires the operant behavior.

The rat doesn't get a pellet for pressing the bar. So after an initial burst of presses, it begins to undergo extinction, and it presses the bar less and less often, until it stops pressing and the total number of bar presses stops increasing.

Once again, the rat receives a reward for pressing the bar. As a result, it resumes pressing the bar, and the total number of bar presses shoots up rapidly as the rat quickly reacquires the operant response.

FIGURE 5.6
Acquisition and Extinction in Operant Conditioning

Just as we saw in classical conditioning, operant responses can also undergo acquisition, extinction, and reacquisition.

Miltenberger, Stricker, & Garlinghouse, 2001). At the very least, you probably would not entirely abandon work until it became very clear that reinforcement would no longer be forthcoming. Extinction tends to occur over a number of trials. Each time the organism emits the operant response without being reinforced, its tendency to repeat the response diminishes (see Figure 5.6).

Because extinction removes responses, it has many practical applications. One way to stop someone from engaging in an annoying behavior is to extinguish it by removing the reinforcement for that behavior. Take the example of a parent and child shopping together in a department store. The child sees a toy that he wants, but his parent refuses to buy it. At this refusal, the child begins to whine and cry, but instead of punishing the child for this behavior, the parent ignores the child. By not reinforcing the whining and crying, the parent begins to extinguish this annoying behavior. Once the child learns that crying and whining do not lead to reward, the child will stop using this behavioral strategy to get what he wants.

The trick to using extinction to reduce unwanted behaviors is figuring out what is actually reinforcing the behavior, removing that reinforcement, and then making sure that no other reinforcement of the unwanted behavior is occurring (Martin & Pear, 2007). If Dad ignores the child's tantrums when he takes the child shopping but Mom gives in and buys the child toys, then the behavior will not be completely extinguished.

Schedules of Reinforcement

Acquisition and extinction of operant behavior seem simple enough, but numerous Skinner box studies have taught us that many factors can affect the rate at which responses are acquired or extinguished. One extremely important factor is the **schedule of reinforcement**—the timing and the consistency of the reinforcement.

extinction burst a temporary increase in a behavioral response that occurs immediately after extinction has begun
schedule of reinforcement the frequency and timing of the reinforcements that an organism receives

CONTINUOUS REINFORCEMENT

Conceptually, the simplest type of reinforcement schedule is **continuous reinforcement**, in which each and every instance of the desired behavior is rewarded. In a Skinner box study, every time the rat presses the bar, a pellet of food is delivered to the rat. In real life, many simple behaviors are reinforced on a continuous schedule. One example is when we reach for objects. The act of reaching is reinforced when we actually grasp the object we were trying to get. Except in unusual circumstances, such as reaching for an object on a shelf that is too high, reaching is rewarded every time we reach (Skinner, 1953). Unfortunately, continuous schedules of reinforcement are often not very helpful when using operant conditioning to modify behavior.

There are two main reasons that continuous reinforcement is often not very helpful. The first drawback is a practical one. Let's say that you were going to use continuous reinforcement to change a child's behavior. You want your child to be polite when speaking to others, so you decide to use a continuous schedule and reinforce your child with praise *every time* she is polite. Would this be feasible? We doubt it. A continuous schedule of reinforcement would mean that you would have to be around your child every time she was polite, and you would have to praise or otherwise reward her for this politeness. This just isn't practical or possible.

The second problem is that continuously reinforced behaviors are vulnerable to extinction. What happens when your children are not in your presence, and you are not there to continually reinforce their good behavior? As we have already seen, when reinforcement is withheld, behavior often starts to extinguish. The problem with using continuous schedules of reinforcement is that they lead to behaviors that extinguish very quickly once the reinforcement ceases (Nevin & Grace, 2005).

Why would this be true? When a behavior has been continuously reinforced, there is a very clear *contingency* between the behavior and the reward. The organism learns that the behavior should *always* lead to a reward. When the reinforcement stops, a clear signal is sent that the contingency no longer holds true, and extinction occurs relatively rapidly. If the behavior is reinforced only *some* of the time, the child or animal is less likely to see the lack of reinforcement as a sign that the contingency is no longer operating. Schedules of reinforcement that reinforce a behavior only some of the time are called **partial reinforcement schedules**. *Ratio schedules* of partial reinforcement are based on the number of responses, whereas *interval schedules* are based on the timing of the responses.

RATIO SCHEDULES OF REINFORCEMENT

In a **fixed ratio schedule**, a set number of responses must be emitted before a reward is given. For example, suppose every third response is rewarded. A rat in a Skinner box would have to press the bar three times to get a food pellet. In the real world, some people are paid on fixed ratio schedules. A person who works in a manufacturing plant and is paid a bonus for every 100 parts assembled is being reinforced on a fixed ratio, as are agricultural workers who are paid per bushel of fruit picked, garment workers who are paid per piece sewn, and so on.

Besides producing slower extinction than continuous reinforcement, fixed ratio schedules also lead to fairly high response rates (■ FIGURE 5.7a). High rates of responding are especially likely if it takes many responses to get a reward (Collier, Hirsch, & Hamlin, 1972; Stephens, Pear, Wray, & Jackson, 1975). If your goal is to produce many instances of the behavior, such as many filled boxes of raspberries, in a short time frame, a fixed ratio schedule may just do the trick.

The second type of ratio schedule is the **variable ratio schedule**, in which the exact number of responses that are required to receive a reward varies around some average. For example, the rat may have to press the bar two times to receive the first reward, one time to receive the second reward, and then six times to receive the third reward.

By ignoring this child's tantrum, the parent is placing the child on an extinction schedule. If the parent does not reward the child for this behavior, the behavior should be less likely to occur in the future, at least for this parent.

© Bob Daemmrich/PhotoEdit

continuous reinforcement a schedule of reinforcement in which the organism is rewarded for every instance of the desired response

partial reinforcement schedule a schedule of reinforcement in which the organism is rewarded for only some instances of the desired response

fixed ratio schedule a schedule of reinforcement in which the organism is rewarded for every *x*th instance of the desired response

variable ratio schedule a schedule of reinforcement in which the organism is rewarded on average for every *x*th instance of the desired response

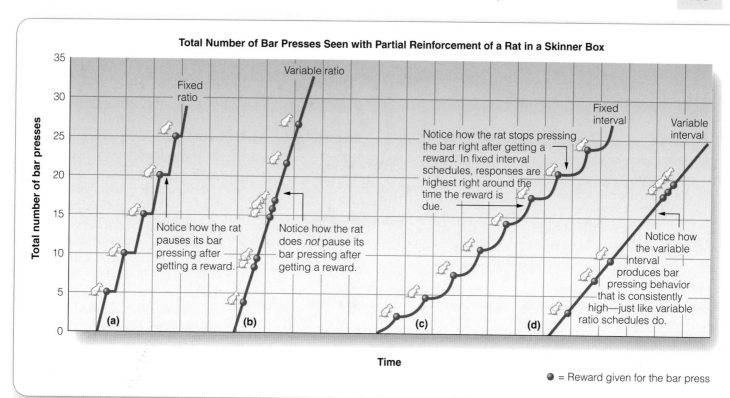

Total Number of Bar Presses Seen with Partial Reinforcement of a Rat in a Skinner Box

Fixed ratio

Variable ratio

Fixed interval

Variable interval

Notice how the rat pauses its bar pressing after getting a reward.

Notice how the rat does *not* pause its bar pressing after getting a reward.

Notice how the rat stops pressing the bar right after getting a reward. In fixed interval schedules, responses are highest right around the time the reward is due.

Notice how the variable interval produces bar pressing behavior that is consistently high—just like variable ratio schedules do.

Total number of bar presses (y-axis: 0, 5, 10, 15, 20, 25, 30, 35)

(a)   (b)   (c)   (d)

Time

● = Reward given for the bar press

FIGURE 5.7 Partial Reinforcement of a Rat in a Skinner Box

This graph plots the rates of response for different schedules of reinforcement and the points at which the rat is reinforced. Notice how the rat's bar-pressing behavior changes before and after it receives a pellet on the different schedules of reinforcement. Which schedule would you use if you were going to use positive reinforcement to train your dog?

Variable ratio schedules of reinforcement yield higher rates of response (Figure 5.7b) and even slower rates of extinction than fixed ratio schedules. A good example of this resistance to extinction comes from a real-world example of variable ratio reinforcement. Slot machines pay off on a variable ratio schedule of reinforcement. You never know how many pulls of the handle it will take to lead to the reward of a payoff. Consequently, people will play slot machines for long periods of time, even when they haven't hit the jackpot. One of us once knew a person who claimed to have lost $2,000 in slot machines during a weekend in Las Vegas. That type of resistance to extinction keeps many a casino owner very happy!

© Bonnie Kamin/Photo Edit

Slot machines pay off on a variable ratio schedule of reinforcement. Because it is hard to predict when the next reward is due, people playing the machine are likely to show high rates of responding and very slow rates of extinction. This translates into big profits for the casinos!

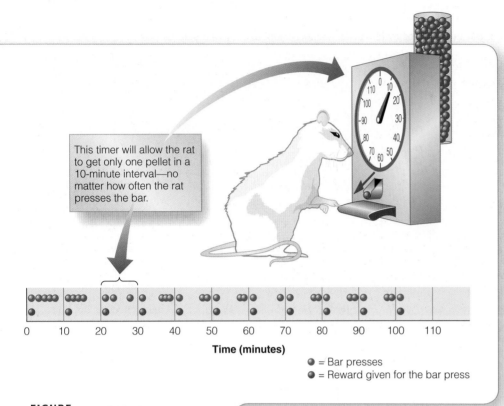

This timer will allow the rat to get only one pellet in a 10-minute interval—no matter how often the rat presses the bar.

Time (minutes)

● = Bar presses
● = Reward given for the bar press

FIGURE 5.8

Fixed Interval Schedule of Reinforcement

This is an example of an FI 10-minute schedule of reinforcement for a rat in a Skinner box. The blue dots indicate when the rat pressed the bar, and the orange dots indicate when the rat was rewarded for its bar-pressing behavior. On an FI of 10 minutes, the rat will receive a maximum of one reinforcement during any one 10-minute interval. Over time, the rat learns to press the bar only when a reward is due—right around the 10-minute interval mark. Yes, rats do have some sense of time!

fixed interval schedule a schedule of reinforcement in which the organism is rewarded for the first desired response in an *x*th interval of time

variable interval schedule a schedule of reinforcement in which the organism is rewarded for the first desired response in an average *x*th interval of time

INTERVAL SCHEDULES OF REINFORCEMENT

Ratio schedules of reinforcement are based on the number of responses emitted by the organism. In interval schedules of reinforcement, the organism is rewarded only once per some interval of time. In a **fixed interval schedule**, the organism is rewarded for the first instance of the desired response, after which a set interval of time must pass before any other instances of the response will be rewarded. For example, if a rat in a Skinner box is reinforced on a fixed interval of 10 minutes, it will be rewarded for its first bar press, but not again until after 10 minutes has passed—no matter how many more times it presses the bar. Then the first bar press after the 10-minute mark has passed will be rewarded (■ FIGURE 5.8).

The typical pattern of responding with a fixed interval schedule is to see most of the responding right around the time at which the reward is due. Then once the organism has received its reward for an interval, it usually stops responding for most of the remainder of the interval. One example of a fixed interval schedule is a yearly performance review at work. If an employee knows that she is going to be evaluated every January, she might be tempted to work her hardest in December. Immediately after being reviewed, the employee may be tempted to reduce her performance because she knows that she will not be reviewed again for another year. But as the end of the interval approaches and the next performance evaluation looms near, we can expect to see another increase in the employee's performance. This characteristic pause after reinforcement on a fixed interval schedule has been seen in rats (Innis, 1979) as well as humans (see Figure 5.7c; Shimoff, Cantania, & Matthews, 1981).

One way to avoid this pause in the behavior immediately after reinforcement is to make the interval *variable*. Similar to what we saw in the variable ratio schedule, in a **variable interval schedule**, the length of the interval varies. What if our employee from the previous example did not know when to expect her next evaluation? What if she could be evaluated during any month of the year? Under these circumstances, her only choice would be to always perform well—assuming, of course, that she wanted to do well on her evaluation. Pop quizzes also reward students on a variable interval schedule for keeping up with their reading and studying! As you can see from Figure 5.7d, variable interval schedules produce steady rates of responding in rats. Another benefit of variable interval schedules is that they produce behaviors that are more resistant to extinction than those produced with fixed interval schedules.

In summary, when it comes to the effects that these different schedules have on operant conditioning:

1. Continuous reinforcement leads to high rates of responding but the quickest extinction.

2. Ratio schedules of reinforcement lead to higher rates of responding than do interval schedules of reinforcement.

3. Variable schedules of reinforcement lead to behaviors that are the most resistant to extinction.

Discrimination and Generalization

Just as classically conditioned responses undergo discrimination and generalization, so do operantly conditioned responses. In operant conditioning, discrimination occurs when the organism learns to distinguish among similar stimulus situations and to offer a particular response only in those specific situations in which reinforcement will be forthcoming. For example, at work we learn to do our job because it leads to reward in the form of pay, but this doesn't mean that we will also do a coworker's job for which we do not expect pay.

Equally important is our ability to generalize our operant responses. Generalization occurs when the same operant behavior is emitted in response to different but similar stimuli. For example, if studying in a particular manner leads to a lot of learning in your psychology class, you may also try this study method in your math class where it may also pay off.

In the previous examples, discrimination and generalization led to positive outcomes. Unfortunately, this is not always the case. One example of the negative aspects of discrimination and generalization is found in prejudice and discrimination against certain groups of people (see Chapter 10). In prejudice, one's negative feelings about a few members of a group generalize to most or all members of that group. Similarly, one may discriminate by treating members of some groups in a kind manner and treating all or most members of a disliked group in an unkind manner. Here what we commonly refer to as discrimination in the social sense is also an example of what psychologists refer to as discrimination in learning.

Shaping New Behaviors

Before a behavior can be operantly conditioned, the organism must first engage in the behavior spontaneously. Before Thorndike's cat learned to quickly receive its reward by stepping on the foot-release in the puzzle box, it first had to accidentally or spontaneously step on the pedal and open the box. Learning occurs only *after* the behavior has been emitted and the organism has been either punished or rewarded. Given this, how can operant conditioning explain the development of novel behaviors? For example, how could an animal trainer use operant conditioning to teach a dog to do a trick that involves walking on its hind legs? If you wait for a dog to spontaneously stand up on its hind legs and begin to walk so that you can reinforce this behavior with a treat, you are going to be waiting for a long time!

Animal trainers use an operant conditioning technique called **shaping**, in which a novel behavior is slowly conditioned by reinforcing *successive approximations* of the final desired behavior. In the case of training the dog, the trainer will reinforce *any* spontaneous behavior that is in the direction of the final desired behavior. The trainer may start by rewarding the dog for looking at him. Once the dog learns to pay attention, it may expand on this behavior by sitting up. This will also lead to a treat. Then the dog must sit up to get the treat. Once the dog learns to sit up, it may go a bit further and rear up a bit on its hind legs. This will also earn the dog a treat. Now that the dog can rear up, it must do so to get a treat. After rearing up for a time, the dog may spontaneously go up all the way onto its hind legs. The trainer responds with more treats. Soon the dog will progress to standing on its hind legs, and the trainer will reciprocate with more treats every time the dog stands up on its hind legs. The final step comes when the dog spontaneously takes its first steps after being conditioned to stand on its hind legs. At this point, all the trainer has to do is reward the dog for walking on its hind legs.

Shaping has many useful purposes in the real world. A parent could use shaping to help a child become more successful in school. At first the parent could reward the child for any study-related behavior, such as doing reading assignments or homework. Then the parent could progress to rewarding the child for earning good grades on individual assignments,

shaping using operant conditioning to build a new behavior in an organism by rewarding successive approximations of the desired response

Animal trainers use shaping to get animals to perform behaviors that they would not typically perform in the wild.

followed by a reward only for good grades on individual exams. Then the parent could reward the child for making good grades in individual courses. Finally, the parent could reward the child only for making good grades in *all* courses. By slowly rewarding closer and closer approximations of the final desired behavior, the parent can shape a behavior in the child that would, perhaps, have never occurred on its own.

These last examples point to the usefulness of operant conditioning in the real world. If used correctly, operant conditioning can be very effective in modifying a child's behavior. This is not to say that operant conditioning can be used only with children. Operant conditioning can be used with any person or animal. However, the use of operant conditioning as a parental tool provides a nice backdrop for discussing some of the choices one must make before implementing an operant conditioning program of behavior modification with any person or animal.

Decisions That Must Be Made When Using Operant Conditioning

One of the first decisions that has to be made when using operant conditioning to change behavior is which type of consequence to use. Recall that there are two basic types of consequences that follow behavior—reinforcement and punishment. When designing an operant conditioning program of behavior modification, one must first decide whether to punish or reinforce the behavior. Sometimes this choice will be a very clear one, but often it will not be.

PUNISHMENT OR REINFORCEMENT?

At times, a parent will have a choice either to *reinforce* a child's *good* behavior or to *punish* the child's *bad* behavior. For example, suppose your child is not studying. You can punish the child for *not* studying, or you can reward the child for studying. Which of these methods do you think will be more successful and cause fewer problems? If you guessed that reinforcement is the safer, more effective route, you guessed correctly. In fact, one of the most effective ways of controlling children's behavior is to show them how you want them to respond and then reward them for behaving that way (Kochanska, 1995; Zahn-Waxler & Robinson, 1995). So what makes punishment riskier and less effective?

- *Punishment doesn't teach the correct behavior in a given situation.* Think about it for a moment. Let's say you hear your daughter getting frustrated with the family dog and cussing at the dog. As a result, you immediately yell at her. What have you taught her? You have taught her not to use whatever cuss word she uttered at the dog. What you have *not* taught her, however, is how she *should have responded* in this situation. The next time she is frustrated with the dog, she will not know how to express her frustration appropriately. Because punishment does not teach the correct response, any use of punishment should include a discussion of appropriate behavior and reinforcement of that behavior (Martin & Pear, 2007).
- *Harsh punishment, especially physical punishment, teaches aggressive behavior.* Harsh punishment provides an aggressive model for the child. When a parent spanks a child, the parent is teaching the child two things: first, that the child's behavior has had aversive consequences; and second, that being aggressive is a powerful means of controlling other people's behavior. In later sections of this chapter, we will see that children often imitate the behavior of others (Bandura, 1977). Therefore, while harsh punishment may stop an unwanted behavior, it may also teach the child to be aggressive. The next time the child feels frustrated or upset with another person, he or she may try using aggression to express those feelings. This is rarely the goal most parents have in mind!
- *Harsh punishment is often ineffective at producing behavior change* (Strassberg, Dodge, Pettit, & Bates, 1994). When punished, children often stop engaging in the undesired behav-

ior, but only for as long as their parents are around. When the parents are out of sight—and the threat of immediate punishment is gone—the undesired behavior returns. Because the goal is usually to ensure that the child behaves even when the parents are not around, punishment is not always effective.

- *Harsh punishment often leads to negative emotional reactions* (Skinner, 1953). These negative reactions include anger, fear, and anxiety. If a child experiences fear and anxiety when a parent punishes him, he may come to fear the parent. Just as Little Albert came to associate the white rat with loud, frightening noises, a child can come to associate a parent with pain and humiliation. Through classical conditioning, the parent can become a conditioned stimulus that evokes negative emotions in the child. This conditioned fear can lead to a psychologically unhealthy, fear-based parent–child relationship in which the child seeks to avoid the parent and the parent becomes resentful toward the child (■ FIGURE 5.9).

Harsh punishment, in particular, is riskier and less effective than reinforcement. If you do choose to use punishment on your children, how can you ensure its effectiveness? Before we begin, let us first state that *physical* punishment or spanking should be avoided. Years of research have shown us that children who experience physical punishment are more likely to be aggressive and experience lower levels of mental health than children who are not hit (Gershoff, 2002). Having experienced physical punishment as a child is also correlated with relationship problems in college students (Leary, Kelley, Morrow, & Mikulka, 2008). Similarly, parents who use physical punishment have been shown to be more hostile and to have higher levels of conflict in their marriages (Kanoy, Ulku-Steiner, Cox, & Burchinal, 2003).

There are a number of alternatives to physical punishment, many of which are listed in ■ TABLE 5.2. If used properly, these techniques will most likely prove effective. Here are a few tips for making punishments like the ones in Table 5.2 more effective in general:

1. Tell the child what the appropriate behavior is, and then reinforce that behavior.

2. Minimize situations that tempt the child to engage in bad behavior.

3. Use a punishment that really is punishing. If the child does not find the punishment aversive, it will fail to control the behavior.

4. Punishment must occur immediately after the bad behavior occurs.

5. Punishment must occur each and every time the bad behavior occurs. Otherwise, the bad behavior is partially reinforced when the child escapes the punishment.

6. Remain calm while you are punishing a child. This will help ensure that you do not abuse the child.

As you can see, punishment, especially physical punishment, is riddled with possible dangers. Some countries, including England, are currently discussing whether to limit or even outlaw a parent's right to spank a child (O'Neill, 2004). When you have a choice, it is much safer and often more effective to use reinforcement of good behavior to control behavior. However, there are things to consider if you want to be sure your program of reinforcement has the desired effect on the behavior you are trying to change.

CHOOSING A REINFORCER THAT IS REINFORCING

It may seem like a trivial issue, but the first consideration in developing a program of reinforcement is to choose a reinforcer that is actually reinforcing for the person you are trying to condition. If the reinforcer is not something the person likes or values, it will not work. For example, if your significant other cleans the whole house, and you reward him by cooking a meal that he does *not* like, then he will not be more likely to clean the house

The pain of spanking   Fear

Parent   The pain of spanking   Fear

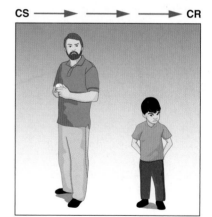

Parent   Fear

FIGURE 5.9 Classical Conditioning of Fear During a Spanking

Even though a parent may only intend to use operant conditioning when spanking a child, it is possible that the child may also experience classical conditioning. Because the parent is delivering the punishment, the parent can become a conditioned stimulus that elicits fear in the child.

Table 5.2 Alternatives to Physical Punishment

METHOD	EXAMPLE
PUNISHMENT METHODS	
Timeout: The child is sent to sit in a quiet place.	Devon, 5 years old, is sent to sit in the laundry room for 5 minutes after hitting his sister. There are no toys, friends, or other reinforcements present.
Restitution: The child has to give up something.	Sabina broke her sister's toy on purpose. Now Sabina has to give one of her own toys to her sister.
Fines: The child has to pay a fine.	Every time a family member uses inappropriate language, he or she has to put 50 cents in the "swear jar."
Loss of privileges: The child loses a privilege.	Giorgio is grounded for 2 weeks for breaking curfew and talking back to his parents.
NONPUNISHMENT METHODS	
Empathy training: Teach the child to empathize with others. If the child hurts another, she is encouraged to imagine what that person might have felt as a result of being hurt. The ability to empathize reduces the motivation to hurt others.	Suzy intentionally breaks Jimmy's toy. To teach her empathy, Suzy's mother asks her to think about how she felt when Bobby broke her toy last week. Then Suzy is asked to think about whether Jimmy might be feeling the same way now that Suzy broke his toy. This should make Suzy feel bad about having hurt Jimmy.
Differential reinforcement of incompatible responses (DRI): The child is rewarded for engaging in a desirable behavior that cannot be emitted at the same time as the undesirable behavior.	Marya's parents reward her for being quiet in church as opposed to punishing her for being loud in church.

again. Your attempt at operant conditioning will have failed. When in doubt, it's a good idea to discuss with the person the consequences that he or she would find reinforcing before conditioning begins.

PRIMARY AND SECONDARY REINFORCERS

Reinforcers can be categorized as either primary or secondary reinforcers. A **primary reinforcer** is one that is directly reinforcing. Examples of primary reinforcers are food, water, a warm bed, and sexual pleasure. These reinforcers are primary because they are pleasurable in and of themselves. If you are hungry, then food will reinforce you by removing your hunger.

In contrast, **secondary reinforcers** are rewarding only because they lead to primary reinforcers. A wonderful example of a secondary reinforcer in Western society is money. By itself, a dollar bill is not reinforcing. What makes a dollar reinforcing is what you can buy with it—food, water, shelter, and other primary reinforcers. When you get right down to it, you don't go to work for money per se. You go to work to ensure that you will be able to purchase an adequate supply of primary reinforcers.

One method of secondary reinforcement is to use a *token economy*. A **token economy** reinforces desired behavior with a token of some sort (e.g., a poker chip or a gold star) that can later be cashed in for primary reinforcers (see Martin, England, Kaprowy, Kilgour, & Pilek, 1968). Token economies are often used to control the behavior of groups of people such as

primary reinforcer a reinforcer that is reinforcing in and of itself

secondary reinforcer a reinforcer that is reinforcing only because it leads to a primary reinforcer

token economy a system of operant conditioning in which participants are reinforced with tokens that can later be cashed in for primary reinforcers

Mrs. Alvarez's Class

Participants	Paying attention in class, +5 tokens	On time for class, +3 tokens	Homework completely done, +7 tokens	B or better on daily quiz, +10 tokens	Talking in class, −5 tokens	Fighting, −10 tokens	Calling people names −10 tokens
Franco							
Mary							
Lou							
Billy							
George							
Eddie							
Latesha							

Token values
  25 tokens = 1 sticker, eraser, or pencil
  50 tokens = 1 small toy
  75 tokens = 1 medium-size toy
100 tokens = 1 coupon for free pizza
125 tokens = 1 DVD

FIGURE 5.10 A Sample Point System From a Token Economy

schoolchildren (Salend, 2001), mental hospital patients, or prisoners. Token economies can also be used in the context of a family (Kazdin, 1977).

To set up a token economy, the first step is to draw up a list of desired and undesired behaviors that you will try to control. The next step is to decide how many tokens to give (or take away) for each of the behaviors, and develop some sort of recordkeeping system to keep track of each participant's tokens. One recordkeeping approach is to draw a chart like the one shown in ■ FIGURE 5.10 and hang it on the wall in a prominent place.

There are two main advantages to using token economies. One is that a token economy is effective when trying to simultaneously modify a number of behaviors in a group of people. For example, a token economy can be used with an entire class, which is easier than trying to develop an individual operant conditioning program for each student.

The second major advantage is that token economies allow for immediate reinforcement with a token, even when it is not practical to immediately present the primary reinforcer. For example, it's disruptive for a teacher to stop the class to give a child a toy as a reinforcer. However, the teacher can immediately hand the child a token that can be used at week's end to purchase a toy. The use of tokens helps to bridge the gap between the behavior and the eventual primary reinforcement of the behavior.

A potential problem with token economies is that they often place the behavior on a continuous schedule of reinforcement. As we saw in previous sections, continuous reinforcement can lead to behavior that is vulnerable to extinction. It is possible that a token economy may lessen a person's desire to engage in a behavior when the behavior is not likely to lead to a token or some other reward. This potential problem may be outweighed, however, by the usefulness of the token economy in controlling the immediate behavior of the people in the program. For instance, in a prison you may be more worried about controlling the immediate, day-to-day behavior of the prison population. Facilitating the future motivation of the inmates to behave in a particular way once they are out of the token economy is likely to be less of a concern.

The Role of Cognition in Learning

So far in this chapter, we have discussed three major types of learning—habituation, classical conditioning, and operant conditioning—that have some important things in common. One common feature is that all of these types of learning require that the person or animal *do something* before learning can occur. In habituation, the organism must emit an orienting reflex. In classical conditioning, the organism must have an unconditioned response. In operant conditioning, the organism must first engage in some random behavior that is either reinforced or punished.

Another common feature of these learning theories is that they do not emphasize the role that mental or cognitive processes play in learning. Researchers such as Ivan Pavlov, John B. Watson, E. L. Thorndike, and B. F. Skinner did not discuss thoughts and feelings and how these may affect the learning process. B. F. Skinner, in particular, argued that psychology should not seek to study the cognitive aspects of behavior because he believed that these things could not be studied scientifically and objectively. Skinner did not deny that humans and animals had thoughts and feelings; he simply held that they could not be studied adequately. Skinner subscribed to the psychological perspective of **behaviorism** (see Chapter 1), which states that the *only* aspect of living things that can and should be studied scientifically is behavior. Therefore, Skinner tried to explain behavior without discussing cognitive or mental processes (Skinner, 1953).

Because strict behaviorism totally ignores the influence of cognitive processes, it does not explain some of the learning we see in the real world, or in the lab. In the early 1900s, some researchers, including Wolfgang Köhler, became aware that cognitive processes must play a role in learning. Köhler observed that chimpanzees did not always attempt to solve problems in a trial-and-error fashion as predicted by the law of effect. Rather, they often seemed to study a problem for a long time as if formulating a mental plan—before attempting to solve it. In one experiment, Köhler placed a banana just out of reach on the outside of a chimpanzee's cage, and he placed a stick inside the cage. The law of effect would predict that the chimpanzee would try many random behaviors—like shaking the bars and jumping up and down—before picking up the stick and using it to reach the banana. But this is not what Köhler observed. Instead, the chimpanzee studied the situation and then appeared to suddenly come up with the solution. After this flash of **insight** into how to solve its dilemma, the chimpanzee picked up the stick and used it to scoot the banana to a point where it could be reached (Köhler, 1925).

Köhler's work shows that learning can be a purely cognitive task. The chimpanzee did not have to wait for the consequences of its behavior to rule out behavioral strategies that would not accomplish the goal of obtaining the banana. Rather, the chimpanzee appeared to reason its way to a solution *before* acting.

In the 1930s, Edward Tolman found additional support for the idea that cognition plays a role in learning. Tolman discovered that rats would learn to run through a maze even when they were not rewarded for doing so (Tolman & Honzik, 1930). In Tolman's experiment, one group of rats was allowed to wander through the maze, and they were rewarded with food if they found their way to the end of the maze. Another group of rats was also allowed to explore the maze, but they were not rewarded even if they found their way to the end. As you might expect, after 10 days of training in the maze, the group that was rewarded could run through the maze more quickly than the unrewarded group could. On the 11th day, Tolman began to give rats in *both* groups a reward at the end of the maze. After just a few rewarded trials, the previously unrewarded rats could run through the maze just as fast as the rats that had been rewarded all along. This rapid learning in the previously unrewarded rats indicates that these rats had been learning even when they were not being rewarded!

Tolman's findings cannot be explained by operant conditioning alone because learning occurred *without* reinforcement. Tolman interpreted his results as being evidence that the rats

behaviorism a school of thought in psychology that emphasizes the study of observable behavior over the study of the mind

insight a sudden realization about how to solve a problem that occurs after an organism has studied the problem for a period of time had engaged in **latent learning**, or learning that cannot be directly observed through behavior. He proposed that while the unrewarded rats were wandering through the maze, they were developing a **cognitive map**, or mental representation of the maze in their heads. Once the reward was presented, they used this map to help them get to the reward more quickly.

Although Tolman's experiments pointed to cognitive processes at work during learning, many psychologists ignored the impact of cognition on learning because of behaviorism's dominance in psychology at the time. It was not until the 1960s that learning researchers really began to look at the role of cognition in learning and behavior.

Let's Review!

This section has given you a quick overview of some of the important issues in operant conditioning, including the law of effect, the factors that affect operant conditioning, the differences between operant conditioning and classical conditioning, and B. F. Skinner's contributions to operant conditioning. As a quick check of your understanding, answer these questions.

1. Denzel wants to increase his son Mario's tendency to mow the yard on Saturday mornings without having to repeatedly ask him. To do this, Denzel tells Mario that he will pay Mario $5 when he mows the yard without first having been told to do so. Denzel is using which schedule of reinforcement?
   a. Fixed ratio
   b. Variable interval
   c. Variable ratio
   d. Continuous

2. Which of the following is an example of operant conditioning?
   a. Byron doesn't go to the dentist because the last time he did, it was very painful.
   b. Byron is afraid of dentists because the last time he went to the dentist, it was very painful.
   c. Byron wants to go to the dentist because when his friend Gina went to the dentist, the dentist gave Gina a toy.
   d. All of the above are examples of operant conditioning.

3. Which of the following is a primary reinforcer?
   a. Receiving good grades
   b. Food, when you're hungry
   c. Receiving a large sum of money
   d. Winning a free plane ticket in a radio contest

Answers 1. d; 2. a; 3. b

Social Learning or Modeling

Learning Objectives

- Describe Albert Bandura's Bobo doll experiments.
- Describe social learning theory.
- Describe the role that cognition plays in social learning.

As we saw in the previous discussion, learning can occur without reinforcement, but even Tolman's unrewarded rats had at least engaged in the behavior of moving through the maze. Does all learning require that we actually engage in the behavior? As it turns out, we can learn by simply observing the behaviors of others. In this type of learning, called **social learning**, we *observe* others and imitate, or *model*, their behavior. For that reason, social learning is sometimes referred to as *observational learning* or *modeling*.

As you read the following sections, keep in mind that social learning departs from the behaviorism that Skinner so forcefully advocated on two major points. First, it acknowledges that learning can occur without an overt change in behavior; second, it takes into account the role of cognition in the learning process.

latent learning learning that cannot be directly observed in an organism's behavior
cognitive map a mental representation of the environment that is formed through observation of one's environment
social learning learning through observation and imitation of others' behavior

Albert Bandura and the Bobo Doll Experiments

In the 1960s, psychologist Albert Bandura (b. 1925) conducted several experiments on social learning, now considered classic psychological experiments, that contributed to his development of *social learning theory*. Collectively, these experiments are referred to as the *Bobo doll experiments* because the experimental procedure utilized a blow-up plastic "Bobo" doll, a popular children's toy.

In the Bobo doll experiments, children watched films in which a woman beat up the Bobo doll. She hit him with a mallet, sat on him, threw him in the air, and so on (Bandura, Ross, & Ross, 1961). After the children viewed the films, Bandura and his colleagues placed them in a room alone with the Bobo doll and observed their behavior without their knowledge. If the children imitated the characteristic behaviors of the model, then Bandura knew that learning had occurred (■ FIGURE 5.11).

In one of the Bobo doll experiments (Bandura, 1965), three groups of children watched three different films. In the *reward* film condition, the model was rewarded after beating up on Bobo. In the *punishment* film condition, she was punished after beating up on Bobo. In the *no consequences* film condition, nothing happened to the model after she beat up Bobo.

After viewing one of these films, the children were observed with Bobo, and their aggressive behaviors were recorded. As you might expect, the children who had seen the model rewarded for beating up Bobo were most likely to beat up on him themselves. However, an unexpected finding of the study was that the children who had seen the *no consequences* film were equally likely to beat up on Bobo! This means that seeing someone merely get away with aggressive behavior is just as likely to lead to modeling as seeing aggression rewarded. The only thing that deterred the children's aggression toward Bobo was having seen the film in which the model was punished for treating Bobo badly. Only these children were more hesitant to beat up on Bobo when they were left alone with him in the observation room.

By leaving the children alone with Bobo and recording their aggressive behavior, Bandura was able to assess how willing the children were to beat up on Bobo as a function of the consequences they expected would follow such aggression. But what about what they learned about how to be aggressive toward Bobo? Is it possible that some of the children who did *not* beat up Bobo had still learned *how* to beat up Bobo? To test the children's level of *learning*, Bandura (1965) asked the children to show him exactly what they had seen in the films. Here, the children were free to model the behavior without fear of any type of punishment. Under these conditions, Bandura found that there were no significant differences across the three groups. All of the groups exhibited equal levels of learning when it came to knowing how the model had beat up Bobo.

The Bobo doll experiments show us two things. First, you don't have to engage in a behavior or experience reinforcement for learning to occur. Second, just as Tolman discovered with his rats in the mazes, learning can be latent. The children who viewed the punishment film had *learned* how to beat up Bobo, but

FIGURE

5.11 Bandura's Bobo Doll Experiments

These photos, taken from the Bobo doll experiments, clearly show the children (panels B and C) modeling what they saw the model (panel A) doing to Bobo.

© Albert Bandura

they were reluctant to beat him up because they feared there would be negative consequences for them if they did. We hope that the Bobo doll experiments make you think about the potential impact that violent movies, video games, and television may have on the children who view them because some very recent research seems to underscore the notion that kids do not merely watch TV—rather, they learn from TV.

Researchers Donna Mumme and Anne Fernald (2003) have found that children as young as 12 months old pay attention to how a televised model reacts to certain stimuli, and they model their own reaction to the stimulus after the model's reaction. In this study, 12-month-old infants watched a televised actress interacting with certain toys. The actress responded either positively, neutrally, or negatively to certain toys. Later, the infants were allowed to play with the same toys. The results showed that the infants were most likely to react favorably to the toys that the actress had either been neutral about or liked. Conversely, the infants were less likely to want to play with the toys to which the actress had reacted negatively. It seems that the infants disliked these toys simply because they had seen the actress reacting negatively toward them. Thus, the social learning that occurs when watching TV may have the power to influence the attitudes that even very young children hold about the objects in their world.

Think about the impact that this process may have on learning stereotypes and prejudices. If a child is subjected to models (in real life or on TV) who react negatively to specific groups of people, could this lead to modeling in which the child comes to react negatively to certain types of people simply because they have seen this reaction in others? It seems likely that it could, and perhaps at a very young age! Later in this text, we will explore the causes of aggression and prejudice in our discussions of social psychology in Chapter 10. But for now, let's take a closer look at this process of social learning and the variables that affect it.

Social Learning Theory and Cognition

The role of cognition in social learning can be clearly seen when you examine the conditions that are necessary for modeling to occur. According to Bandura (1986), modeling is a four-step process.

What do we learn from watching TV and playing video games?

1. *Attention.* The observer must first pay attention to the model's behavior before he or she can model it. Research shows that children tend to model their behavior after people who are warm, nurturant, or powerful (Bandura, 1977). For example, a child may pay attention to the behavior of loving parents, a nurturant teacher, or a popular and seemingly powerful classmate. As we have already seen, another type of model that is particularly good at grabbing our attention is televised models (Bandura, Grusec, & Menlove, 1966). As a result, it is quite common to see children on the playground modeling the behavior of their favorite TV cartoon character. As we age and mature, however, we tend to seek out models that seem similar to us in some way (Bandura, 1986). For example, we may model our behavior after people of the same sex, ethnicity, or occupation.

2. *Retention in memory.* The observer must retain a cognitive representation or memory of the model's behavior. For children on the playground to model the behavior of TV characters, they must have memories of what they have previously seen on TV.

3. *Reproduction of the behavior.* The observer must have a mental representation of the behavior stored in memory that can be retrieved and used to reproduce the behavior. Of course, the person must have the physical abilities to actually reproduce the behavior if modeling is to occur. For instance, a child may remember seeing a cartoon superhero flying. Although the child may be able to model an approximation of this behavior, he will not be able to model the behavior precisely.

4. *Motivation.* After retrieving the memory of the behavior and figuring out how to produce the behavior, the observer must be motivated to actually execute the behavior. As we saw in the Bobo doll experiments, the observer may sometimes not *want* to execute the behavior. This is especially true if the observer believes that execution of the behavior may lead to punishment.

Bandura's social learning theory brings an additional element to the study of learning, in that it addresses the role of cognition in the learning process. In the next two chapters, we will look more carefully at cognitive processes, looking at how memory works in Chapter 6 and at the cognitive processes involved in solving problems and making decisions and judgments in Chapter 7.

Let's Review!

This section has given you a brief overview of some important aspects of social learning theory, including Bandura's Bobo doll experiments, the steps involved in modeling, and the role that cognition plays in social learning. As a quick check of your understanding, answer these questions.

1. Social learning differs from operant conditioning in that _____.
   a. in social learning, the person is less aware that learning is taking place
   b. in operant conditioning, the person is less aware that learning is taking place
   c. in social learning, the person does not have to engage in the response
   d. in operant conditioning, the person does not have to engage in the response

2. Which of the following is an example of social learning?
   a. Henri can cook because as a child he spent a lot of time playing in the kitchen while his mother cooked dinner.
   b. Shalitha slaps another child for taking her toy away.
   c. Javier likes toy trains because they remind him of his childhood days.
   d. Billy is able to study with the neighbor's TV playing at full volume.

3. Tyrone watches a violent TV show, but he has never imitated any of the behaviors he has seen on the show. Which of the following statements is true regarding Tyrone's learning?
   a. Tyrone has not learned anything from watching the show.
   b. Tyrone has definitely learned something from watching the show.
   c. Tyrone may have learned something from watching the show.
   d. At some point in time, Tyrone's behavior will definitely change as a result of watching the show.

Answers 1. c; 2. a; 3. c

Studying THE Chapter

Key Terms

learning (158)
orienting reflex (158)
habituation (159)
dishabituation (160)
unconditioned stimulus (US) (163)
unconditioned response (UR) (163)
neutral stimulus (NS) (163)
conditioned stimulus (CS) (163)
conditioned response (CR) (163)
classical conditioning (164)
contiguity (165)
contingency (166)
stimulus generalization (167)
stimulus discrimination (167)
taste aversion (168)

aversion therapy (169)
extinction (170)
acquisition (170)
spontaneous recovery (171)
operant conditioning (173)
law of effect (174)
reinforcement (174)
positive reinforcement (174)
negative reinforcement (174)
punishment (174)
positive punishment (174)
negative punishment (175)
Skinner box (176)
extinction burst (177)
schedule of reinforcement (177)

continuous reinforcement (178)
partial reinforcement schedules (178)
fixed ratio schedule (178)
variable ratio schedule (178)
fixed interval schedule (180)
variable interval schedule (180)
shaping (181)
primary reinforcer (184)
secondary reinforcer (184)
token economy (184)
behaviorism (186)
insight (186)
latent learning (187)
cognitive map (187)
social learning (187)

What Do You Know? Assess Your Understanding

Test your retention and understanding of the material by answering the following questions.

1. Roman just started working in a day-care center and he is having a hard time adjusting to the noisy environment. Every time a child yells, Roman finds himself snapping to attention. In psychological terms, Roman is exhibiting a(n) _____ to the children's screams.
   a. orienting reflex
   b. habituation
   c. dishabituation
   d. conditioned response

2. After two days working at the day-care center, Roman no longer snaps to attention every time a child screams. The change in Roman's behavior is most likely due to _____.
   a. orienting reflexes
   b. habituation
   c. dishabituation
   d. classical conditioning

3. _____ is responding to a stimulus to which you have previously habituated.
   a. Habituation
   b. Classical conditioning
   c. Dishabituation
   d. Operant conditioning

4. Getting an injection causes Marla to flinch. In classical conditioning terms, the needle stick is a(n) _____.
   a. conditioned stimulus
   b. conditioned response
   c. unconditioned response
   d. unconditioned stimulus

5. In classical conditioning, the neutral stimulus is the same as the _____.
   a. conditioned stimulus
   b. conditioned response
   c. unconditioned response
   d. unconditioned stimulus

6. In Pavlov's original studies, the unconditioned stimulus was _____.
   a.   the buzzer
   b.   salivation
   c.   food
   d.   the tube inserted into the dog's salivary gland

7. The last time Mike ate fried fish, he became very sick from food poisoning. Now, whenever Mike smells frying fish, he feels sick to his stomach. Mike's nausea is likely due to _____.
   a.   habituation
   b.   classical conditioning
   c.   operant conditioning
   d.   social learning

8. For strong classical conditioning to occur, there usually has to be _____ between the unconditioned stimulus and the neutral or conditioned stimulus.
   a.   contiguity and contingency
   b.   contiguity
   c.   contingency
   d.   similarity

9. Classical conditioning best explains the conditioning of what type of responses?
   a.   Behavioral
   b.   Emotional
   c.   Physiological
   d.   b & c

10. The law of effect was written by _____.
   a.   Ivan Pavlov
   b.   E. L. Thorndike
   c.   B. F. Skinner
   d.   Albert Bandura

11. "Learning from the consequences of our behavior" would best describe _____.
   a.   habituation
   b.   classical conditioning
   c.   operant conditioning
   d.   social learning

12. Thelma rewards her son for making his bed by telling him that he doesn't need to mow the grass. Thelma is using _____ with _____ to condition her son's behavior.
   a.   classical conditioning; positive reinforcement
   b.   operant conditioning; positive reinforcement
   c.   classical conditioning; negative reinforcement
   d.   operant conditioning; negative reinforcement

13. _____ is responding to similar stimuli in a similar fashion.
   a.   Stimulus generalization
   b.   Stimulus discrimination
   c.   Extinction
   d.   Shaping

14. _____ involves reinforcing successive approximations of the final desired behavior.
   a.   Extinction
   b.   Shaping
   c.   Secondary reinforcement
   d.   Primary reinforcement

15. Money is an example of a _____.
   a.   primary reinforcer
   b.   secondary reinforcer
   c.   token
   d.   continuous reinforcer

16. Professor Kearns awards five extra credit points to students for every week that they attend all three lectures. Professor Kearns is rewarding her students' attendance on a _____ schedule of reinforcement.
   a.   continuous
   b.   fixed interval
   c.   fixed ratio
   d.   variable ratio

17. A token economy is an example of _____.
   a.   secondary reinforcement
   b.   operant conditioning
   c.   positive reinforcement
   d.   all of the above

18. Which of the following is *not* a true statement about using physical punishment on children?
   a.   Physical punishment may teach children to be aggressive.
   b.   Physical punishment may teach children correct behaviors.
   c.   Physical punishment is often less effective than positive reinforcement.
   d.   Physical punishment may result in classical conditioning of negative emotions in children.

19. Learning to make pizza by watching the cooking channel on TV is an example of what type of learning?
    a. Habituation
    b. Classical conditioning
    c. Operant conditioning
    d. Social learning

20. Which of the following learning theorists would be *most* likely to acknowledge the role that memory plays in learning?
    a. John B. Watson
    b. B. F. Skinner
    c. Albert Bandura
    d. Ivan Pavlov

Answers: 1. a; 2. b; 3. c; 4. d; 5. a; 6. c; 7. b; 8. a; 9. d; 10. b; 11. c; 12. d; 13. a; 14. b; 15. b; 16. c; 17. d; 18. b; 19. d; 20. c.

Online Resources

CENGAGENOW™ Personalized Study

www.cengage.com/login

Go to www.cengage.com/login to link to CengageNOW, your online study tool. First take the **Pre-Test** for this chapter to get your **Personalized Study Plan**, which will identify topics you need to review and direct you to online resources. Then take the **Post-Test** to determine what concepts you have mastered and what you still need work on.

 What Is Psychology? Essentials Book Companion Website

www.cengage.com/psychology/pastorino

Visit your book companion website, where you will find more resources to help you study. Resources include learning objectives, Internet exercises, quizzing, flash cards, and a pronunciation glossary.

CHAPTER 5

Learning is a relatively permanent change in behavior or the potential for behavior that results from experience.

Look Back AT **WHAT** YOU'VE **LEARNED**

Why Do We Orient? What Is Habituation?

- **Dishabituation** allows us to re-respond to a stimulus to which we were previously habituated.

- **Orienting reflexes** allow us to respond to unexpected stimuli.

- **Habituation** allows us to stop responding to stimuli that are repeated over and over.

© isobel flynn/Alamy

© Arclight/Alamy

Carlos Davila/Getty Images

What Is Classical Conditioning?

- Ivan Pavlov discovered classical conditioning while studying salivation in dogs.

- **Classical conditioning** occurs when a **neutral stimulus** is paired with an **unconditioned stimulus** that reliably causes an **unconditioned response**, and because of this association, the neutral stimulus loses its neutrality and becomes a **conditioned stimulus** that elicits the **conditioned response**.

- Classical conditioning is most effective when the NS/CS and US are separated by only a brief period of time (**contiguity**), and the pairing must reliably predict the response (**contingency**).

- In the Little Albert experiments, John B. Watson and Rosalie Rayner studied how emotional responses could be classically conditioned in humans.

- **Stimulus generalization** occurs when we respond to similar stimuli with the same conditioned response.

- **Stimulus discrimination** occurs when the conditioned response is only elicited by a particular CS.

- **Taste aversion** occurs when a particular food is associated with some other ailment or condition that causes nausea and the food becomes a conditioned stimulus for nausea.

- The elimination of a conditioned response is known as **extinction**.

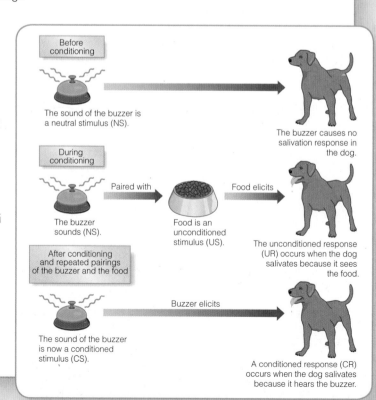

Before conditioning

The sound of the buzzer is a neutral stimulus (NS).

The buzzer causes no salivation response in the dog.

During conditioning

The buzzer sounds (NS). Paired with Food is an unconditioned stimulus (US). Food elicits

The unconditioned response (UR) occurs when the dog salivates because it sees the food.

After conditioning and repeated pairings of the buzzer and the food

The sound of the buzzer is now a conditioned stimulus (CS). Buzzer elicits

A conditioned response (CR) occurs when the dog salivates because it hears the buzzer.

HOW DO WE LEARN?

What Is Operant Conditioning?

- In **operant conditioning**, we learn from the consequences of our actions.

- E. L. Thorndike developed the **law of effect**, which emphasized the negative and positive consequences of behavior.

The Four Consequences of Behavior

	ADD TO ENVIRONMENT	REMOVE FROM ENVIRONMENT
Increase Behavior	+ Reinforcement	− Reinforcement
Decrease Behavior	+ Punishment	− Punishment

- B. F. Skinner, a strong proponent of behaviorism, coined the term *operant conditioning* to refer to how certain behavior operates on the environment to produce some consequence. The **Skinner box** is a chamber used to study animal learning.

- Five schedules of **reinforcement—continuous, fixed ratio, variable ratio, fixed interval**, and **variable interval**—describe the timing and number of responses required to receive reinforcement.

- In **shaping**, a novel behavior is slowly conditioned by reinforcing successive approximations of the final desired behavior.

- **Primary reinforcers** are reinforcing in themselves. **Secondary reinforcers** are rewarding because they lead to primary reinforcers.

- A **token economy** reinforces desired behavior with a token of some sort that can later be cashed in for primary reinforcers.

How Do We Learn Through Social Learning or Modeling?

- **Social learning** is learning that occurs by observing others and modeling their behavior.

  - Albert Bandura's Bobo doll experiments showed that you do not have to engage in a behavior or experience for learning to occur, and that learning can be latent.

- In contrast to behaviorists such as Skinner, social learning theorists emphasize the role that cognitive processes (attention and retention in memory), reproduction of the behavior, and motivation play in learning.

6

How Does Memory FUNCTION?

the phenomenon of **implicit memory**, or the *unconscious* use of memory (Graf & Schacter, 1985; Squire, Knowlton, & Musen, 1993). During the trip home, you were using stored knowledge of how to drive your car, how to find your house, how to read street signs, and so on. The trick is that you did all of these things without conscious awareness. Every day, we execute many behaviors at the implicit level of memory. If we had to execute everything explicitly, we would literally not be able to think and walk at the same time! As we'll see in the coming sections, our cognitive resources for memory are limited. We simply can't do everything explicitly.

Let's Review!

In this section, we discussed the functions of memory and described the difference between implicit and explicit use of memory. For a quick check of your understanding, answer these questions.

1. Printing a document from your computer is analogous to which function of memory?
   a. Encoding
   b. Storage
   c. Retrieval
   d. Forgetting

2. Which of the following *best* illustrates the use of explicit memory?
   a. Forgetting to get eggs at the grocery store
   b. Trying to remember the name of a woman you once met at a party

   c. Automatically thinking of a cat when you see a dog on TV
   d. Guessing the correct answer on a multiple-choice test

3. Which of the following *best* illustrates the use of implicit memory?
   a. Knowing the correct answer on a multiple-choice test
   b. Trying to remember where you left your car keys
   c. Forgetting where you left your car keys
   d. Tying your shoe

Answers 1. c; 2. b; 3. d

How Do We Process New Memories?

- Describe the three stages model of memory.
- Describe the function and characteristics of sensory, short-term, and long-term memory.
- Describe the newer conception of working memory and how it relates to the three stages model's concept of short-term memory.

Learning Objectives

As you may recall from Chapter 1, the study of cognition grew in psychology from the 1960s to the 1980s. As it did, the information processing approach to understanding memory also became more prominent as psychologists began to develop theories of memory that described memory using a computer analogy for the mind. In this section, we'll look at two of these models—the *three stages* and *working memory* models of memory.

The Traditional Three Stages Model of Memory

Traditionally, memory has been explained as having three distinct stages of storage (Atkinson & Shiffrin, 1968). When information enters memory, its first stop is **sensory memory**. In sensory memory, information that comes in from our eyes, ears, and other senses is briefly stored in a sensory form, such as a sound or a visual image. If we pay attention to the

implicit memory the unconscious use of memory

sensory memory a system of memory that very briefly stores sensory impressions so that we can extract relevant information from them for further processing

FIGURE

6.1

The Traditional Three Stages Model of Memory

The traditional three stages model of memory proposes that in forming new memories, information passes sequentially from sensory memory to short-term memory to long-term memory.

short–term memory (STM) a system of memory that is limited in both capacity and duration; in the three stages model of memory, short-term memory is seen as the intermediate stage between sensory memory and long-term memory

long–term memory (LTM) a system of memory that works to store memories for a long time, perhaps even permanently

information in our sensory memory, the information is sent on to the second stage, **short-term memory (STM)**, for further processing. Short-term memory functions as a temporary holding tank for a limited amount of information. We can hold information in short-term memory for only a few seconds before we must act either to send it further on in the memory system or to keep it in short-term memory by refreshing it. If we decide to further process the information, we can move it from temporary storage in short-term memory to the permanent storage system of **long-term memory (LTM)** (■ FIGURE 6.1).

SENSORY MEMORY: ICONIC AND ECHOIC MEMORY

All of the information that enters our memory from the outside world must first pass through our senses. The information we receive from our sense organs lasts for a very brief time after the sensory stimulation has ended. This holding of sensory information after the sensory stimulus ends is sensory memory. Perhaps you have noticed your sensory memory at work. Have you ever heard a fire engine's siren and then found that you could still hear the sound of the siren in your head for a short time after you could no longer actually hear the siren? If so, you caught your sensory memory at work.

Of all our senses, sight (*iconic memory*) and hearing (*echoic memory*), the two most studied by psychologists, are also the primary means through which we acquire information. But they are not the only useful senses. We also learn through our senses of taste, smell, and touch (haptic memory). Psychologists assume that we have sensory memories for each of the senses (see ■ FIGURE 6.2).

The function of sensory memory is to hold sensory information just long enough for us to process it and send it on to short-term memory for further processing. If we do not send the information on to short-term memory within seconds (or less), it will be lost forever as our sensory memories decay. So, how do we transfer information from sensory memory to short-term memory? It's simple, actually. To transfer information from sensory memory to short-term memory, all we have to do is pay attention to the sensory information. In paying attention to a sensory stimulus,

FIGURE

6.2   Sensory Memory

Psychologists believe that we have sensory memory for each of our senses. In sensory memory, we store a brief sensory impression of the object we are sensing.

we focus our consciousness on that stimulus. For example, as you read a phone number in a phone book, you pay attention to the number and bring it into your consciousness. As you do this, you ensure that the image of the phone number will be transferred from iconic memory into short-term memory (see ■ FIGURE 6.3a & b). If you are distracted or unmotivated, you may gaze at the page without paying attention to the number. In that case, the image will be lost as it decays from iconic memory. As you can see, if you don't pay attention to what you are reading, you are wasting your time!

FIGURE

6.3 The Three Stages Model of Memory

(a) As Juanita looks up the phone number of a pizza shop, the information enters into her visual sensory memory. (b) As she focuses her attention on the phone number, the information now moves to her short-term memory. (c) To keep the number in mind while she goes to the phone and dials it, Juanita uses maintenance rehearsal, repeating the number over and over to herself. (d) As Juanita continues to think about the number, she engages in elaborative rehearsal by associating the number with the idea of pizza in her mind; as a result, the number is now stored in her long-term memory. (e) Later, Juanita retrieves the number from long-term memory when once again she wants to order a pizza.

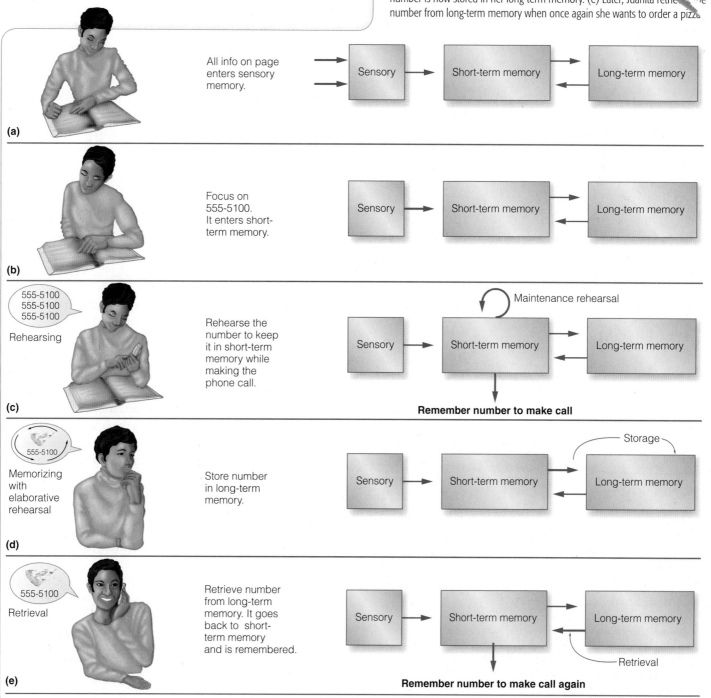

Attention is a necessary step in encoding memories, but there is more to it than that. Once information makes it to your short-term memory, you have to take active steps to keep this information in memory.

SHORT-TERM MEMORY: WHERE MEMORIES ARE MADE (AND LOST)

The three stages view of memory conceptualizes short-term memory as a temporary holding tank for information that has been transferred in from sensory memory. Short-term memory uses a **dual coding system** in which memories can be stored either visually or acoustically (with sound) (Paivio, 1982). Although short-term memory serves us well, it is another point in the system where information can be lost. Because short-term memory is designed for temporary storage, both its capacity and its duration are limited. It can hold only a small amount of information, and only for a short time. If you've ever tried to hold a phone number in your head while you make it to the phone, then you know just how limited short-term memory is and how susceptible it is to forgetting!

The Capacity of Short-Term Memory: Seven (Plus or Minus Two) In 1956, psychologist George Miller published a landmark paper on the capacity of short-term memory. In this research, Miller had participants try to remember as many items from a list as they could. He found that the average person could hold about seven, plus or minus two, items in short-term memory. This 7 ± 2 capacity applies to such items as numbers, words, and other small bits of information.

YOUR TURN – ACTIVE LEARNING

To illustrate the capacity of short-term memory, read the following list of numbers {1, 7, 3, 0, 6, 2, 4, 1, 8, 6, 7, 4, 0, 8, 1, 3, 5, 2, 8, 9, 1} to a friend and then immediately ask the person to recall as many of the numbers as possible in the same order you read them. We bet you'll find that your friend is able to remember only around 7 ± 2 of them.

Given this 7 ± 2 capacity, we can easily hold a phone number, a short grocery list, or the name of a person we just met in our short-term memory. But, if we need to, can we hold more information in our short-term memory? Maybe. One technique for extending the amount of information we can hold in short-term memory is called **chunking** (Simon, 1974). Chunking involves grouping information together into meaningful units, or *chunks*. For example, many of the important numbers in our culture—Social Security numbers, phone numbers, license plates, credit card numbers, and so on—are usually presented in a prechunked form so as to facilitate our remembering them. It would be harder to recall your Social Security number as nine separate digits rather than three chunks.

However, there is also a limit to how much information can be chunked. The number of chunks we can store in short-term memory decreases as the chunks gets larger. In other words, you can hold more three-digit numbers in short-term memory than you can eight-digit numbers (Simon, 1974). In a sense, short-term memory is like a short bookshelf. It may hold seven skinny books of poetry, but only three thick dictionaries.

You Asked...

How long does short-term memory last?   NICK TATUM, STUDENT

dual coding system a system of memory that encodes information in more than one type of code or format

chunking a means of using one's limited short-term memory resources more efficiently by combining small bits of information to form larger bits of information, or chunks

The Duration of Short-Term Memory: It's Yours for 30 Seconds Duration is the second major limitation on short-term memory. Once information passes into short-term memory, it can only be kept there for around 30 seconds without some type of rehearsal or refreshing of the material (J. A. Brown, 1958; Peterson & Peterson, 1959).

So, what if you have to keep some information in short-term memory for more than 30 seconds? Suppose you look up a phone number and have to remember it while you take a 2-minute walk to the pay phone. If you can't write the phone number down, you need to find a way to keep it in your short-term memory for longer than 30 seconds. What do you think you would you do in this situation? One simple solution would be to repeat the phone number over and over out loud as you walk to the phone (Figure 6.3c). This repetition of the material in short-term memory, called **maintenance rehearsal**, is useful for extending the duration of short-term memory (Nairne, 2002). When you repeat the information over and over again, you resupply it to short-term memory before it can decay, extending its retention for another 30 seconds or so before you must repeat the number to yourself again. You can keep this up all day, as long as no one interrupts or distracts you!

HOW WE TRANSFER INFORMATION FROM SHORT-TERM TO LONG-TERM MEMORY

Maintenance rehearsal may be useful for keeping information in short-term memory, but what if you want to move information from short-term memory into permanent, long-term memory storage? Unfortunately, you will likely have to do more than merely repeat the information if you want to store it permanently in long-term memory. Maintenance rehearsal accomplishes only a *weak* transfer of information into long-term memory (Glenberg, Smith, & Green, 1977; Lockhart & Craik, 1990). You may have learned this lesson the hard way if repetition is your primary means of studying material for exams. If you simply repeat information over and over in your head, or repeatedly read over the information in your text and notes, your studying will not accomplish strong transfer of information into long-term memory, and you may find yourself in trouble on test day.

Elaborative Rehearsal Repetition of information is merely maintenance rehearsal. As we just saw, the main function of maintenance rehearsal is to keep information in short-term memory—and information in short-term memory is only temporary. To really get information into your long-term memory, you have to use another technique, called **elaborative rehearsal** (Craik & Lockhart, 1972). Elaborative rehearsal (Figure 6.3d) involves forming *associations*, or mental connections, between the information in short-term memory that you want to store and information you already have stored in your permanent long-term memory. To get customers to recall a business's phone number, for example, advertisers often use jingles. Associating the phone number with the melody serves to elaborate it in memory.

Another powerful type of elaboration is to generate personally relevant examples of the material you are learning. Every time you generate an example from your own life that demonstrates a psychological principle, you are engaging in elaborative rehearsal and increasing the chances of retrieving the material later (Figure 6.3e). For example, thinking about how you used repetition to memorize your multiplication tables in grade school as an example of maintenance rehearsal will help you retain this concept in long-term memory.

Levels of Processing This notion that the more thoroughly or deeply you process information, the more strongly you transfer it to long-term memory is referred to as the **levels-of-processing model** of memory (Craik & Lockhart, 1972). When Fergus Craik and Robert Lockhart (1972) first proposed the levels-of-processing approach, it was assumed that the only way to get information into long-term memory was to use elaborative rehearsal. Subsequent research has shown that this isn't necessarily the case. Although maintenance rehearsal is a shallow form of processing that doesn't involve much elaboration of the material, it does allow for some transfer of information into long-term memory (Lockhart & Craik, 1990). For example, you may eventually remember your checking account number if you have to write it, and thus repeat it, frequently enough. However, the type of transfer to long-term memory that occurs with maintenance rehearsal doesn't really help students pass an exam in which they actually have to understand what they are talking or writing about. One study

maintenance rehearsal repeating information over and over again to keep it in short-term memory for an extended period of time

elaborative rehearsal forming associations or links between information one is trying to learn and information already stored in long-term memory so as to facilitate the transfer of this new information into long-term memory

levels-of-processing model a model that predicts that information that is processed deeply and elaboratively will be best retained in and recalled from long-term memory found that if you increase the amount of maintenance rehearsal by 9 times (900%), you increase your recall of the information by only 1.5% (Glenberg et al., 1977). Elaborative rehearsal, in contrast, involves a very deep level of processing. To elaborate material, you must access information stored in long-term memory and associate it with the new information you are trying to learn. This requires much more effort and thought than merely repeating the information over and over. The good news is that this effort pays off in terms of better memory for the information. Elaborative rehearsal is clearly your best bet if you want to successfully master material, whether it be in a course or in life.

As an example, let's say that you attend a multicultural fair at your school in which students bring foods from their native cultures for everyone to try (one of the author's schools regularly holds such an event). You sample a West African dish called a *puff-puff*, a type of slightly sweet, fried bread that is often eaten with kidney bean stew. Finding the puff-puff delicious, you decide to commit it to memory so that you can later find some means of obtaining more—trust us, they're that good!

If you want to commit information about the puff-puff to long-term memory, you must associate it with what you already know. You might think about how a puff-puff looks very much like an American donut-hole. You may note that the puff-puff contains nutmeg, which reminds you of drinking eggnog with nutmeg during the winter. You might associate the puff-puff with similar fried breads in other cultures, such as Native American fry bread or beignets from New Orleans. Or you might associate puff-puffs with your friend Denis from West Africa. Do you see what we're doing here? We are finding ways to *associate* and *link* the puff-puff to concepts that you already have stored in long-term memory, such as donuts, nutmeg, and a friend. This is what elaborative rehearsal is all about. You go beyond simply repeating information to actually *thinking* about the information, and in doing so, you process the information deeply enough to efficiently transfer it to long-term memory.

When you use elaborative rehearsal as you learn, you will retain the information in the permanent storage system of long-term memory in a way that maximizes the chances of being able to retrieve it when you need it—whether on test day or when searching online for West African recipes.

Puff-puffs are a type of West African fried bread traditionally eaten with kidney bean stew.

© Susann Doyle-Portillo

DOES SHORT-TERM MEMORY REALLY EXIST?

Recall that the three stages model proposes short-term memory as a separate, intermediate stage of memory that is limited in capacity and duration (see Figure 6.1, p. 200). As you learned in Chapter 1, any scientific theory must be supported by the results of scientific experiments before we place much stock in it. As you will shortly see, not all of the available research supports the three stages model, particularly in its conception of short-term memory. Let's take a look at the evidence that supports and that calls into doubt the three stages model.

The Serial-Position Curve, Primacy, and Recency Some support for the three stages model comes from *serial-position experiments*. In a typical experiment, participants listen to a list of around 20 words slowly read aloud by the experimenter, after which they immediately try to recall the words in any order they can. The experimenter then plots the *serial-position curve*, or the tendency for participants to recall each word correctly plotted as a function of the position of the word in the original list. ■ FIGURE 6.4 shows a typical serial-position curve. You will notice in Figure 6.4 that not all of the words in the list have an equal chance of being recalled. Rather, words at the beginning and the end of the list are recalled better than words in the middle of the list.

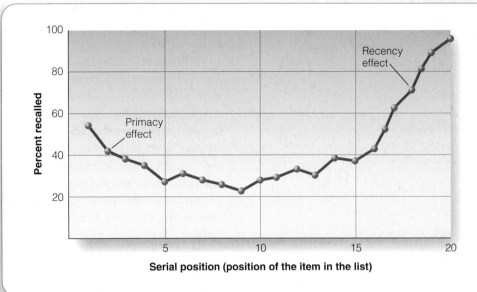

The overall shape of the serial-position curve fits well with the three stages view of memory. In fact, the three stages model predicts that you will obtain a curve like that shown in Figure 6.4. The tendency for words at the beginning of the list to be better recalled, called the **primacy effect**, can be explained in terms of long-term memory. As participants listen to the list of words, they spend considerable time rehearsing the words at the beginning of the list in their short-term memory. While they are doing this, they have no short-term memory capacity left to rehearse the words in the middle of the list. Therefore, words in the middle of the list are lost from short-term memory, but the words at the beginning of the list are moved to long-term memory and thus are remembered well at recall.

The words at the end of the list are also well remembered, in what is called the **recency effect**. The recency effect is thought to occur because participants still have these words in short-term memory at the time they are asked to recall the list. Therefore, all the participants have to do is dump these words from their short-term memory before going on to retrieve the other words (from the beginning of the list) from long-term memory. In the serial-position experiment, participants should be able to recall the last two or three words they heard (Glanzer & Cunitz, 1966). The recency effect does not extend to the full 7 ± 2 capacity of short-term memory because some of the capacity of short-term memory is taken up in rehearsing the words from the start of the list and in continuing to hear new words.

> ### You Asked...
> *Do new memories take the place of old memories?* BROOKE LANDERS, STUDENT

Interestingly, recency memory is one of the aspects of memory that is most affected by normal aging (Wingfield & Kahana, 2002). As we get older, our short-term memory tends to suffer more than our distant long-term memories. One of your authors, who is only 46, often stops by the grocery store without a list and many times leaves the store without buying everything she needs. This type of forgetting almost never occurred in her 20s. However, not all short-term memory suffers as we age. In one study, participants of different ages were shown a series of three pictures in rapid succession. Seconds later, they were shown a test picture and asked to determine if the test picture was one of the pictures they had just seen. In this case, younger and older participants showed serial-position curves that were strikingly similar. The older participants did *not* have poorer recency memory than the younger participants (Sekuler, McLaughlin, Kahana, Wingfield, & Yotsumoto, 2006). It appears that aging negatively affects recency memory for verbal information much more than for visual information. Perhaps your author should *visualize* what she needs to buy at the store instead of naming the items—maybe she'd avoid so many return trips!

Although numerous serial-position experiments like these support the three stages model of memory, some scientists still express doubts about the model, especially its conception of short-term memory. For example, one potential problem with the three stages model

FIGURE

6.4 Serial-Position Curve

In a serial-position experiment (Murdoch, 1962), participants are asked to remember a list of words that are read aloud to them. In such experiments, words at the beginning of the list (primacy effect) and words at the end of the list (recency effect) are remembered best.

primacy effect the tendency for people to recall words from the beginning of a list better than words that appeared in the middle of the list

recency effect the tendency for people to recall words from the end of a list better than words that appeared in the middle of the list has to do with how we process information in memory. The three stages model proposes that the only route by which information can reach long-term memory is through short-term memory. There is some doubt as to whether this is true (Logie, 1999).

If information must pass from sensory memory into short-term memory without having made contact with long-term memory, then long-term memory is activated only *after* information is processed in short-term memory. The problem is that this is not always the case. If you are given a list of seven words to remember, you will likely use maintenance rehearsal (repeating the words over and over to yourself) to keep these words in short-term memory. To do so, however, you will have to know how to pronounce the words, which you can only know by accessing your knowledge (from long-term memory) of how to pronounce the words. You must access and retrieve information in long-term memory *before* you have processed the information into long-term memory (Logie, 1999). The fact that the three stages model cannot account for this type of common behavior calls into doubt the traditional three stages model of memory and led to the development of alternative views of memory. One of the most influential alternatives to the three stages model is the *working memory* view of memory (Baddeley, 1986; Baddeley & Hitch, 1974).

The Working Memory Model: Parallel Memory

Today, many researchers reject the notion that information passes sequentially through the three stages of memory and instead propose a new type of memory called **working memory** (for a review, see Richardson et al., 1996). The working memory model views the memory stages in more of a *parallel* fashion as opposed to a *serial* fashion. In other words, the working memory model assumes that we process different aspects of memory at the same time, rather than in a series of stages as predicted by the three stages model.

In this view, working memory and short-term memory are parts contained within long-term memory (■ FIGURE 6.5). Working memory moves information into and out of long-term memory, whereas short-term memory operates as the part of working memory that briefly stores the information we are using at any particular time.

working memory a multifaceted component of long-term memory that contains short-term memory, a central executive, a phonological loop, and a visuospatial sketch pad; the function of working memory is to access, move, and process information that we are currently using

Suppose a bee stings you. Your haptic (touch) sensory memory registers the pain of the sting, and your visual sensory memory captures the sight of the bee. These sensory impressions are then sent to working memory, where they are combined into an integrated memory representation of being stung by the bee (see Kessler & Meiran, 2006). At the same time, your working memory may activate a long-term memory of what you learned in first-aid class about

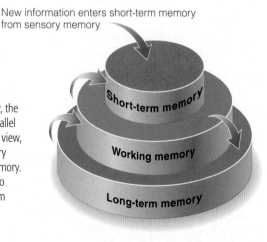

FIGURE
6.5

The Working Memory View of Memory

In the working memory view of memory, the stages of memory work in more of a parallel fashion than a sequential fashion. In this view, short-term memory and working memory are both contained within long-term memory. Working memory moves information into and out of both short-term and long-term memory as necessary.

New information enters short-term memory from sensory memory

Short-term memory

Working memory

Long-term memory

• Working memory retrieves information from long-term memory to help process information in short-term memory; for example, the meaning of words stored in short-term memory may be accessed from long-term memory.

• Working memory also retrieves stored information when you need it—for an exam, your address, directions to your aunt's house—and sends it to short-term memory.

• Working memory also moves information from short-term memory into long-term memory for storage; for example, when you are studying, working memory will move the information you want to remember into long-term memory.

allergic reactions to bee stings. Working memory pulls this information on allergic reactions into short-term memory, and you now consciously think about the signs of an allergic reaction as you check to see if you are having one. You conclude that you are not having an allergic reaction. So you cease to think about the possibility of an allergic reaction, and working memory transfers the new knowledge that you are not allergic to bee stings to long-term memory.

As you can see, in this view of memory, information does not flow sequentially from sensory to short-term to long-term memory. Rather, working memory plays several roles. The short-term memory part of working memory acts as a storage system for information that is currently being used. At the same time, other parts of working memory act to retrieve information, process new information, and send new and revised information on to long-term memory. The order in which the different memory stages are activated can vary depending on the circumstances.

One advantage of the working memory model is that it can explain why we sometimes seem to access long-term memory before we process information in short-term memory. For instance, as you read this page, you must access information that you have stored in long-term memory about the English language in order to pronounce and understand the words. As the words on the page enter your short-term memory, you already know what they mean and how they sound. The working memory view of memory can explain this, but the three stages model cannot. In the working memory model, you can go to your long-term memories to help you process perceptual information in a top-down (see Chapter 3) fashion (Logie, 1999).

THE CENTRAL EXECUTIVE

One of the more prominent theories of a multicomponent working memory proposes that working memory contains a **central executive** component and two subordinate systems: the **phonological loop**, which processes auditory information (e.g., the buzzing of a bee), and the **visuospatial sketch pad**, which processes visual and spatial information (e.g., the sight of a bumblebee) (Baddeley, 1992; Baddeley & Hitch, 1974). These systems are called subordinate systems because they fall under the control of the central executive (■ FIGURE 6.6).

The central executive functions as an attention-controlling mechanism within working memory. The central executive must coordinate the actions of the subordinate systems and integrate information that comes in from these systems (e.g., directing you to pay attention to how close a bee gets to your arm). This makes the central executive component especially important when we are engaged in tasks that require attention and the coordination of visual and auditory information, such as when playing a video game (Baddeley, 1992). Recently, some researchers have proposed that faulty executive functioning—an inability to direct one's attention while using working memory—may be one of the underlying mechanisms in attention deficit hyperactivity disorder (ADHD) in children (Sonuga-Barke, Dalen, & Remington, 2003).

Interestingly, there is also evidence to suggest that one of the results of Alzheimer's disease, which is characterized by progressive memory loss, is a loss of central executive functioning (Crowell, Luis, Vanderploeg, Schinka, & Mullan, 2002). This loss of central executive functioning can be seen when Alzheimer's patients are asked to do visual and auditory tasks at the same time. Because their central executive is not functioning properly, Alzheimer's patients have trouble coordinating and integrating information from visual and auditory sources, and they experience more problems

central executive the attention-controlling component of working memory

phonological [foe-no-LOJ-ih-cull] **loop** in the working memory model, the part of working memory that processes the phonological, or sound, qualities of information

visuospatial [viz-you-oh-SPAY-shall] **sketch pad** in the working memory model, the part of working memory that processes the visual and spatial aspects of information

© Masterfile

FIGURE 6.6

Baddeley's Central Executive Model of Working Memory

In Baddeley's model of working memory, the central executive integrates visual information from the visuospatial sketch pad and auditory information from the phonological loop. The integration of information that the central executive provides is crucial when we are engaged in activities that require us to use both visual and auditory information—as in deciding how to react when you both see and hear nearby bumblebees.

than a healthy person does on the simultaneous tasks. However, when Alzheimer's patients are tested on a single task that is scaled to their ability, such as recalling a list of numbers, they do not perform more poorly than control participants (Baddeley, Logie, Bressi, Della Sala, & Spinnler, 1986). This pattern of results supports the notion that the structure of working memory has multiple components, with at least one component that integrates information.

The working memory view offers a more complex model than the traditional three stages model, one that explains more of what researchers observe about memory. This does not mean, however, that psychologists have a complete understanding of how memory works. There is disagreement even among working memory theorists as to exactly what role working memory plays in the memory system (Richardson et al., 1996). Theorists also disagree as to whether working memory is separate from long-term memory. Not all researchers are convinced that working memory is composed of multiple components, and those who are convinced of its multiplicity do not agree on the number of components. Future research will have to sort out some of these issues before we have a full understanding of how memory is temporarily stored and processed as it passes to and from long-term memory.

Differences Between the Traditional Three Stages Model of Memory and the Working Memory Model

You Review 6.1

THREE STAGES MODEL	WORKING MEMORY MODEL
Memory consists of three separate stages: sensory memory, STM, and LTM.	Memory consists of several interacting components: sensory memory, working memory, and LTM.
STM is a single component of memory that is separate from LTM.	Working memory is a multicomponent part of LTM that includes STM, the central executive, the phonological loop, and the visuospatial sketch pad.
Memory operates in a serial fashion.	Memory operates in a parallel fashion.
The three stages model cannot easily explain some cognitive processes such as top-down perceptual processing.	Because the working memory model is a parallel model of memory, it can better account for processes such as top-down perceptual processing.

Let's Review!

In this section, we described the three stages model of memory and its limitations. We also introduced the newer idea of working memory that deals with some of the limits of the three stages model. For a quick check of your understanding, answer these questions.

1. Which view of memory holds that information must pass through the memory storage systems in a serial fashion?
   a. The three stages model
   b. The working memory view of memory
   c. The parallel processing view of memory
   d. All of the above

2. When you are listening to classical music, which component of working memory are you *least* likely to be using?
   a. The phonological loop
   b. The central executive

   c. The visuospatial sketch pad
   d. Short-term memory

3. Which of the following is the *best* example of elaborative rehearsal?
   a. Reading and outlining a chapter in your text
   b. Relating the material to your personal experiences
   c. Using flashcards of key concepts in the chapter
   d. Repeatedly reading over your lecture notes

Answers 1. a; 2. c; 3. b

How Does Memory Function?

- We are capable of **encoding**, **storing**, and **retrieving** information in an **explicit** or **implicit** fashion.

- The **three stages model** of memory proposes that **memory traces** are processed in a serial fashion from **sensory memory** to **short-term memory** to **long-term memory**.

- The **working memory** view of memory proposes a parallel processing view of memory.

Long-Term Memory: Permanent Storage

- Explain how information is organized in long-term memory.

- Describe the different types of long-term memory and their characteristics.

According to both of the two memory models we've explored—the three stages model and the working memory model—long-term memory is our largest and most permanent memory storage system (Figures 6.3 and 6.6). Long-term memory is where we store information that we wish to keep for a long period of time. Information there is not conscious until we activate it and call it into working memory or short-term memory. Let's begin by getting a better understanding of the nature of long-term memory.

The Capacity of Long-Term Memory

For all practical purposes, long-term memory seems to have a limitless capacity. To date, psychologists have not found any reason to believe that long-term memory has a limited capacity, as short-term memory and working memory do. It is safe to say that you are unlikely to ever run out of room in your long-term memory. It may sometimes feel as though your brain is full, but you still have the capacity to store more information in long-term memory. What

Although you may sometimes feel as if your long-term memory is "full," you always have the capacity to store information–provided that you are not too tired, distracted, or unmotivated to rehearse and elaborate the material you wish to learn.

you are feeling is more likely to be related to a problem in focusing your attention or a lack of available capacity in short-term or working memory. If you can pay enough attention to move the information through sensory memory to short-term/working memory, and then rehearse the material enough to get it to long-term memory, you will find that you have ample storage space for the information.

Encoding in Long-Term Memory

Information is encoded in long-term memory in several forms. As in the other parts of memory storage, information in long-term memory can be stored in both acoustic (sound) and visual forms (Paivio, 1986). However, we more often encode long-term memories semantically, in terms of the meaning of the information. **Semantic encoding** stores the gist, or general meaning, of the stimulus rather than storing all of the sensory details (Anderson, 1974; Gernsbacher, 1985; Wanner, 1968).

Semantic encoding offers some distinct advantages over acoustic and visual encoding in long-term memory even though it sacrifices a lot of the details, because all of the features of the original stimulus are not stored in memory. For example, if you read a description of a West African puff-puff in a cookbook, you could store information about the sound of the word *puff-puff* or the visual image of a puff-puff in your long-term memory, but this wouldn't really help you make a puff-puff. In fact, you could memorize an exact picture of a puff-puff and still not know what it is. On the other hand, if you stored semantic information about the puff-puff—that it is a West African food consisting of a fried ball of dough made of flour, eggs, sugar, nutmeg, shortening, milk, and baking powder—you would potentially have enough understanding of a puff-puff to actually make one. A picture couldn't give you that.

Organization in Long-Term Memory

One aspect of encoding information in long-term memory is how we organize it. Over the years, psychologists have proposed various means by which we organize our knowledge categorically (that is, by category; for a review, see Anderson, 2000). One of these strategies involves the use of a generalized knowledge structure called a **schema** (Bartlett, 1932; Rumelhart, 1980). We have *schemata* (plural of *schema*) for people, places, concepts, events, groups of people, and just about everything else we know.

Schemata can be thought of as filing systems we use for knowledge about particular concepts. Schemata contain general information on the characteristics of the concept's category, its function, and so on. For each of these general characteristics, the schema has slots for information specific to the concept. For example, let's look at a portion of a hypothetical schema for a puff-puff. On the left are the names of the slots in the schema found for *breads*. On the right are the specific bits of information that would be placed in these slots for the puff-puff.

Puff-Puff

Is a:	bread
Contains:	flour, sugar, shortening, nutmeg, eggs, etc.
Method of preparation:	fried
Uses:	energy source; eaten with kidney bean stew
Appearance:	small, donut-hole sized
Origin:	West Africa

semantic encoding encoding memory traces in terms of the meaning of the information being stored

schema [SKEE-ma] an organized, generalized knowledge structure in long-term memory

These slots can also have default values that are used when information is missing from our perception. For instance, if you did not read that the puff-puff is fried, you might assume that because a puff-puff is bread, it must be baked. One of the default values for the slot "method of preparation" may be "baked." We probably rely on these default values in schemata when we engage in *top-down perceptual processing* (Chapter 3).

Obviously, breads are not the only objects for which we have schemata. In fact, we have schemata for many different types of information. In addition to schemata for objects, we have schemata for abstract concepts such as love, hate, and psychology. We also have schemata to categorize our social world. We use *person schemata* for specific people, such as best friend, mother, or brother; *stereotypes* for groups of people, such as Asians, Catholics, football fans, or artists; and *scripts* for events, such as going to the doctor, eating at a fancy restaurant, or going on a date. In Chapter 10, we will take a closer look at how schemata affect our behavior in social situations.

Types of Long-Term Memory

Most research on memory has concerned itself with a type of explicit memory called **declarative memory**. Declarative memory is memory for knowledge that can be easily verbalized: names, dates, events, concepts, and so on. Declarative memory can be divided into two subtypes: **semantic memory**, which is memory for concepts, and **episodic memory**, which is memory for the events in one's life.

Right now, as you read this chapter, you are adding to your semantic memory by increasing your knowledge of psychology and memory processes. In doing this, you will add to the schemata you have stored in long-term memory for these (and other) concepts in the chapter. For example, you may think of semantic and episodic memories from your own life and tie your growing knowledge of psychology to the well-formed schemata you have for the world. By building and strengthening these schemata, you are helping to build a knowledge base for psychology that will later enable you to apply this information to problems that require some understanding of psychology, including the exam on test day.

As you attend school and go about the business of your everyday life, you are also adding to your episodic memory (Tulving, 1972; Wheeler, Stuss, & Tulving, 1997). Episodic

declarative memory a type of long-term memory that encompasses memories that are easily verbalized, including episodic and semantic memories

semantic memory long-term, declarative memory for conceptual information

episodic [epp-uh-SOD-ick] **memory** long-term, declarative memory for autobiographical events

Episodic memory gives us our past—such as these childhood memories.

Michael Dunning/Getty Images

memory, sometimes referred to as autobiographical memory, contains your memories of what has happened in your life. You store memories of your conversations with others, events you have attended, and your activities in your episodic, or autobiographical, memory. Episodic memories are associated with a unique sense of personal awareness (Wheeler et al., 1997). Later, when you remember reading this chapter, you'll think: I was there; I remember reading that chapter. This self-awareness makes episodic memory the most personal part of our long-term memory. It is because of episodic memory that we have cherished memories

of childhood, our first date, or days spent with close friends. In fact, if you think about it, our entire sense of history is largely based on the episodic memories that have been stored both in our mind and in the minds of others who have gone before us (Cappelletto, 2003).

GENDER AND AUTOBIOGRAPHICAL MEMORY

Take a moment now to recall some of your own episodic memories. What comes to mind when you think of your past? Is it easy to recall the events of your life, or is it a struggle? Interestingly, researchers have found that how easily you recall episodic memories may be a function of your gender (Colley, Ball, Kirby, Harvey, & Vingelen, 2002; Niedzwienska, 2003). Penelope Davis (1999) found that compared to men, women are better at recalling emotional childhood memories, such as a happy birthday party or an angry conflict with a childhood friend. Davis hypothesized that gender differences are evident only for emotional memories because females' greater tendency to elaborate is particular to emotional event memories. To test this notion, Davis first had all participants retrieve emotion-laden childhood memories. Then they were asked to sort their memories into categories of memories that seemed to go together—for example, happy memories, memories associated with school, memories associated with family, and so on. The participants were free to use as many or as few categories as they chose. As predicted, the females sorted their memories into significantly more categories than the males did. From these data, Davis concluded that females' enhanced autobiographical memory for emotional events is due to the fact that women tend to organize their autobiographical memories into more diverse categories. In other words, women have been socialized to do more elaborative processing of emotion-laden autobiographical memories, and this processing pays off in terms of better recall.

ARE SEMANTIC AND EPISODIC MEMORY SEPARATE SYSTEMS?

Given that semantic and episodic memory are both enhanced by elaborative rehearsal, does this mean that they are stored in the same fashion in the brain? Currently, there is some debate on this issue. Although the findings are controversial, a number of recent studies suggest that episodic and semantic memory may indeed be separate memory systems (Graham, Simons, Pratt, Patterson, & Hodges, 2000; Wheeler et al., 1997). Some of the most persuasive research on this issue comes from studies utilizing the PET scan technology that you learned about in Chapter 2 (p. 65). PET scans allow researchers to see which parts of the brain are most active while the participant is engaged in certain activities. By taking PET scans of participants while they perform semantic and episodic memory tasks, researchers can get a feel for which parts of the brain are involved in these two types of memory.

The results of such PET scan studies suggest that the prefrontal cortex of the frontal lobe (Figure 2.14a, p. 60) plays a much larger role in episodic memory than it does in semantic memory. Given that episodic memory and semantic memory seem to stem from activity in different parts of the brain, it is not a far leap to assume that they must be separate memory systems. However, the interpretation of the PET scan findings in these studies is controversial. At present, all we can say is that the available data *suggest* that episodic and semantic memory are separate memory systems, but more research is needed to further assess the validity of this suggestion.

Research suggests that relative to males, females are better at recalling emotionally charged episodic memories. Later in life, this girl may recall this happy graduation day better than her male classmates do.

Realistic Reflections/Getty Images

PROCEDURAL MEMORY: MEMORY FOR SKILLS

Regardless of whether or not semantic and episodic memory are part of the same memory system, they share the characteristic of being easily verbalized. This is not true of all of our knowledge. **Procedural memory**, our memory for skills, is not readily put into words. To illustrate the difference between declarative and procedural memories, take a moment to try the following demonstration.

YOUR TURN – ACTIVE LEARNING

First, think of a skill that you know very well, such as walking, riding a bike, or driving a car; then attempt to tell someone else how to execute that skill without showing him or her how to do it. You can use only words to describe the skill. Now, choose something about which you have declarative memory—the directions to your favorite music store or the plot of your favorite movie—and try to communicate that using only words.

Which task did you find to be more difficult? We bet that you found the first task to be much harder than the second! The first task asked you to verbalize a *procedural* memory, whereas the second asked you to verbalize a *semantic* memory. As we said before, procedural memories are not easily verbalized, and we've demonstrated just how hard it can be to find words to describe even everyday skills.

Another defining characteristic of procedural memory is that it is often *implicit* memory (Cohen, 1984; Squire et al., 1993). Recall that implicit memory is memory that is used unconsciously (p. 199). We remember without being aware that we are remembering. For the most part, the skills we execute every day are done in an unconscious, implicit fashion. As you walk to your classes, are you consciously aware of what you need to do to get your body to walk? When you take notes in class, are you aware of what you need to do to get your hand to write? Of course not! We walk, write, drive a car, and perform many other skills without thinking about them. The fact that procedural memories are implicit may also help explain why we have a difficult time verbalizing them. How can you verbalize your execution of a behavior when you are not aware of how you do it? You can't.

A final aspect of procedural memory that separates it from declarative memory is its longevity. Procedural memories tend to last for a long time in long-term memory. You've probably heard the saying "It's like riding a bike. You never forget how to do it." There is a great deal of truth in this folk wisdom—once we have mastered a skill, it does stay with us for a long time. For example, one of your authors recently purchased a bike. She hadn't ridden one in almost 10 years, but when she tried it, it was as if she had ridden just yesterday. Declarative memory, on the other hand, does not enjoy the same longevity as procedural memory. If you put aside your study of psychology and never thought about it, how much psychology do you think you would be able to recall 10 years from now? Probably not much.

As you can see, procedural memory seems to differ substantially from declarative memory. The degree of disparity between these two types of memory brings up the question of whether they are separate memory systems. Strong evidence to support the notion that procedural memory is a separate memory system comes from studies done with people suffering from *amnesia*.

Amnesia: What Forgetting Can Teach Us About Memory

Amnesia is a condition in which a person cannot recall certain declarative memories. Amnesia can be classified as retrograde or anterograde (■ FIGURE 6.7). **Retrograde amnesia** is an inability to recall previously stored declarative memories; **anterograde amnesia** is an inability

procedural memory long-term memory for skills and behaviors

retrograde amnesia a type of amnesia in which one is unable to retrieve previously stored memories from long-term memory

anterograde [an-TARE-oh-grade] **amnesia** a type of amnesia in which one is unable to store new memories in long-term memory

Retrograde:
People with retrograde amnesia cannot remember what they have done in the past.

Anterograde:
People with anterograde amnesia cannot form new memories even though they experience new events.

© Chris Hendrickson/Masterfile

FIGURE

6.7

Amnesia Affects a Person's Memory in Dramatic Ways

to encode new declarative memories in long-term memory. In short, retrograde amnesia is amnesia for one's past, and anterograde amnesia is amnesia for one's present and future.

There are several causes of amnesia, but of most interest to us here is amnesia that is caused by brain injury or illness. In particular, studies of brain-injured people with anterograde amnesia have taught us much about the distinction between declarative and procedural memory. One of the most famous cases of anterograde amnesia involved H.M. (Corkin, 1968), who suffered from severe epilepsy that was centered in the vicinity of his hippocampal regions in the temporal lobe (p. 55) and did not respond to medication. In an effort to curb H.M.'s seizures, doctors removed the hippocamal regions in both hemispheres of his brain (Squire, 1992). The surgery was successful, in that H.M.'s seizures were drastically reduced. However, in another sense, the operation was a serious failure. After H.M. recovered from the surgery, it became apparent that he could no longer store new declarative memories. He could not remember seeing his doctor seconds after the doctor left the room. He was also unable to read an entire magazine article. By the time he got to the end of a long paragraph, he would have forgotten what he'd just read. It was clear that H.M. had severe anterograde amnesia.

Interestingly, however, H.M. did not completely lose his ability to store new long-term memories. After the surgery, he could still store procedural memories. For instance, H.M. could learn to do certain perceptual-motor tasks, such as tracing a stimulus while looking at its image in a mirror. Furthermore, he was seen to improve on these tasks with time (Milner, 1962). Results similar to those found in H.M. have also been found in other people with amnesia (for example, Cermak, Lewis, Butters, & Goodglass, 1973). The fact that H.M. and other people with amnesia can still learn new skills indicates that procedural memory is not stored in long-term memory in the same way as declarative memory.

For people with amnesia, the ability to learn new skills is very fortunate. They can still use their procedural memory to learn new skills that may allow them to perform certain jobs, such as making furniture or knitting sweaters, although they will not remember where they acquired these new skills. If they also lost their ability to encode procedural memories, they would be even more impaired. They would not be able to add anything to their long-term memory.

Most of us will never face amnesia to the degree that H.M. did. However, amnesia may be more common than you think. One study reported that in the United States, some 50,000 to 300,000 athletes can be expected to suffer a concussion during a given sports season. Many of these injured athletes will suffer at least mild, temporary amnesia (Collins et al., 2003). If you add to these numbers the people who suffer from other forms of brain injury—from car accidents, illnesses, drug overdoses, and falls—you can see how amnesia may be more common than you might think. This is why it is important to always follow safety procedures, such as wearing a helmet while bicycling.

Even without brain injury or amnesia, you may still encounter mild problems with your memory from time to time. Normal, everyday forgetting can be an annoyance. In the next sections, we will discuss how we retrieve information from long-term memory and theories of why we sometimes forget the information we have encoded in our memory.

Let's Review!

In this section, we described the characteristics, types, and the organization of long-term memory. For a quick check of your understanding, answer these questions.

1. Remembering the definition of *elaborative rehearsal* is an example of a(n) _____ memory.
   a. semantic
   b. procedural
   c. episodic
   d. sensory

2. You know how to behave when you go to a fast-food restaurant because you have a(n) _____ stored in long-term memory for this event.
   a. episode
   b. icon
   c. schema
   d. proposition

3. Which of the following is the *best* example of semantic encoding in long-term memory?
   a. Remembering how to play the tune to your favorite song on a guitar
   b. Remembering the name of the artist who sings your favorite song
   c. Hearing the tune to your favorite song in your head
   d. Seeing the face of the artist who sings your favorite song in your head

Answers 1. a; 2. c; 3. b

Retrieval and Forgetting: Random Access Memory?

- Explain retrieval processes in memory.
- Describe and give examples of the various theories of forgetting in long-term memory.

We store memories so that we can later retrieve them. *Retrieval* is the act of moving information from long-term memory back into working memory or consciousness. Retrieval occurs when we send a *probe* or *cue* into long-term memory in search of *memory traces*, or encoded memories that we have stored there. A probe or cue can be many things—a test question, the sight of a playground, the sound of a roller coaster, or even a particular smell.

Recall Tamara Stewart from the opening case study. When Tamara's husband, Darryl, was sent to Iraq with his military unit, Tamara found a creative way to cope with the stressful situation. She saved one of Darryl's unlaundered T-shirts wrapped up in a tight ball in the bottom of her dresser drawer. When she felt lonely, she would take out the shirt, which smelled like her husband, and smell it. Darryl's scent acted like a powerful memory probe for the memories of Darryl that Tamara had stored in long-term memory, making her feel closer to him. When Darryl returned home safely and their son, Blaine, was sent to Iraq with his unit, Tamara was quick to save one of Blaine's shirts as well. What types of things are powerful memory probes for you?

Recognition and Recall

Think for a moment about the types of exams you have had in the past—for example, multiple-choice, essay, fill-in-the-blank, and true/false. An essay question is an example of a **recall** task. In a recall task, the probe is relatively weak; it does not contain a great deal of information to go on as you search your memory for the answer. You can't guess your way through an essay test. You must really know the information to answer the question. If you have not elaborated the material in long-term memory, you will likely find it difficult to recall.

recall a type of retrieval process in which the probe or cue does not contain much information

A multiple-choice question, on the other hand, is an example of a **recognition** task. In recognition, the probe is stronger and contains much more information than does a recall cue. Several researchers have proposed theories to explain why recognition is typically easier than recall (for example, Gillund & Shiffrin, 1984; Tulving, 1983). One theory proposes that recognition is easier because of the overlap between the content of the probe and the content of the memory trace (Tulving, 1983). Think about it for a minute: In a multiple-choice question, the answer is actually part of the probe. Because recall is the harsher test of memory, you should always study as if you are going to take an essay exam. This way, you'll be sure to be prepared for your professor's questions. For some helpful hints on how to study more effectively, see *Psychology Applies to Your World*.

recognition a type of retrieval process in which the probe or cue contains a great deal of information, including the item being sought

> **You Asked...**
>
> *Why do we usually forget information we are trying to learn if we cram study?*   HOLLY SOSEBEE, STUDENT

Psychology Applies to Your World:

Tips for Improving Your Memory

Much of your academic performance relies on your ability to remember information. Now that you have learned a bit about how your memory works, you can apply this knowledge to your own life. Yes, you too can have a better memory! To be a successful student, you have to study in a way that works with these processes, not against them. We'll outline some strategies that will help maximize your memory.

Pay Attention

Attention is the first step in getting information into memory. If you are distracted while studying, you won't be able to devote your full attention to the information you are trying to learn, and your ability to recall the information later may be affected (Iidaka, Anderson, Kapur, Cabeza, & Craik, 2000). Therefore, you should study when and where you can focus your full attention on your studies. Try studying in a quiet, distraction-free environment.

Do Not Cram for Exams

Cramming is one of the worst ways to study for an exam! Unfortunately, many students procrastinate and then try to make up for it by pulling an all-nighter right before the exam. If this is the way you approach your studies, you are asking for failure. Even if you manage to pull it off, and you actually pass the exam, the information you stored in long-term memory is likely to become inaccessible shortly after the exam. In short, you waste your time when you cram.

Studies have shown that *massed practice*—when you try to learn a great deal of information in one study session—results in poor recall of the information. Recall suffers because massed practice results in fatigue, which leads to a lack of attention, and the shortened time frame does not give you time

You can't learn well if you don't pay attention!

© Bill Aron/PhotoEdit

to adequately rehearse information. Without adequate attention and elaborative rehearsal, information will not be efficiently stored in long-term memory. A better way to study is to use *distributed practice*, distributing your study time across several days rather than bunching it up on one day (or night). The beauty of distributed practice is that you don't necessarily have to study longer, you just need to space out the time you spend studying.

Use Elaborative Rehearsal

To study efficiently, you must process the information at a deeper level, finding ways to elaborate on the *meaning* of the material in your memory. This means you must form connections or associations among the bits of information you are trying to learn and the information you already know. Outlining is one way to do this. Take all of the material you are trying to learn, and organize it into an outline. When you create an outline, you must elaborate the material because you have to think about the relationships among concepts. It also helps to come up with your own original examples of the concepts you are learning—a technique we've encouraged you to use throughout this text. By generating examples, you once again elaborate the material. If the examples are from your own life, this is even better because it ties the material to your *self*, and we remember information that relates to the self better than information that does not (Symons & Johnson, 1997).

Use Overlearning

Overlearning is a technique in which you learn the material until you feel that you have mastered it, and then you *continue* to study it some more. By doing this, you help ensure that you will be able to retrieve it at a later date, because every time you activate information in long-term memory, you help to make it more available for retrieval. Overlearning can also make you feel more confident as you sit down to take an exam. Knowing that you really know the material, as opposed to "sort of" knowing it, can lessen the anxiety that you feel during an exam, which in turn can improve your performance.

Use the SQ3R Method

SQ3R is an acronym for Survey, Question, Read, Recite, and Review. Using this method when studying a chapter, you first *survey* the whole chapter, noting the section headings. As you survey them, you formulate *questions* based on these headings. Then, as you *read* the chapter, you search for answers to your questions. After you read the chapter, you reread the material and *recite*, or summarize, the meaning of each section. Finally, you *review* what you have learned from reading and reciting the material. The SQ3R seems to foster memory because it encourages elaboration and integration of the material. Give it a try when you read the next chapter.

Mnemonics Make Your Memory Mighty

If you find it difficult to elaborate the material, you might try using *mnemonic devices*, memory tricks that help you recall information. A few that you might try include *acronyms*, taking the first letter of each word you want to remember and use these first letters to form a word; and *acrostics*, creating a rhyme or saying in which each word starts with the first letter of each of the to-be-remembered words. For example, *ESR* could be an acronym for the three memory processes of *encoding*, *storage*, and *retrieval*. And, *Ellen steals rabbits* could be an acrostic to help you remember the three memory processes of *encoding*, *storage*, and *retrieval*.

© Bill Aron/PhotoEdit

On exam day, you really hope that your retrieval methods work!

Unfortunately, no method of study is foolproof. Despite your best efforts at studying, there will always be times when retrieval is difficult. We've all known times when the probes and cues we sent into long-term memory were not successful in retrieving the desired information. For a memory to actually be retrieved from long-term memory, two conditions must be met: the memory must be both *available* and *accessible*. A memory is available when it has been encoded in long-term memory and the memory trace is still present in long-term memory. Obviously, if you never encoded the memory in long-term memory, you won't be able to retrieve it later.

You Asked...

If you can't remember something, is it like never learning it?

CAROLANNE PARKER, STUDENT

However, availability by itself is not enough to ensure retrieval. Accessibility of the memory trace is also important. If the probe cannot reach the memory trace in long-term memory, the memory will not be retrieved, even if it is available. As we will see in the next section, there are a variety of circumstances in which the probe fails to retrieve an available, but inaccessible, memory.

Theories of Forgetting: Decay, Interference, Context, and Repression

What student hasn't asked herself this question: "I studied that material, so why did I forget it on the test?" Forgetting occurs when we cannot, for some reason, retrieve information from long-term memory. One theory of forgetting, **decay theory**, maintains that once a memory trace is stored in long-term memory, it must be routinely activated to keep it there (Ebbinghaus, 1885/1913). If we store a memory and then fail to recall it periodically, the memory trace weakens and decays. If the decay is not stopped by recalling the memory, the memory trace will be lost forever.

Although decay theory seems to make sense, there are some good reasons to doubt that memory traces decay from disuse. One is that memories seem to last a very long time, even when we do not routinely access them. For example, in one study, participants' recognition of English–Spanish vocabulary words was tested anywhere from 1 to 50 years after they had studied Spanish. The results showed that recognition memory for these vocabulary words declined little over the years (Bahrick, 1984).

Interference is another reason for forgetting. In interference, the memory trace is still available, but it has become temporarily inaccessible. **Proactive interference** occurs when older information inhibits our ability to retrieve other, newer information from memory. For example, one of your authors spells her first name in an unusual way that often causes proactive interference in others. Her name is pronounced *Suzanne*, but it is spelled *Susann*. Because of its spelling, people often pronounce her name as *Susan* when they first see it in print. Then, no matter how many times she corrects them, they seem to always want to call her *Susan*. This example is one of proactive interference because the *older* (people's original) pronunciation of her name inhibits the *newer* (correct) pronunciation in people's memory. (It's also the reason she started going by *Sue* early in childhood!)

We can also experience **retroactive interference**, in which *newer* information inhibits the retrieval of *older* information in memory. Suppose you move to a new home and work very hard to memorize your new address and phone number. Chances are, you will soon find

decay theory a theory of forgetting that proposes that memory traces that are not routinely activated in long-term memory will degrade

proactive interference a type of forgetting that occurs when older memory traces inhibit the retrieval of newer memory traces

retroactive interference a type of forgetting that occurs when newer memory traces inhibit the retrieval of older memory traces it hard to recall your old address and phone number. This is an example of retroactive interference, because the new phone number and address interfere with your ability to retrieve the old phone number and address from long-term memory.

Unfortunately, our susceptibility to both proactive (Jacoby, Debner, & Hay, 2001) and retroactive interference (Hedden & Park, 2003) tends to increase as we age. One explanation for why interference increases with age is that our central executive function tends to decline with advancing age. As the central executive becomes less efficient, it is also less able to suppress interfering memory traces (Hedden & Yoon, 2006).

Interference theory does seem to describe one way in which we forget information, but there is reason to suspect that interference may not occur as often in the real world as it does in laboratory experiments (Slameka, 1966). **Cue-dependent forgetting** may be a better explanation of forgetting in the real world. Cue-dependent forgetting (Tulving, 1974) asserts that the amount of information we can retrieve from long-term memory is a function of the type of cue or probe we use. If the memory cues we use are not the right ones, we may experience forgetting.

The cue-dependent forgetting theory is part of the *encoding specificity principle* developed by Endel Tulving (Wiseman & Tulving, 1976). According to this principle, we encode aspects of the context in which we learn information, later using these contextual aspects as cues to help us retrieve the information from long-term memory. If the encoding specificity principle is correct, then we should have better memory when we retrieve information in the same setting that we learned it.

Nicole Duplaix/Getty Images

Studies show that we remember information best when we retrieve it in the same context in which it was learned. Godden and Baddeley (1975) found that divers who learned a list of words while under water recalled more of the words while submerged than they did on the dock. Studies like these suggest that a change in context may be one of the reasons we sometimes forget.

In one distinctive study, researchers asked divers to learn a list of words while they were either on shore or 20 feet under the water (Godden & Baddeley, 1975). Later, researchers tested the divers' recall for the words in either the context in which they studied the words or the context in which they did not study the words. Consistent with the encoding specificity principle, the researchers found that when the divers recalled the words in the same context in which they had learned the words, their recall was better.

Encoding specificity has also been shown to hold true for mood states and states of consciousness. People can recall information they learned while drinking alcohol better when they have been drinking (Eich, Weingartner, Stillman, & Gillin, 1975). Information learned while smoking marijuana is better recalled while smoking marijuana (Eich, 1980). And information learned while in a bad mood is better recalled in a negative mood state than when one is happy (Teasdale & Russell, 1983). These findings do not mean that it is better to learn while in these states. For example, alcohol can reduce one's ability to encode information in the first place (Parker, Birnbaum, & Noble, 1976).

The final theory of forgetting we will discuss is Sigmund Freud's (1915, 1943) proposal that the emotional aspects of a memory can affect our ability to retrieve it. According to Freud, when we experience emotionally threatening events, we push or *repress* these memories into an inaccessible part of our mind called the *unconscious* (Chapter 1). This **repression** results in amnesia for this information.

Repression of memories has become a very controversial subject because of its relationship to cases of childhood sexual abuse. Some people have claimed that they suddenly "remembered" abuse that had occurred many years before. After many years have passed, there is often no corroborating evidence to support such claims. Furthermore, some experiments indicate that the details of memories for past events can be incorrect, and that this may be especially true for children (Brainerd & Reyna, 2002; Howe, 2000). In one study, researchers found that preschool children could not distinguish memories for fictitious events from memories for real events after 10 weeks of thinking about the events. Even more

cue-dependent forgetting a type of forgetting that occurs when one cannot recall information in a context other than the context in which it was encoded

repression a type of forgetting proposed by Sigmund Freud in which memories for events, desires, or impulses that we find threatening are pushed into an inaccessible part of the mind called the unconscious alarming, the children were able to give detailed accounts of the fictitious events, and they seemed to really believe that the fictitious events had happened (Ceci, 1995).

The frequent lack of corroborating evidence for recovered memories, along with experimental evidence that questions the accuracy of memory, has led some to charge that these are in fact *false memories*. The debate is further fueled by the lack of experimental data to support the notion that repression can occur. To test the theory of repression, researchers would have to traumatize participants and then see whether they repressed their memories of the trauma. Obviously, this type of study cannot be done for ethical reasons. So, for now, psychologists cannot say for sure whether or not repression is one of the reasons we forget.

You Review 6.2

Theories of Forgetting

THEORY	DEFINITION	EXAMPLE
Decay	Memory traces that are not routinely activated erode and disappear over time	You haven't thought of your best friend from kindergarten in 15 years. When you meet him/her, you cannot recall his/her name.
Proactive interference	Older memory traces inhibit the retrieval of newer memory traces.	You can't seem to remember your friend's new, married name, but you can recall her maiden name.
Retroactive interference	Newer memory traces inhibit the retrieval of older memory traces.	You can't recall your old phone number, but you can recall your new phone number.
Cue-dependent forgetting	Memories are not as easily retrieved when the retrieval cues do not match the cues that were present during encoding.	You run into a classmate at the grocery store, and you can't recall her name. But you do recall her name when you see her at school.
Repression	Threatening memories are pushed into the inaccessible unconscious part of the mind.	You are in a horrible car accident in which other people are seriously injured. Although you are uninjured, you later cannot recall details of the accident.

Let's Review!

In this section, we discussed how information is retrieved from long-term memory and some theories of why we sometimes forget information that we have stored in long-term memory. As a quick check of your understanding, answer these questions.

1. You meet an old friend on the street and search your memory for his name. This is an example of which type of retrieval task?
   a. Recall
   b. Recognition
   c. Implicit retrieval
   d. Retrieval based on encoding specificity

2. Decay theory states that forgetting is due to a lack of _____, whereas interference theory states that forgetting is due to a lack of _____.
   a. availability; accessibility
   b. accessibility; availability

   c. encoding; accessibility
   d. encoding; availability

3. Mary was married six months ago. Much to her dismay, her friends continue to call her by her maiden name even though she has legally taken her husband's name. Mary's friends are experiencing which memory phenomenon?
   a. Encoding specificity
   b. Repression
   c. Proactive interference
   d. Retroactive interference

Answers 1. a; 2. a; 3. c

Is Memory Accurate?

- Describe the accuracy of memory and its implications for eyewitness memory.

Even when we are successful in retrieving memories, a lingering question is just how accurate they are. Many people report experiencing **flashbulb memories**, or unusually detailed memory for emotionally charged events (R. Brown & Kulik, 1977). Perhaps you have, as well. For example, can you remember what you were doing when you heard that terrorists had attacked the World Trade Center on September 11, 2001? Do you recall watching the live TV coverage as the tragedy was taking place? If so, answer this question: How long after the plane hit the first tower did it take for both towers to fall?

Researchers interviewed 690 people 7 weeks after the attack and asked them this same question. On average, the participants reported that it took 62 minutes for the towers to collapse—when in reality it took almost 2 hours. On the day of the attack, do you remember watching news coverage of the first plane hitting the towers? If so, you are not alone—despite the fact that this video footage did not air until the next day (Perina, 2002) . So how did you do on this task? How accurate (or inaccurate) is your memory of that day?

Interestingly, some researchers now suspect that stress hormones that act on the amygdala (p. 55) may be responsible for certain aspects of flashbulb memories. A current theory is that when you experience an emotional event, such as watching a horrific terrorist attack, your body releases stress hormones that direct your brain's amygdala to initiate storage of a long-term memory of that event (see *Neuroscience Applies to Your World*). However, these stress hormones also seem to block the formation of accurate memories for what was happening immediately before the emotional event. Therefore, you may end up with a memory for the emotional event that may not be entirely accurate because you have something of a "gap" in your memory (Bower, 2003).

Steve McCurry/Magnum Photos

Do you remember what you were doing when you heard about the September 11th attacks?

Memory Is Not a Videotape

Does it surprise you to know that memory is often inaccurate? But think about it: Even when we store memories of the everyday events in our lives, we do not store memory traces for every detail. Memory does not work like a video recorder. It's more like a construction project. We store the gist of the information in long-term memory with the help of schemata (p. 210), but we do not store all of the details. This means that when we retrieve a memory, we do not recall all of the details and then use them to *reconstruct* the event. Memory is more than just **reconstructive**, or based on actual events; it is also *constructive*.

Memory is **constructive** in that we use the knowledge and expectations that we have stored in our schemata to help us fill in the missing details in our stored memories. It is very possible that you filled in the gaps in your memory of September 11, 2001—such as what

> **You Asked...**
>
> *How is memory stored?*
>
> JONATHAN GANTES, STUDENT

flashbulb memory an unusually detailed and seemingly accurate memory for an emotionally charged event

reconstructive memory memory that is based on the retrieval of memory traces that contain the actual details of events we have experienced

constructive memory memory that utilizes knowledge and expectations to fill in the missing details in retrieved memory traces

Neuroscience Applies to Your World:

Finding Ways to Forget in Treating People With Post-Traumatic Stress Disorder

Experiencing traumatic events such as war, violent crime, and natural disasters can sometimes result in victims' developing post-traumatic stress disorder (PTSD), a condition in which they have many troubling symptoms including sleep disturbances and flashbacks. Flashbacks are memories of the traumatic event that are so emotionally intense that it is as if the victim is reliving the event. Recently, memory researchers have discovered some interesting things about the role that stress hormones play in the encoding of emotionally charged memories. Studies have suggested that certain hormones, such as adrenalin, that

are released during times of stress may also serve to facilitate the encoding of these episodic memories in long-term memory (Maheu, Joober, Beaulieu, & Lupien, 2004). The presence of these hormones in the bloodstream during and after a traumatic event tends to burn the event into our memory. Under some circumstances, this might be a good thing—for example, if we learn to avoid certain dangerous situations. However, these intense memories can also be very debilitating if they are retrieved frequently and unpredictably, causing the person to relive the trauma in the midst of normal activities.

Researchers have been investigating the possibility that drugs, such as the beta-blocker *propranolol*, that block adrenergic hormones in the body may be useful in preventing and perhaps even treating PTSD. Studies suggest that if a person is given propranolol within hours of experiencing a traumatic event, his or her later recall of the event may be less emotionally intense (Maheu et al., 2004). Very recently, other researchers have found that giving propanolol to participants with preexisting PTSD and then asking them to recall memories of the trauma tends to reduce the amount of emotion they feel on subsequent retrievals of these traumatic memories (Brunet et al., 2008). The hope is that through such training, people with PTSD may someday be able to recall these memories without experiencing debilitating levels of emotion.

you were wearing that day, the setting in which you first heard the news, or specific details of the news coverage that you watched that day. Most of the time, it makes little difference whether or not we recall such details accurately. But sometimes the details of our recollections can be extremely important, even a matter of life and death.

Eyewitness Memory

Psychologist Elizabeth Loftus has spent a good part of her career showing that eyewitness memory can be manipulated by the expectations we hold about the world. For example, in one experiment (Loftus & Palmer, 1974), Loftus showed participants a film of a car accident. After viewing the film, the participants were randomly divided into several groups and questioned about their memory of the film. In one group, the participants were asked, "About how fast were the cars going when they *smashed into* each other?" In another group, the participants were asked, "About how fast were the cars going when they *hit* each other?" In the control group, the participants were not asked to estimate the speed of the cars. The results showed that the verb used in the question affected participants' estimates of the speed of the cars. Participants in the "smashed into" group estimated the speed of the cars, on average, at 41 mph; the average estimate for participants in the "hit" group was 34 mph.

It seems that the words *smashed* and *hit* activated different expectations that were used to fill in the missing details in the participants' memories of the film, and the result was that they remembered the film differently. Imagine how a lawyer's choice of words might influence a witness's memory on the witness stand.

Even more dramatic is the fact that our memories can be permanently altered by things that happen *after* we encode the memories. In another study (Loftus & Zanni, 1975), Loftus showed participants a film of a car crash and then asked them a series of questions about the accident. The participants in one group were asked, "Did you see *a* broken headlight?" In a second group, the participants were asked," Did you see *the* broken headlight?" Although there had been no broken headlight in the film, of those who were asked about *a* broken headlight, 7% reported that they had seen a broken headlight in the film. Of the participants who were asked about *the* broken headlight, 17% said they had seen it. By subtly suggesting to these participants that there *had* been a broken headlight, Loftus caused more of them to remember seeing something that they had not seen. She created a false memory in her participants.

These false memories do not seem to be motivated by a participant's desire to please the researcher. In another study, Loftus offered participants $25 if they could recall an event accurately. Even with this motivation to be accurate, the participants could not prevent their memories from being distorted by the misleading information they heard *after* viewing the incident (Loftus, 1979).

Although it is clear that eyewitness memory is susceptible to errors, there is some disagreement as to why these errors occur. According to Elizabeth Loftus (2000), we accept subsequent misinformation as being correct, and this information becomes part of our memory for the original event. Others propose that eyewitness memory becomes faulty when we make errors in identifying the source of information we have stored in long-term memory (Johnson, Hashtroudi, & Lindsay, 1993). According to this view, when we retrieve a memory for a particular event from long-term memory, we also retrieve information from other sources relevant to the event. For instance, we might retrieve information from times when we discussed the event with others, from comments others made about the event, from things we read about the event in the newspaper, and so on. Because there is considerable overlap between our memory for the original event and our memories of information related to the event, it is easy for us to get confused about the source of these bits of information. We might misattribute the source of a particular detail to our memory of the original event, when we actually encoded it in another situation.

Regardless of which interpretation is correct, after we witness the original event, the more information we are faced with, the more likely it is that our memory will become faulty.

Let's Review!

In this section, we discussed the accuracy of memories we retrieve from long-term memory—in particular, eyewitness accounts of events. For a quick check of your understanding, answer these questions.

1. In recalling his date from last Saturday night, Juan assumes that she was wearing shoes, even though he did not encode the details of what her shoes looked like. Juan's memory is an example of _____.
   a. constructive memory
   b. reconstructive memory
   c. procedural memory
   d. encoding specificity

2. In question number 1, Juan's recollection of his date is *most* likely to be the result of _____.
   a. reconstructive memory
   b. constructive memory
   c. constructive and reconstructive memory

   d. memory that is like a videotape—an exact copy of what he experienced on the date

3. Which of the following events is most likely to produce a flashbulb memory?
   a. Taking a hard math test
   b. Being in a serious car accident
   c. Having a heated discussion with your best friend
   d. Going to a very scary movie on a date

Answers *1. a; 2. c; 3. b*

The Biology of Memory

Learning Objective

• Describe what is known about the biology of memory.

You Asked...

Why is the brain able to store short-term and long-term memory at the same time? REBECCA MBOH, STUDENT

Much of what we know about the role that the brain plays in memory comes from studies of people with amnesia. People with amnesia often experience severe memory problems that can be traced to damage or disease in particular parts of the brain. Recall the case of H.M., discussed earlier in this chapter. H.M.'s hippocampal regions were removed in an attempt to control his epilepsy, and as a result of the surgery, he lost his ability to move new declarative memories from short-term to long-term memory (■ FIGURE 6.8). Other amnesic cases, too, have supported the notion that the hippocampus plays a significant role in the storage of declarative memories (Parkin & Leng, 1993).

Scientists also use brain-imaging technology, discussed in Chapter 2, to study the function of the brain during memory tasks (for example, see Finn, 2004). These studies indicate that the hippocampus plays an important role in the declarative memory function of people without amnesia. For instance, PET scans show that blood flow in the normal brain is higher in the right hippocampal region during declarative memory tasks, but not during procedural memory tasks (Schacter, Alpert, Savage, Rauch, & Alpert, 1996; Squire et al., 1992).

Research on both animals (Iso, Simoda, & Matsuyama, 2006) and humans (Maguire et al., 2006) suggests that the degree to which we use our memory may have implications for the structure of our brain, particularly in the area of the hippocampus. Do you recall the study of London taxi drivers from Chapter 2 (p. 58)? That study used MRI technology to show that London cab drivers have specific hippocampal regions that are larger than those found in London bus drivers. London's street system is old and complicated, and taxi drivers

Cerebral cortex

Hippocampus
(processes
declarative
memory)

Left frontal lobe
(processes verbal
memory)

Cerebellum
(processes
procedural
memory)

© JLP/Jose Luis Pelaez/zefa/Corbis

FIGURE

6.8

**Brain Structures
That Are Important
to Memory**

The hippocampus processes declarative
memories, the left frontal lobe processes verbal
memories, and the cerebellum processes
procedural memories.

must memorize the entire city, not just a single bus route, in order to be licensed. Is it possible that these drivers experienced greater hippocampal development because they relied on their memory so much in doing their job? No one can say for sure at this time, but consistent with this notion, the researchers did find that the taxi drivers who had been driving the longest tended to have the biggest hippocampal regions (Maguire et al., 2006).

Because the hippocampus appears to play an important role in the formation of new memories, researchers are currently investigating whether drugs that stimulate neural growth and function in the hippocampus may also provide useful treatments for people suffering from memory-robbing diseases such as Alzheimer's disease (e.g., Frielingsdorf, Simpson, Thal, & Pizzo, 2007).

Like the hippocampus, the frontal lobe also seems to play a significant role in the processing of declarative memory. Evoked response potential (ERP) recordings have revealed that the left frontal lobe is very active during the processing of verbal information. This makes sense because one of the language centers of the brain, Broca's area (Chapter 2, p. 60), is in the left frontal lobe (Anderson, 2000). Similarly, PET scans of the brain in action have revealed that the amount of left frontal lobe activation seems to be related to the degree to which the participant is processing the material. Left frontal lobe activity is especially likely to occur when participants are *deeply* processing the material. In fact, the more activation there is in the participants' left frontal lobe, the better they tend to recall the information (Kapur et al., 1994). Findings like these seem to suggest that the levels-of-processing approach to memory may have some biological correlate.

It appears that the hippocampus and the frontal lobes play a crucial role in the processing of declarative memory, but what about procedural memory? How is it that a person with severe hippocampal damage, like H.M., can still learn new skills? Declarative memory is usually explicit, but procedural memory is typically executed in an implicit, unconscious manner. Therefore, we may gain some insight into how the brain processes procedural memory by examining the brain function that underlies implicit memory.

To examine brain function during implicit memory processing, researchers took PET scans of participants while they completed implicit and explicit memory tasks. As expected, the explicit memory task was associated with increased blood flow in the hippocampal regions of the brain. However, when the participants used their implicit memory, all of the blood flow changes that occurred were *outside* of the hippocampal regions of the brain (Schacter et al., 1996). It appears that the hippocampus is not involved when memory is processed implicitly, or when we process procedural memories.

Other brain-imaging studies have shown that procedural memory is linked to brain structures outside the hippocampus. For instance, motor skill memory seems to rely, in part, on the cerebellum (Sanes, Dimitrov, & Hallett, 1990; Figure 6.8). This explains why people like H.M. are able to acquire new skills, because procedural memories do not rely on the hippocampus.

Let's Review!

In this section, we discussed the biological bases of memory. Research indicates that the frontal lobes, the hippocampus, and the cerebellum each play a role in certain aspects of memorial processing. For a quick check of your understanding, answer these questions.

1. Which of the following tasks would be most difficult for a person with amnesia like H.M.?
   a. Learning to jump rope
   b. Learning to play a new video game
   c. Recalling his fifth birthday party
   d. Learning psychology

2. Sarah is learning a list of new words. If you took a PET scan of Sarah's brain as she completed this task, where would you expect to see the greatest brain activity?
   a. The cerebellum
   b. The hypothalamus

   c. The hippocampus
   d. The right frontal lobe

3. José was in a car accident and he damaged his cerebellum. Which of the following tasks would be most difficult for José after his accident?
   a. Learning to play piano
   b. Learning psychology
   c. Recalling his childhood
   d. Remembering what he had for breakfast

Answers 1. d; 2. c; 3. a

Studying THE Chapter

Key Terms

encoding (198)
memory traces (198)
storage (198)
retrieval (198)
consciousness (198)
attention (198)
explicit memory (198)
implicit memory (199)
sensory memory (199)
short-term memory (STM) (200)
long-term memory (LTM) (200)
dual coding system (202)
chunking (202)
maintenance rehearsal (203)

elaborative rehearsal (203)
levels-of-processing model (203)
primacy effect (205)
recency effect (205)
working memory (206)
central executive (207)
phonological loop (207)
visuospatial sketch pad (207)
semantic encoding (210)
schema (210)
declarative memory (211)
semantic memory (211)
episodic memory (211)

procedural memory (213)
retrograde amnesia (213)
anterograde amnesia (213)
recall (215)
recognition (216)
decay theory (218)
proactive interference (218)
retroactive interference (218)
cue-dependent forgetting (219)
repression (219)
flashbulb memory (221)
reconstructive memory (221)
constructive memory (221)

What Do You Know? Assess Your Understanding

Test your retention and understanding of the material by answering the following questions.

1. Adding information to memory is known as
   _____.
   a. retrieval
   b. encoding
   c. tracing
   d. attention

2. Buttoning your shirt in the morning most likely involves the use of which type of memory?
   a. Explicit
   b. Implicit
   c. Episodic
   d. Semantic

3. As you read a book, which is the first stage of memory into which the information that you are reading is processed?
   a. Short-term
   b. Working memory
   c. Iconic memory
   d. Semantic memory

4. Which of the following types of memory has the shortest duration?
   a. Long-term memory
   b. Short-term memory
   c. Sensory memory
   d. Working memory

5. How many single-digit numbers should the average person be able to hold in her short-term memory?
   a. 3
   b. 5
   c. 7
   d. 10

6. You likely store information in your short-term memory in what type of format or code?
   a. Visual
   b. Acoustic
   c. Semantic
   d. a or b

7. Which of the following would be the best example of maintenance rehearsal?
   a. Reading your notes over and over as you study for an exam
   b. Thinking about how the material you are studying relates to chapters that you have previously studied
   c. Developing mnemonics to help you remember the material
   d. Thinking about how the material relates to your own life

8. According to the working memory model, which of the following is not a component of working memory?
   a. Short-term memory
   b. The phonological loop
   c. The central executive
   d. Iconic memory

9. The working memory model is to _____ as the three stages model is to _____.
   a. serial processing; explicit memory
   b. parallel processing; explicit memory
   c. serial processing; parallel processing
   d. parallel processing; serial processing

10. As you read the words on this page, which component of working memory is likely processing the shape, size, and spacing of the letters and words on this page?
    a. Short-term memory
    b. The phonological loop
    c. The central executive
    d. The visuospatial sketch pad

11. Your knowledge of *animals* is most likely stored in _____.
    a. short-term memory as acoustic memory traces
    b. short-term memory as semantic memory traces
    c. long-term memory as acoustic memory traces
    d. long-term memory as semantic memory traces

12. Glenn suffered a concussion in a terrible car accident, after which he could no longer recall the events of the week leading up to the accident. Glenn seems to be suffering from _____.
    a. retrograde amnesia
    b. anterograde amnesia
    c. repression
    d. cue-dependent forgetting

13. Your knowledge of cars and trucks is an example of _____ memory.
    a. long-term
    b. semantic
    c. declarative
    d. All of the above

14. Compared to declarative memory, procedural memory is often _____.
    a. more likely to be processed in the hippocampus
    b. more explicit
    c. less verbal
    d. less implicit

15. In _____, the memory probes and cues are stronger and contain more information.
    a. recall
    b. recognition
    c. short-term memory
    d. long-term memory

16. When you first met your classmate, he was introduced to you as Calvin. However, Calvin never uses his first name and goes by just his initials (C. D.). Now, after a few years, you find that you cannot recall C. D.'s first name. This is most likely an example of _____.
    a. retroactive interference
    b. proactive interference
    c. memory trace decay
    d repression

17. According to the available research, which of the following is not a true statement about flashbulb memories?
    a. They are emotionally charged memories.
    b. They are in part a function of the stress hormones that are released at the time the memory trace is encoded.
    c. They are very accurate in their detail.
    d. Many people experience flashbulb memories at some point in their lives.

18. Recalling the actual details of your first birthday party in an accurate manner would be an example of _____ memory.
    a. reconstructive
    b. constructive
    c. semantic
    d. procedural

19. The phrase *please excuse my dear aunt Sally*, used as a tool to help people recall the order of mathematical operations, is an example of _____.

a. an acronym
b. a mnemonic
c. massed practice
d. All of the above

20. While walking into the grocery store, Shana calls her roommate to find out what they need. The roommate tells Shana to buy eggs, flour, bacon, apples, toilet paper, soap, napkins, lettuce, bread, salt, jam, pickles, coffee, milk, lemons, peanut butter, and pears. Having no pen, Shana has to keep these items in memory. Based on what you know about memory, which of the following items is Shana most likely to forget to buy?

a. Pears
b. Eggs
c. Bacon
d. Soap

Answers: 1. b; 2. b; 3. c; 4. c; 5. c; 6. d; 7. a; 8. d; 9. d; 10. d; 11. d; 12. a; 13. d; 14. c; 15. b; 16. a; 17. c; 18. a; 19. b; 20. d.

Online Resources

CENGAGENOW™ Personalized Study

www.cengage.com/login

Go to www.cengage.com/login to link to CengageNOW, your online study tool. First take the **Pre-Test** for this chapter to get your **Personalized Study Plan**, which will identify topics you need to review and direct you to online resources. Then take the **Post-Test** to determine what concepts you have mastered and what you still need work on.

 What Is Psychology? Essentials Book Companion Website

www.cengage.com/psychology/pastorino

Visit your book companion website, where you will find more resources to help you study. Resources include learning objectives, Internet exercises, quizzing, flash cards, and a pronunciation glossary.

Look Back AT WHAT YOU'VE LEARNED

How Does Memory Function?

- The human brain **encodes**, stores, and processes information. We can use memory both **explicitly** (consciously) and **implicitly** (unconsciously).

- What is the traditional three stages model of memory?

Information → Sensory memory → Short-term memory ⇄ Long-term memory

- Many researchers today reject the rigid **three stages model** of memory and suggest a different type of memory, called **working memory**, that is important in moving information in and out of **long-term memory**.

New information enters short-term memory from sensory memory

Short-term memory

Working memory

Long-term memory

How Is Information Stored in Long-Term Memory?

Declarative memory		Procedural memory
Semantic memory	+	
Episodic memory		

How Is Long-Term Memory Organized?

Long-term memory is organized into **schemata**, which allow us to quickly and efficiently use our memory. In a sense, schemata are like a filing system for the library of knowledge we have stored in our long-term memory.

PhotoSpin, Inc/Alamy

Retrieval and Forgetting: Random Access Memory?

Despite our best efforts to retain information, sometimes forgetting occurs. Forgetting may be due to **decay** of memory traces, **interference**, **cue-dependent forgetting**, or perhaps even **repression**.

HOW DOES MEMORY FUNCTION?

© Bill Arony/PhotoEdit

How Can You Improve Your Memory?

- Pay attention to what you are trying to remember; avoid distractions.

- Do not cram for exams.

- Use elaborative rehearsal to reinforce retention of information.

- Use **overlearning**.

- **Mnemonics** make your memory mighty.

- The SQ3R method encourages a process of Survey, Question, Read, Recite, Review.

Is Memory Accurate?

© Steve McCurry/Magnum Photos

- **Flashbulb memories** are unusually detailed memories for emotionally charged events—memories that are quite powerful but not always accurate.

- In general, we are prone to many memory errors. In cases of eyewitness testimony, these errors can have serious consequences.

What Do We Know About the Biology of Memory?

- Brain-imaging research shows that people who use their memory a great deal may have structural differences in their hippocampal regions. The hippocampus and frontal lobe seem to play significant roles in processing declarative memory.

- Studies suggest that procedural memory is linked to the cerebellum.

Cerebral cortex

Hippocar (processe declarativ memory)

Frontal lobe (cesses verbal ory)

Cerebellun (processes procedural memory)

© JLP/Jose Luis Pelaez/zefa/Corbis

7

Cognition, Language, AND Intelligence: HOW DO WE THINK?

Blend Images/Getty Images

When one of our students, Franco Chevalier, immigrated with his family to the United States from their native Dominican Republic, he faced many challenges. Franco had to adapt to a new culture, a new school, new friends, new customs, and so on. Most challenging was the fact that Franco came to the United States speaking Spanish and some French, but only a few words of English. In school, Franco was very anxious to make the most of his new educational opportunities, but he had difficulty understanding his English-speaking teachers. Some of Franco's classmates mistakenly assumed that his poor English meant that he was unintelligent. In fact, when Franco excelled in math, a less verbal subject, they told him that the teachers gave him good grades because they felt sorry for him. However, despite the difficulty and the prejudice, Franco was determined to succeed. He knew that he was intelligent and that he could master English. In high school, he enrolled in advanced placement courses (including English!) and worked nonstop to learn.

Today, Franco speaks fluent English. He graduated in the top 5% of his high school class and is now a very successful premed major in college. In his college psychology course, Franco learned about how humans develop language and the role that language plays in thinking and intelligence—knowledge that no doubt gave him insight into his own experiences with language and learning. As you read about these same topics in this chapter, consider the important and intertwined roles that thinking, language, and intelligence play in both your life and the lives of others.

© Susann Doyle-Portillo

Franco Chevalier

233

Thinking: How We Use What We Know

- Describe the process of thinking and the manner in which we represent knowledge in our memory.

cognition the way in which we use and store information in memory

thinking the use of knowledge to accomplish some sort of goal

knowledge information stored in our long-term memory about the world and how it works

mental representation memory traces that represent objects, events, people, and so on that are not present at the time

FIGURE

7.1 An Image-Scanning Task

In this task, participants were asked to imagine a black dot moving across the map to the points indicated by the *X*s. The average amount of time to do this was proportionate to the distance between the starting point and the ending point on the map.

Source: © Stephen Kosslyn 1978.

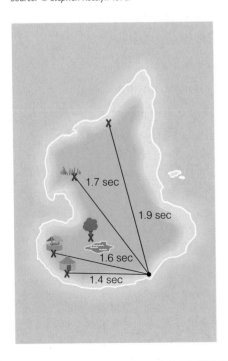

Psychologists define **cognition** as the way in which we store and use information. We engage in some sort of cognition every waking moment. Each day, we do a lot of thinking, but most of us would have difficulty defining what it is that we actually *do* when we think. Psychologists define **thinking** as the use of **knowledge**, the information we have stored in long-term memory, to accomplish some sort of goal. So defined, thinking includes the ability to perceive and understand our world, to communicate with others, and to solve the problems we encounter in our lives (R. E. Mayer, 1983).

Thinking involves the use of all types of knowledge. We store our knowledge in long-term memory as **mental representations**—bits of memory that represent objects, events, people, and so on that are not actually present now. For instance, most of us can close our eyes and think about what our best friend looks like, the smell of her perfume, and her likes and dislikes. To do this, we call on the many mental representations of our friend that we have stored in long-term memory.

In general, thinking involves the use of two broad classes of mental representations: those based on *sensory* aspects of the object, such as its visual appearance, smell, taste, and so forth; and those based on the *meaning* of the object, such as its name, definition, and properties. We will now turn our attention to a discussion of the best-studied forms of these mental representations: *visual images* and *concepts*.

Visual Images: How Good Is the Mental Picture?

The ability to "see" a friend's face in our mind or to visualize a map of our hometown in our head can be very useful in everyday life, but do we really store "pictures" in our memory? Over the years, psychologists have studied this question by examining how people perform on certain tasks in which they must mentally manipulate visual images (Denis & Cocude, 1999; Kosslyn, Ball, & Reiser, 1978).

In a typical *image-scanning* experiment, like the one done by Stephen Kosslyn and colleagues (Kosslyn et al., 1978), participants are asked to memorize a map of a fictitious island with several objects depicted on it (see ■ FIGURE 7.1). After the participants have memorized the map, they are asked to mentally scan the path that a black dot would take as it travels from one point on the map to another. Because the points are at various distances from one another, researchers can correlate the time it takes participants to mentally scan the image with the distance between the points on the actual map. If the participants' visual images of the map are copies of the actual map, then the time it takes to scan longer distances should be longer than the time it takes to scan shorter distances on the map. This is exactly what Kosslyn found: The time it took to scan distances increased proportionately with the increase in the actual distances on the map. The results of this and numerous other experiments (see Shepard, 1978, for a review) suggest that visual images may have all of the spatial properties of the real stimulus. In other words, the visual image we store is essentially a *copy* of the stimulus we see in the world.

As convincing as image-scanning experiments are in supporting the argument that visual images have spatial properties that mimic those of the actual stimulus, the question still remains: Do we actually store photographic images of the things that we see?

As it turns out, there are reasons to suspect that we generally do not. For example, try the following demonstration.

YOUR TURN — ACTIVE LEARNING

Let's look at your ability to answer questions about a visual stimulus that you have seen many times, a map of North America.

Which is farther east: Reno, Nevada, or San Diego, California?

Which is farther north: Montreal, Canada, or Seattle, Washington?

Which is farther west: the Atlantic or the Pacific entrance to the Panama Canal?

The answers seem obvious, but researchers have found that most people answer them incorrectly (Stevens & Coupe, 1978). The correct answers are *San Diego*, *Seattle*, and the *Atlantic entrance*. Are you surprised? Take a look at ■ FIGURE 7.2, which shows that these are the correct answers.

FIGURE

7.2

A Map of North and South America

Most people answer many questions about this map incorrectly even though they have seen it many times before. It is highly unlikely that we have an exact visual image of this map stored in our long-term memory.

The fact that so many of us answer these questions incorrectly argues that we do not store an exact visual image of the U.S. map in memory. Rather, we store an approximate visual image of the map as well as some general knowledge about the geography of the area. Furthermore, when we try to visualize maps in our heads, we tend to think of geographical locations in terms of larger units (Stevens & Coupe, 1978), and we use this knowledge to help us deduce the needed geographical information (B. Tversky, 1981). In response to the first question, for example, we know that San Diego is in California, and we know that California is west of Nevada. Therefore, when we recall our knowledge of the United States, we assume that Reno, Nevada, must be east of San Diego, and we visualize a map in which this is true. In fact, it is not true, as you can see in Figure 7.2.

You Asked...

Do you actually think in a language? TAYLOR EVANS, STUDENT

So, where does all of this research leave us with respect to visual images? Isn't it a bit contradictory? Some studies suggest that visual images are precise mental copies of the actual stimuli (e.g., Shepard, 1978), but other studies show that visual images may deviate significantly from the actual stimuli (e.g., Boden, 1988; Chambers & Reisberg, 1992). According to Stephen Kosslyn (1994), our mental representation of visual stimuli relies on *both* visual images and verbal knowledge. In other words, we use both types of mental representations—sensory (pictures) and meaning (words)—to fully represent visual stimuli. The pictures represent parts of the stimulus, and the words describe the stimulus and tell us how the pieces of the picture fit together. For example, when you look at a flower, you might store, among other things, a visual image of the shape of a petal, the stem, and the center, along with words describing the fact that the petals are placed around the center and the stem descends from the bottom of the flower. In Kosslyn's view, we do not store a carbon copy of the flower. Instead, we use this mixture of verbal and pictorial pieces to *construct* our visual image of the flower. Recall from Chapter 6 that memory is, after all, *constructive*. Unfortunately, the constructive nature of memory does sometimes lead to inaccuracies. So, don't feel bad if you thought Reno was east of San Diego!

Concepts: How We Organize What We Know

As we saw in Chapter 6, we have a tendency to organize our knowledge in long-term memory. We store mental representations for related objects together in the same mental category. For example, we would store our knowledge of cats, dogs, and elephants together in the category for *animals*, and apples, oranges, and grapes together in the category for *fruits*. This tendency to organize information based on similarity shows the *conceptual* nature of human cognition. **Concepts**, the mental categories that contain related bits of knowledge, are organized around the *meaning* of the information they represent. For instance, *animal* is a concept. In our mind we know what it means to be an animal. Animals must be animate, but we also distinguish animals from humans, and so on.

We store conceptual information in a verbal or semantic form (recall Chapter 6), and we use this information to perceive, think about, and deal with our world. Conceptually organizing our knowledge helps us use that knowledge more efficiently. Concepts can be viewed as a type of mental shorthand that both organizes and saves space in our cognitive system. Let's look at an example of a well-known concept: oranges. Close your eyes and picture an orange in your mind's eye. Can you see it clearly? Can you describe it in detail? Most of us can do this easily for something as familiar as an orange. Now look carefully at your mental orange. Is this concept that you have stored in your mind an *actual* orange that you have seen? In other words, is this orange number 123,675 that you saw one Sunday morning at the local market? Not likely! Instead, your concept of an orange is an abstraction, or a general idea, of what an orange is. You don't have to store mental representations for each and every orange you have seen. Rather, you only need to store a generalized concept of what an orange is and what it looks like. This is a great cognitive space-saver when you think about all of the oranges you'll see in your lifetime.

ORGANIZING CONCEPTS INTO CATEGORIES

Another benefit of mental concepts is that we can organize them into hierarchical categories (Markman & Ross, 2003). Psychologists have found that we tend to organize our knowledge into three levels of categorization (Rosch, Mervis, Gray, Johnson, & Boyes-Braem, 1976). The highest, most general level is called the **superordinate category**. The superordinate level

concept mental category that contains related bits of knowledge

superordinate category the highest, most general level of a concept contains concepts that are broad and general in their description. For example, fruit would be considered to be a superordinate category. The intermediate level of categorization is the **basic level category**. The basic level seems to be the level that we use most often to think about our world. For example, when we write out a shopping list, we probably list basic level concepts, such as oranges rather than fruit.

The third level in the hierarchy is the **subordinate category**. Concepts at the subordinate level are less general and more specific than those at the basic level. When speaking of oranges, the subordinate category would contain items like Valencia oranges, navel oranges, and blood oranges. Although the subordinate level is the most specific, it is not the first level that springs to mind when we think about our world. You would be much more likely to place the basic level concept—oranges—on your shopping list than you would be to place Valencia oranges. Interestingly, the basic level is also the first level of knowledge young children acquire (Rosch et al., 1976).

FORMAL AND NATURAL CATEGORIES

So, how do we acquire concepts in the first place? Simply put, we acquire concepts from an early age as we observe and learn from our world. We acquire **formal concepts** as we learn the rigid rules that define certain categories of things. For example, for an animal to be considered a member of the category *female*, it must possess certain attributes or characteristics. All females are genetically designed to produce either offspring or eggs. If an animal does not have this attribute, it cannot be a female.

The lines that define formal categories are very clear-cut. Unfortunately, life is not always so neat and tidy as to provide us with formal rules for everything, and much of our knowledge of the world does not fit cleanly into only one category. For example, do you consider a tomato to be a fruit or a vegetable? How do you categorize cucumbers? Many people consider tomatoes and cucumbers to be vegetables, whereas others—including botanists—categorize them as fruits. Why the confusion? Perhaps because we associate fruits with sweetness, we tend not to classify cucumbers and tomatoes as fruit even though they do contain seeds, which is a defining attribute of fruit. Most of us are aware of the rules for membership as a female, but not aware of the botanical definition of a fruit. We have organized our fruit and vegetable concepts in a less distinct and orderly fashion based on our own experiences with them.

Concepts that develop naturally as we live our lives and experience the world are referred to as **natural concepts**. We do not learn formal rules for these concepts; rather, we intuit and create the rules as we learn about our world. As such, the boundaries defining natural concept categories are often blurry, or "fuzzy" (Rosch, 1973). Our example of the tomato is a good illustration of this. You can classify the tomato as a vegetable, a fruit, or both depending on your experience. Because many of us see tomatoes in the vegetable section of the supermarket, we include them in the vegetable category. However, botanists scientifically classify tomatoes as fruits. How do you see them?

Because natural concepts are a by-product of our day-to-day experience, they develop in a relatively effortless and *natural* manner as we live our lives. Curiously, when researchers try to force people to develop new natural concepts in the laboratory, people have a lot of trouble doing so (Makino & Jitsumori, 2007). In such situations, we may overthink the situation and try to develop clear-cut rules for concepts that are inherently fuzzy. For example, if you were asked to define the criteria for identifying real-world examples of "love," you would likely find this to be a very difficult task.

basic level category the intermediate level of categorization that seems to be the level that we use most to think about our world

subordinate category the lowest level of categorization, which contains concepts that are less general and more specific than those at the basic level

formal concept concept that is based on learned, rigid rules that define certain categories of things

natural concept concept that develops naturally as we live our lives and experience the world

The basic level category *apple* falls under the superordinate category *fruit*. The label *Granny Smith* is a subordinate category of the basic level concept *apple*.

© Athol Franz; Gallo Image/Corbis

© Paul Poplis/Jupiter Images

© Corbis

YOUR TURN – ACTIVE LEARNING

In the real world, we tend to do better with the fuzzy boundaries of natural concepts, but we are not perfect. The difficulty involved in deciding which items to include and which to exclude from a category varies considerably. Sometimes it's an easy task, and other times it's not. Take a look at ■ FIGURE 7.3, and answer the questions as quickly as you can. Which of the questions were you able to answer quickly? Which ones took longer? Why do you think some of them were easier than others?

FIGURE 7.3 Natural Concept Categories

Answer these questions as fast as you can.

Question	Yes	No
Is a bat a mammal?	Yes ☐	No ☐
Is a dolphin a mammal?	Yes ☐	No ☐
Is a penguin a bird?	Yes ☐	No ☐
Is a cat a mammal?	Yes ☐	No ☐
Is a robin a bird?	Yes ☐	No ☐
Is a whale a mammal?	Yes ☐	No ☐
Is an eagle a bird?	Yes ☐	No ☐

All answers are "Yes."

Most people find it easier to decide that a robin is a bird than that a penguin is a bird. But why? One possibility is that a robin is a more typical example of the category bird than a penguin is. According to some researchers, we form what are called **prototypes** for natural concept categories, much like the mental image of the orange we examined on page 236. A prototype is our concept of the most typical member of the category—in essence, a summary of all the members of the category. When we judge whether or not something belongs in a natural concept category, we compare it to the prototype of the category (Minda &

prototype our concept of the most typical member of the category

Smith, 2002). The more similar the object is to the prototype, the faster we judge it to be a member of the concept category.

However, other researchers argue that instead of using abstracted prototypes, we judge category membership by comparing an item to the memories that we have stored for actual examples or **exemplars** of that concept category (Nosofsky & Zaki, 2002; Rehder & Hoffman, 2005). In this view, you would determine that the robin in your backyard is a bird by comparing this robin to the memories or exemplars of the actual birds you have seen during your lifetime. Unless you live where penguins are common, you are likely to have many more songbird exemplars than penguin exemplars available in your memory. Because robins resemble the songbird exemplars that quickly come to mind more closely than penguins do, you are quicker to decide that a robin belongs in the category of birds.

The debate over whether we use prototypes or exemplars to judge category membership is ongoing. Some argue that we may even use both (Storms, DeBoeck, & Ruts, 2001). Regardless of how we go about making category judgments, these judgments are crucial to our ability to think about our world. In the next section, we will see just what we can accomplish with all of our thinking. But first, take a moment to test your knowledge of this last section.

Let's Review!

In this section, we discussed thinking and how we represent information in memory. We discussed not only the format of stored knowledge, but also its organizational structure. For a quick check of your understanding, answer these questions.

1. Which of the following is evidence indicating that our visual images contain all the properties of the actual stimulus?
    a. Memory for images is near perfect in children.
    b. The time it takes to mentally scan an image of an object is related to the actual size of the object.
    c. Most people can visualize familiar objects in great detail.
    d. Our mental maps of the world are perfect in their detail.

2. Which of the following would be a superordinate concept for the category *hammer*?
    a. Ball-peen hammer   c. Tool
    b. Saw   d. Screwdriver

3. In an experiment, Dr. Kelly asks participants to name the first example of a "vehicle" that comes to mind. Based on what you know about concepts, which of the following vehicles would the average participant be *most* likely to name?
    a. A tractor   c. An airplane
    b. A train   d. A truck

Answers 1.b; 2.c; 3.d

Problem Solving: Where Does Our Thinking Get Us?

- Describe the different types of problems we face and the ways in which we may try to solve them.
- Describe common obstacles to problem solving.

Learning Objectives

Imagine that you get into your car one morning, only to find that it won't start. It's 7:30 and you have an 8:00 class. Today of all days, you don't need this because you have a final exam in your psychology class. You have a problem! As you can see from this example, we never know when a problem will arise. What would you do in this situation? Call a friend for a

exemplar [ig-ZEM-plar] a mental representation of an actual instance of a member of a category

Table 7.1 The Steps to Problem Solving

PROBLEM-SOLVING STEP	EXAMPLE
Identify the problem.	The car won't start, and I have a final exam.
Represent the problem.	If I miss this exam without permission, I'll fail the course.
Plan a solution.	I will call a taxi.
Execute the plan.	Call the taxi.
Evaluate the plan.	The taxi will get me to school, but I will be late. Maybe I should also have called my professor?
Evaluate the solution.	I did make it to school, and I took the exam. My professor was a bit angry that I didn't call to say I'd be late, but I did pass the exam. I handled this situation adequately, but next time I'll call my professor.

Source: Hayes, 1989.

ride? Walk to school? Call your professor and arrange to take a makeup final? Or fix your own car? In general, when we solve problems, we go through a series of six stages (Hayes, 1989), outlined in ■ TABLE 7.1.

Although the prospect of missing a final exam is frightening, there are a variety of obvious solutions to this problem. This is not the case for all problems, however. If it were, we would have ended hunger, war, and pollution long ago. Why do some problems seem to have obvious possible solutions whereas others do not? The answer lies in the type of problem we are facing.

Well-Structured and Ill-Structured Problems

Well-structured problems are problems for which there is a clear pathway to the solution. We face well-structured problems every day. Learning to use your new cell phone, balancing your checkbook, and finding the cheapest hotel at your vacation destination are all examples of well-structured problems. When we solve well-structured problems, we tend to go about it in one of two ways. We use either an algorithm or a heuristic to achieve a solution.

An **algorithm** is a method of solving a particular problem that always leads to the correct solution; a **heuristic** is a shortcut or rule of thumb that may or may not lead to a correct solution. Imagine that you're going to paint your bedroom, but you don't know how much paint to buy. The algorithmic solution to this problem is to measure the height and width of all your walls, calculate the area, and look up how many gallons of paint are required to cover this area. This algorithm will lead to the correct answer, and as a result, you will buy just the right amount of paint. However, this strategy also takes considerable time. You must measure the walls, find the formula for paint coverage, and calculate the required figures. If you are in a hurry (or impatient), this strategy may not be your first choice. Instead, you might use a heuristic, such as simply guessing how much paint you will need to do the job. Guessing is quick, but you do run the risk of not buying the right amount of paint. You might have

well-structured problem a problem for which there is a clear pathway to the solution

algorithm [AL-go-rih-thum] a method of solving a particular problem that always leads to the correct solution

heuristic [hyur-RISS-tick] a shortcut or rule of thumb that may or may not lead to a correct solution to the problem to go back to the store for more paint, or you might have a lot of paint left over. *Guessing* and repeated guessing, or *trial and error*, are two very common heuristics.

As you look at this example, you may think that it seems foolish to guess at the amount of paint to buy when a clear algorithm exists for this problem. Why would anyone approach a problem in this seemingly haphazard fashion? There are at least two reasons that one might choose a heuristic over an algorithm. First, heuristics can save time. You might guess correctly that you need 2 gallons of paint to cover your room. Second, we do not always know the correct algorithm for the problem we are facing. What if you lack the mathematical knowledge to calculate the surface area of your bedroom walls? Even though there is a formula for calculating the surface area and paint coverage, if you don't know what it is, you cannot implement the algorithm, and you would have to use a heuristic.

In contrast, when attempting to solve an *ill-structured problem*, we have no choice but to use a heuristic. **Ill-structured problems** are problems for which there is no known algorithm, such as trying to end global warming or effect world peace. However, this does not mean that there is no chance the problem will be solved. Keep in mind that heuristics do sometimes lead to viable solutions to problems. For example, a man lost at sea might randomly plug a hole in his boat by shoving a shoe in the hole. Of course, to implement this problem-solving strategy, he would first have to think about trying the shoe. The danger is that we may not even *think* of certain possible solutions to our problems.

This is often the case with ill-structured problems. Often we get stuck in particular ways of trying to solve problems, and we lack the **insight** required to find a true solution. Insight occurs when we find a new way of looking at the problem that leads to a sudden understanding of how to solve it (Dominowski & Dallob, 1995). Because of its perceived suddenness, insight is often referred to as the "Aha!" experience. Insight often feels as if a lightbulb has turned on, illuminating the answer for us. But current research indicates that insight isn't such a sudden process. Insight often occurs only after we have thought about the problem for a while (C. A. Kaplan & Simon, 1990). Truly understanding a problem and how to solve it often occurs only as the result of much thought and gradual acquisition of knowledge about the problem (Hamel & Elshout, 2000).

Deciding how much paint to buy for a home improvement project is an example of a task that can be most accurately solved using an algorithm.

Creativity: Overcoming Obstacles to Problem Solving

We do not need to tell you that some problems in life are more difficult to face than others. At times, all of us may encounter problems that challenge even our best problem-solving skills. Solving difficult problems often requires *creativity*.

For more than 50 years, psychologists have been trying to define exactly what creativity is and what abilities or traits creative people possess (Mumford, 2003). To date, the major agreement among researchers has been that **creativity** involves the ability to combine mental elements in new and useful ways (e.g., Sternberg, 1999; Vartanian, Martindale, & Kwiatkowski, 2003). Creativity may mean finding a novel solution to a problem or coming up with a unique approach to creating some new product—a piece of music, a painting, or a scientific theory that is widely recognized as being creative (Gelade, 2002).

Certainly all of us can think of people we believe are creative. But what makes one person more creative than another? Are there special traits or abilities that creative people possess? Over the years, psychologists have proposed several variables that may underlie creativity,

ill-structured problem a problem for which an algorithm is not known

insight a new way of looking at a problem that leads to a sudden understanding of how to solve it

creativity the ability to combine mental elements in new and useful ways but the one that has received the most attention is a skill called *divergent thinking* (Vartanian et al., 2003). Divergent thinking is the ability to generate many ideas quickly in response to a single prompt (Eysenck, 1995). For example, a divergent thinker can quickly come up with many different ways to tie a scarf or many different uses for an ink pen.

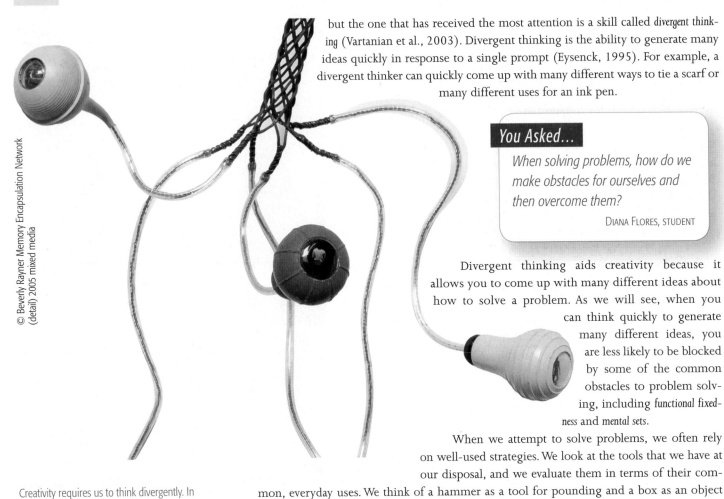

© Beverly Rayner Memory Encapsulation Network (detail) 2005 mixed media

Creativity requires us to think divergently. In creating this piece of art, the artist has found a new use for these common items.

Divergent thinking aids creativity because it allows you to come up with many different ideas about how to solve a problem. As we will see, when you can think quickly to generate many different ideas, you are less likely to be blocked by some of the common obstacles to problem solving, including *functional fixedness* and *mental sets.*

When we attempt to solve problems, we often rely on well-used strategies. We look at the tools that we have at our disposal, and we evaluate them in terms of their common, everyday uses. We think of a hammer as a tool for pounding and a box as an object for holding other objects. We often cannot conceive of using these tools in new, novel ways. This limitation of being able to see objects only in their familiar roles is called **functional fixedness**. Functional fixedness can prevent us from solving problems that otherwise could be solved. For example, if your author could only think of her MP3 player as a device for listening to music, she might not have realized that she could use its illuminated video display to light up a darkened room during a recent power outage, allowing her to find some matches and candles!

Another obstacle to problem solving is a **mental set**. A mental set is a tendency to habitually use the methods of problem solving that have worked for you in the past. Mental sets become an obstacle when we persist in trying solutions that may have worked in the past but are not working in the current situation. If you find yourself having little success in solving a problem, stop working on the problem for a while and let it *incubate*. **Incubation**, or a period of not thinking about the problem, sometimes helps us solve a problem (Ohlsson, 1992). When we incubate, the unproductive strategies recede from memory, and we are better able to attack the problem from a fresh, more productive perspective when we return to it. If we are locked in a mental set, incubation may be just what is needed to solve the problem.

As we've seen in this section, problem solving is a matter of generating possible solutions and then selecting the one that will ultimately solve the problem. If your car broke down tomorrow, how would you decide which course of action to take? Would you call in absent to school? Call a mechanic? Call a taxi? Walk to school? Go back to bed and forget it? Many times, choosing the *best* solution from among all the possibilities is the real task. In the next section, we take a closer look at the cognitive processes that we engage in when we reason, make decisions, and make judgments.

functional fixedness being able to see objects only in their familiar roles

mental set the tendency to habitually use methods of problem solving that have worked for you in the past

incubation [in-cue-BAY-shun] a period of not thinking about a problem that helps one solve the problem

Let's Review!

In this section, we discussed the process of problem solving, including the types of problems we might face, the manner in which we tend to solve such problems, and common obstacles to problem solving. For a quick check of your understanding, answer these questions.

1. Which of the following is the *best* example of an ill-structured problem?
   a. Balancing your monthly checking account statement
   b. Losing weight
   c. Reducing crime in your neighborhood
   d. Solving a crossword puzzle

2. Incubation sometimes aids problem solving because it _____.
   a. reduces fatigue
   b. allows insight
   c. allows us to forget unproductive strategies
   d. allows us to work out a solution subconsciously

3. Sue used a chair with wheels to carry a load of books to her car. She piled the books in the seat of the chair and pushed it to her car. Trina, on the other hand, carried her books by hand, even though she also had a chair with wheels in her office. Trina was most likely suffering the effects of _____.
   a. functional fixedness
   b. an ill-structured problem
   c. insight
   d. stupidity

Answers 1. c; 2. c; 3. a

Reasoning, Decision Making, and Judgment

- Describe the processes of making decisions and judgments.

- Describe the availability and representativeness heuristics and how they may bias our decisions and judgments.

Reasoning, decision making, and judgments are cognitive processes that use some of the same strategies as problem solving. We engage in *reasoning* when we draw conclusions based on certain assumptions about the world. For example, you might reason that your friend Jamal is a nice person because he has many friends. *Decision making* is choosing among several options, as in our example of what you might do if your car breaks down. *Judgments* are also related to solving problems, often using two particular heuristics that we'll discuss.

Deductive and Inductive Reasoning

We engage in **reasoning** when we draw conclusions that are based on certain assumptions about the world. For example, you might reason that your friend Elva has money because she wears nice clothes. Or, based on your experiences, you might reason that studying leads to better grades. Psychologists who study reasoning have traditionally looked at two types of reasoning processes: *deductive reasoning* and *inductive reasoning*. **Deductive reasoning** involves reasoning from the *general* to the *specific*. In other words, you start with a general rule and apply it

You Asked...

What reasoning do we normally use to come to a decision or to solve a problem? PAM LIVELY, STUDENT

reasoning drawing conclusions about the world based on certain assumptions
deductive reasoning reasoning from the general to the specific

to particular cases. For example, you might *deduce* that because studying leads to good grades, your friend Melissa, who makes good grades, must study hard.

Inductive reasoning is the opposite approach. When using inductive reasoning, one reasons from the *specific* to the *general*. Here the object is to begin with specific instances and to discover what general rule fits all of these instances. For example, as children, we may have noticed time and time again that our classmates who did well were also those who seemed to study the most, so we reasoned that studying hard leads to good grades. We used these specific instances to help us *induce* the general rule that studying hard leads to good grades.

We hope you see the parallels between inductive reasoning and the *scientific method* that psychologists use to conduct research (see Chapter 1). When conducting studies to test theories, psychologists try to induce the general rules that explain mental processes and behavior. Once these rules have been induced, they can then be applied to individual situations to help deduce, or predict, how people and animals are likely to behave. This, of course, does not mean that reasoning is just for scientists. Deductive and inductive reasoning are equally important in everyday life. Effective reasoning can be a very important aspect of making good decisions in our lives.

Decision Making: Outcomes and Probabilities

Decision making involves choosing from among several alternatives. We must first choose a course of action before we can implement a solution to a problem. Two factors that influence our decisions are the perceived *outcomes* of our decisions and the *probability* of achieving these outcomes. For example, when you consider a major, you weigh the expected outcomes of choosing that major. How interesting is the subject area to you? What kind of job will it lead to? How difficult will the course work be? What is the pay like in this field? You also temper these judgments with your perception of how likely it is that these outcomes will actually occur. There may be high-salaried jobs in your major area, but if you see little chance of actually getting one of them, then you will be less likely to choose that major.

Logically, we would seek to make decisions that we believe have a good chance of leading to favorable outcomes. However, our decision-making processes are a bit more complex than this. Another factor that affects our decisions is how the possible courses of action are presented, or *framed* (Kahneman & Tversky, 1984). For example, which of the following options would you choose? Would you choose to take a class in which you had a 60% chance of passing? Or one in which you had a 40% chance of failing? Many people would choose the first option because it is framed positively, even though the chance of succeeding in the course is the same in both cases. Whether you prefer a positively framed option or a negatively framed one depends on your orientation. Sometimes we exhibit *loss aversion*, or a tendency to focus on what a certain decision could cost us in terms of potential gain—for example, worrying that your choice of major may limit your future employment opportunities. Other times, we exhibit *risk aversion*, or concern over losing what we already have—for example, worrying that the time you need to devote to your chosen major may force you to give up your current job.

Judgments: Estimating the Likelihood of Events

inductive reasoning reasoning from the specific to the general

decision making making a choice from among a series of alternatives

judgment the act of estimating the probability of an event

Judgment can be seen as a type of problem solving in which we estimate the probability of an event. If you don't know what the probability of a certain event is, and you need to have this probability to make a decision, what do you do? As with all problems, you can solve this one using either an algorithm or a heuristic. An algorithm would involve somehow looking up or calculating the exact probability of the event's occurring, but this is often neither possible nor practical, as in the case of trying to figure out what the stock market will do in the coming months. So, as we saw before, we tend to rely on heuristics when we make judgments.

THE AVAILABILITY HEURISTIC

Many people are afraid to fly, even though air travel is statistically safer than traveling by car ("Air Travel Remains Safe," 1999). Why would people be afraid to choose a *safer* form of travel? The answer lies in the manner in which we make judgments about the frequency of events. When we estimate the frequency of events, we heuristically base our judgments on the ease with which we can recall instances of the event in memory. The more easily we can recall a memory for an event, the more frequent we estimate the event to be. This memory shortcut is called the **availability heuristic** (Tversky & Kahneman, 1974).

The availability heuristic explains the previous example of fearing air travel more than driving. Although fatal car accidents occur every day, they are not as widely covered by the media as plane crashes are. A fatal car crash may result in one or a few deaths, but a plane crash usually involves a larger number of fatalities. Therefore, when a plane goes down, the news coverage is graphic, horrifying, and prolonged. This leaves us with a strong, easily accessible memory for the plane crash. The result is that when we think of ways to travel, we more readily recall memories of plane crashes, and we may mistakenly overestimate the risk associated with air travel. The upshot of this is that many people fear flying, when they really ought to be more afraid of traveling by car.

THE REPRESENTATIVENESS HEURISTIC

We also make heuristic judgments when deciding whether or not an object, event, or person belongs in a particular category by relying on the degree to which the person or thing in question is representative of the category. This tendency, called the **representativeness heuristic**, explains some of the mistakes we make in judgment (Tversky & Kahneman, 1974).

For instance, we often ignore the true probability, or *base rate*, of events in favor of our heuristic judgments. In one experiment on the representativeness heuristic, participants were told that a group of 100 people contained 70 engineers and 30 lawyers. They were also given a description of one of the group members—a man—that included the following traits: conservative, ambitious, nonpolitical, likes carpentry, and enjoys solving mathematical puzzles. Then they were asked to judge the probability that he was an engineer or a lawyer. If we were to approach this question logically, we would base our judgment on the base

availability heuristic a heuristic in which we use the ease with which we can recall instances of an event to help us estimate the frequency of the event

representativeness heuristic a heuristic in which we rely on the degree to which something is representative of a category, rather than the base rate, to help us judge whether or not it belongs in the category

© Cardinale Stephane/Corbis Sygma

According to the availability heuristic, the ease with which we can retrieve memories of events from long-term memory biases our judgments of how frequently the event occurs in real life. Seeing news coverage of air disasters like this one leaves us with vivid memories of plane crashes that cause us to overestimate the probability of a plane crash occurring in the future. As a result, air traffic often falls off immediately following a crash, although in general flying is still safer than driving to your destination.

rate and say that there is a 70% chance that the man is an engineer and a 30% chance that he is a lawyer. The participants, however, did not approach this task logically. Instead, they based their judgments on the representativeness of the description that they were given and ignored the base rate information. As a result, the participants judged that there was a 90% chance that the man was an engineer (Kahneman & Tversky, 1973). Clearly, we often place more confidence in irrational judgments based on heuristics than in rational ones based on more factual probabilities (Tversky & Kahneman, 1980).

Heuristics like representativeness can contribute to serious problems like prejudice. For example, one of your authors once met a man who had little personal contact with African Americans. His exposure to African Americans was mostly limited to watching episodes of the TV show *Cops*, in which he saw many African Americans being arrested for crimes. This left the man with the false impression that most African Americans are representative of the category *criminal*. As a result, the man grew uneasy when he encountered any African American—a clear and unfortunate expression of a racial prejudice. Media depictions of people can interact with our tendency to use heuristics like representativeness, making them powerful influences on our judgments of others.

If all of this sounds as though humans are incapable of making good judgments, don't despair. This is not the case. Often heuristics do lead to correct judgments. In addition, we do not always behave in a heuristic way. Sometimes we do pay attention to probabilities (Cosmides & Tooby, 1996). Whether we make judgments algorithmically or heuristically is a product of both the situation (Cosmides & Tooby, 1996) and the characteristic way that we as individuals tend to think (Stanovich & West, 1998). When the conditions are right, we do make good and logical judgments. This is especially true when we are making judgments in everyday, real-life situations (Anderson, 2000). Take a moment to test your knowledge of this section before moving on to learn about language and its relationship to thought.

Let's Review!

This section described how people make decisions and judgments, and some of the shortcomings of using heuristics. For a quick check of your understanding, answer these questions.

1. It has been unseasonably hot and dry for the last month. Today, you are asked to predict the probability that prolonged heat and drought will occur in the next century as a result of global warming. You are likely to _____ this probability because of the _____.
   a. underestimate; availability heuristic
   b. overestimate; availability heuristic
   c. underestimate; representativeness heuristic
   d. overestimate; representativeness heuristic

2. When we make decisions, we base our decisions in part on _____.
   a. the likely outcomes of the decision
   b. the probability of obtaining certain outcomes
   c. our aversion to risk and loss
   d. All of the above

3. Of the 100 people in Harry's psychology class, 60 are education majors and 40 are psychology majors. Yet when Harry first met a classmate named Sally, he guessed that there was a 90% chance that she was a psychology major because she had a poster of Sigmund Freud on her dorm room wall. Harry likely based his judgment on _____.
   a. the base rate
   b. an algorithm
   c. representativeness
   d. availability

Answers 1. b; 2. d; 3. c

Cognition, Language, and Intelligence: How Do We Think?

Cognition

| **Thinking:** How do we represent **knowledge** in memory? | → | We seem to use both visual and verbal **mental representations** of knowledge. | + | We organize **concepts** into hierarchical **formal** and **natural concepts**. | + | We may store both **prototypes** and **exemplars** for these concept categories. |

Problem Solving
- **Well-Structured Problems** → Use an **algorithm** or **heuristic** to solve. → Obstacles: **mental sets** and **functional fixedness**.
- **Ill-Structured Problems** → Must use a heuristic to solve. **Creativity, incubation,** and **insight** help us overcome these obstacles.

More Thinking! → **Deductive** and **inductive reasoning** + **Decision making** utilizes outcomes and probabilities. Framing also matters! + **Judgments** often ignore base rates in favor of heuristics such as **availability** and **representativeness**.

Language: Communication, Thought, and Culture

- Describe how children acquire language.
- Explain the usefulness of language.
- Describe current research on the issue of nonhuman language.

Learning Objectives

Our capacity for **language** is one of the most spectacular human abilities. No other species has such a well-developed, syntactical verbal system for representing its world. As you learned in Chapter 2 (see p. 60), *Broca's* and *Wernicke's areas* are specialized structures in the left hemisphere of the human brain that help us produce and comprehend speech. We put these brain areas to good use in that we use words in just about every aspect of our lives. As we have seen, much of our knowledge is represented in memory using words. Without words, our ability to mentally represent our world, solve problems, and make decisions would be drastically altered.

How Humans Acquire Language

Some researchers have proposed that humans are born with an innate tendency to acquire language (Bohannon & Bonvillian, 1997; Chomsky, 1957). According to this view, we are born with a *language acquisition device*, or a biological makeup that gives us an innate knowledge of the syntax of a language (Chomsky, 1965). Some disagree with this idea of innate

language a well-developed, syntactical verbal system for representing the world language, believing instead that children are natural problem solvers and that language is a means of solving one of their greatest problems—the need to communicate with others (see Helmuth, 2001).

Deciding which perspective is correct has challenged psychologists for decades. A complicating factor in settling this debate is that it is practically impossible to isolate the effects that our biology and environment have on language development. How can we determine if children are born with innate knowledge of language, when nearly all children in the world are exposed to language immediately after birth? When children begin speaking (at about 1 year), it could be due to some innate, biological mechanism, or it could be that they learned to speak from interacting with others who use language. In normal children, it is impossible to tell exactly why language develops, but what if we could find children who were never exposed to spoken language? What could these children teach us about the development of human language?

During the 1970s researchers documented such a case of deaf children in Nicaragua who had never been exposed to sign language and were unable to hear spoken Spanish. The children's teachers did not know sign language. So, they tried to teach the children to read and write in Spanish. However, when left to their own devices, such as on the playground, the children began to develop their own spontaneous form of sign language. Their language, Nicaraguan Sign Language, is today recognized as a true language complete with gestural vocabulary and its own syntactical and grammatical rules (Senghas & Coppola, 2001). Cases like this one are consistent with the notion that the drive to develop some form of language is innate.

But, what about spoken language? Is there any evidence that hearing children also have an innate capacity for language? Well, yes there is. Evidence for the innate nature of language also comes from cross-cultural studies on language development in hearing children. These studies show that regardless of the culture, language seems to develop in children at about the same age and in the same sequence of stages. This similarity in the developmental process, which occurs despite cultural differences, argues for some biological mechanism that underlies language.

COOING AND BABBLING: BABY STEPS TO LEARNING ONE OR MORE LANGUAGES

> **You Asked...**
>
> *Why is language easier to learn at a young age?*
>
> CLINTON BLAKE ROBERTS, STUDENT

Most of us acquire our first language beginning in the first couple of years of life. Research indicates that newborns from birth to 1 month are capable of categorizing vowel sounds in an adultlike manner (Alderidge, Stillman, & Bower, 2001), and by about 2 months, infants begin **cooing**. Cooing involves making vowel sounds, such as "ooo" and "ah." By 4 months, infants begin to engage in **babbling**, which adds consonant sounds to the vowel sounds they emitted during cooing. For example, an infant might repeat the sound "ka, ka, ka" over and over. Infants' first babbles are very similar across cultures, but this soon changes (Stoel-Gammon & Otomo, 1986). By 7 months, infants begin to emit babbles that contain sounds that are part of the language they have been exposed to in their environment. In this fashion, the infant's language system apparently tunes itself to the language or languages that the infant hears on a regular basis. By 1 year, children's babbling contains the sounds and intonations of their native language (Levitt & Utmann, 1992).

Perhaps because the infant's language system appears to tune itself to the sounds of the language the child hears, children who grow up in bilingual households, where adults speak two languages to the children, tend to acquire both languages at high levels of proficiency. But this does not mean that a child cannot learn a second language later in life. A child who is not exposed to a second language until elementary school can still develop near-native proficiency in the language (Hakuta, 1999). However, from childhood to adulthood, it seems to become steadily more difficult for us to become bilingual. For example, an adolescent who

cooing the vowel sounds made by infants beginning at 2 months

babbling the combinations of vowel and consonant sounds uttered by infants beginning around 4 months is just beginning to learn Spanish may never speak Spanish as fluently as a child who began learning Spanish in elementary school (Hakuta, Bailystok, & Wiley, 2003). Therefore, if true bilingualism is desired, it is best to begin learning the second language as early as possible.

Once a child achieves the stage of babbling the basic sounds, or **phonemes**, of her native tongue, the next step in language development is learning to communicate. At around 12 months, children begin trying to communicate in earnest with others. This communication is often based on gestures before it is based on words. For example, a child may point at a toy that he wants. When parents learn to interpret these *preverbal gestures*, communication is accomplished. As they catch on to their child's preverbal gestures, parents often verbalize the meaning of the gesture for the child. Parents say things like, "Oh, do you want this toy?" This verbalization of the child's intention allows the child to begin to learn **morphemes**, or the smallest sounds in a language that have meaning. As a result, by the end of the first year or so, children begin to speak their first words.

FROM "MAMA" AND "DADA" TO FULL CONVERSATIONS

A child's first words are usually the names of familiar objects, people, actions, or situations, ones with which they have had a great deal of contact. Typically, these words are *Dada, Mama, hi, hot,* and the like. Between 12 to 18 months of age, children utter only one word at a time, and often they convey tremendous meaning with these one-word sentences. For example, the utterance "Milk!" may stand for "I want some milk, please!"

As young children begin to speak, they may exhibit **overextension** in their language, using one word to symbolize all manner of similar instances. For instance, the word *dog* may be used to symbolize any animal. During this period, the opposite problem may also occur when children exhibit **underextension** of language. In this situation, children inappropriately restrict their use of a word to a particular case, such as when a child uses the word *dog* to refer only to the family pet.

By the time children reach 20–26 months, they begin to combine words into two-word sentences in what is called **telegraphic speech**. Telegraphic speech is often ungrammatical, but it does convey meaning, such as "Doggie bad," meaning "The dog was bad." From here, children rapidly acquire vocabulary and the grammatical rules of the language, such as word order in a sentence and tense. By age 6, the average child has an impressive vocabulary of around 10,000 words and a fairly competent mastery of grammar (Tager-Flusberg, 2005).

As children's vocabularies grow, so does their understanding of **grammar**, or the rules that govern sentence structure in their language. From the simple subject–verb combinations of telegraphic speech, English-speaking children progress to more complex subject–verb–object sentences between ages 2 and 3. Children who speak other languages adopt the relevant grammatical patterns of their native language. As children develop throughout the preschool years, their knowledge and use of grammar becomes increasingly complex. By age 4 or 5, children can use most of the grammatical structures of their native language (Tager-Flusberg, 2005).

As children develop better vocabularies and acquire the grammatical rules of language, they exercise these abilities during social interactions with others. It's during these social interactions with peers and adults that children begin to learn **pragmatics**, or the rules of conversation operating in their culture. Pragmatics may include rules about turn taking, eye contact, tone of voice, and other aspects of conversation.

These hard-earned linguistic abilities will be very valuable to the child, as they are to us all. Let's take a closer look at what, exactly, language does for us.

The Function of Language in Culture and Perception

It is not difficult to see that language affects us in many ways. Obviously, one of language's main functions is to facilitate communication. We use language to describe our world, our thoughts, and our experiences to others. Without language, we would lead lives of social isolation.

phoneme [FOE-neem] the smallest unit of sound in a language

morpheme [MORE-feem] the smallest unit of sound in a language that has meaning

overextension when a child uses one word to symbolize all manner of similar instances (e.g., calling all birds *parakeet*)

underextension when a child inappropriately restricts the use of a word to a particular case (e.g., using the word *cat* to describe only the family pet)

telegraphic speech two-word sentences that children begin to utter at 20–26 months

grammar the rules that govern the sentence structure in a particular language

pragmatics the rules of conversation in a particular culture

LANGUAGE AND THE DEVELOPMENT OF CULTURE

Because language brings us together and allows us to share ideas and experiences, language also plays a role in the development of *culture*. Russian psychologist Lev Vygotsky (1896–1934) noted the influence of language in the development of culture in his *sociocultural theory* (Vygotsky, 1934/1987) (see Chapter 9). According to sociocultural theory, older and more knowledgeable members of a society pass on the values, beliefs, and customs of their culture to children by telling the children stories and by engaging in conversations with them. The children store these dialogues in their memory and later use this knowledge to guide their behavior. Just as you learned from the stories of your elders, someday you too will pass down elements of your culture as you converse with younger people.

Language may facilitate the transmission of culture from generation to generation, but does the language we speak also affect the way we view the world? In the next section, we'll take a look at this interesting issue.

LINGUISTIC RELATIVITY: THE INFLUENCE OF LANGUAGE ON THOUGHT

One of the most intriguing theories about language came from an unlikely source. Benjamin Whorf was a Connecticut fire insurance inspector whose unusual hobby was *linguistics*, or the study of language. After intensive studies of the languages of Native Americans, Whorf became convinced that one's language could directly determine or influence one's thoughts (Whorf, 1956). This notion has since come to be called the **Whorfian hypothesis** or the **linguistic relativity hypothesis**.

In its strongest form, the linguistic relativity hypothesis states that one's language actually determines one's thoughts and one's perception of the world. According to this view, people who have different native languages think differently and perceive the world in a different light. For example, Whorf argued that Eskimos would understand "snow" differently than Europeans because the Eskimos' native language has more words for snow than English has. Whorf claimed that differences among languages make it impossible to express all thoughts equally in all languages. Therefore, you can think and see the world only in terms of the language that you know. According to Whorf, your language *determines* what you think and how you perceive the world.

Whorfian [WORE-fee-un] **hypothesis / linguistic relativity hypothesis**
the theory that one's language can directly determine or influence one's thoughts

To date, the bulk of the evidence does not support the strong form of Whorf's linguistic relativity hypothesis (see ■ TABLE 7.2). However, there is reason to think that a modified, or weaker, interpretation of the Whorfian hypothesis may hold true. The weaker version states that instead of language *determining* thought processes, language merely *influences* them. For example, when Spanish speakers were compared to Mayan speakers, differences were seen in their ability to remember colors. Furthermore, these memory differences were related to how easy it is to verbally label colors in Spanish and Mayan (Stefflre, Castillo-Vales, & Morley, 1966). It appears that how easily you can label a color in your language does affect your memory for that color.

It is also likely that language can influence our perception of the world. In one study involving the sorting of color samples, participants who spoke Setswana were more likely to group blues and greens together than were those who spoke English or Russian. This finding was attributed to the fact that in Setswana, one word describes both blue and green colors (Davies, 1998). The idea that humans do not all categorize color the same way is an important premise of the linguistic relativity hypothesis.

Table 7.2 Different Words for Snow

CONTRARY TO WHORF'S HYPOTHESIS, LIKE THE ESKIMO, ENGLISH SPEAKERS DO HAVE SEVERAL WORDS FOR SNOW.

ESKIMO	ENGLISH
qanuk: "snowflake"	snowflake
qanir: "to snow"	snow
kanevvluk: "fine snow/rain particles"	snowfall
muruaneq: "soft deep snow"	powder
pirta: "blizzard, snowstorm"	blizzard, snowstorm
nutaryuk: "fresh snow"	powder
qengaruk: "snow bank"	snowbank

Psychology Applies to Your World:

Are Humans the Only Animals to Use Language?

For centuries, humans believed that they alone had the ability to use language. It was assumed that only the advanced human mind was capable of dealing with the complexities of a language. Remarkably, this assumption has been called into question. Although it is very controversial, today some researchers believe that some other animals may possess linguistic abilities (e.g., Shanker, Savage-Rumbaugh, & Taylor, 1999).

In looking at the linguistic abilities of other species, we first have to make a distinction between *language* and *communication*. Language is a system of communication that has a set vocabulary and a set structure, or grammar. For instance, English sentences generally follow a subject–verb–object pattern. Though many languages reverse the order of the verb and the object, most of the world's languages place the subject at the beginning of the sentence—for example, *Mike ran home* (Ultan, 1969). Languages also differ with respect to the placement of adjectives and adverbs. English places the adjective before the noun, *blue dress*; Spanish places it after, *vestido azul*. As you can see, each language has its own set of rules.

In contrast to the structure and order of language, communication can be very unstructured. All that is required in a communication system is that your meaning be conveyed to others. There is little argument that animals can communicate. For example, a rooster will emit an alarm cry to warn other chickens of danger (Marler, Duffy, & Pickert, 1986) and domestic dogs respond to specific play signals of their owners (Rooney, Bradshaw, & Robinson, 2001). But, does this ability of some animals to communicate equate with the capacity for language?

Some of the best evidence for animal language comes from studies done on Bonobo chimpanzees. Bonobos, also known as pygmy chimpanzees, are perhaps our closest genetic relatives, even more closely related to us than the common chimpanzee. During the 1980s, researcher Sue Savage-Rumbaugh and others attempted to teach English to a Bonobo named Matata. Because Bonobos do not have vocal cords that produce human-like speech, they cannot actually speak. To get around this problem, the researchers used a special computer keyboard during the language training. On the surface of the keyboard were pictures, and when a picture was pressed, a computer-generated voice spoke the name of the object in the picture. Using this keyboard, Savage-Rumbaugh tried to teach Matata the meaning of certain words, but Matata did not catch on well (Wise, 2000, p. 223). However, Matata's infant stepson, Kanzi, had been observing his mother's lessons. Although Savage-Rumbaugh and her colleagues never attempted to teach Kanzi to use the keyboard, he picked up this skill on his own (Savage-Rumbaugh, McDonald, Sevcik, Hopkins, & Rupert, 1986). By age 2$\frac{1}{2}$, Kanzi had begun to use some of the symbols his mother was trying to learn on the keyboard. When experimenters gave up trying to teach Matata to use the keyboard, they separated her from Kanzi. The day Matata left, Kanzi approached the keyboard and began to use it to make requests and express himself. In fact, he used it a total of 120 times on that first day (Wise, 2000).

(Continued)

Much like a young child, Kanzi appeared to have learned some vocabulary just by observing language being used around him. Kanzi's acquisition of language seemed to occur quite naturally (Shanker et al., 1999). For example, a patch of wild strawberries grew outside of Kanzi's laboratory, and when he discovered them, Kanzi began to eat them. He overheard researchers referring to them by the word *strawberries* and soon appeared to understand what the word *strawberries* meant. After apparently learning the meaning of the word *strawberries*, Kanzi would head for the berry patch whenever he heard someone speak the word (Savage-Rumbaugh, 1987).

Overall, Kanzi's use of language is quite impressive. He uses the keyboard to make requests, such as to visit another chimpanzee named Austin. If he is told that he cannot visit because it's too cold to go outside, Kanzi modifies his request to ask to see a picture of Austin on TV (Savage-Rumbaugh, 1987). Furthermore, Kanzi seems to be able to respond to very unusual and novel requests, such as "Put the pine needles in the refrigerator" or "Put the soap on the ball."

As an infant, Kanzi learned to use a language keyboard like this one to communicate with humans just by watching researchers who were working with his mother, Matata.

© Michael Nichols/Magnum Photos

Language abilities have been shown in species other than the Bonobos as well. Researcher Irene Pepperberg (1993, 1999) has had some success in training an African gray parrot named Alex to speak some English. Unlike the Bonobo, a parrot has the physical ability to produce speech as well as comprehend it. Before his death in 2007, Alex was able to speak some words in English, and identify the shape, color, and material of many objects (Pepperberg, 1991).

Dolphins have also shown some linguistic promise. Researcher Louis Herman and his colleagues have had some success in training dolphins to understand a language that the researchers created. This created language is based on gestures, but it has a set vocabulary in which certain gestures stand for certain words, and a specific set of grammatical rules that dictate how gestures can be combined into phrases. One of the dolphins, named Phoenix, was shown to follow a complex sequence of instructions delivered in this gestured language (Herman & Uyeyama, 1999). Furthermore, another dolphin, Ake, seemed to notice when the grammatical laws of the language had been violated (Herman, Kuczaj, & Holder, 1993).

As impressive as the linguistic abilities of Kanzi, Alex, Ake, and Phoenix are, not everyone is convinced that animals truly have the capacity for language. Some argue that these animals are

Although controversial, studies of animals like Alex, the African gray parrot, challenge the presumption that language is a solely human attribute.

© Rick Friedman/Corbis

merely highly trained (Pinker, 1994). Skeptics propose that rather than actually using language, the animals are engaging in trained behaviors that they hope will lead to some reward. Certainly, Alex, Ake, and Phoenix were trained to use language, but what about Kanzi, who was never trained to use language? He learned it on his own during his early years, just as children learn language (Shanker et al., 1999).

Another criticism of animal language research directly questions the linguistic abilities of animals. Some argue that animal language researchers have not adequately demonstrated that animals can follow all of the grammatical and syntactical rules of human language (Kako, 1999). Animal language researchers counter that their critics have unfairly focused on the linguistic abilities that animals lack and have largely ignored the linguistic abilities that animals *do* have (Shanker et al., 1999).

You can see that this is a very passionate debate—as well it should be, for there is a great deal at stake here. If we ultimately determine that animals do have linguistic capacities, then we may have to reconsider what separates humans from the rest of the animal kingdom! This possibility brings up a whole host of ethical questions concerning animals and the manner in which we treat them in human society (Wise, 2000).

Let's Review!

In this section, we covered many aspects of language, including how we acquire language, what it does for us, and the debate over language as a purely human attribute. For a quick check of your understanding, answer these questions.

1. Babies begin _____ when they begin to make _____ sounds.
   a. cooing; consonant
   b. babbling; vowel
   c. cooing; vowel and consonant
   d. babbling; vowel and consonant

2. Which of the following people would be the most likely to agree with the statement "Language facilitates the development of culture"?

   a. Lev Vygotsky   c. Sue Savage-Rumbaugh
   b. Benjamin Whorf   d. Eleanor Rosch

3. One's language can influence one's _____.
   a. speech   c. perception
   b. memory   d. All of the above

Answers 1. d; 2. a; 3. d

Defining and Measuring Intelligence

- Describe historical and modern attempts to measure intelligence, and some of the advantages and disadvantages of these methods.

- Describe the various ways that researchers have conceptualized intelligence.

- Describe the nature versus nurture debate as it applies to intelligence.

Learning Objectives

What makes a person intelligent? Is it earning good grades? Knowing how to survive in the wilderness? Having good social skills? Today, many psychologists view **intelligence** broadly as having abilities that allow you to adapt to your environment and behave in a goal-directed

You Asked...

What is the actual definition of intelligence?   BREDRON LYTLE, STUDENT

intelligence abilities that enable you to adapt to your environment and behave in a goal-directed way

way. But over the years, psychologists have found that developing a precise definition of intelligence is not as easy as it may seem, and our conception of intelligence has undergone several revisions in the history of psychology. Equally challenging has been finding ways of measuring intelligence.

Measuring Intelligence by Abilities and IQs

One of the first people to study the measurement of intelligence was British psychologist Sir Francis Galton (1822–1911). Galton claimed that intelligence is an inherited trait that is correlated with having superior physical abilities. As such, he believed that intelligence could be measured by measuring traits like reaction time, eyesight, and so on. However, early studies failed to find much support for Galton's ideas (Schultz & Schultz, 2000), and they soon fell out of favor.

ALFRED BINET: MEASURING INTELLIGENCE BY MEASURING COGNITIVE ABILITIES

The modern intelligence test is credited to Alfred Binet (1857–1911). In 1904, the French government appointed Alfred Binet and psychiatrist Théodore Simon to a commission charged with developing a means of measuring the intelligence of French schoolchildren so that the government could identify children who would not likely profit from traditional education.

Binet saw intelligence as our capacity to *find and maintain a purpose, adapt our strategy to reach that purpose, and evaluate the strategy so it can be adjusted as necessary* (Terman, 1916). In essence, Binet suggested that having intelligence makes one a good problem solver. As such, he developed an intelligence test that assessed general cognitive abilities such as the individual's attention, judgment, and reasoning skills (Binet & Simon, 1905).

Binet prepared a set of 30 tasks that measured these skills and arranged them in order of difficulty with the easiest questions first and the hardest questions last. Not surprisingly, the brighter students could answer more of the questions than the not-so-bright students could. Also, not surprisingly, the older children tended to answer more questions correctly than the younger children. In fact, Binet noticed that the brighter younger children could sometimes answer correctly as many questions as the average child of an older age. For example, a very smart 6-year-old might be able to answer as many questions as the average 10-year-old child could. So Binet began to quantify children's intelligence in terms of **mental age**, or the age that reflects a child's mental abilities in comparison to the "average" child. In Binet's scheme, a mental age that exceeds one's chronological age indicates above-average intelligence, and a mental age that is below a child's actual age indicates a below-average level of intelligence. Binet's concept of mental age became the foundation for the IQ score, and his test became the basis for modern intelligence tests.

LEWIS TERMAN: THE INTELLIGENCE QUOTIENT AND THE STANFORD-BINET

In 1916, Stanford psychologist Lewis Terman completed an American revision of the intelligence test that Binet and Simon had developed. He named his version of the test the Stanford Revision of the Binet-Simon Scale, which became known as the Stanford-Binet. Perhaps his most significant contribution to the test was to introduce an **intelligence quotient**, or **IQ score**, as the measure of an individual's intelligence. An IQ score is calculated as follows:

$$IQ = (MA/CA) \times 100$$

where

$$MA = \text{mental age}$$

and

$$CA = \text{chronological, or actual, age}$$

mental age the age that reflects the child's mental abilities in comparison to the average child of the same age

intelligence quotient (IQ score) one's mental age divided by one's chronological age times 100

Using the concept of an IQ, a person of average abilities has, by definition, an IQ of 100 or, in other words, a mental age equal to her or his actual age. IQs over 100 indicate above-average intelligence, and IQs below 100 indicate below-average intelligence.

The Stanford-Binet has undergone four major revisions since 1916 and is still in wide use today. The most recent edition, the Stanford-Binet Intelligence Scales, Fifth Edition (SB5), was released in 2003. However, a modern IQ test developed by psychologist David Wechsler (1896–1981) and first released in 1939 has greatly challenged the popularity of the Stanford-Binet.

DAVID WECHSLER'S INTELLIGENCE SCALES

Wechsler (1939) developed an intelligence test in response to shortcomings he saw in the Stanford-Binet. Wechsler objected to the fact that the Stanford-Binet test tried to sum up intelligence in a single score. He believed that one number could not adequately express something as complex as intelligence. Furthermore, Wechsler objected to the use of the mental age concept for adults (R. M. Kaplan & Saccuzzo, 1989). After all, would you necessarily expect a 40-year-old to correctly answer more questions than a 35-year-old? The concept of mental age doesn't apply as well to adults as it does to children because adults do not change as much from year to year as children do. Therefore, mental age has little significance in adulthood.

To correct these problems, Wechsler developed an intelligence test that yields scores on individual *subscales* that measure different mental abilities. Furthermore, instead of using mental age to determine IQ, Wechsler's tests compare a participant's performance to the average person's performance to determine IQ. The Wechsler tests are devised so that an average person's performance on the test results in an IQ of 100. Using this number as a benchmark, people who score above average on the test are given IQ scores above 100, and people who perform below average are given IQ scores below 100. Most people can expect to score near this average IQ, somewhere in the range of 85–115 (■ FIGURE 7.4).

FIGURE

7.4

The Normal Distribution of IQ Scores

IQs tend to be normally distributed across the population. This means that when a frequency distribution of IQ scores is plotted, it forms a bell-shaped curve, with most people scoring near the average of 100 on the IQ test and very few scoring extremely high or low.

Today there are three separate Wechsler intelligence tests. The Wechsler Preschool and Primary Scale of Intelligence, Third Edition (WPPSI-III) is administered to children ages 2½–7. The Wechsler Intelligence Scale for Children, Fourth Edition (WISC-IV) is used for children ages 6–16. And the Wechsler Adult Intelligence Scale, Third Edition (WAIS-III) is used for people over age 15.

The WAIS-III yields three separate scores: a *verbal* score, a *performance* score, and an *overall* score. The verbal score is based on the individual's performance on tests of six types of verbal ability: comprehension, vocabulary, information, similarities, arithmetic, and digit span. The performance score is based on five types of performance ability: object assembly, block design, picture comprehension, picture arrangement, and digit symbol. The third score, the overall score, is a combination of the verbal and performance scores. The design of the WAIS-III makes it flexible. Testers can administer the verbal scale, the performance scale, or both. ■ TABLE 7.3 further describes these scales.

TESTING THE TEST: WHAT MAKES A GOOD INTELLIGENCE TEST?

So far, we have looked at two widely accepted tests that psychologists and educators use to measure intelligence. These are but two of a great many tests that have been devised to

© Bob Daemmrich/The Image Works

The WISC and WAIS use different types of tasks to assess IQ.

Table 7.3 The Wechsler Adult Intelligence Scale (WAIS-III) and Its Subscales

The test items shown are examples—they do not appear in the actual test.

CONTENT AREA	EXPLANATION OF TASKS/QUESTIONS	EXAMPLES OF A POSSIBLE TASK/QUESTION
VERBAL SCALE		
Comprehension	Answer questions of social knowledge.	What does it mean when people say, "A stitch in time saves nine"? Why are convicted criminals put into prison?
Vocabulary	Define the meaning of the word.	What does **persistent** mean? What does **archaeology** mean?
Information	Supply generally known information.	Who is Chelsea Clinton? What are six New England states?
Similarities	Explain how two things or concepts are similar.	In what ways are an ostrich and a penguin alike? In what ways are a lamp and a heater alike?
Arithmetic	Solve simple arithmetical word problems.	If Paul has $14.43, and he buys two sandwiches that cost $5.23 each, how much change will he receive?
Digit span	Listen to a series of digits (numbers), then repeat the numbers either forward, backward, or both.	Repeat these numbers backward: "9, 1, 8, 3, 6."
PERFORMANCE SCALE		
Object assembly	Put together a puzzle by combining pieces to form a particular common object.	Put together these pieces to make a square.
Block design	Use patterned blocks to form a design that looks identical to a design shown by the examiner.	Assemble the blocks on the left to make the design on the right.
Picture completion	Tell what is missing from each picture.	What is missing from this picture ?
Picture arrangement	Put a set of cartoonlike pictures into chronological order, so they tell a coherent story.	Arrange these pictures in an order that tells a story, and then tell what is happening in the story.
Digit symbol	When given a key matching particular symbols to particular numerals, copy a sequence of symbols, transcribing from symbols to numerals, using the key.	Look carefully at the key. In the blanks, write the correct numeral for the symbol below each symbol.

measure intelligence and other psychological traits. When choosing which test to administer or when interpreting the scores yielded by these tests, we have to ask, "Is this a good test?" If psychologists never worried about the quality of their measurements, they could well find themselves making many faulty judgments about the people they measure. Think about it: How would you feel if someone gave you an IQ test and then told you that your score would determine whether or not you got a job? Wouldn't you want some assurance that the test actually reflected your true intellectual ability? Most of us would.

Before a test is used to make decisions about anyone's life, the test itself must be tested and evaluated. Psychologists must be assured that the test is both *reliable* and *valid* before it can be put into widespread use. The **reliability** of a test refers to the degree to which the test yields consistent measurements over time. Although intelligence can change over time, it usually does so very slowly. In general, if you are intelligent today, you will be intelligent 6 months from now. So, if we use a test to measure your IQ today and then again in 6 months, the scores should be comparable. This doesn't mean that the test has to yield *exactly* the same score, but the scores should be close.

Establishing the reliability of an intelligence test is very important, but the **validity** of the test is an equally important characteristic. Validity is the degree to which the test measures what it was designed to measure. In the case of an intelligence test, one must show that the test actually measures intelligence!

One way to establish a test's validity is to show that scores on the test reliably predict future behavior. For example, if we expect that intelligence is related to doing well in school, then scores on a *valid* IQ test should predict who does well in school—and who does not. If the test is valid, IQ and GPA should correlate. Students with higher IQ scores should tend to also have higher GPAs and students with lower IQ scores should tend to have lower GPAs. If they do not, the IQ test is not a valid predictor of academic success, and it should not be used as such.

YOUR TURN – ACTIVE LEARNING

You might be thinking that validity seems like a trivial issue. After all, if you create an IQ test that asks people questions that *seem* to require intelligence to answer, won't the test tell you who is smart and who is not? As it turns out, it is quite easy to devise tests that are invalid. For example, questions that require specific cultural knowledge may not assess the intelligence of people unfamiliar with that culture—even though they may be very intelligent. This validity problem is referred to as **cultural bias**. Some people have argued that intelligence tests are often biased and invalid for cultural minority members (Reynolds & Brown, 1984). To illustrate this point, try to answer the following sample IQ test question.

Choose the term that best completes this analogy:

Chayote is to soup as scissors are to _____.

a. a drawer
b. paper
c. eggs
d. a bird

Was the answer immediately apparent to you? If you are from a culture that is not familiar with the word *chayote*, which is a type of squash eaten in some Latin American cultures, you might not realize that you put scissors *into* a drawer the way you put chayote *into* soup. Does this mean you are unintelligent? Of course not—but an incorrect answer would count against you if it were on an IQ test! Some people contend that IQ tests can't help reflecting the cultural values, language, and knowledge of the people who develop them, and therefore all IQ tests carry some form of cultural bias (Greenfield, 1997). We should always keep in mind that IQ tests do not measure all human abilities, and our cultural environment can affect our performance on these tests (Sternberg, 1997a).

reliability the degree to which a test yields consistent measurements of a trait

validity the degree to which a test measures the trait that it was designed to measure

cultural bias the degree to which a test puts people from other cultures at an unfair disadvantage because of the culturally specific nature of the test items

The Nature of Intelligence: The Search Continues

Back in the early 1900s, psychological historian E. G. Boring noted that "intelligence is what the tests test" (quoted in Gardner, 1999, p. 13). By this, Boring meant that psychologists had placed a great deal of emphasis on developing tests to measure intelligence, but they had not spent adequate time exploring what intelligence actually is.

INTELLIGENCE AS A SINGLE FACTOR

A century ago, British statistician Charles Spearman argued that because test scores of separate mental abilities (e.g., verbal skills, mathematical ability, deductive reasoning skills) tend to correlate, there must be one general level of intelligence that underlies these separate mental abilities (Spearman, 1904). Spearman referred to this **general intelligence** as *g*. In Spearman's view, one's level of *g* would determine how well he or she functioned on any number of cognitive tasks. The idea that intelligence is a single, unitary factor helped lead to the rapid expansion of intelligence testing in schools, the workplace, and the military. But the notion of *g* would soon be challenged.

INTELLIGENCE AS A COLLECTION OF ABILITIES

Is intelligence really a single factor? Can't a person be smart in some areas, but not in others? By the 1930s, some theorists were beginning to challenge the idea of a single intelligence. The notion of *g* fell from favor as psychologists proposed theories that described intelligence as a set of abilities rather than a single trait. In 1938, psychologist L. L. Thurstone argued that intelligence was made up of seven distinct mental abilities: reasoning, associative memory, spatial visualization, numerical fluency, verbal comprehension, perceptual speed, and word fluency. Others would eventually propose as many as 120 different factors underlying intelligence (Guilford, 1967).

However, not everyone was convinced that intelligence was made up of many different factors. In the 1960s, Raymond Cattell (1963) revived the idea of *g*. Cattell proposed that *g* does exist, but in two different forms, which he called **crystallized intelligence** and **fluid intelligence**. Crystallized intelligence refers to our accumulation of knowledge. For example, your knowledge of psychology is part of your crystallized intelligence. Fluid intelligence refers to the speed and efficiency with which we learn new information and solve problems. For instance, the higher your fluid intelligence, the more quickly you will learn the material in this chapter.

There is both good and bad news when it comes to our levels of fluid and crystallized intelligence over a lifetime. The evidence shows that crystallized intelligence can continue to grow well into late adulthood (Horn, Donaldson, & Engstrom, 1981), but fluid intelligence tends to decrease across adulthood (Schaie, 1994). The degree to which we retain these abilities throughout life is affected by our environment and our physical well-being, although environment is much more important in the case of crystallized intelligence (Horn, 1982; see *Neuroscience Applies to Your World*).

As you can see, there has been much disagreement as to exactly what intelligence is. Today, many psychologists still favor the idea of a general intelligence, especially those psychologists who focus on its measurement (Gardner, 1999, p. 14). However, other psychologists have gone on to develop newer theories that conceptualize intelligence as a multifaceted set of abilities or *intelligences*.

HOWARD GARDNER'S MULTIPLE INTELLIGENCES

In the early 1980s, Harvard psychologist Howard Gardner proposed a theory of intelligence that views humans as possessing many different intelligences (Gardner, 1983). According to Gardner, an intelligence is "a biopsychological potential to process information that can

general intelligence (*g*) Charles Spearman's notion that there is a general level of intelligence that underlies our separate abilities

crystallized intelligence our accumulation of knowledge

fluid intelligence the speed and efficiency with which we learn new information and solve problems

Neuroscience Applies to Your World:

Health and Age-related Changes in Intelligence

As we age, we tend to experience some declines in fluid intelligence, but how much decline we experience is in part related to our overall health. In one study, researchers compared middle-aged and older adults who were healthy (healthy group) with middle-aged and older adults who suffered from high blood pressure and/or vascular disease (vascular risk group) over a 5-year period (Raz, Rodrigue, Kennedy, & Acker, 2007). They found that relative to the healthy group, the vascular risk group experienced more negative brain changes. For example, the vascular risk group suffered more brain lesions and increased shrinkage in the prefrontal cortex and hippocampus of the brain relative to the healthy participants. Recall from Chapters 2 and 6 that the hippocampus and prefrontal cortex play important roles in the processing of memories. The vascular risk group also experienced more decline in their working memory, an important aspect of fluid intelligence. These findings suggest that cardiovascular disease and cardiovascular risk factors (such as high blood pressure and diabetes) may increase your risk of suffering declines in fluid intelligence as you age. Therefore, doing what you can to limit your cardiovascular risk—such as exercising, maintaining a healthy weight, eating well, and avoiding smoking—may also reduce your chances of suffering cognitive declines in older age.

© Enigma/Alamy

be activated in a cultural setting to solve problems or create products that are of value in a culture" (Gardner, 1999, pp. 33–34). This definition emphasizes the fact that intelligence allows us to function efficiently in our own environment, and it also highlights the fact that different cultures and environments place different demands on our intelligence.

For example, in the United States today, we might consider the ability to understand and predict fluctuations in the stock market as a sign of intelligence. In an unindustrialized, nomadic culture, however, the ability to seek out a source of water may be a more highly valued intelligence. After carefully considering the different human abilities that allow us to function in our environment, Gardner developed a strict set of criteria for identifying an intelligence (Gardner, 1999). Using these criteria, Gardner has identified nine different intelligences and allowed for the possibility that more may someday be identified (Gardner, 2004). Gardner's theory of **multiple intelligences** is summarized in ■ TABLE 7.4.

As you look at Table 7.4, can you see that you have more of some types of intelligence and less of others? Most of us do not possess equal levels of all types of intelligence. Rather, we each have our own strengths and weaknesses. Therefore, Gardner doesn't have much use for tests that seek to measure general intelligence. For Gardner, it is far more important to look at a person's intelligence *profile*—his or her level of ability across the different types of intelligence.

ROBERT STERNBERG'S TRIARCHIC THEORY OF INTELLIGENCE

Psychologist Robert Sternberg has taken an approach somewhat similar to Howard Gardner's. Like Gardner, Sternberg rejects the usefulness of trying to measure a single, general intel-

multiple intelligences the idea that we possess different types of intelligence rather than a single, overall level of intelligence

Table 7.4 Gardner's Multiple Intelligences

INTELLIGENCE	DESCRIPTION	EXAMPLES
Linguistic	The ability to learn and use languages	An author has a good command of language and can express ideas well in written form.
Spatial	The ability to recognize and manipulate patterns of space	A surveyor is very good at judging distances. A seamstress designs a pattern for a jacket.
Logical-mathematical	The ability to attack problems in a logical manner, solve mathematical problems, and in general exhibit scientific thought	A psychologist can develop and test theories in a scientific manner. A physician examines a patient and makes a diagnosis.
Musical	The ability to perform, compose, and appreciate music	A songwriter can create unique melodies and perform them.
Bodily-kinesthetic	The ability to use one's body to solve problems and create products	A gymnast can perform intricate maneuvers on the balance beam.
Interpersonal	The ability to understand the intentions, motivations, and desires of others	A manager is good at working with others, and can inspire others to perform at their optimal level of performance.
Intrapersonal	The ability to understand oneself	A student knows what she wants in terms of her career and future life, and she uses this information to choose an appropriate major.
Naturalistic	Paying attention to nature and understanding environmental issues	A homemaker recycles her trash and avoids using household cleaners that are harmful to the environment.
Existential	Being concerned with "ultimate" issues; seeking higher truths	A philosophy student ponders the meaning of life.

From Intelligence Reframed: Multiple Intelligences for the 21st Century *by Howard Gardner (New York: Basic Books/Perseus). Reprinted by permission of BASIC BOOKS, a member of Perseus Books Group.*

ligence. However, Sternberg doesn't subscribe to the idea that we possess many separate intelligences. Sternberg considers some of Gardner's intelligences as *talents* that some people possess. For example, it's hard to see why musical intelligence would be important in many cultures. Even if you have little or no musical ability, you could still function very well in many cultures, including American society. However, in the United States and many other cultures, the ability to think logically would be very important to your survival and well-being.

Sternberg suggests that *successful intelligence*, or intelligence that helps us function in our world, is composed of three types of cognitive abilities. Accordingly, Sternberg calls his theory the **triarchic theory of intelligence** (Sternberg, 1985, 1997b). According to the triarchic theory, intelligence is composed of analytical, practical, and creative abilities that help us adapt successfully to our environment.

Analytical intelligence is seen in our ability to use logic to reason our way through problems—for example, finding a way to fix your car when it breaks down. Analytical intelligence is also important as we implement and evaluate problem-solving strategies, allowing us to evaluate whether or not a particular problem-solving strategy is working well.

Practical intelligence is our ability to adapt to our environment. This is the type of intelligence that we see in people who have a great deal of common sense. People who are high in practical intelligence exhibit savvy. They know how to function efficiently within their environment. For example, a Central American farmer may be able to predict the weather by noticing changes in the environment. Or someone who lives in New York City may be

triarchic [tri-ARK-ic] **theory of intelligence** a theory that proposes that intelligence is composed of *analytical*, *practical*, and *creative* abilities that help us adapt to our environment very good at finding the quickest way across town during rush hour. Both of these people, although they possess very different skills, exhibit practical intelligence. Keep in mind that behaviors and skills may be intelligent in some environments, but not in others.

Creative intelligence is our ability to use our knowledge of the world in novel situations. For example, suppose you found yourself in a foreign culture where you did not know the language or the customs. Would you be able to function? People who are high in creative intelligence can adapt what they know about the world to meet the unique demands of new situations. In this case, you might use pantomime skills learned while playing charades to help you communicate without words.

DANIEL GOLEMAN'S THEORY OF EMOTIONAL INTELLIGENCE

Yet another way of conceptualizing intelligence comes from psychologist Daniel Goleman. In his best-selling book *Emotional Intelligence*, Goleman (1995) argues that a concept of intelligence that is based solely on cognitive abilities is too limiting. He notes that even people with relatively high IQs can fail to succeed in life and sometimes do things that appear to be downright unintelligent. For example, a gifted student with a perfect score on the SAT may turn out to be a poor college student who fails most of his classes (Goleman, 1995). According to Goleman, the reason for this is that many times our actions are guided not by our intellectual abilities, but by our emotions. Goleman contends that just as some of us are intellectually gifted, some of us are endowed with emotional prowess—an ability he calls *emotional intelligence.*

In Goleman's view, emotional intelligence includes awareness of your own emotional states, accurate assessment of your own abilities, self-confidence, self-control, trustworthiness, conscientiousness, the ability to adapt to changes, innovation or creativity, achievement motivation, commitment to completing goals, initiative or self-motivation, and a sense of optimism (Goleman, 1998; Petrides, Furnham, & Martin, 2004). In other words, an emotionally intelligent person is a confident self-starter who is ethical and adaptable—the kind of person who sets a goal and works toward it without letting minor obstacles derail his or her progress. With this sort of determination, confidence, and ability to adapt, a person with only an average IQ might be able to go far. Likewise, a bright person with low emotional intelligence might become overwhelmed with self-doubt or lack of motivation and, as a result, fail to perform well in life.

Today, the concept of emotional intelligence is sparking interest among researchers and in the workplace (Yunker & Yunker, 2002). For instance, Goleman and his colleagues have suggested that one way to increase effective leadership in the corporate world is to teach personnel to achieve higher levels of emotional intelligence (Goleman, Boyatzis, & McKee, 2002).

With an eye toward such practical applications, researchers John Mayer, Peter Salovey, and David Caruso have developed a test of emotional intelligence, the *Mayer-Salovey-Caruso Emotional Intelligence Test*, or MSCEIT. The MSCEIT measures four different aspects of emotional intelligence: perceiving emotions accurately, using emotions to facilitate thought, understanding emotions, and managing emotions in oneself and others (Mayer, Salovey, Caruso, & Sitarenios, 2003). In one study, MSCEIT scores were found to be positively correlated with measures of social competence in relationships with friends—but only for men. Men who scored low in emotional intelligence were found to engage in more behaviors that were harmful to their friendships than men who scored high in emotional intelligence. No such correlation was found for women (Brackett, Rivers, Shiffman, Lerner, & Salovey, 2006). At this time, the meaning of this finding is unclear, and there are doubts about the validity of the MSCEIT as a measure of emotional intelligence (Roberts et al., 2006). Researchers still have much work to do before we fully understand the nature of emotional intelligence and its importance to the everyday lives of men and women.

Nature, Nurture, and IQ: Are We Born Intelligent, or Do We Learn to Be?

The issue of *what* intelligence is has certainly stimulated a great deal of debate among researchers, but another issue has captured the attention of the public even more. Where does intelligence come from? Are we born with a predestined level of intelligence, or do we acquire intelligence as we develop (Gardner, 1999)?

NATURE VERSUS NURTURE AND INTERACTIONISM

Explaining how and why we develop as we do is the central issue in the age-old **nature–nurture debate**. On the nature side of this debate is the claim that individual characteristics (such as intelligence) are largely determined by one's genes and are not learned. On the nurture side, individual characteristics are thought to be molded by environmental influences such as parents, the educational opportunities you have, and the TV shows you watch. From the nurture point of view, our traits and characteristics are acquired totally by experience.

You Asked...

Are there "smart genes"?

TAYLOR EVANS, STUDENT

There is little doubt that genes exert a powerful influence on the development of an organism. All living organisms develop according to a "blueprint" or plan contained in the genes that an organism inherits from its parents.

Genes are strands of deoxyribonucleic acid (DNA) that are found in the nuclei of all living cells and direct the development of the organs and systems of the body. In 2003, scientists working on the *Human Genome Project*, a large-scale scientific project aimed at identifying the entire set of genes that are found in the DNA of the human body, completed this mapping. One of the most surprising findings of the project was that the total number of genes in the human genome is about 30,000. Originally, scientists had predicted that they would find approximately 100,000 genes. The fact that a mere 30,000 genes direct the development of something as complex as humans was a surprise (U.S. Department of Energy, 2007). So, why do humans possess these specific 30,000 genes and the characteristics that they govern? To answer this question, you should think back to a concept we discussed in Chapter 1—*natural selection*.

In 1859 Charles Darwin published *On the Origin of Species by Means of Natural Selection* (Darwin, 1859/1936) in which he outlined the process of **natural selection**. Natural selection is a simple but powerful process that can change, kill, or create a species over time. The central principle of natural selection is that for characteristics to be retained in a species, genes for these traits must be passed on to offspring. If an organism does not reproduce, its genes die with it. If a specific trait is *maladaptive* and tends to prevent an organism from surviving and procreating, then the genes for this trait are not as likely to be passed on to offspring. Over time, these maladaptive genes should die out in the species. In contrast, *adaptive* genes, which give rise to traits that help an organism reproduce, will be passed on to future generations. Through *natural selection*, these adaptive genes will become more widespread in the species over time. From this perspective, the genes of the human genome are present in us today because they aided our ancestors' ability to thrive and reproduce.

Even though our human genes direct our bodies to develop as human bodies, we are not all the same. As individuals, we have unique characteristics because we inherited a particular mix of genes for specific traits from our parents. At conception, we get half of our genes from each of our parents. From this combination of genes, we develop our characteristics. The genetic code that we inherit for a particular trait is called the **genotype**. But the genotypes we inherit, such as genes for dark hair, only partly determine the traits we actually acquire. The environment plays a role as well. The actual trait or characteristic we develop is referred

nature–nurture debate age-old debate over whether we are mostly a product of our genes or of environmental influences

genes strands of DNA found in the nuclei of all living cells

natural selection cornerstone of Darwin's theory of evolution, which states that genes for traits that allow an organism to be reproductively successful will be selected or retained in a species and genes for traits that hinder reproductive success will not be selected and therefore will die out in a species

genotype [JEAN-oh-type] inherited genetic pattern for a given trait to as the **phenotype**. The phenotype is a product of the genotype an organism inherits and the environment in which it lives. For example, the exact shade of your hair, the level of your intelligence, the speed with which you run—all are phenotypes, which are the expression of inherited genotypes *and* environmental influences.

Today, the dominant perspective on the nature–nurture debate is **interactionism**. Most psychologists now believe that genetic influences interact with environmental influences to produce our traits and behavior. For example, a child can inherit very "smart" genes, but if education is not provided, the child will not be as "smart" as he or she could have been. Interactionism does not end the nature–nurture debate, however. Today, many psychologists are attempting to understand the relative contributions of nature and nurture to specific traits, asking whether a trait such as intelligence is *mostly* genetic or *mostly* environmental.

TWIN STUDIES

To answer questions about the relative contributions of nature and nurture, researchers often focus on *twin studies*. Twin studies compare specific traits between pairs of *identical twins* (twins who share 100% of their genetic code) and pairs of nonidentical or *fraternal twins* (twins no more genetically related than other siblings). If identical twins have a similar trait more often than fraternal twins do, a genetic basis for the trait is implied. In contrast, if identical twins and fraternal twins do not differ in similarity, there is less support for the existence of a genetic influence on the trait because if the trait were genetic, we would expect the genetically identical twins to be more alike in the trait than the fraternal twins, who are not genetically identical to one another. Other valuable comparisons include comparing identical twins raised in different environments to identical twins raised in the same household. Dissimilarities between identical twins reared together and identical twins raised apart would be a powerful argument for environmental influence on the trait being measured. In doing such comparisons, psychologists can isolate the influence of nature and nurture on the development of specific traits.

INTELLIGENCE AND RACE

The nature–nurture debate is never more contentious than when it's applied to the issue of intelligence. Most recently, this debate was brought into the public eye with the publication of *The Bell Curve* (Herrnstein & Murray, 1994). The title of this book refers to the fact that IQ scores tend to follow a normal distribution, which is shaped like a bell (see Figure 7.4, p. 255). In *The Bell Curve*, the authors argued that intelligence is primarily encoded in our genes and that environmental influences do little to change it. This extreme position was largely denounced by scholars (Gardner, 1999), but the public became engaged in heated discussions about the merits of this position, as well as the implications of the authors' claims. Of particular concern was the implication that some minority groups may be genetically inferior with respect to intelligence. Though the authors never stated that minorities were genetically inferior, this conclusion appeared to follow from their arguments and the data that have been collected on IQ differences across racial groups.

Generally speaking, studies have shown that *average* IQ scores tend to vary across racial groups in America. As a group, African Americans tend to score about 10 to 15 points lower on IQ tests than European Americans, who are in turn outscored, on average, by Asian Americans (Nisbett, 1995; Rushton & Jensen, 2005). Although it has traditionally received less research attention, Hispanic Americans also tend to score below non-Hispanic European Americans on IQ tests (Dickens & Flynn, 2006). If we are to believe the message of *The Bell Curve*, the inference would be that these differences exist mostly because of genetic inheritance. Furthermore, some may be tempted to conclude that if these differences are genetically based, then any attempt to raise children's IQ scores by improving their environment would be a waste of time and money. It is this sort of offensive assertion that has kept the debate on race, genetics, and intelligence ignited for decades (see Rushton & Jensen, 2005,

phenotype [FEEN-oh-type] actual characteristic that results from interaction of the genotype and environmental influences

interactionism perspective that our genes and environmental influences work together to determine our characteristics and Sternberg, Grigorenko, & Kidd, 2005, for thorough reviews of the research from opposing points of view).

Overall, the results of twin studies (and other studies) on the inheritance of traits in families have not supported the strong nature claims made in *The Bell Curve*. Rather, these studies support an *interactionist* perspective that intelligence seems to stem from both our genes and our environment (Chipuer, Rovine, & Polmin, 1990; Polmin, 1994). In fact, the results of such studies suggest that genetics account for about 50% of a person's intelligence; the remaining 50% is the result of environmental influence (Bouchard, 2004). Therefore, it is just as likely that racial differences in IQ are due to environmental differences as genetic ones.

Compared to European Americans, a disproportionate number of minority members live in poverty. An impoverished environment may contribute to lesser performance on IQ tests for a number of reasons. Poorer parents cannot afford educational toys, good schools, computers, and so on for their children. Poorer parents may themselves not be highly educated and therefore may be less able to stimulate their children in the ways that highly educated parents can. Poverty-stricken children may not receive adequate nutrition and medical care, and this may affect neural development. We could go on listing the possibilities for pages, but a stronger argument can be made by looking at what happens when minority children are placed in a different environment. One study (Moore, 1986) showed that African American middle-schoolers who had been placed in affluent European American families as infants had average IQs that were not only above average for African American children but also above average for European American children. This suggests that the environment in which one grows up contributes significantly to one's IQ.

It is also worth noting that there is more variability in intelligence within racial groups than there is between racial groups. In other words, the range of IQ scores among European Americans or among African Americans is wider than the average difference between these groups. Furthermore, keep in mind that *group* characteristics do not predict individual characteristics. For example, knowing that the class average on your last psychology exam was 73 does not mean that *you* made a 73. You may have scored above or below average.

GENDER AND INTELLECTUAL ABILITIES: ARE WE REALLY ALL THAT DIFFERENT?

Just as we saw in our discussion on race and IQ, data are at times open to different interpretations. Another area in which the interpretation of data has been varied and sometimes contentious is in the study of how gender relates to intellectual abilities. Beliefs or stereotypes about male and female intellectual abilities abound. For example, in the United States (and many other cultures), people tend to believe that men are better at math and women are better at verbal tasks. Another common stereotype is that men are more intelligent than women and women are more emotional than men. But are there truly gender differences in intelligence?

The answer to this question has proved to be somewhat complicated. Over the last several decades, many researchers have investigated the issue of gender differences in intelligence, and often their results have been difficult to interpret (Galliano, 2003). In part, the confusion has to do with how individual researchers have defined specific abilities. For example, to evaluate mathematical ability, you could look at a person's ability to solve equations, the speed with which he or she can solve word problems, whether the person succeeds in math classes, and so on. Another problem is that studies that fail to find predicted gender differences are often not published. Therefore, if we look only at published studies that do show gender differences in intelligence, we may falsely conclude that gender differences are more prevalent than they actually are (Galliano, 2003).

After examining the available research, many psychologists have concluded that men and women do not differ in general intelligence, or *g* (Halpern & LeMay, 2000). On the other hand, some gender differences have been indicated with respect to specific multiple intelligences. We have summarized some of these suspected differences in ■ YOU REVIEW 7.1.

Keep a few things in mind as you read this summary table. First, many gender differences are small (e.g., Galliano, 2003; Hyde, Fennema, & Lamon, 1990). Second, finding such differences often depends on how they were measured. For example, females tend to earn better grades in math classes, but males tend to do better on standardized tests of mathematical ability (Hyde & McKinley, 1997). Third, gender differences can vary by culture, age, and race. For instance, in Thailand girls outperform boys in math, but in France boys do better than girls (Galliano, 2003). And in the United States, male superiority on math SAT scores occurs only among European Americans (Robinson, Abbott, Berninger, & Busse, 1996). Finally, gender differences are at times a product of bias in the tests used to measure different abilities. For example, David Share and Phil Silva (2003) found that in a sample of New Zealand students, boys were more likely to be labeled as having reading disabilities because of a statistical bias in the way that reading disability scores were calculated.

Gender Differences on Some Cognitive Tasks

You Review 7.1

TASKS ON WHICH WOMEN OFTEN HAVE HIGHER AVERAGE SCORES	TASKS ON WHICH MEN OFTEN HAVE HIGHER AVERAGE SCORES
VERBAL TASKS	VISUAL MEMORY TASKS
Verbal fluency Writing Synonym generation Foreign languages Spelling Tongue twisters Anagrams Knowledge about literature Reading comprehension	Mental rotation tasks
PERCEPTUAL TASKS	SPATIAL TASKS
Searching for letters within lines of text Detecting touch, taste, odor, and sound at low levels of intensity	Making judgments about moving objects—for example, judging how far away a moving object is
MOTOR SKILL TASKS	MOTOR SKILL TASKS
Fine motor skill tasks like tracing the mirror image of a stimulus on a piece of paper	Motor skills that involve aiming, such as throwing a baseball or darts
ACADEMIC PERFORMANCE	KNOWLEDGE AREAS
Most subject areas at school	General knowledge Knowledge about math, geography, and science
	FLUID REASONING TASKS
	Mechanical reasoning Scientific reasoning Quantitative reasoning Proportional reasoning Verbal analogies

Source: Adapted from Halpern, 1996.

Given these types of complexities in the data, it is difficult to conclude that there are broad-based, global differences between men and women when it comes to intelligence. Despite the lack of clarity concerning the differences, it is fairly clear that we tend to believe the stereotypes we have about men's and women's abilities. Belief in these stereotypes has been well documented in studies that ask men and women to assess their own intellectual abilities. For example, in one study, Adrian Furnham and colleagues found that parents tended to estimate their sons' IQs as being higher than their daughters', indicating that they had more confidence in their sons' overall intelligence, or *g*. When asked to rate their children on specific multiple intelligences, the parents tended to rate their sons higher on mathematical and spatial intelligence and their daughters higher on verbal and musical intelligences (Furnham, Reeves, & Budhani, 2002).

These biases also seem to extend to how we view our own levels of intelligence. In cultures as diverse as the United States, Poland, Argentina, China, Iran, New Zealand, and Slovakia, men's self-ratings of intelligence are higher than women's (see Furnham, Wytykowska, & Petrides, 2005, for a review). Men also rate themselves as having lower levels of emotional intelligence (Petrides et al., 2004), better general knowledge, and more skill on tasks of visual perception (Pallier, 2003). Studies like these seem to suggest that both men and women have (perhaps misguidedly) bought into the commonly held stereotypes about their respective abilities. This can be problematic. If a woman believes that she is less intelligent, this may actually work to lower her performance (Chamorro-Premuzic & Furnham, 2004). Furthermore, even if she performs well, stereotypes like these can be the basis for prejudice and discrimination—topics that we will discuss more in Chapter 10.

Let's Review!

In this section, we discussed intelligence. We looked at ways psychologists attempt to test, measure, and define intelligence, and the controversy concerning influences that affect an individual's level of intelligence. As a quick check of your understanding, answer these questions.

1. Which psychologist would be *most* likely to agree with the following statements: "Intelligence is not a single ability. We do not possess intelligence. We possess many intelligences."
   a. Robert Sternberg
   b. Francis Galton
   c. Howard Gardner
   d. Daniel Goleman

2. Gilbert recently developed a new intelligence test that he plans to administer to second-grade children, but when Gilbert wrote the questions, he used an adult-level vocabulary. Based on your understanding of intelligence tests, what would you predict the test to be?
   a. Valid and reliable
   b. Unreliable
   c. Invalid
   d. Valid, but not reliable

3. One day, Sabrina's front door started squeaking at the hinges. She was out of the spray lubricant that she would normally use for this purpose, so she went to her kitchen and got a bottle of cooking oil. She dabbed a bit of the corn oil on the hinge, and the squeak went away. Sabrina *best* exhibits a high level of _____ intelligence.
   a. analytical
   b. existential
   c. practical
   d. creative

Answers 1. c, 2. c, 3. d

Studying THE Chapter

Key Terms

cognition (234)
thinking (234)
knowledge (234)
mental representation (234)
concept (236)
superordinate category (236)
basic level category (237)
subordinate category (237)
formal concept (237)
natural concept (237)
prototype (238)
exemplar (239)
well-structured problem (240)
algorithm (240)
heuristic (240)
ill-structured problem (241)
insight (241)
creativity (241)
functional fixedness (242)

mental set (242)
incubation (242)
reasoning (243)
deductive reasoning (243)
inductive reasoning (244)
decision making (244)
judgment (244)
availability heuristic (245)
representativeness heuristic (245)
language (247)
cooing (248)
babbling (248)
phoneme (249)
morpheme (249)
overextension (249)
underextension (249)
telegraphic speech (249)
grammar (249)
pragmatics (249)

Whorfian hypothesis/linguistic relativity
   hypothesis (250)
intelligence (253)
mental age (254)
intelligence quotient (IQ score) (254)
reliability (257)
validity (257)
cultural bias (257)
general intelligence (g) (258)
crystallized intelligence (258)
fluid intelligence (258)
multiple intelligences (259)
triarchic theory of intelligence (260)
nature-nurture debate (262)
genes (262)
natural selection (262)
genotype (262)
phenotype (263)
interactionism (263)

What Do You Know? Assess Your Understanding

Test your retention and understanding of the material by answering the following questions.

1. _____ is the way in which we store and use information.
   a. Thinking
   b. Memory
   c. Cognition
   d. Knowledge

2. A concept is an example of a(n) _____.
   a. mental representation
   b. image
   c. judgment
   d. heuristic

3. The available evidence most strongly suggests that we store mental representations of stimuli that are _____ of what we see.
   a. exact visual copies
   b. only verbal descriptions
   c. both verbal descriptions and visual images
   d. only prototypes

4. Given the concepts *crab*, *seafood*, *King crab*, and *Opilio crab*, which one represents the basic level category?
   a. Crab
   b. Seafood
   c. Opilio crab
   d. King crab

5. Which of the following is *most* likely an example of a natural concept?
   a. Vehicles
   b. Tools
   c. Foods
   d. Friends

6. Using a combination to open a lock is an example of a(n) _____.
   a. algorithm
   b. heuristic
   c. exemplar
   d. judgment

7. Determining the best color to paint your living room is *most* likely an example of a(n) _____.
   a. well-structured problem
   b. ill-structured problem
   c. judgment
   d. insight

8. Which of the following is *not* an aid to problem solving?
   a. A mental set
   b. Incubation
   c. Creativity
   d. Insight

9. Reasoning that because many larger cars and trucks get poorer gas mileage, a Hummer must get very poor mileage is an example of _____.
   a. inductive reasoning
   b. deductive reasoning
   c. decision making
   d. problem solving

10. After watching a show on global warming, Mitch overestimates the average yearly temperature for his hometown. Mitch's error is most likely due to _____.
    a. the availability heuristic
    b. the representativeness heuristic
    c. framing
    d. poor decision making

11. The English suffix *-ed* is an example of a(n) _____.
    a. phoneme
    b. morpheme
    c. pragmatic
    d. overextension

12. Lamond is 5 months old. At which stage of language development would you most expect him to be?
    a. Cooing
    b. Babbling
    c. One-word speech
    d. Telegraphic speech

13. Who would most agree with the statement, "A Spanish-speaking person and an English-speaking person will necessarily have different perceptions of the world"?
    a. Robert Sternberg
    b. Noam Chomsky
    c. Benjamin Whorf
    d. Howard Gardner

14. According to the text, which of the following species have *not* been shown to possibly possess linguistic skills?
    a. Parrots
    b. Chimpanzees
    c. Horses
    d. Dolphins

15. _____ is credited with being the father of the modern intelligence test.
    a. Francis Galton
    b. Alfred Binet
    c. Robert Sternberg
    d. Lewis Terman

16. Six-year-old Tasha scores as well as the average 10-year-old on an intelligence test. Tasha's IQ score is approximately _____.
    a. 100
    b. 134
    c. 167
    d. 182

17. David Wechsler did which of the following?
   a. He developed the first intelligence test.
   b. He moved psychologists away from using the concept of mental age to calculate IQ scores.
   c. He introduced the idea that humans possess multiple intelligences as opposed to a general level of intelligence or *g*.
   d. All of the above

18. An intelligence test must be _____ to be of use to psychologists.
   a. reliable
   b. valid
   c. culturally biased
   d. a & b

19. As we age, _____ intelligence tends to decline, but _____ intelligence tends to increase.
   a. fluid; crystallized
   b. crystallized; fluid
   c. practical; analytical
   d. analytical; practical

20. The exact color of your hair is due to your _____.
   a. genotype
   b. genotype and nurture influences
   c. genotype and nature influences
   d. nature influences

Answers: 1. c; 2. a; 3. c; 4. a; 5. d; 6. a; 7. b; 8. a; 9. b; 10. a; 11. b; 12. b; 13. c; 14. c; 15. b; 16. c; 17. b; 18. d; 19. a; 20. b.

Online Resources

CENGAGENOW™ Personalized Study

www.cengage.com/login

Go to www.cengage.com/login to link to CengageNOW, your online study tool. First take the **Pre-Test** for this chapter to get your **Personalized Study Plan**, which will identify topics you need to review and direct you to online resources. Then take the **Post-Test** to determine what concepts you have mastered and what you still need work on.

 What Is Psychology? Essentials Book Companion Website

www.cengage.com/psychology/pastorino

Visit your book companion website, where you will find more resources to help you study. Resources include learning objectives, Internet exercises, quizzing, flash cards, and a pronunciation glossary.

Look Back AT WHAT YOU'VE LEARNED

What Is Thinking?

- **Cognition** is the way in which we store and use information.

- Our **knowledge** comprises the mental representations of the world that we have stored in long-term memory.

- **Thinking** is the use of knowledge to accomplish a goal.

- Visual images are powerful **mental representations** that allow us to remember a person's face or a map of one's town.

- **Concepts** are mental categories that contain related bits of knowledge and are organized around the meaning of the information they represent.

- We tend to organize our knowledge into three levels of categorization: the general, broad **superordinate category**; the **basic level category**; and the **subordinate category**, which is the most specific.

- We acquire **formal concepts** as we learn the rigid rules that define certain categories of things, but **natural concepts** develop naturally as we live our lives and experience the world.

- A **prototype** is our concept of the most typical member of a category—in essence, a summary of all members of that category.

- **Exemplars** are stored representations of actual category members we have experienced.

© Athol Franz; Gallo Image/Corbis

© Paul Poplis/Jupiter Images

© Corbis

How Do We Reason and Make Decisions and Judgments?

- We engage in **reasoning** when we draw conclusions that are based on certain assumptions about the world. **Deductive reasoning** involves reasoning from the general to the specific, whereas **inductive reasoning** involves reasoning from the specific to the general.

- **Decision making** involves choosing among several alternatives and is often part of the problem-solving process.

- Framing, or how possible courses of action are presented, can affect our decisions.

- Two mental shortcuts that can be useful but that can also lead to mistakes are the **availability** and **representativeness heuristics**.

How Do We Solve Problems?

- An **algorithm** is a method of solving a particular problem that always leads to the correct solution. A **heuristic** is a shortcut, or rule of thumb, that may or may not lead to the solution of a problem.

- **Insight**, **creativity**, and **incubation** help us overcome common obstacles to problem solving like **functional fixedness** and **mental sets**.

Image Source Black/Getty Images

Cognition, Language, AND Intelligence: HOW DO WE THINK?

How Do We Develop and Use Language?

- Human **language** is a well-developed, syntactical, verbal system for representing the world.

- Scientists debate the idea that humans are born with an innate language acquisition device—a programmed capacity for language.

- Research indicates that infants generally proceed from **cooing** to **babbling** to **morphemes** on their road to language skills. By age 2, most children exhibit **telegraphic speech**. Soon after, children learn the rules of **grammar** and **pragmatics** for their language.

- One theory, known as the **Whorfian hypothesis** or the **linguistic relativity hypothesis**, suggests that one's language actually determines one's thoughts and perceptions of the world. A more widely held view is that language influences, rather than determines, our thoughts.

- Although animals communicate, it is hotly debated whether they have the capacity for language.

© Helen King/Corbis

How Do Psychologists Define and Measure Intelligence?

© Bob Daemmrich/The Image Works

- Many modern psychologists broadly view **intelligence** as those abilities that allow you to adapt to your environment and behave in a goal-oriented way.

- Alfred Binet established the measurement of **mental age** that reflected a child's mental abilities compared to those of the "average" child at a specific age.

- Stanford psychologist Lewis Terman revised Binet's testing procedures and introduced the **intelligence quotient**, or **IQ score**, which divided one's mental age by one's chronological age.

- The adult version of David Wechsler's test (WAIS-III) yields three separate scores: a verbal score, a performance score, and an overall score.

- Intelligence tests are frequently criticized for having a **cultural bias**.

- The idea of mental ability as a single unitary factor is known as **general intelligence**, or **g**.

- **Crystallized intelligence** refers to our accumulation of knowledge, whereas **fluid intelligence** refers to the speed and efficiency with which we learn new information and solve problems.

- Some theorists argue that we have **multiple intelligences**. Examples are Robert Sternberg's **triarchic theory** and Howard Gardner's theory of multiple intelligences.

- Daniel Goleman's theory of emotional intelligence argues that emotions are also an important component of successful living.

- Although a heated debate continues over whether intelligence is inherited, most research suggests that an interaction of heredity and environment contributes to our intellectual capabilities.

8

Motivation AND Emotion: WHAT Guides OUR BEHAVIOR?

Kim Steele/Getty Images.

Most of us go through puberty and adolescence without ever questioning the fact that we are sexually attracted to members of the opposite sex. But for Daniel (not his real name), adolescence was a confusing time. Like most young men, Daniel started dating girls and began learning to navigate the emotional twists and turns that characterize romantic relationships. But something didn't feel right. One night, when Daniel and his girlfriend were having an intimate moment, Daniel had an epiphany. Although he was with his girlfriend, he wasn't thinking about her. Rather, he was fantasizing about a football player that he knew—an unwelcome realization at the time.

Having been raised in a culture that thought of homosexuality as a bad thing, Daniel's growing awareness of his homosexuality was at times very difficult to accept. But as time went on and Daniel began to share his feelings with family members and close friends, he began to feel more comfortable with his sexuality. He came to accept that being attracted to men was as natural a motivation for him as being attracted to women is for heterosexual men. Once he better understood the biological forces that govern our sexuality, Daniel realized that being homosexual was not a personal failing or something to feel bad about.

Today, Daniel is in a loving, committed relationship with a man. The only negative emotion Daniel feels in connection with his sexuality comes from the prejudice he and other homosexual and bisexual people sometimes experience from others. It is due to the threat of possible prejudice and not due to shame that Daniel chose to use a pseudonym for this piece. As you read about motivation and emotion in this chapter, we hope that you too will experience a better understanding of your own unique behavior and what drives it.

Although he is proud of who he is, Daniel chose to use an avatar and pseudonym for this piece to protect himself from the possible prejudices of others.

Theories About Motivation

- Describe how psychologists define motivation.
- Describe the different theoretical ways of conceptualizing motivation.

> **You Asked...**
>
> *What motivates us to do something?*   ERICK HERNANDEZ, STUDENT

When we are *motivated*, we are driven to engage in some form of behavior. Just as something motivated you to start to read this chapter, every day we are motivated to do many different things. For example, we are motivated to eat, drink, attend school, go to work, interact with family and friends, and so on. In psychological terms, a **motive** is the tendency to desire and seek out positive incentives or rewards and to avoid negative outcomes (Atkinson, 1958/1983; McClelland, 1987). This means that we are motivated to avoid aversive states and to seek more pleasant states. When we experience the motive of hunger, we eat to avoid this aversive feeling. We are motivated to study because we want the feelings of pride and the opportunities for advancement that accompany academic success. We drink to quench our thirst. Because we are generally motivated to avoid pain and other aversive states, our motives often serve to protect us. Without the motivation to eat, we could suffer from malnutrition or even starvation; without thirst, we would face dehydration; and so on. As you can see, without motivation we would not engage in many behaviors that are necessary for good health and survival.

In an attempt to better understand what motivates us, psychologists have historically viewed motivation in several different ways: as *instincts* that direct our behavior; as uncomfortable biological states called *drives* that motivate us to find ways to feel better; as the desire to maintain an optimal level of *arousal* in our body; or as *incentives* that guide us to seek reward from the world. However, none of these theories seems to fully explain all aspects of motivation. Today psychologists do not expect any single theory to explain all our motivations. Instead, we recognize that each of these theories has its strengths and weaknesses. Let's take a closer look at these different theories of motivation.

motive a tendency to desire and seek out positive incentives or rewards and to avoid negative outcomes

instinct innate impulse from within a person that directs or motivates behavior

drive reduction theory theory of motivation that proposes that motivation seeks to reduce internal levels of drive

drive an uncomfortable internal state that motivates us to reduce this discomfort through our behavior

primary drive a drive that motivates us to maintain homeostasis in certain biological processes within the body

homeostasis [home-ee-oh-STAY-sus] an internal state of equilibrium in the body

negative feedback loop a system of feedback in the body that monitors and adjusts our motivation level so as to maintain homeostasis

secondary drive a learned drive that is not directly related to biological needs

Motivation as Instinct

One of the earliest views on motivation was one that was heavily influenced by the work of Charles Darwin and the theory of natural selection (see Chapter 7; Darwin, 1859/1936). Back in the 1800s, American psychologist William James proposed that motives are, in fact, genetically determined **instincts** that have evolved in humans because they support survival and procreation. According to William James, instincts are impulses from within a person that direct or *motivate* that person's behavior. James proposed that we are motivated by more than 35 different innate instincts, including the impulse to love, fight, imitate, talk, and acquire things (James, 1890).

Over time, the idea that motives are inborn instincts gradually fell out of favor with psychologists. One problem with James's view was that the list of proposed instincts kept getting longer and longer, and it seemed unrealistic to argue that *all* behavior is due to instinct. Furthermore, it is impossible to determine whether many of the proposed instincts are truly inborn. Many of James's so-called instincts, such as being *sympathetic* and being *secretive*, may result from learning.

Motivation as a Drive

Instinct theory was followed by **drive reduction theories** of motivation. According to the drive reduction approach, motivation stems from the desire to reduce an uncomfortable, internal state, called a **drive**, that results when our needs are not fulfilled (Hull, 1943). For instance, when we do not have enough food in our system, we feel the uncomfortable state of *hunger*, which *drives* us to eat until we have taken in the food that our bodies require. Then, when we have taken in enough food, the hunger drive dissipates, and we stop eating. In this fashion, our drives can help us survive by creating what psychologists call a *drive state*, which ensures that we will be motivated to meet our biological needs.

Primary drives, such as needing food, water, and warmth, motivate us to maintain certain bodily processes at an internal state of equilibrium, or **homeostasis**. Obviously, it would be desirable for us to take in just the right amount of food and water, to sleep just enough, and to maintain our body temperature at 98.6 degrees. Without the motivation from drives, we would not keep our bodies at homeostasis because we would not know when to eat, sleep, drink, and so on. But what causes a drive state in the first place?

Primary drives begin in the body when the brain recognizes that we are lacking in some biological need. The brain recognizes need based on the *feedback* that it receives from the body's systems and organs. One type of feedback system is called a **negative feedback loop** (■ FIGURE 8.1). Negative feedback loops are information systems in the body that monitor the level of a bodily process and adjust it up or down accordingly. A good analogy for a negative feedback loop is a thermostat. In your home, you set the thermostat at a desired level. The thermostat monitors the air temperature and compares it to that set level. If the room gets too cold, the heater turns on; if the room gets too warm, the heater turns off. Many primary drives in the body work in the same fashion.

The idea that motivation in the form of primary drives serves to maintain homeostasis makes a great deal of sense. Without primary drives, our biological needs would likely not be met, and we might not survive. But how well does the idea of drive explain some of our other motivations? For example, does drive reduction theory explain academic achievement motivation, or motivation to be loved? To help explain what motivates those behaviors not directly related to survival, drive reduction theorists developed the notion of **secondary drives**, or drives that motivate us to perform behaviors that are not directly related to biological needs.

Secondary drives are presumed to have developed through learning and experience. Back in the 1930s, Henry Murray proposed that human behavior is motivated by a host

© Ashley Cooper/Corbis

FIGURE 8.1 Negative Feedback Loops

Negative feedback loops maintain homeostasis in our bodies by monitoring certain physiological conditions (e.g., glucose levels and fluid levels). When levels drop too low, feedback from the body tells the brain to increase motivation (e.g., hunger or thirst). When levels are too high, feedback from the body tells the brain to decrease motivation.

Need
• food
• water
• body heat

Drive
• hunger
• thirst
• chill

Drive-reducing behavior
• eat
• drink
• put on a sweater

Homeostasis (our needs are met)

According to drive reduction theory, we are motivated to eat when our body sends feedback to the brain indicating that our energy supplies are running low. This need for fuel sets up a primary drive state, which motivates us to eat so that we can reduce our hunger.

of secondary motives such as *need for achievement*, *need for affiliation* (the need to be close to others), and *need for understanding* (the need to understand one's world) (Murray, 1938). According to some psychologists, the need to fulfill certain secondary drives differs from person to person, like any other personality characteristic. For example, some people have a higher need for achievement than others do.

The concept of motivation as a means of reducing drives seems to make more sense for primary drives than for secondary drives, but even here it is not without its faults. There are times when drive reduction theory cannot explain certain aspects of our biological motives. For example, what about overeating? Think about a typical holiday meal in your family. At holiday dinners, do you eat only enough food to satisfy your primary drive of hunger? We bet not. How many times have you eaten until you felt ill because it was a special occasion? If our sole motivation for eating were drive reduction, we would not "pig out" in instances like these.

Drive reduction theories also fail to account for times when we seem to be motivated to *increase* the tension or arousal levels in our bodies. For instance, when you decide to ride a roller coaster at an amusement park or to try skydiving, what possible drive could these behaviors lower? Activities such as these do not appear to reduce any of our primary drives. Rather, the sole purpose of these activities seems to be to *arouse* us physiologically. Clearly, we will have to conceptualize motivation in some other way to account for these types of behavior.

Arousal Theories of Motivation

Arousal theories of motivation state that each of us has a level of physiological arousal at which we operate best, an *optimal* level of arousal. In general, we perform best on tasks when we are moderately aroused (■ FIGURE 8.2); too much or too little arousal generally weakens performance (Berlyne, 1967; Hebb, 1955; Sonstroem & Bernardo, 1982). For example, students who are either sleepy (underarousal) or suffering from test anxiety (overarousal) tend to perform poorly on exams. Students who are relaxed yet alert (optimal arousal) tend to perform better.

According to arousal theories of motivation, each of us is motivated to seek out arousal when we find ourselves underaroused, and to reduce our arousal level when we are overaroused. This doesn't mean, however, that there is a level of arousal that is optimal for all of us. Just as we saw with secondary drives, there are individual differences in how much arousal is optimal or right for us. Some of us are motivated to seek out situations that elicit low arousal (e.g., going to the bookstore) while others tend to crave the excitement of highly arousing activities (e.g., going skydiving).

Incentive Theories of Motivation

Perhaps jumping out of airplanes or hanging out in bookstores is not your cup of tea. Take a moment to think about what does motivate you. What gets you out of bed in the morning? Is it money, material goods, or approval from others? These things are motivating for many of us. As we saw before, drive theory states that nonbiological motives like these are the result of prior learning—that somewhere along the way we learned to associate approval, money, and material goods with our pri-

FIGURE

8.2

Performance as a Function of Arousal

Our best performance often occurs at moderate levels of arousal. You would likely do your best on an exam if you were neither too sleepy nor too anxious.

General relationship between performance and arousal level

mary drives. But researchers have had trouble finding support for this idea, and today many psychologists no longer think of these nonbiological motives in terms of drives. Instead they tend to see things like money, praise, and material goods as **incentives** that can motivate many of us into action (Atkinson, 1958/1983). You can think of incentives as goals or desires that you wish to satisfy or fulfill. For example, someone who desires money will be motivated to engage in behaviors that will likely lead to obtaining money, such as taking a job or buying lottery tickets.

We have discussed instincts, drives, and arousal, which are always *intrinsic* parts of who we are. Incentives, however, can be either *intrinsic* or *extrinsic*. Drives, instincts, and physiological arousal originate from inside our bodies and motivate us to behave in certain ways. In contrast, extrinsic incentives have the power to motivate us in ways that may be unrelated to our internal states. For someone addicted to alcohol, drinking at a party may be the result of the drive to avoid the unpleasant physical symptoms associated with withdrawing from alcohol and the incentive to fit in with others. In this situation, he might be both *pushed* by an internal drive to feel better and *pulled* by the external reinforcement he receives from his drinking buddies. Because this behavior is partly motivated from outside of the person, he is experiencing what psychologists call **extrinsic motivation** (Deci & Ryan, 1985).

Sometimes the goal we wish to accomplish leads to some sort of internal reward. For instance, you may wish to do well on an exam, not because it will lead to a good grade or a better job, but rather because earning a good grade will make you feel good about yourself. The internal feeling of pride can be a powerful incentive in motivating behavior! When we are motivated by *intrinsic* incentives, we are said to be experiencing **intrinsic motivation** (Deci & Ryan, 1985).

Maslow's Hierarchy of Needs

Imagine that you have to miss lunch because you don't have time to stop and eat. On this particular day, you have a paper to write, an exam to study for, and a long list of algebra problems to finish. As you sit down to study, you find that several different motives are all trying to direct your behavior at the same time. You need to study, you are hungry, you are sleepy because you did not sleep well last night, and you really want to go to the movies with your friends. Which of these motives will win? What will your first course of action be in this situation? Will you eat, study, go to the movies, or fall asleep? We often find ourselves pulled in different directions by our motives. Are some types of motives inherently stronger than others? Perhaps.

Psychologist Abraham Maslow recognized that in certain circumstances, some motives have greater influence over our behavior than others do. Maslow conceptualized both our physiological and psychological motives as different classes of *needs* to which we assign different levels of priority. These different classes form a **hierarchy of needs**, in which the lower-level needs have the first priority (Maslow, 1970). Maslow's hierarchy of needs is usually presented as a pyramid, as shown in ■ FIGURE 8.3.

The lowest level of Maslow's hierarchy—the base of the pyramid—is our *physiological needs*. Maslow theorized that we seek to satisfy such basic needs as hunger, thirst, and need for warmth before we are motivated to satisfy any of our other needs. If our physiological needs are met, then our next level of concern is satisfying *safety and security needs*, such as having a safe

© Dennis MacDonald/ PhotoEdit

The incentive theory of motivation states that many of us are motivated by extrinsic rewards such as money, material goods, and praise from others.

incentive a goal or desire that we are motivated to fulfill

extrinsic motivation motivation that comes from outside of the person

intrinsic motivation motivation that comes from within the person

hierarchy of needs Maslow's theory that humans are motivated by different motives, some of which take precedence over others place to live. At the next level, Maslow identified *belongingness and love needs*, the motivation to be with others, to be loved, and to be appreciated by others. At the next levels we would seek to successively satisfy our *esteem needs*, *cognitive needs*, and *aesthetic needs* (see Figure 8.3 for descriptions).

If we meet our aesthetic needs, we may seek to move to even higher levels, toward self-fulfillment. At these levels, motives include *self-actualization needs*, or the motivation to reach our full potential, and the *need for transcendence*, the motivation to achieve spiritual fulfillment. Abraham Maslow had little hope that the average person would actually reach the self-fulfillment level. He believed that most people are unable to fulfill enough of the needs at the lower and middle levels of the pyramid, but that some of us do satisfy enough of our lower-level needs to at least try for self-actualization and transcendence.

For example, Mahatma Gandhi, Martin Luther King, Jr., and Mother Teresa all appeared to be motivated by these higher levels of Maslow's hierarchy during their lifetimes.

At first glance, Maslow's hierarchy seems to make sense. If you are starving, you will probably be less concerned with whether or not people love you and more concerned with finding food. Unfortunately, there is not much evidence to support Maslow's hierarchy of needs (Soper, Milford, & Rosenthal, 1995). In fact, we often seem to behave in ways that contradict Maslow's notion that we must fulfill lower needs before we can be concerned with higher-order needs. For instance, have you ever gone without lunch to pursue some other activity, such as studying for an exam? In that case, you were motivated by esteem needs even though your physiological needs had not been met! Likewise, the research also indicates that

**Pyramid figure labels (top to bottom):**

Transcendence

Self-actualization needs: to find self-fulfillment and realize one's potential

Aesthetic needs: symmetry, order, and beauty

Cognitive needs: to know, understand, and explore

Esteem needs: to achieve, be competent, and gain approval and recognition

Belongingness and love needs: to affiliate with others, be accepted, and belong

Safety needs: to feel secure and safe, out of danger

Physiological needs: hunger, thirst, and so forth

FIGURE 8.3 Maslow's Hierarchy of Needs

Maslow, Abraham H.; Frager, Robert D. (Editor); Fadiman, James (Editor), Motivation and Personality, 3rd, © 1987. Electronically reproduced by permission of Pearson Education, Inc., Upper Saddle River, New Jersey.

According to Abraham Maslow, few of us will ever fulfill enough of our lower-level needs to actually reach the level of self-actualization. During her lifetime, Mother Teresa appeared to have reached the levels of self-actualization and need for transcendence. Similarly, singer Bono of the group U2 appears to be striving for self-actualization, spending much of his time engaged in humanitarian causes.

Tim Graham/Getty Images

Andrew Gombert/Landov

when we have satisfied our needs at a certain level of the hierarchy, we do not always move up to the next level and attempt to satisfy those needs (Hall & Nougaim, 1968).

We have seen that there are many different ways to look at motivation. However, whether you view motivation as an instinct, a drive, a need, or an incentive, one thing is certain: Motivation is what catalyzes our behavior and moves us into action.

Let's Review!

In this section, we defined motivation and discussed some of the theoretical perspectives on motivation. For a quick check of your understanding, answer these questions.

1. Which of the following approaches to motivation is most closely aligned with Darwin's theory of evolution?
   a. Drive theory
   b. Instinct theory
   c. Incentive approaches
   d. Maslow's hierarchy of needs

2. Which of the following approaches to motivation assumes that motivation can come from outside the person?
   a. Instinct theory
   b. Drive theory
   c. Incentive theory
   d. None of the above

3. Which of the following is the best example of intrinsic motivation?
   a. Studying hard to keep your scholarship
   b. Staying late at work to earn overtime
   c. Cleaning your house because you enjoy a tidy home
   d. Dressing up for a job interview because you want to make a good impression

Answers 1. b; 2. c; 3. c

Hunger and Thirst: What Makes Us Eat and Drink?

- Describe the feedback our bodies use to regulate hunger.

- Explain what is known about why some people become obese.

- Describe bulimia, anorexia, and binge eating disorder and explain their possible causes.

- Describe the feedback in the body that leads to thirst.

Learning Objectives

Eating is one of our most fundamental activities, basic to survival. To protect us from starvation, the motivation to eat remains strong even when we have competing or conflicting motivations. But what is it in our bodies that initiates the hunger that motivates us to eat?

The Origins of Hunger

The hunger motive is one of our primary drives that helps us maintain homeostasis in the body. The goal of hunger is to motivate us to eat when our bodies need fuel. Thus, we should feel hungry when we are lacking fuel and nutrients, but we should *not* feel the motivation to eat when we have enough fuel and nutrients in our bodies. Like a thermostat, hunger works on a *negative feedback* loop in the body that allows us to maintain homeostasis in our bodies.

Homeostatic regulation of hunger explains why we seem to have a **set point**, or a weight that our body naturally attempts to maintain. Having a set point may be one reason why the

set point a particular weight that our body seeks to maintain vast majority of people who lose weight tend to regain it. When the body loses weight, the person's hunger increases, the person eats more, and the weight is regained. Although having a set point makes dieting very difficult, experiencing increased hunger when we fall below our set point also protects us from starvation. In environments where people struggle to find enough to eat, this extra motivation may make them work harder to obtain enough food to survive.

To motivate us to eat enough food to maintain homeostasis and thereby our set point, our brain must receive accurate and reliable feedback from the rest of our body. Where in the body does this feedback about the current status of our body's fuel supply originate?

HUNGER FEEDBACK FROM THE BODY

One of the first places psychologists looked for clues to hunger was the stomach, and there is some evidence to suggest that one part of the feedback that initiates hunger is an empty stomach. When our stomachs become empty, the walls of the stomach contract, and these contractions appear to stimulate hunger. Additionally, the stomach appears to release a hormone called **ghrelin** that sends strong hunger signals to the brain (Wu & Kral, 2004).

Just as the stomach signals hunger, it may also play a role in telling our brains when it is time to stop eating. When we eat, our stomach's walls must distend to expand the volume of the stomach and allow room for the food we eat. This distention of the stomach is one source of feedback that signals to our brains that it is time to stop eating (Deutsch, 1990). Additionally, receptors in the walls of the stomach may actually be able to measure the nutritive value of the food we eat, and that this feedback may play a role in regulating hunger. For instance, researchers have shown that the degree to which we feel hungry is directly correlated with the number of calories that we have in our stomach (deCastro & Elmore, 1988).

Although the stomach is an important source of feedback in the hunger process, it is not the only source. Surprisingly, even people who have had their stomachs completely *removed* because of cancer usually still feel hunger (Janowitz & Grossman, 1950).

The liver is another source of feedback for hunger. Our liver has the capacity to help regulate hunger by monitoring the levels of **glucose** and **glycogen** in our body. Glucose is the form of sugar that our bodies burn for energy, and glycogen is the form of starch that we store along with fatty acids. When we have excess glucose in our body, we convert it into glycogen and then store it for future use. The liver determines what our energy requirements are by monitoring our levels of glucose and glycogen. If the liver detects that we are converting glucose into glycogen, indicating that we have too much fuel in our bodies, it will send signals to the brain to shut off hunger. On the other hand, if the liver notices that glycogen is being turned back into glucose, indicating that we are dipping into our energy reserves, it will send signals to the brain to initiate hunger.

The endocrine system also plays a role in regulating hunger. The hormone *insulin* can increase feelings of hunger (see Grossman & Stein, 1948). Made in the pancreas, insulin facilitates the movement of glucose from the blood into our cells, where it is metabolized. When glucose moves into the cells, blood levels of glucose drop, so we begin to dip into our glycogen reserves, and hunger is initiated. In this indirect way, insulin can produce feelings of hunger.

Other hormones affect hunger even more directly. When we eat, the small intestines release the hormone **cholecystokinin (CCK)** into the bloodstream. CCK appears to shut off eating (Canova & Geary, 1991; Holt, Brand, Soveny, & Hansky, 1992). However, the level of hunger that we experience is due to more than just the amount of CCK in our bloodstream. How much food we have recently eaten also seems to influence hunger. In one experiment, participants ate either 100 or 500 grams of soup and were then given either CCK or a placebo substance. Afterward, they were allowed to eat a meal. The dependent variable in the study was how much the participants ate of the meal that followed the soup. The results showed that the amount eaten was a function of both the amount of soup the participants had

ghrelin [GRELL-in] a hunger-stimulating hormone produced by the stomach

glucose the form of sugar that the body burns as fuel

glycogen [GLIE-co-jen] a starchy molecule that is produced from excess glucose in the body; it can be thought of as the body's stored energy reserves

cholecystokinin [coe-lih-cyst-oh-KYE-nin] **(CCK)** a hormone released by the small intestines that plays a role in hunger regulation eaten and whether or not they had received the CCK. Participants who had eaten the larger amount of soup (500 grams) and also received the CCK tended to eat less at the meal. But for participants who had eaten only 100 grams of soup, the CCK did not reduce the amount of food eaten at the meal. It appears that if we have not taken in enough food, CCK by itself may not be enough to stop our hunger and our eating (Muurahainen, Kisileff, Lechaussee, & Pi-Sunyer, 1991).

Fat cells may provide yet another source of feedback for hunger regulation. Fat cells make and secrete a chemical called **leptin**. When fat cells release leptin into the bloodstream, it travels to the brain, where it is picked up by receptors near the brain's *ventricles* (the fluid-filled cavities in the brain) and in the *hypothalamus* (the part of the brain that maintains homeostasis) (McGregor et al., 1996). Leptin is thought to inform the brain about the level of fat reserves available. When the brain senses high leptin levels, this may indicate that a large number of fat cells are full of fat reserves. Therefore, we do not need to take in more fuel, and our hunger may be reduced. In support of this hypothesis, researchers have found that mice that are bred to be genetically fat will lose weight if they are given injections of leptin (Pelleymounter et al., 1995). Unfortunately, we are a long way from understanding the exact role of leptin in motivating human eating. For example, researchers are currently investigating the role that the neurotransmitter *dopamine* (Chapter 2) plays in mediating leptin action in the brain (Benoit et al., 2003). At the moment, we have no body of evidence to support the notion that losing weight is as simple as taking a few tablets of leptin!

HUNGER REGULATION IN THE BRAIN

The brain, of course, plays a significant role in our eating behavior. It receives and processes signals from the stomach about contractions and distention, from the liver about the glucose—glycogen balance, and from leptin. The brain may also directly monitor our energy supplies. There is evidence to suggest that the brain, like the liver, monitors the level of glucose in the blood. There appear to be specialized *glucoreceptors* in the hypothalamus that measure glucose levels in the bloodstream. If an animal is given a substance that makes its hypothalamus unresponsive to glucose, the animal goes on an eating binge (Miselis & Epstein, 1970). Disabling the hypothalamus's glucoreceptors tricks the brain into thinking that the body is critically low on fuel. The brain then signals extreme hunger to quickly replenish the body's glucose.

> ### You Asked...
> *What in the brain controls motivation?* JEFF WRIGHT, STUDENT

Further clues about the role of the hypothalamus in hunger regulation come from animal studies in which surgical lesions are made in the brain. By destroying part of the hypothalamus and observing the effect that this destruction has on behavior, psychologists have uncovered some clues about the role that the different parts of the hypothalamus play in both initiating and stopping eating.

One part of the hypothalamus, the **lateral hypothalamus**, or **LH**, seems to function as an "on switch" for hunger. When the LH is destroyed in a rat, the rat stops eating. As a result, the rat loses weight and eventually dies. Without the LH, the rat simply starves to death (Teitelbaum & Stellar, 1954), which seems to indicate that the LH turns *on* hunger. However, further investigation has shown that the LH is not the only "on switch" for hunger. Curiously, if a rat is force-fed for long enough after having had its LH destroyed, the rat will eventually get some of its appetite back. Its appetite will not be as great as it was prior to losing its LH, but the rat will eat, particularly very tasty foods (Teitelbaum & Epstein, 1962).

Another bit of evidence that suggests an "on switch" for hunger outside of the LH comes from studies using **neuropeptide Y**, the most powerful hunger stimulant known (Gibbs, 1996). When an animal is injected with neuropeptide Y, its strongest effect occurs outside of the LH (Leibowitz, 1991). It stands to reason that if the LH were the primary "on switch" for

leptin a hormone released by fat cells in the body that plays a role in hunger regulation

lateral hypothalamus (LH) a region of the hypothalamus once thought to be the hunger center in the brain

neuropeptide Y the most powerful hunger stimulant known

© Richard Howard

FIGURE

8.4

A Mouse With a Lesion in the Ventromedial Hypothalamus (VMH)

This mouse had its ventromedial hypothalamus damaged. As a result, the mouse has eaten more than normal and gained a great deal of weight. But this mouse will not eat itself to death. Rather, it will now eat just enough to maintain this new, higher set point weight.

hunger, then this powerful stimulant would have its strongest effect in the LH. That this does not appear to be the case suggests that there is an even more important "on switch" for hunger elsewhere in the brain.

The hypothalamus is also thought to play a role in shutting off hunger. Some evidence suggests that a part of the hypothalamus, the **ventromedial hypothalamus**, or **VMH**, plays a role in creating a feeling of *satiety*. When we are sated, we feel full and do not wish to eat more. Rats who have had their VMH destroyed will begin to eat ravenously and will gain enormous amounts of weight (■ FIGURE 8.4). If the VMH were the rat's only satiety center, or hunger "off switch," then destroying its VMH should make the rat eat continuously until it dies. But this doesn't happen. A rat without a VMH will eat a great deal of food and gain a great deal of weight, but after a certain amount of weight gain, its appetite will level off and the rat will then eat only enough food to maintain its new, higher weight. It's as if losing the VMH changes the rat's set point. In other words, the weight that the rat's body tries to maintain through homeostatic regulation has been shifted upward to a new, higher weight. So, although the VMH may not be the only "off switch" for hunger, it does appear to play a role in obesity (see Levin & Routh, 1996). When the VMH is damaged, the endocrine system's control over insulin release is disturbed. The result is an increased release of insulin into the bloodstream, which produces great hunger and subsequent increases in eating. Loss of the VMH doesn't remove the satiety center, but rather causes disturbances in the endocrine system that result in increased eating.

What we have learned from studies of the hunger centers in the brain is that many mechanisms turn on and shut off feelings of hunger. There does not appear to be a single "on" or "off" switch for hunger. Rather, hunger seems to be regulated by a complex network of feedback to the brain from various sources in the body, as well as direct signaling in the brain (see ■ YOU REVIEW 8.1).

OTHER CUES THAT INFLUENCE EATING: CULTURE AND CONSUMERISM

Have you ever eaten until you felt as if you were going to burst? Have you ever eaten a big bag of popcorn at the movies just minutes after you finished a large meal? If so, your behavior has shown that eating is often more than just satisfying biological needs and maintaining homeostasis in the body. Recently, psychologists have begun to discriminate between *intuitive eating*, or eating that is motivated by physiological hunger and satiety feedback, and eating that is motivated by emotional and situational cues that have little connection to energy requirements (Avalos & Tylka, 2006). For example, the smell of popping popcorn at a theater can make you want to eat popcorn, even shortly after you've had a full meal. Or you may be tempted to indulge in a big bowl of ice cream after a stressful day.

Such eating occurs for reasons other than supplying fuel for our bodies. In many cultures, food and feasting are an integral part of cultural customs. This is especially true in the United States, where our holiday celebrations—including Christmas, Thanksgiving, Halloween, Hanukkah, Passover, Kwanzaa, and New Year's—are all associated with special foods in large quantities. The same holds true for more personal celebrations—birthdays, weddings, reunions, and even funerals. Americans and many other peoples around the world use food and eating to celebrate. This connection between joy and food can lead to eating when we do not really need to. Whereas intuitive eating is associated with lower body mass in college women (Tylka, 2006), eating that is motivated by emotion and situational cues can lead to a major health concern—obesity.

ventromedial hypothalamus (VMH)
a region of the hypothalamus that plays an indirect role in creating a feeling of satiety

You Review 8.1

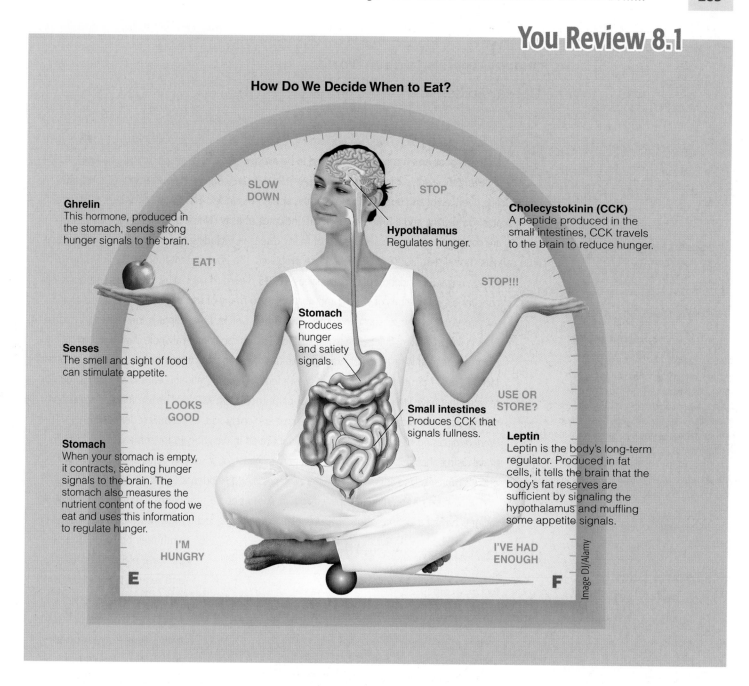

How Do We Decide When to Eat?

Ghrelin
This hormone, produced in the stomach, sends strong hunger signals to the brain.

SLOW DOWN

STOP

Hypothalamus
Regulates hunger.

Cholecystokinin (CCK)
A peptide produced in the small intestines, CCK travels to the brain to reduce hunger.

EAT!

STOP!!!

Stomach
Produces hunger and satiety signals.

Senses
The smell and sight of food can stimulate appetite.

LOOKS GOOD

USE OR STORE?

Small intestines
Produces CCK that signals fullness.

Leptin
Leptin is the body's long-term regulator. Produced in fat cells, it tells the brain that the body's fat reserves are sufficient by signaling the hypothalamus and muffling some appetite signals.

Stomach
When your stomach is empty, it contracts, sending hunger signals to the brain. The stomach also measures the nutrient content of the food we eat and uses this information to regulate hunger.

I'M HUNGRY

I'VE HAD ENOUGH

E

F

Image DJ/Alamy

The Battle of the Bulge: Why Is Dieting So Hard?

In light of the obesity epidemic, many people spend a good deal of their time dieting. In an attempt to bring about weight loss, diets restrict the dieter's eating to varying degrees. Unfortunately, depriving yourself of food is also one reason that most diets fail. When we reduce our caloric intake to the point that we begin to lose weight, our bodies try to counteract the diet. Recall that our motivation to eat is designed to keep us from starving. When we begin to draw on our fat reserves while dieting, our body takes steps to avoid "starvation." At first, we may feel increased hunger as our body tries to avoid burning up fat reserves by urging us to eat. Later, our metabolic rate—the rate at which we burn energy in our bodies—may drop as the body tries to conserve energy, again in order to avoid burning up its fat reserves. The

Psychology Applies to Your World:

The Obesity Epidemic

Americans are obsessed with weight. Collectively we spend millions and millions of dollars each year on diets, exercise equipment, diet pills, and gym memberships, yet roughly two-thirds of all Americans are considered to be *overweight*, and almost a third are **obese** (■ FIGURE 8.5). Sadly, among children ages 9–19, 16% are considered overweight (Kaplan, 2007). One way to define overweight and obesity is to look at the *body mass index* (*BMI*; ■ FIGURE 8.6). A BMI of 25 or higher indicates overweight, and a BMI of 30 or more indicates obesity (National Institutes of Health, 2000). BMIs over 30 are correlated with higher incidences of many diseases, including type II diabetes, heart disease, and some cancers (Kopelman, 2000). In light of these problems, the government-funded Medicare program recently began considering obesity a disease (CBS News, 2004). Why, then, despite our great concern over the issues of weight and health, are so many of us losing the battle of the bulge?

Poor diet is one reason that some people gain weight. One culprit is the high-fat diet common in many Western cultures. A typical fast-food lunch can contain a whole day's worth of fat and calories. Coupled with a lack of exercise, this diet leads to weight gain in many people. Another factor comes from the way our society views food. As we mentioned earlier, we tend to eat for reasons that have little to do with maintaining homeostasis. Many of us use food as a means of dealing with emotions, such as eating when we are lonely, sad, or nervous (Edelman, 1981). This *emotional eating* may be one of the factors involved in weight gain for some people, but emotional distress has not been shown to be a general cause of obesity. In general, overweight people are *not* more likely to suffer from anxiety or depression (Wadden & Stunkard, 1987).

Biological factors may also play a role in some people's problems with weight. One such factor is having a *low metabolic rate*. People differ with respect to how much energy is required to run their bodies. Some people have high metabolic rates and require large amounts of fuel; others have low metabolic rates and require relatively little energy to survive. A person with a very low metabolic rate who eats the same number of calories and exercises just as much as a person with a normal metabolic rate will still gain more weight than the normal person will. Over time, this weight gain could lead to obesity (Friedman, 1990).

Ironically, having a low metabolic rate isn't always a disadvantage. In fact, across

obese having a body mass index of 30 or over

FIGURE

8.5

The Obesity Epidemic in the United States

In the United States, almost one-third of all adults are obese. This map shows the percentage of obese people county by county throughout the United States. The highest concentrations of obese people (shown in red) seem to be in the southern states. The reasons for this epidemic are the subject of much debate, but it is likely that several causes are at work—including genetic, lifestyle, and diet factors.

Source: From TIME, 6/7/2004. Reprinted with permission.

United States Obesity

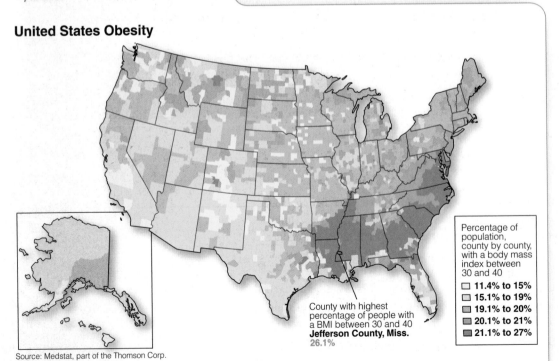

Percentage of population, county by county, with a body mass index between 30 and 40

☐ **11.4% to 15%**
☐ **15.1% to 19%**
☐ **19.1% to 20%**
☐ **20.1% to 21%**
☐ **21.1% to 27%**

County with highest percentage of people with a BMI between 30 and 40
Jefferson County, Miss.
26.1%

Source: Medstat, part of the Thomson Corp.

our evolutionary history, a low metabolic rate was probably a decided advantage. Our ancestors had to hunt and forage for enough food to eat. Those early humans who required less energy to survive probably had an easier time finding enough food to meet their needs. Therefore, those with low metabolic rates probably survived better and procreated more than their counterparts with high metabolic rates. This advantage could have led to some members of our modern society having "thrifty genes" that conserve energy.

For example, in one study that compared European American and African American girls, the African American girls were found to have higher rates of obesity and a resting metabolism that on average burned 71 *fewer* calories per day (Kimm, Glynn, Aston, Poehlman, & Daniels, 2001). This suggests that thrifty genes may have evolved to become more common in African Americans, predisposing them to higher rates of obesity.

Keep in mind that thrifty genes are not confined to any one race of people. In fact, having thrifty genes may predispose many people to obesity in a world in which hunting and gathering high-calorie foods is as simple as a trip to the grocery store or fast-food drive-through. The typical American diet is far different from that of our ancestors. Americans today consume large amounts of red meat, fat, eggs, and dairy products, but few fruits and vegetables. In contrast, the diets of some cultures, such as the Japanese and certain Mediterranean cultures, are much lower in red meat and contain significantly larger proportions of fruits and vegetables.

By examining cultural groups that have recently adapted to the American high-fat diet, we can see more clearly the impact of that diet on health. For example, ethnic Hawaiians have the shortest life span of any ethnic group on the Hawaiian Islands. As a group, ethnic Hawaiians show high rates of high blood pressure, diabetes, obesity, and high cholesterol. One major culprit in these health problems appears to be the fat-heavy American diet they have taken on. When ethnic Hawaiians return to their native diet of sweet potatoes, taro root, breadfruit, fish, chicken, and vegetables, their health significantly improves. In one study, after only 21 days of eating their native diet instead of the typical American diet, Hawaiians showed significant drops in blood pressure, weight, and cholesterol (Shintani, Hughes, Beckham, & O'Connor, 1991). Perhaps many native Hawaiians are biologically unsuited to eat the American diet. The same may be true of many other obese Americans.

Multiply your weight in pounds by 703	Example
_____ × 703 = _____	155 lbs × 703 = 108,965
Multiply your height in inches by itself (squared)	
_____^{2} = _____	68 × 68 [inches] = 4,624
Divide the first number by the second:	
$\dfrac{\text{_____}}{\text{Weight } 703} \div \dfrac{\text{_____}}{\text{Height squared}} = \dfrac{\text{_____}}{\text{BMI}}$	$\dfrac{108,965}{4,624} = 23.6$ BMI

BMI	Weight status
below 18.5	Underweight
18.5–24.9	Normal
25.0–29.9	Overweight
30.0 and above	Obese

FIGURE

8.6 **Calculating Your BMI**

This chart shows how to calculate your own body mass index (BMI). To do so, you will need a calculator, your weight in pounds, and your height in inches.

drop in metabolic rate may offset the reduction in calories on the diet, with the end result being little or no weight loss. Even more discouraging is the fact that our metabolism may drop even lower with each successive diet we go on (Brownell, 1988). This means that the more you diet, the harder it may become to lose weight. Our bodies appear inclined to fight against weight loss and to maintain our typical, or set point, weight.

There are psychological factors in dieting, too. Depriving yourself of food often leads to bingeing on food. It appears that when a dieter strays from his diet program, he feels as if he might as well *really* go off the diet. In one study that illustrated this reaction, dieters and nondieters were given a liquid drink. Half of each group was told that the drink was very high in calories; the other half was told that the drink was very low in calories. In reality, all the drinks were the same in caloric and nutritional content. After the drink, all participants were allowed to eat as much ice cream as they wanted. The nondieters ate the same amount of ice cream regardless of whether they thought they had just consumed a high- or low-calorie drink. This was not true, however, for the dieters. The dieters who thought they had had a high-calorie drink were more likely to eat more ice cream than the dieters who thought their drink had been low-calorie. It appears that the dieters felt that having already "ruined" their diet with the high-calorie drink, there was little point in restraining themselves when it came to the ice cream (Spencer & Fremouw, 1979).

People who restrain their eating are most at risk for this bingeing when they are emotionally aroused. Emotional distress can make a dieter more likely to cheat on her diet (Ruderman, 1985), but so can positive emotions (Cools, Schotte, & McNally, 1992). Whether one is happy or sad, it seems that dieting makes eating binges more likely.

The recipe for dieting success involves two factors. First, you have to make permanent changes in your eating behavior. "Dieting" is forever, and it is probably a mistake to think of losing weight as dieting. It's generally better to focus on eating healthy, balanced meals that are lower in calories than on how many pounds you can lose in a week. The best way to lose weight is to do it *slowly*. People don't typically gain 15 pounds in a week, so why should we expect to lose weight that fast?

The second aspect of successful weight loss is exercise. Cultural changes that reduce physical activity, such as driving to work or school, sedentary jobs, television, and computer games, are also major contributing factors to the growing obesity epidemic. Any weight loss plan that does not include exercise is likely to fail. Exercise not only burns extra calories and causes weight loss, it also increases your metabolism. Recall that when we diet, our body adjusts its metabolic rate downward to prevent starvation. You can help keep your metabolism higher by exercising, which will lead to a more permanent weight loss as your set point moves to a lower weight. So next time you see an advertisement for some miracle diet that allows you to eat all you want without exercising and still promises to safely take off 10 pounds a week, save your money and possibly your health. There are no quick fixes when it comes to shedding pounds. Even people who undergo *gastric bypass* surgery to drastically reduce the size of their stomach must adhere to a strict diet regimen and make lifestyle changes to achieve and sustain long-term weight loss (Powell, Calvin, & Calvin, 2007).

Which of these meals would you rather eat? Unhealthy eating habits contribute to obesity and health problems in many people.

© Michael Newman/PhotoEdit

© Felicia Martinez/PhotoEdit

Culture and Weight-Based Prejudice

People who are overweight do not just face health threats. Being overweight also exacts an emotional toll. Americans abhor fat. Overweight Americans are often ridiculed, socially isolated, and even discriminated against in the workplace. Shockingly, studies have shown that even health care professionals who specialize in the treatment of obesity sometimes demonstrate negative attitudes toward the overweight. In one study, health care professionals, including psychologists, were found to have used words such as *lazy* and *stupid* to refer to overweight persons (Schwartz, O'Neal Chambliss, Brownell, Blair, & Billington, 2003). Similarly, researcher Kristen Davis-Coelho and her colleagues found that some members of the American Psychological Association displayed a negative bias in their perceptions of overweight versus normal weight women. This tendency to perceive overweight people less favorably was most evident in younger and less experienced mental health care professionals (Davis-Coelho, Waltz, & Davis-Coelho, 2000).

Prejudice against the obese seems to also extend to children. In fact, studies have shown that children's prejudice against other overweight children has grown significantly since the 1960s. This is very unfortunate because children who are teased by their peers for being overweight are at higher risk for having a negative self-image, fewer friends, and an increased likelihood of suicide (see DeAngelis, 2004).

This negative attitude about obesity is not worldwide, however. For example, one of the authors once had an overweight friend from Iceland. After living in the United States for a few years, she observed that although there were fewer obese people in her native country, she was treated more normally there than she was in the United States, where so many people are overweight. In yet other cultures, such as the African country of Mauritania, overweight women are valued for their beauty—so much so, that young girls are often force-fed to make them obese. Because of health concerns, we do not advocate intentionally creating obesity in anyone. However, such cultural differences suggest that just as our perceptions of beauty and weight vary cross-culturally, so do our levels of prejudice against the overweight.

Our cultural fear of fat exacts a heavy toll on the many people who suffer weight-based prejudice. And, our attitudes about weight may also play a role in the development of certain eating disorders—our next topic.

Eating Disorders: Bulimia Nervosa, Anorexia Nervosa, and Binge Eating Disorder

Obesity is not the only problem that involves eating. Some people also suffer the devastating toll that *eating disorders*, or mental health disorders that are associated with eating, can take on a person's health and life. Why would food be such an issue for some of us?

BULIMIA NERVOSA

Bulimia nervosa is an eating disorder that is characterized by alternating bouts of *bingeing* and inappropriate compensatory behaviors such as *purging*, fasting, or excessive exercise. People who are bulimic gorge on large quantities of food, sometimes as much as 20,000 calories at a time; then they either go on a very rigid starvation diet or purge the food from their system (Schlesier-Stropp, 1984). Purging is achieved by self-induced vomiting or the abuse of laxatives (in the *mistaken* belief that laxatives prevent weight gain after overeating).

One of the authors once met a girl with bulimia who spent an entire semester's tuition on a 2-week cycle of bingeing and purging. She would go out at night and travel from one drive-through restaurant to another buying large quantities of tacos, hamburgers, and other

bulimia nervosa an eating disorder in which a person alternately binges on large quantities of food and then engages in some inappropriate compensatory behavior to avoid weight gain

© AP Photo/The Grand Island Independent, Barnett Stinson

Anorexia nervosa is a devastating disorder in which people are motivated to drastically restrict their eating while simultaneously increasing their level of exercise. The result is extreme weight loss, but this weight loss is never enough to please the anorectic. Anorectics like this woman still look in the mirror and feel that they need to lose more weight.

anorexia [an-or-EX-ee-uh] **nervosa** an eating disorder in which a person has an intense fear of gaining weight, even though he or she is actually underweight. This irrational fear motivates the person to lose unhealthy amounts of weight through self-starvation.

FIGURE

8.7 Too Thin?

Many models and actresses are *very* thin. The steady parade of these women in the media may have contributed to the increase in eating disorders seen in the 1980s and 1990s.

fast food. She would take the food back to her dorm room, where she would quickly eat all of it and then purge it through vomiting. Luckily, this 2-week binge probably saved her life. When she was unable to explain the missing tuition money, her parents insisted she enter a treatment program. After intense treatment, she regained some measure of normalcy in her eating behavior.

Like this woman, the typical victim of bulimia is a young female who is of average to slightly above average weight. Approximately 1% of American women will suffer from bulimia at some point in their lifetime (Williams, Goodie, & Motsinger, 2008). Bulimia is especially likely among college-age females, almost 4% of whom are estimated to suffer from the disorder (ANRED, 2008). Bulimia can be a socially isolating disorder. A college student who spends her evenings gathering up large quantities of food and bingeing and purging usually does so alone. Aside from its social toll, bulimia can sometimes be fatal. The frequent purging of food can lead to dehydration and electrolyte imbalances, which can lead to serious cardiac problems as well as other problems such as holes and erosions in the esophagus.

Given the devastating toll that bulimia can take on one's life, what would motivate anyone to engage in bulimic behavior? At this time, no one can say for sure why people become bulimic. However, many bulimic people are troubled by low self-esteem and depression (Perez, Joiner, & Lewisohn, 2004). Bulimics tend to be perfectionists who have negative views of their bodies. They tend to have grown up in families that were troubled somehow (Bardone, Vohs, Abramson, Heatherton, & Joiner, 2000). For some bulimics, bingeing and purging become a means of coping with negative emotions such as anxiety and a sense that one has no control over the events of one's own life.

ANOREXIA NERVOSA

Anorexia nervosa is an eating disorder that is characterized by self-starvation, intense fear of gaining weight, and a distorted body image. Unlike people suffering from bulimia, anorexics can be easily spotted by their very low body weight. Anorexics can get down to astonishingly low weights (e.g., 50 lb), and 5–10% of anorexics die as a result of the disorder (Wilson, Grilo, & Vitousek, 2007). The most bizarre aspect of anorexia is that even at a life-threateningly low weight, an anorexic can look in the mirror and *see* herself as fat (Grant & Phillips, 2004).

Most anorexics are females from middle- and upper-class families in industrialized countries. Anorexia is rarely found in men (although less than 15% of people suffering from anorexia and bulimia are male, there is some concern that eating disorders may be a bigger problem in the gay community, where body image concerns appear to be heightened; Russell & Keel, 2002). Anorexia is also less common in cultures that hold a fuller-figured woman up as the standard of beauty. It appears that one of the contributing factors in the development of anorexia is societal pressure on young women to be very thin—unrealistically thin. If you pick up just about any American fashion magazine or watch just about any American television show, you will find that most of the females depicted are extremely thin. Sometimes they actually look anorexic (■ FIGURE 8.7). Many television stars and models wear size 0 or 2 clothes, whereas many American women wear size 10 or 12 (or larger)! If you do the math, you'll see that many American women fall short of the standard of beauty depicted in the media.

Evan Agostini/Getty Images

What do you do if you are a young girl who aspires to look like the actors you see on TV, and a healthy diet and exercise do not allow you to meet your goals? Some girls take drastic steps to reach their "ideal" body image, and anorexia may be the result.

Researchers have found wide cultural variations in women's perceptions of their ideal body image. For example, in one study that compared U.S., Israeli, Spanish, and Brazilian women, the American women were found to be the least satisfied with their bodies. The American women also reported that they felt the most pressure to be thin (Joliot, 2001). This is significant because in cultures that portray beautiful women as being somewhat plumper—for example, in Jamaica (Smith & Cogswell, 1994) or even in American culture prior to the 1970s—anorexia is uncommon. Pre-1970, women who were considered beautiful were considerably heavier than those who are considered beautiful today. For example, Marilyn Monroe was considered to be the standard of beauty in the 1950s and early 1960s, and before her, Mae West—these two women were not the ultra-thin models of today (■ FIGURE 8.8). Still, despite being bombarded with images of very thin women, most American girls do *not* become anorexic. Why would this be?

At one time, anorexia was thought to be correlated with ethnicity. Because the thin standard of female beauty is most frequently portrayed as a White woman in American culture, many predicted that White women suffer greater pressure to be unrealistically thin and therefore suffer from higher rates of anorexia. Indeed, studies conducted in the 1980s seemed to confirm this hypothesis. However, this situation seems to have changed. A recent study conducted in the United States did not find White women to have more symptoms and predictors of eating disorders than Black, Hispanic, and Asian women. The authors concluded that ethnic women have caught up to White women in this domain and are now equally susceptible to risk factors for eating disorders such as dissatisfaction with one's body (Shaw, Ramirez, Trost, Randall, & Stice, 2004).

Other characteristics that do seem to be correlated with anorexia include perfectionism and faulty thinking about food (Steinhausen & Vollrath, 1993), as well as certain biochemical abnormalities (Ferguson & Pigott, 2000). Additionally, many people suffering from eating disorders also suffer from *personality disorders*—characteristic, maladaptive ways of dealing with the world (see Chapter 13; Marañon, Echeburúa, & Grijalvo, 2004). We do not yet know if these are *causal* factors or merely factors that *correlate* with eating disorders.

Another piece of the puzzle may be genetics (Keel & Klump, 2003). Some scholars have argued that genes for anorexia evolved to allow our ancestors to survive famine by helping them to ignore food while migrating to better environments (Guisinger, 2003). Indeed, there is evidence to support the idea of a genetic basis for anorexia. If one identical twin is anorexic, the other twin's chances of becoming anorexic are drastically increased. However, having a fraternal twin who is anorexic only modestly increases one's chances of becoming anorexic (Holland, Sicotte, & Treasure, 1988). This pattern of results supports the

FIGURE
8.8
Standards of Female Beauty

Standards of beauty in the United States have changed over time, and they also differ across cultures. In the 1930s, Mae West was considered to be an icon of feminine beauty. In the 1950s and early 1960s, it was Marilyn Monroe. Today, women like Angelina Jolie are the standard of beauty.

In cultures like Jamaica, Fiji, and Mexico the standard of beauty leans toward heavier women. Cultures such as these have far lower rates of eating disorders than the United States.

existence of a genetic predisposition to anorexia. It is also common to see family members, particularly mothers and daughters, who both suffer from eating disorders. However, this doesn't necessarily indicate a genetic basis for the disorders as family members tend to also have shared environmental influences. At present, it appears that both bulimia and anorexia may result from a complex mix of cultural factors, personality characteristics, environmental issues, and biological factors.

Binge Eating Disorder

Although bulimia and anorexia nervosa are both incapacitating illnesses, they are not the most common eating disorders (see Stice, Telch, & Rizvi, 2000). **Binge eating disorder** is an eating disorder characterized by recurrent episodes of binge eating, such as those seen in bulimia nervosa, but without regular use of the inappropriate compensatory measures that bulimics employ to avoid weight gain. Because binge eaters do not compensate for their overeating, they may be overweight. As we've already seen, obesity and being overweight are at epidemic levels in the United States. Just how many obese and overweight people suffer from binge eating disorder is not precisely known at this time. However, one estimate suggests that up to 30% of people who seek professional treatment for weight control may meet the criteria for this disorder (Brody, Walsh, & Devlin, 1994) (see ■ YOU REVIEW 8.2).

Thirst

As we have seen, the hunger motive drives us to take in food to meet our nutritional requirements. Yet for most of us a typical meal will include both food and a beverage. Does this mean that hunger motivates us to eat *and* drink? It appears not. Maintaining homeostasis of our fluid level is made possible by another motive—thirst, which is in some ways a more important motivation than hunger. If deprived of food and water, we would die from dehydration before we starved to death.

To function well, our bodies must have enough fluid. Fluid is critical because it allows ions to travel into and out of cells. As we saw in Chapter 2, ions such as potassium and sodium are absolutely essential to the functioning of the nervous system. If we were to become dehydrated, these ions would not be able to flow across the cell membranes during the firing of neural impulses, which could mean nervous system collapse and death! In fact, you can live for quite some time without food, but you would not be able to live 1 week without water. Even anorexics, who may go for days without eating, must take in fluids regularly.

Given that water is so crucial to survival, how do you know when you are thirsty? Many people would say that thirst is a feeling of having a parched throat or a dry mouth. Certainly, these characteristics are indicative of thirst, but just as the stomach plays only a partial role in the sensation of hunger, the mouth and throat play only a partial role in thirst. Even people who have had their larynx (part of the throat containing the vocal cords) removed still feel thirst and still drink (Miyaoka, Sawada, Sakaguchi, & Shingai, 1987).

To understand thirst, you must first understand where the body stores fluids. Fluid that is stored inside cells is called **intracellular fluid**. Fluid that is stored in the spaces between cells is called **extracellular fluid**. To maintain optimum fluid levels, the brain's hypothalamus monitors the levels of intracellular and extracellular fluid in and around its neurons. If we eat a salty meal, the sodium concentration in our extracellular fluid increases, which causes intracellular fluid from inside the hypothalamic neurons to cross the cell membrane into the extracellular space. This dilutes, or lowers, the sodium content of the extracellular fluid, but it also decreases the pressure inside the hypothalamic neurons. When this transition begins, and the hypothalamic neurons begin to lose their intracellular fluids, the hypothalamus signals thirst to motivate fluid intake (Memmler, Cohen, & Wood, 1992).

binge eating disorder an eating disorder characterized by recurrent episodes of binge eating, as in bulimia nervosa, but without regular use of compensatory measures to avoid weight gain

intracellular fluid the fluid found inside the cells of the body, which is used to regulate thirst

extracellular fluid the fluid found in the spaces between the cells of the body, which is used to regulate thirst

You Review 8.2

A Summary of the Diagnostic Criteria for Bulimia Nervosa, Anorexia Nervosa, and Binge Eating Disorder

BULIMIA NERVOSA

A. Recurrent episodes of bingeing in which the person eats unusually large amounts of food. The person must have the sense of being unable to control his/her eating during these binges.

B. Recurrent inappropriate compensatory behavior aimed at preventing weight gain (e.g., purging; enemas; misuse of laxatives, diuretics, or other medicines; fasting; excessive exercise).

C. Bingeing and inappropriate compensatory behaviors must both occur, on average, twice a week for a period of at least three months.

D. Self-evaluation is unduly influenced by one's body shape or weight.

E. These behaviors do not occur exclusively during episodes of anorexia nervosa.

ANOREXIA NERVOSA

A. Refusal to maintain a minimally normal body weight (usually defined as 85% of the normal weight for one's height).

B. Intense fear of gaining weight, even though underweight.

C. A disturbed perception of one's body weight or shape, denial of the seriousness of one's low weight, or undue influence of one's body weight or shape on his/her self-evaluation.

D. In females, having missed at least three consecutive menstrual periods.

BINGE EATING DISORDER

A. Recurrent episodes of binge eating (as defined for bulimia nervosa) without regularly engaging in inappropriate compensatory behaviors to avoid weight gain.

Another mechanism of thirst comes from cells that monitor the body's extracellular fluid levels outside of the brain. As we sweat, exhale, and urinate, we lose fluid from our extracellular fluid. As we become dehydrated, this loss of fluid causes a drop in blood volume and a corresponding drop in blood pressure. Specialized *pressure receptors* in the heart, kidneys, and blood vessels detect this slight drop in blood pressure, and they send signals to the brain that will eventually initiate thirst. These pressure receptors also signal the start of measures to conserve the water that is already inside our body (Pinel, 1997).

Dehydration results in the loss of extracellular fluid in the body. This loss of fluid causes a drop in blood pressure that signals the brain to initiate thirst. This athlete will likely feel tremendous thirst, which will motivate her to replace the fluids she has lost through sweating.

© Neal Preston/Corbis

Let's Review!

In this section, we covered eating disorders, obesity, and healthy motivation to eat and drink. As a quick check of your understanding, answer these questions.

1. A friend of yours was recently in a car accident and suffered damage to his ventromedial hypothalamus. What effect would you expect this damage to have on your friend's behavior?

a. He will likely stop eating.

b. He will likely die.

c. He will likely gain a great deal of weight.

d. He will likely gain a great deal of weight, but then he will lose the pounds and return to his normal weight.

2. Which of the following is the hormone that the small intestines release to shut off hunger?

a. Insulin   c. Leptin

b. CCK   d. Serotonin

3. You just ran a 10-mile marathon, and you are now very thirsty. Which of the following is the most likely reason for your excessive thirst?

a. Loss of intracellular fluid

b. Loss of extracellular fluid

c. Loss of sodium in the body

d. Loss of potassium in the body

Answers 1. c; 2. b; 3. b

Stop, LOOK, and LEARN

Theories of Motivation

- **Instinct** theory
- **Drive** theory
- Arousal theory
- **Incentive** theories of motivation
- Maslow's **hierarchy of needs**

Hunger Feedback

Turns Hunger On	**Turns Hunger Off**
• Empty stomach	• A stomach full of nutritive food
• **Ghrelin**	• **CCK**
• Low **glucose** levels (**glycogen** converting to glucose)	• High glucose levels (glucose converting to glycogen)
• The **lateral hypothalamus**	• High **leptin** levels
• The sight and smells of food	• The **ventromedial hypothalamus**

Food-Related Problems

- **Obesity** is on the rise in many cultures, posing health risks and subjecting the obese to prejudices.
- **Anorexia nervosa** is seen in people (mainly females) who starve themselves to the point of emaciation and sometimes death.
- **Bulimia nervosa** is seen in people (mainly females) who binge on food followed by purging or dietary restriction to compensate for the bingeing.
- **Binge eating disorder** is seen in people who binge on food without engaging in compensatory purging or restricting.

Sexual Motivation

Another fundamental motive is the motivation to engage in sexual activity. Although sexual motivation is not necessary for life in the same manner as hunger and thirst are, sexual motivation does help ensure survival of the species through procreation.

Sexual Desire: A Mixture of Chemicals, Thoughts, and Culture

Sexual desire is our motivation and interest in engaging in sexual activity. It is the first step in experiencing **sexual arousal**, a heightened state of sexual interest and excitement. Like many other behaviors that we have discussed, sexual desire is influenced by our biology as well as our learning experiences and cultural expectations.

> **You Asked...**
>
> *What makes us so (sexually) attracted to others?*
>
> HOLLY SOSEBEE, STUDENT

Biological and psychological processes influence sexual desire. The physical desire to have sex, or **libido**, is affected by both the hypothalamus and certain hormones of the endocrine system. As discussed in Chapter 2, the brain's hypothalamus works with the master gland of the body, the pituitary gland, to release hormones into the bloodstream. In this way, the hypothalamus plays a key role in regulating sexual behavior. The hypothalamus continually monitors the level of sex hormones in the bloodstream and directs the endocrine system to either increase or decrease the release of these hormones as required.

In mammals, **estrogens** are female hormones that regulate the female animal's desire to mate. Female animals' estrogen levels increase dramatically during a period called *estrus* ("being in heat"), in which the female is receptive to males' attempts to mate with her. Estrus coincides with ovulation in the female. During ovulation, the female's egg (or eggs) matures, so that it can be fertilized by the male sperm during mating. If fertilization does not occur, the female will pass out of estrus, and she will shed the egg along with the lining of her uterus during *menstruation*. If a pregnancy is going to occur, estrus is when it will happen. Therefore, it is in both the male and female animals' best interest to mate during estrus. To ensure that mating will occur, estrus is usually marked by some physical change in the female that signals to males of the species that she is in estrus and ready to mate. For example, many female chimpanzees have sexual swelling, or engorgement, of the external female genitals that indicate to male chimpanzees that it is time to mate.

Humans are a bit different from other mammals in that for a human, there is no defined period of estrus. Human females can mate at any time in the menstrual cycle, and although female estrogen levels do fluctuate during the menstrual cycle, estrogen is not closely related to human female libido. Evidence for the limited role of estrogen in sexual desire comes from cases of women who have had hysterectomies that involved removal of their ovaries. **Ovaries** are organs that produce eggs and estrogen in a woman's body. Without ovaries, a woman's estrogen levels plummet. Despite the drastic loss of estrogen, some women do not experience a loss of sexual desire after a hysterectomy (Sherwin & Gelfand, 1987). And

sexual desire one's motivation and interest in engaging in sexual activity

sexual arousal a heightened state of sexual interest and excitement

libido [leh-BEE-doe] one's physical desire, or drive, to have sex

estrogens a class of female hormones that regulate many aspects of sexuality

ovaries the organs in a female's body that produce eggs, or ova

Some female mammals show visible signs when they are receptive to mating.

© Gallo Images/Corbis

Simcock Texier/Getty Images

Human sexuality is more than just a matter of hormones.

testosterone a male hormone that plays a role in many aspects of sexuality, including sexual desire

testes the organs in a male's body that produce both sperm and testosterone

erogenous [eh-ROJ-en-ous] **zones** areas of the skin that are sensitive to touch

for those women who do experience loss of desire, taking estrogen alone does not always increase desire or improve sexual response (El-Matary, Kemball, & Feteha, 2006).

In humans, the hormone that seems to govern libido is **testosterone**. Testosterone is part of a class of male hormones called androgens. Although testosterone is a male hormone, it is also found in females (likewise, males have estrogen). In males, the **testes** produce testosterone (in addition to sperm). In women, it is produced by the adrenal glands that sit above the kidneys. Adequate testosterone levels seem to be important in maintaining sexual desire. If testosterone levels fall too low, both males and females experience disinterest in sex. Testosterone may not be the only hormone that drives our desire, however. Another hormone, called *gonadotropin-releasing hormone* (GnRH), may also play some role. GnRH has been shown to increase libido in men who lack testosterone (Dornan & Malsbury, 1989).

Are hormones the sole cause of sexual desire? No. Although hormones play a significant role in our libido, sexual desire is not merely a function of chemicals in our bodies. Our senses, our thoughts, and our culture also influence human sexual desire. Visual cues can increase or decrease sexual desire. Erotic photographs or movies may be a sexual turn-on to some, but not to others. Seeing a lover nude or in sexy lingerie may be stimulating for some. Such visual stimulation seems to have a greater effect on men than on women (Reinisch, 1991). Sounds, such as a lover's voice or romantic music, may be appealing to some. Research also suggests that our sense of smell may play a role in sexual arousal (K. N. Stern & McClintock, 1998). For some it may be the scent of a particular cologne or perfume, whereas for others it may be natural body scents such as sweat. When fertile or at mid-cycle, women prefer the scent of males who have more masculine-looking faces. Similarly, men find the scent of women who are ovulating especially attractive (Gangestad, Thornhill, & Garver-Apgar, 2005). Such findings suggest an evolutionary role of our sense of smell in sexual desire. However, people vary greatly in the types of smells they find arousing. For example, one study found that the aromas of pumpkin pie and lavender evoked the greatest sexual response in males, whereas the smell of candy-coated licorice, cucumbers, and baby powder elicited the greatest sexual response in females (Hirsch et al., 1998).

Our sense of touch plays a more direct role in sexual desire. Because nerve endings are unevenly distributed throughout the body, some areas of the skin are more sensitive to touch than others. These areas, called **erogenous zones**, include the genitals, buttocks, breasts, armpits, ears, navel, mouth, and the inner surfaces of the thighs. However, areas that may be highly stimulating to one person may produce a negative reaction in another. Hence, our preferences in reaction to touch differ.

Many of the differences in our reactions to sensory cues exist because we all think differently about what should be or should not be sexually stimulating. Such expectations may be learned or reflect the larger influence of gender roles and culture on our behavior. For instance, in the United States we emphasize cleanliness and the masking of natural body odors with perfumes and deodorants. Americans may learn to associate such odors as more sexually appealing than body sweat. Similarly, a particular age group may find jazz or rock music sexually stimulating because such sounds are associated with dating. In contrast, funeral music or the sound of a baby crying may dampen sexual desire. These learned experiences and cultural influences, along with biology, shape our sexual desire. Once we are willing to engage in sexual activity, a predictable cycle of physical responses occurs, which we detail in the next section.

The Sexual Response Cycle

In the 1960s, William Masters, a gynecologist, and Virginia Johnson, a nurse, were the first researchers to directly observe and measure the sexual responses of men and women engaged in a variety of activities. Electronic sensors were placed on the bodies of the participants to directly measure physical responses. The participants were also interviewed in detail about their experiences. The information gathered in this study, subsequently published in Masters and Johnson's *Human Sexual Response* (1966), described the common physical changes that we experience in our sexual encounters. The model includes four successive phases: excitement, plateau, orgasm, and resolution (■ FIGURE 8.9). Men and women were remarkably similar in their physical responses.

During the **excitement phase**, men and women experience an increase in heart rate and blood pressure. The nipples may become erect and blood flow is increased to the genital area. Males experience penile erection, and the scrotal sac thickens. Females produce vaginal lubrication, and the inner two-thirds of the vagina expands. The clitoris, the female sex organ that is extremely sensitive to sensation, swells. During the **plateau phase**, excitement peaks and remains somewhat constant. Breathing becomes rapid, and blood pressure and heart rate continue to rise. Men experience a full penile erection and the testes are fully elevated. A few droplets of fluid that can contain sperm may appear at the tip of the penis. In women, the inner part of the vagina expands fully and the uterus becomes elevated. The clitoris shortens and withdraws.

During the **orgasm phase**, breathing, blood pressure, and heart rate peak. Contractions of the pelvic muscles and the anal sphincter produce the sensation of orgasm. Certain parts of the brain are activated and deactivated (Georgiadis et al., 2006), and muscles throughout the body may spasm. In the male, the internal bodily contractions propel seminal fluid through the penis, causing ejaculation. Hence, in the male, the orgasm phase consists of two processes: orgasm and ejaculation. However, males' and females' subjective experience of orgasm is actually quite similar (Proctor, Wagner, & Butler, 1974; Vance & Wagner, 1976; Wiest, 1977). Men and women describe the experience in much the same way.

excitement phase the first stage of the sexual response cycle, in which males get erections and females produce vaginal lubrication

plateau phase the second stage of the sexual response cycle, in which excitement peaks

orgasm phase the third stage of the sexual response cycle, in which the pelvic and anal muscles contract

Masters and Johnson pioneered field research on the sexual response of males and females.

© Bettmann/Corbis

FIGURE

8.9 The Sexual Response Cycle

Masters and Johnson identified three basic patterns of response in females. A female may experience one or more orgasms (A); an extended plateau with no orgasm (B); or a rapid rise to orgasm with a quick resolution (C). Males show less variability in their sexual responses because of the refractory period. *(From* Human Sexual Response *by W. H. Masters and V. E. Johnson. Copyright © 1966 Little, Brown & Co. Reprinted by permission of Lippincott, Williams & Wilkins.)*

Female Sexual Response

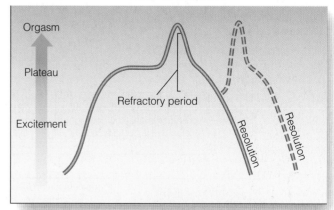

Male Sexual Response

The sexual response cycle concludes with the **resolution phase**, in which the body returns to its prearoused state. Breathing, heart rate, and blood pressure return to normal. The male loses his erection, and in the female the vagina, clitoris, and uterus return to their normal size and position. Yet a distinct gender difference occurs in sexual response during the resolution phase. Unlike women, men experience a **refractory period**, or a time during which they are physically incapable of experiencing another orgasm or ejaculation. This measure of time increases as men age. For an adolescent male, the refractory period may last only a few minutes, whereas for men over age 50, it may last from several minutes to a day. Because women do not undergo a refractory period, they can more easily be rearoused after orgasm, leading some women to experience repeated or multiple orgasms. Hence, compared to males, who experience refractory periods of varying lengths, there is greater variability in the female sexual response pattern (Figure 8.9; Masters, Johnson, & Kolodny, 1993).

Whom Do We Desire? Sexual Orientation

Sexual desire and sexual arousal are states that most of us experience. Yet there are individual differences in sexuality. Some people experience higher levels of sexual desire than others, and there is great variability in whom we desire to have sex with. **Sexual orientation**—one's sexual attraction for members of the same and/or other sex—is one of the factors that influences our choice of sexual partners.

Many people never question their sexual orientation, whereas others may be in doubt as they grapple with the developmental task of establishing their identity in adolescence (Chapter 9). There are three types of sexual orientation. **Heterosexuals** are attracted to members of the other sex, **homosexuals** are attracted to members of the same sex, and **bisexuals** are attracted to members of both sexes. However, sexual orientation is not as fixed as these three terms suggest. Heterosexuality and homosexuality more often represent endpoints on a broad spectrum of behaviors that Kinsey and his colleagues (Kinsey, Pomeroy, & Martin, 1948) identified as a continuum of sexual orientation (■ FIGURE 8.10). Moreover, sexual orientation may change over time, with women reporting greater change in orientation than men (Kinnish, Strassberg, & Turner, 2005). Let's take a look at some aspects of sexual orientation, possible causes of it, and current attitudes toward gay males and lesbians.

SEXUAL ORIENTATION AND SEXUAL BEHAVIOR

When speaking of sexual orientation, one must be careful to distinguish between attraction and behavior. Sexual orientation is not simply a matter of with whom you have sex. A man could be married to a woman, never have had sex with a man, but still be gay because he is truly attracted only to men. A woman could have sex with other women but still consider herself to be heterosexual.

resolution phase the final stage of the sexual response cycle, in which the body returns to homeostasis

refractory period a time during the resolution phase in which males are incapable of experiencing another orgasm or ejaculation

sexual orientation one's sexual attraction for members of the same and/or other sex

heterosexual one who is sexually attracted only to members of the other sex

homosexual one who is sexually attracted only to members of the same sex

bisexual one who is sexually attracted to members of both sexes

FIGURE 8.10 Kinsey's Continuum of Sexual Orientation

Sexual orientation may be expressed along a continuum of behaviors.

Source: Adapted from Kinsey et al., 1948, p. 638.

In the late 1940s, Alfred Kinsey (Kinsey et al., 1948; Kinsey, Pomeroy, Martin, & Gebhard, 1953) began a series of studies on sexual behavior in which he surveyed people on many aspects of their sexuality. Kinsey found that 37% of men and 13% of women had had at least one same-sex sexual encounter, but not all of these people identified themselves as gay males or lesbians. If this sounds confusing, it is. When trying to determine just how many people are homosexual, bisexual, or heterosexual, researchers have had some problems (Savin-Williams, 2006). Kinsey and his colleagues (1948) estimated that roughly 3% of the general population are exclusively homosexual. More modern figures, however, indicate that the rate of homosexuality could be more like 4–6% for males and 2–4% for females (LeVay, 1996). The negative attitudes that many hold about homosexuality make it difficult to get accurate data. It could well be that some people are reluctant to admit their true sexual feelings because they fear reprisals or they themselves feel stigmatized by their sexuality.

ATTITUDES TOWARD GAY MALES AND LESBIANS: DIFFERING VIEWS ACROSS THE WORLD

American attitudes toward gays and lesbians have become somewhat less negative over the last few decades. Television shows such as *Will and Grace, Brothers and Sisters,* and *The L Word* suggest that the public is becoming more comfortable with homosexuality. Some corporations now extend employee benefits to same-sex couples. In 1973 the American Psychological Association (APA) eliminated homosexuality from its list of mental illnesses, and in 1980 dropped it from its *Diagnostic and Statistical Manual (DSM)* (discussed in Chapter 13). Moreover, based on evidence that gay and lesbian relationships are influenced by the same set of variables that influence heterosexual marriages, the APA passed a resolution declaring it unfair and discriminatory to deny same-sex couples legal access to civil marriage (APA, 2004).

But **homophobia**, or prejudice against homosexuals, has not disappeared. The Netherlands, Belgium, Spain, Canada, and South Africa are the only countries that allow same-sex marriage. In the United States, Massachusetts became the first state to legalize same-sex marriage in 2004. Other states vary in their legal recognition of same-sex relationships. Gays and lesbians do not have the same legal protection against discrimination as other minority groups in the United States, and gays and lesbians continue to be the victims of hate crimes. Approximately 80% of gay, lesbian, and bisexual youth are verbally abused, and 17% are physically abused (Meyer, 1999). As of 2007, 32 states and the District of Columbia had enacted laws against hate crimes motivated by sexual orientation (National Gay and Lesbian Task Force, 2007). In 2007, the U.S. Congress introduced federal hate crime legislation called the Matthew Shepard Act in honor of Matthew Shepard, the gay college student who died after he was beaten and tied to a fence in Wyoming in 1998.

Many religions condemn homosexual behavior as immoral. It is quite possible to turn on the television to see a preacher warning of the dangers of homosexual sin. Others see homosexuality as a mental illness that should be cured. However, there is little evidence to support the view that homosexuality is a mental health problem. Gay males and lesbians are no less well adjusted than their heterosexual counterparts (Weinrich, 1994). Moreover, decades of research show that children of gay and lesbian parents do not differ in adjustment or development when compared to children raised by heterosexual couples (Patterson, 2006).

homophobia prejudicial attitudes against homosexuals and homosexuality

Gays, lesbians, and bisexuals face many prejudices in today's society. Yet their relationships are influenced by the same variables that influence heterosexual relationships.

Thinkstock/Getty Images

Kayte M. Deioma/PhotoEdit

Curiously, the negative attitudes that many Americans hold toward gays and lesbians are not shared by all cultures. In fact, many cultures openly accept homosexuality as a natural part of life. One study of 190 societies across the world found that approximately two-thirds of the world's societies accepted homosexuality (Ford & Beach, 1951). A historical study of 225 Native American tribes found that more than half of them accepted male homosexuality and 17% accepted female homosexuality (Pomeroy, 1965). Why do some people abhor homosexuality or see it as a mental illness, whereas others see it as a normal variation of human sexuality? Perhaps these differing points of view stem from beliefs about what causes sexual orientation.

WHAT CAUSES ONE'S SEXUAL ORIENTATION?

One common mistake that people make when trying to answer this question is to confuse sexual orientation with gender. Gender is the collection of personality traits that your society typically associates with either males or females. Gender is not the same thing as sexual orientation. For instance, a gay male may be very masculine or very feminine. Likewise, a heterosexual woman may be either masculine or feminine. In other words, not all feminine men are gay, and not all masculine women are lesbians.

Having said that, there is some indication in the research that early gender-related behavior may be a predictor of later sexual orientation for *some*. Some studies have shown that gender-nonconforming behavior (masculine behavior in girls, feminine behavior in boys) during childhood is correlated with later homosexuality in both men and women (Rieger, Gygax, & Bailey, 2008). Be careful about how you interpret these findings, though. Not all boys who prefer feminine activities become gay; nor do all girls who prefer masculine activities become lesbian. In fact, in one study, approximately half of the adult gay male participants had a preference for traditionally masculine activities in childhood (A. R. Bell, Weinberg, & Hammersmith, 1981). Also, even if some gays and lesbians showed a preference for gender-nonconforming activities in childhood, this does not indicate that the activities made them homosexual. It is just as likely that their homosexuality stemmed from other causes. In fact, in less stereotyped cultures in which children are not pressured to be masculine or feminine, there is less tendency for gay males to have exhibited feminine behavior in childhood (M. W. Ross, 1980).

Another reasonable question is to ask whether homosexuality could be encoded in our genes. A genetic link for homosexuality has been investigated in the traditional way—by examining pairs of identical and fraternal twins who are gay. Such studies find a higher *concordance rate* (percentage of pairs in which both twins are homosexual) among identical twins than fraternal twins (Bailey, Dunne, & Martin, 2000; Bailey & Pillard, 1991). A similar pattern was found for females (Bailey at al., 2000; Bailey, Pillard, Neale, & Agyei, 1993). Such findings suggest a hereditary component in sexual orientation in some people.

Other investigations have found that gay men have a greater number of older brothers than heterosexual men (Blanchard, Zucker, Siegelman, Dickey, & Klassen, 1998; Ridley, 2003), suggesting that some mothers may become increasingly immune to prenatal male hormones. In other words, their bodies produce more antibodies to such male hormones, creating a different prenatal hormonal environment that may affect succeeding male fetuses. Similarly, research has found that homosexuals have a greater chance of being left-handed than heterosexuals, an attribute that is believed to be established prior to birth (Lippa, 2003). Such findings suggest that prenatal factors are related to sexual orientation.

In conclusion, data indicate a strong biological role in sexual orientation. However, as of this moment, no one can say for sure just what causes our sexual orientation. The continuum of sexual orientation is in all likelihood related to the interaction among biological, psychological, and environmental forces that results in different pathways for every person. In any case, the causes of sexual orientation are likely to remain a controversial and emotional issue for some time to come.

Let's Review!

In this section, we discussed sexual desire, the sexual response cycle, and sexual orientation. For a quick check of your understanding, answer these questions.

1. Which is true of animals, but not of humans?
   a. Testosterone regulates sex drive.
   b. Menstruation follows ovulation.
   c. Mating occurs only during estrus.
   d. Hormones influence sexual behavior.

2. While dancing with his girlfriend, Malik notices that he has an erection. Malik is in which stage of the sexual response cycle?
   a. Excitement   **c.** Orgasm
   b. Plateau   **d.** Resolution

3. Paul has been married for five years to Lisa. However, Paul is primarily sexually attracted to men and not to women. What is Paul's sexual orientation?
   a. Heterosexual   **c.** Bisexual
   b. Homosexual   **d.** Both a and b

Answers 1. c; 2. a; 3. b

Theories and Expression of Emotion

- Describe the various theoretical perspectives on emotion.
- Describe how we express our emotional states through facial expressions.

If you ask people to define emotion, you will get a variety of answers. Most will probably say that emotions are *feelings*. Some will give examples, such as *happiness*, *sadness*, or *anger*, but few will be able to produce a good definition of what an emotion actually is. Even psychologists have had trouble defining what is meant by an emotion. One definition is that an **emotion** is a complex reaction to some internal or external event that involves physiological reactions, behavioral reactions, facial expressions, cognition, and affective responses (see Lazarus, 1991). For example, let's imagine that you are walking through the woods and you hear some rustling up ahead. You look up to see a large bear in your path. This event would likely cause an emotional reaction of *fear*. Your experience of fear would have several aspects to it:

Physiological reactions: Your heart rate would increase, your respiration would increase, your pupils would dilate, and your muscles would tense.

Behavioral reactions: You might freeze in your tracks. You might run (an unwise choice in this situation). You might yell at the bear.

Facial expressions: Fear would show on your face. If someone were to observe you at this moment, they would likely recognize that you were afraid.

Cognition: You might think about the TV show you saw on bears last week and what the experts said that you should do in this situation. You might wonder if this is a female bear with cubs just out of sight in the brush. You might think about what you will do if the bear charges.

Affective responses: You would have some subjective reaction to this situation. For example, "I am scared," "I am terrified," or—if you are an animal lover—"I'm thrilled!"

As you can see, emotions are complex. Perhaps that is why psychologists have had a difficult time defining exactly what an emotion is. Another confusing aspect of emotion is that emotion is very similar to motivation. In fact, emotions can produce motivation (e.g.,

emotion a complex reaction to some internal or external event that involves physiological reactions, behavioral reactions, facial expressions, cognition, and affective responses

How would you *feel* if you came across a bear while hiking in the woods?

© Renee Lynn/Corbis

Zaalberg, Manstead, & Fischer, 2004). In our previous example, your fear of the bear might motivate you to run or to yell at the bear. So what separates emotions from motivation? What makes *fear* different from *hunger*? One unique element is the **affective component of emotion**, the subjective experience of what you are *feeling* that fills your consciousness during the emotion. When you are scared, you know that you are scared because you *feel* the affective state of fear. This affective quality of emotion allows us to clearly know when we are feeling an emotion.

Emotions can also be distinguished from motivation in that they are usually (but not always) sparked by things outside of our bodies. For instance, when we see a depressing movie, we may feel sad. Or when we see a baby, we may feel happy. Motivation, on the other hand, often comes from some internal source—hunger may be initiated by low blood sugar or thirst by low blood pressure. Motives tend to be sparked by a specific need or goal, but emotions can be elicited by many stimuli. For instance, many things can make us happy, but only a few conditions will lead to hunger.

Although psychologists have struggled with the concept of emotion, several notable theories of emotion have been set out over the years. Let's take a look at some of them now.

The James-Lange Theory of Emotion

affective component of emotion
the subjective experience of what you are *feeling* during the emotion

James–Lange theory a theory of emotion that defines an emotion as a unique pattern of physiological arousal

American psychologist William James and Danish physiologist Carl Lange each proposed one of the earliest theories of emotion at approximately the same point in history (James, 1884). Their theory, now called the **James-Lange theory** of emotion, states that emotion is *equal to* the pattern of physiological arousal that the person experiences during an emotion. In short, emotion is a physiological response to some stimulus. In our example of meeting the bear in the woods, from the James-Lange point of view, the emotion you feel is the pattern of physical and physiological reactions you have as you see the bear. Your physiological reactions—the increased heart rate, the increased respiration, the running—*are* the emotion of fear that you would experience in this situation. In the James-Lange view, emotion is a purely physiological event.

WALTER CANNON'S CRITICISMS OF THE JAMES-LANGE THEORY

The James-Lange view of emotion has had many critics. One important critic was Walter Cannon, who noted that for the James-Lange theory to adequately explain emotion there would have to be a *different* bodily response for each emotion we experience. If emotion is simply a physiological and bodily response, the only way to discriminate among emotions would be if there were different physical reactions for each emotion. Walter Cannon doubted that this was true and, in fact, offered three good reasons to doubt the James-Lange view (Cannon, 1927). His first criticism, which we just mentioned, is that the physiological experience of emotion does not appear to vary from emotion to emotion to the degree that would be necessary to distinguish one emotion from another based purely on our physiological reaction. For example, the physiological experience of anger is not very different from that of terror—both involve increased heart rate, muscle tension, and so forth.

Second, Cannon argued that the physiological, bodily aspect of emotion sometimes follows our subjective experience of the emo-

According to the James-Lange theory of emotion, this woman is experiencing anger because her body has reacted with a characteristic pattern of physiological changes in response to this event.

© LA Daily News/David Crane/Corbis Sygma

tion. For example, we may know that we are afraid *before* we feel our heart pounding and our muscles tensing. In the James-Lange view, there can be no emotion before there is a physiological response.

Cannon's third criticism was that artificially created physiological responses do not give rise to emotions. For example, drinking a lot of coffee may increase your physiological arousal, but it does not cause you to experience fear, excitement, love, or any other emotion. If emotion were nothing more than a physiological response, it would stand to reason that artificially caused physiological responses would also cause emotional responses.

In light of these criticisms, Cannon proposed that emotion does not originate in the body; rather, it originates in the brain. According to Cannon, when you see a bear in the woods, your fear is not due to the increased heart rate and rapid breathing you experience. Instead, when you see the bear, your brain causes you to feel fear. You may even be aware that you are afraid *before* you become aware of your rapidly beating heart and your panting breath. Cannon's cognitive explanation of emotion was later extended by a man named Philip Bard, and today this theory is called the **Cannon-Bard theory** of emotion.

SOME VALIDATION OF THE JAMES-LANGE THEORY

Of Cannon's three criticisms, by far the most problematic was the first one—that physiological responses are too similar to allow us to adequately discriminate among the many emotions we feel. For many years this criticism was seen as a fatal blow to the James-Lange theory. Things change, however, and in the 1990s, some new evidence gave the James-Lange theory new life. By the 1990s, psychologists had new tools for studying bodily reactions. In addition to precisely measuring heart rate, researchers could now measure minute changes in skin temperature and in the electrical conductivity of the skin that indicate small changes in the moisture of the skin. With these measurement techniques, it was now possible to examine the physiological response that accompanies emotions in greater detail than was possible in Walter Cannon's time (see also *Neuroscience Applies to Your World*).

Cannon–Bard theory a theory of emotion that states that emotions originate in the brain, not the body

Neuroscience Applies to Your World:

Emotion, the Brain, and Attention

Using sensitive instruments, researchers have shown that different emotional states produce different patterns of physiological reaction in the body. Other studies suggest that the brain reacts differently to different emotional states. For example, positive emotions (e.g., happiness) tend to be related to activity in the left hemisphere of the brain: negative emotions (e.g., anger, sadness) tend to be associated with activity in the right hemisphere.

Given that the information we see, hear, and feel is processed *contralaterally* in the brain (see Chapter 2), does processing positive or negative emotions affect our tendency to pay more attention to things on our right or left sides? In one very recent study, Paul Foster and colleagues tested this notion and found that participants were more likely to place pegs labeled with positive emotions on the left side of a pegboard and pegs labeled with negative emotions toward the right side of the board (Foster et al., 2008). These findings suggest that emotion may affect how much attention we pay to different areas of our world. Does this mean that when you are in a good mood, you are less likely to see a car approaching from your right? It's far too soon to say. More research needs to be done to determine the significance of this intriguing finding.

Ron Koeberer/Getty Images

Patrik Stollarz/Bongarts/Getty Images

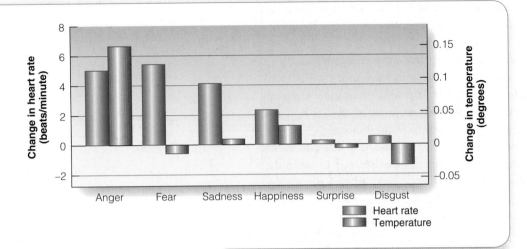

FIGURE

8.11

Physiological Changes for Six Different Emotions

Note the varying degrees of change for these different emotions.

Source: Levenson, Ekman, & Friesen, 1990.

Using measures such as these, researchers have been able to show that some emotions do indeed involve different bodily reactions. In one particularly clever study (Levenson, Ekman, & Friesen, 1990), participants were asked to make facial expressions for the emotions of fear, anger, happiness, disgust, sadness, and surprise and to hold these expressions for 10 seconds. While the participants held these expressions, their physiological reactions were measured very precisely. Just as the James-Lange theory predicts, there were slight but noticeable differences in heart rate, skin temperature, and other physiological reactions for the different emotions. Although all of the emotions caused changes in heart rate and skin temperature, it was the *degree* of change that separated the emotions from one another (■ FIGURE 8.11).

These results indicate that there may be some merit to the James-Lange approach, but they do not necessarily support the entire theory. These results do not address Walter Cannon's other two criticisms—that physiological reactions sometimes follow our awareness of emotions and that artificially created arousal does not seem to directly cause the experience of emotion. Even if patterns of physiological arousal do help us discriminate among emotions, there still may be other factors involved in the experience of emotion. One of these factors could be feedback from our faces.

The Facial Feedback Hypothesis

You may have noticed that in the experiment we just described, the researchers induced the different emotions in an unusual way (Levensen et al., 1990): having the participants make and hold facial expressions of the desired emotion for 10 seconds. In other words, they induced the emotional state through the facial expression of the emotion. How does this work? Doesn't the emotion come *before* the facial expression? Well, maybe not entirely, according to the **facial feedback hypothesis** (McIntosh, 1996). This theory proposes that our experience of an emotion is affected by the feedback our brain gets from our facial muscles. Thus, smiling can influence us to feel happy, and frowning can influence us to feel bad. In one study, participants were asked to smell and rate a series of odors while either smiling or frowning. Consistent with the facial feedback hypothesis, they rated the smells more positively when they were smiling and less positively when they were frowning (Kraut, 1982). Based on this and other studies (e.g., Soussignan, 2002), it appears as if the configuration of your facial muscles does influence your mood. But why would this be true?

One possibility is that the configuration of your facial muscles affects the blood flow to your brain, which in turn affects the temperature of your brain. Certain configurations, such as frowns, may change blood flow to the brain in a way that increases the temperature of the brain. Other facial configurations, such as smiles, may result in blood flow changes that decrease the brain's temperature. Brain temperature, in turn, may affect the release of certain neurotransmitters that affect mood. As wild as this sounds, there is some evidence to suggest that it might be true. In one study, one group of participants was asked to read a story that contained words that forced them to repeatedly hold their mouths in a position that was similar to smiling (Zajonc, Murphy, & Inglehart, 1989). The other group of participants was

facial feedback hypothesis a theory that states that our emotional state is affected by the feedback our brain gets from facial muscles asked to read a story that did not contain such words. Both stories were of similar emotional tone. As the participants read the stories, the temperature of their forehead was measured, providing a crude measure of their brain's internal temperature.

After they had read the stories, the participants were asked to rate the stories for pleasantness. As the facial feedback hypothesis would predict, those who read the story that forced them to use their facial muscles in a manner consistent with a smile rated their story more positively than the other participants rated theirs. Furthermore, when researchers looked at the participants' forehead temperatures, those who read the story that forced them to approximate a smile had lower forehead temperatures! It appears that when we smile, we hold our facial muscles in such a way as to promote blood flow that reduces brain temperature, which somehow improves mood. There may after all be something to being a "hothead" or keeping a "cool head"!

The Schachter-Singer Two-Factor Theory of Emotion

So far, the theories of emotion we have looked at see emotion in physiological terms. Certainly physiological responses and facial expressions are part of an emotional experience—but what about cognition? Do our thoughts play a role in our emotions? Some theorists, including psychologists Stanley Schachter and Jerome Singer, believe that they do. Their **two-factor theory** of emotion states that emotions are a product of both physiological arousal and cognitive interpretations of this arousal. Schachter and Singer agreed with Walter Cannon that we do not have a separate pattern of physiological arousal for each emotion we experience; rather, when we experience an emotion, we experience a nondistinct, general physiological arousal. We then use the situational context to help us cognitively interpret the meaning of this arousal. This cognitive interpretation leads to the experience of an emotion. Going back to our example of the bear in the woods, when we see the bear, we become aroused and our heart begins to beat faster. Next, we interpret why we are reacting this way, given the context of the situation. Because we are faced with a potentially dangerous wild animal, our arousal is likely to be interpreted as stemming from fear. Therefore, we label our emotional experience as fear.

In one of their studies, Schachter and Singer (1962) gave participants an injection of epinephrine, a stimulant that causes increased heart rate, respiration, and nervousness. Some of the participants were accurately informed about what to expect from the injection. Others were told that the injection was a harmless shot that would produce no symptoms. After receiving the injection, all of the participants were asked to wait in a waiting room with another participant. But the "participants" they were sent to wait with were *confederates*, or actors playing a part in the experiment. In one condition, the confederate acted angry. He complained, stomped his feet, and eventually left the waiting room in a huff. In the other condition, the confederate acted happy. He appeared joyful, tossed paper airplanes, and generally acted a bit silly.

The dependent variable in the experiment was the mood of the participants *after* their time in the waiting room with the confederate. Schachter and Singer reasoned that the mood of the informed participants would not be influenced by the mood of the confederate. Because the informed participants would interpret their arousal as being due to the drug and not due to some emotional state, there was no reason for their mood to be influenced by the confederate. On the other hand, Schachter and Singer predicted that the mood of the uninformed participants would indeed be influenced by the mood of the confederate. Because they did not have a ready (cognitive) explanation for their arousal, the uninformed participants would look to the situation to help them interpret their reactions. If the confederate was happy, the participants would interpret their arousal as part of a positive emotional state. If the confederate was angry, then the participants would interpret their arousal as part of a negative emotional state.

two-factor theory a theory that states that emotions result when we cognitively interpret our physiological reactions in light of the situation

The results confirmed Schacter and Singer's predictions. The mood of the informed participants was not influenced by the confederate's mood, but the confederate did influence the mood of the uninformed participants. The uninformed participants who waited with the angry confederate reported feeling angrier than did the informed participants. The uninformed participants who waited with the happy confederate reported feeling happier than did the informed participants. It appears that the uninformed participants used the situation to help them figure out their own emotions.

Although Schachter and Singer produced experimental evidence to support their theory, the two-factor theory has not stood the test of time well. Decades of research on the two-factor theory show that there is little reason to believe that emotions require physiological arousal or that emotions necessarily come from labeling unexplained physiological arousal. For example, people who've been given beta-blocking drugs that prevent autonomic nervous system arousal still report experiencing emotions that are relevant to their current environment (Reisenzein, 1983). Despite doubts about the two-factor theory, Schachter and Singer's contribution to the study of emotion is significant. They introduced the idea that cognition plays an important role in emotion, and many theorists recognize that thoughts are part of the emotional experience.

Lazarus's Cognitive-Mediational Theory of Emotion

According to Richard Lazarus (1995), cognition is the most important part of emotion. Unlike Schacter and Singer, who thought that emotion results from the cognitive interpretation of preexisting physiological arousal, Lazarus's **cognitive-mediational theory** of emotion states that our initial *cognitive appraisal* of a situation determines what emotion we will feel in the situation. Going back to the bear example, if you see a bear in the woods one day after having seen a show on TV about some hikers who were killed by a bear, you would likely feel a lot of fear! On the other hand, you might feel less fear on encountering the bear if your only knowledge of bears came from a TV show about a boy and his pet bear. According to cognitive-mediational theory, your appraisal of the situation determines your specific emotion.

Differing appraisals are one reason different people react with different emotions in the same situation. Cognitive-mediational theory also suggests that the best way to control our emotions is by controlling how we perceive situations in life. For instance, a student who perceives that she received a poor grade because the teacher doesn't like her will likely get angry. A calmer student may simply see the grade as a challenge to work harder and not get mad. Teaching yourself to appraise events like this as opportunities and not as threats may help you become a happier, more successful student.

Although it is clear that cognitive appraisals do influence our emotional states (e.g., van-Reekum, Johnstone, Etter, Wehrle, & Scherer, 2004), not everyone agrees that cognition is an essential part of emotion. Robert Zajonc has argued that we can have an emotional reaction to something that is completely independent of our thoughts. In one study, Zajonc (1980) showed English-speaking participants Japanese ideographs (the symbols of the Japanese language). Each ideograph was presented either frequently or infrequently. Later, the participants were asked to rate their preference for ideographs. Despite having no knowledge about the meaning of the ideographs, the participants showed a clear preference for some of them. They preferred the ideographs that they had seen more frequently to the ones they had seen infrequently. Zajonc called this phenomenon of preferring things to which we have had the most exposure the **mere exposure effect**. He reasoned that because the participants did not know the meaning of the ideographs, their emotional reactions to them could not have been influenced by cognition. Rather, their emotions were purely physiological. We will examine the mere exposure effect again in Chapter 10 when we look at its implications for romantic attraction.

cognitive-mediational theory a theory of emotion that states that our cognitive appraisal of a situation determines what emotion we will feel in the situation

mere exposure effect the idea that the more one is exposed to something, the more one grows to like it

Communicating Emotions: Culture, Gender, and Facial Expressions

Imagine that you have traveled to a place where you do not speak the local language at all. You do not recognize any of the words being spoken all around you. In fact, you can't even tell how many words are being spoken in each sentence, because they all seem to run together as the

people speak. You are all alone in this place, and you have to survive somehow. How will you communicate with these people? Perhaps you will try to use pantomime to communicate with someone, but how will you choose *which* person? How will you tell if a particular person is likely to react kindly to your attempts at communication? One way would be to read the emotional expression on the person's face. Does she look happy? Does he look angry? This could be a crucial source of information for you. But what about the cultural differences in this situation? Can we read the emotional expressions of someone from an unfamiliar culture? This is another question psychologists have tried to answer.

basic emotion a proposed set of innate emotions that are common to all humans and from which other higher-order emotions may derive

YOUR TURN – ACTIVE LEARNING

Before you read any further, look at the pictures in ■ FIGURE 8.12. Can you identify the emotions that these people are feeling? These pictures represent the facial expressions of what psychologists call **basic emotions**. Basic emotions are defined as emotions that all humans are thought to have, regardless of cultural background. The idea behind basic emotions is that the capacity for these emotions is genetically programmed in us as a result of evolution. Many psychologists believe that anger, happiness, fear, and sadness are basic emotions, but there is disagreement about what other emotions might be basic. Some add disgust, shame, interest, surprise, and anxiety to the list (Turner & Ortony, 1992). But others do not. Furthermore, some believe that basic emotions can blend together to give us more complex emotions like guilt, pride, and disappointment (Plutchik, 1984). So, were you able to accurately identify the facial expressions? From left to right, top to bottom, they were: *happiness, anger, sadness, surprise, disgust,* and *fear.*

Paul Ekman (1973) showed pictures like these to people from Argentina, Brazil, Chile, Japan, and the United States and asked participants to identify the emotions being expressed. He found that people were generally able to identify the emotions regardless of their culture, although some emotions appeared to be more universal than others. Happiness appeared to be the easiest emotion to identify. People from the different cultures disagreed the most when identifying fear and anger. Other studies have shown that fear and surprise are also easily confused, but curiously women are better at discriminating between these emotions. This may be due to women's greater concern for relating to others and a greater tendency for women to look at other people's faces (McAndrew, 1986).

Very recently, researchers have found that people from different cultures may have slightly different ways of displaying emotions through facial expressions—somewhat similar to how speakers of the same language can have different accents or dialects. In one study, participants from the French-speaking cultures of Quebec (a province of Canada) and Gabon (a country in West Africa) were asked to pose facial expressions for several different emotions. Their expressions were carefully coded by the experimenters, who found

FIGURE

8.12

Can You Identify These Emotions?

Source: Ekman & Friesen, 1984.

that Quebecois and Gabonese participants used slightly different facial muscles to express the same emotions. Furthermore, these "dialects" of facial expressions seemed to account for the errors that participants made in judging each other's facial expressions. As you might expect, participants tended to make more errors when judging the facial expressions of participants from the other culture who had the strongest "accents" (Elfenbein, Beaupre, Levesque, & Hess, 2007).

Does the fact that some emotions translate fairly well across cultures guarantee that these emotions are basic emotions? Perhaps not. Some cultures list "basic" emotions that may be recognizable to people from other cultures but would not be considered by those people to be basic emotions in their culture. Hindus list *peace, wonder, amusement,* and *heroism* as basic emotions (Hejmadi, Davidson, & Rozin, 2000). Americans may be able to feel these emotions and recognize them in others, but may not consider them to be basic emotions. For reasons like these, some people have begun to question whether basic emotions truly exist (Ortony & Turner, 1990).

Whether or not we humans have basic emotions is an open question. An even more open question is: If we do have basic emotions, what are they? Regardless of whether basic emotions exist, emotions are powerful tools of communication. A smile can signal friendliness to many people—regardless of background or culture.

Let's Review!

In this section, we defined emotion and discussed some theories of emotion. We also looked at how humans tend to show emotions through facial expressions. For a quick check of your understanding, answer these questions.

1. Which of the following is not typically thought of as a basic emotion?
   a. Fear
   b. Sadness
   c. Pride
   d. Happiness

2. Derrick and Monique each went out on blind dates. Derrick took his date to dinner. Monique took her date to a football game. According to the two-factor theory of emotion, who is more likely to go out on a second date with his or her partner?
   a. Derrick
   b. Monique

   c. Monique and Derrick are equally likely to go out on a second date.
   d. Two-factor theory makes no predictions about this situation.

3. Mohammed and Betty are each stuck in a traffic jam. Mohammed remains calm, but Betty begins to get very angry. Which theory of emotion best explains Mohammed's and Betty's different emotions in this situation?
   a. Cognitive-mediational theory
   b. Two-factor theory
   c. Facial feedback theory
   d. James-Lange theory

Answers 1. c; 2. b; 3. a

Studying THE Chapter

Key Terms

motive (274)
instinct (274)
drive reduction theory (275)
drive (275)
primary drive (275)
homeostasis (275)
negative feedback loop (275)
secondary drive (275)
incentive (277)
extrinsic motivation (277)
intrinsic motivation (277)
hierarchy of needs (277)
set point (279)
ghrelin (280)
glucose (280)
glycogen (280)
cholecystokinin (CCK) (280)
leptin (281)
lateral hypothalamus (LH) (281)

neuropeptide Y (281)
ventromedial hypothalamus
  (VMH) (282)
obese (284)
bulimia nervosa (287)
anorexia nervosa (288)
binge eating disorder (290)
intracellular fluid (290)
extracellular fluid (290)
sexual desire (293)
sexual arousal (293)
libido (293)
estrogens (293)
ovaries (293)
testosterone (294)
testes (294)
erogenous zones (294)
excitement phase (295)
plateau phase (295)

orgasm phase (295)
resolution phase (296)
refractory period (296)
sexual orientation (296)
heterosexual (296)
homosexual (296)
bisexual (296)
homophobia (297)
emotion (299)
affective component of emotion (300)
James-Lange theory (300)
Cannon-Bard theory (301)
facial feedback hypothesis (302)
two-factor theory (303)
cognitive-mediational theory (304)
mere exposure effect (304)
basic emotion (305)

What Do You Know? Assess Your Understanding

Test your retention and understanding of the material by answering the following questions.

1. According to William James, motives are best characterized as _____.
   a. drives
   b. instincts
   c. desires
   d. needs

2. Which of the following is not a primary drive?
   a. Hunger
   b. Thirst
   c. Sleepiness
   d. Need for achievement

3. Most of us perform best at a _____ level of arousal.
   a. low
   b. moderate
   c. high
   d. very high

4. Which of the following is an example of a negative feedback loop?
   a. Scratching a mosquito bite, making it itch more
   b. Sexual arousal, leading one to desire more stimulation
   c. Drinking water when thirsty
   d. All of the above

5. Which of the following is an example of intrinsic motivation?
   a. Studying hard because you want to feel proud of your test performance
   b. Going to work to earn a paycheck
   c. Wanting to look good to impress your significant other
   d. Being nice to your grandmother in hopes that she will loan you some money

6. According to Abraham Maslow, which of the following is the highest level of motivation we experience?
   a. Belonginess
   b. Safety needs
   c. Aesthetic needs
   d. Physiological needs

7. A person with a high level of ghrelin in his or her bloodstream would likely _____.
   a. feel no hunger
   b. feel very hungry
   c. feel slight hunger
   d. Ghrelin has no relationship with hunger.

8. If you injected a hungry rat with CCK, what would likely happen?
   a. The rat would become even hungrier.
   b. The rat would stop eating immediately.
   c. The rat would stop eating only if it had already ingested sufficient food.
   d. The rat would slow down its eating, but it would continue to eat.

9. Damage to which area of the brain would most likely result in anorexic behavior in a rat?
   a. The ventromedial hypothalamus (VMH)
   b. The lateral hypothalamus (LH)
   c. The thalamus
   d. The hippocampus

10. Being obese is defined as _____.
    a. being at least 20 lb overweight
    b. having a BMI of 30
    c. being at least 100 lb overweight
    d. having a BMI of 50

11. Belinda often binges by eating large quantities of food. After these binges, she feels bad about herself, but does little to change her eating behavior. As a result of these binges, Belinda is overweight. Belinda most closely meets the criteria for which eating disorder?
    a. Anorexia nervosa
    b. Bulimia nervosa
    c. Binge eating disorder
    d. Obesity

12. Eating a salty meal will cause thirst due to its effect on _____.
    a. intracellular fluid
    b. extracellular fluid
    c. blood pressure
    d. heart rate

13. When a female mammal is receptive to sexual intercourse, she is said to be in _____.
    a. estrus
    b. resolution
    c. the refractory period
    d. the plateau phase

14. Immediately after experiencing an orgasm, females enter the _____.
    a. refractory period
    b. resolution phase
    c. plateau phase
    d. excitement phase

15. Male and female sexual response cycles differ most significantly in which stage?
    a. Excitement phase
    b. Orgasm phase
    c. Plateau phase
    d. Resolution phase

16. Sabrina is married with two kids. What do we know about Sabrina's sexual orientation?
    a. She's homosexual.
    b. She's bisexual.
    c. She's heterosexual.
    d. We cannot tell from this information.

17. Which theory of emotion best explains why one student panics before an exam and another remains calm?
   a. James-Lange theory of emotion
   b. Cannon-Bard theory of emotion
   c. Cognitive-mediational theory
   d. Two-factor theory

18. Which theory of emotion best explains why someone would feel more sexual attraction to his or her partner while at a concert than with the same partner in a library?
   a. James-Lange theory of emotion
   b. Cannon-Bard theory of emotion
   c. Cognitive-mediational theory
   d. Two-factor theory

19. Which of the following theories of emotion defines emotion as a pattern of physiological response in the body?
   a. James-Lange theory of emotion
   b. Cannon-Bard theory of emotion
   c. Cognitive-mediational theory
   d. Two-factor theory

20. Which of the following is a basic emotion?
   a. Guilt
   b. Pride
   c. Disappointment
   d. Sadness

Answers: 1. b; 2. d; 3. b; 4. c; 5. a; 6. c; 7. b; 8. c; 9. b; 10. b; 11. c; 12. a; 13. a; 14. b; 15. d; 16. d; 17. c; 18. d; 19. a; 20. d.

Online Resources

CENGAGENOW™ **Personalized Study**
www.cengage.com/login
Go to www.cengage.com/login to link to CengageNOW, your online study tool. First take the **Pre-Test** for this chapter to get your **Personalized Study Plan**, which will identify topics you need to review and direct you to online resources. Then take the **Post-Test** to determine what concepts you have mastered and what you still need work on.

 What Is Psychology? Essentials Book Companion Website
www.cengage.com/psychology/pastorino
Visit your book companion website, where you will find more resources to help you study. Resources include learning objectives, Internet exercises, quizzing, flash cards, and a pronunciation glossary.

Look Back AT WHAT YOU'VE LEARNED

A **motive** is the tendency to desire and seek out positive incentives and rewards and to avoid negative outcomes.

How Do Psychologists Define Motivation?

- William James believed that motives tend to be inborn **instincts**.

- According to the **drive reduction theory**, **primary drives** maintain **homeostasis**.

- **Arousal theories** of motivation suggest that each of us has an optimal level of arousal.

- According to **incentive theories** of motivation, motivation is directed at attaining certain incentives.

- Abraham Maslow proposed a **hierarchy of needs** in which some needs take priority over others.

© Ashley Cooper/Corbis

Transcendence

Self-actualization needs: to find self-fulfillment and realize one's potential

Aesthetic needs: symmetry, order, and beauty

Cognitive needs: to know, understand, and explore

Esteem needs: to achieve, be competent, and gain approval and recognition

Belongingness and love needs: to affiliate with others, be accepted, and belong

Safety needs: to feel secure and safe, out of danger

Physiological needs: hunger, thirst, and so forth

Maslow, "Hierarchy of Needs," from *Motivation and Personality*. Copyright © 1954 by Harper and Row Publishers, Inc. (Reprinted by permission of Pearson Education, Inc., Upper Saddle River, NJ.)

Why Do We Feel Hunger and Thirst?

- Receptors in the stomach monitor the intake of food and contractions of the stomach, and signal the brain when to make us hungry or to shut off hunger.

- Liver cells, hormones, fat cells, and glucoreceptors in the hypothalamus all play a role in signaling hunger or shutting it off.

- External cues such as advertisements and the sight or smell of food can also trigger hunger.

- **Obesity** can be caused by biological factors, such as a slow metabolism, as well as a number of behavioral factors, including a poor diet, excessive food intake, and emotional eating.

- **Anorexia nervosa** is a serious eating disorder that involves extreme concern about gaining weight and reduction in caloric intake that leads to drastic weight loss.

- **Bulimia nervosa** involves bingeing on food followed by purging or drastic reduction in caloric intake to rid the body of the extra calories.

- **Binge eating disorder** involves bingeing on food without compensatory measures to rid the body of extra calories.

- The body uses two mechanisms to regulate and signal thirst: a drop in **intracellular fluid** pressure, and a drop in **extracellular fluid** pressure.

© Neal Preston/Corbis

© AP Photo/The Grand Island Independent, Barnett Stinson

Motivation AND Emotion: WHAT Guides OUR BEHAVIOR?

Thinkstock/Getty Images

What Causes Sexual Orientation?

- **Sexual orientation** is not just a matter of with whom you have sex. Surveys show that some people may have some same-sex encounters but not consider themselves gay or lesbian.

- Sexual orientation falls along a continuum from **heterosexual** (attracted to the other sex) to **bisexual** (attracted to both sexes) to **homosexual** (attracted to the same sex).

- **Homophobia**, prejudice against homosexuals and bisexuals, is still a big problem in some cultures including the United States.

What Is Sexual Arousal and Response?

- **Sexual desire** is influenced by hormones, sensory cues, and cultural attitudes about what is sexually appealing.

- Masters and Johnson's research examined the physiological changes that men and women undergo during sexual activity. Their results indicate that the sexual response cycle involves **excitement**, **plateau**, **orgasm**, and **resolution** phases.

Female Sexual Response

Orgasm
Plateau
Excitement
Resolution
A B C
C
A
B

Male Sexual Response

Orgasm
Plateau
Excitement
Refractory period
Resolution
Resolution

What Is Emotion?

- Components of **emotion** include physiological reactions, behavioral reactions, facial expressions, cognition, and **affective** response.

- The **James-Lange theory** of emotion proposes that emotion can be understood as a physiological response to some stimulus.

- The **Cannon-Bard theory** of emotion holds that emotion is the brain responding to some stimulus or situation, then prompting an emotional reaction.

- In the **facial feedback hypothesis**, the experience of an emotion is affected by the feedback the brain receives from muscles in the face. Thus, smiling can influence us to feel happy, and frowning can influence us to feel bad.

- The Schachter-Singer **two-factor theory** of emotion states that emotions are a product of both physiological arousal and cognitive interpretations of this arousal.

- **Cognitive-meditational theory** states that our cognitive appraisal of a situation determines what emotion we will feel in the situation; thus, different people react with different emotions in the same situation.

- **Basic emotions**, include happiness, sadness, anger, and fear, have been found to be present across cultures.

9

HOW DO **People** Grow, Change, AND **DEVELOP?**

© Hill Street Studios/Getty Images

At 35 years of age, Michelle Lewis decided to leave her job in the hotel industry and take some courses at the local college. However, after a year in school, Michelle became pregnant, giving birth to Morgan, and two years later, another son, Matthew. Morgan and Matthew joined her two stepchildren Rachel and Nick, now teenagers. Michelle could no longer afford to go to school and returned to work at a child care center. While at school, Michelle had enrolled in a general psychology course. Little did she know how helpful the information on child and adult development would be to her personal and professional life.

Michelle now looks at kids differently. Her knowledge of child development has allowed her to more appropriately tailor activities and tasks to a child's developmental level. She is more likely to encourage and praise the children she takes care of as well as her own, and less likely to just expect that the children will know what to do. Michelle has changed as a parent and wife too. She provides a structured environment for her two young sons and tries to be firm as a parent. She tries to communicate better with her husband by not criticizing him and accepts him for who he is.

This chapter outlines the processes of development. **Development** consists of changes in behavior and abilities. In this chapter, we will see that human development is complicated. Physical changes are occurring along with emotional, social, and mental (or cognitive) development. At the same time, social forces (such as people around us) and our environment also affect these processes. We hope that by understanding the physical, cognitive, and social aspects of development, you, like Michelle, will be able to appreciate the many forces that make each child, teenager, and adult unique.

© Ellen Pastorino

Knowing about child and adult development has helped Michelle Lewis in her personal and professional life.

Nature–Nurture Revisited: Biology and Culture

● Explain the nature–nurture issue.

Psychologists study development in order to understand the changes that humans experience from conception to the end of life. Because this period covers such a large time span, developmental psychologists typically further specialize by limiting their investigations to a particular age group, such as infancy, childhood, adolescence, or adulthood. Within any one of these age stages, psychologists may focus on different aspects of development: physical, mental, social, or personality development. One developmental psychologist may study how language develops in infants while another may research how peer pressure affects drug use in adolescents.

Recall from Chapter 1 that psychology seeks to describe, predict, control, and explain behavior. If psychologists can accomplish these goals, then we can promote healthy development and prevent or alter maladaptive patterns of development. For example, if we understand how children think, we can then create appropriate educational environments, thus maximizing each child's potential. Understanding the dynamics of peer pressure during adolescence may suggest strategies to reduce drug use, delinquency, and teenage pregnancy. Knowing about developmental processes, therefore, has numerous real-world applications.

However, explaining developmental changes is not easy. Think about all the variables that can potentially influence how a person grows and changes. In addition to a unique biological foundation (genetics), every person is also influenced by a multitude of environments: family, school, friends, neighborhoods, religion, and culture. The potential contribution of these biological and environmental factors to development has become a central issue for developmental psychologists. Recall from Chapter 7 that this is referred to as the **nature–nurture issue**. Psychologists are interested in how much one's biology, or *nature*, contributes to a person's development versus how much one's environment and culture, or *nurture*, influence this process.

development changes in behavior and/or abilities

nature–nurture issue the degree to which biology (nature) or the environment (nurture) contributes to one's development

Genetics or *nature* influences almost every aspect of development, from personality and physical development to cognitive processes such as language development and intelligence (Bouchard, 2004; Gottlieb, Wahlsten, & Lickliter, 1998; Rose, 1995). Nurture is the total effect of all the external environmental events and circumstances that influence your development. It includes your family, friends, how others perceive and behave toward you, events that happen to you, television programs that you watch, music that you listen to, the customs and rituals of your ethnic background, your gender, your culture, your schooling, and so on.

Recall that it is not really a case of nature *or* nurture. Rather, it is the *interaction* of these two forces that influences behavior. As you read about the various types of development that we experience, keep this nature–nurture issue in mind, as the influences of nature and nurture seem to interact in a complex fashion.

Both nature and nurture influence every aspect of development.

© Tom Stewart/Corbis

Let's Review!

In this section, we reviewed the nature–nurture issue. As a quick check of your understanding, answer these questions.

1. Studying identical twins to assess the degree to which they are similar focuses most on the _____ side of a key developmental issue.
   a. nature
   b. nurture
   c. development
   d. learning

2. Current thinking on the nature–nurture issue suggests that _____.
   a. nature is more important than nurture in determining development
   b. nurture is more important than nature in determining development
   c. neither nature nor nurture is important in determining development
   d. nature and nurture interact in determining development

Answers 1. a; 2. d

Prenatal Development: Conception to Birth

Learning Objective

- Identify and describe the three stages of prenatal development—germinal, embryonic, and fetal—and explain the importance of a positive prenatal environment.

From the outside, all we see is a woman with a swollen belly who walks with a waddle. We may even have the opportunity to see or feel movement occurring inside her belly. Any woman who has been pregnant has experienced having some people want to touch her stomach or to treat her more delicately because of her "condition." Both tendencies speak to our fascination with the developments going on inside.

All the genetic material for development is inherited from your biological parents at the time of conception. The male sperm cell, containing 23 single chromosomes, fertilizes the female ovum, also containing 23 single chromosomes, to create a fertilized egg, called a **zygote**, that has 23 pairs of chromosomes. Over the next 38 to 40 weeks, the average gestation period for a human, the zygote will experience dramatic changes as it evolves into a baby. So many changes occur during this time that scientists divide the prenatal period into three stages: the germinal or zygotic stage, the embryonic stage, and the fetal stage.

You Asked...

How does a baby develop in the mother's womb?

MELISSA TYNDALE, STUDENT

Don W. Fawcett/Photo Researchers, Inc.

Human sperm and egg at the moment of penetration. The sperm cell fertilizes the female ovum to create a zygote.

Changes in the Prenatal Period

The first 14 days after conception are the **germinal stage** of development. The major characteristic of this stage is cell division. Following conception, the zygote starts to replicate itself and divide. This ensures that all the cells of the organism contain the same genetic material. It divides into 2 cells, which then replicate and divide again, creating a 4-cell organism. The cells continue replicating and dividing, and around the 5th day after conception the zygote has become a 100-cell organism, called a *blastocyst*. During this process of cell division, the

zygote [ZIE-goat] a fertilized egg
germinal stage the first stage of prenatal development, from conception to 14 days

Micro-MRI, reconstructed with 3D imagery, actual size of embryo 4.0 mm. The image depicts a human embryo during its 4th week of development. Age is calculated from the day of fertilization. In this image, the fusing tubes of the heart are highlighted in red. Early growth of the cardiovascular system begins during the 3rd week, when blood vessels form, and continues into the following weeks of development. Image from the book *From Conception to Birth: A Life Unfolds.*

At 14 weeks, the fetus's lungs and external sex organs have developed.

embryonic [em-bree-AH-nik] **stage** the second stage of prenatal development, lasting from the 2nd through the 8th week

fetal stage the stage of prenatal development from the 9th week through the 9th month

Down syndrome a genetic birth disorder resulting from an extra 21st chromosome, characterized by distinct facial features and a greater likelihood of heart defects and mental retardation

mass of cells also travels down the fallopian tube to the uterus. On approximately the 9th day after conception, the blastocyst implants itself in the lining of the uterine wall. Cell division continues through the 2nd week.

The **embryonic stage** covers development of the organism, now called an *embryo*, from the 2nd through the 8th week. After the blastocyst attaches to the uterine wall, its outside cells develop into the support structures: the placenta, umbilical cord, and amniotic sac. The inner cells become the embryo.

The major characteristic of the embryonic period is the formation and development of the major organs and systems. Cells start to specialize into bone, muscle, and body organs. All the major biological systems—the cardiovascular system, the digestive system, the skeletal system, the excretory system, the respiratory system, and the nervous system—are forming. Given the importance of these systems for survival and well-being, the embryonic stage is perhaps the most precarious stage of prenatal development. Most miscarriages and genetic defects surface during this stage. The embryo's development may also be harmed by outside environmental factors, producing devastating effects. We will return to these topics in a moment.

By the end of the embryonic stage, all basic bodily structures and systems have formed. About 4 weeks after conception, the heart is beating, the spinal cord is forming, the liver is producing red blood cells, and ovaries or testes have formed (but the embryo's sex is not apparent by ultrasound until between 12 and 18 weeks). Although only an inch long, the embryo already looks human. Facial features, such as the eyes, lips, nose, and jaw, have taken shape. Short stubs represent arms and legs, and the beginnings of fingers and toes are apparent.

The third prenatal development period, the **fetal stage**, begins the 9th week after conception. From now until birth, the organism is referred to as a *fetus*. The major characteristic of the fetal stage is continued growth and maturation. The fetus grows larger and starts to move. By 14 weeks, the fetus can kick, open its mouth, swallow, and turn its head. Its lungs and external sex organs have developed. By the end of the 6th month (24 weeks), the organs are sufficiently formed that the fetus has reached *viability*—the possibility of surviving outside the womb (but only in a neonatal intensive care unit). During the last 3 months, the fetus is responsive to sound, light, and touch.

From the union of a single sperm cell and egg, the fetus has undergone significant and complex changes over the course of 40 weeks. However, not all zygotes experience these changes. About half of all fertilized eggs die and are miscarried, usually before the woman knows she is pregnant. Of pregnancies that the mother knows about (because of a missed menstrual cycle), approximately 10 to 20% end in miscarriage (Mortensen, Sever, & Oakley, 1991).

The Importance of a Positive Prenatal Environment

You Asked...

What are some birth defects that can occur?   NIESHA HAZZARD, STUDENT

The support structures of the intrauterine environment are designed to protect the developing organism. However, internal and external forces can still interfere with this natural defense system and cause birth defects.

When internal chromosomal abnormalities are present at conception, their effects typically arise during the embryonic stage. For example, **Down syndrome** results from an extra 21st chromosome. Babies with Down syndrome are characterized by distinct facial features and are more likely to experience heart defects and varying degrees of mental retardation. Medical tests can identify the presence of

Down syndrome and more than 450 inherited genetic disorders so that parents can prepare themselves or terminate the pregnancy (Painter, 1997). This highlights the importance of regular prenatal consultations with a physician.

Birth defects may also be caused by outside environmental forces. Any environmental agent that has the potential to harm the embryo is referred to as a **teratogen**. It may be a drug that the mother takes, such as cocaine or alcohol; a disease, such as German measles (rubella); or chemicals that the mother inhales, such as cleaning fluids. All of these substances have the potential to cause birth defects. The critical factor seems to be when the mother is exposed to these agents. These **sensitive periods** emphasize the complex interplay of nature and nurture on development. Certain organs and systems are more vulnerable to the effects of teratogens during particular stages of prenatal development (■ FIGURE 9.1). Notice that the most severe effects are most likely to occur during the embryonic stage of development. Because a woman usually does not discover that she is pregnant until the embryo is already formed and developing, she may unknowingly expose her developing baby to harm.

Women who use any type of drug during pregnancy can potentially affect their babies. Women who smoke during pregnancy reduce the flow of oxygen to the fetus; their babies tend to be irritable, have respiratory problems, and have lower birth weight (Lester, Andreozzi, & Appiah, 2004; Rosenblith, 1992). Women who drink alcohol heavily during pregnancy put their unborn children at risk for **fetal alcohol syndrome (FAS)**. Children suffering from FAS tend to have low birth weight, exhibit limb, head, and facial deformities, and suffer brain abnormalities. FAS is the leading cause of mental retardation (Ikonomidou et al., 2000; Niccols, 1994; Young, 1997). Even moderate drinking can affect the embryo's brain development, resulting in lowered levels of intellectual functioning later (Kraft, 1996). Prenatal alcohol exposure has also been linked to an increased risk of low birth weight and poorer visual acuity in infancy (Carter et al., 2005; Mariscal et al., 2006).

teratogen [tur-RAH-tuh-jun] an environmental substance that has the potential to harm the developing organism

sensitive period in prenatal development, a time when genetic and environmental agents are most likely to cause birth defects

fetal alcohol syndrome (FAS) a birth condition resulting from the mother's chronic use of alcohol during pregnancy; it is characterized by facial and limb deformities and mental retardation

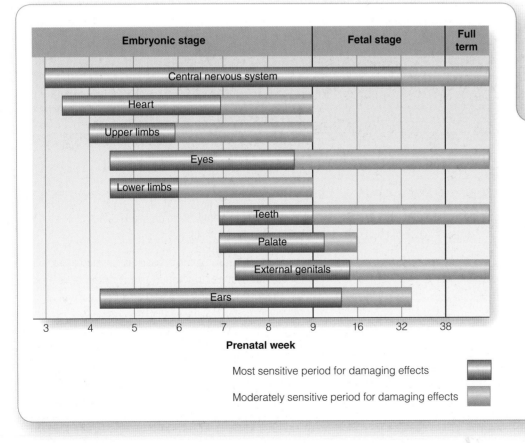

FIGURE 9.1 **Sensitive Periods and Effect on Prenatal Development**

The darker bars indicate the most sensitive period for certain organs and structures; the lighter bars indicate lessened vulnerability. Sensitivity is greatest during the embryonic period, although some structures remain vulnerable throughout the prenatal period.

Adapted from K. L. Moore and T. V. N. Persaud, Before We Are Born: Essentials of Embryology and Birth Defects. Philadelphia: Saunders. Copyright © 1998 Elsevier Science (USA). All rights reserved. Reprinted by permission.

Illegal drugs also produce damaging effects. If the mother is a heroin addict, the baby will be born addicted and have to undergo withdrawal. Crack or cocaine babies are often born premature, underweight, and irritable, and tend to have poor feeding habits (Inciardi, Surratt, & Saum, 1997; Richardson & Day, 1994).

Prenatal exposure to teratogens may also have long-term effects. Children whose mothers used drugs during pregnancy tend to be more impulsive, be less adaptable, and evidence more behavioral problems later in life than children whose mothers did not use drugs during pregnancy (Espy, Riese, & Francis, 1997). In southern Japan, adults whose mothers took in high levels of methylmercury (found in fish) during pregnancy have shown accelerated rates of aging (Newland & Rasmussen, 2003).

Prescription and over-the-counter medicines may also influence fetal development. Read the warning labels on any over-the-counter medication, and you will see that pregnant women are cautioned to seek a doctor's advice before using any medicine. Whatever the mother takes in during pregnancy or breastfeeding, so does the baby. Proper nutrition and a healthy lifestyle are paramount for a pregnant woman. They increase the chances of producing a healthy newborn who is better prepared to face the developmental and life challenges ahead. These challenges include the enormous changes that occur in infancy and childhood—our next topic of discussion.

Let's Review!

In this section, we described prenatal development and emphasized the importance of a positive prenatal environment. For a quick review, answer these questions.

1. Loretta is in her 5th month of pregnancy. What stage of development is her unborn child in?
   a. Germinal
   b. Zygote
   c. Embryonic
   d. Fetal

2. Which of the following is *most* characteristic of the germinal stage of prenatal development?
   a. Cell division
   b. Viability
   c. Birth defects
   d. Formation of major body systems

3. Environmental substances that can harm the developing organism are called _____.
   a. chromosomes
   b. teratogens
   c. critical periods
   d. miscarriage

Answers 1. d; 2. a; 3. b

Infancy and Childhood

Learning Objectives

- Describe major physical changes that infants and children experience as their brains and bodies develop.

- Describe the perceptual abilities of infants and how these abilities develop in the first weeks and months of life.

- Compare and contrast Piaget's and Vygotsky's theories of cognitive development.

- Compare and contrast Kohlberg's and Gilligan's theories of moral reasoning.

- Define temperament, and distinguish among the three temperamental styles of infants.

- Describe behaviors that indicate that an attachment has been formed, distinguish among different attachment patterns, and describe the three parenting styles that Baumrind documented.

- Describe Erikson's theory of psychosocial development as it applies to infants and children.

- Explain gender-schema theory and describe how nature and nurture influence gender-role behavior and gender identity.

Can you remember what you were like as a baby? What memories do you have of your childhood? Which people influenced you the most? Did you think the same way then as you do now? Recalling such experiences will help you apply the material as we outline the major developmental changes in infancy and childhood. Child development includes changes in physical, emotional, social, and cognitive behavior and abilities over time. We will start by examining important physical aspects of development.

Physical Development: Growing, Moving, and Exploring

The average **neonate**, or newborn up to 28 days old, enters the world 20 inches long, weighing 7 pounds. One year later, the average infant is 29 inches long and will have tripled in weight, emphasizing how rapidly babies grow during infancy. Physical growth and developmental changes result from the complex interaction of the forces of nature and nurture. Our genetic program lays the foundation for how tall we grow and how our body fat is distributed. The environmental factors of nutrition, health care, and lifestyle also influence our height and build. A similar interplay of nature and nurture is seen in brain and motor development.

BRAIN DEVELOPMENT

What is your very first childhood memory? How old were you then? Most people do not recall events in infancy or before 3 years old. This lack of memory may be related to the development of the nervous system. At birth, an infant's brain has billions of neurons, but the connections between the neurons are very limited, and myelin (see p. 39) is incomplete. Experience and learning, however, mix with heredity to shape brain development. Neural pathways grow rapidly, and by the time a child is 3 years old, 1,000 trillion synapses have formed (Garlick, 2003). A 2-month-old has very few neural connections compared to the billions a 2-year-old has. More experience plus increased activity equals more neural connections.

During childhood and early adolescence, the brain prunes and discards unnecessary connections, reducing the total number of synapses (Cook & Cook, 2005; Seeman, 1999; Thompson et al., 2000). Those connections that are used repeatedly become permanent, whereas those that are used infrequently or not at all are unlikely to survive (Greenough et al., 1993). This discovery has altered researchers' thinking on infant care and early education. Providing stimulating age-appropriate activities fosters and strengthens brain development. Impoverished environments weaken neural connections—fewer connections are made, and unexercised connections are likely to be discarded.

A young child's brain is highly plastic, or changeable, and very dense with neurons when compared to adults' brains. If a certain area of the brain is damaged in infancy, other areas of the brain can compensate by reorganizing neural connections (Kolb, 1989; Rakic, 1991). However, there are individual inherited differences in this process; some brains may be better able to adapt than others (Garlick, 2002). As children age, the brain is less able to change and adapt because neural connections have already been formed, and in some cases discarded, although some plasticity remains throughout adulthood (Huttenlocher, 2002). The plasticity and density of the brain ensures a child's best chance of adapting to his or her environment. This adaptation is also evident in the development of children's motor skills.

neonate a newborn during the first 28 days of life

Juergen Berger, Max-planck Institute/Photo Researchers, Inc.

Synaptic connections proliferate during infancy and early childhood. The brain then selectively prunes and discards unused connections during childhood and early adolescence.

REFLEXES AND MOTOR DEVELOPMENT

Infants are born relatively helpless creatures. They cannot feed themselves and are unable to walk. Infants do have certain sensory abilities, a good set of lungs that enable them to cry, and a set of reflexes, all of which biologically prepare them to get the help they need to survive.

A **reflex** is an *automatic* response to a particular stimulus. Reflexes enable infants to learn about their environment, thus establishing important neural connections for *voluntary* motor behaviors. Hence, reflexes serve as the foundation for behaviors such as walking, eating, crying, smiling, and grasping. For example, infants are born with a sucking reflex. They will automatically suck on any object that touches their lips. Infants also have a *rooting reflex*. When you touch the side of infants' cheeks, they will turn in that direction and open their mouth. These two reflexes teach infants how to use their mouths to get food. Infants are also born with a grasping reflex. When an object is placed on their palm, they will automatically grasp it. From this reflex, infants learn to handle items with their hands, an ability referred to as *prehension*. Their brains and bodies learn, through grasping, the necessary skills that will later be used to write with a pen, play a musical instrument, tie their shoes, or give a parent a hug.

Infants are also biologically prepared to communicate, despite lacking formal language skills. A crying reflex—automatically crying when distressed—alerts the caretaker to the infant's needs. In a matter of weeks, the baby learns to use crying to get the caretaker's attention. Luckily, infants are also born with a smiling reflex to use when they are pleased. This reflex evolves into a *social smile* during the second month of life, when the infant smiles at everybody. Their smiles then become more discriminating by 6 months of age, when infants reserve their smiles for familiar voices and faces.

Reflexes also initiate *locomotive* ability, or the ability to move around, preparing the brain and body for motions involved in pulling oneself up, crawling, and walking. These abilities develop in much the same sequence for all infants around the world, evidence of our genetic heritage. However, experience may speed up this process, and lack of opportunities may slow it down (Thelen, 1995).

By age 2, most infants are walking, running, and getting into everything. However, motor development, the changes in a child's body activities, does not end there. As children age, gross motor skills become more proficient. **Gross motor skills** refer to behaviors that involve large muscle groups such as the biceps or quadriceps. These include running, walking, jumping, and hopping. This proficiency is apparent when you watch a toddler, a preschooler, and an 8-year-old run. The toddler waddles and is unsteady on her feet. The preschooler is more coordinated compared to the toddler, but less fluid and not as fast as the 8-year-old.

Similar changes occur in **fine motor skills**, which involve small muscle groups. Fine motor skills include such activities as writing, using utensils, and playing a musical instrument. Toddlers and preschoolers are less adept at tasks involving fine motor skills, but as the school years approach, children become much more proficient. ■ TABLE 9.1 details average age ranges for specific gross and fine motor skills achieved in infancy and childhood. Notice that the achievement of a particular task lays the foundation for attaining the subsequent, more difficult, task. In other words, babies must be able to sit up before they can crawl. Children must walk before they learn to jump rope.

Enormous changes occur in physical development through the infancy and childhood years. The same magnitude of change characterizes cognitive development, or how children think, which we'll turn to next.

reflex an automatic response to a specific environmental stimulus

gross motor skills motor behaviors involving the large muscles of the body

fine motor skills motor behaviors involving the small muscles of the body

Cognitive Development: Perception and Thinking

Television shows, movies, and comic strips capitalize on the unique way in which children develop mentally. What is it about children's thinking that makes adults laugh? This section reviews psychological research into how infants first learn to conceptualize the world and

Table 9.1 Motor Milestones in Infancy and Childhood

3 MOS.	6 MOS.	1 YR.	18 MOS.	2 YRS.	3 YRS.	4 YRS.	5 YRS.	6–8 YRS.	9–11 YRS.
Lifts head & chest when lying on stomach	Reaches for & grasps objects	Sits alone	Pulls & pushes objects	Drinks from a straw	Puts on shoes	Runs, jumps, hops, & skips	Rides a bicycle with training wheels	Ties shoelaces	Body strength increases
Grasps rattle	Helps hold a bottle	Crawls	Turns pages in a book	Tosses a ball	Dresses self with help	Jumps over objects	Balances on one foot	Good sense of balance	Increased hand dexterity
Waves arms	Shakes a rattle	Pulls self up	Scribbles	Opens drawers	Kicks a ball	Brushes teeth	Cuts with scissors	Prints name	Faster reaction time
Kicks legs	Sits with little support	Uses finger to point	Stacks a few blocks	Feeds self with a spoon	Hops on one foot	Catches, bounces, & throws a ball	Jumps rope	Catches small balls	Better coordination
	Rolls over	Grasps objects with thumb & index finger	Walks	Bends over without falling	Pedals		Capable of swimming & skating	Copies designs & shapes	
			Runs stiffly	Takes backward steps	Climbs		Copies simple designs		

how this thinking changes as they proceed through childhood. We will start with perceptual development.

PERCEPTUAL DEVELOPMENT

Infants are hard to study. They sleep most of the time, and they can't talk much. We can't remember what it's like to be an infant. Researchers must therefore study infants when they are awake and active, and devise clever ways to measure what infants know. The best way to gather information about what infants can and cannot perceive seems to be to measure certain behaviors and see how those behaviors change under particular conditions. For example, researchers may measure how long an infant spends looking at a stimulus or how long an infant sucks when exposed to different sounds. As researchers create more precise ways of measuring infant behavior, we are discovering that infants know a lot more than we once believed.

Vision Babies are very nearsighted at birth. Objects need to be close in order for babies to see them, and even then, the objects look blurry. In addition, a baby's eyes lack *convergence*, or the ability to focus both eyes on an object. This may be why newborns typically look cross-eyed in photographs. However, as the structure of the eyes and the neural connections in the brain mature, babies attain visual convergence.

Newborns show a preference for looking at complex, high-contrast stimuli. If given a choice of various complex visual stimuli, infants will spend most of their time looking at faces (Turati, 2004; Turati & Simion, 2002; Valenza, Simion, Cassia, & Umilta, 1996). This preference is adaptive, as it helps foster a social bond with the primary caretaker. By 3 months old, a baby can tell the difference between its primary caretaker's face and that of a stranger and more easily recognizes faces from her own race (Bar-Haim, Ziv, Lamy, & Hodes, 2006; Burnham, 1993; Kelly et al., 2007; Sangrigoli & de Schonen, 2004). Infants also have more difficulty processing male faces than female faces (Ramsey-Rennels & Langlois, 2006).

© Corbis

YOUR TURN – ACTIVE LEARNING

Our brains are predisposed to recognize a face, and this predisposition is present in babies. Look closely at the upside down image of Lincoln on this page before looking at it right side up. Notice a difference? Even when presented with an inverted portrait, we ignore the distortions and recognize that it is a face. When you look at Lincoln's portrait right side up, you notice all the distortions.

Depth Perception During their first year, infants develop depth perception. In a classic experiment conducted in 1960, researchers Eleanor Gibson and Richard Walk created an apparatus called a "visual cliff" (■ FIGURE 9.2). They then observed at what age infants would or would not cross over the surface where it appeared to drop off. Infants as young as 6 months of age hesitated when approaching this perceived cliff. Again, we see that biology prepares us for developmental challenges. Babies acquire depth perception at about the same time they become mobile. Because depth perception and body coordination may not yet be developed in some infants, it is extremely important to never leave a baby unattended on a bed, a changing table, or any other elevated surface. Immature depth perception, as well as inadequate body control, makes it more likely that infants will fall and hurt themselves.

FIGURE

9.2

Depth Perception in Infancy

Eleanor Gibson and Richard Walk's visual cliff apparatus tests depth perception in infants.

© Mark Richards/Photo Edit

Hearing Unborn babies react to sounds in the intrauterine environment at around the 20th week. A mother's voice is one of those sounds, which may explain why babies are likely to recognize their mothers' voice soon after birth (DeCasper & Fifer, 1980). Infants can locate the direction of sounds. They readily learn the difference between similar consonant sounds, such as /d/ and /p/, and appear to remember simple speech sounds a day after hearing them (Swain, Zelazo, & Clifton, 1993). Research suggests that these abilities to discriminate sounds and familiar voices from unfamiliar ones may also be present in fetuses (Kisilevsky et al., 2003; Lecanuet, Manera, & Jacquet, 2002).

Babies prefer soft and rhythmic sounds, which explains why they enjoy lullabies so much. They prefer most to listen to voices, specifically the rising tones used by women and children (Sullivan & Horowitz, 1983) and the exaggerated, high-pitched sounds typically used in baby talk. Infants do not like loud noises, which may explain why some children become classically conditioned to fear thunderstorms (see Chapter 5).

The Other Senses Taste, touch, and smell are other ways that infants gather meaning from their environment. Infants' taste buds are functional at birth, and infants prefer sweet tastes. Infants are also born with an acute sense of smell. As soon as 3 days after birth, breastfed infants can discriminate the smell of their own mother from that of other mothers (Cernoch & Porter, 1985).

Infants are also very responsive to touch. Touching and caressing infants stimulates their growth and can improve brain development and cognitive development (Diamond & Amso, 2008). In one study, two groups of premature infants were given the same neonatal care with one exception—half the infants were routinely massaged, and the other half were not. Those receiving the massages gained weight faster, developed faster neurologically, and were therefore able to leave the hospital sooner than those in the control group (Field et al., 1986). Today, it is standard practice to encourage parents of preterm babies to hold them often. Holding and touching infants also fosters their social development.

Infants' perceptual abilities allow them to gather much needed information from the environment—how their caretakers look, sound, and smell, where the food is, and what sounds contribute to language. From these beginnings, infants develop the abilities to know, think, and remember, a process called **cognition**. Perhaps no one has advanced our understanding of children's thinking more than Jean Piaget, whose ideas and research are presented next.

PIAGET'S THEORY OF COGNITIVE DEVELOPMENT

> **You Asked...**
>
> *How does a young mind absorb its environment?* DIERDRA TORRES, STUDENT

Swiss psychologist Jean Piaget (1896–1980) interviewed and observed infants and children, including his own, to discover and describe the changes in thinking that occur in childhood. Piaget gave children certain tasks to perform, observed their problem-solving strategies, and then asked them how they came to their conclusions.

From these observations and interviews, Piaget (1929, 1952) developed a theory about how children acquire their mental abilities. His theory traces the shifts in thinking from infants' reflexes to a teenager's reasoning abilities. He believed that cognition advances in a series of distinct stages, and that how a preschooler thinks differs dramatically from how an elementary school student thinks. Three concepts central to his theory are *schema*, *assimilation*, and *accommodation*.

cognition the ability to know, think, and remember

Piaget observed children's problem-solving strategies to discover and describe the changes in thinking that they experience.

© Bill Anderson/Photo Researchers, Inc.

To Piaget, any mental idea, concept, or thought is a **schema**. We form these schemas based on our experiences of the world. For example, a baby may have a sucking schema, "Is this object suckable?" or a mother schema, "Does this person fit with my cognitive framework of mother?" A preschooler may have the schema "The sun follows me wherever I go." Adults' schemas may be very simple—"A key will start a car"—or more complex, such as individual ideas of justice, morality, or love.

Piaget believed that our brains are biologically programmed to seek understanding of our world. So we form schemas to fit with our perceptions of the world. When we achieve this fit, so that our cognitions correspond with the environment, we have *mental equilibrium*. However, when there is not a fit between our schemas and the world, we experience *mental disequilibrium*, an uncomfortable state that we are motivated to get rid of so our mental harmony can be restored. The processes of assimilation and accommodation explain how we use existing schemas and create new ones to fit our experiences and, therefore, maintain mental equilibrium.

Assimilation is the process by which we apply an existing schema to our understanding of the environment. For example, a young child is traveling in a car with her parents. As they pass an open field, the child sees some cows. The only schema the child has for a four-legged animal is dog. So the child points and says, "Doggies!" The parents may correct the child—"No, those are called cows"—but she may persist in calling them "doggies" because that is her framework for understanding four-legged animals. The child has assimilated her experience of "cow" into her existing schema of "dog." However, many times our existing schemas will not fit our new experiences. At times like these, the process of accommodation takes center stage.

Accommodation is the process we use to change or modify our existing schemas—or even create new ones—to adapt to some change in the environment. For example, suppose the child in the previous example sees a dog and a cow side by side. The differences in the animals cannot be ignored and will create disequilibrium in the child's mental state. In this situation, she may come to call the new animal "cow." Her existing schema for four-legged animals has now been modified. The child will go through the same process when she sees a horse, a cat, or a hippopotamus.

According to Piaget, assimilation and accommodation create shifts in mental thinking that allow the child to progress through four stages of cognition: sensorimotor, preoperational, concrete operations, and formal operations (1952; summarized in ■ YOU REVIEW 9.1). Each stage has characteristics that permit the child to conceptualize the world in a unique fashion.

schema [SKI-muh] a mental idea, concept, or thought

assimilation [uh-sim-uh-LAY-shun] the process by which an existing schema is used to understand something new in the environment

accommodation [uh-com-muh-DAY-shun] the process by which a schema is changed, modified, or created anew in order to understand something new in the environment

Characteristics of Piaget's Stages of Cognitive Development

You Review 9.1

SENSORIMOTOR (BIRTH–2 YRS.)	PREOPERATIONAL (2–6/7 YRS.)	CONCRETE OPERATIONS (6/7 YRS.–11/12 YRS.)	FORMAL OPERATIONS (12 YRS.–ADULT)
Reflexes	Egocentrism	Conservation	Abstract reasoning
Object permanence	Illogical thinking	Logical thinking	
	Centration	Decentration	
	No conservation		

© Bill Anderson/Photo Researchers, Inc.

Sensorimotor Stage During the first cognitive stage, the **sensorimotor stage**, from birth to 2 years, Piaget suggested that infants acquire knowledge through their senses and through their motor abilities—hence the name *sensorimotor*. For example, infants quickly recognize and prefer to look at their mothers' faces. Similarly, infants use their hearing to form schemas of what certain utterances mean, establishing the foundation for language. Taste, touch, and smell are also used to gather information and to form schemas as infants explore objects with their hands, mouth, and feet.

Piaget believed that during this stage infants can only form schemas of objects and actions that are in their immediate perception—in other words, what they currently see, hear, or touch. They learn by doing and by acting on objects. They lack the ability to represent an object when it is not present. For infants, it is truly "out of sight, out of mind," according to Piaget. The baby thinks of his pacifier when it is present by manipulating it with his mouth or hands. An infant can think about her "blankie" only when it is present. If these objects are not present, they no longer exist for the infant. However, as the infant grows and the brain matures, babies begin to have mental representations. One sign of this milestone is object permanence.

Object permanence is the understanding that an object continues to exist even when it is not present. We can see this in infants' behavior when they start to search for hidden objects. For example, Piaget would show a baby an interesting toy and then cover it. Before the age of 6 months, infants would not search for the toy, lacking the understanding that the toy still existed. The infant could not keep a mental representation of the object and its location in mind. However, by 8 months, infants will begin to search for the toy, suggesting the beginnings of object permanence. This ability steadily improves through 24 months, when infants will search long and hard for hidden objects, indicating that they have fully achieved object permanence.

Although Piaget accurately described the process of object permanence in infancy, he may have underestimated infants' abilities. Current research suggests that infants as young as 1 month old (Kaye & Bower, 1994) and infants 3 to 5 months old have a rudimentary understanding of object permanence and that they gradually develop stronger mental representations of objects through experience (Bailargeon & DeVos, 1992; Bremner, Bryant, & Mareschal, 2006; Johnson, Amso, & Slemmer, 2003; Ruffman, Slade, & Redman, 2005; Shinskey & Munakata, 2005; Wang, Baillargeon, & Brueckner, 2004). Moreover, infant abilities that Piaget observed at 18 months of age are now being seen as early as 6 to 8 months of age, depending on the testing method (Hayne & Rovee-Collier, 1995; Mareschal, 2000).

Once infants acquire object permanence, they are on their way to **symbolic thinking**. This is the understanding that an object can be represented with symbols such as gestures or language (Ganea, Shutts, Spelke, & DeLoache, 2007). This ability to use symbols propels the child to the second stage of cognitive development: the preoperational stage.

Preoperational Stage During the **preoperational stage**, from about age 2 to age 6 or 7, preschoolers are actively acquiring and using symbols (DeLoache, 2001). Being able to use symbols opens up a new world to the preschooler. It is the foundation of a child's language development. A word symbolizes or stands for an object that may or may not be present. A child's vocabulary and understanding of language dramatically increase during these years. For example, when a mother asks, "Do you want some juice?" the preoperational child knows what juice is and may even go to the refrigerator to get it. Young children's pretend play also demonstrates their use of symbols, such as a stick to represent a sword or children taking on family roles when they play "house." However, the child's new ability to symbolize objects is still illogical and does not always make sense to adults. For example, a child may believe that a switch turns on ocean waves, or that there are monsters hiding under the bed.

The illogical thinking of preschoolers is due to cognitive limitations that include centration and egocentrism. **Centration** occurs when the child focuses on only one feature or

sensorimotor stage Piaget's first stage of cognitive development, in which infants learn schemas through their senses and motor abilities

object permanence the understanding that an object continues to exist even when it is not present

symbolic thinking the understanding that an object can be represented with a symbol such as bodily gestures or language

preoperational stage Piaget's second stage of cognitive development, characterized by the use of symbols and illogical thought

centration the act of focusing on only one aspect or feature of an object aspect of an object. For instance, a child who sees a man with long hair or an earring may conclude that the man is a woman. She focuses on one feature, the man's hair length, and this man's hair length fits with her schema for females. For preschoolers, if it looks like a duck, it is a duck; they have difficulty distinguishing between appearance and reality. Centration so dominates children's thinking at this stage that they do not realize that something can remain the same if its appearance changes, an ability called **conservation**.

In classic experiments, Piaget tested preschoolers and school-age children's conservation abilities (see photo). Children were shown two equal-sized glasses containing the same amount of liquid. In front of the child, Piaget poured the liquid from one of the glasses into a taller, thinner glass. Children were then asked whether the glasses had equal amounts of liquid or whether one glass had more liquid than the other. Children in the preoperational stage were most likely to reply that the tall, thin glass had more. Centering on the height of the liquid in the glass, it looked as though it had more, so it must have more. For preschoolers at a party, then, adults should be aware that it must *look* as though the children all have the same amount of cake or punch. Otherwise the preschoolers will think they are receiving different amounts—which can create havoc!

Lacking the ability of conservation, young children are likely to believe that the amount of liquid has changed when it is poured into the thinner, taller glass. Centering on the height of the liquid, they believe the taller, thinner glass has more.

An additional limitation to the preschooler's thinking is **egocentrism**, or the belief that everyone else thinks as you do. For example, when one of your authors was playing hide-and-seek with her then 3-year-old son, he hid in his room in the corner. His face was turned into the wall, much like a child who is sent to stand in a corner for misbehaving. On entering the room, your author said, "I see you." Her son replied, "No, you don't." From her son's perspective, he could not see his mother; therefore she could not see him. Preschoolers believe that others see things as they do, and therefore think as they do, a finding that has been repeatedly replicated using a range of different methods (Wellman, Cross, & Watson, 2001).

Although adults may find it frustrating, the illogical thinking of a preschooler lends an almost magical quality to their thought processes. For example, they believe in monsters, bad-dream catchers over their beds to prevent nightmares, the tooth fairy, imaginary friends, and fantasy. However, current research suggests that here, too, Piaget's ideas probably underestimate children's thinking abilities. Egocentrism, centration, and the inability to tell the difference between appearance and reality do not *always* characterize preschoolers' thoughts (Jenkins & Astington, 1996; Siegel & Hodkin, 1982). Rather, these limitations are sometimes present in children's thinking and gradually fade as the child matures and develops more logical thought processes.

ROSE IS ROSE

conservation the understanding that an object retains its original properties even though it may look different

egocentrism [ee-go-SEN-trih-zum] the belief that everyone thinks as you do

Table 9.2 Piaget's Conservation Experiments

Mastery of conservation tasks begins gradually during the concrete operations stage. Children typically master conservation of number by age 6 or 7. Conservation of area may not be grasped until age 8 or 9.

Typical tasks used to measure conservation	Typical age of mastery
Conservation of number Two equivalent rows of objects are shown to the child, who agrees that they have the same number of objects.	6–7
One row is lengthened, and the child is asked whether one row has more objects.	
Conservation of mass The child acknowledges that two clay balls have equal amounts of clay.	7–8
The experimenter changes the shape of one of the balls and asks the child whether they still contain equal amounts of clay.	
Conservation of length The child agrees that two sticks aligned with each other are the same length.	7–8
After moving one of the sticks to the left or right, the experimenter asks the child whether the sticks are of equal length.	
Conservation of area Two identical sheets of cardboard have wooden blocks placed on them in identical positions; the child confirms that the same amount of space is left on each piece of cardboard.	8–9
The experimenter scatters the blocks on one piece of cardboard and again asks the child whether the two pieces of cardboard have the same amount of unoccupied space.	

Concrete Operations Stage During Piaget's third cognitive stage, **concrete operations**, from about age 6 or 7 through age 12, schoolchildren become logical thinkers. They no longer center on one feature or facet of an object as the preschooler did, and their conservation abilities improve (■ TABLE 9.2). Children realize that although the tall, thin glass looks as though it has more liquid, in reality the glasses have equivalent volume. Changes in these abilities force the child to recognize that previous beliefs may be mistaken, so accommodation occurs. It also brings about a reduction in egocentrism as the child can now consider the perspectives of others. This enables empathy, persuasion, and a sense of humor to grow.

Although the concrete operational child thinks more logically, these schemas are limited to actual experience or concrete objects and situations. School-age children have difficulty reasoning abstractly about what may be or what could be without being able to test their ideas in an observable way. This is why hands-on activities and class demonstrations of abstract ideas for school subjects such as geometry and science are necessary in elementary and middle school. Being able to think about situations that are not present occurs in the final stage of Piaget's theory, formal operations.

concrete operations Piaget's third stage of cognitive development, characterized by logical thought

Formal Operations Stage According to Piaget, as children approach their teenage years, they may achieve the final cognitive stage, **formal operations**. They are no longer limited to concrete objects and situations; they can now engage in abstract reasoning. Teenagers can imagine and hypothesize what *may* be. This ability expands their horizons. They are able to understand more abstract, scientific, and mathematical concepts. They can imagine potential careers and envision future consequences for current behavior.

Piaget's theory revolutionized our understanding of children's thinking abilities and stimulated much research in cognition. The changes in thinking that Piaget proposed do not always proceed according to the precise stages and timetable he originally suggested (Haith & Benson, 1998). Children's mental abilities develop at different ages. Nurture, culture, or experience can facilitate growth and change in these abilities. However, Piaget very accurately described the *sequence* in which these changes occur, even in diverse societies (Dasen, 1994; Lourenco & Machado, 1996). One final criticism of Piaget's theory is that it overlooks the important effects of culture on cognitive development. The ideas of Lev Vygotsky explore this connection between culture and cognition.

VYGOTSKY'S THEORY OF COGNITIVE DEVELOPMENT: CULTURE AND THINKING

Lev Vygotsky (1896–1934) was a Russian psychologist whose ideas have influenced how psychologists and educators think about children's cognitive development, providing an alternative to Piaget's theory (John-Steiner & Mahn, 1996). In contrast to Piaget's emphasis on the internal origin of schemas, Vygotsky (1978, 1986) emphasized that mental processes begin externally with our social interactions with others. For example, babies smile at caretakers or toddlers raise their arms to signal that they want to be picked up. A child internalizes these mental processes to create a cognitive framework for understanding the world. Young children often talk to themselves as they play, a behavior Vygotsky called **private speech**. For Vygotsky, private speech represents an internal monitor that guides the child's actions. Private speech, or self-talk, as it is sometimes called, is common among preschoolers, and peaks around 5 to 7 years of age. Around 9 years of age, these spoken words are internalized as silent lip movements. Eventually, children just think the thoughts rather than saying them. However, private speech can return at any age when we are confused or having difficulties in problem solving. Such inner speech cues and guides our thinking. Much research supports Vygotsky's ideas on private speech, even in deaf children using sign language (Berk & Spuhl, 1995; Diaz & Berk, 1992; Kelman, 2001). It makes sense, therefore, to allow and even encourage children to use private speech to talk or sign themselves through a problem.

According to Vygotsky, because cognition is so intimately tied to our social interactions, culture has a profound influence on our mental processing. The language, measurement systems, rituals, beliefs, and technology of a culture both limit and support certain ways of thinking (Tomasello, 2000). For instance, if your language does not have a word to capture an idea or expression, it is difficult to imagine or understand that concept. Similarly, children who have the opportunity to read books, use the Internet, travel, and attend cultural events will be more capable of conceptualizing ideas than children without such tools. According to Vygostsky, cognitive development does not occur in fixed stages as Piaget theorized. Rather,

Vygotsky emphasized the importance of culture and social interactions in his theory of cognitive development.

formal operations Piaget's final stage of cognitive development, characterized by the ability to engage in abstract thought

private speech Vygotsky's term describing when young children talk to themselves to guide their own actions cognitive development may proceed in any number of directions, depending on our culture, social interactions with others, and the environment we live in.

Representing concepts is not achieved simply by having these tools. Conceptual thinking is taught to children by parents, teachers, siblings, coaches, and other important people in their lives. This instruction is most helpful when it is within a child's **zone of proximal development (ZPD)**—the gap between what a child can already do and what he or she is not yet capable of doing without help. Through collaborative interaction, the adult initially guides and supports the child's efforts to master a task. The less able a child is to do a task, the more direction and guidance an adult must give. The adult then gradually minimizes the guidance and support until the child can do it alone, in a process called **scaffolding**. For example, when a child is learning to ride a bicycle, an adult first supports the child on the bicycle and walks or runs alongside as the child pedals. When the child seems ready, less support is given until the child is riding on his or her own. It is through these interactions with others that children internalize strategies, reasoning skills, and problem-solving abilities. For this reason, Vygotsky believed that children's cognitive development benefits most when they interact with people who are more capable or advanced in their thinking than they are.

zone of proximal development (ZPD) according to Vygotsky, the gap between what a child is already able to do and what he or she is not yet capable of doing without help

scaffolding [SKAH-fol-ding] a process in which adults initially offer guidance and support in helping a child to reason, solve a problem, or master a task; as the child becomes more proficient and capable, the adult helps less and less until the child can master it on his or her own

moral reasoning how you decide what is right and what is wrong

Moral Reasoning: How We Think About Right and Wrong

Consider the following situation. Your bank's ATM dispenses $10,000 to you, and there is no way that this error would ever be discovered. You keep the money, but you donate half of it to the soup kitchen in your town. Should you have kept the money? How did you decide what to do? Your answer to this situation would provide clues to psychologists about your level of **moral reasoning**, or how you distinguish right from wrong.

KOHLBERG'S THEORY OF MORAL REASONING

Lawrence Kohlberg (1927–1987) developed moral dilemmas or situations like the one we posed to you, and then asked participants to detail what the main character should do and why. After analyzing data from thousands of participants, Kohlberg created a theory of how people morally reason and the changes in this reasoning that they experience as they develop (Kohlberg, 1969; Kohlberg, Levine, & Hewer, 1983). Kohlberg proposed that our moral reasoning develops in six stages, which he arranged in three levels: preconventional, conventional, and postconventional (■ TABLE 9.3).

At the *preconventional level* of reasoning, children make decisions about right or wrong based on their ability to avoid punishment or to gain rewards. For example, it is wrong to take the money because you may get caught and then punished. It is right to take the money because you can use it and no one will find out about it. Recall that at this age, children are egocentric and have difficulty understanding the

Table 9.3 Kohlberg's Stages of Moral Reasoning

PRECONVENTIONAL LEVEL (MOST CHILDREN)

Stage 1: Obedience and Punishment Orientation. Children obey rules to avoid punishment. "Taking a cookie without asking is wrong because you get a timeout."

Stage 2: Naively Egoistic Orientation. Children view morally right action as that which increases their personal rewards and meets their needs. "You scratch my back, and I'll scratch yours."

CONVENTIONAL LEVEL (MOST ADOLESCENTS AND ADULTS)

Stage 3: Good Boy/Good Girl Orientation. Moral rightness is based on maintaining the approval and/or avoiding the disapproval of others such as family and friends. "I will return the rest of the money so my parents won't be disappointed in me."

Stage 4: Law and Order Orientation. Moral rightness is based on following the rules or laws of the society. Exceptions to the rules are not allowed. "Stealing is wrong because it is against the law."

POSTCONVENTIONAL LEVEL (SOME BUT NOT ALL ADULTS)

Stage 5: Contractual/Legalistic Orientation. Exceptions to rules can now be considered, as the protection of individual rights is emphasized over societal laws. "I confessed to the crime, but I was not read my rights, so the confession does not stand."

Stage 6: Universal Principles Orientation. Individuals develop their own set of universal principles that guide their judgments of right and wrong across all situations and all societies.

nature of rules. Consequently, children are centered on the immediate consequences of their actions.

With the ability to think logically and to understand another person's perspective, children at the *conventional level* of reasoning can now understand rules and expectations that others may have for them. Therefore, their moral reasoning is based on the standards of the group or society. They believe behaviors are right or wrong because they gain the approval or avoid the disapproval of parents, teachers, or peers. You may not take the money because you don't want your parents to be disappointed in you, or you may take the money to gain acceptance from your friends. Children can appreciate society's rules or laws for moral behavior. However, because they lack the ability to reason abstractly, children apply these laws to every situation and every person very rigidly. Exceptions based on circumstances are not considered.

At the *postconventional level* of moral reasoning, people base their judgments of right or wrong on contractual or universal principles of morality. The person can appreciate extenuating circumstances and realizes that external standards handed down from society cannot always be applied to all the situations in the same manner. The person develops internal standards of right and wrong to guide moral behavior. These abstract principles may include the Golden Rule (Do unto others as you would have them do unto you) or values such as respecting the dignity of all persons regardless of race, creed, or culture. You may not take the money because you did not earn it and you may be financially hurting someone else.

Kohlberg's theory has stimulated much research—as well as much criticism and controversy. Kohlberg-like studies in 27 cultures support Kohlberg's stage sequence of moral reasoning. People typically move through these stages in the way that Kohlberg proposed (Damon, 1999; Helwig, 1997; Walker, 1989; Walker & Taylor, 1991). By adulthood, most people have progressed to conventional moral reasoning, but few people move on to post-conventional reasoning, especially the highest stage. Postconventional reasoning treats the individual as the basic source of moral values. Such reasoning may apply more to people from Western cultures. In other parts of the world, moral systems tend to emphasize the group in regulating values (Haidt, 2008; Snarey, 1995). Another area in which Kohlberg's theory has been criticized is that of gender, a controversy initiated by a student of Kohlberg's, Carol Gilligan.

GILLIGAN'S THEORY: GENDER AND MORAL REASONING

Carol Gilligan hypothesized that males and females do not judge right and wrong in the same manner. She believed that Kohlberg's model emphasized the male perspective on moral reasoning more than the female view. In her book *A Different Voice* (1982), Gilligan speculated that males and females focus on different principles for deciding what is right and wrong. Males tend to be more focused on concepts of fairness and justice. Females are more likely to emphasize concern, care, and relations with others in making judgments about right and wrong. Gilligan asserts that women's ethic of care is a different, but not a less valid, basis for moral reasoning.

Research evaluating gender differences in moral reasoning has not strongly supported Gilligan's claims. On hypothetical dilemmas, *both* males and females emphasize themes of justice and caring in their responses (Jadack, Hyde, Moore, & Keller, 1995; Jaffee & Hyde, 2000; Walker, 1995). Thus, moral reasoning may be based on justice or caring independent of gender (Jorgensen, 2006).

Psychosocial Development: Connecting With Others

An intimate connection between nature and nurture also influences a child's social and personality development. Children come into the world with a biological tendency to behave in a certain way. How parents and others respond to these behaviors can influence the child's personality as well as the relationships the child develops with others. We explore these issues as we look at the topics of temperament, attachment, Erik Erikson's theory of psychosocial development, and gender-role development.

TEMPERAMENT: THE INFLUENCE OF BIOLOGY

Babies come into the world showing a general disposition to behave in certain ways in response to their surroundings. These differences are believed to be due more to the child's biological makeup than to his or her environment, especially because the child has not yet been exposed to any environment other than the womb. These differences at birth in behavioral style are referred to as **temperament**. In pioneering research, Stella Chess and Alexander Thomas (Chess & Thomas, 1984; Thomas & Chess, 1977, 1986) gathered information on numerous infant behaviors such as

- General activity level
- General mood
- Ability to establish a regular pattern of eating and sleeping
- Likelihood of approaching or withdrawing from new people and new situations
- Ability to adapt to changes from their normal routine

From observing babies' tendencies on these variables, three temperamental styles of behavior emerged: easy infants, difficult infants, and slow-to-warm-up infants.

As the label implies, *easy infants* are generally in a good mood, establish a regular pattern of eating and sleeping, readily approach new objects and people, and adapt readily to changes in their routines. *Difficult infants*, in contrast, show more intense negative emotions such as crying. They have a more irregular pattern of eating and sleeping and are not as likely to approach new people and situations. Parents may even call such babies "colicky." *Slow-to-warm-up infants* are in between these two extremes. They are not as negative in response as difficult infants, but it takes them some time to adapt to new situations.

A child's temperament and the parents' responses to this temperament influence the parent–child bond called *attachment*.

ATTACHMENT: LEARNING ABOUT RELATIONSHIPS

Attachment, the emotional tie between the infant and the primary caretaker, is usually firmly established by 8 to 9 months. Initially, psychologists believed that feeding provided the basis for building the attachment relationship: the baby feels connected to the primary caretaker because the parent satisfies the infant's hunger. However, animal research by Harry Harlow in the 1950s changed the way we view the attachment process today.

> ### You Asked...
> *How much impact do parents have on their child's development?*
> ANGEL ROSA, STUDENT

In a classic study, Harlow and Zimmerman (1959) wanted to investigate the nature of attachment. They used infant rhesus monkeys as subjects because ethical principles would prohibit such a study with human infants. They designed two artificial monkeys to act as surrogate mothers for the babies. One of the "surrogate mothers" was covered with a soft terry cloth fabric. The other "surrogate mother" was made of wire and had a feeding tube attached. The researchers wanted to see which "surrogate mother" the infants preferred. The infant monkeys went to the wire "surrogate mother" for food, but they clung to and spent most of their time with the cloth-covered "surrogate mother." This showed that feeding was not the reason the monkeys attached; rather, it was the close, warm contact that facilitated this bond. Establishing close, warm contact through holding and caressing facilitates attachment. Human infants can easily attach to multiple people and objects, including fathers, grandparents, siblings, and teddy bears.

Courtesy of Harlow Primate Lab, U. of Wisconsin (both)

Harlow's studies showed that close, warm contact facilitates the attachment bond.

temperament a person's general pattern of attention, arousal, and mood that is evident at birth

attachment the emotional bond between caretaker and infant that is established by 8 or 9 months

The attachment bond is readily seen in specific infant behaviors by the end of the first year. For example, most babies reserve certain behaviors for their parents. The infants smile when the parent approaches them, raise their hands toward the parent to be picked up, and nestle closer when the parent holds them. Two additional signs of attachment include separation anxiety and stranger anxiety. **Separation anxiety** is a fear the infant expresses when separated from the primary caretaker. This normally appears at about 6 or 7 months of age, and peaks at about 14 to 18 months. Separation anxiety gradually becomes less frequent and less intense through the toddler and preschool years. However, it is not uncommon for even older children to become anxious and fearful when separated from their parents for a long period of time (Thurber, 1995). In **stranger anxiety**, the infant becomes distressed when approached by unfamiliar people. Stranger anxiety typically appears between 8 and 10 months of age. It may intensify through the end of the first year, but usually subsides over the second year. Therefore, it is not unusual for a 1- or 2-year-old to cry or cling to a parent when approached by a doctor, an unfamiliar relative, or a new babysitter.

Although most infants will establish an attachment with a caregiver by the end of the first year, the quality of these attachments is not necessarily the same from infant to infant. Mary Ainsworth and her colleagues (Ainsworth, Blehar, Waters, & Wall, 1978) designed a research tool called the *strange situation* procedure to try to measure qualitative differences in infant attachments. In the strange situation, infants and their parents are placed in an unfamiliar playroom. The infant's behavior is observed and measured as certain events occur. For example, does the infant explore the new situation and the toys when left in the playroom with the parent? How does the infant behave when a stranger enters the room? What is the baby's response when the parent leaves the room? What is the infant's reaction when the parent returns?

Observations of infants under these circumstances uncovered several patterns, or styles of attachment. Ainsworth and others (Ainsworth et al., 1978; Hesse & Main, 2006; Main & Solomon, 1990) described four patterns of attachment: secure, avoidant, resistant, and disorganized/disoriented.

- *Secure attachment.* Infants who are securely attached use the parent as a supportive base from which to operate and explore. They explore the toys while in the new situation, paying attention to any new strangers that may enter the room. They may or may not cry when the parent leaves, but this emotional upset quickly subsides once the parent returns.

- *Avoidant attachment.* Infants who show avoidant attachment appear to ignore the parent. They pay the parent little attention. They do not appear to be distressed when the parent leaves, and they show little emotional response when the parent reappears.

- *Resistant attachment.* Infants who display resistant attachment resemble a "clinging" baby. They remain close to the parent and do not actively explore the new situation. They show extreme distress when the parent leaves and appear to be angry when the parent returns. They may hit and push at the parent and are less easily consoled.

- *Disorganized/disoriented attachment.* Infants showing disorganized attachment seem confused or disoriented. They look away from the mother while being held by her and have a blank facial expression after being calmed by her.

Although most children worldwide appear to have secure attachments to their caretakers, we must be cautious in interpreting the "insecure" patterns of attachment. Different child-rearing practices and cultural attitudes influence how we interact with our children, and these interactions as well as the larger social context appear to influence attachment. In some countries, children's independence is encouraged; in other countries, a closeness with the caretaker is emphasized. However, these same styles of attachment have generally emerged when infants are observed in natural, nonexperimental surroundings (Vaughn et al., 1992), suggesting that these styles of attachment are common worldwide.

separation anxiety the fear an infant expresses when separated from the primary caretaker

stranger anxiety the distress an infant expresses when faced with unfamiliar people

Many psychologists endorse the notion that the quality of this first attachment relationship lays the foundation for the quality of all other relationships with friends and lovers. Research supports this reasoning to a certain degree. Securely attached infants are more likely to become curious, resilient, and self-controlled preschoolers. Such children are more likely to persist in problem-solving tasks, do well in school, and interact more skillfully with their peers during the school years (Elicker, Englund, & Sroufe, 1992; Jacobsen & Hofmann, 1997; Kerns, Abraham, Schlegelmilch, & Morgan, 2007; Simpson, Collins, Tran, & Haydon, 2007).

However, being securely attached at an early age does not guarantee an absence of problems later. Moreover, research has not been able to consistently document a negative or unfavorable picture of development for the other attachment patterns. Some studies suggest that insecurely attached infants are more prone to behavioral and adjustment problems in their social relations with others, whereas other studies do not (Fagot & Kavanaugh, 1990; C. E. Hamilton, 2000; Rothbaum, Schneider Rosen, Pott, & Beatty, 1995). Bonds with individuals other than the caretaker can compensate for insecure attachments at home. Moreover, given the number of variables that can influence attachment, an early pattern of insecure attachment does not guarantee a lifelong pattern of insecure relationships. As family circumstances improve, so too may the quality of the attachment. Similarly, social relationships *after* infancy must also be considered when we evaluate children's psychological adjustment.

PARENTING STYLES

Parents' responses to their infants and children also influence the parent–child relationship. Diana Baumrind (1967, 1971) investigated these responses by observing parents' interactions with their children. From her observations, three styles of parenting emerged.

Authoritarian parents tend to exhibit a high level of control and a low level of affection toward their children. They set high expectations for their children but without communicating the reasons behind their expectations. "It's my way or the highway" would be a characteristic attitude of authoritarian parents. The children are not included in discussions of family issues, rules, or roles. They are to do what they are told. If they do not obey, force and physical punishment are used to ensure compliance. Baumrind found that children from authoritarian households tended to be more withdrawn, anxious, and conforming than other children.

Authoritative parents tend to exhibit moderate control and are warm toward their children. Authoritative parents are least likely to spank or hit their children. Rules—and the consequences for violating them—are established in a democratic manner, and children are included in family discussions. Reasonable expectations and demands are made of the children, and the children respond accordingly. Baumrind found that parents who use this style of parenting tended to have competent, happy, and self-confident children. It appears to be the most effective approach to parenting. Although Baumrind's sample was predominantly restricted to European Americans, these benefits of authoritative parenting have also been found to apply to several U.S. ethnic groups including African Americans, Korean Americans, and Hispanic Americans (H. Kim & Chung, 2003; Querido, Warner, & Eyberg, 2002; Steinberg, Lamborn, Dornbusch, & Darling, 1992).

Permissive parents tend to show warmth and affection to their children, but have very little control over them. Discipline is lax. Children make their own decisions even when they may not be capable of doing so. Very few demands are made of the children in terms of rules or chores. Baumrind found that children of permissive parents tended to be the most immature. They were disobedient, lacked impulse control, and were most likely to be rebellious.

Do parents always *cause* children to act a certain way? Certainly not! Recall that these are correlations and causal connections cannot be made from corre-

authoritarian [ah-thor-uh-TARE-ee-an] **parent** a parenting style characterized by high levels of control and low levels of affection

authoritative [ah-thor-uh-TAY-tive] **parent** a parenting style characterized by moderate levels of control and affection

permissive parent a parenting style characterized by moderate levels of affection but low levels of control

Authoritarian parents discipline their children with a high level of control.

© Michael Newman/PhotoEdit

lational data. A parent–child relationship is not a one-way street. Children's temperaments influence the way parents treat them just as much as parents' responses influence the development of their children. Moreover, other variables such as the quality of the parents' relationship or the level of family functioning can influence how parents and children interact (Caldera & Lindsey, 2006; Schoppe-Sullivan, Mangelsdorf, Brown, & Sokolowski, 2007). How a child develops socially and emotionally will depend in part on the *goodness of fit* between the child's temperament and his or her surrounding social relationships, including those with parents (Chess & Thomas, 1984; Kochanska, 1995; Reiss, 2005; Roisman & Fraley, 2006; Stright, Gallagher, & Kelley, 2008).

ERIKSON'S STAGES OF PSYCHOSOCIAL DEVELOPMENT: THE INFLUENCE OF CULTURE

After studying child-rearing practices in several cultures, Erik Erikson (1902–1994) believed that children and adults progress through eight stages, or developmental crises (Erikson, 1963, 1968, 1980). At each stage, the environment and the person's responses to the environment influence the development of either a healthy or an unhealthy personality characteristic. At each stage, the person incorporates a new quality into his or her personality. Resolving earlier stages with healthy outcomes makes it easier to resolve later stages with positive outcomes. An unhealthy resolution of a stage can have potential negative effects throughout life, although damage can sometimes be repaired at later stages. Four of Erikson's eight stages pertain to the childhood years and are discussed here. The other four stages focus on the adolescent and adult years and are discussed later in the chapter. ■YOU REVIEW 9.2 summarizes all eight stages.

According to Erikson, cultures and social environments influence personality development in children and adults by meeting or not meeting basic psychological and emotional needs.

1. *Trust versus mistrust.* This stage occurs during the first year of life, when infants are totally dependent on others in their environment to meet their needs. An infant whose needs are met is more likely to develop trust in others than one whose needs are not met. Developing a sense of trust also fosters the development of a secure attachment.

2. *Autonomy versus shame and doubt.* From 1 to 3 years of age, toddlers struggle with separating from the primary caretaker. They must negotiate an appropriate balance between autonomy, or independence, and dependence. If people in the toddler's environment belittle the child's efforts at independence or encourage dependence by being overly protective, then Erikson believed the child will be more likely to develop shame and doubt.

3. *Initiative versus guilt.* During the preschool years, Erikson believed that children's environments encourage the development of either initiative or guilt. When children develop initiative, they are motivated to take the first step, to start something on their own, and to be ambitious. Preschoolers are actively exploring their environments through trial and error. At the same time, they start to understand that others have expectations for their behavior, and they learn to read people's reactions to their explorations. From these explorations and observations, they begin to develop schemas of what they "ought to do." If these schemas conflict with what others in their environment expect from them, guilt may develop.

Erik Erikson's stages of psychosocial development emphasize how children's personalities grow and develop as they are influenced by those around them.

You Review 9.2

Erikson's Stages of Psychosocial Development

AGE	STAGE	DEVELOPMENTAL CHALLENGE
birth–1 year	Trust versus mistrust	Sense of security
1–3 years	Autonomy versus shame and doubt	Independence
3–6 years	Initiative versus guilt	Trying new things
6–12 years	Industry versus inferiority	Sense of mastery and competence
Adolescence	Identity versus role confusion	Sense of self, personal values and beliefs
Young adulthood	Intimacy versus isolation	Committing to a mutually loving relationship
Middle adulthood	Generativity versus stagnation	Contributing to society through one's work, family, or community services
Late adulthood	Ego integrity versus despair	Viewing one's life as satisfactory and worthwhile

Archives of the History of American Psychology, University of Akron, Akron, Ohio

4. *Industry versus inferiority.* During the elementary school years, children receive a great deal of feedback on their performance. They are in school 6 hours a day, where they receive a steady stream of information on their abilities. Their papers may have stars, red marks, or numbers on them. They may be grouped according to ability. Because children this age can think logically, they can compare their performance on a task with that of their peers. In this way, they form opinions about which activities make them feel industrious, masterful, or competent, as well as ideas about activities or tasks that make them feel inferior or less capable of performing.

According to Erikson, by the time children approach adolescence, their personality has been shaped by the resolution of each of these developmental challenges. How the child resolves these issues has encouraged the development of either a healthy or a not-so-healthy personality.

GENDER-ROLE DEVELOPMENT

By 2 or 3 years old, children know whether they are a boy or a girl and can label the gender of others. These labels then provide a framework for understanding what clothes, toys, colors, jobs, and behaviors are "appropriate" for each sex. Thus, children at a very early age are processing and developing schemas about **gender roles**, or society's expectations for how a female and a male should behave.

Gender permanence or constancy is the knowledge that our assigned gender will not change. Typically, children under the age of 6 years do not yet understand that their gender is permanent (De Lisi & Gallagher, 1991; Szkrybalo & Ruble, 1999). Recall that at this age children center in on only one aspect of a situation or an object. If one of your features or behaviors looks like that of a male, then you are a male. If the feature fits with the child's concept of a female,

gender roles society's expectations for how male and females should behave

gender permanence the understanding that one's gender will not change

Playing dress-up allows young children to explore gender roles.

© Ellen Pastorino

then you are a female. Consequently, if a little boy puts on his mother's dress, he may believe that he is now a girl.

The process by which a child develops gender roles and comes to label specific behaviors and activities as either masculine or feminine is not completely understood. Psychologists currently endorse a perspective that combines elements of social learning theory and cognitive development, called **gender–schema theory**. Gender-schema theory suggests that the social learning processes of modeling and reinforcement work together with a child's developing mental abilities to facilitate the child's understanding of gender (Martin & Halverson, 1981, 1987). From a very early age, children are keen observers of their environment. They see which behaviors men and women engage in, and which of those behaviors are reinforced or punished. With these observations, children actively construct schemas on gender behaviors. These schemas then guide children's decisions about how they and others should behave (Martin & Ruble, 2004).

The schemas for gender-role behavior are culturally defined and vary from society to society. In the United States, males are seen as aggressive, unemotional, and dominant, whereas females are seen as passive and emotional. Yet even within U.S. society, one's ethnic background may convey different gender stereotypes. For example, traditional Hispanic American gender roles stress the faithful, self-giving female who is subordinate to her husband and is seen as the preserver of family and tradition. The male is strong, dominant, and the head of the household who is responsible for the safety and honor of the family (McNeill et al., 2001; Reid & Bing, 2000). Among African Americans, females assume the dominant role in the family. Strong extended family bonds and high levels of adaptability in gender roles are emphasized (Reid & Bing, 2000). Asian Americans value group solidarity. For females, family obligations are expected to be of higher priority than individual achievement, and males are seen as dominant (Pyke & Johnson, 2003).

Psychologists have explored the extent to which gender-role behavior is due to nature and/or nurture, and evidence for both exists. For example, research suggests that many gender differences appear across cultures and in other species, such as the preference to develop same-sex friendships and the higher level of activity and aggressiveness in males (Beatty, 1992). These findings suggest that gender differences may be influenced in part by hormonal or genetic differences between males and females. On the other hand, the child's environment is filled with messages about gender. These messages come from parents, teachers, peers, and the larger society and illustrate the powerful impact of nurture on gender behavior (Bussey & Bandura, 1999).

Moms and dads are the first source of information for babies on gender. An extensive analysis of more than 150 studies on parenting suggest that in many ways, sons and daughters are treated similarly (Lytton & Romney, 1991). Mothers and fathers encourage both sons and daughters to be independent. Parents are equally warm to their children regardless of gender. However, it is in

gender–schema theory the idea that gender roles are acquired through modeling and reinforcement processes that work together with a child's mental abilities

Parents' interactions with their children influence their developing gender schemas.

© Karen Kasmauski/Corbis

© Blend Images/Alamy

the area of gender roles that parents are most likely to respond differently to their daughters and sons. For example, parents hold different expectations for their children depending on their gender. Parents expect their children to play with gender-appropriate toys. Boys play with guns, cars, blocks, and balls. Girls are expected to play with dolls and tea sets and to enjoy activities such as dress-up, house, and school. Parents assign different household chores to their sons and daughters. Girls wash the dishes and do chores inside the house such as vacuuming and dusting. Boys take out the trash and do outdoor chores such as mowing the lawn, washing cars, and cleaning out the garage. Fathers are much more likely to hold to these gender stereotypes and tend to be less accepting of cross-gender behaviors, especially in their sons (Lytton & Romney, 1991).

Parents who are less likely to hold these gender expectations tend to have children who are less gender-typed (Warner & Steel, 1999; Weisner & Wilson-Mitchell, 1990). Moreover, children who *see* their parents behave in a less stereotypical fashion—moms taking out the trash or dads performing household tasks—also tend to be less gender-typed (Turner & Gervai, 1995). Parents, however, are not the only ones who influence children's gender roles. Once children begin school, teachers and peers influence gender schemas as well.

Boys tend to receive both more positive and more negative attention from teachers, and are called on more often (Beal, 1994; Hamilton, Blumenfield, Akoh, & Miura, 1991). Teachers even respond differently to boys' and girls' schoolwork. Girls are praised when their work is orderly and neat. Boys are praised for their problem-solving ability (Sadker & Sadker, 1986). Teachers may also be more likely to accept wrong answers from girls but encourage boys to try harder when they make errors (Horgan, 1995). Even when it comes to career counseling, boys are more likely to be encouraged to enter higher status professions in math and science, such as engineering, whereas girls are encouraged to pursue education, nursing, and social work (Sadker, 2000).

Children's notions about gender are also reinforced within their peer groups, starting as early as 3 years old. Same-sex peers praise the child for engaging in gender-appropriate behaviors. Children who engage in gender-inappropriate behavior may be teased, laughed at, and even isolated from the group. Boys are particularly critical of same-sex peers who engage in "girlish" behavior, resulting in harsher punishment for their activities (Levy, Taylor, & Gelman, 1995.)

© David Young-Wolff/PhotoEdit, Inc.

Society encourages stereotypical gender schema by prescribing what are appropriate "boy" and "girl" toys, as indicated by this obviously girl-oriented display.

Although sexism in general has decreased in the United States over the past 50 years, gender stereotypes have remained relatively stable over the last 25 years (Spence & Buckner, 2000). Society in many ways still contributes to children's gender stereotypes. Fast-food chains offer boy and girl toys with their children's meals. Some toy stores still have aisles marked "Boys" and "Girls." Many television shows still hold to traditional gender stereotypes (Aucoin, 2000). Males appear more frequently and tend to be the dominant characters. Only one-third of all television roles are for women. Male characters are more likely than female characters to engage in active tasks such as climbing or riding a bike. Females are more often depicted as passive, dependent, and emotional. Many of the female characters on television are not employed. When they do have jobs, they are often stereotypical ones such as teachers, nurses, and secretaries (Huston & Wright, 1998; Signorielli & Bacue, 1999). Not surprisingly, children—especially children who watch television frequently—adopt these gender-role stereotypes (Kimball, 1986; Signorielli & Lears, 1992).

Let's Review!

This section dealt with the major physical, cognitive, and psychosocial changes that infants and children undergo as they develop. For a quick review, answer these questions.

1. Which of the following infants is most likely to have the *fewest* neural connections?

   a. A 1-month-old   **c.** A 3-month-old

   b. A 2-month-old   **d.** A 4-month-old

2. Simone sees a military tank on the highway and calls it a "truck." According to Piaget, Simone is engaging in _____.

   a. disequilibrium   **c.** assimilation

   b. private speech   **d.** accommodation

3. Which of the following cognitive abilities *most* characterizes a child in Piaget's preoperational stage of development?

   a. Logical thought   **c.** Object permanence

   b. Conservation   **d.** Egocentrism

4. Kayla, a 4-year-old, shares her toys with June so that June will also share her toys. Kayla is operating at what level of Kohlberg's theory?

   a. Preconventional   **c.** Conventional

   b. Preoperational   **d.** Postconventional

5. In the strange situation procedure, a baby who clings to the mother while she is present and who shows extreme distress when the mother leaves would be exhibiting which style of attachment?

   a. Secure   **c.** Disorganized

   b. Avoidant   **d.** Resistant

6. Jose is a very active toddler who prefers to do things by himself. According to Erikson, Jose appears to be successfully resolving which developmental crisis?

   a. Trust versus mistrust

   b. Autonomy versus shame and doubt

   c. Initiative versus guilt

   d. Industry versus inferiority

7. Which of the following statements about gender-role development is *false*?

   a. At 2 years old, toddlers can label their gender.

   b. At 4 years old, preschoolers have gender permanence.

   c. At 6 years old, children have gender roles.

   d. At 8 years old, children have gender permanence.

Answers 1. a; 2. c; 3. d; 4. a; 5. d; 6. b; 7. b

Stop, LOOK, and LEARN

Prenatal Development

Don W. Fawcett/Photo Researchers, Inc.

Germinal stage
(0–14 days): cell division

Anatomical Travelogue/Photo Researchers, Inc.

Embryonic stage
(2–8 weeks): organs and systems form

Claude Edelmann/Photo Researchers, Inc.

Fetal stage
(week 9–birth): organs and systems more fully develop

Infant & Child Development

Development: The Influence of Nature and Nurture

Brooklyn Photo Group/Getty Images

PHYSICAL

- Brain growth
- **Reflexes**
- **Gross** and **fine motor skills**

COGNITION

- Piaget
  - **Sensorimotor stage** (object permanence)
  - **Preoperational stage** (symbolic thought; egocentrism)
  - **Concrete operations** (logical thought; conservation)
  - **Formal operations** (abstract thought)
- Vygotsky: stressed importance of culture and social interactions

MORAL REASONING

- Kohlberg
  - Preconventional (punishment & rewards)
  - Conventional (standards of group)
  - Postconventional (individual principles)

PSYCHOSOCIAL

- **Temperament** (easy, difficult, or slow-to-warm-up)
- **Attachment** (secure, resistant, avoidant, disorganized)
- Parenting style (**authoritarian**, **authoritative**, or **permissive**)

- Erikson's stages:
  - Trust vs. mistrust
  - Autonomy vs. shame and doubt
  - Initiative vs. guilt
  - Industry vs. inferiority
- Understanding **gender roles** (**gender-schema theory**)

Adolescence and Adulthood

- Describe the physical changes that occur in adolescence and adulthood.
- Describe cognitive changes in adolescence and adulthood.
- Detail Erikson's psychological transitions in adolescence and adulthood.

- Describe the varieties of social relations in adolescence and adulthood.
- Describe the new roles and responsibilities of being a parent.
- Explain the predictable changes people experience in career development.

Development is not limited to the childhood years; changes continue during the adult years, too. In adulthood, however, these changes are much more variable than in childhood. For some people, adulthood may be marked by abrupt changes due to divorce, illness, or death. Others may coast through adulthood experiencing few such disruptions. Here we describe the physical, cognitive, and psychosocial changes that characterize adolescence and adulthood. As in childhood, both nature and nurture influence our development.

Physical Changes: Maturation and Aging

During adolescence and adulthood we both peak and decline in terms of our physical development. How much and how rapidly we decline are very much influenced by both nature and nurture. Genes affect how we age, but so do the degree to which we exercise mind and body and the experiences we have as we age. What we think of as aging is an incremental and gradual process, but growing into our sexual maturation can be abrupt and actually quite dramatic. We are referring, of course, to the onset of puberty.

PUBERTY: BIG CHANGES, RAPID GROWTH

Puberty is the process of sexual maturation. These developmental changes involve overall body growth and maturation of sex characteristics that enable people to sexually reproduce.

> **You Asked...**
>
> *What kinds of changes occur to the sexuality of an adolescent?*
>
> RICHARD NIEVES, STUDENT

Puberty generally occurs 2 years earlier in girls than in boys, with an average onset at age 10 in females and age 12 for males, but the timing of puberty varies greatly from one person to another and from one culture to another (Rice, 1992). Over the past 100 years, the age at which puberty begins has dropped in the United States, Western Europe, and Japan. Even within the United States, African American girls tend to enter puberty a year earlier, on average, than European American girls (Kaplowitz et al., 1999).

A growth spurt shortly after age 10 for girls and after age 12 for boys adds almost 10 inches in height and about 40 pounds in weight to the average adolescent's body. Girls' hips broaden relative to their shoulders, and boys' shoulders widen relative to their hips. Both sexes gain muscle and fat during puberty; however, girls gain more fat and boys gain more muscle. Because these changes are abrupt and uneven at times, early adolescence is regarded as an especially awkward phase of development (Malina, 1990).

In addition to overall growth, puberty also includes internal and external signs of sexual maturity, caused by the release of sex hormones. In girls, sex hormones cause the breasts, ovaries, uterus, and vagina to mature, and initiate the start of their first menstrual cycle, or **menarche**. Pubic hair and underarm hair also develop. In boys, sex hormones cause the

puberty [PEW-bur-tee] the process of sexual maturation

menarche [MEN-ar-kee] a girl's first menstruation

Greg Ceo/Getty Images

penis, scrotum, and testes to mature. These changes are accompanied by the growth of body hair and a deepening of the voice as the larynx enlarges. On average, males and females complete the process of puberty within 4 to 5 years (Wheeler, 1991). ■ FIGURE 9.3 summarizes the physical changes that boys and girls experience during puberty.

Puberty has a definite emotional and psychological impact, particularly on the adolescent's self-image and mood. Typically, adolescents' reactions to these physical changes are mixed, but if they are prepared for the upcoming changes and have a supportive family, psychological adjustment to puberty is better (Koff & Rierdan, 1995; Moore, 1995; Stein & Reiser, 1994). Many adults attribute teenagers' moodiness to "raging hormones." Yet the link between higher hormone levels and moodiness is not strong (Nottelmann, Inoff-Germain, Susman, & Chrousos, 1990). Mood swings are very much influenced by adolescents' changing social environments as they frequently move from one activity to another.

The timing of puberty also has a psychological impact on the self-image of an adolescent, one that differs for boys and girls. For boys who mature early, the growth in stature and muscle brings with it a better self-image than for boys who mature later. In contrast, early-maturing females experience more adjustment difficulties and are more likely to smoke and drink alcohol during adolescence than those who mature later (Alsaker, 1995; Bratberg, Nilsen, Holmen, & Vatten, 2005; Ge, Conger, & Elder, 1996; Graber, Seeley, Brooks-Gunn, & Lewinsohn, 2004). Girls whose breasts develop early may find the attention they receive hard to cope with and fraught with pressures to become sexually active when they may not be ready cognitively and emo-

FIGURE

9.3

Physical Changes in Adolescent Males and Females During Puberty

Hormonal changes during puberty cause the development of sexual characteristics. These include physical changes to the organs directly involved in reproduction.

The physical changes of puberty and the cognitive ability to think abstractly often make teenagers self-conscious about their appearance.

tionally to do so. Girls who develop later are better adjusted to these changes because the pressure to become sexually active occurs at an older age, when their cognitive abilities are better able to handle such pressures. However, long-term studies suggest that the effects of early versus late maturation in puberty may be short-lived. In addition, some studies suggest a benefit to the turmoil caused by puberty. Many early-maturing females and late-maturing males who experienced difficulties during their teenage years exhibited more effective coping skills in adulthood (Livson & Peskin, 1980).

BRAIN CHANGES IN ADOLESCENCE AND ADULTHOOD

Medical technology such as magnetic resonance imaging (MRI and fMRI; see Chapter 2, p. 65) has allowed researchers to examine teenage brains. These studies indicate dynamic changes in brain anatomy throughout adolescence and into early adulthood (Ashtari et al., 2007; Galvan, Hare, Voss, Glover, & Casey, 2007). These changes appear to start at the back of the brain and move toward the front, as you can see in ■ FIGURE 9.4. The number of neurons and the complexity of their connections increase in the cerebellum. Recall that the cerebellum is necessary for balance, muscle tone, and performance of motor skills (p. 54). The amygdala is more active in teens than in adults, and is larger in males (Baird et al., 1999; Durston et al., 2001). As we saw in Chapter 2, the amygdala regulates our emotional reactions. Nerve fibers in the corpus callosum—the band of nerves that connects the two cerebral hemispheres—also thicken before and during puberty (Thompson et al., 2000).

> **You Asked...**
>
> *When is the brain fully developed or mature?*   LESLEY MANZANO, STUDENT

Just prior to puberty there appears to be a second wave of overproduction of cortical gray matter—the tissue that covers the outside of the cerebral hemispheres that appears gray because of the absence of myelin on the axons (Durston et al., 2001; Giedd et al., 1999; Sowell, Thompson, Tessner, & Toga, 2001). The brain then prunes these connections as it did

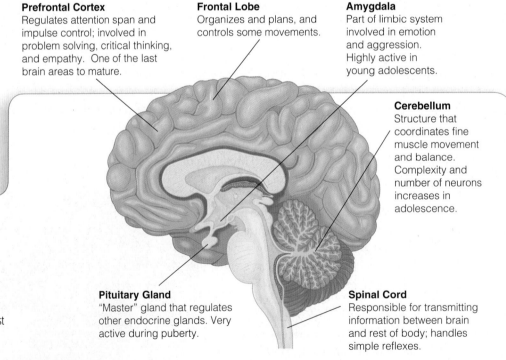

Prefrontal Cortex
Regulates attention span and impulse control; involved in problem solving, critical thinking, and empathy. One of the last brain areas to mature.

Frontal Lobe
Organizes and plans, and controls some movements.

Amygdala
Part of limbic system involved in emotion and aggression. Highly active in young adolescents.

Cerebellum
Structure that coordinates fine muscle movement and balance. Complexity and number of neurons increases in adolescence.

Pituitary Gland
"Master" gland that regulates other endocrine glands. Very active during puberty.

Spinal Cord
Responsible for transmitting information between brain and rest of body; handles simple reflexes.

FIGURE
9.4   **Changes in the Adolescent Brain**

Changes in the adolescent brain generally start at the back of the brain and move toward the front. Hence the areas of the brain that are most involved in problem solving, planning, and critical thinking are the last areas to mature.

earlier in life—keeping the connections that are used while those that are not used wither away (see ■ FIGURE 9.5). This gray matter growth spurt predominates in the prefrontal cortex—the area that plays a major role in cognitive processes such as problem solving, judgment, reasoning, impulse control, and the planning and execution of behavior. This is among the latest brain areas to mature, not reaching adult dimensions until the early 20s (Casey, Giedd, & Thomas, 2000; Giedd, 2004).

Is the brain completely developed at adolescence? No. Under normal conditions, stem cells in some regions of the brain continuously generate neurons throughout life (Schmidt-Hieber, Jonas, & Bischofberger, 2004). The brain remains highly plastic—able to adapt in response to new experiences such as new jobs, marriage, divorce, children, new friends, and financial responsibilities.

Nerve Proliferation...
By age 11 for girls and 12 for boys, the neurons in the front of the brain have formed thousands of new connections. Over the next few years most of these links will be pruned.

...and Pruning
Those that are used and reinforced—the pathways involved in language, for example—will be strengthened, while the ones that aren't used will die out.

FIGURE

9.5 Neural Growth and Pruning

During early adolescence, new neural connections are formed. In a process called pruning, those that are used are strengthened, whereas those that are not wither away. Hence engaging in stimulating and interesting activities during adolescence is good for our brains.

From TIME, 5/10/2004. Reprinted with permission.

Neuroscience Applies to Your World:

Are Teenagers Responsible for Their Criminal Behavior?

Research on the adolescent brain has had an impact on our legal system. In some court cases, lawyers have argued that the immaturity of the prefrontal cortex may explain why teenagers' judgment and reasoning may not always be sound. Although structural changes in the brain correlate with teenage behavior, that does not mean they cause the behavior. Brain data do not take into account other aspects of development, such as cognitive abilities and the psychosocial challenge of forming an identity. Moreover, adolescent behavior is also influenced by environmental and cultural factors, such as parenting, peer pressure, the influence of the media, and other factors that contribute to brain processing. Adolescents all over the world experience roughly the same process of brain development, yet teenagers in different cultures and environments do not all behave the same way. Attributing a teenager's criminal behavior solely to brain changes ignores the complex interaction of nature and nurture in development.

PHYSICAL CHANGES FROM EARLY TO LATER ADULTHOOD

We hit our biological prime during early adulthood when all major biological systems reach full maturation. Both women and men peak during their late 20s and early 30s in terms of physical strength, stamina, coordination, dexterity, and endurance (Whitbourne, 1996). These abilities gradually decline in middle and late adulthood.

A similar process occurs in our sensory abilities. Visual acuity, or the ability to focus vision, peaks in our early 20s and remains fairly high until middle adulthood. As we age, we lose the ability to focus on close objects (*presbyopia*), so that reading glasses or bifocals may become necessary in middle or late adulthood. Age-related hearing loss is also not uncommon among older adults, especially for high-pitched tones such as a distant telephone or a doorbell. However, people's senses of taste, smell, and touch remain fairly stable until late adulthood.

We see additional signs of the aging process in people's physical appearance as they approach their 40s and 50s. The skin starts to show wrinkles, and the hair may thin and turn gray. Weight gain is likely as metabolism slows, causing noticeable "love handles" or a "pot belly." Then, as people approach their 60s, they typically begin to lose weight and muscle, which may result in a sagging of the skin (Haber, 1994). The compression of vertebrae combined with a loss of bone tissue result in a loss of height as people age.

Although many physical abilities decline over the adult years, it is not clear that these declines are inevitable. As we discuss in more detail in Chapter 11, lifestyle factors such as poor diet, smoking, drinking alcohol, and lack of exercise contribute to the decline in physical functioning for some people. Moreover, culture markedly influences the way we think about aging and our expectations of our physical abilities in middle and later adulthood. In Western cultures such as the United States, becoming old is associated with being frail, useless, and ill, so that many people attempt to push back the aging process. Yet in countries such as Brazil, China, Japan, and Russia, where older people are more valued, aging is viewed more positively and is perceived as a time to look forward to rather than to dread (Gardiner, Mutter, & Kosmitzki, 1998). People with positive perceptions of aging engage in more preventive health behaviors, such as exercising, and tend to live longer (Levy & Myers, 2004; Levy, Slade, Kunkel, & Kasl, 2002). Across the world, many older people, despite changes in physical functioning, still lead active lifestyles (Baltes, 1997). As people age, they can usually continue their daily activities by making some adjustments and allowing themselves more time.

GENDER AND REPRODUCTIVE CAPACITY

Our reproductive capacity also changes during the adulthood years. Women's fertility steadily decreases from age 15 to age 50 (McFalls, 1990; Rowe, 2006). Sometime around age 50, on average, women undergo changes associated with the process of **menopause**. Menopause signals the end of a woman's childbearing years. Her body produces less and less estrogen, affecting the number of eggs that are released from the ovaries. Eventually ovulation and menstruation stop altogether. Decreasing levels of estrogen also cause the breasts and the uterus to shrink. The vaginal walls produce less lubrication, which may make sexual intercourse somewhat painful.

Although men do not experience a "male menopause," they too undergo hormonal changes after age 60, termed *andropause* (Finch, 2001; Whitbourne, 2001). They gradually produce fewer male hormones as they age, which lowers the concentration of sperm in the semen and results in hair loss on the legs and face. However, men are still capable of producing offspring into their 70s, 80s, and 90s.

Despite these reproductive changes, most older adults remain sexually active. For example, in one national survey of U.S. adults between the ages of 57 and 85, 73% of 57- to 64-year olds reported regular sexual activity, more than half of the 65- to 74-year-olds reported regular sexual activity, and 26% of the 75- to 85-year olds reported regular sexual activity (Lindau et al., 2007).

menopause the period when a female stops menstruating and is no longer fertile

Because many cultures equate "looking old" with being unattractive, especially for women, middle age and later life may not seem very appealing. However, despite the effects of aging, almost 70% of people over 65 report being in good to excellent health (Hobbs, 1996). Although older adults may not be pleased with certain aspects of physical aging, they are no less content with their lives. Happiness and contentment perhaps have more to do with people's ability to adjust to these changes than with the changes themselves.

Cognitive Changes in Reasoning and Mental Abilities

One important ingredient of adapting to change is how an adolescent or adult thinks and processes information. This section examines these changes in cognition. As we saw earlier in this chapter, children think and reason in ways that are qualitatively different from the thinking of adolescents and adults. Similarly, teenagers do not necessarily think like adults, but they are beginning to practice the reasoning skills and the ability to think outside themselves that characterize later cognitive development.

FORMAL OPERATIONS REVISITED

Recall that Piaget (1952) proposed that teenagers begin to think abstractly during the formal operations stage. This ability to reason abstractly allows them to imagine what could be and to hypothesize about future events and future outcomes. As a result, adolescents experience what they believe are—and often are—tremendous insights into how things could be rather than how they are. This phenomenon is often labeled the idealism of youth (Elkind, 1984, 1998). Adolescents believe that they have the answers to problems such as world hunger or conflicts. This mental ability also helps adolescents in discovering who they are as individuals—a topic that will be detailed later in this chapter.

Formal operational thinking also allows teenagers to tackle more challenging academic subjects (science, geometry, calculus) that rely on abstract visualization and reasoning powers. It also enables adolescents to argue more effectively, a power that may not be seen positively by their parents! They are more capable of suggesting hypothetical scenarios ("What if . . .") to justify their position, making them more effective debaters (Elkind, 1984, 1998). However, along with this ability to think abstractly comes the return of *egocentrism*.

Egocentrism in adolescence involves teenagers' imagining what others must be thinking. However, teens believe that other people are concerned with the same things they are. Because adolescents' ideas focus mainly on themselves, they believe that others are equally concerned about them (Elkind & Bowen, 1979). For example, a teen with a pimple on his face may imagine that his peers and teachers are thinking only about the pimple on his face. Teenagers may not ask or answer questions in class because they are so sure that everyone is talking about them and thinking about them. They are newly and acutely aware of their own being. Because teens believe that others are focused on them, they behave as if they are on stage—playing to an audience—a phenomenon referred to as the **imaginary audience** (Elkind, 1984, 1998). They may laugh especially loudly or behave dramatically because of their belief that they are being constantly watched. Although the

imaginary audience the belief held by adolescents that everyone is watching what they do

The ability to think abstractly allows teenagers to successfully tackle complex academic topics.

BLONDIE

imaginary audience and egocentrism are most associated with the teenage years, they may still be somewhat present later in life as young adults choose clothing, jobs, or interests to impress an audience that is largely imaginary (Frankenberger, 2000).

Another feature of adolescents' thought that relates to egocentrism is the **personal fable** (Elkind, 1984, 1998). Teenagers develop the "personal fable" that they are special and unique, that their thoughts and feelings cannot be adequately understood by others (Elkind, 1994). Reflect back on your first love. When that relationship broke up, you may have felt as if no one in the world could identify with what you were feeling. You may have hated hearing your peers and parents try to cheer you up with phrases such as "There are other fish in the sea" or "This too shall pass." You thought they were insensitive, or at least totally useless and beside the point. How could they understand what you were going through? The story you tell yourself is that this person, who is the only person in the world for you, has now gone away, and your life will never be happy again. This is one personal fable of adolescence.

Personal fables may contribute to adolescent risk taking. Because teenagers feel that they are special and unique, they often feel that their own risks are less than those of their peers. For example, they may engage in unprotected sexual intercourse, believing that they won't be the ones to contract a sexually transmitted disease or conceive a child. They may experiment with drugs, believing that they will not become addicted. In their minds, addiction happens to other people. However, recent research suggests that this *optimistic bias* is no more prevalent in adolescents than it is in adults (Reyna & Farley, 2006). Moreover, research by Vartanian (2000, 2001) suggests that both the imaginary audience and the personal fable are biased views of adolescent social cognition that have not been empirically validated.

Although formal operational thinking is often perceived as the hallmark of adolescent thinking, this does not mean that *all* adolescents think abstractly in this way. Cross-cultural research (Hollos & Richards, 1993; Rogoff & Chavajay, 1995) suggests that the development of formal operational thinking is very much influenced by experience and culture. If abstract thought is necessary to "get by" in one's society or for a particular task, then humans may learn it. This thinking is more likely to be found in youths who are formally educated and in societies with more specialized and technical occupations (Flieller, 1999). In addition to Piaget's stage of formal operations, research has documented that adolescents think in other ways that are qualitatively different from adults. One such discovery is from research studies on postformal thought.

POSTFORMAL THOUGHT

When adolescents and adults are asked to solve complex social problems like homelessness, abortion, or poverty, differences emerge in their thinking. Adolescents often reason in terms of black or white, right or wrong, good or bad—what is called **dualistic thinking** (Perry, 1981). They tend to believe that there is only one solution. However, as people enter adulthood, they are more capable of **relativistic thinking**, the idea that in many situations there is not necessarily one right or wrong answer. As adults we become aware that sometimes solutions and answers are relative to the situation or to the people in the situation.

personal fable the belief held by adolescents that they are unique and special

dualistic [do-uhl-LIS-tik] **thinking** reasoning that divides situations and issues into right and wrong categories

relativistic [rell-uh-tah-VIS-tik] **thinking** the idea that in many situations there is not necessarily one right or wrong answer

Numerous research investigations support the notion that relativistic thinking represents a qualitative change beyond formal operations (King & Kitchener, 1994; Sinnott, 1998). In this context, it has been termed **postformal thought**. It is characterized by the appreciation that a correct solution or answer may vary from situation to situation and that there may be multiple solutions, each equally viable, to a given problem.

CHANGES IN MENTAL ABILITIES

The most comprehensive research to date, undertaken by Schaie (1983, 1994, 1996; Schaie & Willis, 2000), reveals that patterns of aging differ for different mental abilities. Recall from Chapter 7 that there are two broad categories of skills called *fluid intelligence* and *crystallized intelligence*.

Fluid intelligence, which develops during early childhood, relies heavily on processing skills such as reaction time, attention, and working memory. It is presumed to be based primarily on nature or biology, peaking when brain maturity has been reached (Li et al., 2004). Within the category of fluid intelligence, some mental abilities remain stronger than others. For example, perceptual speed and numeric ability tend to decline in one's late 20s and early 30s. Yet fluid skills such as spatial orientation and inductive reasoning remain strong and steady through one's 50s, declining after that (Salthouse, 2004). **Crystallized intelligence**, in contrast, involves the use of knowledge, expertise, and good judgment. Crystallized intelligence depends more on nurture or experience, such as educational background and occupational expertise. These abilities increase into adulthood and then decline somewhat after one's mid-60s (Li et al., 2004; Salthouse, 2004; van Hooren et al., 2007; Willis & Schaie, 1999). Crystallized skills include vocabulary, verbal memory, and responses to social situations. These age-related trends in mental abilities are summarized in ■ FIGURE 9.6.

postformal thought the idea that a correct solution (or solutions) may vary, depending on the circumstances

fluid intelligence abilities that rely on information-processing skills such as reaction time, attention, and working memory

crystallized intelligence abilities that rely on knowledge, expertise, and judgment

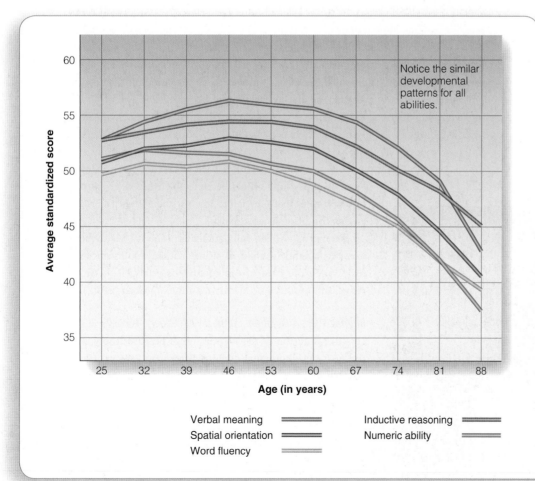

FIGURE

9.6 Age Trends in Mental Abilities

In his ongoing study of mental abilities, Schaie (1983, 1994, 1996) has documented that most mental abilities remain strong through early and middle adulthood. Eighty percent showed no declines by age 60, and almost two-thirds were still stable through age 80.

From "The Course of Adult Intellectual Development," by K. W. Schaie, 1994, American Psychologists, *49, 304–313. Copyright © by the American Psychological Association. Reprinted by permission of the author.*

Many factors other than age shape how well we function mentally. Poor health, diseases, and prescription medications contribute to a rapid decline in mental abilities. Older adults can benefit cognitively from regular physical exercise (Colcombe & Kramer, 2003). A mentally inactive lifestyle is also a potential factor in cognitive decline and Alzheimer's disease (Schaie, 1996; Wilson & Bennett, 2003). The motto "Use it or lose it!" seems most appropriate in this context. Doing crossword puzzles, watching *Jeopardy*, and continuing to read, travel, or participate in educational pursuits are all activities that help sustain cognitive functioning (Stine-Morrow, Parisi, Morrow, Greene, & Park, 2007).

Psychosocial Transitions: Personality, Relationships, and Parenting

How people's individuality and character develop and change in adolescence and adulthood, and how people navigate their social environment are challenging research areas in contemporary psychology. Erik Erikson sees adolescence and adulthood as a process of building, modifying, and sustaining a personal identity.

ERIKSON'S PSYCHOSOCIAL STAGES OF ADOLESCENCE AND ADULTHOOD

Recall Erikson's psychosocial stages of development (You Review 9.2, p. 335) in which children, adolescents, and adults face developmental events that establish their individuality. Successfully mastering each stage strengthens the person's capacity to confront and negotiate the next stages. Here we examine the four stages Erikson attributed to the adolescent and adult years.

Identity Versus Role Confusion: Know Who You Are   For Erikson (1956, 1958, 1959), adolescence represents the integration and summation of the previous crises of childhood into an appropriate identity. It is a time when teenagers must figure out who they are and what they believe in, what their values are, and how they may be similar to or different from peers and parents. This search for personal identity is thought to be very much influenced by both the biological changes of puberty and the newly acquired cognitive ability of abstract reasoning. Teenagers begin to imagine what they want to be and experiment with new roles and responsibilities as they figure out their personal identity. For example, teenagers may try out different styles of clothing or listen to many types of music. They may join different peer groups or try out different college courses to explore various career options. Sometimes adolescents and young adults become so involved in constantly trying out new roles that they fail to form a stable identity. Erikson referred to this condition as *role confusion*.

Even when a teen fully attains an identity, his or her identity is not permanently etched in stone. Rather, adolescence represents a time when the core of our identity is established. We continue to refine and modify our identity as adults (Marcia, 2002).

Intimacy Versus Isolation: Connect With Others   In Erikson's model, successful resolution of the identity crisis prepares the young adult for the next developmental crisis: *intimacy versus isolation*. Having formed a stable identity, the person is now prepared to make a permanent commitment to a partner. Intimacy requires that people refine and modify their identity to accommodate the values and interests of another. In successfully meeting this challenge, neither partner's identity would be sacrificed. For Erikson, *intimacy* is characterized by cooperation, tolerance, and an acceptance of others' different views

Participating in career fairs allows students to explore identity options.

© Kim Kulish/Corbis

and values. This secure sense of intimacy may be expressed through marriage or long-term romantic partnerships, close friendships, or through work relationships. Some people may lose their sense of identity—or fear losing it—and therefore be reluctant to connect with others. Erikson referred to this state as *isolation*. Isolated individuals are easily threatened by close relations with others and hesitate to establish close ties. They are more defensive in the relationships they do form, and they have less tolerance for the varying views and opinions of others.

Generativity Versus Stagnation: Make the World a Better Place According to Erikson, resolving the intimacy versus isolation stage prepares adults for the developmental crisis of the middle adulthood years: *generativity versus stagnation*. This stage of development has to do with our feeling that we have made significant and meaningful contributions to our society. Middle adulthood is often the time when people become aware of their mortality. They recognize that their time here on earth is limited. As a result, they then begin to think about their accomplishments and effect on society. Erikson believed that if a middle-aged adult feels that he or she has contributed something worthwhile to society, then a sense of *generativity* has been achieved. Marriage, child rearing, career accomplishments, and service to the community may all contribute to this sense of having lived a productive life (Westermeyer, 2004). On the other hand, middle-aged adults who conclude that they have contributed very little to improve society will experience *stagnation*, a sense of failure, and an absence of meaningful purpose in life.

People cope with feelings of stagnation in a variety of ways. Some remain disenchanted and bitter. Others attempt to change their lives to regain a sense of generativity and identity. Society often perceives such attempts as a *midlife crisis*. Yet, the number of people who actually experience such dramatic shifts in their life structure is actually quite small (Wrightsman, 1988, 1994). For example, in a 12-year study of people over age 40, Sadler (2000) found that a significant number of middle-aged adults are productive, enjoy their close relationships, and have begun to take risks. They experience what Sadler calls a "second growth" in midlife, characterized by enjoyment of life.

Integrity Versus Despair: No Regrets At the end of the life span, adults begin to review their lives and judge their satisfaction with the choices they have made and the direction that their lives have taken. Erikson believed that the issue facing people in their 60s and beyond was one of *integrity versus despair*. When this evaluation is generally positive and satisfying, individuals have achieved a sense of *integrity*, which allows them to face their eventual death without fear or regret. However, if this life review results in dissatisfaction and a sense of regret over roads not taken, the person is more likely to experience *despair* or hopelessness stemming from the knowledge that one cannot relive one's life. In such a case, the person may become fearful of death.

SOCIAL RELATIONS IN ADOLESCENCE AND ADULTHOOD

In many cultures there are prescribed social roles that determine whom one can date, when one can date, and under what conditions intimate relationships may occur. In Western cultures, today's adolescents and adults express intimacy in relationships in a wide range of lifestyles, including dating, marriage, cohabitation, divorce, and parenthood.

Dating and Singlehood On average, American boys and girls begin to date at age 15 (Zimmer-Gembeck, 2002). However, this is not true for all cultural subgroups. Asian American and Hispanic American teenagers, especially females, tend to begin dating at a later age (Raffaelli, 2005; Xiaohe & Whyte, 1990). Dating serves several functions for teenagers. Besides being an outlet for fun and recreation, dating gives teenagers a chance to learn how to cooperate and

© John Henley/Corbis

For older adults, reminiscing about their experiences provides a sense of integrity and life satisfaction.

compromise with people in a variety of situations (Lambeth & Hallett, 2002). For example, choosing a movie or a restaurant entails listening to the other person's wishes and then resolving any differences. Teens can discover more about themselves and how others' needs may differ from their own. Sexual experimentation may also be involved (Sanderson & Cantor, 1995; Smetana, Campione-Barr, & Metzger, 2006; Zani, 1993). Dating and romantic relationships during adolescence pave the way for establishing adult intimate relationships.

It is typical to start one's adulthood as unmarried—and the number of young single adults is growing. In 2006, about 55% of 20- to 34-year-olds and 19% of 35- to 44-year-olds had never married (U.S. Census Bureau, 2006a). Among African American women, 35% remain unmarried into their late 30s, compared to 14% of Hispanic, 12% of Asian, and 13% of European American women (Teachman, Tedrow, & Crowder, 2000; U.S. Census Bureau, 2006a). Worldwide, young adults are delaying marriage (■ FIGURE 9.7). In the United States, the average age for first marriages is 27.5 for men and 25.9 for women; in 1980, it was 24.7 for men and 22 years for women (U.S. Census Bureau, 2006a). Being single allows young adults a chance to explore different types of friendships and relationships as well as to continue refining and defining their identities. Young single adults also may be moving or traveling as part of building careers, which can make it harder to start or maintain a relationship.

Dating gives teenagers a chance to learn how to cooperate and compromise with people in a variety of situations.

Nancy Ney/Getty Images

Cohabitation Some adults choose to live together, or *cohabit*, with an intimate partner with whom they enjoy a sexual relationship. Cohabitation rates have been increasing steadily over the past 20 years in the United States (U.S. Census Bureau, 2000). Currently, unmarried partner households in the U.S. number 5.5 million, of which 4.9 million are heterosexual partnerships. Yet these unions tend to be short-lived. About half of cohabiting couples either get married or break up within a year (Bumpass & Lu, 2000; Lichter, Qian, & Mellott, 2006). The increased rate of cohabiting couples is not unique to the United States—an even higher level exists in many other countries, such as Sweden and Denmark (Seltzer, 2001). However, cohabitation is rarer in more traditional societies. It is frowned on in Asian societies and severely discouraged in Islamic societies.

Couples cohabit for various reasons. Many gay and lesbian couples cohabit because their states' laws do not recognize civil unions or marriages. Heterosexual couples may feel that cohabiting before marriage gives them the opportunity to see whether they are truly compatible before undertaking the serious commitment of marriage. Some couples cohabit after divorce as an alternative to remarriage (Brown, Lee, & Bulanda, 2006; Coleman, Ganong, & Fine, 2000).

World Marriage Patterns by Region

Average Age at First Marriage

Region	Women	Men
Africa	22.0	26.9
Northern America	25.9	29.7
Southern America	23.9	26.8
Asia	23.3	26.6
Europe	26.1	29.0
Oceania	25.5	28.3

■ Women ■ Men

FIGURE

9.7

World Trends in Age at First Marriage for Men and Women

Worldwide, the average age when men and women first marry is rising, resulting in a larger number of singles in young adulthood.

(Source: United Nations, 2003)

Marriage: Adaptation, Satisfaction, and Gender Differences More than 95% of Americans choose to get married at some point in their lives (U.S. Census Bureau, 2000). Survey research indicates that married couples in the United States are as happy today as they were 20 years ago (Amato, Johnson, Booth, & Rogers, 2003). Yet 60% of marriages worldwide are arranged (Mackay, 2000). In Japan, 25% to 30% of marriages are still arranged (Applbaum, 1995). Parents, relatives, and friends choose marriage partners based on their finances, family values, social status, and perceived compatibility with the potential bride or groom (Batabyal, 2001).

Marriage, like any other lifestyle choice, involves adaptation. A new role as husband or wife has been added, and people must adjust to living as a couple rather than as an individual. Researchers have found that many aspects of the marital relationship change after the first year. The "I love you's" become less frequent, sexual activity becomes less frequent, and couples spend more time performing daily chores and tasks together rather than talking and having fun (Huston & Vangelisti, 1991). Despite these changes, many couples continue to report satisfaction in their marital relationships.

Research has discovered many factors that are related to marital satisfaction. For example, when both people are similar in family background, social class, education, and religion, couples report more satisfying relationships (Gaunt, 2006). Couples who wait to marry until after age 20 are more likely to report happier marriages than those who marry before age 20. Warm and positive extended family relationships, supportive spouse behavior, a willingness to sacrifice, and secure financial circumstances also increase the chances of a satisfying marital relationship (Bramlett & Mosher, 2002; Karney & Bradbury, 2005; Stanley, Whitton, Sadberry, Clements, & Markman, 2006). Perhaps the biggest detriments to a healthy, happy, and long-lasting relationship are negative comments, contempt, defensiveness, and criticism (Gottman, 1999a, 1999b; Levenson, Carstensen, & Gottman, 1993; Robles & Kiecolt-Glaser, 2003).

Research also shows some interesting gender differences in marital satisfaction. Although women report being as happy in marriage as men (Myers, 2000), marriage is associated with better mental and physical health for men. In contrast, single women are emotionally and physically healthier than married women (Levenson et al., 1993; Kaslow, Hansson, & Lundblad, 1994). Today, more married women are employed, but they still perform the majority of household tasks and have more responsibility for child rearing than married men (Bianchi, Kilkie, Sayer, & Robinson, 2000). In dual-earner couples, wives average almost three times as many hours per week on household tasks as their husbands (Coltrane, 2001; Starrels, 1994). Given these circumstances, it is not surprising that when divorce does occur, it is more likely to be initiated by the female (Amato & Rogers, 1997).

Divorce About 1 in 5 adults will at some time in their lives experience divorce. First marriages that end in divorce last, on average, about eight years (Kreider, 2005). Divorce rates are higher among couples who do not have children, who marry at a young age, or whose parents divorced (Amato & DeBoer, 2001; Faust & McKibben, 1999). Divorce rates are also higher among African Americans, Asian and Pacific Islanders, and Hispanics than among European Americans, and higher among lower-income couples than higher-income couples (Rank, 2000; U.S. Census Bureau, 2001).

Like other lifestyle changes, divorce brings with it stresses and adaptations

More than 95% of people in the United States choose to get married at some point in their lives.

that the couple and the family must negotiate. Typically, divorce is preceded by a period of conflict and dissatisfaction (Lucas, 2005). Emotional, economic, legal, and practical difficulties follow. What was once one household must now be divided into two. If there are children involved, custody arrangements must be made. Identities are reshaped and redefined as the couple mentally shifts from thinking in terms of "us" to "me." Friendships with other couples may fade. Simultaneously, each member of the couple is resolving feelings of anger, rejection, disappointment, or loneliness (Amato, 2000). Given these changes, it is not surprising that divorced people are more likely to report higher levels of psychological distress or experience physical health problems (Lorenz et al., 1997; Lorenz, Wickrama, Conger, & Elder, 2006). Perhaps for these reasons, many divorced adults, especially young people, choose to marry again. This is more common for men than for women (Kreider, 2005).

Divorce also affects the family. Previous styles of parenting may change, as the custodial parent must assume more responsibility for disciplining the children. The noncustodial parent may become more permissive because he or she spends less time with the children. Children experience many of the same emotions as their parents, such as loss, grieving for the family that was, and anger that their parents were not able to make the marriage work. As a result, they are more likely to misbehave. Children of divorce may be more aggressive, disrespectful, disobedient, withdrawn, or moody. School performance may deteriorate. Their misbehavior makes it even more difficult for parents to be effective. Studies suggest that it is this breakdown in parenting and children's exposure to marital conflict both prior to and following a divorce that are most detrimental to a child's development (Amato, 1993; Amato & Booth, 1996). Hence, a two-parent household filled with strife and discord is as difficult for a child as the experience of divorce (Booth & Amato, 2001; Harold, Fincham, Osborne, & Conger, 1997).

PARENTING

At one time marriage was synonymous with becoming a parent, but that is not necessarily the case today. With increasing numbers of birth control options available, parenthood is more of a choice today than it used to be. About 19% of U.S. women ages 40 to 44 in 2004

Parenting may bring changes in gender roles and the division of labor in the home. Such changes may increase or decrease marital satisfaction.

Barbara Peacock/Getty Images

had never had a child (U.S. Census Bureau, 2005). At the same time, more single women and cohabitating couples are having or adopting children (Manning, 2001; Teachman et al., 2000). For those who choose to have children, parenthood becomes another life transition that includes adaptation to new roles and responsibilities.

Although most prospective parents look forward to the birth of their child, children radically change people's lives. With the joy and elation of a newborn baby comes less sleep, leisure time, and time spent together as a couple. Life becomes a juggling act as the couple tries to keep an eye on all the responsibilities of work and family at the same time. Although fathers today are more involved in child care and housework than ever before (Coley, 2001), mothers, even working mothers, are more likely to become the primary caregiver of the child as the man intensifies his role as provider (Cowan & Cowan, 2000; Deutsch, 2001).

Other variables also influence life satisfaction following the birth of a baby. For example, the baby's temperament (see p. 331) may create less or more stress on new parents (Schoppe-Sullivan et al., 2007). Difficult babies who cry all the time are more of a challenge than babies who are quiet or who are generally cheerful. The parent makes a difference too. Generally, older parents who have waited longer after marrying to have children are better able to adjust to parenthood (Belsky & Rovine, 1990; Umberson, Williams, Powers, Meichu, & Campbell, 2005). Younger couples who have children right away are adjusting to marriage at the same time that they are coping with being new parents. The levels of income, spousal support, and support from extended family and friends also increase or decrease the amount of stress that comes with parenting (Levy-Shiff, 1994).

As the child grows older, the demands of parenting do not ease up. Parents adjust their styles of discipline to meet the new challenges their children pose as they grow older and become established (O'Brien, 1996). As the child enters early adolescence, parenthood may become even more stressful, and marital satisfaction tends to hit an all-time low (■ FIGURE 9.8; Kurdek, 1999; Waldron-Hennessey & Sabatelli, 1997). Parent–child conflicts increase as adolescents achieve formal operational abilities and begin defining their own identity (Steinberg & Morris, 2001). At the same time, parents, who are typically middle-aged at this time, may also be evaluating and questioning the direction of their own lives. As a result of this conflict and tension, parents may relinquish some control and move toward more shared decision making with their teenagers.

Once the last child has left the family home for college or has moved out to be on her own, parents are left with what is referred to as the *empty nest*. Parents may be lonely at times and feel that a major chapter in their family life is over. The parents are also aware of their own aging. Yet this stage represents lots of opportunity, too. Most parents, especially women, enjoy the changes brought about by the empty nest. Marital satisfaction tends to increase, and women generally feel better about themselves as the stress and responsibilities of parenthood decrease (White & Edwards, 1990).

So what happens to parents if their children don't leave—or if they come back because of divorce, limited finances, or extended schooling? This is more common today, when 25% to 30% of young adults in the United States live with their parents into their late 20s (Gitelson & McDermott, 2006; Ward, Logan, & Spitze, 1992). This phenomenon is referred to as the *full nest*, or the *boomerang generation*. It is more common among Hispanic Americans, African Americans, and Asian Americans, perhaps because of the greater emphasis on family closeness in these ethnic groups (Arnett, 2004). If these young adults act responsibly, going to school or working, parents appear to adjust well. However, some parents do find living with their young adult children stressful (Gitelson & McDermott, 2006; White & Rogers, 1997).

We see, then, that children complicate the lives of adults. Parenthood tends to correlate with lower rates of marital satisfaction and higher levels of stress. Yet despite these negative effects, most parents don't regret the experience. Children also bring many joys and experiences that enrich their parents' lives.

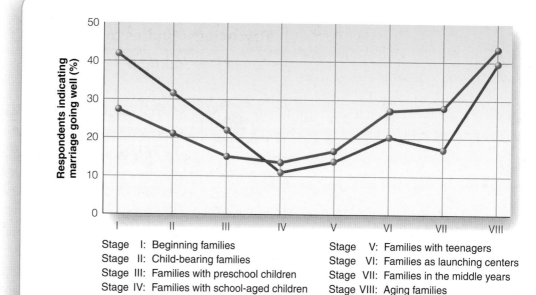

Stage I: Beginning families
Stage II: Child-bearing families
Stage III: Families with preschool children
Stage IV: Families with school-aged children
Stage V: Families with teenagers
Stage VI: Families as launching centers
Stage VII: Families in the middle years
Stage VIII: Aging families

Wives
Husbands

FIGURE 9.8   Marital Satisfaction and Stages of Parenting

First documented by Rollins and Feldman (1975) and later replicated in many studies, the graph shows the percentage of husbands and wives who said their marriage was going well "all the time" at various stages while raising children.

Adapted from Boyd C. Rollins and Harold Feldman, "Marital Satisfaction Over the Family Cycle," Journal of Marriage and the Family, 32 (February), 25. Copyrighted 1975 by the National Council on Family Relations, 3989 Central Ave., N.E., Suite 550, Minneapolis, MN 55421. Reprinted by permission.

Psychology Applies to Your World:

Career Development

What do you want to be when you grow up? As a child, you have been asked this question thousands of times, with the expectation that you will answer it with some type of career choice. What we do for a living, or what we hope to do for a living, becomes an integral part of our identity. It may also determine who we socialize with and where we live. For the past five decades, Donald Super (1957, 1976, 1980, 1991) has addressed such issues, outlining a progression of career development.

In early adolescence, as teenagers form their identities, they experiment with how various career options fit with their ideas of who they are and what they want to be. During this *crystallization phase*, potential career options are reduced to a few choices. For example, a teenager who views himself as outgoing, quick thinking, and motivated may imagine himself in a marketing or law career. Teenagers and young adults further explore career options by testing out prospective career choices in the *specification stage*. For example, a young woman who is considering becoming a doctor may volunteer at a hospital or take a part-time job in a physician's office to determine whether medicine fits her interests and abilities.

Young people enter the workforce and begin to learn about jobs firsthand in the *implementation phase*. The young adult learns both the actual tasks of the job and job-related skills such as getting along with coworkers, getting to work on time, and responding to authority figures. The reality of the work may not meet the person's initial expectations. For example, a teacher's aide may discover that working with children 6 hours a day is not what he expected it to be. Everyone experiences this sort of *reality shock* in some form. However, it is the degree of reality shock that typically determines our willingness to stay on a particular career path. For this reason, the implementation phase can be quite unsettling and unstable. Young adults may find themselves changing positions frequently as they attempt to adjust their expectations to the realities of a particular career.

When a young adult decides on a specific occupation, he or she enters the *establishment phase*. Career expectations continue to be adjusted as the person settles into an occupation and advances in his or her career. Today, however, it is unlikely that this establishment will be with one company or on one career path (Cascio, 1995). The establishment phase may also be more characteristic of men's career pathways. Women's careers may be interrupted during these years for childbearing and child rearing (Betz, 1993; Ornstein & Isabella, 1990).

During the establishment phase, young adults settle into an occupation or a career.

© Peter Beck/Corbis

During middle adulthood, career development is characterized by a *maintenance phase*. Although some people may question their career choices and opt for a career change, most middle-aged adults strengthen their commitment to their careers and are more likely to find personal meaning from their work. This personal meaning more often focuses on internal factors such as job satisfaction and contentment than on external factors such as salary and benefits (Warr, 1994).

Workers enter the *deceleration phase* when they begin planning for their upcoming retirement. Older adults consider such things as finances, where they want to live, and how they want to spend their retirement years. When people stop working full-time, the *retirement phase* begins. Most Americans choose to retire sometime in their 60s and look forward to retirement living. As with other developmental processes that we have discussed, retirement is a process of adjustment that is influenced by many factors such as one's health, one's control over the decision to retire, one's finances, and the ability to maintain social ties with others (J. E. Kim & Moen, 2001, 2002; Reitzes & Mutran, 2004; van Solinge & Henkens, 2005).

Let's Review!

This section detailed the physical, cognitive, and psychosocial changes of adolescence and adulthood. As a quick check of your understanding, answer these questions.

1. Which of the following is *not* a physical change associated with puberty in males?
   a. Growth of the testes   **c.** Widening hips
   b. Voice change   **d.** Broadening shoulders

2. Andre, a 65-year-old man, is likely to experience all of the following as the result of aging *except* _____.
   a. weight loss   **c.** loss in visual acuity
   b. thinning of the hair **d.** faster reaction time

3. When at the mall with her friends, Maria acts as if everyone is watching her. Maria's behavior is an example of _____.
   a. egocentrism   **c.** idealism
   b. imaginary audience   **d.** personal fable

4. According to Erikson, feeling that you have made important contributions to society will lead to a sense of _____.
   a. integrity   **c.** industry
   b. generativity   **d.** identity

5. Which of the following is *false* in regard to social relations in adulthood?
   a. Cohabitation rates have increased over the past decade.
   b. More males than females report being happily married.
   c. Singlehood is associated with better mental and physical health for males.
   d. Divorced people are more likely to experience physical health problems.

6. "Reality shock" is most likely to happen during which phase of career development?
   a. Specification phase   **c.** Implementation phase
   b. Establishment phase   **d.** Deceleration phase

Answers 1. c; 2. d; 3. b; 4. b; 5. c; 6. c

Death and Dying

- Describe how people cope psychologically with their own impending death and the death of their loved ones.

You Asked...

How does death affect us?

SHEILA QUINONES, STUDENT

Death is a process rather than a point in time. Decades ago it was a process that took place at home, with family members present. Today, it is more likely to occur in a hospital or medical facility, surrounded by doctors, nurses, and machines. In our society, death is more removed from our everyday experiences. As a result, when we face death, we and our families are often unprepared for it. Nevertheless, loss is an inevitable part of our development. Knowing what happens when a loved one is dying and how people respond to the death of a loved one may better prepare us for this final journey.

Reactions to Death: Kübler-Ross's Stages

If you were told today that you only had 6 months to live, how would you react? Elisabeth Kübler-Ross (1969, 1974), a pioneer researcher on death and dying, interviewed more than 200 terminally ill people to address this question. She wanted to investigate any predictable emotional and psychological changes that people might experience as they confront their own death. From her research, she noted five reactions that may characterize dying people: denial, anger, bargaining, depression, and acceptance.

When people first learn that they have a terminal illness, a typical reaction is *denial*. They behave as if they have not just been told that they are going to die. For example, they may insist on a second or third medical opinion. Others may continue in their normal activities, behaving as if they had never received this news. Denial is an effective coping strategy that allows the person time to come to terms with impending death.

As denial dwindles, it is replaced by the emotional reaction of *anger*. People lash out at loved ones and medical personnel over the unfairness of death. "Why me?" may be a common response during this stage. Looking for others to blame may also be an expression of this anger.

Following denial and anger, some dying people may also express emotions indicative of *bargaining*. They attempt to strike a deal for more time with the doctors, God, or the universe. For example, a man may want to live just long enough to see his daughter get married. Another person may bargain to make it through a particular holiday. These bargains may be unrealistic and impossible to fulfill.

People who are dying may become *depressed*, or extremely sad, when denial, anger, and bargaining fail to delay the progress of their illness. They may lose interest in their usual activities or refuse to participate. This depression may be one way for those who are near the end of life to mourn their own death.

The final emotional state described by Kübler-Ross is *acceptance*. A peace and calm characterize the dying as they

Given three to six months to live after being diagnosed with pancreatic cancer, Carnegie Mellon University computer science professor Randy Pausch's "Last Lecture," on living rather than dying, inspired millions. Pausch died on July 25, 2008, at the age of 47.

AP Photo/Daily Progress/Kaylin Bowers

face the end of life. They may separate themselves from all but a few of their loved ones as they prepare for life's ending.

Research confirms the legitimacy of Kübler-Ross's reaction stages (Kalish, 1985; Samarel, 1995). However, not every dying person experiences all these reactions. Moreover, not all dying persons go through these reactions in the same order. Death, like many other developmental processes, is influenced by a variety of factors, including one's personality and coping style, the type of support received from family members and health professionals, and the nature of the terminal illness. Yet Kübler-Ross's model is useful for understanding the emotions of dying people and for supporting anyone suffering from loss. People may also experience similar reactions when they face a divorce, unemployment, or the impending death of a loved one.

Bereavement and Grief: How We Respond to Death

When a loved one dies, bereavement and grief follow. **Bereavement** is the experience of losing a loved one; **grief** is our emotional reaction to that loss. Just as death is a highly personal experience, so too is grief. However, research on bereaved people has identified common themes and emotional reactions within three phases: impact/shock, confrontation, and accommodation/acceptance (Bowlby, 1980; Parkes, 1986, 1991; Rando, 1995).

Most people's first reaction to the loss of a loved one is shock. This *impact phase* may include disbelief on hearing that a loved one has died. It may feel as if a numbness has settled within one's body or mind. This numbness is adaptive, dulling the painful emotions of loss. People in this stage may perform such actions as picking out a casket, making arrangements for a funeral or a burial, and even calling friends and relatives to inform them of the death, as if in a dream. This shock is particularly intense if the person's death was sudden.

Deep despair and agony may soon follow the numbness and shock in the *confrontation phase*. Uncontrollable weeping, anxiety, and feelings of guilt and anger are not uncommon as the grieving person yearns for the loved one to return. The survivor must confront the reality of the loss, and this can be especially painful. The person may have difficulty concentrating, sleeping, and eating. By confronting each wave of despair, the person moves closer to realizing that the loved one is gone.

As the pain of the confrontation phase subsides, the survivors begin to accept the death of the loved one in the *accommodation phase*. The survivors reengage with life, and the memories of the deceased are internalized. People are now able to refocus their emotional energies on normal daily events and relationships with the living.

bereavement [bee-REEVE-munt] the experience of losing a loved one

grief one's emotional reaction to the death of a loved one

© Mark Richards/Photo Edit

Shock, disbelief, and numbness are common emotional reactions to the loss of a loved one.

How long does this grieving process take? A definitive answer is not possible. The course and intensity of these phases differ from person to person. Personality traits, cultural background, and the circumstances surrounding the death of the loved one are all factors that influence one's grief responses. Some people function considerably better after a year or two; others may take several years. Some may never recover, especially from the death of a child (Klass, 1993; Rubin, 1993). Research also suggests that women may be better able to handle grief, as they are more likely than men to seek social support and express their feelings more openly (Rando, 1995; Stroebe & Stroebe, 1993).

In this chapter, we examined the many different ways in which people develop. We hope that as you read this chapter, you were able to see how nature and nurture interact and influence physical, cognitive, and social aspects of development. As you look through the key terms and summary that follow, relate the material to your own life by generating personal examples that illustrate these concepts. Many of these concepts will be reinforced in later chapters as we explore social psychology, coping, and personality.

Let's Review!

In this section, we discussed how people cope with their own impending death and the death of loved ones. For a quick check of your understanding, answer these questions.

1. Caryn has just been diagnosed with cancer and has been given 6 months to live. The next week she signs a 2-year lease on a car. Which stage of dying is Caryn most likely in?
   a. Acceptance
   b. Bargaining
   c. Anger
   d. Denial

2. Our emotional reaction to the loss of a loved one is called _____.
   a. bereavement
   b. grief
   c. bargaining
   d. reality shock

3. The most intense emotional reactions to the loss of a loved one typically occur during which grief phase?
   a. Impact
   b. Shock
   c. Confrontation
   d. Accommodation

Answers 1. d; 2. b; 3. c

Studying THE Chapter

Key Terms

development (313)
nature–nurture issue (314)
zygote (315)
germinal stage (315)
embryonic stage (316)

fetal stage (316)
Down syndrome (316)
teratogen (317)
sensitive period (317)
fetal alcohol syndrome (FAS) (317)

neonate (319)
reflex (320)
gross motor skills (320)
fine motor skills (320)
cognition (323)

schema (324)
assimilation (324)
accommodation (324)
sensorimotor stage (325)
object permanence (325)
symbolic thinking (325)
preoperational stage (325)
centration (325)
conservation (326)
egocentrism (326)
concrete operations (327)
formal operations (328)
private speech (328)

zone of proximal development
    (ZPD) (329)
scaffolding (329)
moral reasoning (329)
temperament (331)
attachment (331)
separation anxiety (332)
stranger anxiety (332)
authoritarian parent (333)
authoritative parent (333)
permissive parent (333)
gender roles (335)
gender permanence (335)

gender-schema theory (336)
puberty (340)
menarche (340)
menopause (344)
imaginary audience (345)
personal fable (346)
dualistic thinking (346)
relativistic thinking (346)
postformal thought (347)
fluid intelligence (347)
crystallized intelligence (347)
bereavement (357)
grief (357)

What Do You Know? Assess Your Understanding

Test your retention and understanding of the material by answering the following questions.

1. Enrique believes that the environment is primarily responsible for development. Enrique is emphasizing the _____.
   a.   nurture side of the nature–nurture issue
   b.   nature side of the nature–nurture issue
   c.   influence of genetics
   d.   influence of unconscious desires

2. Organs and systems form during the _____ stage of prenatal development.
   a.   zygote   c.   embryonic
   b.   germinal   d.   fetal

3. _____ are environmental factors, such as alcohol or cleaning fluids, that may cause birth defects.
   a.   Chromosomes   c.   Sensitive periods
   b.   Teratogens   d.   Myelins

4. _____ serve as the foundation for behaviors such as walking, eating, crying, smiling, and grasping.
   a.   Temperaments   c.   Formal operations
   b.   Attachments   d.   Reflexes

5. Learning how to zip up your pants or button your coat are examples of _____ motor skills.
   a.   gross   c.   big
   b.   fine   d.   scaffolding

6. Which of the following stimuli do infants prefer to look at?
   a.   Circles   c.   Faces
   b.   Colors   d.   Machines

7. Pablo sees a porpoise for the first time and exclaims, "Fishy, Daddy!" Pablo is engaging in the cognitive process of _____.
   a.   assimilation
   b.   accommodation
   c.   scaffolding
   d.   formal operations

8. Ms. Lucy, the kindergarten teacher, tries her best to coach her students by making each task somewhat more difficult than the last and modeling how best to approach each task. Ms. Lucy's practice is consistent with _____.
   a.   assimilation
   b.   accommodation
   c.   scaffolding
   d   sensorimotor thought

9. Some students think it is wrong to cheat because it violates the student code of conduct. Such students are operating at the _____ level of moral reasoning.
   a.   preconventional
   b.   conventional
   c.   postconventional
   d.   preoperational

10. Jamal sees two differently shaped glasses filled with liquid. He recognizes that even though they look different, the glasses hold the same amount of liquid. Piaget would say that Jamal is operating at the _____ stage of cognitive development.
   a. sensorimotor
   b. preoperational
   c. concrete operational
   d. preconventional

11. As a baby, Reece did not cry a lot, regularly approached new people and situations, and had a regular pattern of eating and sleeping. Reece's temperament is best described as _____.
   a. easy
   b. slow-to-warm-up
   c. difficult
   d. avoidant

12. While at the state fair, Cicily remains close to her dad and does not explore the games or rides. She shows *extreme* distress if her dad leaves her side. Cicily most likely has a(n) _____ attachment style.
   a. avoidant
   b. resistant
   c. secure
   d. disorganized

13. Which part of the brain is among the last to fully develop during adolescence and young adulthood?
   a. Cerebellum
   b. Amygdala
   c. Pituitary gland
   d. Prefrontal cortex

14. Middle-aged adults evaluate how productive their lives have been in Erikson's psychosocial crisis of _____.
   a. identity vs. role confusion
   b. intimacy vs. isolation
   c. generativity vs. stagnation
   d. integrity vs. despair

15. _____ refers to the changes in the female when she stops menstruating and is no longer fertile.
   a. Puberty
   b. Menopause
   c. Menarche
   d. Andropause

16. Tomas believes that there is only one right answer or single solution to a situation. Tomas is engaging in _____.
   a. dualistic thinking
   b. relativistic thinking
   c. postformal thought
   d. all of the above

17. The development of one's personal values and character is referred to as _____.
   a. industry
   b. integrity
   c. generativity
   d. identity

18. How are teenagers and preschoolers similar in their thinking?
   a. Both cannot think abstractly.
   b. Both have developed conservation abilities.
   c. Both are egocentric in their thinking.
   d. Teenagers and preschoolers are not similar in their thinking.

19. Marital satisfaction is associated with _____.
   a. similar educational background
   b. warm and positive extended family relationships
   c. secure financial circumstances
   d. All of the above

20. Pilar's partner died a week ago. She feels numb and in shock. Pilar is most likely in the _____ phase of grief.
   a. impact
   b. confrontation
   c. accommodation
   d. acceptance

ANSWERS: 1. a; 2. c; 3. b; 4. d; 5. b; 6. c; 7. a; 8. c; 9. b; 10. c; 11. a; 12. b; 13. d; 14. c; 15. b; 16. a; 17. d; 18. c; 19. d; 20. a

Online Resources

CENGAGENOW™ Personalized Study
www.cengage.com/login

Go to www.cengage.com/login to link to CengageNOW, your online study tool. First take the **Pre-Test** for this chapter to get your **Personalized Study Plan**, which will identify topics you need to review and direct you to online resources. Then take the **Post-Test** to determine what concepts you have mastered and what you still need work on.

 What Is Psychology? Essentials Book Companion Website
www.cengage.com/psychology/pastorino

Visit your book companion website, where you will find more resources to help you study. Resources include learning objectives, Internet exercises, quizzing, flash cards, and a pronunciation glossary.

Development includes changes in physical, emotional, social, and cognitive behavior and abilities over time through an interaction of **nature** (one's biology) and **nurture** (one's environment and culture).

Look Back
AT WHAT YOU'VE LEARNED

What Happens During Prenatal Development?

How Do We Develop in Infancy and Childhood?

Juergen Berger, Max-planck Institute/Photo Researchers, Inc.

- **Germinal stage** (0–14 days): The zygote undergoes rapid cell division and duplication.

- **Embryonic stage** (2–8 weeks): Major organs and organ systems form.

- **Fetal stage** (week 9–birth): Body organs and systems more fully develop.

Claude Edelmann/Photo Researchers, Inc.

- Infants' and children's brains are highly plastic, or changeable.

- According to Jean Piaget, infants and children apply **schemas (assimilation)** to understand their environment and adapt to change through **accommodation** when existing schemas are changed or modified in four stages of cognitive development: **sensorimotor**, **preoperational**, **concrete operations**, and **formal operations**.

- Lev Vygotsky stressed the importance of culture and social interactions in cognitive development.

- Kohlberg's research on **moral reasoning** suggests that children's understanding of right and wrong progressively develops from a focus on the self to the external world.

- An infant's **temperament** can influence the **attachment** or the emotional tie between the infant and the primary caregiver.

- Diana Baumrind identified three styles of parenting: **authoritarian**, **authoritative**, and **permissive**.

- Psychologist Erik Erikson proposed that the environment and the child's responses to the environment influence the development of either a healthy or an unhealthy personality.

- At a very early age, children process and develop schemas about **gender roles**, or society's expectations for how a female and a male should behave.

© Blend Images/Alamy

HOW DO **People** Grow, **Change,** AND **DEVELOP?**

Greg Ceo/Getty Images

How Do We Develop In Adolescence and Adulthood?

- **Puberty** involves maturation of sex characteristics that enable us to reproduce. At around age 50, women experience **menopause** and hormonal changes that eventually bring an end to reproductive capacity.

- During adolescence and throughout life, the brain remains highly plastic, allowing us to adapt to changing conditions.

- Teenagers tend to be **egocentric**, believing that others are concerned with the same things that they are.

- **Postformal thought** is characterized by **relativistic thinking**, an appreciation that the correct solution or answer may vary from situation to situation.

- Remaining cognitively active helps adults avoid steep declines in mental abilities.

- Erik Erikson considered adolescence the key stage for developing identity, but he believed adults continue to develop when they establish intimacy, generativity, and integrity.

- Adolescent and adult relationships are expressed in a wide range of lifestyles, including dating, cohabitation, marriage, divorce, and parenthood.

- Finding satisfying work and holding a job are part of adult development.

© Susan Van Etten/Photo Edit

How Do People Cope With Death and Dying?

- Death is a process rather than a point in time that is an inevitable part of our development.

- Elizabeth Kübler-Ross, a researcher on death and dying, identified five reactions that may characterize people who know they are dying: denial, anger, bargaining, depression, and acceptance.

AP Photo/Daily Progress/ Kaylin Bowers

363

10

Social Psychology:
HOW DO WE Understand
AND Interact WITH
OTHERS?

When our student Diana Flores and her family immigrated to the United States from their native Mexico, they were the first Hispanic family to settle in their new neighborhood. At first, it appeared that they were welcomed by their new neighbors. Diana made friends at school, and her parents made new acquaintances as well. However, as time passed, Diana began to notice subtle signs indicating that they may not have been as accepted by some people as she had thought. At times, when she visited friends' homes after school, she felt as if their parents were uncomfortable with her presence. And as other Hispanic families began to move into the area, Diana began to hear some of her friends say disturbing things about "those people" and how "they" were ruining the area. Diana would quickly point out to her friends that she, herself, was one of "those people"—only to be told that she was different. "You're not like those people," her friends would say. "You're our friend."

Later, as Diana began to cultivate friendships with other Hispanics, she found that some of her non-Hispanic friends began to withdraw from their friendship. It was upsetting. Diana didn't understand how her friends could show so much disdain for Hispanics while at the same time professing to like her. Couldn't they see that their comments hurt Diana as well? And why did they appear to dislike Diana's Hispanic friends simply because they were Hispanic?

Possible answers to these questions lie in an understanding of the social psychological processes that guide our social behavior. As you study the chapter, you will gain insight into why people sometimes think and behave the way Diana's friends did. You will also learn about the thought processes and social pressures that influence our behavior in a variety of social situations—perhaps even gaining a deeper understanding of yourself in the process.

Christopher Robbins/Getty Images

© Susann Doyle-Portillo

Diana Flores's understanding of psychology helps her understand why some people discriminate against those who are different from themselves.

365

Attitudes and Attitude Change

- Describe attitudes, how they develop, and how they affect behavior.

- Describe dissonance theory, and explain the role of dissonance in attitude change.

- Describe the major theories of persuasion and how the communicator, the message, and the audience affect persuasion.

Social psychology is the study of how we think and behave in the vast array of social situations that we experience. One area of social psychology, **social cognition**, investigates the ways in which we think (cognition) about ourselves and others—for example, studying how we develop **attitudes**, our liking or disliking for the people, places, and things in our world. We all have attitudes about a multitude of things that represent the evaluative beliefs we hold about the contents of our world (e.g. liking country music or disliking lazy people). But how do we acquire these attitudes?

Acquiring Attitudes Through Learning

As with many of our beliefs, we *learn* to have many of the attitudes we hold. One learning process that affects our attitudes about the world is *classical conditioning*. Recall that classical conditioning is often responsible for the development of certain learned *emotional* and *physiological* responses in humans (■ FIGURE 10.1). Because classical conditioning has the power to change the way we *feel* about certain stimuli, it also has the power to influence our attitude toward these stimuli. For example, if man is robbed by a gang member, he may be classically conditioned to fear (CR) people who wear gang colors and clothes (CS). In short, classical conditioning can often explain the gut-level emotional and physiological aspects of our attitudes (Grossman & Till, 1998).

Operant conditioning, or learning through the consequences of our behavior, also affects our attitudes. If you are rewarded for having certain attitudes, the attitude will be strengthened. But if you are punished for having certain attitudes, the attitude will be weakened. For example, if your friends applaud your efforts to "go green" and recycle your trash, then your pro-green attitude is likely to strengthen.

Operant conditioning can also influence our attitudes through the consequences of our direct interaction with the objects of our attitude. For example, if you try a Jamaican dish with lots of very hot peppers that burns your mouth so badly your eyes water, you might develop a negative attitude about eating hot Jamaican food. As a result, the next time you visit a Jamaican restaurant, your behavior will likely change—you'll order one of the blander dishes!

At times, we also model the attitudes of others. Recall that in *social learning* we learn by watching the actions of others and storing mental representations of their behavior in memory. Take a minute to think about your attitudes and the attitudes of those who are closest to you. How do your attitudes compare to theirs? If you are like most people, you will find that

> **You Asked...**
>
> *Is it possible to influence others without intending to do so?*
>
> TAMARA STEWART, STUDENT

social psychology the branch of psychology that studies how we think and behave in social situations

social cognition the area of social psychology that deals with the ways in which we think about other people and ourselves

attitude an evaluative belief that we hold about something

overall, your attitudes are quite similar to those of your parents (Rohan & Zanna, 1996) and those around you (Kowalski, 2003). There will, of course, be some notable differences, but overall we tend to be more like those we love when it comes to attitudes. In fact, such similarity in attitudes is a factor in attraction, which we'll discuss later in this chapter.

As you can see, we learn attitudes the way that we learn everything in life—through experience. Once we form our attitudes about the world, they then have the power to affect what we know, how we feel, and how we behave toward just about everything we encounter in our lives. But is this always the case—do our attitudes always predict our behavior?

The Link Between Attitudes and Behavior

Do you ever find yourself behaving in a manner that contradicts your attitudes? For example, have you ever laughed at a joke you didn't find very funny? Do you sometimes engage in behavior that you know is harmful to you? If so, your behavior is not unusual. We often behave in ways that go against our attitudes. This lack of *attitude–behavior consistency* has intrigued researchers because it seems so counterintuitive and illogical.

If social pressures can make it difficult for us to behave consistently with our attitudes, what factors make it *more* likely that we will behave in ways that are consistent with our attitudes? Answers to this question have great practical value in society. For instance, under what circumstances might people's positive attitudes toward safer sex actually lead them to engage in protected sex? When might political attitudes accurately predict voting behavior? And in which situations can a company assume that consumer attitudes toward their products will actually translate into sales? Researchers have been diligently trying to answer such questions. ■ TABLE 10.1 describes variables that have been shown to influence attitude–behavior consistency.

Given that our attitudes develop through experience and that once in place they influence our behavior at least part of the time, many psychologists are interested in how attitudes can be changed. This information also has great practical value. If we knew how to change attitudes, we might be able to reverse social problems such as prejudice and alcoholism. These and other pragmatic concerns have fueled a great deal of research on attitude change.

Whether we like it or not, we often take on the attitudes of our parents through social learning.

© Mark Richards/Photo Edit

Mom shows fear.   Child is afraid.

Dog+Mom shows fear.   Child is afraid.

Dog   Child is afraid.

FIGURE

10.1

Classical Conditioning a Negative Attitude Toward Dogs

For a young child, a fear response in her mother (US) will naturally cause fear in the child (UR). On the other hand, the sight of a dog will not reliably elicit fear in a small child. Therefore, the dog is initially a neutral stimulus (NS). When the sight of the dog (NS) is repeatedly paired with a fear response in the mother (US), the child can easily acquire a conditioned fear of dogs (CR) that is elicited by the mere sight of a dog (CS).

Table 10.1 Factors That Affect Attitude–Behavior Consistency

FACTOR	EXAMPLE
Attitudes best predict behaviors that are measured at the same level of specificity.	Liking spinach predicts that you will eat spinach better than liking vegetables does.
If the cognitive and affective aspects of the attitude are both positive (or both negative), the attitude will be a better predictor of behavior.	Both enjoying spinach and knowing that it is good for you increases the chances that you will eat it.
Attitudes that are quickly and automatically retrieved from long-term memory are better predictors of behavior.	If the first thing you think of when ordering dinner is your love of spinach, you are more likely to order it.
When the norms of the situation require us to behave counter to our attitudes, attitude–behavior consistency is likely to be lacking.	If your dinner companions talk about how much they hate spinach, you may be less likely to order it.
Attitudes that are learned through direct experience with the attitude object are likely to be better predictors of behavior.	If you first learned to love spinach by actually eating it, you are more likely to eat it again.

Cognitive Consistency and Attitude Change

Throughout our lifetime, our attitudes will change as we acquire new knowledge and have different experiences. For example, a favorable attitude toward a particular restaurant may change if you read in the paper that the restaurant failed its last health inspection. In light of this new information, the old attitude may be discarded in favor of a less favorable one. In this example, the attitude change was motivated from *within* the attitude holder. The change was not the result of a concerted effort on the part of others. It was motivated more by your desire to maintain what psychologists refer to as **cognitive consistency**, or the desire to avoid contradictions in our attitudes and behaviors (Festinger, 1957). Cognitive consistency theories (Festinger, 1957; Heider, 1946) propose that humans find it uncomfortable when there is inconsistency among their attitudes or between their attitudes and their behavior. Most of us believe that we are intelligent, logical beings. This attitude about being intelligent and logical would be inconsistent with the attitude that an unhealthy restaurant is a good place to eat. So we adjust one of our attitudes (the one concerning the restaurant) to avoid such an inconsistency. But why does inconsistency make us uncomfortable and therefore motivate attitude change?

One explanation of how cognitive inconsistency motivates attitude change is **dissonance theory** (Festinger, 1957). According to dissonance theory, inconsistencies among attitudes or between attitudes and behavior cause an unpleasant physical state called *dissonance*. Think of dissonance as a state of unease much like being hungry or being anxious. It stems from the realization that we have behaved in a way that is contrary to our self-concept (Aronson, 1998). Because dissonance makes us feel bad, we are motivated to stop this unpleasant feeling, which can lead to attitude and/or behavior change (Wood, 2000). For example, a health-conscious person who smokes is likely to experience dissonance because smoking is inconsistent with being health conscious. Once the person experiences dissonance, she will be motivated to stop the dissonance by removing the inconsistency.

In general, there are three ways to remove the inconsistencies that cause dissonance. First, she can change her behavior (stop smoking). Second, she can change her attitudes (decide that she is not health conscious after all). Or third, she can remove the inconsistency by bringing new beliefs and attitudes to bear on the situation (convince herself that smok-

cognitive consistency the idea that we strive to have attitudes and behaviors that do not contradict one another

dissonance theory a theory that predicts that we will be motivated to change our attitudes and/or our behaviors to the extent that they cause us to feel dissonance, an uncomfortable physical state ing has never really been *proven* to cause health problems). Any of these three methods will reduce the dissonance felt by the person and restore a state of *consonance*, in which there is no inconsistency among attitudes and behavior.

Persuasion and Attitude Change

Dissonance theory can explain certain aspects of how we change and grow as human beings, but dissonance is not the only means through which our attitudes change. We also encounter frequent **persuasion** situations in which others directly attempt to change our attitudes. Every day we face persuasive attempts from friends, family members, politicians, the media, and advertisers. By some estimates, the average American encounters a whopping 3,000 advertisements per day (Stanton, 2004)! With all of these persuasive attempts being hurled at us on a daily basis, an understanding of how persuasion occurs becomes almost a necessity.

Obviously, not all of the persuasive attempts we are subjected to actually produce attitude change. We do not become loyal to every product we see advertised on TV. We do not vote for every political candidate we hear speak. So just what makes persuasion successful—or what makes it fail?

One very important factor in the effectiveness of persuasion is the type of *cognitive processes* that we engage in during the persuasive attempt. The degree to which we analyze persuasive arguments can influence whether or not those arguments are effective in changing our attitudes (Petty & Cacioppo, 1986; Stephenson, Benoit, & Tschida, 2001). When we process on the **central route to persuasion**, we carefully and critically evaluate the logic of the persuasive arguments we encounter. When we process on the **peripheral route to persuasion**, we do not attempt to critically evaluate the arguments and are instead persuaded by superficial aspects of the arguments such as the likability of the person making them.

Other variables also affect the success of persuasion. These variables fall into three categories: variables associated with the *communicator* of the message, variables associated with the persuasive *message* itself, and variables associated with the *audience* that receives the persuasive message.

COMMUNICATOR VARIABLES

We tend to be most persuaded when the person communicating the message to us is attractive (Eagly & Chaiken, 1975), appears to be credible (Hovland & Weiss, 1951; Petty, Wegener, & Fabrigar, 1997), and appears to be expert (Petty, Cacioppo, & Goldman, 1981). This is one reason that advertisers hire well-respected, attractive actors and actresses to sell their products. They know that we will be more likely to be persuaded because we place our trust in such people—especially if we are processing on the peripheral route (Petty et al., 1981).

MESSAGE VARIABLES

When the arguments given by the communicator do not seem like attempts to persuade us, we are more easily persuaded (Petty & Cacioppo, 1986). Similarly, we are more likely to be persuaded if the communicator effectively presents both the pros (why we should accept the

Because smoking is inconsistent with being health conscious, this person is likely to experience dissonance that may lead to attitude or behavior change.

persuasion a type of social influence in which someone tries to change our attitudes

central route to persuasion a style of thinking in which the person carefully and critically evaluates persuasive arguments and generates counterarguments; the central route requires motivation and available cognitive resources

peripheral route to persuasion a style of thinking in which the person does not carefully and critically evaluate persuasive arguments or generate counterarguments; the peripheral route ensues when one lacks motivation and/or available cognitive resources

Attractiveness of a communicator can be one factor that makes you more likely to accept an argument. This is especially true when you are processing on the peripheral route to persuasion.

Neal Hamberg/Bloomberg News /Landov

arguments) and cons (why we might not accept the arguments) of the proposal. Of course, for a two-sided argument to be effective, the communicator must be able to effectively argue against objections to accepting the proposal (Crowley & Hoyer, 1994). The superiority of two-sided arguments over one-sided arguments (only the pros) occurs in part because we tend to trust a communicator who is willing to openly discuss the drawbacks of a proposal.

AUDIENCE VARIABLES

Effective persuasion is heavily dependent on who is being persuaded. In general, all of us are easier to persuade on the peripheral rather than the central route to persuasion. However, some of us are habitually more persuadable than others are. People who are low in IQ have sometimes been shown to be more easily persuaded than those who have moderate or high IQ levels (Rhodes & Wood, 1992). Presumably, those low in IQ do not have the cognitive ability to critically evaluate a persuasive message and generate effective counterarguments. Therefore, they are more easily persuaded to accept the message at face value.

However, under certain conditions, people high in IQ are more easily persuaded than those who are low in IQ. For instance, research has shown that when the arguments given are complex and valid, people of high IQ are more likely to be persuaded than people of lesser IQ (Eagly & Warren, 1976). Presumably, if complex, valid arguments are to work, they have to be appreciated by the audience. People of higher intelligence have the ability to understand and appreciate the logic of such arguments, so they are more easily persuaded.

A person's age can also predict the person's likelihood of being persuaded. Confidence in one's own attitudes often comes with age. Adolescence is a crucial time in people's lives—they are trying to develop the attitudes they will hold as adults (Erikson, 1968; Marcia, 1980). Young people in this process of developing their own attitudes are more vulnerable to persuasive attempts. By the time we reach young adulthood, we are less vulnerable to persuasive attempts than we once were (Krosnick & Alwin, 1989).

The last characteristic of the audience that we will discuss is mood. When people are in a good mood, they seem unwilling to do anything that might disrupt their good mood. This apparently includes thinking hard (Bless, Bohner, Schwarz, & Strack, 1990). When people are in a neutral or negative mood, they do not seem to have reservations about engaging in careful evaluation of the persuasive arguments delivered by the communicator. As a result, they tend to process more centrally and will be persuaded only if the arguments are based on sound logic.

Let's Review!

In this section, we covered ways in which our attitudes can change. For a quick check of your understanding, answer these questions.

1. If Mike wishes to make the best possible decision about how to vote in the upcoming presidential election, he should watch the presidential debates while processing on the _____.
   a. central route
   b. peripheral route
   c. algorithmic route
   d. shortest route

2. A politician is attempting to persuade people to vote for her in an upcoming election. All other things being equal, with which group of voters would you expect her to have the most success?
   a. Middle-aged health care workers
   b. Senior citizens
   c. Housewives 25–45 years old
   d. Young voters 18–21 years old

3. Thelma recently discovered that her favorite actress supports a radical political group that Thelma despises. According to dissonance theory, what is most likely to happen in this situation?
   a. She will begin to like the actress more.
   b. She will begin to like the actress less.
   c. She will begin to dislike the political group more.
   d. Her attitudes toward the actress and the group will not change.

Answers 1. a; 2. d; 3. b.

How We Form Impressions of Others

- Describe how we form impressions about ourselves and others, and explain the attribution process.

One of the most important aspects of social cognition is **impression formation**, or how we understand and make judgments about others. When we meet someone for the first time, we usually attempt to determine what type of person he is. Is this person kind, smart, aggressive, or untrustworthy? We want to know. Why do we want to know what other people are like?

In short, if we have a good understanding of other people's traits and abilities, we can predict how they will behave in certain situations. This allows us to guide our own behavior in social situations. Without some understanding of others, social interactions would be much more awkward and uncertain.

> **You Asked...**
>
> *What gives us a perception of other people?*   JOSHUA KENNEDY, STUDENT

The Attribution Process

It appears that one of our basic social cognitive tendencies is to try to explain the behavior of ourselves and others, but how do you determine the traits and characteristics of someone you've just met? If you're thinking that we pay attention to what the person says and does, you're correct. When we judge a person, we observe his behavior, and then we attempt to determine the cause of this behavior (Heider, 1958). This process of assigning cause to behavior is called **attribution**. For example, imagine that you enter a local café and see a man yelling at a woman in the corner booth. Witnessing his outburst, you would likely try to determine why the man is yelling. Is it because he is an aggressive person? Or did the woman somehow provoke this type of outburst in an otherwise kind man? Questions like these may pass through your mind as you watch the scene unfold.

In this example, we can attribute the man's behavior to one of two types of causes. We can attribute the behavior to his traits, abilities, or characteristics, in which case we are making a **trait attribution**. Or we may attribute the behavior to something in the environment, in which case we are making a **situational attribution**. If we make a trait attribution about the yelling man, we assume that he is yelling because he is an aggressive person. If we make a situational attribution, we assume that something happened in the environment that caused the man to yell—perhaps his companion accidently spilled hot coffee in his lap. Note that when we make a situational attribution, we do *not* attribute the man's behavior to his personality.

Heuristics and Biases in Attribution

Ideally, we would weigh all the available evidence before making either a trait attribution or a situational attribution. Unfortunately, the realities of the world do not always allow us to make careful, analytic attributions. Humans are *cognitive misers*, meaning that we try to conserve our cognitive resources whenever we can (Fiske & Taylor, 1991). We have seen evidence of our miserliness in earlier discussions. As we saw in Chapter 7, when we have to quickly solve a problem, we often use shortcuts, or *heuristics*, in hopes of finding a solution. Heuristics may lead to quick answers, but they do not always lead to accurate answers. People have been shown to employ several time-saving heuristics while making attributions, and these shortcuts often lead to errors and biases in the attribution process.

impression formation the way that we understand and make judgments about others
attribution the act of assigning cause to behavior
trait attribution an attribution that assigns the cause of a behavior to the traits and characteristics of the person being judged
situational attribution an attribution that assigns the cause of a behavior to some characteristic of the situation or environment in which the behavior occurs

YOUR TURN — ACTIVE LEARNING

Try the following demonstration. Look at the photos in ■ FIGURE 10.2 and follow the instructions. What type of personality traits did you list for these people? How confident were you in these judgments? Now ask yourself this question: What evidence do I have that these people actually possess these personality traits? If you're like most people, your perceptions of these celebrities are based on the roles they play on TV or in the movies. Most of us assume that their behavior on TV is indicative of their personality *traits* in real life. Did you? If so, what *situational* explanations for these people's TV behavior did you fail to take into account? Did you take into account that on TV, these celebrities are acting? Did you think about the fact that even "reality shows" involve someone directing the actors' behavior and the actors are aware that they are being watched by millions of people? Probably not. The bottom line is that unless you've spent time with these celebrities in real life, you've never really seen their natural behavior; therefore, it's somewhat illogical to draw firm conclusions about their personality traits. If you did just that, don't feel bad. This tendency to rely on trait attributions and to discount situational explanations of behavior is so common that it is called the **fundamental attribution error**.

fundamental attribution error our tendency to overuse trait information when making attributions about others

Mike Rowe of *Dirty Jobs*	Will Smith of the movie *Hancock*	America Ferrrera of *Ugly Betty*	Kyra Sedgwick of *The Closer*
Trait:	Trait:	Trait:	Trait:
Trait:	Trait:	Trait:	Trait:
Trait:	Trait:	Trait:	Trait:
Confidence rating:	Confidence rating:	Confidence rating:	Confidence rating:

Scott Gries/Getty Images · Jim Spellman/WireImage/Getty Images · Soul Brother/FilmMagic/Getty Images · Peter 'Hopper' Stone/© TNT/Courtesy: Everett Collection

FIGURE

10.2

What Do You Think About These Celebrities?

Take a look at these celebrities. Would you like to be friends with these people? What kind of people do you think they are? In the spaces below each photo, write down some of the traits you think this person possesses. Then rate your confidence in the accuracy of your judgments on a scale from 1 to 10, where 1 = not at all confident that your judgment is correct and 10 = very confident that your judgment is correct.

FUNDAMENTAL ATTRIBUTION ERROR

Why we tend to engage in the fundamental attribution error is not entirely clear. Perhaps it reflects our preference to know more about a person's traits than about a person's environment. After all, the goal of forming attributions is to understand the person, not the environment (Jones, 1979). Another explanation is that when we view someone in a social setting, we tend to focus our attention on the person and her behavior, paying less attention to the situation. If we don't pay much attention to the situation, we are unlikely to give situational factors much weight when making our attributions.

Engaging in the fundamental attribution error varies with the degree to which our culture emphasizes individual behavior over group behavior. Some cultures, such as those in North America and Western Europe, are **individualistic cultures**, emphasizing the behavior and success of individuals rather than groups. Some other cultures, such as those in India and Japan, are **collectivistic cultures**, emphasizing the behavior and success of groups more than individuals (Triandis, 1994). Research has shown that people from individualistic cultures are more likely to engage in the fundamental attribution error (Choi & Nesbitt, 1998). Presumably, the Western focus on the individual accounts for this difference in attribution, but more research needs to be done to pinpoint the difference between individualistic and collectivistic cultures.

ACTOR/OBSERVER BIAS

What kind of attributions do we make when we are examining our own behavior? What if you found yourself yelling at a companion in a café? Would you be as likely to label yourself as a mean person as you would the man in the previous example? Probably not. When we observe our own behavior, we tend to take situational factors more into account than we do for others. This tendency has been called the **actor/observer bias** because we make different attributions as *actors* than we make as *observers* of others (Choi & Nesbitt, 1998; Jones & Nesbitt, 1971). The actor/observer bias predicts that you are likely to attribute your own yelling to some situational factor. Perhaps your significant other angered you, or you had a bad day. The explanation you would likely use for others, being a mean person, would be low on your list of attributions for your own behavior.

The actor/observer bias may seem self-serving, but this is not always the case. You would also be more likely to attribute a classmate's unexpected "A" on an exam to his traits than you would your own unexpected "A." In this case, the actor/observer bias predicts that you would consider situational causes, such as an easy exam, more for yourself than for others. So why do we treat ourselves differently from others when it comes to attribution?

One potential reason for the actor/observer bias is that when we are the actor, we cannot literally see our own behavior, and our attention is generally focused outward on the environment. But when we are the observer, our attention is generally focused on the other person's behavior. Therefore, because we are relatively unaware of our own behavior and very aware of the environment, we are more likely to consider situational factors in making attributions for ourselves (Storms, 1973).

The actor/observer bias may also stem from the different knowledge we have about ourselves and other people (Eisen, 1979). When we are making attributions about our own behavior, we are usually very aware of the way in which the environment influences it. Because we do not typically know other people's thoughts, we usually do not know how other people perceive the situation and whether it indeed influences their behavior.

SELF-SERVING BIAS

Although the actor/observer bias does not stem from a desire to enhance one's self-esteem, this does not mean that we never seek to make ourselves look better. Often we do make self-esteem-boosting attributions. The **self-serving bias** refers to our tendency to make trait attributions for our successes and situational attributions for our failures (Miller & Ross, 1975).

individualistic culture a culture, like many Western cultures, in which individual accomplishments are valued over group accomplishments

collectivistic culture a culture, like many Asian cultures, in which group accomplishments are valued over individual accomplishments

actor/observer bias our tendency to make the fundamental attribution error when judging others, while being less likely to do so when making attributions about ourselves

self-serving bias our tendency to make attributions that preserve our own self-esteem—for example, making trait attributions for our success and situational attributions for our failures

If you were to earn an "A" on your next psychology exam, you would likely attribute this grade to your ability or your study habits. However, if you were to fail your next psychology exam (and we hope that you do not!), you would be more likely to attribute your grade to some situational factor, such as your professor's teaching or the fact that your roommate interfered with your studying.

The major reason for the self-serving bias appears to be our desire to feel good about ourselves (Brown & Rogers, 1991; Trafimow, Armendariz, & Madsen, 2004). This bias helps protect our self-esteem, although it can also cause problems if we become too self-serving. For instance, not taking responsibility for our failures can lead others to like us less (Carlston & Shovar, 1983).

As we have seen in this section, we often take shortcuts, or heuristics, when making attributions about others. Heuristics may save time, but often they lead to incorrect attributions and judgments. As we will see in the next section, our tendency to use mental shortcuts can also lead to bigger problems, including prejudice and discrimination.

Let's Review!

In this section, we discussed how we form impressions of ourselves and others. For a quick check of your understanding, answer these questions.

1. Our tendency to overuse trait attributions and to ignore the situational influences on behavior is known as the _____.
   a. fundamental attribution error
   b. self-serving bias
   c. social desirability bias
   d. actor/observer bias

2. Which of the following people would be least likely to exhibit the fundamental attribution error?
   a. Henri from Canada
   b. Kiko from Japan
   c. Lamont from the United States
   d. Greta from Germany

3. Jasper was quick to assume that Susan was intelligent when he saw that she earned an "A" on her last psychology exam. However, when Jasper earned an "A" on his history test, he was not so quick to assume that he was intelligent. Which of the following biases in social cognition best explains Jasper's behavior?
   a. The fundamental attribution error
   b. The self-serving bias
   c. The social desirability bias
   d. The actor/observer bias

Answers 1. a; 2. b; 3. d

Prejudice: How It Occurs, and How to Reduce It

Learning Objective

● Define and distinguish among prejudice, stereotypes, and discrimination, and explain how prejudice develops.

Prejudices based on race, gender, sexual orientation, age, religion, country of origin, and other perceived differences still hamper many people's ability to live a productive and happy life. People have been harassed and belittled, lost jobs, and even been killed because of prejudice. In 2005, the FBI reported a total of 7,163 incidents of hate crimes. Most of these incidents were motivated by racial prejudice, with religious prejudice and prejudice based on sexual orientation the next most frequent motives for hate crimes (Federal Bureau of Investigation, 2006a).

Besides violent crimes and crimes against property, there are subtler forms of discrimination. One study found that African American loan applicants in Columbus, Ohio, were more likely to have their loan applications denied when they were trying to buy homes in White neighborhoods than when they attempted to secure financing for homes in Black neighborhoods (Holloway, 1998). And despite gains in equal rights over the last several decades, women have still not achieved equal status in the workforce, academia, or the government (Fischer, 1992; Smith, 2002). Prejudice remains a serious social problem. Because prejudice poses a threat to all of us, understanding where prejudice comes from is essential.

We can view prejudice as an extension of normal cognitive processes, in that prejudices are attitudes that develop like all other attitudes. At the same time, prejudices are unique because they are especially problematic and divisive attitudes that can cause upheaval in a society. As we look at the development of prejudice, we will examine the similarities between normal cognition and prejudiced thought.

Prejudice and Stereotypes

You will recall from Chapter 6 that as we acquire knowledge about the world, we store that information in generalized knowledge structures called *schemata*. Schemata reside in our long-term memory and allow us to more efficiently encode, store, and retrieve information (Fiske & Taylor, 1991). When we form a schema for a particular group of people, that schema is referred to as a **stereotype**. All of us have stereotypes for the various groups of people—such as professors, children, or females—we encounter in life. Our stereotypes allow us to make assumptions about others and to have certain expectations about how others will behave.

Although stereotypes are generally helpful to us, they are related to the prejudices that cause untold difficulties for humankind. One way to conceptualize a **prejudice** is as a stereotype gone awry. A stereotype can be thought of as the *cognitive* component of an attitude (Aronson, Wilson, & Akert, 2005) or the knowledge you have stored in memory about some group of people. Stereotypes become problematic when we generically apply them to all members of a group without regard to those individuals' unique characteristics. Furthermore, when a stereotype contains biased and negative information about a particular group of people, the stereotype begins to look like a prejudice (e.g., Chory-Assad & Tamborini, 2003). Finally, when a biased, negative stereotype becomes coupled with a negative *affective* or emotional reaction toward all (or most) people belonging to that group, a prejudice results.

In the mind of the prejudiced person, members of a particular group are disliked and labeled as having negative characteristics, regardless of their individual qualities. Additionally, prejudice can affect how the prejudiced person *behaves* toward others. All too often, prejudice motivates people to treat others poorly. **Discrimination** is the behavioral expression of a prejudice. For example, not considering a woman for a job as a forklift operator simply because she is female would be an act of discrimination.

Stereotype Threat

Like a woman seeking employment in a male-dominated field, many people live with the fear that others may harbor prejudices about them. Psychologist Claude Steele proposes that some victims of prejudice actually end up reinforcing certain aspects of the prejudices held against them because of a phenomenon called *stereotype threat*. Stereotype threat exists when a person fears that others will judge her not on her own qualities, but rather on prejudicial stereotypes held about the group(s) to which she belongs (Steele, 1997). Understandably, this fear can lead to considerable anxiety in minorities because of the negative nature of the prejudices they face. For example, women often suffer stereotype threat in the workplace. Because of widespread negative stereotyping of women in the workplace, females expect

stereotype a schema for a particular group of people

prejudice a largely negative stereotype that is unfairly applied to all members of a group regardless of their individual characteristics

discrimination the behavioral expression of a prejudice

their coworkers to give them less credit for successes and more blame for failures (e.g., Heilman & Kram, 1983).

Studies have shown that stereotype threat can actually inhibit performance on a task. For example, normally high-achieving females tend to score less well on mathematics problems, but not on verbal tasks, when they are asked to perform these tasks in an environment where they are outnumbered by men (Inzlicht & Ben-Zeev, 2000). In this situation, females presumably become aware of the negative stereotypes that many people hold—that men are better at math—and the fear of being perceived to be mathematically inept (stereotype threat) then impairs their math performance. Females are not stereotyped as being poor at verbal tasks, so there is no stereotype threat for verbal tasks, and females exhibit no impairment in performance even when they are outnumbered by males. Stereotype threat can thus become a *self-fulfilling prophecy*, in which a woman behaves in a manner that actually reinforces negative stereotypes about females (e.g., Davies, Spencer, Quinn, & Gerhardstein, 2002; Quinn & Spencer, 2001; J. Steele, James, & Barnett, 2002).

Stereotype threat has also been shown to impair African Americans' academic performance (e.g., Steele & Aronson, 1995), and may contribute to some African Americans' experiencing *disidentification* with certain aspects of European American culture. For example, if young African Americans experience stereotype threat in school (they perceive that others expect them to fail), one way they may protect themselves emotionally is by devaluing education. If one does not feel that academic achievement is important, then if one fails at academics, it is not damaging to his or her self-esteem (Steele, 1997). Unfortunately, this not only prevents some African Americans from achieving academically, it may also place pressure on those African Americans who do wish to pursue academic success. If your friends devalue your dreams, you must either abandon your plans or distance yourself from your friends—both of which can be painful. One thing is certain: As long as negative stereotypes persist, it's a safe bet that many people will suffer as a result.

Social Transmission of Prejudice

© Mark Peterson/Corbis

This child is likely to adopt the prejudices of her parents through modeling.

Like other attitudes, prejudices can develop through the processes of classical conditioning, operant conditioning, and social learning (Duckitt, 1992). As you can see in ■ YOU REVIEW 10.1, these types of learning allow prejudices to develop and also be passed from person to person within a culture. The experiences we have with other groups of people, the models we are exposed to (Kowalski, 2003), and the rewards and punishments we receive in life all have the power to mold our stereotypes and prejudices.

How easily prejudices can be learned was dramatically demonstrated in one of the most famous classroom exercises ever done on prejudice. In the 1970s, grade school teacher Jane Elliot decided to teach her third-grade class an important lesson about prejudice. She believed that her students, who were all rural White children, could benefit from learning about prejudice from both sides of the fence.

One day in class, Elliot told her students that she had recently heard that scientists had determined that brown-eyed people were inferior to blue-eyed people. She told the class that brown-eyed people were less intelligent, trustworthy, and nice than the "superior" blue-eyed people. To make the group differences very salient, Elliot had all the brown-eyed children wear brown cloth collars over their clothing so they could be immediately identified as members of the "inferior" group of students.

Within hours of her announcement concerning eye color, Elliot had created a strong prejudice in her classroom. The blue-eyed children made fun of the brown-eyed children. The blue-eyes called the brown-eyes names, ostracized them, and in general treated them cruelly. A fight even occurred on the playground as a result of the prejudice. In less than a day, Elliot turned a peaceful, egalitarian classroom into a hotbed of prejudice and discrimination (Monteith & Winters, 2002).

You Review 10.1

Learning to Be Prejudiced Against Men

TYPE OF LEARNING	SITUATION	OUTCOME
Classical conditioning	Marlita is robbed at knifepoint (US) by a man (CS). During the attack, she feels terror and anger (UR/CR).	After the attack, Marlita feels anger and terror when she sees men. She has been classically conditioned to feel negative emotions in response to men.
Operant conditioning	Bobbi makes fun of some boys at her school. She calls them "stupid crybabies" (behavior). All of Bobbi's friends laugh when they see her behaving this way (reward).	Bobbi is more likely to make fun of boys in the future because in the past she has been rewarded for doing so. Her friends have operantly conditioned her prejudiced, discriminatory behavior.
Social learning	From a young age, Jackie hears her mother frequently say that men are sloppy, stubborn, insensitive creatures.	Jackie is likely to model her mother's prejudices and adopt her mother's belief that men are sloppy, stubborn, and insensitive.

Elliot's demonstration showed how quickly prejudice can be learned. Admittedly, the environment Elliot created in her classroom was deliberately designed to create prejudice. What other types of environments may contribute to the development of prejudices? Can prejudice be developed within a family, for instance? There is some evidence to suggest that we do adopt the prejudices of our parents, but having prejudiced parents does not guarantee that we will become prejudiced. In one study that examined the match between parental values and those held by their children, it was found that children are most likely to have attitudes similar to their parents when the parents hold egalitarian beliefs. When parents hold prejudicial attitudes, the match between their values and their children's values is less strong (Rohan & Zanna, 1996).

It appears that when parents hold strong prejudices, the children may pick up these prejudices but later find that their peers do not reinforce them for holding such negative views. Because they are not reinforced and may even be punished by their peers for holding prejudices, they experience a decline in prejudice that distances them from their parents' values. But when parents hold egalitarian values, their children may pick up these values and be reinforced by their peers for having them. Their values then remain more like those of their parents (Aronson et al., 2005). This line of research makes a powerful argument for teaching tolerance in schools and in society because if tolerance becomes prevalent in a culture, it may have the power to override what happens in the home.

Intergroup Dynamics and Prejudice

We all belong to certain groups: families, schools, clubs, states, countries, religions, and races. These groups and the roles we play in them help define who we are as individuals (e.g., Gergen & Gergen, 1988). Because we tend to identify with the groups to which we belong, we also tend to prefer the groups of which we are members.

IN-GROUP BIAS: US VS. THEM

We tend to like the people in our group a little more than we like the people who are not members. In other words, we exhibit an **in-group bias** (Hewstone, Rubin, & Willis, 2002). We tend to like our family members more than strangers. We like those who attend our

in-group bias our tendency to favor people who belong to the same groups that we do school more than those who do not. We have a bias toward liking our country's citizens a little more than foreigners.

Think of the groups of spectators at a sporting event. Each group sits on its team's side, and at times the rivalry between the two sides erupts into name-calling and even violence. If these same people met under other conditions in which their team affiliations were not obvious, such as at the grocery store or library, do you think they would be as likely to call each other names and fight? Probably not. Why do we sometimes allow our group affiliations to bias how we feel about and treat others? It appears to boil down to self-esteem.

We apparently derive some of our self-esteem from the groups of which we are members. One way to enhance self-esteem is by belonging to a group we perceive as good and desirable. For example, if you perceive your religion as being the *best* religion, then belonging to this religious group increases your self-esteem. Unfortunately, one way to perceive your particular group as being good is to believe that other groups are not as good (Tajfel, 1982). When our group succeeds at something, we tend to be especially proud (Cialdini et al., 1976). In the absence of meaningful victory, we still tend to view our in-group members as superior to **out-group** members (Brewer, 1979; Molero, Navas, Gonzalez, Aleman, & Cuadrado, 2003; Tajfel, 1982).

> ### You Asked...
>
> *Why do people have the tendency to generalize?*   DIANA FLORES, STUDENT

The in-group bias tends to make us prejudiced against those who are not part of our social groups. Further, the in-group bias tends to affect the way we *perceive* out-group members, causing us to see members of an out-group as being pretty much all alike. Researchers call this tendency the **out-group homogeneity bias** (Linville, Fischer, & Salovey, 1989). Individual characteristics are perceived not to differ much from the stereotype that defines the group. So once we have knowledge about one member of an out-group, we tend to apply it to all people in that group (Quattrone & Jones, 1980).

INTERGROUP CONFLICT AND PREJUDICE: IT'S THEIR FAULT

Realistic-conflict theory (Levine & Campbell, 1972) proposes that conflict among groups for resources motivates the development of prejudice. In the United States, immigrants are often the targets of prejudice because they are perceived as coming here "to steal jobs away from hard-working Americans" (Esses, Dovidio, Jackson, & Armstrong, 2001). One of the authors lives in a predominantly White town that has recently experienced large influxes of Latino immigrants from Mexico and Central and South America. At times, she has heard comments reflecting anti-Latino sentiments in her community. Typically these comments mention the loss of jobs to immigrants, even though unemployment is low in her community, and most of the immigrants hold low-paying jobs in poultry-processing plants that many community members do not want. Minority out-group members often play the role of *scapegoat* when times are hard (Allport, 1954/1979). In modern America, as you might expect, racial prejudice most often exists when groups are in direct competition for the same jobs (Simpson & Yinger, 1985).

Possibly the most famous study ever conducted on conflict and prejudice is Muzafer Sherif's Robber's Cave experiment (Sherif, Harvey, White, Hood, & Sherif, 1961). Sherif and his colleagues conducted this experiment in a naturalistic setting, a summer boys' camp at Robber's Cave State Park in Oklahoma (hence the experiment's nickname). The participants were normal, healthy, middle-class, White, Protestant, 11- to 12-year-old boys who attended Boy Scout camp at the park. Prior to participation in the camp, the boys were all strangers to one another.

out-group a group that is distinct from one's own and so usually an object of more hostility or dislike than one's in-group

out-group homogeneity [home-uh-juh-NEE-it-tee] **bias** our tendency to see out-group members as being pretty much all alike

realistic-conflict theory the theory that prejudice stems from competition for scarce resources

As they arrived at the camp, the boys were randomly assigned to one of two cabins, Eagles' cabin or Rattlers' cabin. The cabins were situated fairly far apart to ensure that the two groups would not have much contact with each other. The boys in each group lived together, ate together, and spent much of their time together. Under these conditions of isolation from each other, the Eagles and the Rattlers became separate, tight-knit in-groups. Once each group bonded, the experimenters placed the Eagles and Rattlers together under conditions of conflict.

In this next phase, the experimenters had the Eagles and Rattlers compete with each other in sporting events. The winning group would get prizes that 12-year-old boys find attractive, such as pocketknives. The losers got nothing for their efforts except defeat. As a result of this competition, the Eagles and the Rattlers began to call each other names, sabotage each other's cabins and belongings, and even engage in physical violence against one another. In short, the Eagles hated the Rattlers, and the Rattlers hated the Eagles. A prejudice based on the relatively meaningless distinctions of being Eagles or Rattlers was fully developed in the boys. When the prejudice between the Eagles and Rattlers reached the point of physical violence, the experimenters stopped the competition between the boys and sought ways to reduce the prejudice that had developed.

Does Social Contact Reduce Prejudice?

One of Sherif's strategies to reduce prejudice was to increase noncompetitive contact between the Eagles and the Rattlers (e.g., watching movies together). In fact, the idea that contact between groups is enough to reduce prejudice, the so-called **contact hypothesis**, has been around for quite some time (Lee & Humphrey, 1943, cited in Allport, 1954/1979). If people from different in-groups see a lot of each other, won't they realize that the prejudices they hold about one another are unfounded and abandon them?

As Sherif found out, mere contact often does little to reduce prejudice (e.g., Poore et al., 2002). One reason contact doesn't work is that when people from different groups are thrown together, they tend to self-segregate. A drive through any big city illustrates this point. Neighborhoods are often well defined on the basis of ethnicity and race—even though people are legally free to live where they choose. If contact is to reduce prejudice, it has to be of a certain kind—it has to be *cooperative contact*.

After experimenting with increased contact between the Eagles and the Rattlers, Sherif and his colleagues (1961) did find a way to reduce the prejudice between the two groups of boys. The key was a special type of contact. Sherif and his colleagues created superordinate

contact hypothesis the theory that contact between groups is an effective means of reducing prejudice between them

Superordinate goals are an effective means of reducing prejudice. These people are likely to see themselves as members of the same in-group as they work together to survive this challenge. As a result, they are likely to experience less prejudice toward one another.

Alistair Berg/Getty Images

goals for the Eagles and the Rattlers. A **superordinate goal** is a goal that both groups want to accomplish but cannot without the help of the other group. For instance, the researchers disrupted the water supply that both groups used by tampering with the water pipes. To reestablish water to the camp, the Eagles and Rattlers had to work together to find the source of the trouble. While they were trying to solve their mutual problem, the Eagles and Rattlers did not seem to have much time to hate one another. In another instance, a food supply truck broke down, and the two groups had to work together to push-start the truck. Without their combined efforts, both groups would have gone hungry. After a series of such contacts, the prejudice between the groups began to dissolve, perhaps because the Eagles and Rattlers now saw themselves as part of the same group—the group that was trying to find food and water. Without clear lines between the boys, there was no basis for in-group or out-group bias or prejudice. The researchers noted that friendships began to form between individual Eagles and Rattlers, and as a whole, the Rattlers and Eagles began to cooperate, spend time together, and even share their money. The prejudice that was once so strong was dramatically reduced (Sherif, 1966).

Based in part on the results of the Robber's Cave study, researchers have attempted to outline the characteristics of the type of contact between groups that reduces prejudice. The most effective strategies are ones in which:

- The different groups need each other.
- The different groups have a common, superordinate goal that requires everyone's effort to achieve.
- The different groups work shoulder to shoulder on an equal playing field to accomplish the goal.
- The contact is hospitable, informal, and free from negative emotional interaction.
- Contact with out-group members lasts for a significant period of time.
- The norms governing the contact situation must promote harmony and mutual respect.

One practical application of these conditions is called a *jigsaw classroom* (Aronson, 2000). A jigsaw classroom is one in which students from diverse ethnic groups are asked to work together on a project in a cooperative way. Each child is responsible for a different piece of the project, which forces the children to be interdependent. Because they must rely on each other, the children begin to focus more on the tasks at hand and less on their differences. According to psychologist Elliot Aronson (2000), research on the outcomes of jigsaw classrooms over the last 25 years consistently indicate that as participants begin to identify as members of the same in-group, prejudice and hostility among the children are reduced, and self-esteem and academic performance are increased. These findings further underscore the message of the Robber's Cave experiment—that cooperation rather than competition can work to lower prejudice in the world.

We have seen that prejudices can affect the judgments we make about other people. When we attribute negative characteristics to people simply because they belong to a certain social group, we are behaving prejudicially. Our prejudices can, in turn, affect the way we treat other people. Regardless of whether we base our impressions on a prejudice or on actual behavior, we tend to want to spend more time with people we *like*. We may decide to enter into a friendship or a romantic relationship with someone about whom we have formed a positive impression. The relationship may turn out to be wonderful, or it may fail. In the aftermath of the breakup of a relationship, we often ask ourselves, "What did I ever see in this person?" This is the question that we will tackle next as we look at what attracts us to others.

superordinate goal a goal that is shared by different groups

Let's Review!

In this section, we discussed prejudice and ways to reduce it. As a quick check of your understanding, answer these questions.

1. Kelly is a manager at a firm that has been troubled by considerable prejudice between its male and female employees. Kelly wants to institute a program that will reduce the level of prejudice between the sexes. Which of the following plans has the best chance of working?
   a. Appoint opposite-sex managers to supervise workers.
   b. Have a "battle of the sexes" to see which sex can outperform the other on the job.
   c. Form work teams to solve company problems, and make sure that the teams contain both male and female members.
   d. Threaten to fire anyone who says or does anything prejudicial, and post this message around the workplace to ensure that everyone knows about the policy.

2. Relative to in-group members, we tend to view out-group members as being _____.
   a. less like us   c. less favorable
   b. more homogeneous   d. All of the above

3. Which of the following is the best example of cooperative contact?
   a. Teachers supervising students taking a math test
   b. A manager meeting with employees to discuss sales figures
   c. A police officer speaking to an elementary school class about the dangers of drugs
   d. A citizen's group meeting to find ways to reduce crime in their neighborhood

Answers 1. c; 2. d; 3. d

The Nature of Attraction

- Describe the factors affecting attraction: exposure, proximity, similarity, balance, and physical attractiveness.

Learning Objective

The attitudes that we form about a person determine whether or not we will be attracted to this person as a friend or as a romantic partner. The affective component of the attitudes we hold about someone is particularly important. If a person produces positive emotional reactions in us, we are much more likely to find him or her attractive. Think about the people closest to you. How do you *feel* about your best friend and your significant other? We are betting that most of you generally feel positive emotions about those you love. Most of us do. When it comes to attraction, the most important question is: What makes us feel good about another person?

Proximity

One of the most intriguing findings in the area of attraction concerns how much exposure we have to certain people and how the exposure affects our feelings of attraction for them. Recall from Chapter 8 that the more often we see a person or an object, the more we tend to like it. This trend, called the *mere exposure effect* (Lee, 2001; Zajonc, 1968), appears to be true for a variety of stimuli. One study found that participants liked Japanese ideographs (written characters) more if they had been repeatedly exposed to them (Moreland & Zajonc, 1977).

Students who sit in close proximity to each other in the classroom are more likely to be friends and lovers.

Another study found that participants preferred tones that they had heard repeatedly over those they had heard only a few times (W. R. Wilson, 1979).

Mere exposure also seems to play a role in our liking for others (Zebrowitz, White, & Wieneke, 2008). Many studies have shown that we tend to be friends and lovers with those who live and work close to us (Clarke, 1952; Festinger, 1951; Festinger, Schachter, & Back, 1950; Ineichen, 1979; Segal, 1974). The more **proximity**, or geographical closeness, we have to someone in our daily lives, the more exposure we have to them, and the more we tend to like them. For example, within an apartment building, the closer a person's apartment is to yours, the higher the probability that you will be friends with that person (Festinger, 1951). This is true even when apartments are assigned on a random basis, as you might find in university housing (Festinger et al., 1950). Attraction to those who live and work nearby seems to hold across cultures as well. Studies have found evidence supporting a relationship between proximity and liking in both Africa (Brewer & Campbell, 1976) and France (Maisonneuve, Palmade, & Fourment, 1952).

Think about the people you sit close to in your classes. You may not have realized it, but your seat in a classroom may have an impact on your social relationships. The closer you sit to someone in a classroom, the more likely you are to be friends (and perhaps more) with that person (Segal, 1974). The effects of proximity also indicate that the architecture of apartment buildings and office buildings may influence the social relationships we form.

> ### You Asked...
> *Is it true that opposites attract?*
> CAROLANNE PARKER, STUDENT

If, for example, you live or work on a busy hallway, you may have more relationships than someone who is on a less traveled hallway. So a smart person would choose his or her classroom seat, apartment, or office wisely!

Similarity

There are two old adages about the people we tend to choose as friends or romantic partners. One says, "Birds of a feather flock together," and the other says, "Opposites attract." You probably know some couples who demonstrate both views of attraction. But what does the average person look for? Do we want someone who is similar to us, or are we looking for someone who is different to complement our personality?

Research on this issue indicates that indeed, "Birds of a feather flock together." When choosing a romantic partner, we tend to gravitate to people who are of similar age, socioeconomic status, education, intelligence, race, religion, attitudes, power, and physical attractiveness (Brehm, 1992; Browning, Kessler, Hatfield, & Choo, 1999; Hendrick & Hendrick, 1983). Furthermore, similarity seems to predict attraction across a variety of cultures, including Mexico, India, and Japan (Byrne et al., 1971). Similarity also seems to be a factor in the friends we choose (Kandel, 1978; Newcomb, 1961; Rubin, Lynch, Coplan, Rose-Krasnor, & Booth, 1994).

Physical Attractiveness

One of the first things we notice about a potential romantic partner is his or her physical attractiveness. Although standards of physical attractiveness vary across cultures (see ■ FIGURE 10.3),

proximity physical closeness

© Les Gibbon/Alamy Images

it is an important factor in determining our attraction to others. In a classic study that examined physical attractiveness and attraction in a blind-date scenario, physical attractiveness was the only factor found to predict whether a person wanted to go out on a second date (Walster, Aronson, Abrahams, & Rottman, 1966).

When it comes to choosing potential partners, physical attractiveness seems to be important to both men and women, but men seem to place particular emphasis on how attractive their potential romantic partners are (Green, Buchanan, & Heuer, 1984; Woll, 1986). This special emphasis that men place on physical attractiveness seems to hold for both homosexual and heterosexual men. Heterosexual and homosexual women, on the other hand, place more importance on the psychological traits of their potential partners. So it seems that although physical attractiveness is important to women, it is not the *most* important aspect of a partner (Deaux & Hanna, 1984).

Female or male, we tend to be romantically involved with people whose level of physical attractiveness is comparable to our own. This tendency, called the **matching hypothesis**, seems to be true of both dating and married couples (Zajonc, Adelmann, Murphy, & Neidenthal, 1987).

Interestingly, the influence of physical attractiveness on romantic relationships seems to be mirrored in our same-sex friendships. The matching hypothesis predicts that our same-sex friends will be, on average, about as attractive as we are (McKillip & Reidel, 1983). And although both men and women seem to choose their friends on the basis of their physical attractiveness, again men place more emphasis on this characteristic than do women (Berscheid, Dion, Walster, & Walster, 1971; Feingold, 1988; Perlini, Bertolissi, & Lind, 1999). The

matching hypothesis the theory that we are attracted to people whose level of physical attractiveness is similar to our own

FIGURE

10.3

Cultural Differences in Physical Attractiveness

Which of these people do you find attractive? Standards of physical attractiveness vary across cultures.

importance of physical attractiveness in social relationships isn't surprising in light of findings that we tend to perceive attractive people differently from the unattractive. For example, attractive people are perceived to be more interesting, sociable, kind, sensitive, and nurturing than unattractive people (Dion, Berscheid, & Walster, 1972). With all these *perceived* qualities, no wonder we want to be friends and lovers with attractive people!

However, there may also be another reason why we prefer attractive people. Perhaps being attracted to others is in part biological and instinctive (see *Neuroscience Applies to Your World*). In an interesting study, researchers found that babies as young as 2 months old looked longer at attractive faces than they did at unattractive ones (Langlois et al., 1987), indicating that they preferred the attractive faces. Because it is hard to imagine that 2-month-old babies have had time to *learn* to be biased toward attractive people, these findings suggest that we are born with an instinctive preference for good-looking people. Perhaps this instinct has evolved in humans because certain features that are found in attractive people (e.g., symmetrical facial features) indicate good health. In terms of natural selection and evolution, it makes sense for us to be sexually attracted to people who are healthy and therefore able to facilitate our ability to produce offspring.

Pure attraction is not the only reason that we are drawn to others, however. Sometimes our desire to be with others serves a purpose other than sex and reproduction. In the next section, we will further explore our social nature by examining some of the reasons we are driven to be with others in the form of social groups.

Neuroscience Applies to Your World:

The Chemistry of Romance

When it comes to love and romance, is there anything to the notion of "chemistry" between people? Perhaps. Psychologists have identified three separate emotional systems involved in romantic relationships. *Lust* is our sex drive or desire for sexual gratification. *Romantic attraction* is our physical and emotional desire for a specific person. *Attachment* is companionate love, or our desire to be close with our partner. Interestingly, psychologists have discovered that each of these emotional systems seems to be related to the action of different chemicals in the body. Lust is governed by hormones, in particular, estrogens and androgens. Experiencing romantic attraction is related to increased dopamine and norepinephrine, but lowered serotonin in the brain. Experiencing attachment or love is associated with the action of other neurotransmitters and hormones, including neuropeptides, oxytocin, and vasopressin (Fisher, 2000).

© RI/Alamy

If love and romance are related to chemical action in the brain, does this mean that altering the chemical environment of the brain can affect our romantic feelings for our partner? Some researchers believe so. Psychologist Dixie Meyer suggests that antidepressant drugs such as selective serotonin reuptake inhibitors that increase serotonin action in the brain may also interfere with the brain chemicals that support romantic attraction, resulting in the person's experiencing reduced satisfaction with his/her romantic relationship (Meyer, 2007). According to Meyer, therapists should be aware that satisfaction with one's romantic life is affected by many things, including perhaps one's biochemistry and the medications he or she is taking.

Let's Review!

In this section, we discussed what attracts us to others. For a quick assessment of your understanding, answer these questions.

1. Based on the available psychological research, you are most likely to end up in a romantic relationship with _____.
   a. a neighbor who shares your values
   b. a person from another state who shares your values
   c. a fellow student who does not share your values
   d. a coworker who has opposite views

2. Attractive people are assumed to be all of the following things, *except* _____.
   a. interesting
   b. sociable
   c. nurturant
   d. proud

3. Which of the following statements is true?
   a. Women are unconcerned with physical attractiveness when choosing a romantic partner.
   b. Women and men are equally interested in physical attractiveness when choosing a romantic partner.
   c. Neither men nor women pay that much attention to physical attractiveness when choosing a romantic partner.
   d. Men pay more attention to physical attractiveness when choosing a romantic partner.

Answers 1. a; 2. d; 3. d

Social Psychology: How Do We Understand and Interact With Others?

Stop, LOOK, and LEARN

ATTITUDES

Attitudes
develop and change through
Learning
Dissonance
Persuasion

IMPRESSION FORMATION

Impression formation
sometimes involves heuristics
such as the **fundamental attribution error**,
actor/observer bias, and **self-serving bias**
to make **attributions** about the causes of behavior.

PREJUDICE

Stereotypes become **prejudices**
when they are over-applied and biased.
Learning, **in-group/out-group bias**, and **realistic conflict**
contribute to the development of prejudice.
Cooperative contact is an effective means
of reducing prejudice.

ATTRACTION

Attraction to potential romantic partners is influenced by
proximity,
their similarity to us,
physical attractiveness,
and biochemicals.

Groups and Group Influence

- Describe the factors that affect our tendency to conform to the norms of a group, and how this affects group decision making.

Throughout our lifetime, we will belong to a multitude of groups—some of which we join and some of which we belong to by circumstance—families, communities, clubs, teams, professional organizations, and so on. For many of us, belonging to such groups is something that we value, but why? Psychologists suggest several potential explanations for why we join groups (Baumeister & Leary, 1995; Paulus, 1989). Groups may give us companionship, make us feel safe, make us feel proud, provide us with information, or help us achieve our goals in life. Regardless of why we join a group, once we do join, the group and its collective members then have the power to influence our behavior.

Social Forces Within Groups: Norms and Cohesiveness

Groups are characterized by the expectations and attitudes of their members. Group **norms** are the laws that guide the behavior of group members. Norms can be explicitly stated rules or unwritten expectations that members have for behavior within the group. Norms tell us how to dress, how to behave, how to interact with each other, and so on. Virtually every group has its own unique set of norms—each family, culture, workplace, and group of friends may have different expectations for how its members should behave. For an example of how norms can vary across ethnic groups in the United States, take a look at ■ TABLE 10.2.

In general, we do not like to break the norms of the groups to which we belong. When we do, we may face several unpleasant consequences. Group members may ridicule us or try to persuade us to change our behavior, or—perhaps most threatening—we might be thrown out or ostracized from the group. Recall that groups often fulfill social needs and give us a sense of security and identity. Because of these benefits, we often value our group memberships and wish to protect them. The degree to which members wish to maintain membership in the group is referred to as **cohesiveness**. In groups in which members tend to have very positive attitudes about their membership in the group, cohesiveness is high, and the group tends to be close-knit. When cohesiveness is high, the pressure we feel to meet group norms is also high. This means that as our attraction for certain groups increases, so does the influence these groups have over us. The more we value our membership in a group, the less willing we are to risk losing that membership. Therefore, group cohesiveness helps ensure **conformity** within a group as group members modify their behavior to avoid breaking the group's norms (Crandall, 1988; Latané & L'Herrou, 1996; Schachter, 1951).

norm unwritten rule or expectation for how group members should behave

cohesiveness [coe-HEE-sive-ness] the degree to which members of a group value their group membership; cohesive groups are tight-knit groups

conformity behaving in accordance with group norms

We are likely to conform to the norms of groups because we do not want to be ostracized or ridiculed.

Seth Goldfarb/Getty Images

Table 10.2 Some Cross-Cultural Differences in Norms Governing Conversation Within the United States

CULTURE → NORM ↓	NATIVE AMERICAN CULTURE	EUROPEAN AMERICAN CULTURE	ASIAN AMERICAN CULTURE	AFRICAN AMERICAN CULTURE	HISPANIC AMERICAN CULTURE
LEVEL OF EYE CONTACT	Direct eye contact is seen as invasive and disrespectful.	Direct eye contact is generally expected—especially when being spoken to.	Direct eye contact that lasts more than a second or two is considered disrespectful—especially with one's superiors.	Direct eye contact is expected and prolonged during speaking, but less when listening.	Direct eye contact is often viewed as disrespectful—especially when one is being spoken to.
LEVEL OF EMOTION DISPLAYED	Conversations are often unemotional and dispassionate.	Highly emotional, animated conversation is not preferred in public settings.	Controlling one's display of emotion is very important.	Conversations are often passionate and animated.	Conversations that take place among Hispanics only may be very emotional and animated. Conversations that occur in ethnically mixed settings tend to be more low-key.
LEVEL OF GESTURE USE	In daily conversation, gesture use tends to be restrained.	Moderate gesture use is typical.	Gesture use is restrained. Asian Americans tend to use fewer gestures than European Americans.	Frequent and large gestures are the norm.	Moderate to high use of gestures is typical.

Comma Image/Jupiter Images

© PYMCA/Alamy

© Masterfile

Source: Adapted from Elliott, C. E. (1999). Cross-cultural communication styles. Available online at http://www.awesomelibrary.org/multiculturaltoolkit-patterns.htm

Conformity Within a Group

One of the most influential psychologists to formally study the process of conformity was Solomon Asch. During the 1950s, Asch conducted a series of classic experiments on conformity and the factors that make us more or less likely to conform in a given situation. Asch (1951) had male participants engage in a perceptual task with eight other men. The participants were unaware that the eight other men in the experiment were *confederates*, or actors posing as participants. Each participant, along with the eight confederates, was shown a series of lines and asked to match the length of a test line to one of three other comparison lines (■ FIGURE 10.4). The experiment was set up so that the confederates made their judgments first. The participant heard all of the confederates in turn choose—aloud—the wrong line. By the time the true participant's turn came, he had heard all the others choose what was clearly the wrong line. A norm had formed in the group, the norm

Test line	Comparison lines		
8"	6 1/4"	8"	6 3/4"

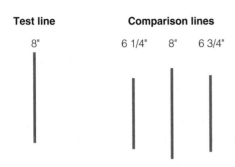

FIGURE

10.4   The Asch Procedure for Testing Conformity

In Asch's study, 74% of the subjects conformed and chose the 6¼-inch line as the match for the comparison line after hearing the confederates make this obviously incorrect choice.

Source: Based on Asch, 1951.

normative conformity conformity that occurs when group members change their behavior to meet group norms but are not persuaded to change their beliefs and attitudes

informational conformity conformity that occurs when conformity pressures actually persuade group members to adopt new beliefs and/or attitudes

Nonconformists seem to enjoy violating the norms of the majority group.

of choosing the wrong line. The *dependent variable* in Asch's study was whether the participant would conform to the norm or whether he would go with his own perception and choose the correct comparison line.

What do you think Asch found? What would you have done in this situation? In fact, Asch found that 74% of his participants conformed at least once during the experiment. Apparently, many people can be easily made to conform. Only 26% of the participants consistently stood by their convictions and refused to conform.

Asch also found that as the *majority group* (the number of confederates who choose the wrong line) increased, so did the participants' tendency to conform. However, Asch found that maximum conformity was reached in the participants when only three confederates were present.

Since Asch's original experiments, others have studied the factors that affect conformity in groups. Overall, the picture that emerges from the research on conformity is that we are most likely to conform if:

- We do not feel confident of our abilities.
- Cohesiveness is high in the group.
- Our responses are made public (we are not anonymous).
- The group has at least three members who are unanimous in their dedication to the norm.
- The idea that one *should* conform is itself a norm in our culture and/or we do not feel a personal need to be individuated.

EXPLAINING CONFORMITY: THE EFFECTS OF CULTURE AND CONFIDENCE

Asch showed us that conformity is rather easy to obtain, but why are so willing to adhere to group norms? As part of his *debriefing* at the end of his experiments, Asch asked participants why they had chosen the wrong line. Their answers were interesting.

Some participants indicated that they chose the wrong line even though they knew it was wrong. This type of conformity, involving a change of behavior to fit a norm but no real attitude change or persuasion, is called **normative conformity**. The primary motive for normative conformity seems to be a desire to fit in with the group and be liked by others. This is one reason that cohesiveness tends to increase conformity. When we like being in the group, we want others to like us as well (Sakari, 1975). Research has shown that people in cultures that value individualism (such as the United States) are less likely to conform than are people from cultures that place more value on being part of a group (such as Japan; Bond & Smith, 1996; Hamilton & Sanders, 1995; Killen, Crystal, & Watanabe, 2002). In cultures in which nonconformists are admired, you can expect to see less conformity.

Yet some of Asch's participants had other reasons for conforming. Some reported that they chose the wrong line because they became convinced that it was the correct choice. These participants were actually persuaded by the majority group. Recall that persuasion leads to attitude change. The way these participants perceived the lines and what they believed to be true about the lines changed as a function of the majority opinion. The majority opinion *informed* these participants of what the correct choice was. For this reason, conformity that results in actual attitude change is referred to as **informational conformity**. Informational conformity is heightened when people are unsure of their opinions and insecure about their abilities (Cacioppo & Petty, 1980).

The Dark Side of Conformity: The Stanford Prison Experiment

In 1971, Stanford University psychologist Phillip Zimbardo set out to conduct an experiment on the effects of a prison setting on the behavior of prisoners and guards. Twenty-four healthy male participants were randomly assigned to play the role of either a prisoner or a guard in a mock prison set up in the basement of a campus building. All participants wore uniforms appropriate to their roles as guards or prisoners. The prisoners wore prison uniforms and were referred to by serial numbers rather than their names. The guards had dark sunglasses, wore khaki uniforms, and carried clubs.

The experiment was slated to last two weeks, with the prisoners remaining in the "prison" for the entire experiment. Within days, some very disturbing behavior began to emerge. The men assigned to play the guards became abusive toward the mock prisoners. The men assigned to play the prisoners became docile and depressed, allowing the so-called guards to abuse and manipulate them. The mock guards hooded the prisoners, called them names, and subjected them to a host of demeaning, humiliating activities. Their behavior got so out of hand that Zimbardo had to cancel the experiment before the end of the first week (Zimbardo, 1972).

Why would 24 healthy young men begin to behave like animals in such a short time? A great deal of their behavior stemmed from the fact that they were isolated from the outside world and the norms of society. Within the prison-like setting, a new set of norms sprang up—ones that called for the guards to be abusive and the prisoners to be submissive. Another factor at work is **deindividuation**. In deindividuation, a person's behavior becomes controlled more by external norms than by the person's own internal values and morals. In short, the roles that the men were playing became stronger determinants of their behavior than their own attitudes and beliefs. Several factors aided the deindividuation process:

- All participants wore uniforms, which heightened their anonymity.
- All participants were "playing" an assigned *social role*. As "actors," the participants' behavior was more controlled by their roles and their ideas about how prison guards and prisoners typically behave than it was by their own internal values and beliefs.
- The guards hid behind dark glasses, which heightened their anonymity.
- The prisoners were referred to by numbers, not names, which made them seem less human.
- The experiment was conducted in a basement, away from the outside world and its norms.
- There was no strong leader who argued for fair treatment of the prisoners.

When deindividuation occurs, dangerous things can happen. All it takes is one person to begin behaving badly, and even good people may blindly conform to this new norm of behavior. Sometimes being part of the group can be problematic, as we will see again in the next section.

Most of us will belong to many different groups in our lifetime, and these groups will have the power to influence our behavior through conformity. It is worthwhile looking at how groups make the decisions that set up an agenda for the group.

deindividuation [DEE-in-dih-vid-you-AYE-shun] a state in which a person's behavior becomes controlled more by external norms than by the person's own internal values and morals

Phillip Zimbardo's Stanford prison experiment shows that when we become deindividuated, we lose track of our own internal values and beliefs, and our behavior comes under the control of the group's norms. When deindividuated, we may find ourselves doing things we never thought we would do.

© Philip Zimbardo

Decision Making in Groups

Based on the old saying "Two heads are better than one," we often seek out others when we have important decisions to make. The assumption is that important decisions are best placed in the hands of many. Ironically, psychological research indicates that in some instances our faith in the wisdom of groups may be misplaced. Group decisions are not necessarily better, more effective, or more logical than decisions made by individuals.

One factor that can contribute to poor group decisions is known as **groupthink**. Groupthink occurs when a group fixates on one decision and members assume that it must be the correct one, without carefully examining other alternatives (Janis, 1982). When groupthink occurs, the group does not weigh all of the options, often resulting in disastrous decisions. For example, in one historical example of groupthink, NASA decided to launch the space shuttle *Challenger* in 1986 despite troubling data from engineers indicating that O-rings on the rocket booster could fail. The result was an explosion that claimed the lives of all aboard and brought intense public and governmental scrutiny of NASA. How is it that a group of intelligent people could fall prey to groupthink, resulting in such a tragic decision?

Group isolation, group cohesiveness, strong dictatorial leadership, and *stress within the group* have all been implicated as factors that promote groupthink (Janis, 1985). Sometimes groups must work in isolation because the issues they are dealing with are secret or confidential. An isolated group is unable to get information from or call on outside sources. Therefore, they are able to consider only solutions that are generated within the group. Because the group cannot consider all possible solutions, some potentially good solutions may be overlooked, and groupthink is more likely.

Group cohesiveness also contributes to groupthink. As we have seen, when a group is very cohesive, members highly value their membership in the group. When this is the case, the group's norms become powerful influences on the members' behavior. In a cohesive group, members may be hesitant to voice their objections to the prevailing group attitude because they do not want to "rock the boat." When members hesitate to voice objections, groupthink becomes more likely because potentially poor decisions are not adequately critiqued and rejected (Esser, 1998).

For the same reason, a dictatorial group leader would also facilitate groupthink. When members are afraid to disagree with a leader, they tend to go along with the leader's position, and groupthink is more likely (Shafer & Crichlow, 1996).

groupthink a situation in which a group fixates on one decision, and members blindly assume that it is the correct decision

A final reason for groupthink is stress. When a group is making decisions under some form of duress, they may not behave in as logical a manner as they would if they were not stressed. Time pressure is one such stressor that can contribute to groupthink. When a group has a very short time in which to generate a solution to some problem, they are less likely to be able to examine all possible options, and groupthink becomes more likely.

Let's Review!

In this section, we explored groups and how they influence us. For a quick check of your understanding, answer these questions.

1. Which of the following would *not* typically increase one's tendency to conform in a group?
   a. High cohesiveness among group members
   b. Unanimity of opinion among other group members
   c. Anonymity of group members
   d. All of the above would increase conformity.

2. Which of the following is an example of conformity?
   a. Donating to a charity after receiving a request for funding in the mail
   b. Driving 55 mph in a 45 mph zone

   c. Wearing fashionable clothes
   d. Helping clean your apartment because your roommate demands that you help

3. Which of the following is *not* typically a benefit that one derives from being in a group?
   a. A sense of security
   b. A sense of social identity
   c. Needed information
   d. Fulfillment of social needs

Answers 1. c; 2. c; 3. c

Requests and Demands: Compliance and Obedience

Learning Objective

- Describe the differences between obedience and compliance, and describe commonly used compliance techniques.

Imagine that you answer the phone one evening and hear a telemarketer on the other end. After she identifies herself as a telemarketer, she asks you to contribute to the local police organization. Would you agree to contribute, or would you refuse? Now compare this situation with a similar one. This time, you answer the phone and hear a police officer on the other end. After identifying herself as a local officer, she asks you to contribute to the police organization. Would you be *more* inclined to agree to the officer's request? Many people would, but why? What makes these two situations different?

One difference is the source of the request. A police officer represents an authority figure to many people. Many of us would perceive a request coming from an authority figure to be more of a *demand* for **obedience**. On the other hand, we are less likely to be intimidated by a telemarketer, and therefore we would likely perceive her request as just that, a simple *request* for **compliance**. Although the differences between compliance and obedience situations may appear to be subtle, they have great implications for how we respond.

Compliance Techniques

Compliance situations are very common in life. For instance, salespeople try to get us to agree to buy their products. Doctors ask us to follow their instructions. Spouses ask their partners to do household chores. Given that pressures to comply are inescapable, psychologists are interested in identifying successful compliance techniques and the reasons that make them work well. Marketers and other professionals also want to understand compliance so that they can create more effective campaigns for changing public behavior. For example, research on direct mail (e.g., catalog) marketing often centers on effective use of compliance techniques (e.g., Weyant, 1996). It's a good idea for us to become familiar with compliance techniques because others will be using them on us.

FOOT-IN-THE-DOOR COMPLIANCE

Suppose a friend asks to borrow a dollar, and you comply. Later, if that same friend asks to borrow $5, would it be harder to refuse the request because you had previously lent him or her the dollar? Research on compliance suggests that it would. Once a person gets a foot in the door, so to speak, by getting us to comply with a small request, it seems to open the way to getting us to comply with another, larger, request. In a classic experiment on **foot-in-the door compliance**, researchers approached some homes and asked the person answering the door to sign a petition to promote safe driving. The researchers also selected other homes in the neighborhood to participate in the study but did not approach them at this time. Two weeks later, the researchers returned to the neighborhood and approached the homes they had previously visited as well as the homes that were not visited on the first day. This time, the researchers asked if they could put up a huge billboard that said "Drive Carefully" in the front yard. The data showed that those people who had complied with the first request to sign the petition were more likely to comply with the request for the billboard (Freedman & Fraser, 1966). Similarly, researchers in Israel found that people who had previously signed a petition for a specific charity were more likely to agree to donate money to the charity at

obedience yielding to a demand
compliance yielding to a simple request
foot-in-the-door compliance increasing compliance by first asking people to give in to a small request, which then paves the way for compliance with a larger request

Compliance techniques such as foot-in-the-door and door-in-the-face can be used to influence our behavior.

a later date (Schwarzwald, Bizman, & Raz, 1983). It appears that giving in to a small request paves the way for us to give in to a larger request.

One explanation for foot-in-the-door's effectiveness is that our general desire to behave in a consistent fashion makes it hard for us to refuse subsequent requests. When you give in to the initial small request, your self-image changes ever so slightly. Having already complied, you are now the type of person who complies with requests made by this person or group. Because your self-image has changed, you now feel compelled to behave consistently with this new self-image. Recall that to not act in accordance with one's attitudes would likely produce *dissonance*. So when the person or group makes a subsequent request, to deny it would mean going against one's self-image and perhaps feeling dissonance. Therefore, compliance is more likely. When a clever manipulator gets a person to give in on a small matter, it does indeed seem to lead to future compliance (Cialdini, 2001; Girandola, 2002).

DOOR-IN-THE-FACE COMPLIANCE

In **door-in-the-face compliance**, a very large request is followed by a smaller target request. For example, researchers asked college students whether they would agree to commit to volunteering two hours a week for the next two years in a program to help juvenile delinquents. As you might guess, all the students declined. Then the researchers asked if the students would be willing to volunteer to take the juveniles to the zoo for a couple of hours. A full 50% of the students agreed to take the trip to the zoo *after* they had refused to volunteer weekly. This number was significantly higher than the 17% of students in a control group who agreed after being asked only whether they would take the trip to the zoo (Cialdini, Vincent, Catalan, Wheeler, & Darby, 1975). It appears that if we figuratively "slam the door" in the face of a person's request, we are more likely to comply if she makes a more reasonable request later.

One explanation for door-in-the-face compliance centers on the *perceptual contrast* between the two requests. After the extremity of the first request, the second, smaller, request may seem more reasonable to you than if it had been the only request you received (Cialdini et al., 1975).

Another explanation for door-in-the-face compliance centers on **reciprocity**, a very strong norm in many cultures that requires that we reciprocate others' behavior (Mowen & Cialdini, 1980). For example, if we are nice, others should be nice to us. If we are mean, others may be mean in return. Reciprocity explains in part why we feel more obligated to comply in a door-in-the-face situation than with a single request. In a door-in-the-face situation, after you refuse the initial request, the requester then concedes the initial position and makes a more reasonable request. Because the requester has made a concession, we feel as though we must reciprocate and also make a concession. The easiest way to do this is to comply with the second request. If we don't make this concession, then we may feel as if we are breaking an important social norm.

door-in-the-face compliance increasing compliance by first asking people to give in to a very large request and then, after they refuse, asking them to give in to a smaller request

reciprocity [reh-cih-PRAH-cih-tee] a strong norm that states that we should treat others as they treat us

Finally, some researchers (e.g., O'Keefe & Figge, 1997) propose that emotion plays a role in compliance. When we turn down the initial large request, we feel negative emotions, such as guilt. Because we do not enjoy feeling bad, we look for a way to reduce these negative emotions. With the opportunity to comply when a second, more reasonable, request is presented, we are more likely to comply to relieve our guilt and make ourselves feel better (Millar, 2002).

The research on compliance shows that we are fairly likely to give in to simple requests from others. Given this, how do we respond when others demand our obedience?

Obedience

In a famous set of experiments, Yale psychologist Stanley Milgram set out to discover just how likely the average person is to obey demands from others—even when their obedience may cause others pain. Milgram ran an ad in a New Haven, Connecticut, newspaper that solicited participants for an experiment that would investigate the role of punishment in learning. In actuality, the experiment would measure the participants' willingness to obey an order to administer a very painful electric shock to another person. The participants weren't told this until *after* the experiment was over. As far as the participants knew, they were participating in a study on learning, not obedience.

In all, 40 men participated in Milgram's first study (Milgram, 1963). These men ranged from 20 to 50 years of age, and they represented a variety of professions, including teachers, engineers, and postal clerks. All of the men were paid $4.50 (approximately $30 in today's money) for their participation *before* the experiment began.

When they arrived at the lab, the participants were told that they would be playing the role of a teacher in the experiment. As the teacher, their job would be to administer electric shocks, using an apparatus that delivered shocks ranging from 15 volts to 450 volts, to a participant playing the role of the learner (■FIGURE 10.5). The learner was supposed to learn a list of words, and the teachers were told that the purpose of the experiment was to see whether the shocks would improve the learner's rate of learning. In actuality, the learner was a confederate, an actor who only pretended to be shocked, but the participants did not know this until after the experiment ended.

During the procedure, the experimenter, a 31-year-old high school biology teacher dressed in a lab coat, stood slightly behind the seated teacher. Throughout the experiment, the teacher and learner communicated via an intercom system, but they did not have visual contact. The teacher was instructed to read a list of words to the learner over the intercom, and then to listen as the learner recalled the words from memory. Every time the learner made a mistake, the teacher was told to deliver a shock to the learner by flipping one of the switches on the apparatus. The procedure began with the 15-volt switch, and the teacher was instructed to move progressively up the scale toward the 450-volt switch as the learner made more and more mistakes.

Stanley Milgram was primarily interested in seeing how far up the scale the teachers would go before they refused to obey orders to shock the learner further. At the 300-volt mark, the learner began to pound on the wall as if in great pain, protesting the continued shocking. At this point, most participants began to question the experimenter as to whether they should continue to shock the learner, who was obviously in pain. The teachers began to show clear signs of distress, including shaking, stuttering, sweating, nervous laughter, and biting their lips and fingernails. The teachers often protested verbally and indicated that they didn't feel good about continuing to shock the learner.

In response to such displays and protests, the experimenter calmly prodded the participants to continue with the procedure. The experimenter never yelled. He never made verbal or physical threats. He never threatened to take away their $4.50. The experimenter merely requested that the participants continue following orders. The strongest statement by the experimenter was, "You have no other choice, you must go on" (Milgram, 1963, p. 374).

After the 315-volt mark, the learner fell completely silent and unresponsive, as if he had lost consciousness or was injured. Because the learner missed all the words on the trial by not responding, the experimenter instructed the teacher to continue delivering the shocks. At this point, it is likely that the teacher believed that he was being asked to shock an injured—or even unconscious—man! What would you do in this situation? What do you think the teachers did?

The results of Milgram's study were nothing short of shocking. A full 65% of the teachers continued to shock the learner all the way up to the 450-volt mark.

FIGURE

10.5

The Apparatus Used by Milgram in His Famous Obedience Studies

How far would you go before you refused to obey?

Obedience © 1965, Stanley Milgram

Despite believing the learner to be ill or worse, most of the teachers continued to follow the experimenter's orders. Even Stanley Milgram was surprised by his findings. Prior to the experiment, Milgram had surveyed psychology students and behavioral science professionals to get a feel for how many participants they thought would go all the way to 450 volts (Milgram, 1963, 1974). Most people believed that only 1−3% would. The results showed, of course, a very different picture. Approximately 65% of the participants did go all the way to 450 volts, and no participant refused to obey before the 300-volt mark had been reached!

As you might imagine, Milgram's findings generated a great deal of skepticism. Some people questioned whether the participants in Milgram's (1963) study were abnormal in some way. To answer such skepticism and to further investigate the variables that affect the rate of obedience, Milgram repeated his procedure with different participants. He replicated the study in another town (Bridgeport, CT) and found similar results (Milgram, 1965). Milgram also conducted the study using female participants and again found high rates of obedience (Milgram, 1974).

> ## You Asked...
>
> *When others try to influence us, what factors make it more likely that we will do what they want?*
>
> PAIGE REDMON, STUDENT

Other researchers have since replicated Milgram's findings. High school students were found to be even *more* willing to obey orders (Rosenhan, 1969). Cross-cultural research in other Western cultures has also yielded high rates of obedience using Milgram's procedure (Triandis, 1994). Unfortunately, it seems as though Milgram's results were not flukes. So what accounts for our tendency to obey orders to hurt others?

FACTORS THAT AFFECT OBEDIENCE

One factor that contributed to the high rate of obedience in the Milgram studies was the presence of a perceived *authority figure*. During the procedure, the experimenter, dressed in a lab coat and looking official, stood close by the participant and issued orders to deliver the shocks. Authority figures work in two ways to ensure obedience. First, the fact that the authority figure is ultimately in charge may seem to relieve the person following orders from responsibility for his actions. A person can always tell himself that he was only following orders. Second, the presence of official-looking authority figures tends to intimidate us, and we are therefore more likely to obey their orders (Bushman, 1988). Sometimes it makes sense to be intimidated by authority figures because some authority figures have true power (for example, police officers). If you perceive that authority figures can observe your behavior and that you may suffer negative consequences for disobeying, you might obey out of fear alone.

In later experiments, Milgram found that he could reduce obedience in his participants by increasing the physical distance between the experimenter and the teacher. If the experimenter was not physically present to watch the teacher's behavior, the teachers were much less likely to obey the orders to shock the participant. ■ TABLE 10.3 summarizes some of the later experimental manipulations that Milgram (1965) used to test variables that affect rates of obedience. From Table 10.3, you can see that when the experimenter telephoned his orders to the teachers, obedience dropped to 27.5%.

Another reason for the high rates of obedience in Milgram's studies is the *timing of the requests* made by the experimenter. When the participants arrived at the lab, they very quickly found themselves faced with orders from an authority figure to shock another human being. Because the orders began almost immediately after the participants arrived, they did not have much time to think about their actions. As we saw earlier, when we do not have time to think things through, we are more susceptible to persuasive attempts.

Another factor that contributed to high rates of obedience was the fact that the shock levels were increased incrementally. In essence, Milgram's procedure was a textbook example

Table 10.3 Some Experimental Conditions in Milgram's Experiments and Their Resultant Rates of Obedience

EXPERIMENTAL MANIPULATION	PERCENTAGE OF PARTICIPANTS WHO OBEYED ALL THE WAY TO THE 450-VOLT LEVEL
The learner was seated in the same room with the teacher.	40%
The teacher had to hold the learner's hand down on the shock plate.	30%
The experimenter delivered his orders by telephone instead of in person.	27.5%
The teacher was tested with two *confederates* who pretended to be participants also playing the role of teacher. Halfway through the experiment, the two confederates refused to shock the learner any further.	10% of participants continued to obey after the confederates refused to further shock the learner.
The teacher was tested with two *confederates* who pretended to be participants also playing the role of teacher. One of the confederates was the one who actually flipped the switch to shock the learner. The real participant only played an auxiliary role in shocking the learner.	92.5%
Female participants played the role of teacher.	65%

Source: Milgram, 1965.

of foot-in-the-door compliance in action. The first orders were for the teachers to deliver a 15-volt shock, a mere tingle compared to the final shock level of 450 volts. Few people would have qualms about following an order to deliver an almost painless shock, so why not obey? What the participants did not know was that by obeying the order to deliver the 15-volt shock, they were paving the way for their own obedience to further orders to shock the learner. Every time the participants obeyed an order to shock, it became harder for them to refuse to continue. Some have likened this type of incremental obedience to standing on a **slippery slope**. Once you begin to obey, it's like beginning to slide down the slope. The farther you go, the more momentum you gain, and the harder it is to stop obeying. If Milgram's procedure had begun with an order to deliver the potentially dangerous shock of 450 volts, it is unlikely that he would have obtained such high rates of obedience.

A final factor that affects obedience is the **psychological distance** we feel between our actions and the results of those actions. In Milgram's first experiment (Milgram, 1963), the teacher could not see the learner during the procedure. In this type of condition, psychological distance is large, meaning that it was relatively easy for the teachers to not think about the consequences of their actions. If you don't think about the consequences of your actions, then you don't have to consciously come to terms with and take responsibility for those actions. This allows you to obey even in situations in which your actions may harm others.

In one dramatic experiment, Milgram had the teacher and learner sit side by side during the procedure. In this variation of the experiment, the teacher had to reach over and hold the learner's hand down on the shock plate. As you might guess, this procedure dramatically reduced the psychological distance for the teacher. It's hard to dissociate yourself from the consequences of your actions when you're actually touching your victim. Under these con-

slippery slope the use of foot-in-the-door compliance in an obedience situation to get people to obey increasing demands

psychological distance the degree to which one can disassociate oneself from the consequences of his/her actions ditions, only 30% of the participants delivered the maximum 450-volt shock. Note, however, that although obedience was cut in half by reducing the psychological distance, obedience was not eliminated. Almost one-third of participants still continued to obey the experimenter, even under these conditions.

Are Milgram's results troubling to you? They are for many. His studies suggest that the average person has the capacity to obey orders even when doing so hurts others. Some researchers have termed this type of obedience **destructive obedience**, to distinguish it from obedience that does not lead to harming others. In many instances, obedience is a good thing. For instance, we want people to obey the laws of our society; otherwise, chaos would ensue. Therefore, you should not conclude from Milgram's studies that all obedience is bad.

Another aspect of Milgram's work that may have bothered you is the obvious discomfort Milgram inflicted on his research participants. Milgram's use of *deception* to convince his participants that they were hurting another person has been heavily criticized by other psychologists (e.g., Baumrind, 1964). Milgram did *debrief* his participants afterward, explaining that they had never actually hurt the learner and that the purpose of the experiment was to study obedience, not learning. Recall our discussion of ethics in psychological research from Chapter 1 and the ethical mandate that all human participants in psychological experiments should leave the experiment in *at least as good a condition as they were prior to the experiment*. Critics maintain that the participants left the Milgram studies knowing that they were capable of hurting another human being simply because they were told to do so. This is not a very positive thing to learn about oneself. Additionally, critics have asserted that exposing participants to the trauma of the procedure itself was an ethical violation of their rights (Baumrind, 1964). Today, at most universities in the United States, it would be virtually impossible to get approval to do an experiment such as Milgram's because of the possible ethical problems associated with it. Modern psychologists are extremely protective of the rights of research participants.

Despite the criticisms, Milgram's work remains one of the most powerful statements ever made about human behavior. Aside from demonstrating our obedience to authority, Milgram's work also brings up some important and perhaps frightening questions about basic human nature. For instance, how can psychologists explain the tendency of some people to behave aggressively? We will look at this issue next.

destructive obedience obedience to immoral, unethical demands that cause harm to others

Let's Review!

In this section, we examined the social influence that occurs in compliance and obedience. As a quick check of your understanding, answer these questions.

1. You want your friend to lend you $50. If you want to use the door-in-the-face compliance technique to ensure that your friend will comply with your request, what should you do?
   a. First ask for $1,000 before asking for the $50.
   b. First ask for $10 before asking for the $50.
   c. Wash your friend's car before you ask for the $50.
   d. Tell your friend that you will pay the money back in one week.

2. In Milgram's original experiment, what percentage of participants went all the way to 450 volts when "shocking" the learner?
   a. 35%   c. 65%
   b. 55%   d. 75%

3. Which of the following compliance techniques best explains Milgram's findings in his study on obedience?
   a. Foot-in-the-door   c. Reciprocity
   b. Door-in-the-face   d. Low-balling

Answers 1. a; 2. c; 3. a

Aggression

- Describe the factors that affect the tendency to behave aggressively.

Psychologists define aggression as an action that is intended to cause harm to another person who does not want to be harmed (Baron & Richardson, 1992; Brehm, Kassin, & Fein, 2002; Huesmann, 1994). Aggressive acts can be classified as *instrumental* or *hostile*. **Instrumental aggression** is aimed at achieving some goal. For example, a child may hit a playmate to distract her so the child can grab her toy. **Hostile aggression** is motivated solely by a desire to hurt others. For example, a bully may punch another child on the playground just to see the child cry.

Although both types of aggression are widespread in many cultures, the overall prevalence of aggression varies across cultures. Among developed countries, the United States is considered to be an aggressive society (see Osterman et al., 1994). Pick up a major American metropolitan newspaper any day of the week, and you will see abundant evidence of this in the daily crime reports. In 2006, New York, Los Angeles, Chicago, and Dallas reported a combined total of 1,678 murders and many more rapes, assaults, and robberies (Federal Bureau of Investigation, 2007).

Besides the almost daily reports of violent crime in the United States, it appears that even noncriminals have aggression on their minds. Researchers surveyed 312 college students at a U.S. university about whether they had ever thought about killing someone. Fully 73% of male students and 66% of female students reported that they had (Kenrick & Sheets, 1993)! What could account for such numbers? Could aggressive feelings be more natural than we like to think?

> *You Asked...*
>
> *What causes aggression?*
>
> JONATHAN GANTES, STUDENT

Instrumental aggression is aimed at achieving some goal. This child is being aggressive to obtain a toy.

© Barbara Stitzer/PhotoEdit

Biological Theories of Aggression

It has been widely documented that among many species, including humans, males tend to be more aggressive than females (e.g., Eagly & Steffen, 1986). In 2006, males accounted for 89% of those arrested for murder, and they represented 82.1% of those arrested for all violent crimes (Federal Bureau of Investigation, 2006b). Because males have more of the hormone testosterone in their bodies, researchers have long suspected that testosterone and aggressive behavior are related. But the research on the relationship between aggression and testosterone has yielded a somewhat confusing picture. Sometimes higher levels of testosterone are associated with higher levels of aggression in animals (Wagner, Beuving, & Hutchinson, 1980), and sometimes they are not (Eaton & Resko, 1974). Likewise, human studies sometimes show a correlation between high testosterone levels and aggression (Dabbs & Morris, 1990; Van Goozen, Frijda, & de Poll, 1994), and sometimes they fail to find a clear relationship (Archer, Birring, & Wu, 1998; Tremblay et al., 1998).

instrumental aggression aggression used to facilitate the attainment of one's goals
hostile aggression aggression that is meant to cause harm to others

Even if the correlation between testosterone and aggressive behavior were more consistent in the literature, it would still be difficult to determine the actual cause(s) of aggressive behavior. Recall that *correlation does not imply causation*. Higher levels of testosterone are associated with muscularity and strength, which may simply give one the physical ability to be a bully. Some researchers have found that in adolescent boys, aggression is correlated with physical size, but not correlated with levels of testosterone (Tremblay et al., 1998).

A POSSIBLE ROLE FOR SEROTONIN

Research has suggested that another chemical, serotonin, may also play a role in regulation of aggressive behavior (Libersat & Pflueger, 2004). Researchers measured levels of the neurotransmitter serotonin in the bloodstream of three groups of people: survivors of suicide attempts, people institutionalized since childhood for aggressive behavior, and a normal control group (Marazzitti et al., 1993). They found that the suicide survivors and the aggressive patients had *lower* levels of serotonin than those in the normal control group.

Low levels of serotonin are associated with disorders such as *obsessive-compulsive disorder*, in which the person has difficulty controlling his or her behavior and feels compelled to repeat certain actions (see Chapter 13). If we extend this thinking to the relationship between serotonin and aggression, we can speculate that people with lower levels of serotonin may have difficulty in controlling their aggressive impulses toward themselves (as in suicide) and toward others (as in the institutionalized patients). However, more research is needed before any firm conclusions can be drawn about the role of serotonin in aggression.

CHILDHOOD ABUSE AND AGGRESSION

Another connection between biology and aggression comes from research into the backgrounds of incarcerated criminals. During the 1980s and 1990s, psychiatrist Dorothy Otnow Lewis interviewed more than 100 murderers in an attempt to discover whether they had experienced physical abuse as children (Lewis, 1992). During these interviews, Lewis discovered that an overwhelming majority of these murderers had suffered extreme abuse during childhood. In particular, many had suffered severe head injuries as a result of the abuse, which led Lewis and her colleagues to hypothesize that the murderers' aggressive tendencies may have resulted from brain damage (Lewis, Picus, Feldman, Jackson, & Bard, 1986).

More recent research seems to reinforce Lewis's notions. It is now thought that childhood abuse and neglect are related to the development of several brain abnormalities. Using some of the techniques for studying the brain that we discussed in Chapter 2 (such as EEG, MRI, and fMRI), researchers have found that childhood abuse and neglect correlate with having structural abnormalities in the amygdala, hippocampus, corpus callosum, left frontal lobe, left temporal lobe, and cerebellum (Teicher, 2002).

Virtually no one would disagree that an end to child abuse would be good for society. Aside from a possible link between the physical damage caused by child abuse and later aggression, psychologists have other reasons to fear the destructive influence of child abuse. An aggressive model, such as an aggressive, punitive parent or a violent TV character, can teach a child to be aggressive.

Learning Theories of Aggression

In Chapter 5, we described Albert Bandura's *Bobo doll* experiments, in which children who watched an adult model beat up a plastic Bobo doll were likely to mimic the model's aggression when later left alone with the doll (Bandura, Ross, & Ross, 1963). After being exposed to an *aggressive model*, the children acquired new and aggressive behaviors. Many psychologists believe that aggression is often learned through this type of *social learning*.

However, exposure to violence and aggression may promote more than just modeling of aggressive behavior. Such exposure may actually influence the cognitive, emotional, and behavioral responses we have to events in our daily lives. One model of aggression, the *cognitive neoassociation theory*, proposes that cues present during an aggressive event can become associated in memory with the thoughts and emotions experienced during that event (Anderson & Bushman, 2002; Berkowitz, 1990). For example, if you see many instances (real or televised) in which people use guns to shoot and hurt those who have humiliated them, you may begin to associate concepts from these events in your memory. You may begin to associate guns with anger, hurt, fear, and humiliation; or you may begin to associate conflict with shooting. Because these concepts become tightly linked in memory, activation of one of them can *prime* other related concepts and cause them to become active. In other words, merely seeing a gun may cause you to have aggressive thoughts. Being humiliated may activate feelings of anger and the desire to use a gun to retaliate against those who hurt you. Indeed, research participants have been shown to have aggressive thoughts after simply being shown pictures of weapons (Anderson, Benjamin, & Bartholow, 1998).

If our behavior is heavily influenced by the cues we perceive to be associated with aggression and violence, then the nature of such perceptions is very important. Given that many of our ideas about the world are influenced by the media, it is worthwhile to ask the question, does television portray violence and its consequences accurately? For a look at this issue, see *Psychology Applies to Your World*.

Psychology Applies to Your World:
Does Television Portray Violence Accurately?

TV has been shown to portray many aspects of life unrealistically, including marriage (Segrin & Nabi, 2002), the medical profession (Chory-Assad & Tamborini, 2001), and violence. One study reported a total of 2,126 antisocial acts in 65.5 hours of so-called reality television programming, or shows that are supposed to document real life, such as *Cops*. The problem is that these "reality shows" do not give an accurate picture of real life. They portray acts of aggression at rates that are far above the actual rates at which they occur in U.S. society (Potter et al., 1997).

Even more disturbing is that many televised acts of aggression are ones in which the aggressor experiences no negative repercussions for his or her actions. Criminals and other aggressors often go unpunished on TV, and victims are typically not shown to suffer realistic consequences as a result of their victimization. Movies and television shows often do not accurately show the physical pain, mental anguish, and economic costs that victims suffer. In 1996, a report sponsored by the National Cable Television Association indicated that perpetrators went unpunished in 73% of all violent scenes on TV and that only 16% of all violent acts on TV portrayed long-term negative consequences for the victim. Worse yet, the genre that was least likely to portray the long-term consequences of aggression was children's programming (Mediascope, Inc., 1996). These figures indicate that not only is television programming violent, it may also leave children with the false impression that aggression often goes unpunished and that victims do not really suffer painful consequences. These false impressions may increase the likelihood that children will actually model the behavior they see on TV (Bandura, 1965; Hogben, 1998).

Are these children learning to be aggressive as they watch television?

Situations That Promote Aggressive Behavior

When are you most likely to behave aggressively? Are there circumstances in which you might behave in a physically aggressive manner toward another? What would it take?

One key factor in aggression appears to be frustration. According to the **frustration-aggression hypothesis** (Dollard, Doob, Miller, Mowrer, & Sears, 1939), when we become frustrated, we activate a motive to harm other people or objects. These motives are likely to be directed at those people or objects that we perceive to be the source of our frustration. For example, most physically abusive parents never *intend* to threaten or harm their children. But in the heat of the moment some parents take out their frustration on their children. Parents in high-stress situations—such as extreme poverty—who do not have good coping skills are most at risk for becoming abusive (Garbarino, 1997). Recall from Chapter 8 that motives drive and catalyze behavior. Consequently, when we are frustrated, our chances of behaving aggressively increase. Therefore, during stressful, frustrating situations, we have to be on guard for possible aggressive behavior in ourselves and in others.

Let's Review!

In this section, we explored the nature of aggression. As a quick check of your understanding, answer these questions.

1. Which neurotransmitter has been implicated as possibly playing a role in aggressive behavior?
   a. Testosterone
   c. Dopamine
   b. Serotonin
   d. Estrogen

2. Road rage incidents are more likely to occur in heavy traffic. This fact can *best* be explained as due to the increase in _____ that occurs among drivers in heavy traffic.
   a. frustration
   c. fear
   b. fatigue
   d. anxiety

3. Little Sabina wants to play with her sister's doll, but her sister will not let Sabina have the doll. So Sabina hits her sister and takes the doll away while her sister cries. Sabina's behavior is *best* characterized as an example of _____.
   a. hostile aggression
   b. instrumental aggression
   c. biological aggression
   d. learned aggression

Answers 1. b; 2. a; 3. b

Helping Behavior: Will You, or Won't You?

Learning Objective

- Describe helping behavior and the factors that influence helping, including the bystander effect.

By now you might be thinking that humans are pretty rotten creatures. We seem to be easily biased against others, easily influenced by others, aggressive, and even easily convinced to do real harm to others. In fact, humans are often very generous as well. Sometimes we demonstrate **altruism**, or a willingness to help others without considering any possible benefit for ourselves. Just as we have the capacity for violence, we also have the capacity for kindness and compassion.

frustration–aggression hypothesis
the idea that frustration causes aggressive behavior

altruism helping another without being motivated by self-gain

helping behavior another term for altruism

The Murder of Kitty Genovese

As was the case with the study of obedience, the psychological study of altruism, or **helping behavior**, was prompted by a tragedy, the murder of Kitty Genovese in New York City on

March 13, 1964. Kitty Genovese, age 28, was returning to her apartment in Queens at 3:20 A.M. when she was approached and stabbed by a man in a prolonged assault that lasted 30 minutes. During the attack, Kitty's screams were heard by 38 of her neighbors. Tragically, the neighbors' reactions did not lead to Kitty getting the help she needed, and Kitty died from her injuries. A *New York Times* article that reported the murder claimed that although 38 people witnessed Kitty's murder, none of them called the police until after she was dead (Gansberg, 1964). As you might imagine, people reacted with shock and outrage to this news. Further reports of interviews with some of the witnesses only fanned the flames. Some of the witnesses explained their inaction by saying, "I didn't want to get involved." Even a man who did call the police first called a friend for advice because he was so afraid of getting involved (Mohr, 1964).

Today, some people allege that these early reports misrepresented some of the facts of the case and overstated the witnesses' apathy. For example, many of the witnesses may not have been in a position to actually see the attack, and may have only heard some commotion on the street. It is also possible that some witnesses may have tried to call the police immediately after Kitty was attacked but for unknown reasons the calls were ineffective (De May, 2006). Perhaps we will never know exactly how the 38 witnesses, many of whom have since passed away, actually responded that night. However, what is certain is how the public *perceived* the situation back in 1964—they perceived that the 38 witnesses were apathetic and callous.

Soon after Kitty's murder and the uproar that followed, researchers Bibb Latané and John Darley (1969) set out to determine which factors influence whether or not we help others in need. They found that apathy or lack of concern is *not* the reason that people fail to help in situations like the Genovese murder. They also discovered that deciding whether or not to help someone is not necessarily a single decision, nor is it a simple decision to make. You must first *notice* that something out of the ordinary is occurring. Second, you must correctly *interpret* the situation as one that requires your aid. It is very possible that some of those who heard Kitty Genovese's cries did not realize that they were anything other than the normal sounds of a New York City street at night. Third, you must feel that you have a *responsibility* to intervene in the situation. Some of the 38 witnesses may have believed that someone else was coming to Kitty Genovese's aid. Fourth, you must decide *how to help* the person in distress. If you don't know what to do, you cannot offer help to someone in need. And, finally, you must *implement* your helping strategy, and actually help the person in need.

> ### You Asked...
> *Why do we help others?*
> DIANA FLORES, STUDENT

bystander effect the idea that the more witnesses there are to an emergency, the less likely any one of them is to offer help

Humans often do come to the aid of others.

The Bystander Effect

Because deciding to help is a multistep process, failure can occur at any of the five steps. Early studies of helping behavior focused on responsibility and the thought processes that might contribute to one person's feeling responsible to help another in need. Latané and Darley hypothesized what they called the **bystander effect**. As the number of bystanders *increases* in an emergency situation, the probability that any one of the bystanders will actually intervene *decreases*.

To test their theory, Latané and Darley conducted a number of experiments (Latané & Darley, 1969). In one study, participants worked on a questionnaire either alone or in the presence of two other people. Halfway through the questionnaire, smoke began to filter into the room through a wall vent, as if there were a fire nearby. The dependent variable in the study was whether or not the participant got up to investigate the source of the smoke and how quickly he or she did so. The results of this experiment supported the idea of the bystander effect. When participants were in the room alone, 75% of them got up to investigate the source

© Tom Stewart/Corbis

of the smoke. When there were two other people in the room, only 10% of the participants got up to investigate. It appears that even when you may be helping yourself, the presence of other bystanders can reduce your tendency to help! Why would this be the case?

One explanation for the bystander effect is **diffusion of responsibility**, or the idea that all bystanders *equally* share the responsibility for helping in an emergency. Each of the 38 witnesses would have borne only a fraction of the responsibility for helping Kitty Genovese. As the number of bystanders *decreases*, the amount of responsibility any one bystander bears *increases*. When you are the only witness, you bear all of the responsibility for helping. So what can you do if you need help and there are several bystanders present? You can reduce the bystander effect by clearly identifying one bystander and requesting his or her help. By singling out one person, you eliminate the diffusion of responsibility, placing all of the responsibility on that one person. Remembering this could save your life someday!

Diffusion of responsibility is not the only factor that prevents people from helping others. Another possible explanation for a bystander's failure to help is **pluralistic ignorance**, or the failure of a group of witnesses to perceive there is a problem that requires their help (Latané & Darley, 1969). When the witnesses saw the others doing nothing to help Kitty, this lack of action and excitement on the part of the other witnesses may have caused the individual witnesses to inaccurately perceive that Kitty did not need help (Sexton, 1995). In other words, when we see that others are not interpreting a situation as an emergency, we are less likely to interpret the situation as an emergency, and therefore we are less likely to help.

Researchers now believe that the number of witnesses to an emergency is only one factor that influences helping. Several other variables that have been shown to influence helping behavior are summarized in ■ TABLE 10.4. As you read through Table 10.4, you'll notice that, unfortunately, not all people are equally likely to receive help.

diffusion of responsibility the idea that responsibility for taking action is diffused across all the people witnessing an event

pluralistic ignorance the idea that we use the behavior of others to help determine whether a situation is really an emergency requiring our help; if no one else is helping, we may conclude that help isn't needed

When People Choose to Help

By this time, it may seem as if humans are callous, uncaring creatures. Take heart. Although we do fail to help in some cases, there are also many examples of people who have helped others both in heroic ways and through simple, everyday acts of kindness. For example, when the I-35 bridge across the Mississippi River in Minneapolis collapsed on August 1, 2007, many bystanders rushed to help pull people from the trapped vehicles and debris. *New York*

Table 10.4 Variables That Affect Helping Behavior

VARIABLE	DESCRIPTION
Level of bystander's hurry	Bystanders who are in a hurry are less likely to stop and help someone in distress.
Bystander's relationship to other bystanders	When bystanders are friends, they are more likely to help a stranger in need.
Relationship between victim and bystander	A bystander who knows the victim is more likely to help.
Bystander's perceived ambiguity	If the situation is ambiguous, bystanders will tend to see it as a nonemergency and therefore be less likely to help.
Bystander's fear for own safety	If bystanders are afraid they will be harmed, they are less likely to help.
Bystander's prejudice against the victim or belief that the victim is an out-group member	Bystanders who are prejudiced against the victim or see the victim as an out-group member are less likely to help.
Victim's level of dependency	Bystanders are more likely to help a victim they perceive to be dependent—for example, a child.
Victim's responsibility for own plight	Bystanders are less likely to help if they perceive the emergency to be the victim's own fault.

Times reporter Susan Orr Braudy (2003) has also documented what she calls "urban altruism," everyday acts of kindness among New Yorkers. Her examples include a doctor who helped homeless people get access to social services, an antique dealer who spontaneously helped a woman who was short on cash buy a gift for her friend, an apartment dweller who spent days watching over a fellow tenant who she feared might become suicidal, a passersby who immediately stopped to help a woman after she fell on a icy sidewalk, an office worker who quickly stepped in to stop a coworker's diabetic reaction, and an artist who volunteered once a month at a homeless shelter. In similar fashion, people from all over the world selflessly exhibit concern for the well-being and comfort of others on a daily basis—in other words, *altruism*.

When we fail to help, it is usually not out of a sense of apathy or cruelty, but rather out of misunderstanding, confusion, or fear (Latané & Darley, 1969). Perhaps by becoming aware of the factors that affect our tendency to help others, we can find ways to make the world a more altruistic place.

Let's Review!

In this section, we discussed altruism, or helping behavior. As a quick check of your understanding, answer these questions.

1. What did Darley and Latané conclude about the witnesses in the Kitty Genovese murder case?
   a. Many of the witnesses were uncaring people, and that is why they failed to help.
   b. The witnesses were not really witnesses; they did not actually see or hear Kitty being attacked.
   c. Many of the witnesses did not help because they assumed that someone else would help.
   d. Fear was the best explanation for why the witnesses did not help.

2. Recently, one of the authors was sitting in her office when the fire alarms in her building went off. To her amazement, everyone seemed to ignore the sirens, and no one evacu-ated the building until security forced them to leave. Which of the following best explains their reluctance to leave the building?
   a. Diffusion of responsibility   c. Apathy
   b. Pluralistic ignorance   d. A lack of conformity

3. If you are ever the victim of an accident, and there are many witnesses, what should you do to help ensure that one of the witnesses helps you?
   a. Scream for help.
   b. Remain quiet so as not to scare the witnesses.
   c. Single out one of the witnesses, and request that he or she help you.
   d. Yell "Fire!"

Answers 1. c; 2. b; 3. c

Studying THE Chapter

Key Terms

social psychology (366)	cognitive consistency (368)	central route to persuasion (369)
social cognition (366)	dissonance theory (368)	peripheral route to persuasion (369)
attitude (366)	persuasion (369)	impression formation (371)

attribution (371)

trait attribution (371)

situational attribution (371)

fundamental attribution error (372)

individualistic culture (373)

collectivistic culture (373)

actor/observer bias (373)

self-serving bias (373)

stereotype (375)

prejudice (375)

discrimination (375)

in-group bias (377)

out-group (378)

out-group homogeneity bias (378)

realistic-conflict theory (378)

contact hypothesis (379)

superordinate goal (380)

proximity (382)

matching hypothesis (383)

norm (386)

cohesiveness (386)

conformity (386)

normative conformity (388)

informational conformity (388)

deindividuation (389)

groupthink (390)

obedience (391)

compliance (391)

foot-in-the-door compliance (391)

door-in-the-face compliance (392)

reciprocity (392)

slippery slope (395)

psychological distance (395)

destructive obedience (396)

instrumental aggression (397)

hostile aggression (397)

frustration-aggression hypothesis (400)

altruism (400)

helping behavior (400)

bystander effect (401)

diffusion of responsibility (402)

pluralistic ignorance (402)

What Do You Know? Assess Your Understanding

Test your retention and understanding of the material by answering the following questions.

1. Which of the following is not an attitude?
   a. Liking rap music
   b. Believing that honesty is the best policy
   c. Believing that Atlanta is the capital of Georgia
   d. All of the above are attitudes.

2. _____ is a direct attempt to change a person's attitudes.
   a. Dissonance   c. Conformity
   b. Persuasion   d. Compliance

3. If you are in the market for a new car, you should process television ads from car dealers on the _____ route to persuasion.
   a. central   c. cognitive
   b. peripheral   d. emotional

4. Complex, valid arguments have the best chance of persuading people who are of _____ intelligence.
   a. very low   c. moderate
   b. low   d. high

5. Assuming that your professor is a happy person because she was smiling today in class is likely an example of _____.
   a. dissonance
   b. fundamental attribution error
   c. actor/observer bias
   d. in-group/out-group bias

6. Believing that your roommate is to blame for your poor performance on your history exam is likely an example of _____.

   a. a trait attribution
   b. the fundamental attribution error
   c. the actor/observer bias
   d. the self-serving bias

7. Believing that in general firefighters are brave, strong, and intelligent is an example of a _____.
   a. stereotype   c. situational attribution
   b. prejudice   d. All of the above

8. Jane Elliott's study of prejudice in brown-eyed and blue-eyed grade school students showed us that _____.
   a. prejudices are already present in us
   b. prejudices develop easily in us
   c. prejudices develop slowly over time
   d. children do not form prejudices as easily as adults do

9. The fact that Mary slightly prefers talking to other women over talking to men best exemplifies _____.
   a. stereotyping
   b. prejudice
   c. in-group/out-group bias
   d. the fundamental attribution error

10. Muzafer Sherif's study of the Eagles and Rattlers indicated that _____ is the most useful way to reduce prejudice.
    a. punishment
    b. mere contact with out-group members
    c. cooperative contact between groups
    d. competition between groups

11. Living and working in close proximity to someone is likely to increase our liking for that person because of _____.
    a. in-group/out-group bias
    b. the mere exposure effect
    c. similarity
    d. the out-group homogeneity effect

12. Being in love with someone is associated with increased _____ in the brain.
    a. dopamine   c. GABA
    b. serotonin   d. acetylcholine

13. When group members value their group membership, the group is said to be high in _____.
    a. cohesiveness   c. unanimity
    b. conformity   d. groupthink

14. Informational conformity is most closely related to _____.
    a. compliance   c. attribution
    b. obedience   d. persuasion

15. Which of the following would be least likely to reduce the risk of groupthink in a group?
    a. Having a strong group leader
    b. Allowing ample time for discussion of ideas
    c. Allowing visitors to attend group meetings
    d. Having low cohesiveness

16. The destructive obedience that Stanley Milgram demonstrated in his experiments is most closely related to which of the following social psychological phenomena?
    a. Realistic conflict
    b. Attribution
    c. Foot-in-the door compliance
    d. The frustration-aggression hypothesis

17. Which of the following has not been linked to aggressive behavior?
    a. Low serotonin levels
    b. High testosterone
    c. Frustration
    d. High norepinephrine levels

18. The bystander effect predicts that you are most likely to receive help from an individual when he or she _____.
    a. is the only witness to your plight
    b. is one of many witnesses to your plight
    c. is knowledgeable about helping
    d. is a compassionate person

19. Altruism is helping someone _____.
    a. without concern for your own gain
    b. because you expect a reward
    c. because you are afraid you'll be sued if you fail to help
    d. because other people are watching

20. Pluralistic ignorance prevents helping because _____.
    a. everyone decides that someone else is responsible for helping
    b. no one knows how to help
    c. no one recognizes that help is needed
    d. no one cares enough to help

Answers: 1. c; 2. b; 3. a; 4. d; 5. b; 6. d; 7. a; 8. b; 9. c; 10. c; 11. b; 12. a; 13. a; 14. d; 15. a; 16. c; 17. d; 18. a; 19. a; 20. c

Online Resources

CENGAGENOW™ Personalized Study

www.cengage.com/login

Go to www.cengage.com/login to link to CengageNOW, your online study tool. First take the **Pre-Test** for this chapter to get your **Personalized Study Plan**, which will identify topics you need to review and direct you to online resources. Then take the **Post-Test** to determine what concepts you have mastered and what you still need work on.

What Is Psychology? Essentials Book Companion Website

www.cengage.com/psychology/pastorino

Visit your book companion website, where you will find more resources to help you study. Resources include learning objectives, Internet exercises, quizzing, flash cards, and a pronunciation glossary.

Look Back AT WHAT YOU'VE LEARNED

Social psychology is the study of how we think and behave in social situations. **Social cognition** refers to the ways in which we think about ourselves and others.

© Mark Richards/Photo Edit

How Do Attitudes Change and Develop?

- **Attitudes** are evaluative beliefs that contain affective, behavioral, and cognitive components.

- Attitudes develop through learning processes, including classical conditioning, operant conditioning, and social learning or modeling.

- Attitudes sometimes predict how we will behave in certain situations.

- **Dissonance** results from a lack of **cognitive consistency**, and it motivates us to change either our attitudes or our behavior.

- **Persuasion** occurs when someone makes a direct attempt to change our attitudes.

- We tend to be most persuaded by people who appear to be attractive, credible, and expert.

- Typically, people are easier to persuade when they are processing on the **peripheral route** rather than the **central route**.

Neal Hamberg/Bloomberg News /Landov

How Do We Form Impressions of Others?

- In forming impressions of others, we make **trait** or **situational attributions** when we assign cause to their behavior.

- The **fundamental attribution error** is the tendency to discount situational explanations during attribution.

- The **actor/observer bias** and the **self-serving bias** are two other sources of mistaken or biased attributions.

What Is Prejudice?

© Mark Peterson/Corbis

- **Prejudices** are negatively biased **stereotypes** that are applied to all members of a social group regardless of the members' individual characteristics.

- Like most attitudes, prejudices are learned.

- Intergroup dynamics such as **in-group bias** and **out-group homogeneity bias** often play a role in prejudice.

- The **contact hypothesis** states that mere contact between in-group and out-group members can reduce prejudice. Cooperative contact and **superordinate goals** have been shown to be more effective in reducing prejudice.

What Attracts Us to Others?

- Some of the factors that affect our attraction to others include **proximity**, similarity of their attitudes and characteristics to ours, physical attractiveness, and biochemicals.

Jorgen Schytte/
Peter Arnold, Inc.

Social Psychology: HOW DO WE Understand AND Interact WITH OTHERS?

How Do Groups Influence Us?

- **Conformity** is the tendency to behave in ways that are consistent with the **norms** or expectations of a group.

- In **normative conformity**, we conform just to avoid breaking norms. In **informational conformity**, we conform because we are persuaded by conformity pressure to believe the group's stance is correct.

- Conformity is influenced by such factors as majority group size, unanimity of the majority group, anonymity, group cohesion, and self-esteem.

- **Groupthink** occurs when groups working under conditions of isolation, high **cohesiveness**, stress, and dictatorial leadership make poor decisions after failing to examine all possible solutions to a problem.

Why Do We Comply and Obey?

- **Compliance** is giving in to a simple request.

  - In **foot-in-the-door compliance**, one is more likely to yield to a second larger request after having already complied with a first, smaller request.

  - In **door-in-the-face compliance**, one is more likely to yield to a second, smaller request after having refused an earlier large request.

  - **Reciprocity**, or feeling obligated to return others' favors, is a major reason why we comply.

- **Obedience** is giving in to a demand. Factors that make us more likely to obey orders, even when they direct us to behave destructively, include:

  - the presence of an authority figure,

  - the foot-in-the door compliance of the **slippery slope**, and

  - **psychological distance**.

Obedience © 1965, Stanley Milgram

Why Are Some People Aggressive?

- Aggression is causing harm or injury to someone who does not wish to be harmed.

- **Instrumental aggression** is goal-directed aggression; **hostile aggression** is aimed solely at hurting others.

- Potential causes of aggression include high levels of testosterone, a lack of serotonin, brain damage caused by child abuse, social learning or modeling the aggression of others, cognitive neoassociation theory, and the **frustration-aggression hypothesis**.

When Are People Likely to Help Others?

- **Helping behavior**, or **altruism**, is the tendency to help others in need with little concern for our own gain.

- One of the factors affecting helping behavior is the **bystander effect**, in which **diffusion of responsibility** reduces your chance of obtaining help when there are many witnesses. **Pluralistic ignorance** may also ensure that we do not correctly perceive the situation as an emergency.

11

Health, Stress, AND Coping:
HOW CAN YOU Create a HEALTHY LIFE?

BananaStock/Jupiter Images

Because all of us cope with stress on a daily basis, this chapter offers much psychological research that will be relevant to your day-to-day living, as our student Crystal Athas Thatcher discovered. Crystal, 23, lives on an Army base with her 4-year-old daughter, Nevaeh. Her husband of four years, Brian, 25, has been stationed in Iraq for the past four months. This situation has created quite a lot of stress for Crystal. However, Crystal has applied her knowledge of health psychology to cope better.

To reduce her worry and anxiety over Brian's being at war, Crystal videoconferences with Brian almost every day. Seeing him and talking to him makes her feel more connected and in control. It has also helped Nevaeh maintain a relationship with her father. When Brian first left, Nevaeh would not speak to Brian on the phone. But when she sees Brian on the video, she will speak with him. Crystal has also postponed her own education to reduce her stress level so that she can be a better mom to Nevaeh, as she is essentially raising her daughter on her own. Neveah asks many questions and frequently complains that she misses her daddy. Crystal copes by relying on family and friends—for advice, companionship, or a shoulder to cry on. She has an optimistic attitude and tries not to "sweat the small stuff." Although she is sometimes overwhelmed by emotions, she waits until she puts Nevaeh to bed at night before she allows herself to express them.

These strategies have by no means made Crystal stress-free. What they have done is helped her cope during a very difficult time. In this chapter we'll explore the field of **health psychology**. Health psychologists study how a person's behavior, thoughts, personality, and attitudes influence his or her health for better and for worse.

In this regard, health is seen as a result of the interaction among biological, psychological, and social forces (Brannon & Feist, 2004; S. E. Taylor, 2003). The main topics of this chapter are stress, coping, and health. We hope that, like Crystal, you will be able to apply the information in this chapter to your life and realize how some of your personal habits, thoughts, or daily actions may be unhealthy. Hopefully, this analysis will encourage you to live a healthier, longer life!

Lisa Athas

Crystal Athas Thatcher does her best to cope with raising her daughter, Nevaeh, while her husband, Brian, is serving in the military.

What Is Stress? Stress and Stressors

● Define stress, and identify stressors and conflict situations.

> **You Asked...**
>
> *What causes stress?*
>
> JUSTEN CARTER, STUDENT

You are running late for school and your car breaks down—today of all days, when you have a major project due in one class and a midterm in another. Or maybe you're a working parent, trying to get the kids off to school in the morning, when your youngest can't find her shoes and the dog just got into the garbage. Perhaps you have just fallen in love and are contemplating getting married. Or maybe you have grown dissatisfied with your relationship and are contemplating ending it. All of these situations have one thing in common. They all include *stress*, an inevitable and unavoidable fact of life.

Stress can be defined as any event or environmental stimulus (stressor) that we respond to because we perceive it as challenging or threatening. This definition implies three aspects to stress. First, we all encounter stressors—stimuli in our lives that we perceive as challenges or threats, such as traffic, an approaching midterm exam, or a hurricane. Second, our reactions to these stressors include bodily reactions. Third, by perceiving and then reacting, we cope with the challenges or threats (successfully or not, as we will see). This chapter explores these three aspects of stress.

Briefly reflect on an ordinary day in your life. There are probably many events or stimuli that you perceive as provoking or annoying: a long line at the fast-food drive-through, a confrontation with your boss, or having several errands to run in a limited amount of time. There probably have also been events in your life that you found to be particularly trying or traumatic, such as the death of a loved one, dealing with an unplanned pregnancy, or being fired from your job. Stressors come in all shapes and sizes. Psychological research classifies these stressors into four types:

● Major life events
● Catastrophes
● Daily hassles
● Conflict

Let's take a look at how each of these stressors is defined.

Life Events: Change Is Stressful

How do we know which events in our life qualify as major, rather than minor, stressors when they all *feel* stressful? Believe it or not, psychologists have tried to measure this difference.

health psychology the subfield of psychology that investigates the relationship between people's behaviors and their health

stress any event or environmental stimulus (stressor) that we respond to because we perceive it as challenging or threatening

Ralph Dunagin & Dana Summers.
© 1999 Tribune Media Services, Inc.
Reprinted with permission.

Pioneering research by Thomas Holmes and Richard Rahe in 1967 set out to measure the impact of particular stressors on people's health. They asked a large sample group to rate **life events**, or changes in one's living, both good and bad, that require us to adjust to them. In other words, which life events did the respondents perceive as more or less stressful? From these ratings, Holmes and Rahe developed the Social Readjustment Rating Scale (SRRS), reprinted in ■ TABLE 11.1.

life event a change in one's life, good or bad, that requires readjustment

Table 11.1 Holmes & Rahe's Social Readjustment Rating Scale

Rank	Life Event	Life Change Units	Rank	Life Event	Life Change Units
1	Death of spouse	100	23	Son or daughter leaving home	29
2	Divorce	73	24	Trouble with in-laws	29
3	Marital separation	65	25	Outstanding personal achievement	28
4	Jail term	63	26	Spouse begins or stops work	26
5	Death of a close family member	63	27	Begin or end school	26
6	Personal injury or illness	53	28	Change in living conditions	25
7	Marriage	50	29	Revision of personal habits	24
8	Fired at work	47	30	Trouble with boss	23
9	Marital reconciliation	45	31	Change in work hours or conditions	20
10	Retirement	45	32	Change in residence	20
11	Change in health of family member	44	33	Change in school	20
12	Pregnancy	40	34	Change in recreation	19
13	Sex difficulties	39	35	Change in church activities	19
14	Gain of new family member	39	36	Change in social activities	18
15	Business readjustment	39	37	Take out loan less than $20,000	17
16	Change in financial state	38	38	Change in sleeping habits	16
17	Death of a close friend	37	39	Change in number of family get-togethers	15
18	Change to different line of work	36	40	Change in eating habits	15
19	Change in number of arguments with spouse	35	41	Vacation	13
20	Take out mortgage or loan for major purchase	31	42	Christmas	12
21	Foreclosure of mortgage or loan	30	43	Minor violation of the law	11
22	Change in responsibilities at work	29			

Reprinted with permission from T. H. Holmes & R. H. Rahe (1967), "The Social Readjustment Rating Scale," in Journal of Psychosomatic Research, *Vol. 11, No. 2, pp. 213–218. Copyright © 1967 Elsevier Science.*

Note: In Holmes and Rahe's Social Readjustment Rating Scale, each major life event is assigned a numerical value. The higher the number, the more stressful the life event is perceived to be. Add up the life change units for all those events you have experienced in the past year. Then compare your total to the standards indicated in the text.

Holmes and Rahe assigned each major life event a numerical value, referred to as a *life change unit*. The higher the number, the more stressful this life event was rated by Holmes and Rahe's sample. Notice that the life events on the scale include positive as well as negative changes—for example, marriage, a new family member, and outstanding personal achievement. However, it is not just experiencing one of these events that is at issue. Rather, it is reacting to several of these events within a year that Holmes and Rahe found may influence one's health.

YOUR TURN – ACTIVE LEARNING

Take a moment to look at the Social Readjustment Rating Scale (Table 11.1). Add up the life change units for all those events you have experienced in the last year. Compare your total to the standards devised by Holmes and Rahe:

0–150	No significant problems
150–199	Mild life crisis
200–299	Moderate life crisis
300 or more	Major life crisis

Holmes and Rahe (1967) found that the higher people scored on the SRRS, the more prone they were to illness. Of those who scored within the mild life crisis range, 37% had experienced deteriorated health. This figure rose to 51% for those whose scores indicated they were experiencing a moderate life crisis, and 79% for those in the major life crisis range. Follow-up studies have supported Holmes and Rahe's findings (Gruen, 1993; Scully, Tosi, & Banning, 2000). If you scored high on the scale, you may want to consider adjusting your lifestyle in ways that reduce your chances of becoming ill. However, keep in mind that these are correlations and, as we discussed in Chapter 1, correlation does not mean causation. Life events do not directly cause illness, but they may make a person more vulnerable to illness and disease.

Subsequent research (Pearlin, 1993) evaluating Holmes and Rahe's scale indicates that the impact of these life changes is not simply a matter of how many of them one experiences. We need to take several other variables into account, including:

- The voluntary or involuntary nature of the life change
- How desirable or undesirable the life change is perceived to be
- Whether the life change is scheduled or unscheduled

Life events, both good and bad, can be perceived as stressful and require us to adjust to them.

Consider as an example a heterosexual couple about to divorce. Typically, the partner who asks for a divorce feels less stress after she has informed her mate of her decision. In this context, the divorce is seen as voluntary, desirable, and scheduled. At the same time, her husband may experience increased stress, as the divorce for him may be involuntary (not of his choosing), undesirable, and unscheduled. As this example illustrates, the amount of stress one experiences when faced with life changes may vary across people. We can consider Holmes and Rahe's scale as a rough index of how susceptible some may be to illness, given the number of major stressors the person encounters.

You may have noticed that the scale has very few life events that are likely to be experienced by college students and younger people. The SRRS has been criticized for not adequately defining stress events among younger age groups. Yet research supports the notion that major changes, such as the breakup of a relationship, academic pressure, or even college itself, may influence the health of college students (Crandall, Preisler, & Aussprung, 1992). This is important because perceived stress also seems to predict how well students perform academically. High levels of perceived stress in college students correlate with lower grade point averages (Lloyd, Alexander, Rice, & Greenfield, 1980). You may find that the Undergraduate Stress Questionnaire (■ TABLE 11.2) includes more of the stressors that you typically face than does Holmes and Rahe's SRRS. It was specifically designed to measure life event stress in college students. Undergraduates who have experienced more of these life events are more likely to report more physical symptoms and are less likely to report a positive mood (Crandall et al., 1992). It may therefore provide a more accurate assessment of your stress level and hence your susceptibility to illness.

Catastrophes: Natural Disasters and Wars

Unexpected traumatic events or catastrophes that almost all people perceive as threats also qualify as stressors. Catastrophes may affect one's physical and psychological health. After catastrophic events such as floods, earthquakes, hurricanes, tornadoes, or fires, people are generally more likely to experience depression or anxiety (Brende, 2000; Davidson, 2000; Rubonis & Bickman, 1991). We have for a long time recognized the stress of war on soldiers, as evidenced by the various names we have given to the pattern of symptoms that soldiers experience when they return. It was called shell shock in World War I, battle fatigue in World War II, and *posttraumatic stress disorder* (PTSD) following the Vietnam War and Operation Desert Storm. Soldiers experienced nightmares, flashbacks, and vivid memories as they relived their war experiences. They evidenced intense startle responses to loud noises and had difficulty concentrating and getting along with others. Rape victims report similar physical and psychological symptoms that may meet the criteria for what is referred to as *rape trauma syndrome*, more evidence that unexpected events may take their toll on one's health. Given that these events are often involuntary, undesirable, and somewhat unscheduled in that we typically don't have a lot of time to prepare for them, it is relatively easy to see how they might influence our health and well-being. We'll discuss PTSD in more detail in Chapter 13.

daily hassles the everyday irritations and frustrations that individuals face

Unexpected traumatic events also cause stress and can affect one's physical and psychological health.

Daily Hassles: Little Things Add Up!

When psychologists evaluate the relationship between stress and health, they not only measure life changes and analyze the influence of catastrophes, they also evaluate the impact of everyday irritations and frustrations. These **daily hassles** also appear to play a role in our health. At times these irritants add to the stress of major life changes and catastrophic events, such as the daily planning for a wedding or getting stuck in traffic during an evacuation due to a natural disaster. But for most of us, the routine annoyances and frustrations we experience on a daily basis are stressful in themselves. Can you think of any examples of daily hassles? Waiting in lines, lack of money, losing your keys, or fights with loved ones may be a few that come to mind. Such daily hassles may in fact be the most significant source of stress, placing a great burden on our immediate health and well-being (Kohn & Macdonald, 1992; Lazarus, 1990; S. M. Roberts, 1995; Ruffin, 1993). As daily hassles increase, our physical and mental health decreases

© Tony Arruza/Corbis

Table 11.2 Undergraduate Stress Questionnaire

Have any of the following stressful events happened to you at any time during the past semester? If any has, check the space next to it.
If an item has not occurred, leave it blank. Stressful life events are listed in descending order of severity.
Students with more checkmarks are more likely to need health care than students with fewer checkmarks.

___ 1. Death (family member or friend)	___ 42. Crammed for a test
___ 2. Had a lot of tests	___ 43. Feel unorganized
___ 3. It's finals week	___ 44. Trying to decide on major
___ 4. Applying to graduate school	___ 45. Feel isolated
___ 5. Victim of a crime	___ 46. Parents controlling with money
___ 6. Assignments in all classes due the same day	___ 47. Couldn't find a parking space
___ 7. Breaking up with boy/girlfriend	___ 48. Noise disturbed you while trying to study
___ 8. Found out boy/girlfriend cheated on you	___ 49. Someone borrowed something without your permission
___ 9. Lots of deadlines to meet	___ 50. Had to ask for money
___ 10. Property stolen	___ 51. Ran out of toner while printing
___ 11. You have a hard upcoming week	___ 52. Erratic schedule
___ 12. Went into a test unprepared	___ 53. Can't understand your professor
___ 13. Lost something (especially wallet)	___ 54. Trying to get into your major or college
___ 14. Death of a pet	___ 55. Registration for classes
___ 15. Did worse than expected on test	___ 56. Stayed up late writing a paper
___ 16. Had an interview	___ 57. Someone you expected to call did not
___ 17. Had projects, research papers due	___ 58. Someone broke a promise
___ 18. Did badly on a test	___ 59. Can't concentrate
___ 19. Parents getting a divorce	___ 60. Someone did a "pet peeve" of yours
___ 20. Dependent on other people	___ 61. Living with boy/girlfriend
___ 21. Having roommate conflicts	___ 62. Felt need for transportation
___ 22. Car/bike broke down, flat tire	___ 63. Bad haircut today
___ 23. Got a traffic ticket	___ 64. Job requirements changed
___ 24. Missed your menstrual period and waiting	___ 65. No time to eat
___ 25. Thoughts about future	___ 66. Felt some peer pressure
___ 26. Lack of money	___ 67. You have a hangover
___ 27. Dealt with incompetence at the Registrar's Office	___ 68. Problems with your computer
___ 28. Thought about unfinished work	___ 69. Problem getting home when drunk
___ 29. No sleep	___ 70. Used a fake I.D.
___ 30. Sick, injury	___ 71. No sex in a while
___ 31. Had a class presentation	___ 72. Someone cut ahead of you in line
___ 32. Applying for a job	___ 73. Checkbook didn't balance
___ 33. Fought with boy/girlfriend	___ 74. Had a visit from a relative and entertained him/her
___ 34. Working while in school	___ 75. Decision to have sex on your mind
___ 35. Arguments, conflict of values with friends	___ 76. Spoke with a professor
___ 36. Bothered by not having family's social support	___ 77. Change of environment (new doctor, dentist, etc.)
___ 37. Performed poorly at a task	___ 78. Exposed to upsetting TV show, book, or movie
___ 38. Can't finish everything you need to do	___ 79. Got to class late
___ 39. Heard bad news	___ 80. Holiday
___ 40. Had confrontation with an authority figure	___ 81. Sat through a boring class
___ 41. Maintaining a long-distance boy/girlfriend	___ 82. Favorite sports team lost

Source: C. S. Crandal et al., *"Measuring Life Event Stress in the Lives of College Students: The Undergraduate Stress Questionnaire (USQ),"* in Journal of Behavioral Medicine, *15(6), pp. 627–662,* © 1992. Reprinted with kind permission of Springer Science and Business Media.

(Chamberlain & Zika, 1990; O'Connor, Jones, Conner, McMillan, & Ferguson, 2008; Sim, 2000). However, whether we perceive these frustrations as stressful is of prime importance in determining our susceptibility to illness. Some people easily shrug off these annoyances, whereas others find them particularly perturbing.

Gender, race, age, socioeconomic status, and education seem to influence our perception of stress from daily hassles (Almeida, 2005; H. Taylor, 2002). Women are more likely than men to perceive stress from concerns about money, having too many things to do, health concerns, and having trouble relaxing. In general, younger people report more daily hassles in their lives than older people. Those with more money and more education also report lower levels of perceived stress from daily hassles than do those with lower income and less education. Although people who make more money and have more education may lead full and hectic lives, they generally perceive that they have more control over their lives and report having more fun. They are less likely to experience hassles concerning health, illness of a family member, trouble relaxing, problems at work, and exposure to excessive noise than are people with less education and lower incomes. Racial differences also appear in reports on daily hassles. African Americans are more likely than Hispanic or European Americans to report economic hassles, exposure to noise, feeling lonely, and invasion of personal privacy as frequent day-to-day hassles. Hispanics are more likely than European or African Americans to report problems with aging parents as a hassle of daily living.

Everyday irritations and frustrations increase our stress level and can influence our health.

© Michael Newman/PhotoEdit

Conflict: Approach and Avoidance

Conflict, or having to choose between two or more needs, desires, or demands, can also place stress on us. Should you take the required science course or the required math course? Should you wear the blue or the gray suit to the job interview? Whether we perceive these options as positive or negative results in four basic forms of conflict (■ FIGURE 11.1).

FIGURE

11.1 Four Common Conflict Situations

In an approach–approach conflict, a person must choose between two appealing choices—in this example, two movies one would like to see. In an avoidance–avoidance conflict, a person must choose between two undesirable choices—in this example, two disliked vegetables. In an approach–avoidance conflict, a person faces a decision that has both positive and negative features—in this example, owning a pet that cuddles yet also makes messes. Multiple conflicts involve several choices that have both positive and negative qualities—in this example, choosing among three jobs.

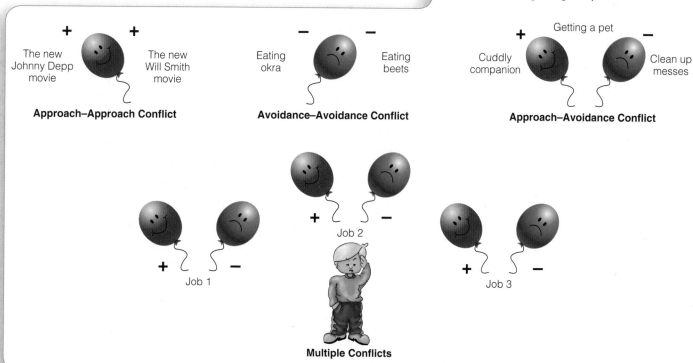

+ The new Johnny Depp movie   + The new Will Smith movie
Approach–Approach Conflict

− Eating okra   − Eating beets
Avoidance–Avoidance Conflict

+ Cuddly companion   Getting a pet   − Clean up messes
Approach–Avoidance Conflict

+ − Job 1
+ − Job 2
+ − Job 3
Multiple Conflicts

1. *Approach–approach conflicts.* The easiest conflict to resolve, and therefore the conflict that is accompanied by the least amount of perceived stress, is the **approach–approach conflict**, in which a person must choose between two likable, or positive, events. Choosing between seeing an old friend who is passing through town or going out on a date with someone you've been hoping would ask you out is an example of an approach–approach conflict. A more stressful approach–approach example could be liking and being challenged in your job and being offered another attractive and challenging position in the same company. In this type of conflict you really can't lose, because both options are favorable.

2. *Avoidance–avoidance conflicts.* The opposite of the approach–approach conflict is the **avoidance–avoidance conflict**, in which a person has to choose between two undesirable, or negative, events. You can think of this type of conflict as a "Catch-22" situation. For example, do you spend the morning in line to register your car, or do you get your car towed because the registration has expired? Because both options in an avoidance–avoidance conflict are unappealing, many people remain undecided and inactive, or "frozen." They don't do anything. Consequently, avoidance–avoidance conflicts are accompanied by a greater degree of perceived stress than are approach–approach conflicts.

3. *Approach–avoidance conflicts.* Another stressful conflict to resolve is the **approach–avoidance conflict**, in which a person is faced with a desire or need that has both positive and negative qualities. He or she is drawn to the situation because of its positive features (approach), but is also repelled by and would rather not experience the negative aspects of the situation (avoidance). For example, think of a home fire with your dog trapped inside the burning structure. You don't want to lose your lifelong friend and therefore want to save the dog, but attempting to do so may put your own life at risk. As with avoidance–avoidance conflicts, these situations may immobilize people so that they cannot make a decision or resolve the conflict, which leads to the experience of stress.

4. *Multiple conflicts.* In real life, many conflicts involve several alternatives, each with both positive and negative features. These **multiple approach–avoidance conflicts** can contribute to the amount of stress we feel. In deciding which college to attend, you may have been faced with several choices. Each school may have had its good points and bad points (distance from home, tuition cost, program of studies, social life). Deciding on a major or a career, choosing between two job offers, and deciding which house or car to buy are other examples of multiple conflicts. This may account for *buyer's remorse*, which some people experience after making a major purchase. They bought, or approached, an item because of its attractive features but afterward felt regret as they contemplated the item's negative features or alternatives that they should have considered more seriously.

conflict having to choose between two or more needs, desires, or demands

approach–approach conflict a situation in which a person must choose between two likable events

avoidance–avoidance conflict a situation in which a person must choose between two undesirable events

approach–avoidance conflict a situation in which a person is faced with a need that has both positive and negative aspects

multiple approach–avoidance conflict a situation that poses several alternatives that each have positive and negative features

Let's Review!

In this section, we defined stress and described four types of stressors. For a quick check of your understanding, answer these questions.

1. You go to the dentist and find out that you have to get a tooth extracted. The only time the dentist can schedule your appointment is at the same time as a traffic court appointment. This situation is an example of a(n) _____.
   a. approach–approach conflict
   b. approach–avoidance conflict
   c. avoidance–avoidance conflict
   d. multiple conflict

2. Which of the following does the Social Readjustment Rating Scale consider to be the most stressful major life event?
   a. A jail term   c. Divorce
   b. Death of a spouse   d. Pregnancy

3. Getting stuck in traffic on your way to a job interview is an example of a _____.
   a. daily hassle   c. catastrophe
   b. major life event   d. stress response

The Stress Response: Is This Stress? How Do I React?

- Discuss the concept of appraisal in the stress response.

- Explain how the body responds to stress and how that response influences immunity to disease.

Now that we have looked at the types of stressors that may influence health, we will examine the second feature of stress: the reactions that accompany stress. This analysis will further your understanding of the relationship between stress and health.

Appraisal: Assessing Stress

We all experience stressors, especially daily hassles. We all wait in lines, sit in traffic, and pay bills. Yet not all of us interpret these events as equally stressful. Some people view giving blood as less stressful than others. You may feel excited about giving a speech, whereas others cringe at the same prospect. Therefore, the first step in experiencing stress is how you think about or interpret an event or situation. Our initial interpretation of an event is called **primary appraisal** (Lazarus, 1991, 1993). Primary appraisal can be irrelevant, positive, or stressful.

If your primary appraisal of an event is *irrelevant*, you interpret the situation as immaterial or unrelated to your happiness or safety. For example, the number of students in a particular course you are taking may not make a difference to you one way or another. Class size may be appraised as not relevant to your performance in the class, and therefore viewed as not stressful. Primary appraisals also can be *positive*. For example, you may take a class in which there is a small number of students and view this situation as something good. Again, we typically don't feel much stress in situations such as these. However, when we appraise a situation as *stressful*, we believe it will require a great deal of our emotional and psychological resources. For example, you may view a small class size as stressful if you fear speaking in front of a group and you are expected to participate in class discussion.

Our primary appraisal of an event as stressful can lead to positive or negative emotions that either increase or decrease our perceived stress levels (Barlow, 2002). How much stress we experience will depend on whether we see the situation as a threat, a harm, or a challenge. If we appraise a stressful event as a *threat*, we believe that the situation will cause us some harm in the future. When we interpret an event in this manner, we typically feel fear, anxiety, or anger—negative emotions that increase our stress levels. For example, having to give an oral presentation on a project later in the term may be perceived as threatening by a student. He may fear negative evaluations by the professor or other students or be anxious that his voice may crack or that he will stammer. If we appraise an event as *harmful*, we believe it will do us some damage or injury. For example, one of the authors of your textbook appraised putting holiday lights up on her house as stressful because she believed that getting on the roof of her house could lead to injury. Again, such appraisals typically lead to feelings of fear and anxiety that increase our feelings of stress. However, situations can also be appraised as *challenging*, as a means toward personal growth or personal gain. For example, taking a new job may be appraised as an opportunity for career growth, or getting married may be appraised as an opportunity to deepen and expand the nature of an intimate relationship. Challenge appraisals typically elicit positive emotions such as excitement and happiness, and are therefore perceived as less stressful.

primary appraisal [uh-PRAY-zull] our initial interpretation of an event as either irrelevant, positive, or stressful

Do you perceive an oral presentation as a threat or a challenge? A primary appraisal of threat will make you feel more stressed than viewing it as a challenge.

Not all primary appraisals break down easily into the categories of threat, harm, or challenge. A situation or event may involve a combination of appraisals. For example, starting a relationship, finding a job, or having a baby are complex situations that may involve appraisals of both threat and challenge. Also, the appraisal process is a personal one. Not everyone appraises the same situation in the same manner. For example, some students may perceive course exams as threats, whereas other students may see them as challenges. Yet for everyone, primary appraisal is the first step in experiencing stress. Once you appraise a situation or event as stressful, your body changes to deal with the stressor.

Selye's General Adaptation Syndrome: The Body's Response to Stress

general adaptation syndrome (GAS) the general physical responses we experience when faced with a stressor

alarm reaction the first phase of the general adaptation syndrome, characterized by immediate activation of the nervous and endocrine systems

> ### You Asked...
> *What does stress do to the body?*
>
> CHARLOTTE ANDERSON, STUDENT

Many of us recognize stressful situations because of the bodily reactions that accompany them. For example, if you perceive giving a speech as a stressor, when faced with doing so, you may feel shaky, perspire more, feel your heart race, or even experience difficulty breathing. You may experience these same reactions when accepting an award or before an important job interview. These reactions are a part of a general bodily pattern termed the **general adaptation syndrome** (**GAS**; Selye, 1976). ■ FIGURE 11.2 shows the GAS as three phases that we all experience when we face a stressor in the environment: an initial *alarm reaction, resistance,* and *exhaustion.*

ALARM REACTION

The **alarm reaction** consists of those bodily responses that are immediately triggered when we initially appraise an event as stressful. It is much like the car alarm that goes off the moment an intruder tries to open the car door. In the body, this involves activation of the nervous system and the endocrine system (■ FIGURE 11.3).

Recall from Chapter 2 that your nervous system has two branches: the central nervous system, consisting of the brain and the spinal cord, and the peripheral nervous system, including the somatic and autonomic divisions (see p. 50). The autonomic division includes two systems: the parasympathetic branch, which operates when we are calm and relaxed, and the sympathetic nervous system, our fight-or-flight mechanism that prepares us to face a threat in the environment. This sympathetic branch of the nervous system is at the heart of the stress response.

When a person perceives a threat in the environment—or what we have now referred to as a stressor—the sympathetic nervous system is activated. In order to prepare the body to deal with the stressor, the sympathetic nervous system works in conjunction with the endocrine (or hormonal) system. It stimulates the adrenal gland to secrete two hormones: adrenalin and corticosteroids. These hormones travel to the major organs (liver, heart, lungs) to prepare the body for fight or flight. Our heart rate and blood pressure increase, our lungs expand, and our liver releases stored sugars that can be used for energy. At the same time, the brain also stimulates the pituitary gland to release endorphins, the body's natural painkillers. The body continues to expend these resources for as long as the stressor

FIGURE 11.2 **General Adaptation Syndrome**

According to Hans Selye, the biological stress response consists of three phases. In the *alarm reaction,* the body releases chemicals to deal with a stressor. These chemicals lower the body's resistance. In the *resistance stage,* the body shores up additional resources to cope with the stressor. If the stressor persists, the body enters the *exhaustion stage,* in which bodily resources dwindle and we function at less than normal capacity. Wear and tear on the body begin.

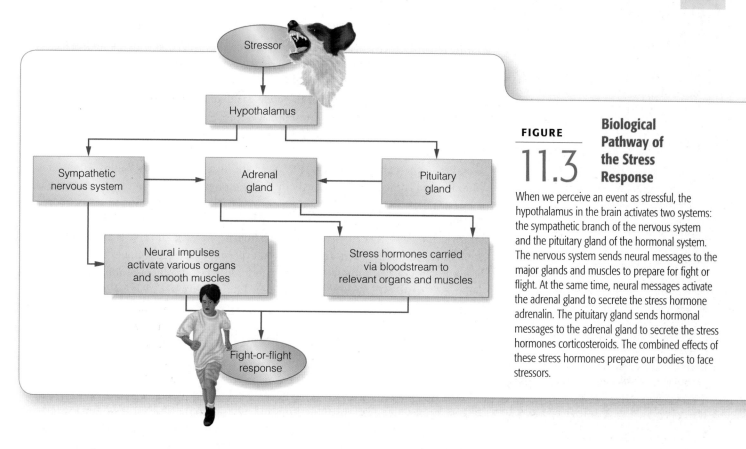

FIGURE

11.3

Biological Pathway of the Stress Response

When we perceive an event as stressful, the hypothalamus in the brain activates two systems: the sympathetic branch of the nervous system and the pituitary gland of the hormonal system. The nervous system sends neural messages to the major glands and muscles to prepare for fight or flight. At the same time, neural messages activate the adrenal gland to secrete the stress hormone adrenalin. The pituitary gland sends hormonal messages to the adrenal gland to secrete the stress hormones corticosteroids. The combined effects of these stress hormones prepare our bodies to face stressors.

persists. Once the stressor passes, the brain turns off the sympathetic nervous system, which in turn shuts off the release of these stress hormones, and the body returns to its parasympathetic mode of calm and relaxation. However, if the stressor continues, the body enters the resistance stage.

Neuroscience Applies to Your World:

Loneliness & Health

As social animals, humans are motivated to maintain social connections with others. As a result, feeling lonely has a major impact on health and well-being. Higher levels of loneliness and smaller social networks in college students have been found to be associated with higher levels of cortisol (a corticosteroid secreted during the stress response) and a lower antibody response to flu shots. High levels of cortisol are not good for one's health. Poor antibody response means the body's immune system produces fewer protective antibodies and puts the person at greater risk for illness (Pressman et al., 2005).

RESISTANCE STAGE

During the **resistance stage**, the body continues its efforts to cope with the stressor. The sympathetic nervous system and endocrine system continue to be activated. However, the bodily reactions associated with resistance are less intense than the alarm reaction, as the body's resources begin to dwindle. When the body has drained its resources so that energy is no longer available, we enter the exhaustion stage.

EXHAUSTION STAGE

It is during the **exhaustion stage** that wear and tear on the body begins. High levels of adrenalin and corticosteroids in the body over a prolonged period of time damage the heart and lessen the effectiveness of the immune system. The result is that you become more vulnerable to heart disease, ulcers, high blood pressure, and colds and flus (Cohen, 1996; Doctor & Doctor, 1994; Kiecolt-Glaser, McGuire, Robles, & Glaser, 2002; G. E. Miller & Blackwell, 2006; Rice, 2000). Excessive and prolonged exposure to stress hormones may also produce headaches, backaches, indigestion, constipation, diarrhea, fatigue, insomnia, mood swings, and muscle tension (B. Brown, 1980; De Benedittis, Lorenzetti, & Pieri, 1990).

Stress and the Immune System: Resistance to Disease

As we have seen, our body's reaction to stress, particularly during the exhaustion phase, can influence the effectiveness of our immune system. The immune system is our body's best defense against illness because it destroys and fights bacteria, viruses, and other foreign substances that may invade our bodies. If this system is impaired, as in the case of prolonged stress, we are more prone to illness and disease (Webster Marketon & Glaser, 2008).

The corticosteroids and endorphins that are released into our body during the stress response actually reduce and dampen the activity of our immune system. This is referred to as **immunosuppression**. Consequently, turning on our stress response, which ensures our ability to survive immediate danger, comes at the expense of our immune system, our long-term survival mechanism.

Much research supports the notion that stress suppresses the functioning of the immune system, which then increases the chances of developing infections such as the common cold (Anderson, 2003; Cohen, Tyrrell, & Smith, 1991; Kiecolt-Glaser et al., 2002; Rice, 2000). During final exam time and other periods of academic pressure, students show a weakened immune system (D. G. Gilbert, Stunkard, Jensen, & Detwiler, 1996; Jemmott, Borysenko, McClelland, Chapman, & Benson, 1985). This may explain why you catch a cold or are more likely to experience allergies and sinus infections during finals week or when you have several projects or papers due at the same time. Immunosuppression also occurs in both men and women following the death of a spouse or partner (Schleifer, Keller, Camerino, Thornton, & Stein, 1983) and in people going through separation and divorce (Kiecolt-Glaser & Glaser, 1992). There is evidence that when people experience high levels of stress as a result of caring for a relative or friend with a terminal disease or dementia, they also experience immunosuppression (Kiecolt-Glaser, Marucha, Malarkey, Mercado, & Glaser, 1995; Vitaliano, Young, & Zhang, 2004).

More serious, though, is the correlation between stress, the

resistance stage the second phase of the general adaptation syndrome, in which the nervous and endocrine systems continue to be activated

exhaustion stage the third and final phase of the general adaptation syndrome, in which bodily resources are drained and wear and tear on the body begins

immunosuppression [im-mew-no-suh-PREH-shun] the reduction in activity of the immune system

Caring for a loved one is a highly stressful experience that can reduce the effectiveness of our immune system and make us more vulnerable to illness.

David Grossman/Photo Researchers, Inc.

immune system, and cancer. For example, cancer occurs more often than usual in people who are divorced, separated, or widowed (Schleifer, Keller, McKegney, & Stein, 1979). Moreover, our response and attitude toward having cancer may influence the eventual spread and fatality of the disease. Most people's initial reaction to a cancer diagnosis is panic, anger, or depression—emotions that activate the stress response and momentarily retard immune system functioning (Ader, 2001).

Our long-term attitude toward a disease may also influence our health. For example, emotional distress in breast cancer patients is associated with a lower survival rate (Luecken & Compas, 2002; Osborne et al., 2004). Patients who express their emotions about the disease—both positive and negative—tend to have a higher chance of survival than patients who hold in their emotions (O'Leary, 1990; Temoshok, 1992). Similarly, cancer patients with an optimistic attitude who are determined to beat the disease often outlive patients with a less positive attitude (Carver et al., 2000; Shen, McCreary, & Myers, 2004). Notice that this research does not say that stress causes cancer but, rather, that stress may influence the rate at which cancer cells grow. If your immune system is functioning at reduced levels during times of stress, it is less available to fight these life-threatening cells.

We are by no means saying that surviving or not surviving cancer is totally up to the individual. The onset, course, and magnitude of cancer in patients are influenced by variables that include the type of cancer, when it is detected, social support, and the treatments available. Our attitude about developing cancer and receiving cancer treatment is only one factor among many to consider when examining the connection between stress and health. Moreover, there is virtually no scientific evidence that our mental state *causes* cancer or that our mental state *cures* cancer.

We don't yet understand the exact relationship between stress, cancer, and immune system functioning. Some research suggests that low to moderate stress can *enhance* immune system functioning (Bosch et al., 2001; Dhabhar, Miller, McEwen, & Spencer, 1995). Current studies also speculate that chronic stress leads to an imbalance in our immune system, in which some immune responses are suppressed while others are enhanced; it is this disruption of the normal balance in our immune system that increases our vulnerability to illness and disease (Robles, Glaser, & Kiecolt-Glaser, 2005; Segerstrom, 2007). Moreover, the exact nature of our physical response to stress depends on the specific stressors and our cognitive appraisals of those stressors (Kemeny, 2003). We look to future research to fill in the blanks and make our knowledge more complete.

Let's Review!

This section detailed how we appraise stress, the body's response to stress, and the relationship between stress and immune system functioning. As a quick check, answer these questions.

1. You are more vulnerable to illness during which stage of Selye's stress response model?
   a. Alarm reaction
   b. Resistance
   c. Rejuvenation
   d. Exhaustion

2. Immunosuppression refers to _____.
   a. the activation of the immune system when we are faced with a stressor
   b. a reduction in the activity of the immune system
   c. the immune system's ability to survive immediate danger
   d. the release of endorphins and corticosteroids to help the immune system function

3. The first step in experiencing stress is _____.
   a. the alarm reaction
   b. resistance
   c. primary appraisal
   d. exhaustion

Answers 1.d; 2.b; 3.c

Stop, LOOK, and LEARN

Health, Stress, and Coping: How Can You Create a Healthy Life?

Learning Objectives

How Can I Cope With Stress?

● Distinguish between problem-focused and emotion-focused coping styles.

● Indicate adaptive ways to manage stress.

> ### You Asked...
>
> *What are some ways to deal with stress without "blowing up" or getting angry?* BRITTANY TELLER, STUDENT

Think of the exam or exams you will take for this course. Does your body evidence the telltale signs of the stress response when thinking about your exam? What do you do when faced with stress like this? Are you likely to react emotionally, becoming very anxious and worrying about what the test will be like? Are you likely to tackle the stressor directly, focusing all your energy on studying and preparing for the exam? Or do you simply ignore your stress, hoping for a miracle such as postponement or cancellation of the exam? Maybe you experience some or all of these reactions.

Whatever you do to manage an event or stimulus that you perceive as threatening is part of **coping**. How we cope with stress influences the way stress affects us. We will discuss two broad types of strategies for coping: *problem-focused coping* and *emotion-focused coping* (Folkman & Lazarus, 1988). You may use one or both types of coping when you're faced with a stressor. Each has its benefits and costs (Lazarus & Folkman, 1984; Roth & Cohen, 1986).

Problem-Focused Coping: Change the Situation

Problem-focused coping is aimed at controlling or altering the environment that is causing the stress. Let's say, for example, that you are working while going to school and your boss just increased your work hours. You now feel that you don't have enough time for school or your social life. A problem-focused approach to coping with this increased workload may include finding another job without as many required hours, or reducing the number of credit hours you are taking in school. Both of these strategies are aimed at changing the

coping the behaviors that we engage in to manage stressors

problem-focused coping behaviors that aim to control or alter the environment that is causing stress situation to reduce the amount of perceived stress. One benefit of either of these problem-focused coping strategies would be eliminating the perceived stressor. At the same time, you benefit by experiencing more control over your environment, which may also enhance your self-esteem. However, it is also possible that you have misdiagnosed the problem, which is a cost of problem-focused coping. Maybe the number of work hours isn't affecting your college work so much as your motivation or your social schedule is. You may actually increase your long-term level of stress by choosing an inappropriate course of action. For example, reducing your college hours increases the time it will take to complete your college education. Alternately, changing jobs may result in lower wages, making it more difficult to pay for your education.

Generally, problem-focused coping tends to be most useful when we feel that we can actually do something about a situation (Folkman & Moskowitz, 2000). Under these circumstances, problem-focused coping is more likely to lead to a more positive health outcome (Largo-Wight, Peterson, & Chen, 2005; Penley, Tomaka, & Wiebe, 2002; M. C. Smith & Dust, 2006). However, when we do not feel that a situation is controllable, we often rely more on emotion-focused coping strategies (Lazarus, 1993).

Emotion-Focused Coping: Change Your Reaction

Emotion-focused coping is aimed at controlling your internal, subjective, emotional reactions to stress. You alter the way you feel or think in order to reduce stress. Stressors activate a variety of emotions, including anxiety, worry, guilt, shame, jealousy, envy, and anger. Because these emotions are usually experienced as unpleasant, we are motivated to reduce or avoid them. For example, suppose that a young woman is anticipating the arrival of her boyfriend at a party where they planned to meet, and he is already an hour late. The stress of this situation not only activates the physical sensations that we have discussed previously but also triggers emotional reactions. She may be angry with him because she feels that he is purposely ignoring her wants and desires. She may take her anger out on a friend, or she may turn all of her emotional energy into being the life of the party. Conversely, she may experience anxiety and worry, fearing that something harmful has happened to him. When he arrives, she may express her anger by complaining about his lateness or ignoring him altogether, or she may be especially loving and attentive. Either way, her coping behavior is directed at reducing the emotions that she is experiencing.

We attempt to lessen the effects of these emotions in two ways: by engaging in *cognitive reappraisal* and through the use of psychological *defense mechanisms*. **Cognitive reappraisal** is an active and conscious process in which we alter our interpretation of the stressful event. In the previous example, the young woman has appraised her boyfriend's lateness in a negative manner (he's ignoring her or something bad has happened to him). These appraisals have led to feelings of anger and anxiety. She can reappraise or reinterpret his lateness in a more realistic manner—he got caught in traffic or he had to work late. These reappraisals are less likely to lead to emotional distress. Thus, cognitive reappraisal can be an emotionally constructive way of coping with a stressful event (Mauss, Cook, Cheng, & Gross, 2007; Ray, Wilhelm, & Gross, 2008). In one study, positive reappraisal even led to less immunosuppression during a chronic stress period (Koh, Choe, Song, & Lee, 2006).

emotion-focused coping behaviors aimed at controlling the internal emotional reactions to a stressor

cognitive reappraisal [re-uh-PRAY-zull] an active and conscious process in which we alter our interpretation of a stressful event

Taking your anger out on someone to relieve stress is an example of emotion-focused coping.

© David Madison/Corbis

A more automatic and unconscious way in which we lessen the effects of our emotions is by using **defense mechanisms**. Sigmund Freud was one of the first theorists to identify psychological defense mechanisms. You will learn more about Freud's ideas on personality and coping in the next chapter. For now, what is relevant is that Freud suggested that coping strategies are employed unconsciously to allow us to reduce our anxiety and maintain a positive self-image and self-esteem. Because of these features, we now consider these defense mechanisms as emotion-focused coping strategies. We use them to avoid or reduce the emotions associated with a stressor, but they do not necessarily eliminate the source of stress. For example, you might use the defense mechanism of *displacement* to deal with your anger toward a boss, a parent, or a significant other. You take your anger out on a friend by yelling at her, or on an object by throwing it against the wall. Afterward, you may *feel* better, but it does not resolve the issue that made you angry in the first place. The stressor is still present and may resurface again in the future.

Everyone uses defense mechanisms from time to time. Some of these defense mechanisms are adaptive. Directing your anger into a more constructive activity such as washing your car is more productive than hurting someone else (see sublimation in ■ TABLE 11.3). Other defense mechanisms, especially when we use them to excess, can prevent us from developing effective ways of coping. For example, the student who fails to study for a test may decide that his roommate who watches television is at fault. Such a defense on the part of the student does not promote an adaptive way of coping with failure. The more common defense mechanisms are displayed in Table 11.3. See if you can identify the defense mechanisms that you tend to use.

defense mechanisms unconscious, emotional strategies that are engaged in to reduce anxiety and maintain a positive self-image

Table 11.3 Common Defense Mechanisms

DEFENSE MECHANISM	DEFINITION	EXAMPLES
Denial	Refusing to accept or acknowledge the reality of a situation or idea	Going out partying the night before an exam denies how this behavior will affect your exam performance. Having unprotected sex denies the possibility of an unwanted pregnancy or contracting an STI.
Rationalization	Devising a plausible reason or motive to explain one's behavior	You rationalize your excessive consumption of alcohol by saying it makes you more sociable or improves your personality.
Reaction formation	Engaging in a behavior or attitude that is at the opposite extreme of one's true motive or impulse	A young boy pulls the ponytail of the girl sitting in front of him, behaving aggressively to cover up the opposite emotion—liking her. After bumping into someone at the mall whom you dislike, you approach and say warmly, "Hi. How have you been? You look great!"
Regression	Returning to an earlier stage of development in one's behavior, thinking, or attitudes	Adults who throw tantrums, pout, or whine are engaging in childlike behaviors. An older child may react to the birth of a sibling by wetting the bed or sucking her thumb again.
Sublimation	Directing emotions into an activity that is more constructive and socially acceptable	Some people exercise or clean their room when they are angry or upset. Others direct their emotions into writing, sculpting, music, or painting.
Repression	Excluding wishes, impulses, ideas, or memories from consciousness	A person may forget the details of an accident, crime, or other situation associated with trauma or harm.
Projection	Attributing one's own ideas, feelings, or attitudes to other people	You accuse another student of brown-nosing the professor when in reality it is you who engage in this behavior. A person in a relationship may accuse his partner of wanting to date other people when this is his own desire.
Displacement	Directing emotions toward a less threatening source	You yell at your partner after an argument with your boss. An athlete throws objects or kicks the bench after a missed play.

The use of defense mechanisms involves costs and benefits. The main reason we use them is to restore our self-image. We also benefit because defense mechanisms reduce anxiety. They may also give us the confidence to handle additional stressors. However, the benefits of defense mechanisms are typically outweighed by the costs. Defense mechanisms often inhibit our ability to resolve a problem. Using our emotions to cope with stressors may impede our functioning in other daily activities—yelling at our friends too often may drive them away. Most important, using defense mechanisms keeps us in a state of unawareness as to the true source of any stress-related symptoms. Given these disadvantages, why do we continue to use defense mechanisms? Basically, they are easier and produce quicker results in reducing our feelings of anxiety. Unfortunately, this is often at the expense of our well-being as we may experience more distress and negative mood over the long run (Littleton, Horsley, John, & Nelson, 2007; O'Brien, Terry, & Jimmieson, 2008).

Psychology Applies to Your World:

Resisting the Harmful Effects of Stress: Stress Management Techniques

Because stress affects our health, considerable research has addressed what strategies may reduce our risk of illness and disease. These techniques all focus on changing one or more aspects of the stress response.

1. *Exercise*. Some form of regular aerobic exercise, such as swimming, walking, or dancing, can be an effective strategy for reducing physical stress reactions (Anshel, 1995; Langreth, 2000; Stear, 2003). Exercise reduces negative emotions such as depression and anxiety that we often feel in response to stress (Brugman & Ferguson, 2002; Long & van Stavel, 1995). Exercise raises energy levels, strengthens the heart, and lowers muscle tension. We sleep more soundly after exercise and also feel better as the body increases its production of natural mood elevators like serotonin and endorphins (Chapter 2).

2. *Relax*. One of the most successful nonchemical ways to manage stress is through the application of relaxation techniques. This may include **progressive relaxation training**, in which you learn to alternately tense and then relax each muscle group of the body in a systematic fashion. This gives you an awareness of when and where you feel tension when you're under stress. You then learn to manage and control the tension that you feel by relaxing on command. Other relaxation techniques may include regular massages, meditation, yoga, deep breathing exercises, engaging in a hobby, or listening to music. Daily use of relaxation procedures are effective in lessening symp-

progressive relaxation training a stress management technique in which a person learns how to systematically tense and relax muscle groups in the body

Having close relationships with others helps us weather stress.

Leonora Hamill/Getty Images

(continued)

toms of asthma, insomnia, tension headaches, migraine headaches, high blood pressure, intestinal problems, and chronic anxiety (Astin, 2004; Benson, 1996; Meissner, Blanchard, & Malamood, 1997; Smyth, Litcher, Hurewitz, & Stone, 2001).

3. *Develop social support.* Having friends, a shoulder to cry on, or someone to discuss an issue or trying event with are all examples of **social support**—having close and positive relationships with others. Social support buffers the effects of stress (Cohen, Doyle, Turner, Alper, & Skoner, 2003; Diener & Seligman, 2004; Ornish, 1998; Shields, 2004; Wills & Fegan, 2001). Family stability, a partner's support, or simply having friends to confide in is related to a longer life span, as well as a longer survival rate for those with cancer or heart disease (Antoni & Lutgendorf, 2007; Case, Moss, Case, McDermott, & Eberly, 1992; Hawkley & Cacioppo, 2007; Krantz & McCeney, 2002; Schwartz et al., 1995; Shen et al., 2004). Even giving social support to others appears to buffer the effects of stress (S. L. Brown, Nesse, Vinokur, & Smith, 2003). Social support also may act to decrease the release of stress hormones and reverse stress-induced immune responses (Eisenberger, Taylor, Gable, Hilmert, & Liberman, 2007; Koh et al., 2006; Pressman et al., 2005; Uchino, Cacioppo, & Kiecolt-Glaser, 1996).

4. *Be spiritual.* Spiritual faith, prayer, church or temple membership, and strong value systems promote physical health and well-being (Hawks, Hull, Thalman, & Richins, 1995; W. R. Miller & Thoresen, 2003; Powell, Shahabi, & Thoresen, 2003). Spirituality often means having a purpose in life, self-awareness, and connectedness with self, others, and a larger community. Religiousness is typically defined as participation in an institutionalized doctrine. For example, several studies have found that prayer and spirituality are associated with reduced symptoms of distress in cancer patients (Laubmeier, Zakowski, & Bair, 2004; E. J. Taylor & Outlaw, 2002). Religiousness and spirituality have also been shown to be significantly associated with reduced symptoms in people with serious mental illness (Corrigan, McCorkle, Schell, & Kidder, 2003). One study found a relationship between prayer and better health, but only among less educated and, to a lesser extent, lower-income people (Banthia, Moskowitz, Acree, & Folkman, 2007).

Religion, spirituality, and health are correlated. We cannot conclude that religiousness or spirituality causes better health. Many of the studies have significant flaws (Hill & Pargament, 2003; Sloan & Bagiella, 2002). As more sound research is conducted, psychologists will be able to uncover the distinct contribution of religion and spirituality to health and well-being.

Guided imagery involves using your mind to achieve a state of relaxation.

5. *Imagine a calm environment.* **Guided imagery** is a technique in which you learn to use your mind to achieve a state of relaxation. You imagine that you are in a safe, pleasant, calming environment, perhaps walking along a beach or in a forest. You maintain your focus on this image as you feel the tensions associated with stress leave your body. Similar to progressive relaxation, you become trained to automatically summon up this image when you feel stressed. For some people, guided imagery is just as effective as the relaxation techniques discussed previously (Astin, 2004). Can you think of your own image, scene, or memory that would provide these benefits for you? How does your body feel as you think about it?

social support having close and positive relationships with others

guided imagery a technique in which you focus on a pleasant, calming image to achieve a state of relaxation when you feel stressed

© Jochen Schlenker/Masterfile

6. *Meditate*. **Meditation** in the form of yoga, Zen, or transcendental meditation also may reduce tension and anxiety caused by stress (Andresen, 2000). They are mental exercises in which people consciously focus their attention to heighten awareness and bring their mental processes under more control. The person sits in a comfortable position with her eyes closed and silently focuses her attention on a specially assigned word that creates a resonant sound. Meditation appears to decrease heart rate, respiration, and oxygen consumption (Carrington, 1993; D. S. Holmes, 1987). Some studies have also found that meditation can improve mood, lessen tiredness, and enhance immune system response (Solberg, Halvorsen, & Holen, 2000). Isolating the key element common to the different meditation practices may help us draw more solid conclusions on the specific health benefits of meditation (Doraiswamy & Xiong, in press).

7. *Be optimistic*. Simply expecting good things to happen may influence your health. For example, in a study on first-year law students, those students who endorsed optimistic beliefs, such as believing they could succeed and having confidence about their abilities, had better immune system functioning at mid-semester than did students with a more pessimistic outlook (Segerstrom, Taylor, Kemeny, & Fahey, 1998). Optimists report lower stress levels and have fewer stress-related physical complaints (Finkelstein, Kubzansky, Capitman, & Goodman, 2007; Peterson, 2000; Peterson & Bossio, 2001; Pritchard, Wilson, & Yamnitz, 2007; Wiebe & Smith, 1997). Cancer and heart disease patients with an optimistic attitude often show a better response to treatment than patients with a less positive attitude (Carver et al., 2000; Shen et al., 2004). Focusing on the half of the glass that is full is better for your health than focusing on the half that is empty.

8. *Laugh*. Laughter promotes relaxation, which may explain why good-humored people perceive less stress when faced with life's challenges (Lefcourt, 2001; Lefcourt & Davidson-Katz, 1991). Laughter may buffer stress by reducing blood pressure, increasing deep breathing, boosting the immune system, increasing feelings of well-being, and raising energy levels (Bennett, Zeller, Rosenberg, & McCann, 2003; Christie & Moore, 2005). Any one or all of these factors may be responsible for the positive health effects.

9. *Manage your time wisely*. Many of us experience stress because we feel that there is not enough time to accomplish all the tasks, errands, and work that we have established for ourselves. One way to minimize the stress resulting from such pressures is to organize your time better. Keeping a daily planner or formal time schedule to record your obligations, commitments, and deadlines for study, work, and leisure activities can ease tension. Writing out a formal time schedule also allows you to evaluate the number and importance of your commitments. One of the most common time management mistakes that college students make is not allowing enough time to study all of the assigned material (Buehler, Griffin, & Ross, 1994). The key to effective time management is to treat each responsibility—whether work, study, or play—as a serious commitment.

(continued)

meditation mental exercises in which people consciously focus their attention to heighten awareness and bring their mental processes under more control

By using these methods, you have the opportunity to reduce the ill effects of stress on your health right now, as well as the cumulative effect of stress on your body in the future. However, if you sometimes feel that you cannot manage the stress in your life, or you aren't coping well with your stressors, then it may be time to seek professional help. Chapter 14 describes the different types of mental health professionals who can help us cope more effectively.

Let's Review!

This section distinguished between problem-focused and emotion-focused coping and described some stress management techniques. For a quick check, answer these questions.

1. Organizing your time better would be best classified as a(n) _____ coping skill.
   a. problem-focused
   b. emotion-focused
   c. avoidance-focused
   d. encounter-focused

2. It is common for young children to react to the birth of a sibling by regressing to earlier behaviors such as sucking their thumb again or wanting to feed from a bottle. Such behaviors exemplify _____ coping skills.
   a. problem-focused
   b. emotion-focused
   c. avoidance-focused
   d. encounter-focused

3. Which of the following is the *least* effective stress management technique?
   a. Guided imagery
   b. Physical exercise
   c. Defense mechanisms
   d. Relaxation techniques

Answers 1. a; 2. b; 3. c

Personality and Health

Learning Objective

- Discuss the relationship between personality and health.

Health psychologists have also been interested in how personality influences our health. A number of personality dimensions have been related to health—specifically, to the functioning of our cardiovascular and immune systems (Segerstrom, 2000; T. W. Smith, 2006). We consider three such avenues of research here: the *Type A personality*, *learned helplessness*, and the *hardy personality*.

Type A Personality: Ambition, Drive, and Competitiveness

Take a moment to look at ■ TABLE 11.4. Which of these descriptions more accurately reflects your personality? Would you consider yourself more of a **Type A personality**, a person who is aggressive, competitive, and driven to achieve? Do you characterize yourself as more of a

Type A personality a personality that is aggressive, ambitious, and competitive

Table 11.4 The ABCs of Personality: Which Type Are You?

TYPE A	TYPE B	TYPE C
competitive	easygoing	cautious
verbally aggressive	calm	careful
overcommitted to achieving	relaxed	detached
impatient	patient	introspective
hostile attitude when frustrated	trusting	sensitive to criticism
sense of time urgency	good-natured	serious
workaholic	lower need for achievement	results oriented
easily angered	supportive	suppressed emotion

Type B personality, a person who is more relaxed, easygoing, patient, and flexible? Or do you consider yourself more like a **Type C personality**, a relatively new category describing a person who is cautious, careful, overly patient and nice, one who avoids conflict and suppresses negative emotions such as anger?

At one time, having a Type A personality was considered a risk factor for heart disease. Cardiologists Meyer Friedman and Ray Rosenman (1974) were the first to examine the connection between personality and heart disease. They suspected that personality or behavior patterns might play a role in the lives of men who were more likely to develop heart disease or more likely to die from a heart attack. To test their idea, the researchers gathered a sample of 3,000 men between the ages of 35 and 59 with no known health problems. Each man was interviewed, and based on his behavior during the interview, each was designated as a Type A personality, a Type B personality, or somewhere in between. A label of Type A or Type B was given to those men who very much exemplified those traits listed in Table 11.4. The majority of the sample fell somewhere in between, but in comparing the two types, Friedman and Rosenman found that over the next decade those with Type A personalities were two to three times more likely to suffer a heart attack. Keep in mind that the majority of the sample could not easily be categorized as either Type A or Type B.

Friedman and Rosenman's landmark study stimulated additional research on how personality factors may place people at risk for disease. However, subsequent research on the connection between Type A personality and the risk of heart disease has not been able to replicate these results (Booth-Kewley & Friedman, 1987; T. Q. Miller, Turner, Tindale, Posavac, & Dugoni, 1991).

Later research attempted to isolate which specific aspects of the Type A personality might predispose a person to heart problems. The key features include anger, mistrust, and hostility. People who are frequently angry, suspicious, bitter, antagonistic, and distrustful of others seem more likely to experience heart-related health problems and have a shorter life span (Denollet, 1993; Krantz & McCeney, 2002; T. Q. Miller, Smith, Turner, Guijarro, & Hallet, 1996; B. W. Roberts, Kuncel, Shiner, Caspi, & Goldberg, 2007; T. W. Smith, Glazer, Ruiz, & Gallo, 2004; J. E. Williams et al., 2000; R. Williams, 1993). People with a Type A personality who do not show these specific behaviors appear to be no more at risk for heart disease than their Type B counterparts.

Research on the Type C or cancer-prone personality has proceeded in a similar fashion. That is, at one time having a Type C personality was suggested as a major factor in the devel-

Type B personality a personality characterized by patience, flexibility, and an easygoing manner

Type C personality a personality that is cautious, serious, sensitive to criticism, results oriented, and suppresses negative emotions such as anger opment of cancer, specifically breast cancer in women (see Scheier & Bridges, 1995, for review). However, subsequent research suggests that it is the suppression or denial of anger, one specific aspect of the Type C personality, that may put a woman more at risk for breast cancer. There is little evidence for a so-called cancer-prone personality; yet a modest to weak relationship has been found between not expressing one's negative emotions and the risk of breast cancer (Bleiker, Hendriks, Otten, Verbeek, & van der Ploeg, 2008; Bleiker, van der Ploeg, Hendriks, & Ader, 1996; Butow et al., 2000; McKenna, Zevon, Corn, & Rounds, 1999).

Learned Helplessness: I Can't Do It

Do you believe that you have no control over stressful life events? Do you believe that even your best efforts will result in failure? When you blame yourself for any failure you experience, are you more likely to attribute your failure to a specific factor—you're just not good at soccer—or to a more global feature—you're just too uncoordinated to do any athletic activity? These questions illustrate the key features of a personality factor called **learned helplessness**, in which people develop a passive response to stressors based on their exposure to previously uncontrolled, negative events.

Learned helplessness was first demonstrated in dogs in a psychological laboratory (Seligman & Maier, 1967). The dogs were placed in a cage that was equipped with an electrified grid. When the dogs received shock they could not escape from, after repeated trials the dogs' escape responses slowly decreased. Recall from Chapter 5 that this decrease in responding is called extinction (see p. 169). Even when they were later given the opportunity to escape the shock, the dogs remained in the cage. The dogs had learned to be helpless. Experiments using human participants (not using shock) have produced similar results (Hiroto, 1974; W. R. Miller & Seligman, 1975). Consequently, when previous experiences lead you to believe that you cannot "fix" the problems facing you, you may approach new situations with this perceived lack of control and passively endure whatever comes your way (Dweck, Chiu, & Hong, 1995; Peterson, Maier, & Seligman, 1993). You are likely to view stressors as threats rather than as challenges. As a result, your levels of stress increase, and you are more likely to develop stress-related physical illnesses (Stern, McCants, & Pettine, 1982).

learned helplessness   a passive response to stressors based on exposure to previously uncontrolled, negative events

Research supports the notion that college students who feel helpless about their studies are less likely to persist and more likely to give up easily; as a result, they earn poor grades and report unhappiness (McKean, 1994). Adults and adolescents who react to stress by feeling at a loss to do anything about the situation are more prone to depression and other stress problems (Haack, Metalsky, Dykman, & Abramson, 1996; Waschbusch, Sellers, LeBlanc, & Kelley, 2003). Learned helplessness has also been documented in children with a history of reading failure (Fowler & Peterson, 1981). It can develop in elderly people in nursing homes who are not given choices about their daily activities and routines (Seligman, 1989). In all of these situations, the *expectation* of failure and lack of control is what influences one's perceived level of stress, one's subsequent response to stress, and ultimately, one's mental and physical health.

Digital Vision/Getty Images

If you fail an exam, do you go and get help, or do you just assume that you'll never understand the material and withdraw from the class? Expecting to fail and believing you have no control over the outcome of events are key qualities of learned helplessness.

The Hardy Personality: Control, Commitment, and Challenge

Do you view stressors as challenges rather than as threats? For example, if you try out for the tennis team one year and don't make it, do you try out again the next year, or do you simply give up? Do you stay committed to the pursuit of your goals and values? If you fail an exam, do you go and get help, or do you just assume that you'll never understand the material and withdraw from the class—possibly spoiling your chance at a college degree? Do you believe that your actions influence the outcome of a situation? Your answers to these questions outline three factors that appear to be related to health: challenge, commitment, and control.

- The tendency to see life as a series of *challenges*
- A sense of personal *commitment* to self, work, family, and other values
- A perception of *control* over life and work

The "three Cs" taken together were labeled by psychologists Salvatore Maddi and Suzanne Kobasa (1984) as the **hardy personality**.

This term resulted from Kobasa's (1982) research on upper-level executives and attorneys who had experienced considerable stress over a three-year period. Those who exemplified hardy traits were less likely to get ill during this time of stress. Even Type A people who scored high on measures of hardiness were less likely to get ill than Type A people who scored low on hardiness. This led Kobasa to conclude that hardiness traits may decrease stress levels, thereby decreasing one's chances of developing illness.

Psychological research confirms that hardy people seem to be unusually resistant to stress. They endorse a positive worldview in which stressors are appraised as challenges rather than threats, so they feel less potential harm from them (Wiebe, 1991). Notice that these qualities are in direct contrast to learned helplessness. This positive attitude appears to promote more problem-focused coping, enabling such people to handle conflict better and be more willing to rely on the help of others when weathering stress (Scheir & Carver, 1992). Hardy people also report higher levels of personal satisfaction with their work (Rush, Schoel, & Barnard, 1995) and show greater immune system responses to bacteria (Dolbier et al., 2001).

What does all this research on personality tell us? First, we can recognize that how one expresses negative emotions such as anger and hostility can influence one's health. Frequent anger and hostility as well as suppressing one's negative emotions do not promote good health. Similarly, negative cognitions such as expecting failure or a lack of control do not appear to be good for our health. In contrast, the "three Cs" of hardiness—a sense of control, being comfortable with challenge, and maintaining commitment—appear to be most beneficial to our ability to deal with stress and therefore most advantageous to our health.

hardy personality   a personality, high in the traits of commitment, control, and challenge, that appears to be associated with strong stress resistance

Let's Review!

This section described the relationship between personality and health. As a quick check of your understanding, answer these questions.

1. Donald is described by his friends as easygoing, calm, and patient. Donald would most likely be classified as a _____.
   a. Type A personality   **c.** Type C personality
   b. Type B personality   **d.** learned helpless personality

2. Which of the following personality factors has been strongly linked to depression and other stress problems?
   a. Type A traits   **c.** Hardiness
   b. Type B traits   **d.** Learned helplessness

3. After working on a project for more than three years, Zilmarie is told by her boss to redesign the project in a new way. Zilmarie considers such a task a challenge and commits herself to the new project with gusto. Zilmarie is probably high on which personality dimension?
   a. Type A personality   **c.** Hardiness
   b. Type B personality   **d.** Type C personality

Answers 1. b; 2. d; 3. c

Lifestyle and Health

- Identify health-defeating and health-promoting behaviors.

- Discriminate among the various sexually transmitted infections, their causes, modes of transmission, and treatment options.

> **You Asked...**
>
> *How can you try to be healthy?*
>
> EMMANUEL COTTO, STUDENT

Health psychologists also examine lifestyle and environmental factors that may play a role in our susceptibility to illness and disease. Because these behaviors should be easier to change or prevent, considerable research has examined those behaviors that have been found to put us at higher risk for illness and disease and those behaviors or lifestyle choices that have been linked to healthier living.

health–defeating behaviors behaviors that increase the chance of illness, disease, or death

Health-Defeating Behaviors

We already have seen that high levels of stress may increase our chances of illness. Some of these events may or may not be under your control. Health psychologists define **health-defeating behaviors** as those behaviors that increase the chance of illness, disease, or death. They include risky behaviors such as driving at excessive speeds, carrying a weapon, or being a passenger in a car with a driver who is under the influence of drugs or alcohol. Risky behaviors endanger your health because you place yourself in a situation in which you have a higher risk of physical injury. Many of the leading causes of death are related to unsafe health practices (■ FIGURE 11.4). More than 45% of all deaths are in some way related to personal habits that damage our health (McGinnis & Foege, 1993). This is our focus in this section. We will examine behavior patterns, usually engaged in over a long period of time, that *are* controllable and that seriously put your health at risk. These behaviors include alcohol consumption, smoking, and unsafe sex practices that can lead to contracting a sexually transmitted infection (STI).

ALCOHOL

Recall from Chapter 4 the specific effects that alcohol has on the body and brain. These effects can be seen within a larger context by detailing the social and physical ramifications of alcohol abuse on people's health and well-being. Consider that the majority of manslaughter convictions, assaults, and domestic violence incidents involve alcohol. Nearly half of all U.S. highway deaths involve alcohol. Fetal alcohol syndrome (FAS), caused by a mother's excessive ingestion of alcohol during pregnancy, is the leading cause of mental retardation (Adler & Rosenberg, 1994). In one national survey (Johnston, O'Malley, Bachman, & Schulenberg, 2007), 29% of high school seniors admitted to being drunk in the past month. The students reported this behavior despite being underage! For college men and women, the rate is even higher.

Alcohol abuse not only leads to social problems, but also is associated with major health problems including heart disease, stroke, cancer, liver disease, memory blackouts, and erectile dysfunction in males. These statistics convey the drastic impact that alcohol abuse has on our nation's health and suggest that alcohol should be used only in moderation, if at all.

SMOKING

Another easily preventable behavior is cigarette smoking. Recall from Chapter 4 that nicotine affects several neurotransmitters in the brain that act as stimulants, increasing

FIGURE 11.4

Leading Causes of Death in the United States

In 2004, heart disease, cancer, stroke, respiratory diseases, and accidents were the top five causes of deaths in the United States. (The top two causes of death, heart disease and cancer, were the same for males and females and for Whites, Blacks, and American Indians; for Asian/Pacific Islanders, cancer was the leading cause of death with heart disease second.) Many of these deaths could have been prevented by engaging in better health practices.

Source: National Vital Statistics Report, *Vol. 55, No. 19, August 21, 2007.*

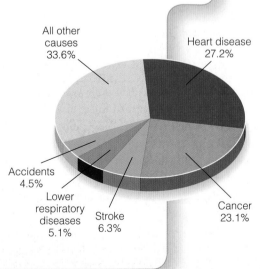

All other causes 33.6%

Heart disease 27.2%

Accidents 4.5%

Lower respiratory diseases 5.1%

Stroke 6.3%

Cancer 23.1%

arousal, feelings of pleasure and reward, and metabolic rate, which is why smokers tend to be thinner than nonsmokers. However, in high doses, nicotine causes vomiting, diarrhea, sweating, and dizziness. Most first-time users report nausea and dizziness from smoking cigarettes. Yet users quickly develop nicotine dependence and cravings for cigarettes (Rose et al., 2007).

In some developing countries, smoking is the norm. In the United States, smoking has declined over the past 30 years, yet one in five adults over the age of 18 still smoke. The percentage of current smokers in the United States is higher for men (24%) than for women (18%); higher for American Indian/Alaskan Native (27%), African Americans (22%), and Whites (21%) than for Hispanic/Latino Americans (15%) and Asian Americans (11%); and lower among adults aged 65 and older, perhaps because many longtime smokers die (Pleis & Lethbridge-Ceiku, 2007). Level of education and income level also differentiate smokers from nonsmokers, with people living below poverty level and people with lower levels of education having higher smoking rates (Wetter et al., 2005).

Why do people smoke? Many adolescents experiment with smoking in middle and high school. In 2005, 11% of 12- to 17-year-olds were current cigarette smokers (Substance Abuse and Mental Health Services Administration, 2006). Many of these young people are aware of the health hazards associated with smoking, yet they begin anyway. Smoking initiation is related to both biological and environmental factors. On the side of biology, there is considerable evidence that specific genes and gene combinations are involved in smoking and nicotine dependence (Erblich, Lerman, Self, Diaz, & Bovbjerg, 2005; Kremer et al., 2005; Ling, Niu, Feng, Xing, & Xu, 2004). However, social pressure also contributes to smoking. For example, peer pressure is often cited as a reason why young people start smoking (Hayes & Plowfield, 2007). Seeing their favorite celebrities or music idols smoke also glamorizes smoking (Cin, Gibson, Zanna, Shumate, & Fong, 2007; Distefan, Pierce, & Gilpin, 2004; Pierce, 2005). For this reason, many antismoking programs are aimed at teenagers because this seems to be the prime age when smoking begins. Health officials have determined that the cost of treating the health problems associated with smoking far outweighs the cost of prevention programs.

Today, antismoking ads aimed at young people attempt to prevent teenagers from smoking.

Unsafe Sex and the Risk of Sexually Transmitted Infections (STIs)

Sexually transmitted infections (STIs) are infections that are passed from one person to another, usually through sexual contact. However, some STIs may be spread by nonsexual contact as well as from a mother to her unborn child. Every day we hear news accounts of the spread of AIDS and the HIV virus. Yet AIDS and the HIV virus are not the only types of STIs, many of which are more widespread, especially in the United States.

The Centers for Disease Control and Prevention (2007b) estimate that more than 19 million people in the United States become infected each year, and almost half of them are young people between the ages of 15 and 24 (Weinstock, Berman, & Cates, 2004). The United States has the highest rates of STIs in the industrialized world. At least one in four Americans will contract an STI by the age of 21 (Feroli & Burstein, 2003).

Why are STIs so widespread? One reason is that younger people today are more likely to engage in sexual intercourse. At least 25% of new cases of STIs occur among teenagers, who may not use condoms or use them infrequently, or in women "on the pill" using oral contraceptives, which do not prevent STIs (Feroli & Burstein, 2003; Kamb et al., 1998). A second reason is that many STIs often have no symptoms, so they are unknowingly passed from one person to the next (Bowie, Hammerschlag, & Martin, 1994). A third reason is the social stigma attached to those infected with an STI. Such negative perceptions may prevent

sexually transmitted infection (STI)
an infection that is passed from one person to another primarily through sexual contact

people from openly discussing their conditions with medical personnel, partners, and other loved ones.

Women, teenagers, and some ethnic groups are more likely to have an STI in the United States. Men and women between the ages of 15 and 25 are most at risk (Calvert, 2003; Gilson & Mindel, 2001). Young people are at increased risk because they engage in many high-risk sexual behaviors, such as having multiple partners and engaging in unprotected sexual intercourse. Women are at higher risk for contracting an STI than men because the warm, moist environment of the vagina renders women more susceptible to infection. It is twice as easy for a male to transmit an STI to a female as it is for a female to transmit one to a male (Laumann, Gagnon, Michael, & Michaels, 1994). Younger women are especially vulnerable as viruses and bacteria can more easily invade immature cervical cells than mature ones (Farley et al., 1997; Parker-Pope, 2002). According to data from the Centers for Disease Control and Prevention (2007b), higher rates of STIs are found among all ethnic minority populations except Asians/Pacific Islanders when compared to European Americans.

Engaging in certain sexual behaviors also puts one at a higher risk for contracting an STI. High-risk sexual behaviors include oral–genital sex without a condom or dental dam, semen in the mouth, and vaginal or anal intercourse without a condom (Hatcher et al., 1994). Sex with multiple partners also increases one's chances of contracting an STI. Moreover, some STIs are contracted through nonsexual means. Certain forms of drug use increase the risk, as sharing contaminated needles can directly transmit organisms such as HIV. An infected pregnant woman also risks transmitting the infection to her unborn child and causing serious birth defects.

STIs can cause irreparable damage. The financial cost to our health care system is enormous. Left untreated, STIs can cause pelvic inflammatory disease (PID), chronic pelvic pain, and infertility in women (Eng & Butler, 1997; Howell, Kassler, & Haddix, 1997). They can also result in arthritis, heart problems, brain damage, and even death. The human cost to partners, families, and infected persons is incalculable. It's a cost that does not necessarily have to be paid, as many STIs are easily treated.

■ YOU REVIEW 11.1 shows the main types of sexually transmitted infections, modes of transmission, symptoms, and treatment. There are three basic categories of STIs: bacterial infections, viral infections, and parasitic infections.

Bacterial infections include chlamydia, gonorrhea, and syphilis. Bacteria are microorganisms or germs that can quickly reproduce and cause disease in the body. Chlamydia, gonorrhea, and syphilis are transmitted primarily through vaginal, anal, or oral sexual activity. If present in the vagina, these infections also can be transmitted from a mother to a newborn during delivery. An unusual discharge, sore, or painful urination are common symptoms of these infections. However, many men and women show no symptoms during the early stages and therefore do not seek treatment until more serious symptoms develop. Antibiotics are typically used to treat bacterial infections (Cates, 1998).

Viral infections include genital herpes, genital human papillomavirus (HPV), and HIV/AIDS. Viruses are incapable of reproducing on their own. They invade a normal cell and direct that cell to make new viral copies. These copies then invade other healthy cells, causing infection. Many of the symptoms of these infections can be treated, but the virus remains in the body and is yours for life. Viral infections are transmitted primarily through genital contact.

Most people with genital herpes or HPV do not initially develop symptoms or health problems. When symptoms do occur in genital herpes, noticeable sores appear. Most people who become infected with any of the more than 40 strains of HPV do not know they have it. However, certain types of HPV can cause genital warts, small bumps, or groups of bumps, usually in the genital area. Approximately 20 million people in the United States are currently infected with HPV. It is estimated that at least 50% of sexually active men and women will get infected with HPV at some point in their lives, making it the most common sexually transmitted infection (STI) in the United States (Centers for Disease Control and Prevention,

Is this couple at risk for an STI?

Stuart McClymont/Getty Images

Sexually Transmitted Infections (STIs)

STI	TRANSMISSION MODES	SYMPTOMS	TREATMENTS
BACTERIAL			
Chlamydia	Vaginal, oral, or anal sexual activity, or from an infected mother to her newborn during a vaginal birth	In females: frequent and painful urination, lower abdominal pain, and vaginal discharge. In males: burning or painful urination, and slight penis discharge. However, many people show no symptoms.	Antibiotics
Gonorrhea	Vaginal, oral, or anal sexual activity, or from an infected mother to her newborn during a vaginal birth	In females: increased vaginal discharge, burning urination, or irregular menstrual bleeding (many women show no early symptoms). In males: yellowish, thick penile discharge, or burning urination.	Antibiotics
Syphilis	Vaginal, oral, or anal sexual activity, or by touching an infected chancre or sore	A hard, round, painless chancre or sore appears at site of infection within 2 to 4 weeks.	Penicillin or other antibiotics for pencillin-allergic patients
VIRAL			
Genital Herpes	Vaginal, oral, or anal sexual activity	Painful, reddish bumps around the genitals, thighs, or buttocks, and for females on the vagina or cervix. Other symptoms may include burning urination, flu-like symptoms, or vaginal discharge in females.	No cure, although certain drugs can provide relief and help sores heal
HPV	Vaginal, oral, or anal sexual activity	Some strains cause painless warts to appear in the genital area or anus; other strains may cause abnormal cell changes in the cervix.	Cryotherapy (freezing), acid burning, or surgical removal of warts
HIV/AIDS	Sexual contact, infusion with contaminated blood, or from mother to child during pregnancy, childbirth, or breast-feeding	May develop flu-like symptoms that may disappear for many years before developing full-blown AIDS. AIDS symptoms include fever, weight loss, fatigue, diarrhea, and susceptibility to infection.	No cure; treatment includes a combination of antiviral drugs
PARASITES			
Pubic Lice	Sexual contact or contact with infested linens or toilet seats	Intense itching in hairy regions of the body, especially the pubic area	Prescription shampoos or nonprescription medications
Scabies	Sexual contact or contact with infested linens or toilet seats	Intense itching, reddish lines on skin, welts, and pus-filled blisters in affected area	Prescription shampoos

2007a). A controversial vaccine can be administered to young females to protect them from four types of HPV that cause most cervical cancers and genital warts. There is currently no vaccine licensed to prevent HPV-related diseases in men.

Being HIV-positive means that a person has been infected with the human immunodeficiency virus (HIV). In HIV/AIDS, the HIV attacks the immune system, resulting in mild flu-like symptoms that may then disappear for years before developing into a full-blown case of AIDS. Although symptoms may not be present, a person still carries the virus and is therefore capable of transmitting it to a partner during sexual activity. HIV/AIDS can also be contracted through the exchange of contaminated blood, to a fetus during pregnancy, or to an infant during breastfeeding.

It is estimated that more than 1 million people are currently living with HIV in the United States (Glynn & Rhodes, 2005). In 2006, males accounted for more than 74% of all HIV/AIDS cases among adults and adolescents. People with HIV tend to come from lower socioeconomic groups, are more likely to be uneducated, and are more likely to be African American (Centers for Disease Control and Prevention, 2008). However, anyone—regardless of age, income, or race—can contract this potentially deadly disease.

Today, treatment to suppress HIV/AIDS infection typically consists of a steady regime of antiretroviral drugs. This treatment offers AIDS patients the *chance* of a longer life (Katz et al., 2002; Rabkin & Ferrando, 1997). Unfortunately, the drugs are costly, and not everyone responds to them. For this reason, health psychologists try to prevent the spread of HIV and AIDS mainly through educational prevention programs (Carey et al., 1997). Success in these efforts with adolescents, however, is hampered by the tendency of adolescents to believe it can't happen to them.

Parasitic infections include pubic lice and scabies. A parasite lives off of another organism or host. Pubic lice, or "crabs," survive by feeding on human blood. Scabies are tiny mites that burrow under the skin and lay eggs. Both infections can be spread through sexual contact or by contact with infested towels, linens, or clothing. The most common symptom is intense itching in the genital area. Parasitic infections are typically treated with a solution that kills the lice or mites and their eggs. It is important to carefully reexamine the body 4 to 7 days after treatment to ensure that all the eggs have been killed. Towels, linens, and clothing also need to be treated to prevent reinfection (Reinisch, 1991).

Eye of Science/Photo Researchers, Inc.

Pubic lice are often called "crabs" because of the organism's resemblance to a crab.

Health-Promoting Behaviors

It is only fitting to end this chapter by exploring health-promoting behaviors. Health psychologists define **health-promoting behaviors** as those that decrease the chance of illness, disease, or death. Throughout this chapter we have indicated behaviors that you can engage in that appear to be related to better physical and psychological functioning. Take a moment to reflect on all that you have learned from our discussion of behavior and health.

What behaviors would you suggest to promote health and well-being? Now read the following list to see how many behaviors you were able to correctly identify.

- Commit yourself to a value and belief system.
- View stressors as challenges rather than threats.
- Perceive events as controllable.
- Do not rely exclusively on one or two defense mechanisms for coping.
- Engage in problem-focused coping.
- Cultivate an optimistic, positive attitude.
- Develop a social support network.

health–promoting behaviors behaviors that decrease the chance of illness, disease, or death

- Don't expect failure.
- Be patient and flexible.
- Laugh.
- Manage your time wisely.
- Engage in relaxing activities.
- Get regular physical exercise.
- Avoid being hostile, bitter, and resentful.
- Avoid the use of cigarettes.
- Use alcohol in moderation.
- Avoid substance use and abuse.
- Engage in safe sex.

In addition to the behaviors we've discussed, health research suggests a number of other behaviors that promote healthier living (Glik, Kronenfeld, & Jackson, 1996; Motivala & Irwin, 2007).

- Sleep 7 to 8 hours a night.
- Maintain your ideal body weight.
- Avoid a high-fat diet.
- Receive regular medical check-ups.

This list will undoubtedly grow as we discover more about the intimate connection between our bodies and minds. This knowledge will enable health psychologists to continue their efforts at understanding stress, preventing illnesses, and promoting lifelong well-being.

Let's Review!

This section examined behaviors that put us at higher risk for illness and disease, and those that have been linked to healthier living. For a quick check, answer these questions.

1. Which of the following is not a health-promoting behavior?
   a. Viewing stressors as challenges rather than as threats
   b. Perceiving events as controllable
   c. Relying exclusively on one defense mechanism for coping
   d. Engaging in problem-focused coping

2. Pedro has experienced an intense, burning sensation during urination and a thick, yellowish penile discharge. Pedro most likely has which STI?
   a. Gonorrhea   **c.** Genital warts
   b. Genital herpes   **d.** HPV

3. Which of the following is a low-risk sexual behavior for contracting a STI?
   a. Semen in the mouth
   b. Vaginal intercourse while the woman is "on the pill"
   c. Sex with multiple partners
   d. Oral sex with a dental dam

Answers 1. c; 2. a; 3. d

Studying THE Chapter

Key Terms

health psychology (409)
stress (410)
life event (411)
daily hassles (413)
conflict (415)
approach–approach conflict (416)
avoidance–avoidance conflict (416)
approach–avoidance conflict (416)
multiple approach–avoidance
    conflict (416)
primary appraisal (417)
general adaptation syndrome
    (GAS) (418)

alarm reaction (418)
resistance stage (420)
exhaustion stage (420)
immunosuppression (420)
coping (422)
problem-focused coping (422)
emotion-focused coping (423)
cognitive reappraisal (423)
defense mechanisms (424)
progressive relaxation training (425)
social support (426)
guided imagery (426)
meditation (427)

Type A personality (428)
Type B personality (429)
Type C personality (429)
learned helplessness (430)
hardy personality (431)
health-defeating behaviors (432)
sexually transmitted infection (STI) (433)
health-promoting behaviors (436)

What Do You Know? Assess Your Understanding

Test your retention and understanding of the material by answering the following questions.

1. Which of the following events is likely to produce the most stress for the average person?
   a. Losing your job after months of talk about a buyout
   b. Losing your job without any warning
   c. Quitting your job to look for a different line of work
   d. Keeping your job after others have lost their jobs due to downsizing

2. Which of the following is NOT considered a major life event?
   a. Marriage   c. Buying a home
   b. Losing your job   d. Being late to work

3. The adrenal gland secretes which two hormones during the stress response?
   a. Adrenalin and corticosteroids
   b. Adrenalin and GABA
   c. Corticosteroids and insulin
   d. Insulin and GABA

4. Cecilia feels stressed from her full-time job and taking care of her two children. Cecilia finds a more flexible job that allows her to spend more time with her children. Which style of coping does Cecilia's behavior illustrate?
   a. Emotion-focused
   b. Problem-focused
   c. Defensive
   d. Both a and c

5. Which one of the following behaviors best promotes health and well-being?
   a. Perceiving events as controllable
   b. Engaging in emotion-focused coping
   c. Expecting failure
   d. All of the above

6. Ryan can't decide which of two sound speakers to buy with his birthday money. Ryan is experiencing a(n) _____.
   a. approach–avoidance conflict
   b. approach–approach conflict
   c. avoidance–avoidance conflict
   d. multiple approach–avoidance conflict

7. Matresha is driving when a van pulls out in front of her and almost causes an accident. Matresha's heart begins to pound, and her blood pressure shoots up. Matresha is likely in the _____ phase of the general adaptation syndrome.
   a. alarm
   b. resistance
   c. exhaustion
   d. final

8. A weakened immune system and vulnerability to disease are most likely to occur in which stage of the general adaptation syndrome?
   a. Alarm
   b. Resistance
   c. Exhaustion
   d. Resilience

9. Jariel is a workaholic. He never takes a vacation. He won't even speak to friends and family on the phone when they call him at work. He is often angry and impatient with others. What type of personality does Jariel appear to have?
   a. Type A
   b. Type B
   c. Type C
   d. A hardy personality

10. April recently lost her high-paying job. While talking to a friend about her job loss, April told her that she was looking forward to finding a job in a new field. April appears to be most exhibiting the hardy trait of _____.
   a. challenge
   b. commitment
   c. control
   d. resistance

11. Which of the following is not a means of managing stress?
   a. Exercise
   b. Relaxation techniques
   c. Talking to friends
   d. Throwing away your planner

12. Tom views his new job as a positive and challenging change. Tom's appraisal of stress in this situation is most likely to elicit the emotion of _____.
   a. anger
   b. fear
   c. excitement
   d. anxiety

13. Lucinda believes she has no control over what happens to her. She expects failure and often feels stressed out. What type of personality does Lucinda appear to have?
   a. Learned helplessness
   b. A hardy personality
   c. Type A personality
   d. Type B personality

14. Which of the following is an accurate statement concerning the relationship between stress and the immune system?
   a. Stress always decreases the effectiveness of our immune system.
   b. Stress always increases the effectiveness of our immune system.
   c. If stress disrupts normal immune system functioning, we increase our vulnerability to illness and disease.
   d. If stress disrupts normal immune system functioning, we decrease our vulnerability to illness and disease.

15. The events of Hurricane Katrina powerfully illustrate the stressful nature of _____.
   a. daily hassles
   b. major life events
   c. catastrophes
   d. both a and b

16. Jeffrey has been feeling like he has the flu. He also has noticed reddish bumps around his genital area. Jeffrey most likely has which STI?
   a. Gonorrhea
   b. Genital herpes
   c. Syphilis
   d. Chlamydia

17. The two leading causes of death in the United States are _____.
   a. accidents and stroke
   b. respiratory diseases and cancer
   c. accidents and heart disease
   d. heart disease and cancer

18. Mickey feels really stressed. His car got a flat on the way to work. His boss did not like his proposal for a new account, and his new leather shoes got soaked in the rain. Mickey's high stress level is most due to _____.
    a. major life events
    b. daily hassles
    c. catastrophes
    d. approach–approach conflict

19. When Alexandra gets in a fight with her partner, she stomps her feet, covers her ears, and refuses to listen. Alexandra's behavior best illustrates the defense mechanism called _____.
    a. regression
    b. repression
    c. reaction formation
    d. displacement

20. Health-defeating behaviors _____.
    a. are not controllable
    b. are engaged in over a short period of time
    c. make us more susceptible to illness and disease
    d. All of the above

Answers: 1. b; 2. d; 3. a; 4. b; 5. a; 6. b; 7. a; 8. c; 9. a; 10. a; 11. d; 12. c; 13. a; 14. c; 15. c; 16. b; 17. d; 18. b; 19. a; 20. c

Online Resources

CENGAGENOW™ Personalized Study

www.cengage.com/login

Go to www.cengage.com/login to link to CengageNOW, your online study tool. First take the **Pre-Test** for this chapter to get your **Personalized Study Plan**, which will identify topics you need to review and direct you to online resources. Then take the **Post-Test** to determine what concepts you have mastered and what you still need work on.

 What Is Psychology? Essentials Book Companion Website

www.cengage.com/psychology/pastorino

Visit your book companion website, where you will find more resources to help you study. Resources include learning objectives, Internet exercises, quizzing, flash cards, and a pronunciation glossary.

Look Back AT **WHAT** YOU'VE **LEARNED**

Health psychologists study how people's behavior influences their health for better and for worse.

What Is Stress?

- **Stress** is any event or environmental stimulus (stressor) that we respond to because we perceive it as challenging or threatening.

- Catastrophes and significant **life events**, such as the death of a loved one or a new job, are major stressors. Everyday frustrations—called **daily hassles**—are less serious stressors, but can have a negative effect on health.

- **Conflict** also produces stress.

Digital Vision/Getty Images

© Michael Newman/Photo Edit

How Do I React to Stress?

- If our initial interpretation or **primary appraisal** of an event is one of stress, we may view it as a threat, as harmful, or merely as a challenge.

- Our body responds to stress in a three-phase **general adaptation syndrome**:

  - The **alarm reaction** consists of those bodily responses, including the nervous system and endocrine system, that are immediately triggered when we initially appraise an event as stressful.

  - In the **resistance stage**, the body continues to cope with the stressor, but the bodily reactions are less intense than during the alarm reaction.

  - In the **exhaustion phase**, wear and tear on the body begins, causing serious damage if stress continues over an extended period of time.

- The corticosteroids and endorphins that are released into our body during the stress response actually dampen the activity of our immune system, making us more vulnerable to health problems.

Health, Stress, AND Coping: HOW CAN YOU Create a HEALTHY LIFE?

How Can I Cope with Stress?

© Jochen Schlenker/Masterfile

- **Coping** is how we manage a threatening event or stimulus.

- **Problem-focused coping** controls or alters the environment that caused the stress. It is most useful when we feel that we can do something about the stressor.

- **Emotion-focused coping** controls our internal, subjective, emotional responses to stress. We alter the way we feel or think in order to reduce stress.

- **Defense mechanisms** are unconscious coping strategies that allow us to reduce our anxiety and maintain a positive self-image and self-esteem.

- A number of strategies can be used to reduce stress in one's life, including exercise, having strong **social support**, **guided imagery**, **meditation**, laughter, and time management.

Leonora Hamill/Getty Images

Does Your Personality Influence Your Health?

- A person with a **Type A personality** is aggressive, competitive, and driven to achieve; a person with a **Type B personality** is relaxed, easygoing, patient, and flexible; a person with a **Type C personality** is careful and patient and suppresses negative emotions such as anger. The Type A personality trait of hostility is related to a higher incidence of heart disease.

- **Learned helplessness** results from believing that you have no control over stressful life events. You view stressors as threats, your level of stress increases, and you are more likely to develop stress-related illnesses.

- The **hardy personality** is resistant to stress; it includes characteristics such as

  - A tendency to see life as a series of challenges

  - A sense of personal commitment to self, work, family, and other values

  - A perception of control over one's life and work

What Behaviors Promote Health and Well-Being?

- **Health-defeating behaviors**, such as alcohol and substance abuse, smoking, driving recklessly, and unsafe sex, increase the chance of illness, disease, or death.

- **Sexually transmitted infections** are passed from one person to another primarily through sexual contact. One in four Americans will contract an STI by the age of 21.

- Young people are at greater risk for contracting STIs because they are more likely to engage in high-risk sexual behaviors.

- Regular exercise, adequate sleep, an appropriate body weight, a healthy diet, good time management, a strong social support network, an optimistic outlook, and avoiding health-defeating behaviors are **health-promoting behaviors**; they decrease the chance of illness, disease, or death.

© David Madison/Corbis

12

WHAT IS Personality, AND HOW Do We MEASURE IT?

© Ariel Skelley/Corbis

- The Psychoanalytic Approach: Sigmund Freud and the Neo-Freudians

- The Trait Approach: Describing Personality

- The Social Cognitive Approach: The Environment and Patterns of Thought

- The Humanistic Approach: Free Will and Self-Actualization

- Measuring Personality

Mayra Rosario is a 28-year-old college student working on a bachelor's degree in business management. Mayra never thought that her course in general psychology would be of use to her, but working primarily with young adults as an enrollment counselor for a southern university has changed her opinion. As a part of her job, Mayra gets to know each student's personality to build rapport. She has to question them to assess what "type" of student they are in order to help prepare them to be successful in college. She looks at their past personal and academic behavior to gauge how they will most likely react in the future. Students are often fearful about enrolling in college, so she tries to understand the students' situations and to put herself in their shoes. Once she builds a relationship with a student, she can find the best solution and course of action for that student. She's not always right. Some students present one side of their personality during the enrollment process and then change their behaviors once they've enrolled. But Mayra's success in her job illustrates how relevant psychology can be for any career.

This chapter's topic is **personality**, or the unique collection of attitudes, emotions, thoughts, habits, impulses, and behaviors that define how a person typically behaves across situations. Where does this unique way of responding come from? Psychologists do not agree on a single, specific answer to this question—personality is difficult to define, difficult to measure, and influenced by many factors (Schultz & Schultz, 2005). Four dominant perspectives have emerged to explain our personalities: the psychoanalytic approach, the trait approach, the social cognitive approach, and the humanistic approach. No single theoretical approach can explain all facets of personality development in all people. Each perspective has its advantages and disadvantages.

© Ellen Pastorino

Understanding the nature of personality has helped Mayra Rosario in her job as an enrollment counselor.

445

As we describe each approach, consider your own ideas about personality. Do you think that you inherit your personality, or that it is formed from your experiences? Do you think that your behavior is influenced by your unconscious? Do you think that people strive to be all that they can be? Examining such ideas will allow you to connect the material to your values, experiences, and current way of thinking, as Mayra has done.

The Psychoanalytic Approach: Sigmund Freud and the Neo-Freudians

Learning Objectives

- Discuss Freud's perspective on personality, detailing how the levels of consciousness, resolution of psychosexual stages, and component parts of the personality interact to generate behavior.

- Detail neo-Freudian perspectives on personality, indicating their differences from and similarities to Freud's theory.

The **psychoanalytic perspective** on personality originated with Sigmund Freud. We introduced his approach to understanding behavior in Chapter 1 (see p. 8). Recall that Freud practiced medicine, specializing in nervous diseases. However, soon after beginning private practice, Freud moved away from physical explanations of nervous disorders and focused more on investigating psychological causes of these disorders. His ideas about personality were based on case studies of his patients, his reading of literature, and his own self-analysis. Freud saw personality as the product of driving forces within a person that were often conflicting and sometimes unconscious. As we saw in Chapter 4, Freud believed that dreams were one of the ways these unconscious forces expressed themselves. Freud's theory is unique in that it strongly emphasizes unconscious aspects of personality.

personality the unique collection of attitudes, emotions, thoughts, habits, impulses, and behaviors that define how a person typically behaves across situations

psychoanalytic [psi-co-an-uh-LIH-tic] **perspective** a personality approach developed by Sigmund Freud that sees personality as the product of driving forces within a person that are often conflicting and sometimes unconscious

conscious [CON-shus] **level** the level of consciousness that holds all the thoughts, perceptions, and impulses of which we are aware

preconscious [pre-CON-shus] **level** the level of consciousness that holds thoughts, perceptions, and impulses of which we could become aware

The Levels of Awareness

Freud (1940/1964) proposed that human personality operates at three different levels of awareness or consciousness, and that each level of awareness influences behavior. Freud viewed consciousness as being like an iceberg (■ FIGURE 12.1). When we look at behavior, all we usually see is the tip of the iceberg, or the **conscious level**: the thoughts, perceptions, and explanations of behavior of which the person is aware. The major portion of the iceberg, according to Freud, is below the surface. These impulses, memories, and thoughts are unseen but have a huge impact on personality. Because so large a portion of one's personality lies below the surface of consciousness, or awareness, Freud believed, any explanation of personality and behavior must focus on these unconscious forces.

Below the surface of the conscious level are the *preconscious* and *unconscious* levels. The preconscious level comes right before your conscious level. Your conscious level, as previously stated, includes any memories, thoughts, or urges of which you are currently aware. You know you want the new Beyonce or Maroon 5 CD, or you know that it is important to read this chapter and study for the test next week. But the things you could potentially be aware of at any one time are infinite, and you cannot hold more than a couple of thoughts, urges, and memories in consciousness at any one time. So, according to Freud, it is necessary to have a holding place for easily accessible memories, thoughts, or impulses of which you could become aware. This is the role of the **preconscious level**.

The psychoanalytic perspective on personality originated with Sigmund Freud. Freud saw personality as the product of driving forces within a person that were often conflicting and sometimes unconscious.

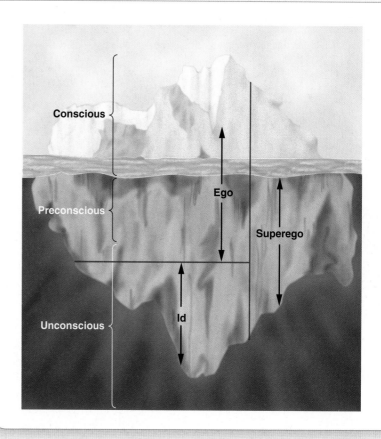

FIGURE

12.1

Iceberg Analogy of Freud's Levels of Awareness

In Freud's "iceberg" analogy of the mind, the id, superego, and parts of the ego are submerged below the water in the unconscious. Parts of the ego and superego show in the conscious and preconscious.

The **unconscious level** contains all those thoughts, impulses, memories, and behaviors of which you are unaware. However, although you are unaware of them, they always influence your behavior. Consider the 4-year-old boy who stops his parents from hugging or inserts himself between them to prevent them from kissing. He is not aware that this behavior stems from a need or wish to bond with his mother, yet it is still influencing his behavior.

The Structure of Personality

To Freud (1940/1964), human personality is an energy system comprised of three major personality structures: the id, the *ego*, and the *superego*. At birth, all of the energy of the personality is contained within a structure called the **id**. The id is an unconscious energy force that seeks pleasure and gratification. Hungry infants cry for food or because they are wet or tired. The id operates according to the **pleasure principle**; it drives people to feel good and to maximize pleasure and gratification. Freud saw the impulses driving the id as sexual and aggressive in nature. In this way, he viewed humans as very similar to animals—unconsciously and selfishly motivated by basic sexual and aggressive instincts. Such basic instincts ensure and promote the survival of the individual, and therefore the survival of the species as a whole. When we grow and begin to interact with our environment, we realize that our demands cannot always be immediately fulfilled. As such, part of the energy of the id becomes directed to the ego.

The **ego**, the second personality structure, acts as a negotiator between the instinctual needs of the id and the demands of membership in human society. Children learn that their id demands can be fulfilled only when they behave appropriately. The ego operates according to the **reality principle**. It realizes that the desires of the id can be met only by successfully dealing with the environment, by finding appropriate or attainable means by which to fulfill id impulses. Suppose a 4-year-old wants something to eat. Does he immediately cry like a baby? Not typically. The 4-year-old with a functioning ego knows that there are more appropriate and acceptable ways of getting something to eat. He will probably ask for something to eat and be willing to wait (at least for a little while) for his caregiver to prepare it for him. We see the ego functioning in the child's ability to delay his desire for food, for example. But the ego's job is still to fulfill the instinctual demands of the id—the unseen force beneath the tip of the iceberg (see Figure 12.1).

As the child continues to grow, parents and other important people impart their values and standards of behavior to the child. Parents convey the right and wrong ways to feel, think, and behave. The child incorporates these standards as the energy of the personality

unconscious [un-CON-shus] **level** the level of awareness that contains all the thoughts, perceptions, and impulses of which we are unaware

id the unconscious part of the personality that seeks pleasure and gratification

pleasure principle the basis on which the id operates; to feel good and maximize gratification

ego the conscious part of the personality that attempts to meet the demands of the id by successfully dealing with the environment

reality principle the basis on which the ego operates; finding socially appropriate means to fulfill id demands

It is a child's superego that drives feelings of guilt after wrongdoing.

superego the part of the personality that represents your moral conscience

further divides into a third personality structure. The **super-ego** typically emerges during the resolution of the phallic stage (discussed shortly) and represents your moral conscience. Your superego judges the rightness or wrongness of your actions. When you have the sense that you did something wrong, your superego is talking. The moral directives of the superego must also be taken into account by the ego. Just like id demands, superego demands must be met realistically by the ego in order to function in society.

The energy that these three personality components use cannot be cut apart. For Freud, personality is a dynamic, or active, process. The id, ego, and superego are not fixed entities but rather parts of our personality that serve different functions. A healthy personality will have developed a strong ego that appropriately releases and controls instinctual energy. However, problems may arise in personality functioning if id energy or superego energy overwhelms the functioning of the ego.

To Freud, all adult behaviors are a reflection of the interplay among these three structures (■ FIGURE 12.2). When examining behavior, we see only the functioning of the ego, but this ego is simultaneously being influenced by the unconscious demands of the id and the superego. *Freudian slips* help explain this interaction. A Freudian slip is the expression of an unconscious impulse from the id before the ego controls the impulse. The ego may then state that it did not mean to say something and corrects the slip to conform to socially approved behavior. For example, one might say to a rival businessperson at a meeting, "Would you like to hit in this chair?" instead of "Would you like to sit in this

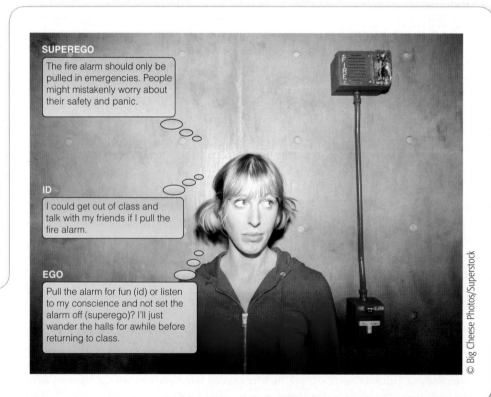

FIGURE

12.2

Freud's Personality Structures

chair?" and then quickly correct the error. Freud would state that what "slipped out" was meant. It just hadn't yet been socially screened by the ego.

You can see that the demands of the id and the superego are often in direct opposition to one another. This internal conflict sometimes overwhelms the ego, creating anxiety. The ego handles this anxiety by using **defense mechanisms** (A. Freud, 1936). Defense mechanisms, discussed in Chapter 11 (see p. 424), protect the ego by reducing the anxiety it feels when faced with the conflicting demands of the id and the superego. We all make use of these *coping mechanisms*, as they are now familiarly called. We tend to use those defense mechanisms that have been previously reinforced or that successfully reduce anxiety. For example, if you rationalized behavior as a child, you probably continue to use this defense mechanism as an adult.

Differences in personality, then, arise from internal energy conflicts among the id, ego, and superego (called *intrapsychic conflicts*). Freud further believed that personality is shaped by differences in how we resolve psychosexual stages of development.

Psychosexual Development

According to Freud (1940/1964), personality develops through a series of five psychosexual stages. These stages represent a complex interaction between natural shifts of pleasure from one part of the body to another and the environmental factors that influence how we handle these sexual desires. From birth through adolescence, children must resolve numerous unconscious conflicts that arise from sexual pleasure associated with stimulation of certain body parts, or what Freud called *erogenous zones*. For example, the infant nursing (from the mother's breast or from a bottle) derives a great deal of sensual pleasure from the feel of the nipple on his or her lips, and the satisfaction of hunger the milk brings. However, the pleasure received from any erogenous zone must be balanced with parental restrictions or permissiveness placed on one's behavior. This creates an internal struggle, or "conflict," that significantly influences the resulting personality. Freud uses the term *psychosexual* to refer to the psychological significance of these sexual drives in the formation of a healthy personality. Because environmental circumstances vary in terms of how we are parented or how we respond to these socialization experiences, the result is individual differences in personality. Let's take a brief look at each of Freud's psychosexual stages.

> ### You Asked...
> *There is a common perception that we model our lives after our parents—for example, the idea that heterosexual men seek out women like their mother. Is this an accurate perspective?* MICHAEL HORSFALL, STUDENT

defense mechanism a process used to protect the ego by reducing the anxiety it feels when faced with the conflicting demands of the id and the superego

oral stage Freud's first psychosexual stage of development, which occurs during the first year of life, in which the handling of the child's feeding experiences affects personality development

anal stage Freud's second psychosexual stage, which occurs from approximately 18 months to 3 years, in which the parents' regulation of the child's biological urge to expel or retain feces affects personality development

Parents' toilet-training practices influence a toddler's attempt to resolve the anal psychosexual stage, according to Freud.

ORAL STAGE

The **oral stage** lasts from birth until approximately 18 months of age. The mouth, tongue, and lips are the erogenous zones, or focus of pleasure. Babies receive pleasure from sucking, licking, biting, and chewing.

ANAL STAGE

The **anal stage** lasts from approximately 18 months to 3 years. The anus and rectum are the erogenous zones. Freud viewed production of feces in particular as a creative act. The toddler typically feels quite proud of them, either holding them in or spreading them around. How the parent then responds to this or how the parent attempts to control this production through toilet-training practices is the key to adequately resolving this stage.

Ryan McVay/Getty Images

PHALLIC STAGE

During the **phallic stage**, from 3 to 6 years of age, the genitals are the primary erogenous zones, and children receive pleasure from self-stimulation. This stage is particularly important for personality development as it represents the time when the **Oedipus complex** and the **Electra complex** occur. Freud believed that at this age, young children develop unconscious sexual urges for the parent of the other sex. The child wants to bond with the parent of the other sex as the child sees the parents bonding. Using the terms *Oedipus* and *Electra* from two ancient Greek tragedies, Freud believed that at this psychosexual stage little boys unconsciously fall in love with their mothers and experience hostile feelings toward their fathers much as Oedipus (unknowingly) married his mother and killed his father. Like Electra, little girls unconsciously fall in love with their fathers and feel jealousy toward their mothers.

For example, children at this age may prevent their parents from hugging or be jealous of the parents' spending time alone together. Children then resolve these complexes by identifying with and behaving more like the same-sex parent. The child incorporates the values and standards of the same-sex parent, thus ending the rivalry. The child's psychic energy is then redirected to the growth of the superego (discussed earlier). A young boy may start to imitate the way his father eats, or a young girl may mimic the way her mother brushes her hair.

LATENCY STAGE

The **latency stage** occurs from age 6 until puberty. During the latency stage, sexual impulses are pushed into the background. The child's energy focuses on other demands of the environment, most noticeably school and peer relations. Sexuality reappears at puberty as reflected in the final psychosexual stage, the genital stage.

GENITAL STAGE

The **genital stage** occurs during puberty. The genitals again become the source of pleasure, as the adolescent must revisit the sexual urges that first appeared during the phallic stage. Recall that during the phallic stage, children developed unconscious attractions to the other-sex parent. Recognizing now that the love for the parent cannot be fulfilled, the adolescent seeks resolution of the genital stage through transference of this love onto an other-sex mate. Consequently, for Freud, adult heterosexual intimate relations reflect the unconscious desire to choose a mate in the image of one's other-sex parent. If during the phallic stage the child develops unconscious attractions to the same-sex parent, then during the genital stage, homosexual intimate relations arise from the transference of love onto a same-sex partner.

As Freud saw it, children develop through these predictable stages that are primarily sexual but are psychologically significant in forming a healthy personality. Successfully resolving these stages entails receiving an optimal amount of gratification at each stage—not too much and not too little. A child who receives too much satisfaction at one stage may be reluctant to move on to the next stage. Too little satisfaction may result in frustration for the child, who may continue to seek gratification instead of moving on. These examples of inadequate resolution of a stage result in what Freud called a *fixation*. Those who fixate at one stage remain stuck, and their personalities remain immature or underdeveloped. Part of the psychic energy of the personality remains focused on the concerns of this stage.

For Freud, problems in adult personality reflect these unresolved issues

phallic [FAH-lick] **stage** Freud's third psychosexual stage of development, which occurs between 3 and 6 years of age, in which little boys experience the Oedipus complex and little girls the Electra complex

Oedipus [ED-uh-puss] **complex** in the male, an unconscious sexual urge for the mother that develops during the phallic psychosexual stage

Electra complex in the female, an unconscious sexual urge for the father that develops during the phallic psychosexual stage

latency [LATE-an-see] **stage** Freud's fourth psychosexual stage of development, which occurs from around age 6 to puberty, in which the child's sexuality is suppressed due to widening social contacts with school, peers, and family

genital stage Freud's final psychosexual stage of development, which occurs during puberty, in which sexual energy is transferred toward peers of the other sex (heterosexual orientation) or same sex (homosexual orientation)

According to Freud, the genital stage of psychosexual development unconsciously motivates teens to interact with potential sexual partners.

© Adrian Sherratt/Alamy

or fixations from childhood. For example, a person whose oral urges were not adequately satisfied in infancy would develop an *oral fixation*. An oral fixation might be expressed in the adult behaviors of overeating, nail biting, constantly chewing on pens or pencils, or boasting. More serious behaviors reflecting oral fixations include smoking, alcoholism, and binge eating. Fixation at the anal stage may express itself in the adult personality as *anal-retentiveness* or *anal-expulsiveness*. Being overly neat, stingy, or orderly (anal-retentive) or being excessively sloppy, generous, or carefree (anal-expulsive) both result from inadequate resolution of the anal stage. These are just two examples of how fixations might manifest themselves in an adult personality.

personal unconscious according to Jung, the part of the unconscious that consists of forgotten memories and repressed experiences from one's past

collective unconscious according to Jung, the part of the unconscious that contains images and material universal to people of all time periods and cultures

archetypes [ARE-kuh-types] according to Jung, mental representations or symbols of themes and predispositions to respond to the world in a certain way that are contained in the collective unconscious

Neo-Freudians: Carl Jung, Alfred Adler, and Karen Horney

Freud's work created much controversy among professionals in the developing field of psychology. Many physicians and psychologists were initially intrigued by Freud's ideas but had their differences with aspects of his theory and eventually separated from Freud. These *neo-Freudians* agreed with Freud that unconscious conflicts were important to understanding personality, but they placed less emphasis on the role of the instinctual impulses of sex and aggression in motivating behavior. We have already introduced one neo-Freudian, Erik Erikson, whose theory of psychosocial development we discussed in Chapter 9. His eight stages detailed the influence of the environment on the developing ego over the life span. Three other examples of neo-Freudian theories are presented here, in the ideas of Carl Jung, Alfred Adler, and Karen Horney.

Carl Jung and the Collective Unconscious

Carl Jung was a student of Freud's who came to reject his ideas about personality, particularly the sexual aspects of his theory. Like Freud, Jung maintained that personality was a function of the interplay between conscious and unconscious processes. However, Jung (1917/1967) divided the unconscious into the personal unconscious and the collective unconscious. The **personal unconscious**, much like Freud's unconscious, consisted of forgotten memories and repressed experiences. The **collective unconscious** is universal to all people of all time periods and cultures. The collective unconscious represents the collected images and ideas from the earliest development of the human psyche. In particular, the collective unconscious includes **archetypes**, mental representations or symbols of themes and predispositions to respond to the world in a certain way. According to Jung, two of the major archetypes of the personality are the *anima* and the *animus*, the female and male aspects of each person. Among the other archetypes Jung identified are the *persona* and the *shadow*. The persona is the appearance we present to the world, the role or character we assume when relating to others, such as the martyr, the rebel, or the teacher. The shadow includes those negative tendencies or qualities of the self that a person tries to deny or hide from the world. Jung's emphasis on the collective unconscious and his belief that spiritual and religious drives are just as important as sexual ones continue to draw attention. He also stressed the importance of enduring personality traits such as introversion and extraversion.

Hulton Archive/Getty Images

Jung divided the unconscious into the personal unconscious (forgotten memories and repressed experiences) and the collective unconscious (the collected images and ideas from the earliest development of the human psyche).

Adler believed that it is the child's desire to overcome feelings of helplessness and to master the environment that directs behavior.

Imagno/Getty Images

Alfred Adler and the Inferiority Complex

Alfred Adler also began as a student of Freud's but disagreed with Freud's emphasis on aggressive and sexual urges as the major force in personality development. Adler (1928) believed that it is the child's desire to overcome feelings of helplessness and to master the environment that directs behavior. In the world of adults, children are small and helpless and feel inadequate and weak. Children have to be bathed by a parent and hold a parent's hand when crossing the street. These feelings of inferiority motivate the child—and later the adult—toward achievement. For Adler, personality develops from our attempts to compensate for inferiority feelings. Moderate feelings of inferiority will result in constructive achievement and creative growth, but deep feelings of inferiority will impede positive growth and development and result in an *inferiority complex*.

Adler also emphasized the importance of birth order as a factor in personality development. He argued that firstborns, middle-borns, and youngest children grow up in differing family environments and are not necessarily treated the same by parents. These different experiences are likely to affect personality development. Adler's ideas have resulted in hundreds of studies on the effects of birth order. These studies have generally not found any reliable relationships between birth order and personality (Abdel-Khalek & Lester, 2005; Harris, 2000). Yet people generally believe that birth order affects personality, which may then actually encourage those in various birth ranks to differ in their personalities (Herrera, Zajonc, Wieczorkowska, & Cichomski, 2003).

KAREN HORNEY AND BASIC ANXIETY

Although Karen Horney agreed with Freud on the significance of early childhood in personality development, she rejected his belief that this development arose from instinctual conflicts. Instead, Horney (1937, 1939) suggested that family environments and disturbances in early relationships lead to **basic anxiety**, or a feeling of helplessness in children. Children cope with this basic anxiety by pursuing love, power, prestige, or detachment. Horney further argued, in contrast to Freud, that culture plays a larger role in personality development than biology and instinct. For Horney, personality is not merely the result of psychosexual conflicts, as Freud would argue, but rather is influenced by all the events and people in the culture that make a child feel unsafe and unloved, giving rise to basic anxiety.

© Bettmann/Corbis

Karen Horney argued that culture plays a larger role in personality development than biology and suggested that family environments and disturbances in early relationships lead to basic anxiety in children. Children cope with this basic anxiety by pursuing love, power, prestige, or detachment.

Contributions and Criticisms of the Psychoanalytic Approach

Freud's contributions to psychology have been immense (Erwin, 2002). He is regarded as one of the most influential thinkers of the 20th century (Gedo, 2002). His presence is still felt among the general public through literature, arts, and the movies. His theory on dreams stimulated much research on the nature of sleep. His notion of defense mechanisms was extensively elaborated on by his daughter, Anna Freud, and his focus on coping and well-being sparked interest and research in health psychology. His ideas are evident in tests designed to measure personality (discussed later in this chapter) and in therapy approaches to help people with psychological problems (Chapter 14). Freud's basic notion of the unconscious influencing our behavior also has merit (Bargh & Morsella, 2008; Gedo, 2002; Greenwald & Draine, 1997; Kihlstrom, 1993; Westen, 1999). How many of us can say that we know why we have engaged in every single behavior we have ever produced? Isn't it possible that there are unconscious forces influencing our behavior?

Furthermore, Freud was one of the first to see the importance of early development in later adult behavior (Gedo, 2002). In the early 1900s, children were seen as mini-adults. People did not believe as strongly as we do now that how infants and children are treated influences their adult behavior. Although we know that infancy and childhood experiences do not *determine* adult behavior, as Freud asserted, his emphasis on the importance of these early years was a critical departure from accepted beliefs at that time. Through his psychosexual stages, Freud placed much emphasis on explaining the developmental nature of personality, probably more so than any other theorist.

Freud's perspective has been criticized on several counts. First, many believe that Freud placed too much emphasis on sexual and aggressive instincts. His perspective shines very little light on environmental and social conditions that may affect personality functioning. We have just seen that many neo-Freudians diverged from Freud on this point, creating alternate

basic anxiety according to Horney, the feeling of helplessness that develops in children from early relationships views of the ego and personality that take our interactions with others into account (Horgan, 1996). His ideas and themes have also been attacked for his focus on male development and perpetuation of the idea of male superiority (Person, 1990).

Much more problematic are Freud's method of data collection and the fact that his theories cannot be readily tested experimentally (Crews, 1996). His theories are based almost entirely on case study research and his own self-analysis. His observations may not have been objective, and his case studies involved patients who were diagnosed with nervous disorders. What his patients told him may not have been accurate, and their statements were not corroborated by other sources. These issues make it difficult to generalize Freud's observations. Scientifically testing Freud's theoretical concepts is also quite challenging. Measuring the unconscious is impossible if participants are unaware of these impulses. It is equally difficult to measure psychosexual stages of development. For this reason, we cannot prove that Freud's theory is true, but we also cannot disprove it. Thus, it remains a possible explanation of personality functioning, though not as popular as it was in the past. Freud's ideas have not been supported by data from other cultures, possibly because his theories reflect the Western cultural value of individualism. They may not apply in collectivist cultures that emphasize the importance of the group (Matsumoto, 1994).

Let's Review!

This section outlined the psychoanalytic perspective on personality. For a quick check of your understanding, answer these questions.

1. The psychoanalytic perspective emphasizes the influence of _____ on personality.
   a. unconscious desires   c. self-actualization
   b. traits   d. environmental factors

2. Maria often feels guilty when she engages in even the slightest offensive behavior. Freud would say that Maria has a strong _____.
   a. id   c. superego
   b. ego   d. collective unconscious

3. One of the major criticisms of Freud's theory is its _____.
   a. overemphasis on environmental and cognitive factors in explaining behavior
   b. difficulty in being experimentally tested and validated
   c. emphasis on the conscious
   d. assumption that all people are good

Answers 1. a; 2. c; 3. b

The Trait Approach: Describing Personality

- Define traits, and compare the various trait approaches to understanding personality (Allport, Cattell, Eysenck, and the five factor theory).
- Discuss genetic contributions to personality, and address whether personality is consistent and stable over time.

A second major perspective on personality is called the **trait approach**. The trait approach, like the psychoanalytic approach, focuses on internal aspects of personality. Whereas the psychoanalytic approach attempts to explain personality by focusing on unconscious forces, the trait perspective describes personality and emphasizes its biological aspects. Trait theory assumes that we all have internal **traits**, or tendencies to behave in a certain way across most situations. These traits remain relatively stable as we age and explain why people generally behave the same way across a variety of situations. Yet because people differ in the degree to which they possess various traits, we develop unique personalities. We will describe four major approaches to understanding these personality traits in the theories of Gordon Allport, Raymond Cattell, Hans Eysenck, and the five factor theory.

trait approach a personality perspective that attempts to describe personality by emphasizing internal, biological aspects of personality called traits

trait tendency we have across most situations to behave in a certain way

BEETLE BAILEY

Psychology Applies to Your World:

Are You a Sensation Seeker?

One trait of particular interest to psychologists is that of sensation seeking. Some people seem to crave arousal, seeking out higher levels of arousal than the rest of us. In fact, sometimes they seek out levels of arousal that the rest of us would find *aversive*. For example, think of contestants on the television show *Fear Factor*, the stunts engaged in by actors in the movie *Jackass*, or extreme sports enthusiasts who try to ski off dangerous mountainsides, climb skyscrapers without protective gear, or bungee jump off bridges. Some people are what psychologists call **sensation seekers**, those who habitually tend to seek out high levels of physiological arousal by engaging in intensely stimulating experiences (Zuckerman, 1978, 1994). Some sensation seekers pursue daring activities such as mountain climbing, skydiving, and fast driving, whereas others may be stimulated by travel to new places, taking drugs, having multiple sexual experiences, or gambling.

One theory that seeks to explain the causes of sensation seeking looks at biological differences in the brains of sensation seekers. Psychologist Marvin Zuckerman found that sensation seekers tend to have low levels of a substance called *monoamine oxidase*, or *MAO* (Zuckerman, 1994). MAO is an enzyme that breaks down neurotransmitters like serotonin, dopamine, and norepinephrine (see Chapter 2). One of these neurotransmitters, dopamine, seems to be responsible for motivating us to obtain rewards. The low level of MAO in the brains of sensation seekers may mean that they experience more dopamine activity than do non–sensation seekers. This increased dopamine action may motivate sensation seekers to look for more and more rewards in the form of arousal.

According to psychologist Marvin Zuckerman, some people are high in the trait of sensation seeking. They engage in highly energizing and stimulating activities such as skydiving and extreme sports.

sensation seeker a person who by trait tends to seek out arousing activities

Chuck Karcher/Jupiter Images

Are you a sensation seeker? To get a feel for your level of sensation seeking, take the questionnaire in ■ TABLE 12.1. Just keep in mind that this questionnaire is a brief version of the full Zuckerman Sensation Seeking Scale (Zuckerman, 1994). Therefore, your true level of sensation seeking may differ from your test results.

Table 12.1 Brief Sensation-Seeking Questionnaire

Are you a sensation seeker? This questionnaire will give you some insight into your sensation-seeking tendencies, but please recognize that this test gives you only a rough idea of where you fall on this dimension.

Measuring sensation seeking

Answer "true" or "false" to each item listed below by circling "T" or "F." A "true" means that the item expresses your preference most of the time. A "false" means that you do not agree that the item is generally true for you. After completing the test, score your responses according to the instructions that follow the test items.

T F   1. I would really enjoy skydiving.
T F   2. I can imagine myself driving a sports car in a race and loving it.
T F   3. My life is very secure and comfortable—the way I like it.
T F   4. I usually like emotionally expressive or artistic people, even if they are sort of wild.
T F   5. I like the idea of seeing many of the same warm, supportive faces in everyday life.
T F   6. I like doing adventurous things and would have enjoyed being a pioneer in the early days of this country.
T F   7. A good photograph should express peacefulness creatively.
T F   8. The most important thing in living is fully experiencing all emotions.
T F   9. I like creature comforts when I go on a trip or vacation.
T F 10. Doing the same things each day really gets to me.
T F 11. I love snuggling in front of a fire on a wintry day.
T F 12. I would like to try several types of drugs as long as they didn't harm me permanently.
T F 13. Drinking and being rowdy really appeals to me on weekends.
T F 14. Rational people try to avoid dangerous situations.
T F 15. I prefer figure A to figure B.

Give yourself 1 point for answering "true" to the following items: 1, 2, 4, 6, 8, 10, 12, and 13. Also give yourself 1 point for answering "false" to the following items: 3, 5, 7, 9, 11, 14, and 15. Add up your points, and compare your total to the following norms: 11–15, high sensation seeker; 6–10, moderate sensation seeker; 1–5, low sensation seeker. Bear in mind that this is a shortened version of the Sensation Seeking Scale and that it provides only a rough approximation of your status on this personality trait.

(Source: A. F. Grasha & D. S. Kirschenbaum (1986). Adjustment and competence: Concepts and applications. St. Paul, MN: West Publishing. Reprinted by permission of Anthony F. Grasha.)

Gordon Allport's Trait Theory

Psychologist Gordon Allport (1961) believed that three types of traits help us understand a person's uniqueness: *central traits*, *secondary traits*, and *cardinal traits*. **Central traits** include those tendencies we have across most situations; they are the core qualities your friends would state if they were asked to describe you. For example, if you are friendly in most situations, then friendly would be considered a central trait. We all have central traits, yet the qualities that are considered a central trait may differ from person to person.

Secondary traits describe how we behave in certain situations; they are tendencies that are less consistent and more situation-specific. Many of us behave aggressively in certain situations, such as when we are frustrated or when we see others behave aggressively. Again, we all have secondary traits, but whether a specific quality is considered a secondary trait may differ from person to person.

Cardinal traits describe how we behave across all situations. Allport considered these a very basic and dominant element of our personalities—but he had difficulty in finding cardinal traits in all people that he studied. Consequently, the validity of cardinal traits became

central traits according to Allport, those tendencies we have to behave in a certain way across most situations

secondary traits according to Allport, the tendencies we have that are less consistent and describe how we behave in certain situations

cardinal traits according to Allport, those dominant elements of our personalities that drive all of our behaviors

Using factor analysis, Cattell reduced the number of core personality traits to 16 basic traits, referred to as source traits.

surface traits basic traits that describe people's personalities, according to Cattell

source traits universal tendencies that underlie and are at the core of surface traits, according to Cattell

suspect. Recall from Chapter 5 on learning and Chapter 10 on social psychology the powerful effect the environment can have on our behavior. This effect often makes us behave differently across situations.

Allport's goal in describing traits was to understand the behavior of a specific individual. Other research focused on identifying and understanding core or universal traits that direct the behavior of people in general, relying heavily on the use of statistics. This set the stage for Raymond Cattell's statistical analysis of personality traits.

Raymond Cattell's Factor Analytic Trait Theory

Raymond Cattell (1943) attempted to document relationships among traits using a sophisticated statistical technique called *factor analysis*. In contemporary factor analysis, data are entered into a computer. The computer is then asked to find shared qualities among the data and to group these shared relationships into factors. For example, suppose we perform a factor analysis on soups. All the ingredients for all soups are entered into the computer database. The computer is then instructed to generate a list of any shared ingredients among all the soups. If it finds a shared "quality" among them—perhaps salt or water was in every soup—then these items would be called soup factors. Psychologists can do the same thing with personality traits. All traits that are used to describe people are entered into a computer, then the computer is instructed to find any shared qualities or factors. In this way, Cattell reduced the number of personality traits that could be used to describe all people.

Cattell's research (1965) originally yielded 36 **surface traits** that could describe personality. He hypothesized that there must be common underlying factors that account for the 36 surface traits. Cattell referred to these qualities or dimensions as **source traits**. Source traits are basic, broad, and relatively universal tendencies at the core of our personalities. We may differ in the amount or quality of these traits, but they are present in everyone's personality to some degree. Through subsequent analysis and research, Cattell identified 16 source traits (■ TABLE 12.2). However, Cattell's 16 source traits did not easily lend themselves to research. Research led by British psychologist Hans Eysenck would further reduce the number.

Table 12.2 Cattell's 16 Personality Factors

FACTOR	DESCRIPTION
	(Extremes of each factor from low to high levels)
Warmth	Reserved - - - - - - - - - - - - - - - -Warm
Reasoning	Less intelligent - - - - - - - - - - -More intelligent
Emotional Stability	Easily upset - - - - - - - - - - - - -Emotionally stable
Dominance	Submissive- - - - - - - - - - - - - -Dominant
Liveliness	Serious - - - - - - - - - - - - - - -Expressive
Rule Consciousness	Nonconforming - - - - - - - - -Conforming
Social Boldness	Shy - - - - - - - - - - - - - - - - -Venturesome
Sensitivity	Tough-minded - - - - - - - - - -Sensitive
Vigilance	Trusting - - - - - - - - - - - - - -Suspicious
Abstractedness	Practical- - - - - - - - - - - - - - -Imaginative
Privateness	Open- - - - - - - - - - - - - - - - -Shrewd
Apprehension	Unworried - - - - - - - - - - - - -Worried
Openness to Change	Conservative - - - - - - - - - - -Experimenting
Self-Reliance	Dependent- - - - - - - - - - - - -Self-sufficient
Perfectionism	Undisciplined- - - - - - - - - - -Precise
Tension	Relaxed - - - - - - - - - - - - - - -Tense

Hans Eysenck Narrows Down the Traits: The PEN Model

Building on Cattell's factor analytic studies, Eysenck and Rachman (1965) found two factors that they believed measured people's key characteristics: introversion/extraversion and emotional stability/neuroticism (■ FIGURE 12.3). Introversion and extraversion define where a person's energy is directed. **Introversion** means that the person's energy is directed inward. This could include being rigid, reliable, sober, or controlled. **Extraversion** means that the person's energy is directed outward. This could include being easygoing, lively, or excitable. Emotional *stability* and *neuroticism* refer to control over one's emotions. Being even-tempered, calm, or a leader are traits that include more control over emotions, whereas moody and touchy describe traits that represent **neuroticism**. We all are somewhere on the introversion/extraversion scale and somewhere on the emotional stability/neuroticism continuum; we just differ in the degree to which we express the two factors.

In the 1970s, Eysenck in collaboration with his wife, Sybil Eysenck, added a third dimension called psychoticism to the model (Eysenck & Eysenck, 1969, 1976). **Psychoticism** includes tendencies toward recklessness, disregard for common sense and cultural norms, inconsideration, hostility, anger, and impulsivity. Eysenck originally characterized impulsivity as a dimension of extraversion. However, once the dimension of psychoticism was added, he moved this trait from extraversion to psychoticism. Eysenck's three factor model of personality is referred to as the PEN (Psychoticism, Extraversion, Neuroticism) model (■ TABLE 12.3).

	Unstable	
moody		touchy
anxious		restless
rigid		aggressive
sober		excitable
pessimistic		changeable
reserved		impulsive
unsociable		optimistic
quiet		active
Introverted		**Extraverted**
passive		sociable
careful		outgoing
thoughtful		talkative
peaceful		responsive
controlled		easygoing
reliable		lively
even-tempered		carefree
calm	leadership	
	Stable	

Table 12.3 Eysenck's PEN Model

PSYCHOTICISM	EXTRAVERSION	NEUROTICISM
Aggressive	Sociable	Anxious
Assertive	Irresponsible	Depressed
Impulsive	Expressive	Guilt feelings
Manipulative	Active	Moody
Tough-minded	Dominant	Obsessive
Hostile	Lack of reflection	Tense

FIGURE

12.3 Eysenck's Trait Theory

British psychologist Hans Eysenck arrived at two universal traits using factor analysis. The stable–unstable axis defines one's emotionality; the introversion–extraversion axis defines the degree to which a person's energy is directed inward or outward. The traits in each quadrant indicate where they are placed with respect to these two factors.

Source: H. J. Eysenck and S. Rachman (1965), The Causes and Curses of Neurosis. Copyright © 1965 by J. J. Eysenck and R. Rachman. Reprinted by permission of EdiTS.

Neuroscience Applies to Your World:

Why Am I an Introvert?

Livia Corona/Getty Images

Eysenck (1967, 1982, 1991) proposed that introverts inherit the tendency toward higher levels of physical arousal than extraverts. Introverts are more likely to avoid social situations because such experiences will elevate their arousal and lead to overstimulation and discomfort. Hence, they are more likely than extraverts to turn inward and become introverted. Research has generally supported Eysenck's theory; several studies confirm that introverts tend to show higher levels of physical arousal than extraverts (Beauducel, Brocke, & Leue, 2006; Bullock & Gilliland, 1993; LeBlanc, Ducharme, & Thompson, 2004; Kumari, ffytche, Williams, & Gray, 2004).

© Gail Mooney/Masterlife

introversion [in-tro-VER-shun] personality traits that involve energy directed inward, such as being calm or peaceful

extraversion [ex-tra-VER-shun] personality traits that involve energy directed outward, such as being easygoing, lively, or excitable

neuroticism [nur-RAH-tuh-siz-um] the degree to which one is emotionally unstable

psychoticism [psi-COT-uh-siz-um] the degree to which one is hostile, nonconforming, impulsive, and aggressive

The Five Factor Trait Theory

Currently, the most widely accepted trait theory derived from factor analysis is Paul Costa and Robert McCrae's (1992) five factor theory. This theory proposes five core dimensions that can be measured along a continuum in all people.

- *Extraversion*: the degree to which energy is directed inward or outward. People high in extraversion are talkative, sociable, and prefer to be around others. At the other end of the continuum are people low in extraversion (introverts), who are quiet, reserved, and comfortable on their own.

- *Neuroticism*: the degree to which one is emotionally stable or unstable. People high in neuroticism are temperamental, worrisome, and pessimistic. People who score low on this factor tend to be more even-tempered and calm.

- *Openness*: the degree to which one is thoughtful and rational in considering new ideas. People who score high in openness tend to be imaginative, creative, and curious and to prefer variety; those who score low in openness prefer routine and are more narrow-minded in their ideas and experiences.

- *Agreeableness*: the degree to which one gets along well with others. Being easygoing and trusting are traits characteristic of one high in agreeableness. At the other end of the spectrum are people who are unfriendly, antagonistic, and suspicious (low agreeableness).

- *Conscientiousness*: the degree to which one is aware of and attentive to other people and/or the details of a task. People who are high in conscientiousness tend to be hardworking, ambitious, reliable, and self-controlled, whereas individuals low in this dimension are more often described as unreliable, lazy, and spontaneous.

These five dimensions appear in all cultures, suggesting that these five factors may represent universal personality components (Katigbak, Church, Guanzon-Lapeña, Carlota, & del Pilar, 2002; McCrae & Costa, 1998; Yamagata et al., 2006). An easy way to remember the five factors is with the acronym OCEAN. Each letter in OCEAN stands for one of the five factors: O = openness, C = conscientiousness, E = extraversion, A = agreeableness, and N = neuroticism.

■ YOU REVIEW 12.1 compares the four trait theories. Notice that the main difference in these theories is the number of basic traits that are proposed. Allport's theory proposes 3, Eysenck's theory proposes 3, Cattell's theory proposes 16, and Costa and McCrae's model proposes 5.

You Review 12.1

Summary of Trait Theories

THEORIST/THEORY	METHOD OF COLLECTION	RESULTS
Allport	Subjectively collected traits	3 trait levels: central, secondary, and cardinal
Cattell	Factor analysis	36 surface traits; 16 source traits
Eysenck's PEN model	Factor analysis	3 basic traits labeled PEN: psychoticism, extraversion, and neuroticism
Costa & McCrae's five factor theory	Factor analysis	5 basic dimensions that form the acronym OCEAN: openness, conscientiousness, extraversion, agreeableness, and neuroticism

Genetic Contributions to Personality

The trait perspective assumes that people have internal dispositions to behave consistently across situations. Thus, some researchers have speculated that we inherit some aspects of our personalities. Recall that newborn infants do show differences in behavior that we refer to as temperament (see Chapter 9), that these

You Asked...

Is personality hereditary?

TIFFANY SLOWEY, STUDENT

temperamental differences appear strongly related to genes (Braungart, Plomin, DeFries, & Fulker, 1992), and that they are quite stable over time (Jaffari-Bimmel, Juffer, van Ijzendoorn, Bakermans-Kranenburg, & Mooijaart, 2006; Majdandzic & van den Boom, 2007; McCrae et al., 2000; Rothbart, Ahadi, & Evans, 2000). It seems possible that other characteristics or personality dispositions are also inherited.

One way to study genetic contributions—the nature side of personality—is to look at children who are adopted. Because adopted children have no genes in common with their adoptive family members, any similarities in personality characteristics between these children and their adoptive parents are likely due to learning or modeling. On the other hand, because these children have genes in common with their biological parents but do not share a family environment, any similarities to them are likely due to genetics. These research studies have found more personality similarities between adoptive children and their biological parents (Carey & DiLalla, 1994). These findings suggests a strong genetic component to personality.

Another method for investigating the contribution of genes—or nature—is to study identical twins. Research on identical twins provides even more compelling evidence that at least some personality tendencies may be inherited (Bouchard, 2004; Weiss, Bates, & Luciano, 2008). Identical twins reared in separate environments appeared to show remarkable similarities in behavior years later when they were reunited (Bouchard, Lykken, McGue, Segal, & Tellegen, 1990; Holden, 1980; Lykken, McGue, Tellegen, & Bouchard, 1992). One of the more famous separated pairs is the "Jim twins." Both drove Chevrolets and chain-smoked Salem cigarettes. They both worked as sheriff's deputies and listed stock-car racing, carpentry, and mechanical drawing as interests and hobbies (Holden, 1980). Studies have found more similarities between the personalities of identical twins than of non-identical twins (Buss, 1995; Plomin, DeFries, McClearn, & McGuffin, 2001; Saudino, McQuire, Reiss, Heatherington, & Plomin, 1995). Such evidence indicates a significant genetic role in the personalities we exhibit.

Mel Yates/Getty Images

Studies have found more similarities between the personalities of identical twins than of nonidentical twins, indicating a significant genetic role in the personalities we exhibit.

Stability and Change in Personality

The trait approach not only assumes that traits are inherited, it also assumes that these internal tendencies are consistent and stable over time. What does the research indicate? Research does support the stability of *some* personality traits over the course of adulthood. However, age,

You Asked...

Do people's personalities change over time?   YANILSA OSORIA, STUDENT

culture, and gender are important when considering stability and change in personality.

After the age of 30, changes in personality traits are smaller than in childhood and young adulthood (Costa & McCrae, 1997; Roberts & DelVecchio, 2000; Roberts, Walton,

& Viechtbauer, 2006; Terracciano, Costa, & McCrae, 2006). As a part of the developmental process, children, adolescents, and young adults experiment with new identities and ways of behaving. They may adopt new values and attitudes or revise existing ones. Changes in personality, therefore, are more frequent during these periods.

Some studies suggest that at least for some traits, there is a consistency from childhood to adulthood (Roberts, Caspi, & Moffitt, 2001). For example, McCrae and colleagues (2002) found stability in the factors of extraversion, agreeableness, and conscientiousness from age 12 to age 18. Hampson and Goldberg (2006) found stability for the traits of extraversion and conscientiousness from elementary school to midlife. Shiner, Masten, and Roberts (2003) found modest continuity in the traits of motivation, academic conscientiousness, and agreeableness from childhood to adulthood. Another study (Robins, Fraley, Roberts, & Trzesniewski, 2001) found consistency in the five factor personality traits when following the same people from the beginning to the end of their college years.

Age differences in personality have also been investigated in other cultures, and a similar picture has emerged. Data from Germany, Britain, Spain, Italy, Portugal, Croatia, Turkey, South Korea, and the Czech Republic are consistent with findings on the five factor model of personality in U.S. samples (McCrae et al., 1999, 2000). Older men and women in these cultures also tended to be lower in extraversion and openness to experience and higher in agreeableness and conscientiousness. Such findings appear to support the universality of some personality traits. These societies differ dramatically in language, culture, and historical experiences from each other and from the experiences of most people in the United States. Yet the cultural differences seemed to have little impact on age differences in personality traits.

However, other research suggests substantial *changes* in personality even during the course of adulthood (Jones & Meredith, 1996; Ravenna, Jones, & Kwan, 2002; Scollon & Diener, 2006; Whitbourne, Zuschlag, Elliot, & Waterman, 1992). People generally become more introspective, cautious, and conforming as they approach late adulthood (Reedy, 1983). In one study, conscientiousness and agreeableness showed increases throughout early and middle adulthood (Srivastava, John, Gosling, & Potter, 2003). Many people also become more androgynous, exhibiting both male and female traits, as they age (Fiske, 1980). Even McCrae and colleagues' (1999, 2000) cross-cultural research did not find consistency across all of the five factor traits. Only two cultures looked similar to U.S. samples on the neuroticism dimension.

Gender differences in personality traits also show evidence of both stability and change. Across cultures and for both college-age and adult samples, women report themselves to be higher in neuroticism, extraversion, agreeableness, conscientiousness, and openness to feelings, whereas men report themselves higher in assertiveness and openness to ideas (Costa, Terracciano, & McCrae, 2001; Schmitt, Realo, Voracek, & Allik, 2008). Neuroticism also tends to decrease in women as they age but stay the same for men (Srivastava et al., 2003). Moreover, the research demonstrates that not all people change at the same rate over their lives. Some people's traits may be stable whereas other people's traits may change (Mroczek & Spiro, 2003; Roberts & Mroczek, 2008; Small, Hertzog, Hultsch, & Dixon, 2003).

> ### You Asked...
>
> *Does personality always describe how a person acts all the time?*
>
> JAELYNN PACKER, STUDENT

Situational factors also influence the stability and consistency of traits. Many of us display the same trait (behave the same way) when faced with similar circumstances—that is, when the environmental cues are the same. However, when the situation is different, our behavior may change. This is referred to as the **person–situation interaction** (Mischel & Shoda, 1995). For example, the students of one of the authors of this textbook are always surprised to hear that she has a fear of public speaking. They see her speak every week in class

person–situation interaction the influence of the situation on the stability of traits; when in the same situation, we display similar behavior, but when the situation is different, behavior may change with little anxiety. They know that she has been teaching for more than 20 years. From such knowledge, they predict that she would not fear public speaking in other situations, such as at a research conference or at a community function. But in these different situations, she is extremely anxious, panicked, and nauseated at the thought of speaking in front of a group. The cues of the two different situations evoke different behaviors and reactions. Thus, our traits do not always predict how we will behave across different situations.

How do psychologists reconcile these seemingly contradictory findings? Psychologists recognize that personality is both stable *and* changeable. Some traits are probably more consistent across the life span and from culture to culture, whereas others are more easily influenced by one's society, gender, environment, and daily situations (Fleeson, 2004).

Contributions and Criticisms of the Trait Approach

The trait perspective has contributed to our understanding of personality by providing psychologists with a common vocabulary to describe people's personalities. Because this common language facilitates communication within the field, the trait approach has been particularly useful in the area of personality assessment, a topic we will turn to shortly. Knowing a person's tendencies or traits also helps psychologists predict future behavior. These predictions, however, will be influenced by the nature of the situation (Johnson, 1997). The assumptions of the trait perspective—that traits are internal and stable—have also fueled research investigating the biological aspects of personality and the consistency and stability of personality traits across the life span.

However, the objective of personality research is to uncover how we differ from one another. Although the trait perspective does a good job of *describing* people's personalities, it is criticized for not *explaining* why we behave in a particular way (Digman, 1997; Funder, 1993). Critics further argue that it portrays personality too simplistically and fails to reflect its complexity and depth (Block, 1995; Epstein, 1994; Gladwell, 2004). Can everyone really be reduced to 3, 5, or 16 dimensions? Can we cleanly divide personality into biological and environmental components without taking into account the complex interactions among them? We have also seen its shortcomings in predicting people's behavior across different situations (Wiggins, 1997). This should not be surprising, though, given the powerful influence of situational forces on behavior.

Often our personality interacts with our environment. A behavior we display in one context (texting on one's cell phone when the teacher is not looking) may not be the same behavior we exhibit at other times (studious and engaged when the teacher is attentive).

© LWA-Sharie Kennedy/Corbis

Let's Review!

This section presented the trait approach to personality and discussed genetic aspects of personality and its stability over time. For a quick check of your understanding, answer these questions.

1. The trait perspective emphasizes the influence of _____ on personality.

   a. unconscious impulses   **c.** self-actualization

   b. internal tendencies   **d.** environmental factors

2. Terrence is outgoing in most situations. Allport would describe this tendency in Terrence as a _____.

   a. source trait   **c.** cardinal trait

   b. secondary trait   **d.** central trait

3. Which of the following is not considered one of the five factor traits of personality?

   a. Achievement   **c.** Conscientiousness

   b. Extraversion   **d.** Agreeableness

Answers 1.b; 2.d; 3.a

Stop, LOOK, and LEARN

What Is Personality, and How Do We Measure It?

Psychoanalytic Theories

Emphasize unconscious aspects of personality

Sigmund Freud

- Levels of awareness
  - Unconscious
  - Preconscious
  - Conscious
- Personality structure
  - Id: pleasure principle
  - Ego: reality principle
  - Superego: moral compass
- Psychosexual development
  - Oral stage
  - Anal stage
  - Phallic stage
  - Latency stage
  - Genital stage

Neo-Freudians

- Carl Jung: collective unconscious
- Alfred Adler: inferiority complex
- Karen Horney: basic anxiety
- Erik Erikson: life crises

Trait Theories

Emphasize inherited or biological aspects of personality

Gordon Allport

- Central, secondary, and cardinal traits

Raymond Cattell

- 16 source traits

Hans Eysenck (PEN)

- Psychoticism, extraversion, and neuroticism

Five Factor Theory (OCEAN)

- Openness, conscientiousness, extraversion, agreeableness, and neuroticism

Stability of personality over time

- Some traits are consistent from childhood to adulthood, but the situation influences the consistency of traits.

The Social Cognitive Approach: The Environment and Patterns of Thought

The **social cognitive approach** sees personality as influenced by both the environment and one's thoughts. Whereas Freud focused on how unconscious forces influence behavior and the trait perspective investigates internal dispositions, the social cognitive approach looks at the characteristic ways a person perceives and interprets events in the environment. For example, the person who assumes that others are unlikely to treat her fairly is more likely to have a quarrelsome personality than a person who tends to assume that things generally happen for the best. These patterns of thoughts are established through our interactions with and observations of other people. Two examples of this approach are Albert Bandura's *reciprocal determinism* and Julian Rotter's *locus of control* theory.

Bandura speculates that personality is the product of reciprocal determinism, or the mutual interaction between one's environment, behavior, and thoughts.

Reciprocal Determinism: Albert Bandura's Interacting Forces

Albert Bandura (1986) speculates that personality is the product of three interacting forces: environment, behavior, and thoughts. Bandura called the constant interaction among these three factors **reciprocal determinism** (■ FIGURE 12.4). We choose to place ourselves in certain environments, and these environments

> *You Asked...*
>
> *Is one's personality due to one's environment?*   RAMON VELEZ, STUDENT

then influence our behavior and the way we think. However, the way we think—our goals, values, and perceptions—may guide which environments we choose to be in as well as the behavior we exhibit. Our behavior, in turn, may change the environment as well as the way we think. All three variables influence each other in a reciprocal manner.

For example, when we were children, we were placed in a family environment that modeled specific child-rearing techniques. We tend to think that everything we experienced

social cognitive approach a personality perspective that emphasizes the influence of one's thoughts and social experiences in formulating personality

reciprocal determinism [ree-SIP-pra-cull dee-TER-min-iz-um] according to Bandura, the constant interaction among one's behavior, thoughts, and environment determines personality

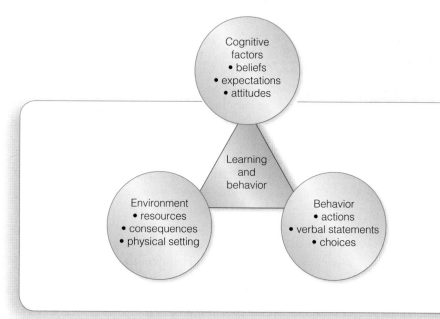

FIGURE

12.4 Bandura's Reciprocal Determinism

Albert Bandura speculates that the constant interaction between our behavior, thoughts, and environment determines our personalities.

in our home was normal, and that these same experiences occurred everywhere else, too. We tend to think that everyone else grew up with the parental discipline style we had. When we ourselves have children, if we have not learned anything different, we tend to behave in the same way toward our children. The family environment and our understanding of the way we were raised have now influenced our own parenting behavior.

A critical cognitive element in this interplay is what Bandura (1997) termed **self-efficacy**, or one's expectation of success in a given situation. Self-efficacy can differ among different domains in one's life. People with high self-efficacy in a certain domain believe that they will be successful in that domain. Approaching a situation with this belief is more likely to result in actual success. On the other hand, people with low self-efficacy in a particular domain are more likely to approach a task believing that they won't succeed at it. This mind-set then decreases their chance of succeeding by causing them to give up too easily or not even really try in the first place.

Returning to our previous example, if you believe that you will be a successful parent by using the same discipline techniques that your parents used on you, you will be more likely to use such measures. If such practices are successful—in other words, your children behave as you would like—you feel even better as a parent. However, if you do not believe that you will be a successful parent, you may constantly change the methods you use to discipline your children. Such inconsistency will make it even more likely that your children will not behave the way you want, which only reinforces your lack of confidence in your parenting ability.

Julian Rotter's Locus of Control: Internal and External Expectations

self-efficacy [self-EF-fuh-kah-see] the expectation that one has for success in a given situation

locus [LOW-cus] **of control** the expectation of control we have over the outcome of an event; an internal locus expects some degree of personal control, whereas an external locus expects little personal control

Julian Rotter provides another example of a social cognitive approach to personality. His theory (Rotter, 1982) is referred to as **locus of control**, or *location of control*. Rotter believes that we all have expectations regarding how much control we have over the outcome of an event. These expectations fall on a continuum from internal to external. For example, you probably enter the testing room on exam day already expecting to do well, average, or poorly on the exam. This is your expectation of the event. Some people attribute the outcome of an event to internal forces, such as hard work. If you expect to do well on an exam because you studied hard, you are exhibiting an *internal locus of control*. You are attributing the outcome of the event to factors within your control. However, other people attribute the outcome of an event to external forces, such as good luck, fate, or environmental factors. If you believe you will do well on the exam because the course or test is easy or because the professor likes you, these expectations demonstrate an *external locus of control*. You attribute the outcome to factors outside your control. Not surprisingly, internals demonstrate higher academic achievement than externals. Externals tend to believe that only fate or the luck of a sympathetic teacher will get them a good grade, so they do not study as much as internals (Schultz & Schultz, 2005).

Rotter suggests that these varying expectations of control lead to differences in personality. Think about your health. Who would be more likely to exercise regularly and maintain a healthy lifestyle? Externals are more likely to attribute their weight, health, or medical condition to fate. "What will be, will be" could be their motto. They feel that when their time is up, their time is up. Internals, however, believe that they can control their health and are therefore more likely to exercise, follow doc-

People who exercise may be more likely to believe that they can control their health—an example of an internal locus of control.

© Image Source Black/Alamy

tors' directions, get regular checkups, and eat wisely, behaviors that actually contribute to better health (Phares, 1991; Strickland, 1989).

Contributions and Criticisms of the Social Cognitive Approach

The social cognitive approach has made major contributions to the field of psychology. By detailing the influence on behavior of cognitive processes such as thinking, expectations, and other mental events, it has expanded our conceptualization and understanding of personality. This in turn has stimulated an enormous amount of research focusing on how environmental and cognitive factors influence behavior. Our knowledge of memory, attributions, and problem solving stem directly from this perspective, which easily lends itself to research, specifically experimental testing. Objectively measuring social and cognitive processes is easier than measuring unconscious forces or biological tendencies. Despite these contributions, the social cognitive approach has been criticized for not addressing biological, unconscious, and emotional factors that influence personality (Liebert & Spiegler, 1998). It also has been criticized for not detailing the exact nature of personality development.

Let's Review!

This section described social cognitive approaches to personality. For a quick check of your understanding, answer these questions.

1. The social cognitive perspective emphasizes the influence of _____ on personality.
   a. unconscious impulses   c. self-actualization
   b. internal tendencies   d. patterns of thoughts

2. Dylan is sure he will do poorly on his next psychology exam. Dylan often thinks this way in regard to his academic studies. Bandura would say that Dylan has _____.
   a. low self-esteem   c. an internal locus of control
   b. low self-efficacy   d. reciprocal determinism

3. Juanita believes that finding a job is a matter of being in the right place at the right time. Rotter would classify Juanita as having _____.
   a. low self-efficacy
   b. low determinism
   c. an internal locus of control
   d. an external locus of control

Answers 1.d; 2.b; 3.d

The Humanistic Approach: Free Will and Self-Actualization

- Define self-actualization, and describe how the humanistic views of Maslow and Rogers propose that it can be achieved.

- Compare and contrast the four perspectives on personality, indicating the strengths and weaknesses of each approach.

Learning Objectives

The fourth and final personality perspective we will discuss is the humanistic approach. Humanistic psychology viewed itself as a "third force" in American psychology, following behavioral (the first force) and psychoanalytic (the second force) views. The **humanistic approach** emphasizes the individual, personal choice, and free will in shaping personality. The individual is seen as an active participant in his or her growth as a person. The humanistic view further assumes that humans have a built-in drive toward fulfilling their own

humanistic approach a personality perspective that emphasizes the individual, personal choice, and free will in shaping personality; assumes that humans have a built-in drive toward fulfilling their own natural potential natural potential. The attainment of this potential is referred to as **self-actualization**. Two well-known humanistic theorists have charted somewhat different paths to achieving self-actualization. One is Abraham Maslow, whose hierarchy of needs theory was introduced in Chapter 8. The other is Carl Rogers and his self theory.

Abraham Maslow and the Hierarchy of Needs Theory

Recall from Chapter 8 that Maslow (1968, 1970, 1971) believed that the pathway to achieving self-actualization was in the form of a hierarchy, with physical or biological needs at the bottom and more psychological or social needs at the top. According to Maslow, a person must satisfy lower-level needs before higher-level needs can be attained. At the bottom of the hierarchy are basic physiological needs, such as the need for food and water. Without food and water, we cannot proceed to the next rung of the ladder. At this next level, safety becomes the concern: the need to be free from harm and to feel secure. Once this safety need is met, the person focuses on psychological needs, such as feeling a sense of belongingness (the need to fit in) and feeling esteem or respect from others. Once these needs have been satisfied, self-actualization can be attained. Maslow estimated that only 1 person in 10 operates from self-actualization needs.

Unfortunately, Maslow's hierarchy does not explain why some people would deprive themselves of lower food and safety needs in favor of higher needs, such as esteem or self-actualization. For example, Nelson Mandela preferred to remain imprisoned in South Africa for many years than to lose his right to criticize the apartheid government. Salman Rushdie was forced into exile under threat from an Islamic *fatwah* and other death threats he received for publishing *The Satanic Verses*, a critique of life in Islamic countries. Perhaps Maslow's hierarchy is too simple a view of personality (Neher, 1991). Another view of self-actualization is Carl Rogers's self theory.

People who meet the criteria for self-actualization, such as Mother Teresa, might actually deprive themselves of lower-level needs, such as food or shelter.

self-actualization [self-ack-shu-lih-ZAY-shun] the fulfillment of one's natural potential

actualizing [ACK-shu-lies-ing] **tendency** according to Rogers, the natural drive in humans to strive for fulfillment and enhancement

self-concept one's perception or image of his/her abilities and uniqueness

Carl Rogers and Self Theory

Carl Rogers (1942, 1951, 1961, 1970, 1980) believed that understanding human personality required an understanding of how people view themselves and how they interpret events around them. He believed that human beings naturally strive for fulfillment and enhancement, a basic motive that he referred to as the **actualizing tendency**.

Rogers's proposed actualizing tendency is set at birth and moves the infant to recognize that she is separate from the mother and an independent being. The infant begins to experience the self as "I" or "me." This self gradually evolves into the person's self-concept. **Self-concept** is our perception or image of our abilities and our uniqueness. At first

one's self-concept is very general and changeable, as in the 4-year-old who describes herself as a girl with brown hair or the 3-year-old who states in one moment that he is happy but five minutes later that he is sad. As we grow older, these self-perceptions become much more organized, detailed, and specific. For example, a 15-year-old is more likely to describe himself in terms of his academic abilities, athletic abilities, social abilities, and talents. For example, he may say, "I'm a decent second baseman, a B student, and I have a lot of friends."

Rogers believed that understanding human personality requires an understanding of how people view themselves and how they interpret events around them.

Underlying Rogers's actualizing tendency is an *organismic valuing process*. Experiences that maintain or enhance the person are valued, and therefore preferred and liked. Experiences that do not maintain or enhance the person are not valued, and therefore are rejected (Sheldon, Arndt, & Houser-Marko, 2003). An infant's valuing process is direct and simple. We know as infants what we like and what we dislike. We value food because it reduces the sensation of hunger. We value being held in a parent's arms because it makes us feel secure. However, such an internal evaluation of our values is soon influenced by our interactions with others and our basic need for love and acceptance.

As children, we come to realize that other important people in our lives (such as parents, teachers, siblings, or other relatives) also place value on our experiences. They communicate to us the "right" and "wrong" ways to think, feel, and behave. Because we desire their love and affection, we incorporate these messages into our valuing process. Experiences that meet these imposed values tend to be incorporated into our self-concept. For example, if a parent has communicated to a child that good grades are valued and the child gets good grades, she may describe herself as a good student. A child may come home every day from school reporting on how well she did in school. This gives the child the opportunity to gain acceptance and love from the parent. On the other hand, suppose the child does not get good grades at school. This child may hide test scores from parents for fear of being rejected and unloved. This example illustrates the enormous influence of others' standards and values on our self-concepts. We may no longer listen to our own internal valuing system but pay more attention to the views and values of loved ones. Our worth and regard are now judged on the basis of the imposed opinions, judgments, and values of others, rather than our own internal organismic valuing process. We have come to see ourselves as others see us.

What determines the degree to which we "listen" to, or incorporate, these parental and other outside norms and standards? For Rogers, it is the degree of **unconditional positive regard**, or acceptance and love with no strings attached, that we receive from others. Our good points as well as bad points are accepted. People accept us and love us for who we are. This does not mean that a person's *actions* always receive approval. For example, suppose a youngster kicks the dog because the dog chewed a cherished toy. A parent can express displeasure at the child's actions, yet still let the child know that the angry behavior is understood and that the child is still loved by the parent despite the behavior. However, if the parent attacks the child's self, calling the child "bad," the parent has now communicated *conditional* positive regard. The child will believe that feeling angry is wrong because feeling angry will lose his parent's love and acceptance. In other words, unconditional positive regard communicates respect for a person's thoughts and feelings.

If a child, especially during the early years of life, experiences unconditional positive regard, he or she is less likely to lose contact with the organismic valuing process established at birth. In this way, the child grows into an adult who chooses to act, feel, or think on the basis of his or her inner evaluations, taking into consideration the effect of his or her behavior on others. For Rogers, this represented a healthy personality. On the other hand, if a child experiences primarily conditional positive regard during these years, he or she is more likely to develop a self-concept that is based on how others see him or her and disregard the inner guiding voice in his or her behavior. Such people think, act, or behave in a certain way in hope of ensuring the continued love and acceptance of others. In such situations, healthy development of the personality is hindered, and psychological discomfort may occur (Assor, Roth, & Deci, 2004).

unconditional positive regard acceptance and love of another's thoughts and feelings without expecting anything in return

The approval (or disapproval) we receive from others influences our self-concept, according to Rogers.

© Jeff Greenberg/PhotoEdit

Contributions and Criticisms of the Humanistic Approach

Many humanistic ideas have been incorporated into individual, family, and group therapy approaches, as we will see in Chapter 14. The humanistic approach has encouraged many people to become more aware of themselves and their interactions with others. However, the humanistic perspective has been criticized for its seemingly naïve and optimistic view of behavior: it assumes that all people are good and are motivated toward good in attaining self-actualization. Critics argue that all people are not necessarily good and pure in their intentions. They believe that humanists underestimate the capacity for evil in some individuals (Coffer & Appley, 1964; Ellis, 1959). Equally problematic is the difficulty in validating through experiments many of the humanistic concepts such as actualizing tendency, organismic valuing process, and unconditional positive regard (Burger, 2004). The major source of data for Rogers's self theory has been under scrutiny as well, as it was derived from clients' self-statements. How reliable and valid are such statements? It's possible that clients did not always present their "true" selves to Rogers, and that as a listener Rogers was biased. As a result, humanistic psychology has not become as major a force in psychology as Maslow once hoped.

Let's Review!

This section presented the humanistic view of personality. For a quick check of your understanding, answer these questions.

1. The humanistic perspective emphasizes the influence of _____ on personality.
   a. unconscious impulses
   b. internal tendencies
   c. an actualizing tendency
   d. environmental and cognitive factors

2. Which of the following elements does Rogers believe promotes self-actualization?
   a. Unconditional positive regard
   b. Esteem
   c. Sympathy
   d. Adaptability

3. SuLing was recently mugged. Since the mugging, she has been suspicious and paranoid. She locks her doors at night and sleeps with a night-light. Maslow would attribute Su-Ling's behavior to _____.
   a. esteem needs
   b. safety needs
   c. belongingness needs
   d. biological needs

Answers 1. c; 2. a; 3. b

Measuring Personality

Learning Objective

- Detail the various methods psychologists use to measure personality and the theoretical perspective that gave rise to each method. Compare the advantages and disadvantages of each measure.

We have described four approaches to personality. Each perspective tends to employ certain tools to measure or assess personality. As with any tool or measuring device, it is important that the test be *reliable* and *valid*. **Reliability** refers to the consistency of a measurement tool. If we were to assess your height as an adult with a tape measure, we would want to get a consistent "reading" every time we measured your height. Personality tests also need to be

reliability the consistency of a test's measurements over time reliable, or yield similar results over time. This reliability will not be perfect as we are not consistent in our behavior at all times. However, personality tests should report similar trends if they are reliable.

Measurement tools like personality tests also need to be valid. **Validity** refers to the ability of a test to measure what it says it is measuring. If a test states that it is measuring your intelligence and it does so by measuring your foot size, this test would not be valid. There is no relationship between foot size and intelligence. Notice that this test would be reliable (that is, yield a consistent measure from time to time), but it does not measure what we think of as intelligence. Therefore, personality tests should measure what we believe personality to be.

Each of the four major perspectives has developed its own way of measuring personality. These measures include *personality inventories, projective tests, rating scales,* and *clinical interviews.*

> **You Asked...**
>
> *How can you tell what kind of personality a person has?*
>
> BRITTANY BRYANT, STUDENT

Personality Inventories: Mark Which One Best Describes You

Personality inventories are objective paper-and-pencil self-report forms. You are typically asked to indicate how well a statement describes you or to answer true or false to a specific statement. For example, in college settings many students have completed the *Myers-Briggs Personality Inventory.* This test details an individual's personality on four different dimensions. In clinical settings, the most frequently used personality inventory is the **Minnesota Multiphasic Personality Inventory (MMPI-2)**.

The MMPI-2 is a 567-item true–false questionnaire that takes about 1 hour to complete. The questions describe a wide range of behaviors (■ TABLE 12.4). The purpose of the MMPI-2 is to identify problem areas of functioning in a person's personality. It is organized into 10 groups of items, called *clinical scales*. These scales measure patterns of responses or traits associated with specific psychological disorders such as depression, paranoia, and schizophrenia. A person's response patterns are reviewed to see whether they resemble the pattern of responses from groups of people who have specific mental health disorders. Interpreting the MMPI-2 involves comparing the test taker's responses to those of the norming population.

As part of its construction, the MMPI-2 was given to thousands of people, called a *norming group*. Individuals in the norming group included people who had no psychological disorders and people who had particular disorders. In this way the test constructors could see how frequently someone without the disorder would respond "true" to these items and how frequently someone with the psychological disorder would respond "true." The first group established the average, or "normal," number of items for each of these clinical scales, whereas the second group gave an indication of what would be considered problematic functioning. A psychologist is interested in examining any areas of your personality that fall outside the normal range. These areas would be considered problem areas of your personality and might suggest issues for therapy. One of the main problems with self-report measures such as the MMPI-2 is the test taker's honesty or truthfulness. For this reason, the MMPI-2 also contains four *validity scales* to assess the truthfulness of the individual's responses.

validity the ability of a test to measure what it says it is measuring

personality inventory objective paper-and-pencil self-report form that measures personality on several dimensions

Minnesota Multiphasic [mul-tee-FAZE-ick] **Personality Inventory (MMPI-2)** a personality inventory that is designed to identify problem areas of functioning in a person's personality

Table 12.4 Sample MMPI-2 Items

I have trouble with my bowel movements.	T	F
I do not sleep well.	T	F
At parties, I sit by myself or with one other person.	T	F
A lot of people have it in for me.	T	F
In school, I was frequently in trouble for acting up.	T	F
I am anxious most of the time.	T	F
I hear strange things that others do not hear.	T	F
I am a very important person.	T	F

FIGURE

12.5   **Sample Rorschach Inkblot**

After being shown an inkblot like this one, the person indicates what he or she sees on the card.

projective test an unstructured and subjective personality test in which an individual is shown an ambiguous stimulus and is asked to describe what he or she sees

Rorschach [ROAR-shock] **inkblot test** a projective personality test consisting of ten ambiguous inkblots in which a person is asked to describe what he or she sees; the person's responses are then coded for consistent themes and issues

Thematic Apperception [Thee-MAT-ick ap-per-SEP-shun] **Test (TAT)** a projective personality test consisting of a series of pictures in which the respondent is asked to tell a story about each scene; the responses are then coded for consistent themes and issues

Projective Tests: Tell Me What You See

Another type of tool used to measure personality, the **projective test**, is unstructured compared to the personality inventory. When taking this test, you are shown an ambiguous image and then asked to describe what you see or to tell a story about the picture. Such tests rely on the idea that whatever stories, motives, or explanations are offered by the person reflect his or her own issues and concerns, projected onto the image.

One of the most famous projective tests is the **Rorschach inkblot test**. The Rorschach test consists of ten inkblots on cards. As each card is presented, you indicate what images you see. Your responses are then coded according to specific guidelines to decrease subjectivity and enhance the validity of the results. A sample card is shown in ■ FIGURE 12.5.

Another widely used projective test is the **Thematic Apperception Test (TAT)**. In the TAT, you are shown images that are not as ambiguous as inkblots yet still allow for a variety of interpretations. You are asked to tell a story about the image, and your responses are then coded for any consistent themes, emotions, or issues. A sample TAT image is depicted in ■ FIGURE 12.6. After being shown this image, a client might relate the following story: "It's a picture of a young man who has been waiting several hours at a park for his girlfriend to arrive. He is tired, anxious, and angry. He is hoping that nothing bad has happened to his girlfriend. He is also hoping that she didn't just stand him up."

The purpose of projective tests is similar to that of personality inventories. Psychologists want to pinpoint healthy and unhealthy areas of functioning in the person. However, unlike personality inventories, projective tests are derived from the psychoanalytic perspective; the images and stories described are thought to reflect underlying unconscious urges and desires. Because projective tests are more subject to the interpretation of the clinician than are personality inventories, coding systems have been devised to decrease variation in interpretation. However, research suggests that they are less reliable than objective tests in measuring personality (Aiken, 1996; Lilienfeld, Wood, & Garb, 2000; T. B. Rogers, 1995). Projective tests are most useful for identifying themes in a person's life or for delineating an individual's problem-solving style.

Rating Scales and Direct Observation

A third type of tool used by psychologists to measure personality is *rating scales*. Rating scales are formatted similarly to checklists. You check off the statements or behaviors that most apply to you. Because the person being evaluated may not answer the statements truthfully, teachers, parents, partners, and clinicians can also complete rating scales on the person being evaluated. These alternate perspectives minimize the self-distortions that are associated with self-report instruments.

Psychologists may also rely on directly observing a client's behavior and interactions with others to assess personality. Closely watching how you behave in particular situations can be helpful in determining what happens before and after your responses. Such information is particularly important to clinicians from a social cognitive approach who want to understand the social or environmental factors that may be influencing problem behavior.

FIGURE

12.6   **Sample Thematic Apperception (TAT) Card**

In taking the TAT, a person is asked to tell a story about a scene such as this one.

YOUR TURN – ACTIVE LEARNING

Psychologists may find rating scales on self-esteem and self-concept useful to understanding how a person perceives reality and the degree to which one's real self is congruent with one's ideal self. Take a moment to complete the self-esteem scale provided in ■ TABLE 12.5.

Table 12.5 Rosenberg Self-Esteem Scale

Below is a list of statements dealing with your general feelings about yourself. If you Strongly Agree, circle SA. If you Agree with the statement, circle A. If you Disagree, circle D. If you Strongly Disagree, circle SD.

		STRONGLY AGREE	AGREE	DISAGREE	STRONGLY DISAGREE
1.	I feel that I'm a person of worth, at least on an equal plane with others.	SA	A	D	SD
2.	I feel that I have a number of good qualities.	SA	A	D	SD
3.	All in all, I am inclined to feel that I am a failure.	SA	A	D	SD
4.	I am able to do things as well as most other people.	SA	A	D	SD
5.	I feel I do not have much to be proud of.	SA	A	D	SD
6.	I take a positive attitude toward myself.	SA	A	D	SD
7.	On the whole, I am satisfied with myself.	SA	A	D	SD
8.	I wish I could have more respect for myself.	SA	A	D	SD
9.	I certainly feel useless at times.	SA	A	D	SD
10.	At times I think I am no good at all.	SA	A	D	SD

Scoring:

For items 1, 2, 4, 6, 7 Strongly Agree=3; Agree=2; Disagree=1; Strongly Disagree=0
For items 3, 5, 8, 9, 10 Strongly Agree=0; Agree=1; Disagree=2; Strongly Disagree=3
The scale ranges from 0 to 30, with 30 indicating the highest score possible. There are no discrete cutoff points for high and low self-esteem. Higher scores indicate more positive feelings toward the self while lower scores indicate more negative feelings toward the self.

Source: Rosenberg, M. (1989). Society and the adolescent self-image. *Middletown, CT: Wesleyan University Press.*

Clinical Interviews

One tool used by all clinical psychologists is the **clinical interview**. This interview typically takes place during the first meeting between the client and the clinician and involves the clinician asking the client questions to identify the client's difficulty in functioning. The format and length of the interview, as well as the questions that are asked during the interview, may differ from clinician to clinician. These differences again relate to the alternate views on personality that were discussed in this chapter. For example, a clinician who favors the social cognitive approach is more likely to ask specific questions about social situations and patterns of thoughts. This clinician may want to know what you were thinking about prior to, during, and after a particular behavior occurred. A humanist is more likely to focus on the client's interpretation and perception of reality. The focus of any clinical interview, however, is to identify as

A clinical interview typically takes place during the first meeting between the client and the clinician. The focus is on identifying as clearly as possible the difficulty in functioning that the person is experiencing.

Zigy Kaluzny/Getty Images

clinical interview the initial meeting between a client and a clinician in which the clinician asks questions to identify the difficulty in functioning that the person is experiencing

clearly as possible the difficulty in functioning that the person is experiencing. This difficulty is often given a name, or diagnosis. The exact nature of these diagnoses is the subject of the next chapter.

This chapter presented four different views of personality: the psychoanalytic perspective, the trait approach, the social cognitive perspective, and the humanistic approach. Rather than debating which of these perspectives is "right," many psychologists prefer instead to see these viewpoints as complementary. Just as a photographer may take the same picture from many different angles, psychologists, too, like to understand personality from varying viewpoints. When taken together, these theories provide a much more complex and richer view of the forces that make us unique than any single perspective could do.

Let's Review!

This section detailed the various methods psychologists use to measure personality. For a quick check of your understanding, answer these questions.

1. Tamara goes to see a clinical psychologist. The psychologist asks her to look at some vague pictures and report what she sees. Most likely Tamara is taking a _____.
   a. personality inventory   c. rating scale
   b. projective test   d. clinical interview

2. The major disadvantage of self-report instruments, such as the MMPI-2, is _____.
   a. the subjective interpretation of the results by the clinician
   b. the respondents may not tell the truth

   c. the scoring criteria are vague and unreliable
   d. there are no norms to compare one's responses against

3. When one goes to a clinical psychologist, the first session is most likely to involve _____.
   a. personality testing   c. hypnosis
   b. a physical examination   d. a clinical interview

Answers 1. b; 2. b; 3. d

Studying THE Chapter

Key Terms

personality (445)
psychoanalytic perspective (446)
conscious level (446)
preconscious level (446)
unconscious level (447)
id (447)

pleasure principle (447)
ego (447)
reality principle (447)
superego (448)
defense mechanism (449)
oral stage (449)

anal stage (449)
phallic stage (450)
Oedipus complex (450)
Electra complex (450)
latency stage (450)
genital stage (450)

personal unconscious (451)
collective unconscious (451)
archetypes (451)
basic anxiety (452)
trait approach (453)
trait (453)
sensation seeker (454)
central traits (455)
secondary traits (455)
cardinal traits (455)
surface traits (456)
source traits (456)
introversion (456)

extraversion (456)
neuroticism (457)
psychoticism (457)
person–situation interaction (460)
social cognitive approach (463)
reciprocal determinism (463)
self-efficacy (464)
locus of control (464)
humanistic approach (465)
self-actualization (466)
actualizing tendency (466)
self-concept (466)
unconditional positive regard (467)

reliability (468)
validity (469)
personality inventory (469)
Minnesota Multiphasic
    Personality Inventory
    (MMPI-2) (469)
projective test (470)
Rorschach inkblot test (470)
Thematic Apperception
    Test (TAT) (470)
clinical interview (471)

What Do You Know? Assess Your Understanding

Test your retention and understanding of the material by answering the following questions.

1. Which perspective suggests that human beings naturally strive for fulfillment and enhancement?
   a. Psychoanalytic perspective
   b. Trait perspective
   c. Humanistic perspective
   d. Social cognitive perspective

2. Meera's friends describe her as warm and giving across most situations. According to Allport, warm and giving are _____ of Meera's.
   a. central traits
   b. secondary traits
   c. cardinal traits
   d. primary traits

3. Which personality perspective emphasizes genetic contributions to personality?
   a. Psychoanalytic perspective
   b. Trait perspective
   c. Humanistic perspective
   d. Social cognitive perspective

4. Timothy feels very confident about his writing abilities. Bandura would say that Timothy has high _____ for his writing.
   a. extraversion
   b. self-efficacy
   c. determinism
   d. self-concept

5. Even though her mother told her not to, Gretchen had a second piece of chocolate cake. Which personality structure, according to Freud, motivated Gretchen's behavior?
   a. Superego
   b. Ego
   c. Id
   d. The preconscious

6. Which of the following is not one of the traits of the five factor theory?
   a. Openness
   b. Extraversion
   c. Conformity
   d. Agreeableness

7. Defense mechanisms are used to handle intrapsychic conflict between which two personality structures?
   a. Id and ego
   b. Id and superego
   c. Ego and superego
   d. The ego and the preconscious

8. Which theory examines the influence of one's environment, behaviors, and thoughts on personality?
   a. Hierarchy of needs
   b. Locus of control
   c. Self theory
   d. Reciprocal determinism

9. The Oedipus and Electra complexes occur during which psychosexual stage?
a. Phallic   c. Anal
b. Latency   d. Genital

10. Which of the following individuals will most likely undergo the most personality change in the future?
a. Carver, a 30-year-old
b. Tracy, a 15-year-old
c. Gene, a 45-year-old
d. Winston, a 60-year-old

11. Melinda believes that her hard work and determination have led to her successful career. According to Rotter, Melinda has a(n) _____.
a. positive self-concept
b. external locus of control
c. internal locus of control
d. overactive superego

12. You take a personality test in which you are asked to look at vague drawings and tell a story about what you see. Most likely you are taking which of the following personality tests?
a. MMPI-2
b. Aptitude test
c. Self-esteem scale
d. TAT

13. Your long-term memories most likely reside in which level of consciousness?
a. Unconscious   c. Preconscious
b. Subconscious   d. Conscious

14. Wally is described as hostile, impulsive, and aggressive. According to Eysenck, Wally is high in _____.
a. extraversion   c. openness
b. neuroticism   d. psychoticism

15. Marley is in high school and very much wants to be a part of the in-crowd. According to Maslow, Marley is trying to fulfill _____ needs.
a. physical   c. belongingness
b. safety   d. esteem

16. Donny's mother is very upset when Donny's grades slip below a B level. Donny feels that he must make good grades in order to receive his mother's love and acceptance. According to Rogers, Donny perceives _____ from his mother.
a. unconditional positive regard
b. conditional positive regard
c. actualizing tendency
d. self-actualization

17. Shanique takes a personality test in which she is asked to solve math problems and draw pictures of animals. This personality test most lacks _____.
a. validity   c. consistency
b. reliability   d. norming

18. In what way did Karen Horney agree with Freud on personality development?
a. Development arises from instinctual conflicts.
b. Personality is the result of psychosexual conflicts.
c. Culture plays a large role in personality development.
d. Early childhood is a significant time for personality development.

19. The humanistic approach has been criticized for _____.
a. not detailing personality development
b. relying too heavily on experimental data
c. its optimistic view that all people are good
d. All of the above

20. Which of the following is *not* a contribution of the psychoanalytic perspective?
a. Stimulated research on sleep and dreaming
b. Stimulated research on coping and health
c. Created personality tests and therapy approaches
d. Experimentation on the unconscious

Answers: 1. c; 2. a; 3. b; 4. b; 5. c; 6. c; 7. b; 8. d; 9. a; 10. b; 11. c; 12. d; 13. c; 14. d; 15. c; 16. b; 17. a; 18. d; 19. c; 20. d.

Online Resources

CENGAGE**NOW**™ **Personalized Study**

www.cengage.com/login

Go to www.cengage.com/login to link to CengageNOW, your online study tool. First take the **Pre-Test** for this chapter to get your **Personalized Study Plan**, which will identify topics you need to review and direct you to online resources. Then take the **Post-Test** to determine what concepts you have mastered and what you still need work on.

  What Is Psychology? Essentials Book Companion Website

www.cengage.com/psychology/pastorino

Visit your book companion website, where you will find more resources to help you study. Resources include learning objectives, Internet exercises, quizzing, flash cards, and a pronunciation glossary.

Look Back AT WHAT YOU'VE LEARNED

Personality is the unique collection of attitudes, emotions, thoughts, habits, impulses, and behaviors that defines how a person typically behaves across situations.

How Does the Psychoanalytic Approach Explain Personality?

- Emphasizes unconscious aspects of personality. It proposes that personality operates at the **conscious**, **preconscious**, and **unconscious** levels.

- According to Freud, personality is comprised of the unconscious **id** that operates according to the **pleasure principle**, the conscious **ego** that operates according to the **reality principle**, and the moral directives of the **superego**.

- For Freud, personality develops through a series of five psychosexual stages (**oral**, **anal**, **phallic**, **latency**, **genital**) that represent a complex interaction between natural sexual urges and our socialization experiences.

- Neo-Freudians such as Jung, Adler, and Horney placed less emphasis on the role of the sexual impulses in motivating behavior.

Hulton Archive/Getty Images

How Does the Trait Approach Explain Personality?

- Attempts to describe personality by identifying the internal **traits**, or tendencies that we have across most situations.

- Allport classified traits into three types: **central**, **cardinal**, and **secondary** traits.

- Cattell's factor analysis of traits yielded 16 **source traits** that could be measured in everyone. Eysenck proposed three universal traits in his PEN model: **psychoticism**, **extraversion**, and **neuroticism**.

- Costa and McCrae's five factor theory proposes five core universal dimensions of personality: openness, conscientiousness, extraversion, agreeableness, and neuroticism (OCEAN).

- Research suggests a complex interaction between genes and the environment in producing personality. Some traits remain stable over the course of adulthood, but situational factors also influence the consistency of traits.

© LWA-Sharie Kennedy/Corbis

WHAT IS Personality, AND HOW Do We MEASURE It?

How Does the Social Cognitive Approach Explain Personality?

- Evaluates environmental and cognitive factors that influence personality.

- Bandura's **reciprocal determinism** speculates that personality is due to the constant interaction between one's environment, one's behavior, and one's thoughts. A critical cognitive element is **self-efficacy**, or the expectation one has for success in a given situation.

- Rotter believes that one's **locus of control**, or one's expectations of whether the outcome of an event is due to internal or external forces, influences personality.

- The **social cognitive approach** is comprehensive, has many applications, and is easily tested experimentally.

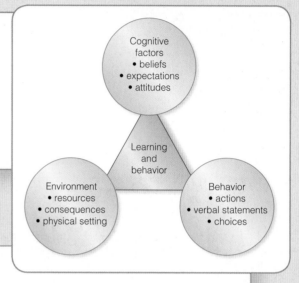

Cognitive factors
- beliefs
- expectations
- attitudes

Learning and behavior

Environment
- resources
- consequences
- physical setting

Behavior
- actions
- verbal statements
- choices

How Does the Humanistic Approach Explain Personality?

© Roger Ressmeyer/Corbis

- Emphasizes one's tendency to strive toward uniqueness and **self-actualization**.

- Maslow believed that the pathway to self-actualization lies in fulfilling a hierarchy of needs, with physical needs at the bottom and psychological needs at the top.

- Rogers' self theory emphasizes how one's **self-concept**, or perception of self, is influenced by the standards and values of others, most notably the degree to which we perceive and receive **unconditional positive regard** from others.

- The **humanistic approach** promotes self-awareness and positive interactions with others, and its ideas have been incorporated into several therapy approaches.

How Do We Measure Personality?

- Tools that assess personality should be **reliable** and **valid**.

- **Personality inventories** such as the **MMPI-2** are objective paper-and-pencil self-report forms that can reliably detail a person's traits if answered honestly.

- **Projective tests** such as the **Rorschach inkblot test** and the **Thematic Apperception Test** are unstructured tests in which a person is shown an ambiguous image and asked to describe it. A person's responses are believed to reflect underlying unconscious concerns, according to the psychoanalytic perspective.

- Psychologists may also use rating scales and direct observation to measure behaviors and interactions with others.

- The focus of the **clinical interview** is to identify the difficulty in functioning that a person is experiencing.

13

WHAT ARE Psychological Disorders, AND How CAN WE UNDERSTAND Them?

After years of working at a bank, Tawnya Brown decided to enroll in college to pursue a nursing degree. One of the first classes she took was a general psychology course. Although Tawnya could see the usefulness of some course topics such as development or biology, she didn't think that learning about psychological disorders would be of much value—it's not like she was going into psychiatry or counseling. Since then she has noticed how much she relies on this information in several areas of her life.

Tawnya serves on a hospital advisory board as an advocate for patients, many of whom have psychological disorders. By understanding the nature of these disorders, Tawnya can make sure that appropriate mental health services are included as a part of their patient care. Tawnya also volunteers as a facilitator for a women's support group in the community. Many of these women have experienced significant trauma in their lives and as a result experience depression and/or abuse drugs. Tawnya's knowledge of psychological disorders helps her better understand these women. She can now recognize the different symptoms of the psychological disorders and see the impact of negative life experiences on mental health.

This chapter outlines several major categories of psychological disorders and explains the symptoms used to diagnose each disorder. For each type of disorder, we will consider the possible reasons why a person behaves this way. Although the research presented may seem overwhelming at times, keep in mind that these explanations are closely tied to topics with which you are already familiar. For example, many of the symptoms of psychological disorders are physical in nature, focusing on brain functioning, neurotransmitters, hormones, and genetics— biological factors that were introduced in Chapter 2. Many of the symptoms also focus

Jean-Noel Reichel/Getty Images

© Ellen Pastorino

Tawnya Brown's knowledge of psychological disorders has helped her in several areas of her life.

on psychological concepts such as learning, cognitions, personality, and emotions—again, topics that have been addressed in previous chapters. Furthermore, we will see that certain disorders are more common among certain segments of the population. Your familiarity with previous discussions on gender, race, and culture will assist you in understanding the influence of these social factors on mental health.

What Is Abnormal Behavior?

Learning Objectives

- Identify the criteria that psychologists use for determining abnormal behavior.

- Compare and contrast the varying perspectives on explaining psychological disorders, and formulate a biopsychosocial or integrated perspective to explain a particular behavior.

Psychologists use four main criteria when distinguishing normal from abnormal behavior.

1. **Statistical Infrequency.** If we judge normal as what most people do, then one criterion that may be used to gauge abnormality is engaging in a behavior a lot less or more frequently than others. For example, it is considered crucial for survival to ingest a minimum amount of food per day. People who engage in this behavior a lot less than everyone else—as in the case of people with anorexia—would qualify as abnormal. Persons with autism engage in social communication far less than everyone else does. As such, their behavior may be considered abnormal. Statistical infrequency can also include engaging in a behavior that most people do not. For example, believing that you are from another planet or galaxy is a thought that most people do not have. It represents an unusual, or statistically infrequent, thought and therefore may be judged as abnormal. However, there are problems with using the criterion of statistical infrequency. For example, only one person holds the record for running a mile the fastest; this person is certainly atypical but not necessarily abnormal.

2. **Violation of Social Norms.** Another measure of abnormality is to assess whether the behavior violates social norms of how people are supposed to behave. However, it is extremely important to emphasize that social norms vary widely across cultures, within cultures, and across historical times. What is considered socially acceptable in San Francisco may be considered unacceptable in Keokuk, Iowa. Similarly, what was deemed unacceptable in the 1950s may be considered acceptable today. For example, changing views on homosexuality in part influenced the American Psychiatric Association to remove homosexuality from its list of psychological disorders in 1973. Because social norms vary so widely, judging the abnormality of behavior on this criterion alone is especially problematic.

3. **Personal Distress.** This criterion focuses on whether a behavior causes great personal distress to the individual. Often people seek treatment when a behavior causes such suffering. However, problems can also arise from judging a behavior by this criterion alone. A person may abuse one or more people and not be distressed by this behavior, even though it causes great harm to others.

4. **Level of Impairment.** Because each of these criteria by itself is not adequate in defining abnormality, many psychologists find that combining them and assessing whether a behavior *interferes with a person's ability to function and/or causes distress to oneself or others* may best define abnormality (Wakefield, 1992).

Autism is a childhood disorder that is marked by disordered communication.

© Michael Macor/San Francisco Chronicle/Corbis

Prevalence of Psychological Disorders

An estimated 26% of Americans 18 and older will suffer from a diagnosable psychological disorder in any given year (Kessler, Chiu, Demler, & Walters, 2005). Lifetime prevalence estimates are quite a bit higher, with 46% of Americans meeting the criteria for a mental health disorder at some time in their lives (Kessler, Berglund, Demler, Jin, & Walters, 2005; see ■ FIGURE 13.1). Psychological disorders are the leading cause of disability in the United States and Canada for people between the ages of 15 and 44 (World Health Organization, 2004). Although there is little overall gender difference in the lifetime risk of a psychological disorder, males and females do show differences in the types of psychological disorders they are more likely to experience (Kessler et al., 1994; see ■ FIGURE 13.2). Consequently, it is likely that you or someone close to you will at some time experience a mental health disorder. Being familiar with psychology's current understanding of such behavior may help you manage such a situation.

> ### You Asked...
> *What are the most common psychological disorders for men and women?*   KIARA SUAREZ, STUDENT

Explaining Psychological Disorders: Perspectives Revisited

> ### You Asked...
> *What are the causes of psychological disorders?* DAVID MELENDEZ, STUDENT

Since the beginning of time, doctors and philosophers have tried to understand why people behave abnormally. Today, Western cultures predominantly lean toward three main approaches for understanding psychological disorders: biological theories, psychological theories, and social or cultural theories.

FIGURE

13.1 Lifetime Prevalence of Psychological Disorders

Almost half of U.S. adults will suffer from a psychological disorder at some time in their lives.

(Source: Kessler, Berglund, et. al., 2005)

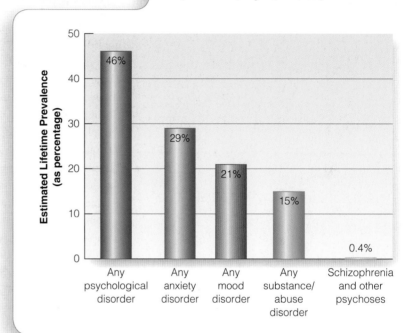

FIGURE

13.2 Prevalence of Depression, Anxiety, Substance Abuse, and Antisocial Personality Disorder in Women and Men

Males and females differ in the types of psychological disorders they are more likely to experience.

(Source: Kessler et al., 1994)

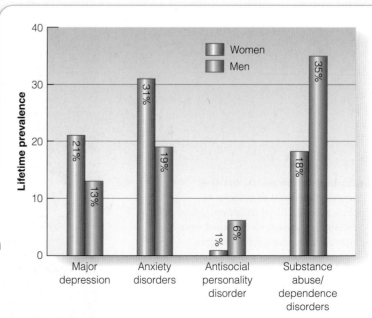

BIOLOGICAL THEORIES: THE MEDICAL MODEL

Biological theories attribute abnormal behavior to some physical process: genetics, an imbalance in hormones or neurotransmitters, or some brain or bodily dysfunction. This perspective is also known as the **medical model** because psychological disorders are viewed as similar to physical diseases. As such, they can be diagnosed, treated, or cured in much the same way as other physical illnesses by prescribing medications or through surgery.

PSYCHOLOGICAL THEORIES: HUMANE TREATMENT AND PSYCHOLOGICAL PROCESSES

Psychological theories attribute abnormal behavior to internal or external stressors. Recall from the previous chapter on personality that four predominant perspectives resulted, which we briefly review here.

- **The psychoanalytic perspective.** This perspective attributes abnormal behavior to unresolved unconscious conflicts. According to Freud, psychological disorders result from the conflict between the unconscious sexual and aggressive instinctual desires of the id and the outward demands of society. Newer theories, referred to as psychodynamic theories, developed by Freud's followers such as Alfred Adler and Karen Horney, downplay the role of sexual and aggressive instincts and instead emphasize the role of the ego and interpersonal relationships in maintaining or restoring psychological health.

- **The social learning perspective.** Learning theorists (particularly B. F. Skinner and his successors) explain abnormal behavior as a result of the same learning processes that produce normal behavior—classical conditioning, operant conditioning, and social learning. A person's responses to stimuli in the environment and the consequences of these behaviors are what lead to abnormal behavior. A person's past learning and modeling along with current experiences can explain psychological disorders.

- **The cognitive perspective.** This perspective emphasizes the role of thoughts, expectations, assumptions, and other mental processes in abnormal behavior. Think about the little voice inside of you that comments on your behavior. Does it encourage you to do well, or does it criticize you for your stupidity? Is it possible that such internal messages influence your behavior? The cognitive perspective maintains that they do.

- **The humanistic perspective.** Humanists like Carl Rogers see abnormal behavior as resulting from a distorted perception of the self and reality. When people lose touch with their personal values and their sense of self, or when they fail to fulfill their basic

medical model perspective that views psychological disorders as similar to physical diseases; they result from biological disturbances and can be diagnosed, treated, and cured like other physical illnesses

Poverty and adverse environments are important sociocultural factors that must be looked at when evaluating abnormal behavior.

© Owen Franken/Corbis

biological and psychological needs, they cannot attain self-actualization. Instead, they experience personal distress and are more likely to engage in maladaptive behavior.

SOCIOCULTURAL THEORIES: THE INDIVIDUAL IN CONTEXT

Sociocultural theories emphasize social or cultural factors that may play a role in psychological disorders. Such a perspective argues that internal biological and psychological processes can be understood only in the context of the larger society and culture that shape and influence people's behavior. Abnormal behavior, therefore, can be fully understood only when social factors such as age, race, gender, and socioeconomic status are taken into account. In addition, social conditions such as poverty, discrimination, and environmental stressors must be looked at when evaluating abnormal behavior.

A BIOPSYCHOSOCIAL MODEL: INTEGRATING PERSPECTIVES

No single theory or perspective is correct. It is only by integrating all the perspectives that our explanations of abnormality become comprehensive. We often hear in the popular press and in television commercials that a psychological disorder such as depression or anxiety is caused by "a specific gene" or "a chemical imbalance." But such reports are too simplistic to explain the complexity of mental illness. Most psychological disorders result from a combination of biological, psychological, and social factors (hence the name of the *biopsychosocial model*); they do not have just one cause.

For example, as we will soon see, people diagnosed with major depression often show changes in brain chemistry—a biological factor. They also are likely to engage in a negative pattern of thinking, a psychological factor. In addition, major depression is more likely to be diagnosed in women—a sociocultural factor. Current research in psychology focuses on understanding how these forces operate together, much like the way pieces of a jigsaw puzzle fit together.

Although our understanding of the *causes* of abnormality may be in its infancy, we can *describe* fairly well the specific behaviors that accompany psychological disorders. Such descriptors allow us to diagnosis a mental health disorder in a person who is having difficulty functioning.

Let's Review!

In this section, we outlined the criteria used to define abnormal behavior, indicated the prevalence of psychological disorders, and reviewed perspectives on explaining abnormal behavior. For a quick check of your understanding, answer these questions.

1. Susan enjoys eating garbage when she is hungry. By which criteria can Susan's behavior be considered abnormal?
   a. Danger to others
   b. Violates social norms
   c. Personal distress
   d. All of the above

2. Judging abnormality by social norms is especially problematic because social norms _____.
   a. may be atypical or rare, but not abnormal
   b. cause great distress to the individual
   c. interfere with a person's ability to function
   d. vary widely across and within cultures

3. What is the likelihood that you or someone close to you will be diagnosed with a psychological disorder sometime in your life?
   a. 15%
   b. 26%
   c. 46%
   d. 75%

4. Dr. Kwan believes that Ken's abnormal behavior has resulted from a distorted sense of self and a loss of personal values. Dr. Kwan is adopting which perspective?
   a. Humanistic
   b. Psychoanalytic
   c. Learning
   d. Cognitive

5. Environmental conditions such as poverty, discrimination, and violent crime are most likely to be considered important causes of abnormal behavior by which perspective?
   a. Psychoanalytic
   b. Sociocultural
   c. Learning
   d. Supernatural

Answers 1. b; 2. d; 3. c; 4. a; 5. b

The *DSM* Model for Classifying Abnormal Behavior

- Describe the nature of the *DSM* model, and identify its strengths and weaknesses.

> ## You Asked...
>
> What do psychologists look at in order to diagnose someone with a psychological disorder?
>
> CARLA BELLIARD, STUDENT

In 1952, the American Psychiatric Association (APA) published a book listing the symptoms that must be shown for a person to be diagnosed with a specific psychological disorder. More than 50 years later, the **Diagnostic and Statistical Manual of Mental Disorders (DSM)** is in its fourth edition, published in 1994. In 2000, the APA revised the text (but not the criteria) to clarify the diagnosis of some psychological disorders. This most recent edition, known as the *DSM-IV-TR*, lists specific and concrete criteria for diagnosing nearly 400 disorders in children, adolescents, and adults. It also indicates the length of time that a person must show these symptoms to qualify for a diagnosis. These criteria require that the symptoms interfere with the person's ability to function, adopting the maladaptive criterion that we discussed at the start of this chapter and that is accepted by many professionals today. However, the current version of the DSM does not speculate as to the causes of the individual's behavior—it is *atheoretical*. This atheoretical position underscores the complex nature of the causes of mental illness.

The *Diagnostic and Statistical Manual (DSM)* describes the specific symptoms that must be present in order for someone to be diagnosed with a specific psychological disorder.

A Multidimensional Evaluation

> ## You Asked...
>
> What types of mental health disorders are there? KATIRIA MEJIA, STUDENT

With the third edition of the *DSM*, published in 1980, clinicians began to evaluate patients along five dimensions or *axes*, listed in ■ TABLE 13.1. Notice that Axis I includes 15 major categories of psychological disorders. These disorders are the focus of this chapter and are listed in ■ TABLE 13.2. The multiaxial system of the *DSM* attempts to provide as comprehensive a picture as possible of a person's behavior.

How Good Is the *DSM* Model?

How *reliable* and *valid* is the DSM model? Recall from Chapter 12 that *reliability* refers to the consistency of a measurement system. We would expect two different clinicians to give a similar judgment or a consistent rating when presented with the same symptoms. Similar diagnoses should also be made when different people exhibit the same symptoms.

Validity refers to how well a rating system does what it was intended to do; it refers to the accuracy of the test. We would expect that the DSM model should be accurate in diagnosing people who are having difficulty functioning. In addition, it should be accurate in the label it applies to a person's condition. People who are depressed should be diagnosed as depressed, and people addicted to drugs should be diagnosed as having a substance abuse problem.

The numerous revisions of the DSM have attempted to improve its reliability and validity. As a result, the reliability and validity for many of the Axis I clinical disorders are very high (Brown, DiNardo, Lehman, & Campbell, 2001; Foa & Kozak, 1995; Hasin, Hatzenbuehler,

Diagnostic and Statistical Manual of Mental Disorders (DSM) a book published by the APA that lists the criteria for close to 400 psychological disorders

Keyes, & Ogburn, 2006; Lahey et al., 2004). However, the reliability of Axis II personality disorders is considered extremely low, calling into question the validity of diagnosing the personality disorders (Jablensky, 2002; Livesley, Jang, & Vernon, 1998; Widiger, 2003; Zanarini et al., 2000). Future revisions of the DSM model will need to address such inadequacies. The preparatory work for the next edition of the DSM (*DSM-V*) has begun, and it is due to be published around 2011 or later.

Having a standard system such as the DSM does not guarantee an accurate diagnosis. Making diagnostic judgments will always involve some subjectivity and personal bias on the part of the clinician, as people's symptoms often do not fit neatly into one category. Biases having to do with gender, race, or culture—whether conscious or unconscious—can also skew a diagnosis (Hartung & Widiger, 1998; Jane, Oltmanns, South, & Turkheimer, 2007; Skodol & Bender, 2003; Widiger, 1998; Widiger & Chaynes, 2003).

Critics of the DSM model also point out the possible negative effects of labeling someone with a psychological disorder (Baumann, 2007; Grover, 2005). A diagnostic label may serve as a *self-fulfilling prophecy*, encouraging a person to behave in a way that is consistent with the disorder. Others in the person's environment may also treat the person in a way that encourages the symptoms of the disorder. We as a society tend to treat people with any diagnostic label negatively, perhaps increasing their maladaptive functioning through prejudice and discrimination. Such negative treatment may persist even after the person's behavior returns to normal (Rosenhan, 1973; Szasz, 1987).

Table 13.1 *DSM-IV-TR* Diagnostic Axes

Axis I	
CLINICAL DISORDERS	Major categories of mental disorders, including depression, anxiety disorders, phobias, amnesia, substance abuse, and schizophrenia. (See Table 13.2.)
Axis II	
PERSONALITY DISORDERS; MENTAL RETARDATION	Lifelong conditions that negatively affect a person's ability to function. Divided into two major classes: *mental retardation* and *personality disorders*. (See Table 13.6.)
Axis III	
GENERAL MEDICAL CONDITIONS	Physical problems or conditions—such as cancer diagnosis and treatment, diabetes, and arthritis—that may influence the person's mental health and that must also be considered when medication is prescribed.
Axis IV	
PSYCHOSOCIAL AND ENVIRONMENTAL PROBLEMS	*Psychosocial* problems might include problems holding a job or staying in school, or lack of social support. *Environmental* problems might include physical or sexual abuse, or experiencing a traumatic event.
Axis V	
GLOBAL ASSESSMENT FUNCTIONING	A numerical scale for evaluating the person's level of functioning. A rating of 90 indicates a person who is functioning very well in all areas of life, has minimal symptoms, if any, and is experiencing only everyday problems. At a rating of 50, a person shows serious symptoms or one or more problems with relationships, work, or school, including possible suicidal thoughts and obsessional behavior.

Table 13.2 *DSM-IV-TR* Axis I Major Categories of Clinical Disorders

AXIS I MAJOR CATEGORY	SOME INCLUDED DISORDERS	EXAMPLES
Disorders usually first diagnosed in infancy, childhood, or adolescence	• Learning disorders • Pervasive developmental disorders • Disruptive behavior and attention deficit disorders • Tic disorders • Communication disorders	Attention deficit disorder, autism, enuresis (bedwetting), stuttering, difficulty in academic skills
Delirium, dementia, amnesia, and other cognitive disorders	• Deliria • Amnesic disorders • Dementias	Delirium (due to a general medical condition or substance induced), dementia (Alzheimer's), amnesia (due to a general medical condition or substance induced)
Substance-related disorders (see Chapter 4)	• Alcohol use disorders • Inhalant use disorders • Cocaine use disorders • Polysubstance use disorders	Alcoholism, cocaine or crack addiction, use of inhalants (sniffing glue or paint)
Schizophrenia and other psychotic disorders (see Table 13.3)	• Schizophrenia • Delusional disorder • Brief psychotic disorder (1 major symptom of psychosis that lasts less than 1 month; often in reaction to a stressor) • Psychotic disorder due to a general medical condition	Paranoid type, catatonic
Mood disorders	• Depressive disorders • Substance-induced mood • Bipolar disorders disorder	Major depressive disorder, dysthymic disorder, bipolar disorder, cyclothymic disorder
Anxiety disorders (see You Review 13.1)	• Panic disorder • Obsessive-compulsive disorder • Agoraphobia without • Posttraumatic stress disorder history of panic disorder • Generalized anxiety disorder • Specific phobia (simple phobia)	Panic disorder without agoraphobia, acrophobia
Somatoform disorders (see Table 13.5)	• Conversion disorder • Body dysmorphic disorder • Hypochondriasis • Pain disorder	
Dissociative disorders (see Table 13.4)	• Dissociative amnesia • Dissociative identity disorder • Dissociative fugue	
Sexual and gender identity disorders	• Sexual dysfunction • Gender identity disorder • Paraphilias	Sexual aversion disorder, male erectile disorder, fetishism, pedophilia
Eating disorders (see Chapter 8)	• Anorexia nervosa • Bulimia nervosa	Binge eating disorder
Sleep disorders (see Chapter 4)	• Primary sleep disorders • Dyssomnia not otherwise specified	Sleepwalking disorder, narcolepsy, primary insomnia
Factitious disorders	• Factitious disorder (deliberately faking a physical or psychological disorder)	
Impulse control disorders not elsewhere classified	• Kleptomania (recurrent failure to control the urge to steal things that are not needed) • Pyromania (recurrent failure to control the urge to set fires) • Pathological gambling	
Adjustment disorder	• Adjustment disorder with anxiety • Adjustment disorder with disturbance of conduct (maladaptive reactions to a known stressor such as a family crisis that begins within 3 months of the stressor but does not last longer than 6 months)	
Other conditions that may be a focus of clinical attention	• Medication-induced movement disorders • Relational problems • Problems related to abuse or neglect	Parent–child relational problem, occupational problem, borderline intellectual functioning

Reprinted with permission from the Diagnostic and Statistical Manual of Mental Disorders, *Fourth Edition, Text Revision, Copyright 2000. American Psychiatric Association.*

The DSM model is not perfect, and can provide only a general description of the problem a person is experiencing. It does not take into account the uniqueness of each individual, nor can it tell us how this person will behave in the future. The effects of labeling a person's disorder should also be kept in mind as we review some of the psychological disorders, starting with the anxiety disorders.

Let's Review!

This section presented the general structure of the DSM model and reviewed its strengths and weaknesses. For a quick check of your understanding, answer these questions.

1. The purpose of the DSM is to _____.
   a. explain the causes of psychological disorders
   b. describe the symptoms of psychological disorders
   c. indicate the frequency of psychological disorders
   d. prescribe treatment methods for psychological disorders

2. The DSM model relies mainly on which criterion of abnormality?
   a. Statistical infrequency
   b. Violation of social norms
   c. Inability to function
   d. Mental insanity

3. Which of the following is *not* information gained by using the multiaxial system of the current DSM?
   a. Presence of mental retardation
   b. Degree of social support
   c. Medical conditions
   d. Future behavior

Answers 1. b; 2. c; 3. d

Anxiety Disorders: It's Not Just "Nerves"

Learning Objective

- Distinguish among the symptoms of the five anxiety disorders, and discuss our current understanding of the causes of anxiety disorders.

We all experience anxiety from time to time. Many students are anxious when they have to make an oral presentation. Other people are nervous when they have to meet new people or fly in an airplane. In these examples, however, the anxiety tends to decrease once the situation is over. People with **anxiety disorders** are different in that they experience chronic anxiety that seriously interferes with their ability to function.

Components of the Anxiety Disorders

Typically, anxiety disorders can be characterized by four components: physical, cognitive, emotional, and behavioral. These components interact powerfully, creating an unpleasant experience of fear or dread, although there may not be a specific fear-producing stimulus present.

The physical components of anxiety include dizziness, elevated heart rate and blood pressure, muscle tension, sweating palms, and dry mouth. These physical symptoms stem from the activation of the sympathetic nervous system (Chapter 2). The hormonal system is also activated as adrenalin is released into the bloodstream. Recall that this is referred to as the fight-or-flight response. This fight-or-flight response occurs every time we perceive a threat in our environment.

anxiety disorder a disorder marked by excessive apprehension that seriously interferes with a person's ability to function

Our bodies are designed to react to realistic threats in our environment, but people with anxiety disorders have concerns that are unrealistic and disproportionate to the amount of harm that could occur. Cognitive components of anxiety may include worrying, fearing loss of control, exaggerating (in one's mind) the danger of a situation, exhibiting paranoia, or being extremely wary and watchful of people and events. These thoughts may lead to emotional reactions such as a sense of dread, terror, panic, irritability, or restlessness. These thoughts and emotions propel the person to behave in ways meant to cope with the anxiety.

Coping with abnormal anxiety may include escaping or fleeing from the situation, behaving aggressively, "freezing" such that they cannot move, or avoiding the situation in the future. Again, these symptoms are so intense that they interfere with people's ability to function and disrupt the quality of their lives.

Types of Anxiety Disorders

You Asked...

What are the different types of anxiety disorders? KAYLA CAMPANA, STUDENT

Approximately 18% of Americans over 18 years of age are diagnosed with an anxiety disorder in a given year (Kessler, Chiu, et al., 2005). African Americans have a lower lifetime risk of anxiety disorders than European Americans and Hispanic Americans (Breslau, Kendler, Su, Gaxiola-Aguilar, & Kessler, 2005). We will discuss five anxiety disorders: *generalized anxiety disorder, panic disorder, phobic disorder, obsessive-compulsive disorder,* and *posttraumatic stress disorder* (see ■ FIGURE 13.3).

generalized anxiety disorder (GAD)
an anxiety disorder characterized by chronic, constant worry in almost all situations

GENERALIZED ANXIETY DISORDER (GAD)

Some people are anxious all the time in almost all situations. These individuals may be diagnosed with **generalized anxiety disorder (GAD)**. Symptoms of GAD include excessive anxiety, worry, and difficulty in controlling such worries. The person may be easily fatigued, restless, and irritable, and may experience difficulty concentrating or sleeping (APA, 2000a). The worrying and anxiety are chronic; many people report having felt this way their entire lives. They worry not only about major issues, such as which car or house to buy, their children's health, or their job performance, but also about minor issues such as being late, wearing the right outfit, or what to make for dinner. It is estimated that about 3% of American adults experience GAD in any given year (Kessler, Chiu, et al., 2005). European Americans are at higher risk of GAD than African Americans and Hispanic Americans (Breslau et al., 2006).

PANIC DISORDER

Imagine that you are attending a party given by a good friend. When you arrive at the party, a feeling of panic suddenly overwhelms you. Your heart begins to pound, you hear ringing in your ears, your skin feels tingly and numb, and it becomes harder and harder to breathe. These are common symptoms that occur during a *panic attack,* a short but intense episode of severe anxiety. As many as 30–40% of young adults in the United States report occasional panic attacks (Ehlers, 1995; King, Gullone, Tonge, & Ollendick, 1993). However, when panic attacks are more common, and a person begins to fear

FIGURE

13.3

Prevalence of Anxiety Disorders in a Given Year

Among adults 18 or older, social and specific phobias are the most commonly diagnosed anxiety disorders in any given year because the age of onset for phobias is typically earlier than for other anxiety disorders.

(Source: Kessler, Chiu, et al., 2005)

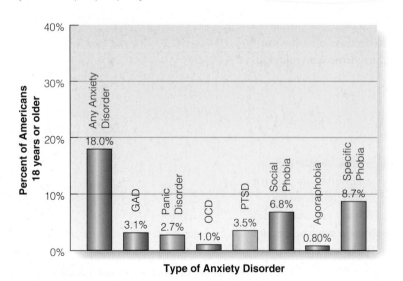

having panic attacks to the extent that it interferes with the ability to function, a diagnosis of **panic disorder** may be given (APA, 2000a).

It is estimated that between 1.5% and 4% of people will develop panic disorder at some time in their lives (APA, 2000a). It typically develops in late adolescence or early adulthood, and is twice as common in women as in men (Craske & Barlow, 2001; Kessler, Berglund, et al., 2005). African Americans tend to have a lower risk of panic disorder than European Americans and Hispanic Americans (Breslau et al., 2006).

People with panic disorder often feel so overwhelmed by the feelings of panic that they think they are having a heart attack or a seizure. They may believe that they are "going crazy" or going to die, and many seek medical attention to find out what is wrong with them. The panic attacks may occur frequently or only sporadically. Most people with panic disorder cannot identify any specific thing that they were doing or thinking at the time that might have triggered the attack. However, when a panic attack occurs, the same situation may then trigger a future attack. Fear of having another panic attack may lead to **agoraphobia**, or fear of being in places from which escape may be difficult or where help may not be available if one were to experience panic. People affected with agoraphobia avoid any place—the mall, the grocery store, or the theater—in which they believe a panic attack may occur. They may also fear that no one will help them, or that they may embarrass themselves. Such fears can leave people housebound for years. At least 75% of those who suffer from agoraphobia are women (Barlow, 2002). Note that people without panic disorder can experience agoraphobia (Eaton & Keyl, 1990). When agoraphobia occurs in the absence of panic disorder, it is characterized as a phobic disorder, our next topic of discussion.

Phobic Disorders

All of us have fears. Some of us get anxious when we think of or see a snake or a spider. Others may fear public speaking or eating in public. As children, we may have been afraid of the dark or the dentist. These are normal fears. However, when our fears become so intense that they cause severe anxiety, possibly even panic attacks that interfere with our ability to function, then a diagnosis of **phobic disorder** is made (APA, 2000a). We have already mentioned one type of phobic disorder, *agoraphobia*. Two other types of phobic disorders are *specific phobias* and *social phobias*.

Specific phobias involve a persistent fear and avoidance of a specific object or situation—animals, heights, bridges—or other specific stimuli. These are the most common phobias, affecting approximately 8% of American adults at some time in their lives (Kessler, Chiu, et al., 2005). Specific phobias typically begin in childhood (Kessler, Berglund, et al., 2005).

Social phobias include an irrational, persistent fear of being negatively evaluated by others in a social situation. A person with a social phobia may have an extreme fear of embarrassment or humiliation. This may include fear of public speaking, fear of eating or undressing in front of others, or fear of using public restrooms. Social phobias tend to develop in the early preschool years and in adolescence, and are somewhat more likely to develop in women than in men (Lang & Stein, 2001; Kessler, Berglund, et al., 2005; Turk, Heimberg, & Hope, 2001). African Americans and Hispanic Americans tend to have a lower lifetime risk of social phobias than European Americans (Breslau et al., 2006).

People with phobic disorders typically recognize that their fears are irrational, but they cannot stop the overwhelming anxiety they feel when faced with the feared object or situation. People with agoraphobia are more likely to seek

panic disorder an anxiety disorder characterized by intense fear and anxiety in the absence of danger that is accompanied by strong physical symptoms

agoraphobia [agg-or-uh-FOE-bee-uh] an excessive fear of being in places from which escape might be difficult or where help might not be available if one were to experience panic

phobic [FOE-bick] **disorder** an anxiety disorder characterized by an intense fear of a specific object or situation

specific phobia a persistent fear and avoidance of a specific object or situation

social phobia an irrational, persistent fear of being negatively evaluated by others in a social situation

For many college students, giving a speech or presentation is an anxiety-producing event.

Barbara Stitzer/Photo Edit

treatment than are people with specific or social phobias, perhaps because agoraphobia is more likely to severely impair normal functioning (Kessler, Stein, & Berglund, 1998).

OBSESSIVE-COMPULSIVE DISORDER (OCD)

Obsessions are recurrent thoughts or images that intrude on a person's consciousness or awareness. **Compulsions** are repetitive behaviors that a person feels a strong urge to perform. All of us experience intrusive thoughts and strong urges. For example, you leave your house in the morning to go to school or work. On the way, the thought pops into your head that you left the coffeepot on, or that you forgot to lock the front door. Immediately, thoughts of the house on fire or ransacked by thieves follow. Many of us feel compelled to turn the car around to check that everything is okay. However, what if this scenario occurred each and every time you got in the car, and you spent hours going back and forth to make sure that everything was fine? In such a case, you might be diagnosed with **obsessive-compulsive disorder (OCD)**.

Obsessive-compulsive disorder is an anxiety disorder in which a person experiences recurrent obsessions or compulsions that he or she feels cannot be controlled (APA, 2000a). Obsessions often center on dirt and contamination, doing harm to oneself or others, sexual thoughts, or repeated doubts (such as not having locked the house). Common compulsions include cleaning, checking, counting things, or arranging and straightening things in a particular fashion. The compulsions are often performed with the hope of preventing the obsessive thoughts or making them go away. However, performing these "rituals" provides only temporary relief. Not performing the rituals increases the person's anxiety.

Recurrent obsessions cause great personal distress, and compulsions can be time-consuming and in some cases harmful—as when a person washes his or her hands so frequently that they bleed. It is estimated that between 1% and 3% of individuals will develop OCD at some time in their lives, and in the United States, the rates are higher among European Americans than among Hispanic Americans and African Americans (Hewlett, 2000; Kessler, Chiu, et al., 2005). Males and females are equally affected by this disorder (Karno & Golding, 1991).

POSTTRAUMATIC STRESS DISORDER (PTSD)

Another type of anxiety disorder is **posttraumatic stress disorder (PTSD)**. PTSD develops after exposure to a terrifying event or ordeal in which grave physical harm occurred or was threatened. Traumatic events may include:

- Violent personal assaults such as rape, physical abuse, or sexual abuse
- Natural or human-caused disasters such as an earthquake, a hurricane, a terrorist attack, or an outbreak of an infectious disease
- Military combat
- Events that anyone might experience—the sudden, unexpected death of a loved one or witnessing a violent crime or a deadly traffic accident

A diagnosis of PTSD requires that the person repeatedly reexperience the ordeal in the form of distressing memories, nightmares, frightening thoughts, or flashback episodes, especially when exposed to situations that are similar to the original trauma. For example, a car backfire might trigger a flashback to a combat trauma or being the victim of an armed robbery. Anniversaries of the event also can trigger symptoms. In addition, people diagnosed with PTSD may experience emotional numbness or withdrawal from themselves or others such that they lose interest in usual activities or are regarded as distant and emotionally unavailable. Lastly, people with PTSD are always on guard—showing *hypervigilance*, having difficulty concentrating, or having difficulty sleeping (APA, 2000a). They may experience depression, anxiety, irritability, or outbursts of anger; physical symptoms such as headaches, dizziness, or chest pain; or feelings of intense guilt. For some people, such symptoms can seriously disrupt the ability to work or to meet social and family obligations.

obsession a recurrent thought or image that intrudes on a person's awareness

compulsion repetitive behavior that a person feels a strong urge to perform

obsessive–compulsive disorder (OCD) an anxiety disorder involving a pattern of unwanted intrusive thoughts and the urge to engage in repetitive actions

posttraumatic stress disorder (PTSD) an anxiety disorder, characterized by distressing memories, emotional numbness, and hypervigilance, that develops after exposure to a traumatic event

Approximately 3.5% of U.S. adults are diagnosed with PTSD in a given year (Kessler, Chiu, et al., 2005). More than twice as many females as males experience PTSD following exposure to a trauma (J. R. T. Davidson, 2000; Tolin & Foa, 2006). Women's higher PTSD risk has been attributed to a number of biological, psychological, and social factors. For example, sex differences in the responses of the *amygdala*, the brain structure that mediates fear, have been documented (Hamann, 2005). Moreover, women are more likely to perceive threat and loss of control than men—psychological factors that may influence the risk of PTSD (Olff, Langeland, Draijer, & Gersons, 2007). Women are more likely to be victims of sexual abuse and experience these traumas at younger ages than men—social factors that also play a role in PTSD (Cortina & Kubiak, 2006; Olff et al., 2007; Tolin & Foa, 2006).

Soldiers (male or female) are also at high risk for developing PTSD, as military conflict is a source of trauma. About 19% of Vietnam veterans developed PTSD at some point after the war (Dohrenwend et al., 2006). The disorder has also been reported among Persian Gulf war veterans, with estimates running as high as 8% (Wolfe, Erickson, Sharkansky, King, & King, 1999). After two decades of conflict in Afghanistan, 42% of participants in a national population-based survey reported PTSD symptoms (Cardozo et al., 2004). Studies on U.S. military personnel in Iraq also indicate problems in mental health, most notably PTSD (Felker, Hawkins, Dobie, Gutierrez, & McFall, 2008; Hoge et al., 2004; Milliken, Auchterlonie, & Hoge, 2007).

Research on the effects of the September 11 attacks on mental health revealed a remarkable degree of PTSD, at least initially (Calderoni, Alderman, Silver, & Bauman, 2006; Grieger, Fullerton, & Ursano, 2004; Lating, Sherman, Everly, Lowry, & Peragine, 2004). New Yorkers who viewed more television images in the days after September 11 were more likely to report symptoms of PTSD (Ahern, Galea, Resnick, & Vlahov, 2004). A comprehensive mental health screening of more than 11,000 rescue and recovery workers and volunteers at the World Trade Center revealed that more than 20% of the participants experienced symptoms of PTSD and 13% met the diagnostic criteria for PTSD (Centers for Disease Control and Prevention, 2004). Years later, many of these individuals are faring better; however, people who were directly exposed to the attacks are more likely to have persistent symptoms of PTSD (Bonanno, Galea, Bucciarelli, & Vlahov, 2006; Laugharne, Janca, & Widiger, 2007).

Similar statistics emerged following Hurricane Katrina's effects on the U.S. Gulf Coast in 2005. More than 19% of people from the largest employer in New Orleans evidenced PTSD symptoms six months after the hurricane (Desalvo et al., 2007). ■ You Review 13.1 summarizes the anxiety disorders that we have discussed.

Robert Essel NYC/Corbis

Exposure to a trauma can lead to the development of PTSD.

Explaining Anxiety Disorders

What causes anxiety disorders? Research on people with anxiety disorders suggests biological, psychological, and sociocultural factors that may contribute to such behavior, underscoring the biopsychosocial nature of psychological disorders presented at the beginning of the chapter.

BIOLOGY AND THE BRAIN

From a biological perspective, the functioning of several neurotransmitters has been linked to anxiety disorders. For example, some research suggests that abnormal activity of norepi-

Symptoms of the Main Anxiety Disorders

DISORDER	SYMPTOMS
Panic disorder	Abrupt experiences of unexpected intense fear accompanied by physical symptoms such as heart palpitations, shortness of breath, or dizziness that interfere with a person's functioning.
Phobic disorder	Persistent fear of a specific object or social situation that is excessive and unreasonable, and interferes with a person's ability to function.
Posttraumatic stress disorder	Exposure to a traumatic event during which one feels helplessness or fear followed by recurrent and intrusive memories or nightmares of the event, avoidance of stimuli associated with the event, numbing of emotions, and increased arousal that impair the person's functioning.
Obsessive-compulsive disorder	A pattern of recurrent, persistent, intrusive thoughts or images that are followed by repetitive behaviors or mental acts that a person feels driven to perform to reduce stress or to prevent some event from happening. The thoughts or behaviors are time-consuming and interfere with the person's functioning.
Generalized anxiety disorder	Excessive worry for at least 6 months about a number of events accompanied by physical symptoms such as muscle tension, mental agitation, and irritability that impair a person's functioning.

nephrine, serotonin, and/or GABA is involved in panic attacks (Bell & Nutt, 1998; Bourin, Baker, & Bradwejn, 1998; Charney et al., 2000). Abnormal activity of GABA has been linked to people with GAD, and problems in serotonin regulation have been suggested as a cause for OCD (Sanders & Shekhar, 1995; Saxena, Brody, Schwartz, & Baxter, 1998). Moreover, twin and family studies have found that panic disorder and OCD appear to run in families, suggesting a genetic link (Biederman et al., 2001; Grados, Walkup, & Walford, 2003; Hettema, Neale, & Kendler, 2001; Samuels & Nestadt, 1997; Scherrer et al., 2000).

Studies on animals and humans have focused on specific brain areas that are involved in anxiety and fear (LeDoux, 1998; Rosen, 2004; Rosen & Donley, 2006). As stated previously, our fear response is coordinated by the amygdala, a small structure deep inside the brain that also plays a role in our emotional memories (LaBar, 2007). Neuroimaging research on humans with PTSD suggests dysfunction in the amygdala that may contribute to their emotional and memory-related symptoms (Kolassa & Elbert; 2007; Liberzon et al., 1999; Rauch, Shin, & Phelps, 2006; Shin, Rauch, & Pitman, 2006). Specifically, people who have PTSD show overactivity in the amygdala. In one study, for example, Vietnam veterans with PTSD had exaggerated responses in their amygdala after hearing combat sounds reminiscent of the trauma that gave rise to their PTSD symptoms. Healthy individuals and veterans without PTSD did not show this intense amygdala response (Liberzon et al., 1999).

Research on OCD suggests abnormal functioning of a part of the forebrain called the *striatum* (Choi et al., 2007; Rauch et al., 1997). For example, in one study (Rauch et al., 1997), PET scans of individuals with OCD showed different brain circuitry in the striatum when performing a cognitive task than did the PET scans of people without OCD. Other research suggests that an overactive monitoring system in the brain is related to the symptoms of OCD (Gehring, Himle, & Nisenson, 2000; Ursu, Stenger, Shear, Jones, & Carter, 2003).

PSYCHOLOGICAL FACTORS

Psychological factors also help in explaining anxiety disorders. The social learning perspective suggests that phobias are learned in the same way that Watson and Rayner were able to condition Little Albert to fear a white rat (see p. 167; Field, 2006). A neutral stimulus (the phobic object) gets paired with a stimulus that naturally elicits fear. So, when a thunderstorm gets paired with a loud noise (thunder) that naturally evokes fear, we learn to be fearful of thunderstorms.

Direct experience is not always necessary to develop a phobia. We may acquire fears simply by observing or hearing about others' negative experiences (Kelly & Forsyth, 2007; Kleinknecht, 1991). How many of us have come face to face with a shark? But after seeing the classic *Jaws* movies, we may be more cautious and fearful when swimming in the ocean. In either case, our behavior toward the feared object is then often reinforced. We avoid or run away from objects or situations that cause fear. If we fear a shark attack in the ocean, we avoid swimming in the sea. Avoiding or running away reduces our anxiety and thereby helps maintain our fear of the object or situation.

Reinforcement also helps explain compulsions. If you engage in a certain behavior following an anxiety-provoking obsession, your anxiety is often reduced. The next time the obsession occurs, you feel more compelled to engage in the behavior so that you can reduce your anxiety (Barlow, 2002). Learning and conditioning theories have also been useful in understanding PTSD. Sights, sounds, or images of the trauma all become conditioned stimuli that trigger the fear reaction.

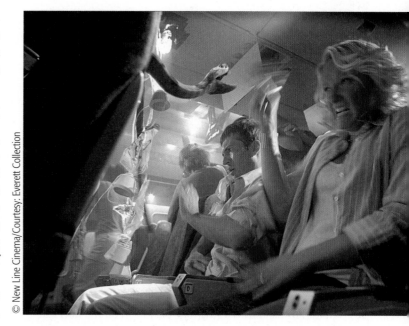

© New Line Cinema/Courtesy: Everett Collection

We may acquire fears by observing others' negative experiences either in real life or through media portrayals.

Cognitive research suggests that our thinking processes play a role in developing an anxiety disorder. In particular, people who perceive situations and objects as uncontrollable, unpredictable, dangerous, and disgusting are more vulnerable to anxiety disorders (Armfield, 2006; Bryant & Guthrie, 2005). For example, studies show that people with panic disorder sometimes misinterpret their bodily sensations, thinking they are beginning a panic attack. Their negative and catastrophic thinking then heightens their anxiety (Barlow, 2000; Craske & Barlow, 2001). People diagnosed with GAD tend to anticipate that something bad will happen to them and that they will feel out of control. While driving in a car, they may worry that they will get lost or in an accident. In an airplane, they may worry that it will crash. These worries become constant and almost automatic in their thought processes (Beck, 1997; Riskind, Williams, Gessner, Chrosniak, & Cortina, 2000).

Research has found that the shattering of certain basic assumptions about life may bring on PTSD. An unpredictable trauma—such as a rape, an earthquake, or an automobile accident—may make us question our assumptions that the world is safe and just and that events happen for a reason. It dispels our illusion of control and invincibility, and our assumption that bad things only happen to bad people (Janoff-Bulman, 1992; Terr, 1983). Some research suggests that people with OCD are less able to turn off the intrusive, negative thoughts that we all experience from time to time (Salkovskis, Westbrook, Davis, Jeavons, & Gledhill, 1997).

SOCIOCULTURAL FACTORS

Sociocultural factors must also be considered when explaining anxiety disorders. For example, in cultures experiencing rapid social change or war, people are more likely to exhibit anxiety symptoms than are people in more stable countries (Compton et al., 1991). Similarly, people who have been abused as children or who have had other previous traumatic or stressful experiences are more likely to develop anxiety disorders (Hyman & Rudorfer, 2000; Widom, 1999). We have also seen that European Americans and women are more likely than men to be diagnosed with an anxiety disorder. More research will have to examine the role of gender and culture in anxiety disorders before we fully understand their influence.

Let's Review!

This section described the main anxiety disorders and detailed our current understanding of what causes them. For a quick check of your understanding, answer these questions.

1. Marilu is anxious and nervous all the time. She constantly worries over her family, her job, and her schoolwork. Which anxiety disorder *best* describes Marilu's behavior?
   a. Panic disorder
   b. Generalized anxiety
   c. Phobic disorder
   d. Obsessive-compulsive disorder

2. Learning theories suggest that obsessive-compulsive disorder is the result of _____.
   a. reinforcement   c. low self-esteem
   b. faulty cognitions   d. unconscious impulses

3. Abdul was involved in a four-car pileup on the interstate 8 months ago. Since then, he has been having nightmares and flashback episodes of the accident. He has difficulty concentrating and has withdrawn from his family and friends. Abdul would most likely be diagnosed with which anxiety disorder?
   a. Panic disorder
   b. Posttraumatic stress disorder
   c. Phobic disorder
   d. Generalized anxiety disorder

4. Which of the following neurotransmitters has *not* been linked to anxiety disorders?
   a. GABA   c. Serotonin
   b. Norepinephrine   d. Acetylcholine

Answers 1. b; 2. a; 3. b; 4. d

Stop, LOOK, and LEARN

What Are Psychological Disorders, and How Can We Understand Them?

What Is Abnormal Behavior?

Abnormality is best explained when a behavior interferes with a person's ability to function.

Explaining Psychological Disorders: A Biopsychosocial Model

Jean-Noel Reichel/Getty Images

Biological Factors
- Genetics
- Hormones
- Neurotransmitters
- Brain functioning

Sociocultural Factors
- Environmental stressors
- Age
- Race
- Gender
- Culture

Psychological Factors
- Unresolved unconscious conflicts
- Learning processes
- Cognitions
- Perception of self

Psychological disorders result from a combination of biological, psychological, and social factors. They do not have just one cause.

Diagnosing Psychological Disorders: The *DSM* Model

Axis I   Clinical disorders

Axis II   Personality disorders; mental retardation

Axis III   General medical conditions

Axis IV   Psychosocial and environmental problems

Axis V   Global assessment of functioning

Anxiety Disorders

Anxiety Components

- Physical: fight or flight
- Cognitive: worry, paranoia
- Emotional: dread, panic, restlessness
- Behavioral: fleeing, avoiding, aggressing

Anxiety Disorders

- Generalized anxiety disorder
- Panic disorder
- Phobic disorder
- Obsessive-compulsive disorder
- Posttraumatic stress disorder

Possible Causes of Anxiety Disorders

- Biological: genetics, neurotransmitters, amygdala dysfunction
- Psychological: learning, maladaptive cognitions
- Sociocultural: rapid social change, stress, low social status, gender

Mood Disorders: Beyond the Blues

Learning Objectives

- Distinguish between the symptoms of unipolar and bipolar depressive disorders, and discuss our current understanding of the causes of mood disorders.

- Detail common misconceptions that people hold about suicide.

A second major category of disorders described in the DSM-IV-TR is mood disorders. **Mood disorders** involve a significant change in a person's emotional state. This may include feeling depressed or extremely elated for an extended time. Following anxiety disorders, mood disorders are one of the more common psychological disorders, affecting approximately 9.5% of adult Americans in a given year (Kessler, Chiu, et al., 2005).

Many of us experience sadness, but typically this period of sadness lasts only a few days. In clinical depression, the mood change is persistent and interferes significantly with a person's ability to function. Also, normal periods of sadness are usually brought on by environmental events—the loss of a loved one, the breakup of a relationship, or a disappointment in one's life. People with clinical depression are sad over a longer period, in the absence of such external events or long after most people would have adjusted to such changes. Mood disorders can be devastating to personal relationships and to the ability to work or go to school. Many people think that the symptoms are not "real" and that the person should be able to "snap out of it." These inaccurate beliefs may cause shame, which discourages people from seeking appropriate treatment. We will discuss two basic types of mood disorders: *unipolar depression* and *bipolar depression*.

mood disorder a disorder marked by a significant change in one's emotional state that seriously interferes with one's ability to function

Unipolar Depressive Disorders: A Change to Sadness

The DSM-IV-TR indicates two categories of unipolar depressive disorder: *major depression* and *dysthymic disorder*. A diagnosis of **major depression** requires that a person experience either extreme sadness—referred to as **dysphoria**—or extreme apathy (loss of interest in usual activities) plus at least four other symptoms of depression for a period of at least two weeks. These symptoms must be severe enough that they interfere with the person's ability to function (APA, 2000a). In addition to the emotional symptoms of dysphoria and apathy, people diagnosed with major depression show four or more of the following symptoms nearly every day during the two-week period:

Physical and Behavioral Symptoms

- Change in sleep patterns—either sleeping too much (hypersomnia) or too little (insomnia)
- Change in appetite—either eating too much (resulting in weight gain) or too little (resulting in weight loss)
- Change in motor functioning—either moving slowly and sluggishly or appearing agitated in movement
- Fatigue, or loss of energy

Cognitive Symptoms

- Inability to concentrate or pay attention
- Difficulty in making decisions
- Low self-esteem
- Exaggerated feelings of worthlessness or guilt
- Thoughts of suicide
- Delusions (believing something that is not true) and hallucinations (perceiving things that are not there) with depressing themes

major depression a mood disorder involving dysphoria, feelings of worthlessness, loss of interest in one's usual activities, and changes in bodily activities such as sleep and appetite that persists for at least two weeks

dysphoria [dis-FOR-ee-uh] an extreme state of sadness

dysthymic [dis-THIGH-mik] **disorder** a mood disorder that is a less severe but more chronic form of major depression

Major depression may occur as a single episode or as repeated episodes over the course of years. Some episodes may be so severe that the person requires hospitalization, especially in the presence of frequent suicide attempts or delusional thinking.

Dysthymic disorder is a less severe but more chronic form of major depression. The person seems sad and downcast over a longer time. A diagnosis of dysthymic disorder requires the symptom of depressed mood plus at least two other symptoms of depression for a period of at least two years. Dysthymic disorder generally begins in childhood, adolescence, or early adulthood (APA, 2000a). Typically, the symptoms of dysthymic disorder are not severe enough to require hospitalization. However, most people with dysthymic disorder eventually experience a major depressive episode (Klein, Lewinsohn, & Seeley, 2001; Regier et al., 1993).

Worldwide, major depression is the leading cause of disability (C. J. Murray & Lopez, 1996; World Health Organization, 2004). In the United States, 17% of adults will experience an acute episode of depression at some time in their lives, and 6% will experience more chronic depression (Kessler, Chiu, et al., 2005). Although major depression can develop at any age, the average age of onset is 32 (Kessler, Berglund, et al., 2005). People between 15 and 24 years of age are at high risk for experiencing a major depressive episode, whereas 45- to 54-year-olds experience the lowest rates of major depressive episodes (Blazer, Kes-

Major depression is marked by physical, behavioral, and cognitive symptoms, in addition to depressed mood.

Benelux Press/Getty Images

sler, McGonagle, & Swartz, 1994; Kessler et al., 2003). Most studies have also found gender differences in adult depression rates. Women are twice as likely as men to experience both mild and more severe depression, a difference found in many different countries, ethnic groups, and across adult age groups (Bradley & Hopcroft, 2007; Culbertson, 1997; Kessler et al., 2003; Nolen-Hoeksema, 2002; Weissman & Olfson, 1995; D. R. Williams et al., 2007). Although African Americans and Hispanic Americans have a lower lifetime risk for a major depressive disorder, when they do have one, it tends to be more chronic and severe (Breslau et al., 2005, 2006; D. R. Williams et al., 2007).

Bipolar Depressive Disorders: The Presence of Mania

A second major group of mood disorders is the bipolar depressive disorders. The DSM-IV-TR indicates two categories of bipolar depressive disorders: *bipolar disorder* and *cyclothymic disorder*.

Bipolar disorder involves a shift in mood between two states, or *poles*. One of these shifts is to a depressed state, with symptoms similar to those of major depression. The person feels sad, lacks self-worth, and may show changes in sleeping and eating over a two-week period. The second mood change is to the opposite extreme—to a "high" or euphoric state, called **mania**. During a manic state, people feel elated and have high self-esteem, have a decreased need for sleep, are more talkative than usual, and are highly distractible. Much energy is directed at achieving goals, although many projects may be started and few finished. People in this state have an inflated sense of self, feeling confident and able to accomplish anything. This may result in delusional thinking or hallucinations. Also, their boundless energy often results in more impulsive and risk-taking behaviors. When such symptoms of mania and depression interfere with a person's ability to function, a diagnosis of bipolar disorder is appropriate (APA, 2000a).

Cyclothymic disorder is a less severe but more chronic form of bipolar disorder. In cyclothymic disorder, a person alternates between milder periods of mania and more moderate depression over a two-year period (APA, 2000a). The person functions reasonably well during the mild mania but is likely to be more impaired during the depressive phase.

Bipolar disorders are less common than unipolar disorders, with 2.6% of adult Americans experiencing an episode of bipolar disorder at some time in their lives (Kessler, Chiu, et al., 2005; Lewinsohn, Klein, & Seeley, 2000). Men are just as likely as women to be diagnosed with bipolar disorder. The median age of onset for bipolar disorder is late adolescence and early adulthood (Angst & Sellaro, 2000; Kessler, Berglund, et al., 2005).

Explaining Mood Disorders

What causes mood disorders? Not surprisingly, research has identified biological, psychological, and sociocultural factors that may contribute to mood disorders. Again, this highlights the biopsychosocial nature of psychological disorders.

BIOLOGICAL FACTORS: GENES, NEUROTRANSMITTERS, AND STRESS HORMONES

The evidence from family history studies, twin studies, and adoption studies suggests that mood disorders may be genetically transmitted, especially in the case of bipolar disorder. For example, first-degree relatives (parent, child, or sibling) of persons with bipolar disorder are much more likely to develop the disorder than are relatives of people without the disorder (Saunders, Scott, McInnis, & Burmeister, 2007). Similarly, if an identical twin is diagnosed as having bipolar disorder, the other identical twin has a higher probability of developing the disorder than if they were fraternal twins (MacKinnon, Jamison, & DePaulo, 1997; Wallace,

bipolar disorder a mood disorder characterized by both depression and mania

mania a period of abnormally excessive energy and elation

cyclothymic [sigh-clo-THIGH-mik] **disorder** a mood disorder that is a less severe but more chronic form of bipolar disorder

Psychology Applies to Your World:

Suicide Facts and Misconceptions

Suicidal thoughts are one symptom of depression. Research suggests that nearly 90% of all people who commit suicide have some diagnosable mental disorder, commonly a depressive disorder or a substance abuse disorder (National Institute of Mental Health, 2002; Wulsin, Vaillat, & Wells, 1999). In 2005, suicide was the 11th leading cause of death in the United States (higher than homicide). Among 25- to 34-year-olds, it was the second leading cause of death; among 35- to 44-year-olds, it was the fourth leading cause of death. Among 15- to 24-year-olds, suicide was the third leading cause of death, although these rates are probably grossly underestimated given the negative stigma attached to suicide in this country (Anderson & Smith, 2003; Heron & Smith, 2007; Kung, Hoyert, Xu, & Murphy, 2008). Women are two to three times more likely than men to *attempt* suicide, but four times as many men actually kill themselves, in part because of the means chosen (Denning, Conwell, King, & Coz, 2000; Hoyert, Heron, Murphy, & Kung, 2006; Kung et al., 2008). Men tend to shoot, hang, or stab themselves. Women are more likely to choose less lethal means, such as drug overdoses. This gender difference appears in many countries across the world (Weissman et al., 1999; Welch, 2001) except China, where more women commit suicide than men (Phillips, Li, & Zhang, 2002). As seen in ■ FIGURE 13.4, in the United States, Whites and American Indian/Alaskan Natives have higher rates of suicide than other ethnic groups (Heron & Smith, 2007; Kung et al., 2008). All of these statistics highlight the importance of understanding and preventing suicide, because many of us will or already have encountered someone who is suicidal. So let's take a moment to dispel some of the more common misconceptions concerning suicide.

Misconception: People who talk of suicide will not kill themselves.

Although most people who talk of suicide do not go on to attempt suicide, people who commit suicide typically have expressed their intentions at some time to family members or friends before their attempt (Shneidman, 1987). They may have talked about "going away" or be preoccupied in general with the notion of death. Therefore, any talk of suicide should be taken seriously. A suicidal person should not be left alone. You may need to contact a mental health professional, call 911, or call a suicide crisis hotline in your area.

Misconception: If you ask someone who is depressed whether he or she has thoughts of suicide, it will only plant the idea of suicide in his or her head.

Asking direct questions about a person's plan for suicide is the only way to assess the person's risk for commit-

---

FIGURE

13.4

U.S. Death Rates for Suicide by Gender and Ethnicity in 2005

Although women attempt suicide more often, men across all ethnic groups are more likely to commit suicide.

Source: National Vital Statistics Reports, *Vol. 56, no. 10, January 2008.*

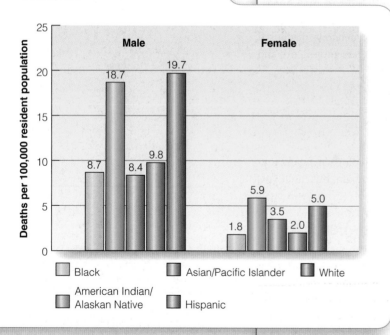

ting suicide. Bringing up the subject can also give the person an opportunity to talk about his or her problem. People who have a concrete plan in mind for when or how they will end their life are more likely to attempt suicide than those whose plans are less specific (Clark, Gibbons, Fawcett, & Scheftner, 1989).

Misconception: People who have unsuccessfully attempted suicide will not try again.

Only 10% of people who unsuccessfully attempt suicide try again and succeed (Clark & Fawcett, 1992). Yet among adolescents, a previous history of suicide attempts is the single best predictor of future suicide attempts and completions (Lewinsohn, Rohde & Seeley, 1994). Therefore, a previous suicide attempt puts adolescents in particular at a higher risk for future suicide attempts.

Misconception: A better mood means the risk of suicide is gone.

Suicide does not typically happen when a person is in the depths of a deep depression. Rather, suicide attempts are more likely to occur when people with depression have energy and can think more clearly and make decisions. This energy and clearer thinking make it appear to loved ones that the person is getting better and is therefore at a lower risk of suicide. However, this energy and decision-making ability allow the individual to make and carry out plans for suicide. So a better mood does not always mean a decreased risk of suicide, and sometimes actually indicates an increased risk of suicide.

Misconception: Only people who are depressed attempt suicide.

Although suicidal thoughts are a symptom of depression, people with other serious psychological disorders, including bipolar disorder, substance abuse disorder, dissociative disorders, and schizophrenia, are also at risk for suicide (Foote, Smolin, Neft, & Lipschitz, 2008; Statham et al., 1998; Tsuang, Fleming, & Simpson, 1999). A number of other events and situations also increase one's risk of suicide, including economic hardship, serious illness, loss of a relationship, childhood sexual or physical abuse, and the presence of a firearm in the home (Brent et al., 1991; Crosby, Cheltenham, & Sacks, 1999; Fergusson, Horwood, & Lynskey, 1996; Kaplan, Pelcovitz, Salzinger, Mandel, & Weiner, 1997; Lester, 1992; Welch, 2001). Suicide occurs among people who have psychological disorders as well as those who face environmental stressors. The majority of suicide attempts are expressions of extreme distress and helplessness, and not just "harmless" bids for attention.

Schneider, & McGuffin, 2002; Winokur, Coryell, Keller, Endicott, & Leon, 1995). In one twin study, the heritability of bipolar disorder was estimated as high as 85% (McGuffin et al., 2003). Even people who are adopted who have blood relatives with bipolar disorder are much more likely to develop the disorder than adoptees whose blood relatives do not have mood disorders (Wender et al., 1986).

The evidence for genetic factors in major depression is less clear. The trend toward genetic transmission is present, particularly in women, but it is not as strong as the evidence in bipolar disorders (Abkevich et al., 2003; Bierut et al., 1999; Sullivan, Neale, & Kendler, 2000). Specific regions of chromosomes have been identified that may contribute to one's risk for depression, but a specific gene mechanism has not yet been identified (Holmans et al., 2007; Levinson et al., 2007).

The malfunctioning of certain neurotransmitters has also been linked to mood disorders, specifically serotonin and norepinephrine (Soares & Mann, 1997; Thase, Jindal, & Howland, 2002). Antidepressant drugs that act on serotonin and norepinephrine to relieve the symptoms of depression seem to offer evidence for the role of these neurotransmitters in depression. The role of the neurotransmitters norepinephrine, dopamine, and glutamate in bipolar disorder has been investigated, although their contribution to the bipolar disorders is less clear (Dixon & Hokin, 1998; Goodwin & Jamison, 1990). However, dysfunction in the serotonin system may also account for the depressive phase of bipolar disorder (Oquendo et al., 2007).

Neuroscience Applies to Your World:

Let the Sun Shine In!

Sunlight helps regulate several hormones and neurotransmitters that have strong effects on mood and behavior. Two critical chemicals appear to be melatonin and serotonin. As the sun goes down, the level of sleep hormone called melatonin naturally increases, signaling the body that it is time to sleep. In the morning as the sun rises, your eyes transmit light information to the brain that signals a decrease in melatonin levels and an increase in serotonin levels. Serotonin wakes us up and keeps us in a good mood. Therefore, it is very important to get an adequate amount of sunlight each day. So, spend time outdoors during daylight hours, sit by open windows when you are unable to be outside, and use full spectrum lightbulbs in your living and work areas. Sunlight not only supplies us with Vitamin D, but it elevates our mood as well.

Stockbyte/Getty Images

The connection between depression and hormones has also been researched. Hormones regulate functions such as sleep, appetite, sexual desire, and pleasure. Symptoms of depression relate to these bodily functions (McClung, 2007). People who are depressed tend to show higher than usual levels of stress hormones (Young & Korzun, 1998). These stress hormones tend to inhibit the activity of neurotransmitters that are related to mood. Hence, repeated activation of the hormonal stress system may lay the groundwork for depression (Arborelius, Owens, Plotsky, & Nemeroff, 1999; Gillespie & Nemeroff, 2007). Excessive levels of stress hormones have been linked to the shrinkage of certain brain areas that may also be related to depression (Sapolsky, 2000b; Sheline, 2000). Research is also investigating how changes in the brain (specifically in the limbic system) may be associated with depressive symptoms (Gotlib & Hamilton, 2008; Jacobs, 2004; Jacobs, van Praag, & Gage, 2000).

Because of the connection between neurotransmitter dysregulation and depressive conditions, more recent investigations have focused on genes that regulate the activity of neurotransmitters, specifically serotonin. However, the results of such studies indicate a complex relationship between genes, neural activity, and depression (Dannlowski et al., 2007; Kraft et al., 2007; Rao et al., 2007; Vergne & Nemeroff, 2006). Future technologies may assist us in sorting out the precise relationship between biology and mood disorders.

PSYCHOLOGICAL FACTORS: ABANDONMENT, LEARNED HELPLESSNESS, AND NEGATIVE THINKING

Psychological factors also help in explaining mood disorders, especially depression. For example, psychoanalytic theory suggests that depression is linked to unresolved childhood issues of abandonment, rejection, and loss. Freud (1917) believed that depression was a symbolic expression of anger. A child who perceives that he or she has been abandoned or rejected by loved ones is afraid to express anger outwardly. Instead, the child redirects this anger onto the self, resulting in self-blame, self-hatred, and other symptoms of depression. As the child enters adolescence and adulthood and forms new relationships, these feelings of abandonment and separation may resurface. When they do, the person falls into another depression.

Some research is consistent with this view. A history of early adverse experiences such as insecure attachments, separations, and losses can make one vulnerable to depression (Heim, Plotsky, & Nemeroff, 2004; Vergne & Nemeroff, 2006; Weissman, Markowitz, & Klerman, 2000). People who are depressed do show low self-esteem, and some do have difficulty expressing anger (Bromberger & Matthews, 1996; Klein, Durbin, Shankman, & Santiago, 2002). So it is possible that early feelings of abandonment and rejection may play a role in depression, but this idea has not been thoroughly investigated.

Social learning theories suggest that mood disorders are related to levels of positive reinforcement, learned helplessness, and ruminative coping styles. Peter Lewinsohn's (1974) theory of depression links depression to a reduction in the number of positive reinforcers we receive from others. This reduction is more likely in people with poor social skills. Imagine for a moment that you pass an acquaintance on your campus, someone who is in one of your courses. As you pass by, what do you do? Most people nod, say hello, or express some form of acknowledgment; this is a social skill. Imagine further that the classmate fails to respond, continues walking, and does not reciprocate your casual greeting. What happens the next time that you walk by this person? In all likelihood, you will ignore the person, giving her or him no positive reinforcement. As this example illustrates, people with poor social skills or those who tend to withdraw receive less positive reinforcement from others. Lewinsohn suggests that such a pattern may result in depression.

Another psychological explanation of depression is **learned helplessness**. Learned helplessness involves the belief that you cannot control the outcome of events or what is going to happen (see Chapter 11). Therefore, you do not respond even when your response could lead to success. Initial evidence for learned helplessness came from studies in which dogs were administered controllable shock, uncontrollable shock, or no shock (Overmier & Seligman, 1967; Seligman & Maier, 1967). The dogs in the controllable shock situation had to learn to jump a barrier in order to turn off the shock. They quickly learned this behavior. The dogs in the uncontrollable shock situation could not turn off the shock. Later, when the dogs who had been in the uncontrollable shock situation were given the opportunity to jump the barrier to avoid the shock, they failed to respond. They had learned to be helpless and just sat there taking the shock *even when they could escape* it. Such research suggests that people who are depressed may respond similarly—they do not take steps to solve or even prevent problems when such action could be helpful because they believe that life is uncontrollable. Thus, people with depression may have an increased sensitivity to uncontrollable stress (Ilgen & Hutchison, 2005).

Research by Susan Nolen-Hoeksema and her colleagues (Nolen-Hoeksema, 2001, 2002; Nolen-Hoeksema, Larson, & Grayson, 1999; Nolen-Hoeksema, Parker, & Larson, 1994; Nolen-Hoeksema, Stice, Wade, & Bohon, 2007) indicates that coping styles play a role in depression. People who are depressed are more likely to engage in what is called a **ruminative coping style**. To ruminate means to focus on your thoughts. People who are depressed spend a lot of time thinking about their depression and why they are depressed. They do not do anything about their depression or its causes, but rather remain focused on repetitively analyzing their feelings and concerns. This focus makes it more likely that they will become more severely depressed and also stay depressed longer. Several studies support an association between rumination and vulnerability to depression (Donaldson & Lam, 2004; Hong, 2007; Ito, Takenaka, Tomita, & Agari, 2006; McLaughlin, Borkovec, & Sibrava, 2007).

learned helplessness the belief that one cannot control the outcome of events

ruminative [RUE-muh-nay-tive] **coping style** the tendency to persistently focus on how one feels without attempting to do anything about one's feelings

Cognitive research highlights the role of negative thinking patterns and attributions in the development of mood disorders. People who are depressed are more likely to engage in negative thinking errors, called **cognitive distortions**, according to research by Aaron Beck (1967, 1976). For example, people who are depressed tend to reject positive experiences and focus only on the negative aspects of a situation. Beck believes that these people engage in a negative view so automatically that they may not even realize their errors in thinking.

YOUR TURN – ACTIVE LEARNING

To help you understand the impact of negative thinking errors on mood, try this demonstration. Before you go to bed tonight, write down how you feel generally—for example, happy, sad, or stressed. Tomorrow, carry a pad of paper around with you all day. Every time you have a positive thought or experience, write it down. At the end of the day, again write down how you feel generally. It is likely that noting positive feelings all day will create a more positive overall feeling. If we had asked you to note negative thoughts for an entire day, how do you think that would affect your outlook on your day?

Research on the *attributions* of people who are depressed further supports Beck's model. An attribution is an explanation of why an event happened. People who are depressed tend to attribute negative environmental events to factors within themselves (Alloy, Abramson, & Francis, 1999; Peterson & Seligman, 1984). For instance, failing an exam is interpreted to mean that one is stupid, will always be stupid, and will probably fail more exams. A relationship breakup is interpreted to mean that one is not lovable and will always be unlovable. These negative attributions and cognitive distortions appear related to depressed mood (Abramson et al., 2002; Gibb, Alloy, Abramson, Beevers, & Miller, 2004).

SOCIOCULTURAL FACTORS: SOCIAL STATUS AND GENDER

Sociocultural factors must also be considered when explaining mood disorders. Depression is more likely among people of lower social status (Blazer et al., 1994), especially those from adverse neighborhoods (Cutrona, Wallace, & Wesner, 2006). Explaining such differences is further complicated by the worldwide gender difference in depression.

You Asked...

Why are women more likely to get depressed? ERIKA LARKINS, STUDENT

Forces that are unique to women may explain their higher vulnerability to depressive disorders (see ■ FIGURE 13.5; Gorman, 2006; Mazure, Keita, & Blehar, 2002). We have already seen that the genetic risk of depression appears stronger in women than in men. Research has also investigated—over many years and many studies—the relationship between the female ovarian hormones, estrogen and progesterone, and mood in an effort to understand pathways to depression. However, it is not as simple as saying ovarian hormones cause depression. Research has not linked depression solely to an imbalance in female hormones (Steiner & Born, 2000). Rather, research suggests that women's estrogen and progesterone levels may influence the functioning of the neurotransmitter serotonin, which plays a central role in mood. However, researchers don't yet understand the precise actions by which estrogen and progesterone influence serotonin functioning (Lu, Eshleman, Janowsky, & Bethea, 2003; Parker & Brotchie, 2004; Steiner, Dunn, & Born, 2003).

Psychological factors unique to women must also be considered when examining gender differences in depression. For example, females are more likely than males to engage in a ruminative coping style (Li, DiGiuseppe, & Froh, 2006; Nolen-Hoeksema, 2001; Nolen-

cognitive distortion thought that tends to be pessimistic and negative

FIGURE

13.5 Women and Depression

Biological, psychological, and sociocultural forces unique to women may explain their higher vulnerability to depressive disorders.

Biological: Women are genetically at risk for depression, and ovarian hormones may influence serotonin levels.

Psychological: Women tend to ruminate about problems, and relationships are a key part of a woman's self worth.

Sociocultural: Women's lower social status is a risk factor for stressors, and the female gender role encourages dependence and passivity.

© Masterfile

Hoeksema et al., 1999; Papadakis, Prince, Jones, & Strauman, 2006). That is, women tend to focus on how they feel and to fret about their feelings. Even co-rumination, or excessively talking about problems with friends, while offering women social support, can also amplify or increase one's depressive symptoms (Byrd-Craven, Geary, Rose & Ponzi, 2008; Rose, Carlson, & Waller, 2007). In contrast, men are more likely to engage in some activity to take their minds off their feelings, to withdraw, or to abuse drugs. As Nolen-Hoeksema and her colleagues (1999) put it, "Women think and men drink." Women are also more likely to have an interpersonal orientation that puts them at risk for depression (Mazure et al., 2002). Relationships are more important to a woman's sense of self-worth than they are to a man's. As a result, women are more likely to silence their own demands in order to maintain a positive relationship and are more likely to place their needs secondary to those of others. This relational style may also predispose women to depression.

Tied to these biological and psychological factors are the social circumstances that women face. Women are at a disadvantage in society: they earn less and have less power than men. They report less satisfaction with work and family and are more likely to be victims of violence, discrimination, abuse, and poverty (Klonoff, Landrine, & Campbell, 2000; Koss & Kilpatrick, 2001). Negative life events such as these put women more at risk for depression. They foster feelings of uncontrollability and helplessness, perceptions that are intimately connected to mood disorders (Browne, 1993; Fitzgerald, 1993; Ilgen & Hutchison, 2005). These perceptions also relate to female gender-role socialization, which encourages women to base their self-worth and self-esteem on the quality of relationships and discourages women from expressing anger (Helgeson, 1994; Jack, 1991). Traditional gender roles also discourage women from being masterful, independent, and assertive and encourage them to be dependent and passive. These prescribed roles may increase women's feelings of uncontrollability and helplessness (Barlow, 2002).

For both men and women, depression is a complex behavior affected by biological, psychological, and sociocultural variables. Each of us probably has *some* biological vulnerability to mood disorders. However, social and psychological factors may act to protect us from such vulnerability, or make us more likely to express this vulnerability. Research continues to explore the exact role these factors play. People's lives depend on it.

Let's Review!

This section outlined the major types of mood disorders and described our current understanding of their causes. For a quick check of your understanding, answer these questions.

1. Maria has been sad for three weeks. She can't sleep, eat, or concentrate, and is constantly crying. She has lost interest in her usual interests and activities. Maria would most likely be diagnosed with which disorder?
   a. Bipolar disorder   c. Major depression
   b. Manic depression   d. Cyclothymic disorder

2. Last week, Tyrone had little sleep but felt confident, exhilarated, and excessively happy. He talked fast and felt that he could accomplish anything. Now his energy has evaporated. He sleeps most of the time, feels worthless, and lacks his usual vitality. Tyrone would most likely be diagnosed with which disorder?
   a. Major depression
   b. Bipolar disorder
   c. Dysthymic disorder
   d. Unipolar depressive disorder

3. Research on depression has found that people who are depressed are more likely to _____.
   a. engage in negative thinking
   b. engage in rumination
   c. believe they have little control over events
   d. All of the above

4. Dysthymic disorder is a less severe but more chronic form of _____.
   a. major depression   c. dysphoria
   b. bipolar disorder   d. apathy

5. Which of the following statements about suicide is true?
   a. People who talk of suicide will not kill themselves.
   b. Among adolescents, previous suicide attempts are a predictor of future attempts.
   c. A better mood means the risk of suicide is gone.
   d. Only people who are depressed commit suicide.

Answers 1. c; 2. b; 3. d; 4. a; 5. b

Learning Objective

Schizophrenic Disorders: Disintegration

- Identify and describe the symptoms of schizophrenia, discriminate between the types of schizophrenia, and discuss our current understanding of the causes of schizophrenia.

Schizophrenia is a chronic, disabling psychological disorder that affects roughly 1–2% of the general population worldwide (Ho, Black, & Andreasen, 2003). It involves the disintegration of one's personality.

Is schizophrenia the same thing as multiple personalities? No. Multiple personalities involve the existence of several *intact* personalities within a person. In schizophrenia, the one personality is no longer intact, or held together and connected. If we think of someone's personality as a related set of cognitive, emotional, perceptual, and motor behaviors, then in schizophrenia we see the disconnection between these personality elements. As these elements lose their connections with one another, the person loses his or her connection with reality. This results in impaired functioning.

Onset, Gender, Ethnicity, and Prognosis

schizophrenia [skit-sue-FREE-nee-uh]
a severe disorder characterized by disturbances in thought, perceptions, emotions, and behavior

Symptoms of schizophrenia typically appear in adolescence or young adulthood. In some cases, the symptoms come on gradually; in others, they appear more abruptly. Schizophrenia affects men and women with equal frequency, although it typically appears earlier in men than in women. Men tend to develop the disorder in their late teens or early 20s, and women are generally affected in their 20s or early 30s (Robins & Regier, 1991). Perhaps because of the earlier onset, men with schizophrenia tend to be more chronically impaired (Goldstein & Lewine, 2000; Ho et al., 2003). Although schizophrenia appears with equal frequency among various ethnic groups, it is more prevalent in lower socioeconomic groups (Escobar, 1993; Kirkbride et al., 2007).

Symptoms of schizophrenia are often shocking and confusing to family members and friends. Most people with schizophrenia suffer throughout their adult lives, losing opportunities for careers and relationships (Harrow, Sands, Silverstein, & Goldberg, 1997). Several factors contribute to this suffering: the negative stigma that a schizophrenia diagnosis brings, the lack of public understanding, and inaccurate media portrayals of people with schizophrenia as criminally violent. Most people with schizophrenia are not violent toward others but are withdrawn and prefer to be left alone (Steadman et al., 1998). Although there currently is no cure, a diagnosis of schizophrenia does not necessarily mean progressive deterioration in functioning, as most people believe. Rather, for reasons we don't yet understand, schizophrenic symptoms and episodes tend to decline as a person ages, with 20–30% of people with schizophrenia showing only minor impairment 20 or 30 years later (Breier, Schreiber, Dyer, & Pickar, 1991; Eaton, Thara, Federman, & Tien, 1998; Jablensky, 2000). However, recovery is very much related to social factors such as economic and social support. Most people with schizophrenia continue to experience difficulties throughout their lives.

Symptoms of Schizophrenia

Schizophrenia can express itself in many forms, depending on which symptoms are present. Symptoms of schizophrenia may include disordered thoughts, perceptions, affect, and/or motor behavior.

DISORDERED THOUGHTS: LOOSE ASSOCIATIONS AND DELUSIONS

Thought disorder and *delusions* are two examples of symptoms that characterize the disorganized thinking that many people with schizophrenia experience (APA, 2000a). **Thought disorder** involves a lack of associations between ideas and events. Because the ideas of people with schizophrenia lack connection, we refer to this as *loose associations. Poverty of content* describes their communications: their ideas seem unrelated to one another, and their speech is often characterized as a *word salad* (words seem tossed together without any apparent syntax or organization). They may be saying a lot, but what they say is not communicating anything to the receiver.

Delusions are thoughts and beliefs that the person believes to be true but that have no basis in reality. For example, *persecutory delusions* involve beliefs about being followed or watched, usually by agents of authorities such as the FBI or the government. *Grandiose delusions* involve beliefs about being a famous or special person. For instance, a person with schizophrenia may believe that he is the president of France. People with schizophrenia may also hold *delusions of reference* (believing that others are talking about them) or *delusions of thought control* (believing that their thoughts are controlled by another person or force).

DISORDERED PERCEPTIONS: HALLUCINATIONS

People who are diagnosed with schizophrenia also may experience hallucinations. **Hallucinations** represent a disorder in perception because the person sees,

thought disorder a symptom of schizophrenia that involves a lack of associations between one's ideas and the events that one is experiencing

delusion a thought or belief that a person believes to be true but in reality is not

hallucination perceiving something that does not exist in reality

Schizophrenia is a severe mental disorder marked by disordered thoughts, perceptions, emotions, and/or motor behavior, as depicted in this drawing by someone with schizophrenia.

© Jean-Michel Girand/Photo Researchers, Inc.

In catatonic schizophrenia, the person may remain totally motionless and rigid for hours on end in a catatonic stupor.

hears, tastes, smells, or feels something that others do not perceive. In schizophrenia, hearing voices or other sounds (called *auditory hallucinations*) is the most common altered perception, followed by *visual hallucinations* (seeing things that aren't there). The hallucinations may tell the person to perform certain acts or may be frightening in nature.

DISORDERED AFFECT: LAUGHING AT ALL THE WRONG THINGS

Disordered emotional expression is another symptom of schizophrenia. **Affect**, in psychological terms, refers to expressing emotions. Some people with schizophrenia show *blunted* or *flat affect*, or a lack of emotional expression. They appear passive and immobile. They do not respond to events in their environment with any emotion. Their speech lacks the inflection that usually communicates a speaker's mood. Others with schizophrenia may show *inappropriate affect*. They laugh at sad things, as when they are told that someone has died, or they may react with anger when they are given a gift. They do not show the emotion that we consider typical and appropriate to the event. They may laugh and giggle all the time, or they may switch from one emotional extreme to another for no apparent reason.

DISORDERED MOTOR BEHAVIOR: AGITATION AND STUPOR

Disordered behavior may also characterize some people with schizophrenia. This may take the form of unusual, odd, or repetitive behaviors and gestures. Head banging, finger flapping, or tracing a pattern over and over again are examples. Some people with schizophrenia may show an absence of all motor behaviors, remaining totally motionless and rigid for hours on end. Such behavior is referred to as a **catatonic stupor**. Alternatively, other people with schizophrenia may show **catatonic excitement**, in which they are suddenly agitated, fidgety, shouting, swearing, or moving around rapidly.

Types of Schizophrenia: Positive and Negative Symptoms

The *DSM-IV-TR* recognizes five subtypes of schizophrenia, classified according to which symptoms are most prevalent. These five types—*paranoid, disorganized, catatonic, undifferentiated,* and *residual schizophrenia*—are described in ■ TABLE 13.3.

Researchers have moved toward understanding schizophrenia in terms of *positive* and *negative symptoms* (Andreasen, Arndt, Alliger, Miller, & Flaum, 1995; Nicholson & Neufield, 1993). *Negative symptoms* of schizophrenia are those that represent losses in a domain of behavior. These would include the flattened affect, social withdrawal, and catatonic stupor described previously. Approximately 25% of persons with schizophrenia display these symptoms (Ho et al., 2003). *Positive symptoms* of schizophrenia are those that represent an increase, or addition, in a domain of behavior. These would include unusual perceptions, thoughts, or behaviors, including the symptoms of hallucinations and delusions discussed previously.

Although many people with schizophrenia exhibit both positive and negative symptoms, those who show predominantly positive symptoms tend to have a less severe course of schizophrenia and respond better to medication. For instance, positive symptoms predominate in *paranoid schizophrenia*, which may partly explain why people with paranoid schizophrenia tend to have a more favorable prognosis than those with other types of schizophrenia (Fenton & McGlashan, 1994; Kendler, McGuire, Gruenberg, & Walsh, 1994). Such findings have led researchers to believe that positive symptoms of schizophrenia may have a different cause than negative symptoms. So let's look at our current understanding of the development of schizophrenia.

affect one's expressed emotion toward an action at a given time

catatonic [cat-uh-TAWN-ick] **stupor** a disorder in motor behavior involving immobility

catatonic excitement a disorder in motor behavior involving excited agitation

Photo credit: © Grunnitis Studio/Photo Researchers, Inc.

Table 13.3 *DSM-IV-TR* Types of Schizophrenia

TYPE	MAJOR FEATURES
Catatonic schizophrenia	Disordered movement: total unresponsiveness to the environment (stupor) or agitated excitement
Disorganized schizophrenia	Delusions, hallucinations, incoherent thought and speech, flat or inappropriate emotions
Paranoid schizophrenia	Delusions of grandeur or persecution, hallucinations
Undifferentiated schizophrenia	Schizophrenic symptoms present but does not meet criteria for other subtypes
Residual schizophrenia	Prior schizophrenic episodes but does not currently display symptoms

Reprinted with permission from the Diagnostic and Statistical Manual of Mental Disorders, *Fourth Edition, Text Revision, Copyright 2000. American Psychiatric Association.*

Explaining Schizophrenia: Genetics, the Brain, and the Environment

To date, biological factors account for the strongest evidence in the development of schizophrenia, although environmental factors must also be considered. It is likely that environmental conditions interact with biological factors to make a person either more or less susceptible to the illness. Biological research has focused on three main areas: genetics, brain abnormalities, and the malfunctioning of specific neurotransmitters in the brain. Environmental research has focused on prenatal and development factors, as well as the role of family and the environment.

A STRONG GENETIC FACTOR

Family, twin, and adoption studies have routinely demonstrated a high heritability of schizophrenia (NIMH Genetics Workgroup, 1998; Parnas et al., 1993). As ■ FIGURE 13.6 shows, although the incidence of schizophrenia in the general population is 1–2%, the more genetically similar a person is to someone with schizophrenia, the more likely he or she will also develop the disorder (Cardno & Gottesman, 2000). In identical twin pairs, if one twin develops schizophrenia, the other twin has about a 48% chance of developing the disorder. However, in fraternal twins (who are not genetically identical), the probability is only 17%. Adoption studies show a similar pattern (Heston, 1966; Kety et al., 1994; Tienari et al., 2003). Adopted children who have biological parents with schizophrenia are 10 times more likely to develop the disorder than are adopted children whose biological parents are not diagnosed with schizophrenia.

Yet despite these results, it is unlikely that a single gene is responsible for the illness; if it were, the rates would be

> **You Asked...**
>
> *If schizophrenia runs in the family, how likely is it that someone from a later generation will inherit the disorder?*
>
> KRISTIN MACPHERSON, STUDENT

FIGURE 13.6

Risk of Schizophrenia and Genetic Relatedness

The incidence of schizophrenia in the general population is 1–2%. However, the more closely one is genetically related to a person with schizophrenia, the higher the risk of developing the disorder.

(Source: Reprinted by permission of Irving I. Gottesman)

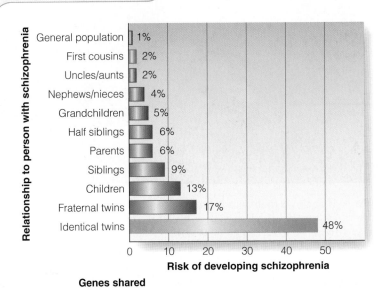

higher. Research has therefore moved toward exploring several chromosomal regions that may work together to increase a person's vulnerability to schizophrenia (Norton, Williams, & Owen, 2006; Rapoport, Addington, Frangou, & Psych, 2005; Walker & Tessner, 2008). The exact nature of these pathways has yet to be identified and detailed.

Another genetic explanation for schizophrenia stems from the association between advanced paternal age and an increased risk of schizophrenia: Some people with schizophrenia are more likely to have had older fathers (45 years or older) at birth. Such an association has led to the hypothesis that mutations in male sperm cells (which are more likely to occur as a male ages) may be in part a genetic mechanism for schizophrenia, at least in some people (Byrne, Agerbo, Ewald, Eaton, & Mortensen, 2003; Dalman & Allebeck, 2002; Malaspina et al., 2001).

THE BRAIN: NEUROTRANSMITTERS AND STRUCTURAL ABNORMALITIES

A second area of research on the development of schizophrenia looks at neurotransmitters. It was originally believed that schizophrenia was caused by excess activity of the neurotransmitter dopamine in the brain. The drugs that are prescribed for schizophrenia, called *phenothiazines*, reduce dopamine activity in the brain and are typically more effective in reducing the positive symptoms of schizophrenia. However, many people with schizophrenia do not respond to treatment with phenothiazines. One of the newer drugs used to treat schizophrenia, called *clozapine*, does not block the same dopamine receptors as the phenothiazines, clearly indicating that dopamine is involved, but in a more complex way (Conklin & Iacono, 2002).

Other research suggests a potential role for the neurotransmitter glutamate (Coyle, 2006; Goff & Coyle, 2001). Drugs such as PCP and ketamine (see Chapter 4) that block the action of glutamate can cause normal subjects to exhibit cognitive impairments and negative symptoms similar to those found in people with schizophrenia (Deakin et al., 2008). Current research is focused on how glutamate and dopamine dysfunction may interact to contribute to the development of schizophrenia (Javitt, 2007; Stahl, 2007; Stone, Morrison, & Pilowsky, 2007). Obviously, the relationship between neurotransmitters and schizophrenia remains a complex one.

Abnormalities in certain brain structures have also been investigated for their links to schizophrenia. The most consistent abnormality found in people with schizophrenia is enlarged ventricles (Andreasen, Swayze, Flaum, & Alliger, 1990; Lieberman et al., 2001; Zorrilla et al., 1997). A ventricle is a fluid-filled cavity in the brain. Enlarged ventricles reduce the overall size of the brain, which in turn may contribute to the development of schizophrenia (Wright et al., 2000). Brain dysfunction in the frontal and temporal lobes has also been implicated in the development of schizophrenia (Mitelman, Buchsbaum, Brickman, & Shihabuddin, 2005; Weinstein, Woodward, & Ngan, 2007; Wolf et al., 2007). The frontal lobe is responsible for language, emotions, and social behavior, and the temporal lobe plays an important role in memory. The symptoms of schizophrenia (disordered cognitions, emotions, and motor behavior) are associated with these brain areas.

PRENATAL AND DEVELOPMENTAL FACTORS

How do people with schizophrenia develop these neurochemical or brain abnormalities? In addition to possible hereditary factors, these abnormalities have been linked to birth complications and the mother's exposure to prenatal viruses (Cannon, 1998; Goldstein et al., 2000; Jones & Cannon, 1998; Mednick et al., 1998), although many other causes could exist. Some

Dr. Nancy C. Andreasen/Photo Researchers, Inc.

Dr. Nancy C. Andreasen/Photo Researchers, Inc.

The most consistent brain abnormality that has been found in people with schizophrenia is enlarged ventricles. Shown here are 3-D magnetic resonance images (MRI) of a brain of a person with schizophrenia (bottom) and the brain of a person without schizophrenia (top). The hippocampus (yellow, at center) is shrunken and the fluid-filled ventricles (white) enlarged in the brain of a person with schizophrenia.

researchers propose that schizophrenia results from abnormal neural development during the prenatal period (R. M. Murray, O'Callaghan, Castle, & Lewis, 1992). A genetic predisposition to schizophrenia interacts with prenatal environmental agents such as a maternal virus or poor nutrition, causing changes in normal brain development. Then, as the brain reaches maturation (during adolescence), a natural trimming away of brain synapses occurs. It is hypothesized that in people with schizophrenia, the brain trims away too many synapses, resulting in the expression of the disorder in the teenage years. Symptoms of schizophrenia are particularly likely to appear if the person has a strong genetic disposition, or if environmental circumstances have encouraged the expression of the disorder in those with even a mild genetic link (McGlashan & Hoffman, 2000; Rapoport et al., 2005).

THE ROLE OF FAMILY AND ENVIRONMENT

Two critical psychological factors appear to contribute to the onset and course of schizophrenia: family support and exposure to stressful living conditions. Studies on the families of people with schizophrenia have found that the quality of family communication and interactions may either encourage or discourage the onset of schizophrenia in people who are genetically at high risk. The quality of family interactions may also influence whether future psychotic episodes are triggered. Families that are critical, harsh, hostile, and poor communicators may make a high-risk person more susceptible to the disorder (Butzlaff & Hooley, 1998; Hooley & Hiller, 1998). Chronic stress from living a low-income lifestyle or within a family with poor communication also appears to influence future relapses (Dohrenwend et al., 1987; Norman & Malla, 1993; Ventura, Nuechterlein, Subotnik, Hardesty, & Mintz, 2000). Although it appears that family and lifestyle do not *cause* schizophrenia, they are especially critical factors in people's susceptibility to the disorder and must be taken into account when designing prevention or treatment programs for those with schizophrenia.

Let's Review!

In this section we described the symptoms and types of schizophrenia, and outlined our current understanding of the factors that play a role in its development. For a quick check of your understanding, answer these questions.

1. Schizophrenia has been linked most strongly to which neurotransmitter?
   a. Dopamine
   b. GABA
   c. Serotonin
   d. Acetylcholine

2. People with _____ schizophrenia show predominantly positive symptoms, such as delusions and hallucinations.
   a. disorganized
   b. catatonic
   c. paranoid
   d. undifferentiated

3. The most consistent brain abnormality found among people with schizophrenia is _____.
   a. a small frontal lobe
   b. a small temporal lobe
   c. enlarged ventricles
   d. an enlarged frontal lobe

4. Loose associations, poverty of content, and word salad characterize which symptom of schizophrenia?
   a. Thought disorder
   b. Catatonic stupor
   c. Delusions
   d. Flat affect

Answers 1. *a*; 2. *c*; 3. *c*; 4. *a*

Dissociative and Somatoform Disorders

● Describe the nature of dissociative and somatoform disorders.

Dissociative and somatoform disorders are quite rare in the general population, but often are of the most interest to students. Here we outline the general nature of these disorders and the psychological factors that may a play a role in their development.

Dissociative Disorders: Flight or Multiple Personalities

To *dissociate* means to break or pull apart. Thus, the **dissociative disorders** involve a loss of awareness of some part of our self, our surroundings, or what is going on around us. Mild dissociative experiences are common (Aderibigbe, Bloch, & Walker, 2001; Ross, 1997). For instance, have you ever driven somewhere and on arrival did not remember driving there? Have you ever missed a part of a conversation but can tell from the speaker's demeanor that you appeared to have been listening the whole time? Have you ever appeared attentive in class while you were daydreaming about your plans for the weekend? All of these are common everyday dissociative experiences.

However, when loss of awareness becomes more extreme, a diagnosis of a dissociative disorder may apply. Such extreme dissociation is typically linked to severe stress or a series of emotionally traumatic events (Classen, Koopman, & Spiegel, 1993; Isaac & Chand, 2006; Spiegel, 1997). ■ TABLE 13.4 provides a brief description of the dissociative disorders listed in the *DSM-IV-TR*. Here we will confine our discussion to two: *dissociative fugue* and *dissociative identity disorder*.

In 2006, a 57-year-old husband and father of two left work at his New York law firm and disappeared. Six months later he was found living under a new name in a homeless shelter in Chicago. He didn't know who he was or where he came from. During the same year, another man left his Washington home to visit a friend in Canada who was dying from cancer. Four days later, he was walking around Denver asking people for help because he didn't know who he was. Both of these men were diagnosed with *dissociative fugue disorder* (Brody, 2007).

Dissociative fugue involves one or more episodes of amnesia in which a person is unable to recall some or all of his or her past and is confused about his or her identity. A new identity may be formed in which the person suddenly and unexpectedly travels away from

dissociative [dih-SEW-she-ate-ive] **disorder** a disorder marked by a loss of awareness of some part of one's self or one's surroundings that seriously interferes with the person's ability to function

dissociative fugue [dih-SEW-she-ate-ive FYOUG] a disorder marked by episodes of amnesia in which a person is unable to recall some or all of his or her past and is confused about his or her identity; a new identity may be formed in which the person suddenly and unexpectedly travels away from home

Table 13.4 Types of Dissociative Disorders

DISORDER	MAJOR FEATURES
Dissociative identity disorder	Separate multiple personalities in the same individual.
Dissociative fugue	Person unexpectedly travels away from home and may assume a new identity with amnesia of previous identity.
Dissociative amnesia	Memory loss of important personal information, not due to organic problems or brain injury.
Depersonalization disorder	Frequent episodes in which the person feels detached from own mental state or body.
Dissociative trance disorder	Temporary alterations in one's state of consciousness or loss of personal identity that causes significant distress and is not accepted as a normal part of a cultural or religious practice.

home (APA, 2000a). In this fugue state the person appears normal. He or she may adopt a new name, identity, and residence, and engage in normal social interactions. The fugue state may last hours, weeks, or months. However, at some point confusion about one's identity or the return of the original identity may surface, leading to personal distress. Once the person has returned to the prefugue identity, he or she may or may not remember what happened during the fugue state, which may cause additional confusion and distress.

Dissociative identity disorder (DID), formerly called multiple personality disorder, involves the existence of two or more separate personalities in the same individual (APA, 2000a). The separate personalities—referred to as *alters* (for alternate personalities)—may or may not be known to the "core," or "host," personality—the person who asks for treatment. Each personality has its own perceptions, thoughts, mannerisms, speech characteristics, and gestures. Each alter appears to have a specific function. For example, one alter may arise to deal with romantic relationships, whereas another alter deals with academic work. The alter personalities may be of different ages, gender, or ethnicities. The majority of people diagnosed with DID are women (APA, 2000a).

Frequent blackouts or episodes of amnesia are common in people with dissociative identity disorder. They may notice money missing from their bank accounts that they don't remember spending, or find objects in their home that they do not recognize. Self-mutilating behavior is also common in people with this disorder. They may repeatedly burn or cut themselves, and have a history of suicide attempts (Foote et al., 2008; Ross, 1997). Often they have been previously diagnosed with other disorders such as major depression, PTSD, substance abuse disorder, or schizophrenia, especially if they have reported hearing voices (Ellason, Ross, & Fuchs, 1996).

One striking similarity among people with DID is their backgrounds. Almost all have experienced chronic, horrific childhood physical and/or sexual abuse at the hands of family members (Coons, 1994; Ellason et al., 1996; Putnam, Guroff, Silberman, & Barban, 1986). Many clinicians believe that in an attempt to deal with such trauma, these people defensively dissociate, developing alter personalities that can protect them from experiencing such events in life or in memory. Research has found that people with DID have a high level of hypnotic susceptibility (Kihlstrom, Glisky, & Angiulo, 1994). Thus, the ability to dissociate may have become an effective coping mechanism early in life.

Some psychologists question the validity of the dissociative identity disorder (Piper & Merskey, 2004). There has been a great increase in the number of reported cases since 1980 (APA, 2000a). Only one-third of a sample of U.S. psychiatrists believed it should have been included in the *DSM-IV* (Pope, Oliva, Hudson, Bodkin, & Gruber, 1999). Verifying the claims of amnesia and blackouts is difficult, and people with DID have often been diagnosed with other psychological disorders (Ellason & Ross, 1997; Kluft, 1999). Some believe that DID may represent an extreme form of posttraumatic stress disorder (Butler, Duran, Jasiukaitis, Koopman, & Spiegel, 1996). Future research may help us better understand the nature of this disorder.

Somatoform Disorders: Doctor, I'm Sure I'm Sick

Somatic means related to the body. The **somatoform disorders** involve physical complaints for which there is no apparent physical cause. The physical symptoms are real to the person, but physicians can find no medical reason why they are experiencing such symptoms. For example, a person may complain of constant hip pain. Numerous medical tests are completed, but there is no apparent physical cause for the hip ache. Because no physical cause can be found, it is assumed that psychological distress underlies the physical problem. ■ TABLE 13.5 describes the somatoform disorders listed in the *DSM-IV-TR*. Our discussion in this section will focus on one of them, *hypochondriasis*.

dissociative identity disorder (DID) a disorder in which two or more personalities coexist within the same individual; formerly called multiple personality disorder

somatoform [sew-MA-tih-form] **disorder** a disorder marked by physical complaints that have no apparent physical cause

Table 13.5 Types of Somatoform Disorders

DISORDER	MAJOR FEATURES
Conversion disorder	Loss of functioning in some part of the body, but no physical cause can be found.
Somatization disorder	Long history of physical complaints affecting several areas of the body. The person has sought medical attention, but no physical cause can be found.
Pain disorder	Long history of pain complaints. The person has sought medical attention, but no physical cause can be found.
Hypochondriasis	Persistent worry over having a physical disease. The person frequently seeks medical attention, but no physical disease can be found.
Body dysmorphic disorder	Extreme preoccupation and obsession with a part of the body that is believed to be defective. The person makes elaborate attempts to conceal or change the body part.

hypochondriasis [hi-po-con-DRY-uh-sis]
a somatoform disorder in which the person believes he or she has a disease, without any evident physical basis

Somatoform disorders involve physical complaints with no apparent physical cause. Numerous medical tests may be completed, but no physical cause can be found for the patient's complaint.

© David Young-Wolff/PhotoEdit

In **hypochondriasis**, a person believes that he or she has a serious medical disease despite evidence to the contrary (APA, 2000a). Many of us tend to think that someone in our family has hypochondriasis because that person frequently complains about physical ailments. However, people with hypochondriasis are convinced that they have a disease, not just one or two specific symptoms. People with hypochondriasis may undergo extensive medical testing by several doctors to confirm the existence of their disease. When a doctor suggests that they may have a psychological problem, people with hypochondriasis are likely to seek out another physician rather than seek psychological treatment. People with hypochondriasis often have a family history of depression or anxiety (Escobar et al., 1998), leading some researchers to speculate that hypochondriasis is an intense form of health anxiety related to panic disorder and obsessive-compulsive disorder (Abramowitz & Moore, 2007; Braddock & Abramowitz, 2006).

Let's Review!

This section described the nature of the dissociative and somatoform disorders. For a quick check of your understanding, answer these questions.

1. Dissociative disorders involve _____.
    a. the disintegration of one's personality
    b. physical symptoms without any physical cause
    c. a splitting off of one's conscious mind
    d. a numbness or paralysis in some part of the body

2. Alphonsia has recurrent abdominal pain. Her doctors have conducted numerous medical tests and can find no physical cause for her symptom. Alphonsia appears to have a _____.
    a. personality disorder
    b. somatoform disorder
    c. dissociative disorder
    d. depressive disorder

Answers 1. c; 2. b

Personality Disorders: Maladaptive Patterns of Behavior

- Describe the nature of personality disorders.

Recall from our discussion on the DSM model that the **personality disorders** are represented on Axis II (see Table 13.1). They consist of lifelong or longstanding patterns of malfunctioning. All of us have personality "quirks." Some people may be excessively neat. Others may be somewhat suspicious and mistrustful of others. However, these traits do not necessarily qualify someone for a personality disorder. In personality disorders, the person's behavior (1) is maladaptive to self or others and (2) has been stable across a long period of time and across many situations, typically since childhood or adolescence.

People with personality disorders also can be diagnosed with any of the clinical disorders previously discussed, and they typically seek treatment for these clinical disorders or because someone else has a problem with their behavior and encourages them to undergo therapy. Individuals with a personality disorder often don't see a problem with their behavior and, therefore, seldom seek treatment on their own. The list of personality disorders is long, and space considerations prohibit a discussion of all of them, but we give a brief description of the DSM personality disorders in ■ TABLE 13.6. Here we will confine our discussion to two: *antisocial personality disorder* and *borderline personality disorder*.

personality disorder a disorder marked by maladaptive behavior that has been stable across a long period of time and across many situations

Table 13.6 Types of Personality Disorders

Disorder	Major Features
Paranoid personality disorder	Excessive suspicion and mistrust of others.
Schizoid personality disorder	Lack of desire to form close relationships with others. Emotional detachment and coldness toward others.
Schizotypal personality disorder	Considered a mild version of schizophrenia. The person shows inappropriate social and emotional behavior, and unusual thoughts and speech.
Antisocial personality disorder	Chronic pattern of impulsive behavior. Violates rights of others and does not show remorse or guilt for actions.
Borderline personality disorder	Instability in mood, self-concept, and interpersonal relationships.
Histrionic personality disorder	Intense need for attention. Always wants to be the center of attention. Excessively dramatic behavior. Rapidly changing moods.
Narcissistic personality disorder	Preoccupation with own sense of importance and view of self as above others. Typically ignores the needs and wants of others.
Avoidant personality disorder	Intense and chronic anxiety over being negatively evaluated by others, so avoids social interactions
Dependent personality disorder	Excessive need to be cared for by others. Denies own thoughts and feelings and clings to others.
Obsessive-compulsive personality disorder	Pattern of rigid and perfectionist behavior. Preoccupied with details, rules, order, and routine. (This is *not* the same as the anxiety disorder, OCD.)

Antisocial Personality Disorder: Charming and Dangerous

> ### You Asked...
> *Is ignoring the thoughts and feelings of others a symptom of a psychological disorder?*
>
> VICTOR OCASIO, STUDENT

People who are impulsive and disregard the rights of others without showing any remorse or guilt are diagnosed with **antisocial personality disorder** (APA, 2000a). A person with this disorder is commonly referred to as a psychopath, or a sociopath. People who have antisocial personalities are callous and malicious, blame others for their problems, and frequently have difficulty maintaining social relationships. They can also be superficially charming and sociable, typically in order to manipulate others into doing what they want. Such antisocial behavior has often been present since childhood or adolescence (Loney, Taylor, Butler, & Iacono, 2007). Serial murderers such as Charles Manson, Gary Gilmore, Andrew Cunanan, and Ted Bundy come to mind when thinking about antisocial personality disorder, as they have received much media attention. It is one of the more common personality disorders, and men are five times more likely than women to be diagnosed with this disorder (Cloninger, Bayon, & Przybeck, 1997).

People with antisocial personality disorder are more often sent to prison than to treatment. However, this does not mean that all criminals have antisocial personality disorder. Although antisocial behavior is highly correlated with criminal behavior, not all criminals are antisocial. One of the key features distinguishing the two is the lack of remorse and guilt for one's actions. A person can commit armed robbery yet afterward regret his actions. The antisocial person does not experience such regret or remorse. People with antisocial personality disorder may not be violent. They may be "con artists," and more of them may live outside of prison than in it. They may function successfully in business, politics, or entertainment fields (Stout, 2005).

What causes antisocial personality disorder? Some research suggests biological factors. Twin studies, adoption studies, and family studies support a genetic influence (Carey & Goldman, 1997; Cloninger & Gottesman, 1987). For example, family members of people with antisocial personality disorder have higher rates of the disorder than the general population. Other research suggests low levels of the neurotransmitter serotonin (Moffitt et al., 1998); deficits in brain areas that control impulsivity, attention, and decision making (Henry & Moffitt, 1997; Kiehl, Bates, Laurens, Hare, & Liddle, 2006); elevated levels of the hormone testosterone (van Honk & Schutter, 2007); and low arousal of the nervous system (Raine, 1997; Raine, Lencz, Bihrle, LaCasse, & Colletti, 2000). However, psychological and social variables cannot be ruled out. People with antisocial personality disorder often experi-

WANTED BY THE FBI
Andrew Phillip Cunanan
Unlawful Flight to Avoid Prosecution - Murder

Race: White; Sex: Male; Height: 5'9" - 5'11"; Weight: 160-185 lbs.
Date of Birth: 8/31/69; Hair: Brown (short); Eyes: Brown; Wears glasses and/or contact lenses
CAUTION: CONSIDER ARMED AND DANGEROUS
Please contact the nearest FBI office if you have any information on Andrew Phillip Cunanan.

AP Photo/FBI

antisocial personality disorder a personality disorder marked by a pattern of disregard for and violation of the rights of others with no remorse or guilt for one's actions

Andrew Cunanan murdered famous clothes designer Gianni Versace in 1997 after killing several others. He was described by many as a charming and bright young man.

ence conflict-filled childhoods. Their parents may be neglectful, inconsistent in discipline, harsh, hostile, or less warm. As a result, they often learn to expect such treatment from others and adopt a mistrustful and aggressive stance toward others (Crick & Dodge, 1994; Dishion & Patterson, 1997; Feinberg, Button, Neiderhiser, Reiss, & Hetherington, 2007).

Borderline Personality Disorder: Living on Your Fault Line

Borderline personality disorder (BPD) is characterized by instability in moods, interpersonal relationships, self-image, and behavior (APA, 2000a). This key feature of instability often disrupts people's relationships, career, and identity. Their unstable emotions result in intense bouts of anger, depression, or anxiety that may occur for hours or for a day. Their unstable self-concepts are reflected in extreme insecurity at some times and exaggerated feelings of importance at other times. This instability may prompt frequent changes in goals, jobs, friendships, and values because people with borderline personalities lack a clear definition of themselves. They have little idea of who they are. Their interpersonal relationships are also characterized by instability. They may admire, idealize, and cling to loved ones at first, but when conflict occurs, feelings of abandonment and rejection surface, and their feelings quickly turn to anger and dislike. They then seek out new friends or loved ones, and the cycle repeats itself. People with this disorder often feel unworthy, bad, or empty inside. At times of extreme insecurity and depression, self-injury and suicide attempts are common (Black, Blum, Pfohl, & Hale, 2004; Soloff, Lis, Kelly, Cornelius, & Ulrich, 1994).

People with borderline personality disorder are often diagnosed with other clinical disorders such as major depression, substance abuse, or anxiety (Weissman, 1993). It is estimated that approximately 2% of the population will be diagnosed with BPD at some point in their lives, and it is diagnosed more often in young women than in men (Swartz, Blazer, George, & Winfield, 1990). Extensive mental health services are often needed to treat people with BPD.

Research on borderline personality disorder has focused on biological, psychological, and social factors. Low levels of serotonin are related to impulsive behaviors (Ni et al., 2007; Siever & Koenigsberg, 2000). Difficulty in regulating emotions may be related to abnormal brain functioning (R. J. Davidson, Jackson, & Kalin, 2000; R. J. Davidson, Putnam, & Larson, 2000; L. M. Williams, Sidis, Gordon, & Meares, 2006). However, many people with BPD report a history of abuse, neglect, or separation as young children, making environment a probable factor (Bornovalova, Gratz, Delany-Brumsey, Paulson, & Lejuez, 2006; Zanarini & Frankenburg, 1997). For example, in one study (Zanarini, 2000), 40–71% of patients with BPD had reported being sexually abused. Such social stressors may impede normal attachment patterns, identity development, and the ability to express appropriate emotions.

In this chapter, we have outlined 6 of the major categories of psychological disorders listed in the DSM-IV-TR. Each disorder meets the criterion of abnormality endorsed at the beginning of the chapter—inability to function. Although research continues into the exact origins of each disorder, we have seen that in many cases, a person's biological vulnerability appears to combine with psychological and sociocultural factors—learning experiences, thinking patterns, family interactions, cultural attitudes, gender roles—to trigger the onset of the disorder. Many people with psychological disorders seek help in the form of therapy. So keep the symptoms of these disorders in mind. It will assist you in mastering the material of the next chapter, where we explore the different therapies psychologists and psychiatrists use to treat psychological disorders.

borderline personality disorder (BPD) a personality disorder marked by a pattern of instability in mood, relationships, self-image, and behavior

Let's Review!

This section described the nature of personality disorders, in particular antisocial and borderline personality disorders. As a quick check of your understanding, answer these questions.

1. Felicia is extremely insecure and lacks a clear sense of identity. She often clings to new friends and then hates them two weeks later. She has an intense fear of abandonment and rejection. Felicia's behavior best fits which personality disorder?

   a. Narcissistic   c. Borderline
   b. Antisocial   d. Paranoid

2. Personality disorders _____.

   a. do not coexist with clinical disorders such as depression or anxiety
   b. generally appear in early or middle adulthood
   c. are stable patterns of malfunctioning
   d. do not pose any threat to others

Answers 1. c; 2. c

Studying THE Chapter

Key Terms

medical model (482)
Diagnostic and Statistical Manual of Mental Disorders (DSM) (484)
anxiety disorder (487)
generalized anxiety disorder (GAD) (488)
panic disorder (489)
agoraphobia (489)
phobic disorder (489)
specific phobia (489)
social phobia (489)
obsession (490)
compulsion (490)
obsessive-compulsive disorder (OCD) (490)

posttraumatic stress disorder (PTSD) (490)
mood disorder (495)
major depression (496)
dysphoria (496)
dysthymic disorder (496)
bipolar disorder (497)
mania (497)
cyclothymic disorder (497)
learned helplessness (501)
ruminative coping style (501)
cognitive distortion (502)
schizophrenia (504)
thought disorder (505)
delusion (505)

hallucination (505)
affect (506)
catatonic stupor (506)
catatonic excitement (506)
dissociative disorder (510)
dissociative fugue (510)
dissociative identity disorder (DID) (511)
somatoform disorder (511)
hypochondriasis (512)
personality disorder (513)
antisocial personality disorder (514)
borderline personality disorder (BPD) (515)

What Do You Know? Assess Your Understanding

Test your retention and understanding of the material by answering the following questions.

1. Allison can't help feeling sad most of the time. It upsets her that she can't be happy and seem "normal." Allison's behavior best fits which criterion of abnormality?
   a. Violation of social norms
   b. Personal distress
   c. Danger to others
   d. All of the above

2. Which psychological disorder is characterized by a persistent fear and avoidance of a specific object or situation?
   a. Phobic disorder   c. Major depression
   b. Conversion disorder   d. Schizophrenia

3. Dr. Sanchez believes that mental illness is the result of unresolved, unconscious conflicts. Dr. Sanchez views mental illness from the _____ perspective.
   a. social learning   c. psychoanalytic
   b. biological   d. cognitive

4. Julissa repeatedly complains about stomach pains and nausea. Numerous medical tests and procedures cannot find a physical cause for Julissa's symptoms. Julissa may be diagnosed with what type of psychological disorder?
   a. A mood disorder
   b. An anxiety disorder
   c. A somatoform disorder
   d. A dissociative disorder

5. Delusions and hallucinations represent _____ symptoms of schizophrenia.
   a. positive   c. neutral
   b. negative   d. undifferentiated

6. Some clinicians question the validity of dissociative identity disorder and suggest that it represents an extreme form of the anxiety disorder called

   _____.
   a. phobic disorder
   b. panic disorder
   c. generalized anxiety disorder
   d. posttraumatic stress disorder

7. Men are more likely than women to be diagnosed with _____.
   a. anxiety disorders   c. mood disorders
   b. substance abuse   d. schizophrenia

8. A young woman was picked up by police after she was found wandering the streets alone and confused. She asked the police to help her discover her identity. This woman is most likely to be diagnosed with which psychological disorder?
   a. Dissociative fugue disorder
   b. Hypochondriasis
   c. Agoraphobia
   d. Borderline personality disorder

9. Which psychological disorder is characterized by delusions, hallucinations, incoherent thought and speech, and inappropriate emotions?
   a. Dissociative identity disorder
   b. Schizophrenia
   c. Panic disorder
   d. Bipolar disorder

10. For the last month, Dimitri has been dysphoric, has felt worthless, has been losing weight, can't concentrate, and constantly feels tired. Dimitri is most likely to be diagnosed with which psychological disorder?
    a. Bipolar disorder
    b. Major depression
    c. Cyclothymic disorder
    d. Manic depression

11. Jayne was shopping at the local mall when all of a sudden her chest felt tight, she couldn't catch her breath, her heart began to pound, and she felt shaky and dizzy. Since that day, Jayne has had several more episodes like this. They always strike without warning and in different types of situations. It is most likely that Jayne has _____.
    a. generalized anxiety disorder
    b. a phobic disorder
    c. panic disorder
    d. agoraphobia

12. Which of the following symptoms distinguishes bipolar disorder from major depression?
  a. Mania
  b. Dysphoria
  c. Apathy
  d. Delusions

13. Betta is always worried. She worries that her kids will get sick. She worries that she will lose her job. She worries that her husband will get cancer. Sometimes she is worried without even knowing why she is worried. Betta is most likely to be diagnosed with _____.
  a. posttraumatic stress disorder
  b. obsessive-compulsive disorder
  c. generalized anxiety disorder
  d. agoraphobia

14. Which personality disorder is characterized by instability in moods, interpersonal relationships, self-image, and behavior?
  a. Histrionic
  b. Narcissistic
  c. Antisocial
  d. Borderline

15. Which of the following information is not covered by the five axes of the current DSM?
  a. Medical conditions
  b. Causes of the disorder
  c. Personality disorders
  d. Environmental problems

16. Which brain structure is most involved in anxiety and fear?
  a. Frontal lobe
  b. Temporal lobe
  c. Hippocampus
  d. Amygdala

17. When depressed, Katelyn constantly thinks about her depression and why she is depressed. This often results in Katelyn being even more depressed. Katelyn's behavior is most consistent with _____.
  a. learned helplessness
  b. negative attributions
  c. a ruminative coping style
  d. compulsions

18. The most consistent brain abnormality found in people with schizophrenia is _____.
  a. a damaged frontal lobe
  b. enlarged ventricles
  c. less white matter
  d. larger brain size

19. Ozzie has an excessive need to be cared for by others. He denies his own thoughts and feelings and clings to others. Which personality disorder best fits Ozzie's behavior?
  a. Dependent personality disorder
  b. Antisocial personality disorder
  c. Schizoid personality disorder
  d. Borderline personality disorder

20. Social learning theorists emphasize the role of _____ in explaining psychological disorders.
  a. thoughts
  b. unconscious conflicts
  c. unrealistic self-images
  d. reinforcement processes

Answers: 1. b; 2. a; 3. c; 4. c; 5. a; 6. d; 7. b; 8. a; 9. b; 10. b; 11. c; 12. a; 13. c; 14. d; 15. b; 16. d; 17. c; 18. b; 19. a; 20. d

Online Resources

CENGAGE**NOW**™ **Personalized Study**

www.cengage.com/login

Go to www.cengage.com/login to link to CengageNOW, your online study tool. First take the **Pre-Test** for this chapter to get your **Personalized Study Plan**, which will identify topics you need to review and direct you to online resources. Then take the **Post-Test** to determine what concepts you have mastered and what you still need work on.

What Is Psychology? Essentials Book Companion Website

www.cengage.com/psychology/pastorino

Visit your book companion website, where you will find more resources to help you study. Resources include learning objectives, Internet exercises, quizzing, flash cards, and a pronunciation glossary.

Look Back AT WHAT YOU'VE LEARNED

Psychologists use several criteria, including statistical infrequency, violation of social norms, and personal distress, to define abnormal behavior. However, abnormality is best defined by a behavior that interferes with a person's ability to function.

How Can We Explain Abnormal Behavior?

Jean-Noel Reichel/Getty Images

- Biological theories suggest that mental illness is a disease resulting from physical causes.

- Psychological theories propose that psychological factors lead to abnormal behavior.

- Sociocultural theories suggest that environmental stressors and social factors such as age, race, gender, and culture influence abnormal behavior.

- Psychological disorders result from a combination of biological, psychological, and social factors (biopsychosocial model). They do not have just one cause.

How Do We Diagnose Psychological Disorders?

DIAGNOSTIC AND STATISTICAL MANUAL OF MENTAL DISORDERS

FOURTH EDITION

TEXT REVISION

DSM-IV®-TR

AMERICAN PSYCHIATRIC ASSOCIATION

- The **Diagnostic and Statistical Manual of Mental Disorders (DSM)**, currently in its fourth edition, is an atheoretical, multiaxial system that details specific criteria for a diagnosis of a psychological disorder.

- Labeling someone with a psychological disorder can have negative effects because it may encourage the person to behave in a way that is consistent with the disorder.

What Are Anxiety Disorders?

- **Anxiety disorders** include physical, cognitive, emotional, and behavioral components.
- **Generalized anxiety disorder** is characterized by excessive anxiety, worry, and difficulty in controlling such worries.
- **Panic disorder** is characterized by recurrent panic attacks or the persistent fear of having a panic attack.
- **Phobic disorder** is a persistent fear of a specific object or social situation.
- In **obsessive-compulsive disorder**, a person experiences recurrent **obsessions** or **compulsions** that cannot be controlled.
- **Posttraumatic stress disorder** develops after exposure to a terrifying event. The person experiences distressing memories, nightmares, thoughts, or flashback episodes of the event that interfere with functioning.
- Potential causes of anxiety disorders include:

  - Biological factors such as genetics, neurotransmitter imbalances, and abnormal brain functioning

  - Psychological factors such as conditioning and maladaptive cognitions

  - Social factors such as rapid social change, stress, low social status, and gender

© Barbara Stitzer/Photo Edit

WHAT ARE **Psychological** Disorders, AND **How** CAN WE UNDERSTAND Them?

What Are Mood Disorders?

- **Mood disorders** are characterized by a significant change in one's emotional state over an extended period of time.

- In unipolar depression, the person experiences extreme or chronic sadness or apathy.

- **Bipolar disorder** involves a shift in mood between two states: sadness and **mania**.

- Potential causes of mood disorders include

  - Biological factors such as genetics, neurotransmitter imbalances, and hormones

  - Psychological factors such as unresolved issues of loss and rejection, low positive reinforcement, **learned helplessness**, **ruminative coping style**, **cognitive distortions**, and pessimistic attributions

  - Social factors such as lower social status, stressful life events, and gender

Benelux Press/Getty Images

What Are Schizophrenic Disorders?

- **Schizophrenia** is a chronic mental health disorder characterized by disordered thought (**delusions**, **thought disorder**), perception (**hallucinations**), emotion, and/or motor behavior (**catatonic stupor** and **catatonic excitement**).

- Types of schizophrenia include paranoid, disorganized, catatonic, undifferentiated, and residual.

- Positive symptoms of schizophrenia involve excesses of a behavior, whereas negative symptoms represent losses in a domain of behavior.

- Potential causes of schizophrenia are primarily biological, including genetics, dopamine and glutamate activity, and abnormal brain functioning. However, family support and interactions, and stressful living conditions may influence the course of the disorder.

What Are Dissociative and Somatoform Disorders?

- **Dissociative disorders** are characterized by the splitting off of one's conscious mind. In **dissociative fugue**, a person unexpectedly travels away from home and may assume a new identity with amnesia of the previous identity. In **dissociative identity disorder**, separate multiple personalities exist in the same person. Both disorders are believed to be related to the repression of psychological pain or trauma.

- **Somatoform disorders** are characterized by physical complaints or symptoms with no apparent physical cause, as in **hypochondriasis**.

- Psychological distress appears to underlie the physical complaints of the somatoform disorders.

What Are Personality Disorders?

- The **personality disorders** consist of longstanding patterns of malfunctioning typically evident in childhood or adolescence.

- People who disregard the rights of others without showing any remorse or guilt are diagnosed with **antisocial personality disorder**.

- **Borderline personality disorder** is characterized by instability in moods, interpersonal relationships, self-image, and behavior.

- Personality disorders are related to biological factors (genetics, neurotransmitters, abnormal brain functioning) and psychosocial factors (inconsistent parenting practices, gender, conflict-filled childhood).

© Grunnitis Studio/Photo Researchers, Inc.

WANTED BY THE FBI
Andrew Phillip Cunanan
Unlawful Flight to Avoid Prosecution - Murder

Race: White; Sex: Male; Height: 5'9" - 5'11"; Weight: 160-185 lbs.
Date of Birth: 8/31/69; Hair: Brown (short); Eyes: Brown; Wears glasses and/or contact lenses
CAUTION: CONSIDER ARMED AND DANGEROUS
Please contact the nearest FBI office if you have any information on Andrew Phillip Cunanan.

AP Photo/FBI

521

14

WHAT **Therapies** ARE USED TO **Treat Psychological PROBLEMS?**

- Providing Psychological Assistance

- Psychoanalytic Therapies: Uncovering Reasons for Psychological Problems

- Humanistic Therapy: Empathizing to Empower

- Behavior Therapies: Learning Healthier Behaviors

- Cognitive Therapies: Thinking Through Problems

- Group Therapy Approaches: Strength in Numbers

- Effective Psychotherapy: What Treatments Work?

- Biomedical Therapies: Changing the Chemistry

© Don Hammond/Design Pics/Corbis

Angel Rosa Rivera, a 28-year-old veteran of the Marines, served two tours in the infantry before accepting a position as a combat instructor in Virginia. Now in college, Angel enrolled in a general psychology course to satisfy requirements for a nursing degree. After learning about the different types of therapy approaches, Angel can see how relevant this knowledge is to his previous military experiences.

As a section leader of enlisted men, Angel encountered many soldiers who had been diagnosed with PTSD. The soldiers had been in combat in Iraq and had witnessed ambushes, bombings, and the deaths and injuries of friends and fellow enlistees. Many had been away from loved ones for an extended period of time. Upon returning to the states, many of these men had difficulty adjusting after the stressful conditions in Iraq as they could not erase many of their combat experiences. The men saw a psychologist during group therapy sessions once a week, although some stopped going after one or two sessions. Looking back, Angel realizes that the men who continued group therapy were more likely to function better than those who were resistant to group therapy. Often those who were resistant were more likely to get drunk or get into trouble. He also understands why the men were instructed to routinely fire off rounds from their guns—a desensitization therapy approach that you will soon learn about. Many of these men were also prescribed medications such as Zoloft and Xanax by a psychiatrist. Learning about biomedical therapies helped Angel understand what these medications do, and how they facilitate sleep and control rage responses.

© Ellen Pastorino

Angel Rosa Rivera can relate the various therapy approaches to his military service.

This chapter explores the principal approaches to therapy common today. **Therapy** consists of techniques that are used to help people with psychological or interpersonal problems. All therapies attempt to change a person's behavior. But the techniques that are used differ, because each therapy approach stems from one of the main theoretical perspectives introduced in the first chapter and explained in more detail in subsequent chapters. We will begin by defining therapy, examining who is qualified to give it, and addressing when it is appropriate for a person to seek therapy.

Providing Psychological Assistance

- Identify when a person should consider seeking therapy, who is qualified to give therapy, and the ethical standards that psychotherapists must follow.

> **You Asked...**
>
> *How does biomedical therapy differ from psychological therapy?*
>
> SARAH KNYCH, STUDENT

Mental health professionals today use two broad forms of therapy to help people who are having difficulty functioning: *psychotherapy* and *biomedical therapy*. **Psychotherapy** is the use of psychological principles and techniques to treat the symptoms of psychological disorders, such as depression, or to treat interpersonal problems, such as troubled relationships. Psychotherapy is a general term that encompasses hundreds of different forms of therapy. However, all psychotherapies are based on the central assumption that underlying psychological factors such as emotions, cognitions, behavior, or relationships are at the root of interpersonal problems and psychological disorders.

In contrast, **biomedical therapy** uses medications or other medical interventions to treat the symptoms of mental health problems. Biomedical therapy assumes that biological factors, such as abnormal brain functioning or chemistry, are at the root of mental illness. As we saw in the previous chapter on psychological disorders, both assumptions are supported by substantial research. Many people, like the soldiers that Angel interacted with, receive therapy that combines both psychological and biomedical approaches.

Who Is Qualified to Give Therapy?

Trained professionals administer psychotherapy and biomedical therapy. A variety of educational and experiential backgrounds characterize psychotherapists (■ TABLE 14.1). These include clinical psychologists, psychoanalysts, licensed counselors or social workers, and marital or family therapists. A master's degree is the minimum educational requirement for any of these professions, and some require doctorate-level degrees. Many therapists receive training in specialty areas or in specific forms of psychotherapy. For example, a psychoanalyst is trained in Freud's methods of treatment. Often their backgrounds include internships in which they have been supervised in administering treatment. In addition, most states require licensing and/or certification of mental health professionals.

In contrast, only licensed psychiatrists or other medical doctors can legally administer biomedical therapies. A degree in psychiatry requires completion of medical school before specializing in psychiatry. For the most part, a psychiatrist is the only mental health profes-

therapy techniques that are used to help people with psychological or interpersonal problems

psychotherapy the use of psychological principles and techniques to treat psychological disorders

biomedical therapy the use of medications or other medical interventions to treat psychological disorders

Table 14.1 Types of Mental Health Professionals

PROFESSION	EDUCATION	TRAINING
Clinical Psychologist	• College degree • Graduate school in clinical psychology to earn a doctorate (Ph.D. or Psy.D.; requires 5–8 years after college degree)	Supervised research and/or training in psychotherapy techniques, psychological testing, and the diagnosis of psychological disorders
Counseling Psychologist	• College degree • Graduate school in counseling psychology or education to earn a doctorate (Ph.D. or Ed.D.; requires 4–6 years after college degree)	Supervised training in assessment, counseling, and therapy techniques
Licensed Professional Counselor	• College degree • Graduate school to earn a master's degree in counseling (requires 3–5 years after college degree)	Supervised training in assessment, counseling, and therapy techniques
Licensed Social Worker	• College degree • Graduate school in social work to receive a master's degree (M.S.W.; requires 3–5 years after college degree)	Supervised training in a social service agency or a mental health center; may or may not include training in psychotherapy
Couple or Family Therapist	• College degree • Graduate school to receive a master's degree in counseling, psychology, or social work (requires 3–5 years after college degree)	Supervised training in family and couple therapy; may also include training in individual psychotherapy methods
Psychiatrist	• College degree • Medical school to receive a medical degree (M.D. or D.O.) and then specialize in psychiatry (requires 5–10 years after college degree)	Training in the diagnosis and prevention of psychological disorders with a focus on pharmaceutical treatment approaches; may include training in psychotherapy methods

sional who can prescribe medication. However, the right of clinical psychologists to administer medications is currently the subject of a hot debate. For example, the state of New Mexico recently passed legislation allowing prescription privileges for clinical psychologists who have completed additional training.

Ethical Standards for Psychotherapists

In addition to being adequately trained and educated, mental health professionals are required to behave ethically and according to certain professional standards when conducting treatment. These are not legal statutes but rather standards established by the American Psychological Association (2002) indicating how psychotherapists should behave toward their clients. Violations of these standards should be reported to professional review boards that oversee the licensing of psychotherapists. Four essential ethical principles are competent treatment, informed consent, confidentiality, and appropriate interactions.

COMPETENT TREATMENT AND INFORMED CONSENT

The primary responsibility of the clinician toward a client is to provide *appropriate and adequate treatment*. Such a guideline prevents clinicians from merely warehousing clients in a treatment center, a practice that was common in previous decades and centuries. When providing treatment, psychotherapists must get *informed consent* from their clients. This involves fully informing clients of the nature of treatment and the details of their participation, including any potential side effects or consequences of treatment. These requirements are especially critical if any experimental types of treatment will be used.

CONFIDENTIALITY

Psychotherapists must respect the *confidentiality* of their communications with clients. They do not repeat to family members or friends any client discussions that occur within the context of therapy. Consultations with other professionals are permitted only when the client has agreed. Using client stories or experiences in a published work is not permitted without the express permission of the client. This ensures trust within the therapist–client relationship.

However, there are exceptions to this guideline. One exception is when the therapist believes that the client should be committed to a treatment facility. In this circumstance, the therapist will have to break confidentiality to convince a court that the client is a danger to him- or herself or to others. Another exception to maintaining confidentiality is when others might be in danger. For example, if during therapy a client expresses violent intent toward another person, therapists are legally required to inform the potential victim of this potential harm. In addition, if a therapist suspects child abuse, partner abuse, or elder abuse, he or she is legally required to report such cases to the appropriate authorities.

APPROPRIATE INTERACTIONS

Therapists must *interact appropriately* with clients for successful therapy to occur. For example, psychotherapists are forbidden from becoming sexually involved with any client, and are not to date their clients either. Psychotherapists do not drink alcohol with their clients or engage in intimate demonstrations of affection such as an arm around the waist. Psychotherapists are not to go into business with clients or establish any other form of social relationship that would impede the course of therapy. Unfortunately, when therapists are depicted in movies and on television, they often do not maintain these ethical standards. Such media portrayals confuse the public as to the appropriate behavior of therapists.

> **You Asked...**
>
> *What are the different types of psychotherapy?*   ALLY BURKE, STUDENT

How do you find a therapist? Talk to family and friends for recommendations, consult your local or state psychological association, or inquire at your community mental health center. Your church, temple, mosque, physician, or local college may also be useful resources for finding a therapist. Given the hundreds of psychotherapy approaches, which one should you choose? The next five sections of this chapter describe the main psychotherapy approaches. After reading about them, you may find that you are more comfortable with the philosophy, goals, and techniques of some over others. This information will assist you in understanding the nature of therapy, and in choosing a therapist if the need ever arises.

Psychology Applies to Your World:

When Does One Need to Consider Psychotherapy?

People seek psychotherapy for a variety of reasons. Many come to therapy because they are suffering from one of the many psychological disorders discussed in the previous chapter. Their behavior is maladaptive, or they are experiencing difficulty in functioning in everyday life. They may be dealing with depression, extreme anxiety, or schizophrenia. Others who seek treatment have a history of mental illness and exhibit significant symptoms of a disorder. Some people are legally mandated to receive therapy by the court system. Yet only about half of the people receiving therapy in a given year can be diagnosed with a psychological disorder (Narrow, Regier, Rae, Manderscheid, & Locke, 1993). People with severe mental illness are at an economic disadvantage because they are more likely to be uninsured, so many do not receive adequate mental health care (McAlpine & Mechanic, 2000).

You do not have to be suffering from a psychological disorder in order to benefit from psychotherapy. Millions of people seek professional help to cope with other life problems. For example, couples and families in conflict may consider counseling to deal with their troubled relationships. People who have experienced major life transitions such as divorce, unemployment, retirement, or the death of a loved one may seek therapy to help them adjust to these changes. People are more likely to receive therapy if they have medical insurance and are educated. Females are also more likely than males to seek therapy (Olfson & Pincus, 1996; see ■ FIGURE 14.1).

You may want to consider therapy if you feel helpless, sad, blue, or nervous for a prolonged period or if such feelings do not improve despite several efforts to change them. You also may want to consider therapy if you are having difficulty carrying out your everyday activities. Therapy may also be useful if you want to make decisions differently, improve the functioning of important relationships, or change your life to feel more satisfied.

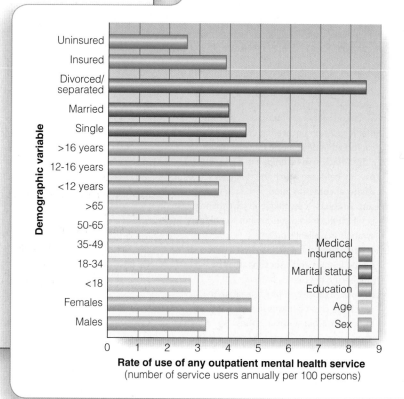

FIGURE

14.1 **Who Uses Therapy?**

People are more likely to enter therapy if they have medical insurance and are educated. Therapy is also more likely to be used by people who are divorced or separated, people between the ages of 35 and 49, and females.

Source: Olfson & Pincus, 1996.

Let's Review!

This section discussed who is qualified to give therapy, the ethical standards that psychotherapists must follow, and when one should consider psychotherapy. As a quick check of your understanding, answer these questions.

1. Psychotherapy should be considered when _____.
   a. you get in trouble with your boss
   b. you are having difficulty functioning in some aspect of your life
   c. you have physical problems
   d. All of the above

2. Michael is seeing a social worker to help him with his interpersonal problems. Michael is undergoing _____.
   a. psychiatric counseling
   b. medical treatment

   c. psychotherapy
   d. biomedical therapy

3. Which of the following professionals is most likely to administer medication as a form of therapy?
   a. Clinical psychologist
   b. Social worker
   c. Biological psychologist
   d. Psychiatrist

Psychoanalytic Therapies: Uncovering Reasons for Psychological Problems

- Describe the aim of psychoanalytic therapies, and distinguish between traditional and modern psychoanalysis.

As we have seen from previous chapters, Sigmund Freud originally developed the psychoanalytic approach based on his ideas about different levels of consciousness and personality formation. Recall that Freud theorized that each of us has an unconscious level that contains desires, urges, thoughts, and memories of which we are unaware or that have been repressed or hidden. These unconscious conflicts psychologically threaten the functioning of the ego by causing us distress and anxiety. Over the years, we continue to defend our ego by erecting more barriers to keep these conflicts hidden.

Freud assumed that symptoms of psychological disorders stem from these unresolved unconscious issues. Consequently, the goal of psychoanalytic therapies is to change maladaptive behavior by uncovering unconscious conflicts so that clients can gain insight into the real source of their problems (Wolitzky, 1995). Freud named this approach **psychoanalysis**. Professionals who administer this type of therapy are called *psychoanalysts*. Here we will describe two forms of psychoanalysis: *traditional psychoanalysis* and the more *modern psychodynamic approach*.

psychoanalysis [sigh-co-uh-NAL-uh-sis] a method of therapy formulated by Freud that focuses on uncovering unconscious conflicts that drive maladaptive behavior

free association a technique in psychoanalysis in which the client says whatever comes to mind

dream analysis a technique in psychoanalysis in which the therapist examines the hidden symbols in a client's dreams

interpretation the psychoanalyst's view on the themes and issues that may be influencing the client's behavior

resistance a process in psychoanalysis in which the client behaves in such a way as to deny or avoid sensitive issues

In psychoanalysis, the patient lies down on a couch away from the therapist so that the patient may freely associate and express whatever comes to mind.

© Jose Luis Pelaez, Inc./Corbis

Traditional Psychoanalysis

In traditional psychoanalysis as developed by Freud, the client lies down on a couch and talks about his/her concerns. It is the psychoanalyst's job to listen carefully and attentively to the client and discover what unconscious conflicts, themes, or concerns may be affecting the person. Uncovering unconscious conflicts is not an easy task. Therefore, the psychoanalyst uses several methods to help clients gain insight and uncover critical issues from their pasts (Freud, 1949). These methods include free association, dream analysis, interpretation, resistance, and transference.

Free association involves talking freely about a subject without censoring any thoughts. The client is fully awake and is asked to talk about a specific topic. The client says whatever comes to mind. The psychoanalyst makes very few comments during free association, instead focusing on important themes or issues that may be revealed.

Dream analysis is a tool that some psychoanalysts use to reveal unconscious conflicts (Pesant & Zadra, 2004). Dreams do not directly represent unconscious conflicts but rather are comprised of symbols that reflect these underlying unconscious impulses (see Chapter 4). It is the psychoanalyst's job to decipher the true meaning, or *latent content*, of these dreams and thereby reveal important unconscious issues. Free association and dream content provide the psychoanalyst with information on the unconscious workings of the client's mind. The psychoanalyst can then make interpretations to the client. **Interpretations** are the psychoanalyst's views on the themes and issues that may be influencing the client's behavior. These interpretations may help the client gain insight into his or her problems. However, if the client is not psychologically ready to deal with these issues, he or she may resist these interpretations.

Resistance occurs when a client behaves in such a way as to deny or avoid certain topics or issues. A client may resist a psychoanalyst's interpretation because it is too close to the truth and therefore creates anxiety. Clients may miss appointments or arrive late as a way of resisting the revealing nature of the therapy session. Clients may laugh or joke about topics that are actually quite painful for them. These resistant behaviors provide the psychoanalyst an additional clue to the unconscious conflicts affecting the client.

The process of **transference** also provides a clue to a client's unconscious conflicts. Freud (1949) believed that at some point during therapy, clients would unconsciously react to the therapist as if the therapist were his or her parent, friend, sibling, or lover. Freud termed this unconscious reaction *transference* because the client was unknowingly transferring feelings and emotions toward a loved one onto the therapist. The psychoanalyst can explore such instances of transference to reveal how the dynamics of clients' relationships may be influencing their behavior.

Traditional psychoanalysis was a dominant treatment approach through the 1950s. However, uncovering unconscious conflicts often took years and called for as many as five sessions per week. This long-term nature of traditional psychoanalysis made it increasingly impractical and expensive for the average person and for the growing involvement of the health insurance industry. The development of other psychotherapies as well as the advent of drug therapy (discussed later) also led to the demise of traditional psychoanalysis (Henry, Strupp, Schacht, & Gaston, 1994). Hence, psychoanalysis was forced to move in a new direction.

Modern Psychoanalysis

Modern psychoanalysis, often referred to as **psychodynamic therapy**, or *short-term dynamic therapy*, is evident in many different forms. Such therapies are consistent with the views of Freud and the psychoanalytic approach. They continue to rely on the therapist's interpretations of the client's feelings and behavior, and on identifying instances of transference and resistance. However, modern psychoanalysis tends to focus less on the client's past. Current problems and the nature of interpersonal relationships are seen as more important in improving the client's behavior. The therapist also plays a more direct role, rapidly interviewing and questioning the client to uncover unconscious issues and themes in a shorter time. Then the therapist and client agree to focus on a limited set of problems that are seen as causing the client the most trouble. Modern psychoanalysis tends to be more short term, lasting no more than a few months, and appears to be effective in improving clients' symptoms (Blagys & Hilsenroth, 2000; Blatt & Shahar, 2004; Crits-Christoph, 1992; Leichsenring & Leibing, 2007; Reynolds, Stiles, Barkham, & Shapiro, 1996; Schottenbauer, Glass, Arnkoff, & Gray, 2008).

transference a process in psychoanalysis in which the client unconsciously reacts to the therapist as if the therapist were a parent, friend, sibling, or lover

psychodynamic therapy modern psychoanalysis delivered in a shorter time that focuses less on the client's past and more on current problems and the nature of interpersonal relationships

Let's Review!

This section discussed the aim of psychoanalytic therapies and described traditional and modern psychoanalysis. As a quick check, answer these questions.

1. The goal of psychoanalysis is to change behavior by _____.
   a. uncovering unconscious conflicts so that the client can gain insight into the source of his or her problems
   b. uncovering negative cognitive patterns that impede the client's ability to function
   c. examining environmental conditions and how they influence the client's responses
   d. providing the client with unconditional support and love so that he or she makes adaptive and healthy behavioral choices

2. Song often arrives late for her psychoanalysis appointment and sometimes forgets her appointments altogether. Her psychoanalyst might interpret Song's behavior as a sign of _____.
   a. transference   c. resistance
   b. interpretation   d. free association

3. Modern psychoanalysis differs from traditional psychoanalysis in that _____.
   a. it is shorter in duration
   b. it is focused less on the client's past and more on present relationships and issues
   c. the therapist is more direct
   d. All of the above

Answers 1. a; 2. c; 3. d

Humanistic Therapy: Empathizing to Empower

- Describe humanistic therapy approaches.

The *humanistic approach* focuses less on unconscious forces and more on the conscious actions we take in controlling our behavior. Humanists believe that behavior is driven not by unconscious impulses, but rather by how we interpret the world and our awareness of our feelings. The only way to understand a person's behavior, therefore, is to connect with and understand the person's worldview. Humanism further assumes that people will naturally strive toward personal growth and achieving their full potential when raised in a positive and accepting environment. When a person holds distorted perceptions or lacks self-awareness, psychological problems arise, preventing the person from becoming self-actualized. Yet people are capable of healing themselves, if only the right environment is provided. The therapist's role is to create this safe environment for self-exploration and facilitate the journey toward self-fulfillment (Greenberg & Rice, 1997). One of the most influential and best known of the humanistic therapies is client-centered therapy.

Client-Centered Therapy

Disillusioned with the goals, methods, and assumptions of psychoanalysis, Carl Rogers (1902–1987) developed a different therapy approach that exemplifies the humanistic perspective. Whereas Freud saw the analyst as all-knowing and responsible for client change, Rogers believed that the therapist should serve more as a facilitator or coach to help move the client in the direction of change. Such a viewpoint resulted in **client-centered therapy**, or *person-centered therapy*. As the names imply, in client-centered therapy, the focus and direction of therapy comes from the person, or client. The client decides what to talk about, without interpretation or judgment from the therapist. The therapist, according to Rogers (1951, 1980, 1986), creates a positive and accepting environment to facilitate self-awareness and personal growth by providing three key characteristics: *empathy*, *genuineness*, and *unconditional positive regard*.

EMPATHY: UNDERSTANDING THE CLIENT

Are you a good listener? Do friends and family frequently confide in you? If so, then maybe you possess empathy. According to Rogers, **empathy** is the ability to understand a client's feelings and thoughts without being judgmental. The therapist does not express disapproval toward the client but rather indicates understanding of the client's feelings. Conveying empathy involves actively listening to the client—making eye contact, nodding as the client speaks, and assuming an interested and attentive pose. Empa-

client-centered therapy a humanistic psychotherapy approach formulated by Carl Rogers that emphasizes the use of empathy, genuineness, and unconditional positive regard to help the client reach his/her potential

empathy the ability of a therapist to understand a client's feelings and thoughts without being judgmental

In humanistic therapy, therapist and client sit face to face as they work together in solving the client's problems.

© Tom Stewart/Corbis

thy also involves *reflection*. The therapist restates, repeats, or summarizes the thoughts and feelings that he or she hears the client express. Reflected statements communicate to the client the active attention of the therapist and mirror the client's perceptions and views of reality. Consider this example of empathy and reflection from Irvin Yalom's work, *Love's Executioner and Other Tales of Psychotherapy* (1989).

> Client: I believe he is intentionally trying to drive me to suicide. Does that sound like a crazy thought?
>
> Therapist: I don't know if it's crazy, but it sounds like a desperate and terribly painful thought. (p. 29)

Notice in this example that the therapist does not judge the client's thoughts as crazy and reflects the emotions underlying the statement of suicide. Ideally, empathy and reflection will help clients see themselves and their problems more clearly, promoting a realistic self-image and greater self-acceptance.

GENUINENESS: SHARING THOUGHTS, FEELINGS, AND EXPERIENCES

A second key therapist quality in client-centered therapy is genuineness. **Genuineness** is the ability to openly share one's thoughts and feelings with others. The therapist expresses his or her true feelings and thoughts to the client and does not hide behind the mask of being the "professional," "doctor," or authority figure. The therapist self-discloses a fair amount to the client, which allows the client to see the therapist as a real, living person. It also creates an open environment that promotes trust and an honest expression of thoughts and feelings. Rogers believed that such an environment would model to the client how relationships can be built on a foundation of trust and honesty.

UNCONDITIONAL POSITIVE REGARD: VALUING THE CLIENT

The third key quality in client-centered therapy, unconditional positive regard, was introduced in the chapter on personality (Chapter 12). Recall that Rogers defined **unconditional positive regard** as the ability to accept and value a person for who he or she is, regardless of his or her faults or problems. Rogers believed that receiving unconditional positive regard in one's childhood is a key factor in healthy personality adjustment. A therapist who offers unconditional positive regard to a client does not indicate shock, dismay, or disapproval to any client statements. Instead, the therapist communicates caring and respect toward the client regardless of what the client says. This does not mean that the therapist has to personally *agree* with everything the client states. Rather, the therapist's job is to reflect the client's feelings and thoughts in order to further the client's self-knowledge and enable the client to solve problems in his or her own way. Unconditional positive regard enables the client to believe that he or she has value and is competent at making decisions. Such attitudes foster self-confidence and self-acceptance that lead to healthier growth choices.

For Rogers, a therapist who demonstrates all three qualities—empathy, genuineness, and unconditional positive regard—establishes a positive and nurturing environment. A person feels accepted, understood, and valued. These feelings help the client self-explore a more realistic self-image and perception of the world. This in turn removes the obstacles to personal growth so that self-actualization can be realized.

Do these therapist qualities actually have an effect on changing people's behavior? Each quality by itself does not appear to help clients change (Beutler, Machado, & Neufeldt, 1994). Yet when used together, they lead to more promising results, emphasizing the importance of a positive client–therapist relationship. Compared to no-treatment control groups, people in client-centered therapy do change their behavior (Greenberg & Rice, 1997; Hill & Nakayama, 2000). Compared to more structured therapy approaches, client-centered therapy is equally effective (Borkovec & Mathews, 1988; Greenberg, Elliot, & Lietaer, 1994). However, it may not be appropriate for people who are seriously distressed (Bohart, 1990).

genuineness the ability of a therapist to openly share his or her thoughts and feelings with a client

unconditional positive regard the ability of a therapist to accept and value a client for who he or she is, regardless of his or her faults or problems

Let's Review!

This section described humanistic approaches to therapy. As a quick check of your understanding, answer these questions.

1. The goal of humanistic therapy is to change behavior by _____.
   a. uncovering unconscious conflicts so that the client can gain insight into the source of his or her problems
   b. uncovering negative cognitive patterns that impede the client's ability to function
   c. examining environmental conditions and how they influence the client's responses
   d. providing the client with a safe environment for self-exploration and facilitating the journey toward self-fulfillment

2. Which of the following is *not* one of the elements used in client-centered therapy to help the client achieve self-fulfillment?
   a. Genuineness
   b. Obedience
   c. Unconditional positive regard
   d. Empathy

3. Marcos is receiving client-centered therapy. His therapist openly shares his thoughts and feelings with Marcos, relating his own experiences. Marcos' therapist is exhibiting which quality of client-centered therapy?
   a. Genuineness
   b. Reflection
   c. Unconditional positive regard
   d. Empathy

Answers 1.d; 2.b; 3.a

Behavior Therapies: Learning Healthier Behaviors

Learning Objective

- Describe the aim of behavior therapy approaches, and explain how they operate through classical or operant conditioning processes.

Behavior therapy focuses directly on changing current problem behaviors rather than delving into the client's past. Behavior therapies, also called *behavior modification*, consist of techniques and methods that use learning principles to change problem behavior. Chapter 5 described the learning processes of classical conditioning and operant conditioning. The behavioral perspective relies on these principles to modify behavior. Recall that the *behavioral perspective* assumes that behavior is a result of environmental variables such as stimuli and consequences in the environment. It further assumes that people learn maladaptive behavior in the same way that they learn adaptive behavior. So, changing behavior involves changing the environmental circumstances that seem to elicit negative behavior. Learning principles that focus on *extinction* are used to stop disruptive behaviors. Similarly, learning principles that focus on *shaping* or acquiring behaviors are used to replace undesirable behaviors with more adaptive ones. Behavior therapy can take many forms. Here we discuss two broad categories of behavior therapy: classical conditioning techniques and operant conditioning techniques.

Classical Conditioning Techniques

behavior therapy therapy that applies the principles of classical or operant conditioning to help people change maladaptive behaviors

Some behavior therapies rely on the principles of classical conditioning outlined in Chapter 5. Briefly, classical conditioning occurs when stimuli in the environment become associated so that both produce the same response. For example, as a child, one of the authors was bitten by a dog twice within a two-year period. In both instances, the dog was a German shepherd. Following those incidents, she developed an intense fear of large dogs. Her dog-biting experiences became associated with pain, so that now she feared pain from all large dogs and routinely avoided them. Her fear was a learned behavior. Behavior therapy would focus on having her unlearn her response to dogs. Two behavior therapy techniques that rely on principles of classical conditioning are *systematic desensitization* and *aversion therapy*.

SYSTEMATIC DESENSITIZATION: RELAX AND HAVE NO FEAR

One effective tool for treating phobias and anxiety is systematic desensitization (Wolpe, 1958). **Systematic desensitization** involves replacing a fear or anxiety response with an incompatible response of relaxation. Anxiety and relaxation are *competing responses*. You cannot feel both at the same time; you can only feel one or the other. So the aim of systematic desensitization is to have a client learn how to relax and then slowly and systematically introduce the feared object, situation, or thought while the client maintains this state of relaxation.

Systematic desensitization is accomplished in three basic steps. First, the client is trained in *progressive muscle relaxation*. This method involves alternately tensing and relaxing different muscle groups, beginning with the head and working down to the toes, so that the client learns to distinguish when muscles are tense and when they are relaxed.

YOUR TURN – ACTIVE LEARNING

Try progressive muscle relaxation training on your own. Close your eyes and take deep breaths for a minute. Then tighten your jaw muscles and clench your teeth. Hold the tension for a few moments and then relax and take several deep breaths. Do the same for your eyes, forehead, neck, and shoulders, alternating between tensing your muscles and then relaxing them. You will be pleasantly surprised by how a few minutes of this procedure can reduce tension.

Once the client has learned progressive relaxation, the client and therapist develop an anxiety hierarchy. An **anxiety hierarchy** (■ FIGURE 14.2) outlines, according to the degree of fear, the threatening images elicited when the client is faced with the feared object or situation. The hierarchy starts with the least frightening images and progresses to the most distressing.

In the third step, progressive relaxation and the anxiety hierarchy are combined. Relaxation is paired with each item in the hierarchy. As the client becomes able to imagine a feared situation and remain relaxed, the next item in the hierarchy is addressed. Over several therapy sessions, this systematic process continues until the client has become desensitized to all items in the hierarchy.

You may be skeptical at this point, unconvinced that thinking about a feared stimulus is similar to actually encountering the object or situation. Once the client has mastered the mental images, behavior therapists can extend systematic desensitization to a simulated or actual environment. For many fears, this is when systematic desensitization is most effective (Antony & Barlow, 2002; Menzies & Clark, 1993). For example, flight simulators can be used to help desensitize people to a fear of flying. Combining systematic desensitization with the actual situation, called *in vivo exposure*, is also a very effective tool in treating a variety of anxiety disorders (Choy, Fyer, & Lipsitz, 2007; Follette & Hayes, 2000; Gould, Otto, Pollack, & Yap, 1997).

Virtual reality computer technology also can be used to simulate a feared situation. The client wears a head-mounted display with small video monitors and stereo earphones that integrate visual and auditory cues to immerse the client in a computer-generated virtual

systematic desensitization [sis-tuh-MAT-ick de-sen-sih-tuh-ZAY-shun] a behavior therapy technique in which a client is desensitized to a fear in a gradual, step-by-step process

anxiety hierarchy a list, according to the degree of fear, of threatening images elicited by a feared object or situation; starts with the least frightening images and progresses to the most distressing

An Anxiety Hierarchy for Systematic Desensitization

Degree of fear

5	I'm standing on the balcony of the top floor of an apartment tower.
10	I'm standing on a stepladder in the kitchen to change a light bulb.
15	I'm walking on a ridge. The edge is hidden by shrubs and treetops.
20	I'm sitting on the slope of a mountain, looking out over the horizon.
25	I'm crossing a bridge 6 feet above a creek. The bridge consists of an 18-inch-wide board with a handrail on one side.
30	I'm riding a ski lift 8 feet above the ground.
35	I'm crossing a shallow, wide creek on an 18-inch-wide board, 3 feet above water level.
40	I'm climbing a ladder outside the house to reach a second-story window.
45	I'm pulling myself up a 30-degree wet, slippery slope on a steel cable.
50	I'm scrambling up a rock, 8 feet high.
55	I'm walking 10 feet on a resilient, 18-inch-wide board which spans an 8-foot-deep gulch.
60	I'm walking on a wide plateau, 2 feet from the edge of a cliff.
65	I'm skiing an intermediate hill. The snow is packed.
70	I'm walking over a railway trestle.
75	I'm walking on the side of an embankment. The path slopes to the outside.
80	I'm riding a chair lift 15 feet above the ground.
85	I'm walking up a long, steep slope.
90	I'm walking up (or down) a 15-degree slope on a 3-foot-wide trail. On one side of the trail the terrain drops down sharply; on the other side is a steep upward slope.
95	I'm walking on a 3-foot-wide ridge. The slopes on both sides are long and more than 25 degrees steep.
100	I'm walking on a 3-foot-wide ridge. The trail slopes on one side. The drop on either side of the trail is more than 25 degrees.

FIGURE

14.2

Sample Anxiety Hierarchy

An anxiety hierarchy like the one shown here is used during systematic desensitization. This hierarchy was developed for a woman who had a fear of heights.

From K. E. Rudestam, Methods of Self Change: An ABC Primer, *© 1980 Wadsworth. Reprinted with permission of the author.*

Virtual reality exposure therapy allows clients to experience their fears in a simulated, nonthreatening environment.

AP Photo/Bebeto Matthews

environment. For example, a person with a fear of flying may be exposed to stimuli that simulate sitting in a plane and hearing the plane's engines revving for takeoff. A person with a fear of public speaking may experience simulation of standing at a podium. The therapist can control the images the client receives while monitoring heart rate, respiration, and skin temperature to assess the client's fear responses during the session (Bender, 2004).

Virtual reality technology provides an effective treatment for people who have a fear of heights and of flying (Krijn, Emmelkamp, Olafsson, & Biemond, 2004; Rothbaum, Hodges, Kooper, Opdyke, & Williford, 1995; Rothbaum, Hodges, Watson, Kessler, & Opdyke, 1996; Wiederhold, Jang, Kim, & Wiederhold, 2002). It also has had some success in treating driving phobia (Wald & Taylor, 2003), social phobia (Klinger et al., 2005), fear of public speaking (P. L. Anderson, Zimand, Hodges, & Rothbaum, 2005; Harris, Kemmerling, & North, 2002), panic disorders (Botella et al., 2004), and posttraumatic stress disorder (J. G. Beck, Palyo, Winer, Schwagler, & Ang, 2007; Difede & Hoffman, 2002). However, to date the results of such research are not conclusive.

AVERSION THERAPY: WE WON'T DO SOMETHING IF WE DISLIKE IT

Do you bite your nails? As a child, did you suck your thumb? Did loved ones try to get you to stop such behaviors? Many parents put a foul-tasting or spicy liquid such as Tabasco sauce on their child's nails or thumb to stop nail-biting or thumb-sucking. These parents unknowingly are performing *aversion therapy*, another example of a behavior therapy that relies on classical conditioning principles. **Aversion therapy** involves pairing an unpleasant stimulus (foul or spicy taste) with a specific behavior such as biting one's fingernails. Ideally, the aversive stimulus becomes associated with the undesirable response so that the person is less likely to engage in the response again.

Aversive conditioning occurs frequently in everyday life. Food poisoning is a prime example. If a particular food has ever made you sick, normally it will be months or even years before you touch that food again. The food (stimulus) becomes associated with being sick (response) so that you avoid it at all costs. Therapists use this knowledge to treat a variety of undesirable habits and behaviors. For example, an aversion therapy method for treating alcoholism involves taking a drug called Antabuse (Cannon & Baker, 1981). Antabuse interacts with alcohol, causing nausea and vomiting. If a person with alcoholism drinks while using Antabuse, it makes him or her ill. The unwanted stimulus (alcohol) becomes associated with the response of feeling ill and nauseated. The person with alcoholism learns to avoid alcohol in order to avoid the associated unpleasant response. Unfortunately, the person can also simply avoid taking the medication, thereby nullifying the effectiveness of the procedure. In clinical trials, Antabuse has demonstrated mixed results in helping people abstain from alcohol use. When Antabuse is given under supervision and in conjunction with a drug that specifically reduces alcohol cravings, its effectiveness is improved (Johnson, 2008; Suh, Pettinati, Kampman, & O'Brien, 2006).

Aversion therapy also has been used to eliminate a variety of other behaviors, including compulsive hair pulling, gambling, smoking (tobacco, marijuana, or crack cocaine), and maladaptive sexual behaviors such as pedophilia (child molestation) and fetishism (sexual arousal to objects) (Emmelkamp, 1994; Laws, 2001).

At this point, you may be disturbed by the knowledge that therapists use such unpleasant procedures in treatment. Keep in mind, though, that therapists are ethically bound to get informed consent from clients. Clients are informed of the procedure and must agree before such a method can be used. An alternative form of aversion therapy is called **covert sensitization therapy**. In this procedure, graphic imagery is used to create unpleasant associations with specific stimuli. For example, a person who smokes cigarettes may have to repeatedly imagine black and diseased lungs when faced with the stimulus of a cigarette.

Operant Conditioning Techniques

Whereas systematic desensitization and aversion therapy rely on classical conditioning principles, some behavior therapies rely on the principles of operant conditioning outlined in Chapter 5. Briefly, operant conditioning focuses on the consequences of a behavior. It assumes that reinforced behavior will be maintained and punished behavior will be extinguished. For instance, in the previous example in which your author developed a fear of large dogs, recall that following the dog-biting episodes she responded by avoiding large dogs. The consequence of this response was reinforcing—it reduced her fear. She learned that the next time she encountered a large dog, avoiding it would quickly rid her of any anxiety. This example illustrates how operant conditioning principles often operate to maintain problem behaviors.

Changing undesirable behavior, therefore, involves changing the consequences of a behavior. These changes can be accomplished in a variety of ways (Thorpe & Olson, 1997):

1. *Positive reinforcement.* Positive reinforcement is used to encourage or maintain a behavior. For example, every time a child complies with a parental request, verbal praise follows. After the child's compliance increases, verbal praise need not occur every single time.

2. *Nonreinforcement and extinction.* To discourage unwanted behavior, any reinforcers of the behavior are removed. For instance, to discourage a child from throwing tantrums at

aversion [uh-VER-shun] **therapy** a behavior therapy technique in which a specific behavior is paired with an unpleasant stimulus in order to reduce its occurrence

covert sensitization [co-VERT sen-sih-tuh-ZAY-shun] **therapy** a milder form of aversion therapy in which graphic imagery is used to create unpleasant associations with specific stimuli home, the child's parents ignore the behavior so that no attention (even negative attention, such as a reprimand) reinforces the behavior. If a reinforcer does not follow a behavior, the behavior will occur less frequently. Eventually the behavior will be eliminated or extinguished. However, keep in mind that often the unwanted behavior will increase before it goes away because a person is expecting the reinforcer. The child's tantrums will be longer or more frequent in an attempt to get a reaction from the parents. Misbehavior may continue because all subtle forms of reinforcers have not been eliminated. For example, consider what happens when the same child acts up in school. Although the teacher may scold or reprimand the child, the child still receives a form of attention, and therefore the behavior may not subside. Even if the teacher ignores the child's misbehavior, classmates may reinforce the behavior by laughing and paying attention to him or her.

3. *Punishment.* Sometimes punishment is used to decrease undesirable behaviors. Recall that punishment occurs when an undesired behavior is immediately followed by a negative or aversive consequence such as loss of a privilege. But also remember the side effects of punishment. It can produce negative emotions such as anger, fear, or escaping the situation altogether. For these reasons, punishment is used sparingly.

4. *Shaping.* Recall from Chapter 5 that shaping involves positively reinforcing each successive attempt at a behavior. It is used to teach a person new, desired behaviors. For example, shaping may be used to teach children with autism how to speak. If the child makes a "t" sound to say *toy*, this attempt is rewarded. Shaping has also been successfully used to teach people with mental retardation self-help skills, such as washing their face or brushing their teeth.

5. *Token economy.* A **token economy** involves rewarding people with tokens, or symbolic rewards, for desired behavior. Because not everyone is influenced by the same reward, tokens—such as chips, points, or stars—are given each time a person engages in a desired behavior. These tokens can then be exchanged for a variety of reinforcers such as food, privileges, goods, phone time, and so on.

You may recall having had a treasure chest or goody box in elementary school. Students who had acquired a certain number of points or tokens could visit the prize box at the end of the week. Today, your consumer behavior may be unknowingly reinforced by a token economy. Many credit card companies offer points for purchases. These points can then be exchanged for a variety of merchandise. Airlines do the same thing with frequent flyer points. Their aim is to increase your consumption of their services.

The same principle can be used in hospitals, halfway houses, prisons, drug abuse treatment centers, and other institutional settings. People earn tokens for desired behavior and constructive activities, and then exchange them for passes, free time, meals, access to television, or private rooms. In some institutions, patients may lose or be charged tokens for undesired behavior such as fighting, noncompliance, or not completing their chores. A token economy can be a very effective tool for managing behavior in a group setting (Adams, Girolami, Joseph, Sauvageot, & Slater, 2002; Comaty, Stasio, & Advokat, 2001; Morisse, Batra, Hess, & Silverman, 1996; Mottram & Berger-Gross, 2004; Petry et al., 2004; Sullivan & O'Leary, 1990).

Although the behavior therapies have been very successful in treating a variety of psychological and behavioral problems, particularly in children, they do not address the thoughts and perceptions that often accompany behavior. For this reason, behavioral strategies have been increasingly used in conjunction with cognitive therapy (Wilson, Hayes, & Gifford, 1997), our next topic of discussion.

token economy a behavioral therapy technique in which people are rewarded with tokens for desired behavior; the tokens can then be exchanged for what is reinforcing to them

Let's Review!

This section described behavior therapy approaches and the ways in which classical and operant conditioning techniques are used to change behavior. For a quick check of your understanding, answer these questions.

1. Behavior therapies change behavior by _____.
   a. uncovering unconscious conflicts so that the client can gain insight into the source of his or her problems
   b. uncovering negative cognitive patterns that impede the client's ability to function
   c. examining and then changing the environmental circumstances that seem to elicit negative behavior
   d. providing the client with a safe environment for self-exploration and facilitating the journey toward self-fulfillment

2. Celia goes to a therapist to try to reduce her fear of driving. The therapist teaches Celia how to relax and then has her imagine those aspects of driving that make her fearful while maintaining her relaxed mode. Celia is most likely undergoing _____.
   a. aversion therapy
   b. a token economy
   c. systematic desensitization
   d. client-centered therapy

3. Which of the following is *not* a therapy approach based on the principles of operant conditioning?
   a. Token economies
   b. Shaping
   c. Positive reinforcement
   d. Aversion therapy

Answers 1. c; 2. c; 3. d

Cognitive Therapies: Thinking Through Problems

- Describe the aim of cognitive therapy approaches, and distinguish between rational-emotive therapy and Beck's cognitive therapy.

Many psychological problems such as anxiety and depression may stem from negative and distorted thought patterns. *Cognitive therapies* focus on changing these maladaptive patterns of thinking and perceiving, and replacing them with more adaptive ways of interpreting events. Two of the most widely used cognitive therapies are Albert Ellis's *rational-emotive therapy* and Aaron Beck's *cognitive therapy*.

Ellis's Rational-Emotive Therapy

Developed by Albert Ellis (1973, 1995), **rational-emotive therapy** is based on the premise that many psychological problems stem from how people think about and interpret events in their lives. It is not the actual event that causes the emotional upset, but rather the person's *interpretation* of the event that results in emotional distress. Specifically, it identifies the client's faulty or irrational beliefs that lead to self-defeating behaviors, anxiety, depression, anger, or other psychological problems. Several studies support Ellis's notion that people who think more irrationally exhibit more psychological distress (Solomon, Arnow, Gotlib, & Wind, 2003; Ziegler & Leslie, 2003; Ziegler & Smith, 2004).

Ellis identified common irrational beliefs (1991) that often impede people's functioning, as listed in ■ TABLE 14.2. Identifying such irrational beliefs is the first step in rational-

Albert Ellis developed rational-emotive therapy to deal with clients' faulty or irrational beliefs that lead to self-defeating behaviors such as anxiety, depression, or anger.

rational–emotive therapy a cognitive therapy approach created by Albert Ellis that focuses on changing the irrational beliefs that people hold that seem to impede healthy psychological functioning

Courtesy of Ellis Institute

Table 14.2 Examples of Irrational Assumptions

1. I must be loved by or approved of by everyone.

2. I must be competent and achieving in all things I do; otherwise I am worthless.

3. Some people are bad and should be severely blamed and punished for it. I should be extremely upset over the wrongdoings of others.

4. It is awful and upsetting when things are not the way I would like them to be.

5. Unhappiness is caused by external events, and I cannot control my bad feelings and emotional reactions.

6. If something unpleasant happens, I should dwell on it.

7. Avoiding difficulties, rather than facing them, will make you happy.

8. Always rely on someone who is stronger than you.

9. Your past will indefinitely affect your present life.

10. There is a perfect solution for every problem, and it is awful and upsetting if this solution is not found.

emotive therapy. For example, one client may have an excessive need for approval because she believes that she "must be loved by everyone." Another client may irrationally believe that there is a "right" solution for every problem and become frustrated or depressed because a problem recurs. Once these beliefs have been identified, the therapist challenges their validity. The therapist confronts and disputes these fallacies in a logical and persuasive manner, pushing the client to recognize that such beliefs are irrational and unhealthy. The therapist might make statements such as "What evidence do you have to support this belief?" or "In what other ways could this evidence be interpreted?" Additionally, the client may be asked "What is the worst thing that could happen?" and "If that happened, what could you do?" Asking such questions forces the client to consider alternative viewpoints, face his fears and anxieties, and explore possible problem-solving methods. After a client's irrational beliefs have been recognized and refuted, they can then be replaced with more realistic and rational beliefs. These beliefs may be reflected in such statements as "Not everyone will like me, but that is okay and not a measure of my worth" or "There are several ways to solve a problem, and if I fail I can try another approach."

Rational-emotive therapy is a very direct and confrontational approach. Admitting that our way of thinking is irrational and unhealthy and radically changing our interpretation of events in our lives is not an easy task. Yet despite these obstacles, rational-emotive therapy has generally been effective in treating depression, social phobias, and other anxiety disorders (David, Szentagotai, Lupu, & Cosman, 2008; Gould et al., 1997; Lewinsohn, Clark, Hops, & Andrews, 1990; Robinson, Berman, & Neimeyer, 1990).

Beck's Cognitive Therapy

A second illustration of focusing on thought patterns in therapy is Aaron Beck's **cognitive therapy**. Noticing that many of his clients who were depressed expressed a negative view of themselves and the world almost habitually, Beck turned his attention to the role cognitions play in emotional distress. He developed a cognitive therapy based on the principle that distorted thinking, in the form of **cognitive distortions** and negative, automatic thought patterns, leads to depression, anxiety, and low self-esteem (Beck, Rush, Shaw, & Emery, 1979). For example, do you ever notice that you make critical remarks to yourself such as "Oh, I am so stupid" or "I am such an idiot"? Such personal negative statements depress mood and lower self-esteem. Beck believed that such maladaptive patterns could be identified and changed, resulting in more adaptive behavior. ■ TABLE 14.3 illustrates some of the more common cognitive distortions that Beck identified in people who are depressed.

Beck's cognitive therapy is not as confrontational in its approach as rational-emotive

cognitive therapy a therapy created by Aaron Beck that focuses on uncovering negative automatic thought patterns that impede healthy psychological functioning

cognitive distortions distorted thinking patterns, such as overgeneralization or all-or-none thinking, that, according to Beck, lead to depression, anxiety, and low self-esteem

Aaron Beck developed cognitive therapy based on the principle that distorted thinking and negative, automatic thought patterns lead to depression, anxiety, and low self-esteem.

Courtesy of Beck Institute for Cognitive Therapy and Research

Table 14.3 Examples of Cognitive Distortions

COGNITIVE ERROR	DESCRIPTION	EXAMPLE
All-or-nothing thinking	Seeing each event as completely good or bad, right or wrong, a success or a failure	"If I don't get this job, I am a failure."
Arbitrary inference	Concluding that something negative will happen or is happening even though there is no evidence to support it	"My neighbor did not say hello to me. She must be mad at me."
Disqualifying the positive	Rejecting positive experiences	"Anyone can paint. It's no big deal."
Emotional reasoning	Assuming that negative emotions are accurate without questioning them	"I feel fat, so I must be fat."
Labeling	Placing a negative, global label on a person or situation	"I can't do anything right, so why should I try?"
Magnification and minimization	Overestimating the importance of negative events and underestimating the impact of positive events	"In my job evaluation, my boss said I need to work on my time management skills. She only said I was a productive worker and good team manager to be nice."
Overgeneralization	Applying a negative conclusion of one event to other unrelated events and areas of one's life	"I messed up on my math test, so I won't do well in history or Spanish. I should drop out of school."
Personalization	Attributing negative events to oneself without reason	"My parents are in a bad mood because they have an idiot for a son."
Selective abstraction	Focusing on a single, irrelevant, negative aspect of a situation, while ignoring the more relevant and important aspects of the situation	"It doesn't matter that I got a raise and promotion. I have to go to work an hour earlier."

therapy. Rather, Beck (1991) saw the client and therapist as a collaborative team, working together to identify and evaluate the accuracy and biases of the client's thought patterns. At first, the therapist teaches the client how to recognize and keep track of her negative automatic thoughts such as "I never do anything right" or "I always fail at whatever I do." The therapist and client then test the validity or accuracy of these thoughts. For example, a client may be asked to list all the tasks assigned to him in a week and then indicate whether each task was completed or not. The therapist hopes that such an exercise will not only point out the inaccuracy of the client's beliefs, but also train him how to evaluate negative automatic thoughts in the future.

Cognitive therapy, like rational-emotive therapy, has been very effective in treating depression and anxiety disorders (David et al., 2008; Resick, Nishith, Weaver, Astin, & Feuer, 2002; Wampold, Minami, Baskin, & Callen Tierney, 2002). In some studies, it has been just as effective as drugs (Abramowitz, 1997; Gould et al., 1997). More important, clients who have adopted new and more adaptive patterns of thinking are less likely to become depressed in the future—a benefit that drugs cannot provide (G. A. Fava, Grandi, Zielezny, & Rafanelli, 1996; Jarrett et al., 2001; Teasdale et al., 2001).

Currently, the elements of cognitive therapy are often combined with the techniques of behavioral therapy (discussed previously), called *cognitive-behavior therapy* (CBT). CBT has been shown to be highly effective in treating anxiety and depression (Hofmann & Smits, 2008; McEvoy & Nathan, 2007; Norton & Price, 2007) and a variety of other disorders, including eating disorders and substance abuse (Dobson, Backs-Dermott, & Dozois, 2000; Pike, Devlin, & Loeb, 2004; Schmidt et al., 2007).

Let's Review!

This section discussed the aim of cognitive therapy approaches and described rational-emotive therapy and cognitive therapy. For a quick check of your understanding, answer these questions.

1. Svetlana goes to a therapist who focuses on her negative automatic statements. Svetlana is most likely undergoing what type of therapy?
   a. Rational-emotive therapy
   b. Cognitive therapy
   c. Systematic desensitization
   d. Client-centered therapy

2. The goal of cognitive therapy approaches is to change behavior by _____.
   a. uncovering unconscious conflicts so that the client can gain insight into the source of his or her problems

   b. uncovering negative cognitive patterns that impede the client's ability to function
   c. examining and then changing the environmental circumstances that seem to elicit negative behavior
   d. providing the client with a safe environment for self-exploration and facilitating the journey toward self-fulfillment

3. The cognitive therapies have been most effective in treating which type of disorders?
   a. Schizophrenia   c. Depression
   b. Personality disorders   d. Autism

Answers 1.b; 2.b; 3.c

Stop, LOOK, and LEARN

What Therapies Are Used to Treat Psychological Problems?

© Tom Stewart/Corbis

Psychotherapy: the use of psychological principles and techniques to treat the symptoms of mental health disorders.

- *Qualifications:* A master's degree is the minimum educational requirement. There are a variety of mental health professionals, including clinical psychologists, psychoanalysts, licensed counselors or social workers, and marital or family therapists.

- *Ethical Principles:*
  1. Competent treatment   3. Confidentiality
  2. Informed consent   4. Appropriate interactions

- *Psychotherapy Approaches:*

Psychological Perspective	Therapy Approaches	Goals	Techniques
Psychoanalytic	**Traditional psychoanalysis; modern psychodynamic therapy**	Insights and resolution regarding unconscious conflicts	**Free association, dream analysis, interpretation**
Humanistic	**Client-centered therapy**	Acceptance of genuine self and personal growth	**Genuineness, empathy,** and **unconditional positive regard**
Behavioral/learning	Behavior modification	Eliminate maladaptive behaviors and acquire adaptive behaviors	**Systematic desensitization, aversion therapy,** shaping, reinforcement, extinction, **token economies**
Cognitive	**Rational-emotive therapy; Beck's cognitive therapy**	Reduce negative thinking and irrational beliefs, develop more realistic thinking	Challenge irrational beliefs, record automatic thoughts

Group Therapy Approaches: Strength in Numbers

● Describe the advantages and disadvantages of group therapy approaches.

The psychotherapies we have described so far focus on a one-to-one relationship between a client and a therapist. This is known as individual psychotherapy. However, therapy can be administered to many people at one time with one or more therapists, in a process called **group therapy**. Group therapy approaches are often used in psychiatric facilities, group homes, the military, addiction centers, and mental institutions. They are also frequently offered by community mental health centers and outpatient treatment programs. Group therapy often centers on one type of problem (such as addiction or depression) or is offered for a specific type of client (such as women who have been battered, teenagers, or sex offenders). Group therapy may be administered by any of the different types of professionals discussed at the beginning of this chapter.

> ### You Asked...
>
> *What types of group therapy are there?*   BIANCA VAUGHAN, STUDENT

David Harry Stewart/Getty Images

Group therapy can be a less expensive alternative to individual psychotherapy.

The Benefits of Group Therapy

Group therapy has several distinct advantages over individual therapy (Dies, 1993; Yalom & Leszcz, 2005). First, group therapy tends to be less expensive than individual therapy. The cost of one or more therapists is shared by several people. However, clients do receive less one-on-one or individualized treatment in a group therapy setting. Second, group therapy offers therapists a view into the client's social interactions with others. Because many people receive therapy to address interpersonal problems, group therapy offers a safe mini-environment in which to explore new social behaviors or to understand how our interactions with others may be impeding our psychological health. Group therapy also enables clients to recognize that they are not the only ones struggling with difficulties. Group members can offer acceptance, trust, and support for someone who is having problems. They can offer ideas or suggestions for solving problems and can learn from one another. Studies on group therapy have found it to be generally comparable in outcomes to individual psychotherapy (Forsyth & Corazzini, 2000; Nevonen & Broberg, 2006).

The Nature and Types of Group Therapy

Group therapy, like individual psychotherapy, can take many forms. Any one of the four approaches previously described can be used for treating groups of people (Alonso & Swiller, 1993). For example, group behavior therapy can be used to reduce people's fear of flying. Group psychoanalysis or group cognitive therapy can be adapted to work with people who are depressed or to improve interpersonal relations. Three unique forms of group therapy are *family therapy*, *couple therapy*, and *self-help groups*.

group therapy therapy that is administered to more than one person at a time

FAMILY THERAPY: THE WHOLE SYSTEM

In **family therapy**, the family unit is the group. Often families come to therapy with an "identified patient," such as a misbehaving or rebellious teenager. Yet the focus of family therapy is not on the functioning of the individual, but rather on the functioning of the family as a whole system. The goal of family therapy is to create balance and restore harmony within the family system to improve its functioning. If one person in the family is having problems, these problems are seen as a symptom of disharmony within the family unit (Lebow & Gurman, 1995).

Think of your own family for a moment. All members of a family have roles, expectations, or labels placed on them, usually at a very young age. One member of the family may be considered "the brain." Another family member may be viewed as "the peacemaker." These roles are not spoken but rather are communicated within the interactions we have with our family members. If a family member does not conform to his or her assigned role, then the rest of the family system will be disrupted. Many times we try to make family members behave in a way that is consistent with our expectations of their perceived roles. Do you ever feel that your family does not know the "real" you? Have you ever tried to step out of your assigned role, only to find family members so concerned or shaken by your new behavior that it is easier to just go back to your old pattern of behaving? If so, you have experienced the power of the family system.

Family therapists view the "identified patient" as merely the focus for problems in the family system. As such, they explore and analyze the interactions and communications between family members. They address sources of conflict and note how unspoken rules or expected roles may be interfering with healthy family functioning.

COUPLE THERAPY: IMPROVING COMMUNICATION

Couple therapy focuses on improving communication and intimacy between two people in a committed relationship. The unspoken rules that couples use to communicate, and the ways in which they miscommunicate, are identified and addressed. The couple therapist then replaces ineffective or unhealthy patterns of communicating with more adaptive ones (Gurman & Jacobson, 2002). For example, each partner is encouraged to paraphrase what the other has said to confirm that the correct message has been heard. Criticism and

family therapy therapy that focuses on creating balance and restoring harmony to improve the functioning of the family as a whole system

couple therapy therapy that focuses on improving communication and intimacy between two people in a committed relationship

The goal of family therapy is to improve the functioning of the family system.

© Nancy Sheehan/Photo Edit

derogatory labels or names are discouraged. These are just two examples of the "new rules" therapists suggest to improve communication and intimacy within couples.

SELF-HELP GROUPS: HELPING EACH OTHER COPE

Self-help groups are comprised of people who share the same problem who meet to help one another. Self-help groups differ from other forms of group therapy in that they are organized and led by nonprofessionals. Self-help organizations are becoming increasingly popular, and you, a family member, or a friend may have attended one of their meetings. It is estimated that as many as 20 million people belong to one of these groups and that perhaps 2–3% of the U.S. population is involved in a self-help group at any one time (Borkman, 1997). In one study of Michigan and Massachusetts psychiatrists, 75% reported referring clients with depression to a self-help group (Powell, Silk, & Albeck, 2000). Self-help groups can be found for anything from addictions and eating disorders to people who have undergone a medical procedure such as a mastectomy or open heart surgery. The main purpose of these groups is to offer social support and help one another cope, but they often provide useful information and advice as well.

The format and purpose of self-help groups vary widely. For example, group meetings may be highly structured or conducted more loosely. Many self-help groups adopt a 12-step program format originated by the well-known Alcoholics Anonymous (AA). Such a format includes admitting that you have a problem and that you are powerless over the problem. It encourages people to seek strength from a "greater power," to admit one's shortcomings, and to make amends to people they have harmed. Although such 12-step programs are not therapy, mental health professionals often encourage clients to participate in such groups to receive additional emotional support and encouragement. They can increase a patient's adherence to treatment and reduce the severity of psychological symptoms (Depression and Bipolar Support Alliance, 2002; Magura, Laudet, Mahmood, Rosenblum, & Knight, 2002). Some research suggests that self-help groups can be just as effective as therapy with a mental health professional (Christensen & Jacobson, 1994). However, research has been unable to specify what elements of self-help groups make them effective or what types of people they benefit most.

self-help group group comprised of people who share the same problem who meet to help one another

Let's Review!

This section discussed the advantages and disadvantages of group therapy approaches. For a quick check of your understanding, answer these questions.

1. Which of the following is not an advantage of group therapy approaches?
   a. Less expensive
   b. More individual attention
   c. Focus on interpersonal interactions
   d. None of the above

2. The goal of family therapy is to _____.
   a. fix the person with the most problems
   b. improve communication between the parents
   c. create harmony and balance within the family unit
   d. understand the past problems of the family

3. Many self-help groups, such as Alcoholics Anonymous and Narcotics Anonymous, assume that _____ is a critical factor in improving one's psychological health.
   a. social support
   b. physical health
   c. financial status
   d. medication

Answers 1. b; 2. c; 3. a

Effective Psychotherapy: What Treatments Work?

● Examine the effectiveness of psychotherapy and the factors that contribute to effective therapy.

After reading about all these different forms of psychotherapy, you may be asking yourself, "Does psychotherapy work? And if it does work, which approach is the best?" Researchers analyzing the effectiveness of therapy have asked themselves similar questions. As we shall soon see, the answers to these questions are neither simple nor straightforward. Many factors influence and contribute to the effectiveness of therapy.

Which Type of Psychotherapy Is Most Effective?

To answer the question "Does psychotherapy work?" research typically compares clients who are receiving therapy with clients who are receiving a placebo treatment or no treatment at all. Such studies have generally shown that psychotherapy has positive effects and is better than a placebo treatment or no treatment at all. They also suggest that the different approaches—psychodynamic, humanistic, behavioral, and cognitive—produce relatively equivalent results in terms of client improvement (Asay & Lambert, 1999; Chambless & Ollendick, 2001; Kopta, Lueger, Saunders, & Howard, 1999; Lambert & Bergen, 1994; Nathan, Stuart, & Dolan, 2000; Robinson et al., 1990; Smith & Glass, 1977; Smith, Glass, & Miller, 1980; Wampold et al., 1997; Westen & Bradley, 2005). This finding has been termed the *Dodo Bird verdict* after the Dodo Bird in *Alice in Wonderland* who, following the race, stated, "Everyone has won, and all must have prizes." The Dodo Bird verdict implies that it doesn't matter which therapy approach a therapist selects because all are equivalent in effectiveness.

Are all psychotherapies equally effective? Some reviews suggest that the standard psychotherapies have similar success rates (Kopta et al., 1999; Nathan et al., 2000; Wampold et al., 1997, 2002). However, other research suggests that certain forms of therapy work better for certain types of disorders (Chambless & Ollendick, 2001; Crits-Christoph, 1997; Engels, Garnefski, & Diekstra, 1993; Lambert & Bergen, 1994). For example, panic disorder may respond best to cognitive therapy, whereas phobias may respond best to behavioral methods (Chambless & Ollendick, 2001; Hollon & Beck, 1994; Seligman, 1995).

> **You Asked...**
>
> *When using therapy to help with a psychological disorder, does one therapy over the other work better, or does a combination work best?*
>
> JESSE MADONNA, STUDENT

Such mixed results underscore the complexity of conducting research on therapy effectiveness. Perhaps a more appropriate question to ask about therapy is "Which treatment is most effective for this person, with this problem, under these circumstances?" Such a personalized approach to treatment is becoming more common as many therapists are adopting an *eclectic approach* to treatment (Kopta et al., 1999). An **eclectic approach** involves an integrated and diverse use of therapeutic methods. For example, a therapist may combine cognitive therapy with specific psychoanalytic and client-centered methods to help a client who is depressed.

Factors That Contribute to Effective Psychotherapy

eclectic [ee-KLECK-tick] **approach** therapy that incorporates an integrated and diverse use of therapeutic methods

Although research has provided mixed results on the question "Which psychotherapy is most effective?" evidence suggests that all successful psychotherapies share certain common elements, even when the specific methods used differ greatly. Over the last decade, the term **therapeutic alliance** has surfaced to describe the interactive and collaborative relationship between the client and the therapist. The nature and development of this relationship influence the effectiveness of therapy (Barber, Connolly, Crits-Christoph, Gladis, & Siqueland, 2000; Kozart, 2002; Martin, Garske, & Davis, 2000).

> ### You Asked...
>
> *Is the therapist giving the treatment really the one behind client change, or are the results based on a client's willingness to change?*
>
> TAKESE McKENZIE, STUDENT

Therapists contribute to a successful alliance in many ways. First, they establish a positive relationship with the client. This involves an atmosphere of mutual respect and trust. Clients who trust their therapist are more likely to believe that they will benefit from therapy. The clients, therefore, are more likely to engage in the therapy process by revealing important information about themselves and by trying the new skills, behaviors, or techniques that the therapist suggests. Second, effective therapists are empathetic and warm, evidencing a caring attitude toward the client and the ability to listen (Beutler et al., 1994; Crits-Christoph, Baranackie, Kurcias, & Beck, 1991; Teyber & McClure, 2000). Third, successful therapists offer an explanation or interpretation of why the client is having a problem and encourage clients to confront painful emotions (Garfield, 1992; Ingram, Hayes, & Scott, 2000; Snyder, Ilardi, Michael, & Cheavens, 2000). Finally, effective therapists are sensitive to any cultural differences between them and their clients (Yutrzenka, 1995). Given that most providers of psychological services come from the majority culture and clients may be members of minority cultures, it is important to the success of therapy that counselors acknowledge and understand the experiences and values of diverse ethnocultural populations in the United States (Pedersen, 2002).

Therapist characteristics are not the only determinant of a successful alliance. Client attitudes and behaviors also make a difference (Garfield, 1994; Leon, Kopta, Howard, & Lutz, 1999). Clients who are motivated and committed to therapy tend to experience more positive results. Those who are actively involved in the therapy process and optimistic about the benefits of therapy also fare better. Moreover, clients who can express their feelings and thoughts and who are more psychologically mature experience more gains from therapy. Clients who have no previous history of psychological disorders also tend to benefit more. The social environment of the client is also important. Clients who have supportive loved ones and stable, rather than chaotic, living conditions tend to benefit more from therapy.

Notice that none of these characteristics is specific to any one of the therapy approaches we have described. So if you or a loved one is in need of a therapist, it is important to find a therapist and an approach that make you comfortable. If you are more comfortable with the philosophy behind psychoanalysis, find a warm and caring psychoanalyst. If you lean more toward a cognitive approach, seek a therapist who is trained in cognitive methods. Believing in the therapist and his or her approaches will establish a positive therapeutic alliance, thereby enhancing the effectiveness of your therapy.

Modern Delivery Methods of Therapy: Computer Technology and Cybertherapy

In recent years, the rapid development of computer technology and the Internet has started to influence psychotherapy (C. B. Taylor & Luce, 2003). Computer-based programs can now be used to administer psychological assessments such as the MMPI-2. Personal digital assistants (PDAs) can be used to collect data from clients on their thoughts, behaviors, and mood, allowing clinicians to analyze a client's behavior across many situations. Effective computer

therapeutic alliance [thair-uh-PEW-tick uh-LIE-unce] the interactive and collaborative relationship between the client and the therapist programs have been developed to reduce symptoms in people with anxiety, depressive, and substance dependence disorders (Carroll et al., 2008; Kenardy et al., 2003; Proudfoot, 2004; Selmi, Klein, Greist , Sorrell, & Erdman, 1990). Videoconferencing can provide clients who live too far away a link to therapists. These are just some of the computer tools that can enhance the delivery of psychotherapy.

Are there online psychological services? You bet! The Internet has produced psychological treatment by e-mail, real-time online counseling, professionally assisted chat rooms, self-help groups, and mental health information and education sites. However, Internet-based interventions present a number of professional and ethical issues (Hsiung, 2001; Humphreys, Winzelberg, & Klaw, 2000). Online psychological services lack the close, personal contact of face-to-face interactions. Establishing a therapeutic alliance is more difficult when you cannot hear the tone of someone's voice or read his or her body language and facial expressions. "Cybershrinks" may or may not have adequate training or be appropriately licensed (Bloom, 1998). Client confidentiality is of great concern because information on the Internet can be easily accessed. Moreover, the effectiveness of these programs has not been demonstrated. Studies on Internet-based treatments for grief and anxiety suggest improved client functioning (Hirai & Clum, 2005; Richards, Klein, & Carlbring, 2003; Wagner, Knaevelsrud, & Maercker, 2006). Yet controlled studies are needed to evaluate all the benefits and disadvantages of these new communication tools. At this time, technology and the Internet appear to be valuable resources that can be added to traditional psychotherapy (Castelnuovo, Gaggioli, Mantovani, & Riva, 2003). However, caution should be exercised if they are the only type of treatment used.

© Artiga Photo/Corbis

Videoconferencing can provide mental health services to people who live a long distance away such as in large rural areas.

Let's Review!

This section discussed the effectiveness of psychotherapy and described those factors that contribute to effective therapy. As a quick check, answer these questions.

1. Which of the following statements about the effectiveness of psychotherapy is true?
   a. Cognitive therapy is considerably more effective than other forms of therapy.
   b. Psychoanalysis is considerably more effective than other forms of therapy.
   c. The main types of therapy appear to be equally effective.
   d. Receiving any type of therapy appears to be no more effective than no therapy.

2. Which of the following is an element associated with successful therapy?
   a. Free association
   b. Chaotic living conditions of the client
   c. Being forced to receive therapy
   d. A positive therapist–client relationship

3. An eclectic approach to therapy refers to _____.
   a. an integrated and diverse use of therapeutic methods
   b. a reliance on free association and interpretation
   c. a mutual bond of respect and warmth between the therapist and client
   d. deepening the client's knowledge of psychology

Answers 1. c; 2. d; 3. a

Biomedical Therapies: Changing the Chemistry

- Describe the aim of biomedical therapies, and distinguish among the various drug therapies.

Now that we have described psychological treatments for psychological disorders, it is time to turn our attention to biomedical approaches. The two dominant biomedical approaches are drug therapy and electroconvulsive therapy (ECT). Far less used, but still a dramatic last resort, is psychosurgery.

Drug Therapies

Today, the most common biomedical therapy used to treat mental health problems is medications. Recall that medications must be prescribed by a physician or a psychiatrist and are generally not prescribed by psychologists. As with any prescribed medication, side effects can occur and must be considered in any treatment plan. Medication cannot cure a psychological disorder. Rather, it reduces the symptoms of the disorder while the person is taking the medication. Often, therefore, medications are prescribed jointly with psychotherapy. The medication stabilizes the person so that psychological issues can be addressed. Here we present the major types of medications that are prescribed for specific psychological disorders.

> **You Asked...**
>
> *What are the different drugs that are prescribed to people with psychological disorders?*
>
> JENNIFER DEANE, STUDENT

ANTIANXIETY DRUGS

As the name implies, **antianxiety medications** are sedatives prescribed to reduce tension and anxiety. The best-known antianxiety drugs are the *benzodiazepines* such as Valium, Ativan, and Xanax. These medications reduce tension, relax the muscles, and promote sleep by depressing the central nervous system. They influence the functioning of three neurotransmitters: GABA, serotonin, and norepinephrine. They are fast-acting drugs, calming feelings of anxiety within an hour or so. These medications are useful in treating people who are diagnosed with generalized anxiety disorder, panic disorder, posttraumatic stress disorder, agoraphobia, and insomnia (Barlow, 2002; Greenblatt, Harmatz, & Shader, 1993).

The benzodiazepines are highly addictive if taken over a long period. People quickly build up a tolerance to these medications, requiring higher and higher dosages to achieve a reduction in anxiety. If dependence does occur, the person must be gradually weaned from the drug because abrupt withdrawal can be life threatening. Withdrawal symptoms can include tremors, irritability, insomnia, tingling sensations, a return of intense anxiety, and in rare cases even seizures and paranoia.

A second drawback of taking benzodiazepines is the effect on cognitive and motor functioning. As a depressant drug, the benzodiazepines reduce coordination, alertness, and reaction time (van Laar, Volkerts, & Verbaten, 2001). These impairments can affect a person's ability to drive a car or perform tasks at work or school. These effects are even more severe when alcohol is used with these medications.

Finally, *relapse rates* for patients taking benzodiazepines are high. This means that many patients taking these drugs experience the anxiety

antianxiety medications minor tranquilizers, such as Valium, that are prescribed to reduce tension and anxiety

The most common form of biomedical therapy is prescribing medications for psychological disorders.

© Brian Pieters/Masterfile

Neuroscience Applies to Your World:

Treating Drug Addictions

The high produced by many legal (alcohol, tobacco) and illegal (cocaine, Ecstasy) drugs results ultimately from the boost in the activity of the brain's reward or pleasure system—the same system that makes us feel good after eating, exercise, or sex. Activating this system makes us feel good and encourages us to do it again, and again. But repeated drug use actually changes the structure and function of the brain in ways that can last for weeks, months, or years. These changes then lessen the pleasure one gets from the drug while at the same time increases one's cravings for the drug. This is the brain trap of drug dependence.

Many treatments for drug addiction attempt to address these biological forces. For example, medications may be prescribed that block the drug's pleasurable effects. Other medications mimic the drug's effects in order to decrease cravings long enough for a person to kick the habit. For example, nicotine gum or the nicotine patch may be used to help

people stop smoking. Still other medications (such as sedatives or antidepressants) are prescribed to help people cope with the anxiety or depression that often accompanies drug withdrawal. Unfortunately, not one of these biomedical therapies by itself is successful for most people. Substance abusers tend to relapse at a high rate. However, any comprehensive treatment program aimed at helping people with substance abuse must dampen the intense biological forces—the dependence, the cravings—that drive addiction.

symptoms again when they discontinue treatment or are taken off the drugs. The drugs appear to provide only short-term relief from anxiety symptoms. Long-term benefits are more likely when benzodiazepine treatment is combined with cognitive-behavioral therapies (Spiegel, 1998).

Because of the disadvantages of benzodiazepine treatment, a nonbenzodiazepine drug, called *buspirone* (trade name BuSpar), is sometimes prescribed to treat anxiety (Asnis, Kohn, Henderson, & Brown, 2004; Laakmann et al., 1998; Rickels et al., 2000; Varley & Smith, 2003). A modest success, buspirone has a lower risk of dependence, but it takes considerably longer for the drug to reduce anxiety. The person must take this medication for several days or weeks before a noticeable reduction in anxiety symptoms is achieved.

ANTIPSYCHOTIC DRUGS

Over the centuries, many medical treatments had been unsuccessful in treating psychotic symptoms, especially in people diagnosed with schizophrenia. Such treatments included brain surgery (lobotomy), insulin injections, and shock treatment. Because these treatments were ineffective, most people with schizophrenia were merely warehoused in mental hospitals. Then, in the 1950s, *chlorpromazine* (trade name Thorazine) was discovered as an effective drug in treating psychosis, or a loss of touch with reality. Thorazine and the numerous drugs that followed, such as Mellaril and Haldol, are conventional or first-generation antipsychotic medications. **Antipsychotic medications** are major tranquilizers prescribed to relieve psy-

antipsychotic medications major tranquilizers, such as Haldol, that are prescribed to relieve psychotic symptoms such as delusions and hallucinations chotic symptoms such as agitation, delusions, disordered thinking, and hallucinations. They may be prescribed for people with schizophrenia, bipolar disorder, or major depression when such individuals have lost touch with reality. These drugs appear to work by reducing the action of the neurotransmitter dopamine in the brain (Sanyal & vanTol, 1997). Recall that dopamine has long been suspected as a major link in understanding psychotic behavior.

Although conventional antipsychotic drugs dramatically decreased the number of patients in mental hospitals, they are effective for only 60% of persons who try them (American Psychiatric Association, 2000b). They are more effective in treating the positive symptoms of schizophrenia (delusions, hallucinations) than the negative symptoms (catatonic stupor) (see Chapter 13). The conventional antipsychotic medications also have significant side effects, including sleepiness, dry mouth, blurred vision, weight change, drooling, constipation, sexual dysfunction, and depression. Motor side effects also occur, including tremors, spasms, frozen facial expressions, and motor agitation, causing people with schizophrenia to pace. These motor side effects often look like Parkinson's disease. This should not be surprising given that Parkinson's disease has been related to a reduced functioning of dopamine in the brain, precisely the effect of conventional antipsychotic medications.

Long-term use of such drugs can lead to an irreversible motor disorder called **tardive dyskinesia** that involves involuntary motor movements of the mouth, tongue, and face. People experiencing this side effect may repeatedly smack their lips, stick out their tongues, puff out their cheeks, or make other odd facial movements. It is estimated that this serious side effect occurs in 15–20% of people with long-term use of conventional antipsychotic drugs (Chakos, Alvir, Woerner, & Koreen, 1996; Morgenstern & Glazer, 1993).

New drugs, called *atypical antipsychotics* or second-generation antipsychotics, have renewed hope of successfully treating schizophrenia. These drugs influence the action of serotonin and dopamine in the brain and cause less serious side effects. They are effective in reducing both the positive and negative symptoms of schizophrenia (Buchanan, Breier, Kirkpatrick, Ball, & Carpenter, 1998; Lieberman et al., 2003; Lindenmayer, Khan, Iskander, Abad, & Parker, 2007; Stahl, 2001a, 2001b). Side effects such as sedation, nausea, seizures, and dizziness may occur, but for people who do not respond to conventional antipsychotic medications, these newer drugs can be a lifesaver. As such, they have become the most commonly used antipsychotic drugs in clinical practice. Examples of such drugs include *clozapine, risperidone*, and *aripiprazole*. Emerging data indicate that atypical antipsychotic medications may also be useful in the treatment of bipolar disorder (Vieta & Goikolea, 2005) and dementia-related behaviors (Daiello, 2007).

ANTIDEPRESSANTS

Antidepressants are prescribed to alter mood and alleviate the symptoms of major depression. Antidepressants have also been effective in treating people with obsessive-compulsive disorders, panic disorders, eating disorders, and cigarette cravings (Barlow, 2002). As shown in ■ TABLE 14.4, there are three main classes of antidepressants: *tricyclics, MAO inhibitors*, and *selective serotonin reuptake inhibitors*.

Tricyclics   Tricyclic antidepressants, such as Tofranil and Elavil, elevate mood and reduce the symptoms of depression by influencing the action of norepinephrine and serotonin in the brain (Stahl, 1998). However, it takes from 4 to 8 weeks on such medication before noticeable relief from depression occurs. Tricyclics are effective in relieving depressive symptoms in 60–85% of people who are depressed (Fawcett, 1994; Guze & Gitlin, 1994). As with any drug, tricyclics have a number of side effects, including dry mouth, weight gain, dizziness, blurred vision, constipation, and sexual dysfunction. The tricyclics can also be fatal in overdose amounts, which is why they are seldom prescribed to patients who are suicidal.

MAO Inhibitors   The monoamine oxidase (MAO) inhibitors are a class of antidepressants that elevate mood by increasing the monamine neurotransmitters in the brain (Stahl, 1998). They

tardive dyskinesia [TAR-div dis-kuh-NEE-juh] a side effect of antipsychotic medications involving involuntary motor movements of the mouth, tongue, and face

antidepressants medications prescribed to alleviate the symptoms of depression, eating disorders, and some anxiety disorders

Table 14.4 Antidepressant Drugs

GENERIC NAME	TRADE NAME	COMMON SIDE EFFECTS
TRICYCLIC ANTIDEPRESSANTS		
Amitriptyline	Elavil	Dizziness, drowsiness, constipation, dry mouth, water retention, low blood pressure, hair loss, blurred vision
Desipramine	Norpramin Pertofrane	Dizziness, drowsiness, dry mouth, low blood pressure, headache, increased appetite/weight, nausea, tiredness, unpleasant taste
Doxepin	Adepin Sinequan	Dizziness, drowsiness, diarrhea, dry mouth, water retention, low blood pressure, blurred vision
Imipramine	Tofranil	Dizziness, drowsiness, diarrhea, dry mouth, water retention, low blood pressure
Nortriptyline	Aventyl Pamelor	Dizziness, drowsiness, constipation, dry mouth, water retention, low blood pressure, blurred vision
MAO INHIBITORS		
Phenelzine	Nardil	Dizziness, drowsiness, change in appetite, low blood pressure, constipation, dry mouth, headache, liver problems, sexual problems, sleep disturbances, stomach and intestinal problems, water retention, weight gain
Tranylcypromine	Parnate	Dizziness, drowsiness, dry mouth, diarrhea, change in appetite, insomnia, nausea, rapid or irregular heartbeat, water retention, weakness, weight loss
SELECTIVE SEROTONIN REUPTAKE INHIBITORS (SSRIs)		
Fluoxetine	Prozac	Headache, insomnia, drowsiness, tremor, dizziness, fatigue, poor concentration, abnormal dreams, agitation, nausea, diarrhea, dry mouth, change in appetite, constipation, cramps, vomiting, flatulence, sweating, rash, nasal congestion, cough, heart palpitations, muscle pain, decreased sexual desire, urinary frequency
Paroxetine	Paxil	Nausea, prolonged sleepiness, headache, dry mouth, constipation, dizziness, insomnia, diarrhea, sweating
Sertraline	Zoloft	Insomnia or prolonged drowsiness, dizziness, headache, tremor, fatigue, male sexual dysfunction, diarrhea, nausea, constipation, change in appetite, dry mouth, vomiting, flatulence
OTHER ANTIDEPRESSANTS		
Bupropion	Wellbutrin, Zyban	Headache, agitation, dizziness, confusion, insomnia, tremors, hypertension, nausea, vomiting, dry mouth, constipation, menstrual irregularities, rash, sweating, blurred vision, weight loss or gain

are just as effective as the tricyclic antidepressants but are less frequently prescribed because of their more serious side effects (M. Fava & Rosenbaum, 1995). These include lowered blood pressure, liver damage, and weight gain. These drugs also interact with substances high in an amino acid called tyramine. Tyramine is present in common foods such as cheese, smoked meats, and chocolate, liquids such as beer and wine, and even over-the-counter medications. This interaction can produce a sudden rise in blood pressure that is potentially fatal. Simply check the caution statements on the back of any over-the-counter cold medication and you will notice that it is not to be used by a person who is taking an MAO inhibitor. Yet MAO inhibitors may be more effective in the treatment of severe depression than the newer antidepressants (Parker, Roy, Wilhelm, & Mitchell, 2001).

Selective Serotonin Reuptake Inhibitors (SSRIs)   Currently, the most frequently prescribed antidepressant medications are the **selective serotonin reuptake inhibitors (SSRIs)** such as

selective serotonin reuptake inhibitor (SSRI) a type of antidepressant drug that inhibits the reuptake of the neurotransmitter serotonin, thereby improving mood

Prozac and Zoloft. Recall from Chapter 2 that reuptake is the process whereby the neurotransmitters that are left over in the synapse of the neuron are recycled back into the presynaptic neuron. SSRIs elevate mood by leaving the neurotransmitter serotonin in the synapse longer. SSRIs are just as effective as the other classes of antidepressants (Mulrow et al., 2000; Thase, 2003; Thase, Jindal, & Howland, 2002; Thase & Kupfer, 1996) and have several advantages.

The side effects of SSRIs are less severe and are not fatal in overdose. These include increased nervousness, headaches, insomnia, nausea, stomach cramps, decreased sexual drive, and sexual dysfunction (Fisher, Kent, & Bryant, 1995; Michelson, Bancroft, Targum, Kim, & Tepner, 2000). Some of these side effects may diminish after a few weeks of treatment, however. As stated previously, the SSRIs are useful in treating other disorders besides depression, including anxiety disorders, eating disorders, and substance abuse, especially alcohol dependence (Abramowitz, 1997; Barlow & Durand, 2005; Bell & Nutt, 1998). For all of these reasons, the SSRIs are quite popular. Other antidepressants, such as Zyban and Wellbutrin, that are similar to the SSRIs but influence the norepinephrine and dopamine systems, are also being prescribed (Stahl, 1998). These antidepressants do not decrease one's sexual drive and are therefore sometimes used in conjunction with SSRI drugs.

However, antidepressant medication has been associated with an increased risk of suicidal thoughts and behaviors in children and adolescents, especially in the first few months of treatment (FDA Public Health Advisory, 2004). In October 2004, the Food and Drug Administration directed that manufacturers of antidepressants include a "black box" warning—the FDA's strongest—on all antidepressant medication for children and adolescents.

ANTIMANICS

The **antimanic medications** are prescribed to alleviate manic symptoms of bipolar disorder. The first mood-stabilizing drug approved by the FDA was **lithium**, a naturally occurring mineral salt. Lithium has the advantage of controlling both manic and depressive symptoms in people with bipolar disorder, although it is far more effective in treating mania (Barondes, 1993; Kahn, 1995). For this reason, people with bipolar disorder may be prescribed antidepressant drugs in addition to lithium to stabilize their moods. Lithium achieves its effect by influencing several neurotransmitters in the brain: glutamate, serotonin, and dopamine (Dixon & Hokin, 1998; Lenox & Manji, 1995). It is taken even when people have no symptoms of mania to prevent future manic episodes.

Research on the effectiveness of lithium is controversial. Some research reports a success rate of 80–90%, whereas other research indicates a considerably lower level of success (30–50%; Goodwin & Jamison, 1990; Moncrieff, 1997; Shou, 1993). This controversy in success rate may be related to the extreme variability in people's absorption of lithium. Some people absorb lithium rather quickly and can therefore tolerate only small dosages, whereas others absorb the chemical more slowly. Lithium dosage amounts, therefore, vary considerably from one person to the next. Too little lithium can lead to manic episodes, whereas too much can lead to lithium poisoning, involving vomiting, nausea, slurred speech, and impaired muscle coordination. For any one person, the difference between the correct, or "therapeutic," amount of lithium and a toxic amount is a very fine line. For this reason, lithium levels must be carefully monitored in people with bipolar disorder.

Lithium, like all the drugs discussed so far, also has side effects, including nausea, vomiting, diarrhea, blurred vision, reduced concentration, weight gain, and increased risk of diabetes and kidney problems (Maj, Pirozzi, Magliano, & Bartoli, 1997). It can also lead to birth defects if taken by pregnant women during their first trimester.

For those people with bipolar disorder who do not respond to lithium or who cannot tolerate its side effects, other drug options are available. For example, *anticonvulsant drugs* such as carbamazepine (Tegretol) and valproate (Depakote) are effective in treating severe mania and produce fewer side effects than lithium. Valproate, approved by the FDA to treat mania in 1995, has recently overtaken lithium as the most frequently prescribed mood-stabilizing

antimanic medications drugs that are prescribed to alleviate manic symptoms of bipolar disorder

lithium a naturally occurring mineral salt prescribed to control manic symptoms in people with bipolar disorder; it influences several neurotransmitters in the brain, including glutamate, serotonin, and dopamine drug. However, the anticonvulsant drugs are less effective than lithium in preventing suicide (Goodwin & Goldstein, 2003; Thies-Flechtner, Muller-Oerlinghausen, Seibert, Walther, & Greil, 1996). Moreover, there is some evidence that valproate may lead to adverse hormone changes in women who began taking the drug before age 20 (Vainionpaa et al., 1999). The anticonvulsant drugs can also cause birth defects when taken by pregnant women. Yet, when compared to placebo, both lithium and the anticonvulsant drugs have been shown to be effective treatments for bipolar disorder (Bowden et al., 2003; Calabrese et al., 2005; Goldberg, 2007; Keck & McElroy, 2002). More recently, drugs called *calcium channel blockers* have proven effective in treating manic symptoms in some cases (Goodnick, 2000; Levy & Janicak, 2000; Post et al., 1998; Yingling, Utter, Vengalil, & Mason, 2002). Although their effectiveness is uncertain, these drugs are advantageous in that they have fewer side effects and do not lead to birth defects when taken by pregnant women. When a person with bipolar disorder experiences a manic state that progresses to the point of psychosis, antipsychotic medications (discussed previously) may be prescribed.

The effectiveness of medications for treating bipolar disorder is further complicated by patient compliance (Sachs & Rush, 2003). Some people with bipolar disorder miss the euphoric feelings of the manic state and, against the advice of their physicians, go off their medications when they are feeling better. They often believe that they can control their symptoms without medication. For example, in one large study of patients with bipolar disorder receiving treatment in VA settings, almost 50% did not take their medications as prescribed (Sajatovic, Valenstein, Blow, Ganoczy, & Ignacio, 2007). Unfortunately, manic symptoms often return, thus requiring a recalibration of appropriate medication levels (Cookson, 1997). ■ YOU REVIEW 14.1 summarizes which medications are typically prescribed for specific psychological disorders.

Drug Therapy and Psychological Disorders   You Review 14.1

Medication Type	Type of Drug	Examples	Symptoms Treated
Antianxiety drugs	Benzodiazepines	Valium, Xanax	Anxiety and tension; insomnia
	Nonbenzodiazepines	BuSpar	
Antipsychotic drugs	Conventional antipsychotics	Thorazine, Mellaril, Haldol	Psychotic symptoms such as agitation, delusions, disordered thinking, and hallucinations
	Atypical antipsychotics	Clozaril, Risperdal, Zyprexa	Psychotic symptoms such as agitation, delusions, disordered thinking, and hallucinations; negative symptoms of schizophrenia
Antidepressant drugs	Tricyclics	Elavil, Tofranil	Depressed mood; anxiety
	MAO inhibitors	Nardil, Parnate	
	Selective serotonin reuptake inhibitors (SSRIs)	Prozac, Paxil, Zoloft	
Antimanic drugs	Lithium	Lithium carbonate	Relieves manic symptoms and taken to prevent future manic episodes
	Anticonvulsants	Tegretol, Depakote	
	Calcium channel blockers	Nimodipine, Verapamil	

Electroconvulsive Therapy (ECT)

Before the birth of drug therapy in the 1950s, the most common form of biomedical therapy consisted of administering electrical shocks to the brains of patients to induce seizures. This procedure, called **electroconvulsive therapy (ECT)**, was a routine therapy approach used on people with schizophrenia. It was believed that producing a seizure would calm the hallucinations, agitation, and delusions that people with schizophrenia experience. In fact, ECT was not effective in treating people with schizophrenia. However, for reasons that aren't clear, it can be effective in treating people with severe depression.

Although still highly controversial, ECT today consists of a series of treatments, usually performed in a hospital, in which electrical current is passed through the brain, causing a seizure. After administration of anesthesia and a muscle relaxant, metal electrodes are placed on the head of the now unconscious patient. A current of 70–130 volts is passed through one side of the brain for roughly one-half second. A seizure occurs, causing the patient to have muscle tremors for about 1 minute. Violent convulsions do not occur because of the administration of the muscle relaxant prior to the procedure. The patient undergoes this procedure about every other day for 6 to 12 sessions. It is a quick and painless medical procedure.

Many students are appalled and even frightened by ECT. It seems so archaic and primitive. These are natural and common reactions. However, keep in mind that ECT is not the first treatment for depression, but rather a last resort. It is administered to patients who are depressed and are not responding to psychotherapy or drug therapy and remain in a severely depressed state. These patients may be suicidal or even psychotic. For these patients, ECT may be the only form of treatment that is effective (Nemeroff, 2007).

ECT is effective for 50–80% of people who are severely depressed, and it is very effective in treating psychotic depression (Coryell, 1998; Maxmen & Ward, 1995; Parker et al., 2001). It also relieves depression faster than drug therapy. Most patients improve within a few days. We currently don't understand how ECT lifts depression. It is speculated that the seizure may alter the functioning of brain structures (S. M. Taylor, 2008). Alternatively, the seizure may alter the functioning of neurotransmitters in the brain (O'Connor, 1993). Identifying the precise effect of shock on all brain functions is rather like finding a needle in a haystack. So we continue to investigate the power of ECT on depression.

ECT does have its drawbacks. It can lead to cognitive impairments, such as memory loss, learning difficulties, or disturbances in verbal abilities. A second concern in using ECT is the high relapse rate. As many as 85% of ECT patients relapse into depression. This relapse may occur as soon as four months after treatment. Thus, the effects of ECT seem to be short-lived (Swartz, 1995). Despite ECT's short-term effectiveness, these concerns—as well as people's fears about administering electrical shock to the brain—continue to make ECT a very controversial treatment approach. Given this controversy, research is currently investigating more focused brain stimulation techniques that have the same effectiveness as ECT but without the risks and side effects (Holtzheimer & Nemeroff, 2006).

© Najlah Feanny/Corbis

Electroconvulsive therapy (ECT) is a last-resort treatment option administered to patients who are depressed and are not responding to psychotherapy or drug therapy and remain in a severely depressed state.

Psychosurgery

A dramatic last resort for the treatment of psychological disorders is *psychosurgery*. **Psychosurgery** involves surgically altering the brain to alleviate symptoms in someone with a mental health disorder. First introduced in the 1940s and 1950s, probably the best-known psycho-

electroconvulsive therapy (ECT) a series of treatments in which electrical current is passed through the brain, causing a seizure; used to alleviate severe depression

psychosurgery a biomedical treatment approach involving neurosurgery to alleviate symptoms in someone with a psychological disorder surgery is the *prefrontal lobotomy*, in which the neurons connecting the frontal lobe to the rest of the brain were surgically disconnected. However, with the rise and success of drug therapies, psychosurgery declined considerably, as lobotomies were generally ineffective and produced seizures and a loss in intellectual functioning (Swayze, 1995).

Is psychosurgery still used today? Yes. Many neurosurgeons continue to use psychosurgery for treating people with mental illness who do not respond to conventional biological or psychological treatments. Today, psychosurgery methods are more precise, thanks to recent improvements in surgical techniques. For example, a neurosurgeon may lesion (destroy) a small target area of the brain to reduce symptoms of obsessive-compulsive disorder. Research suggests that approximately 25–30% of patients who have undergone this procedure improve significantly (Baer et al., 1995; Dougherty et al., 2002; Jenike et al., 1991). Since 1993, neurosurgeons have been implanting deep brain stimulators in people who have Parkinson's disease (Benabid et al., 2001). It is the most commonly practiced surgical treatment for this disease, improving motor function by at least 60%, leading to a significant improvement in the quality of life for people with Parkinson's (Ashcan, Wallace, Bell, & Benabid, 2004). Yet keep in mind that such operations are performed very infrequently and only as a last resort. Psychosurgery continues to be a controversial biomedical technique (Anderson & Arciniegas, 2004).

This chapter outlined the major types of psychotherapies and biomedical therapies. We have seen that each therapeutic approach stems from one of the main psychological perspectives introduced in the beginning of this textbook: biological, psychoanalytic, cognitive, behavioral, and humanistic. We have also seen that therapy is generally effective, regardless of the specific techniques endorsed. Of course, the effectiveness of therapy will be directly related to the characteristics of the therapist and the client.

We hope that you have enjoyed your journey through psychology. Moreover, we hope that you have found the material relevant to your life. Being aware of the complex interaction among biological, psychological, and social variables will further your understanding of not only your behavior but the behavior of those around you. Good luck!

Let's Review!

This section described biomedical approaches to therapy, including drug therapies, electroconvulsive therapy, and psychosurgery. For a quick check of your understanding, answer these questions.

1. Electroconvulsive therapy is most effective for the treatment of _____.
   a. schizophrenia
   b. panic attacks
   c. severe depression
   d. bipolar disorder

2. Which of the following is the most serious side effect of taking conventional antipsychotic medication?
   a. Rebound anxiety
   b. Physical dependence
   c. Hallucinations
   d. Tardive dyskinesia

3. Prozac is what type of antidepressant drug?
   a. SSRI
   b. MAO inhibitor
   c. Tricyclic
   d. Benzodiazepine

Answers 1. c; 2. d; 3. a

Studying
THE **Chapter**

Key Terms

therapy (524)
psychotherapy (524)
biomedical therapy (524)
psychoanalysis (528)
free association (528)
dream analysis (528)
interpretation (528)
resistance (528)
transference (529)
psychodynamic therapy (529)
client-centered therapy (530)
empathy (530)
genuineness (531)

unconditional positive regard (531)
behavior therapy (532)
systematic desensitization (533)
anxiety hierarchy (533)
aversion therapy (534)
covert sensitization therapy (535)
token economy (536)
rational-emotive therapy (537)
cognitive therapy (538)
cognitive distortions (538)
group therapy (541)
family therapy (542)
couple therapy (542)

self-help group (543)
eclectic approach (544)
therapeutic alliance (545)
antianxiety medications (547)
antipsychotic medications (548)
tardive dyskinesia (549)
antidepressants (549)
selective serotonin reuptake
 inhibitor (SSRI) (550)
antimanic medications (551)
lithium (551)
electroconvulsive therapy (ECT) (553)
psychosurgery (553)

What Do You Know? Assess Your Understanding

Test your retention and understanding of the material by answering the following questions.

1. Most psychotherapists hold at least a _____ degree and in most states hold an appropriate license or certificate.
   a. bachelor's
   b. associate's
   c. master's
   d. doctorate

2. Which of the following are exceptions to the ethical guideline of confidentiality?
   a. When the therapist believes the client is a danger to herself
   b. When a client expresses violent intent toward another
   c. If a therapist suspects some type of abuse
   d. All of the above

3. _____ uses techniques such as free association and dream analysis to uncover hidden conflicts.
   a. Psychoanalysis
   b. Cognitive therapy
   c. Behavior therapy
   d. Client-centered therapy

4. Which psychotherapy would use systematic desensitization to treat a person with a phobic disorder?
   a. Psychoanalysis
   b. Cognitive therapy
   c. Behavior therapy
   d. Client-centered therapy

5. In which psychotherapy does the therapist challenge the irrational beliefs of the client?
   a. Behavior therapy
   b. Rational-emotive therapy
   c. Client-centered therapy
   d. Psychodynamic therapy

6. Dr. Ramon expresses genuineness and empathy to her client. Dr. Ramon is most likely engaging in _____.
   a. psychoanalysis
   b. cognitive therapy
   c. behavior therapy
   d. client-centered therapy

7. Dr. Andrews reinforces appropriate client behavior and ignores inappropriate behavior. Dr. Andrews is engaging in _____ .
   a. psychoanalysis
   b. cognitive therapy
   c. behavior therapy
   d. client-centered therapy

8. Dr. Shu reflects her client's thoughts and feelings so that she can better understand the client's problems. Dr. Shu is engaging in _____.
   a. behavior modification
   b. client-centered therapy
   c. rational-emotive therapy
   d. free association

9. Which type of therapy pairs an unpleasant stimulus with the problem behavior in the hopes of reducing its occurrence?
   a. Aversion therapy
   b. Systematic desensitization
   c. Token economy
   d. Client-centered therapy

10. Dr. Tyler teaches his client how to recognize negative automatic thought patterns. Dr. Tyler is engaging in _____.
    a. rational-emotive therapy
    b. systematic desensitization
    c. cognitive therapy
    d. psychodynamic therapy

11. Which of the following is *not* a benefit of group therapy?
    a. It is less expensive than individual psychotherapy.
    b. Therapists can view clients' social interactions.
    c. It offers more one-on-one treatment.
    d. It provides social support from others experiencing the same problem.

12. Dr. Mendel encourages Maurice to paraphrase what his partner says to confirm that he has understood the comment. It is most likely that Maurice is engaged in _____.
    a. psychoanalysis   c. couple therapy
    b. family therapy   d. drug therapy

13. The "Dodo Bird" verdict refers to _____.
    a. the effect of psychotherapy on the brain
    b. how the main psychotherapy approaches are equivalent in effectiveness
    c. the high relapse rates among people with psychological disorders
    d. the higher effectiveness of group therapy over individual therapy

14. Dr. Garfield and his client have an interactive and collaborative relationship, commonly referred to as a(n) _____.
    a. eclectic approach
    b. therapeutic alliance
    c. psychotherapeutic effect
    d. transference

15. Which of the following is a disadvantage of cybertherapy?
    a. The increased client confidentiality
    b. Provides clients who live far away from therapists access to psychological services
    c. Lacks the close personal contact of face-to-face interactions
    d. It costs more than face-to-face therapy.

16. Juanita has been diagnosed with bipolar disorder. A psychiatrist is most likely to prescribe _____ to treat Juanita's manic symptoms.
    a. lithium   c. Prozac
    b. Xanax   d. Clozapine

17. Antipsychotic medications affect which neurotransmitter?
    a. Endorphins   c. GABA
    b. Glutamate   d. Dopamine

18. Craig has been diagnosed with PTSD. His psychiatrist has prescribed Xanax to help Craig function. Which of the following side effects might Craig experience from taking this medication?
    a. Dizziness and drowsiness
    b. Tardive dyskinesia
    c. Fluid retention and rash
    d. Kidney problems

19. Electroconvulsive therapy has been shown to be particularly effective for the treatment of _____.
   a. schizophrenia
   b. severe depression
   c. panic attacks
   d. obsessive-compulsive disorder

20. Which of the following medications has been associated with an increased risk of suicidal thoughts and behaviors in children and adolescents?
   a. Antianxiety drugs
   b. Lithium
   c. SSRI drugs
   d. Antipsychotic drugs

Answers: 1. c; 2. d; 3. a; 4. c; 5. b; 6. d; 7. c; 8. b; 9. a; 10. c; 11. c; 12. c; 13. b; 14. b; 15. c; 16. a; 17. d; 18. a; 19. b; 20. c

Online Resources

CENGAGENOW™ **Personalized Study**

www.cengage.com/login

Go to www.cengage.com/login to link to CengageNOW, your online study tool. First take the **Pre-Test** for this chapter to get your **Personalized Study Plan**, which will identify topics you need to review and direct you to online resources. Then take the **Post-Test** to determine what concepts you have mastered and what you still need work on.

 What Is Psychology? Essentials Book Companion Website

www.cengage.com/psychology/pastorino

Visit your book companion website, where you will find more resources to help you study. Resources include learning objectives, Internet exercises, quizzing, flash cards, and a pronunciation glossary.

Look Back AT WHAT YOU'VE LEARNED

Therapy consists of techniques that are used to help people with psychological or interpersonal problems.

Who Is Qualified to Give Psychotherapy?

- **Psychotherapy** is administered by clinical psychologists, licensed counselors, social workers, or therapists.

- Psychotherapists abide by ethical standards of confidentiality, competent treatment, informed consent, and appropriate interactions.

- You should consider therapy if you feel helpless, sad, or nervous for a prolonged period of time or if such feelings do not improve despite several efforts to change them.

© Nancy Sheehan/Photo Edit

What Are the Main Types of Psychotherapy?

© Tom Stewart/Corbis

- Traditional **psychoanalysis** has clients gain insight into the real source of their problems.

- Modern **psychodynamic therapy** also relies on the therapist's **interpretations** of the client's feelings and behaviors but places more emphasis on current problems and interpersonal relations and less on the client's past.

- Humanistic therapy such as **client-centered therapy** connects with and understands the client's worldview. The therapist offers **genuineness**, **empathy**, and **unconditional positive regard** to encourage self-exploration and self-fulfillment.

- **Behavior therapies** use learning principles to change maladaptive behavior. In classical conditioning therapies such as **systematic desensitization**, the use of virtual reality technology, and **aversion therapy**, the client's responses to stimuli are changed. Operant conditioning therapies use techniques such as shaping, extinction, positive reinforcement, and **token economies** to change behavior.

- In cognitive therapies, maladaptive patterns of thinking and perceiving are replaced with more adaptive ways of interpreting events. In **rational-emotive therapy**, the therapist confronts, questions, and challenges the validity of client's irrational beliefs. In Beck's **cognitive therapy**, the therapist identifies and tracks negative automatic thoughts and has the client test the accuracy of these **cognitive distortions**.

WHAT **Therapies** ARE USED TO **Treat** **Psychological** **PROBLEMS?**

David Harry Stewart/Getty Images

What Happens In Group Therapy?

- The goal of **group therapy** is to improve the functioning and interactions of individuals, couples, families, or other groups.

- Group therapy tends to be less expensive than individual therapy and offers a safe mini-environment in which to explore new social behaviors or to understand how our interactions with others may be impeding our psychological health.

What Treatments Work?

© Jose Luis Pelaez, Inc./Corbis

- Generally, the different psychotherapy approaches produce relatively equivalent results in terms of client improvement.

- A personalized approach to treatment is becoming more common as many therapists adopt an **eclectic approach** that involves an integrated and diverse use of therapeutic methods.

- The effectiveness of modern delivery methods of therapy such as cyber-therapy has not been demonstrated.

What Are the Biomedical Therapies?

© Najlah Feanny/Corbis

- **Biomedical therapies** are administered by psychiatrists and other medical professionals.

- The most common biomedical therapy used to treat psychological disorders is medications. Drug therapies influence brain neurotransmitters to alter behavior.

  - **Antianxiety medications** are prescribed to reduce tension and anxiety.

  - **Antipsychotic medications** are prescribed to relieve psychotic symptoms such as agitation, delusions, disordered thinking, and hallucinations.

  - **Antidepressants** are prescribed for mood and anxiety disorders, eating disorders, and substance dependence.

  - **Antimanic medications** are used primarily to treat mania.

- More controversial biomedical therapies include **electroconvulsive therapy (ECT)** and **psychosurgery**. In ECT, a seizure is created in the brain to treat severe depression. Psychosurgery involves surgically altering the brain to alleviate severe symptoms of Parkinson's disease or obsessive-compulsive disorder.

Appendix A

How ARE Statistics Used IN PSYCHOLOGY?

- Statistics in Psychology
- Using Statistics to Describe Data
- Inferential Statistics

Statistics in Psychology

- Define the terms data and statistics, and explain how they are used in science.
- Explain the difference between samples and populations, as well as the importance of obtaining representative samples through random selection.

data information gathered in scientific studies

population all the members of a group that we wish to draw inferences about in a scientific study

sample the subset of the population that is actually studied in a piece of research

As you learned in Chapter 1, psychology is the scientific study of behavior and mental processes. Psychologists develop hypotheses about behavior and mental processes and then test these hypotheses using experiments, case studies, surveys, naturalistic observations, or other research methods. In the course of their research, psychologists collect a variety of information, or **data**, from their research participants.

For example, many people believe that when it comes to romance, opposites attract. Is this really true, or is it just a bit of ill-conceived folk wisdom? A psychologist would rely on science to answer this question. One way to test this idea would be to collect data from couples concerning each partner's personal characteristics and then examine these data to see whether couples tend to be more similar or dissimilar on these characteristics. After numerous studies that have taken this scientific approach to romance (for a review, see Aronson, Wilson, & Akert, 2004, pp. 342–344), psychologists have concluded that the folk wisdom of "opposites attract" does *not* seem to be true. Rather, when seeking romantic partners, we tend to gravitate toward people who are similar to us. Without scientific data to point us in the right direction, it would be impossible to separate fact from fiction in the world.

In another example of how a scientist might use data, imagine that you are a health psychologist interested in whether the legal drinking age in a country affects the rate of underage drinking in that society. More specifically, you might ask questions like "Does having a lower legal drinking age encourage drinking among 15-year-olds? And if so, does legal drinking age affect both male and female 15-year-olds equally?" To see whether such relationships exist, you must first collect data on the number of 15-year-olds who drink in particular countries along with each country's legal drinking age.

Obviously, it would be impractical for any researcher to survey the entire **population** of 15-year-olds in the world. So, instead of trying to collect data from the entire population, you would measure the characteristics of a subset, or **sample**, of the population. However, if your sample is to be useful in answering your questions, you must use a **representative sample**, or a sample in which the participants are representative of the entire population about which you are trying to draw conclusions. For instance, you would not wish to sample and test only 15-year-olds from wealthy families. Likewise, it would be a mistake to limit your sample to White 15-year-olds or to those growing up in rural areas. So, how can you ensure that your sample of 15-year-olds is representative and accurately reflects the behavior of the entire population of 15-year-olds?

One way to do this is to use **random selection** when choosing participants for your study. Random selection involves selecting participants so that each person in the population has an equal chance of being chosen to participate in the study. Randomly selecting 15-year-olds in each country you are studying makes it highly unlikely that your sample will be limited to any specific type of 15-year-old. Therefore, your sample will be unbiased and representative of the whole population. This is important because only a representative sample will allow you to draw conclusions about the entire population—not just those 15-year-olds who participated in your study. ■ TABLE A.1 shows data from a representative sample of male and female 15-year-olds for 28 selected countries.

Take a moment to look at the data in Table A.1. By just looking at the table, can you tell whether a relationship exists between the percentage of 15-year-old students who drink and a country's minimum legal drinking age? If you cannot, don't feel bad. You are in good company—it's impossible to tell from just a table whether the data support one's hypothesis. Instead, psychologists must use a type of applied mathematics called **statistics** to describe and analyze their data. Only then can researchers determine what the data say about their hypothesis.

Table A.1 Percent of Students Who Report Drinking Alcohol Weekly at Age 15, Selected Countries

Country	Minimum Legal Drinking Age	Males	Females
Austria	16	39%	23%
Belgium	16	38	22
Canada	18	22	17
Czech Republic	18	32	19
Denmark	15	46	38
England	18	47	36
Estonia	18*	21	10
Finland	18	11	8
France	16	31	15
Germany	16	29	22
Greece	16*	52	31
Greenland	18	13	10
Hungary	16	29	11
Ireland	18	27	12
Israel	18	26	10
Latvia	18	28	12
Lithuania	21	16	9
Northern Ireland	18	33	20
Norway	18	16	12
Poland	18	20	8
Portugal	16	29	9
Russia	18	28	24
Scotland	18	37	33
Slovakia	18	32	16
Sweden	18	17	11
Switzerland	16	19	9
United States	21	23	15
Wales	18	53	36

Source: Except where noted, data taken from Kaul, C. (2002). Statistical Handbook on the World's Children (p. 447). Westport, CT: Oryx Press.

*These data taken from http://www2.potsdam.edu/alcohol-info/LegalDrinkingAge.html#worlddrinkingages on 11/6/03

representative sample a sample, or subset, of the population that is representative of the entire population (i.e., the participants in the sample have the same characteristics as the larger population from which they are taken)

random selection a method of obtaining a representative sample from a population in which all members of the population have an equal chance of being selected to be in the sample

statistics a type of applied mathematics used to describe data and test hypotheses

Using Statistics to Describe Data

Learning Objectives

- Interpret the different types of graphs and distributions used in statistical analyses, including frequency distributions, frequency polygons, histograms, and scatter plots.

- Calculate and interpret the different measures of central tendency and variability used in statistics—

the mean, median, mode, range, sample variance, and standard deviation.

- Explain what a normal and a standard normal distribution are.

- Calculate and interpret a z score and the correlation coefficient.

Graphs: Depicting Data Visually

Take another look at the data in Table A.1. Where would you start if you wanted to see whether the legal drinking age is related to drinking rates among 15-year-olds? Well, have you ever heard that *a picture is worth a thousand words*? One way to start would be to create a **graph**, or pictorial representation, of the data. Psychologists use many different types of graphs to help analyze their data. One of the more common graphs is a **frequency distribution**. A graph of a frequency distribution is a two-dimensional illustration that plots how frequently certain events occur. For example, it might be useful to see the frequency, or rate, at which countries have set certain minimum drinking ages. This information could be depicted using several types of graphs to illustrate the frequency distribution; two of the more common ones are **frequency polygons** (a line graph) and **histograms** (a bar graph). ■ FIGURE A.1 shows the frequency distribution of legal drinking age depicted in a frequency polygon; ■ FIGURE A.2 shows the same frequency distribution using a histogram. By looking at either one of these graphs, we can see that most of these selected governments have set their minimum drinking age below 21 and that the most commonly set drinking age is 18.

An even more useful type of graph for this investigation would be a **scatter plot**. In a scatter plot, two variables are plotted as a function of each other. For example, we could plot

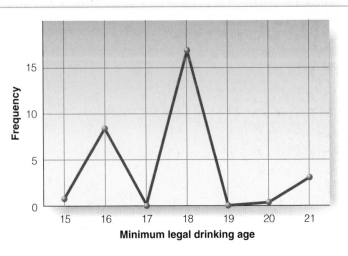

FIGURE

A.1   Frequency Polygon

Frequency polygon showing the frequency distribution for minimum drinking age in 28 countries (data from Table A.1).

graph a visual depiction of data

frequency distribution a graph of data that plots the frequency of data points on the y-axis and the data points themselves on the x-axis

frequency polygon a line graph that is used to illustrate a frequency distribution

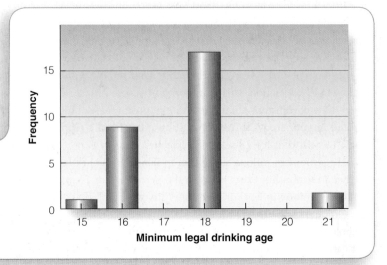

FIGURE

A.2   Histogram

Histogram showing the frequency distribution for minimum drinking age in 28 countries (data from Table A.1).

the percentage of 15-year-old drinkers as a function of the country's minimum drinking age. ■ FIGURE A.3 shows such plots separately for males and females. By looking at the scatter plots in Figure A.3, you can get a *very crude* picture of the relationship between drinking age and the rate of underage drinking at age 15. Looking at Figure A.3, as the minimum drinking age decreases, does the rate of underage drinking increase? Do these data confirm or discount our hypothesis that lowering the drinking age encourages underage drinking? Although it is true that countries with a minimum drinking age of 16 or younger have relatively high levels of underage drinking, there are also a number of countries with a minimum drinking age of 18 that have even higher levels of underage drinking by 15-year-olds. ■ FIGURE A.4 is another scatter plot, this time relating male and female rates of drinking. It appears from this graph that as more males drink, more females also engage in drinking—but if you look closely at the scatter plot, this isn't always true. Therefore, these plots only give us a crude picture of the relationship between our variables. It's impossible to say for sure whether our hypotheses about teenage drinking have merit simply by looking at these plots. To truly examine our hypotheses, we will have to delve deeper into our statistical analysis.

histogram a bar graph that is used to illustrate a frequency distribution

scatter plot a graph of data that plots pairs of data points, with one data point on the *x*-axis and the other on the *y*-axis

descriptive statistics statistics that are calculated to summarize or describe certain aspects of a data set

Measures of Central Tendency: Means, Medians, and Modes

To get to the heart of the matter, we are going to have to use **descriptive statistics**. Descriptive statistics are numerical values that are calculated on the data to summarize and describe the data as a whole. For example, you could calculate the percentage of these 28 countries that have a minimum drinking age of 18 or higher. This percentage would be 19 of the 28 countries, or 67.9%. Or you could calculate the percentage of countries with a minimum drinking age under 18 in which more than 25% of their male sample indicated that they drank weekly (8 out of 9 countries, or 88.9%). Although such percentages can sometimes be helpful, there are other, better statistical methods to use in this situation.

Some of the most useful descriptive statistics are those that describe the average, or most typical, entry in a data set; in other words, a statistic

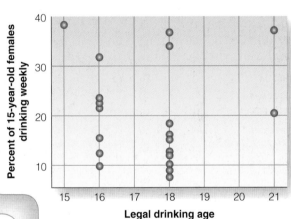

FIGURE

A.3   **Drinking at Age 15 as a Function of Minimum Legal Drinking Age**

Scatter plots of the percentage of 15-year-olds who drink weekly as a function of minimum legal drinking age in 28 countries (data from Table A.1).

FIGURE

A.4   **Drinking at Age 15 of Males Versus Females**

Scatter plot relating the percentage of 15-year-old males and females who drink alcohol weekly in 28 countries (data from Table A.1).

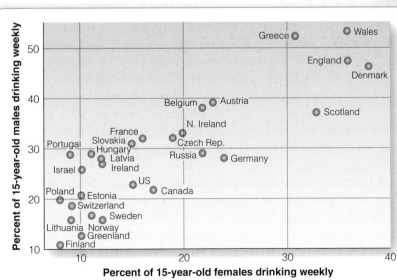

Table A.2 Average Minimum Drinking Age and Average Percent of Students Who Report Drinking Alcohol Weekly at Age 15, Selected Countries

COUNTRY	MINIMUM LEGAL DRINKING AGE	MALES	FEMALES
Austria	16	39%	23%
Belgium	16	38	22
Canada	18	22	17
Czech Republic	18	32	19
Denmark	15	46	38
England	18	47	36
Estonia	18*	21	10
Finland	18	11	8
France	16	31	15
Germany	16	29	22
Greece	16*	52	31
Greenland	18	13	10
Hungary	16	29	11
Ireland	18	27	12
Israel	18	26	10
Latvia	18	28	12
Lithuania	21	16	9
Northern Ireland	18	33	20
Norway	18	16	12
Poland	18	20	8
Portugal	16	29	9
Russia	18	28	24
Scotland	18	37	33
Slovakia	18	32	16
Sweden	18	17	11
Switzerland	16	19	9
United States	21	23	15
Wales	18	53	36
ΣX	491	814	498
$\bar{X} = \Sigma X/N$	491/28 = 17.5	814/28 = 29.1	498/28 = 17.8

Source: Except where noted, data taken from Kaul, C. (2002). Statistical Handbook on the World's Children (p. 447). Westport, CT: Oryx Press.

*These data taken from http://www2.potsdam.edu/alcohol-info/LegalDrinkingAge .html#worlddrinkingages on 11/6/03

measures of central tendency descriptive statistics that describe the most central, or typical, data points in the frequency distribution

mean a descriptive statistic that describes the most average, or typical, data point in the distribution

median a descriptive statistic that identifies the center of the frequency distribution; 50% of the scores are above and 50% are below this point in the distribution

that shows what a *typical* country's legal drinking age is. These measures are collectively referred to as **measures of central tendency** because they tell us something about the center of the frequency distribution (in this case, what minimum drinking age is most common, or most typical). Look again at Figures A.1 and A.2. What do you think is the most common minimum drinking age? To answer this question, we have three different measures of central tendency: the *mean*, *median*, and *mode*.

The **mean** is the average of a distribution. To calculate the mean, you add up all of the data points and then divide the total by the number of data points. This formula can be expressed with this equation:

$$\bar{X} = \Sigma X/N$$

Where

$\bar{X}$ is the symbol for the mean

Σ is a mathematical symbol that means to sum up the items that follow it

X = the individual data points in the distribution

N = the total number of data points or scores in the distribution

The calculations for the average minimum drinking age and the average percentages of males and females who drink weekly at age 15 are shown in ■ TABLE A.2.

Another measure of central tendency is the **median**, or the score that is at the center of a frequency distribution. To find the median, you must first list all of the scores in ascending order. Once this is done, simply find the score that is at the center of this ordered list of scores. The calculation of the median legal drinking age is shown in ■ FIGURE A.5. As you can see by comparing Figure A.5 and Table A.2, the median and the mean are not the same number. This shows one advantage of the median over the mean. The mean is highly affected by unusual scores, or **outliers**, in the distribution. In this case, one country, Denmark, has an unusually low drinking age of 15. Although Denmark's minimum drinking age of 15 does not differ very much from the more common limit of 16, Denmark is the only country to set the age this low, and this outlying score works to lower the mean somewhat. However, because the median is simply the center score of the distribution, it is unaffected by unusual scores. So, whereas the mean drinking age is 17.5, the median drinking age is somewhat higher at 18.

When a distribution contains outliers, the median is the better choice for measuring central tendency. This is especially true for situations in which the outliers are more extreme than in our drinking-age example. For instance, assume that in a class of 10 students, 9 students score a 75 on an exam, and 1 student scores a 15. The mean for the class would be 69, but the median would be 75. That's a difference of more than half a letter grade between these two measures of central tendency, with the median more accurately reflecting how most students scored on the exam.

FIGURE

A.5

**Calculation
of the
Median Legal
Drinking Age**

First take all of the minimum legal drinking ages for the countries and list them in ascending order:

15, 16, 16, 16, 16, 16, 16, 16, 16, 18, 18, 18, 18, 18,
18, 18, 18, 18, 18, 18, 18, 18, 18, 18, 18, 18, 21, 21

Now find the score at the center of this distribution. In this case, because there is an even number of scores ($N = 28$) the center of this distribution would be between the 14th and 15th score in the list. Therefore, to find the median or X_{50}, we would average the 14th and 15th score:

$$(18 + 18)/2 = 18$$

$$X_{50} = 18$$

The final measure of central tendency is the **mode**, or the most frequent score in the distribution. If you look again at Figure A.1 (or Figure A.2), you will see that the most frequent, or most common, drinking age is 18. Therefore, like the median, the mode is also 18. The mode is an especially useful measure of central tendency when the data being examined are not numerical (for example, the most typical car color in the student parking lot).

Measures of central tendency tell us something about the most representative scores at the center of the frequency distribution, but they do not tell us anything about the range, or breadth, of the scores in the distribution. To determine this characteristic of the distribution, we will have to look at *measures of variability*.

Measures of Variability: Analyzing the Distribution of Data

Variability refers to the degree to which the individual scores of the distribution tend to differ from the central tendency of the distribution. In other words, variability measures how spread out the frequency distribution is. Look back at Figure A.1. As we just saw, the mean drinking age is 17.5. As you would expect, most of the scores in the frequency distribution are clustered around 18, but that does not mean that *all* of the scores are close in value to 18. Some scores are as low as 15, and some are as high as 21. Measures of variability tell us about the degree to which these more extreme scores differ from the mean. The simplest measure of variability is the **range** of the distribution, or the difference between the highest and lowest values in the distribution. In this case, the range of drinking ages would be $21 - 15 = 6$ years.

Although the range is a measure of variability, it is fairly crude in that it doesn't really tell us how much most scores differ from the mean. Another measure of variability, called **sample variance**, takes into account the difference between the individual scores of the distribution and the mean of the distribution. The first step to calculating the sample variance is to calculate the mean of the distribution. The next step is to calculate the **sum of squares** of the distribution. Here, *squares* refers to the difference between each score in the distribution and the mean of the distribution, with this difference being taken to the second power (that is, squared, or multiplied by itself). So, the sum of squares (SS) can be calculated using the following equation:

$$SS = \Sigma \, (X - \bar{X})^2$$

Once you have calculated SS, to calculate the sample variance (S^2), simply divide by the total number of scores (N):

$$S^2 = \Sigma(X - \bar{X})^2/N$$

outliers unusual data points that are at the extremes of the frequency distribution and either far above or below the mean

mode a measure of central tendency that identifies the most common, or frequent, score in the distribution

range a measure of variability that is the difference between the high score and the low score of the distribution

sample variance a measure of variability that shows on average how much the scores vary from the mean

sum of squares the sum of the squared errors, or deviations, from the mean for the scores in the distribution; the numerator of the sample variance equation

Country N = 28	X = Percent of 15-Year-Old Males Drinking	$X - \bar{X} =$ $X - 29.1$	$(X - \bar{X})^2 =$ $(X - 29.1)^2$
Austria	39	9.9	98.01
Belgium	38	8.9	79.21
Canada	22	– 7.1	50.41
Czech Republic	32	2.9	8.41
Denmark	46	16.9	285.61
England	47	17.9	320.41
Estonia	21	– 8.1	65.61
Finland	11	–18.1	327.61
France	31	1.9	3.61
Germany	29	– .1	.01
Greece	52	22.9	524.41
Greenland	13	–16.1	259.21
Hungary	29	– .1	.01
Ireland	27	– 2.1	4.41
Israel	26	– 3.1	9.61
Latvia	28	– 1.1	1.21
Lithuania	16	–13.1	171.61
Northern Ireland	33	3.9	15.21
Norway	16	–13.1	171.61
Poland	20	– 9.1	82.81
Portugal	29	– .1	.01
Russia	28	– 1.1	1.21
Scotland	37	7.9	62.41
Slovakia	32	2.9	8.41
Sweden	17	–12.1	146.41
Switzerland	19	–10.1	102.01
United States	23	– 6.1	37.21
Wales	53	23.9	571.21
	$\Sigma X = 814$		$\Sigma(X - \bar{X})^2 =$ 3407.88
	$\bar{X} = \Sigma X/N =$ 814/28 = 29.1		$S^2 = \Sigma(X - \bar{X})^2 / N =$ 3407.88/28 = 121.71
			$S = \sqrt{\Sigma(X - \bar{X})^2 / N} =$ $\sqrt{121.71} = 11.03$

Legend: $\bar{X}$ = the mean; S^2 = the sample variance; S = the standard deviation; Σ = a symbol that means sum up the items that follow; N = the total number of scores or data points

FIGURE

A.6

Calculation of the Standard Deviation for the Percentage of Males Drinking Weekly at Age 15

Another measure of variability is the **standard deviation** (S), or the square root of the sample variance:

$$S = \sqrt{\Sigma(X - \bar{X})^2/N}$$

All three measures of variability indicate the degree to which the scores in the distribution are dispersed. The higher these measures are, the more dispersion, or spread, there is among the scores. Although it may be difficult to see why you would want to know the variability of a distribution, one reason is that you can use the standard deviation as a ruler, or guideline, for judging how atypical or typical a score in the distribution is.

To see how this works, take a look at ■ FIGURE A.6. Figure A.6 shows the calculation of the standard deviation for the male drinking percentages across the 28 countries. As you can see, the standard deviation for the distribution of male drinking scores is 11.03. We can use this figure to gauge how unusual a specific score in the distribution is. Using the standard deviation and the mean of the distribution, we can calculate a **z score**. A z score expresses the degree to which an individual score differs from the mean of the distribution in terms of the standard deviation of the distribution.

$$z = (X - \bar{X})/S$$

For example, in Germany, 29% of 15-year-old males drink weekly. This means that Germany's score would be:

$$z = (29 - 29.1)/11.03 = -.009$$

Germany's z score indicates that the percentage of German 15-year-old boys who drink is far less than one standard deviation below the mean of 29.1 for all of the 28 countries. This is illustrated graphically in ■ FIGURE A.7.

On the other hand, look at the figure reported for Wales. In Wales, 53% of the 15-year-old males surveyed were drinking. Wales's z score of 2.17 indicates that their score of 53% is more than 2 standard deviations above the mean. This indicates that Wales's experience is not very typical of the average country's experience with male underage drinking at age 15. Wales *seems* to have a bigger problem with this issue than the average country does, but is this deviation from the mean enough of a problem to worry about? To answer this, we have to assess the probability that a given country would have a particular percentage of its young men drinking alcohol on a weekly basis. Luckily, we might be able to do this.

Many variables, such as height, weight, IQ, and so on, have a **normal distribution**. In other words, if you measured these characteristics for a very large number of people and plotted them in a frequency distribution, the resulting graph would be bell-shaped and symmetrical, like the one in Figure A.7. If we assume that drinking behavior is normally distributed, then we can also assume

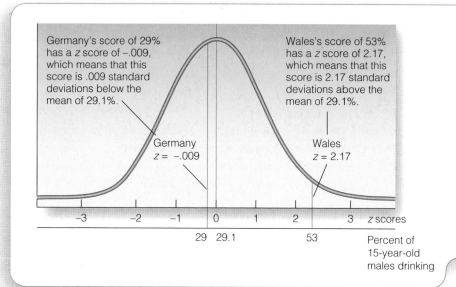

FIGURE

A.7 z Scores for Germany and Wales

The mean, or average, percentage of 15-year-old males who drank was 29.1% and the standard deviation was 11.03 across the 28 countries. This figure shows the individual z scores for the percentage of 15-year-old males drinking in Germany and Wales. Z scores indicate how many standard deviations away from the mean a particular score falls. As you can see, Germany has a slightly below average percentage of 15-year-old male drinkers, with a raw score of 29% and a z score of −.009. Wales is quite a bit above average in its male underage drinking, with a raw score of 53% and a z score of 2.17.

Germany's score of 29% has a z score of −.009, which means that this score is .009 standard deviations below the mean of 29.1%.

Wales's score of 53% has a z score of 2.17, which means that this score is 2.17 standard deviations above the mean of 29.1%.

Germany
z = −.009

Wales
z = 2.17

29   29.1   53

Percent of 15-year-old males drinking

that if we calculated the z scores for all of the different countries and plotted them in a frequency distribution, that distribution of z scores would also be a normal distribution, with $\bar{X} = 0$ and $S = 1$.

When a distribution of z scores is normal in shape, it is referred to as the **standard normal distribution**. The great thing about the standard normal distribution is that we know exactly what percentage of the distribution falls between any two scores, as shown in ■ FIGURE A.8. As you can see, 68.26% of the z scores should fall within the range of z scores from −1 to +1, whereas only .26% of the scores will be above a z score of +3 or below a z score of −3. The probability that a country would have a z score of +2.17 or higher is on the order of a mere 1.5%. So, indeed, Wales seems to have some possible cause for concern here because the number of 15-year-old boys consuming alcohol on a weekly basis is unusual compared to other countries.

The Correlation Coefficient: Measuring Relationships

Take a look again at Figure A.4, the scatter plot for underage drinking in males versus females in the 28 countries. Do you notice anything interesting about this scatter plot? Don't the data points of the scatter plot tend to fall along a line that slopes up to the right of the graph?

standard deviation a measure of variability equal to the square root of the sample variance; often used to gauge the degree to which an individual score deviates from the mean of a distribution

z score a measure of relative standing that measures the distance of a score from the mean of the distribution in standard deviation units

normal distribution a bell-shaped, symmetric frequency distribution

standard normal distribution a bell-shaped, symmetric distribution ($\bar{X} = 0$, $S = 1$) for which we know the exact area under the curve

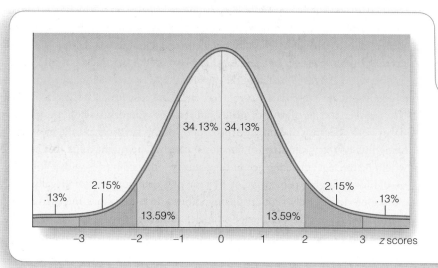

34.13%   34.13%

.13%   2.15%   2.15%   .13%

13.59%   13.59%

−3   −2   −1   0   1   2   3   z scores

FIGURE

A.8 The Standard Normal Distribution of z Scores

The standard normal distribution is a symmetric, bell-shaped distribution of z scores with $\bar{X} = 0$ and $S = 1$. The z score is the number of standard deviations from the mean that the score is.

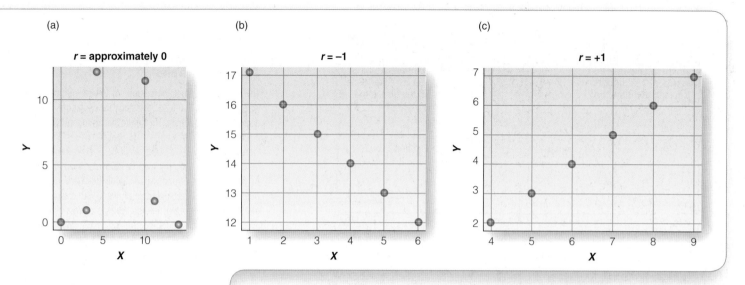

FIGURE

A.9

The Correlation Coefficient (*r*)

Graphic depictions of different values of the correlation coefficient: (a) *r* = approximately 0; (b) *r* = −1; (c) *r* = +1.

Doesn't this seem to indicate that there might be a linear relationship between the percentage of 15-year-old males and females drinking alcohol in a country? As one sex drinks more, doesn't the other seem to generally follow suit? To examine the degree to which such a relationship might exist, psychologists would use yet another statistic to describe these data—the **correlation coefficient**. Simply put, the correlation coefficient measures the degree to which pairs of data points fall along a straight line on a scatter plot. The formula for the correlation coefficient is:

$$r = (\Sigma\, z_x z_y)/N$$

Where

r = the correlation coefficient

z_x = the z score for one of the variables in a pair

z_y = the z score for the other variable of the pair

N = the total number of pairs of scores

The correlation coefficients that can be calculated with this formula have a possible range of $-1 \leq r \leq +1$. See ■ FIGURE A.9 for an interpretation of these values. As you can see, an r value of 0 (Figure A.9a) indicates no linear relationship between the two variables. As r approaches either −1 (Figure A.9b) or +1 (Figure A.9c), the linear relationship between the two variables becomes stronger. Positive r values indicate a *direct* relationship between the variables—as one variable increases, so does the other. Negative r values indicate an *indirect* relationship between the variables—as one variable increases, the other decreases.

Now let's return to our question of a relationship between the percentage of males and females in a country who at age 15 drink weekly. ■ FIGURE A.10 shows the calculation of the correlation coefficient for these data. As you can see, there is a strong positive correlation (r = .8715) between the percentage of males and females who drink alcohol weekly at age 15. This makes sense, because one might expect many of the factors that influence male underage drinking in a country to influence females similarly. One might think that one of these factors would be the legal drinking age in the country—that countries with a younger drinking age would have a higher percentage of 15-year-olds drinking alcohol illegally.

The data, however, do not fully support this hypothesis. In our sample, the correlation between legal drinking age and the percentage of males drinking at 15 is r = −.412. This moderately negative correlation indicates that countries with a lower legal drinking age tend

correlation coefficient the average product of z scores calculated on pairs of scores; describes the degree to which the scores in the pairs are linearly related

Country	Percent of Males	z score for Percent of Males	Percent of Females	z score for Percent of Females	$z_{male}z_{female}$
Austria	39	.90027	23	.56263	.50652
Belgium	38	.80961	22	.45464	.36808
Canada	22	–.64098	17	–.08531	.05468
Czech Republic	32	.26564	19	.13067	.03471
Denmark	46	1.53490	38	2.18251	3.34994
England	47	1.62557	36	1.96652	3.19671
Estonia	21	–.73164	10	–.084125	.61549
Finland	11	–1.63826	8	–1.05724	1.73203
France	31	.17498	15	–.30130	–.05272
Germany	29	–.00635	22	.45464	–.00289
Greece	52	2.07888	31	1.42657	2.96565
Greenland	13	–1.45694	10	–.84125	1.22565
Hungary	29	–.00635	11	–.73326	.00465
Ireland	27	–.18767	12	–.62527	.11734
Israel	26	–.27833	10	–.84125	.23415
Latvia	28	–.09701	12	–.62527	.06066
Lithuania	16	–1.18495	9	–.94924	1.12481
Northern Ireland	33	.35630	20	.23866	.08504
Norway	16	–1.18495	12	–.62527	.74091
Poland	20	–.82230	8	–1.05724	.86937
Portugal	29	–.00635	9	–.94924	.00602
Russia	28	–.09701	24	.67063	–.06506
Scotland	37	.71895	33	1.64255	1.18091
Slovakia	32	.26564	16	–.19330	–.05135
Sweden	17	–1.09429	11	–.73326	.80240
Switzerland	19	–.91296	9	–.94924	.86663
United States	23	–.55032	15	–.30130	.16581
Wales	53	2.16954	36	1.96652	4.26644
					$\Sigma z_{male}z_{female} =$ 24.403
					$r = \Sigma z_{male}z_{female} / N$ $= 24.403/28 = .8715$

Recall that the formula for a z **score is:** $z = (X - \bar{X})/S$, where $\bar{X} =$ the mean and S = the standard deviation.

FIGURE

A.10

Calculation of the Correlation Coefficient for the Percentage of Males and Females Who Drink Alcohol Weekly in 28 Countries

to have higher rates of males drinking illegally at age 15. However, such a clear relationship was not found for females. Therefore, we can conclude that having a lower drinking age is *related* to higher rates of drinking at age 15 for males only. Recall from Chapter 1 that correlation does not imply causation here. We cannot say that a lower drinking age *causes* males to drink at 15. We can only say that the two variables are related in a linear fashion.

Inferential Statistics

- Explain the logic behind inferential statistics, hypothesis testing, and statistical significance.

Inferential statistics are statistics that psychologists use to test hypotheses about their data. In short, inferential statistics help psychologists judge whether observed differences in their data are large enough to be **significant** or meaningful. To illustrate this issue, let's look at the difference in the average rate of drinking for males and females across the 28 countries (see Table A.2). The mean percentage of males drinking at 15 is 29.1%, but the mean percentage of females who report drinking at 15 is only 17.8%. Thus, it appears that males and females are not equally likely to drink at age 15. But is this difference ($29.1 - 17.8 = 11.3$) large enough to convince us that males really differ from females in their underage drinking? Is it possible that these data are merely a fluke or coincidence? How big a difference must we see between the sexes before we can say that our results are *significant*? These are the questions that inferential statistics tackle.

The first step to understanding inferential statistics is to understand the nature of hypotheses. In all studies that use inferential statistics, the researcher sets forth two hypotheses. The first one, called the **null hypothesis (H_0)**, is a statement of what the researcher does *not* believe to be true about the variables. The second one, called the **alternative hypothesis (H_1)**, is a statement of what the researcher *does* believe to be true about the variables. In our example, these would be:

$$H_0: \mu_{males} = \mu_{females}$$
$$H_1: \mu_{males} \neq \mu_{females}$$

Where

μ_{males} = the mean percent of males drinking in the entire population of all 15-year-old males

$\mu_{females}$ = the mean percent of females drinking in the entire population of all 15-year-old females

In other words, we do *not* believe that the rate of drinking is the same for males and females across the world at age 15. Rather, we believe that 15-year-old males drink at a different rate than 15-year-old females. Although it may seem odd, the way that scientists proceed from this point is to try to show that the null hypothesis is correct. Rather than directly testing the notion set forth in the alternative hypothesis, we instead test the hypothesis that contains the statement of what we do *not* believe to be true about our variables. So for the moment, we will assume that there is no difference between the rates of drinking for males and females at age 15. We will analyze our data to see whether they support this notion or whether we must reject this null hypothesis in favor of the alternative hypothesis that at age 15, males and females do indeed differ in their rates of drinking alcohol.

To test the null hypothesis, we must determine the probability of finding our results (that 29.1% of males and 17.8% of females were drinking), given the *assumption* that there is no real difference between the males and females when it comes to drinking at age 15. This is where a standard distribution comes in handy. If we can calculate a statistic on our data for which we know the distribution and the probabilities of obtaining certain values of the statistic, then we can determine how likely or unlikely it would be to get our results simply by accident or fluke. In a sense, we did this earlier when we looked at the probability of finding that Wales had a rate of drinking for males that was 2.17 standard deviations above the

inferential statistics statistics that psychologists use in hypothesis testing to tell them when they should reject or accept their hypotheses about the population

significant results are considered significant when there is a very small chance (usually less than 5%) of finding those results given the assumption that the null hypothesis is true

null hypothesis (H_0) the hypothesis that contains a statement of what we do *not* believe is true about our variables in the population

alternative hypothesis (H_1) the hypothesis that contains a statement of what we do believe is true about our variables in the population mean. When we found that the probability of a country's having a z score of 2.17 was only 1.5%, we were then fairly confident that the rate of male drinking in Wales was significantly different from most of the other countries. So, how low a probability is low enough for us to say that our results are significant? Generally speaking, psychologists are comfortable dealing with results that have probabilities less than 5%, although in some cases the significance level might be placed at a lower percentage.

Going back to our current example, the question now is this: "Is there a 5% or less probability of finding that 29.1% of the males and 17.8% of the females in our sample drink, if there is indeed *no* difference between 15-year-old males and females in the population at large?" If we find that the probability of obtaining our results is less than 5%, then we can safely conclude that our null hypothesis is likely incorrect, and we should *reject* it in favor of the alternative hypothesis. If we find that the probability of obtaining our results is greater than 5%, then we must accept our null hypothesis and admit that we were likely wrong in formulating our alternative hypothesis.

So how do we go about finding the probability of our results? Unfortunately, a detailed explanation of how we would determine this probability is beyond the scope of this text. If you ever take a statistics class, you will learn how this number is determined. However, so as not to leave you in suspense, we will tell you how the story ends. If the null hypothesis is true and there is no difference between male and female drinking in the population, the probability of finding our results (that 29.1% of males and 17.8% of females drink at age 15) is close to 0. This means that it is highly unlikely that males and females drink equally at age 15, and we can safely reject our null hypothesis in favor of the alternative hypothesis.

Summary

We hope that this appendix has helped you get a very basic understanding of how psychologists use statistics. Statistics are the major tool through which we as scientists judge the validity of our research results. Without statistics, we would have no way to separate the flukes and coincidences of life from the true, meaningful differences that exist in the world. We use statistics to describe our data, and in doing so, we use graphs or plots to visually depict data. We use measures of central tendency, such as the mean, median, and mode, to describe the center, or most typical, score in a frequency distribution. We use measures of variability, such as the range, sample variance, or standard deviation, to describe the dispersion, or spread, of the scores within the frequency distribution.

Another descriptive statistic that is commonly used is the correlation coefficient. The correlation coefficient describes the degree to which two variables are linearly related. A linear relationship between variables indicates that as one variable changes in magnitude, the other variable also experiences some change. The range of the correlation coefficient is $-1 \leq r \leq +1$. Positive correlations indicate a direct relationship between the variables: as one variable increases, so does the other. Negative correlations indicate an indirect relationship between the variables: as one variable increases, the other tends to decrease. As the correlation coefficient approaches -1 and $+1$, the described relationship between the variables is stronger or more linear.

Statistics are also used to test hypotheses about variables in the population being studied using a representative sample. When statistics are used to test hypotheses and thus to draw inferences about the population, they are referred to as inferential statistics. In testing hypotheses, researchers always set up two competing hypotheses. The null hypothesis contains a statement of what the researcher does not believe about the variables. The alternative hypothesis contains a statement of what the researcher believes to be true about the variables. The researcher then uses inferential statistics to test the null hypothesis.

To do this, the researcher must calculate some statistic on the data in the sample, and this statistic must be one for which we know what its distribution looks like. For instance, if the variable being studied is normally distributed in the population, then one could calculate z scores on the data and know that the distribution of these z scores in the population would be the standard normal distribution. The standard normal distribution is a bell-shaped, symmetric curve that has a mean of 0 and a standard deviation of 1. Because we know the shape, mean, and variance of the standard normal distribution, we also know exactly how much of the distribution falls between any two z scores. This allows us to determine the exact probability of obtaining any particular z score in our data.

In practice, z scores are not used very often to test hypotheses because psychologists frequently study more than one variable, and z scores can help us determine only the probability of obtaining a single data point in a sample. Therefore, psychologists often use other inferential statistics. The principle is still the same, however. You calculate an inferential statistic with a known distribution on your sample data. Next, you use the distribution to determine the probability of obtaining this particular value of the statistic, given the assumption that the null hypothesis is true. If the probability of obtaining this value of the inferential statistic when the null hypothesis is true is less than 5%, then you can safely say that within an acceptable margin of error, it appears that the null hypothesis is not true and it should be rejected in favor of the alternative hypothesis. In other words, your results are significant, and your data support your hypothesis.

In conclusion, please realize that this appendix has just skimmed the surface of what statistics is all about. All psychologists must undergo fairly extensive training in statistics before completing their degrees so that they have all the tools they need to discover the true nature of mental processes and behavior.

Studying
THE Appendix

Key Terms

data (560)
population (561)
sample (561)
representative sample (561)
random selection (561)
statistics (561)
graph (562)
frequency distribution (562)
frequency polygon (562)
histogram (562)

scatter plot (562)
descriptive statistics (563)
measures of central tendency (564)
mean (564)
median (564)
outliers (564)
mode (565)
range (565)
sample variance (565)
sum of squares (565)

standard deviation (566)
z score (566)
normal distribution (566)
standard normal distribution (567)
correlation coefficient (568)
inferential statistics (570)
significant (570)
null hypothesis (H_0) (570)
alternative hypothesis (H_1) (570)

What Do You Know? Assess Your Understanding

Test your retention and understanding of the material by answering the following questions.

1. _____ are bits of information gathered in scientific studies.
   a. Data
   b. Probabilities
   c. Samples
   d. Statistics

2. The statistic that describes the degree to which two variables are linearly related is the _____.
   a. mean
   b. median
   c. z score
   d. correlation coefficient

3. The mean, median, and mode are all measures of _____.
   a. correlation
   b. variance
   c. central tendency
   d. probability

4. A very unusual score in a distribution is called a(n) _____.
   a. standard deviation
   b. mode
   c. outlier
   d. variance

5. The mean of the standard normal distribution is equal to _____.
   a. the variance of the distribution
   b. one
   c. zero
   d. the sum of squares of the data points

6. If you are doing a scientific study, it is important to use _____ when selecting your participants to ensure that your sample is representative of the population.
   a. random assignment
   b. random selection
   c. probability sampling
   d. All of the above

7. A z score of 2.33 means that the raw score in question is _____ standard deviations above the mean of the distribution.
   a. 1
   b. 0
   c. 2.33
   d. 4.66

8. The hypothesis that contains a statement of what the researcher believes to be true about the world is called the _____ hypothesis.
   a. null
   b. alternative
   c. correct
   d. rejected

9. In doing research, scientists actually test the _____ hypothesis.
   a. null
   b. alternative
   c. correct
   d. rejected

10. A(n) _____ distribution is a bell-shaped, symmetric frequency distribution.
    a. skewed
    b. sampling
    c. normal
    d. population

Answers: 1. a; 2. d; 3. c; 4. c; 5. c; 6. b; 7. c; 8. b; 9. a; 10. c

Appendix B

How DO WE Apply Psychology IN THE WORKPLACE?

KATHY A. HANISCH, IOWA STATE UNIVERSITY

- Industrial and Organizational Psychology

- Selecting Employees

- Socializing Employees: Culture, Groups, and Leadership

- Attitudes and Behaviors at Work

You have applied for a job, submitted your resume, and taken a series of tests. You have been interviewed by your potential supervisor and given a tour of the company. You now find yourself sitting across from the co-owners, who have just offered you a position. They tell you that their organization is a great place to work. As evidence, they tell you that no one has quit a job at the company in the last five years and employees *are rarely absent. They also tell you that they have flexible policies. You can work whatever hours you like and take vacation whenever you want. And if you decide to work for them, you'll have access to spending cash as well as keys to the company.*

You try to maintain your composure. You'd heard interesting things about this company but didn't really believe them. Finally, the co-owners ask you what you are worth, indicating they will pay you whatever you wish. Now you're really dumbfounded and wonder what the catch is but sit quietly while they talk about other issues. Does this sound too good to be true? Wouldn't this be ideal?

Almost this exact scenario played out in an organization owned and managed by an Oakland appliance dealer in the 1970s. His name was Arthur Friedman, and he had decided to change how he ran his business. Art, as reported in the *Washington Post* (Koughan, 1975), announced at one of his staff meetings that employees could work the hours they wanted, be paid what they thought they were worth, take vacation time when they wanted, and help themselves to petty cash if they were in need of spending money. New employees would be allowed to set their own wages too. As you might imagine, the employees weren't sure how to take this news. It was reported that no one said anything during the meeting when Art first described his plan (Koughan, 1975).

When asked why he was changing his business practices, Art replied, "I always said that if you give people what they want, you get what you want. You have to be willing to lose, to stick your neck out. I finally decided that the time had come to practice what I preached" (Koughan, 1975). In the final analysis, Art's experiment worked. The organization was profitable. Friedman signed union contracts without reading them (the employees didn't need a union with Art in charge). Employees didn't quit, they didn't steal from the company, and they were rarely absent. Net profits increased, and the company was a success. The employees realized that to make the organization work and remain in business, they had to be reasonable in their requests and behavior (Koughan, 1975).

A present-day company with similar enticing work perks is Google. In 2007, *Fortune* magazine rated it the number one company to work for. Included among its many perks are free gourmet meals, snack rooms, free haircuts, gyms, massages, subsidized exercise classes, classes to learn another language, child care, on-site doctors for free employee checkups, a pet-friendly facility, and a traveling library for book checkout. In addition, they offer free shuttle bus transportation to work or, if you drive, free on-site car washes and oil changes. If you have a baby, they provide up to $500 reimbursement for takeout food to ease your transition home. They give you extra cash if you refer a friend to work at Google and the person is hired. They even provide washers and dryers so you can do your laundry at work for free (they provide the detergent too!). In addition to all these benefits, they reward innovation, both high-tech and otherwise, and allow employees such as engineers to spend some time on independent work projects.

Google provides many employee perks, including free meals and haircuts, exercise classes, child care, and on-site doctors. Would you want to work for Google?

© Catherine Karnow/Corbis

Industrial and Organizational Psychology

Learning Objectives

- Discuss the importance of work in people's lives.
- Describe the different types of jobs available.

Organizations like Google and Friedman's company are interesting because of how they deal with their employees and how that affects the employees' behaviors. Psychologists who study people's behavior at work using psychological principles are called *industrial and organizational psychologists*, and their field of study is **industrial and organizational (I/O) psychology**. I/O psychologists study employee selection, performance appraisal, training, job design, communication, work stress, motivation, leadership, groups and teams, organizational culture, human factors, job attitudes, well-being, and work behavior. This appendix will introduce you to the field of I/O psychology. You will experience many of the topics discussed here when you seek, obtain, and keep a job.

Work in Our Lives

You have learned about work since you were a small child. You may have asked where your mother was going when she took you to day care or why your father left the house before 8 A.M. and did not return until after 5 P.M. You likely "played" at different jobs by dressing up as an astronaut, firefighter, teacher, chef, or construction worker. As you got older, other sources of information about work may have come from your friends, other family members, school, and the media. In high school, more education and a part-time job may have given you additional details about the meaning of work. As you pursue a college degree, you may receive information about the work and jobs available in your chosen field through classes, internships, or other job experiences.

Work is an important part of life for many people. We often ask people we meet what they "do," which translates into "What is your job and whom do you work for?" Many people identify with their work because they spend so much of their waking lives at work. Work is important because it provides many of the things people need and value. Work for pay provides us with the money to satisfy our basic needs for food, shelter, and security (e.g., health care, retirement income); any "leftover" money provides us with discretionary funds to use as we see fit. These funds may be used to buy a round of golf, an iPod, or a fancy place to live; to support charities or attend athletic or fine art performances; or to save money for college. Essentially, money, typically from work, provides us with a standard of living that varies from person to person depending on our income and how we choose to spend it. In addition, work provides much more. It provides a source of social interactions and friendships, independence, a sense of accomplishment, satisfaction, a reason to get up in the morning, happiness, a sense of identity, recognition, and prestige (see ■ TABLE B.1).

Although most researchers and practitioners agree that money and recognition are nearly universal motivators (R. Clark, 2003),

industrial and organizational (I/O) psychology the study of people's behavior at work using psychological principles

Table B.1 Jobs With the Highest and Lowest Prestige (2006)

Job Description	Percent Rating Job as High Prestige
HIGHEST PRESTIGE	
Firefighter	63%
Doctor	58%
Nurse	55%
Scientist	54%
Teacher	52%*
LOWEST PRESTIGE	
Stockbroker	11%
Business Executive	11%
Real estate broker/agent	6%

*The prestige ratings for teachers rose from 29% in 1977 to 52% in 2006, the only job surveyed to show a positive change in prestige over 29 years.

Source: www.harrisinteractive.com.

many of the things we value or seek from work vary from person to person. For example, the prestige of a job may not be important to you, but might be important to your best friend. Perhaps you want your work to provide you with a sense of accomplishment or a source of social interaction, while those may not be valued by your friend. It is important to understand what you want from your work as well as what a job can provide.

From an employer's perspective, it is useful to determine what employees want because satisfied employees are more likely than dissatisfied employees to work to meet organizational goals. Part of a supervisor's job is to ascertain what employees value because those values can be used to motivate employees to perform well in their jobs.

Courtesy of K. Hanisch

Perhaps these are future electrical workers!

Types of Jobs

There are many types of work, in many types of jobs, in many different organizational settings. These settings include multinational conglomerates, public and private companies, nonprofits, federal, state, and local government organizations, and home businesses.

People in the United States work a variety of schedules, from extended workweeks (45–99 hours) to standard workweeks (35–44 hours) to part-time workweeks (less than 35 hours). Some people, such as police officers, medical personnel, and factory workers, because of the nature of their jobs, work shifts other than the typical 8 A.M. TO 5 p.m. shift. Others are offered flexible working schedules that best fit their lives as long as they work the required number of hours and accomplish the work. Telecommuting is becoming more and more popular with an increase in appropriate technology. Some people work for virtual organizations that use communication technologies to outsource the majority of their functions.

Regardless of the type of job or your work schedule, you will spend most of your waking hours in some type of employment for many years. Many people spend their weekends working, too. Because work is critical to who we are and what we do, studying the psychological principles and some of the topics examined by I/O psychologists will provide you with information that may be useful to you in your future careers.

Let's Review!

This section provided an introduction to industrial and organizational psychology and highlighted the importance of work in our lives. As a quick check of your understanding, answer these questions.

1. Nearly all people value _____ and _____ from their work.
   a. money; prestige
   b. prestige; social interactions
   c. money; recognition
   d. satisfaction; prestige

2. Which of the following would an I/O psychologist be *least* likely to study?
   a. Leadership
   b. Employee selection
   c. Life satisfaction
   d. Performance appraisal

Answers 1. c; 2. c

Selecting Employees

- Describe how employers decide which job applicants to hire.

Industrial and organizational psychologists first became involved in the process of selecting employees when the United States government needed help selecting and placing officers and soldiers in World War I (Aamodt, 2007). They used mental ability tests to determine who would become officers and who would be in the infantry. The process many employers use now to hire employees is very detailed, typically consisting of five components: *job analysis, testing, legal issues, recruitment,* and the *selection decision.*

Job Analysis

Job analysis is the identification of the critical elements of a job. I/O psychologists have helped devise effective strategies for determining three basic aspects of any job: (1) What tasks and behaviors are essential to the job? (2) What knowledge, skills, and abilities are needed to perform the job? (3) What are the conditions (such as stress, safety, and temperature) under which the job is performed? A job analysis can be conducted in many ways. An analyst may interview current employees, have them complete questionnaires, observe people in the job, or talk to people knowledgeable about the job (Gael, 1988).

The information from a job analysis is used in many types of personnel functions, including employee selection, performance appraisal, training, and human resources planning. Within the hiring process, job analysis is used to write job descriptions; to determine what tests might be used to assess the relevant knowledge, skills, and abilities of job applicants; and to assist in meeting legal requirements that affect the selection process.

Testing

You are familiar with tests and taking tests. **Tests** are defined here as the measurement of carefully chosen samples of behavior. These include the standard paper-and-pencil tests used to measure specific skills or abilities in a class, or more general abilities as in the SAT or ACT. They also include vocational interest inventories and personality assessments (see Chatper 12), such as conscientiousness and honesty tests. In addition, work samples, in which applicants do a replica of the work they will be asked to do on the job, are useful tests. Tests are vital to the success of organizations. They are used to ascertain differences between people. The goal of these tests is to help employers choose the person best suited for the job and the organization. Regardless of the type of test or how it is administered, the *reliability* and *validity* of a test are very important (see Chapter 7).

Another type of test is the *employee interview*. Nearly all organizations use some type of interview in their selection of employees (Salgado, Viswesvaran, & Ones, 2003), even though interviews are often viewed as subjective and worthless. More than 85 years of research has provided evidence regarding when interviews are useful and when they are not.

Selection interviews can be broadly classified as unstructured and structured. **Unstructured interviews** are informal and unplanned. They are conducted by an untrained interviewer, with random questions and no scoring key. **Structured interviews** are conducted by a trained interviewer. They have standardized questions, a specific question order, and a predetermined scoring or answer key. Some typical questions asked during an informal

job analysis identification of the critical elements of a job, including tasks, skills required, and working conditions

test the measurement of a carefully chosen sample of behavior

unstructured interview informal, unplanned interview, using random questions and no scoring key, and conducted by an untrained interviewer

structured interview interview using standardized questions, a specific question order, and a predetermined scoring or answer key, and conducted by a trained interviewer

Table B.2 Typical Unstructured Interview Questions

1. What are your weaknesses?
2. Why should we hire you?
3. Why do you want to work here?
4. What are your goals?
5. Why did you leave (or why are you leaving) your job?
6. When were you most satisfied in your job?
7. What can you do for us that other candidates can't?
8. What are three positive things your last boss would say about you?
9. What salary are you seeking?
10. If you were an animal, which one would you want to be?

Source: C. Martin, 2006, Monster.com.

Table B.3 Structured Behavior-Based Interview Questions

1. Tell me in specific details about a time when you had to deal with a difficult customer.
2. Give me an example of a time when you had to make a decision without a supervisor present.
3. Give me a specific example of when you demonstrated your initiative in an employment setting.
4. Give me an example of a time when you had to work with a team.
5. Describe a time when you had to be creative at solving a problem.

Source: Adapted from The Job Centre, Niagara College Canada, 2005, http://jobs.niagarac.on.ca/.

interview are listed in ■ TABLE B.2. Examples of structured interview questions are listed in ■ TABLE B.3. Structured interviews, based on a job analysis, have greater validity than unstructured interviews (Huffcutt & Arthur, 1994).

Legal Issues

One of the most important pieces of legislation regarding employment, and specifically the hiring of employees, is **Title VII of the Civil Rights Act of 1964** (Equal Employment Opportunity Commission, 2002). Title VII "prohibits discrimination based on race, color, religion, sex, and national origin," known as the "Big 5." Providing protection for people comprising the Big 5 helps to ensure that they have equal employment opportunities. Exceptions to this provision include national security, seniority systems, and bona fide occupational qualifications (BFOQs). BFOQs permit organizations to discriminate in hiring persons in a protected class if the qualification is determined to be reasonably necessary to the operation of the business. For example, women can be discriminated against when hiring someone to model men's swimwear, and vice versa. It is reasonably necessary to the marketing and selling of swimwear that organizations hire men to model male swimwear and women to model female swimwear; sex is a BFOQ. It is not reasonably necessary, however, that a secretary in a church who does office work and not church or religious work be of the same religion as the employing church; religion in this case could not be used as a BFOQ.

It is important for employers to abide by laws that protect people against discrimination, as the costs of litigation can be very high, both monetarily and in terms of an organization's reputation. This applies to discrimination based not only on the Big 5, covered under the Civil Rights Act, but also on age (Age Discrimination in Employment Act) and disability (Americans with Disabilities Act). Employment law in the United States is meant to protect and provide equal opportunities for all individuals (see *Psychology Applies to Your World*).

Title VII of the Civil Rights Act of 1964 law that prohibits discrimination based on race, color, religion, sex, or national origin

How effective would this advertisement be if the model were male?

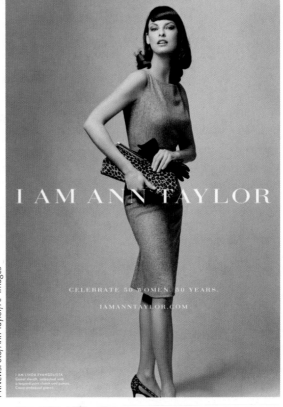

PRNewsFoto/Ann Taylor/AP Images

Psychology Applies to Your World:

Legal Issues in Employment Vary in Different Countries

This advertisement (shown here as it appeared in print) for a support staff position in Thailand would not be legal in the United States. It specifies that the applicant must be female, which would be illegal under Title VII of the Civil Rights Act. It also specifies an upper age limit of 29, which would be illegal in most states. U.S. federal law prohibits discrimination based on age once a person reaches the age of 40 (Age Discrimination in Employment Act). It is obvious the employer is seeking a very young person, which is likely not related to expected job performance; people older than 29 could perform just as well in the job.

Nondiscrimination offers fair treatment for people looking for a job. In the United States, organizations with several employees are required to abide by the employment laws. These laws have changed the employment process over the last 50 years, affording equal opportunities for those seeking a position. Equal opportunity laws in the United States today make the job market a fairer place than in many countries.

Post Date:	Sunday, June 10, 2007 Location: Suvintawong Rd., Minburi
Salary:	20,000-25,000
Business Type:	Our client is Manufactoring of VDO, VTR Camera, Printer, Auto Part and now is looking for qualified candidates for the following position
Qualification:	Be handle procedure of Import-Export such as P/O, D/O, etc. Be arrange delivery process and coordinate delivery schedule and most support Malaysian customer

****

- Female, age not over 29, able to working at Minburi (nearest Carrefour-Minburi)
- Bachelor's Degree in any field
- 2-3 year experience in Sales Coordinate or Export-Import, most preferred if from Factory, Electronics but any related business are welcome
- Good command of written and spoken in English and PC
- Good personality, business manners and able to work under pressure

Source: http://www.pasona.co.th/en/hotjob.aspx.

Recruitment

The process organizations use to identify potential employees for a job defines **recruitment**. Depending on the job, an organization may recruit from inside the company or seek someone outside the organization. They may advertise on their company web page or on a website for specific types of jobs. In addition, websites like monster.com and careerbuilder.com link potential employees and employers in a variety of jobs and locations. Other recruitment sources include newspapers, radio and television advertisements, trade magazines, professional publications, and employee referrals.

Research indicates that employees recruited through inside sources such as employee referrals or rehires work for the organization longer and have better job performance than

recruitment the process organizations use to identify potential employees for a job those recruited through outside sources, including advertisements, employment agencies, or recruiters (Zottoli & Wanous, 2000). Studies have supported the idea that those recruited using inside sources receive more accurate information about the job than those recruited through external sources (Conrad & Ashworth, 1986; McManus & Baratta, 1992).

A survey of the 50 best small and medium organizations to work for in the United States found that 92% use employee referrals and more than 30% of all hires were referred by a current employee (Pomeroy, 2005). Because of their effectiveness, some companies provide rewards to employees who recommend an applicant who is hired. These rewards include cash, vacations, and raffles for prizes such as televisions and free cleaning service for a year (Stewart, Ellenburg, Hicks, Kremen, & Daniel, 1990). Typically, the new employee must work for the organization a set period of time for the referring employee to receive the award (Stewart et al., 1990). Google rewards an employee with a $2,000 bonus if his or her referral accepts Google's offer and remains employed for at least 60 days.

can–do factors factors that determine the maximum performance an employee can exhibit

will–do factors factors that determine the normal or typical performance by an employee

Based on these photos, would you hire these job candidates?

After applicants have submitted either a resume or an application, someone from the organization such as the human resources manager or supervisor will determine which applicants should be considered further. In that process, he or she may make telephone inquiries of previous employers or other references and conduct criminal background checks.

© Louis Quail/Corbis

A growing phenomenon is employers' use of social networking sites such as Facebook, MySpace, Xanga, and Friendster to learn about job candidates (Finder, 2006). On these sites, recruiters and company presidents have found promising candidates reporting on their own drug use, sexual exploits, and drinking, along with suggestive photographs (Finder, 2006). These are considered "red flags" by employers. They assume that these applicants are lacking in good judgment and therefore remove them from their selection process (Finder, 2006). Information that students thought would only be viewed by their peers is making its way into the public arena at all levels, with future employers and relatives viewing the information without the students' knowledge.

© David Young-Wolff/PhotoEdit

Making the Decision

When selecting employees, employers are looking for a good match between the employee and the organization. They would like to match the requirements for excellent performance in the job with the person's knowledge, skills, abilities, personality, and motivation for the job. They attempt to accomplish this by using the different types of tests discussed earlier.

Researchers have posited two groups of factors that determine an employee's performance in a job: the **can-do factors** and the **will-do factors** (Schmitt, Cortina, Ingerick, & Wiechmann, 2003). Can-do factors include knowledge, skills, and abilities; they suggest what an employee is capable of doing on the job if he is working to the best of his ability. Will-do factors include personality traits such as conscientiousness and need for achievement as well as integrity (Schmitt et al., 2003); they suggest the time and effort an employee is willing to exert for the organization. A person's can-do and will-do factors may change as she moves from organization to organization. Once a person is selected, the important process of being accepted and socialized into the organization at all levels, including a work group or team, begins.

Let's Review!

This section discussed the process of employee selection, including the five components of job analysis, testing, legal issues, recruitment, and the decision of whom to hire. As a quick check of your understanding, answer these questions.

1. Asking employees to describe their job is one way of conducting a _____.
   a. job evaluation
   b. job analysis
   c. performance appraisal
   d. job review

2. Alexander, a television reporter, wants access to the women's locker room right after basketball games to conduct interviews with the team members. The team lets female reporters in to interview them, but wants Alexander to wait until after they have showered and changed because they think he is too critical in his reporting style. Alexander argues that he needs to be treated the same as the female reporters. What would be the likely outcome if this issue goes before a court?
   a. The team would win because sex is a BFOQ in this case.
   b. The team members would win because they can discriminate against Alexander because they don't like his reporting style.
   c. Alexander would win because the team members can't discriminate against him because they don't like his reporting style.
   d. Alexander would win because sex is not a BFOQ in this case.

3. Zachary is usually a conscientious and hardworking employee, but the company has hired a new boss who is really lazy and doesn't motivate his employees. It is likely that Zachary's _____ will be compromised in this situation.
   a. try-to factors
   b. will-do factors
   c. can-do factors
   d. must-do factors

Answers 1.b; 2.d; 3.b

Socializing Employees: Culture, Groups, and Leadership

Learning Objective

- Describe how new employees become adapted to their work and organization.

When you report for your first day of work in an organization, there are many things you will need to learn to be successful in your job. The process of learning these things is called **organizational socialization**; it has been defined as "the process by which organizational members become a part of, or are absorbed into, the culture of the organization" (Jablin, 1982, p. 255). Organizational socialization consists of people learning how the organization operates by using information provided by management, coworkers, observation, and company handbooks or memos.

Nowadays, electronic communication is an important part of how you and your coworkers are socialized (Flanagin & Waldeck, 2004). Employees communicate through e-mail, company websites, chat groups, and blogs. Job applicants also use these resources to learn about the organization before submitting their applications.

Supervisors and coworkers are also important sources of socialization information. **Mentoring** is a form of training in which a current and often long-term employee (the mentor) is paired with a new employee. The mentor's role is to help the new employee adapt to the job by assisting with advice or resources. The mentor may provide information about how the organization works and career advancement opportunities. Good mentoring helps new employees become successful on the job and learn the formal and informal rules of the organization (Aamodt, 2007).

organizational socialization the process by which members of an organization become a part of, or are absorbed into, the culture of the organization

mentoring the pairing of a current and often long-term employee (the mentor) with a new employee

Research indicates that both mentors and those they mentor often benefit from the relationship. For example, in one study of health care employees, it was found that those who were mentored reported higher salaries, greater promotion rates, and more positive career success than those who did not receive mentoring (T. D. Allen, Lentz, & Day, 2006). Employees who have been mentored experience more effective socialization and better compensation, advancement, career satisfaction, job satisfaction, job involvement, and organizational commitment than those with no mentoring (Greenhaus, 2003).

Organizational Culture and Climate

Organizational culture includes the shared assumptions and beliefs of the organization. These cognitions then influence the **organizational climate**, or actions and behaviors of the people in the group or organization (Schein, 1985). These behaviors are considered the norm for the organization; they represent the "normal behaviors" expected by its members. Because culture and climate generally operate in concert, our discussion will refer to these elements collectively as culture (Ostroff, Kinicki, & Tamkins, 2003). Organizational culture is important because it lets employees know what is expected of them and affects how they think and behave. Culture is often determined by the founders of the organization, and may be modified over time by the successes and failures of an organization.

There have been several case studies of organizations that have successfully changed their culture. Remember Arthur Friedman from the beginning of this appendix? Arthur Friedman allowed his employees to set their own wages and decide the hours they worked; he also required employees to belong to the union. After Friedman made these changes, employee grumbling stopped. The organizational culture changed, resulting in better morale, increased productivity, and employee longevity. No one wanted to quit working in a culture where the employees got to make their own decisions that affected the organization's bottom line. Finding an organizational culture that fits your working style will have consequences for your morale, performance, and tenure in an organization. Work teams and the leadership of an organization have a large influence on the culture of an organization.

"I don't know how it started, either. All I know is that it's part of our corporate culture."

Groups and Teams

Work teams and **groups** can be defined as two or more employees who have common goals, have tasks that are interdependent, interact socially, and work on relevant organizational tasks within specific requirements and rules (Kozlowski & Bell, 2003). Just as there can be a culture in an organization, groups or teams also exhibit cultures that may encourage or discourage certain types of work-related behaviors and attitudes. These cultures then form the basis for the socialization of new group or team members.

Although most organizations provide formal means of socializing new employees, the group or team dynamics have immediate and direct effects on employees' socialization (N. Anderson & Thomas, 1996). The outcomes of informal and formal socialization may be different. Teams may have leaders or may be self-managing. Self-managing teams tend to show better productivity, an increase in work quality, improved quality of life for employees, decreased absenteeism, and decreased turnover (S. G. Cohen & Ledford, 1994). When teams fail, often the failure is linked to the team leader, who may be too autocratic, wielding too much power or influence. As a result, the team does not realize the autonomy and control levels it needs to be successful (Stewart & Manz, 1995).

organizational culture the shared cognitive assumptions and beliefs of an organization

organizational climate the behavioral norms of an organization

work teams/groups two or more employees who together perform organizationally relevant tasks, share one or more common goals, interact socially, exhibit task interdependencies, and maintain and manage boundaries within an organizational context

leadership a social influence process in which a person steers others toward a goal

transformational leadership a leader with high ethical standards, inspirational motivation, intellectual stimulation, and individual consideration

Oprah Winfrey is a modern-day transformational leader. She is probably best known as host of the *Oprah Winfrey Show*. In addition, she has started multiple charity groups, donating millions of dollars across the globe.

Peter Kramer/Getty Images

Leadership

Leadership has many definitions, including one person influencing another person or a team toward a goal (Bryman, 1996). Leadership has received a lot of research attention in industrial/organizational psychology. Yet it is still difficult to describe how to make or select the ideal leader. Many theories exist, and most have been useful in helping us understand what makes a good leader and how to improve leadership style.

Personality plays a role in many leadership theories. Certainly, it is an important aspect of successful or unsuccessful leaders. Kirkpatrick and Locke's (1991) review suggests that drive, honesty and integrity, self-confidence, cognitive abilities, and knowledge are associated with successful leaders. Leaders with poor cognitive abilities and social skills and those who are indecisive, low in self-confidence and self-esteem, dishonest, and lacking in ambition tend to be less successful (R. E. Kaplan, Drath &, Kofodimos, 1991).

Art Friedman's integrity likely made him a successful leader. He decided to give employees what he would want, providing them with the capabilities to make major decisions that could either make or break the organization. In his case, he created a self-managing group that had no need for external assistance from unions or other entities. As a result, Friedman demonstrated the **transformational leadership** approach (Bass, 1990). Transformational leadership is characterized by high ethical standards, inspirational motivation, intellectual stimulation, and individual consideration—all clearly evident in Arthur Friedman's leadership style.

Leaders today must contend with information-based team environments requiring the capacity for sifting large amounts of information coming from computer networks (Avolio, Kahai, & Dodge, 2000). The widely varying working environments that result from global competition require leaders to be adaptable (R. D. Mann, 1959), capable of handling stress (D. Goleman, 1998), knowledgeable about competitors and products (Kirpatrick & Locke, 1991), and able to solve complex problems quickly (Zaccaro, Mumford, Connelly, Marks, & Gilbert, 2000).

Let's Review!

This section discussed employee socialization within an organization and its work groups. Leadership and the type of work group will affect employees' job performance. As a quick check of your understanding, answer these questions.

1. Mentoring of new employees, in general, has been found to have positive outcomes or consequences for _____.
   a. both the mentor and the employee
   b. the mentor
   c. the employee
   d. organizations with autocratic leaders

2. Spencer, a new employee, has learned most of the behaviors required to do his job effectively. This means that Spencer has learned the _____ of the organization.
   a. organizational climate
   b. organizational culture
   c. transformational culture
   d. transformational climate

3. Carol is part of a successful self-managing team in an organization that produces handcrafted furniture. Compared to her coworkers in traditional leader-led teams, Carol and her work team should have _____.
   a. better productivity, lower work quality, and a decrease in absenteeism
   b. an increase in work quality, decrease in work quantity, and better quality of life
   c. an increase in absenteeism, lower work quality, and higher work quantity
   d. better productivity, better work quality, and a better quality of life

Answers 1. *a*; 2. *b*; 3. *d*

Attitudes and Behaviors at Work

- Describe the impact of employees' attitudes on their behaviors at work.

One of the most important factors influencing whether you will be motivated to do a good job hinges on your attitudes at work (see Chapter 10). The causes and consequences of work attitudes have been extensively researched. Some of the outcomes of attitudes include volunteering for a project, helping out a coworker, quitting, absenteeism, tardiness, early retirement, and performance.

Attitudes at Work

Attitudes at work include satisfaction with the work itself, pay and benefits, supervision, coworkers, promotion opportunities, working conditions, and job security. In general, you can be satisfied or dissatisfied with the tasks and conditions at work, the people in your work environment, and the rewards you get from work. Employee satisfaction is important because it has been shown to be related to employee behaviors at work (Hanisch, 1995). Two of the most commonly studied work attitudes are *job satisfaction* and *organizational commitment*.

JOB SATISFACTION

The positive or negative *affect* associated with a job defines **job satisfaction** (Thurstone, 1931). Some of the ways organizations can create satisfied employees include flexible working hours, professional growth opportunities, interesting work (Hackman & Oldham, 1976), autonomy, job security, a good supervisor, good benefits, competitive pay, and opportunities for promotion (Cranny, Smith, & Stone, 1992). It is important to note that what makes one worker satisfied may not make another worker satisfied. For some people, interesting work is paramount. Others place higher emphasis on having coworkers they like. Still others feel that the pay and benefits they receive is most important. Just as in selection, a match between what you want and what the organization can provide will result in a successful outcome for both parties.

Table B.4 Work on Present Job

Think of the work you do at present. How well does each of the following words or phrases describe your job? In the blank beside each word or phrase below, write:

Y for "Yes" if it describes your work
N for "No" if it does NOT describe it
? if you cannot decide

_____ 1. Fascinating	_____ 10. Useful
_____ 2. Routine	_____ 11. Tiring
_____ 3. Satisfying	_____ 12. Healthful
_____ 4. Boring	_____ 13. Challenging
_____ 5. Good	_____ 14. Too much to do
_____ 6. Creative	_____ 15. Frustrating
_____ 7. Respected	_____ 16. Simple
_____ 8. Uncomfortable	_____ 17. Repetitive
_____ 9. Pleasant	_____ 18. Gives sense of accomplishment

Scoring Key:

1. Y=3, N=0, ?=1	7. Y=3, N=0, ?=1	13. Y=3, N=0, ?=1
2. Y=0, N=3, ?=1	8. Y=0, N=3, ?=1	14. Y=0, N=3, ?=1
3. Y=3, N=0, ?=1	9. Y=3, N=0, ?=1	15. Y=0, N=3, ?=1
4. Y=0, N=3, ?=1	10. Y=3, N=0, ?=1	16. Y=0, N=3, ?=1
5. Y=3, N=0, ?=1	11. Y=0, N=3, ?=1	17. Y=0, N=3, ?=1
6. Y=3, N=0, ?=1	12. Y=3, N=0, ?=1	18. Y=3, N=0, ?=1

To interpret your score on the work scale, 27 is considered the neutral value (Balzer, et al., 1997). Values considerably higher would be evaluated as very satisfied, and values considerably lower would be evaluated as very dissatisfied, with the work on your present job.

YOUR TURN – ACTIVE LEARNING

One measure often used to assess employee work attitudes, and specifically different facets of job satisfaction, is the Job Descriptive Index (JDI; P. C. Smith, Kendall, & Hulin, 1969). This index has been improved upon based on years of research (e.g., Balzer et al., 1997; Hanisch, 1992). The JDI measures five facets of satisfaction: Work on Present Job, Supervisor, Coworkers, Present Pay, and Opportunities for Promotion. Test your own level of job satisfaction by filling out the Work on Present Job scale shown in ▪ TABLE B.4.

attitudes at work satisfaction with the work itself, pay and benefits, supervision, coworkers, promotion opportunities, working conditions, and job security

job satisfaction the positive or negative affect associated with a job

Employees report that their job satisfaction and productivity increase if they are allowed privileges such as listening to music while they work.

© Digital Vision/Photolibrary

affective commitment an employee's emotional attachment to the organization

normative commitment commitment to the organization based on feelings of obligation

continuance commitment remaining with an organization because of the high cost, monetary and/or social, of losing organizational membership

A recent survey found that listening to music at work leads to higher levels of reported employee satisfaction. About one-third of those participating in a Spherion Workplace Snapshot survey conducted by Harris Interactive in 2006 reported they listened to an iPod, MP3 player, or other personal music device while working (www.spherion.com). Seventy-nine percent of the participants reported that listening to music improved their job satisfaction and/or productivity at work. Allowing workers to listen to music may become more and more popular in jobs where music does not interfere with coworkers, safety, or job performance. Having happy workers contributes to an organization's success.

ORGANIZATIONAL COMMITMENT

Employee commitment to an organization is related to employee retention within the organization. There are three types of organizational commitment: *affective, normative,* and *continuance* (J. P. Meyer & Allen, 1991). Meyer and Allen define **affective commitment** as an employee's emotional attachment to the organization that makes the employee want to stay in the organization. **Normative commitment** is based on feelings of obligation. **Continuance commitment** results when an employee remains with a company because of the high cost of losing organizational membership, including monetary (e.g., pension benefits) and social (e.g., friendships) costs. J. P. Meyer and Herscovitch (2001) argue that employees have an organizational commitment profile at any given time in their job, with high or low values on each of the three types of commitment. In other words, an employee may have high scores on normative and continuance commitment, but be lower on affective commitment. Depending on the profile, the employee may engage in different behaviors such as quitting or helping out the organization.

Students may experience these different types of commitment to their college. Affective commitment means that a student feels an emotional attachment to the school because she really likes the school, including classes, the football team, and the town. The student wants to stay in that school because of her attachment to it. Normative commitment might be evidenced by a student whose parents attended that college and who feels obligated to do the same thing regardless of whether it is the best school for him. Staying at a college because your friends are there and you have already paid for two years of college would typify someone acting under continuance commitment. The three levels of commitment could be represented as a commitment profile for a student.

One of the causes of organizational commitment is job satisfaction. People who are satisfied with their job are more committed to their organization than those who are less satisfied (Mueller, Boyer, Price, & Iverson, 1994). Other causes of organizational commitment include trust in one's supervisor and human resources practices that are supportive of employees (Arthur, 1994). The organizational commitment of Friedman's employees was very high, as evidenced by no turnover in five years.

© 1996 Carol Simpson. Reprinted with permission.

"Employee morale is at an all-time high. We must be paying them too much."

Behaviors at Work

Employers want their employees to engage in behaviors that will make them successful in the job because their success helps the organization meet its goals, including earning profits and fulfilling its mission. Employees have control over two aspects of their work: their time and their effort (Naylor, Pritchard, & Ilgen, 1980). Having employees at work instead of late or absent is important to performance and productivity. Positive behaviors generally help an organization meet its goals while negative behaviors detract from goal attainment.

ORGANIZATIONAL CITIZENSHIP BEHAVIORS

Organizational citizenship behaviors (OCBs), or prosocial behaviors, are often described as extra-role behaviors because they are behaviors not specifically required by the job and not usually evaluated during performance reviews. These behaviors go beyond what is expected by the organization (C. A. Smith, Organ, & Near, 1983). Examples include staying late to finish a project, mentoring a new employee, volunteering for work, and helping a coworker. Some reasons why people engage in organizational citizenship behaviors are job satisfaction, high job autonomy, a positive organizational culture, high agreeableness (as a personality dimension; Witt, Kacmar, Carlson, & Zivnuska, 2002), and high conscientiousness (Borman, Penner, Allen, & Motowidlo, 2001). However, males who engage in OCBs are viewed positively while females are viewed as just doing their jobs (Heilman & Chen, 2005; Kidder & Parks, 2001)—a difference that may result in gender disparity in performance ratings. OCBs have positive consequences for the organization and for employees in their day-to-day interactions with others in the organization.

ORGANIZATIONAL WITHDRAWAL AND COUNTERPRODUCTIVE BEHAVIORS

Unhappy employees cause problems for organizations because they sometimes engage in behaviors that researchers refer to as **organizational withdrawal** (Hanisch, Hulin, & Roznowski, 1998) and counterproductive behaviors (Sackett & DeVore, 2003). Organizational withdrawal has been defined as behaviors employees use to avoid their work (**work withdrawal**) or their job (**job withdrawal**) (Hanisch, 1995; Hanisch & Hulin, 1990, 1991). Examples of work withdrawal are being absent from work, leaving work early, arriving to work late, missing meetings, and using work equipment for personal purposes without permission. Examples of job withdrawal are quitting one's job, transferring to another department within an organization, and retiring.

College students are familiar with withdrawal behaviors when it comes to certain college courses. Some classes may fail to keep your attention, and you may find yourself taking a nap in class or reading the newspaper. You may even look for legitimate reasons not to attend class, such as offering to fill in for another employee at work or deciding to attend an optional session for another class.

Counterproductive behaviors, although similar in some ways to withdrawal behaviors, are defined as "any intentional behavior on the part of an organizational member viewed by the organization as contrary to its legitimate interests" (Sackett & DeVore, 2003). An example of a counterproductive behavior would be an intentional violation of safety procedures that puts the employee and the organization at risk. Other examples of counterproductive behavior are theft, destruction of property, unsafe behavior, poor attendance, drug use, and inappropriate physical actions such as attacking a coworker.

Relation Between Attitudes and Behavior

Organizational citizenship behaviors are positively related to job satisfaction and organizational commitment. In other words, employees with good attitudes and who feel committed to their organization are more likely to do positive things to assist the organization (LePine, Erez, & Johnson, 2002). Research indicates that those employees who demonstrate organizational citizenship behaviors are less likely to engage in counterproductive behaviors (Dalal, 2005). Researchers have found strong links between job satisfaction and specific withdrawal

organizational citizenship behaviors (OCBs) employee behaviors that go beyond what is expected by the organization
organizational withdrawal work withdrawal or job withdrawal
work withdrawal behaviors employees use to avoid their work (e.g., lateness, absenteeism)
job withdrawal behaviors employees use to avoid their job (e.g., quitting, retiring)
counterproductive behaviors intentional behaviors on the part of an organizational member viewed by the organization as contrary to its legitimate interests

or counterproductive behaviors such as absenteeism (Hackett, 1989), and even stronger links with job withdrawal (Hanisch & Hulin, 1990).

Employers need to evaluate their work environment and fringe benefit packages and make modifications where necessary to ensure that they have employees who are satisfied and committed. Art Friedman made modifications in the work environment of his organization that resulted in high satisfaction and commitment among his employees. To help with the commute to and from work, Google added a free shuttle service that many employees say is the best fringe benefit, given some of the worst traffic in the Silicon Valley (Helft, 2007). Employees need to learn how to seek out satisfying work and perks that will result in their commitment to the organization. Satisfaction and commitment facilitate OCBs and decrease withdrawal and counterproductive behaviors. Together the right employee attitudes and behaviors will lead to successful organizational functioning.

Let's Review!

This section discussed employee attitudes and behaviors at work, focusing on job satisfaction, organizational commitment, withdrawal, and counterproductive behaviors. As a quick check of your understanding, answer these questions.

1. Quitting one's job would be an example of _____.
   a. normative commitment
   b. job withdrawal
   c. organizational citizenship behavior
   d. work withdrawal

2. Gordon's organizational commitment has been decreasing in the last year. Which of the following is Gordon most likely to do if his organizational commitment doesn't improve soon?
   a. Be absent
   b. Quit
   c. Ask for a raise
   d. Steal from the organization

3. _____ would be an example of an organizational citizenship behavior while _____ would be an example of a counterproductive behavior.
   a. Mentoring a new employee; engaging in safe work practices
   b. Being late; staying late to help a coworker
   c. Missing a meeting; being late for work
   d. Volunteering to serve on a committee; physically attacking your supervisor

Answers 1. b; 2. b; 3. d

Summary

This appendix discussed the role of I/O psychologists in the workplace, including job analysis, employee recruitment and selection, organizational culture, and the effect of employees' work attitudes on their work behaviors.

Now that you have an understanding of the process organizations use to hire successful employees, you have some of the tools necessary to help you in your search for a job. You also learned about the appropriate matches you might strive for in seeking employment that will make your work with an organization fulfilling for both you and the organization.

If you enjoyed learning about I/O psychology and think it might be a possible career for you, education and employment opportunities may interest you. Most I/O psychologists earn a master's or doctoral degree from a graduate school. This may take an additional two to five years beyond a bachelor's degree. Job opportunities are varied and often lucrative. For example, people with master's degrees in I/O psychology may work for an organization in their human resources office or conduct research on the best ways to train their employees. They may also work in a consulting firm or start their own after obtaining some experience in the workplace. Those who earn a doctoral degree may secure the same type of jobs as those with master's degrees but will typically be paid more for their expertise. In addition, they may also work for an academic institution such as a university or college teaching courses and/or conducting research on topics of their choosing. I/O psychology is an excellent career choice for many students interested in business who wish to interact with and help people.

Studying
THE Appendix

Key Terms

industrial and organizational (I/O) psychology (576)
job analysis (578)
test (578)
unstructured interview (578)
structured interview (578)
Title VII of the Civil Rights Act of 1964 (579)
recruitment (580)
can-do factors (581)

will-do factors (581)
organizational socialization (582)
mentoring (582)
organizational culture (583)
organizational climate (583)
work teams/groups (583)
leadership (584)
transformational leadership (584)
attitudes at work (585)
job satisfaction (585)

affective commitment (586)
normative commitment (586)
continuance commitment (586)
organizational citizenship behaviors (OCBs) (587)
organizational withdrawal (587)
work withdrawal (587)
job withdrawal (587)
counterproductive behaviors (587)

What Do You Know? Assess Your Understanding

Test your retention and understanding of the material by answering the following questions.

1. _____ is the shared assumptions and beliefs of employees in an organization.
   a. Organizational climate
   b. Organizational culture
   c. Leadership
   d. Organizational citizenship behavior

2. _____ is (are) the maximum performance an employee can exhibit.
   a. Can-do performance
   b. Will-do performance
   c. Counterproductive behaviors
   d. All of the above

3. _____ has standardized questions, a specific question order, and a predetermined scoring or answer key, and is conducted by a trained interviewer.
   a. Mentoring
   b. Leadership
   c. A structured interview
   d. An unstructured interview

4. _____ are behaviors employees engage in that go beyond what is expected by the organization.
   a. Organizational citizenship behaviors
   b. Counterproductive behaviors
   c. Organizational culture
   d. Organizational socialization

5. _____ are intentional behaviors on the part of an organizational member viewed by the organization as contrary to its legitimate interests.
   a. Organizational citizenship behaviors
   b. Counterproductive behaviors
   c. Will-do behaviors
   d. Can-do behaviors

6. _____ is the normal or typical performance by an employee.
   a. Organizational citizenship behavior
   b. Counterproductive behavior
   c. Will-do behavior
   d. Can-do behavior

7. _____ is the process organizations use to identify potential employees for a job.
   a. An unstructured interview
   b. A structured interview
   c. Mentoring
   d. Recruitment

8. _____ is when a current and often long-term employee teaches a new employee about the operations of the organization.
   a. Recruitment
   b. Leadership
   c. Organizational socialization
   d. Mentoring

9. _____ is the behavioral expectations of employees by their employers.
   a. Organizational climate
   b. Organizational culture
   c. Organizational socialization
   d. Can-do performance

10. _____ is informal, unplanned, with random questions and no scoring key, and is conducted by an untrained interviewer.
   a. Recruitment
   b. Mentoring
   c. A structured interview
   d. An unstructured interview

11. _____ is comprised of work and job withdrawal.
   a. Counterproductive behavior
   b. Organizational withdrawal
   c. Will-do performance
   d. All of the above

12. _____ is the process by which organizational members become a part of, or are absorbed into, the culture of the organization.
   a. Organizational socialization
   b. Organizational culture
   c. Organizational climate
   d. Recruitment

13. _____ is a social influence process in which a person steers members of the group toward a goal.
   a. Organizational socialization
   b. Organizational culture
   c. Leadership
   d. Recruitment

Answers: 1. b; 2. a; 3. c; 4. a; 5. b; 6. c; 7. d; 8. d; 9. a; 10. d; 11. b; 12. a; 13. c

absolute threshold the minimum intensity of a stimulus at which participants can identify its presence 50% of the time

accommodation (1) the process through which the lens is stretched or squeezed to focus light on the retina; (2) the process by which a schema is changed, modified, or created anew in order to understand something new in the environment

acetylcholine (ACh) neurotransmitter related to muscle movement and perhaps consciousness, learning, and memory

acquisition the process of learning a conditioned response or behavior

action potential neural impulse fired by a neuron when it reaches −55 mv

activation-synthesis theory suggests that dreams do not have symbolic meaning, but are the by-product of the brain's random firing of neural impulses during REM sleep

actor/observer bias our tendency to make the fundamental attribution error when judging others, while being less likely to do so when making attributions about ourselves

actualizing tendency according to Rogers, the natural drive in humans to strive for fulfillment and enhancement

adrenal medulla center part of the adrenal gland that plays a crucial role in the functioning of the sympathetic nervous system

adrenal cortex outside part of the adrenal gland that plays a role in the manufacture and release of androgens, and therefore influences sexual characteristics

affect one's expressed emotion toward an action at a given time

affective commitment an employee's emotional attachment to the organization

affective component of emotion the subjective experience of what you are *feeling* during the emotion

agoraphobia an excessive fear of being in places from which escape might be difficult or where help might not be available if one were to experience panic

alarm reaction the first phase of the general adaptation syndrome, characterized by immediate activation of the nervous and endocrine systems

algorithm a method of solving a particular problem that always leads to the correct solution

all-or-none fashion all action potentials are equal in strength; once a neuron begins to fire an action potential, it fires all the way down the axon

alternative hypothesis (H$_1$) the hypothesis that contains a statement of what we do believe is true about our variables in the population

altruism helping another without being motivated by self-gain

amplitude a physical property of some energies that corresponds to the height of wave peaks

amygdala part of the limbic system that plays a role in our emotions of fear and aggression

anal stage Freud's second psychosexual stage, which occurs from approximately 18 months to 3 years, in which the parents' regulation of the child's biological urge to expel or retain feces affects personality development

androgens a class of male hormones

anorexia nervosa an eating disorder in which a person has an intense fear of gaining weight, even though he or she is actually underweight. This irrational fear motivates the person to lose unhealthy amounts of weight through self-starvation.

anterograde amnesia a type of amnesia in which one is unable to store new memories in long-term memory

antianxiety medications minor tranquilizers, such as Valium, that are prescribed to reduce tension and anxiety

antidepressants medications prescribed to alleviate the symptoms of depression, eating disorders, and some anxiety disorders

antimanic medications drugs that are prescribed to alleviate manic symptoms of bipolar disorder

antipsychotic medications major tranquilizers, such as Haldol, that are prescribed to relieve psychotic symptoms such as delusions and hallucinations

antisocial personality disorder a personality disorder marked by a pattern of disregard for and violation of the rights of others with no remorse or guilt for one's actions

anxiety disorder a disorder marked by excessive apprehension that seriously interferes with a person's ability to function

anxiety hierarchy a list, according to the degree of fear, of threatening images elicited by a feared object or situation; starts with the least frightening images and progresses to the most distressing

approach–approach conflict a situation in which a person must choose between two likable events

approach–avoidance conflict a situation in which a person is faced with a need that has both positive and negative aspects

archetypes according to Jung, mental representations or symbols of themes and predispositions to respond to the world in a certain way that are contained in the collective unconscious

assimilation the process by which an existing schema is used to understand something new in the environment

association cortex areas of the cortex involved in the association or integration of information from the motor-sensory areas of the cortex

attachment the emotional bond between caretaker and infant that is established by 8 or 9 months

attention an organism's ability to focus its consciousness on some aspect of its own mental processes and/or its environment

attention conscious awareness; can be focused on events that are taking place in the environment or inside our minds

attitude an evaluative belief that we hold about something

attitudes at work satisfaction with the work itself, pay and benefits, supervision, coworkers, promotion opportunities, working conditions, and job security

attribution the act of assigning cause to behavior

auditory cortex a region of cortex found in the temporal lobe that governs the processing of auditory information in the brain

auditory nerve the nerve that carries information from the inner ear to the brain

authoritarian parent a parenting style characterized by high levels of control and low levels of affection

authoritative parent a parenting style characterized by moderate levels of control and affection

autonomic nervous system branch of the peripheral nervous system that primarily governs involuntary organ functioning and actions in the body

availability heuristic a heuristic in which we use the ease with which we can recall instances of an event to help us estimate the frequency of the event

aversion therapy a behavior therapy technique in which a specific behavior is paired with an unpleasant stimulus in order to reduce its occurrence

avoidance–avoidance conflict a situation in which a person must choose between two undesirable events

axon the long tail-like structure that comes out of the cell body of the neuron and carries action potentials that convey information from the cell body to the synapse

babbling the combinations of vowel and consonant sounds uttered by infants beginning around 4 months

basic anxiety according to Horney, the feeling of helplessness that develops in children from early relationships

basic emotion a proposed set of innate emotions that are common to all humans and from which other higher-order emotions may derive

basic level category the intermediate level of categorization that seems to be the level that we use most to think about our world

basilar membrane the structure in the cochlear duct that contains the hair cells, which convert sound waves into action potentials

behavior therapy therapy that applies the principles of classical or operant conditioning to help people change maladaptive behaviors

behavioral perspective focuses on external, environmental causes of behavior

behaviorism a psychological perspective that emphasizes the study of observable responses and behavior

bereavement the experience of losing a loved one

binge eating disorder an eating disorder characterized by recurrent episodes of binge eating, as in bulimia nervosa, but without regular use of compensatory measures to avoid weight gain

binocular depth cues depth cues that utilize information from both eyes

biological perspective focuses on physical causes of behavior

biomedical therapy the use of medications or other medical interventions to treat psychological disorders

bipolar disorder a mood disorder characterized by both depression and mania

bisexual one who is sexually attracted to members of both sexes

blindspot the point where the optic nerve leaves the retina, where there are no rods or cones

borderline personality disorder (BPD) a personality disorder marked by a pattern of instability in mood, relationships, self-image, and behavior

bottom-up perceptual processing perception that is not guided by prior knowledge or expectations

brightness the intensity of light; it corresponds to the amplitude of the light waves

Broca's area a region in the left frontal lobe that plays a role in the production of speech

bulimia nervosa an eating disorder in which a person alternately binges on large quantities of food and then engages in some inappropriate compensatory behavior to avoid weight gain

bystander effect the idea that the more witnesses there are to an emergency, the less likely any one of them is to offer help

can-do factors factors that determine the maximum performance an employee can exhibit

Cannon-Bard theory a theory of emotion that states that emotions originate in the brain, not the body

cardinal traits according to Allport, those dominant elements of our personalities that drive all of our behaviors

case study an in-depth observation of one person

catatonic excitement a disorder in motor behavior involving excited agitation

catatonic stupor a disorder in motor behavior involving immobility

causal hypothesis an educated guess about how one variable will influence another variable

cell body the part of the neuron that contains the nucleus and DNA

central executive the attention-controlling component of working memory

central nervous system (CNS) the brain and the spinal cord

central route to persuasion a style of thinking in which the person carefully and critically evaluates persuasive arguments and generates counterarguments; the central route requires motivation and available cognitive resources

central traits according to Allport, those tendencies we have to behave in a certain way across most situations

centration the act of focusing on only one aspect or feature of an object

cerebellum hindbrain structure that plays a role in balance, muscle tone, and coordination of motor movements

cerebral cortex thin, wrinkled outer covering of the brain in which high-level processes such as thinking, planning, language, interpretation of sensory data, and coordination of sensory and motor information take place

cerebral hemispheres right and left sides of the brain that to some degree govern different functions in the body

cholecystokinin (CCK) a hormone released by the small intestines that plays a role in hunger regulation

chunking a means of using one's limited short-term memory resources more efficiently by combining small bits of information to form larger bits of information, or chunks

circadian rhythm changes in bodily processes that occur repeatedly on approximately a 24- to 25-hour cycle

classical conditioning learning that occurs when a neutral stimulus is repeatedly paired with an unconditioned stimulus; because of this pairing, the neutral stimulus becomes a conditioned stimulus with the same power as the unconditioned stimulus to elicit the response in the organism

client-centered therapy a humanistic psychotherapy approach formulated by Carl Rogers that emphasizes the use of empathy, genuineness, and unconditional positive regard to help the client reach his/her potential

clinical interview the initial meeting between a client and a clinician in which the clinician asks questions to identify the difficulty in functioning that the person is experiencing

closure a Gestalt principle of perception that states that when we look at a stimulus, we tend to see it as a closed shape rather than lines

cochlea the curled, fluid-filled tube that contains the basilar membrane in the inner ear

cognition the ability to know, think, and remember; the way in which we use and store information in memory

cognitive consistency the idea that we strive to have attitudes and behaviors that do not contradict one another

cognitive distortions distorted thinking patterns, such as overgeneralization or all-or-none thinking, that, according to Beck, lead to depression, anxiety, and low self-esteem

cognitive map a mental representation of the environment that is formed through observation of one's environment

cognitive perspective focuses on how mental processes influence behavior

cognitive psychology the study of mental processes such as reasoning and problem solving

cognitive reappraisal an active and conscious process in which we alter our interpretation of a stressful event

cognitive therapy a therapy created by Aaron Beck that focuses on uncovering negative automatic thought patterns that impede healthy psychological functioning

cognitive-mediational theory a theory of emotion that states that our cognitive appraisal of a situation determines what emotion we will feel in the situation

cohesiveness the degree to which members of a group value their group membership; cohesive groups are tight-knit groups

collective unconscious according to Jung, the part of the unconscious that contains images and material universal to people of all time periods and cultures

collectivistic culture a culture, like many Asian cultures, in which group accomplishments are valued over individual accomplishments

color blindness a condition in which a person cannot perceive one or more colors because of a lack of specific cones in the retina

compliance yielding to a simple request

compulsion repetitive behavior that a person feels a strong urge to perform

concept mental category that contains related bits of knowledge

concrete operations Piaget's third stage of cognitive development, characterized by logical thought

conditioned response (CR) the response that is elicited by a conditioned stimulus

conditioned stimulus (CS) a stimulus that elicits a conditioned response in an organism

cones the cells of the retina that are sensitive to specific colors of light and send information to the brain concerning the colors we are seeing

confidentiality researchers do not reveal which data were collected from which participant

conflict having to choose between two or more needs, desires, or demands

conformity behaving in accordance with group norms

confounding variable any factor other than the independent variable that affects the dependent measure

conscious level the level of consciousness that holds all the thoughts, perceptions, and impulses of which we are aware

consciousness feelings, thoughts, and aroused states of which we are aware

conservation the understanding that an object retains its original properties even though it may look different

constructive memory memory that utilizes knowledge and expectations to fill in the missing details in retrieved memory traces

contact hypothesis the theory that contact between groups is an effective means of reducing prejudice between them

contiguity the degree to which two stimuli occur close together in time

contingency the degree to which the presentation of one stimulus reliably predicts the presentation of the other

continuance commitment remaining with an organization because of the high cost, monetary and/or social, of losing organizational membership

continuous reinforcement a schedule of reinforcement in which the organism is rewarded for every instance of the desired response

cooing the vowel sounds made by infants beginning at 2 months

coping the behaviors that we engage in to manage stressors

corpus callosum a thick band of neurons that connect the right and left hemispheres of the brain

correlation the relationship between two or more variables

correlation coefficient the average product of z scores calculated on pairs of scores; describes the degree to which the scores in the pairs are linearly related

counterproductive behaviors intentional behaviors on the part of an organizational member viewed by the organization as contrary to its legitimate interests

couple therapy therapy that focuses on improving communication and intimacy between two people in a committed relationship

covert sensitization therapy a milder form of aversion therapy in which graphic imagery is used to create unpleasant associations with specific stimuli

creativity the ability to combine mental elements in new and useful ways

crystallized intelligence abilities that rely on knowledge, expertise, and judgment

cue-dependent forgetting a type of forgetting that occurs when one cannot recall information in a context other than the context in which it was encoded

cultural bias the degree to which a test puts people from other cultures at an unfair disadvantage because of the culturally specific nature of the test items

cycle a physical characteristic of energy defined as a wave peak and the valley that immediately follows it

cyclothymic disorder a mood disorder that is a less severe but more chronic form of bipolar disorder

daily hassles the everyday irritations and frustrations that individuals face

dark adaptation the process through which our eyes adjust to dark conditions after having been exposed to bright light

data information gathered in scientific studies

debriefing after an experiment, participants are fully informed of the nature of the study

decay theory a theory of forgetting that proposes that memory traces that are not routinely activated in long-term memory will degrade

decibels (dB) the unit of measure used to determine the loudness of a sound

decision making making a choice from among a series of alternatives

declarative memory a type of long-term memory that encompasses memories that are easily verbalized, including episodic and semantic memories

deductive reasoning reasoning from the general to the specific

defense mechanism (1) a process used to protect the ego by reducing the anxiety it feels when faced with the conflicting demands of the id and the superego; (2) unconscious, emotional strategies that are engaged in to reduce anxiety and maintain a positive self-image

deindividuation a state in which a person's behavior becomes controlled more by external norms than by the person's own internal values and morals

delusion a thought or belief that a person believes to be true but in reality is not

dendrites branchlike structures on the head of the neuron that receive incoming signals from other neurons in the nervous system

dependent variable the variable in an experiment that measures any effect of the manipulation

depressants drugs that inhibit or slow down normal neural functioning

dermis the inner layer of the skin

descriptive statistics statistics that are calculated to summarize or describe certain aspects of a data set

destructive obedience obedience to immoral, unethical demands that cause harm to others

development changes in behavior and/or abilities

Diagnostic and Statistical Manual of Mental Disorders (DSM) a book published by the APA that lists the criteria for close to 400 psychological disorders

diffusion of responsibility the idea that responsibility for taking action is diffused across all the people witnessing an event

discrimination the behavioral expression of a prejudice

dishabituation to begin re-responding to a stimulus to which one has been habituated

dissociation theory Hilgard's proposal that hypnosis involves two simultaneous states: a hypnotic state and a hidden observer

dissociative disorder a disorder marked by a loss of awareness of some part of one's self or one's surroundings that seriously interferes with the person's ability to function

dissociative fugue a disorder marked by episodes of amnesia in which a person is unable to recall some or all of his or her past and is confused about his or her identity; a new identity may be formed in which the person suddenly and unexpectedly travels away from home

dissociative identity disorder (DID) a disorder in which two or more personalities coexist within the same individual; formerly called multiple personality disorder

dissonance theory a theory that predicts that we will be motivated to change our attitudes and/or our behaviors to the extent that they cause us to feel dissonance, an uncomfortable physical state

DNA the chemical found in the nuclei of cells that contains the genetic blueprint that guides development in the organism

door-in-the-face compliance increasing compliance by first asking people to give in to a very large request and then, after they refuse, asking them to give in to a smaller request

dopamine neurotransmitter that plays a role in movement, learning, and attention

Down syndrome a genetic birth disorder resulting from an extra 21st chromosome, characterized by distinct facial features and a greater likelihood of heart defects and mental retardation

dream analysis a technique in psychoanalysis in which the therapist examines the hidden symbols in a client's dreams

drive an uncomfortable internal state that motivates us to reduce this discomfort through our behavior

drive reduction theory theory of motivation that proposes that motivation seeks to reduce internal levels of drive

dual coding system a system of memory that encodes information in more than one type of code or format

dualistic thinking reasoning that divides situations and issues into right and wrong categories

duplicity theory proposes that a combination of volley and place theory explains how our brain decodes pitch

dysphoria an extreme state of sadness

dysthymic disorder a mood disorder that is a less severe but more chronic form of major depression

eclectic approach (1) an approach to explaining behavior that integrates and combines several perspectives; (2) therapy that incorporates an integrated and diverse use of therapeutic methods

ego the conscious part of the personality that attempts to meet the demands of the id by successfully dealing with the environment

egocentrism the belief that everyone thinks as you do

elaborative rehearsal forming associations or links between information one is trying to learn and information already stored in long-term memory so as to facilitate the transfer of this new information into long-term memory

Electra complex in the female, an unconscious sexual urge for the father that develops during the phallic psychosexual stage

electroconvulsive therapy (ECT) a series of treatments in which electrical current is passed through the brain, causing a seizure; used to alleviate severe depression

embryonic stage the second stage of prenatal development, lasting from the 2nd through the 8th week

emotion a complex reaction to some internal or external event that involves physiological reactions, behavioral reactions, facial expressions, cognition, and affective responses

emotion-focused coping behaviors aimed at controlling the internal emotional reactions to a stressor

empathy the ability of a therapist to understand a client's feelings and thoughts without being judgmental

encoding the act of inputting information into memory

endocrine glands organs of the endocrine system that produce and release hormones into the blood

endorphins neurotransmitters that act as a natural painkiller

enuresis a condition in which a person over the age of 5 shows an inability to control urination during sleep

epidermis the outer layer of the skin

episodic memory long-term, declarative memory for autobiographical events

erogenous zones areas of the skin that are sensitive to touch

estrogens a class of female hormones that regulate many aspects of sexuality

evolutionary perspective focuses on how evolution and natural selection cause behavior

excitation when a neurotransmitter depolarizes the postsynaptic cell and it becomes more likely to fire an action potential

excitement phase the first stage of the sexual response cycle, in which males get erections and females produce vaginal lubrication

exemplar a mental representation of an actual instance of a member of a category

exhaustion stage the third and final phase of the general adaptation syndrome, in which bodily resources are drained and wear and tear on the body begins

experiment a research method that is used to test causal hypotheses

explicit memory the conscious use of memory

extinction the removal of a conditioned response

extinction burst a temporary increase in a behavioral response that occurs immediately after extinction has begun

extracellular fluid the fluid found in the spaces between the cells of the body, which is used to regulate thirst

extraversion personality traits that involve energy directed outward, such as being easygoing, lively, or excitable

extrinsic motivation motivation that comes from outside of the person

facial feedback hypothesis a theory that states that our emotional state is affected by the feedback our brain gets from facial muscles

family therapy therapy that focuses on creating balance and restoring harmony to improve the functioning of the family as a whole system

feature detection theory a theory of perception that proposes the existence of feature detectors, cortical cells that fire only when we see certain visual stimuli such as shapes, colors of light, or movement

feature detectors specialized cells in the visual cortex that fire only when they receive input that indicates we are looking at a particular shape, color, angle, or other visual feature

fetal alcohol syndrome (FAS) a birth condition resulting from the mother's chronic use of alcohol during pregnancy, characterized by facial and limb deformities and mental retardation

fetal stage the stage of prenatal development from the 9th week through the 9th month

figure–ground a Gestalt principle of perception that states that when we perceive a stimulus, we visually pull the figure part of the stimulus forward while visually pushing backward the background, or ground, part of the stimulus

fine motor skills motor behaviors involving the small muscles of the body

fixed interval schedule a schedule of reinforcement in which the organism is rewarded for the first desired response in an xth interval of time

fixed ratio schedule a schedule of reinforcement in which the organism is rewarded for every xth instance of the desired response

flashbulb memory an unusually detailed and seemingly accurate memory for an emotionally charged event

fluid intelligence abilities that rely on information-processing skills such as reaction time, attention, and working memory

foot-in-the-door compliance increasing compliance by first asking people to give in to a small request, which then paves the way for compliance with a larger request

forebrain brain structures including the limbic system, thalamus, hypothalamus, and cortex that govern higher-order mental processes

formal concept concept that is based on learned, rigid rules that define certain categories of things

formal operations Piaget's final stage of cognitive development, characterized by the ability to engage in abstract thought

free association a technique in psychoanalysis in which the client says whatever comes to mind

frequency a physical characteristic of energy defined as the number of cycles that occur in a given unit of time

frequency distribution a graph of data that plots the frequency of data points on the y-axis and the data points themselves on the x-axis

frequency polygon a line graph that is used to illustrate a frequency distribution

frequency theory proposes that our brain decodes pitch directly from the frequency at which the hair cells of the basilar membrane are firing

frontal lobe cortical area directly behind the forehead that plays a role in thinking, planning, decision making, language, and motor movement

frustration-aggression hypothesis the idea that frustration causes aggressive behavior

functional fixedness being able to see objects only in their familiar roles

functionalism an early psychological perspective concerned with how behavior helps people adapt to their environment

fundamental attribution error our tendency to overuse trait information when making attributions about others

gamma amino butyric acid (GABA) the body's chief inhibitory neurotransmitter, which plays a role in regulating arousal

gender permanence the understanding that one's gender will not change

gender roles society's expectations for how male and females should behave

gender-schema theory the idea that gender roles are acquired through modeling and reinforcement processes that work together with a child's mental abilities

general adaptation syndrome (GAS) the general physical responses we experience when faced with a stressor

general intelligence (g) Charles Spearman's notion that there is a general level of intelligence that underlies our separate abilities

generalizability how well a researcher's findings apply to other individuals and situations

generalized anxiety disorder (GAD) an anxiety disorder characterized by chronic, constant worry in almost all situations

genes strands of DNA found in the nuclei of all living cells

genital stage Freud's final psychosexual stage of development, which occurs during puberty, in which sexual energy is transferred toward peers of the other sex (heterosexual orientation) or same sex (homosexual orientation)

genotype inherited genetic pattern for a given trait

genuineness the ability of a therapist to openly share his or her thoughts and feelings with a client

germinal stage the first stage of prenatal development, from conception to 14 days

Gestalt approach a psychological school of thought originating in Germany that proposed that the whole of a perception must be understood rather than trying to deconstruct perception into its parts

gestation the sense of taste

ghrelin a hunger-stimulating hormone produced by the stomach

glia cells brain cells that provide support functions for the neurons

glucose the form of sugar that the body burns as fuel

glutamate the chief excitatory neurotransmitter in the brain, found at more than 50% of the synapses in the brain

glycogen a starchy molecule that is produced from excess glucose in the body; it can be thought of as the body's stored energy reserves

good continuation a Gestalt principle of perception that states that we have a preference for perceiving stimuli that seem to follow one another as part of a continuing pattern

grammar the rules that govern the sentence structure in a particular language

graph a visual depiction of data

grief one's emotional reaction to the death of a loved one

gross motor skills motor behaviors involving the large muscles of the body

group therapy therapy that is administered to more than one person at a time

groupthink a situation in which a group fixates on one decision, and members blindly assume that it is the correct decision

guided imagery a technique in which you focus on a pleasant, calming image to achieve a state of relaxation when you feel stressed

habituation the tendency of an organism to ignore repeated stimuli

hair cells neurons that grow out of the basilar membrane and convert sounds waves into action potentials

hallucination perceiving something that does not exist in reality

hallucinogens drugs that simultaneously excite and inhibit normal neural activity, thereby causing distortions in perception

hardy personality a personality, high in the traits of commitment, control, and challenge, that appears to be associated with strong stress resistance

health psychology the subfield of psychology that investigates the relationship between people's behaviors and their health

health-defeating behaviors behaviors that increase the chance of illness, disease, or death

health-promoting behaviors behaviors that decrease the chance of illness, disease, or death

helping behavior another term for altruism

heterosexual one who is sexually attracted only to members of the other sex

heuristic a shortcut or rule of thumb that may or may not lead to a correct solution to the problem

hierarchy of needs Maslow's theory that humans are motivated by different motives, some of which take precedence over others

hindbrain primitive part of the brain that comprises the medulla, pons, and cerebellum

hippocampus part of the brain that plays a role in the transfer of information from short- to long-term memory

histogram a bar graph that is used to illustrate a frequency distribution

homeostasis an internal state of equilibrium in the body

homophobia prejudicial attitudes against homosexuals and homosexuality

homosexual one who is sexually attracted only to members of the same sex

hormones chemical messengers of the endocrine system

hostile aggression aggression that is meant to cause harm to others

hue the color of a light

humanism a psychological perspective that emphasizes the personal growth and potential of humans

humanistic approach a personality perspective that emphasizes the individual, personal choice, and free will in shaping personality; assumes that humans have a built-in drive toward fulfilling their own natural potential

humanistic perspective focuses on how an individual's view of him- or herself and the world influence behavior

hypnosis a state of heightened suggestibility

hypochondriasis a somatoform disorder in which the person believes he or she has a disease, without any evident physical basis

hypothalamus part of the forebrain that plays a role in maintaining homeostasis in the body involving sleep, body temperature, sexual behavior, thirst, and hunger; also the point where the nervous system intersects with the endocrine system

hypothesis an educated guess

id the unconscious part of the personality that seeks pleasure and gratification

ill-structured problem a problem for which an algorithm is not known

imaginary audience the belief held by adolescents that everyone is watching what they do

immunosuppression the reduction in activity of the immune system

implicit memory the unconscious use of memory

impression formation the way that we understand and make judgments about others

incentive a goal or desire that we are motivated to fulfill

incubation a period of not thinking about a problem that helps one solve the problem

independent variable the variable in an experiment that is manipulated

individualistic culture a culture, like many Western cultures, in which individual accomplishments are valued over group accomplishments

inductive reasoning reasoning from the specific to the general

industrial and organizational (I/O) psychology the study of people's behavior at work using psychological principles

inferential statistics statistics that psychologists use in hypothesis testing to tell them when they should reject or accept their hypotheses about the population

informational conformity conformity that occurs when conformity pressures actually persuade group members to adopt new beliefs and/or attitudes

informed consent research participants agree to participate after being told about aspects of the study

in-group bias our tendency to favor people who belong to the same groups that we do

inhibition when a neurotransmitter further polarizes the postsynaptic cell and it becomes less likely to fire an action potential

insight a new way of looking at a problem that leads to a sudden understanding of how to solve it

insomnia a sleep disorder in which a person cannot get to sleep and/or stay asleep

instinct innate impulse from within a person that directs or motivates behavior

Institutional Review Board (IRB) a committee that reviews research proposals to ensure that ethical standards have been met

instrumental aggression aggression used to facilitate the attainment of one's goals

intelligence abilities that enable you to adapt to your environment and behave in a goal-directed way

intelligence quotient (IQ score) one's mental age divided by one's chronological age times 100

interactionism perspective that our genes and environmental influences work together to determine our characteristics

interpretation the psychoanalyst's view on the themes and issues that may be influencing the client's behavior

intracellular fluid the fluid found inside the cells of the body, which is used to regulate thirst

intrinsic motivation motivation that comes from within the person

introspection observing one's own thoughts, feelings, or sensations

introversion personality traits that involve energy directed inward, such as being calm or peaceful

ions charged particles that play an important role in the firing of action potentials in the nervous system

James-Lange theory a theory of emotion that defines an emotion as a unique pattern of physiological arousal

job analysis identification of the critical elements of a job, including tasks, skills required, and working conditions

job satisfaction the positive or negative affect associated with a job

job withdrawal behaviors employees use to avoid their job (e.g., quitting, retiring)

judgment the act of estimating the probability of an event

just noticeable difference (jnd) the minimum change in intensity of a stimulus that participants can detect 50% of the time

kinesthesis the ability to sense the position of our body parts in relation to one another and in relation to space

knowledge information stored in our long-term memory about the world and how it works

language a well-developed, syntactical verbal system for representing the world

latency stage Freud's fourth psychosexual stage of development, which occurs from around age 6 to puberty, in which the child's sexuality is suppressed due to widening social contacts with school, peers, and family

latent content according to Freudian theory, the symbolic meaning of a dream

latent learning learning that cannot be directly observed in an organism's behavior

lateral hypothalamus (LH) a region of the hypothalamus once thought to be the hunger center in the brain

law of effect a principle discovered by E. L. Thorndike, which states that random behaviors that lead to positive consequences will be strengthened and random behaviors that lead to negative consequences will be weakened

leadership a social influence process in which a person steers others toward a goal

learned helplessness a passive response to stressors based on exposure to previously uncontrolled, negative events; the belief that one cannot control the outcome of events

learning a relatively permanent change in behavior, or behavior potential, as a result of experience

lens the part of the eye that lies behind the pupil and focuses light rays on the retina

leptin a hormone released by fat cells in the body that plays a role in hunger regulation

levels-of-processing model a model that predicts that information that is processed deeply and elaboratively will be best retained in and recalled from long-term memory

libido one's physical desire, or drive, to have sex

life event a change in one's life, good or bad, that requires readjustment

light adaptation the process through which our eyes adjust to bright light after having been exposed to darkness

limbic system system of structures, including the amygdala and hippocampus, that govern certain aspects of emotion, motivation, and memory

lithium a naturally occurring mineral salt prescribed to control manic symptoms in people with bipolar disorder; it influences several neurotransmitters in the brain, including glutamate, serotonin, and dopamine

lock-and-key theory proposes that olfactory receptors are excited by odor molecules in a fashion that is similar to how neurotransmitters excite receptor sites

locus of control the expectation of control we have over the outcome of an event; an internal locus expects some degree of personal control, whereas an external locus expects little personal control

long-term memory (LTM) a system of memory that works to store memories for a long time, perhaps even permanently

loudness the psychophysical property of sound that corresponds to the amplitude of a sound wave

maintenance rehearsal repeating information over and over again to keep it in short-term memory for an extended period of time

major depression a mood disorder involving dysphoria, feelings of worthlessness, loss of interest in one's usual activities, and changes in bodily activities such as sleep and appetite that persists for at least two weeks

mania a period of abnormally excessive energy and elation

manifest content according to Freud, what the dreamer recalls on awakening

matching hypothesis the theory that we are attracted to people whose level of physical attractiveness is similar to our own

mean a descriptive statistic that describes the most average, or typical, data point in the distribution

measures of central tendency descriptive statistics that describe the most central, or typical, data points in the frequency distribution

median a descriptive statistic that identifies the center of the frequency distribution; 50% of the scores are above and 50% are below this point in the distribution

medical model perspective that views psychological disorders as similar to physical diseases; they result from biological disturbances and can be diagnosed, treated, and cured like other physical illnesses

meditation mental exercises in which people consciously focus their attention to heighten awareness and bring their mental processes under more control

medulla part of the hindbrain that controls basic, life-sustaining functions such as respiration, heart rate, and blood pressure

melatonin hormone in the body that facilitates sleep

memory traces the stored code that represents a piece of information that has been encoded into memory

menarche a girl's first menstruation

menopause the period when a female stops menstruating and is no longer fertile

mental age the age that reflects the child's mental abilities in comparison to the average child of the same age

mental representation memory traces that represent objects, events, people, and so on that are not present at the time

mental set the tendency to habitually use methods of problem solving that have worked for you in the past

mentoring the pairing of a current and often long-term employee (the mentor) with a new employee

mere exposure effect the idea that the more one is exposed to something, the more one grows to like it

microsleep brief episode of sleep that occurs in the midst of a wakeful activity

midbrain brain structure that connects the hindbrain with the forebrain

Minnesota Multiphasic Personality Inventory (MMPI-2) a personality inventory that is designed to identify problem areas of functioning in a person's personality

mode a measure of central tendency that identifies the most common, or frequent, score in the distribution

monocular depth cues depth cues that require information from only one eye

mood disorder a disorder marked by a significant change in one's emotional state that seriously interferes with one's ability to function

moral reasoning how you decide what is right and what is wrong

morpheme the smallest unit of sound in a language that has meaning

motive a tendency to desire and seek out positive incentives or rewards and to avoid negative outcomes

motor cortex a strip of cortex at the back of the frontal lobe that governs the execution of motor movement in the body

motor neurons neurons that transmit commands from the brain to the muscles of the body

multiple approach–avoidance conflict a situation that poses several alternatives that each have positive and negative features

multiple intelligences the idea that we possess different types of intelligence rather than a single, overall level of intelligence

myelin fatty, waxy substance that insulates portions of some neurons in the nervous system

narcolepsy a rare sleep disorder in which a person falls asleep during alert activities during the day

natural concept concept that develops naturally as we live our lives and experience the world

natural selection cornerstone of Darwin's theory of evolution, which states that genes for traits that allow an organism to be reproductively successful will be selected or retained in a species and genes for traits that hinder reproductive success will not be selected and therefore will die out in a species

naturalistic observation observing behavior in the environment in which the behavior typically occurs

nature–nurture debate age-old debate over whether we are mostly a product of our genes or of environmental influences

nature–nurture issue the degree to which biology (nature) or the environment (nurture) contributes to one's development

negative correlation a relationship in which increases in one variable correspond to decreases in a second variable

negative feedback loop a system of feedback in the body that monitors and adjusts our motivation level so as to maintain homeostasis

negative punishment weakening a behavior by removing something pleasant from the organism's environment

negative reinforcement reinforcing a behavior by removing something unpleasant from the environment of the organism

neonate a newborn during the first 28 days of life

nervous system an electrochemical system of communication within the body that uses cells called neurons to convey information

neurons cells in the central nervous system that transmit information

neuropeptide Y the most powerful hunger stimulant known

neuroticism the degree to which one is emotionally unstable

neurotransmitters chemical messengers that carry neural signals across the synapse

neutral stimulus (NS) a stimulus that does not naturally elicit an unconditioned response in an organism

night terrors very frightening non-REM sleep episodes

nightmare a brief scary REM dream that is often remembered

non-REM sleep relaxing state of sleep in which the person's eyes do not move

norepinephrine (NOR) neurotransmitter that plays a role in regulating sleep, arousal, and mood

norm unwritten rule or expectation for how group members should behave

normal distribution a bell-shaped, symmetric frequency distribution

normative commitment commitment to the organization based on feelings of obligation

normative conformity conformity that occurs when group members change their behavior to meet group norms but are not persuaded to change their beliefs and attitudes

null hypothesis (H_0) the hypothesis that contains a statement of what we do not believe is true about our variables in the population

obedience yielding to a demand

obese having a body mass index of 30 or over

object permanence the understanding that an object continues to exist even when it is not present

obsession a recurrent thought or image that intrudes on a person's awareness

obsessive-compulsive disorder (OCD) an anxiety disorder involving a pattern of unwanted intrusive thoughts and the urge to engage in repetitive actions

occipital lobe cortical area at the back of the brain that plays a role in visual processing

Oedipus complex in the male, an unconscious sexual urge for the mother that develops during the phallic psychosexual stage

olfaction the sense of smell

olfactory epithelium a special piece of skin at the top of the nasal cavity that contains the olfactory receptors

operant conditioning a type of learning in which the organism learns through the consequences of its behavior

opiates painkilling drugs that depress some brain areas and excite others

opponent-process theory proposes that we have dual-action cells beyond the level of the retina that signal the brain when we see one of a pair of colors

optic chiasm the point in the brain where the optic nerve from the left eye crosses over the optic nerve from the right eye

optic nerve the structure that conveys visual information away from the retina to the brain

oral stage Freud's first psychosexual stage of development, which occurs during the first year of life, in which the handling of the child's feeding experiences affects personality development

organizational citizenship behaviors (OCBs) employee behaviors that go beyond what is expected by the organization

organizational climate the behavioral norms of an organization

organizational culture the shared cognitive assumptions and beliefs of an organization

organizational socialization the process by which members of an organization become a part of, or are absorbed into, the culture of the organization

organizational withdrawal work withdrawal or job withdrawal

orgasm phase the third stage of the sexual response cycle, in which the pelvic and anal muscles contract

orienting reflex the tendency of an organism to orient its senses toward unexpected stimuli

out-group a group that is distinct from one's own and so usually an object of more hostility or dislike than one's in-group

out-group homogeneity bias our tendency to see out-group members as being pretty much all alike

outliers unusual data points that are at the extremes of the frequency distribution and either far above or below the mean

ovaries the organs in a female's body that produce eggs, or ova

overextension when a child uses one word to symbolize all manner of similar instances (e.g., calling all birds *parakeet*)

panic disorder an anxiety disorder characterized by intense fear and anxiety in the absence of danger that is accompanied by strong physical symptoms

papillae bumps on the tongue that many people mistake for taste buds

parasympathetic nervous system branch of the autonomic nervous system most active during times of normal functioning

parietal lobe cortical areas on the top sides of the brain that play a role in touch and certain cognitive processes

partial reinforcement schedule a schedule of reinforcement in which the organism is rewarded for only some instances of the desired response

perception the process through which we interpret sensory information

peripheral nervous system all of the nervous system except the brain and spinal cord

peripheral route to persuasion a style of thinking in which the person does not carefully and critically evaluate persuasive arguments or generate counterarguments; the peripheral route ensues when one lacks motivation and/or available cognitive resources

permissive parent a parenting style characterized by moderate levels of affection but low levels of control

person–situation interaction the influence of the situation on the stability of traits; when in the same situation, we display similar behavior, but when the situation is different, behavior may change

personal fable the belief held by adolescents that they are unique and special

personal unconscious according to Jung, the part of the unconscious that consists of forgotten memories and repressed experiences from one's past

personality the unique collection of attitudes, emotions, thoughts, habits, impulses, and behaviors that define how a person typically behaves across situations

personality disorder a disorder marked by maladaptive behavior that has been stable across a long period of time and across many situations

personality inventory objective paper-and-pencil self-report form that measures personality on several dimensions

persuasion a type of social influence in which someone tries to change our attitudes

phallic stage Freud's third psychosexual stage of development, which occurs between 3 and 6 years of age, in which little boys experience the Oedipus complex and little girls the Electra complex

phenotype actual characteristic that results from interaction of the genotype and environmental influences

pheromones airborne chemicals that are released from glands and detected by the vomeronasal organs in some animals and perhaps humans

phobic disorder an anxiety disorder characterized by an intense fear of a specific object or situation

phoneme the smallest unit of sound in a language

phonological loop in the working memory model, the part of working memory that processes the phonological, or sound, qualities of information

photopigments light-sensitive chemicals that create electrical changes when they come into contact with light

pitch the psychophysical property of sound that corresponds to the frequency of a sound wave

pituitary gland master gland of the endocrine system that controls the action of all other glands in the body

place theory proposes that our brain decodes pitch by noticing which region of the basilar membrane is most active

plateau phase the second stage of the sexual response cycle, in which excitement peaks

pleasure principle the basis on which the id operates; to feel good and maximize gratification

pluralistic ignorance the idea that we use the behavior of others to help determine whether a situation is really an emergency requiring our help; if no one else is helping, we may conclude that help isn't needed

pons hindbrain structure that plays a role in respiration, consciousness, sleep, dreaming, facial movement, sensory processes, and the transmission of neural signals from one part of the brain to another

population all the members of a group that we wish to draw inferences about in a scientific study

population of interest the entire universe of animals or people that could be studied

positive correlation a relationship in which increases in one variable correspond to increases in a second variable

positive punishment weakening a behavior by adding something unpleasant to the organism's environment

positive reinforcement strengthening a behavior by adding something pleasant to the environment of the organism

postformal thought the idea that a correct solution (or solutions) may vary, depending on the circumstances

postsynaptic neuron the neuron that is receiving the signal at a synapse in the nervous system

posttraumatic stress disorder (PTSD) an anxiety disorder, characterized by distressing memories, emotional numbness, and hypervigilance, that develops after exposure to a traumatic event

pragmatics the rules of conversation in a particular culture

preconscious level the level of consciousness that holds thoughts, perceptions, and impulses of which we could become aware

prediction an expected outcome of how variables will relate

predictive hypothesis an educated guess about the relationships among variables

prejudice a largely negative stereotype that is unfairly applied to all members of a group regardless of their individual characteristics

preoperational stage Piaget's second stage of cognitive development, characterized by the use of symbols and illogical thought

presynaptic neuron the neuron that is sending the signal at a synapse in the nervous system

primacy effect the tendency for people to recall words from the beginning of a list better than words that appeared in the middle of the list

primary appraisal our initial interpretation of an event as either irrelevant, positive, or stressful

primary drive a drive that motivates us to maintain homeostasis in certain biological processes within the body

primary reinforcer a reinforcer that is reinforcing in and of itself

private speech Vygotsky's term describing when young children talk to themselves to guide their own actions

proactive interference a type of forgetting that occurs when older memory traces inhibit the retrieval of newer memory traces

problem-focused coping behaviors that aim to control or alter the environment that is causing stress

procedural memory long-term memory for skills and behaviors

progressive relaxation training a stress management technique in which a person learns how to systematically tense and relax muscle groups in the body

projective test an unstructured and subjective personality test in which an individual is shown an ambiguous stimulus and is asked to describe what he or she sees

prototype our concept of the most typical member of the category

proximity (1) a Gestalt principle of perception that states that we tend to group close objects together during perception; (2) physical closeness

psychoactive drugs substances that influence the brain and thereby the behavior of individuals

psychoanalysis a method of therapy formulated by Freud that focuses on uncovering unconscious conflicts that drive maladaptive behavior

psychoanalytic perspective a personality approach developed by Sigmund Freud that sees personality as the product of driving forces within a person that are often conflicting and sometimes unconscious

psychoanalytic theory Sigmund Freud's view that emphasizes the influence of unconscious desires and conflicts on behavior

psychodynamic perspective focuses on internal unconscious mental processes, motives, and desires that may explain behavior

psychodynamic therapy modern psychoanalysis delivered in a shorter time that focuses less on the client's past and more on current problems and the nature of interpersonal relationships

psychological distance the degree to which one can disassociate oneself from the consequences of his/her actions

psychology the scientific study of behavior and mental processes

psychophysics the study of how the mind interprets the physical properties of stimuli

psychosurgery a biomedical treatment approach involving neurosurgery to alleviate symptoms in someone with a psychological disorder

psychotherapy the use of psychological principles and techniques to treat psychological disorders

psychoticism the degree to which one is hostile, nonconforming, impulsive, and aggressive

puberty the process of sexual maturation

punishment the weakening of a response that occurs when a behavior leads to an unpleasant consequence

pupil the hole in the iris through which light enters the eye

quasi-experiment a research study that is not a true experiment because participants are not randomly assigned to the different conditions

random assignment participants have an equal chance of being placed in any condition of the study

random selection a method of obtaining a representative sample from a population in which all members of the population have an equal chance of being selected to be in the sample

range a measure of variability that is the difference between the high score and the low score of the distribution

rational-emotive therapy a cognitive therapy approach created by Albert Ellis that focuses on changing the irrational beliefs that people hold that seem to impede healthy psychological functioning

realistic-conflict theory the theory that prejudice stems from competition for scarce resources

reality principle the basis on which the ego operates; finding socially appropriate means to fulfill id demands

reasoning drawing conclusions about the world based on certain assumptions

recall a type of retrieval process in which the probe or cue does not contain much information

recency effect the tendency for people to recall words from the end of a list better than words that appeared in the middle of the list

reciprocal determinism according to Bandura, the constant interaction among one's behavior, thoughts, and environment determines personality

reciprocity a strong norm that states that we should treat others as they treat us

recognition a type of retrieval process in which the probe or cue contains a great deal of information, including the item being sought

reconstructive memory memory that is based on the retrieval of memory traces that contain the actual details of events we have experienced

recruitment the process organizations use to identify potential employees for a job

reflex an automatic response to a specific environmental stimulus

refractory period (1) brief period of time after a neuron has fired an action potential in which the neuron is inhibited and unlikely to fire another action potential; (2) a time during the resolution phase in which males are incapable of experiencing another orgasm or ejaculation

reinforcement the strengthening of a response that occurs when the response is rewarded

relativistic thinking the idea that in many situations there is not necessarily one right or wrong answer

reliability the consistency of a test's measurements over time

REM behavior disorder a condition in which normal muscle paralysis does not occur, leading to violent movements during REM sleep

REM rebound loss of REM sleep is recouped by spending more time in REM on subsequent nights

REM sleep active state of sleep in which the person's eyes move

representative sample a sample, or subset, of the population that is representative of the entire population (i.e., the participants in the sample have the same characteristics as the larger population from which they are taken)

representativeness heuristic a heuristic in which we rely on the degree to which something is representative of a category, rather than the base rate, to help us judge whether or not it belongs in the category

repression a type of forgetting proposed by Sigmund Freud in which memories for events, desires, or impulses that we find threatening are pushed into an inaccessible part of the mind called the unconscious

resistance a process in psychoanalysis in which the client behaves in such a way as to deny or avoid sensitive issues

resistance stage the second phase of the general adaptation syndrome, in which the nervous and endocrine systems continue to be activated

resolution phase the final stage of the sexual response cycle, in which the body returns to homeostasis

response set theory of hypnosis asserts that hypnosis is not an altered state of consciousness, but a cognitive set to respond appropriately to suggestions

resting potential potential difference that exists in the neuron when it is resting (approximately −70 mv in mammals)

reticular activating system (RAS) part of the midbrain that regulates arousal and plays an important role in attention, sleep, and consciousness

retina the structure at the back of the eye that contains cells that convert light into neural signals

retinal disparity a binocular depth cue that uses the difference in the images projected on the right and left retinas to inform the brain about the distance of a stimulus

retrieval the process of accessing information in memory and pulling it into consciousness

retroactive interference a type of forgetting that occurs when newer memory traces inhibit the retrieval of older memory traces

retrograde amnesia a type of amnesia in which one is unable to retrieve previously stored memories from long-term memory

reuptake process through which unused neurotransmitters are recycled back into the presynaptic neuron

rods the light-sensitive cells of the retina that pick up any type of light energy and convert it to neural signals

Rorschach inkblot test a projective personality test consisting of ten ambiguous inkblots in which a person is asked to describe what he or she sees; the person's responses are then coded for consistent themes and issues

ruminative coping style the tendency to persistently focus on how one feels without attempting to do anything about one's feelings

sample the portion of the population of interest that is selected for a study

sample variance a measure of variability that shows on average how much the scores vary from the mean

saturation the purity of light; pure light or saturated light consists of a single wavelength

scaffolding a process in which adults initially offer guidance and support in helping a child to reason, solve a problem, or master a task; as the child becomes more proficient and capable, the adult helps less and less until the child can master it on his or her own

scatter plot a graph of data that plots pairs of data points, with one data point on the x-axis and the other on the y-axis

schedule of reinforcement the frequency and timing of the reinforcements that an organism receives

schema a mental idea, concept, or thought; an organized, generalized knowledge structure in long-term memory

schizophrenia a severe disorder characterized by disturbances in thought, perceptions, emotions, and behavior

scientific method a systematic process used by psychologists for testing hypotheses about behavior

secondary drive a learned drive that is not directly related to biological needs

secondary reinforcer a reinforcer that is reinforcing only because it leads to a primary reinforcer

secondary traits according to Allport, the tendencies we have that are less consistent and describe how we behave in certain situations

selective serotonin reuptake inhibitor (SSRI) a type of antidepressant drug that inhibits the reuptake of the neurotransmitter serotonin, thereby improving mood

self-actualization the fulfillment of one's natural potential

self-concept one's perception or image of his/her abilities and uniqueness

self-efficacy the expectation that one has for success in a given situation

self-help group group comprised of people who share the same problem who meet to help one another

self-serving bias our tendency to make attributions that preserve our own self-esteem—for example, making trait attributions for our success and situational attributions for our failures

semantic encoding encoding memory traces in terms of the meaning of the information being stored

semantic memory long-term, declarative memory for conceptual information

sensation the process through which our sense organs convert environmental energies such as light and sound into neural impulses

sensation seeker a person who by trait tends to seek out arousing activities

sensitive period in prenatal development, a time when genetic and environmental agents are most likely to cause birth defects

sensorimotor stage Piaget's first stage of cognitive development, in which infants learn schemas through their senses and motor abilities

sensory memory a system of memory that very briefly stores sensory impressions so that we can extract relevant information from them for further processing

sensory neurons neurons that transmit information from the sense organs to the central nervous system

separation anxiety the fear an infant expresses when separated from the primary caretaker

serotonin neurotransmitter that plays a role in many different behaviors, including sleep, arousal, mood, eating, and pain perception

set point a particular weight that our body seeks to maintain

sexual arousal a heightened state of sexual interest and excitement

sexual desire one's motivation and interest in engaging in sexual activity

sexual orientation one's sexual attraction for members of the same and/or other sex

sexually transmitted infection (STI) an infection that is passed from one person to another primarily through sexual contact

shaping using operant conditioning to build a new behavior in an organism by rewarding successive approximations of the desired response

short-term memory (STM) a system of memory that is limited in both capacity and duration; in the three stages model of memory, short-term memory is seen as the intermediate stage between sensory memory and long-term memory

significant results are considered significant when there is a very small chance (usually less than 5%) of finding those results given the assumption that the null hypothesis is true

similarity a Gestalt principle of perception that states that we tend to group like objects together during perception

situational attribution an attribution that assigns the cause of a behavior to some characteristic of the situation or environment in which the behavior occurs

Skinner box a device created by B. F. Skinner to study operant behavior in a compressed time frame; in a Skinner box, an organism is automatically rewarded or punished for engaging in certain behaviors

sleep apnea a sleep disorder in which a person stops breathing during sleep

sleep disorder a disturbance in the normal pattern of sleeping

sleepwalking a sleep disorder in which a person is mobile and may perform actions during stage IV sleep

slippery slope the use of foot-in-the-door compliance in an obedience situation to get people to obey increasing demands

social cognition the area of social psychology that deals with the ways in which we think about other people and ourselves

social cognitive approach a personality perspective that emphasizes the influence of one's thoughts and social experiences in formulating personality

social learning learning through observation and imitation of others' behavior

social phobia an irrational, persistent fear of being negatively evaluated by others in a social situation

social psychology the branch of psychology that studies how we think and behave in social situations

social support having close and positive relationships with others

sociocultural perspective focuses on societal and cultural factors that may influence behavior

somatic nervous system branch of the peripheral nervous system that governs sensory and voluntary motor action in the body

somatoform disorder a disorder marked by physical complaints that have no apparent physical cause

somatosensory cortex a strip of cortex at the front of the parietal lobe that governs the sense of touch

source traits universal tendencies that underlie and are at the core of surface traits, according to Cattell

specific phobia a persistent fear and avoidance of a specific object or situation

split brain a brain with its corpus callosum severed; sometimes done to control the effects of epilepsy in patients who do not respond to other therapies

spontaneous recovery during extinction, the tendency for a conditioned response to reappear and strengthen over a brief period of time before re-extinguishing

standard deviation a measure of variability equal to the square root of the sample variance; often used to gauge the degree to which an individual score deviates from the mean of a distribution

standard normal distribution a bell-shaped, symmetric distribution ($\bar{X} = 0$, $S = 1$) for which we know the exact area under the curve

statistics a type of applied mathematics used to describe data and test hypotheses

stereotype a schema for a particular group of people

stimulants drugs that speed up normal brain functioning

stimulus discrimination responding only to particular stimuli

stimulus generalization responding in a like fashion to similar stimuli

storage the place where information is retained in memory

stranger anxiety the distress an infant expresses when faced with unfamiliar people

stress any event or environmental stimulus (stressor) that we respond to because we perceive it as challenging or threatening

structuralism an early psychological perspective concerned with identifying the basic elements of experience

structured interview interview using standardized questions, a specific question order, and a predetermined scoring or answer key, and conducted by a trained interviewer

subliminal when the intensity of a stimulus is below the participant's absolute threshold and the participant is not consciously aware of the stimulus

subordinate category the lowest level of categorization, which contains concepts that are less general and more specific than those at the basic level

substance abuse loss of control over one's drug use

substance dependence a condition in which a person needs a drug in order to maintain normal functioning

sum of squares the sum of the squared errors, or deviations, from the mean for the scores in the distribution; the numerator of the sample variance equation

superego the part of the personality that represents your moral conscience

superordinate category the highest, most general level of a concept

superordinate goal a goal that is shared by different groups

suprachiasmatic nucleus (SCN) a group of brain cells located in the hypothalamus that signal other brain areas when to be aroused and when to shut down

surface traits basic traits that describe people's personalities, according to Cattell

symbolic thinking the understanding that an object can be represented with a symbol such as bodily gestures or language

sympathetic nervous system branch of the autonomic nervous system most active during times of danger or stress

synapse the connection formed between two neurons when the axon bulb of one neuron comes into close proximity with the dendrite of another neuron

systematic desensitization a behavior therapy technique in which a client is desensitized to a fear in a gradual, step-by-step process

tardive dyskinesia a side effect of antipsychotic medications involving involuntary motor movements of the mouth, tongue, and face

taste aversion classical conditioning that occurs when an organism pairs the experience of nausea with a certain food and becomes conditioned to feel ill at the sight, smell, or idea of the food

taste buds the sense organs for taste that are found between the papillae on the tongue

telegraphic speech two-word sentences that children begin to utter at 20–26 months

temperament a person's general pattern of attention, arousal, and mood that is evident at birth

temporal lobes cortical areas directly below the ears that play a role in auditory processing and language

teratogen an environmental substance that has the potential to harm the developing organism

test the measurement of a carefully chosen sample of behavior

testes the organs in a male's body that produce both sperm and testosterone

testosterone a male hormone that plays a role in many aspects of sexuality, including sexual desire

thalamus part of the forebrain that functions as a sensory relay station

THC (tetrahydrocannabinol) the active ingredient in marijuana that affects learning, short-term memory, coordination, emotion, and appetite

Thematic Apperception Test (TAT) a projective personality test consisting of a series of pictures in which the respondent is asked to tell a story about each scene; the responses are then coded for consistent themes and issues

theory an explanation of why and how a behavior occurs

therapeutic alliance the interactive and collaborative relationship between the client and the therapist

therapy techniques that are used to help people with psychological or interpersonal problems

thinking the use of knowledge to accomplish some sort of goal

thought disorder a symptom of schizophrenia that involves a lack of associations between one's ideas and the events that one is experiencing

threat simulation theory (TST) suggests that dreaming is an ancient biological defense mechanism that allows us to repeatedly simulate potentially threatening situations so that we can rehearse our responses to these events

threshold of excitation potential difference at which a neuron will fire an action potential (−55 mv in humans)

Title VII of the Civil Rights Act of 1964 law that prohibits discrimination based on race, color, religion, sex, or national origin

token economy a behavioral therapy technique, based on operant conditioning, in which people are reinforced for desired behaviors with tokens; the tokens can later be exchanged for what is reinforcing to them

tolerance a condition in which after repeated use, more of a drug is needed to achieve the same effect

top-down perceptual processing perception that is guided by prior knowledge or expectations

trait tendency we have across most situations to behave in a certain way

trait approach a personality perspective that attempts to describe personality by emphasizing internal, biological aspects of personality called traits

trait attribution an attribution that assigns the cause of a behavior to the traits and characteristics of the person being judged

transference a process in psychoanalysis in which the client unconsciously reacts to the therapist as if the therapist were a parent, friend, sibling, or lover

transformational leadership a leader with high ethical standards, inspirational motivation, intellectual stimulation, and individual consideration

triarchic theory of intelligence a theory that proposes that intelligence is composed of *analytical, practical,* and *creative* abilities that help us adapt to our environment

trichromatic theory of color vision the idea that color vision is made possible by the presence of three different types of cones in the retina that react respectively to either red, green, or blue light

two-factor theory a theory that states that emotions result when we cognitively interpret our physiological reactions in light of the situation

Type A personality a personality that is aggressive, ambitious, and competitive

Type B personality a personality characterized by patience, flexibility, and an easygoing manner

Type C personality a personality that is cautious, serious, sensitive to criticism, results oriented, and suppresses negative emotions such as anger

unconditional positive regard (1) acceptance and love of another's thoughts and feelings without expecting anything in return; (2) the ability of a therapist to accept and value a client for who he or she is, regardless of his or her faults or problems

unconditioned response (UR) the response that is elicited by an unconditioned stimulus

unconditioned stimulus (US) a stimulus that naturally elicits a response in an organism

unconscious level the level of awareness that contains all the thoughts, perceptions, and impulses of which we are unaware

underextension when a child inappropriately restricts the use of a word to a particular case (e.g., using the word *cat* to describe only the family pet)

unstructured interview informal, unplanned interview, using random questions and no scoring key, and conducted by an untrained interviewer

validity the degree to which a test measures the trait that it was designed to measure

variable interval schedule a schedule of reinforcement in which the organism is rewarded for the first desired response in an average xth interval of time

variable ratio schedule a schedule of reinforcement in which the organism is rewarded on average for every xth instance of the desired response

ventromedial hypothalamus (VMH) a region of the hypothalamus that plays an indirect role in creating a feeling of satiety

vestibular sense the sense of balance

visible spectrum the spectrum of light that humans can see

visual cortex a region of cortex found at the back of the occipital lobe that processes visual information in the brain

visuospatial sketch pad in the working memory model, the part of working memory that processes the visual and spatial aspects of information

volley theory proposes that our brain decodes pitch by noticing the frequency at which groups of hair cells on the basilar membrane are firing

wavelength a physical property of some energies that corresponds to the distance between wave peaks

Weber's law a psychological principle that states that for each of our five senses, the amount of change in the stimulus

that is necessary to produce a jnd depends on the intensity at which the stimulus is first presented

well-structured problem problem for which there is a clear pathway to the solution

Wernicke's area a region of the left temporal lobe that plays a role in the comprehension of speech

Whorfian hypothesis/linguistic relativity hypothesis the theory that one's language can directly determine or influence one's thoughts

will-do factors factors that determine the normal or typical performance by an employee

withdrawal symptoms physical or behavioral effects that occur after a person stops using a drug

work teams/groups two or more employees who together perform organizationally relevant tasks, share one or more common goals, interact socially, exhibit task interdependencies, and maintain and manage boundaries within an organizational context

work withdrawal behaviors employees use to avoid their work (e.g., lateness, absenteeism)

working memory a multifaceted component of long-term memory that contains short-term memory, a central executive, a phonological loop, and a visuospatial sketch pad; the function of working memory is to access, move, and process information that we are currently using

z score a measure of relative standing that measures the distance of a score from the mean of the distribution in standard deviation units

zone of proximal development (ZPD) according to Vygotsky, the gap between what a child is already able to do and what he or she is not yet capable of doing without help

zygote a fertilized egg

Aamodt, M. G. (2007). *Industrial/organizational psychology: An applied approach*. Belmont, CA: Wadsworth.

Abad, V. C., & Guilleminault, C. (2004). Review of rapid eye movement behavior sleep disorders. *Current Neurology Neuroscience Reports, 4,* 157–163.

Abdel-Khalek, A., & Lester, D. (2005). Sibship size, birth order, and personality. *Psychological Reports, 97,* 387–388.

Abkevich, V., Camp, N. J., Hensel, C. H., Neff, C. D., Russell, D. L., Hughes, D. C., et al. (2003). Predisposition locus for major depression at chromosome 12q22–12q23.2. *American Journal of Human Genetics, 73,* 1271–1281.

Abramowitz, J. S. (1997). Effectiveness of psychological and pharmacological treatments for obsessive-compulsive disorder: A quantitative review. *Journal of Consulting and Clinical Psychology, 65,* 44–52.

Abramowitz, J. S., & Moore, E. L. (2007). An experimental analysis of hypochondriasis. *Behaviour Research and Therapy, 45,* 413–424.

Abrams, D. B., & Wilson, G. T. (1983). Alcohol, sexual arousal, and self-control. *Journal of Personality and Social Psychology, 45,* 188–198.

Abramson, L. Y., Alloy, L. B., Hankin, B. L., Haeffel, G. J., MacCoon, D. G., & Gibb, B. E. (2002). Cognitive vulnerability: Stress models of depression in a self-regulatory and psychobiological content. In I. H. Gotlib & C. L. Hammen (Eds.), *Handbook of depression* (pp. 268–294). New York: Guilford Press.

Adams, C. D., Girolami, P. A., Joseph, K. E., Sauvageot, S. A., & Slater, H. (2002). Use of a token reinforcement system to promote appropriate behavior at a pediatric burn summer camp. *Journal of Burn and Care Rehabilitation, 23,* 297–305.

Adan, A., & Natale. V. (2002). Gender differences in morningness–eveningness preference. *Chronobiology International, 19,* 709–720.

Ader, R. (2001). Psychoneuroimmunology. *Current Directions in Psychological Science, 10,* 94–98.

Aderibigbe, Y. A., Bloch, R. M., & Walker, W. R. (2001). Prevalence of depersonalization and derealization experiences in a rural population. *Social Psychiatry and Psychiatric Epidemiology, 36,* 63–69.

Adler, A. (1928). *Understanding human nature.* London: Allen & Unwin.

Adler, J., & Rosenberg, D. (1994, December 19). The endless binge. *Newsweek,* p. 72.

Adolphs, R. (2002). Neural systems for recognizing emotion. *Current Opinion in Neurobiology, 12,* 169–177.

Adolphs, R., Tranel, D., & Damasio, A. R. (1998). The human amygdala in social judgment. *Nature, 393,* 470–474.

Aghajanian, G. K. (1994). Serotonin and the action of LSD in the brain. *Psychiatric Annals, 24,* 137–141.

Ahern, J., Galea, S., Resnick, H., & Vlahov, D. (2004). Television images and probable posttraumatic stress disorder after September 11th: The role of background characteristics, event exposures, and perievent panic. *Journal of Nervous and Mental Disorders, 192,* 217–226.

Aiken, L. R. (1996). *Personality assessment methods and practices* (2nd ed.). Seattle: Hogrefe & Huber.

Ainsworth, M. D., Blehar, M. C., Waters, E., & Wall, S. (1978). *Patterns of attachment.* Hillsdale, NJ: Erlbaum.

Air travel remains safe. (1999, November 5). *Salt Lake City Tribune,* p. A12.

Alderidge, M. A., Stillman, R. D., & Bower, T. G. R. (2001). Newborn categorization of vowel-like sounds. *Developmental Science, 4,* 220–232.

Alexander, G. M. (2003). An evolutionary perspective on sex-typed toy preferences: Pink, blue, and the brain. *Archives of Sexual Behavior, 32,* 7–14.

Allen, T. D., Lentz, E., & Day, R. (2006). Career success outcomes associated with mentoring others: A comparison of mentors and nonmentors. *Journal of Career Development, 32*(3), 272–285.

Alloy, L. B., Abramson, L. Y., & Francis, E. L. (1999). Do negative cognitive styles confer vulnerability to depression? *Current Directions in Psychological Science, 8,* 128–132.

Allport, G. W. (1961). *Pattern and growth in personality.* New York: Holt, Rinehart, & Winston.

Allport, G. W. (1979). *The nature of prejudice.* Reading, MA: Addison-Wesley. (Original work published 1954)

Almeida, D. M. (2005). Resilience and vulnerability to daily stressors assessed via diary methods. *Current Directions in Psychological Science, 14,* 64–68.

Alonso, A., & Swiller, H. I. (1993). Introduction: The case for group therapy. In A. Alonso & H. I. Swiller (Eds.), *Group therapy in clinical practice* (pp. xxi–xxv). Washington, DC: American Psychiatric Press.

Alsaker, F. D. (1995). Timing of puberty and reactions to pubertal changes. In M. Rutter (Ed.), *Psychosocial disturbances in young people* (pp. 37–82). New York: Cambridge University Press.

Amato, P. R. (1993). Children's adjustment to divorce: Theories, hypotheses, and empirical support. *Journal of Marriage and the Family, 55,* 23–38.

Amato, P. R. (2000). The consequences of divorce for adults and children. *Journal of Marriage and the Family, 62,* 1269–1287.

Amato, P. R., & Booth, A. (1996). A prospective study of divorce and parent–child relationships. *Journal of Marriage and the Family, 58,* 356–365.

Amato, P. R., & DeBoer, D. D. (2001). The transmission of marital instability across generations: Relationship skills or commitment to marriage? *Journal of Marriage and Family, 63,* 1038–1051.

Amato, P. R., Johnson, D. R., Booth, A., & Rogers, S. J. (2003). Continuity and change in marital quality between 1980 and 2000. *Journal of Marriage and the Family, 65,* 1–22.

Amato, P. R., & Rogers, S. J. (1997). A longitudinal study of marital problems and subsequent divorce. *Journal of Marriage and the Family, 59,* 612–624.

American Psychiatric Association (APA). (2000a). *Diagnostic and statistical manual of mental disorders* (4th ed., Text Revision). Washington, DC: Author.

American Psychiatric Association (APA). (2000b). Substance use disorders: Alcohol, cocaine, opiods. In *Practice guidelines for the treatment of psychiatric disorders: Compendium 2000* (pp. 139–238). Washington, DC: Author.

American Psychological Association (APA). (1984). *Behavioral research with animals.* Washington DC: Author.

American Psychological Association (APA). (1997). *Visions and transformations.* Washington DC: APA's Commission on Ethnic Minority Recruitment, Retention and Training in Psychology.

American Psychological Association (APA). (2000a). *Psychology careers for the twenty-first century.* Washington DC: Author.

American Psychological Association (APA). (2000b). *Women in academe: Two steps forward, one step back.* Washington, DC: Author.

American Psychological Association (APA). (2002). Ethical principles of psychologists and code of conduct. *American Psychologist, 57,* 1060–1073.

American Psychological Association (APA). (2004). *Resolution on sexual orientation and marriage.* Retrieved May 2, 2007, from http://www.apa.org/releases/gaymarriage.html

Amoore, J. E. (1970). *Molecular basis of odor.* Springfield, IL: Thomas.

Anderson, C. (2003). Social stress and support factors in susceptibility to the common cold. *APS Observer, 16,* 37.

Anderson, C. A., & Arciniegas, D. B. (2004). Neurosurgical interventions for neuropsychiatric syndromes. *Current Psychiatry Reports, 6,* 355–363.

Anderson, C. A., & Bushman, B. J. (2002). Human aggression. *Annual Review of Psychology, 53,* 27–51.

Anderson, C. A., Benjamin, A. J., & Bartholow, B. D. (1998). Does the gun pull the trigger? Automatic priming effects of weapon pictures and weapon names. *Psychological Science, 9,* 308–314.

Anderson, J. R. (1974). Verbatim and propositional representation of sentences in immediate and long-term memory. *Journal of Verbal Learning and Verbal Behavior, 13,* 149–162.

Anderson, J. R. (2000). *Cognitive psychology and its applications* (5th ed.). New York: Worth.

Anderson, N., & Thomas, H.D.C. (1996). Work group socialization. In M. A. West (Ed.), *Handbook of work group psychology* (pp. 423–450). New York: Wiley.

Anderson, P. L., Zimand, E., Hodges, L. F., & Rothbaum, B. O. (2005). Cognitive behavioral therapy for public-speaking anxiety using virtual reality for exposure. *Depression and Anxiety, 22,* 156–158.

Anderson, R. N., & Smith, B. L. (2003). Deaths: Leading causes for 2001. *National Vital Statistics Reports, 52*(9). Hyattsville, MD: National Center for Health Statistics.

Andreasen, N. C., Arndt, S., Alliger, R., Miller, D., & Flaum, M. (1995). Symptoms of schizophrenia. *Archives of General Psychiatry, 52,* 341–351.

Andreasen, N. C., Swayze, V. W., Flaum, M., & Alliger, R. (1990). Ventricular abnormalities in affective disorder: Clinical and demographic correlates. *American Journal of Psychiatry, 147,* 893–900.

Andresen, G. V., Birch, L. L., & Johnson, P. A. (1990). The scapegoat effect on food aversions after chemotherapy. *Cancer, 66,* 1649–1653.

Andresen, J. (2000). Meditation meets behavioural medicine: The story of experimental research on meditation. *Journal of Consciousness Studies, 7*(11–12), 17–73.

Angst, J., & Sellaro, R. (2000). Historical perspectives and natural history of bipolar disorder. *Biological Psychiatry, 48,* 445–457.

Ankey, C. D. (1992). Sex differences in relative brain size: The mismeasure of woman, too? *Intelligence, 16,* 329–336.

Anorexia and Related Eating Disorders, Inc. (ANRED). (2008). Eating disorder statistics. Retrieved July 24, 2008, from http://www.anred.com

Anshel, M. H. (1995). Effect of chronic aerobic exercise and progressive relaxation on motor performance and affect following acute stress. *Behavioral Medicine, 21*(4), 186–196.

Antoni, M. H., & Lutgendorf, S. (2007). Psychosocial factors and disease progression in cancer. *Current Directions in Psychological Science, 16,* 42–46.

Antony, M. M., & Barlow, D. H. (Eds.). (2002). *Handbook of assessment and treatment planning for psychological disorders.* New York: Guilford Press.

APA Research Office. (2001). *2000–2001 Faculty salaries survey.* Washington, DC: APA.

APA Research Office. (2003). *2002–2003 Faculty salaries survey,* American Psychological Association. Retrieved

January 2, 2006, from http://research.apa.org/doctoralfac03.html

APA Research Office. (2004). *2004 Graduate study in psychology.* Retrieved January 2, 2006, from http://research.apa.org/race03.html

Applbaum, K. D. (1995). Marriage with the proper stranger: Arranged marriage in metropolitan Japan. *Ethnology, 34,* 37–51.

Appleby, D. (1997). *The handbook of psychology.* New York: Longman.

Arborelius, L., Owens, M. J., Plotsky, P. M., & Nemeroff, C. B. (1999). The role of corticotropin-releasing factor in depression and anxiety disorders. *Journal of Endocrinology, 160,* 1–12.

Archer, J., Birring, S. S., & Wu, F. C. W. (1998). The association between testosterone and aggression in young men: Empirical findings and a meta-analysis. *Aggressive Behavior, 24,* 411–420.

Arendt, J. (2006). Melatonin and human rhythms. *Chronobiology International, 23,* 21–37.

Arendt, R. E., Short, E. J., Singer, L. T., Minnes, S., Hewitt, J., Flynn, S., et al. (2004). Children prenatally exposed to cocaine: Developmental outcomes and environmental risks at seven years of age. *Journal of Developmental and Behavioral Pediatrics, 25,* 83–90.

Armfield, J. M. (2006). Cognitive vulnerability: A model of the etiology of fear. *Clinical Psychology Review, 26,* 746–768.

Armitage, R. (1995). The distribution of EEG frequencies in REM and NREM sleep stages in healthy young adults. *Sleep, 18*(5), 334–341.

Arnett, J. (2004). *Emerging adulthood: The winding road from the late teens through the twenties.* New York: Oxford University Press.

Aronson, E. (1998). Dissonance, hypocrisy, and the self-concept. In E. Harmon-Jones & J. S. Mills, *Cognitive dissonance theory: Revival with revisions and controversies.* (pp. 103–126). Washington, DC: American Psychological Association.

Aronson, E. (2000). The jigsaw strategy. *Psychology Review, 7,* 2.

Aronson, E., Wilson, T. D., & Akert, R. M. (2004). *Social psychology* (4th ed.). Upper Saddle River, NJ: Prentice Hall.

Aronson, E., Wilson, T. D., & Akert, R. M. (2005). *Social psychology* (5th ed.). Englewood Cliffs, NJ: Prentice Hall.

Arthur, J. B. (1994). Effects of human resource systems on manufacturing performance and turnover. *Academy of Management Journal, 37,* 670-687.

Asay, T. P., & Lambert, M. J. (1999). The empirical case for the common factors in therapy: Quantitative findings. In M. A. Hubble, B. L. Duncan, & S. D. Miller (Eds.), *The heart and soul of change: What works in therapy* (pp. 33–56). Washington, DC: American Psychological Association.

Asch, S. E. (1951). Effects of group pressure upon modification and distortion of judgments. In H. Guetzkow (Ed.), *Groups, leadership, and men* (pp. 117–190). Pittsburgh: Carnegie.

Ashcan, K., Wallace, B., Bell, B. A., & Benabid, A. L. (2004). Deep brain stimulation of the subthalamic nucleus in Parkinson's disease 1993–2003: Where are we ten years on? *British Journal of Neurosurgery, 18,* 19–34.

Ashtari, M., Cervellione, K. L., Hasan, K. M., Wu, J., McIlree, C., Kester, H., et al. (2007). White matter development during late adolescence in healthy males: A cross-sectional diffusion tensor imaging study. *NeuroImage, 35,* 501–510.

Ashwin, C., Baron-Cohen, S., Wheelwright, S., O'Riordan, M., & Bullmore, E. T. (2006). Differential activation of the amygdala and the "social brain" during fearful face-processing in Asperger syndrome. *Neuropsychologia, 45,* 2–14.

Asnis, G. M., Kohn, S. R., Henderson, M., & Brown, N. L. (2004). SSRIs versus non-SSRIs in post-traumatic stress disorder: An update with recommendations. *Drugs, 64,* 383–404.

Assor, A., Roth, G., & Deci, E. L. (2004). The emotional costs of parents' conditional regard: A self-determination theory analysis. *Journal of Personality, 72,* 47–88.

Astin, J. A. (2004). Mind–body therapies for the management of pain. *Clinical Journal of Pain, 20,* 27–32.

Atkinson, J. W. (1983). Towards experimental analysis of human motivation in terms of motives, expectancies, and incentives. In J. W. Atkinson (Ed.), *Personality, motivation, and action: Selected papers* (pp. 81–97). New York: Praeger. (Original work published 1958)

Atkinson, R. C., & Shiffrin, R. W. (1968). Human memory: A proposed system and its control processes. In K. Spence & J. Spence (Eds.), *The psychology of learning and motivation* (Vol. 2, pp. 89–195). New York: Academic Press.

Aucoin, D. (2000, May 25). Feminist report says "sexist stereotypes" abound in prime time. *Oregonian,* E9.

Avalos, L. C., & Tylka, T. L. (2006). Exploring a model of intuitive eating with college women. *Journal of Counseling Psychology, 53,* 486–497.

Avolio, B. J., Kahai, S. S., & Dodge, G. (2000). E-leading in organizations and its implications for theory, research and practice. *Leadership Quarterly, 11,* 615–670.

Azar, B. (1998). A genetic disposition for certain tastes may affect people's food preferences. *American Psychological Association Monitor* [Online], 29. Available from http://www.apa.org/monitor/jan98/food.html

Baddeley, A. D. (1986). *Working memory.* Oxford, UK: Clarendon Press.

Baddeley, A. D. (1992). Working memory. *Science, 255,* 556–559.

Baddeley, A. D., & Hitch, G. J. (1974). Working memory. In G. H. Bower (Ed.), *The psychology of learning and motivation* (Vol. 8, 47–89). London: Academic Press.

Baddeley, A. D., Logie, R., Bressi, S., Della Sala, S., & Spinnler, H. (1986). Dementia and working memory [Special issue: Human memory]. *Quarterly Journal of Experimental Psychology: Human Experimental Psychology, 38*(4-A), 603–618.

Baer, L., Rauch, S. L., Ballantine, T., Martuza, R., Cosgrove, R., Cassem, E., et al. (1995). Cingulotomy for intractable obsessive-compulsive disorder. *Archives of General Psychiatry, 52,* 384–392.

Bagshaw, S. M., Jr. (1985). The desensitisation of chronically motion sick aircrew in the Royal Air Force. *Aviation Space Environmental Medicine, 56,* 1144–1151.

Bahrick, H. P. (1984). Semantic memory content in permastore: Fifty years of memory for Spanish learned in school. *Journal of Experimental Psychology: General, 113,* 1–24.

Bailargeon, R., & DeVos, J. (1992). Object permanence in young infants: Further evidence. *Child Development, 62*(6), 1227–1246.

Bailey, J., Dunne, M., & Martin, N. (2000). Genetic and environmental influences on sexual orientation and its correlates in an Australian twin sample. *Journal of Personality and Social Psychology, 78,* 524–536.

Bailey, J., & Pillard, R. C. (1991). A genetic study of male sexual orientation. *Archives of General Psychiatry, 48,* 1089–1096.

Bailey, J., Pillard, R. C., Neale, M. C., & Agyei, Y. (1993). Heritable factors influence female sexual orientation in women. *Archives of General Psychiatry, 50,* 217–223.

Baird, A. A., Gruber, S. A., Fein, D. A., Maas, L. C., Steingard, R. J., Renshaw, P. F., et al. (1999). Functional magnetic resonance imaging of facial affect recognition in children and adolescents. *Journal of the American Academy of Child and Adolescent Psychiatry, 38,* 195–209.

Baker, T. B., Japuntich, S. J., Hogle, J. M., McCarthy, D. E., & Curtin, J. J. (2006). Pharmacologic and behavioral withdrawal from addictive drugs. *Current Directions in Psychological Science, 15,* 232–236.

Ball, E. M. (1997). Sleep disorders in primary care. *Comprehensive Therapy, 23,* 25–30.

Baltes, P. B. (1997). On the incomplete architecture of human ontogeny: Selection, optimization, and compensation as foundation of developmental theory. *American Psychologist, 52,* 366–380.

Balthazart, J., & Ball, G. F. (2006). Is brain estradiol a hormone or neurotransmitter? *Trends in Neurosciences, 29,* 241–249.

Balzer, W. K., Kihm, J. A., Smith, P. C., Irwin, J. L., Bachiochi, P. D., Robie, C., et al. (1997). *Users' manual for the Job Descriptive Index (JDI, 1997 revision) and the Job in General Scales.* Bowling Green, OH: Bowling Green State University.

Bandura, A. (1965). Influence of model's reinforcement contingencies on the acquisition of imitative responses. *Journal of Personality and Social Psychology, 1,* 589–595.

Bandura, A. (1977). *Social learning theory.* Englewood Cliffs, NJ: Prentice Hall.

Bandura, A. (1986). *Social foundations of thought and action: A social cognitive theory.* Englewood Cliffs, NJ: Prentice Hall.

Bandura, A. (1997). *Self-efficacy: The exercise of control.* New York: W. H. Freeman.

Bandura, A., Grusec, J. E., & Menlove, F. L. (1966). Observational learning as a function of symbolization and incentive set. *Child Development, 37,* 499–506.

Bandura, A., Ross, D., & Ross, S. (1961). Transmission of aggression through imitation of aggressive models. *Journal of Abnormal and Social Psychology, 63,* 575–582.

Bandura, A., Ross, D., & Ross, S. (1963). Imitation of film-mediated aggressive models. *Journal of Abnormal and Social Psychology, 66,* 3–11.

Banich, M. T., & Heller, W. (1998). Evolving perspectives on lateralization of function. *Current Directions in Psychological Science, 74,* 1–2.

Banthia, R., Moskowitz, J. T., Acree, M., & Folkman, S. (2007). Socioeconomic differences in the effect of prayer on physical symptoms and quality of life. *Journal of Health Psychology, 12,* 249–260.

Barbee, J. G. (1993). Memory, benzodiazepines, and anxiety: Integration of theoretical and clinical perspectives. *Journal of Clinical Psychiatry, 54*(10 supplement), 86–101.

Barber, J. P., Connolly, M. B., Crits-Christoph, P., Gladis, L., & Siqueland, L. (2000). Alliance predicts patients' outcome beyond in-treatment change in symptoms. *Journal of Consulting and Clinical Psychology, 68,* 1027–1032.

Bardone, A. M., Vohs, K. D., Abramson, L. Y., Heatherton, T. F., & Joiner, T. E., Jr. (2000). The confluence of perfectionism, body dissatisfaction, and low self-esteem predicts bulimic symptoms: Clinical implications. *Behavior Therapy, 31,* 265–280.

Bargh, J. A., & Morsella, E. (2008). The unconscious mind. *Perspectives on Psychological Science, 3,* 73–79.

Bar-Haim, Y., Ziv, T., Lamy, D., & Hodes, R. M. (2006). Nature and nurture in own-race face processing. *Psychological Science, 17,* 159–163.

Barlow, D. H. (2000). Unraveling the mysteries of anxiety and its disorders from the perspective of emotion theory. *American Psychologist, 55,* 1247–1263.

Barlow, D. H. (2002). *Anxiety and its disorders: The nature and treatment of anxiety and panic* (2nd ed.). New York: Guilford Press.

Barlow, D. H., & Durand, V. M. (2005). *Abnormal psychology: An integrative approach* (4th ed.). Belmont, CA: Wadsworth.

Baron, R. A., & Richardson, D. R. (1992). *Human aggression* (2nd ed.). New York: Plenum Press.

Barondes, S. H. (1993). *Molecules and mental illness.* New York: Scientific American Library.

Bartlett, F. C. (1932). *Remembering.* Cambridge, UK: Cambridge University Press.

Bartoshuk, L. M. (2000). Comparing sensory experiences across individuals: Recent psychophysical advances illuminate genetic variation in taste perception. *Chemical Senses, 25,* 447–460.

Bartoshuk, L. M., & Beauchamp, G. K. (1994). Chemical senses. *Annual Review of Psychology, 45,* 419–449.

Bass, B. M. (1990). From transactional to transformational leadership: Learning to share the vision. *Organizational Dynamics, 18*(3), 19–31.

Batabyal, A. A. (2001). On the likelihood of finding the right partner in an arranged marriage. *Journal of Socio-Economics, 30,* 273–281.

Bates, B. L. (1994). Individual differences in response to hypnosis. In J. W. Rhue, S. J. Lynn, & I. Kirsch (Eds.), *Handbook of clinical hypnosis* (pp. 23–54). Washington, DC: American Psychological Association.

Batsell, W. R., Jr. (2000). Augmentation: Synergistic conditioning in taste-aversion learning. *Current Directions in Psychological Science, 9,* 164–168.

Baumann, A. E. (2007). Stigmatization, social distance and exclusion because of mental illness: The individual with mental illness as a "stranger." *International Review of Psychiatry, 19,* 131–135.

Baumeister, R. F., & Leary, M. R. (1995). The need to belong: The desire for interpersonal attachments as a fundamental human motivation. *Psychological Bulletin, 117,* 497–529.

Baumrind, D. (1964). Some thoughts on ethics of research: After reading Milgram's "Behavioral Study of Obedience." *American Psychologist, 19,* 421–423.

Baumrind, D. (1967). Child care practices anteceding three patterns of preschool behavior. *Genetic Psychology Monographs, 75,* 43–88.

Baumrind, D. (1971). Current patterns of parental authority. *Developmental Psychology Monograph, 4*(1, Pt. 2).

Beach, S. R. H., Sandeen, E. E., & O'Leary, K. D. (1990). Depression in marriage: A model for etiology and treatment. In D. H. Barlow (Ed.), *Treatment manuals for practitioners.* New York: Guilford Press.

Beal, C. R. (1994). *Boys and girls: The development of gender roles.* New York: McGraw-Hill.

Beardsley, T. (1996, July). Waking up. *Scientific American,* pp. 14, 18.

Beatty, W. W. (1992). Gonadal hormones and sex differences in nonreproductive behaviors. In A. A. Gerall, H. Moltz, & I. L. Ward (Eds.), *Handbook of behavioral neurobiology: Vol. 11. Sexual differentiation* (pp. 85–128). New York: Plenum Press.

Beauducel, A., Brocke, B., & Leue, A. (2006). Energetical bases of extraversion: Effort, arousal, EEG, and performance. *International Journal of Psychophysiology, 62,* 212–223.

Beck, A. T. (1967). *Depression: Clinical, experimental, and theoretical aspects.* New York: Harper & Row.

Beck, A. T. (1976). *Cognitive therapy and the emotional disorders.* New York: International Universities Press.

Beck, A. T. (1991). Cognitive therapy: A 30-year retrospective. *American Psychologist, 46,* 368–375.

Beck, A. T. (1997). Cognitive therapy: Reflections. In J. K. Zeig (Ed.), *The evolution of psychotherapy: The third conference* (pp. 55–67). New York: Brunner/Mazel.

Beck, A. T., Rush, A. J., Shaw, B. F., & Emery, G. (1979). *Cognitive therapy of depression.* New York: Guilford Press.

Beck, J. G., Palyo, S. A., Winer, E. H., Schwagler, B. E., & Ang, E. J. (2007). Virtual reality exposure therapy for PTSD symptoms after a road accident: An uncontrolled case series. *Behavior Therapy, 38,* 39–48.

Becker, P. M., Schwartz, J. R., Feldman, N. T., & Hughes, R. J. (2004). Effect of modafinil on fatigue, mood, and health-related quality of life in patients with narcolepsy. *Psychopharmacology, 171,* 133–139.

Beeman, M. J., & Chiarello, C. (1998). Complementary right- and left-hemisphere language comprehension. *Current Directions in Psychological Science, 74,* 2–8.

Békésy, G. von (1960). *Experiments in hearing.* New York: McGraw-Hill.

Bell, A. R., Weinberg, M. S., & Hammersmith, S. K. (1981). *Sexual preference: Its development in men and women.* Bloomington: Indiana University Press.

Bell, C. J., & Nutt, D. J. (1998). Serotonin and panic. *British Journal of Psychiatry, 172,* 465–471.

Belsky, J., & Rovine, M. (1990). Patterns of marital change across the transition to parenthood: Pregnancy to three years postpartum. *Journal of Marriage and the Family, 52,* 5–19.

Belsky, J., Woodworth, S., & Crnic, K. (1996). Trouble in the second year: Three questions about family interaction. *Child Development, 67,* 556–578.

Benabid, A. L., Koudsie, A., Benazzouz, A., Vercueil, L., Fraix, V., Chabardes, S., et al. (2001). Deep brain stimulation of the corpus luysi (subthalamic nucleus) and other targets in Parkinson's disease. Extension to new indications such as dystonia and epilepsy. *Journal of Neurology, 248*(Suppl. 3), III37–III47.

Bender, E. (2004). Virtual reality treatment combats phobias, PTSD. *Psychiatric News, 39,* 45.

Benham, G., Woody, E. Z., Wilson, K. S., & Nash, M. R. (2006). Expect the unexpected: Ability, attitude, and responsiveness to hypnosis. *Journal of Personality and Social Psychology, 91,* 342–350.

Benjamin, L. T., Jr., Henry, K. D., & McMahon, L. R. (2005). Inez Beverly

Prosser and the education of African Americans. *Journal of the History of the Behavioral Sciences, 41,* 43–62.

Bennett, M. P., Zeller, J. M., Rosenberg, L., & McCann, J. (2003). The effect of mirthful laughter on stress and natural killer cell activity. *Alternative Therapies in Health and Medicine, 9,* 38–45.

Bennett, W. I. (1990, December). Boom and doom. *Harvard Health Letter, 16,* 1–3.

Benoit, S. C., McQuade, J.-A., Clegg, D. J., Xu, M., Rushing, P. A., Woods, S. C., et al. (2003). Altered feeding responses in mice with targeted disruption of the dopamine-3 receptor gene. *Behavioral Neuroscience, 117,* 46–54.

Benson, H. (1996). *Timeless healing: The power and biology of belief.* New York: Scribner.

Benton, D., & Donohoe, R. T. (1999). The effects of nutrients on moods. *Public Health Nutrition, 3A,* 403–409.

Berger, A. M., & Hobbs, B. B. (2006). Impact of shift work on the health and safety of nurses and patients. *Clinical Journal of Oncology Nursing, 10,* 465–471.

Berk, L. E., & Spuhl, S. T. (1995). Maternal interaction, private speech, and task performance in preschool children. *Early Childhood Research Quarterly, 10,* 145–169.

Berkowitz, L. (1990). On the formation and regulation of anger and aggression: A cognitive-neoassociationistic analysis. *American Psychologist, 45,* 494–503.

Berlyne, D. E. (1967). Novelty and curiosity as determinants of exploratory behavior. *British Journal of Psychology, 41,* 68–80.

Berry, A. K. (2006). Helping children with nocturnal enuresis: The wait-and-see approach may not be in anyone's best interest. *American Journal of Nursing, 106,* 56–63.

Berscheid, E., Dion, K., Walster, E., & Walster, G. W. (1971). Physical attractiveness and dating choice: A test of the matching hypothesis. *Journal of Experimental Social Psychology, 7,* 173–189.

Betz, N. E. (1993). Women's career development. In F. L. Denmark & M. A. Paludi (Eds.), *Psychology of women* (pp. 627–684). Westport, CT: Greenwood Press.

Beutler, L. E., Machado, P. P., & Neufeldt, S. A. (1994). Therapist variables. In A. E. Bergin & S. L. Garfield (Eds.), *Handbook of psychotherapy and behavior change* (4th ed., pp. 229–269). New York: Wiley.

Bezchlibnyk-Butler, K. Z., & Jeffries, J. J. (Eds.). (1998). *Clinical handbook of psychotropic drugs* (8th ed.). Seattle: Hogrete & Huber.

Bianchi, S. M., Kilkie, M. A., Sayer, L. C., & Robinson, J. P. (2000). Is anyone doing the housework? Trends in the gender division of household labor. *Social Forces, 79,* 191–228.

Biederman, J., Faraone, S. V., Hirschfeld-Becker, D. R., Friedman, D., Robin, J. A., & Rosenbaum, J. F. (2001). Patterns of psychopathology and dysfunction in high-risk children of parents with panic disorder and major depression. *American Journal of Psychiatry, 158,* 49–57.

Bierut, L. J., Heath, A. C., Bucholz, K. K., Dinwiddie, S. H., Madden, P. A. F., Statham, D. J., et al. (1999). Major depressive disorder in a community-based twin sample: Are there different genetic contributions for men and women? *Archives of General Psychiatry, 56,* 557–563.

Binet, A., & Simon, T. (1905). Méthodes nouvelles pour le diagnostics du niveau intéllectuel des anormaux. *L'Année Psychologique, 11,* 191–244.

Black, D. W., Blum, N., Pfohl, B., & Hale, N. (2004). Suicidal behavior in borderline personality disorder: Prevalence, risk factors, prediction, and prevention. *Journal of Personality and Disorders, 18,* 226–239.

Blagys, M. D., & Hilsenroth, M. J. (2000). Distinctive features of short-term psychodynamic-interpersonal psychotherapy: A review of the comparative psychotherapy process literature. *Clinical Psychology: Science and Practice, 7,* 167–188.

Blanchard, R., Zucker, K. J., Siegelman, M., Dickey, R., & Klassen, P. (1998). The relation of birth order to sexual orientation in men and women. *Journal of Biosocial Science, 30,* 511–519.

Blane, H. T. (1988). Prevention issues with children of alcoholics. *British Journal of Addiction, 83(7),* 793–798.

Blatt, S. J., & Shahar, G. (2004). Psychoanalysis—with whom, for what, and how? Comparisons with psychotherapy. *Journal of the American Psychoanalysis Association, 52,* 393–447.

Blazer, D. G., Kessler, R. C., McGonagle, K. A., & Swartz, M. S. (1994). The prevalence and distribution of major depression in a national community sample: The National Comorbidity Study. *American Journal of Psychiatry, 151,* 979–986.

Bleiker, E. M., Hendriks, J. H., Otten, J. D., Verbeek, A. L., & van der Ploeg, H. M. (2008). Personality factors and breast cancer risk: A thirteen-year follow-up. *Journal of the National Cancer Institute, 100,* 213–218.

Bleiker, E. M., van der Ploeg, H. M., Hendriks, J. H., & Ader, H. J. (1996). Personality factors and breast cancer development: A prospective longitudinal study. *Journal of the National Cancer Institute, 88,* 1478–1482.

Bless, H., Bohner, G., Schwarz, N., & Strack, F. (1990). Mood and persuasion: A cognitive response analysis. *Personality and Social Psychology Bulletin, 16,* 331–345.

Blincoe, L., Seay, A., Zaloshnja, E., Miller, T., Romano, E., Luchter, S., et al. (2002). *The economic impact of motor vehicle crashes, 2000.* Washington, DC: National Highway Traffic Safety Administration.

Block, J. A. (1995). A contrarian view of the five-factor approach. *Psychological Bulletin, 117,* 187–215.

Bloom, F., Nelson, C. A., & Lazerson, A. (2001). *Brain, mind and behavior* (3rd ed.). New York: Worth.

Bloom, J. W. (1998). The ethical practice of WebCounseling. *British Journal of Guidance and Counselling, 26,* 53–59.

Boden, M. (1988). *Computer models of the mind.* Cambridge, UK: Cambridge University Press.

Boeri, M. W., Sterk, C. E., & Elifson, K. W. (2004). Rolling beyond raves: Ecstasy use outside the rave setting. *Journal of Drug Issues, 34,* 831–860.

Bohannon, J. N., III, & Bonvillian, J. D. (1997). Theoretical approaches to language acquisition. In J. B. Gleason (Ed.), *The development of language* (4th ed., pp. 259–316). Boston: Allyn & Bacon.

Bohart, A. C. (1990). Psychotherapy integration from a client-centered perspective. In G. Lietaer (Ed.), *Client-centered and experiential psychotherapy in the nineties* (pp. 481–500). Leuven, Belgium: Leuven University Press.

Boivin, D. B., Czeisler, C. A., Kijk, D. J., Duffy, J. F., Folkard, S., Minors, D. S., et al. (1997). Complex interaction of sleep–wake cycle and cicadian phase modulates mood in healthy subjects. *Archives of General Psychiatry, 54,* 145–152.

Bolles, R. C. (1972). Reinforcement, expectancy, and learning. *Psychological Review, 79,* 394–409.

Bonanno, G. A., Galea, S., Bucciarelli, A., & Vlahov, D. (2006). Psychological resilience after disaster: New York City in the aftermath of the September 11th terrorist attack. *Psychological Science, 17,* 181–186.

Bond, R., & Smith, P. B. (1996). Culture and conformity: A meta-analysis of studies using Asch's (1952, 1956) line judgment task. *Psychological Bulletin, 119,* 111–137.

Bonte, M. (1962). The reaction of two African societies to the Mueller-Lyer illusion. *Journal of Social Psychology, 58,* 265–268.

Booth, A., & Amato, P. R. (2001). Parental pre-divorce relations and offspring post-divorce well-being. *Journal of Marriage and the Family, 63,* 197–212.

Booth-Kewley, S., & Friedman, H. S. (1987). Psychological predictions of heart disease: A quantitative review. *Psychological Bulletin, 101,* 343–362.

Bootzin, R. R., & Rider, S. P. (1997). Behavioral techniques and biofeedback for insomnia. In M. R. Pressman & W. C. Orr (Eds.), *Understanding sleep: The evaluation and treatment of sleep disorders* (pp. 315–338). Washington DC: American Psychological Association.

Borkman, T. J. (1997). A selected look at self-help groups in the U.S. *U.S. Health and Social Care in the Community, 5,* 357–364.

Borkovec, T. D., & Mathews, A. M. (1988). Treatment of nonphobic anxiety disorders: A comparison of nondirective, cognitive, and coping desensitization therapy. *Journal of Consulting and Clinical Psychology, 56,* 877–884.

Borman, W. C., Penner, L. A., Allen, T. D., & Motowidlo, S. J. (2001). Personality predictors of citizenship performance. *International Journal of Selection and Assessment, 9,* 52–69.

Bornovalova, M. A., Gratz, K. L., Delany-Brumsey, A., Paulson, A., & Lejuez, C. W. (2006). Temperamental and environmental risk factors for borderline personality disorder among inner-city substance users in residential treatment. *Journal of Personality Disorders, 20,* 218–231.

Bornstein, M. H. (1985). On the development of color naming in young children: Data and theory. *Brain and Language, 26,* 72–93.

Bornstein, M. H., & Marks, L. E. (1982, January). Color revisionism. *Psychology Today, 16,* 64–73.

Bosch, J. A., de Geus, E. J., Kelder, A., Veerman, E. C., Hoogstraten, J., & Amerongen, A. V. (2001). Differential effects of active versus passive coping on secretory immunity. *Psychophysiology, 38,* 836–846.

Botella, C., Villa, H., Garcia Palacios, A., Quero, S., Banos, R. M., & Alcaniz, M. (2004). The use of VR in the treatment of panic disorders and agoraphobia. *Student Health and Technology Information, 99,* 73–90.

Bouchard, T. J. (2004). Genetic influence on human psychological traits: A survey. *Current Directions in Psychological Science, 13,* 148–151.

Bouchard, T. J., Lykken, D. T., McGue, M., Segal, N. L., & Tellegen, A. (1990). Sources of human psychological differences: The Minnesota study of twins reared apart. *Science, 250,* 223–228.

Boulcott, P., & Braithewaite, V. (2005). Ultraviolet light and visual behavior in the three-spined stickleback, gasterosteus aculeatus. *Physiological and Biochemical Zoology, 78,* 736–743.

Bourin, M., Baker, G. B., & Bradwejn, J. (1998). Neurobiology of panic disorder. *Journal of Psychosomatic Research, 44,* 163–180.

Bowden, C. L., Calabrese, J. R., Sachs, G., Yatham, L. N., Asghar, S. A., Hompland, M., et al. (2003). A placebo-controlled 18-month trial of lamotrigine and lithium maintenance treatment in recently manic or hypomanic patients with bipolar I disorder. *Archives of General Psychiatry, 60,* 392–400.

Bower, B. (2003, November 8). Forgetting to remember: Emotion robs memory while reviving it. *Science News, 164,* 293.

Bowers, K. S., & LeBaron, S. (1986). Hypnosis and hypnotizability: Implications for clinical intervention. *Hospital and Community Psychiatry, 37,* 457–467.

Bowie, W., Hammerschlag, M., & Martin, D. (1994). STD's in 1994: The new CDC guidelines. *Patient Care, 28,* 29–53.

Bowlby, J. (1980). *Attachment and loss: Vol. 3. Loss: Sadness and depression.* New York: Basic Books.

Bozarth, M. A., & Wise, R. A. (1984). Anatomically distinct opiate receptor fields mediate reward and physical dependence. *Science, 224,* 516–518.

Brackett, M. A., Rivers, S. E., Shiffman, S., Lerner, N., & Salovey, P. (2006). Relating emotional abilities to social functioning: A comparison of self-report and performance measures of emotional intelligence. *Journal of Personality and Social Psychology, 91,* 780–795.

Braddock, A. E., & Abramowitz, J. S. (2006). Listening to hypochondriasis and hearing health anxiety. *Expert Review of Neurotherapeutics, 6,* 1307–1312.

Bradford, H. F. (1987). Neurotransmitters and neuromodulators. In R. L. Gregory (Ed.), *The Oxford companion to the mind* (pp. 550–560). New York: Oxford University Press.

Bradley, D. B. & Hopcroft, R. L. (2007). The sex difference in depression across 29 countries. *Social Forces, 85,* 1483–1507.

Brainerd, C. J., & Reyna, V. F. (2002). Recollection rejection: How children edit their false memories. *Developmental Psychology, 38,* 156–172.

Bramlett, M. D., & Mosher, W. D. (2002). Cohabitation, marriage, divorce, and remarriage in the United States. *Vital Health Statistics, 23*(22). Hyattsville, MD: National Center for Health Statistics.

Brannon, L., & Feist, J. (2004). *Health psychology: An introduction to behavior and health* (5th ed.) Belmont, CA: Wadsworth.

Bratberg, G. H., Nilsen, T. I., Holmen, T. L., & Vatten, L. J. (2005). Sexual maturation in early adolescence and alcohol drinking and cigarette smoking in late adolescence: A prospective study of 2,129 Norwegian girls and boys. *European Journal of Pediatrics, 164,* 621–625.

Braudy, S. O. (2003, April 13). Small kindness in the big city. *New York Times,* p. 3.

Braungart, J. M., Plomin, R., DeFries, J. C., & Fulker, D. W. (1992). Genetic influence on tester-rated infant temperament as assessed by Bayley's Infant Behavior Record. *Developmental Psychology, 28*(1), 40–47.

Brehm, S. S. (1992). *Intimate relationships* (2nd ed.). New York: McGraw-Hill.

Brehm, S. S., Kassin, S. M., & Fein, S. (2002). *Social psychology* (5th ed.). Boston: Houghton Mifflin.

Breier, A., Schreiber, J. L., Dyer, J., & Pickar, D. (1991). National Institutes of Mental Health longitudinal study of chronic schizophrenia: Prognosis and predictors of outcome. *Archives of General Psychiatry, 48,* 239–246.

Bremner, A. J., Bryant, P. E., & Mareschal, D. (2006). Object-centered spatial reference in 4-month-old infants. *Infant Behavior and Development, 29,* 1–10.

Brende, J. O. (2000). Stress effects of floods. In G. Fink (Ed.), *Encyclopedia of stress* (Vol. 2, pp. 153–157). San Diego: Academic Press.

Brent, D. A., Perper, J. A., Allman, C. J., Moritz, G. M., Wartella, M. E., & Zelenak, J. P. (1991). The presence and accessibility of firearms in the homes of adolescent suicide: A case-control study. *Journal of the American Medical Association, 266,* 2989–2995.

Breslau, J., Aguilar-Gaxiola, S., Kendler, K. S., Su, M., Williams, D., & Kessler, R. C. (2006). Specifying race-ethnic differences in risk for psychiatric disorder in a USA national sample. *Psychological Medicine, 36,* 57–68.

Breslau, J., Kendler, K. S., Su, M., Gaxiola-Aguilar, S., & Kessler, R. C. (2005). Lifetime risk and persistence of psychiatric disorders across ethnic groups in the United States. *Psychological Medicine, 35,* 317–327.

Brewer, M. B. (1979). In-group bias in the minimal intergroup situation: A cognitive-motivational analysis. *Psychological Bulletin, 86,* 307–324.

Brewer, M. B., & Campbell, D. T. (1976). *Ethnocentrism and intergroup attitudes: East African evidence.* New York: Halstead.

Britt, G. C., & McCance-Katz, E. F. (2005). A brief overview of the clinical pharmacology of "club drugs." *Substance Use and Misuse, 40,* 1189–1201.

Broberg, D. J., & Bernstein, I. L. (1987). Candy as a scapegoat in the prevention of food aversions in children receiving chemotherapy. *Cancer, 60,* 2344–2347.

Brody, J. E. (2007, April 17). When a brain forgets where memory is. *New York Times.* Retrieved May 13, 2008, from http://www.nytimes.com/2007/04/17/health/psychology/17brody.html

Brody, M. J., Walsh, B. T., & Devlin, M. (1994). Binge eating disorder: Reliability and validity of a new diagnostic category. *Journal of Consulting and Clinical Psychology, 62,* 381–386.

Bromberger, J. T., & Matthews, K. A. (1996). A longitudinal study of the effects of pessimism, trait anxiety, and life stress on depressive symptoms in middle-aged women. *Psychology and Aging, 11,* 207–213.

Brown, B. (1980). Perspectives on social stress. In H. Selye (Ed.), *Selye's guide to stress research* (Vol. 1, p. 31). New York: Van Nostrand Reinhold.

Brown, J. A. (1958). Some tests of the decay theory of immediate memory. *Quarterly Journal of Experimental Psychology, 10,* 12–21.

Brown, J. D., & Rogers, R. J. (1991). Self-serving attributions: The role of physiological arousal. *Personality and Social Psychology Bulletin, 17,* 501–506.

Brown, R., & Kulik, J. (1977). Flashbulb memories. *Cognition, 5,* 73–99.

Brown, S. L., Lee, G. R., & Bulanda, J. R. (2006). Cohabitation among older adults: A national portrait. *Journals of Gerontology, Series B: Psychological Sciences and Social Sciences, 61,* S71–S79.

Brown, S. L., Nesse, R. M., Vinokur, A. D., & Smith, D. M. (2003). Providing social support may be more beneficial than receiving it: Results from a prospective study of mortality. *Psychological Science, 14,* 320–327.

Brown, T. A., DiNardo, P. A., Lehman, C. L., & Campbell, L. A. (2001). Reliability of DSM-IV anxiety and mood disorders: Implications for the classification of emotional disorders. *Journal of Abnormal Psychology, 110,* 49–58.

Browne, A. (1993). Violence against women by male partners: Prevalence, outcomes, and policy implications. *American Psychologist, 48,* 1077–1087.

Brownell, K. (1988, January). Yo-yo dieting. *Psychology Today, 22,* 22–23.

Browning, J. R., Kessler, D., Hatfield, E., & Choo, P. (1999). Power, gender, and sexual behavior. *Journal of Sex Research, 36,* 342–348.

Brugman, T., & Ferguson, S. (2002). Physical exercise and improvements in mental health. *Journal of Psychosocial Nursing and Mental Health Services, 40,* 24–31.

Brunet, A., Orr, S., Tremblay, J., Robertson, K., Nader, K., & Pitman, R. (2008). Effect of post-retrieval propranolol on psychophysiologic responding during subsequent script-driven traumatic imagery in post-traumatic stress disorder. *Journal of Psychiatric Research, 42,* 503–506.

Bryant, R. A., & Guthrie, R. M. (2005). Maladaptive appraisals as a risk factor for posttraumatic stress: A study of trainee firefighters. *Psychological Science, 16,* 749–752.

Bryman, A. S. (1996). The importance of context: Qualitative research and the study of leadership. *Leadership Quarterly, 7,* 353–370.

Brzezinski, A. (1997). Melatonin in humans. *New England Journal of Medicine, 336,* 186–195.

Buboltz, W. C. Jr., Brown, F., & Soper, B. (2001). Sleep habits and patterns of college students: A preliminary study. *Journal of American College Health, 50,* 131–135.

Buchanan, R. W., Breier, A., Kirkpatrick, B., Ball, P., & Carpenter, W. T. (1998). Positive and negative symptom response to clozapine in schizophrenic patients with and without the deficit syndrome. *American Journal of Psychiatry, 155,* 751–760.

Buckley, K. W. (1989). *Mechanical man: John Broadus Watson.* New York: Guilford Press.

Buehler, R., Griffin, D., & Ross, M. (1994). Exploring the "planning fallacy": Why people underestimate their task completion times. *Journal of Personality and Social Psychology, 67,* 366–381.

Bullock, W. A., & Gilliland, K. (1993). Eysenck's arousal theory of introversion-extraversion: A converging measures investigation. *Journal of Personality and Social Psychology, 64,* 113–123.

Bumpass, L. L., & Lu, H. H. (2000). Trends in cohabitation and implications for children's family contexts in the United States. *Population Studies, 54,* 29–41.

Burger, J. M. (2004). *Personality* (6th ed.). Belmont, CA: Wadsworth.

Burnham, D. (1993). Visual recognition of mother by young infants: Facilitation by speech. *Perception, 22,* 1133–1153.

Bush, S. I., & Geer, J. H. (2001). Implicit and explicit memory of neutral, negative emotional, and sexual information. *Archives of Sexual Behavior, 30,* 615–631.

Bushman, B. J. (1988). The effects of apparel on compliance: A field experiment with a female authority figure. *Personality and Social Psychology Bulletin, 14,* 459–467.

Buss, D. M. (1995). Psychological sex differences. *American Psychologist, 50,* 164–168.

Bussey, K., & Bandura, A. (1999). Social cognitive theory of gender development and differentiation. *Psychological Review, 106,* 676–713.

Butler, L. D., Duran, R. E. F., Jasiukaitis, P., Koopman, C., & Spiegel, D. (1996). Hypnotizability and traumatic experience: A diathesis stress model of dissociative symptomatology. *American Journal of Psychiatry, 153,* 42–63.

Butow P. N., Hiller, J. E., Price, M. A., Thackway, S. V., Kricker, A., & Tennant, C. C. (2000). Epidemiological evidence for a relationship between life events, coping style, and personality factors in the development of breast cancer. *Journal of Psychosomatic Research, 49,* 169–181.

Butzlaff, R. L., & Hooley, J. M. (1998). Expressed emotion and psychiatric relapse. *Archives of General Psychiatry, 55,* 547–552.

Byrd-Craven, J., Geary, D. C., Rose, A. J., & Ponzi, D. (2008). Co-ruminating increases stress hormone levels in women. *Hormones and Behavior, 53,* 489–492.

Byrne, D., Gouaux, C., Griffitt, W., Lamberth, J., Murakawa, N., Prasad, M. B., et al. (1971). The ubiquitous relationship: Attitude similarity and attraction: A cross-cultural study. *Human Relations, 24,* 201–207.

Byrne, M., Agerbo, E., Ewald, H., Eaton, W. W., & Mortensen, P. B. (2003). Parental age and risk of schizophrenia: A case-control study. *Archives of General Psychiatry, 60,* 673–678.

Cacioppo, J. T., & Petty, R. E. (1980). Sex differences in influenceability: Toward specifying the underlying processes. *Personality and Social Psychology Bulletin, 6,* 651–656.

Cain, W. S. (1988). Olfaction. In R. C. Atkinson, R. J. Herrnstein, G. Lindzey, & R. D. Luce (Eds.), *Steven's handbook of experimental psychology* (2nd ed., Vol. 1, pp. 409–459). New York: Wiley.

Calabrese, J. R., Shelton, M. D., Rapport, D. J., Youngstrom, E. A., Jackson, K., Bilali, S., et al. (2005). A 20-month, double-blind, maintenance trial of lithium versus divalproex in rapid-cycling bipolar disorder. *American Journal of Psychiatry, 162,* 2152–2161.

Caldera, Y. M., & Lindsey, E. W. (2006). Coparenting, mother–infant interaction, and infant–parent attachment relationships in two-parent families. *Journal of Family Psychology, 20,* 275–283.

Calderoni, M. E., Alderman, E. M., Silver, E. J., & Bauman, L. J. (2006). The mental health impact of 9/11 on inner-city high school students 20 miles north of Ground Zero. *Journal of Adolescent Health, 39,* 57–65.

Calvert, H. (2003). Sexually transmitted diseases other than human immunodeficiency virus infection in older adults. *Clinical Infectious Diseases, 36,* 609–614.

Camper, J. (1990, February 7). Drop pompom squad, U. of I. rape study says. *Chicago Tribune,* p. 1.

Cannon, D. S., & Baker, T. B. (1981). Emetic and electric shock alcohol aversion therapy: Assessment of conditioning. *Journal of Consulting and Clinical Psychology, 49,* 20–33.

Cannon, T. D. (1998). Genetic and perinatal influences in the etiology of schizophrenia: A neurodevelopmental model. In M. F. Lenzenweger (Ed.), *Origins and development of schizophrenia: Advances in experimental psychopathology* (pp. 67–92). Washington DC: American Psychological Association.

Cannon, W. B. (1927). The James-Lange theory of emotions: A critical examination and an alternative theory. *American Journal of Psychology, 39,* 106–124.

Canova, A., & Geary, N. (1991). Intraperitoneal injections of nanogram CCK-8 doses inhibits feeding in rats. *Appetite, 17,* 221–227.

Caplan, G. A., & Brigham, B. A. (1990). Marijuana smoking and carcinoma of the tongue: Is there an association? *Cancer, 66,* 1005–1006.

Cappelletto, F. (2003). Long-term memory of extreme events: From autobiography to history. *Journal of the Royal Anthropological Institute, 9,* 241–260.

Cardno, A. G., & Gottesman, I. I. (2000). Twin studies of schizophrenia: From bow-and-arrow concordances to Star Wars Mx and functional genomics. *American Journal of Medical Genetics, 97,* 12–17.

Cardozo, B. L., Bilukha, O. O., Crawford, C. A., Shaikh, I., Wolfe, M. I., Gerber, M., et al. (2004). Mental health, social functioning, and disability in postwar Afghanistan. *Journal of the American Medical Association, 292,* 575–584.

Carey, B. (2007, October 23). An active, purposeful machine that comes out at night to play. *New York Times* [Online].

Carey, G., & DiLalla, D. L. (1994). Personality and psychopathology: Genetic perspectives. *Journal of Abnormal Psychology, 103,* 32–43.

Carey, G., & Goldman, D. (1997). The genetics of antisocial behavior. In D. M. Stoff, J. Breiling, & J. D. Maser (Eds.), *Handbook of antisocial personality disorder* (pp. 243–254). New York: Wiley.

Carey, M. P., Maisto, S. A., Kalichman, S. C., Forsyth, A. D., Wright, E. M., & Johnson, B. T. (1997). Enhancing motivation to reduce the risk of HIV infection for economically disadvantaged urban women. *Journal of Consulting and Clinical Psychology, 65,* 531–541.

Carlson, D. E., & Shovar, N. (1983). Effects of performance attributions on others' perceptions of the attributor. *Journal of Personality and Social Psychology, 44,* 515–525.

Carney, C. E., Edinger, J. D., Meyer, B., Lindman, L., & Istre, T. (2006). Daily activities and sleep quality in college students. *Chronobiology International, 23,* 623–637.

Carrington, P. (1993). Modern forms of meditation. In P. M. Lehrer & R. L. Woolfolk (Eds.), *Principles and practice of stress management* (2nd ed., pp. 139–168). New York: Guilford Press.

Carroll, K. M., Ball, S. A., Martino, S., Nich, C., Babuscio, T. A., Nuro, K. F., et al. (2008). Computer-assisted delivery of cognitive-behavioral therapy for addiction: A randomized trial of CBT4CBT. *American Journal of Psychiatry, 165,* 793–795.

Carskadon, M. A., Acebo, C., & Jenni, O. G. (2004). Regulation of adolescent sleep: Implications for behavior. *Annals of the New York Academy of Sciences, 1021,* 276–291.

Carter, R. C., Jacobson, S. W., Molteno, C. D., Chiodo, L. M., Viljoen, D., & Jacobson, J. L. (2005). Effects of prenatal alcohol exposure on infant visual acuity. *Journal of Pediatrics, 14,* 473–479.

Cartwright, R. D. (1993). Who needs their dreams? The usefulness of dreams in psychotherapy. *Journal of the American Academy of Psychoanalysis, 21,* 539–547.

Carver, C. S., Harris, S. D., Lehman, J. M., Durel, L. A., Antoni, M. H., Spencer, S. M., et al. (2000). How important is the perception of personal control? Studies of early stage breast cancer patients.

Personality and Social Psychology Bulletin, 26, 139–149.

Cascio, W. F. (1995). Whither industrial and organizational psychology in a changing world of work? *American Psychologist, 50,* 928–939.

Case, R. B., Moss, A. J., Case, N., McDermott, M., & Eberly, S. (1992). Living alone after myocardial infarction: Impact on prognosis. *Journal of the American Medical Association, 267,* 515–519.

Casey, B. J., Giedd, J. N., & Thomas, K. M. (2000). Structural and functional brain development and its relation to cognitive development. *Biological Psychology, 54,* 241–257.

Castelnuovo, G., Gaggioli, A., Mantovani, F., & Riva, G. (2003). From psychotherapy to e-therapy: The integration of traditional techniques and new communication tools in clinical settings. *Cyberpsychology and Behavior, 6,* 375–382.

Cates, W., Jr. (1998). Reproductive tract infections. In R. A. Hatcher et al. (Eds.), *Contraceptive technology* (17th rev. ed., pp. 179–210). New York: Ardent Media.

Cattell, R. B. (1943). The description of personality: Basic traits resolved into clusters. *Journal of Abnormal and Social Psychology, 38,* 476–506.

Cattell, R. B. (1963). Theory of fluid and crystallized intelligence: A critical experiment. *Journal of Educational Psychology, 54,* 1–22.

Cattell, R. B. (1965). *The scientific analysis of personality.* Baltimore: Penguin.

CBS News. (2004). *Medicare to fund obesity treatment.* Available online at http://www .cbsnews.com/stories/2004/07/16/ health/printable630141.shtml

Ceci, S. J. (1995). False beliefs: Some developmental and clinical considerations. In D. L. Schacter (Ed.), *Memory distortions* (pp. 91–125). Cambridge, MA: Harvard University Press.

Centers for Disease Control and Prevention. (2002). Involvement by young drivers in fatal alcohol-related motor-vehicle crashes—United States, 1982–2001. *Morbidity and Mortality Weekly Report, 51,* 1089–1091.

Centers for Disease Control and Prevention. (2004). Mental health status of World Trade Center rescue and recovery workers and volunteers—New York City, July 2002–August 2004. *Morbidity and Mortality Weekly Report, 53,* 812–815.

Centers for Disease Control and Prevention. (2005). Annual smoking-attributable mortality, years of potential life lost, and productivity losses—United States, 1997–2001. *Morbidity and Mortality Weekly Report, 54,* 625–628.

Centers for Disease Control and Prevention. (2006a). Racial/ethnic differences among youths in cigarette smoking and susceptibility to start smoking—United States, 2002–2004. *Morbidity and Mortality Weekly Report, 55,* 1275–1277.

Centers for Disease Control and Prevention. (2006b). Tobacco use among adults—United States, 2005. *Morbidity and Mortality Weekly Report, 55,* 1145–1148.

Centers for Disease Control and Prevention. (2007a). *CDC Fact Sheet: Genital HPV.* Atlanta, GA: Author.

Centers for Disease Control and Prevention. (2007b). *Sexually transmitted disease surveillance report 2006.* Atlanta, GA: Author.

Centers for Disease Control and Prevention. (2008). *HIV/AIDS Surveillance report, 2006* (Vol. 18). Atlanta, GA: Author.

Cermak, L. S., Lewis, R., Butters, N., & Goodglass, H. (1973). Role of verbal mediation in performance of motor tasks by Korsakoff patients. *Perceptual and Motor Skills, 37,* 259–262.

Cernoch, J., & Porter, R. H. (1985). Recognition of maternal axillary odors by infants. *Child Development, 56*(6), 1593–1598.

Chabas, D., Baranzini, S. E., Mitchell, D., Bernard, C. C. A., Rittling, S. R., Denhardt, D. T., et al. (2001). The influence of the proinflammatory cytokine, oesteopontin, on autoimmune demyelinating disease (Reports). *Science, 294,* 1731–1735.

Chabris, C. F., & Kosslyn, S. M. (1998). How do the cerebral hemispheres contribute to encoding spatial relations? *Current Directions in Psychological Science, 74,* 8–14.

Chakos, M. H., Alvir, J. M., Woerner, M., & Koreen, A. (1996). Incidence and correlates of tardive dyskinesia in first episode of schizophrenia. *Archives of General Psychiatry, 53,* 313–319.

Chamberlain, K., & Zika, S. (1990). The minor events approach to stress: Support for the use of daily hassles. *British Journal of Psychology, 81,* 469–481.

Chambers, D., & Reisberg, D. (1992). What an image depicts depends on what an image means. *Cognitive Psychology, 24,* 145–174.

Chambless, D. L., & Ollendick, T. H. (2001). Empirically supported psychological interventions: Controversies and evidence. *Annual Review of Psychology, 52,* 685–716.

Chamorro-Premuzic, T., & Furnham, A. (2004). A possible model for understanding the personality–intelligence interface. *British Journal of Psychology, 95,* 249–264.

Chandrashekar, J., Hoon, M. A., Ryba, N. J. P., & Zuker, C. S. (2006). The receptors and cells for mammalian taste. *Nature, 444,* 288–294.

Charney, D. S., Nagy, L. M., Bremner, J. D., Goddard, A. W., Yehuda, R., & Southwick, S. M. (2000). Neurobiologic mechanisms of human anxiety. In B. S. Fogel (Ed.), *Synopsis of neuropsychiatry* (pp. 273–288). Philadelphia: Lippincott Williams & Wilkins.

Chaves, J. F. (1994). Recent advances in the application of hypnosis to pain management. *American Journal of Clinical Hypnosis, 37,* 117–129.

Chess, S., & Thomas, A. (1984). *Origins and evolution of behavior disorders: From infancy to early adult life.* New York: Brunner/Mazel.

Chiang, A. A. (2006). Obstructive sleep apnea and chronic intermittent hypoxia: A review. *Chinese Journal of Physiology, 49,* 234–243.

Chipuer, H. M., Rovine, M. J., & Polmin, R. (1990). LISREL modeling: Genetic and environmental influences on IQ revisited. *Intelligence, 14,* 11–29.

Choi, I., & Nesbitt, R. E. (1998). Situational salience and cultural differences in the correspondence bias and actor-observer bias. *Personality and Social Psychology Bulletin, 24,* 949–960.

Choi, J. S., Kim, S. H., Yoo, S. Y., Kang, D. H., Kim, C. W., Lee, J. M., et al. (2007). Shape deformity of the corpus striatum in obsessive-compulsive disorder. *Psychiatry Research, 155,* 257–264.

Chollar, S. (1989, April). Dreamchasers. *Psychology Today,* pp. 60–61.

Chomsky, N. (1957). *Syntactic structures.* The Hague: Mouton.

Chomsky, N. (1965). *Aspects of the theory of syntax.* Cambridge, MA: MIT Press.

Chory-Assad, R. M., & Tamborini, R. (2001). Television doctors: An analysis of physicians on fictional and non-fictional television programs. *Journal of Broadcasting and Electronic Media, 45,* 499–521.

Chory-Assad, R. M., & Tamborini, R. (2003). Television exposure and the public's perceptions of physicians. *Journal of Broadcasting and Electronic Media, 47,* 197–215.

Chou, S. P., Dawson, D. A., Stinson, F. S., Huang, B., Pickering, R. P., Zhou, Y., et al. (2006). The prevalence of drinking and driving in the United States, 2001–2002: Results from the national epidemiological survey on alcohol and related conditions. *Drug and Alcohol Dependence, 83,* 137–146.

Choy, Y., Fyer, A. J., & Lipsitz, J. D. (2007). Treatment of specific phobia in adults. *Clinical Psychology Review, 27,* 266–286.

Christensen, A., & Jacobson, N. S. (1994). Who (or what) can do psychotherapy: The status and challenge of nonprofessional therapies. *Psychological Science, 5,* 8–14.

Christie, W., & Moore, C. (2005). The impact of humor on patients with cancer. *Clinical Journal of Oncology Nursing, 9,* 211–218.

Church, R. M., & Black, A. H. (1958). Latency of the conditioned heart rate as a function of the CS–US interval. *Journal of Comparative and Physiological Psychology, 51,* 478–482.

Cialdini, R. B. (2001). *Influence: Science and practice* (4th ed.). Needham Heights, MA: Allyn & Bacon.

Cialdini, R. B., Borden, R. J., Thorne, A., Walker, M. R., Freeman, S., & Sloan, L. R. (1976). Basking in the reflected glory: Three (football) field studies. *Journal of Personality and Social Psychology, 34,* 366–375.

Cialdini, R. B., Vincent, J. E., Catalan, J., Wheeler, D., & Darby, B. L. (1975). Reciprocal concessions procedure for inducing compliance: The door-in-the-face technique. *Journal of Personality and Social Psychology, 31,* 206–215.

Cin, S. D., Gibson, B., Zanna, M. P., Shumate, R., & Fong, G. T. (2007). Smoking in movies, implicit associations of smoking with the self, and intentions to smoke. *Psychological Science, 18,* 559–563.

Citirik, M., Acaroglu, G., Batman, C., & Zilelioglu, O. (2005). Congenital color blindness in young Turkish men. *Opthalmic Epidemiology, 12,* 133–137.

Clark, D. C., & Fawcett, J. (1992). Review of empirical risk factors for evaluation of the suicidal patient. In B. Bongar (Ed.), *Suicide: Guidelines for assessment, management, and treatment* (pp. 16–48). New York: Oxford University Press.

Clark, D. C., Gibbons, R. D., Fawcett, J., & Scheftner, W. A. (1989). What is the mechanism by which suicide attempts predispose to later suicide attempts? A mathematical model. *Journal of Abnormal Psychology, 98,* 42–49.

Clark, R. E. (2003). Fostering the work motivation of individuals and teams. *Performance Improvement, 42*(3), 21–29.

Clarke, A. C. (1952). An examination of the operation of residential propinquity as a factor in mate selection. *American Sociological Review, 17,* 17–22.

Classen, C. Koopman, C., & Spiegel, D. (1993). Trauma and dissociation. *Bulletin of the Menninger Clinic, 57,* 178–194.

Clay, R. A. (1996, May). Modern hypnosis wins clinical respect, praise. *APA Monitor.*

Cloninger, C. R., Bayon, C., & Przybeck, T. (1997). Epidemiology and axis I comorbidity of antisocial personality disorder. In D. M. Stoff, J. Breiling, & J. D. Maser (Eds.), *Handbook of antisocial personality disorder* (pp. 12–21). New York: Wiley.

Cloninger, C. R., & Gottesman, I. I. (1987). Genetic and environmental factors in antisocial behavior disorders. In S. A.

Mednick, T. E. Moffitt, & S. A. Stack (Eds.), *The causes of crime: New biological approaches* (pp. 92–109). New York: Cambridge University Press.

Coffer, C. N., & Appley, M. (1964). *Motivation: Theory and research.* New York: Wiley.

Cohen, N. J. (1984). Preserved learning capacity in amnesia: Evidence for multiple memory systems. In L. R. Squire & N. Butters (Eds.), *Neuropsychology of memory* (pp. 83–103). New York: Guilford Press.

Cohen, S. (1996). Psychological stress, immunity, and upper respiratory infections. *Current Directions in Psychological Science, 5,* 86–90.

Cohen, S., Doyle, W. J., Turner, R., Alper, C. M., & Skoner, D. P. (2003). Sociability and susceptibility to the common cold. *Psychological Science, 14,* 389–395.

Cohen, S., Tyrrell, D., & Smith, A. (1991). Psychological stress and susceptibility to the common cold. *New England Journal of Medicine, 325,* 606–612.

Cohen, S. G., & Ledford, G. E., Jr. (1994). The effectiveness of self-managing teams: A quasi-experiment. *Human Relations, 47,* 13–43.

Colado, M. I., O'Shea, E., & Green, A. R. (2004). Acute and long-term effects of MDMA on cerebral dopamine biochemistry and function. *Psychopharmacology (Berlin), 173,* 249–263.

Colcombe, S., & Kramer, A. F. (2003). Fitness effects on the cognitive function of older adults: A meta-analytic study. *Psychological Science, 14,* 125–130.

Coleman, M., Ganong, L., & Fine, M. (2000). Reinvestigating marriage: Another decade of progress. *Journal of Marriage and the Family, 62,* 1288–1307.

Coley, R. L. (2001). (In)visible men: Emerging research on low-income, unmarried, and minority fathers. *American Psychologist, 56,* 743–753.

Colley, A., Ball, J., Kirby, N., Harvey, R., & Vingelen, I. (2002, December). Gender-linked differences in everyday memory performance: Effort makes the difference. *Sex Roles: A Journal of Research, 47,* 577–582.

Collier, G., Hirsch, E., & Hamlin, P. H. (1972). The ecological determinants of reinforcement in the rat. *Physiology and Behavior, 9,* 705–716.

Collins, M. W., Field, M., Lovell, M. R., Iverson, G., Johnston, K. M., Maroon, J., et al. (2003). Relationship between postconcussion headache and neuropsychological test performance in high school athletes. *American Journal of Sports Medicine, 31,* 168–173.

Coltrane, S. (2001). Research on household labor: Modeling and measuring the social embeddedness of routine family work. In R. M. Milardo (Ed.), *Understanding families in the new millennium: A decade in review* (pp. 427–452). Minneapolis: National Council on Family Relations.

Comaty, J. E., Stasio, M., & Advokat, C. (2001). Analysis of outcome variables of a token economy in a state psychiatric hospital: A program evaluation. *Research in Developmental Disabilities, 22,* 233–253.

Compton, W. M., Helzer, J. E., Hwu, H., Yeh, E., McEvoy, L., Tipp, J. E., et al. (1991). New methods in cross-cultural psychiatry: Psychiatric illness in Taiwan and the United States. *American Journal of Psychiatry, 148,* 1697–1704.

Conklin, H. M., & Iacono, W. G. (2002). Schizophrenia: A neurodevelopmental perspective. *Current Directions in Psychological Science, 11,* 33–37.

Conrad, M. A., & Ashworth, S. D. (1986). *Recruiting source effectiveness: A meta-analysis* and re-examination of two rival hypotheses. Paper presented at the First Annual Meeting of the Society for Industrial and Organizational Psychology, Chicago.

Conway, B. R. (2003). Colour vision: A clue to hue in V2. *Current Biology, 13,* R308–R310.

Conway, B. R., & Livingstone, M. S. (2005). A different point of hue. *Proceedings of the National Academy of Sciences of the United States of America, 102,* 10761–10762.

Cook, J. L., & Cook, G. (2005). *Child development: Principles and perspectives.* Boston: Allyn & Bacon.

Cookson, J. (1997). Lithium: Balancing risks and benefits. *British Journal of Psychiatry, 171,* 113–119.

Cools, J., Schotte, D. E., & McNally, R. J. (1992). Emotional arousal and overeating in restrained eaters. *Journal of Abnormal Psychology, 69,* 390–400.

Coons, P. M. (1994). Confirmation of childhood abuse in child and adolescent cases of multiple personality disorder and dissociative disorder not otherwise specified. *Journal of Nervous and Mental Disease, 182,* 461–464.

Cooper, M. L. (2002). Alcohol use and risky sexual behavior among college students and youth. *Journal of Studies on Alcohol, 14,* 101–117.

Coren, S., Porac, C., Aks, D. J., & Morikawa, K. (1988). A method to assess the relative contribution of lateral inhibition to the magnitude of visual-geometric illusions. *Perception and Psychophysics, 43,* 551–558.

Coren, S., Ward, L. M., & Enns, J. T. (1999). *Sensation and perception* (5th ed.). Fort Worth, TX: Harcourt Brace.

Corkin, S. (1968). Acquisition of motor skill after bilateral medial temporal-lobe excision. *Neuropsychologia, 6,* 255–265.

Corrigan, P., McCorkle, B., Schell, B, & Kidder, K. (2003). Religion and spirituality in the lives of people with serious mental illness. *Community Mental Health Journal, 39,* 487–499.

Cortina, L. M., & Kubiak, S. P. (2006). Gender and posttraumatic stress: Sexual violence as an explanation for women's increased risk. *Journal of Abnormal Psychology, 115,* 753–759.

Coryell, W. (1998). The treatment of psychotic depression. *Journal of Clinical Psychiatry, 59*(Suppl. 1), 22–27.

Cosmides, L., & Tooby, J. (1996). Are humans good intuitive statisticians after all? Rethinking some conclusions from the literature on judgment under uncertainty. *Cognition, 58,* 1–73.

Costa, P. T., & McCrae, R. R. (1992). Multiple uses for longitudinal personality data. *European Journal of Personality, 6*(2), 85–102.

Costa, P. T., & McCrae, R. R. (1997). Longitudinal stability of adult personality. In R. Hogan, J. A. Johnson, & S. R. Briggs (Eds.), *Handbook of personality psychology* (pp. 269–290). San Diego, CA: Academic Press.

Costa, P. T., Terracciano, A., & McCrae, R. R. (2001). Gender differences in personality traits across cultures: Robust and surprising findings. *Journal of Personality and Social Psychology, 81,* 322–331.

Cowan, C. P., & Cowan, P. A. (2000). *When partners become parents: The big life change for couples.* Mahwah, NJ: Erlbaum.

Cowan, R. L. (2007). Neuroimaging research in human MDMA users: A review. *Psychopharmacology* (Berlin), 189, 539–556.

Cox, J. J., Reimann, F., Nicholas, A. K., Thornton, G., Roberts, E., Springell, K., et al. (2006). An SCN9A channelopathy

causes congenital inability to experience pain. *Nature, 444,* 894–898.

Coyle, J. T. (2006). Glutamate and schizophrenia: Beyond the dopamine hypothesis. *Cellular and Molecular Neurobiology, 26,* 365–384.

Craik, F. I. M., & Lockhart, R. S. (1972). Levels of processing: A framework for memory research. *Journal of Verbal Learning and Verbal Behavior, 11,* 671–684.

Crandall, C. S. (1988). Social contagion of binge eating. *Journal of Personality and Social Psychology, 55,* 588–598.

Crandall, C. S., Preisler, J. J., & Aussprung, J. (1992). Measuring life event stress in the lives of college students: The Undergraduate Stress Questionnaire (USQ). *Journal of Behavioral Medicine, 15*(6), 627–662.

Cranny, C. J., Smith, P. C., & Stone, E. F. (1992). *Job satisfaction: How people feel about their jobs and how it affects their performance.* New York: Lexington Books.

Craske, M. G., & Barlow, D. H. (2001). Panic disorder and agoraphobia. In D. H. Barlow (Ed.), *Clinical handbook of psychological disorders* (3rd ed., pp. 1–59). New York: Guilford Press.

Crawford, H. J., Brown, A. M., & Moon, C. E. (1993). Sustained attentional and disattentional abilities: Differences between low and highly hypnotizable persons. *Journal of Abnormal Psychology, 102,* 534–543.

Crews, F. (1996). The verdict on Freud. *Psychological Science, 7,* 63–68.

Crick, F., & Mitchison, G. (1995). REM sleep and neural nets. *Behavioural Brain Research, 69*(1–2), 147–155.

Crick, N. R., & Dodge, K. A. (1994). A review and reformulation of social information-processing mechanisms in children's social adjustment. *Psychological Bulletin, 115,* 74–101.

Crits-Christoph, P. (1992). The efficacy of brief dynamic psychotherapy: A meta-analysis. *American Journal of Psychiatry, 149,* 151–158.

Crits-Christoph, P. (1997). Limitations of the dodo bird verdict and the role of clinical trials in psychotherapy research: Comment on Wamplod et al. (1997). *Psychological Bulletin, 122,* 216–220.

Crits-Christoph, P., Baranackie, K., Kurcias, J. S., & Beck, A. T. (1991). Meta-analysis of therapist effects in psychotherapy outcome. *Psychotherapy Research, 1,* 81–91.

Crombag, H. S., & Robinson, T. E. (2004). Drugs, environment, brain, and behavior. *Current Directions in Psychological Science, 13,* 107–111.

Crosby, A. E., Cheltenham, M. P., & Sacks, J. J. (1999). Incidence of suicidal ideation and behavior in the United States, 1994. *Suicide and Life-Threatening Behavior, 29,* 131–140.

Crowell, T. A., Luis, C. A., Vanderploeg, R. D., Schinka, J. A., & Mullan, M. (2002). Memory patterns and executive functioning in mild cognitive impairment and Alzheimer's disease. *Aging Neuropsychology and Cognition, 9,* 288–297.

Crowley, A. E., & Hoyer, W. D. (1994). An integrative framework for understanding two-sided persuasion. *Journal of Consumer Research, 20,* 561–574.

Croxford, J. L. (2003). Therapeutic potential of cannabinoids in CNS disease. *CNS Drugs, 17,* 179–202.

Culbertson, F. M. (1997). Depression and gender: An international review. *American Psychologist, 52,* 25–31.

Cutrona, C. E., Wallace, G., & Wesner, K. A. (2006). Neighborhood characteristics

and depression: An examination of stress processes. *Current Directions in Psychological Science, 15,* 188–192.

Dabbs, J. M., Jr., & Morris, R. (1990). Testosterone, social class, and antisocial behavior in a sample of 4,462 men. *Psychological Science, 1,* 209–211.

Dacey, D. M. (2000). Parallel pathways for spectral coding in primate retina. *Annual Review of Neuroscience, 23,* 743–775.

Daiello, L. A. (2007). Atypical antipsychotics for the treatment of dementia-related behaviors: An update. *Medicine and Health, 90,* 191–194.

Dalal, R. S. (2005). A meta-analysis of the relationship between organizational citizenship behavior and counterproductive work behavior. *Journal of Applied Psychology, 90,* 1241–1255.

Dalman, C., & Allebeck, P. (2002). Paternal age and schizophrenia: Further support for an association. *American Journal of Psychiatry, 159,* 1591–1592.

Damak, S., Rong, M., Yasumatsu, K., Kokrashvii, Z., Varadarajan, V., Zou, S., et al. (2003). Detection of sweet and umami taste in the absence of taste receptor T1r3. *Science, 301,* 850–851.

Damasio, H., Grabowski, T., Frank, R., Galaburda, A. M., & Damasio, A. R. (1994). The return of Phineas Gage: Clues about the brain from the skull of a famous patient. *Science, 264,* 1102–1105.

Damon, W. (1999). The moral development of children. *Scientific American, 281,* 73–78.

Dannlowski, U., Ohrmann, P., Bauer, J., Kugel, H., Baune, B. T., Hohoff, C., et al. (2007). Serotonergic genes modulate amygdale activity in major depression. *Genes, Brain and Behavior, 6,* 672–676.

Darwin, C. (1936). *On the origin of species by means of natural selection.* New York: Random House. (Original work published 1859)

Dasen, P. R. (1994). Culture and cognitive development from a Piagetian perspective. In W. J. Lonner & R. Malpass (Eds.), *Psychology and culture* (pp. 141–150). Boston: Allyn & Bacon.

Dasgupta, A. M., Juza, D. M., White, G. M., & Maloney, J. F. (1995). Memory and hypnosis: A comparative analysis of guided memory, cognitive interviews, and hypnotic hyperamnesia. *Imagination, Cognition, and Personality, 14*(2), 117–130.

David, D., Szentagotai, A., Lupu, V., & Cosman, D. (2008). Rational emotive behavior therapy, cognitive therapy, and medication in the treatment of major depressive disorder: A randomized clinical trial, posttreatment outcomes, and six-month follow-up. *Journal of Clinical Psychology, 64,* 728–746.

Davidson, J. R. T. (2000). Trauma: The impact of post-traumatic stress disorder. *Journal of Psychopharmacology, 14,* S5–S12.

Davidson, R. J., Jackson, D. C., & Kalin, N. H. (2000). Emotion, plasticity, context, and regulation: Perspectives from affective neuroscience. *Psychological Bulletin, 126,* 873–889.

Davidson, R. J., Putnam, K. M., & Larson, C. L. (2000). Dysfunction in the neural circuitry of emotion regulation: A possible prelude to violence. *Science, 289,* 591–594.

Davies, I. R. L. (1998). A study of colour grouping in three languages: A test of the linguistic relativity hypothesis. *British Journal of Psychology, 89,* 433–452.

Davies, P. G., Spencer, S. J., Quinn, D. M., & Gerhardstein, R. (2002). Consuming images: How television commercials that elicit stereotype threat can restrain women academically and professionally.

Journal of Personality and Social Psychology, 28, 1615–1628.

Davis, M., & Egger, M. D. (1992). Habituation and sensitization in vertebrates. In L. R. Squire, J. H. Byrne, L. Nadel, H. L. Roediger, D. L. Schacter, & R. F. Thompson (Eds.), *Encyclopedia of learning and memory* (pp. 237–240). New York: Macmillan.

Davis, P. J. (1999). Gender differences in autobiographical memory for childhood emotional experiences. *Journal of Personality and Social Psychology, 76,* 498–510.

Davis-Coelho, K., Waltz, J., & Davis-Coelho, B. (2000). Awareness and prevention of bias against fat clients in psychotherapy. *Professional Psychology: Research and Practice, 31,* 682–684.

De Benedittis, G., Lorenzetti, A., & Pieri, A. (1990). The role of stressful life events in the onset of chronic primary headache. *Pain, 40*(1), 65–75.

de Fonseca, F., Carrera, M. R. A., Navarro, M., Koob, G. F., & Weiss, F. (1997, June 27). Activation of corticotropin-releasing factor in the limbic system during cannabinoid withdrawal. *Science, 276,* 2050–2054.

De Lisi, R., & Gallagher, A. M. (1991). Understanding gender stability and constancy in Argentinean children. *Merrill-Palmer Quarterly, 37,* 483–502.

De May, J. (2006). A critical review of the March 27, 1964, New York Times article that first broke the story. Retrieved July 12, 2007, from http://www.oldkewgardens.com/ss-nytimes-3.html html

de Tommaso, M., Difruscolo, O., Sardaro, M., Losito, L., Serpino, C., Pietrapertosa, A., et al. (2007). Influence of MTHFR genotype on contingent negative variation and MRI abnormalities in migraine. *Headache, 47,* 253–265.

Deakin, J. F., Lees, J., McKie, S., Hallak, J. E., Williams, S. R., & Dursun, S. M. (2008). Glutamate and the neural basis of the subjective effects of ketamine: A pharmaco-magnetic resonance imaging study. *Archives of General Psychiatry, 65,* 154–164.

DeAngelis, T. (2004, January). Size-based discrimination may be hardest on children. *American Psychological Association Monitor on Psychology, 35,* 62.

Deaux, K., & Hanna, R. (1984). Courtship in the personals column: The influence of gender and sexual orientation. *Sex Roles, 11,* 363–375.

DeCasper, A. J., & Fifer, W. P. (1980). Of human bonding: Newborns prefer their mothers' voices. *Science, 208,* 1174–1176.

DeCastro, J. M., & Elmore, D. K. (1988). Subjective hunger relationships with meal patterns in the spontaneous feeding behavior of humans: Evidence for a causal relationship. *Physiology and Behavior, 43,* 159–165.

Deci, E. L., & Ryan, R. M. (1985). *Intrinsic motivation and self-determination in human behavior.* New York: Plenum Press.

Degroot, A. B. (2004). The role of the septo-hippocampal system in fear and anxiety. *Dissertation Abstracts International: Section B: The Sciences and Engineering, 65*(1-B), 475.

DeLacoste-Utamsing, C., & Holloway, R. L. (1982). Sexual dimorphism in the human corpus callosum. *Science, 216,* 1431–1432.

DeLoache, J. (2001). The symbol-mindedness of young children. In W. W. Hartup & R. A. Weinberg (Eds.), *Child psychology in retrospect and prospect* (Vol. 32, pp. 73–101). Mahwah, NJ: Erlbaum.

Dement, W. (1960). The effect of dream deprivation. *Science, 131,* 1705–1707.

Dement, W., & Kleitman, N. (1957). Cyclic variations in EEG during sleep and their relation to eye movements, body motility, and dreaming. *Electroencephalography and Clinical Neurophysiology, 9,* 673–690.

Dement, W., & Vaughan, C. (1999). *The promise of sleep: A pioneer in sleep medicine explains the vital connection between health, happiness, and a good night's sleep.* New York: Delacorte.

Denis, M., & Cocude, M. (1999). On the metric properties of visual images generated from verbal descriptions: Evidence for the robustness of the mental scanning effect. *Journal of Cognitive Psychology, 9,* 353–379.

Denning, D. G., Conwell, Y., King, D., & Coz, C. (2000). Method choice, intent, and gender in completed suicide. *Suicide and Life-Threatening Behavior, 30,* 282–288.

Denollet, J. (1993). Biobehavioral research on coronary heart disease. *Journal of Behavioral Medicine, 16*(2), 115–141.

Depression and Bipolar Support Alliance (DBSA). (2002). *National DMDA support groups: An important step on the road to wellness.* Chicago: Author.

Desalvo, K. B., Hyre, A. D., Ompad, D. C., Menke, A., Tynes, L. L., & Muntner, P. (2007). Symptoms of posttraumatic stress disorder in a New Orleans workforce following Hurricane Katrina. *Journal of Urban Health, 84,* 142–152.

Deutsch, F. M. (2001). Equally shared parenting. *Current Directions in Psychological Science, 10,* 25–28.

Deutsch, J. A. (1990). Food intake. In E. M. Stricker (Ed.), *Handbook of behavioral neurobiology: Vol. 10. Neurobiology of food and fluid intake* (pp. 151–182). New York: Plenum Press.

DeValois, R. L., & DeValois, K. K. (1975). Neural coding of color. In E. C. Carterette & M. P. Friedman (Eds.), *Handbook of perception* (pp. 117–166). New York: Academic Press.

Dhabhar, F. S., Miller, A. H., McEwen, B. S., & Spencer, R. L. (1995). Effects of stress on immune cell distribution. Dynamics and hormonal mechanisms. *Journal of Immunology, 154*(10), 5511–5527.

Diamond, A., & Amso, D. (2008). Contributions of neuroscience to our understanding of cognitive development. *Current Directions in Psychological Science, 17,* 136–141.

Diamond, M. C., Scheibel, A. B., & Elson, L. M. (1985). *The human brain coloring book.* New York: Harper Perennial.

Diaz, R. M., & Berk, L. E. (Eds.). (1992). *Private speech: From social interaction to self-regulation.* Hillsdale, NJ: Erlbaum.

Dickens, W. T. & Flynn, J. R. (2006). Black Americans reduce the racial IQ gap. Evidence from standardization samples. *Psychological Science, 17,* 913–920.

Diener, E., & Seligman, M. E. (2004). Beyond money: Toward an economy of well-being. *Psychological Science in the Public Interest, 5,* 1–31.

Dies, R. R. (1993). Research on group psychotherapy: Overview and clinical applications. In A. Alonso & H. I. Swiller (Eds.), *Group therapy in clinical practice* (pp. 473–518). Washington, DC: American Psychiatric Press.

Difede, J., & Hoffman, H. G. (2002). Virtual reality exposure therapy for World Trade Center post-traumatic stress disorder: A case report. *Cyberpsychology and Behavior, 5,* 529–535.

Digman, J. M. (1997). Higher-order factors of the Big Five. *Journal of Personality and Social Psychology, 73,* 1246–1256.

Dion, K. K., Berscheid, E., & Walster, E. (1972). What is beautiful is good. *Journal of Personality and Social Psychology, 24,* 285–290.

Dishion, T. J., & Patterson, G. R. (1997). The timing and severity of antisocial behavior: Three hypotheses within an ecological framework. In D. M. Stoff, J. Breiling, & J. D. Maser (Eds.), *Handbook of antisocial personality disorder* (pp. 205–217). New York: Wiley.

Distefan, J. M., Pierce, J. P., & Gilpin, E. A. (2004). Do favorite movie stars influence adolescent smoking initiation? *American Journal of Public Health, 94,* 1239–1244.

Dixon, J. F., & Hokin, L. E. (1998). Lithium acutely inhibits and chronically up-regulates and stabilizes glutamate uptake by presynaptic nerve endings on mouse cerebral cortex. *Neurobiology, 95,* 8363–8368.

Dobson, K. S., Backs-Dermott, B. J., & Dozois, D. J. A. (2000). Cognitive and cognitive-behavioral therapies. In C. R. Snyder & R. E. Ingram (Eds.), *Handbook of psychological change: Psychotherapy processes and practices for the 21st century* (pp. 409–428). New York: Wiley.

Doctor, R. M., & Doctor, J. N. (1994). Stress. *Encyclopedia of human behavior* (Vol. 4). San Diego, CA: Academic Press.

Dohrenwend, B. P., Levav, I., Shrout, P. E., Link, B. G., Skodol, A. E., & Martin, J. L. (1987). Life stress and psychopathology: Progress on research begun with Barbara Snell Dohrenwend. *American Journal of Community Psychology, 15,* 677–715.

Dohrenwend, B. P., Turner, J. B., Turse, N. A., Adams, B. G., Koen, K. C., & Marshall, R. (2006). The psychological risk of Vietnam for U.S. veterans: A revisit with new data and methods. *Science, 313,* 979–982.

Dolbier, C. L., Cocke, R. R., Leiferman, J. A., Steinhardt, M. A., Schapiro, S. J., Nehete, P. N., et al. (2001). Differences in functional immune responses of high vs. low hardy healthy individuals. *Journal of Behavioral Medicine, 24,* 219–229.

Dollard, J., Doob, L., Miller, N., Mowrer, O. H., & Sears, R. R. (1939). *Frustration and aggression.* New Haven, CT: Yale University Press.

Dominowski, R. L., & Dallob, P. (1995). Insight and problem solving. In R. J. Sternberg & J. E. Davidson (Eds.), *The nature of insight* (pp. 33–62). Cambridge, MA: MIT Press.

Domjan, M., & Purdy, J. E. (1995). Animal research in psychology: More than meets the eye of the general psychology student. *American Psychologist, 50,* 496–503.

Donaldson, C., & Lam, D. (2004). Rumination, mood, and social problem-solving in major depression. *Psychological Medicine, 34,* 1309–1318.

Doraiswamy, P. M., & Xiong, G. L. (in press). Does meditation enhance cognition and brain longevity? *Annals of the New York Academy of Sciences.*

Dornan, W. A., & Malsbury, C. W. (1989). Neuropeptides and male sexual behavior. *Neuroscience and Biobehavioral Reviews, 13,* 1–15.

Doty, R. L. (2001). Olfaction. *Annual Review of Psychology, 52,* 423–452.

Dougherty, D. D., Baer, L., Cosgrove, G. R., Cassem, E. H., Price, B. H., Nirenberg, A. A., et al. (2002). Prospective long-term follow-up of 44 patients who received cingulotomy for treatment of refractory obsessive-compulsive disorder. *American Journal of Psychiatry, 159,* 269–275.

Driesen, N. R., & Raz, N. (1995). The influence of sex, age, and handedness on corpus callosum morphology: A meta-analysis. *Psychobiology, 23,* 240–247.

Druckman, D., & Bjork, R. A. (1994). *Learning, remembering, believing: Enhancing human performance.* Washington, DC: National Academy Press.

Duckitt, J. (1992). Psychology and prejudice: A historical analysis and integrative framework. *American Psychologist, 47,* 1182–1193.

Durmer, J. S., & Dinges, D. F. (2005). Neurocognitive consequences of sleep deprivation. *Seminars in Neurology, 25,* 117–129.

Durrence, H. H., & Lichstein, K. L. (2006). The sleep of African Americans: A comparative review. *Behavioral Sleep Medicine, 4,* 29–44.

Durston, S., Hulshoff Pol, H. E., Casey, B. J., Giedd, J. N., Buitelaar, J. K., & van Engeland, H. (2001). Anatomical MRI of the developing human brain: What have we learned? *Journal of the American Academy of Child and Adolescent Psychiatry, 40,* 1012–1020.

Dweck, C. S., Chiu, C., & Hong, Y. (1995). Implicit theories and their role in judgments and reactions: A world from two perspectives. *Psychological Inquiry, 6,* 267–285.

Dyer, K. A. (2006). Chocolate: Good for the mind, body, and spirit. *Medical Wellness Journal, 3,* 13–15.

Eagly, A. H., & Chaiken, S. (1975). An attribution analysis of communicator characteristics on opinion change: The case of communicator attractiveness. *Journal of Personality and Social Psychology, 32,* 136–144.

Eagly, A. H., & Steffen, V. J. (1986). Gender and aggressive behavior: A meta-analytic review of the social-psychological literature. *Psychological Bulletin, 100,* 309–330.

Eagly, A. H., & Warren, R. (1976). Intelligence, comprehension, and opinion. *Journal of Personality, 44,* 226–242.

Eaton, A. H., & Resko, J. A. (1974). Plasma testosterone and male dominance in a Japanese macaque (Macca fuscata) troop compared with repeated measures of testosterone in laboratory males. *Hormones and Behavior, 5,* 251–259.

Eaton, W. W., & Keyl, P. M. (1990). Risk factors for the onset of Diagnostic Schedule/DSM-III agoraphobia in a prospective population-based study. *Archives of General Psychiatry, 47,* 819–824.

Eaton, W. W., Thara, R., Federman, E., & Tien, A. (1998). Remission and relapse in schizophrenia: The Madras longitudinal study. *Journal of Nervous and Mental Disease, 186,* 357–363.

Ebbinghaus, H. (1910). *Abriss der psychologie.* Leipzig: Veit & Comp.

Ebbinghaus, H. (1913). *Memory: A contribution to experimental psychology* (H. Ruyer & C. E. Bussenius, Trans.). New York: Teachers College, Columbia University. (Original work published 1885)

Edelman, B. (1981). Binge eating in normal and overweight individuals. *Psychological Reports, 49,* 739–746.

Edenberg, H. J., & Foroud, T. (2006). The genetics of alcoholism: Identifying specific genes through family studies. *Addiction Biology, 11,* 386–396.

Egner, T., Jamieson, G., & Gruzelier, J. (2005). Hypnosis decouples cognitive control from conflict monitoring processes of the frontal lobe. *Neuroimaging, 27,* 969–978.

Ehlers, A. (1995). A 1-year prospective study of panic attacks: Clinical course

and factors associated with maintenance. *Journal of Abnormal Psychology, 104,* 164–172.

Eich, J. E. (1980). The cue-dependent nature of state-dependent retrieval. *Memory and Cognition, 8,* 157–173.

Eich, J. E., Weingartner, H., Stillman, R. C., & Gillin, J. C. (1975). State-dependent accessibility of retrieval cues in the retention of a categorized list. *Journal of Verbal Learning and Verbal Behavior, 14,* 408–417.

Eisen, S. V. (1979). Actor-observer differences in information inference and causal attribution. *Journal of Personality and Social Psychology, 37,* 261–272.

Eisenberger, N. I., Taylor, S. E., Gable, S. L., Hilmert, C. J., & Liberman, M. D. (2007). Neural pathways link social support to attenuated neuroendocrine stress responses. *NeuroImage, 35,* 1601–1612.

Eiser, A. S. (2005). Physiology and psychology of dreams. *Seminars in Neurology, 25,* 97–105.

Ekman, P. (1973). Cross-cultural studies of facial expression. In P. Ekman (Ed.), *Darwin and facial expression* (pp. 169–222). New York: Academic Press.

Ekman, P., & Friesen, W. V. (1984). *Unmasking the face* (2nd ed.). Palo Alto, CA: Consulting Psychologists Press.

Elfenbein, H. A., Beaupre, M., Levesque, M., & Hess, U. (2007). Toward a dialect theory: Cultural differences in the expression and recognition of posed facial expressions. *Emotion, 7,* 131–146.

Elicker, J., Englund, M., & Sroufe, L. A. (1992). Predicting peer competence and peer relationships in childhood from early parent–child relationships. In R. D. Parke & G. W. Ladd (Eds.), *Family–peer relationships: Modes of linkage* (pp. 77–107). Hillsdale, NJ: Erlbaum.

Elkind, D. (1984). *All grown up and no place to go.* Reading, MA: Addison-Wesley.

Elkind, D. (1994). *A sympathetic understanding of the child: Birth to sixteen* (3rd ed.). Boston: Allyn & Bacon.

Elkind, D. (1998). *All grown up and no place to go* (Rev. ed.). Reading, MA: Perseus Books.

Elkind, D., & Bowen, R. (1979). Imaginary audience behavior in children and adolescents. *Developmental Psychology, 15,* 38–44.

Ellason, J. W., & Ross, C. A. (1997). Two-year follow up of inpatients with dissociative identity disorder. *American Journal of Psychiatry, 154,* 832–839.

Ellason, J. W., Ross, C. A., & Fuchs, D. L. (1996). Lifetime Axis I and II comorbidity and childhood trauma history in dissociative identity disorder. *Psychiatry, 59,* 255–266.

Ellenbogen, J. M., Hu, P. T., Payne, J. D., Titone, D., & Walker, M. P. (2007). Human relational memory requires time and sleep. *Proceedings of the National Academy of Science, U.S.A., 104,* 7723–7728.

Ellis, A. (1959). Requisite conditions for basic personality change. *Journal of Consulting Psychology, 23,* 538–540.

Ellis, A. (1973, February). The no cop-out therapy. *Psychology Today, 7,* 56–60, 62.

Ellis, A. (1991). *Reason and emotion in psychotherapy.* New York: Carol Publishing.

Ellis, A. (1995). Changing rational-emotive therapy (RET) to rational emotive behavior therapy (REBT). *Journal of Rational-Emotive and Cognitive Behavior Therapy, 13,* 85–89.

El-Matary, A., Kemball, G., & Feteha, H. (2006). Loss of libido in postmenopausal women. *Journal of Obstetrics and Gynaecology, 26,* 495–500.

Emmelkamp, P. M. (1994). Behavior therapy with adults. In A. E. Bergin & S. L.

Garfield (Eds.), *Handbook of psychotherapy and behavior change* (4th ed., pp. 379–427). New York: Wiley.

Eng, T. R., & Butler, W. T. (1997). *The hidden epidemic: Confronting sexually transmitted diseases.* Washington, DC: National Academy Press.

Engels, G. I., Garnefski, N., & Diekstra, R. F. W. (1993). Efficacy of rational-emotive therapy: A quantitative analysis. *Journal of Consulting and Clinical Psychology, 61,* 1083–1090.

Epley, N., Savitsy, K., & Kachelski, R. A. (1999). What every skeptic should know about subliminal persuasion. *Skeptical Inquirer, 23,* 40–45.

Epping-Jordan, M. P., Watkins, S. S., Koob, G. F., & Markou, A. (1998). Dramatic decreases in brain reward function during nicotine withdrawal. *Nature, 393,* 76.

Epstein, S. (1994). Trait theory as personality theory: Can a part be as great as the whole? *Psychological Inquiry, 5,* 120–122.

Equal Employment Opportunity Commission. (2002, May 24). *Federal laws prohibiting job discrimination questions and answers.*

Equal Employment Opportunity Commission. (2003). *Sexual harassment charges EEOC & FEPAs combined: FY 1992–2002.* Retrieved November 18, 2003, from www.eeoc.gov/stats/harass.html

Erblich, J., Lerman, C., Self, D. W., Diaz, G. A., & Bovbjerg, D. H. (2005). Effects of dopamine D2 receptor (DRD2) and transporter (SLC6A3) polymorphisms on smoking cue-induced cigarette craving among African-American smokers. *Molecular Psychiatry, 10,* 407–414.

Erikson, E. H. (1956). The problem of ego identity. *Journal of American Psychoanalysis Association, 4,* 56–121.

Erikson, E. H. (1958). *Young man Luther.* New York: Norton.

Erikson, E. H. (1959). Identity and life cycle. Selected papers. *Psychological Issues, 1,* 1–171.

Erikson, E. H. (1963). *Childhood and society* (2nd ed.). New York: Norton.

Erikson, E. H. (1968). *Identity, youth and crisis.* New York: Norton.

Erikson, E. H. (1980). *Identity and the life cycle* (2nd ed.). New York: Norton.

Erwin, E. (Ed.). (2002). *The Freud encyclopedia: Theory, therapy, and culture.* London: Routledge.

Escobar, J. I. (1993). Psychiatric epidemiology. In A. C. Gaw (Ed.), *Culture, ethnicity, and mental illness* (pp. 43–73). Washington, DC: American Psychiatric Press.

Escobar, J. I., Gara, M., Waitzkin, H., Cohen Silver, R., Holman, A., & Compton, W. (1998). DSM-IV hypochondriasis in primary care. *General Hospital Psychiatry, 20,* 155–159.

Espy, K. A., Riese, M. L., & Francis, D. J. (1997). Neurobehavior in preterm neonates exposed to cocaine, alcohol, and tobacco. *Infant Behavior and Development, 20,* 297–309.

Essed, N. H., van Staveren, W. A., Kok, F. J., & de Graaf, C. (2007). No effect of 16 weeks flavor enhancement on dietary intake and nutritional status of nursing home elderly. *Appetite, 48,* 29–36.

Esser, J. K. (1998). Alive and well after 25 years: A review of groupthink research. *Organizational Behavior and Human Decision Processes, 73,* 116–141.

Esses, V. M., Dovidio, J. F., Jackson, L. M., & Armstrong, T. L. (2001). The immigration dilemma: The role of perceived group competition, ethnic prejudice, and national identity. *Journal of Social Issues, 57,* 389–412.

Eysenck, H. J. (1967). *The biological basis of personality.* Springfield, IL: Charles C. Thomas.

Eysenck, H. J. (1982). *Personality, genetics, and behavior: Selected papers.* New York: Praeger.

Eysenck, H. J. (1991). Dimensions of personality: 16, 5 or 3? Criteria for a taxonomic paradigm. *Personality and Individual Differences, 12,* 773–790.

Eysenck, H. J. (1995). *Genius: The natural history of creativity.* Cambridge, UK: Cambridge University Press.

Eysenck, H. J., & Eysenck, S. B. G. (1969). *Personality structure and measurement.* London: Routledge.

Eysenck, H. J., & Eysenck, S. B. G. (1976). *Psychoticism as a dimension of personality.* London: Hodder and Stoughton.

Eysenck, H. J., & Rachman, S. (1965). *The causes and cures of neurosis: An introduction to modern behavior therapy based on learning theory and the principle of conditioning.* San Diego: Knapp.

Fagot, B. I., & Kavanaugh, K. (1990). The prediction of antisocial behavior from avoidant attachment classifications. *Child Development, 61,* 864–873.

Farley, E., Loup, D., Nelson, M., Mitchell, A., Esplund, G., Macri, C., et al. (1997). Neoplastic transformation of the endocervix associated with down regulation of lactoferrin expression. *Molecular Carcinography, 20,* 240–250.

Faust, K. A., & McKibben, J. N. (1999). Marital dissolution: Divorce, separation, annulment, and widowhood. In M. B. Sussman, S. K., Steinmetz, & G. W. Peterson (Eds.), *Handbook of marriage and the family* (pp. 475–502). New York: Plenum Press.

Fava, G. A., Grandi, S., Zielezny, M., & Rafanelli, C. (1996). Four-year outcome for cognitive-behavioral treatment of residual symptoms in major depression. *American Journal of Psychiatry, 153,* 945–947.

Fava, M., & Rosenbaum, J. F. (1995). Pharmacotherapy and somatic therapies. In E. E. Beckham & W. R. Leber (Eds.), *Handbook of depression* (2nd ed., pp. 280–301). New York: Guilford.

Fawcett, J. (1994). Antidepressants: Partial response in chronic depression. *British Journal of Psychiatry, 165*(Suppl. 26), 37–41.

FDA Public Health Advisory. (2004, October 15). *Suicidality in children and adolescents being treated with antidepressant medications.* Retrieved October 23, 2004, from www.fda.gov/cder/drug/antidepressants/SSRIPHA200410.htm

Federal Bureau of Investigation. (2006a). *Uniform crime reports.* Retrieved July 13, 2007, from http://www.fbi.gov/ucr/hc2005/table1.htm

Federal Bureau of Investigation. (2006b). *Uniform crime reports.* Retrieved July 24, 2007, from http://www.fbi.gov/ucr/05cius/data/table_33.html

Federal Bureau of Investigation. (2007). *Uniform crime reports.* Retrieved July 24, 2007, from http://www.fbi.gov/ucr/06prelim/ucrtable4index.htm

Feinberg, M. E., Button, T. M., Neiderhiser, J. M., Reiss, D., & Hetherington, E. M. (2007). Parenting and adolescent antisocial behavior and depression: Evidence of genotype × parenting environment interaction. *Archives of General Psychiatry, 64,* 457–465.

Feingold, A. (1988). Matching for attractiveness in romantic partners and same-sex friends: A meta-analysis and theoretical critique. *Psychological Bulletin, 104,* 226–235.

Felker, B., Hawkins, E., Dobie, D., Gutierrez, J., & McFall, M. (2008). Characteristics of deployed Operation Iraqi Freedom military personnel who seek mental health care. *Military Medicine, 173,* 155–158.

Fenton, W. S., & McGlashan, T. H. (1994). Antecedents, symptom progression, and long-term outcome of the deficit syndrome in schizophrenia. *American Journal of Psychiatry, 151,* 351–356.

Ferguson, C. P., & Pigott, T. A. (2000). Anorexia and bulimia nervosa: Neurobiology and pharmacotherapy. *Behavior Therapy, 31,* 237–263.

Fergusson, D. M., Horwood, L. J., & Lynskey, M. T. (1996). Childhood sexual abuse and psychiatric disorder in young adulthood II: Psychiatric outcomes of childhood sexual abuse. *Journal of the American Academy of Child and Adolescent Psychiatry, 35,* 1365–1374.

Feroli, K., & Burstein, G. (2003). Adolescent sexually transmitted diseases. *American Journal of Maternal/Child Nursing, 28,* 113–118.

Festinger, L. (1951). Architecture and group membership. *Journal of Social Issues, 1,* 152–163.

Festinger, L. (1957). *A theory of cognitive dissonance.* Evanston, IL: Row, Peterson.

Festinger, L., Schachter, S., & Back, K. (1950). *Social pressures in informal groups: A study of human factors in housing.* Stanford, CA: Stanford University Press.

Fichna, J., Janecka, A., Piestrzeniewicz, M., Costentin, J., & do Rego, J-C. (2007). Anti-depressant-like effect of endomorphin-1 and endomorphin-2 in mice. *Neuropsychopharmacology, 32,* 813–821.

Field, A. P. (2006). Is conditioning a useful framework for understanding the development and treatment of phobias? *Clinical Psychology Review, 26,* 857–875.

Field, T. M., Schanberg, S. M., Scafidi, F., Bauer, C. R., Vega-Lahr, N., Garcia, R., et al. (1986). Tactile/kinesthetic stimulation effects of preterm neonates. *Pediatrics, 77,* 654–658.

Fields, D. R. (2007). Sex and the secret nerve. *Scientific American Mind, 18,* 20–27.

Fiellin, D. A., Friedland, G. H., & Gourevitch, M. N. (2006). Opioid dependence: Rationale for and efficacy of existing and new treatments. *Clinical Infectious Diseases, 43*(Suppl.), S173–S177.

Finch, C. E. (2001). Toward a biology of middle age. In M. E. Lachman (Ed.), *Handbook of midlife development* (pp. 77–108). New York: Wiley.

Finder, A. (2006, June 11). For some, online persona undermines a resume. *New York Times.*

Finkelstein, D. M., Kubzansky, L. D., Capitman, J., & Goodman, E. (2007). Socioeconomic differences in adolescent stress: The role of psychological resources. *Journal of Adolescent Health, 40,* 127–134.

Finn, R. (2003). Antabuse no panacea for alcoholism. *Clinical Psychiatry News, 31,* 6.

Finn, R. (2004, February 15). Functional MRI offers insights into working memory in Alzheimer's (greater whole-brain activation). *Internal Medicine News, 37,* 29.

Fiorentino, L., Marler, M., Stepnowsky, C., Johnson, S., & Ancoli-Israel, S. (2006). Sleep in older African Americans and Caucasians at risk for sleep-disordered breathing. *Behavioral Sleep Medicine, 4,* 164–178.

Fischer, A. B. (1992, September 21). When will women ever get to the top? *Fortune,* pp. 44–56.

Fisher, C. A., Hoffman, K. J., Austin-Lane, J., & Kao, T. C. (2000). The relationship between heavy alcohol use and work productivity loss in active duty military personnel: A secondary analysis of the 1995 Department of Defense Worldwide Survey. *Military Medicine, 165,* 355–361.

Fisher, H. (2000). Lust, attraction, attachment, biology and evolution of the three primary emotional systems of mating, reproduction, and parenting. *Journal of Sex Education and Therapy, 25,* 96–102.

Fisher, S., Kent, T. A., & Bryant, S. G. (1995). Postmarketing surveillance by patient self-monitoring: Preliminary data for sertraline versus fluoxetine. *Journal of Clinical Psychiatry, 56,* 288–296.

Fiske, M. (1980). Tasks and crises of the second half of life: The interrelationship of commitment, coping, and adaptation. In J. E. Birrent & R. B. Sloane (Eds.), *Handbook of mental health and aging* (pp. 337–373). Englewood Cliffs, NJ: Prentice-Hall.

Fiske, S. T., & Taylor, S. E. (1991). *Social cognition* (2nd ed.). New York: McGraw-Hill.

Fitzgerald, L. F. (1993). Sexual harassment: Violence against women in the workplace. *American Psychologist, 48,* 1070–1076.

Flanagin, A. J. & Waldeck, J. H. (2004). Technology use and organizational newcomer socialization. *Journal of Business Communication, 41*(2), 137–165.

Fleeson, W. (2004). Moving personality beyond the person–situation debate. *Current Directions in Psychological Science, 13,* 83–87.

Flieller, A. (1999). Comparison of the development of formal thought in adolescent cohorts aged 10 to 15 years (1967–1996 and 1972–1993). *Developmental Psychology, 35,* 1048–1058.

Foa, E. B., & Kozak, M. J. (1995). DSM-IV field trial: Obsessive-compulsive disorder. *American Journal of Psychiatry, 152,* 90–96.

Fogel, S. M., & Smith, C. T. (2006). Learning-dependent changes in sleep spindles and stage 2 sleep. *Journal of Sleep Research, 15,* 250–255.

Fogel, S. M., Smith, C. T., & Cote, K. A. (2007). Dissociable learning-dependent changes in REM and non-REM sleep in declarative and procedural memory systems. *Behavior and Brain Research, 180,* 48–61.

Folkman, S., & Lazarus, R. (1988). *Manual for the ways of coping questionnaire.* Palo Alto, CA: Consulting Psychologists Press.

Folkman, S., & Moskowitz, J. T. (2000). Stress, positive emotion, and coping. *Current Directions in Psychological Science, 9,* 115–118.

Follette, W. C., & Hayes, S. C. (2000). Contemporary behavior therapy. In C. R. Snyder & R. E. Ingram (Eds.), *Handbook of psychological change: Psychotherapy processes and practices for the 21st century* (pp. 381–408). New York: Wiley.

Foote, B., Smolin, Y., Neft, D. I., & Lipschitz, D. (2008). Dissociative disorders and suicidality in psychiatric outpatients. *Journal of Nervous and Mental Disease, 196,* 29–36.

Ford, C. S., & Beach, F. A. (1951). *Patterns of sexual behavior.* New York: Harper & Row.

Forsyth, D. R., & Corazzini, J. G. (2000). Groups as change agents. In C. R. Snyder & R. E. Ingram (Eds.), *Handbook of psychological change: Psychotherapy processes and practices for the 21st century* (pp. 309–336). New York: Wiley.

Foster, P. S., Drago, V., Webster, D. G., Harrison, D. W., Crucian, G. P., & Heilman, K. M. (2008). Emotional influences on spatial attention. *Neuropsychology, 22,* 127–135.

Fowler, J., & Peterson, P. (1981). Increasing reading persistence and altering attributional style of learned helpless children. *Journal of Educational Psychology, 73,* 251–260.

Frankenberger, K. D. (2000). Adolescent egocentrism: A comparison among adolescents and adults. *Journal of Adolescence, 23,* 343–354.

Freedman, J. L., & Fraser, S. C. (1966). Compliance without pressure: The foot-in-the-door technique. *Journal of Experimental Social Psychology, 4,* 195–203.

Freud, A. (1936). *The ego and the mechanisms of defense.* London: Hogarth Press.

Freud, S. (1915). Repression. In *Freud's collected papers* (Vol. 4). London: Hogarth.

Freud, S. (1917). *Mourning and melancholia. Collected works.* London: Hogarth Press.

Freud, S. (1943). *A general introduction to psychoanalysis.* New York: Garden City.

Freud, S. (1949). *An outline of psychoanalysis.* New York: Norton.

Freud, S. (1964). An outline of psycho-analysis. In J. Strachey (Ed. and Trans.), *The standard edition of the complete psychological works of Sigmund Freud* (Vol. 23). London: Hogarth Press. (Original work published 1940)

Freud, S. (1980). *The interpretation of dreams* (J. Strachey, Ed. and Trans.). New York: Avon. (Original work published 1900)

Friedman, M. (1990). Body fat and the metabolic control of food intake. *International Journal of Obesity, 14,* 53–67.

Friedman, M., & Rosenman, R. (1974). *Type A behavior and your heart.* New York: Knopf.

Frielingsdorf, H., Simpson, D. R., Thal, L. J., & Pizzo, D. P. (2007). Nerve growth factor promotes survival of new neurons in the adult hippocampus. *Neurobiology of Disease, 26,* 46–55.

Frings, M., Awad, N., Jentzen, W., Dimitrova, A., Kolb., F. P., Diener, H. C., et al. (2006). Involvement of the human cerebellum in short-term and long-term habituation of the acoustic startle response: A serial PET study. *Clinical Neurophysiology, 117,* 1290–1300.

Fry, C., & Miller, P. (2002). *Victorian drug trends 2001: Findings from the illicit drug reporting system (IDRS),* National Drug and Alcohol Research Centre (NDARC) Technical Report No. 129. Sydney: NDARC, University of New South Wales.

Funder, D. C. (1993). Explaining traits. *Psychological Inquiry, 5,* 125–127.

Furnham, A., Reeves, E., & Budhani, S. (2002). Parents think their sons are brighter than their daughters: Sex differences in parents' self-estimations and estimations of their children's multiple intelligences. *Journal of Genetic Psychology, 163,* 24–39.

Furnham, A., Wytykowska, A., & Petrides, K. V. (2005). Estimates of multiple intelligences: A study in Poland. *European Psychologist, 10,* 51–59.

Furumoto, L. (1989). The new history of psychology. In I. S. Cohen (Ed.), *The G. Stanley Hall lecture series* (Vol. 9, pp. 5–34). Washington DC: American Psychological Association.

Gael, S. A. (1988). *The job analysis handbook for business, industry, and government* (Vols. 1 and 2). New York: Wiley.

Gais, S., Hullemann, P., Hallschmid, M., & Born, J. (2006). Sleep-dependent surges in growth hormone do not contribute to sleep-dependent memory consolidation. *Psychoneuroendocrinology, 31,* 786–791.

Gais, S., Lucas, B., & Born, J. (2006). Sleep after learning aids memory recall. *Learning and Memory, 13,* 259–262.

Galensky, T. L., Miltenberger, R. G., Stricker, J. M., & Garlinghouse, M. A. (2001).

Functional assessment and treatment of mealtime behavior problems. *Journal of Positive Behavior Interventions, 3,* 211.

Gallerani, M., Manfredini, R., Dal Monte, D., Calo, G., Brunaldi, V., & Simona, C. (2001). Circadian differences in the individual sensitivity to opiate overdose. *Critical Care Medicine, 29,* 96–101.

Galliano, G. (2003). *Gender: Crossing boundaries.* Belmont, CA: Wadsworth.

Gallopin, T., Luppi, P. H., Rambert, F. A., Frydman, A., & Fort, P. (2004). Effect of the wake-promoting agent modafinil on sleep-promoting neurons from the ventrolateral preoptic nucleus: An in vitro pharmacologic study. *Sleep, 27,* 19–25.

Galvan, A. Hare, T., Voss, H., Glover, G., & Casey, B. J. (2007). Risk-taking and the adolescent brain: Who is at risk? *Developmental Science, 10,* F8–F14.

Ganea, P. A., Shutts, K., Spelke, E. S., & DeLoache, J. S. (2007). Thinking of things unseen: Infants' use of language to update mental representations. *Psychological Science, 18,* 734–739.

Gangestad, S. W., Thornhill, R., & Garver-Apgar, C. E. (2005). Adaptations to ovulation: Implications for sexual and social behavior. *Current Directions in Psychological Science, 14,* 312–316.

Gansberg, M. (1964, March 27). 37 who saw murder didn't call the police: Apathy at stabbing of Queens woman shocks inspector. *New York Times,* p. 1.

Garbarino, J. (1997). The role of economic deprivation in the social context of child maltreatment. In M. E. Helfer, R. S. Kempe, & R. D. Krugman (Eds.), *The battered child* (5th ed., pp. 49–60). Chicago: University of Chicago Press.

Garcia, J. (1992). Taste aversion and preference learning in animals. In L. R. Squire, J. H. Byrne, L. Nadel, H. L. Roediger, D. L. Schacter, & R. F. Thompson (Eds.), *Encyclopedia of learning and memory* (pp. 611–613). New York: Macmillan.

Garcia, J., Ervin, F. R., & Koelling, R. A. (1966). Learning with prolonged delay of reinforcement. *Psychonomic Science, 5,* 121–122.

Garcia, J., & Koelling, R. A. (1966). Relation of cue to consequence in avoidance learning. *Psychonomic Science, 4,* 123–124.

Gardiner, H. W., Mutter, J. D., & Kosmitzki, C. (1998). *Lives across cultures: Cross-cultural human development.* Boston: Allyn & Bacon.

Gardner, H. (1983). *Frames of mind.* New York: Basic Books.

Gardner, H. (1999). *Intelligence reframed: Multiple intelligences for the 21st century.* New York: Basic Books.

Gardner, H. (2004). *Changing minds: The art and science of changing our own and other people's minds.* Boston: Harvard Business School Press.

Garfield, S. L. (1992). Eclectic psychotherapy: A common factors approach. In J. C. Norcross (Ed.), *Handbook of psychotherapy integration* (pp. 169–201). New York: Basic Books.

Garfield, S. L. (1994). Research on client variables in psychotherapy. In A. E. Bergin & S. L. Garfield (Eds.), *Handbook of psychotherapy and behavior change* (4th ed., pp. 190–228). New York: Wiley.

Garlick, D. (2002). Understanding the nature of the general factor of intelligence: The role of individual differences in neural plasticity as an explanatory mechanism. *Psychological Review, 109,* 116–136.

Garlick, D. (2003). Integrating brain science research with intelligence research. *Current Directions in Psychological Science, 12,* 185–189.

Gaunt, R. (2006). Couple similarity and marital satisfaction: Are similar spouses happier? *Journal of Personality, 74,* 1401–1420.

Gawin, F. H. (1991). Cocaine addiction: Psychology and neurophysiology. *Science, 251,* 1580–1586.

Gazzaniga, M. S. (1967). The split brain in man. *Scientific American, 217,* 24–29.

Ge, X., Conger, R. D., & Elder, G. H. (1996). Coming of age too early: Pubertal influences on girls' vulnerability to psychological distress. *Child Development, 67,* 3386–3400.

Gedo, J. E. (2002). The enduring scientific contributions of Sigmund Freud. *Perspective in Biology and Medicine, 45,* 200–212.

Gehring, W. J., Himle, J., & Nisenson, L. G. (2000). Action-monitoring dysfunction in obsessive-compulsive disorder. *Psychological Science, 11,* 1–6.

Gelade, G. (2002). Creative style, personality, and artistic endeavor. *Genetic, Social and General Psychology Monographs, 128,* 213–234.

Gelfand, S. A. (1981). *Hearing.* New York: Marcel Dekker.

Geller, E. S., Russ, N. W., & Altomari, M. G. (1986). Naturalistic observations of beer drinking among college students. *Journal of Applied Behavior Analysis, 19,* 391–396.

Georgiadis, J. R., Kortekaas, R., Kuipers, R., Nieuwenburg, A., Pruim, J., Reinders, A. A., et al. (2006). Regional cerebral blood flow changes associated with clitorally induced orgasm in healthy women. *European Journal of Neuroscience, 11,* 3305–3316.

Gergen, K. J., & Gergen, M. M. (1988). Narrative and self as relationship. In L. Berkowitz (Ed.), *Advances in experimental social psychology* (Vol. 21, pp. 17–56). New York: Academic Press.

Gernsbacher, M. A. (1985). Surface information and loss in comprehension. *Cognitive Psychology, 17,* 324–363.

Gerrish, C. J., & Mennella, J. A. (2001). Flavor variety enhances food acceptance in formula-fed infants. *American Journal of Clinical Nutrition, 73,* 1080–1085.

Gershoff, E. T. (2002). Corporal punishment by parents and associated child behaviors and experiences: A meta-analytic and theoretical review. *Psychological Bulletin, 128,* 539–579.

Geschwind, N. (1975). The apraxias: Neural mechanisms of disorders of learned movements. *American Scientist, 63,* 188–195.

Geschwind, N., & Levitsky, W. (1968). Human brain: Left-right asymmetries in temporal speech region. *Science, 161,* 186–187.

Gibb, B. E., Alloy, L. B., Abramson, L. Y., Beevers, C. G., & Miller, I. W. (2004). Cognitive vulnerability to depression: A taxometric analysis. *Journal of Abnormal Psychology, 113,* 81–89.

Gibbs, W. W. (1996). Gaining on fat. *Scientific American, 275,* 88–94.

Gibson, E. J., & Walk, R. (1960). The visual "cliff." *Scientific American, 202,* 64–71.

Gibson, H. B. (1995, April). Recovered memories. *The Psychologist,* pp. 153–154.

Giedd, J. N. (2004). Structural magnetic resonance imaging of the adolescent brain. *Annals of the New York Academy of Sciences, 1021,* 77–85.

Giedd, J. N., Blumenthal, J., Jeffries, N. O., Castellanos, F. X., Liu, H., Zijdenbos, A., et al. (1999). Brain development during childhood and adolescence: A longitudinal MRI study. *Nature Neuroscience, 2,* 861–863.

Gilbert, D. G., Stunkard, M. E., Jensen, R. A., & Detwiler, F. R. J. (1996). Effects of exam stress on mood, cortisol, and immune functioning. *Personality and Individual Differences, 21*(2), 235–246.

Gilbertson, M. W., Shenton, M. E., Ciszewski, A., Kasai, K., Lasko, N. B., Orr, S. P., et al. (2002). Smaller hippocampal volume predicts pathologic vulnerability to psychological trauma. *Nature Neuroscience, 5*, 1242–1247.

Gillam, B. (1980). Geometrical illusions. *Scientific American, 242*, 102–111.

Gillespie, C. F., & Nemeroff, C. B. (2007). Corticotropin-releasing factor and the psychobiology of early-life stress. *Current Directions in Psychological Science, 16*, 85–89.

Gilligan, C. F. (1982). *In a different voice.* Cambridge, MA: Harvard University Press.

Gillund, G., & Shiffrin, R. M. (1984). A retrieval model for both recognition and recall. *Psychological Review, 91*, 1–67.

Gilson, R. J., & Mindel, A. (2001). Sexually transmitted infections. *British Medical Journal, 322*(729S), 1135–1137.

Girandola, F. (2002). Sequential requests and organ donation. *Journal of Social Psychology, 142*, 171–178.

Gitelson, I. B., & McDermott, D. (2006). Parents and their young adult children: Transitions to adulthood. *Child Welfare League of America, 85*, 853–866.

Givens, B. (1995). Low doses of ethanol impair spatial working memory and reduce hippocampal theta activity. *Alcoholism: Clinical and Experimental Research, 19*(3), 763–767.

Gladwell, M. (2004, September 20). Annals of psychology: Personality plus. *New Yorker*, pp. 42–48.

Glanzer, M., & Cunitz, A. R. (1966). Two storage mechanisms in free recall. *Journal of Verbal Learning and Verbal Behavior, 5*, 351–360.

Glenberg, A. M., Smith, S. M., & Green, C. (1977). Type I rehearsal: Maintenance and more. *Journal of Verbal Learning and Verbal Behavior, 16*, 339–352.

Glik, D. C., Kronenfeld, J. J., & Jackson, K. (1996). Predictors of well role performance behaviors. *American Journal of Health Behavior, 20*, 218–228.

Glynn, M., & Rhodes, P. (2005). *Estimated HIV prevalence in the United States at the end of 2003.* National HIV Prevention Conference, Atlanta, GA. Abstract T1-Bll01.

Godden, D. R., & Baddeley, A. D. (1975). Context dependent memory in two natural environments: On land and underwater. *British Journal of Psychology, 66*, 325–332.

Goeders, N. E. (2004). Stress, motivation, and drug addiction. *Current Directions in Psychological Science, 13*, 33–35.

Goff, D. C., & Coyle, J. T. (2001). The emerging role of glutamate in the pathophysiology and treatment of schizophrenia. *American Journal of Psychiatry, 158*, 1367–1377.

Gold, M. S. (1994). The epidemiology, attitudes, and pharmacology of LSD use in the 1990's. *Psychiatric Annals, 24*(3), 124–126.

Goldberg, J. F. (2007). What psychotherapists should know about pharmacotherapies for bipolar disorder. *Journal of Clinical Psychology, 63*, 475–490.

Goldstein, J. M., & Lewine, R. R. J. (2000). Overview of sex differences in schizophrenia: Where have we been and where do we go from here? In D. J. Castle, J. McGrath, & J. Kulkarni (Eds.), *Women and schizophrenia* (pp. 111–141). Cambridge, UK: Cambridge University Press.

Goldstein, J. M., Seidman, L. J., Buka, S. L., Horton, N. J., Donatelli, J. L., Rieder, R. O., et al. (2000). Impact of genetic

vulnerability and hypoxia on overall intelligence by age 7 in offspring at high risk for schizophrenia compared with affective psychoses. *Schizophrenia Bulletin, 26*, 323–334.

Goleman, D. (1982, March). Staying up: The rebellion against sleep's gentle tyranny. *Psychology Today*, pp. 24–35.

Goleman, D. (1995). *Emotional intelligence.* New York: Bantam.

Goleman, D. (1998). *Working with emotional intelligence.* London: Bloomsbury

Goleman, D., Boyatzis, R. E., & McKee, A. (2002). *Primal leadership: Realizing the power of emotional intelligence.* Boston: Harvard Business School Press.

Goodnick, P. J. (2000). The use of nimodipine in the treatment of mood disorders. *Bipolar Disorders, 2*(3 Pt. 1), 165–173.

Goodwin, F. K., & Goldstein, M. A. (2003). Optimizing lithium treatment in bipolar disorder: A review of the literature and clinical recommendations. *Journal of Psychiatric Practice, 9*, 333–343.

Goodwin, F. K., & Jamison, K. R. (1990). *Manic-depressive illness.* New York: Oxford University Press.

Gorman, J. M. (2006). Gender differences in depression and response to psychotropic medication. *Gender Medicine, 3*, 93–109.

Gorsky, R. D., Schwartz, E., & Dennis, D. (1988). The mortality, morbidity, and economic costs of alcohol abuse: New Hampshire. *Preventative Medicine, 17*, 736–745.

Gotlib, I. H., & Hamilton, J. P. (2008). Neuroimaging and depression: Current status and unresolved issues. *Current Directions in Psychological Science, 17*, 159–163.

Gottlieb, G., Wahlsten, D., & Lickliter, R. (1998). The significance of biology for human development: A developmental psychobiological systems view. In W. Damon & R. M. Lerner (Eds.), *Handbook of child psychology* (Vol. 1, pp. 233–273). New York: Wiley.

Gottman, J. (1999a). *The marriage clinic.* New York: Norton.

Gottman, J. (1999b). *The seven principles of making marriage work.* New York: Crown.

Graber, J. A., Seeley, J. R., Brooks-Gunn, J., & Lewinsohn, P. M. (2004). Is pubertal timing associated with psychopathology in young adulthood? *Journal of the American Academy of Child and Adolescent Psychiatry, 43*, 718–726.

Gould, R. A., Otto, M. W., Pollack, M. H., & Yap, L. (1997). Cognitive behavioral and pharmacological treatment of generalized anxiety disorder: A preliminary meta-analysis. *Behavior Therapy, 28*, 285–305.

Grados, M. A., Walkup, J., & Walford, S. (2003). Genetics of obsessive-compulsive disorders: New findings and challenges. *Brain Development, 25*, S55–S61.

Graf, P., & Schacter, D. L. (1985). Implicit and explicit memory for new associations in normal and amnesiac subjects. *Journal of Experimental Psychology: Learning, Memory, and Cognition, 11*, 501–518.

Graffin, N. F., Ray, W. J., & Lundy, R. (1995). EEG concomitants of hypnosis and hypnotic susceptibility. *Journal of Abnormal Psychology, 104*, 123–131.

Graham, K. S., Simons, J. S., Pratt, K. H., Patterson, K., & Hodges, J. R. (2000). Insights from semantic dementia on the relationship between episodic and semantic memory. *Neurpsychologia, 38*, 313–324.

Graham, R., Devinsky, O., & LaBar, K. S. (2007). Quantifying deficits in the

perception of fear and anger in morphed facial expressions after bilateral amygdale damage. *Neuropsychologia, 45*, 42–54.

Grant, J. E., & Phillips, K.A. (2004). Is anorexia nervosa a subtype of body dysmorphic disorder? Probably not, but read on. . . . *Harvard Review of Psychiatry, 12*, 123–126.

Green, J. P., & Lynn, S. J. (2000). Hypnosis and suggestion-based approaches to smoking cessation: An examination of the evidence. *International Journal of Clinical and Experimental Hypnosis, 48*, 195–224.

Green, S. K., Buchanan, D. R., & Heuer, S. K. (1984). Winners, losers, and choosers: A field investigation of dating initiation. *Personality and Social Psychology Bulletin, 10*, 502–511.

Greenberg, L. S., Elliot, R., & Lietaer, G. (1994). Research on humanistic and experiential psychotherapies. In A. Bergin & S. Garfield (Eds.), *Handbook of psychotherapy and behavior change* (4th ed., pp. 509–542). New York: Wiley.

Greenberg, L. S., & Rice, L. N. (1997). Humanistic approaches to psychotherapy. In P. L. Wachtel & S. B. Messer (Eds.), *Theories of psychotherapy: Origins and Evolution* (pp. 97–129). Washington DC: American Psychological Association.

Greenblatt, D., Harmatz, J., & Shader, R. I. (1993). Plasma alprazolam concentrations: Relation to efficacy and side effects in the treatment of panic disorder. *Archives of General Psychiatry, 50*, 715–732.

Greenfield, P. (1997). You can't take it with you: Why ability assessments don't cross cultures. *American Psychologist, 52*, 1115–1124.

Greenhaus, J. H. (2003). Career dynamics. In W. C. Borman, D. R. Ilgen, & R. J. Klimoski (Eds.), *Handbook of psychology: Industrial and organizational psychology* (Vol. 12, pp. 519–540). New York: Wiley.

Greenough, W. T., Wallace, C. S., Alcantara, A. A., Anderson, B. J., Hawrylak, N., Sirevaag, A. M., et al. (1993). Experience affects the structure of neurons, glia, and blood vessels. In N. J. Anastasiow & S. Harel (Eds.), *At-risk infants: Interventions, family, and research* (pp.175–185). Baltimore: Paul H. Brookes.

Greenwald, A. G., & Draine, S. C. (1997). Do subliminal stimuli enter the mind unnoticed? Tests with a new method. In J. D. Cohen & J. W. Schooler (Eds.), *Scientific approaches to consciousness: Carnegie Mellon Symposia on cognition* (pp. 83–108). Mahwah, NJ: Erlbaum.

Grieger, T. A., Fullerton, C. S., & Ursano, R. J. (2004). Posttraumatic stress disorder, depression, and perceived safety 13 months after September 11th. *Psychiatric Services, 55*, 1061–1063.

Grinspoon, L., & Bakalar, J. B. (1995). Marijuana as medicine: A plea for reconsideration. *Journal of the American Medical Association, 273*(23), 1875–1876.

Grinspoon, L., Bakalar, J. B., Zimmer, L., & Morgan, J. P. (1997). Marijuana addiction. *Science, 277*, 751–752.

Grivetti, L. E. (2000). Food prejudices and taboos. In K. E. Kipple & K. C. Ornelas (Eds.), *The Cambridge world history of food* (Vol. 1, pp. 1495–1513). Cambridge, UK: Cambridge University Press.

Grossman, M. I., & Stein, L. F. (1948). Vagotomy and the hunger-producing action of insulin in man. *Journal of Applied Physiology, I*, 263–269.

Grossman, R. P., & Till, B. D. (1998). The persistence of classically conditioned brand attitudes. *Journal of Advertising, 27*, 23–31.

Grover, S. (2005). Reification of psychiatric diagnoses as defamatory: Implications for ethical clinical practice. *Ethical Human Psychology and Psychiatry*, 7, 77–86.

Gruen, R. J. (1993). Stress and depression: Toward the development of integrative models. In L. Goldberger & S. Breznitz (Eds.), *Handbook of stress: Theoretical and clinical aspects* (pp. 550–569). New York: Free Press.

Gugger, J. J., & Wagner, M. L. (2007). Rapid eye movement sleep behavior disorder. *Annals of Pharmacotherapy*, 41, 1833–1841.

Guilford, J. P. (1967). *The nature of human intelligence*. New York: McGraw-Hill.

Guilleminault, C., Palombini, L., Pelayo, R., & Chervin, R. D. (2003). Sleepwalking and sleep terrors in prepubertal children: What triggers them? *Pediatrics, 111*, e17–25.

Guisinger, S. (2003). Adapted to flee famine: Adding an evolutionary perspective on anorexia nervosa. *Psychological Review, 110*, 745–761.

Gurman, A. S., & Jacobson, N. S. (Eds.). (2002). *Clinical handbook of couple therapy* (3rd ed.). New York: Guilford Press.

Gustavson, C. R., & Garcia, J. (1974, August). Pulling a gag on the wily coyote. *Psychology Today*, pp. 68–72.

Guthrie, J. P., Ash, R. A., & Bendapudi, V. (1995). Additional validity evidence for a measure of morningness. *Journal of Applied Psychology*, 80, 186–190.

Guze, B. H., & Gitlin, M. (1994). New antidepressants and the treatment of depression. *Journal of Family Practice*, 38, 49–57.

Haack, L. J., Metalsky, G. I., Dykman, B. M., & Abramson, L. Y. (1996). Use of current situational information and causal inference: Do dysphoric individuals make "unwarranted" causal inferences? *Cognitive Therapy and Research*, 20, 309–331.

Haber, D. (1994). *Health promotion and aging*. New York: Springer.

Hackett, R. D. (1989). Work attitudes and employee absenteeism: A synthesis of the literature. *Journal of Occupational Psychology*, 62(3), 235–248.

Hackman, J. R., & Oldham, G. R. (1976). Motivation through the design of work: A test of a theory. *Organizational Behavior and Human Performance*, 16(2), 250–279.

Haidt, J. (2008). Morality. *Perspectives on Psychological Science*, 1, 65–72.

Haie, L., & Do, D. P. (2007). Racial differences in self-reports of sleep duration in a population-based study. *Sleep*, 30, 1096–1103.

Haith, M. M., & Benson, J. B. (1998). Infant cognition. In W. Damon & R. M. Lerner (Eds.), *Handbook of child psychology* (Vol. 1, pp. 235–246). New York: Wiley.

Hakuta, K. (1999). The debate on bilingual education. *Developmental and Behavioral Pediatrics*, 20, 36–37.

Hakuta, K., Bailystok, E., & Wiley, E. (2003). Critical evidence: A test of the critical-period hypothesis for second-language acquisitions. *Psychological Science*, 14, 31–38.

Hall, D. T., & Nougaim, K. E. (1968). An examination of Maslow's need hierarchy in an organizational setting. *Organizational Behavior and Human Performance*, 3, 12–35.

Halpern, D. F. (1996). Public policy implications of sex differences in cognitive abilities. *Psychology, Public Policy and Law*, 2(3/4), 564.

Halpern, D. F., & LeMay, M. L. (2000). The smarter sex: A critical review of sex-differences in intelligence. *Educational Psychology Review*, 12, 229–246.

Hamann, S. (2005). Sex differences in the responses of the human amygdala. *Neuroscientist*, 11, 288–293.

Hamel, R., & Elshout, J. (2000). On the development of knowledge during problem solving. *Journal of Cognitive Psychology*, 12, 289–322.

Hamilton, C. E. (2000). Continuity and discontinuity of attachment from infancy through adolescence. *Child Development*, 71, 690–694.

Hamilton, V. L., Blumenfeld, P. C., Akoh, H., & Miura, K. (1991). Group and gender in Japanese and American elementary classrooms. *Journal of Cross-Cultural Psychology*, 22, 317–346.

Hamilton, V. L., & Sanders, J. (1995). Crimes of obedience and conformity in the workplace: Surveys of Americans, Russians, and Japanese. *Journal of Social Issues*, 51, 67–88.

Hampson, S. E., & Goldberg, L. R. (2006). A first large cohort study of personality trait stability over the 40 years between elementary school and midlife. *Journal of Personality and Social Psychology*, 91, 763–779.

Hanisch, K. A. (1992). The Job Descriptive Index revisited: Questions about the question mark. *Journal of Applied Psychology*, 77, 377–382.

Hanisch, K. A. (1995). Behavioral families and multiple causes: Matching the complexity of responses to the complexity of antecedents. *Current Directions in Psychological Science*, 4(5), 156–162.

Hanisch, K. A., & Hulin, C. L. (1990). Job attitudes and organizational withdrawal: An examination of retirement and other voluntary withdrawal behaviors. *Journal of Vocational Behavior*, 37(1), 60–78.

Hanisch, K. A., & Hulin, C. L. (1991). General attitudes and organizational withdrawal: An evaluation of a causal model. *Journal of Vocational Behavior*, 39, 110–128.

Hanisch, K. A., Hulin, C. L., & Roznowski, M. A. (1998). The importance of individuals' repertoires of behaviors: The scientific appropriateness of studying multiple behaviors and general attitudes. *Journal of Organizational Behavior*, 19, 463–480.

Hanson, G., & Venturelli, P. J. (1998). *Drugs and society* (5th ed.). Boston: Jones and Bartlett.

Harlow, H. F., & Zimmerman, R. (1959). Affectional responses in the infant monkey. *Science*, 130, 421–432.

Harold, G. T., Fincham, F. D., Osborne, L. N., & Conger, R. D. (1997). Mom and Dad are at it again: Adolescent perceptions of marital conflict and adolescent psychological distress. *Developmental Psychology*, 33, 335–350.

Harris, J. D. (1943). Habituatory response decrement in the intact organism. *Psychological Bulletin*, 40, 385–422.

Harris, J. R. (2000). Context-specific learning, personality, and birth order. *Current Directions in Psychological Science*, 9, 174–177.

Harris, S. R., Kemmerling, R. L., & North, M. M. (2002). Brief virtual reality therapy for public speaking. *Cyberpsychology and Behavior*, 5, 543–550.

Harris Poll. (2006). Firefighters, doctors and nurses top list as "most prestigious occupations," according to latest Harris Poll. *Harris Poll, 58* [Online]. Available at http://www.harrisinteractive.com/harris_poll/index.asp?PID=685

Harrow, M., Sands, J. R., Silverstein, M. L., & Goldberg, J. F. (1997). Course and outcome for schizophrenia versus other psychotic patients: A longitudinal study. *Schizophrenia Bulletin*, 23, 287–303.

Hartmann, E. (1981, April). The strangest sleep disorder. *Psychology Today*, pp. 14, 16, 18.

Hartung, C. M., & Widiger, T. A. (1998). Gender differences in the diagnosis of mental disorders: Conclusions and controversies of the DSM-IV. *Psychological Bulletin*, 123, 260–278.

Hasin, D., Hatzenbuehler, M. L., Keyes, K., & Ogburn, E. (2006). Substance use disorders: Diagnostic and Statistical Manual of Mental Disorders, fourth edition (DSM-IV) and International Classification of Diseases, tenth edition (ICD-10). *Addiction*, 101(Suppl. 1), 59–75.

Hatcher, R., Trussell, J., Stewart, F., Stewart, G., Kowal, D., Guest, E., et al. (1994). *Contraceptive technology* (16th ed.). New York: Irvington.

Haus, E., & Smolensky, M. (2006). Biological clocks and shift work: Circadian dysregulation and potential long-term effects. *Cancer Causes and Control*, 17, 489–500.

Havermans, R. C., & Jansen, A. (2007). Increasing children's liking of vegetables through flavour–flavour learning. *Appetite*, 48, 259–262.

Hawkley, L. C., & Cacioppo, J. T. (2007). Aging and loneliness: Downhill quickly? *Current Directions in Psychological Science*, 16, 187–191.

Hawks, S. R., Hull, M. L., Thalman, R. L., & Richins, P. M. (1995). Review of spiritual health: Definition, role, and intervention strategies in health promotion. *American Journal of Health Promotion*, 9, 371–378.

Hayes, E. R., & Plowfield, L. A. (2007). Smoking too young: Students' decisions about tobacco use. *American Journal of Maternal Child Nursing*, 32, 112–116.

Hayes, J. R. (1989). *The complete problem solver* (2nd ed.). Hillsdale, NJ: Erlbaum.

Hayne, H., & Rovee-Collier, C. (1995). The organization of reactivated memory in infancy. *Child Development*, 66(3), 893–906.

Hayward, M. D., Schaich-Borg, A., Pintar, J. E., & Low, M. J. (2006). Differential involvement of endogenous opioids in sucrose consumption and food reinforcement. *Pharmacology Biochemistry and Behavior*, 85, 601–611.

Hebb, D. O. (1955). Drives and the C.N.S. (conceptual nervous system). *Psychological Review*, 62, 243–255.

Hedden, T., & Park, D. C. (2003). Contributions of source and inhibitory mechanisms to age-related retroactive interference in verbal working memory. *Journal of Experimental Psychology: General*, 132, 93–122.

Hedden, T., & Yoon, C. (2006). Individual differences in executive processing predict susceptibility to interference in verbal working memory. *Neuropsychology*, 20, 511–528.

Heider, F. (1946). Attitudes and cognitive organization. *Journal of Psychology*, 21, 107–112.

Heider, F. (1958). *The psychology of interpersonal relations*. New York: Wiley.

Heilman, M. E., & Chen, J. J. (2005). Same behavior, different consequences: Reaction's to men's and women's altruistic citizenship behaviors. *Journal of Applied Psychology*, 90, 431–441.

Heilman, M. E., & Kram, K. E. (1983). Male and female assumptions about colleagues' views of their competence. *Psychology of Women Quarterly*, 7, 329–337.

Heim, C., Plotsky, P. M., & Nemeroff, C. B. (2004). Importance of studying the contributions of early adverse experience to neurobiological findings in depression. *Neuropsychopharmacology*, 29, 641–648.

Heiser, P., Dickhaus, B. Schreiber, W., Clement, H. W., Hasse, C., Hennig, J., et al. (2000). White blood cells and cortisol after sleep deprivation and recovery sleep in humans. *European Archives of Psychiatry and Clinical Neuroscience, 250*, 16–23.

Hejmadi, A., Davidson, R. J., & Rozin, P. (2000). Exploring Hindu Indian emotion expressions. *Psychological Science, 11*, 183–187.

Helft, M. (2007, March 10). Google's buses help its workers beat the rush. *New York Times.*

Helgeson, V. S. (1994). Relation of agency and communion to well-being: Evidence and potential explanations. *Psychological Bulletin, 116*, 412–428.

Helmholtz, H. L. F. von. (1930). *The sensations of tone* (A. J. Ellis, Trans.). New York: Longmans, Green. (Original work published 1863)

Helmuth, L. (2001). From the mouths (and hands) of babes. *Science, 293*, 1758–1759.

Helwig, C. C. (1997). Making moral cognition respectable (again): A retrospective review of Lawrence Kohlberg. *Contemporary Psychology, 42*, 191–195.

Helzer, J. E., & Canino, G. J. (Eds.) (1992). *Alcoholism in North America, Europe, and Asia.* New York: Oxford University Press.

Hendrick, C., & Hendrick, S. S. (1983). *Liking, loving, and relating.* Pacific Grove, CA: Brooks/Cole.

Henry, B., & Moffitt, T. E. (1997). Neuropsychological and neuroimaging studies of juvenile delinquency and adult criminal behavior. In D. M. Stoff, J. Breiling, & J. D. Maser (Eds.), *Handbook of antisocial personality disorder* (pp. 280–288). New York: Wiley.

Henry, W. P., Strupp, H. H., Schacht, T. E., & Gaston, L. (1994). Psychodynamic approaches. In A. E. Bergin & S. L. Garfield (Eds.), *Handbook of psychotherapy and behavior change* (4th ed., pp. 143–189). New York: Wiley.

Herman, L. M., & Uyeyama, R. J. (1999). The dolphin's grammatical competency: Comments on Kako (1999). *Animal Learning and Behavior, 27*, 18–23.

Herman, L. M., Kuczaj, S. A., II, & Holder, M. D. (1993). Responses to anomalous gestural sequences by a language-trained dolphin: Evidence for processing of semantic relations and syntactical information. *Journal of Experimental Psychology: General, 122*, 184–194.

Heron, M. P., & Smith, B. L. (2007). Deaths: Leading causes for 2003. *National Vital Statistics Reports, 55*, 1–93.

Herrera, N. C., Zajonc, R. B., Wieczorkowska, G., & Cichomski, B. (2003). Beliefs about birth rank and their reflection in reality. *Journal of Personality and Social Psychology, 85*, 142–150.

Herrnstein, R., & Murray, C. (1994). *The bell curve.* New York: Free Press.

Hesse, E., & Main, M. (2006). Frightened, threatening, and dissociative parental behavior in low-risk samples: Description, discussion, and interpretations. *Development and Psychopathology, 18*, 309–343.

Heston, L. L. (1966). Psychiatric disorders in foster home reared children of schizophrenic mothers. *British Journal of Psychiatry, 112*, 819–825.

Hettema, J. M., Neale, M. C., & Kendler, K. S. (2001). A review and meta-analysis of the genetic epidemiology of anxiety disorders. *American Journal of Psychiatry, 158*, 1568–1578.

Hewlett, W. A. (2000). Benzodiazepines in the treatment of obsessive-compulsive disorder. In W. K. Goodman (Ed.), *Obsessive-compulsive disorder: Contemporary issues in treatment* (pp. 405–429). Mahwah, NJ: Erlbaum.

Hewstone, M., Rubin, M., & Willis, H. (2002). Intergroup bias (social prejudice). *Annual Review of Psychology, 53*, 575–604.

Higbee, K. L., & Clay, S. L. (1998). College students' beliefs in the ten-percent myth. *Journal of Psychology, 132*, 469–476.

Hikosaka, O., Nakamura, K., Sakai, K., & Nakamura, H. (2002). Central mechanisms of motor skill learning. *Current Opinion in Neurobiology, 12*, 217–222.

Hilgard, E. R. (1977). *Divided consciousness: Multiple controls in human thought and action.* New York: Wiley.

Hilgard, E. R. (1982). Hypnotic susceptibility and implications for measurement. *International Journal of Clinical and Experimental Hypnosis, 30*, 394–403.

Hilgard, E. R. (1992). Divided consciousness and dissociation. *Consciousness and Cognition, 1*, 16–31.

Hilgard, E. R., Morgan, A. H., & MacDonald, H. (1975). Pain and dissociation in the old pressor test: A study of "hidden reports" through automatic key-pressing and automatic talking. *Journal of Abnormal Psychology, 84*, 280–289.

Hill, C. E., & Nakayama, E. Y. (2000). Client-centered therapy: Where has it been and where is it going? A comment on Hathaway (1948). *Journal of Clinical Psychology, 56*, 861–875.

Hill, P. C., & Pargament, K. I. (2003). Advances in the conceptualization and measurement of religion and spirituality. Implications for physical and mental health research. *American Psychologist, 58*, 64–74.

Hirai, M., & Clum, G. A. (2005). An Internet-based self-change program for traumatic event related fear, distress, and maladaptive coping. *Journal of Traumatic Stress, 18*, 631–636.

Hiroto, D. S. (1974). Locus of control and learned helplessness. *Journal of Experimental Psychology, 102*, 187–193.

Hirsch, M. S., Conway, B., D'Aquila, R. T., Johnson, V. A., Brun-Vezinet, F., Clotet, B., et al. (1998). Antiretroviral drug resistance testing in adults with HIV infection: Implications for clinical management. *Journal of the American Medical Association, 279*, 1984–1991.

Hirshkowitz, M., Moore, C. A., & Minhoto, G. (1997). The basics of sleep. In M. R. Pressman & W. C. Orr (Eds.), *Understanding sleep: The evaluation and treatment of sleep disorders* (pp. 11–34). Washington, DC: American Psychological Association.

Ho, B.-C., Black, D. W., & Andreasen, N. C. (2003). Schizophrenia and other psychotic disorders. In R. E. Hales & S. C. Yudofsky (Eds.), *Textbook of clinical psychiatry* (4th ed., pp. 379–438). Washington DC: American Psychiatric Publishing.

Hobbs, F. B. (with B. L. Damon). (1996). *65+ in the United States.* Washington DC: U.S. Bureau of the Census.

Hobson, J. A., & McCarley, R. W. (1977). The brain as a dream state generator: An activation-synthesis hypothesis of the dream process. *American Journal of Psychiatry, 134*, 1335–1348.

Hobson, J. A., Pace-Schott, E., & Stickgold, R. (2000). Dreaming and the brain: Toward a cognitive neuroscience of conscious states. *Behavioral and Brain Sciences, 23*, 783–842.

Hodson, N. A., & Linden, R. W. A. (2006). The effect of monosodium glutamate on parotid salivary flow in comparison to the response to representatives of the other four basic tastes. *Physiology and Behavior, 89*, 711–717.

Hoffer, T. B., Welch, V., Jr., Webber, K., Williams, K., Lisek, B., Hess, M., et al. (2006). *Doctorate recipients from United States universities: Summary report 2005.* Chicago: National Opinion Research Center.

Hofmann, S. G., & Smits, J. A. (2008). Cognitive-behavioral therapy for adult anxiety disorders: A meta-analysis of randomized placebo-controlled trials. *Journal of Clinical Psychiatry, 69*, 621–632.

Hogben, M. (1998). Factors moderating the effect of televised aggression on viewer behavior. *Communication Research, 25*, 220–247.

Hoge, C. W., Castro, C. A., Messer, S. C., McGurk, D., Cotting, D. I., & Koffman, R. L. (2004). Combat duty in Iraq and Afghanistan, mental health problems, and barriers to care. *New England Journal of Medicine, 351*, 13–22.

Holden, C. (1980, November). Twins reunited. *Science, 80*, 55–59.

Holland, A. J., Sicotte, N., & Treasure, J. (1988). Anorexia nervosa: Evidence of a genetic basis. *Journal of Psychosomatic Research, 32*, 561–571.

Hollon, S. D., & Beck, A. T. (1994). Cognitive and cognitive-behavioral therapies. In A. E. Bergin & S. L. Garfield (Eds.), *Handbook of psychotherapy and behavior change* (4th ed., pp. 447–492). New York: Wiley.

Hollos, M., & Richards, F. A. (1993). Gender-associated development of formal operations in Nigerian adolescents. *Ethos, 21*, 24–52.

Holloway, S. R. (1998). Exploring the neighborhood contingency of race discrimination in mortgage lending in Columbus, Ohio. *Annals of the Association of American Geographers, 88*, 252–276.

Holmans, P., Weissman, M. M., Zubenko, G. S., Scheftner, W. A., Crowe, R. R., Depaulo, J. R., et al. (2007). Genetics of recurrent early-onset major depression (GenRED): Final genome scan report. *American Journal of Psychiatry, 164*, 248–258.

Holmes, D. S. (1987). The influence of meditation versus rest on physiological arousal: A second examination. In M. A. West (Ed.), *The psychology of meditation* (pp. 81–103). Oxford, UK: Clarendon Press.

Holmes, T. H., & Rahe, R. H. (1967). The Social Readjustment Rating Scale. *Journal of Psychosomatic Research, 11*, 213–218.

Holroyd, J. (2003). The science of meditation and the state of hypnosis. *American Journal of Clinical Hypnosis, 46*, 109–128.

Holt, S., Brand, J. C., Soveny, C., & Hansky, J. (1992). Relationship of satiety to postprandial glycaemic, insulin and cholecystokinin responses. *Appetite, 18*, 129–141.

Holtzheimer, P. E., III, & Nemeroff, C. B. (2006). Advances in the treatment of depression. *NeuroRx, 3*, 42–56.

Hong, R. Y. (2007). Worry and rumination: Differential associations with anxious and depressive symptoms and coping behavior. *Behaviour Research and Therapy, 45*, 277–290.

Hood, D. C., & Finkelstein, M. A. (1986). Sensitivity to light. In K. R. Boff, L. Kaufman, & J. P. Thomas (Eds.), *Handbook of perception and human performance* (pp. 5.1–5.66). New York: Wiley.

Hooley, J. M., & Hiller, J. B. (1998). Expressed emotion and the pathogenesis of relapse in schizophrenia. In M. F. Lenzenweger & R. H. Dworkin (Eds.), *Origins of the development of schizophrenia* (pp. 447–468). Washington, DC: American Psychological Association.

Horgan, D. D. (1995). *Achieving gender equity: Strategies for the classroom.* Boston: Allyn & Bacon.

Horgan, J. (1996, December). Why Freud isn't dead. *Scientific American,* pp. 106–111.

Horn, J. L. (1982). The aging of human abilities. In B. B. Wolman (Ed.), *Handbook of developmental psychology* (pp. 847–870). Englewood Cliffs, NJ: Prentice-Hall.

Horn, J. L., Donaldson, G., & Engstrom, R. (1981). Apprehension, memory, and fluid intelligence decline through the "vital years" of adulthood. *Research on Aging, 3,* 33–84.

Horne, J. A., & Staff, L. H. E. (1983). Exercise and sleep: Body-heating effects. *Sleep, 6,* 36–46.

Horney, K. (1937). *The neurotic personality of our time.* New York: Norton.

Horney, K. (1939). *New ways in psychoanalysis.* New York: Norton.

Hovland, C. I., & Weiss, W. (1951). The influence of source credibility on communication effectiveness. *Public Opinion Quarterly, 15,* 635–650.

Howe, M. L. (2000). *The rate of early memories.* Washington, DC: American Psychological Association.

Howell, M. R., Kassler, W. J., & Haddix, A. (1997). Partner notification to prevent pelvic inflammatory disease in women: Cost effectiveness of two strategies. *Sexually Transmitted Diseases, 24,* 287–292.

Hoyert, D. L., Heron, M. P., Murphy, S. L., & Kung, H. (2006). Deaths: Final data for 2003. *National Vital Statistics Report, 54,* 1–120.

Hsiung, R. C. (2001). Suggested principles of professional ethics for the online provision of mental health services. *Medinfo, 10,* 296–300.

Huang, Y. H., & Bergles, D. E. (2004). Glutamate transporters bring competition to the synapse. *Current Opinions in Neurobiology, 14,* 346–352.

Hubel, D. H. (1990, February). Interview. *Omni,* pp. 74–110.

Hubel, D. H. (1995). *Eye, brain, and vision.* New York: Scientific American Library.

Hubel, D. H., & Weisel, T. N. (1965). Receptive fields of single neurons in two nonstriate visual areas (18 and 19) of the cat. *Journal of Neurophysiology, 28,* 229–289.

Hubel, D. H., & Weisel, T. N. (1979). Brain mechanisms and vision. *Scientific American, 214,* 150–162.

Huber, D., Henrich, G., & Gündel, H. (2005). Psychophysiological response patterns of migraine patients in two habituation tests. *Headache: The Journal of Head and Face Pain, 45,* 1375–1387.

Huesmann, L. R. (Ed.). (1994). *Aggressive behavior: Current perspectives.* New York: Plenum Press.

Huffcutt, A. I., & Arthur, W., Jr. (1994). Hunter and Hunter (1984) revisited: Interview validity for entry-level jobs. *Journal of Applied Psychology, 79,* 184–190.

Hughes, J., Smith, T. W., Kosterlitz, H. W., Fothergill, L. A., Morgan, B. A., & Morris, H. R. (1975). Identification of two related pentapeptides from the brain with potent opiate agonist activity. *Nature, 258,* 577–579.

Hulbert, A. (2003). Colour vision: Primary visual cortex shows its influence. *Current Biology, 13,* R270–R272.

Hull, C. L. (1943). *Principles of behavior.* New York: Appleton-Century-Crofts.

Hummel, M., & Unterwald, E. M. (2002). D1 dopamine receptor: A putative neurochemical and behavioral link to cocaine action. *Journal of Cell Physiology, 191,* 17–27.

Humphreys, K., Winzelberg, A., & Klaw, E. (2000). Psychologists' ethical responsibilities in Internet-based groups: Issues, strategies, and a call for dialogue. *Professional Psychology, Research, and Practice, 31,* 493–496.

Hunt, R. R. (2002). How effective are pharmacologic agents for alcoholism? *Journal of Family Practice, 51,* 577.

Hurt, H., Brodsky, N. L., Roth, H., Malmud, E., & Giannetta, J. M. (2005). School performance of children with gestational cocaine exposure. *Neurotoxicology and Teratology, 27,* 203–211.

Hurvich, L. M., & Jameson, D. (2000). An opponent-process theory of color vision. In S. Yantis (Ed.), *Visual perception: Essential readings* (pp. 129–144). New York: Psychology Press. (Original work published 1957)

Huston, A. C., & Wright, J. C. (1998). Mass media and children's development. In W. Damon (Series Ed.), *Handbook of child psychology* (Vol. 4, pp. 999–1058). New York: Wiley.

Huston, T. L., & Vangelisti, A. L. (1991). Socioemotional behavior and satisfaction in marital relationships: A longitudinal study. *Journal of Personality and Social Psychology, 6,* 721–733.

Huttenlocher, P. R. (2002). *Neural plasticity: The effects of environment on the development of the cerebral cortex.* Cambridge, MA: Harvard University Press.

Hyde, J. S., Fenneman, E., & Lamon, S. (1990). Gender differences in mathematics performance: A meta-analysis. *Psychological Bulletin, 107,* 139–155.

Hyde, J. S., & McKinley, N. M. (1997). Gender differences in cognition: Results from meta-analyses. In P. J. Caplan, M. Crawford, J. S. Hyde, & J. T. E. Richardson (Eds.), *Gender differences in human cognition* (pp. 30–51). New York: Oxford University Press.

Hyman, S. E., & Rudorfer, M. V. (2000). Anxiety disorders. In D. C. Dale & D. D. Federman (Eds.), *Scientific American Medicine* (Vol. 3). New York: Healtheon/WebMD Corp.

Iidaka, T., Anderson, N. D., Kapur, S., Cabeza, S., & Craik, F. I. M. (2000). The effect of divided attention on encoding and retrieval in episodic memory revealed by positron emission tomography. *Journal of Cognitive Neuroscience, 12,* 267.

Ikonomidou, C., Bittigau, P., Ishimaru, M. J., Wozniak, D. F., Koch, C., Genz, K., et al. (2000, February 11). Ethanol-induced apoptotic neurodegeneration and fetal alcohol syndrome. *Science, 287,* 1056–1060.

Ilgen, M. A., & Hutchison, K. E. (2005). A history of major depressive disorder and the response to stress. *Journal of Affective Disorders, 86,* 143–150.

Inciardi, J. A., Surratt, H. L., & Saum, C. A. (1997). *Cocaine-exposed infants: Social legal, and public health issues.* Thousand Oaks, CA: Sage.

Ineichen, B. (1979). The social geography of marriage. In M. Cook & G. Wilson (Eds.), *Love and attraction* (pp. 145–149). New York: Pergamon Press.

Infante-Rivard, C., Fernandez, A., Gauthier, R., David, M., & Rivard, G. E. (1993). Fetal loss associated with caffeine intake before and during pregnancy. *Journal of the American Medical Association, 270*(24), 2940–2943.

Ingram, R. E., Hayes, A., & Scott, W. (2000). Empirically supported treatments: A critical analysis. In C. R. Snyder & R. E. Ingram (Eds.), *Handbook of psychological change: Psychotherapy processes and practices for the 21st century* (pp. 40–60). New York: Wiley.

Innis, N. K. (1979). Stimulus control of behavior during postreinforcement pause of FI schedules. *Animal Learning and Behavior, 7,* 203–210.

Inzlicht, M., & Ben-Zeev, T. (2000). A threatening intellectual environment: Why females are susceptible to experiencing problem-solving deficits in the presence of males. *Psychological Science, 11,* 365–371.

Irwin, M., Clark, C., Kennedy, B., Christian Gillin, J., & Ziegler, M. (2003). Nocturnal catecholamines and immune function in insomniacs, depressed patients, and control subjects. *Brain, Behavior, and Immunity, 17,* 365–372.

Irwin, M., McClintick, J., Costlow, C., Fortner, M., White, J., & Gillin, J. C. (1996). Partial night sleep deprivation reduces natural killer and cellular immune responses in humans. *Journal of the Federation of American Societies for Experimental Biology, 10,* 643–653.

Isaac, M., & Chand, P. K. (2006). Dissociative and conversion disorders: Defining boundaries. *Current Opinion in Psychiatry, 19,* 61–66.

Isenberg, N., Silbersweig, D., Engelien, A., Emmerich, S., Malavade, K., Beattie, B., et al. (1999). Linguistic threat activates the human amygdala. *Proceedings of the National Academy of Sciences, USA, 96,* 10456–10459.

Iso, H., Simoda, S., & Matsuyama, T. (2006). Environmental change during postnatal development alters behavior, cognitions, and neurogenesis of mice. *Behavioural Brain Research, 179,* 90–98.

Ito, T., Takenaka, K., Tomita, T., & Agari, I. (2006). Comparison of ruminative responses with negative rumination as a vulnerability factor for depression. *Psychological Reports, 99,* 763–772.

Iverson, L. (2003). Cannabis and the brain. *Brain, 126,* 1252–1270.

Izac, S. M. (2006). Basic anatomy and physiology of sleep. *American Journal of Electroneurodiagnostic Technology, 46,* 18–38.

Jablensky, A. (2000). Epidemiology of schizophrenia: The global burden of disease and disability. *European Archives of Psychiatry and Clinical Neuroscience, 250,* 274–285.

Jablensky, A. (2002). The classification of personality disorders: Critical review and need for rethinking. *Psychopathology, 35,* 112–116.

Jablin, F. M. (1982). Organizational communication: An assimilation approach. In M. E. Rolff & C. R. Berger (Eds.), *Social cognition and communication* (pp. 255–286). Beverly Hills, CA: Sage.

Jack, D. C. (1991). *Silencing the self: Women and depression.* New York: HarperPerennial.

Jacobs, B. L. (2004). Depression: The brain finally gets into the act. *Current Directions in Psychological Science, 13,* 103–106.

Jacobs, B. L., van Praag, H., & Gage, F. H. (2000). Adult brain neurogenesis and psychiatry: A novel theory of depression. *Molecular Psychiatry, 5,* 262–269.

Jacobsen, T., & Hofmann, V. (1997). Children's attachment representations: Longitudinal relations to school behavior and academic competency in middle childhood and adolescence. *Developmental Psychology, 33,* 701–710.

Jacoby, L. L., Debner, J. A., & Hay, J. F. (2001). Proactive interference, accessibility bias, and process dissociations: Valid subjective reports of memory. *Journal of Experimental Psychology: Learning, Memory, and Cognition, 27,* 686–700.

Jadack, R. A., Hyde, J. S., Moore, C. F., & Keller, M. L. (1995). Moral reasoning about sexually transmitted diseases. *Child Development, 66,* 167–177.

Jaffari-Bimmel, N., Juffer, F., van Ijzendoorn, M. H., Bakermans-Kranenburg, M. J., & Mooijaart, A. (2006). Social development from infancy to adolescence: Longitudinal and concurrent factors in an adoption sample. *Developmental Psychology, 42,* 1143–1153.

Jaffee, S., & Hyde, J. (2000). Gender differences in moral orientation: A meta-analysis. *Psychological Bulletin, 126,* 703–726.

James, W. (1884). What is an emotion? *Mind, 9,* 188–205.

James, W. (1890). *The principles of psychology.* New York: Holt.

Jäncke, L., & Steinmetz, H. (2006). Brain size: A possible source of interindividual variability on corpus callosum morphology. In E. Zaidel & M. Iacobini (Eds.), *The parallel brain: The cognitive neuroscience of the corpus callosum* (pp. 51–63). Cambridge, MA: MIT Press.

Jane, J. S., Oltmanns, T. F., South, S. C., & Turkheimer, E. (2007). Gender bias in diagnostic criteria for personality disorders: An item response theory analysis. *Journal of Abnormal Psychology, 116,* 166–175.

Janis, I. L. (1982). *Victims of groupthink* (2nd ed.). Boston: Houghton Mifflin.

Janis, I. L. (1985). Sources of error in strategic decision making. In J. M. Pennings (Ed.), *Organizational strategy and change* (pp. 157–197). San Francisco: Jossey-Bass.

Janoff-Bulman, R. (1992). *Shattered assumptions: Toward a new psychology of trauma.* New York: Maxwell Macmillan International.

Janowitz, H., & Grossman, M. (1950). Hunger and appetite: Some definitions and concepts. *Journal of Mount Sinai Hospital, 16,* 231–240.

Jarrett, R. B., Kraft, D., Doyle, J., Foster, B. M., Eaves, G. G., & Silver, P. C. (2001). Preventing recurrent depression using cognitive therapy with and without a continuation phase. *Archives of General Psychiatry, 58,* 381–388.

Javitt, D. C. (2007). Glutamate and schizophrenia: Phencyclidine, N-Methyl-d-aspartate receptors, and dopamine-glutamate interactions. *International Review of Neurobiology, 78,* 69–108.

Jemmott, J. B., III, Borysenko, M., McClelland, D. C., Chapman, R., & Benson, H. (1985). Academic stress, power motivation, and decrease in salivary secretory immunoglobulin: A secretion rate. *Lancet, 1,* 1400–1402.

Jenike, M. A., Baer, L., Ballantine, H. T., Martuza, R. L., Tynes, S., Giriunas, I., et al. (1991). Cingulotomy for refractory obsessive-compulsive disorder: A long-term follow up of 33 patients. *Archives of General Psychiatry, 48,* 548–555.

Jenkins, J. M., & Astington, J. W. (1996). Cognitive factors and family structure associated with theory of mind development in young children. *Developmental Psychology, 32,* 70–78.

Jenni, O. G., Achermann, P., & Carskadon, M. A. (2005). Homeostatic sleep regulation in adolescents. *Sleep, 28,* 1446–1454.

Jennings, J. R., Monk, T. H., & van der Molen, M. W. (2003). Sleep deprivation influences some but not all processes of supervisory attention. *Psychological Science, 14,* 473–479.

Johnson, B. A. (2008). Update on neuropharmacological treatments for alcoholism: Scientific basis and clinical findings. *Biochemical Pharmacology, 75,* 34–56.

Johnson, J. A. (1997). Units of analysis for the description and explanation of personality. In R. Hogan, J. Johnson, & S. Briggs (Eds.), *Handbook of personality psychology* (pp. 3–93). New York: Academic Press.

Johnson, M. K., Hashtroudi, S., & Lindsay, D. S. (1993). Source monitoring. *Psychological Bulletin, 114,* 3–28.

Johnson, S. P., Amso, D., & Slemmer, J. A. (2003). Development of object concepts in infancy: Evidence for early learning in an eye-tracking paradigm. *Proceedings of the National Academy of Sciences, USA, 100,* 10568–10573.

John-Steiner, V., & Mahn, H. (1996). Sociocultural approaches to learning and development: A Vygotskian framework. *Educational Psychologist, 31,* 191–206.

Johnston, L. D., O'Malley, P. M., Bachman, J. G., & Schulenberg, J. E. (2006). *Decline in daily smoking by younger teens has ended.* Ann Arbor: University of Michigan News and Information Services. Retrieved January 20, 2007, from www .monitoringthefuture.org

Johnston, L. D., O'Malley, P. M., Bachman, J. G., & Schulenberg, J. E. (2007). *Overall, illicit drug use by American teens continues gradual decline in 2007.* Ann Arbor: University of Michigan News Service [Online]. Retrieved March 8, 2008, from www .monitoringthefuture.org

Joliot, A. E. (2001). A comparative study of body image satisfaction and attitudes among American, Israeli, Spanish, and Brazilian college women (United States). *Dissertation Abstracts International: B. The Physical Sciences and Engineering, 61,* 55–67.

Jones, C. J., & Meredith, W. (1996). Patterns of personality change across the life span. *Psychology of Aging, 11,* 57–65.

Jones, E. E. (1979). The rocky road from acts to dispositions. *American Psychologist, 34,* 107–117.

Jones, E. E., & Nesbitt, R. E. (1971). *The actor and the observer: Divergent perceptions of the causes of behavior.* Morristown, NJ: General Learning Press.

Jones, P., & Cannon, M. (1998). The new epidemiology of schizophrenia. *Psychiatric Clinics of North America, 21,* 1–25.

Jones, S., Casswell, S., & Zhang, J. F. (1995). The economic costs of alcohol-related absenteeism and reduced productivity among the working population of New Zealand. *Addiction, 90,* 1455–1461.

Jordan, A. S., & McEvoy, R. D. (2003). Gender differences in sleep apnea: Epidemiology, clinical presentation and pathogenic mechanisms. *Sleep Medical Review, 7,* 377–389.

Jorgensen, G. (2006). Kohlberg and Gilligan: Duet or duel? *Journal of Moral Education, 35,* 179–196.

Julien, R. M. (1995). *A primer of drug action.* San Francisco: Freeman.

Jung, C. G. (1967). The psychology of the unconscious. In H. Read, M. Fordham, & G. Adler (Eds.), *Collected works of C. G. Jung* (Vol. 7). Princeton, NJ: Princeton University Press, 1967. (Original work published 1917)

Kahn, D. A. (1995). New strategies in bipolar disorder: Part II. Treatment. *Journal of Practical Psychiatry and Behavioral Health, 3,* 148–157.

Kahneman, D., & Tversky, A. (1973). On the psychology of prediction. *Psychological Review, 80,* 237–251.

Kahneman, D., & Tversky, A. (1984). Choices, values, and frames. *American Psychologist, 39,* 341–350.

Kahol, K., Leyba, M. J., Deka, M., Deka, V., Mayes, S., Smith, M., et al. (2008). Effect of fatigue on psychomotor and cognitive skills. *American Journal of Surgery, 195,* 195–204.

Kako, E. (1999). Elements of syntax in the systems of three language-trained animals. *Animal Learning and Behavior, 27,* 1–14.

Kalish, R. A. (1985). The social context of death and dying. In R. H. Binstock & E. Shanas (Eds.), *Handbook of aging and the social sciences* (2nd ed., pp. 149–170). New York: Van Nostrand Reinhold.

Kamb, M. L., Fishbein, M., Douglas, J. M., Jr., Rhodes, F., Rogers, J., Bolan, G., et al. (1998). Efficacy of risk-reduction counseling to prevent human immunodeficiency virus and sexually transmitted diseases: A randomized controlled trial. *Journal of the American Medical Association, 280,* 1161–1167.

Kandel, D. B. (1978). Similarity in real-life adolescent friendship pairs. *Journal of Personality and Social Psychology, 36,* 306–312.

Kanin, E. J., Davidson, D. K. D., & Scheck, S. R. (1970). A research note on male–female differentials in the experience of heterosexual love. *Journal of Sex Research, 6,* 64–72.

Kanoy, K., Ulku-Steiner, B., Cox, M., & Burchinal, M. (2003). Marital relationship and individual psychological characteristics that predict physical punishment of children. *Journal of Family Psychology, 17,* 20–28.

Kaplan, C. A., & Simon, H. A. (1990). In search of insight. *Cognitive Psychology, 22,* 374–419.

Kaplan, R. E., Drath, W. H., & Kofodimos, J. R., (1991). *Beyond ambition: How driven managers can lead better and live better.* San Francisco: Jossey-Bass.

Kaplan, R. M. (2007). Should Medicare reimburse providers for weight loss interventions? *American Psychologist, 62,* 217–219.

Kaplan, R. M., & Saccuzzo, D. P. (1989). *Psychological testing: Principles, applications, and issues.* Pacific Grove, CA: Brooks/Cole.

Kaplan, S. J., Pelcovitz, D., Salzinger, S., Mandel, F., & Weiner, M. (1997). Adolescent physical abuse and suicide attempts. *Journal of the American Academy of Child and Adolescent Psychiatry, 36,* 799–808.

Kaplowitz, P. B., Oberfield, S. E., & the Drug and Therapeutics and Executive Committees of the Lawson Wilkins Pediatric Endocrine Society. (1999). Reexamination of the age limit for defining when puberty is precocious in girls in the United States: Implications for evaluation and treatment. *Pediatrics, 104,* 936–941.

Kapur, S., Craik, F. I. M., Tulving, E., Wilson, A. A., Houle, S., & Brown, G. M. (1994). Neuroanatomical correlates of encoding in episodic memory. *Proceedings of the National Academy of Science, USA, 91,* 2008–2011.

Karney, B. R., & Bradbury, T. N. (2005). Contextual influences on marriage: Implications for policy and intervention.

Current Directions in Psychological Science, 14, 171–174.

Karni, A., Tanne, D., Rubenstein, B. S., Askenasy, J. J. M., & Sagi, D. (1994). Dependence on REM sleep of overnight improvement of a perceptual skill. *Science,* 265, 679–682.

Karno, M., & Golding, J. M. (1991). Obsessive compulsive disorder. In L. R. Robins & D. A. Regier (Eds.), *Psychiatric disorders in America: The Epidemiologic Catchment Area Study* (pp. 204–219). New York: Maxwell Macmillan International.

Kaslow, F. W., Hansson, K., & Lundblad, A. (1994). Long-term marriages in Sweden: And some comparisons with similar couples in the United States. *Contemporary Family Therapy,* 16, 521–537.

Katigbak, M. S., Church, A. T., Guanzon-Lapena, M. A., Carlota, A. J., & del Pilar, G. H. (2002). Are indigenous personality dimensions culture specific? Philippine inventories and the Five-Factor model. *Journal of Personality and Social Psychology,* 82, 89–101.

Katz, M. H., Schwarcz, S. K., Kellogg, T. A., Klausner, J. D., Dilley, J. W., Gibson, S., et al. (2002). Impact of highly active antiretroviral treatment on HIV seroincidence among men who have sex with men. *American Journal of Public Health,* 92, 388–395.

Kaufman, L., & Rock, L. (1989). The moon illusion thirty years later. In M. Hershenson (Ed.), *The moon illusion* (pp. 193–234). Hillsdale, NJ: Erlbaum.

Kaye, K.L., & Bower, T.G.R. (1994). Learning and intermodal transfer of information in newborns. *Psychological Science,* 5, 286–288.

Kazdin, A. E. (1977). *The token economy: A review and evaluation.* New York: Plenum Press.

Keck, P. E., Jr., & McElroy, S. L. (2002). Carbamazepine and valproate in the maintenance treatment of bipolar disorder. *Journal of Clinical Psychiatry,* 63, 13–17.

Keel, P. K., & Klump, K. L. (2003). Are eating disorders culture-bound syndromes? Implications for conceptualizing their etiology. *Psychological Bulletin,* 129, 747–769.

Kelly, D. J., Ge, L., Liu, S., Quinn, P. C., Slater, A. M., Lee, K., et al. (2005). Cross-race preferences for same-race faces extend beyond the African versus Caucasian contrast in 3-month-old infants. *Infancy,* 11, 87–95.

Kelly, M. M., & Forsyth, J. P. (2007). Observational fear conditioning in the acquisition and extinction of attentional bias for threat: An experimental evaluation. *Emotion,* 7, 324–335.

Kelman, C. A. (2001). Egocentric language in deaf children. *American Annals of the Deaf,* 146, 276–279.

Kemeny, M. E. (2003). The psychobiology of stress. *Current Directions in Psychological Science,* 12, 124–129.

Kenardy, J. A., Dow, M. G., Johnston, D. W., Newman, M. G., Thompson, A., & Taylor, C. B. (2003). A comparison of delivery methods of cognitive-behavioral therapy for panic disorder: An international multicenter trial. *Journal of Consulting and Clinical Psychology,* 71, 1068–1075.

Kendall, A. P., Kautz, M. A., Russo, M. B., & Killgore, W. D. (2006). Effects of sleep deprivation on lateral visual attention. *International Journal of Neuroscience,* 116, 1125–1138.

Kendler, K. S., McGuire, M., Gruenberg, A. M., & Walsh, D. (1994). Outcome and family study of the subtypes of

schizophrenia in the west of Ireland. *American Journal of Psychiatry,* 151, 849–856.

Kenrick, D. T., & Sheets, V. (1993). Homicidal fantasies. *Ethology and Sociobiology,* 14, 231–246.

Kerns, K. A., Abraham, M. M., Schlegelmilch, A., & Morgan, T. A. (2007). Mother–child attachment in later middle childhood: Assessment approaches and associations with mood and emotion regulation. *Attachment and Human Development,* 9, 33–53.

Kessler, R. C., Berglund, P. A., Demler, O., Jin, R., Koretz, D., Merikangas, K. R. et al. (2003). The epidemiology of major depressive disorder. Results from the National Comorbidity Survey Replication (NCS-R). *Journal of the American Medical Association,* 289, 3095–3105.

Kessler, R. C., Berglund, P. A., Demler, O., Jin, R., & Walters, E. E. (2005). Lifetime prevalence and age-of-onset distributions of DSM-IV disorders in the National Comorbidity Survey Replication (NCS-R). *Archives of General Psychiatry,* 62, 593–602.

Kessler, R. C., Chiu, W. T., Demler, O., & Walters, E. E. (2005). Prevalence, severity, and comorbidity of twelve-month DSM-IV disorders in the National Comorbidity Survey Replication (NCS-R). *Archives of General Psychiatry,* 62, 617–627.

Kessler, R. C., McGonagle, K. A., Zhao, S., Nelson, C. B., Hughes, M., Eshleman, S., et al. (1994). Lifetime and 12-month prevalence of DSM-III-R psychiatric disorders in the United States: Results from the National Comorbidity Survey. *Archives of General Psychiatry,* 51, 8–19.

Kessler, R. C., Stein, M. B., & Berglund, P. (1998). Social phobia subtypes in the National Comorbidity Survey. *American Journal of Psychiatry,* 155, 613–619.

Kessler, Y., & Meiran, N. (2006). All update-able objects in working memory are updated whenever any of them are modified: Evidence from the memory updating paradigm. *Journal of Experimental Psychology: Learning, Memory, and Cognition,* 32, 570–585.

Kety, S. S., Wender, P. H., Jacobsen, B., Ingraham, L. J., Jansson, L., Faber, B., et al. (1994). Mental illness in the biological and adoptive relative of schizophrenic adoptees: Replication of the Copenhagen study in the rest of Denmark. *Archives of General Psychiatry,* 51, 442–455.

Kidder, D. L., & Parks, J. M. (2001). The good soldier: Who is s(he)? *Journal of Organizational Behavior,* 22, 939–959.

Kiecolt-Glaser, J. K., & Glaser, R. (1992). Psychoneuroimmunology: Can psychological interventions modulate immunity? *Journal of Consulting and Clinical Psychology,* 60, 569–575.

Kiecolt-Glaser, J. K., Marucha, P. T., Malarkey, W. B., Mercado, A. M., & Glaser, R. (1995). Slowing of wound healing by psychological stress. *Lancet,* 346, 1194.

Kiecolt-Glaser, J. K., McGuire, L., Robles, T. F., & Glaser, R. (2002). Emotions, morbidity, and mortality: New perspectives from psychoneuroimmunology. *Annual Review of Psychology,* 53, 83–107.

Kiehl, K. A., Bates, A. T., Laurens, K. R., Hare, R. D., & Liddle, P. F. (2006). Brain potentials implicate temporal lobe abnormalities in criminal psychopaths. *Journal of Abnormal Psychology,* 115, 443–453.

Kihlstrom, J. F. (1993). The continuum of consciousness. *Consciousness and Cognition,* 2, 334–354.

Kihlstrom, J. F., Glisky, M. L., & Angiulo, M. J. (1994). Dissociative tendencies and dissociative disorders. *Journal of Abnormal Psychology,* 103, 117–124.

Kilbride, H. W., Castor, C. A., & Fuger, K. L. (2006). School-age outcome of children with prenatal cocaine exposure following early case management. *Journal of Developmental and Behavioral Pediatrics,* 27, 181–187.

Killen, M., Crystal, D. S., & Watanabe, H. (2002). Japanese and American children's evaluations of peer exclusion, tolerance of differences, and prescriptions for conformity. *Child Development,* 73, 1788–1802.

Kim, H., & Chung, R. H. (2003). Relationship of recalled parenting style to self-perception in Korean American college students. *Journal of Genetic Psychology,* 164, 481–492.

Kim, J. E., & Moen, P. (2001). Moving into retirement: Preparation and transitions in late midlife. In M. E. Lachman (Ed.), *Handbook of midlife development* (pp. 487–527). New York: Wiley.

Kim, J. E., & Moen, P. (2002). Retirement transitions, gender, and psychological well-being: A life-course, ecological model. *Journal of Gerontology, Series B: Psychological Sciences and Social Sciences,* 57, P212–P222.

Kimball, M. M. (1986). Television and sex-role attitudes. In T. M. Williams (Ed.), *The impact of television* (pp. 265–301). New York: Academic Press.

Kimm, S. Y., Glynn, N. W., Aston, C. E., Poehlman, E. T., & Daniels, S. R. (2001). Effects of race, cigarette smoking, and use of contraceptive medications on resting energy expenditure in young women. *American Journal of Epidemiology,* 154, 718–724.

Kimura, D. (2000). *Sex and cognition.* Cambridge, MA: MIT Press.

King, N. H., Gullone, E., Tonge, B. J., & Ollendick, T. H. (1993). Self-reports of panic attacks and manifest anxiety in adolescents. *Behaviour Research and Therapy,* 31, 111–116.

King, P. M., & Kitchener, K. S. (1994). *Developing reflective judgment: Understanding and promoting intellectual growth and critical thinking in adolescents and adults.* San Francisco: Jossey-Bass.

Kinnish, K. K., Strassberg, D. S., & Turner, C. W. (2005). Sex differences in the flexibility of sexual orientation: A multidimensional retrospective assessment. *Archives of Sexual Behavior,* 34, 173–183.

Kinomura, S., Larsson, J., Gulyas, B., & Roland, P. E. (1996). Activation by attention of the human reticular formation and thalamic intralaminar nuclei. *Science,* 271, 512–515.

Kinsey, A. C., Pomeroy, W. B., & Martin, C. E. (1948). *Sexual behavior in the human male.* Philadelphia: Saunders.

Kinsey, A. C., Pomeroy, W. B., Martin, C. E., & Gebhard, P. H. (1953). *Sexual behavior in the human female.* Philadelphia: Saunders.

Kirkbride, J. B., Morgan, C., Fearon, P., Dazzan, P., Murray, R. M., & Jones, P. B. (2007). Neighborhood-level effects on psychoses: Re-examining the role of context. *Psychological Medicine,* 37, 1413–1425.

Kirkpatrick, S. A., & Locke, E. A. (1991). Leadership: Do traits matter? *Academy of Management Executive,* 5, 48–60.

Kirsch, I. (1994). Cognitive-behavioral hypnotherapy. In J. W. Rhue, S. J. Lynn, & I. Kirsch (Eds.), *Handbook of clinical hypnosis* (pp. 151–172). Washington, DC: American Psychological Association.

Kirsch, I. (2000). The response set theory of hypnosis. *American Journal of Clinical Hypnosis, 42*, 274–292.

Kirsch, I., & Lynn, S. J. (1995). The altered state of hypnosis. *American Psychologist, 50*, 846–858.

Kirsch, I., & Lynn, S. J. (1997). Hypnotic involuntariness and the automaticity of everyday life. *American Journal of Clinical Hypnosis, 40*, 329–348.

Kirsch, I., Montgomery, G., & Sapirstein, G. (1995). Hypnosis as an adjunct to cognitive behavioral psychotherapy: A meta-analysis. *Journal of Consulting and Clinical Psychology, 63*, 214–220.

Kisilevsky, B. S., Hains, S. M., Lee, K., Xie, X., Huang, H., Ye, H. H., et al. (2003). Effects of experience on fetal voice recognition. *Psychological Science, 14*, 220–224.

Klass, D. (1993). Solace and immortality: Bereaved parents' continuing bond with their children. *Death Studies, 17*, 343–368.

Klein, D. N., Durbin, C. E., Shankman, S. A., & Santiago, N. J. (2002). Depression and personality. In J. H. Gotlib & C. L. Hammen (Eds.), *Handbook of depression* (pp. 115–140). New York: Guilford Press.

Klein, D. N., Lewinsohn, P. M., & Seeley, J. R. (2001). A family study of major depressive disorder in a community sample of adolescents. *Archives of General Psychiatry, 58*, 13–21.

Klein, S. B. (1987). *Learning.* New York: McGraw-Hill.

Klein, T. W., & Newton, C. A. (2007). Therapeutic potential of cannabinoid-based drugs. *Advances in Experimental Medicine and Biology, 601*, 395–413.

Kleiner, K. (2004). What we gave up for color vision. *New Scientist, 181*, p. 12.

Kleinknecht, R. A. (1991). *Mastering anxiety: The nature and treatment of anxious conditions.* New York: Plenum.

Klinger, E., Bouchard, S., Legeron, P., Roy, S., Lauer, F., Chemin, I., et al. (2005). Virtual reality therapy versus cognitive behavior therapy for social phobia: A preliminary controlled study. *Cyberpsychology and Behavior, 8*, 76–88.

Klonoff, E. A., Landrine, H., & Campbell, R. (2000). Sexist discrimination may account for well-known gender differences in psychiatric symptoms. *Psychology of Women Quarterly, 24*, 93–99.

Kluft, R. P. (1999). Current issues in dissociative identity disorder. *Journal of Practical Psychology and Behavioral Health, 5*, 3–19.

Kobasa, S. C. (1982). Commitment and coping in stress resistance among lawyers. *Journal of Personality and Social Psychology, 42*, 707–717.

Kochanska, G. (1995). Children's temperament, mothers' discipline, and security of attachment: Multiple pathways to emerging internalization. *Child Development, 66*, 597–615.

Koff, E., & Rierdan, J. (1995). Early adolescent girls' understanding of menstruation. *Women and Health, 22*, 1–19.

Koh, K. B., Choe, E., Song, J. E., & Lee, E. H. (2006). Effect of coping on endocrinoimmune functions in different stress situations. *Psychiatry Research, 143*, 223–234.

Kohlberg, L. (1969). Stage and sequence: The cognitive-developmental approach to socialization. In D. A. Goslin (Ed.), *Handbook of socialization theory and research* (pp. 347–480). Chicago: Rand McNally.

Kohlberg, L., Levine, C., & Hewer, A. (1983). *Moral stages: A current formulation and a response to critics.* Basel, Switzerland: Karger.

Köhler, W. (1925). *The mentality of apes.* New York: Harcourt Brace.

Kohn, P. M., & Macdonald, J. E. (1992). The survey of recent life experiences: A decontaminated hassles scales for adults. *Journal of Behavioral Medicine, 15*, 221–236.

Kolassa, I. T., & Elbert, T. (2007). Structural and functional neuroplasticity in relation to traumatic stress. *Current Directions in Psychological Science, 16*, 321–325.

Kolb, B. (1989). Brain development, plasticity, and behavior. *American Psychologist, 44*(9), 1203–1212.

Konkol, R. J., Murphey, L. J., Ferriero, D. M., Dempsey, D. A., & Olsen, G. D. (1994). Cocaine metabolites in the neonate: Potential for toxicity. *Journal of Child Neurology, 9*(3), 242–248.

Koob, G. F., & Bloom, F. E. (1988). Cellular and molecular mechanisms of drug dependence. *Science, 242*, 715–723.

Kopelman, P. G. (2000). Obesity as a medical problem. *Nature, 404*, 635–643.

Kopta, S. M., Lueger, R. J., Saunders, S. M., & Howard, K. I. (1999). Individual psychotherapy outcome and process research: Challenges leading to greater turmoil or a positive transition? *Annual Review of Psychology, 50*, 441–469.

Koslowsky, M., & Babkoff, H. (1992). Meta-analysis of the relationship between total sleep deprivation and performance. *Chronobiology International, 9*, 132–136.

Koss, M. P., & Kilpatrick, D. G. (2001). Rape and sexual assault. In E. Gerrity (Ed.), *The mental health consequences of torture* (pp. 177–193). New York: Kluwer Academic/Plenum Press.

Kosslyn, S. M. (1994). *Image and brain: The resolution of the imagery debate.* Cambridge, MA: MIT Press.

Kosslyn, S. M., Ball, T. M., & Reiser, B. J. (1978). Visual images preserve metric spatial information: Evidence from studies of image scanning. *Journal of Experimental Psychology: Human Perception and Performance, 4*, 47–60.

Koughan, M. (1975, February 23). Arthur Friedman's outrage: Employees decide their pay. *Washington Post.*

Kowalski, K. (2003). The emergence of ethnic and racial attitudes in preschool-aged children. *Journal of Social Psychology, 143*, 677–690.

Kozart, M. F. (2002). Understanding efficacy in psychotherapy. *American Journal of Orthopsychiatry, 72*, 217–231.

Kozlowski, S. W., & Bell, B. S. (2003). Work groups and teams in organizations. In W. C. Borman, D. R. Ilgen, & R. J. Klimoski (Eds.), *Handbook of psychology: Industrial and organizational psychology* (Vol. 12, pp. 333–375). New York: Wiley.

Kraft, J. B., Peters, E. J., Slager, S. L., Jenkins, G. D., Reinalda, M. S., McGrath, P. J., et al. (2007). Analysis of association between the serotonin transporter and antidepressant response in a large clinical sample. *Biological Psychiatry, 61*, 734–742.

Kraft, J. M. (1996). Prenatal alcohol consumption and outcomes for children: A review of the literature. In R. L. Parrott & C. M. Condit (Eds.), *Evaluating women's health messages: A resource book* (pp. 175–189). Thousand Oaks, CA: Sage.

Krantz, D. S., & McCeney, M. K. (2002). Effects of psychological and social factors on organic disease: A critical assessment of research on coronary heart disease. *Annual Reviews of Psychology, 53*, 341–369.

Kraut, R. E. (1982). Social presence, facial feedback, and emotion. *Journal of Personality and Social Psychology, 42*, 853–863.

Kreider, R. M., (2005). Number, timing, and duration of marriages and divorces: 2001. *Current Population Reports, P70–97.* Washington, DC: U.S. Census Bureau.

Kremer, I., Bachner-Melman, R., Reshef, A., Broude, L., Nemanov, L., Gritsenko, I., et al. (2005). Association of the serotonin transporter gene with smoking behavior. *American Journal of Psychiatry, 162*, 924–930.

Krijn, M., Emmelkamp, P. M., Olafsson, R. P., & Biemond, R. (2004). Virtual reality exposure therapy of anxiety disorders: A review. *Clinical Psychology Review, 24*, 259–281.

Kropp, P., Siniatchkin, M., & Gerber, W.-D. (2002). On the pathophysiology of migraine—Links for "empirically based treatment" with neurofeedback. *Applied Psychophysiology and Biofeedback, 27*, 203–213.

Krosnick, J. A., & Alwin, D. F. (1989). Aging and susceptibility to attitude change. *Journal of Personality and Social Psychology, 57*, 416–425.

Krystal, J. H., Staley, J., Mason, G., Petrakis, I. L., Kaufman, J., Harris, R. A., et al. (2006). Gamma-aminobutyric acid type A receptors and alcoholism: Intoxication, dependence, vulnerability, and treatment. *Archives of General Psychiatry, 63*, 957–968.

Kübler-Ross, E. (1969). *On death and dying.* New York: Macmillan.

Kübler-Ross, E. (1974). *Questions and answers on death and dying.* New York: Macmillan.

Kumada, T., Jiang, Y., Cameron, D. B., & Komuro, H. (2007). How does alcohol impair neuronal migration? *Journal of Neuroscience Research, 85*, 465–470.

Kumari, V., ffytche, D. H., Williams, S. C., & Gray, J. A. (2004). Personality predicts brain responses to cognitive demands. *Journal of Neuroscience, 24*, 10636–10641.

Kung, H. S., Hoyert, D. L., Xu, J., & Murphy, S. L. (2008). Deaths: Final data for 2005. *National Vital Statistics Reports, 56*(10).

Kurdek, L. A. (1999). The nature and predictors of the trajectory of change in marital quality for husbands and wives over the first 10 years of marriage. *Developmental Psychology, 35*, 1283–1296.

Kuriyama, K., Stickgold, R., & Walker, M. P. (2004). Sleep-dependent learning and motor-skill complexity. *Learning and Memory, 11*, 705–713.

Laakmann, G., Schuele, C., Lorkowski, G., Baghai, R., Kuhn, K., & Ehrentraut, S. (1998). Buspirone and lorazepam in the treatment of generalized anxiety disorder in outpatients. *Psychopharmacology, 136*, 357–366.

LaBar, K. S. (2007). Beyond fear: Emotional memory mechanisms in the human brain. *Current Directions in Psychological Science, 16*, 173–177.

Lacayo, A. (1995). Neurologic and psychiatric complications of cocaine abuse. *Neuropsychiatry, Neuropsychology, and Behavioral Neurology, 8*(1), 53–60.

Lahey, B. B., Pelham, W. E., Loney, J., Kipp, H., Ehrhardt, A., Lee, S. S., et al. (2004). Three-year predictive validity of DSM-IV attention deficit hyperactivity disorder in children diagnosed at 4–6 years of age. *American Journal of Psychiatry, 161*, 2014–2020.

Lambert, M. J., & Bergen, A. E. (1994). The effectiveness of psychotherapy. In A. E. Bergen & S. L. Garfield (Eds.), *Handbook of psychotherapy and behavior change* (4th ed., pp. 143–189). New York: Wiley.

Lambeth, G. S., & Hallett, M. (2002). Promoting healthy decision making in relationships: Developmental interventions with young adults on college and university campuses. In C. L.

& D. R. Atkinson (Eds.), *Counseling across the lifespan: Prevention and treatment* (pp. 209–226). Thousand Oaks, CA: Sage.

Lancet, D. Ben-Arie, N., Cohen, S., Gat, U., Gross-Isseroff, R., Horn-Saban, S., et al. (1993). Olfactory receptors: Transduction diversity, human psychophysics and genome analysis. In D. Chadwick, J. Marsh, & J. Goode (Eds.), *The molecular basis of smell and taste transduction* (pp. 131–146). New York: Wiley.

Landabaso, M. A., Iraurgi, I., Sanz, J., Calle, R., Ruiz de Apodaka, J., Jimenez-Lerma, J. M., et al. (1999). Naltrexone in the treatment of alcoholism: Two-year follow up results. *European Journal of Psychiatry, 13*, 97–105.

Lang, A. J. & Stein, M. B. (2001). Social phobia: Prevalence and diagnostic threshold. *Journal of Clinical Psychiatry, 62*(Suppl. 1), 5–10.

Lange, T., Dimitrov, S., Fehm, H. L., Westermann, J., & Born, J. (2006). Shift of monocyte function toward cellular immunity during sleep. *Archives of Internal Medicine, 166*, 1695–1700.

Langlois, J. H., Roggman, L. A., Casey, R. J., Ritter, J. M., Rieser-Danner, L. A., & Jenkins, V. Y. (1987). Infant preferences for attractive faces: Rudiments of a stereotype? *Developmental Psychology, 23*, 363–369.

Langreth, R. (2000, May 1). Every little bit helps: How even moderate exercise can have a big impact on your health. *Wall Street Journal*, p. R5.

Largo-Wight, E., Peterson, P. M., & Chen, W. W. (2005). Perceived problem solving, stress, and health among college students. *American Journal of Health Behavior, 29*, 360–370.

Larkin, M. (1998). On the trail of human pheromones. *Lancet, 351*, 809.

Latané, B., & Darley, J. (1969). Bystander "apathy." *American Scientist, 57*, 244–268.

Latané, B., & L'Herrou, T. (1996). Spatial clustering in the conformity game: Dynamic social impact in electronic groups. *Journal of Personality and Social Psychology, 70*, 1218–1230.

Lating, J. M., Sherman, M. F., Everly, G. S., Jr., Lowry, J. L., & Peragine, T. F. (2004). PTSD reactions and functioning of American Airlines flight attendants in the wake of September 11. *Journal of Nervous and Mental Disorders, 192*, 435–441.

Laubmeier, K. K., Zakowski, S. G., & Bair, J. P. (2004). The role of spirituality in the psychological adjustment to cancer. A test of the transactional model of stress and coping. *International Journal of Behavioral Medicine, 11*, 48–55.

Laugharne, J., Janca, A., & Widiger, T. (2007). Posttraumatic stress disorder and terrorism: Five years after 9/11. *Current Opinion in Psychiatry, 20*, 36–41.

Laumann, E. O., Gagnon, J. H., Michael, R. T., & Michaels, S. (1994). *The social organization of sexuality: Sexual practices in the United States*. Chicago: University of Chicago Press.

Lavoie, C., & Desrochers, S. (2002). Visual habituation at five months: Short-term reliability of measures obtained with a new polynomial regression criterion. *Journal of Genetic Psychology, 163*, 261–271.

Laws, D. R. (2001). Olfactory aversion: Notes on procedure, with speculations on its mechanism of effect. *Sex Abuse, 13*, 275–287.

Lazarus, R. S. (1990). Theory-based stress measurement. *Psychological Inquiry, 1*, 3–13.

Lazarus, R. S. (1991). Cognition and motivation in emotion. *American Psychologist, 46*, 352–367.

Lazarus, R. S. (1993). From psychological stress to the emotions: A history of changing outlooks. *Annual Review of Psychology, 44*, 1–21.

Lazarus, R. S. (1995). Vexing research problems inherent in cognitive-mediational theories of emotion—and some solutions. *Psychological Inquiry, 6*, 183–197.

Lazarus, R. S., & Folkman, S. (1984). *Stress, appraisal, and coping*. New York: Springer.

Leary, C., Kelley, M., Morrow, J., & Mikulka, P. (2008). Parental use of physical punishment as related to family environment, psychological well-being, and personality in undergraduates. *Journal of Family Violence, 23*, 1–7.

LeBlanc, J., Ducharme, M. B., & Thompson, M. (2004). Study on the correlation of the autonomic nervous system response to a stressor of high discomfort with personality traits. *Physiology of Behavior, 82*, 647–652.

Lebow, J. L., & Gurman, A. S. (1995). Research assessing couple and family therapy. *Annual Review of Psychology, 46*, 27–57.

Lecanuet, J.-P., Manera, S., & Jacquet, A.-Y. (2002, April). *Fetal cardiac responses to maternal sentences, to playback of these sentences, and to their recordings by another woman's voice.* Paper presented at the XIII International Conference on Infant Studies, Toronto, Ontario, Canada.

LeDoux, J. (1998). Fear and the brain: Where have we been, and where are we going? *Biological Psychiatry, 44*, 1229–1238.

Lee, A. Y. (2001). The mere exposure effect: An uncertainty reduction explanation revisited. *Personality and Social Psychology Bulletin, 27*, 1255–1266.

Lefcourt, H. M. (2001). The humor solution. In C. R. Snyder (Ed.), *Coping with stress: Effective people and processes* (pp. 68–92). New York: Oxford University Press.

Lefcourt, H. M., & Davidson-Katz, K. (1991). The role of humor and the self. In C. R. Synder & D. R. Forsyth (Eds.), *Handbook of social and clinical psychology: The health perspective* (pp. 41–56). New York: Pergamon Press.

Leibowitz, S. F. (1991). Brain neuropeptide Y: An integrator of endocrine, metabolic, and behavioral processes. *Brain Research Bulletin, 27*, 333–337.

Leichsenring, F., & Leibing, E. (2007). Psychodynamic psychotherapy: A systematic review of techniques, indications and empirical evidence. *Psychology and Psychotherapy, 80*(Pt. 2), 217–228.

Leigh, B. C. (1989). In search of the seven dwarves: Issues of measurement and meaning in alcohol expectancy research. *Psychological Bulletin, 105*, 361–373.

Lenox, R. H., & Manji, H. K. (1995). Lithium. In A. F. Schatzberg & C. B. Nemeroff (Eds.), *The American Psychiatric Press textbook of psychopharmacology* (pp. 303–349). Washington, DC: American Psychiatric Press.

Leon, S. C., Kopta, S. M., Howard, K. I., & Lutz, W. (1999). Predicting patients' responses to psychotherapy: Are some more predictable than others? *Journal of Consulting and Clinical Psychology, 67*, 698–704.

LePine, J. A., Erez, A., & Johnston, D. E. (2002). The nature and dimensionality of organizational citizenship behavior: A critical review and a meta-analysis. *Journal of Applied Psychology, 87*(1), 52–65.

Lester, B. M., Andreozzi, L., & Appiah, L. (2004). Substance use during pregnancy: Time for policy to catch up with research. *Harm Reduction Journal, 1*, 5–49.

Lester, B. M., Corwin, M. J., Sepkoski, C., Seifer, R., Peucker, M., McLaughlin, S., et al. (1991). Neurobehavioral syndromes in cocaine-exposed newborn infants. *Child Development, 62*, 694–705.

Lester, D. (1992). Suicide and disease. *Loss, Grief, and Care, 6*, 173–181.

LeVay, S. (1996). *Queer science: The use and abuse of research into homosexuality*. Cambridge, MA: MIT Press.

Levenson, R. W., Carstensen, L. L., & Gottman, J. M. (1993). Long-term marriage: Age, gender, and satisfaction. *Psychology and Aging, 8*, 301–313.

Levenson, R. W., Ekman, P., & Friesen, W. V. (1990). Voluntary facial action generates emotion-specific nervous system activity. *Psychophysiology, 27*, 363–384.

Levin, B. E., & Routh, V. H. (1996). Role fo the brain in energy balance and obesity. *The American Journal of Physiology, 271*, R491–500.

Levine, R. A., & Campbell, D. T. (1972). *Ethnocentrism: Theories of conflict, ethnic attitudes, and group behavior*. New York: Wiley.

Levinson, D. F., Evgrafov, O. V., Knowles, J. A., Potash, J. B., Weissman, M. M., Scheftner, W. A., et al. (2007). Genetics of recurrent early-onset major depression (GenRED): Significant linkage on chromosome 15q25–q26 after fine mapping with single nucleotide polymorphism markers. *American Journal of Psychiatry, 164*, 259–264.

Levitt, A. G., & Utmann, J. G. A. (1992). From babbling towards the sound systems of English and French: A longitudinal two-case study. *Journal of Child Language, 19*, 19–40.

Levy, B. R., & Myers, L. M. (2004). Preventive health behaviors influenced by self-perceptions of aging. *Preventive Medicine, 39*, 625–629.

Levy, B. R., Slade, M. D., Kunkel, S. R., & Kasl, S. V. (2002). Longevity increased by positive self-perceptions of aging. *Journal of Personality and Social Psychology, 83*, 261–270.

Levy, G. D., Taylor, M. G., & Gelman, S. A. (1995). Traditional and evaluative aspects of flexibility in gender roles, social conventions, moral rules, and physical laws. *Child Development, 66*, 515–531.

Levy, N. A., & Janicak, P. G. (2000). Calcium channel antagonists for the treatment of bipolar disorder. *Bipolar Disorders, 2*, 108–119.

Levy-Shiff, R. (1994). Individual and contextual correlates of marital change across the transition to parenthood. *Developmental Psychology, 30*, 591–601.

Lewinsohn, P. M. (1974). A behavioral approach to depression. In R. J. Friedman & M. M. Katz (Eds.), *The psychology of depression: Contemporary theory and research* (pp. 157–185). Washington, DC: Winston-Wiley.

Lewinsohn, P. M., Clark, G. N., Hops, H., & Andrews, J. (1990). Cognitive-behavioral treatment for depressed adolescents. *Behavior Therapy, 21*, 385–401.

Lewinsohn, P. M., Klein, D. N., & Seeley, J. R. (2000). Bipolar disorder during adolescence and young adulthood in a community sample. *Bipolar Disorders, 2*, 281–293.

Lewinsohn, P. M., Rohde, P., & Seeley, J. R. (1994). Psychosocial risk factors for future adolescent suicide attempts. *Journal of Consulting and Clinical Psychology, 62*, 297–305.

Lewis, D. O. (1992). From abuse to violence: Psychophysiological consequences of maltreatment. *Journal of the American Academy of Child and Adolescent Psychiatry, 31,* 383–391.

Lewis, D. O., Picus, J. H., Feldman, M., Jackson, L., & Bard, B. (1986). Psychiatric, neurological, and psychoeducational characteristics of 15 death row inmates in the United States. *American Journal of Psychiatry, 143,* 838–845.

Li, C. E., DiGiuseppe, R., & Froh, J. (2006). The roles of sex, gender, and coping in adolescent depression. *Adolescence, 41,* 409–415.

Li, S., Lindenberger, U., Hommel, B., Aschersleben, G., Prinz, W., & Baltes, P. B. (2004). Transformations in the couplings among intellectual abilities and constituent cognitive processes across the life span. *Psychological Science, 15,* 155–163.

Libersat, F., & Pflueger, H.-J. (2004). Monoamines and the orchestration of behavior. *BioScience, 54,* 17–25.

Liberzon, I., Taylor, S. F., Amdur, R., Jung, T. D., Chamberlain, K. R., Minoshima, S., et al. (1999). Brain activation in PTSD in response to trauma-related stimuli. *Biological Psychiatry, 45,* 817–826.

Lichter, D. T., Qian, Z., & Mellott, L. M. (2006). Marriage or dissolution? Union transitions among poor cohabiting women. *Demography, 43,* 223–240.

Lieberman, J., Chakos, M., Wu, H., Alvir, J., Hoffman, E., Robinson, D., et al. (2001). Longitudinal study of brain morphology in first episode schizophrenia. *Biological Psychiatry, 49,* 487–499.

Lieberman, J., Tollefson, G., Tohen, M., Green, A. I., Gur, R. E., Kahn, R., et al. (2003). Comparative efficacy and safety of atypical and conventional antipsychotic drugs in first-episode psychosis: A randomized, double-blind trial of olanzapine versus haloperidol. *American Journal of Psychiatry, 160,* 1396–1404.

Liebert, R. M., & Spiegler, M. D. (1998). *Personality: Strategies and issues* (8th ed.), Pacific Grove, CA: Brooks/Cole.

Lilienfeld, S. O., Wood, J. M., & Garb, H. N. (2000). The scientific status of projective techniques. *Psychological Science in the Public Interest, 1,* 27–66.

Lindau, S. T., Schumm, L. P., Laumann, E. O., Levinson, W., O'Muircheartaigh, C. A., & Waite, L. J. (2007). A study of sexuality and health among older adults in the United States. *New England Journal of Medicine, 357,* 762–774.

Lindenmayer, J. P., Khan, A., Iskander, A., Abad, M. T., & Parker, B. (2007). A randomized controlled trial of olanzapine versus haloperidol in the treatment of primary negative symptoms and neurocognitive deficits in schizophrenia. *Journal of Clinical Psychiatry, 68,* 368–379.

Ling, D., Niu, T., Feng, Y., Xing, H., & Xu, X. (2004). Association between polymorphism of the dopamine transporter gene and early smoking onset: An interaction risk on nicotine dependence. *Journal of Human Genetics, 49,* 35–39.

Linville, P. W., Fischer, G. W., & Salovey, P. (1989). Perceived distributions of characteristics on in-group and out-group members: Empirical evidence and a computer simulation. *Journal of Personality and Social Psychology, 57,* 165–188.

Liossi, C., White, P., & Hatira, P. (2006). Randomized clinical trial of local anesthetic versus a combination of local anesthetic with self-hypnosis in the management of pediatric procedure-related pain. *Health Psychology, 25,* 307–315.

Lippa, R. (2003). Handedness, sexual orientation, and gender-related personality traits in men and women. *Archives of Sexual Behavior, 32,* 103–114.

Lipsitt, L.P. (2003). Crib death: A biobehavioral phenomenon? *Current Directions in Psychological Science, 12,* 164–170.

Littleton, H., Horsley, S., John, S., & Nelson, D. V. (2007). Trauma coping strategies and psychological distress: A meta-analysis. *Journal of Trauma and Stress, 20,* 977–988.

Livesley, W. J., Jang, K. L., & Vernon, P. A. (1998). Phenotypic and genotypic structure of traits delineating personality disorder. *Archives of General Psychiatry, 55,* 941–948.

Livson, N., & Peskin, H. (1980). Perspectives on adolescence from longitudinal research. In J. Adelson (Ed.), *Handbook of adolescent psychology* (pp. 47–98). New York: Wiley.

Lloyd, G., Alexander, A. A., Rice, D. G., & Greenfield, N. S. (1980). Life events as predictors of academic performance. *Journal of Human Stress, 6,* 15–26.

Lockhart, R. S., & Craik, F. I. M. (1990). Levels of processing: A retrospective commentary on a framework for memory research. *Canadian Journal of Psychology, 44,* 87–112.

Loewenstein, W. R. (1960). Biological transducers. *Scientific American, 203,* 98–108.

Loftus, E. F. (1979). *Eyewitness testimony.* Cambridge, MA: Harvard University Press.

Loftus, E. F. (2000). Remembering what never happened. In E. Tulving (Ed.), *Memory, consciousness, and the brain* (pp. 106–118). Philadelphia: Psychology Press.

Loftus, E. F., & Palmer, J. C. (1974). Reconstruction of automobile destruction: An example of the interaction between language and memory. *Journal of Verbal Learning and Verbal Behavior, 13,* 585–589.

Loftus, E. F., & Zanni, G. (1975). Eyewitness testimony: The influence of the wording of a question. *Bulletin of the Psychonomic Society, 5,* 86–88.

Logie, R. H. (1999). State of the art: Working memory. *Psychologist, 12,* 174–178.

Logue, A. W. (1979). Taste aversion and the generality of the laws of learning. *Psychological Bulletin, 86,* 276–296.

Loney, B. R., Taylor, J., Butler, M. A., & Iacono, W. G. (2007). Adolescent psychopathy features: 6-year temporal stability and the prediction of externalizing symptoms during the transition to adulthood. *Aggressive Behavior, 33,* 242–252.

Long, B. C., & van Stavel, R. (1995). Effects of exercise training on anxiety: A meta-analysis. *Journal of Applied Sport Psychology, 7,* 167–189.

Lorenz, F. O., Simons, R. L., Conger, R. D., Elder, G. H., Jr., Johnson, C., & Chao, W. (1997). Married and recently divorced mothers' stressful events and distress: Tracing change across time. *Journal of Marriage and the Family, 59,* 219–232.

Lorenz, F. O., Wickrama, K. A., Conger, R. D., & Elder, G. H., Jr. (2006). The short-term and decade-long effects of divorce on women's midlife health. *Journal of Health and Social Behavior, 47,* 111–125.

Lourenco, O., & Machado, A. (1996). In defense of Piaget's theory: A reply to 10 common criticisms. *Psychological Review, 103,* 143–164.

Lu, N. Z., Eshleman, A. J., Janowsky, A. & Bethea, C. L. (2003). Ovarian steroid regulation of serotonin reuptake transporter (SERT) binding, distribution, and function in female macaques. *Molecular Psychiatry, 8,* 353–360.

Lucas, R. E. (2005). Time does not heal all wounds: A longitudinal study of reaction and adaptation to divorce. *Psychological Science, 16,* 945–950.

Luecken, L. J., & Compas, B. E. (2002). Stress, coping, and immune function in breast cancer. *Annals of Behavioral Medicine, 24,* 336–344.

Lumer, E. D., Friston, K. J., & Rees, G. (1998, June 19). Neural correlates of perceptual rivalry in the human brain. *Science, 280,* 1930–1934.

Lykken, D. T., McGue, M., Tellegen, A., & Bouchard, T. J. (1992). Emergenesis. *American Psychologist, 47,* 1565–1567.

Lynn, S. J. (1997). Automaticity and hypnosis: A sociocognitive account. *International Journal of Clinical and Experimental Hypnosis, 45,* 239–250.

Lytton, H., & Romney, D. M. (1991). Parents' differential socialization of boys and girls: A meta-analysis. *Psychological Bulletin, 109,* 267–296.

Maas, J. B. (1998). *The sleep advantage: Preparing your mind for peak performance.* New York: Villard.

Macht, M., & Mueller, J. (2007). Immediate effects of chocolate on experimentally induced mood states. *Appetite, 49,* 667–674.

Mackay, J. (2000). *The Penguin atlas of human sexual behavior: Sexuality and sexual practices around the world.* New York: Penguin Putnam.

MacKinnon, D., Jamison, K. R., & DePaulo, J. R. (1997). Genetics of manic depressive illness. *Annual Review of Neuroscience, 20,* 355–373.

Maddi, S. R., & Kobasa, S. C. (1984). *The hardy executive: Health under stress.* Homewood, IL: Dorsey Press.

Maguire, E. A., Woollett, K., & Spiers, H. J. (2006). London taxi drivers and bus drivers: A structural MRI and neuropsychological analysis. *Hippocampus, 16,* 1091–1101.

Magura, S., Laudet, A. B., Mahmood, D., Rosenblum, A., & Knight, E. (2002). Adherence to medication regimes and participation in dual-focus self-help groups. *Psychiatric Services, 53,* 310–316.

Maheu, F. S., Joober, R., Beaulieu, S., & Lupien, S. J. (2004). Differential effects of adrenergic and corticosteroid hormonal systems on human short- and long-term declarative memory for emotionally arousing material. *Behavioral Neuroscience, 118,* 420–428.

Main, M., & Solomon, J. (1990). Procedures for identifying infants as disorganized/disoriented during the Ainsworth Strange Situation. In M. Greenberg, D. Cicchetti, & M. Cummings (Eds.), *Attachment in the preschool years: Theory, research, and intervention* (pp. 121–160). Chicago: University of Chicago Press.

Maisonneuve, J., Palmade, G., & Fourment, C. (1952). Selective choices and propinquity. *Sociometry, 15,* 135–140.

Maj, M., Pirozzi, R., Magliano, L., & Bartoli, L. (1997). Long-term outcome of lithium prophylaxis in bipolar disorder: A 5-year prospective study of 402 patients at a lithium clinic. *American Journal of Psychiatry, 155,* 30–55.

Majdandzic, M., & van den Boom, D. C. (2007). Multimethod longitudinal assessment of temperament in early childhood. *Journal of Personality, 75,* 121–168.

Makino, H., & Jitsumori, M. (2007). Discrimination of artificial categories structured by family resemblances: A comparative study in people (Homo sapiens) and pigeons (Columba livia). *Journal of Comparative Psychology, 121,* 22–33.

Malaspina, D., Harlap, S., Fennig, S., Heiman, D., Nahon, D., Feldman, D., et al. (2001). Advancing paternal age and the risk of schizophrenia. *Archives of General Psychiatry, 58,* 361–367.

Malina, R. M. (1990). Physical growth and performance during the transitional years (9–16). In R. Montemayor, G. R. Adams, & T. P. Gullotta (Eds.), *From childhood to adolescence: A transitional period?* (pp. 41–62). Newbury Park, CA: Sage.

Mann, R. D. (1959). A review of the relationships between personality and performance in small groups. *Psychological Bulletin, 56,* 241–270.

Manning, W. D. (2001). Childbearing in cohabiting unions: Racial and ethnic differences. *Family Planning Perspectives, 33,* 217–223.

Marañon, I., Echeburúa, E., & Grijalvo, J. (2004). Prevalence of personality disorders in patients with eating disorders: A pilot study using the IPDE. *European Eating Disorders Review, 12,* 217–222.

Marazzitti, D., Rotondo, A., Presta, S., Pancioloi-Guasagnucci, M. L., Palego, L., & Conti, L. (1993). Role of serotonin in human aggressive behavior. *Aggressive Behavior, 19,* 347–353.

Marcia, J. E. (1980). Identity in adolescence. In J. Adelson (Ed.), *Handbook of adolescent psychology* (pp. 159–187). New York: Wiley.

Marcia, J. E. (2002). Identity and psychosocial development in adulthood. *Identity, 2,* 7–28.

Mareschal, D. (2000). Object knowledge in infancy: Current controversies and approaches. *Trends in Cognitive Science, 4,* 408–416.

Marijuana as medicine: How strong is the science? (1997, May). *Consumer Reports,* pp. 62–63.

Mariscal, M., Palma, S., Liorca, J., Perez-Iglesias, R., Pardo-Crespo, R., & Delgado-Rodriguez, M. (2006). Pattern of alcohol consumption during pregnancy and risk for low birth weight. *Annals of Epidemiology, 16,* 432–438.

Markman, A. B., & Ross, B. H. (2003). Category use and category learning. *Psychological Bulletin, 129,* 592–613.

Marler, P. R., Duffy, A., & Pickert, R. (1986). Vocal communication in the domestic chicken: II. Is a sender sensitive to the presence and nature of a receiver? *Animal Behavior, 34,* 194–198.

Martin, C. L., & Halverson, C. F. (1981). A schematic processing model of sex typing and stereotyping in children. *Child Development, 52,* 1119–1134.

Martin, C. L., & Halverson, C. F. (1987). The role of cognition in sex role acquisition. In D. B. Carter (Ed.), *Current conceptions of sex roles and sex typing: Theory and research* (pp. 123–137). New York: Praeger.

Martin, C. L., & Ruble, D. (2004). Children's search for gender cues: Cognitive perspectives on gender development. *Current Directions in Psychological Science, 13,* 67–70.

Martin, D. J., Garske, J. P., & Davis, M. K. (2000). Relation of the therapeutic alliance with outcome and other variables: A meta-analytic review. *Journal of Consulting and Clinical Psychology, 68,* 438–450.

Martin, G., England, G., Kaprowy, E., Kilgour, K., & Pilek, V. (1968). Operant conditioning of kindergarten-class

behavior in autistic children. *Behavior Research and Therapy, 6,* 281–294.

Martin, G., & Pear, J. (2007). *Behavior modification: What it is and how to do it* (8th ed.). Englewood Cliffs, NJ: Prentice Hall.

Maslow, A. (1968). *Toward a psychology of being* (2nd ed.). New York: Van Nostrand.

Maslow, A. (1970). *Motivation and personality* (2nd ed.). New York: Harper & Row.

Maslow, A. (1971). *The farther reaches of human nature.* New York: Viking.

Masters, W. H., & Johnson, V. E. (1966). *Human sexual response.* Boston: Little, Brown.

Masters, W. H., Johnson, V. E., & Kolodny, R. C. (1993). *Biological foundations of human sexuality.* New York: HarperCollins.

Mathew, R., Wilson, W., Blazer, D., & George, L. (1993). Psychiatric disorders in adult children of alcoholics: Data from the epidemiologic catchment area project. *American Journal of Psychiatry, 150,* 793–796.

Matlin, M. W., & Foley, H. J. (1997). *Sensation and perception.* Boston: Allyn & Bacon.

Matsuda, L. A., Lolait, S. J., Brownstein, M. J., Young, A. C., & Bonner, T. I. (1990). Structure of a cannabinoid receptor and functional expression of the cloned cDNA. *Nature, 346,* 561–564.

Matsumoto, D. (1994). *People: Psychology from a cross-cultural perspective.* Pacific Grove, CA: Brooks/Cole.

Mauss, I. B., Cook, C. L., Cheng, J. Y., & Gross, J. J. (2007). Individual differences in cognitive reappraisal: Experiential and physiological responses to an anger provocation. *International Journal of Psychophysiology, 66,* 116–124.

Maxmen, J. S., & Ward, N. G. (1995). *Essential psychopathology and its treatment* (2nd ed.). New York: Norton.

Maxwell, J. C., & Spence, R. T. (2003). Profiles of club drug users in treatment. *Substance Use and Misuse, 40,* 1409–1426.

Mayer, J. D., Salovey, P., Caruso, D. R., & Sitarenios, G. (2003). Measuring emotional intelligence with the MSCEIT V2.0. *Emotion, 3,* 97–105.

Mayer, R. E. (1983). *Thinking, problem solving, cognition.* San Francisco: Freeman.

Mayes, L. C., Bornstein, M. H., Chawarska, K., & Haynes, O. M. (1996). Impaired regulation of arousal in 3-month-old infants exposed prenatally to cocaine and other drugs. *Development and Psychopathology, 8*(1), 29–42.

Mazure, C. M., Keita, G. P., & Blehar, M. C. (2002). *Summit on women and depression: Proceedings and recommendations.* Washington, DC: American Psychological Association.

McAlpine, D. D., & Mechanic, D. (2000). Utilization of specialty mental health care among persons with severe mental illness: The roles of demographics, need, insurance, and risk. *Health Services Research, 35,* 277–292.

McAndrew, F. (1986). A cross-cultural study of recognition thresholds for facial expressions of emotions. *Journal of Cross-Cultural Psychology, 17,* 211–224.

McCarley, R. W. (1998). Dreams: Disguise of forbidden wishes or transparent reflections of a distinct brain state? *Annals of the New York Academy of Sciences, 843,* 116–133.

McClelland, D. C. (1987). *Human motivation.* Cambridge, UK: Cambridge University Press.

McClung, C. A. (2007). Circadian genes, rhythms and the biology of mood disorders. *Pharmacology and Therapeutics, 114,* 222–232.

McClure, E. B. (2000). A meta-analytic review of sex differences in facial expression

processing and their development in infants, children, and adolescents. *Psychological Bulletin, 126,* 424–453.

McConkey, K. M. (1995). Hypnosis, memory, and the ethics of uncertainty. *Australian Psychologist, 30,* 1–10.

McCrae, R. R., & Costa, P. T. (1998). Personality trait structure as a human universal. *American Psychologist, 52,* 509–516.

McCrae, R. R., Costa, P. T., Ostendorf, F., Angleitner, A., Hrebickova, M., Avia, M. D., et al. (2000). Nature over nurture: Temperament, personality, and life span development. *Journal of Personality and Social Psychology, 78,* 173–186.

McCrae, R. R., Costa, P. T., Pedroso de Lima, M., Simoes, A., Ostendorf, F., Angleitner, A., et al. (1999). Age differences in personality across the adult life span: Parallels in five cultures. *Developmental Psychology, 35,* 466–477.

McCrae, R. R., Costa, P. T., Terracciano, A., Parker, W. D., Mills, C. J., De Fruyt, F., et al. (2002). Personality trait development from age 12 to age 18: Longitudinal, cross-sectional, and cross-cultural analyses. *Journal of Personality and Social Psychology, 83,* 1456–1468.

McEvoy, P. M., & Nathan, P. (2007). Effectiveness of cognitive behavior therapy for diagnostically heterogeneous groups: A benchmarking study. *Journal of Consulting and Clinical Psychology, 75,* 344–350.

McFalls, J. A., Jr. (1990). The risks of reproductive impairment in the later years of childbearing. *Annual Review of Sociology, 16,* 491–519.

McGehee, D. S., Heath, M. J. S., Gelber, S., Devay, P., & Role, L. W. (1995). Nicotine enhancement of fast excitation synaptic transmissions in CNS by presynaptic receptors. *Science, 269,* 1692–1696.

McGinnis, J. M., & Foege, W. H. (1993). Actual causes of death in the United States. *Journal of the American Medical Association, 270,* 2207–2212.

McGlashan, T. H., & Hoffman, R. E. (2000). Schizophrenia as a disorder of developmentally reduced synaptic connectivity. *Archives of General Psychiatry, 57,* 637–648.

McGregor, G., Desaga, J. F., Ehlenz, K., Fischer, A., Heese, F., Hegele, A., et al. (1996). Radioimmunological measurement of leptin in plasma of obese and diabetic human subjects. *Endocrinology, 137,* 1501–1504.

McGuffin, P., Rijsdijk, F., Andrew, M., Sham, P., Katz, R., & Cardno, A. (2003). The heritability of bipolar affective disorder and the genetic relationship to unipolar depression. *Archives of General Psychiatry, 60,* 497–502.

McIntosh, D. N. (1996). Facial feedback hypotheses: Evidence, implications, and directions. *Motivation and Emotion, 20,* 121–147.

McKean, K. J. (1994). Using multiple risk factors to assess the behavioral, cognitive, and affective effects of learned helplessness. *Journal of Psychology, 128*(2), 177–183.

McKenna, M. C., Zevon, M. A., Corn, B., & Rounds, J. (1999). Psychosocial factors and the development of breast cancer: A meta-analysis. *Health Psychology, 18,* 520–531.

McKillip, J., & Reidel, S. L. (1983). External validity of matching on physical attractiveness for same and opposite sex couples. *Journal of Applied Social Psychology, 13,* 328–337.

McKim, W. A. (1997). *Drugs and behavior.* Upper Saddle River, NJ: Prentice Hall.

McLaughlin, K. A., Borkovec, T. D., & Sibrava, N. J. (2007). The effects of worry and rumination on affect states and cognitive activity. *Behavior Therapy, 38,* 23–38.

McManus, M. A., & Baratta, J. E. (1992). *The relationship of recruiting source to performance and survival.* Paper presented at the annual meeting of the Society for Industrial and Organizational Psychology, Montreal.

McMillen, D. L., Smith, S. M., & Wells-Parker, E. (1989). The effects of alcohol, expectancy, and sensation seeking on driving risk taking. *Addictive Behaviors, 14,* 477–483.

McNaughton, P. A. (1990). The light response of photoreceptors. In C. Blakemore (Ed.), *Vision: Coding and efficiency* (pp. 65–73). Cambridge, UK: Cambridge University Press.

McNeill, B., Prieto, L., Niemann, Y., Pizarro, M., Vera, E., & Gomez, S. (2001). Current directions in Chicana/o psychology. *Counseling Psychologist, 29,* 5–17.

Mediascope, Inc. (1996). *National television violence study.* Studio City, CA: Author.

Mednick, S. A., Watson, J. B., Huttunen, M., Cannon, T. D., Katila, H., Machon, R., et al. (1998). A two-hit working model of the etiology of schizophrenia. In M. F. Lenzenweger & R. H. Dworkin (Eds.), *Origins of the development of schizophrenia* (pp. 27–66). Washington, DC: American Psychological Association.

Meissner, J. S., Blanchard, E. B., & Malamood, H. S. (1997). Comparison of treatment outcome measures for irritable bowel syndrome. *Applied Psychophysiology and Biofeedback, 22,* 55–62.

Meltzer, L. J., & Mindell, J. A. (2006). Sleep and sleep disorders in children and adolescents. *Psychiatric Clinics of North America, 29,* 1059–1076.

Memmler, R. L., Cohen, B. J., & Wood, D. (1992). *Structure and function of the human body* (5th ed.). Philadelphia: J. B. Lippincott.

Mennella, J. A., & Beauchamp, G. K. (1991). Maternal diet alters the sensory qualities of human milk and nursling's behavior. *Pediatrics, 88,* 737–744.

Menzies, R. G., & Clark, J. C. (1993). A comparison of in vivo and vicarious exposure in the treatment of childhood water phobia. *Behaviour Research and Therapy, 31,* 9–15.

Meyer, D. (2007). Selective serotonin reuptake inhibitors and their effects on relationship satisfaction. *Family Journal, 15,* 392–397.

Meyer, J. P., & Allen, N. J. (1991). A three-component conceptualization of organizational commitment. *Human Resource Management Review, 1,* 61–89.

Meyer, L. (1999). Hostile classrooms. *The Advocate, 32*(1), 33–35.

Michael, G. A., Boucart, M., Degreef, J. F., & Goefroy, O. (2001). The thalamus interrupts top-down attentional control for permitting exploratory shiftings to sensory signals. *Neuroreport, 12,* 2041–2048.

Michelson, D., Bancroft, J., Targum, S., Kim, Y., & Tepner, R. (2000). Female sexual dysfunction associated with antidepressant administration: A randomized, placebo-controlled study of pharmacological intervention. *American Journal of Psychiatry, 157,* 239–243.

Milgram, S. (1963). Behavioral study of obedience. *Journal of Abnormal and Social Psychology, 67,* 371–378.

Milgram, S. (1965). Some conditions of obedience and disobedience to authority. *Human Relations, 18,* 57–76.

Milgram, S. (1974). *Obedience to authority: An experimental view.* New York: Harper & Row.

Millar, M. (2002). The effectiveness of the door-in-the-face compliance strategy on friends and strangers. *Journal of Social Psychology, 142,* 295–305.

Miller, D. T., & Ross, M. (1975). Self-serving biases in the attribution of causality: Fact or fiction? *Psychological Bulletin, 82,* 213–225.

Miller, E. (1999). The pheromone androsterol: Evolutionary considerations. *Mankind Quarterly, 39,* 455–466.

Miller, G. A. (1956). The magical number seven, plus or minus two: Some limits on our capacity for processing information. *Psychological Review, 63,* 81–97.

Miller, G. E., & Blackwell, E. (2006). Turning up the heat: Inflammation as a mechanism linking chronic stress, depression, and heart disease. *Current Directions in Psychological Science, 15,* 269–272.

Miller, I. J., Jr., & Bartoshuk, L. M. (1991). Taste perception, taste bud distribution, and spatial relationships. In T. V. Gethell, R. L. Doty, L. M. Bartoshuk, & J. B. Snow, Jr. (Eds.), *Smell and taste in health and disease* (pp. 205–233). New York: Raven.

Miller, N. S., & Gold, M. S. (1994). LSD and Ecstasy: Pharmacology, phenomenology, and treatment. *Psychiatric Annals, 24,* 131–133.

Miller, T. Q., Smith, T. W., Turner, C. W., Guijarro, M. L., & Hallet, A. J. (1996). A meta-analytic review of research on hostility and physical health. *Psychological Bulletin, 119,* 322–348.

Miller, T. Q., Turner, C. W., Tindale, R. S., Posavac, E. J., & Dugoni, B. L. (1991). Reasons for the trend toward null findings in research on Type A behavior. *Psychological Bulletin, 110,* 469–485.

Miller, W. R., & Seligman, M. E. P. (1975). Depression and learned helplessness in man. *Journal of Abnormal Psychology, 84,* 228–238.

Miller, W. R., & Thoresen, C. E. (2003). Spirituality, religion, and health. An emerging research field. *American Psychologist, 58,* 24–35.

Milliken, C. S., Auchterlonie, J. L., & Hoge, C. W. (2007). Longitudinal assessment of mental health problems among active and reserve component soldiers returning from the Iraq war. *Journal of the American Medical Association, 298,* 2141–2148.

Milling, L. S., Reardon, J. M., & Carosella, G. M. (2006). Mediation and moderation of psychological pain treatments: Response expectancies and hypnotic suggestibility. *Journal of Consulting and Clinical Psychology, 74,* 253–262.

Milner, B. (1962). Les troubles de la mémoire accompagnant des lésions hippocampiques bilatérales. In P. Passonant (Ed.), *Physiologie de l'hippocampe* (pp. 257–272). Paris: Centre National de la Recherche Scientifique.

Milton, J., & Wiseman, R. (2001). Does psi exist? Reply to Storm and Ertel (2001). *Psychological Bulletin, 127,* 434–438.

Minda, J. P., & Smith, J. D. (2002). Comparing prototype-based and exemplar-based accounts of category learning and attentional allocation. *Journal of Experimental Psychology: Learning, Memory, and Cognition, 28,* 275–292.

Mischel, W., & Shoda, Y. (1995). A cognitive-affective system theory of personality: Reconceptualizing situations, dispositions, dynamics, and invariance of personality structure. *Psychological Review, 102,* 246–268.

Miselis, R. R., & Epstein, A. N. (1970). Feeding induced by 2-deoxy-D-glucose injections into the lateral ventrical of the rat. *Physiologist, 13,* 262.

Mitelman, S. A., Buchsbaum, M. S., Brickman, A. M., & Shihabuddin, L. (2005). Cortical intercorrelations of frontal area volumes in schizophrenia. *Neuroimage, 27,* 753–770.

Miyaoka, Y., Sawada, M., Sakaguchi, T., & Shingai, T. (1987). Sensation of thirst in normal and laryngectomized man. *Perceptual and Motor Skills, 64,* 239–242.

Mobini, S., Chambers, L. C., & Yeomans, M. R. (2007). Effects of hunger state on flavour pleasantness conditioning at home: Flavour–nutrient learning vs. flavour–flavour learning. *Appetite, 48,* 20–28.

Moffitt, T. E., Brammer, G. L., Caspi, A., Fawcet, J. P., Raleigh, M., Yuwiler, A., et al. (1998). Whole blood serotonin relates to violence in an epidemiological study. *Biological Psychiatry, 43,* 446–457.

Mohr, C. (1964, March 28). Apathy is puzzle in Queens killing. *New York Times,* pp. 21, 40.

Molero, F., Navas, M. S., Gonzalez, J. L., Aleman, P., & Cuadrado, I. (2003). Paupers or riches: The perception of immigrants, tourists and ingroup members in a sample of Spanish children. *Journal of Ethnic and Migration Studies, 29,* 501–517.

Moncrieff, J. (1997). Lithium: Evidence reconsidered. *British Journal of Psychiatry, 171,* 113–119.

Mongrain, V., Lavoie, S., Selmaoui, B., Paquet, J., & Dumont, M. (2004). Phase relationships between sleep–wake cycle and underlying circadian rhythms in Morningness–Eveningness. *Journal of Biological Rhythms, 19,* 248–257.

Monteith, M., & Winters, J. (2002, May–June). Why we hate. *Psychology Today, 35,* 44–51.

Monti-Bloch, L., Diaz-Sanchez, V., Jennings-White, C., & Berliner, D. L. (1998). Modulation of serum testosterone and autonomic function through stimuluation of the male human vomeronasal organ (VNO) with pregna-4, 20-diene-3, 6-dione. *Journal of Steroid Biochemistry and Molecular Biology, 65,* 237–242.

Moore, E. G. J. (1986). Family socialization and the IQ test performance of traditionally and transracially adopted black children. *Developmental Psychology, 22,* 317–326.

Moore, S. M. (1995). Girls' understanding and social constructions of menarche. *Journal of Adolescence, 18,* 87–104.

Moreland, R. L., & Zajonc, R. B. (1977). Is stimulus recognition a necessary condition for the occurrence of mere exposure effects? *Journal of Personality and Social Psychology, 35,* 191–199.

Morgan, W. P. (1987). Reduction of state anxiety following acute physical activity. In W. P. Morgan & S. E. Golston (Eds.), *Exercise and mental health* (pp. 105–109). Washington, DC: Hemisphere.

Morgenstern, H., & Glazer, W. M. (1993). Identifying risk factors for tardive dyskinesia among long-term outpatients maintained with neuroleptic medications: Results of the Yale Tardive Dyskinesia Study. *Archives of General Psychiatry, 50,* 723–733.

Morisse, D., Batra, L., Hess, L., & Silverman, R. (1996). A demonstration of a token economy for the real world. *Applied and Preventive Psychology, 5,* 41–46.

Morlock, R. J., Tan, M., & Mitchell, D. Y. (2006). Patient characteristics and patterns of drug use for sleep complaints in the United States: Analysis of National Ambulatory Medical Survey data, 1997–2002. *Clinical Therapeutics, 28,* 1044–1053.

Mortensen, M. E., Sever, L. E., & Oakley, G. P. (1991). Teratology and the epidemiology of birth defects. In S. G. Gabbe, J. R. Niebyl, & J. L. Simpson (Eds.), *Obstetrics: Normal and problem pregnancies* (pp. 233–268). New York: Churchill Livingstone.

Morton, B. E., & Rafto, S. E. (2006). Corpus callosum size is linked to dichotic deafness and hemisphericity, not sex or handedness. *Brain and Cognition, 62,* 1–8.

Motivala, S. J., & Irwin, M. R. (2007). Sleep and immunity: Cytokine pathways linking sleep and health outcomes. *Current Directions in Psychological Science, 16,* 21–25.

Motivala, S. J., & Irwin, M. R. (2007). Sleep and immunity: Cytokine pathways linking sleep and health outcomes. *Current Directions in Psychological Science, 16,* 21–25.

Mottram, L., & Berger-Gross, P. (2004). An intervention to reduce disruptive behaviors in children with brain injury. *Pediatric Rehabilitation, 7,* 133–143.

Moulton, S., & Kosslyn, S. (2008). Using neuroimagining to resolve the psi debate. *Journal of Cognitive Neuroscience, 20,* 182–192.

Mowen, J. C., & Cialdini, R. B. (1980). On implementing the door-in-the-face compliance technique in a business context. *Journal of Marketing Research, 17,* 253–258.

Mroczek, D. K., & Spiro, A., III. (2003). Modeling intraindividual change in personality traits: Findings from the Normative Aging Study. *Journal of Gerontology: Psychological Sciences, 58B,* P153–P165.

Mueller, C. W., Boyer, E. M., Price, J. L., & Iverson, R. D. (1994). Employee attachment and noncoercive conditions of work: The case of dental hygienists. *Work and Occupations, 21,* 179–212.

Mulrow, C. D., Willaims, J. W., Jr., Chiquette, E., Aguilar, C., Hitchcock-Noel, P., Lee, S., et al. (2000). Efficacy of newer medications for treating depression in primary care patients. *American Journal of Medicine, 108,* 54–64.

Mumford, M. D. (2003). Where have we been, where are we going? Taking stock in creativity research. *Creativity Research Journal, 15,* 107–120.

Mumme, D. L., & Fernald, A. (2003). The infant as onlooker: Learning from emotional reactions observed in a television scenario. *Child Development, 74,* 221–237.

Munch, M., Knoblauch, V., Blatter, K., Schroder, C., Schnitzler, C., Krauchi, K., et al. (2005). Age-related attenuation of the evening circadian arousal signal in humans. *Neurobiology of Aging, 26,* 1307–1319.

Murdoch, B. B., Jr. (1962). The serial position effect of free recall. *Journal of Experimental Psychology, 64,* 482–488.

Murray, C. J., & Lopez, A. D. (Eds.). (1996). *Summary: The global burden of disease: A comprehensive assessment of mortality and disability from diseases, injuries, and risk factors in 1990 and projected to 2020.* Cambridge, MA: Harvard University Press.

Murray, H. A. (1938). *Explorations in personality.* New York: Oxford University Press.

Murray, R. M., O'Callaghan, E., Castle, D. J., & Lewis, S. W. (1992). A neurodevelopmental approach to the classification of schizophrenia. *Schizophrenia Bulletin, 18,* 319–332.

Murray, S. O., Olshausen, B. A., & Woods, D. L. (2003). Processing shape, motion, and three-dimensional shape-from-motion in the human cortex. *Cerebral Cortex, 13,* 508–516.

Muurahainen, N. E., Kisileff, H. R., Lachaussee, J., & Pi-Sunyer, F. X. (1991). Effect of a soup preload on reduction of food intake by cholecystokinin in humans. *American Journal of Physiology, 260,* R672–R680.

Myers, D. G. (2000). The funds, friends, and faith of happy people. *American Psychologist, 55,* 56–67.

Naegele, B., Thouvard, V., Pepin, J. L., Levy, P., Bonnet, C., Perret, J. E., et al. (1995). Deficits of cognitive functions in patients with sleep apnea syndrome. *Sleep, 18*(1), 43–52.

Nairne, J. S. (2002). Remembering over the short term: The case against the standard model. *Annual Review of Psychology, 53,* 53–81.

Narrow, W. E., Regier, D. A., Rae, D., Manderscheid, R. W., & Locke, B. Z. (1993). Use of services by persons with mental and addictive disorders. *Archives of General Psychiatry, 50,* 95–107.

Nash, M. (1987). What, if anything, is regressed about hypnotic age regression? A review of the empirical literature. *Psychological Bulletin, 102,* 42–52.

Nathan, P. E., Stuart, S. P., & Dolan, S. L. (2000). Research on psychotherapy efficacy and effectiveness: Between Scylla and Charybdis? *Psychological Bulletin, 126,* 964–981.

Nathans, J., Merbs, S. L., Sung, C. H., Weitz, C. J., & Wang, Y. (1992). Molecular genetics of human visual pigments. *Annual Review of Genetics, 26,* 403–424.

National Gay and Lesbian Task Force. (2007). *Hate crime laws in the U. S.* Retrieved June 25, 2007, from http://www.thetaskforce.org/downloads/reports/issue_maps/hate_crimes_5_07.pdf

National Highway Traffic Safety Administration (NHTSA). (2003). *Traffic safety facts, 2003: Alcohol.* Washington, DC: U.S. Department of Transportation.

National Institute of Mental Health (NIMH). (2002). *Suicide facts.* Retrieved from http://www.nimh.nih.gov/research/suifact.htm

National Institute on Drug Abuse (NIDA). (2001). *Research report series: Hallucinogens and dissociative drugs.* NIH Publication Number 01-4209.

National Institute on Drug Abuse (NIDA). (2006a). *Research report series: MDMA (Ecstasy) abuse.* NIH Publication Number 06-4728.

National Institute on Drug Abuse (NIDA). (2006b). *Research report series: Methamphetamine abuse and addiction.* NIH Publication Number 06-4210.

National Institute on Drug Abuse (NIDA) & University of Michigan. (2006). *Monitoring the Future national survey results on drug use, 1975–2005: Volume 11. College students and adults ages 19–45.*

National Institutes of Health. (2000). *The practical guide: Identification, evaluation, and treatment of overweight and obesity in adults* (NIH Publication No. 00-4084). Washington, DC: Author.

National Science Foundation (NSF). (2006). *U.S. doctorates in the 20th century.* NSF 06-319. Arlington, VA: Author.

National Sleep Foundation. (2004). *Summary findings: 2004 Sleep in America poll.* Washington, DC: Author.

National Sleep Foundation. (2005). *Summary findings: 2005 Sleep in America poll.* Washington, DC: Author.

National Sleep Foundation. (2006). *Summary findings: 2006 Sleep in America poll.* Washington, DC: Author.

Navarro, M. (1995, December 9). Drug sold abroad by prescription becomes widely abused in U.S. *New York Times,* pp. 1, 9.

Naylor, J. C., Pritchard, R. D., & Ilgen, D. R. (1980). *A theory of behavior in organizations.* New York: Academic Press.

Neher, A. (1991). Maslow's theory of motivation: A critique. *Journal of Humanistic Psychology, 31,* 89–112.

Neitz, J., Neitz, M., & Jacobs, G. H. (1993). More than three different cone pigments among people with normal color vision. *Vision Research, 33,* 117–122.

Nemeroff, C. B. (2007). The burden of severe depression: A review of diagnostic challenges and treatment alternatives. *Journal of Psychiatric Research, 41,* 189–206.

Nestler, E. J. (2006). The addicted brain: Cocaine use alters genes. *Paradigm, 11,* 12–22.

Nestler, E. J., & Carlezon, W. A., Jr. (2006). The mesolimbic dopamine reward circuit in depression. *Biological Psychiatry, 59,* 1151–1159.

Nevin, J. A., & Grace, R. C. (2005). Resistance to extinction in the steady state and in the transition. *Journal of Experimental Psychology: Animal Behavior Processes, 31,* 199–212.

Nevonen, L., & Broberg, A. G. (2006). A comparison of sequenced individual and group psychotherapy for patients with bulimia nervosa. *International Journal of Eating Disorders, 39,* 117–127.

Newcomb, T. M. (1961). *The acquaintance process.* New York: Holt, Rinehart & Winston.

Newland M. C., & Rasmussen, E. B. (2003). Behavior in adulthood and during aging is affected by contaminant exposure in utero. *Current Directions in Psychological Science, 12,* 212–217.

Newman, S. D., & Tweig, D. (2001). Differences in auditory processing of words and pseudowords: An fMRI study. *Human Brain Mapping, 14,* 39–47.

Ni, X., Sicard, T., Bulgin, N., Bismil, R., Chan, K., McMain, S., et al. (2007). Monoamine oxidase A gene is associated with borderline personality disorder. *Psychiatric Genetics, 17,* 153–157.

Niccols, G. A. (1994). Fetal alcohol syndrome: Implications for psychologists. *Clinical Psychology Review, 14,* 91–111.

Nicholson, I. R., & Neufield, R. W. J. (1993). Classification of the schizophrenias according to symptomatology: A two factor model. *Journal of Abnormal Psychology, 102,* 259–270.

Niedzwienska, A. (2003). Gender differences in vivid memories. *Sex Roles: A Journal of Research, 49,* 321–331.

NIMH Genetics Workgroup. (1998). *Genetics and mental disorders* (NIH Publication No. 98-4268). Rockville, MD: National Institute of Mental Health.

Nisbett, R. (1995). Race, IQ, and scientism. In Steven Fraser (Ed.), *The bell curve wars: Race, intelligence, and the future of America* (pp. 36–57). New York: Basic Books.

Noah, T., & Robinson, L. (1997, March 3). OK, OK, cigarettes do kill. *U.S. News & World Report,* pp. 29, 32.

Noble, M., & Harding, G. E. (1963). Conditioning of rhesus monkeys as a function of the interval between CS and US. *Journal of Comparative and Physiological Psychology, 56,* 220–224.

Nolan, R. P., Spanos, N. P., Hayward, A. A., & Scott, H. A. (1995). The efficacy of hypnotic and nonhypnotic response-based imagery for self-managing recurrent headache. *Imagination, Cognition, and Personality, 14*(3), 183–201.

Nolen-Hoeksema, S. (2001). Gender differences in depression. *Current Directions in Psychological Science, 10,* 173–176.

Nolen-Hoeksema, S. (2002). Gender differences in depression. In I. H. Gotlib & C. L. Hammen (Eds.), *Handbook of depression* (pp. 492–509). New York: Guilford Press.

Nolen-Hoeksema, S., Larson, J., & Grayson, C. (1999). Explaining the gender difference in depressive symptoms. *Journal of Personality and Social Psychology, 77,* 1061–1072.

Nolen-Hoeksema, S., Parker, L. E., & Larson, J. (1994). Ruminative coping with depressed mood following loss. *Journal of Personality and Social Psychology, 67,* 92–104.

Nolen-Hoeksema, S., Stice, E., Wade, E., & Bohon, C. (2007). Reciprocal relations between rumination and bulimic, substance abuse, and depressive symptoms in female adolescents. *Journal of Abnormal Psychology, 116,* 198–207.

Nordin, S., Razani, J. L., Markison, S., & Murphy, C. (2003). Age-associated increases in intensity discrimination for taste. *Experimental Aging Research, 29,* 371–381.

Norman, R. M., & Malla, A. K. (1993). Stressful life events and schizophrenia: II. Conceptual and methodological issues. *British Journal of Psychiatry, 162,* 166–174.

Norton, N., Williams, H. J., & Owen, M. J. (2006). An update on the genetics of schizophrenia. *Current Opinion in Psychiatry, 19,* 158–164.

Norton, P. J., & Price, E. C. (2007). A meta-analytic review of adult cognitive-behavioral treatment outcome across the anxiety disorders. *Journal of Nervous and Mental Disease, 195,* 521–531.

Nosofsky, R. M., & Zaki, S. R. (2002). Exemplar and prototype models revisited: Response strategies, selective attention, and stimulus generalization. *Journal of Experimental Psychology: Learning, Memory, and Cognition, 28,* 924–940.

Nottelmann, E. D., Inoff-Germain, G., Susman, E. J., & Chrousos, G. P. (1990). Hormones and behavior at puberty. In J. Bancroft & J. M. Reinisch (Eds.), *Adolescence and puberty* (pp. 88–123). New York: Oxford University Press.

Nowell, P. D., Buysse, D. J., Morin, C. M., Reynolds C. F., III, & Kuper, D. J. (1998). Effective treatments for selected sleep disorder. In P. E. Nathan (Ed.), *A guide to treatments that work* (pp. 531–543). New York: Oxford University Press.

O'Brien, A., Terry, D. J., & Jimmieson, N. L. (2008). Negative affectivity and responses to work stressors: An experimental study. *Anxiety, Stress, and Coping, 21,* 55–83.

O'Brien, M. (1996). Child-rearing difficulties reported by parents of infants and toddlers. *Journal of Pediatric Psychology, 21,* 433–446.

O'Connor, D. B., Jones, F., Conner, M., McMillan, B., & Ferguson, E. (2008). Effects of daily hassles and eating style on eating behavior. *Health Psychology, 27,* S20–S31.

O'Connor, M. K. (1993). Hypotheses regarding the mechanism of action of electroconvulsive therapy, past and present. *Psychiatric Annals, 23,* 15–18.

O'Keefe, D. J., & Figge, M. (1997). A guilt-based explanation of the door-in-the-face influence strategy. *Human Communication Research, 24,* 64–81.

O'Leary, A. (1990). Stress, emotion, and human immune function. *Psychological Bulletin, 108,* 363–382.

O'Neill, B. (2004, April 19). Britain debates: To spank or not to spank. *Christian Science Monitor,* p. 9.

Oginska, H., & Pokorski, J. (2006). Fatigue and mood correlates of sleep length in three age-social groups: School children, students, and employees. *Chronobiology International, 23,* 1317–1328.

Ohlsson, S. (1992). Information processing explanations of insight and related phenomena. In M. T. Keane & K. J. Gihooly (Eds.), *Advances in the psychology of thinking* (pp. 1–44). London: Harvester Wheatsheaf.

Olff, M., Langeland, W., Draijer, N., & Gersons, B. P. (2007). Gender differences in posttraumatic stress disorder. *Psychological Bulletin, 133,* 183–204.

Olfson, M., & Pincus, H. A. (1996). Outpatient mental health care in nonhospital settings: Distribution of patients across provider groups. *American Journal of Psychiatry, 153,* 1353–1356.

Ondersma, S. J., & Walker, C. E. (1998). Elimination disorders. In T. H. Ollendick & M. Hersen (Eds.), *Handbook of child psychopathology* (pp. 355–380). New York: Plenum Press.

Oquendo, M. A., Hastings, R. S., Huang, Y. Y., Simpson, N., Ogden, R. T., Hu, X. Z., et al. (2007). Brain serotonin transporter binding in depressed patients with bipolar disorder using positron emission tomography. *Archives of General Psychiatry, 64,* 201–208.

Ornish, D. (1998). *Love and survival.* New York: HarperCollins.

Ornstein, S., & Isabella, L. (1990). Age vs. stage models of career attitudes of women: A partial replication and extension. *Journal of Vocational Behavior, 36,* 1–19.

Ortony, A., & Turner, T. J. (1990). What's basic about basic emotions? *Psychological Review, 97,* 315–331.

Osborne, R. H., Sali, A., Aaronson, N. K., Elsworth, G. R., Mdzewski, B., & Sinclair, A. J. (2004). Immune function and adjustment style: Do they predict survival in breast cancer? *Psychooncology, 13,* 199–210.

Osterman, K., Bjorkqvist, K., Lagerspertz, K. M. J., Kaukiainen, A., Huesmann, L. R., & Fraczek, A. (1994). Peer and self-estimated aggression and victimization in 8-year-old children from five ethnic groups. *Aggressive Behavior, 20,* 411–428.

Ostroff, C., Kinicki, A. J., & Tamkins, M. M. (2003). Organizational culture and climate. In W. C. Borman, D. R. Ilgen, & R. J. Klimoski (Eds.), *Handbook of psychology: Industrial and organizational psychology* (Vol. 12, pp. 565–593). New York: Wiley.

Overman, W. H., Bachevalier, J., Schuhmann, E., & Ryan, P. (1996). Cognitive gender differences in very young children parallel biologically based cognitive gender differences in monkeys. *Behavioral Neuroscience, 110,* 673–684.

Overmier, J. B., & Seligman, M. E. (1967). Effects of inescapable shock upon subsequent escape and avoidance responding. *Journal of Comparative and Physiological Psychology, 63,* 28–33.

Overstreet, L. S. (2005). Quantal transmission: Not just for neurons. *Trends in Neurosciences, 28,* 59–62.

Özgen, E., & Davies, I. R. L. (2002). Acquisition of categorical color perception: A perceptual learning approach to the linguistic relativity hypothesis. *Journal of Experimental Psychology: General, 131,* 477–493.

Ozturk, L., Pelin, Z., Karadeniz, D., Kaynak, H., Cakar, L., & Gozukirmizi, E. (1999). Effects of 48 hours sleep deprivation on human immune profile. *Sleep Research Online, 2,* 107–111.

Painter, K. (1997, August 15–17). Doctors have prenatal test for 450 genetic diseases. *USA Today.*

Paivio, A. (1982). The empirical case for dual coding. In J. Yuille (Ed.), *Imagery, cognition, and memory* (pp. 307–332). Hillsdale, NJ: Erlbaum.

Paivio, A. (1986). *Mental representations: A dual coding approach.* New York: Oxford University Press.

Pallier, G. (March, 2003). Gender differences in the self-assessment of accuracy on cognitive tasks. *Sex Roles: A Journal of Research, 48(5/6),* 265–276.

Papadakis, A. A., Prince, R. P., Jones, N. P., & Strauman, T. J. (2006). Self-regulation, rumination, and vulnerability to depression in adolescent girls. *Development and Psychopathology, 18,* 815–829.

Parker, E. S., Birnbaum, I. M., & Noble, E. P. (1976). Alcohol and memory: Storage and state dependency. *Journal of Verbal Learning and Verbal Behavior, 15,* 691–702.

Parker, G. B., & Brotchie, H. L. (2004). From diathesis to dimorphism: The biology of gender differences in depression. *Journal of Nervous and Mental Disorders, 192,* 210–216.

Parker, G. B., Roy, K., Wilhelm, K., & Mitchell, P. (2001). Assessing the comparative effectiveness of antidepressant therapies: A prospective clinical practice study. *Journal of Clinical Psychiatry, 62,* 117–125.

Parker-Pope, T. (2002, August 27). A new reason for teens to avoid sex: It could be harmful to their health. *Wall Street Journal,* D1.

Parkes, C. M. (1986). *Bereavement: Studies of grief in adult life* (2nd ed.). London: Tavistock.

Parkes, C. M. (1991). Attachment, bonding, and psychiatric problems after bereavement in adult life. In C. M. Parkes, J. Stevenson-Hinde, & P. Marris (Eds.), *Attachment across the life cycle* (pp. 268–292). London: Tavistock/Routledge.

Parkin, A. J., & Leng, N. R. C. (1993). *Neuropsychology of the amnesic syndrome.* Hove, UK: Psychology Press.

Parnas, J., Cannon, T., Jacobsen, B., Schulsinger, H., Schulsinger, F., & Mednick, S. (1993). Lifetime DSM-III-R diagnostic outcomes in the offspring of schizophrenic mothers. *Archives of General Psychiatry, 50,* 707–714.

Pasquet, P., Obeerti, B., Ati, J. El, & Hladik, C. M. (2002). Relationships between threshold-based PROP sensitivity and food preferences of Tunisians. *Appetite, 39,* 167–173.

Pate, W. E., II. (2001). *Analyses of data from graduate study in psychology: 1999–2000.* APA Research Office. Retrieved December 29, 2006, from http://research.apa.org/grad00contents.html

Patterson, C. J. (2006). Children of lesbian and gay parents. *Current Directions in Psychological Science, 15,* 241–244.

Paulus, P. B. (Ed.). (1989). *Psychology of group influence* (2nd ed.). Hillsdale, NJ: Erlbaum.

Pavlov, I. P. (1960). *Conditioned reflexes: An investigation of the physiological activity of the cerebral cortex* (G. V. Anrep, Trans.). New York: Dover. (Original work published 1927)

Payte, J. T. (1997). Methadone maintenance treatment: The first thirty years. *Journal of Psychoactive Drugs, 29,* 149–153.

Pearlin, L. I. (1993). The social contexts of stress. In L. Goldberger & S. Breznitz (Eds.), *Handbook of stress: Theoretical and clinical aspects* (2nd ed., pp. 303–315). New York: Free Press.

Pedersen, D. M., & Wheeler, J. (1983). The Müller-Lyer illusion among Navajos. *Journal of Social Psychology, 121,* 3–6.

Pedersen, P. B. (2002). Ethics, competence, and other professional issues in culture-centered counseling. In P. B. Pedersen, J. G. Draguns, W. J. Lonner, & J. E. Trimble (Eds.), *Counseling across cultures* (5th ed., pp. 3–28). Thousand Oaks, CA: Sage.

Pelleymounter, M. A., Cullen, M. J., Baker, M. B., Hecht, R., Winters, D., Boone, T., et al. (1995). Effects of the obese gene product on body weight regulation in ob/ob mice. *Science, 269,* 540–543.

Penley, J. A., Tomaka, J., & Wiebe, J. S. (2002). The association of coping to physical and psychological health outcomes: A meta-analytic review. *Journal of Behavioral Medicine, 25,* 551–603.

Pepperberg, I. M. (1991). A communicative approach to animal cognition: A study of conceptual abilities of an African gray parrot. In C. A. Ristau (Ed.), *Cognitive ethology* (pp. 153–186). Hillsdale, NJ: Erlbaum.

Pepperberg, I. M. (1993). Cognition and communication in an African gray parrot (*Psittacus erithacus*): Studies on a nonhuman, nonprimate, nonmammilian, subject. In H. L. Roitblat, L. M. Herman, & P. E. Nachtigall (Eds.), *Language and communication: Comparative perspectives.* Hillsdale, NJ: Erlbaum.[S1]

Pepperberg, I. M. (1999). Rethinking syntax: A commentary on E. Kako's "Elements of syntax in the systems of three language-trained animals." *Animal Learning and Behavior, 27,* 15–17.

Perez, M., Joiner, T. E., Jr., & Lewisohn, P. M. (2004). Is major depressive disorder or dysthymia more strongly associated with bulimia nervosa? *International Journal of Eating Disorders, 36,* 55–61.

Perina, K. (2002). Hot on the trail of flash-bulb memory. *Psychology Today, 35,* 15–16.

Perlini, A. H., Bertolissi, S., & Lind, D. L. (1999). The effects of women's age and physical appearance on evaluations of attractiveness and social desirability. *Journal of Social Psychology, 139,* 343–344.

Perry, C. (1997). Admissibility and per se exclusion of hypnotically elicited recall in American courts of law. *International Journal of Clinical and Experimental Hypnosis, 45,* 266–279.

Perry, E., Walker, M., Grace, J., & Perry, R. (1999). Acetylcholine in mind: A neurotransmitter correlate of consciousness? *Trends in Neurosciences, 22,* 273–280.

Perry, W. G., Jr. (1981). Cognitive and ethical growth. In A. Chickering (Ed.), *The modern American college* (pp. 76–116). San Francisco: Jossey-Bass.

Person, E. S. (1990). The influence of values in psychoanalysis: The case of female psychology. In C. Zanardi (Ed.), *Essential papers in psychoanalysis* (pp. 305–325). New York: University Press.

Pesant, N., & Zadra, A. (2004). Working with dreams in therapy: What do we know and what should we do? *Clinical Psychology Review, 24,* 489–512.

Pesant, N., & Zadra, A. (2006). Dream content and psychological well-being: A longitudinal study of the continuity hypothesis. *Journal of Clinical Psychology, 62,* 111–121.

Peterson, C. (2000). The future of optimism. *American Psychologist, 55,* 44–55.

Peterson, C., & Bossio, L. M. (2001). Optimism and physical well-being. In E. C. Chang (Ed.), *Optimism and pessimism: Implications for theory, research, and practice* (pp. 127–146). Washington, DC: American Psychological Association.

Peterson, C., Maier, S. F., & Seligman, M. E. P. (1993). *Learned helplessness: A theory for the age of personal control.* New York: Oxford University Press.

Peterson, C., & Seligman, M. E. (1984). Causal explanations as a risk factor for depression: Theory and evidence. *Psychological Review, 91,* 347–374.

Peterson, L. R., & Peterson, M. J. (1959). Short-term retention of individual verbal items. *Journal of Experimental Psychology, 58,* 193–198.

Petrides, K. V., Furnham, A., & Martin, G. N. (2004). Estimates of emotional and psychometric intelligence: Evidence for gender-based stereotypes. *Journal of Social Psychology, 144,* 149–162.

Petry, N. M., Tedford, J., Austin, M., Nich, C., Carroll, K. M., & Rounsaville, B. J. (2004). Prize reinforcement contingency management for treating cocaine users: How low can we go, and with whom? *Addiction, 99,* 349–360.

Petty, R. E., & Cacioppo, J. T. (1986). *Communication and persuasion: Central and peripheral routes to attitude change.* New York: Springer-Verlag.

Petty, R. E., Cacioppo, J. T., & Goldman, R. (1981). Personal involvement as a determinant of argument-based persuasion. *Journal of Personality and Social Psychology, 41,* 847–855.

Petty, R. E., Wegener, D. T., & Fabrigar, L. R. (1997). Attitude and attitude change. *Annual Review of Psychology, 48,* 609–647.

Phares, E. J. (1991). *Introduction to personality* (3rd ed.). New York: HarperCollins.

Phillips, M. R., Li, X., & Zhang, Y. (2002). Suicide rates in China, 1995–99. *Lancet, 359,* 835–840.

Phillipson, O. T. (1987). Catecholamines. In R. L. Gregory (Ed.), *The Oxford companion to the mind* (pp. 126–127). New York: Oxford University Press.

Piaget, J. (1929). *The child's conception of the world.* New York: Harcourt Brace.

Piaget, J. (1952). *The origins of intelligence in children.* New York: International Universities Press.

Pidoplichko, V. I., DeBiasi, M., Williams, J. T., & Dani, J. A. (1997). Nicotine activates and desensitizes midbrain dopamine neurons. *Nature, 390,* 401–404.

Pierce, J. P. (2005). Influence of movie stars on the initiation of adolescent smoking. *Pediatric Dentistry, 27,* 149.

Pike, K. M., Devlin, M. J., & Loeb, C. (2004). Cognitive-behavioral therapy in the treatment of anorexia nervosa, and binge eating disorder. In J. K. Thompson (Ed.), *Handbook of eating disorders and obesity* (pp. 130–162). New York: Wiley.

Pinel, J. P. J. (1997). *Biopsychology* (3rd ed.). Boston: Allyn & Bacon.

Pinker, S. (1994). *The language instinct: How the mind creates language.* New York: Morrow.

Pinnell, C. M., & Covino, N. A. (2000). Empirical findings on the use of hypnosis in medicine: A critical review. *International Journal of Clinical and Experimental Hypnosis, 48,* 170–194.

Pion, G. M. (1991). Psychologists wanted: Employment trends over the last decade. In R. R. Kilburg (Ed.), *How to manage your career in psychology* (pp. 229-246). Washington, DC: American Psychological Association.

Piper, A., & Merskey, H. (2004). The persistence of folly: A critical examination of dissociative identity disorder: Part I. The excesses of an improbable concept. *Canadian Journal of Psychiatry, 49,* 592–600.

Plazzi, B., Corsini, R., Provini, R., Pierangeli, G., Martinelli, P., Montagna, P., et al. (1997). REM sleep behavior disorders in multiple system atrophy. *Neurology, 48,* 1094–1097.

Pleis, J. R., & Lethbridge-Ceiku, M. (2007). Summary health statistics for U.S. adults: National health interview survey, 2006. *Vital Health Statistics, 10,* No. 235.

Plomin, R., DeFries, J. C., McClearn, G. E., & McGuffin, P. (2001). *Behavioral genetics* (4th ed.). New York: Worth.

Plutchik, R. (1984). Emotions: A general psychoevolutionary theory. In K. R. Scherer & P. Ekman (Eds.), *Approaches to emotion* (pp. 197–219). Hillsdale, NJ: Erlbaum.

Pollard, R. J., Coyle, J. P., Gilbert, R. L., & Beck, J. E. (2007). Intraoperative awareness in a regional medical system: A review of 3 years' data. *Anesthesiology, 106,* 269–274.

Polmin, R. (1994). The Emanuel Miller Memorial Lecture 1993: Genetic research and identification of environmental influences. *Journal of Child Psychology and Psychiatry, 35,* 817–834.

Polotsky, V. Y., & O'Donnell, C. P. (2007). Genomics of sleep-disordered breathing. *Proceedings of the American Thoracic Society, 4,* 121–126.

Pomeroy, A. (2005). 50 best small and medium places to work: Money talks. *HR Magazine, 50*(7), 44–65.

Pomeroy, W. (1965, May). Why we tolerate lesbians. *Sexology,* 652–654.

Poore, A. G., Gagne, F., Barlow, K. M., Lydon, J. E., Taylor, D. M., & Wright, S. C. (2002). Contact and the personal/group discrimination discrepancy in an Inuit community. *Journal of Psychology, 136,* 371–382.

Pope, H. D., Jr., Oliva, P. S., Hudson, J. I., Bodkin, J. A., & Gruber, A. J. (1999). Attitudes toward DSM-IV dissociative disorders diagnoses among board-certified American psychiatrists. *American Journal of Psychiatry, 156,* 321–323.

Pope, H. G., & Yurgelun-Todd, D. (1996). The residual cognitive effects of heavy marijuana use in college students. *Journal of the American Medical Association, 275*(7), 521–527.

Porkka-Heiskanen, T., Strecker, R. E., Thakkar, M., Bjorkum, A. A., Greene, R. W., & McCarley, R. W. (1997). Adenosine: A mediator of the sleep-inducing effects of prolonged wakefulness. *Science, 276,* 1265–1268.

Porte, H. S., & Hobson, J. A. (1996). Physical motion in dreams: One measure of three theories. *Journal of Abnormal Psychology, 105,* 329–335.

Post, R., Frye, M., Denicoff, K. Leverich, G., Kimbrell, T., & Dunn, R. (1998). Beyond lithium in the treatment of bipolar illness. *Neuropsychopharmacology, 19,* 206–219.

Potter, W. J., Warren, R., Vaughan, M., Howley, K., Land, A., & Hagemeyer, J. (1997). Antisocial acts in reality programming on television. *Journal of Broadcasting and Electronic Media, 41,* 69–89.

Powell, L. H., Calvin, J. E., III, & Calvin, J. E., Jr. (2007). Effective obesity treatments. *American Psychologist, 62,* 234–246.

Powell, L. H., Shahabi, L., & Thoresen, C. E. (2003). Religion and spirituality: Linkages to physical health. *American Psychologist, 58,* 36–52.

Powell, T. J., Silk, K. R., & Albeck, J. H. (2000). Psychiatrists' referrals to self-help groups for people with mood disorders. *Psychiatric Services, 51,* 809–811.

Pratkanis, A. R. (1992). The cargo-cult science of subliminal persuasion. *The Skeptical Inquirer, 16,* 260–272.

Pratkanis, A. R., Epley, N., Savitsky, K., & Kachelski, R. A. (2007). Issue 12: Is subliminal persuasion a myth? In J. A. Nier (Ed.), *Taking sides: Clashing views in social psychology* (2nd ed., pp. 230–255). New York: McGraw-Hill.

Prescott, C. A., Hewitt, J. K., Truett, K. R., Heath, A. C., Neale, M. C., & Eaves, L. J. (1994). Genetic and environmental influences on alcohol-related problems in a volunteer sample of older twins. *Journal of Studies on Alcohol, 55,* 184–202.

Pressman, S. D., Cohen, S., Miller, G. E., Barkin, A., Rabin, B. S., & Treanor, J. J. (2005). Loneliness, social network size, and immune response to influenza vaccination in college freshman. *Health Psychology, 24,* 297–306.

Price, W. F., & Crapo, R. H. (2002). *Cross-cultural perspectives in introductory psychology.* Belmont, CA: Wadsworth.

Pritchard, M. E., Wilson, G. S., & Yamnitz, B. (2007). What predicts adjustment among college students? A longitudinal panel study. *Journal of American College Health, 56,* 15–21.

Proctor, F., Wagner, N., & Butler, J. (1974). The differentiation of male and female orgasm: An experimental study. In N. Wagner (Ed.), *Perspectives on human sexuality.* New York: Behavioral Publications.

Proudfoot, J. G. (2004). Computer-based treatment for anxiety and depression: Is it feasible? Is it effective? *Neuroscience Biobehavior Review, 28,* 353–363.

Prutkin, J., Duffy, V. B., Etter, L., Fast, K., Gardner, E., Lucchina, L. A., et al. (2000). Genetic variation and inferences about perceived taste intensity in mice and men. *Physiology and Behavior, 69,* 161–173.

Purves, D., Augustine, G. J., Fitzpatrick, D., Katz, L., LaMantia, A. S., & McNamara, J. O. (1997). *Neuroscience.* Sunderland, MA: Sinauer.

Putnam, F. W., Guroff, J. J., Silberman, E. K., & Barban, L. (1986). The clinical phenomenology of multiple personality disorder: Review of 100 recent cases. *Journal of Clinical Psychiatry, 47,* 285–293.

Pyke, K., & Johnson, D. (2003). Asian American women and racialized femininities: "Doing" gender across cultural worlds. *Gender and Society, 17,* 33–53.

Quattrone, G. A., & Jones, E. E. (1980). The perception of variability within ingroups and outgroups: Implications for the law of small number. *Journal of Personality and Social Psychology, 38,* 141–152.

Querido, J. G., Warner, T. D., & Eyberg, S. M. (2002). Parenting styles and child behavior in African American families of preschool children. *Journal of Clinical Child and Adolescent Psychology, 31,* 272–277.

Quickfall, J., & Crockford, D. (2006). Brain neuroimaging in cannabis use: A review. *Journal of Neuropsychiatry and Clinical Neurosciences, 18,* 318–332.

Quinn, D. M., & Spencer, S. J. (2001). The interference of stereotype threat with women's generation of mathematical problem-solving strategies. *Journal of Social Issues, 57,* 55–71.

Rabkin, J. G., & Ferrando, S. (1997). A "second life" agenda. *Archives of General Psychiatry, 54,* 1049–1053.

Rabkin, S. W., Boyko, E., Shane, F., & Kaufert, J. (1984). A randomized trial comparing smoking cessation programs utilizing behavior modification, health education, or hypnosis. *Addictive Behaviors, 9,* 157–173.

Raffaelli, M. (2005). Adolescent dating experiences described by Latino college students. *Journal of Adolescence, 28,* 559–572.

Raine, A. (1997). Antisocial behavior and psychophysiology: A biological perspective. In D. M. Stoff, J. Breiling, & J. D. Maser (Eds.), *Handbook of antisocial personality disorder* (pp. 289–304). New York: Wiley.

Raine, A., Lencz, T., Bihrle, S., LaCasse, L., & Colletti, P. (2000). Reduced prefrontal gray matter volume and reduced autonomic activity in antisocial personality disorder. *Archives of General Psychiatry, 57,* 119–127.

Rainville, P., Duncan, G. H., Price, D. D., Carrier, B., & Bushnell, M. C. (1997). Pain affect encoded in human anterior cingulate but not somatosensory cortex. *Science, 277,* 968–971.

Rainville, P., & Price, D. D. (2003). Hypnosis phenomenology and the neurobiology of consciousness. *International Journal of Clinical and Experimental Hypnosis, 51,* 105–129.

Rakic, P. (1991). Plasticity of cortical development. In S. E. Brauth, W. S. Hall, & R. J. Dooling (Eds.), *Plasticity of Development* (pp. 127–161). Cambridge, MA: Bradford/MIT Press.

Ramsey-Rennels, J. L., & Langlois, J. H. (2006). Infants' differential processing of female and male faces. *Current Directions in Psychological Science, 15,* 59–62.

Rando, T. A. (1995). Grief and mourning: Accommodating to loss. In H. Wass & R. A. Neimeyer (Eds.), *Dying: Facing the facts* (3rd ed., pp. 211–241). Washington DC: Taylor & Francis.

Ranganathan, M., & D'Souza, D. C. (2006). The acute effects of cannabinoids on memory in humans: A review. *Psychopharmacology (Berlin), 188,* 425–444.

Rank, M. R. (2000). Poverty and economic hardship in families. In D. H. Demo, K. R. Allen, & M. A. Fine (Eds.), *Handbook of family diversity* (pp. 293–315). New York: Oxford University Press.

Rao, H., Hillihan, S. J., Wang, J., Korczykowski, M., Sankoorikal, G. M., Kaercher, K. A., et al. (2007). Genetic variation in serotonin transporter alters resting brain function in healthy individuals. *Biological Psychiatry, 62,* 600–606.

Rapoport, J. L., Addington, A. M., Frangou, S., & Psych, M. R. (2005). The neurodevelopmental model of schizophrenia: Update 2005. *Molecular Psychiatry, 10,* 434–449.

Rauch, S. L., Savage, C. R., Alpert, N. M., Dougherty, D., Kendrick, A., Curran, T., et al. (1997). Probing striatal function in obsessive-compulsive disorder: A PET study of implicit sequence learning. *Journal of Neuropsychiatry and Clinical Neuroscience, 9,* 568–573.

Rauch, S. L., Shin, L. M., & Phelps, E. A. (2006). Neurocircuitry models of posttraumatic stress disorder and extinction: Human neuroimaging research—past, present, and future. *Biological Psychiatry, 60,* 376–382.

Rauchs, G., Bertran, F., Guillery-Girard, B., Desgranges, B., Kerrouche, N., Denise, P., et al. (2004). Consolidation of strictly episodic memories mainly requires rapid eye movement sleep. *Sleep, 27,* 395–401.

Ravenna, H., Jones, C., & Kwan, V. S. (2002). Personality change over 40 years of adulthood: Hierarchical linear modeling analyses of two longitudinal samples. *Journal of Personality and Social Psychology, 83,* 752–766.

Ray, R. D., Wilhelm, F. H., & Gross, J. J. (2008). All in the mind's eye? Anger rumination and reappraisal. *Journal of Personality and Social Psychology, 94,* 133–145.

Raz, A. (2005). Attention and hypnosis: Neural substrates and genetic associations of two converging processes. *International Journal of Clinical and Experimental Hypnosis, 53,* 237–258.

Raz, N., Rodrigue, K. M., Kennedy, K. M., & Acker, J. D. (2007). Vascular health and longitudinal changes in brain and cognition in middle-aged and older adults. *Neuropsychology, 21,* 149–157.

Reedy, M. N. (1983). Personality and aging. In D. S. Woodruff & J. E. Birren (Eds.), *Aging: Scientific perspectives and social issues* (2nd ed., pp. 112–136). Monterey, CA: Brooks/Cole.

Regier, D. A., Narrow, W. E., Rae, D. S., Manderscheid, R. W., Locke, B. Z., & Goodwin, F. K. (1993). The de facto U. S. mental and addictive disorders service system: Epidemiologic Catchment Area prospective 1-year prevalence rates of disorders and services. *Archives of General Psychiatry, 50,* 85–94.

Rehder, B., & Hoffman, A. B. (2005). Thirty-something categorization results explained: Selective attention, eyetracking, and models of category learning. *Journal of Experimental Psychology: Learning, Memory, and Cognition, 31,* 811–829.

Reid, P., & Bing, V. (2000). Sexual roles of girls and women: An ethnocultural lifespan perspective. In C. Travis & J. White (Eds.), *Sexuality, society, and feminism* (pp. 141–166). Washington, DC: American Psychological Association.

Reinisch, J. M. (1991). *The Kinsey Institute new report on sex: What you must know to be sexually literate.* New York: St. Martin's Press.

Reisenzein, R. (1983). The Schachter theory of emotion: Two decades later. *Psychological Bulletin, 94,* 239–264.

Reiss, D. (2005). The interplay between genotypes and family relationships: Reframing concepts of development and prevention. *Current Directions in Psychological Science, 14,* 139–143.

Reite, M., Sheeder, J., Teale, P., Richardson, D., Adams, M., & Simon, J. (1995). MEG based brain laterality: Sex differences in normal adults. *Neuropsychologia, 33,* 1607–1616.

Reitzes, D. C., & Mutran, E. J. (2004). The transition to retirement: Stages and factors that influence retirement adjustment. *International Journal of Aging and Human Development, 59,* 63–84.

Rescorla, R. A. (1967). Pavlovian conditioning and its proper control procedures. *Psychological Review, 74,* 71–80.

Resick, P. A., Nishith, P., Weaver, T. L., Astin, M. C., & Feuer, C. A. (2002). A comparison of cognitive-processing therapy with prolonged exposure and a waiting condition for the treatment of chronic posttraumatic stress disorder in female rape victims. *Journal of Consulting and Clinical Psychology, 70,* 867–879.

Resta, O., Foschino-Barbaro, M. P., Legari, G., Talamo, S., Bonfitto, P., Palumbo, A., et al. (2001). Sleep-related breathing disorders, loud snoring and excessive daytime sleepiness in obese subjects. *International Journal of Obesity and Related Metabolic Disorders, 25,* 669–675.

Reyna, V. F., & Farley, F. (2006). Risk and rationality in adolescent decision making. *Psychological Science in the Public Interest, 7,* 1–44.

Reynolds, C. R., & Brown, R. T. (Eds.). (1984). *Perspectives on bias in mental testing.* New York: Plenum Press.

Reynolds, S., Stiles, W. B., Barkham, M., & Shapiro, D. A. (1996). Acceleration of changes in session impact during contrasting time-limited psychotherapies. *Journal of Consulting and Clinical Psychology, 64,* 577–586.

Rhodes, N., & Wood, W. (1992). Self-esteem and intelligence affect influencability: The mediating role of message reception. *Psychological Bulletin, 111,* 156–171.

Rice, F. P. (1992). *Intimate relationships, marriages, and families.* Mountain View, CA: Mayfield.

Rice, V. H. (Ed.). (2000). *Handbook of stress, coping and health.* Thousand Oaks, CA: Sage.

Richards, J., Klein, B., & Carlbring, P. (2003). Internet-based treatment for panic disorder. *Cognitive Behaviour Therapy, 32,* 125–135.

Richardson, G. E., & Day, N. L. (1994). Detrimental effects of prenatal cocaine exposure: Illusion or reality. *Journal of the American Academy of Child and Adolescent Psychiatry, 33,* 28–34.

Richardson, J. T. E., Engle, R. W., Hasher, L., Logie, R. H., Stoltzfus, E. R., & Zacks, R. T. (1996). *Working memory and human cognition.* Oxford, UK: Oxford University Press.

Rickels, K., DeMartinis, N., Garcia-Espana, F., Greenblatt, D. J., Mandos, L.A., & Rynn, M. (2000). Imipramine and buspirone in treatment of patients with generalized anxiety disorder who are discontinuing long-term benzodiazepine therapy. *American Journal of Psychiatry, 157,* 1973–1979.

Ridley, M. (2003, May 25). What makes you who you are: Which is stronger, nature or nurture? *Time,* pp. 54–62.

Rieger, G., Gygax, L., & Bailey, J. M. (2008). Sexual orientation and childhood gender non-conformity: Evidence from home videos. *Developmental Psychology, 44,* 46–58.

Riskind, J. H., Williams, N. L., Gessner, T. L., Chrosniak, L. D., & Cortina, J. M., (2000). The looming maladaptive style: Anxiety, danger, and schematic processing. *Journal of Personality and Social Psychology, 79,* 837–852.

Rivers, P. C. (1994). *Alcohol and human behavior.* Englewood Cliffs, NJ: Wiley.

Roberts, B. W., Caspi, A., & Moffitt, T. E. (2001). The kids are alright: Growth and stability in personality development from adolescence to adulthood. *Journal of Personality and Social Psychology, 81,* 670–683.

Roberts, B. W., & DelVecchio, W. F. (2000). The rank-order consistency of personality traits from childhood to old age: A quantitative review of longitudinal studies. *Psychological Bulletin, 126,* 3–25.

Roberts, B. W., Kuncel, N. R., Shiner, R., Caspi, A., & Goldberg, L. R. (2007). The power of personality: The comparative validity of personality traits, socioeconomic status, and cognitive ability for predicting important life outcomes. *Perspectives on Psychological Science, 2,* 313–345.

Roberts, B. W., & Mroczek, D. (2008). Personality trait change in adulthood. *Current Directions in Psychological Science, 17,* 31–35.

Roberts, B. W., Walton, K. E., & Viechtbauer, W. (2006). Patterns of mean-level change in personality traits across the life course: A meta-analysis of longitudinal studies. *Psychological Bulletin, 132,* 1–25.

Roberts, R. D., Schulze, R., O'Brien, K., MacCann, C., Reid, J., & Maul, A. (2006). Exploring the validity of the Mayer-Salovey-Caruso emotional intelligence test (MSCEIT) with established emotions measures. *Emotion, 6,* 663–669.

Roberts, R. E., Roberts, C. R., & Chan, W. (2006). Ethnic differences in symptoms of insomnia among adolescents. *Sleep, 29,* 359–365.

Roberts, S. M. (1995). Applicability of the goodness-of-fit hypothesis to coping with daily hassles. *Psychological Reports, 77(3,* Pt. 1), 943–954.

Robins, L. N., & Regier, D. A. (Eds.). (1991). *Psychiatric disorders in America: The Epidemiologic Catchment Area Study.* New York: Free Press.

Robins, R. W., Fraley, R. C., Roberts, B. W., & Trzesniewski, K. H. (2001). A longitudinal study of personality change in young adulthood. *Journal of Personality, 69,* 617–640.

Robinson, L. A., Berman, J. S., & Neimeyer, R. A. (1990). Psychotherapy for the treatment of depression: A comprehensive review of controlled outcome research. *Psychological Bulletin, 109,* 30–49.

Robinson, N. M., Abbott, R. D., Berninger, V. W., & Busse, J. (1996). The structure of abilities in math-precocious young children: Gender similarities and differences. *Journal of Educational Psychology, 88,* 341–352.

Robles, T. F., Glaser, R., Kiecolt-Glaser, J. K. (2005). Out of balance: A new look at chronic stress, depression, and immunity. *Current Directions in Psychological Science, 14,* 111–115.

Robles, T. F., & Kiecolt-Glaser, J. K. (2003). The physiology of marriage: Pathways to health. *Physiology and Behavior, 79,* 409–416.

Rogers, C. R. (1942). *Counseling and psychotherapy.* Boston: Houghton Mifflin.

Rogers, C. R. (1951). *Client-centered therapy: Its current practice, implications, and theory.* Boston: Houghton Mifflin.

Rogers, C. R. (1961). *On becoming a person.* Boston: Houghton Mifflin.

Rogers, C. R. (1970). *Carl Rogers on encounter groups.* New York: Harper & Row.

Rogers, C. R. (1980). *A way of being.* Boston: Houghton Mifflin.

Rogers, C. R. (1986). Client-centered therapy. In I. L. Kutash & A. Wolf (Eds.), *Psychotherapists' casebook* (pp. 197–208). San Francisco: Jossey-Bass.

Rogers, N. L., Szuba, M. P., Staab, J. P., Evans, D. L., & Dinges, D. F. (2001). Neuroimmunologic aspects of sleep and sleep loss. *Seminars in Clinical Neuropsychiatry, 6,* 295–307.

Rogers, T. B. (1995). *The psychological testing enterprise: An introduction.* Pacific Grove, CA: Brooks/Cole.

Rogoff, B., & Chavajah, P. (1995). What's become of research on the cultural basis of cognitive development? *American Psychologist, 50,* 859–873.

Rohan, M. J., & Zanna, M. P. (1996). Value transmission in families. In C. Seligman & J. M. Olson (Eds.), *The psychology of values: The Ontario symposium* (Vol. 8, pp. 253–276). Mahwah, NJ: Erlbaum.

Roisman, G. I., & Fraley, R. C. (2006). The limits of genetic influence: A behavior–genetic analysis of infant–caregiver relationship quality and temperament. *Child Development, 77,* 1656–1667.

Rolls, E. T. (2000). The representation of umami tastes in the taste cortex. *Journal of Nutrition, 130,* 960–965.

Rooney, N. J., Bradshaw, J. W. S., & Robinson, I. H. (2001). Do dogs respond to play signals given by humans? *Animal Behavior, 61,* 715–722.

Rosch, E. (1973). Natural categories. *Cognitive Psychology, 4,* 328–350.

Rosch, E., Mervis, C. B., Gray, W. D., Johnson, D. M., & Boyes-Braem, P. (1976). Basic objects in natural categories. *Cognitive Psychology, 8,* 382–439.

Rose, A. J., Carlson, W., & Waller, E. M. (2007). Prospective associations of co-rumination with friendship and emotional adjustment: Considering the socioemotional trade-offs of co-rumination. *Developmental Psychology, 43,* 1019–1031.

Rose, J. E., Behm, F. M., Salley, A. N., Bates, J. E., Coleman, R. E., Hawk, T. C., et al. (2007). Regional brain activity correlates of nicotine dependence. *Neuropsychopharmacology, 32,* 2441–2452.

Rose, R. J. (1995). Genes and human behavior. *Annual Review of Psychology, 46,* 625–654.

Rose, S. A. (1980). Enhancing visual recognition memory in preterm infants. *Developmental Psychology, 16,* 85–92.

Rosen, J. B. (2004). The neurobiology of conditioned and unconditioned fear: A neurobehavioral system analysis of the amygdale. *Behavior and Cognitive Neuroscience Reviews, 3,* 23–41.

Rosen, J. B., & Donley, M. P. (2006). Animal studies of amygdala function in fear and uncertainty: Relevance to human research. *Biological Psychology, 73,* 49–60.

Rosenblith, J. F. (1992). *In the beginning.* Newbury Park, CA: Sage.

Rosenhan, D. L. (1969). Some origins of the concerns for others. In P. Mussen & M. Covington (Eds.), *Trends and issues in developmental psychology* (pp. 134–153). New York: Holt, Rinehart & Winston.

Rosenhan, D. L. (1973). On being sane in insane places. *Science, 179,* 250–258.

Ross, C. A. (1997). *Dissociative identity disorder: Diagnosis, clinical features, and treatment of multiple personality.* Toronto: Wiley.

Ross, M. W. (1980). Retrospective distortion in homosexual research. *Archives of Sexual Behavior, 9,* 523–531.

Roth, S., & Cohen, J. L. (1986). Approach, avoidance, and coping with stress. *American Psychologist, 41,* 813–819.

Roth, T., Krystal, A. D., & Lieberman, J. A., 3rd (2007). Long-term issues in the treatment of sleep disorders. *CNS Spectrum, 12,* 1–13.

Roth, T., Schwartz, J. R., Hirshkowitz, M., Erman, M. K., Dayno, J. M., & Arora, S. (2007). Evaluation of the safety of modafinil for treatment of excessive sleepiness. *Journal of Clinical Sleep Medicine, 3,* 595–602.

Rothbart, M. K., Ahadi, S. A., & Evans, D. E. (2000). Temperament and personality: Origins and outcomes. *Journal of Personality and Social Psychology, 78,* 122–135.

Rothbaum, B. O., Hodges, L. F., Kooper, R., Opdyke, D., & Williford, J. (1995). Effectiveness of computer-generated (virtual reality) graded exposure in the treatment of acrophobia. *American Journal of Psychiatry, 152,* 626–628.

Rothbaum, B. O., Hodges, L., Watson, B. A., Kessler, G. D., & Opdyke, D. (1996). Virtual reality exposure therapy in the treatment of fear of flying: A case report. *Behavior Research and Therapy, 34,* 477–481.

Rothbaum, F., Rosen, K. S., Pott, M., & Beatty, M. (1995). Early parent–child relationships and later problem behavior: A longitudinal study. Merrill-Palmer Quarterly, 41, 133–151.

Rothbaum, F., Schneider Rosen, K. S., Pott, M., & Beatty, M. (1995). Early parent–child relationships and later problem behavior: A longitudinal study. Merrill-Palmer Quarterly, 41, 133–151.

Rotter, J. (1982). The development and application of social learning theory. New York: Praeger.

Rouch, I., Wild, P., Ansiau, D., & Marquie, J. C. (2005). Shiftwork experience, age, and cognitive performance. Ergonomics, 48, 1282–1293.

Rowe, T. (2006). Fertility and a woman's age. Journal of Reproductive Medicine, 51, 157–163.

Rubin, K. H., Lynch, D., Coplan, R., Rose-Krasnor, L., & Booth, C. L. (1994). "Birds of a feather . . .": Behavioral concordances and preferential personal attraction in children. Child Development, 65, 1778–1785.

Rubin, S. S. (1993). The death of a child is forever: The life course impact of child loss. In M. Stroebe, W. Stroebe, & R. O. Hansson (Eds.), Handbook of bereavement. Theory, research, and intervention (pp. 285–299). Cambridge, UK: Cambridge University Press.

Rubonis, A. V., & Bickman, L. (1991). Psychological impairment in the wake of disaster: The disaster–psychopathology relationship. Psychological Bulletin, 109, 384–399.

Ruderman, A. J. (1985). Dysphoric mood and overeating: A test of restraint theory's disinhibition hypothesis. Journal of Abnormal Psychology, 94, 78–85.

Rudgley, R. (1998). The encyclopedia of psychoactive substances. New York: Little, Brown.

Ruffin, C. L. (1993). Stress and health: Little hassles vs. major life events. Australian Psychologist, 28(3), 201–208.

Ruffman, T., Slade, L., & Redman, J. (2005). Young infants' expectations about hidden objects. Cognition, 97, B35–B43.

Rumelhart, D. E. (1980). Schemata: The basic building blocks of cognition. In R. Spiro, B. Bruce, & W. Brewer (Eds.), Theoretical issues in reading comprehension (pp. 33–58). Hillsdale, NJ: Erlbaum.

Rush, M. C., Schoel, W. A., & Barnard, S. M. (1995). Psychological resiliency in the public sector: "Hardiness" and pressure for change. Journal of Vocational Behavior, 46(1), 17–39.

Rushton, J. P., & Jensen, A. R. (2005). Thirty years of research on race differences in cognitive ability. Psychology, Public Policy, and Law, 11, 235–294.

Rushton, W. A. H. (1975). Visual pigments and color blindness. Scientific American, 232, 64–74.

Russell, C. J., & Keel, P. K. (2002). Homosexuality as a specific risk factor for eating disorders in men. International Journal of Eating Disorders, 31, 300–306.

Rutherford, W. (1886). A new theory of hearing. Journal of Anatomy and Physiology, 21, 166–168.

Saadat, H., Drummond-Lewis, J., Maranets, I., Kaplan, D., Saadat, A., Wang, S. M., et al. (2006). Hypnosis reduces preoperative anxiety in adult patients. Anesthesia and Analgesia, 102, 1394–1396.

Sachs, G. S., & Rush, A. J. (2003). Response, remission, and recovery in bipolar disorders: What are the realistic treatment goals? Journal of Clinical Psychiatry, 64(Suppl. 6), 18–22.

Sackett, P. R., & DeVore, C. J. (2001). Counterproductive behaviors at work. In N. Anderson, D. S. Ones, H. K. Sinangil, & C. Viswesvaran (Eds.), Handbook of industrial, work and organizational psychology (Vol. 1, pp. 145–165). Thousand Oaks, CA: Sage.

Sadker, D. (2000). Gender equity: Still knocking at the classroom door. Equity and Excellence in Education, 33, 80–83.

Sadker, M., & Sadker, D. (1986). Questioning skills. In J. Cooper (Ed.), Classroom teaching skills (3rd ed., pp. 143–180). Lexington, MA: D. C. Heath.

Sadler, W. A. (2000). The third age: Six principles for growth and renewal after forty. New York: Perseus.

Sah, P., Faber, E. S. L., Lopez De Armentia, M., & Power, J. (2003). The aymgdaloid complex: Anatomy and physiology. Physiological Reviews, 83, 803–834.

Sajatovic, M., Valenstein, M., Blow, F., Ganoczy, D., & Ignacio, R. (2007). Treatment adherence with lithium and anticonvulsant medications among patients with bipolar disorder. Psychiatric Services, 58, 855–863.

Sakari, M. M. (1975). Small group cohesiveness and detrimental conformity. Sociometry, 38, 340–357.

Salend, S. J. (2001). Creating inclusive classrooms: Effective and reflective practices (4th ed.). Upper Saddle River, NJ: Prentice Hall.

Salgado, J. F., Viswesvaran, C., & Ones, D. (2003). Predictors used for personnel selection: An overview of constructs, methods and techniques. In N. Anderson, D. S. Ones, H. K. Sinangil, & C. Viswesvaran (Eds.), Handbook of industrial, work and organizational psychology (Vol. 1, pp. 166–199). Thousand Oaks, CA: Sage.

Salkovskis, P. M., Westbrook, D., Davis, J., Jeavons, A., & Gledhill, A. (1997). Effects of neutralizing on intrusive thoughts: An experiment investigating the etiology of obsessive-compulsive disorder. Behaviour Research and Therapy, 35, 211–219.

Salthouse, T. A. (2004). What and when of cognitive aging. Current Directions in Psychological Science, 13, 140–144.

Samarel, N. (1995). The dying process. In H. Wass & R. A. Neimeyer (Eds.), Dying: Facing the facts (3rd ed., pp. 89–116). Washington DC: Taylor & Francis.

Samuels, J., & Nestadt, G. (1997). Epidemiology and genetics of obsessive-compulsive disorder. International Review of Psychiatry, 9, 61–72.

Sanders, S. K., & Shekhar, A. (1995). Regulation of anxiety by GABA-sub(A) receptors in the rat amygdala. Pharmacology, Biochemistry, and Behavior, 52, 701–706.

Sanderson, C. A., & Cantor, N. (1995). Social dating goals in late adolescence: Implications for safer sexual activity. Journal of Personality and Social Psychology, 68, 1121–1134.

Sanes, J. N., Dimitrov, B., & Hallett, M. (1990). Motor learning in patients with cerebellar dysfunction. Brain, 113, 103–120.

Sangrigoli, S., & de Schonen, S. (2004). Recognition of own-race and other-race faces by three-month-old infants. Journal of Child Psychology and Psychiatry, 45, 1219–1227.

Sanyal, S., & vanTol, H. M. (1997). Review the role of dopamine D4 receptors in schizophrenia and anti-psychotic action. Journal of Psychiatric Research, 31, 219–232.

Sapolsky, R. M. (2000a). Glucocorticoids and hippocampal atrophy in neuropsychiatric disorders. Archives of General Psychiatry, 57, 925–935.

Sapolsky, R. M. (2000b). The possibility of neurotoxicity in the hippocampus in major depression: A primer on neuron death. Biological Psychiatry, 48, 755–765.

Sapolsky, R. M. (2002). Chickens, eggs and hippocampal atrophy. Nature Neuroscience, 5, 1111–1113.

Saskin, P. (1997). Obstructive sleep apnea: Treatment options, efficacy, and effects. In M. R. Pressman & W. C. Orr (Eds.), Understanding sleep: The evaluation and treatment of sleep disorders. Washington DC: American Psychological Association.

Saudino, K. J., McQuire, S., Reiss, D. Heatherington, E. M., & Plomin, R. (1995). Parent ratings of EAS temperaments in twins, full siblings, half siblings, and step siblings. Journal of Personality and Social Psychology, 68, 723–733.

Saunders, E. H., Scott, L. J., McInnis, M. G., & Burmeister, M. (2007, May 24). Familiality and diagnostic patterns of subphenotypes in the National Institute of Mental Health bipolar sample. American Journal of Medical Genetics Part B: Neuropsychiatric Genetics [Online].

Savage-Rumbaugh, E. S. (1987). Communication, symbolic communication and language: Reply to Seidenberg and Petitto. Journal of Experimental Psychology: General, 116, 288–292.

Savage-Rumbaugh, E. S., McDonald, K., Sevcik, R., Hopkins, W., & Rupert, E. (1986). Spontaneous symbol acquisition and communicative use by pygmy chimpanzees (Pan paniscus). Journal of Experimental Psychology: General, 115, 211–235.

Savin-Williams, R. C. (2006). Who's gay? Does it matter? Current Directions in Psychological Science, 15, 40–44.

Saxena, S., Brody, A. L., Schwartz, J. M., & Baxter, L. R. (1998). Neuroimaging and frontal-subcortical circuitry in obsessive-compulsive disorder. British Journal of Psychiatry, 173(Suppl. 35), 26–37.

Schachter, S. (1951). Deviation, rejection, and communication. Journal of Abnormal and Social Psychology, 46, 190–207.

Schachter, S., & Singer, J. E. (1962). Cognitive, social, and physiological determinants of emotional state. Psychological Review, 69, 379–399.

Schacter, D. L., Alpert, N. M., Savage, C. R., Rauch, S. L., & Alpert, M. S. (1996). Conscious recollection and the hippocampal formation: Evidence from positron emission tomography. Proceedings of the National Academy of Science, USA, 93, 321–325.

Schaie, K. W. (1983). The Seattle longitudinal study: A 21-year exploration of psychometric intelligence in adulthood. In K. W. Schaie (Ed.), Longitudinal studies of adult psychological development (pp. 64–135). New York: Guilford Press.

Schaie, K. W. (1994). The course of adult intellectual development. American Psychologist, 49, 304–313.

Schaie, K. W. (1996). Intellectual development in adulthood: The Seattle longitudinal study. New York: Cambridge University Press.

Schaie, K. W., & Willis, S. L. (2000). A stage theory model of adult cognitive development revisited. In B. Rubinstein, M. Moss, & M. Kleban (Eds.), The many dimensions of aging: Essays in honor of M. Powell Lawton (pp. 173–191). New York: Springer.

Scheier, M. F., & Bridges, M. W. (1995). Person variables and health: Personality predispositions and acute psychological states as shared determinants for disease. *Psychosomatic Medicine, 57,* 255–268.

Schein, E. H. (1985). *Organizational leadership and culture: A dynamic view.* San Francisco: Jossey-Bass.

Scheir, M. F., & Carver, C. S. (1992). Effects of optimism on psychological and physical well-being: Theoretical overview and empirical update. *Cognitive Therapy and Research, 16,* 201–228.

Scherrer, J. F., True, W. R., Xian, H., Lyons., M. J., Eisen, S. A., Goldberg, J., et al. (2000). Evidence for genetic influences common and specific to symptoms of generalized anxiety and panic. *Journal of Affective Disorders, 57,* 25–35.

Schleifer, S. J., Keller, S. E., Camerino, M., Thornton, J. C., & Stein, M. (1983). Suppression of lymphocyte stimulation following bereavement. *Journal of the American Medical Association, 250,* 374–377.

Schleifer, S. J., Keller, S. E., McKegney, F. P., & Stein, M. (1979). *The influence of stress and other psychosocial factors on human immunity.* Paper presented at the 36th Annual Meeting of the American Psychosomatic Society.

Schlesier-Stropp, B. (1984). Bulimia: A review of the literature. *Psychological Review, 95,* 247–257.

Schmidt, H. D., & Pierce, R. C. (2006). Systematic administration of a dopamine, but not a serotonin or norepinephrine, transporter inhibitor reinstates cocaine seeking in the rat. *Behavioural Brain Research, 175,* 189–194.

Schmidt, U., Lee, S., Beecham, J., Perkins, S., Treasure, J., Yi, I., et al. (2007). A randomized controlled trial of family therapy and cognitive behavior therapy guided self-care for adolescent with bulimia nervosa and related disorders. *American Journal of Psychiatry, 164,* 591–598.

Schmidt-Hieber, C., Jonas, P., & Bischofberger, J. (2004). Enhanced synaptic plasticity in newly generated granule cells of the adult hippocampus. *Nature, 429,* 184–187.

Schmitt, D. P., Realo, A., Voracek, M., & Allik, J. (2008). Why can't a man be more like a woman? Sex differences in Big Five personality traits across 55 cultures. *Journal of Personality and Social Psychology, 94,* 168–182.

Schmitt, N., Cortina, J. M., Ingerick, M. J., & Wiechmann, D. (2003). Personnel selection and employee performance. In W. C. Borman, D. R. Ilgen, & R. J. Klimoski (Eds.), *Handbook of psychology: Industrial and organizational psychology* (Vol. 12, pp. 77–105). New York: Wiley.

Schoppe-Sullivan, S. J., Mangelsdorf, S. C., Brown, G. L., & Sokolowski, M. S. (2007). Goodness-of-fit in family context: Infant temperament, marital quality, and early coparenting behavior. *Infant Behavior and Development, 30,* 82–96.

Schottenbauer, M. A., Glass, C. R., Arnkoff, D. B., & Gray, S. H. (2008). Contributions of psychodynamic approaches to treatment of PTSD and trauma: A review of the empirical treatment and psychopathology literature. *Psychiatry, 71,* 13–34.

Schuckit, M. A., & Smith, T. L. (1997). Assessing the risk for alcoholism among sons of alcoholics. *Journal of Studies on Alcohol, 58,* 141–145.

Schuh, K. J., & Griffiths, R. R. (1997). Caffeine reinforcement: The role of withdrawal. *Psychopharmacology, 130,* 320–326.

Schultz, D. P., & Schultz, S. E. (2000). *A history of modern psychology* (7th ed.). Fort Worth, TX: Harcourt Brace.

Schultz, D. P., & Schultz, S. E. (2005). *Theories of personality* (8th ed.). Belmont, CA: Wadsworth.

Schwartz, J. E., Friedman, H. S., Tucker, J. S., Tomlinson-Keasey, C., Wingard, D. L., & Criqui, M. H. (1995). Sociodemographic and psychosocial factors in childhood as predictors of adult mortality. *American Journal of Public Health, 85,* 1237–1245.

Schwartz, M., O'Neal Chambliss, H., Brownell, K., Blair, S., & Billington, C. (2003). Weight bias among health professionals specializing in obesity. *Obesity Research, 11,* 1033–1039.

Schwarzwald, J., Bizman, A., & Raz, M. (1983). The foot-in-the-door paradigm: Effects of second request size on donation probability and donor generosity. *Personality and Social Psychology Bulletin, 9,* 443–450.

Scoboria, A., Mazzoni, G., & Kirsch, I. (2006). Effects of misleading questions and hypnotic memory suggestion on memory reports: A signal-detection analysis. *International Journal of Clinical and Experimental Hypnosis, 54,* 340–359.

Scoboria, A., Mazzoni, G., Kirsch, I., & Milling, L. S. (2002). Immediate and persisting effects of misleading questions and hypnosis on memory reports. *Journal of Experimental Psychology, Applied, 8,* 26–32.

Scollon, C. N., & Diener, E. (2006). Love, work, and changes in extraversion and neuroticism over time. *Journal of Personality and Social Psychology, 91,* 1152–1165.

Scott, T. R., & Plata-Salaman, C. R. (1991). Coding of taste quality. In T. V. Gethell, R. L. Doty, L. M. Bartoshuk, & J. B. Snow, Jr. (Eds.), *Smell and taste in health and disease* (pp. 345–368). New York: Raven.

Scoville, W. B., & Milner, B. (1957). Loss of recent memory after bilateral hippocampal lesions. *Journal of Neurology, Neurosurgery, and Psychiatry, 20,* 11–19.

Scully, J. A., Tosi, H., & Banning, K. (2000). Life events checklist: Revisiting the social readjustment rating scale after 30 years. *Educational and Psychological Measurement, 60,* 864–876.

Sebel, P. S., Bowdle, T. A., Ghoneim, M. M., Rampil, I. J., Padilla, R. E., Gan, T.J., et al. (2004). The incidence of awareness during anesthesia: A multicenter United States study. *Anesthesia and Analgesia, 99,* 833–839.

Seeman, P. (1999). Brain development, X: Pruning during development. *American Journal of Psychiatry, 156,* 168.

Segal, M. W. (1974). Alphabet and attraction: An unobtrusive measure of the effect of propinquity in a field setting. *Journal of Personality and Social Psychology, 30,* 654–657.

Segerstrom, S. C. (2000). Personality and the immune system: Models, methods, and mechanisms. *Annals of Behavioral Medicine, 22,* 180–190.

Segerstrom, S. C. (2007). Stress, energy, and immunity: An ecological view. *Current Directions in Psychological Science, 16,* 326–330.

Segerstrom, S. C., Taylor, S. E., Kemeny, M. E., & Fahey, J. L. (1998). Optimism is associated with mood, coping, and immune change in response to stress. *Journal of Personality and Social Psychology, 74,* 6.

Segrin, C., & Nabi, R. L. (2002). Does television viewing cultivate unrealistic expectations about marriage? *Journal of Communication, 52,* 247–263.

Seidler, R. D., Purushotham, A., Kim, S.-G., Ugurbil, K., Willingham, D., & Ashe, J. (2002). Cerebellum activation associated with performance change but not after motor learning. *Science (Washington), 296,* 2043–2046.

Seiffert, A. E., Somers, D. C., Dale, A. M., & Tootell, R. B. H. (2003). Functional MRI studies of human visual motion perception: Texture, luminance, attention, and after-effects. *Cerebral Cortex, 13,* 340–349.

Sekuler, R., McLaughlin, C., Kahana, M. J., Wingfield, A., & Yotsumoto, Y. (2006). Short-term visual recognition and temporal order memory are both well-preserved in aging. *Psychology and Aging, 21,* 632–637.

Seligman, M. E. P. (1970). On the generality of laws of learning. *Psychological Review, 77,* 406–418.

Shimoff, E., Catania, A. C., & Matthews, B. A. (1981). Unstructured human responding: Sensitivity of low-rate performance to schedule contingencies. *Journal of Experimental Analysis of Behavior, 36,* 207–220.

Seligman, M. E. P. (1989). *Helplessness.* New York: Freeman.

Seligman, M. E. P. (1995). The effectiveness of psychotherapy: The Consumer Reports Study. *American Psychologist, 50,* 965–974.

Seligman, M. E. P., & Maier, S. F. (1967). Failure to escape traumatic shock. *Journal of Experimental Psychology, 74,* 1–9.

Selmi, P. M., Klein, M. H., Greist, J. H., Sorrell, S. P., & Erdman, H. P. (1990). Computer-administered cognitive-behavioral therapy for depression. *American Journal of Psychiatry, 147,* 51–56.

Seltzer, J. A. (2001). Families formed outside of marriage. In R. M. Milardo (Ed.), *Understanding families into the new millennium: A decade in review* (pp. 466–487). Minneapolis: National Council on Family Relations.

Selye, H. (1976). *The stress of life.* New York: McGraw-Hill.

Senghas, A., & Coppola, M. (2001). Children creating language: How Nicaraguan sign language acquired a spatial grammar. *Psychological Science, 12,* 323–328.

Seto, M. C., & Barbaree, H. E. (1995). The role of alcohol in sexual aggression. *Clinical Psychology Review, 15,* 545–566.

Sexton, J. (1995, July 25). Reviving Kitty Genovese case, and its passions. *New York Times,* pp. B1, B5.

Shafer, M., & Crichlow, S. (1996). Antecedents of groupthink: A quantitative study. *Journal of Conflict Resolution, 40,* 415–435.

Shallenberger, R. S. (1993). *Taste chemistry.* London: Blackie.

Shanker, S. G., Savage-Rumbaugh, E. S., & Taylor, T. J. (1999). Kanzi: A new beginning. *Animal Learning and Behavior, 27,* 24–25.

Share, D. L., & Silva, P. A. (2003). Gender bias in IQ-discrepancy and post-discrepancy definitions of reading disability. *Journal of Learning Disabilities, 36,* 4–14.

Sharma, L. (2007). Lifestyles, flying and associated health problems in flight attendants. *Journal of the Royal Society of Health, 127,* 268–275.

Shaw, H., Ramirez, L., Trost, A., Randall, P., & Stice, E. (2004). Body image and eating disturbances across ethnic groups: More similarities than differences. *Psychology of Addictive Behaviors, 18,* 12–18.

Sheldon, K. M., Arndt, J., & Houser-Marko, L. (2003). In search of the organismic valuing process: The human tendency to move towards beneficial goal choices. *Journal of Personality, 71,* 835–869.

Sheline, Y. I. (2000). 3D MRI studies of neuroanatomic changes in unipolar major depression: The role of stress and medical comorbidity. *Biological Psychiatry, 48,* 791–800.

Shen, B. J., McCreary, C. P., & Myers, H. F. (2004). Independent and mediated contributions of personality, coping, social support, and depressive symptoms to physical functioning outcome among patients in cardiac rehabilitation. *Journal of Behavioral Medicine, 27,* 39–62.

Shepard, G. M. (2006). Smell images and the flavour system in the brain. *Nature, 444,* 316–321.

Shepard, R. N. (1978). The mental image. *American Psychologist, 33,* 125–137.

Sherif, M. (1966). *In common predicament: Social psychology of intergroup conflict and cooperation.* Boston: Houghton Mifflin.

Sherif, M., Harvey, O. J., White, J., Hood, W., & Sherif, C. (1961). *Intergroup conflict and cooperation: The Robber's Cave experiment.* Norman: University of Oklahoma Press.

Sherwin, B. B., & Gelfand, M. M. (1987). The role of androgen in the maintenance of sexual functioning in oophorectomized women. *Psychosomatic Medicine, 49,* 397–409.

Shields, M. (2004). Stress, health and the benefit of social support. *Health Reports, 15,* 9–38.

Shin, L. M., Rauch, S. L., & Pitman, R. K. (2006). Amygdala, medial prefrontal cortex, and hippocampal function in PTSD. *Annals of the New York Academy of Sciences, 1071,* 67–79.

Shiner, R. L., Masten, A. S., & Roberts, J. M. (2003). Childhood personality foreshadows adult personality and life outcomes two decades later. *Journal of Personality, 71,* 1145–1170.

Shinskey, J. L., & Munakata, Y. (2005). Familiarity breeds searching: Infants reverse their novelty preferences when reaching for hidden objects. *Psychological Science, 16,* 596–600.

Shintani, T., Hughes, C., Beckham, S., & O'Connor, H. (1991). Obesity and cardiovascular risk intervention through the ad libitum feeding of traditional Hawaiian diet. *American Journal of Clinical Nutrition, 53,* 1647S–1651S.

Shneidman, E. S. (1987, March). At the point of no return. *Psychology Today,* 54–58.

Shou, M. (1993). *Lithium treatment of manic-depressive illness: A practical guide* (5th ed.). Basel, Switzerland: Karger.

Siegel, J. M. (2001). The REM sleep-memory consolidation hypothesis. *Science, 294,* 1058–1063.

Siegel, J. M., & Boehmer, L. N. (2006). Narcolepsy and the hypocretin system: Where motion meets emotion. *Nature Clinical Practice Neurology, 2,* 548–556.

Siegel, L. S., & Hodkin, B. (1982). The garden path to the understanding of cognitive development: Has Piaget led us into the poison ivy? In S. Modgil & C. Modgil (Eds.), *Jean Piaget: Consensus and controversy* (pp. 57–82). New York: Praeger.

Siegel, S. (2005). Drug tolerance, drug addiction, and drug anticipation. *Current Directions in Psychological Science, 14,* 296–300.

Siever, L. J., & Koenigsberg, H. W. (2000). The frustrating no-man's-land of borderline personality disorder. *Cerebrum: The Dana Forum on Brain Science, 2*(4).

Signorielli, N., & Bacue, A. (1999). Recognition and respect: A content analysis of prime-time television characters. *Sex Roles, 40,* 527–544.

Signorielli, N., & Lears, M. (1992). Children, television, and conceptions about chores:

Attitudes and behavior. *Sex Roles, 27,* 157–170.

Silva, C. E., & Kirsch, I. (1992). Interpretive sets, expectancy, fantasy proneness, and dissociation as predictors of hypnotic response. *Journal of Personality and Social Psychology, 63,* 847–856.

Sim, H. (2000). Relationship of daily hassles and social support to depression and antisocial behavior among early adolescents. *Journal of Youth and Adolescence, 29,* 647–659.

Simon, H. A. (1974). How big is a chunk? *Science, 183,* 482–488.

Simpson, G., & Yinger, J. M. (1985). *Racial and cultural minorities.* New York: Plenum Press.

Simpson, J. A., Collins, W. A., Tran, S., & Haydon, K. C. (2007). Attachment and the experience and expression of emotions in romantic relationships: A developmental perspective. *Journal of Personality and Social Psychology, 92,* 355–367.

Sinclair, S. (1985). *How animals see.* New York: Facts on File Publications.

Sinnott, J. D. (1998). *The development of logic in adulthood: Postformal thought and its applications.* New York: Plenum.

Skinner, B. F. (1938). *The behavior of organisms.* New York: Appleton-Century-Crofts.

Skinner, B. F. (1953). *Science and human behavior.* New York: Macmillan.

Skodol, A. E., & Bender, D. S. (2003). Why are women diagnosed borderline more than men? *Psychiatry Quarterly, 74,* 349–360.

Slameka, N. J. (1966). Differentiation versus unlearning of verbal associations. *Journal of Experimental Psychology, 71,* 822–828.

Sloan, R. P., & Bagiella, E. (2002). Claims about religious involvement and health outcomes. *Annals of Behavioral Medicine, 24,* 14–21.

Small, B. J., Hertzog, C., Hultsch, D. F., & Dixon, R. A. (2003). Stability and change in adult personality over 6 years: Findings from the Victoria Longitudinal Study. *Journal of Gerontology: Psychological Sciences, 58B,* P166–P176.

Smetana, J. G., Campione-Barr, N., & Metzger, A. (2006). Adolescent development in interpersonal and societal contexts. *Annual Review of Psychology, 57,* 255–284.

Smith, C. (1995). Sleep states and memory processes. *Behavioural Brain Research, 69*(1–2), 137–145.

Smith, C. A., Organ, D. W., & Near, J. P. (1983). Organizational citizenship behavior: Its nature and antecedents. *Journal of Applied Psychology, 68,* 653–663.

Smith, D. E., & Cogswell, C. (1994). A cross-cultural perspective on adolescent girls' body perception. *Perceptual and Motor Skills, 78,* 744–746.

Smith, J. W., Frawley, P. J., & Polissar, N. L. (1997). Six- and twelve-month abstinence rates in inpatient alcoholics treated with either faradic aversion or chemical aversion compared with matched inpatients from a treatment registry. *Journal of Addictive Diseases, 16,* 5–24.

Smith, M. C., Coleman, S. R., & Gormezano, I. (1969). Classical conditioning of the rabbit's nictitating membrane response at backward, simultaneous, and forward CS–US intervals. *Journal of Comparative and Physiological Psychology, 69,* 226–231.

Smith, M. C., & Dust, M. C. (2006). An exploration of the influence of dispositional traits and appraisal on coping strategies in African American college students. *Journal of Personality, 74,* 145–174.

Smith, M. L., & Glass, G. V. (1977). Meta-analysis of psychotherapy outcome studies. *American Psychologist, 32,* 752–760.

Smith, M. L., Glass, G. V., & Miller, T. I. (1980). *The benefits of psychotherapy.* Baltimore: Johns Hopkins University Press.

Smith, P. C., Kendall, L. M., & Hulin, C. L. (1969). *The measurement of satisfaction in work and retirement.* Chicago: Rand McNally.

Smith, R. A. (2002). Race, gender, and authority in the workplace: Theory and research. *Annual Review of Sociology, 28,* 509–542.

Smith, T. W. (2006). Personality as risk and resilience in physical health. *Current Directions in Psychological Science, 15,* 227–231.

Smith, T. W., Glazer, K., Ruiz, J. M., & Gallo, L. C. (2004). Hostility, anger, aggressiveness and coronary heart disease: An interpersonal perspective on personality, emotion, and health. *Journal of Personality, 72,* 1217–1270.

Smyth, J., Litcher, L., Hurewitz, A., & Stone, A. (2001). Relaxation training and cortisol secretion in adult asthmatics. *Journal of Health Psychology, 6,* 217–227.

Snarey, J. (1995). In a communitarian voice: The sociological expansion of Kohlbergian theory, research, and practice. In W. M. Kurtines & J. L. Gewirtz (Eds.), *Moral development: An introduction* (pp. 109–134). Boston: Allyn & Bacon.

Snedecor, S. M., Pomerleau, C. S., Mehringer, A. M., Ninowski, R., & Pomerleau, O. F. (2006). Differences in smoking-related variables based on phenylthiocarbamide "taster" status. *Addictive Behaviors, 31,* 2309–2312.

Snibbe, A. C. (2003). Cultural psychology: Studying the exotic other. *APS Observer, 16*(1), 30–32.

Snyder, C. R., Ilardi, S., Michael, S. T., & Cheavens, J. (2000). Hope theory: Updating a common process for psychological change. In C. R. Snyder & R. E. Ingram (Eds.), *Handbook of psychological change: Psychotherapy processes and practices for the 21st century* (pp. 128–153). New York: Wiley.

Soares, J. C., & Mann, J. J. (1997). The functional neuroanatomy of mood disorders. *Journal of Psychiatric Research, 31,* 393–432.

Solberg, E. E., Halvorsen, R., & Holen, A. (2000). Effect of meditation on immune cells. *Stress Medicine, 16,* 185–190.

Soloff, P. H., Lis, J. A., Kelly, T., Cornelius, J., & Ulrich, R. F. (1994). Self-mutilation and suicidal behavior in borderline personality disorder. *Journal of Personality Disorders, 8,* 257–267.

Solomon, A., Arnow, B. A., Gotlib, I. H., & Wind, B. (2003). Individualized measurement of irrational beliefs in remitted depressives. *Journal of Clinical Psychology, 59,* 439–455.

Somers, V. K., Phil, D., Dyken, M. E., Mark, A. L., & Abboud, F. M. (1993). Sympathetic-nerve activity during sleep in normal subjects. *New England Journal of Medicine, 328,* 303–307.

Sonstroem, R. J., & Bernardo, P. (1982). Intraindividual pregame state anxiety and basketball performance: A re-examination of the inverted-U curve. *Journal of Sport Psychology, 4,* 235–245.

Sonuga-Barke, E. J. S., Dalen, L., & Remington, B. (2003). Do executive deficits and delay aversion make independent contributions to preschool attention-deficit/hyperactivity disorder symptoms? *Journal of the American Academy of Child and Adolescent Psychiatry, 42,* 1335–1342.

Soper, B., Milford, G. E., & Rosenthal, G. T. (1995). Belief when evidence does not support theory. *Psychology and Marketing, 12,* 415–422.

Soussignan, R. (2002). Duchenne smile, emotional experience, and autonomic reactivity: A test of the facial feedback hypothesis. *Emotion, 2,* 52–74.

Sowell, E. R., Thompson, P. M., Tessner, K. D., & Toga, A. W. (2001). Mapping continued brain growth and gray matter density reduction in dorsal frontal cortex: Inverse relationships during postadolescent brain maturation. *Journal of Neuroscience, 21,* 8819–8829.

Soyka, M., Preuss, U. W., Hesselbrock, V., Zill, P., Koller, G., & Bondy, B. (2008). GABA-A2 receptor subunit gene (GABRA2) polymorphisms and risk for alcohol dependence. *Journal of Psychiatric Research, 42,* 184–191.

Spanos, N. P. (1996). *Multiple identities and false memories: A sociocognitive perspective.* Washington, DC: American Psychological Association.

Spanos, N. P., Burnley, M. C. E., & Cross, P. A. (1993). Response expectancies and interpretations as determinants of hypnotic responding. *Journal of Personality and Social Psychology, 65,* 1237–1242.

Spearman, C. (1904). The proof and measurement of association between two things. *American Journal of Psychology, 15,* 72–101.

Spence, J. T., & Buckner, C. E. (2000). Instrumental and expressive traits, trait stereotypes, and sexist attitudes: What do they signify? *Psychology of Women Quarterly, 24,* 44–62.

Spencer, J. A., & Fremouw, W. J. (1979). Binge eating as a function of restraint and weight classification. *Journal of Abnormal Psychology, 88,* 262–267.

Spherion. (2006). *Spherion survey: Workers say listening to music while working improves job satisfaction, productivity* [Online]. Available at http://www.spherion.com/press/releases/2006/IPod_at_Work_Snapshot.jsp

Spiegel, D. (1997). Trauma, dissociation, and memory. *Annals of the New York Academy of Sciences, 821,* 225–237.

Spiegel, D. A. (1998). Efficacy studies of alprazolam in panic disorder. *Psychopharmacology Bulletin, 43,* 191–195.

Squire, L. R. (1992). Memory and the hippocampus: A synthesis from findings with rats, monkeys, and humans. *Psychological Review, 99,* 195–232.

Squire, L. R., Knowlton, B., & Musen, G. (1993). The structure and organization of memory. *Annual Review of Psychology, 44,* 453–495.

Squire, L. R., Ojemann, J. G., Miezin, F. M., Petersen, S. E., Videen, T. O., & Raichle, M. E. (1992). Activation of the hippocampus in normal humans: A functional anatomical study of memory. *Proceedings of the National Academy of Science, USA, 89,* 1837–1841.

Srinivasan, L., Eden, U. T., Miller, S. K., & Brown, E. N. (2007). General-purpose filter design for neural prosthetic devices. *Journal of Neurophysiology, 98,* 2456–2475.

Srivastava, S., John, O. P., Gosling, S. D., & Potter, J. (2003). Development of personality in early and middle adulthood: Set in plaster or persistent change? *Journal of Personality and Social Psychology, 84,* 1041–1053.

Stahl, S. M. (1996). *Essential psychopharmacology.* New York: Cambridge University Press.

Stahl, S. M. (1998). Basic psychopharmacology of antidepressants: Part I. Antidepressants have seven distinct mechanisms of action. *Journal of Clinical Psychiatry, 59*(Suppl. 4), 5–14.

Stahl, S. M. (2001a). Dopamine system stabilizers, aripiprazole, and the next generation of antipsychotics: Part I. "Goldilocks" actions at dopamine receptors. *Journal of Clinical Psychiatry, 62,* 841–842.

Stahl, S. M. (2001b). Dopamine system stabilizers, aripiprazole, and the next generation of antipsychotics: Part II. Illustrating their mechanism of action. *Journal of Clinical Psychiatry, 62,* 923–924.

Stahl, S. M. (2007). Beyond the dopamine hypothesis to the NMDA glutamate receptor hypofunction hypothesis of schizophrenia. *CNS Spectrums, 12,* 265–268.

Stanley, S. M., Whitton, S. W., Sadberry, S. L., Clements, M. L., & Markman, H. J. (2006). Sacrifice as a predictor of marital outcomes. *Family Process, 45,* 289–303.

Stanovich, K. E., & West, R. F. (1998). Individual differences in rational thought. *Journal of Experimental Psychology: General, 127,* 161–188.

Stanton, J. L. (2004). The end of TV advertising: Technologies allow consumers to miss what once were the bedrock of consumer product advertising. *Food Processing, 65,* 26.

Starrels, M. E. (1994). Husbands' involvement in female gender-typed household chores. *Sex Roles, 31,* 473–491.

Statham, D. J., Heath, A. C., Madden, P., Bucholz, K. Bierut, L., Dinwiddie, S. H., et al. (1998). Suicidal behavior: An epidemiological study. *Psychological Medicine, 28,* 839–855.

Steadman, H. J., Mulvey, E. P., Monahan, J., Robbins, P. C., Applebaum, P. S., Grisso, T., et al. (1998). Violence by people discharged from acute psychiatric inpatient facilities and by others in the same neighborhoods. *Archives of General Psychiatry, 55,* 393–401.

Stear, S. (2003). Health and fitness: Series 1. The importance of physical activity on health. *Journal of Family Health Care, 13,* 10–13.

Steele, C. M. (1997). A threat in the air: How stereotypes shape the intellectual identities and performance of women and African-Americans. *American Psychologist, 52,* 613–629.

Steele, C. M., & Aronson, J. (1995). Stereotype threat and the intellectual test performance of African Americans. *Journal of Personality and Social Psychology, 69,* 797–811.

Steele, J., James, J. B., & Barnett, R. C. (2002). Learning in a man's world: Examining the perceptions of undergraduate women in male-dominated academic areas. *Psychology of Women Quarterly, 26,* 46–50.

Steffire, V., Castillo-Vales, V., & Morley, L. (1966). Language and cognition in Yucatan: A cross-cultural replication. *Journal of Personality and Social Psychology, 4,* 112–115.

Stein, J. H., & Reiser, L. W. (1994). A study of white middle-class adolescent boys' responses to "semenarche" (the first ejaculation). *Journal of Youth and Adolescence, 23,* 373–384.

Steinberg, L., Lamborn, S. D., Dornbusch, S. M., & Darling, N. (1992). Impact of parenting practices on adolescent achievement: Authoritative parenting, school involvement, and encouragement to succeed. *Child Development, 63,* 1266–1281.

Steinberg, L., & Morris, A. S. (2001). Adolescent development. *Annual Reviews of Psychology, 52,* 83–110.

Steiner, M., & Born, L. (2000). Diagnosis and treatment of premenstrual dysphoric disorder: An update. *International Clinical Psychopharmacology, 15*(Suppl. 3), S5–S17.

Steiner, M., Dunn, E., & Born, L. (2003). Hormones and mood: From menarche to menopause and beyond. *Journal of Affective Disorders, 74,* 67–83.

Steinhausen, H. C., & Vollrath, M. (1993). The self-image of adolescent patients with eating disorders. *International Journal of Eating Disorders, 13,* 221–229.

Stephan, K. E., Marshall, J. C., Friston, K. J., Rowe, J. B., Ritzl, A., Zilles, K., et al. (2003). Lateralized cognitive processes and lateralized task control in the human brain. *Science, 301,* 384–386.

Stephens, C. E., Pear, J. J., Wray, L. D., & Jackson, G. C. (1975). Some effects of reinforcement schedules in teaching picture names to retarded children. *Journal of Applied Behavior Analysis, 8,* 435–447.

Stephens, R. S., Roffman, R. A., & Simpson, E. E. (1994). Treating adult marijuana dependence: A test of the relapse prevention model. *Journal of Consulting and Clinical Psychology, 62,* 92–99.

Stephenson, M. T., Benoit, W. L., & Tschida, D. A. (2001). Testing the mediating role of cognitive responses in the elaboration likelihood model. *Communication Studies, 52,* 324–337.

Steriade, M., & McCarley, R. W. (1990). *Brainstem control of wakefulness and sleep.* New York: Plenum Press.

Stern, G. S., McCants, T. R., & Pettine, P. W. (1982). Stress and illness: Controllable and uncontrollable life events' relative contributions. *Personality and Social Psychology Bulletin, 8,* 140–143.

Stern, K. N., & McClintock, M. K. (1998). Regulation of ovulation by human pheromones. *Nature, 392,* 177–179.

Sternberg, R. J. (1985). *Beyond IQ: A triarchic theory of human intelligence.* New York: Cambridge University Press.

Sternberg, R. J. (1997a). The concept of intelligence and its role in lifelong learning and success. *American Psychologist, 52,* 1030–1037.

Sternberg, R. J. (1997b). *Successful intelligence.* New York: Plume.

Sternberg, R. J. (1999). *Handbook of creativity.* Cambridge, UK: Cambridge University Press.

Sternberg, R. J., Grigorenko, E. L., & Kidd, K. K. (2005). Intelligence, race, and genetics. *American Psychologist, 60,* 46–59.

Stevens, A., & Coupe, P. (1978). Distortions in judged spatial relations. *Cognitive Psychology, 10,* 422–437.

Stewart, G. L., & Manz, C. C. (1995). Leadership for self-managing work teams: A typology and integrative model. *Human Relations, 48,* 347–370.

Stewart, R., Ellenburg, G., Hicks, L., Kremen, M., & Daniel, M. (1990). Employee references as a recruitment source. *Applied H.R.M. Research, 1*(1), 1–3.

Stice, E., Telch, C. F., & Rizvi, S. L. (2000). Development and validation of the eating disorder diagnostic scale: A brief self-report measure of anorexia, bulimia, and binge-eating disorder. *Psychological Assessment, 12,* 123–131.

Stickgold, R., & Walker, M. P. (2007). Sleep-dependent memory consolidation and reconsolidation. *Sleep Medicine, 8,* 331–343.

Stine-Morrow, E. A., Parisi, J. M., Morrow, D. G., Greene, J., & Park, D. C. (2007). An engagement model of cognitive optimization through adulthood. *Journals of Gerontology, Series B: Psychological Sciences and Social Sciences, 62,* 62–69.

Stoel-Gammon, C., & Otomo, K. (1986). Babbling development of hearing impaired and normal subjects. *Journal of Speech and Hearing Disorders, 51,* 33–41.

Stone, J. M., Morrison, P., & Pilowsky, L. S. (2007). Glutamate and dopamine dysregulation in schizophrenia: A synthesis and selective review. *Journal of Psychopharmacology, 21,* 440–452.

Storms, G., DeBoeck, P., & Ruts, W. (2001). Categorization of novel stimuli in well-known natural concepts. *Psychonomic Bulletin and Review, 8,* 377–384.

Storms, M. D. (1973). Videotape and the attribution process: Reversing actors' and observers' points of view. *Journal of Personality and Social Psychology, 27,* 165–175.

Stout, M. (2005). *The sociopath next door.* New York: Broadway Books.

Strassberg, Z., Dodge, K., Pettit, G. S., & Bates, J. E. (1994). Spanking in the home and children's subsequent aggression toward kindergarten peers. *Development and Psychopathology, 6,* 445–461.

Strickland, B. R. (1989). Internal–external control expectancies: From contingency to creativity. *American Psychologist, 44,* 1–12.

Stright, A. D., Gallagher, K. C., & Kelley, K. (2008). Infant temperament moderates relations between maternal parenting in early childhood and children's adjustment in first grade. *Child Development, 79,* 186–200.

Stroebe, W., & Stroebe, M. S. (1993). Determinants of adjustment to bereavement in younger widows and widowers. In M. S. Stroebe, W. Stroebe, & R. O. Hansson (Eds.), *Handbook of bereavement* (pp. 208–226). New York: Cambridge University Press.

Substance Abuse and Mental Health Services Administration (SAMHSA). (2006). *Results from the 2005 National Survey on Drug Use and Health: National findings.* Rockville, MD: Office of Applied Studies, NSDUH Series H-30, DHHS Publication No. SMA 06-4194.

Substance Abuse and Mental Health Services Administration (SAMHSA). (2007). *Results from the 2006 National Survey on Drug Use and Health: National findings.* Rockville, MD: Office of Applied Studies, NSDUH Series H-32, DHHS Publication No. SMA 07-4293.

Suh, J. J., Pettinati, H. M., Kampman, K. M., & O'Brien, C. P. (2006). The status of disulfiram: A half of a century later. *Journal of Clinical Psychopharmacology, 26,* 290–302.

Sullivan, J. W., & Horowitz, F. D. (1983). The effects of intonation on infant attention: The role of the rising intonation contour. *Journal of Child Language, 10,* 521–534.

Sullivan, M. A., & O'Leary, S. G. (1990). Maintenance following reward and cost token programs. *Behavior Therapy, 21,* 139–149.

Sullivan, P. F., Neale, M. C., & Kendler, S. K. (2000). Genetic epidemiology of major depression: Review and meta-analysis. *American Journal of Psychiatry, 157,* 1552–1562.

Super, D. E. (1957). *The psychology of careers.* New York: Harper & Row.

Super, D. E. (1976). *Career education and the meanings of work.* Washington DC: U.S. Office of Education.

Super, D. E. (1980). A life-span, life-space approach to career development. *Journal of Vocational Behavior, 16,* 282–298.

Super, D. E. (1991). A life-span, life-space approach to career development. In D. Brown, L. Brooks, & Associates (Eds.), *Career choice and development: Applying contemporary theories to practice* (2nd ed., pp. 197–261). San Francisco: Jossey-Bass.

Swain, I. U., Zelazo, P. R., & Clifton, R. K. (1993). Newborn infants' memory for speech sounds retained over 24 hours. *Developmental Psychology, 29*(2), 312–323.

Swartz, C. (1995). Setting the ECT stimulus. *Psychiatric Times, 12*(6).

Swartz, M., Blazer, D., George, L., & Winfield, I. (1990). Estimating the prevalence of borderline personality disorder in the community. *Journal of Personality Disorders, 4,* 257–272.

Swayze, V. W. (1995). Frontal leucotomy and related psychosurgical procedures in the era before antipsychotics (1935–1954): A historical overview. *American Journal of Psychiatry, 152,* 505–515.

Symons, C. S., & Johnson, B. T. (1997). The self-reference effect in memory: A meta-analysis. *Psychological Bulletin, 121,* 371–394.

Szasz, T. S. (1987). *Insanity: The idea and its consequences.* New York: Wiley.

Szentirmai, E., Yasuda, T., Taishi, P., Wang, M., Churchill, L., Bohnet, S., et al. (2007). Growth hormone-releasing hormone: Cerebral cortical sleep-related EEG actions and expressions. *American Journal of Physiology: Regulatory, Integrative and Comparative Physiology, 293,* R922–R930.

Szkrybalo, J., & Ruble, D. N. (1999). "God made me a girl": Sex-category constancy judgments and explanations revisited. *Developmental Psychology, 35,* 392–402.

Tager-Flusberg, H. (2005). Putting words together: Morphology and syntax in the preschool years. In J. B. Gleason (Ed.), *The development of language* (5th ed., pp. 148–190). Boston: Allyn & Bacon.

Tajfel, H. (1982). *Social identity and intergroup relations.* Cambridge, UK: Cambridge University Press.

Tankova, I., Adan, A., & Buela-Casal, G. (1994). Circadian typology and individual Differences: A review. *Personality and Individual Differences, 16,* 671–684.

Taylor, C. B., & Luce, K. H. (2003). Computer- and Internet-based psychotherapy interventions. *Current Directions in Psychological Science, 12,* 18–22.

Taylor, D. J., Jenni, O. G., Acebo, C., & Carskadon, M. A. (2005). Sleep tendency during extended wakefulness: Insights into adolescent sleep regulation and behavior. *Journal of Sleep Research, 14,* 239–244.

Taylor, E. J., & Outlaw, F. H. (2002). Use of prayer among persons with cancer. *Holistic Nursing Practices, 16,* 46–60.

Taylor, H. (2002). Poor people and African Americans suffer the most stress from the hassles of daily living. *The Harris Poll #66.*

Taylor, S. E. (2003). *Health psychology* (5th ed.). New York: McGraw-Hill.

Taylor, S. M. (2008). Electroconvulsive therapy, brain-derived neurotrophic factor, and possible neurorestorative benefit of the clinical application of electroconvulsive therapy. *Journal of ECT, 24,* 160–165.

Teachman, J. D., Tedrow, L. M., & Crowder, K. D. (2000). The changing demography of America's families. *Journal of Marriage and the Family, 62,* 1234–1246.

Teasdale, J. D., & Russell, M. L. (1983). Differential effects of induced mood on the recall of positive, negative, and neutral words. *British Journal of Clinical Psychology, 22,* 163–171.

Teasdale, J. D., Scott, J., Moore, R. G., Hayhurst, H., Pope, M., & Paykel, E. S. (2001). How does cognitive therapy prevent relapse in residual depression? Evidence from a controlled trial. *Journal of Consulting and Clinical Psychology, 69,* 347–357.

Teicher, M. H. (2002). Scars that won't heal: The neurobiology of child abuse. *Scientific American, 286,* 68–75.

Teitelbaum, P., & Epstein, A. N. (1962). The lateral hypothalamic syndrome: Recovery of feeding and drinking after lateral hypothalamic lesions. *Psychological Review, 69,* 74–90.

Teitelbaum, P., & Stellar, E. (1954). Recovery from failure to eat produced by hypothalamic lesions. *Science, 120,* 894–895.

Temoshok, L. (1992). *The Type C connection: The behavioral links to cancer and your health.* New York: Random House.

Terman, L. M. (1916). *The measurement of intelligence.* Boston: Houghton Mifflin.

Terr, L. C. (1983). Chowchilla revisited: The effects of psychic trauma four years after a school-bus kidnapping. *American Journal of Psychiatry, 140,* 1543–1550.

Terracciano, A., Costa, P. T., & McCrae, R. R. (2006). Personality plasticity after age 30. *Personality and Social Psychology Bulletin, 32,* 999–1009.

Teyber, E., & McClure, F. (2000). Therapist variables. In C. R. Snyder & R. E. Ingram (Eds.), *Handbook of psychological change: Psychotherapy processes and practices for the 21st century* (pp. 62–87). New York: Wiley.

Thase, M. E. (2003). Effectiveness of antidepressants: Comparative remission rates. *Journal of Clinical Psychiatry, 64*(Suppl. 2), 3–7.

Thase, M. E., Jindal, R., & Howland, R. H. (2002). Biological aspects of depression. In I. H. Gotlib & C. L. Hammen (Eds.), *Handbook of depression* (pp. 192–218). New York: Guilford Press.

Thase, M. E., & Kupfer, D. J. (1996). Recent developments in the pharmacotherapy of mood disorders. *Journal of Consulting and Clinical Psychology, 64,* 646–659.

Thatcher, G. R. J., Bennett, B. M., & Reynolds, J. N. (2006). NO chimeras as therapeutic agents in Alzheimer's disease. *Current Alzheimer's Research, 3,* 237–245.

Thelen, E. (1995). Motor development: A new synthesis. *American Psychologist, 50,* 79–95.

Thies-Flechtner, K., Muller-Oerlinghausen, B., Seibert, W., Walther, A., & Greil, W. (1996). Effect of prophylactic treatment on suicide risk in patients with major affective disorders. Data from a randomized prospective trial. *Pharmacopsychiatry, 29,* 103–107.

Thomas, A., & Chess, S. (1977). *Temperament and development.* New York: Brunner/Mazel.

Thomas, A., & Chess, S. (1986). The New York longitudinal study: From infancy to early adult life. In R. Plomin & J. Dunn (Eds.), *The study of temperament: Changes, continuities, and challenges* (pp. 39–52). Hillsdale, NJ: Erlbaum.

Thompson, P. M., Giedd, J. N., Woods, R. P., MacDonald, D., Evans, A. C., & Togo, A. W. (2000, March 9). Growth patterns in the developing human brain detected by using continuum-mechanical tensor maps. *Nature, 404,* 190–193.

Thorndike, E. L. (1898). Animal intelligence: An experimental study of associative process in animals. *Psychological Review Monograph, No. 8.*

Thorndike, E. L. (1905). *The elements of psychology.* New York: Seiler.

Thorpe, G. L., & Olson, S. L. (1997). *Behavior therapy: Concepts, procedures, and applications* (2nd ed.). Boston: Allyn & Bacon.

Thorpy, M. (2007). Therapeutic advances in narcolepsy. *Sleep Medicine, 8,* 427–440.

Thurber, C. A. (1995). The experience and expression of homesickness in preadolescent and adolescent boys. *Child Development, 66,* 1162–1178.

Thurstone, L. L. (1931). The measurement of social attitudes. *Journal of Abnormal and Social Psychology, 26,* 249–269.

Tienari, P., Wynne, L. C., Laksy, K., Moring, J., Nieminen, P., Sorri, A., et al. (2003). Genetic boundaries of the schizophrenia spectrum: Evidence from the Finnish Adoptive Family Study of Schizophrenia. *American Journal of Psychiatry, 160,* 1567–1594.

Tolin, D. F., & Foa, E. B. (2006). Sex differences in trauma and posttraumatic stress disorder: A quantitative review of 25 years of research. *Psychological Bulletin, 132,* 959–992.

Tolman, E. C., & Honzik, C. H. (1930). "Insight" in rats. *University of California Publications in Psychology, 4,* 215–232.

Tomasello, M. (2000). Culture and cognitive development. *Current Directions in Psychological Science, 9,* 37–40.

Trafimow, D., Armendariz, M. L., & Madsen, L. (2004). A test of whether attributions provide for self-enhancement or self-defense. *Journal of Social Psychology, 144,* 453–463.

Tremblay, R. E., Schaal, B., Boulerice, B., Arseneault, L., Soussignan, R. G., Paquette, D., et al. (1998). Testosterone, physical aggression, dominance, and physical development in early adolescence. *International Journal of Behavioral Development, 22,* 753–777.

Triandis, H. C. (1994). *Culture and Social Behavior.* New York: McGraw-Hill.

Troisi, J. R., II. (2003). Spontaneous recovery during, but not following, extinction of the discriminative stimulus effects of nicotine in rats: Reinstatement of stimulus control. *The Psychological Record, 53,* 579–592.

Tsai, G., Gastfriend, D. R., & Coyle, J. T. (1995). The glutamatergic basis of human alcoholism. *American Journal of Psychiatry, 152,* 332–340.

Tsuang, M. T., Fleming, J. A., & Simpson, J. C. (1999). Suicide and schizophrenia. In D. G. Jacobs (Ed.), *The Harvard Medical School guide to suicide assessment and intervention* (pp. 287–299). San Francisco: Jossey-Bass.

Tulving, E. (1972). Episodic and semantic memory. In E. Tulving & W. Donaldson (Eds.), *Organisation of memory* (pp. 381–403). London: Academic Press.

Tulving, E. (1974). Cue-dependent forgetting. *American Scientist, 62,* 74–82.

Tulving, E. (1983). *Elements of episodic memory.* Oxford, UK: Oxford University Press.

Turati, C. (2004). Why faces are not special to newborns: An alternative account of the face preference. *Current Directions in Psychological Science, 13,* 5–8.

Turati, C., & Simion, F. (2002). Newborns' recognition of changing and unchanging aspects of schematic faces. *Journal of Experimental Child Psychology, 83,* 239–261.

Turk, C. L., Heimberg, R. G., & Hope, D. A. (2001). Social anxiety disorder. *Clinical handbook of psychological disorders: A step-by-step treatment manual* (3rd ed., pp. 114–153). New York: Guilford Press.

Turner, A. J., & Ortony, A. (1992). Basic emotions: Can conflicting criteria converge? *Psychological Review, 99,* 566–571.

Turner, P. J., & Gervai, J. (1995). A multidimensional study of gender typing in preschool children and their parents: Personality, attitudes, preferences, behavior, and cultural differences. *Developmental Psychology, 31,* 759–772.

Tversky, A., & Kahneman, D. (1974). Judgment under uncertainty: Heuristics and biases, *Science, 185,* 1124–1131.

Tversky, A., & Kahneman, D. (1980). Causal schemas in judgments under uncertainty. In M. Fishbein (Ed.), *Progress in social psychology* (pp. 49–72). Hillsdale, NJ: Erlbaum.

Tversky, B. (1981). Distortions in memory for maps. *Cognitive Psychology, 13,* 407–433.

Tylka, T. L. (2006). Development and psychometric evaluation of a measure of intuitive eating. *Journal of Counseling Psychology, 53,* 226–240.

U.S. Census Bureau. (2000). *Statistical abstract of the United States* (122nd ed.). Washington DC: U.S. Government Printing Office.

U.S. Census Bureau. (2001). *Survey of income and program participation (SIPP), 2001 Panel, Wave 2 Topical Module.* Washington DC: U.S. Department of Commerce.

U.S. Census Bureau. (2005). *Fertility of American women: June 2004.* Washington, DC: U.S. Department of Commerce.

U.S. Census Bureau. (2006a). *2006 American community survey.* Washington, DC: U.S. Department of Commerce.

U.S. Census Bureau. (2006b). Nation's population one-third minority, U.S. Census Bureau News. Retrieved March 24, 2008, from http://www.census.gov/Press-Release/www/releases/archives/population/006808.html

U.S. Department of Education. (2005). *1999 and 2004 National study of postsecondary faculty.* Washington, DC: National Center for Education Statistics.

U.S. Department of Education. (2006). *Digest of education statistics.* Washington, DC: National Center for Education Statistics.

U.S. Department of Energy. (2007). *The human genome project information.* Available online at http://www.ornl.gov/hgmis

Uchino, B. N., Cacioppo, J. T., & Kiecolt-Glaser, J. K. (1996). The relationship between social support and physiological processes: A review with emphasis on underlying mechanisms and implications for health. *Psychological Bulletin, 119,* 488–531.

Ultan, R. (1969). Some general characteristics of interrogative systems. *Working Papers in Language Universals (Stanford University), 1,* 41–63.

Umberson, D., Williams, K., Powers, D. A., Meichu, D. C., & Campbell, A. M. (2005). As good as it gets? A lifecourse perspective on marital quality. *Social Forces, 84,* 493–511.

United Nations. (2003). *World fertility report 2003 (United Nations publication ST/ESA/SER.A/234).*

Ursu, S., Stenger, A., Shear, M. K., Jones, M. R., & Carter, C. S. (2003). Overactive action-monitoring in obsessive-compulsive disorder: Evidence from functional magnetic resonance imaging. *Psychological Science, 14,* 347–353.

Vainionpaa, L. K., Rattya, J., Knip, M., Tapanainen, J. S., Pakarinen, A. J., Lanning, P., et al. (1999). Valproate-induced hyperandrogenism during pubertal maturation in girls with epilepsy. *Annals of Neurology, 45,* 444–450.

Valenza, E., Simion, F., Cassia, V. M., & Umilta, C. (1996). Face preference at birth. *Journal of Experimental Psychology, 33,* 711–723.

Valli, K., Revonsuo, A., Palkas, O., Ismail, K. H., Ali, K. J., & Punamaki, R. L. (2005). The threat simulation theory of the evolutionary function of dreaming: Evidence from dreams of traumatized children. *Consciousness and Cognition, 14,* 188–218.

Van Goozen, S., Frijda, N., & de Poll, N. V. (1994). Anger and aggression in women: Influence of sports choice and testosterone administration. *Aggressive Behavior, 20,* 213–222.

Van Heteren, C. F., Boekkooi, P. F., Jongsma, H. W., & Nijhuis, J. G. (2000). Fetal learning and memory. *Lancet, 356,* 9236–9237.

van Honk, J., & Schutter, D. J. L. G. (2007). Testosterone reduces conscious detection of signals serving social correction: Implications for antisocial behavior. *Psychological Science, 18,* 663–667.

van Hooren, S. A., Valentijn, A. M., Bosma, H., Ponds, R. W., van Boxtel, M. P., & Jolles, J. (2007). Cognitive functioning in healthy older adults aged 64–81: A cohort study into the effects of age, sex, and education. *Neuropsychology, Development, and Cognition, Section B: Aging, Neuropsychology, and Cognition, 14,* 40–54.

van Laar, M., Volkerts, E., & Verbaten, M. (2001). Subcronic effects of the GABA-agonist lorazepam and the 5-HT2A/2C antagonist ritanserin on driving performance, slow wave sleep and daytime sleepiness in healthy volunteers. *Psychopharmacology, 154,* 189–197.

van Solinge, H., & Henkens, K. (2005). Couples' adjustment to retirement: A multi-actor panel study. *Journals of Gerontology, Series B: Psychological Sciences and Social Sciences, 60,* S11–S20.

Vance, E. B., & Wagner, N. N. (1976). Written descriptions of orgasms: A study of sex differences. *Archives of Sexual Behavior, 5,* 87–98.

Vandrey, R. G., Budney, A. J., Hughes, J. R., & Liguori, A. (2008). A within-subject comparison of withdrawal symptoms during abstinence from cannabis, tobacco, and both substances. *Drug and Alcohol Dependence, 92,* 48–54.

vanReekum, C., Johnstone, T., Etter, A., Wehrle, T., & Scherer, K. (2004). Psychophysiological response to appraisal dimensions in a computer game. *Cognition and Emotion, 18,* 663–688.

Varley, C. K., & Smith, C. J. (2003). Anxiety disorders in the child and teen. *Pediatric Clinics of North America, 50,* 1107–1138.

Vartanian, L. R. (2000). Revisiting the imaginary audience and personal fable constructs of adolescent egocentrism: A conceptual review. *Adolescence, 35,* 639–661.

Vartanian, L. R. (2001). Adolescents' reactions to hypothetical peer group conversations: Evidence for an imaginary audience? *Adolescence, 36,* 347–380.

Vartanian, O., Martindale, C., & Kwiatkowski, J. (2003). Creativity and inductive reasoning: The relationship between divergent thinking and performance on Wason's 2-4-6 task. *The Quarterly Journal of Experimental Psychology, 56A,* 641–655.

Vaughn, B. E., Stevenson-Hinde, J., Waters, E., Kotsaftis, A., Lefever, G., Shouldice, A., et al. (1992). Attachment security and temperament in infancy and early childhood: Some conceptual clarifications. *Developmental Psychology, 28,* 463–473.

Ventura, J., Nuechterlein, K. H., Subotnik, K. L., Hardesty, J. P., & Mintz, J. (2000). Life events can trigger depressive exacerbation in the early course of schizophrenia. *Journal of Abnormal Psychology, 109,* 139–144.

Vergne, D. E., & Nemeroff, C. B. (2006). The interaction of serotonin transporter gene polymorphisms and early adverse life events on vulnerability for major depression. *Current Psychiatry Reports, 8,* 452–457.

Vieta, E., & Goikolea, J. M. (2005). Atypical antipsychotics: Newer options for mania and maintenance therapy. *Bipolar Disorders*, 7(Suppl. 4), 21–33.

Vigezzi, P., Guglielmino, L., Marzorati, P., Silenzio, R., De Chiara, M., Corrado, F., et al. (2006). Multimodal drug addiction treatment: A field comparison of methadone and buprenorphine among heroin- and cocaine-dependent patients. *Journal of Substance Abuse and Treatment, 31*, 3–7.

Villaneuva, A. T., Buchanan, P. R., Yee, B. J., & Grunstein, R. R. (2005). Ethnicity and obstructive sleep apnea. *Sleep Medical Review, 9*, 419–436.

Vitaliano, P. P., Young, H. M., & Zhang, J. (2004). Is caregiving a risk factor for illness? *Current Directions in Psychological Science, 13*, 13–16.

Voderholzer, U., Al-Shajlawi, A., Weske, G., Feige, B., & Riemann, D. (2003). Are there gender differences in objective and subjective sleep measures? A study of insomniacs and healthy controls. *Depression and Anxiety, 17*, 162–172.

Volkow, N. D., Gillespie, H., Mullani, N., & Tancredi, L. (1996). Brain glucose metabolism in chronic marijuana users at baseline and during marijuana intoxication. *Psychiatry Research: Neuroimaging, 67*(1), 29–38.

Volkow, N. D., Wang, G. J., Fowler, J. S., Leonido-Yee, M., Franceschi, D., Sedler, M. J., et al. (2001). Association of dopamine transporter reduction with psychomotor impairment in methamphetamine abusers. *American Journal of Psychiatry, 158*, 377–382.

Volterra, A., & Steinhauser, C. (2004). Glial modulation of synaptic transmission in the hippocampus. *Glia, 47*, 249–257.

Vygotsky, L. S. (1978). *Mind in society: The development of higher mental process.* Cambridge, MA: Harvard University Press.

Vygotsky, L. S. (1986). *Thought and language.* Cambridge, MA: MIT Press.

Vygotsky, L. S. (1987). Thinking and speech. In R. W. Reiber & A. S. Carton (Eds.), *The collected works of L. S. Vygotsky: Vol. 1I. Problems of general psychology* (pp. 37–285). New York: Plenum Press. (Original work published 1934)

Wadden, T. A., & Stunkard, A. J. (1987). Psychopathology and obesity, *Annals of the New York Academy of Sciences, 499*, 55–65.

Wagner, B., Knaevelsrud, C., & Maercker, A. (2006). Internet-based cognitive-behavioral therapy for complicated grief: A randomized controlled trial. *Death Studies, 30*, 429–453.

Wagner, G. C., Beuving, L. J., & Hutchinson, R. R. (1980). The effects of gonadal hormone manipulations on aggressive target-biting in mice. *Aggressive Behavior, 6*, 1–7.

Wakefield, J. C. (1992). The concept of mental disorder: On the boundary between biological facts and social values. *American Psychologist, 47*, 373–388.

Wald, G. (1964). The receptors of human color vision. *Science, 145*, 1007–1017.

Wald, J., & Taylor, S. (2003). Preliminary research on the efficacy of virtual reality exposure therapy to treat driving phobia. *Cyberpsychology and Behavior, 6*, 459–465.

Waldron-Hennessey, R., & Sabatelli, R. M. (1997). The parental comparison level index: A measure for assessing parental rewards and costs relative to expectations. *Journal of Marriage and the Family, 59*, 824–833.

Walker, B. R., Diefenbach, K. S., & Parikh, T. N. (2007). Inhibition within the nucleus tractus solitarius (NTS) ameliorates environmental exploration deficits due to cerebellum lesions in an animal model for autism. *Behavioural Brain Research, 176*, 109–120.

Walker, E., & Tessner, K. (2008). Schizophrenia. *Perspectives on Psychological Science, 3*, 30–37.

Walker, L. J. (1989). A longitudinal study of moral reasoning. *Child Development, 60*, 157–166.

Walker, L. J. (1995). Sexism in Kohlberg's moral psychology? In W. M. Kurtines & J. L. Gewirtz (Eds.), *Moral development: An introduction* (pp. 83–107). Boston: Allyn & Bacon.

Walker, L. J., & Taylor, J. H. (1991). Stage transitions in moral reasoning: A longitudinal study of developmental processes. *Developmental Psychology, 27*, 330–337.

Walker, M. P., & Stickgold, R. (2004). Sleep-dependent learning and memory consolidation. *Neuron, 44*, 121–133.

Wallace, J., Schneider, T., & McGuffin, P. (2002). Genetics of depression. In I. H. Gotlib & C. L. Hammen (Eds.), *Handbook of depression* (pp. 169–191). New York: Guilford Press.

Walster, E., Aronson, E., Abrahams, D., & Rottman, L. (1966). Importance of physical attractiveness in dating behavior. *Journal of Personality and Social Psychology, 4*, 508–516.

Walters, S. T., Foy, B. D., & Castro, R. J. (2003). The agony of Ecstasy: Responding to growing MDMA use among college students. *Journal of American College Health, 51*, 139–141.

Wampold, B. E., Minami, T., Baskin, T. W., & Callen Tierney, S. (2002). A meta-(re)analysis of the effects of cognitive therapy versus other therapies for depression. *Journal of Affective Disorders, 68*, 159–165.

Wampold, B. E., Mondin, G. W., Moody, M., Stich, F., Benson, K., & Ahn, H. (1997). A meta-analysis of outcome studies comparing bona fide psychotherapies: Empirically, "All must have prizes." *Psychological Bulletin, 122*, 203–215.

Wang, S. H., Baillargeon, R., & Brueckner, L. (2004). Young infants' reasoning about hidden objects: Evidence from violation-of-expectation tasks with test trials only. *Cognition, 93*, 167–198.

Wanner, H. E. (1968). *On remembering, forgetting, and understanding sentences: A study of the deep structure hypothesis.* Unpublished doctoral dissertation, Harvard University.

Warburton, D. M. (1995). Effects of caffeine on cognition and mood without caffeine abstinence. *Psychopharmacology, 119*, 66–70.

Ward, R., Logan, J., & Spitze, G. (1992). The influence of parent and child needs on coresidence in middle and later life. *Journal of Marriage and the Family, 54*, 209–221.

Warner, R., & Steel, B. (1999). Child rearing as a mechanism for social change: The relationship of child gender to parents' commitment to gender equity. *Gender and Society, 13*, 503–517.

Warr, P. B. (1994). Age and employment. In M. D. Dunnette, L. Hough, & H. Triandis (Eds.), *Handbook of industrial and organizational psychology* (pp. 485–550). Palo Alto, CA: Consulting Psychologists Press.

Waschbusch, D. A., Sellers, D. P., LeBlanc, M., & Kelley, M. L. (2003). Helpless attributions and depression in adolescents: The roles of anxiety, event valence, and demographics. *Journal of Adolescence, 26*, 169–183.

Wasserman, E. A., & Miller, R. R. (1997). What's elementary about associative learning? *Annual Review of Psychology, 48*, 573–607.

Wasserman, G. S. (1978). *Color vision: An historical introduction.* New York: Wiley.

Watson, J. B., & Rayner, R. (1920). Conditioned emotional reactions. *Journal of Experimental Psychology, 3*, 1–14.

Webb, W. B. (1983). Theories in modern sleep research. In A. Mayes (Ed.), *Sleep mechanisms and functions* (pp. 1–17). Wokingham, UK: Van Nostrand Reinhold.

Webb, W. B., & Campbell, S. S. (1983). Relationships in sleep characteristics of identical and fraternal twins. *Archives of General Psychiatry, 40*, 1093–1095.

Webster Marketon, J. I., & Glaser, R. (2008). Stress hormones and immune function. *Cellular Immunology, 252*, 16–26.

Wechsler, D. (1939). *The measurement of adult intelligence.* Baltimore: Williams & Wilkins.

Weidenmayer, C. P., Anderson, G. M., Zhu, H., Amat, J., Whiteman, R., & Peterson, B. S. (2006). Cortisol levels and hippocampus volumes in healthy preadolescent children. *Biological Psychiatry, 60*, 856–861.

Weinrich, J. D. (1994). Homosexuality. In V. L. Bullough & B. Bullough (Eds.), *Human sexuality: An encyclopedia* (pp. 277–283). New York: Garland.

Weinstein, S., Woodward, T. S., & Ngan, E. T. (2007). Brain activation mediates the association between structural abnormality and symptom severity in schizophrenia. *Neuroimage, 36*, 188–193.

Weinstock, H., Berman, S., & Cates, W., Jr. (2004). Sexually transmitted diseases among American youth: Incidence and prevalence estimates, 2000. *Perspectives on Sexual and Reproductive Health, 36*, 6–10.

Weisner, T. S., & Wilson-Mitchell, J. E. (1990). Nonconventional family lifestyles and sex typing in six-year-olds. *Child Development, 61*, 1915–1933.

Weiss, A., Bates, T. C., & Luciano, M. (2008). Happiness is a personal(ity) thing: The genetics of personality and well-being in a representative sample. *Psychological Science, 19*, 205–210.

Weissman, M. M. (1993). The epidemiology of personality disorders: A 1990 update. NIMH Conference: Personality disorders (1990, Williamsburg, Virginia). *Journal of Personality Disorders* (Spr. Suppl. 1), 44–62.

Weissman, M. M., Bland, R. C., Canino, G. J., Greenwald, S., Hwu, H. G., Joyce, P. R., et al. (1999). Prevalence of suicide ideation and suicide attempts in nine countries. *Psychological Medicine, 29*, 9–17.

Weissman, M. M., Markowitz, J. C., & Klerman, G. I. (2000). *Comprehensive guide to interpersonal psychotherapy.* New York: Basic Books.

Weissman, M. M., & Olfson, M. (1995). Depression in women: Implications for health care research. *Science, 269*, 799–801.

Welch, S. S. (2001). A review of the literature on the epidemiology of parasuicide in the general population. *Psychiatric Services, 52*, 368–375.

Welford, A. T. (1987). Ageing. In R. L. Gregory (Ed.), *The Oxford companion to the mind* (pp. 13–14). Oxford, UK: Oxford University Press.

Wellman, H. M., Cross, D., & Watson, J. (2001). Meta-analysis of theory of mind development: The truth about false-belief. *Child Development, 72*, 655–684.

Wells, G. L., & Olson, E. A. (2003). Eyewitness testimony. *Annual Review of Psychology, 54*, 277–295.

Wender, P. H., Kety, S. S., Rosenthal, D., Schulsinger, F., Ortmann, J., & Lunde, I. (1986). Psychiatric disorders in the biological and adoptive families of adopted individuals with affective disorders. *Archives of General Psychiatry, 43,* 923–929.

Wertheimer, M. (1923). Principles of perceptual organization (Abridged trans. by M. Wertheimer). In D. S. Beardslee & M. Wertheimer (Eds.), *Readings in perception* (pp. 115–137). Princeton, NJ: Van Nostrand -Reinhold. (Original work published 1923, *Psychologishe Forschung, 41,* 301–350)

Westen, D. (1999). The scientific status of unconscious processes: Is Freud really dead? *Journal of the American Psychoanalytic Association, 47,* 1061–1106.

Westen, D., & Bradley, R. (2005). Empirically supported complexity: Rethinking evidence-based practice in psychotherapy. *Current Directions in Psychological Science, 14,* 266–271.

Westermeyer, J. F. (2004). Predictors and characteristics of Erikson's life cycle model among men: A 32-year longitudinal study. *International Journal of Aging and Human Development, 58,* 29–48.

Westover, A. N., & Marangell, L. B. (2002). A cross-national relationship between sugar consumption and major depression. *Depression and Anxiety, 16,* 118–120.

Wetter, D. W., Cofta-Gunn, L., Fouladi, R. T., Irvin, J. E., Daza, P., Mazas, C., et al. (2005). Understanding the association among education, employment characteristics, and smoking. *Addictive Behaviors, 30,* 905–914.

Wever, E. G. (1970). *Theory of hearing.* New York: Wiley. (Original work published 1949)

Weyant, J. M. (1996). Application of compliance techniques to direct-mail requests for charitable donations. *Psychology and Marketing, 13,* 157–170.

Wheeler, M. A., Stuss, D. T., & Tulving, E. (1997). Toward a theory of episodic memory: The frontal lobes and autonoetic consciousness. *Psychological Bulletin, 121,* 331–354.

Wheeler, M. D. (1991). Physical changes of puberty. *Endocrinology and Metabolism Clinics of North America, 20,* 1–14.

Whitbourne, S. K. (1996). *The aging individual.* New York: Springer.

Whitbourne, S. K. (2001). The physical aging process in midlife: Interactions with psychological and sociocultural factors. In M.E. Lachman (E d.), *Handbook of midlife development* (pp. 109–155). New York: Wiley.

Whitbourne, S. K., Zuschlag, M. K., Elliot, L. B., & Waterman, A. D. (1992). Psychosocial development in adulthood: A 22-year sequential study. *Journal of Personality and Social Psychology, 63,* 260–271.

White, L. K., & Edwards, J. N. (1990). Emptying the nest and parental well-being: An analysis of national panel data. *American Sociological Review, 55,* 235–242.

White, L. K., & Rogers, S. J. (1997). Strong support but uneasy relationships: Coresidence and adult children's relationships with their parents. *Journal of Marriage and the Family, 59,* 62–76.

Whorf, B. L. (1956). *Language, thought, and reality: Selected writings of Benjamin Lee Whorf.* New York: Wiley.

Wickelgren, I. (1997). Marijuana: Harder than thought? *Science, 276,* 1967–1968.

Widiger, T. A. (1998). Invited essay: Sex differences in the diagnosis of personality disorders. *Journal of Personality Disorders, 12,* 95–118.

Widiger, T. A. (2003). Personality disorder and Axis I psychopathology: The problematic boundary of Axis I and Axis II. *Journal of Personality Disorders, 17,* 90–108.

Widiger, T. A., & Chaynes, K. (2003). Current issues in the assessment of personality disorders. *Current Psychiatry Reports, 5,* 28–35.

Widom, C. S. (1999). Posttraumatic stress disorder in abused and neglected children grown up. *American Journal of Psychiatry, 156,* 1223–1229.

Wiebe, D. J. (1991). Hardiness and stress moderation: A test of proposed mechanisms. *Journal of Personality and Social Psychology, 60,* 89–99.

Wiebe, D. J., & Smith, T. W. (1997). Personality and health: Progress and problems in psychosomatics. In R. Hogan, J. Johnson, & S. Briggs (Eds.), *Handbook of personal psychology* (pp. 891–918). New York: Academic Press.

Wiechman Askay, S., & Patterson, D. R. (2007). Hypnotic analgesia. *Expert Review of Neurotherapeutics, 7,* 1675–1683.

Wiederhold, B. K., Jang, D. P., Kim, S. I., & Wiederhold, M. D. (2002). Physiological monitoring as an objective tool in virtual reality therapy. *Cyberpsychology and Behavior, 5,* 77–82.

Wiest, W. (1977). Semantic differential profiles of orgasm and other experiences among men and women. *Sex Roles, 3,* 399.

Wiggins, J. S. (1997). In defense of traits. In R. Hogan, J. Johnson, & S. Briggs (Eds.), *Handbook of personality psychology* (pp. 97–115). New York: Academic Press.

Wijdicks, E. F. M., Atkinson, J. L. D., & Okazaki, H. (2001). Isolated medulla oblongata function after severe traumatic brain injury. *Journal of Neurology, Neurosurgery, and Psychiatry, 70,* 127.

Williams, D. R., Gonzalez, H. M., Neighbors, H., Neese, R., Abelson, J. M., Sweetman, J., et al. (2007). Prevalence and distribution of major depressive disorder in African Americans, Caribbean Blacks, and non-Hispanic Whites. *Archives of General Psychiatry, 64,* 305–315.

Williams, J. E., Paton, C. C., Siegler, I. C., Eigenbrodt, M. L., Nieto, F. J., & Tyroler, H. A. (2000). Anger proneness predicts coronary heart disease risk: Prospective analysis from the Atherosclerosis Risk in Communities (ARIC) study. *Circulation, 101,* 2034–2039.

Williams, J. M., & Galli, A. (2006). The dopamine transporter: A vigilant border control for psychostimulant action. *Handbook of Experimental Pharmacology, 175,* 215–232.

Williams, L. M., Sidis, A., Gordon, E., & Meares, R. A. (2006). "Missing links" in borderline personality disorder: Loss of neural synchrony relates to lack of emotion regulation and impulse control. *Journal of Psychiatry and Neuroscience, 31,* 181–188.

Williams, P. M., Goodie, J., & Motsinger, L. D. (2008). Treating eating disorders in primary care. *American Family Physician, 77,* 187–195.

Williams, R. (1993). *Anger kills.* New York: Times Books.

Willis, S. L., & Schaie, K. W. (1999). Intellectual functioning in midlife. In S. L. Willis & J. D. Reid (Eds.), *Life in the middle: Psychological and social development in middle age* (pp. 233–247). San Diego, CA: Academic Press.

Wills, T. A., & Fegan, M. (2001). Social networks and social support. In A. Baum, T. A. Revenson, & J. E. Singer (Eds.), *Handbook of health psychology* (pp. 209–234). Mahwah, NJ: Erlbaum.

Wilson, G. T., Grilo, C. M., & Vitousek, K. M. (2007). Psychological treatment of eating disorders. *American Psychologist, 62,* 199–216.

Wilson, K. G., Hayes, S. C., & Gifford, E. V. (1997). Cognition in behavior therapy: Agreements and differences. *Journal of Behavior Therapy and Experimental Psychiatry, 28,* 53–63.

Wilson, R. S., & Bennett, D. A. (2003). Cognitive activity and risk of Alzheimer's disease. *Current Directions in Psychological Science, 12,* 87–91.

Wilson, W. R. (1979). Feeling more than we can know: Exposure effects without learning. *Journal of Personality and Social Psychology, 37,* 811–821.

Wingfield, A., & Kahana, M. J. (2002). The dynamics of memory retrieval in older adulthood. *Canadian Journal of Psychology, 56,* 187–199.

Winokur, G., Coryell, W., Keller, M., Endicott, J., & Leon, A. (1995). A family study of manic-depressive (bipolar I) disease. *Archives of General Psychiatry, 52,* 367–373.

Wise, S. M. (2000). *Rattling the cage: Toward legal rights for animals.* Cambridge, MA: Perseus Books.

Wiseman, S., & Tulving, E. (1976). Encoding specificity: Relations between recall superiority and recognition failure. *Journal of Experimental Psychology: Human Learning and Memory, 2,* 349–361.

Witt, L. A., Kacmar, M., Carlson, D. S., & Zivnuska, S. (2002). Interactive effects of personality and organizational politics on contextual performance. *Journal of Organizational Behavior, 23,* 911–926.

Wolf, D. H., Gur, R. C., Valdez, J. N., Loughead, J., Elliott, M. A., Gur, R. E., et al. (2007). Alterations of fronto-temporal connectivity during word encoding in schizophrenia. *Psychiatry Research, 154,* 221–232.

Wolfe, J., Erickson, D. J., Sharkansky, R. J., King, D. W., & King, L. A. (1999). Course and predictors of posttraumatic stress disorder among Gulf War veterans: A prospective analysis. *Journal of Consulting and Clinical Psychology, 67,* 520–528.

Wolitzky, D. L. (1995). The theory and practice of traditional psychoanalytic psychotherapy. In A. S. Gurman & S. B. Messer (Eds.), *Essential psychotherapies* (pp. 12–54). New York: Guilford.

Woll, S. (1986). So many to choose from: Decision strategies in video dating. *Journal of Social and Personal Relationships, 3,* 43–52.

Wolpe, J. (1958). *Psychotherapy by reciprocal inhibition.* Stanford, CA: Stanford University Press.

Won, J., Mair, E. A., Bolger, W. E., & Conran, R. M. (2000). The vomeronasal organ: An objective anatomic analysis of its prevalence. *Ear, Nose, and Throat Journal, 79,* 800.

Wood, W. (2000). Attitude change: Persuasion and social influence. *Annual Review of Psychology, 51,* 539–570.

World Health Organization. (2004). *The World Health Report 2004: Changing history. Annex Table 3: Burden of disease in DALYs by cause, sex, and mortality stratum in WHO regions, estimates for 2002.* Geneva: Author.

Wright, I. C., Rabe-Hesketh,, S., Woodruff, P. W., David, A. S., Murray, R. M., & Bullmore, E. T. (2000). Meta-analysis of regional brain volumes in schizophrenia. *American Journal of Psychiatry, 157,* 16–25.

Wrightsman, L. S. (1988). *Personality development in adulthood.* Newbury Park, CA: Sage.

Wrightsman, L. S. (1994). *Adult personality development: Vol 1. Theories and concepts.* Thousand Oaks, CA: Sage.

Wu, T., & Kral, J. G. (2004). Gherlin, integrative neuroendocrine peptide in health and disease. *Annals of Surgery, 239,* 464–474.

Wulsin, L. R., Vaillat, G. E., & Wells, V. E. (1999). A systematic review of the mortality of depression. *Psychosomatic Medicine, 61,* 6–17.

Xiao, Y., Wang, Y., & Felleman, D. J. (2003). A spatially organized representation of colour in macaque cortical area V2. *Nature, 421,* 535–539.

Xiaohe, X., & Whyte, M. K. (1990). Love matches and arranged marriages. *Journal of Marriage and the Family, 52,* 709–722.

Xie, T., Tong, L., McLane, M. W., Hatzidimitriou, G., Yuan, J., McCann, U., et al. (2006). Loss of serotonin transporter protein after MDMA and other ring-substituted amphetamines. *Neuropsychopharmacology, 31,* 2639–2651.

Yackinous, C. A., & Guinard, J. (2002). Relation between PROP (6-n-propylthiouracil) taster status, taste anatomy and dietary intake measures for young men and women. *Appetite, 38,* 201–209.

Yalom, I. D. (1989). *Love's executioner and other tales of psychotherapy.* New York: HarperCollins.

Yalom, I. D., & Leszcz, M. (2005). *The theory and practice of group psychotherapy* (5th ed.). New York: Basic Books.

Yamagata, S., Suzuki, A., Ando, J., Ono, Y., Kijima, N., Yoshimura, K., et al. (2006). Is the genetic structure of human personality universal? A cross-cultural twin study from North America, Europe, and Asia. *Journal of Personality and Social Psychology, 90,* 987–998.

Yardley, L., & Kirby, S. (2006). Evaluation of booklet self-management of symptoms in Meniere disease: A randomized controlled trial. *Psychosomatic Medicine, 68,* 762–769.

Yingling, D. R., Utter, G., Vengalil, S., & Mason, B. (2002). Calcium channel blocker, nimodipine, for the treatment of bipolar disorder during pregnancy. *American Journal of Obstetrics and Gynecology, 187,* 1711–1712.

York, J. L., & Welte, J. W. (1994). Gender comparisons of alcohol consumption in alcoholic and nonalcoholic populations. *Journal of Studies on Alcohol, 55,* 743–750.

Young, E., & Korzun, A. (1998). Psychoneuroendocrinology of depression: Hypothalmic-pituitary-gonadal axis. *Psychiatric Clinics of North America, 21,* 309–323.

Young, N. K. (1997). Effects of alcohol and other drugs on children. *Journal of Psychoactive Drugs, 29,* 23–42.

Yunker, G. W., & Yunker, B. D. (2002). Primal leadership (book). *Personnel Psychology, 55,* 1030–1033.

Yutrzenka, B. A. (1995). Making a case for training in ethnic and cultural diversity in increasing treatment efficacy. *Journal of Consulting and Clinical Psychology, 63,* 197–206.

Zaalberg, R., Manstead, A. S. R., & Fischer, A. H. (2004). Relations between emotions, display rules, social motives, and facial behaviors. *Cognition and Emotion, 18,* 183–207.

Zaccaro, S. J., Mumford, M. D., Connelly, M., Marks, M., & Gilbert, J.A. (2000). Assessment of leader abilities. *Leadership Quarterly, 11,* 37–64.

Zadina, J. E., Hackler, L., Ge, L. J., & Kastin, A. J. (1997). A potent and selective endogeneous agonist for the u-opiate receptor. *Nature, 386,* 499–502.

Zadra, A., Desjardins, S., & Marcotte, E. (2006). Evolutionary function of dreams: A test of the threat simulation theory in recurrent dreams. *Consciousness and Cognition, 15,* 450–463.

Zahn-Waxler, C., & Robinson, J. (1995). Empathy and guilt: Early origins of feelings of responsibility. In J. P. Tangney & K. W. Fischer (Eds.), *Self-conscious emotions* (pp. 143–173). New York: Guilford Press.

Zajonc, R. B. (1968). Attitudinal effects of mere exposure. *Journal of Personality and Social Psychology, 9,* 1–27.

Zajonc, R. B. (1980). Feeling and thinking: Preferences need no inferences. *American Psychologist, 35,* 151–175.

Zajonc, R. B., Adelmann, P. K., Murphy, S. T., & Neidenthal, P. M. (1987). Convergence in the physical appearance of spouse. *Motivation and Emotion, 11,* 335–346.

Zajonc, R. B., Murphy, S. T., & Inglehart, M. (1989). Feeling and facial efference: Implications of the vascular theory of emotions. *Psychological Review, 96,* 395–416.

Zanarini, M. C. (2000). Childhood experiences associated with the development of borderline personality disorder. *Psychiatric Clinics of North America, 23,* 89–101.

Zanarini, M. C., & Frankenburg, (1997). Pathways to the development of borderline personality disorder. *Journal of Personality Disorders, 11,* 93–104.

Zanarini, M. C., Skodol, A. E., Bender, D., Dolan, R., Sanislow, C., Schaefer, E., et al. (2000). The Collaborative Longitudinal Personality Disorders Study: Reliability of Axis I and II diagnoses. *Journal of Personality Disorders, 14,* 291–299.

Zani, B. (1993). Dating and interpersonal relationships in adolescence. In S. Jackson & H. Rodriguez-Tome (Eds.), *Adolescence and its social worlds* (pp. 95–119). Hillsdale, NJ: Erlbaum.

Zebrowitz, L. A., White, B., & Wieneke, K. (2008). Mere exposure and racial prejudice: Exposure to other-race faces increases liking for strangers from that race. *Social Cognition, 26,* 259–275.

Zee, P. C., & Manthena, P. (2007). The brain's master circadian clock: Implications and opportunities for therapy of sleep disorders. *Sleep Medicine Reviews, 11,* 59–70.

Zeitzer, J. M., Nishino, S., & Mignot, E. (2006). The neurobiology of hypocretins (orexins), narcolepsy and related therapeutic interventions. *Trends in Pharmacological Sciences, 27,* 368–374.

Zeman, A., Britton, T., Douglas, N., Hansen, A., Hicks, J., Howard, R., et al. (2004). Narcolepsy and excessive daytime sleepiness. *British Medical Journal, 329,* 724–728.

Zhang, B., & Wing, Y. K. (2006). Sex differences in insomnia: A meta-analysis. *Sleep, 29,* 85–93.

Ziegler, D. J., & Leslie, Y. M. (2003). A test of the ABC model underlying rational emotive behavior therapy. *Psychological Reports, 92,* 235–240.

Ziegler, D. J., & Smith, P. N. (2004). Anger and the ABC model underlying rational-emotive behavior therapy. *Psychological Reports, 93,* 1009–1014.

Zimbardo, P. G. (1972, April). Psychology of imprisonment. *Transition/Society,* pp. 4–8.

Zimmer, L., & Morgan, J. P. (1997). *Marijuana myths, marijuana fact: A review of scientific evidence.* New York: Lindesmith Center.

Zimmer-Gembeck, M. J. (2002). The development of romantic relationships and adaptations in the system of peer relationships. *Journal of Adolescent Health, 31,* 216–225.

Zorrilla, L. T., Cannon, T. D., Kronenberg, S., Mednick, S. A., Schulsinger, F., Parnas, J., et al. (1997). Structural brain abnormalities in schizophrenia: A family study. *Biological Psychiatry, 42,* 1080–1086.

Zottoli, M. A., & Wanous, J. P. (2000). Recruitment source research: Current status and future directions. *Human Resource Management Review, 10,* 435–451.

Zuckerman, M. (1978). The search for high sensation. *Psychology Today, 11,* 38–99.

Zuckerman, M. (1994). *Behavioral expressions and biosocial bases of sensation seeking.* Cambridge, UK: Cambridge University Press.

Name Index

Aamodt, M. G., 578, 582
Abad, V. C., 131
Abdel-Khalek, A., 452
Abkevich, V., 499
Abramowitz, J. S., 512, 539, 551
Abrams, D. B., 139
Abramson, L. Y., 502
Adams, C. D., 536
Adan, A., 132
Ader, R., 421
Aderibigbe, Y. A., 510
Adler, A., 451–2
Adler, J., 143, 432
Adolphs, R., 56, 57
Aghajanian, G. K., 149
Ahern, J., 491
Aiken, L. R., 470
Ainsworth, M. D., 332
Alderidge, M. A., 248
Alexander, G. M., 87
Allen, T. D., 583
Alloy, L. B., 502
Allport, G. W., 378, 379, 455–6
Almeida, D. M., 415
Alonso, A., 541
Alsaker, F. D., 341
Altomari, M. G., 20–1
Amato, P. R., 351, 352
Amoore, J. E., 98
Anderson, C., 420
Anderson, C. A., 399, 554
Anderson, J. R., 210, 225, 246
Anderson, N., 583
Anderson, P. L., 534
Anderson, R. N., 498
Andreasen, N. C., 506, 508
Andresen, G. V., 170
Andresen, J., 427
Angst, J., 497
Ankey, C. D., 61
Anshel, M. H., 425
Antoni, M. H., 426
Antony, M. M., 533
Applbaum K. D., 351
Appleby, D., 17
Arborelius, L., 500
Archer, J., 397
Arendt, J., 124

Arendt, R. E., 147
Armfield, J. M., 493
Armitage, R., 127
Arnett, J., 353
Aronson, E., 368, 375, 377, 380, 561
Arthur, J. B., 586
Asay, T. P., 544
Asch, S. E., 387–8
Ashcan, K., 554
Ashtari, M., 342
Ashwin, C., 57
Assor, A., 467
Astin, J. A., 426
Atkinson, J. L. D., 54
Atkinson, J. W., 274, 277
Atkinson, R. C., 199
Aucoin, D., 338
Avalos, L. C., 282
Avolio, B. J., 584
Azar, B., 97
Baddeley, A. D., 206, 207, 208
Baer, L., 554
Bagshaw, S. M. Jr., 161
Bahrick, H. P., 218
Bailargeon, R., 325
Bailey, J., 298
Baird, A. A., 342
Baker, T. B., 139
Ball, E. M., 131
Ball, G. F., 45
Baltes, P. B., 344
Balthazart, J., 45
Balzer, W. K., 585
Bandura, A., 182, 188–90, 398, 399, 463–4
Banich, M. T., 60
Banthia, R., 426
Barbee, J. G., 144
Barber, J. P., 545
Bard, P., 301
Bardone, A. M., 288
Bargh, J. A., 452
Bar-Haim, Y., 322
Barlow, D. H., 417, 489, 493, 503, 547, 551
Baron, R. A., 397
Barondes, S. H., 551
Bartlett, F. C., 210

Bartoshuk, L. M., 94, 97
Bass, B. M., 584
Batabyal, A. A., 351
Bates, B. L., 135, 136
Batsell, W. R., 170
Baumann, A. E., 485
Baumeister, R. F., 386
Baumrind, D., 29, 333, 396
Beach, S. R. H., 24
Beal, C. R., 337
Beardsley, T., 121
Beatty, M., 23
Beatty, W. W., 336
Beauducel, A., 457
Beck, A. T., 502, 538–9
Beck, J. G., 534
Becker, P. M., 131
Beeman, M. J., 60
Békésy, G. von, 92
Bell, A. R., 298
Bell, C. J., 492, 551
Belsky, J., 22, 353
Benabid, A. L., 554
Bender, E., 534
Benjamin, L. T., 15
Bennett, M. P., 427
Bennett, W. I., 89
Benoit, S. C., 281
Benson, H., 426
Benton, D., 48
Berger, A. M., 125
Bergles, D. E., 39
Berk, L. E., 328
Berkowitz, L., 399
Berlyne, D. E., 276
Berry, A. K., 132
Berscheid, E., 383
Betz, N. E., 354
Beutler, L. E., 531, 545
Bezchlibnyk-Butler, K. Z., 147, 148
Bianchi, S. M., 351
Biederman, J., 492
Bierut, L. J., 499
Binet, A., 254
Black, D. W., 515
Blagys, M. D., 529
Blanchard, R., 298
Blane, H. T., 143

Blatt, S. J., 529
Blazer, D. G., 496, 502
Bless, H., 370
Blincoe, L., 143
Block, J. A., 461
Bloom, F., 40
Bloom, J. W., 546
Boden, M., 236
Boeri, M. W., 147
Bohannon, J. N., 247
Bohart, A. C., 531
Boivin, D. B., 121
Bolles, R. C., 166
Bonanno, G. A., 491
Bond, R., 388
Bonte, M., 111
Booth, A., 352
Booth-Kewley, S., 429
Bootzin, R. R., 130
Boring, E. G., 258
Borkman, T. J., 543
Borkovec, T. D., 531
Borman, W. C., 587
Bornovalova, M. A., 515
Bornstein, M. H., 80, 87
Bosch, J. A., 421
Botella, C., 534
Bouchard, T. J., 264, 314, 459
Boulcott, P., 80
Bourin, M., 492
Bowden, C. L., 552
Bower, B., 221
Bowers, K. S., 136
Bowie, W., 433
Bowlby, J., 357
Boycott, B. B., 82
Bozarth, M. A., 145
Brackett, M. A., 261
Braddock, A. E., 512
Bradford, H. F., 45
Bradley, D. B., 497
Brainerd, C. J., 219
Bramlett, M. D., 351
Brandt, Amber, 157
Brannon, L., 409
Bratberg, G. H., 341
Braudy, S. O., 403
Braungart, J. M., 459
Brehm, S. S., 382, 397

Note: the Null hypothesis entry uses H_0.